This Is Who We Were
In The 1980s

This Is Who We Were
In The 1980s

Based on material from Grey House Publishing's
Working Americans Series by Scott Derks

Grey House
Publishing

PUBLISHER:	Leslie Mackenzie
EDITORIAL DIRECTOR:	Laura Mars
EDITORIAL ASSISTANT:	Jennifer Bossert
PRODUCTION MANAGER:	Kristen Thatcher
MARKETING DIRECTOR:	Jessica Moody
COMPOSITION:	David Garoogian

Grey House Publishing, Inc.
4919 Route 22
Amenia, NY 12501
518.789.8700
FAX 845.373.6390
www.greyhouse.com
e-mail: books @greyhouse.com

Publisher's Cataloging-In-Publication Data
(Prepared by The Donohue Group, Inc.)

Names: Derks, Scott. Working Americans. | Grey House Publishing, Inc.
Title: This is who we were. In the 1980s / [edited by] Grey House Publishing.
Other Titles: In the 1980s
Description: [First edition]. | Amenia, NY : Grey House Publishing, [2016] | Edition statement supplied by publisher. | "Based on material from Grey House Publishing's Working Americans Series by Scott Derks." | Includes bibliographical references and index.
Identifiers: ISBN 978-1-61925-934-8 (hardcover)
Subjects: LCSH: United States—Economic conditions—1971-1981. | United States—Economic conditions—1981-2001. | United States—Social conditions—1980- | United States—Civilization—1970- | United States—History—1969- | Nineteen eighties.
Classification: LCC HC106.8 .T45 2016 | DDC 330.973—dc23

TABLE OF CONTENTS

Section One: Profiles

This section contains 28 profiles of individuals and families living and working in the 1980s. It examines their lives at home, at work, and in their communities. Based upon historic materials, personal interviews, and diaries, the profiles give a sense of what it was like to live in the years 1980 to 1989.

Section Two: Historical Snapshots

This section includes lists of important "firsts" in America, from technical advances and political events to new products, books, and movies. Combining American history with fun facts, these snapshots present an easy-to-read overview of the 1980s.

Section Three: Economy of the Times

This section looks at a wide range of economic data, including prices for food, clothing, transportation, and housing, plus reprints of actual advertisements for products and services of the time. It includes comparable figures for expenditures, income, and prices, plus a valuable year-by-year listing of the value of a dollar.

Section Four: All Around Us—What We Saw, Wrote, Read & Listened To

This section offers reprints of newspaper and magazine articles, speeches, and other items designed to help readers focus on what was on the minds of Americans in the 1980s. These 29 original pieces show how popular opinion was formed, and how American life was affected.

Section Five: Census Data

This section includes state-by-state comparative tables, the special report series We the Americans *published in 1993 by the U.S. Census Bureau, and reprints from the 1990 Census.*

ESSAY ON THE 1980s

The 1980s was a decade of transformative change. When Ronald Reagan entered the White House in 1981, he promised to restore faith in the nation by shrinking government and defending America more aggressively against the Soviet Union. During his first term the recession ended, inflation was controlled, and taxes went down. After the instability of the 1970s, Americans felt hopeful that they could make money again, and when they did there were plenty of ways to spend it. With the economy soaring, Americans enjoyed compact discs instead of records. We got cash from ATM machines instead of waiting on long lines at the bank. And personal computers, once only used in colleges and big companies, were set up in almost every home.

Defined by patriotism, prosperity, and peace, the 1980s were vibrant and big, and with the Cold War coming to an end, Americans felt like the country was back to being the world's only superpower.

Economy

Economic principles of the 1980s were focused around tax reduction, allowing Americans to keep more of their paychecks. President Reagan believed that high taxes threatened individual freedom and encouraged wasteful government spending, and that low taxes induced people to work longer and harder, leading to more investments, spending, and overall economic growth.

While the tax cuts served mainly to benefit wealthy Americans, proponents argued that these benefits would eventually trickle down to lower-income people due to new job opportunities and higher wages. The Tax Reform Bill, which slashed tax rates for taxpayers in almost every income bracket, was passed in July 1981. With the resulting economic growth came federal budget deficits of over $100 billion, but most agree that the economic expansion and upswing in the business cycle were an improvement over the dark economy of the 1970s.

Music

The 1980s saw a new form of music called "rap," with words spoken—not sung—over a heavy beat. The 1980s also saw the reinvention of musicians Michael Jackson, Prince, Madonna, Whitney Houston, and Janet Jackson, and their videos played as permanent fixtures on MTV. The resurgence of hard rock bands such as Def Leppard, Kiss, Bon Jovi, Poison, Twisted Sister, and Whitesnake, was a hallmark of the decade. Music of the 1980s is commonly remembered for an increase in the use of digital recording, primarily synthesizers. Surveys since the 1980s reveal that it was the most favored musical decade of the last 50 years.

Television & Movies

Television talk shows also became popular in the 1980s. Guests would appear mostly to talk about themselves, their political views and personal escapades. It was novel to hear Americans talk so publicly about things once considered private. *The Oprah Winfrey Show* aired nationally beginning in 1986, and to this day remains the highest-rated talk show in American television history.

Popular television shows in the 1980s, including *Dallas* and *Dynasty,* showed increased interest in financial success, with characters living in expensive homes, wearing costly clothes, and driving fancy cars. At the movies, *Wall Street* depicted a young, wealthy, dishonest man trading on the New York Stock Exchange. Power was also a popular theme with action films *Rambo* and *Rocky,* where good triumphs over evil.

Social Change

For many, the symbol of the decade was "yup"—short for Young, Urban Professional, which quickly turned into "yuppie." Yuppies typically were college educated with good jobs and expensive tastes, and often self-centered and materialistic. Surveys showed that yuppies were more concerned with making money and buying consumer goods than their parents and grandparents had been. A theory behind this attitude suggested that many of this generation, filled with anxiety and doubt, used material items as a path to happiness.

Americans' appetite during the 1980s also extended to sexually explicit music lyrics and television shows, which many blamed for the AIDS epidemic, unquestionably the most challenging health issue of the 1980s. Originally linked to gay men, the American public learned that anyone could be affected through the exchange of blood and other bodily fluids. The spread of the deadly virus forced a national dialogue about sex education as a means to safe sex. In 1987, hundreds of thousands of activists marched on Washington DC, demanding more federal resources be devoted to the epidemic. In 1988, the World Health Organization declared December 1 as World AIDS day.

Another national concern during the 1980s was the quality of American education. Studies demonstrated poor performance in every subject area when compared to past scores, and to other countries. In an effort to reverse this trend, educators developed tests that limited multiple choice questions in favor of essays, and focused more on at-risk children who were more likely to fail, drop out, or abuse drugs.

INTRODUCTION

This Is Who We Were In The 1980s is an offspring of our 13-volume *Working Americans* series, which is devoted, volume by volume, to Americans by class, occupation, or social cause. This new edition is devoted to the 1980s. It represents various economic classes, dozens of occupations, and all regions of the country. This comprehensive look at this decade is through the eyes and ears of everyday Americans, not the words of historians or politicians.

This Is Who We Were In The 1980s presents 28 profiles of individuals and families—their lives at home, on the job, and in their neighborhood—with lots of photos and historical images. These stories portray struggling and successful Americans, and capture a wide range of thoughts and emotions. From the many government surveys, social worker histories, economic data, family diaries and letters, and newspaper and magazine features, this unique reference assembles a remarkable personal and realistic look at the lives of a wide range of Americans between the years 1980-1989.

The profiles, together with additional sections outlined below, present a complete picture of what it was like to live in America in the 1980s.

Section One: Profiles

Each of the 28 profiles in Section One begins with a brief introduction. Each profile is arranged in three categories: Life at Home; Life at Work; Life in the Community. Photographs and original advertisements support each chapter, and many include industry or social timelines and contemporary articles.

Section Two: Historical Snapshots

Section Two is made up of three long, bulleted lists of significant events and milestones. In chronological order—Early 1980s, Mid 1980s, and Late 1980s—these offer an amazing range of firsts and turning points in American history, including a few "can you believe it?" facts.

Section Three: Economy of the Times

One of the most interesting things about researching an earlier time is learning how much things cost and what people earned. This section offers this information in three categories—Consumer Expenditures, Annual Income of Standard Jobs, and Selected Prices—with actual figures from three specific years for easy comparison and study.

At the end of Section Three is a Value of a Dollar Index that compares the buying power of $1.00 in 2015 to the buying power of $1.00 in every year prior, back to 1860, helping to put the economic data in *This Is Who We Were In The 1980s* into context.

Section Four: All Around Us

There is no better way to put your finger on the pulse of a country than to read its magazines and newspapers. This section offers 29 original articles, book excerpts, speeches, and advertising copy that influenced American thought from 1980-1989.

Section Five: Census Data

This section includes invaluable data to help define the 1980s such as State-by-State comparative tables, and actual reprints from the Census of Population, including a Special Report titled *We the Americans*. Here you will find detailed population, social and economic characteristics. This section also includes dozens of maps and charts for easy analysis.

This Is Who We Were In The 1980s ends with a comprehensive Further Reading section and a detailed Index.

The editors thank all those who agreed to be interviewed and share their personal photos for this book. We also gratefully acknowledge the Prints & Photographs Collections of the Library of Congress.

1980: Alberto Enriquez, Sergeant First Class, Desert One Mission: Iran

When his Delta unit was called to Iran to rescue 53 hostages in the American Embassy, Sergeant First Class Alberto Enriquez was ready and willing to serve his country.

Life at Home

- Alberto Enriquez was a professional and proud of it.
- While many of his friends schemed to avoid the draft, Alberto volunteered to serve his country.
- He enjoyed his time in the 101st Airborne Division, and when the opportunity presented itself, was quick to join the 75th Ranger Regiment—the men called upon for the really tough jobs.
- When he heard a new unit called Delta was being formed to specialize in counter-terrorism, he knew where he belonged.
- He especially loved the challenge of the new unit: The physical requirements were rigorous, only men of sergeant rank and above were eligible, and excellent performance reviews were needed.
- Alberto grew up in the Mexican section of Denver; his grandparents had been illegal immigrants from Mexico.
- His father served in the Second World War, earning a bronze star for bravery.
- A small pair of American flags and a picture of the current American president—Democrat or Republican—always hung in his house.
- In school, Alberto earned better-than-average grades, played some football and ran track.
- After school and most Saturdays he worked in his father's suburban landscaping business, the success of which paralleled the growth of rapidly expanding Denver.
- When Alberto joined the army following graduation, he realized almost immediately that he had found his place, and after a few years set sights on being the best sergeant in the army.
- Yet his father was unhappy; he wanted his son to be an officer.
- Alberto demurred; sergeants, he knew from experience, were the guys who got the real work done in the military.

Sergeant First Class Alberto Enriquez was a professional soldier.

- His wife had grown up in the same neighborhood in Denver, graduated from the University of Colorado and became a nurse.
- Over the years, Alberto had also attended college classes under various training programs, but getting a degree remained secondary to his military career.
- They both loved the military life—its discipline, purpose and focus.
- Most of all, Alberto enjoyed the opportunity to fight on behalf of his country—even for the ones who, he felt, did not fully appreciate what it took to have a great military to protect America.
- The selection process for Delta, or 1st Special Forces Operation D, as it was known, was both exhilarating and the most grueling experience of Alberto's life.
- Each candidate had to perform a 40-yard inverted crawl in 25 seconds, 37 sit-ups in a minute, 33 pushups in a minute, a run-dodge-jump obstacle course in 24 seconds, a two-mile run in 16 minutes, 30 seconds, and a 100-meter swim fully clothed, including boots.
- Those who met these standards were then subjected to an 18-mile speed march followed by an exercise in which each man, equipped with a map, a compass and a 55-pound pack, traversed heavily wooded mountain terrain from one rendezvous point to another in a prescribed time.
- Then there was a psychological evaluation that lasted four hours.
- In addition, each prospective Delta Force member was required to have a special skill.
- Alberto spoke Spanish, Portuguese and Italian; he was also a skilled rock climber.
- His acceptance into Delta was one of the high points of his life.
- His wife arranged for a romantic celebration dinner—without their 10-year-old son—at one of Fayetteville's finest restaurants.
- Even Alberto's father said he was proud, although talked more about son Ricardo, who was now a partner in an insurance company.

Life at Work

- A basic Delta operating group consists of four men armed with light weapons, pistols, rifles, machine guns and grenade launchers.
- Each is given latitude in selecting the weapons that best suit his style and the demands of the mission.
- Alberto preferred a German-made machine gun that can fire fully automatic or single shot at a rate of 900 rounds per minute with an effective range of 1,200 meters.
- Alberto was proud of his efficiency and skill.
- One exercise that demonstrated his judgment involved entering a multi-room structure filled with both "captors" and "captives."
- Without warning, silhouettes pop up representing the enemy or a hostage; Alberto had to make a split-second evaluation of whether to shoot or hold his fire.
- It was a point of great personal pride for Alberto that rarely did a captive take a bullet, while stacks of the enemy were riddled with slugs from his HK-21.
- Alberto believed he was ready for the real thing and just in time to play a role in a world crisis.
- When Iranian students captured the American Embassy in Tehran, Alberto knew immediately that the rescue of the hostages was a job for Delta.
- Since the Shah of Iran was deposed by Islamic fundamentalists led by Ayatollah Khomeini, tensions against anything American escalated in Iran.
- Within days of the embassy invasions, intelligence units delivered detailed drawings of the compound where 53 American hostages were being held, as well as routes to and from the embassy through the city of Tehran.
- They also provided information on the captors, how they were armed, and their possible plans for the hostages.

- Soon Alberto and his unit were assigned to a remote training site in the North Carolina woods dubbed Camp Smoky.
- There, as new information was delivered, they trained, retrained and prepared for the mission ahead.
- Over the next three months, they were called up six times, only to be told to stand down each time.
- As frustration grew, Alberto did not know whether the military or the politicians were calling the shots, and though he tried to remain silent, he often failed.
- Daily, the newspaper and television reports made America and its military look impotent and cowardly while the 53 hostages awaited their fate at the hands of religious fanatics.
- In April, Delta got the seventh call.
- On the plane, the highly trained warriors of Delta said little; there was no need for nervous chatter—the trademark of less seasoned troops, Alberto believed.
- After the plane landed in Egypt for a short stay, Alberto's unit was flown to a small island off the coast of Oman.

The selection process for Delta was both exhilarating and grueling.

- From there, six C-130 transports—three filled with troops and three loaded with fuel—flew into the Iranian desert to a site called Desert One.
- The mission was finally under way.
- There, they unloaded the transport plane and waited to be met by the eight CH-53 Sea Stallion helicopters, which were flying in from the aircraft carrier *USS Nimitz*.
- The helicopters' role was to fly two hours and 13 minutes toward Tehran and place the Delta Force to within 50 miles of their destination.
- Eight trucks were to take the Delta Force into the hostile city; once the hostages were free, the helicopters would get them and their rescuers out.
- In the heat of the desert, a force of 120 men, including 90 from Delta, 12 drivers, an interpreter and 13 other Special Forces, waited silently.
- During the final briefing, Alberto was told that only about 15 student radicals guarded the embassy compound.
- Only three or four guards would be outside, one of whom habitually leaned his rifle against the wall; stories about extensive booby traps and mines appeared to be false.
- After nightfall, he was told, his unit would first be flown by helicopter, then driven through the city to the embassy.
- The hostages would be freed and the captors taken out before sunrise.
- The rescue helicopters were to meet them either in the embassy compound or the soccer field across the road.
- Hostages and soldiers would then be flown by helicopter to a captured Iranian airfield 38 minutes away, where large transport planes would fly them to freedom in Egypt.

- That was the plan; bold, simple and logical.
- At the appointed hour, Alberto was more than ready, waiting in the desert for the first leg of the trip.
- But the helicopters were late.
- When they finally arrived, the mission was already one hour behind schedule.
- Soon, six helicopters landed instead of eight; two had been forced to turn back because of mechanical problems.
- The mission was redesigned around six helicopters.
- Alberto then heard angry voices from the officers in charge.
- As more officers gathered, the shouting increased.
- One of the six helicopters could not fly.
- His commander said the mission was aborted; without explanation, he ordered Alberto and his men to reload the C-130 transports and depart.
- The helicopters would fly empty back to the *Nimitz* in the Coral Sea.
- Disgusted and in shock, Alberto was reloading the transport when, as one of the refueled but empty helicopters attempted to lift off from the desert floor in the dark, it collided with a parked C-130 transport and exploded, shooting flames hundreds of feet into the air.
- The men in the airplane were trapped by the flames; eight servicemen died almost immediately, and more were badly burned.
- Alberto was despondent; the next day the headlines only heralded failure, not courage.
- Even President Jimmy Carter's statement failed to honor the death of the brave men.

Members of the operating group were given latitude in selecting the weapons that best suited their style and the mission.

Life in the Community: Denver, Colorado and Iran

- As the 1980s began, the focus of international attention became centered on the Islamic nations of the Middle East.
- The first spark came in Iran in 1979, where the attempts of the Shah to westernize his fiercely Islamic country led to a religious backlash led by the Ayatollah Khomeini.
- In February 1979, the rebels laid siege to the headquarters of the élite bodyguard of the Shah; the Islamic Republic that replaced it was based on Koranic law.
- With an official blessing, Iranian students captured the staff of the American Embassy on November 4, 1979, then released all non-American and black hostages.
- The students demanded that the ex-Shah, who was living in New York, be returned to Iran to face charges of murder and robbery in exchange for the hostages.

- President Jimmy Carter refused, and instead began deporting Iranians in America and freezing Iranian assets.
- Six months later, after the failed rescue attempt, Iranian troops exhibited the wreckage and bodies left behind.
- In September 1980, Iran and Iraq went to war, ostensibly over disputed territory of the Shatt al Arab on the Gulf of Arabia, though religious differences had inflamed the dispute.

When students demanded that the ex-Shah be returned to Iran to face charges, President Jimmy Carter refused.

Six months after the failed rescue attempt, Iranian troops exhibited the wreckage and bodies left behind.

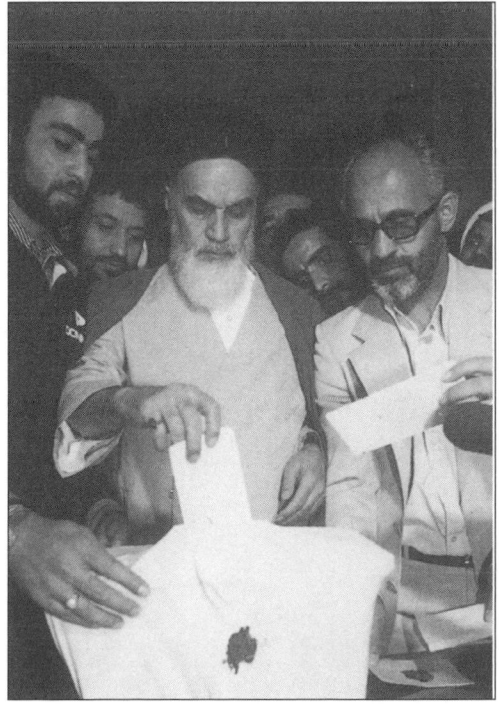

Anti-American tensions in Iran escalated after the Shah was deposed by Islamic fundamentalists led by Ayatollah Khomeini.

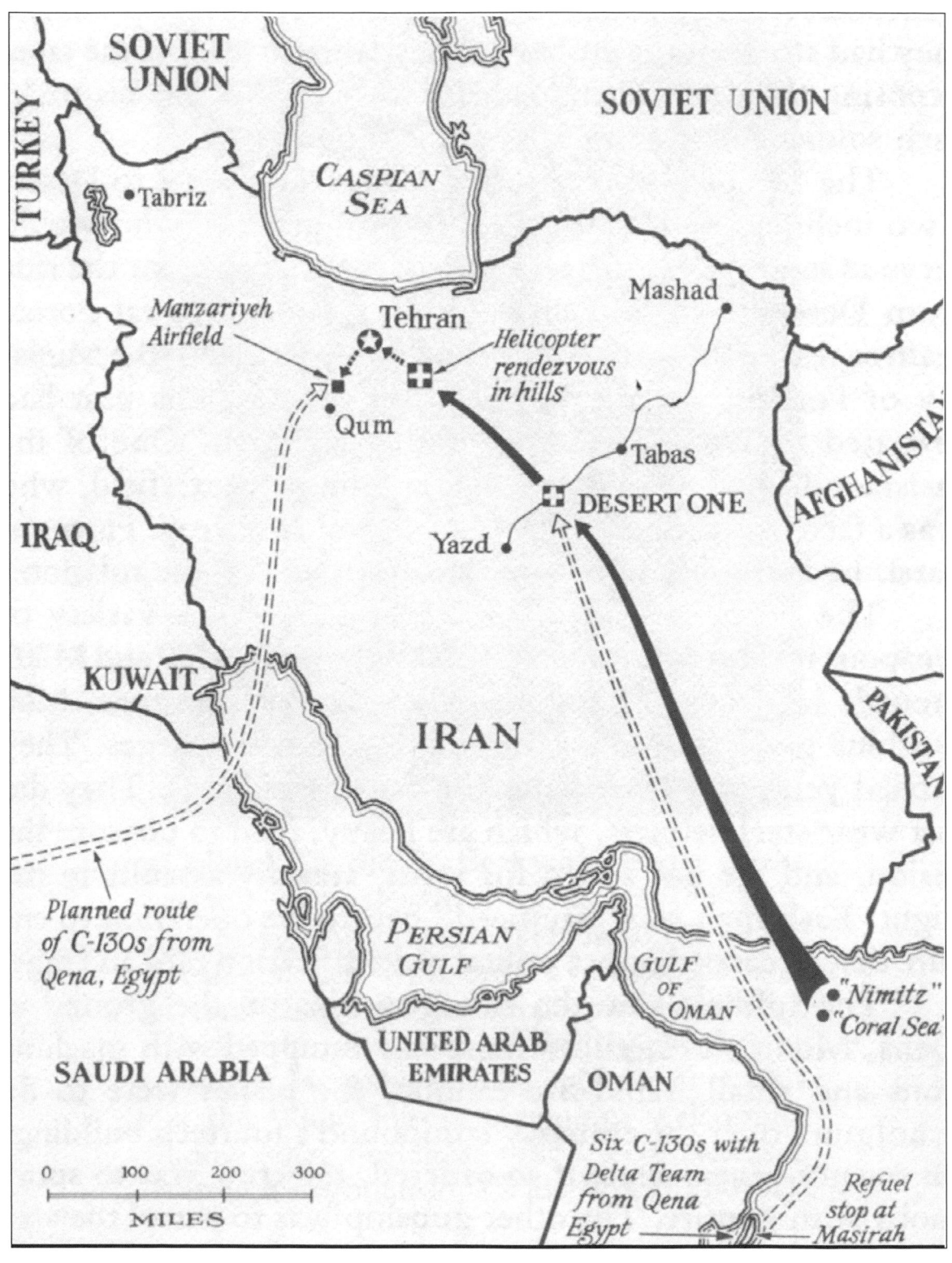

1981: Elizabeth Putnam, 15-Year Old Migrant Worker from New York

Fruit tramp Betty Elizabeth Putnam desperately sought a way out of her migrant life and a chance to stay in one school so she could one day become an English teacher.

Life at Home

- Fifteen-year-old Betty Elizabeth Putnam hated her name and moving around all the time.
- She wanted to live in one house, in one town, and know one group of kids; meeting new people was hard.
- She was named after her grandmother and her mother's favorite actress, Elizabeth Taylor, whom Betty saw in several old movie magazines.
- Betty didn't think she looked like her grandmother or Elizabeth Taylor, and didn't want a used name anymore.
- Sometimes she told her new friends to call her Sugar or Peaches—depending on which school she's attending.
- But at home she was Betty Elizabeth, and in the community she was simply called "a fruit tramp" because her parents were migrant workers and followed the crops.
- Even her parents called themselves fruit tramps, much to her embarrassment.
- Each year, they traveled up the East Coast from Florida to New York picking crops: citrus in Florida; peaches in Georgia; tomatoes, cucumbers and beans in South Carolina; apples, squash and beans in North Carolina; and apples, pears, cherries and cabbage in New York.
- As quickly as one job was finished, the family packed themselves into their ancient Plymouth—with duct tape and paper covering the rear window—and headed up the road looking for more work.
- When the job was big enough and scheduled to take more than a few weeks, the children enrolled in school.
- The little ones were placed in daycare or the older children were given the job of staying home to baby-sit.
- Even the children who attend school had to help in the fields; it took the entire family to make ends meet.
- Betty Elizabeth's oldest sister, Lurken, dropped out of school when she was 14.

Betty Elizabeth Putnam wanted to escape her life as a fruit tramp.

Each year, the family traveled from Florida to New York picking crops.

- Lurken married another fruit tramp and had a baby girl who slept in a makeshift tent during the day while the picking was going on.
- Lurken and her husband often followed the Putnams from place to place seeking work, acting as an extended family work team.
- Betty Elizabeth was determined to graduate from high school, even though she was already at least a year behind her age group.
- Since she was a little girl, she loved language and literature, and dreamt of being a teacher one day.
- The family lived on the beach because, even though they have saved up their money, they couldn't find anyone in the area who will rent to them.
- Betty Elizabeth's father, C. O. Putnam, gained a reputation for heavy drinking, rowdy behavior and a casual attitude toward his financial obligations.
- When it rained, the family huddled under picnic tables in a nearby public park, which also provided them with a bathhouse complete with showers and toilets—if they were not caught trespassing by the police.
- When the weather was turning colder and the Florida citrus season will be starting, C. O. talked about taking the family back down South.
- Besides, more than once the police hinted to him that vagrancy charges were just around the corner.
- He said it didn't matter where they lived because foreigners moved in and took over America; loud and often, he said they were "driving down wages and harming real Americans who are trying to make a living."
- In Florida, the compensation for picking oranges was $0.80 a bushel, but the presence of Latin and Caribbean immigrants drove the wages down to nearly $0.40 a bushel.
- A young, fast picker could gather about 100 bushels a day for about $40 in earnings.
- When the weather was bad, the crops late, or the family is traveling, they earned nothing.
- One year, C. O. and his wife Alfeda earned about $2,800.

- Betty Elizabeth loved her school in Olcott and did not want to leave, but arguing with her father was dangerous.
- C. O. thinks that "Queen Liz," as he called his high-minded daughter when he was drinking, had enough education and should not only move to Florida, but drop out of school and earn her keep in the fields.
- Besides, he knew that Skeeter Matuse, a 26-year-old divorced fruit tramp who often travels the same route as the Putnams, would be happy to take her off his hands.
- Betty Elizabeth's mother, who can sign her name and read street signs, wanted her daughter to chase dreams and get an education, but couldn't cross her husband.

Migrant workers followed the crops, moving from place to place.

Life at School

- By Betty Elizabeth's count, this is the fourth time she had attended a school in Olcott.
- Her English teacher, Mrs. Agardy, was very excited about teaching English and enjoys the girl's enthusiasm, loaning her books and creating a reading list of library books for her, knowing she may leave abruptly.
- After class, they read poems together and discussed what makes a good novel. Betty Elizabeth loved her family, but if they go to Florida when the winter weather arrives, she wanted to stay in New York.
- With the encouragement of Mrs. Agardy, she spent more time in front of the mirror at the bathhouse, combing her hair and pressing her clothes to look like the other children.
- Her teacher bought her some outfits from the local thrift store, and showed her how to do alterations.
- Even though they know she was a fruit tramp and will be gone soon, several girls in the class were nice to her, sharing their makeup and chatting with her during lunch.
- A cute boy even spoke to her several days in a row and wanted to see her outside of school, but she was terrified that he will come to the migrant camp looking for her and see how she lives.
- She first realized she didn't want to be a fruit tramp when she was nine years old and the family was spending Christmas at a large migrant camp where the local people staged a large Christmas Party, complete with food and someone playing Santa Claus.
- During the gift-giving, Betty Elizabeth was given a doll with long, blond hair, rosy-red cheeks and an innocent expression on her face.
- She fell in love with the plastic doll, even though it was missing a leg.
- She got her mother to show her how to make a doll's dress from a piece of light purple cloth, a lilac color that made the doll beautiful and covered the missing leg.
- Then, she tied a cord around the doll's neck and hung it on the wall to make sure everyone knew it was hers alone, and that no one should mess with it.
- Having the one-legged doll made her wonder why her family worked so hard and had so little; she kept thinking, "Is this all there is to life?"
- Almost immediately, she and her doll began to take imaginary journeys together to faraway places where children had bedrooms and friends, and received Christmas presents that didn't include hand-me-down dolls with one leg.

Life in the Community: Olcott, New York

- Olcott's year-round population of about 1,000 swelled significantly in the summer when the community becomes a center for boating and fishing on Lake Ontario.
- New York was unique in that it is the only state which touches both the Atlantic Ocean and the Great Lakes.
- The coastline meanders 127 miles along the ocean, and borders 371 miles of Lake Ontario and Lake Erie.
- Although only about four percent of New York's 18 million-plus people are engaged in farming, it is a leading source of the state's revenues.
- Primary crops included clover, timothy grass, apples and grapes, while secondary crops comprise corn, oats, wheat, peas, peaches, cherries, melons, beans, beets, onions, cauliflower and potatoes.
- Much of this harvest goes directly into the state's canneries and freezing plants; New York was where Clarence Birdseye, of frozen-food fame, developed his technology.

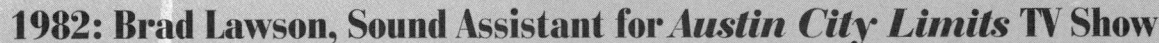

1982: Brad Lawson, Sound Assistant for *Austin City Limits* TV Show

Brad Lawson, who loved music and understood the history of the television music show Austin City Limits, *wanted a job assisting in sound production.*

Life at Home

- Brad Lawson was a certified sound geek—not that anyone really wanted to certify such a thing.
- He felt least alone when nestled beneath a set of headphones listening to music, recordings of truck noise, birds chirping or the noise of city traffic.
- His life's work, as he saw it, was to isolate each sound into its component parts and worship the purity of each tone.
- His real job—the one that paid the rent and put gas in his four-year-old Honda—was working at Music World helping musical neophytes track down the newest album by Judas Priest, Eric Clapton, or U2.
- With an eagerness Brad almost found charming, customers invariably forgot the band's name and were therefore forced to describe, sing or hum the song they had heard and now wished to buy.
- Often he knew in a flash the recording they wanted, but waited patiently to see what the customer was willing to say or sing before Brad provided the solution.
- After work, Brad had begun slowly and meticulously combing through his taped recordings of the first six seasons of the weekly PBS breakout hit *Austin City Limits*, filmed just up the street at a University of Texas studio in his home town of Austin.
- Their sound, he believed, was better and he wanted to know why.
- Ever since Brad got tickets and attended his first show three years earlier at 16, he had been mesmerized by the possibility of accurately reproducing a band's sound for broadcast on television.
- Television's traditional inability to accurately capture the energy and intensity of a rock concert was traceable to TV's poor audio quality.
- Programs were exclusively broadcast via single-channel monophonic transmission, and the speakers on most television sets—even the most expensive—were no larger than an automobile speaker.

Brad Lawson's love of music led to a job on the TV music show, Austin City Limits.

Brad wanted to bring the rock concert experience to the home viewer.

- Brad was interested in inventing the perfect broadcast; he wanted to reinvent the personal experience of attending a rock concert while sitting at home.
- He knew his father would help him with the technical aspects—if he could get his father's attention.
- Four marriages, six children, two jobs and a new relationship with the mother of one of his high school friends—how embarrassing!—kept his father fairly busy.
- Brad's father shared his son's joy at listening to and accurately recording live music; the elder Lawson became a high school band director because he discovered an innate facility for talking to teenagers and he needed a job.
- Brad knew that to be effective, he had to get organized.
- He drew up a list of topics to discuss, including mixing techniques that added texture to the sound, microphone positioning to capture not just the sound, but also the magic that inhabited every well-performed song and the appropriate separation of instrumental tones.
- That's why he had turned his highly focused brain on the qualities of sound that made *Austin City Limits* different.
- He had also begun attending church so he could assist with recording and broadcasting services using the church's new sound equipment.
- That's also where he met a University of Texas sound technician who was often assigned to help out at *Austin City Limits* performances.
- It was Brad's first real chance to peek into the technical side of a commercial studio and explore the creation of *Austin City Limits*—a bold experiment in 1974 even for freethinking public television.

- Not only did the producers initiate the broadcast of long, uninterrupted musical acts before a live audience, but they audaciously booked promising performers who were not necessarily recognized stars.
- Historically, television had devoted relatively little time to live music beyond the lip-synched choreography of American Bandstand.
- To handle the sound quality limitations of television, many music programming efforts such as The Midnight Special emphasized quantity over quality and featured a parade of rotating acts who played two or three songs each.
- Further handicapping its appeal, *Austin City Limits* was not about the hottest music around; its focus was on the traditional R&B and country music favored in Central Texas.
- While the entire music industry was changing and embracing punk, *Austin City Limits* was looking back to its roots, critics charged.
- Austin resident Willie Nelson was the first featured artist on the pilot episode of *Austin City Limits* broadcast in 1975.

Lyle Lovett was a regular on Austin City Limits *and very much appreciated the genuine quality of its music and musicians.*

- At that time, Austin was not widely recognized for its musical heritage.
- In 1976, the original members of Bob Wills' Texas Playboys reunited for the first time in 30 years for their performance on *Austin City Limits*; three members of the band would pass away later in the year.
- *Austin City Limits'* theme song, "London Homesick Blues," which included the line "I wanna go home with the armadillo," became a regular feature of the show in 1977, the same year that Fleetwood Mac's album Rumours held the #1 spot on the Billboard 200 for 31 weeks, and performer Kenny Rogers re-emerged with his hit "Lucille."
- When the soundtrack to the movie Saturday Night Fever by the Bee Gees swept disco into dominance in 1978, *Austin City Limits* showcased Nashville country stars Chet Atkins and Merle Haggard.

Bonnie Raitt performed on Austin City Limits.

- A new producer of *Austin City Limits* ushered in a more diverse lineup in 1979: Tom Waits, Taj Mahal, Lightnin' Hopkins, and the Neville Brothers, and in 1980 inaugurated the first "Songwriter's Special," including performances by Ray Charles, Jerry Jeff Walker, and Carl Perkins.
- The following year, when the 24-hour music video channel MTV debuted, *Austin City Limits* held an "Instrumental Showcase" featuring the mandolin playing Tiny Moore, Jethro Burns, Johnny Gimble and David Grisman.

- Then, in 1982 the skyline of Austin appeared as the show's painted backdrop, giving the image of the Texas capital an added boost and prompting viewers worldwide to fret about how possible rain showers would impact the show.
- Austin's skyline was modest in height and spread out to preserve the view of the Texas State Capitol Building from various locations around Austin, but it established a mood—a home—for the weekly performances.
- Since the show was taped six to nine months in advance of broadcast, the featured performers' tour schedule often dictated when the recording would be made.
- The free tickets were precious.
- Crowds lined up around the block for the limited seating; having Lone Star beer as a sponsor didn't hurt.
- At one point, University officialdom objected to free beer, but relented when it became clear that the audience was packed with music lovers, not party animals.

Life at Work

- For Brad Lawson the news from *Austin City Limits* could not have been better; sound quality would be a high priority in the 1982 season, recorded in 1981.
- The nationwide success of *Austin City Limits* had made the booking of talent—Kris Kristofferson, Emmylou Harris, Crystal Gayle—much easier.
- Concurrently, sound technology as a craft was improving and was now a priority.
- As a first step, 40 stations, including those in the trendsetting markets of Los Angeles, Chicago, and Atlanta, would be broadcasting the show in stereo.
- Discussion was also underway concerning the purchase of an additional two-inch, 16-track mixer and the addition of high-caliber microphones that could more accurately capture the authentic sound.
- A mixer was designed to mesh an array of inputs into a few controllable outputs; Brad was overwhelmed by the oceans of knobs when he was allowed to attend his first *Austin City Limits* taping as an assistant's assistant with instructions to touch nothing.
- With a dozen microphones ringing the area, all the musicians were required to do was to play their best.
- One of the show's greatest assets was its four-story ceiling, which enhanced the sound.
- *Austin City Limits* had long distinguished itself with its emphasis on a limited number of acts who were privileged to play for one hour to 90 minutes before a receptive audience.
- The tape would then be edited and broadcast eight months to a year later—after sign-off from the artist.
- Band members always worked well below their usual scale: $500 per show, half that for sidemen; the famous and the obscure toiled for the same minimum wage.
- Thanks to the meticulous care and production quality, the show had earned its place on the TV schedule: 90 percent of all PBS stations carried the show, comprising over 260 stations and reaching 10 million viewers each week.

The success of Austin City Limits *made booking talent–like Emmylou Harris–easier.*

As an assistant's assistant, Brad was overwhelmed by the sound board on the set of the show.

- In addition, an 11-part PBS series entitled Southbound had ignited considerable interest in Southern roots music featuring gospel music, Cajun, bluegrass, fiddling, Mex-Tex, ballad singing and mouth music.
- Brad soon learned that musicians loved the rhythms of *Austin City Limits* because they were asked to perform to an audience, not the red light on a bulky television camera.
- The show was about live music; even the long, lingering shots of the audience—featured in the early years—were shrunk to showcase the performance itself.
- Mishaps were inevitable: Following an afternoon of flawless rehearsals with singer/songwriter Kris Kristofferson, all the lights in the building went out.
- Trapped in the windowless building, the audience and performers alike had to feel their way to the exits in absolute darkness.
- The trouble had been caused by a rat eating through an electrical wire; the audience was readmitted the next night for the taping.
- As an assistant's assistant, Brad was earning more experience than money, and had to keep his sales job at Music World.
- But since the taping schedule ran from July to January, with most PBS stations broadcasting the shows in January through April, he could schedule paid work around heart work.

Life in the Community: Austin, Texas

- Home of the University of Texas, the state legislature, and a more bohemian mindset than most of Texas, Austin became the center of the state's laissez-faire, go-with-the-flow artisans and musicians.
- Local historians trace Austin's musical heritage to the post-World War II decision by booking agent and band manager Johnny Holmes to open the Victory Grill on the city's East Side to showcase local and touring blues and R&B musicians.
- By the 1970s, Austin had room for the city's most psychedelic nightclub, the Vulcan Gas Company, and R&B clubs such as Ernie's Chicken Shack and Charlie's Playhouse.

Home of the University of Texas, the state legislature, and a more bohemian mindset than most of Texas, Austin became the center of the state's artisans and musicians.

- The city developed a gumbo-flavored musical palette, or as one tunes man described it, "freeform-country-folkrock-science-fiction-gospel-gum-bluegrass-opera-cowjazz music."
- The official city slogan promoted Austin as "The Live Music Capital of the World" to honor the live music venues within the area and the long-running PBS TV concert series *Austin City Limits*.
- Many Austinites have also adopted the unofficial slogan "Keep Austin Weird" in defense of the proudly eclectic, liberal lifestyles of many Austin residents, plus a desire to protect small, unique, local businesses from being overrun by large corporations.
- The centrally located Austin was settled in the 1830s on the banks of the Colorado River by pioneers who named the village Waterloo.
- In 1839, Waterloo was chosen to become the capital of the newly independent Republic of Texas and was renamed for Stephen F. Austin, known as the father of Texas.
- Bitter Texas politics, Indian uprisings, Mexican army incursions and the wholesale movement of government documents repeatedly threatened the city's designation as the capital of Texas until 1846.
- In 1860, even though 38 percent of Travis County residents were slaves, voters in Austin and other Central Texas communities voted against secession at the outbreak of the Civil War.
- The opening of the Houston and Texas Central Railway (H&TC) in 1871 vaulted Austin into a major trading center for the region with the ability to transport both cotton and cattle.
- Austin was also the terminus of the southernmost leg of the Chisholm Trail and "drovers" pushed cattle north to the railroad.
- The University of Texas held its first classes in 1883, and the state capital building was completed in 1888.
- In the late nineteenth century, Austin expanded its city limits to more than three times its former area, and the first granite dam was built on the Colorado River to power a new streetcar line and the new "moon towers," which illuminated areas of the city at night.
- In the early twentieth century, the Texas Oil Boom took hold, creating tremendous economic opportunities in Southeast Texas and North Texas.
- The growth generated by this boom largely passed by Austin at first, with the city slipping from fourth largest to tenth largest in Texas between 1880 and 1920.
- Beginning in the 1920s and 1930s, Austin launched a series of civic development and beautification projects that created much of the city's infrastructure and parks.
- In addition, the state legislature established the Lower Colorado River Authority that, along with the City of Austin, created the system of dams along the Colorado River to form the Highland Lakes.
- These projects were enabled in large part because Austin received more Depression-era relief funds than any other Texas city.
- After the mid-twentieth century, Austin became established as one of Texas' major metropolitan centers, attracting companies focused on semiconductors and software.
- The 1970s also saw Austin's emergence in the national music scene, with artists such as Willie Nelson and venues such as the Armadillo World Headquarters.

1982: Greg Tilsner, Software Company Executive from California

Greg Tilsner was chief operating officer of Softec, a software company for personal computers in Los Angeles. His wife, Yukiko, who was second-generation Japanese, worked alongside him.

Life at Home

- Softec was this couple's life; together all day at work, they rarely went home to the apartment they rented nearby.
- All of their friends worked at Softec; occasionally, Yukiko would take a break and fly to see her father in San Francisco, where she grew up.
- Most of Greg's waking hours were spent on the job.
- Working at Softec was like living in a college dormitory; the average age of the employees was 30 years old, and they were crammed into tiny offices two at a time.
- Blue jeans and work shirts were common, and most of the men wore beards and have sideburns.
- The company refrigerator was stocked with Coke, Pepsi, and an assortment of natural fruit juices.
- Every employee, including receptionists, had a computer terminal.
- All the interoffice mail was sent through the company's newest Prime minicomputer.
- Dozens of personal computers, Apples, Radio Shacks, IBMs, and others, were scattered throughout the office, most with their innards permanently exposed.

Most of Greg Tilsner's life revolved around Softec.

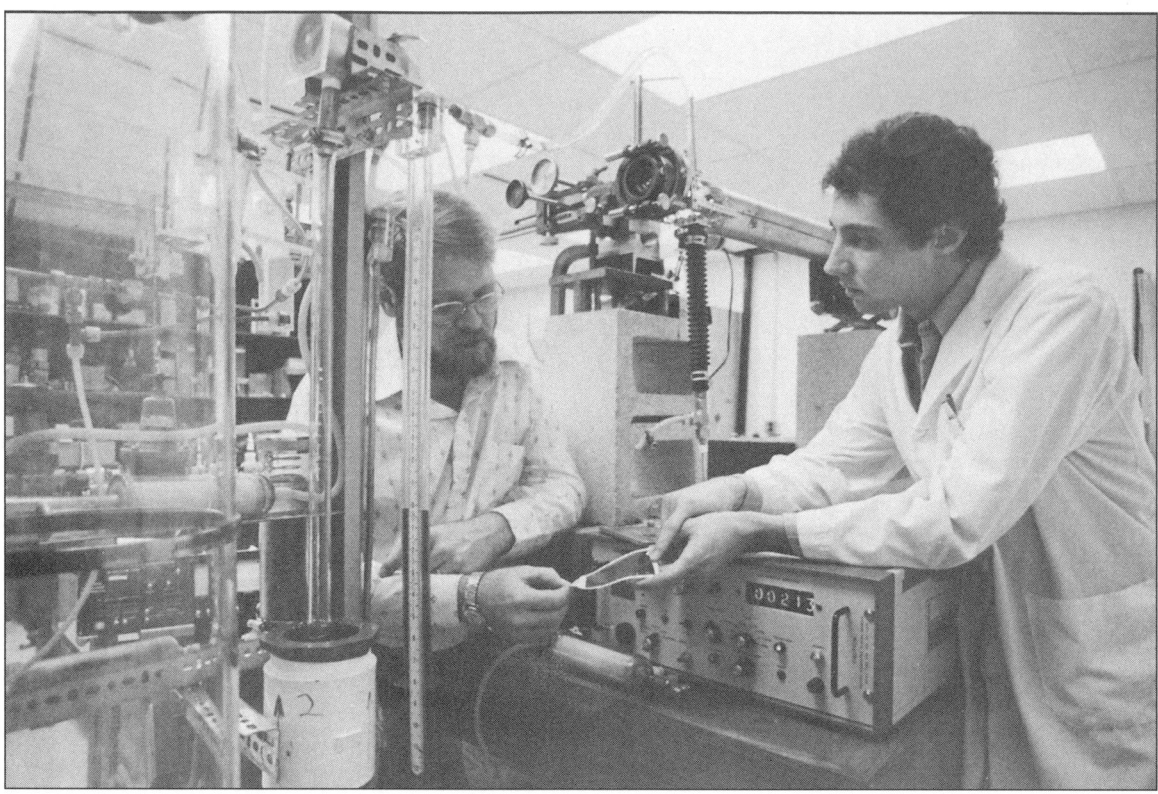

Greg's biggest worry was finding the type of management to help the company grow.

Life at Work

- Greg served as the chief financial officer and day-to-day manager of a Los Angeles-based software company called Softec, which was focused exclusively on providing products for the personal computer market.
- His biggest worry at the moment was finding the type of management the company will need in a year if Softec continues to grow as quickly.
- The company's principal product was a home budgeting program that effectively crunches and organizes a large quantity of numbers; more than 200,000 copies have been sold.
- Initially, the program was designed exclusively for Apple computers; Apple believed the software had helped promote its hardware.
- All of the management was under 30 years old.
- The revenues of Softec were $1 million; the company planned for $2 million and ended with $3 million.
- Management was unsure of how to plan for this year, because in a company only three years old in an industry only five years old, there were few precedents to draw upon.
- The number of employees had grown from four to 35 in the first year, and this year stood at 50.
- Management was trying to grow the company in a controlled way, but felt it was constantly out of control.
- Cautious about making public sales projections, they didn't want too much hype to spoil their progress.

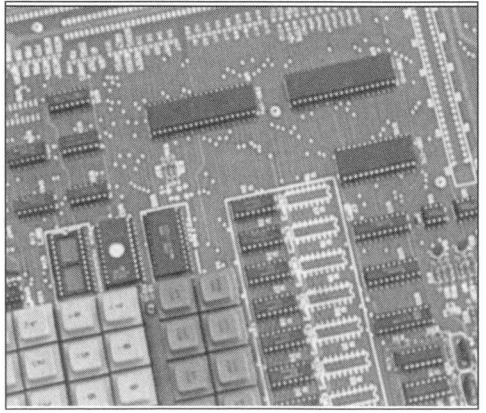

- Greg had a sense that time has sped up; he works 18-hour days, rarely accomplishing as much as he had hoped.
- He began development of the software during college with two partners, slowly developing the concept, often borrowing computers or renting time-sharing terminals to complete the programming.
- After several computer dealers showed little interest in their prototype, Greg and his partners scraped up $20,000 in cash, pledged a loan for $65,000, and bought a Prime 550 minicomputer for the final development of the Softec program.

Life in the Community: Los Angeles, California

- Despite the success of Softec, the general economy was battered.
- The auto industry was burdened with debt, housing activity was slow, and retailers reported sluggish sales.
- Gasoline prices were moving up again as OPEC attempts to push the price of oil to $34 a barrel.
- However, high tech was booming; both California's Apple Computer and New Jersey's Matrix, maker of diagnostic imaging systems, registered seven-fold increases in sales from 1977 to 1981.
- Los Angeles, the largest city area in the country, encompassed 450 square miles and boasted more than 10 million population in the metropolitan area.
- It was the city of cars; day and night, the freeways and highways are choked with traffic.
- It was also a city of diversity.
- A report indicated that its large Spanish-speaking population was switching to English at about the same rate as the German, Italian, and Polish immigrants who came before them.

"Oh, no. . . . It's Sunday."

1983: Anna Delgado, Anti-Nuclear Weapons Movement Protestor

The daughter of Vietnam War protestors, Anna Delgado first became involved in the Anti-Nuclear Weapons Movement through her activity in rallies held to put a freeze on the growth of nuclear weapon stockpiles.

Life at Home

- Though only 21 years old, Anna Delgado spent two years actively working for the nuclear freeze movement-an effort to stop the development of weapons that could potentially destroy the world's population.
- As a result, she saw the inside of a jail for the first time, had long political talks with her parents and found a cause she felt was worth fighting for.
- Throughout the Cold War, the United States competed with the Soviet Union to develop thousands of Intercontinental Ballistic Missiles, or ICBMs, capable of delivering nuclear warheads across the world.
- This growth in potential nuclear destruction disturbed Anna, and she vehemently disagreed with the media's assertion that the growth of nuclear weapons was a method for peace.
- The United States was currently promoting new weapons to maintain the peace, such as the MX missile and the Space Defense Initiative.
- The MX missile would allow the United States to send 10 nuclear warheads in one missile halfway around the world with deadly accuracy.
- The Space Defense Initiative-a satellite system that would destroy incoming missiles attacking America-was nicknamed "Star Wars" and attacked by critics as unlikely to succeed.
- This was in addition to the thousands of Minuteman missiles already in place and prepared to be launched at targets around the world in the event of a nuclear attack.
- While attending the University of Pennsylvania, Anna first got involved in the nuclear movement by participating in several rallies intended to persuade the U.S. and other governments to freeze the number of nuclear weapons.
- Finding the time to participate in protests was a challenge-her obligations to her college

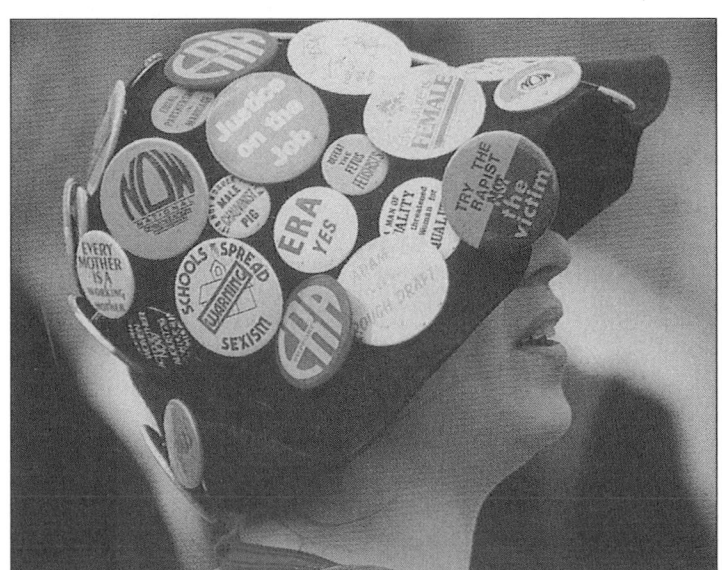

Anna Delgado worked for the nuclear freeze movement.

coursework in elementary education and her part-time job left little time to be involved in the movement.

- But by attending the protests, she discovered a strong connection to what her parents believed in and the need to thwart the growing war establishment.
- Both her mother and father had protested the Vietnam War, especially after her older brother went "missing in action" in 1972.
- She vividly remembered attending anti-war rallies with her mother a decade earlier.
- Regretfully, it did nothing to help bring her brother back home.
- At nuclear weapons rallies, Anna carried one of her two protest picket signs designed by her father: "End the Arms Race NOW!" and "Women for Peace."
- Anna saw this movement as a "New Abolitionist Movement" and was proud of being part of a national effort.
- This concept was reinforced when she read a *Rolling Stone Magazine* article on the subject in March.

- At the protest rallies off-campus in the city, Anna was one of the youngest protesters; the vast majority were working professionals 10 or 20 years older, often with families.
- Also at these rallies were religious people, especially those with Christian backgrounds, who viewed the development of nuclear weapons as immoral.
- Some of the older protestors had worked to elect politicians in Congress who would support a bilateral freeze of nuclear weapons with the Russians and stop the proliferation of nuclear devices, weapons, and generating plants, all nicknamed "nukes."
- During the prior year's elections, these activists worked nationwide to support candidates in 45 election races in the House of Representatives on this issue.
- Pro-freeze candidates won 36 of the races.
- Over 1,500 different peace groups across the country were backing the freeze.
- Yet the majority of Americans still believed that the best way to be safe from Communist domination was to build the biggest weapons.
- At the rallies Anna attended in Philadelphia, she was often confronted by supporters of the government's nuclear arms policy, who called her a "dupe of the Kremlin."
- They insisted that the American Pro-Freeze rallies were hurting the United States' effort to negotiate with the Soviets.
- They were also called "freezeniks," along with other references of being communists and traitors to America.
- During one of the protests, an older woman told Anna about a women-only protest at the Seneca Army Depot in New York planned for the summer.
- The summer protest was called the Women's Encampment for a Future of Peace and Justice and would operate from July 4 to Labor Day.

- Through the summer, the encampment would condemn the nuclear weapons the U.S government was storing on-site, including the Pershing cruise missiles for shipment to Western Europe.
- The location was also chosen for its close proximity to Seneca Falls, where the first women's rights convention occurred in 1848.
- Anna knew immediately that she wanted to participate.
- With help from friends, she arranged to sublease her apartment during the summer and saved money to cover expenses for six weeks.
- Anna packed her Ford Pinto with camping gear, her "comfy" sleeping pillow, her protest signs, several changes of clothes, three milk gallon jugs of water, four cartons of Virginia Slims cigarettes and three grocery bags full of rice, beans and canned vegetables.
- By the end of June, Anna left her parents' home in Columbia, Maryland, and traveled to Romulus, New York-the location of the women's encampment.

Life at Work

- When Anna Delgado arrived in Romulus, New York, at the Women's Encampment for a Future of Peace and Justice, the grounds were already full of women from all over the United States.
- Many saw this protest as a way to protect their families from nuclear war, but others supported a range of feminist and peace issues.
- Some believed that women-centered protests enabled the world to see women as the caretakers of the world and of families.
- All women were encouraged to volunteer for many duties; Anna decided to help prepare the vegetarian meals for the attendees during her stay.
- The opening day of protest on July 4 was full of excitement and debate.
- One early controversy was whether to accept an American flag from a local community leader for the women to fly on the encampment property.

SIERRA CLUB RADIOACTIVE WASTE CAMPAIGN

- Many of the women were conflicted because the American flag held mixed symbols of militaristic nationalism and of benevolence.
- Some felt that an international peace camp should not fly any nation's flag.
- The women decided not to fly the flag, but to permit the women to create their own flags the size of a pillowcase to hang on a clothesline.
- The local community did not receive the decision favorably.
- Anna was thrilled with the first day's activities, which started with approximately 500 women gathered to pledge their allegiance to the earth, for the life it provides and for peace and beauty for all.
- Later she and the others followed a Buddhist woman beating her drum while they walked slowly, chanting "All we are saying is give peace a chance."
- As the women marched past the Seneca Army Depot gate, they planted two rose bushes-one red, one white-as symbols of life.
- Later, the women lined up holding up their hands in a triangular shape known as a "yoni," or ancient goddess symbol, which became the sign of the women's resistance to the Depot.
- Four local veterans planted little American flags by the two rose bushes outside the depot, saluted and walked away.
- The opening day's protest was peaceful and viewed as a successful beginning.
- Peaceful protest continued daily at the Seneca Army Depot with other symbols that showed the strength of women.
- Women formed in circles or webs-both signs of unification, strength, and the world's connectivity.
- The interconnected web was painted on a number of the structures around the camp.
- In another symbolic act, the protestors tied onto the Army Depot's fence possessions they did not want to lose in the event of a nuclear war.
- Items included photos of families and children.
- Anna tied a number of webs to the fence with photos of her parents, her friends and the family dog.
- She wanted to put her missing brother's photo on the fence, but she was afraid of losing one of her few remaining mementos of him.
- Anna shared her grief of losing her brother in Vietnam with some of the friends she made at camp; they encouraged her to hold on to the photo until he was found.
- Over the next couple of weeks of protests, hundreds of women arrived to condemn the nuclear weapons on the base.
- Over time, the women expanded their civil disobedience by climbing over the Seneca Army Depot's fence to protest.
- Anna was a bit hesitant at first to participate in this aggressive form of protest.
- The women who climbed over were arrested by military police and detained on the post, fingerprinted, photographed and given letters barring them from re-entering the property.
- Anna climbed over the fence one hot summer morning.

- Immediately she was arrested by a military police sergeant and handcuffed while chanting "Peaceful women wanting peace."
- After a couple of hours of military arrest, Anna was fingerprinted and awarded her "bar letter" prohibiting her from re-entering the site.
- Anna was excited and immediately went to a pay phone to call her parents about the arrest, receiving her bar letter and the good she was doing for the world.
- They were happy for her but cautioned her not to do anything that would hurt her professionally in the long run.
- After the call, she jumped up and down with glee.
- She now had documented proof that her protests were impacting the military, and it further validated her efforts in the Freeze Movement.

Life in the Community: Seneca, New York

- Local residents in the Seneca, New York area had issues with the women protesters.
- Some tried to welcome the women but received little community support.
- Residents were also concerned about the added cost and attention the protest brought to the community and feared that it might cause the closure of the military base.
- Anna and the women did not want the base to close, but to be used for something peaceful to the community.
- Regardless of how often the protesters communicated this message, the residents were worried that jobs would be lost.
- Times had been tough and didn't need to get tougher.
- Also, the community was shocked by the broad feminist nature of the protests, which ranged from nuclear weapons to sexuality, religion and the concerns of oppressed women.
- A large number of the residents were simply offended by the alternative lifestyles the women were supporting and viewed the protest as un-American.
- Anna often spent time discussing these concerns with the other women: Would the locals come to see their point of view or should the women attempt to improve relations with the local community?
- Most in the discussion agreed that there was little that could be done to improve the situation.
- The community's wariness exploded during a planned 15-mile feminist walk from Seneca Falls to the Peace Camp on Saturday, July 30.
- The women communicated this planned march to local officials along the route, including the town of Waterloo near the women's encampment.
- On that Saturday, when Anna and hundreds of women entered Waterloo, they wore white bibs printed with historically important women's names, such as Elizabeth Cady Stanton and Susan B. Anthony.
- At the Waterloo Bridge, they encountered 300 local residents waving American flags with a 20-foot banner in front saying, "Many Men and Women Have Earned the Right for Anyone to Protest in America. Respect Them, Our Flag, and Our Country."
- Some of the local residents were holding American flags or cardboard signs that said, "Go Home," "We're Proud to Be Americans," and "Pinko Lesbians, Go Home."
- They were also chanting "America" and screaming at the women, "Go home" and "Go protest in Russia."
- The local citizens' counter-protest blocked traffic and the flow of the women marchers for a period of time.
- Local law enforcement was fearful of a riot at the bridge.
- Anna was concerned; she had never seen so much anger and hatred from those who opposed her.
- Instead of trying to cross the bridge, the women decided to stop and sit in the road.

- Many of the women were becoming angry at the comments and expletives coming from the bridge.
- Within a short time, both sides were yelling at each other.
- The moment became extremely frightening when a man with a rifle approached the women.
- Fortunately the police apprehended the man and arrested him immediately.
- After two hours of tension between the two groups, the officers instructed the women to leave and return to the encampment.
- The women refused because the local citizens, not the women, were illegally blocking the road.
- The police disagreed.
- A number of the women, including Anna, held their ground until the police dragged them away and arrested them.
- As each was hauled away, the local citizens cheered and encouraged the police.
- The authorities charged 53 women from the encampment for disorderly conduct at the bridge.
- The only local resident arrested was the man with the rifle.
- Because there was little space in the sheriff's department jail, a makeshift jail was established at a school away from Waterloo in Seneca County.
- It was stuffy, confusing and maddening.
- The women supported each other during the next several days while in prison at the school.
- Anna thought about calling her parents for help, but the other women convinced her that she had done nothing wrong and should go free.
- Each day when she thought she should call, she decided to wait one more day.
- She even thought of trying to escape as two women did while imprisoned at the school.
- After several days, the local authorities dropped all charges on the women.
- While Anna was under arrest, approximately 2,000 women protested at the Seneca Army Depot.
- Over 200 were arrested for peacefully trespassing onto the federal property.
- Upon returning to the women's encampment, Anna heard rumors that the locals may cause further harm to the women.
- Rumors of bombings or burnings were bruited for a couple of days.
- With all the excitement and stress over the past several weeks, Anna's time at the camp came to an end.
- She headed home and prepare for her final year at the University of Pennsylvania and the next confrontation with the military establishment.

1983: Maggi Taylor, 23-year-old Boom Operator in NYC

At age 23, Maggi Taylor arrived in America from Australia with her husband, Richard, a New York City foreign correspondent. When Richard went back to Australia, Maggi chose to stay in America.

Life at Home

- Maggi Taylor was born in 1943 in Sydney, New South Wales, Australia; her sister Jenny was born two years later.
- Her parents split up shortly after Jenny's birth; her mother, with her two daughters, moved in with her parents.
- Her mother left for long periods of time to find work, and "Margaret" and her sister were left almost entirely in the care of their grandmother.
- Maggi was sent to boarding school at age 12, and although she came home for holidays and summer break, The Glennie School for Girls, in Toowoomba, Queensland, was her home until she graduated at age 18.
- Although she was a very bright and friendly girl, Maggi almost always felt alone.
- After graduation, and against her mother's wishes, she defiantly ran off and married Richard, a young writer she had met just a year before while on school break.
- It was 1962, and Maggi and Richard moved to New Zealand, where he had a job; she found work there on a radio station, something an inexperienced young woman could not have done in Australia.
- New Zealand needed educated workers of all kinds, and businesses were willing to hire women.
- The job away from home helped prepare her for her move to America in 1966.
- Since childhood, Maggi had been called by her given name, Margaret.
- On her first day in New York, when asked her name, she said, "It's Maggi"; she knew right then that America was the beginning of a new life.
- As a foreigner in a foreign land, she could truly be herself—not her mother's daughter, not the lonely girl in boarding school, and not just her ambitious husband's wife.

Maggi Taylor left Australia when she was 23.

Glennie School for Girls, Queensland.

- Twenty-three-year-old Maggi and husband Richard lived in New York, where Richard worked as a foreign correspondent from 1966 to 1968, and then both returned home to Australia.
- It wasn't until she was back in Australia, faced with the old familiar attitudes and inhibitions, that Maggi realized she wanted to return to America.
- Then in 1973, after five years away from the United States and her first taste of America, to Maggi's delight, Richard was again assigned to New York.
- As a foreign journalist, he entered the country on an H-1 visa, giving him the right to work and stay in the U.S.
- Spouses, mostly wives of H-1 workers, were technically visitors, but were given a complimentary H-2 visa, so that they would not have to exit and re-enter the country every six months to renew a visitor's visa.
- The H-2 visa was not exactly a working visa, but near enough.
- A much-Xeroxed copy of a notice from the Immigration and Naturalization Service (INS) circulated among the wives that stated that as long as the H-1 visa holder was legally employed, the INS permitted the spouse to work, too.
- Through her connections with the Australian community, Maggi got a job in the Australian Consul as a receptionist.
- She then worked at the UN for United Nations English Language Radio, which eventually led to her career as a boom operator in the film and television industry.

- When in 1980, after seven years in America, Richard returned to Australia, Maggi chose to remain behind.
- Since the late 1970s, Maggi and Richard had been navigating very rocky marital terrain.
- Maggi often worked late on a movie or television shoot or was on location for days, sometimes weeks at a time.
- As a news reporter, Richard had a schedule that was even more erratic and which included lots of out-of-town trips and lots of hotel bars.
- Richard was becoming an alcoholic, and there were other women.
- After his trips, often marked by unaccounted-for absences from his hotel room, Richard would return home contrite, affectionate, and determined to tell almost all to soothe his conscience, regardless of how much it hurt Maggi.
- She forgave him each time and they drifted back to their fractured home life.
- In the spring of 1980, Richard quit his job in order to work full-time on a novel.
- He had a publisher and a contract, but the writing wasn't going well; he said he needed to devote more time to the writing.
- He said he needed to be alone.

Maggi and Richard in NYC.

- Soon afterward, in June, he left for Newport, Rhode Island, where he met Joan, a visiting, well-off Australian widow.
- She was there enjoying the sunny days; it was, after all, winter in Australia, but she planned to go back to Sydney at the end of August.
- Maggi was working on a film in New Hampshire, and she and Richard talked on the phone every couple of days and even met up when she could get a day off.
- She sensed that something was wrong—more wrong than usual.
- He said the writing wasn't going very well.
- At the end of August, Richard returned to New York, but within a month he left for Australia, claiming research for his book.
- While paying the past month's phone bill, Maggi noticed an unusual number of calls to an unknown number in Australia.
- She called the number and got Joan and Richard at the other end.
- After many heart-wrenching calls back and forth, he and Maggi decided to separate; with or without Joan, he wanted to stay in Australia.
- With or without Richard, Maggi wanted to stay in America.

Life at Work

- By the time Maggi and Richard Taylor decided to break up, she found that she was surprisingly relieved, and realized that she did not want him to come back.
- She had started building a career and a life, and in his absence, she realized that she had been lonelier when they were together than she was now.

- She began the long, arduous, and expensive process to get a work permit and then a Green Card so that she could stay in America on her own as a permanent legal immigrant.
- This legal journey would take many letters of inquiry, many phone calls, many forms to fill out, a second set of lawyers, a trip back to Australia, and four years of appointments and paperwork to reach her goal.
- Because of the nature of her work, there were more than the normal delays; she often had to be out of town on location for a shoot, and had to postpone appointments.
- Sometimes she spent 14 straight hours on the set, and could do nothing when she got off work but sleep.
- She never knew on the job how long a sequence would take, or how many takes it would require.
- A missed appointment could mean a long wait before another could be scheduled; government bureaucracies, she came to understand, did not operate on "show biz" time.
- She had to wait for downtime between shoots to write letters, fill out forms, and meet with lawyers or government officials.
- The process dragged on.
- To start the process, she first needed to submit an Application for Alien Employment Certification to the U.S. Department of Labor, Employment and Training Administration; this application had to identify a potential employer and describe the job to be performed.
- Maggi checked all of her film connections and The National Association of Broadcast Engineers and Technicians (NABET) bulletin board; she needed a Sound Man looking for an assistant.
- She heard through the grapevine that Joseph Neeland was looking for someone with multimedia sound experience.
- She had worked on a free-lance project with him in the past, and he was willing to be her sponsor and ready to offer her a full-time job as his assistant.

At United Nations English Radio.

- He needed a boom person with production skills, and she fit the bill.
- Along with the application, she had to show proof that extensive recruitment efforts made by Neeland had produced no qualified U.S. workers.
- He was required to advertise the position in a newspaper of general circulation, such as The New York Times, to run for three consecutive days (not on a Saturday).
- She also had to post the same ad on the NABET bulletin board, and had to formally apply for the job herself.
- She then had to include a copy of the ad, and all of the responses, with her application to the Department of Labor.
- The application required a full job description, work hours and salary.
- The description read: "Applicant must be responsible for correlating materials, processing and dubbing in cassette production. Responsible for supervising transfer of sound material, editing and mixing. Must be familiar will all aspects of sound recording, including studio, motion picture and video techniques, post-production, signal processing editorial procedures, boom work and equipment maintenance."
- The position paid $15,000 per year.
- Her labor certification was filed with the Department of Labor in November 1981, and she was hired by Neeland, using her complimentary H-1 visa, based on her H-2 visa, while she waited.
- She was advised that she should expect to wait another year for permanent residence status, and her application for preference status would have to be submitted to the Immigration Service and to the American Consul in Australia.
- When she was called for a visa appointment, she had to leave the U.S. and report to the American Consul in Sydney.
- She had to produce her birth certificate; the Police/Character Clearance Certificate, attesting that she did not have a police record; and a set of her Non-Criminal Fingerprints taken in New York.
- She also needed four copies of a recent photograph, 11/2 x 11/2 inches, and an update of her job offer, written on her employer's business stationery, and notarized.
- It was a long and costly process, involving lawyers.
- Maggi also had to have a medical examination, including X-rays and blood tests, from a physician who had been approved of in the consular district.
- When everything was in order, her papers were stamped and accepted; her health was perfect, and her past good citizenship was certified—plus, her interview went very, very well.
- She had been coached on what to say to immigration officials, advised to cover up her tattoos—she had several—and had to provide a clean police record from Australia.
- Because of the time difference between the U.S. and Australia, Maggi spent one whole night on the phone (at great expense), and finally got a promise from someone in the police department to send a fax saying that she did not have a police record.
- On the day of the interview she remembered to wear slacks and a turtleneck sweater with long sleeves, and a pleasing smile.
- Once Maggi's application for alien labor certification was accepted, she was free to work and live in the U.S.
- Thanks to her past work in radio, and the fact that she had apprenticed on the set of Contract on Cherry Street, Maggi continued to get work as a boom operator while she applied for a Green Card.
- A boom operator is an assistant of the production sound mixer.
- The principal responsibility of the boom operator is microphone placement, often using a "fishpole" with a microphone attached to the end.
- Sometimes, when the situation permitted, the boom operator used a "Fischer boom," a special piece of equipment that the operator stands for more precise control of the microphone at a much greater distance away from the actors.

- The boom operator also placed wireless microphones on actors when necessary.
- The boom operator was part of the film's crew, employed during the production or photography phase for the purpose of producing a motion picture.
- Crew are distinguished from cast, consisting of the actors who appear in front of the camera or provide voices for characters in the film.
- The crew is also distinct from the production staff, consisting of producers, managers, their assistants, and those whose responsibility falls in pre-production or post-production phases, such as writers and editors.

Maggi had a successful career as a boom operator.

- Communication between production and crew generally passes through the director and his/her staff.
- Medium to large crews are generally divided into departments with well-defined hierarchies and standards for interaction and cooperation among the departments.
- Other than acting, the crew handles everything in the photography phase: props and costumes, cameras, sound, lighting, sets, and special effects.
- Caterers (known in the film industry as "craft services") are usually not considered part of the crew.
- Within a short time, Maggi gained a reputation for excellence and was soon in great demand.
- *Eddie and the Cruisers,* an independent, underground hit, was one of her first feature films; she also worked on the full first season of *Law & Order.*
- Maggi had to put in long hours on various film sets, often six days a week during intensive shooting, and traveled wherever she was needed.
- In 1980 she worked on *Imposters,* directed by Mark Rappaport, which was presented at the Museum of Modern Art's New Directors/New Films series.
- She worked on TV commercials, including ones for BMW and Jumping Jack Shoes, and even an independent horror film, *You Better Watch Out,* starring Brandon Maggart and Jeffrey DeMunn.
- She worked on the American segments of foreign films, traveling to Philadelphia, Ohio and Canada.
- As a woman in a man's business, she knew it was important to establish a reputation of being not only good at her job, but also reliable and available.
- Her made-for-TV movies included *Summer,* part of the Edith Wharton Project for PBS, shot in Keene, New Hampshire, and *We're Fighting Back,* a TV movie based on the Guardian Angels with Ellen Barkin.
- Maggi traveled to Minnesota for the videotaping of a performance for television of *The Wonderful World of Oz,* which was produced by the Children's Television Theatre Company, staged at the Guthrie Center in Minneapolis.
- In 1983 she did *Over the Brooklyn Bridge,* directed by Menahem Golan and starring Elliott Gould, Margaux Hemingway, Sid Caesar and Shelley Winters.

Life in the Community: New York City

- Maggi Taylor found a small apartment in Manhattan on East 22nd Street.
- Although she kept in touch with the friends she had made in the foreign press and the Australian Consul when she had first arrived with Richard, she quickly made friends in the film industry, and spent most of her free time with them because of the odd hours they all worked.
- New York as a city was once again reinventing itself.

- In Greenwich Village, Tower Records was attracting 6,000 to 8,000 customers on an average Saturday to shop, watch MTV on 17 large video screens and learn about emerging groups like Human Sexual Response.
- The New York City Council was addressing potential birth defects by requiring liquor stores, bars and restaurants to post signs saying that pregnant women who drink alcohol were in danger of harming their babies.
- All of this while many New York 11th grade students were sitting through interdisciplinary seminars on "Nuclear Issues."

INS gave Maggi permission to work in America.

1983: Alicia Burack, Civilian (Medical Student), Invasion of Grenada

Alicia Burack's efforts to become a doctor led her through two attempts at the Medical College Admission Test, life on a Caribbean island, a government coup and a military invasion.

Life at Home

- Alicia Burack, known to all as Cia, wanted to be a doctor since she was a small child.
- Cia grew up in a very small town high in the Rockies of southwestern Wyoming near the continental divide.
- There, everyone counted on Dr. Robert McMullen—Dr. Bob—for all their healthcare needs.
- He had been there when Cia broke her right leg, left wrist, and battled the mumps, measles and severe acne.
- Once, when heavy snow kept the vet at bay, he had even nursed Cia's mare Sally through a difficult delivery.
- The Dr. Bob tales involved late night visits, miraculous recoveries and waived fees.
- Cia felt it was her destiny to step into his shoes when he finally decided to retire.
- After graduating from high school as valedictorian, she attended the University of Wyoming, where her grades were strong, particularly in the sciences.
- Her extracurricular activities included forestry rescue, EMT training and time with the local Rescue Squad during summer breaks.
- Everything she did prepared her to become a doctor, until she took the MCAT, the Medical College Admission Test.
- She never did exceptionally well on standardized tests, and this time was no different.
- Though she thought she could handle it if her score was not great, she wasn't ready for the dismal results.
- Two days of tears, three more months of study and another shot at the MCAT brought no improvement.
- Her advisor told her to apply to her chosen medical schools anyway, but add to her list the University of St. George's Medical School in the Caribbean island nation of Grenada.

Cia pursued her dream of being a doctor at the University of St. George's Medical School in Grenada.

- He said the admission standards might be less rigorous and tended to consider the whole person, not just the test scores.
- Cia bristled at the idea of going to a "cop-out" school, but in the end, the only acceptance letter came from the University of St. George's Medical School; she would become a doctor after all, via Grenada.
- There, she discovered the unexpected: a beautiful island paradise controlled by a Marxist government.
- Cia settled down to work in a lush seascape far removed from the mountains of Wyoming.
- She took long swims in the morning, enjoyed rides on a rented horse twice a week, and most important, thrived in the academic, often challenging atmosphere.
- By the time her third year rolled around, she was near the top of her class.
- Dr. Bob had even proposed that he hand over his practice to her once she had the word "doctor" placed before her name.
- The stars were truly aligned this time.

Life at Work

- In early October, third-year medical student Cia Burack heard the first rumors of major political unrest in Grenada.
- According to the stories, the conflict was pitting Prime Minister Maurice Bishop against the Deputy Prime Minister Bernard Coard and his influential wife, Phyllis Coard, Minister for Women's Affairs.
- The two were accusing the charismatic Bishop of not practicing a pure form of Marxism.
- Cia wasn't interested; her thoughts were focused entirely on finishing school.
- Even word that Bishop had been placed under arrest had little impact on her.
- On Wednesday morning, October 19, rumors began to circulate that a large crowd had freed Bishop and was marching on Fort Rupert just a few miles up the coast.
- This development brought more notice on campus; some students began checking the airline schedules.
- Then, word arrived that Bishop and several of his key supporters were dead.
- Immediately, some of the American students started packing, assuming classes would be cancelled, anyway.
- Cia decided to stay in her room, keep her head down and study.
- She was unaware that the execution of Bishop set into motion a chain of events in America; the safety of the students of the University of St. George's Medical School was now a major concern in Washington.
- On short notice, a large-scale mission was assembled, ostensibly to rescue Cia and her fellow students.
- A naval task force carrying a Marine Amphibious Unit was diverted from Lebanon to Grenada.
- Special Forces, including SEALs, Rangers and Delta Force, were called up, along with two brigades of the 82nd Airborne Division.
- Cia got her first real alert of the brewing storm after her usual morning swim, when her parents called to say they were concerned about the unrest.

Aware of the political unrest, some students began packing when they heard that Cuban and Russian soldiers were arriving to fortify the island.

- Then, Dr. Bob called, saying he had waited for retirement this long, and did not wish his replacement to be shot out of the saddle.
- Cia told everyone all was well in Grenada, and that the media were exaggerating the danger, as usual.
- The next day, she heard that Cuban or even Russian soldiers would soon be arriving to fortify the island.
- The only Cubans she had seen were construction workers near True Blue campus; most were friendly and quick to wave hello.
- By Monday, the Grenadians who worked on-campus were becoming increasingly tense, but there seemed to be no threat of violence.
- Early Tuesday morning, when Cia heard booms and thuds to the south, she realized fighting was under way—but who was fighting whom? Were Soviets involved? The Cubans? Where were the Americans? Would she be safe?
- Later that morning, word came from True Blue campus that American troops had landed, and that the students at that campus would be first flown to Barbados and then to the U.S.
- To prepare for the invasion, Navy SEALs had landed before dawn, followed by Army Rangers parachuting into the airport, where 250 Cubans were captured.
- Shortly thereafter, they secured the 500 American students on True Blue campus on the eastern tip of the island.
- The plan was for the soldiers to secure the Grand Anse campus next, though Cia was still unsure of what she was being saved from.
- Movement off of campus was prohibited, and telephone service became intermittent; fortunately, one of the students was a hand radio operator and able to send messages through civilian operators.

To rescue the American medical students, Navy SEALS landed at dawn, followed by parachuting Army Rangers.

- To outsiders in the states, Cia realized her situation appeared desperate.
- According to reports, as the Rangers moved northward to Frequente, west of the Grand Anse campus, they encountered stiff opposition.
- In a metal warehouse near Frequente, American soldiers discovered a large cache of Cuban and Soviet weapons.
- Cia understood little of the politics and knew next to nothing about the principal players, so she was unsure of whom to trust, and pleased that the soldiers would secure the campus in the morning.
- The students reacted in a variety of ways to the situation; two women cried quietly, several made a great production out of packing, while others were angry that anyone would threaten their safety.
- While the sound of battle continued in the distance, few slept.
- Throughout the night, Cia learned about troop movements, shootings, bombings and enemy positions via the hand radio.
- She also heard that some of the medical students at True Blue campus were being asked to help treat the wounded.

Throughout the conflict, Cia became aware of troop movements, shootings, bombings and enemy positions.

- It was very confusing, but clearly American troops were battling Cuban troops, who were on the island to help defend the new Marxist government.
- Dawn brought increased excitement.
- One older student, who claimed ties to the State Department and West Point, instructed everyone to wear long pants and running shoes to make their rescue and evacuation easier.
- He then tore sheets into strips to create white armbands so all 224 students could be easily identified.
- Mattresses were placed in front of the glass doors and windows to protect against flying glass.
- As the hours passed, the rooms became hot; tempers tweaked by fear also flared.
- At 4:30 a.m., intense explosions drove shattered glass into the mattresses; the sound of frequent gunfire was shockingly loud.
- Cia, like many of the students, felt helpless, huddled in the dark waiting for a rescue team.
- Twelve students took refuge in the safest room in the dorm—the bathroom.
- Others kept up their spirits by singing, "The Star-Spangled Banner," "God Bless America" and "You're a Grand Old Flag."
- At noon, the students were instructed to move into 12 dorm rooms close to the beach.
- This required that some people lie two deep on the floor, packed body over body like canned fish.
- The air conditioning no longer functioned, and the heat was stifling.
- Thirty hours had passed since the liberation of True Blue campus.
- Suddenly, Cia could hear the faint sound of a helicopter.
- As it approached, the sound became deafening; the helicopter seemed to be on top of the dorm.
- The door shattered and a huge, fully camouflaged military man toting a giant weapon burst through the opening, fully filling the space.
- "U.S. soldier, freeze!" he barked. "Friend or foe?"
- Cia was the first to respond, "Friend, friend!"
- The soldier quickly organized the students into single-file lines of 40, directing them toward the beach and the military rescue helicopters.
- Cia helped organize the evacuation; she was the last to leave, supporting one woman who sobbed uncontrollably.

- The path to the beach was guarded by a phalanx of armed troopers.
- The 224 students piled aboard the Chinook helicopters, which took them to Point Salines, near True Blue campus; there, a C-141 transport flew them to Charleston, South Carolina.
- At Point Salines, the students paused to drink fruit juice and eat K rations, some of them captured from the Cubans.
- Only after she landed in Charleston and had an opportunity to read a newspaper did Cia understand the size and intensity of the invasion of Grenada.
- Early reports showed that 160 Grenadian soldiers and 71 Cubans died in the fighting, while American deaths totaled 18.
- When she spoke to her parents this time, she made sure everyone knew she was safe, but not as cavalier about the dangers of a Marxist revolution.

Life in the Community: Grenada
- The University of St. George's Medical School in Grenada is located on two campuses several miles apart.
- True Blue campus is near the new airport being constructed by several hundred Cuban workers.
- The 10,000-foot airstrip is costing $71 million to build.
- Cia lived in a dorm near the beach on the Grand Anse campus.
- In addition, some students lived off-campus in an apartment complex.

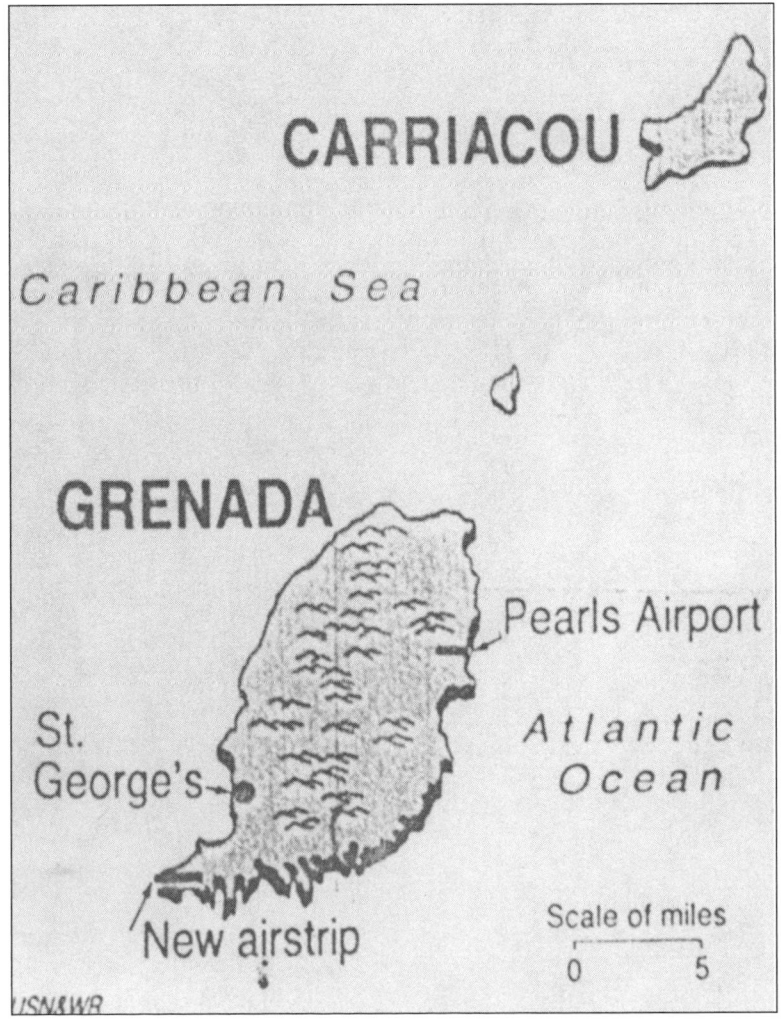

1983: Jim Rosser, National Football League Referee

Jim Rosser was a National Football League referee on weekends, on top of his full-time position as director of personnel for American Furniture Company in Martinsville, Virginia.

Life at Home

- In 1960, Jim Rosser got his first taste of officiating during a newly formed midget league football game in Mooresville, North Carolina.
- The league was formed following a disastrous 0-10 season, and Mooresville High School had hired a new football coach who believed in building a solid foundation for the future.
- He wanted to develop a midget age (six to 12 years old) football program that would supply him with quality players and he needed referees; Jim gave it a try and loved it.
- He earned $10 for calling the first game.
- A year later he was calling high school football games every Friday night, and by 1967 he had broken into the college ranks, refereeing freshman games in the Atlanta Coast Conference.
- By 1970, he was elevated to Atlantic Coast Conference (ACC) varsity games, traveling each week to a different setting and rivalry.
- His regular Saturday stage was a stadium filled with thousands of screaming fans desperate for another win.
- The college ranks, he quickly learned, was a place where the speed of the players and the pace of the game accelerated dramatically.
- "One of the first things I learned was to swivel my head"; otherwise, he would miss a call, and Jim hated to make mistakes or draw attention to himself.
- Football officials always wanted to be invisible, even wearing stripes.
- Major games between in-state rivals could be nerve wracking.
- But as a gangly 6'4", 175-pound tackle for the 1952 Anniston High School football team in Alabama, Jim got some advice to live by from his coach: "if you ever pull on your jockstrap and don't have butterflies in your stomach, take it right back off."

Jim Rosser juggled a full-time job with refereeing for the NFL.

41

The officiating crew was a tight-knit group.

- Nervousness was simply part of the players' preparation.
- When he graduated high school, Jim was an all Calhoun County, Alabama footballer, captain of the Anniston basketball team and sixth man on the golfing team.
- At Auburn University he played freshman basketball, but a bad shoulder ended his collegian athletic career and the scholarship; Jim waited tables to pay the $31-a-quarter tuition.
- After graduation, he was off to Quantico, Virginia, and Camp Pendleton, California, for a stint as a Marine Corps reconnaissance officer.
- In civilian life he found his calling as a personnel director and referee.
- Life was good.
- Jim served seven years as a football official in the Atlantic Coast Conference and was first scouted by the NFL during the 1974 Bluebonnet Bowl and again in the 1977 Orange Bowl.
- On the third play of the Orange Bowl game, Jim was accidentally knocked to the ground; he was then helped to his feet by Ohio State coach Woody Hayes, one of the toughest taskmasters in the game.
- But referees are often remembered best for their mistakes, and Jim had one he would always recall.
- In 1974 he was suspended for a game for blowing a call at Duke.
- He had counted twice and was convinced there were 12 men on the field before he threw the flag.
- The film showed only 11 men on the field.
- So the next week he watched the University of North Carolina-North Carolina State game from the stands instead of the field.
- "It was one of the hardest things I've ever had to do," he said.

Life at Work

- Jim Rosser's first assignment as a National Football League referee was in St. Louis on August 2, 1977-a pre-season game.
- As a rookie referee, he made $325 a game.
- Just as it was the job of 22 highly paid professional football players to do bodily harm to each other on over 100 plays a game, it was Jim's job to control the chaos one play at a time.
- "You have to consciously think about every play. You try to get set mentally on every play. Before the play starts you review what can happen. The first time you don't, something weird happens."
- The NFL first began scouting Jim as a NFL referee four years earlier, conducting extensive background checks, psychiatric testing, FBI-style investigation and comprehensive interviewing.
- He also had a veteran NFL mentor guiding him through the rigorous process.
- Every year more than 120 college referees were considered for five or six slots.
- Initially, Jim was told his application had been rejected; two months later Jim received a phone call from Art McNally, supervisor for NFL officials, who informed him that he been selected to fill aposition which had opened unexpectedly.
- To prepare for his first game as a back judge, Jim watched game films provided by the NFL until deep into the night.
- "First I watched clips of a rookie back judge making key calls; then I watched films of their best back judge making calls. The NFL trains its officials well."
- Back judge is one of the most physically demanding positions in officiating, especially as the pass has come to dominate the professional game.
- Normally, he started 17 yards beyond the line of scrimmage and went full length down the field with the receiver and some of the fastest players in the league.
- Yet, he was supposed to beat them to the goal line.
- During an average game, a back judge will run up to 11 miles.
- Unlike baseball umpires, whose crews rotated positions from game to game, football officials specialized.
- When Jim joined the NFL in 1977, there were six on-field officials: the referee, who lines up behind the offensive backfield; the umpire, who is positioned in the middle of the field behind the defensive line; the head linesman and the line judge, who are on opposite sidelines on the line of scrimmage; the field judge, who stands on the sideline in the defensive backfield, and the back judge, who is positioned in midfield behind the defensive backs.
- A seventh official, the side judge, an across-thefield complement to the field judge, was added in 1978.
- The additional judge provided assistance to Jim and passing plays, whose area of responsibility was 18 to 20 yards ahead of scrimmage.

Jim was excited to make the move from college football to the NFL.

Referees had to be physically and mentally fit.

- Each official played a particular role on every play; officials had to wait for the play to come to them.
- Every call was graded, including his no calls.
- Jim's part-time role as arbitrator in one of professional sports' most violent pastimes was on top of his full-time position as director of personnel for American Furniture Company in Martinsville, Virginia.
- Typically he worked a five-day week and dropped by the office on Saturday mornings to clean up paperwork before flying off to whatever NFL city he was assigned that week.
- Game assignments and locations were made on a weekly basis; Jim was never able to plan his travel in advance.
- Once in the NFL city of the week, he would join the rest of the officiating crew for a meeting, break for dinner and meet again at 9 p.m. to go over game film from the previous week's game.
- The crew, who worked together all season, also ate breakfast together on Sunday mornings to once again go over the basic mechanics of the game.
- Jim then returned home late Sunday night or early Monday morning, after attempting to get some sleep on the plane so he could report to work on Monday morning.
- The NFL flew referees first-class, which was seldom heavily booked on Sunday nights, so he could stretch out across two seats and get some sleep.
- It was the same routine for 107 referees, most of them holding full-time jobs.
- Only 10 NFL officials played pro football themselves.
- Their average age was 48, with 24 years of officiating experience; the NFL required a minimum of 10 years' experience to even be considered.
- To remain eligible, NFL referees were required to complete an exhausting battery of tests annually.
- In addition, a four-day clinic was held each summer that included game films of each official, which were reviewed and offered for critique.

- A 175-question test was taken each spring; the first year Jim missed 18 of the first 20 questions.
- "The test was open book, so you might guess how in-depth each question must be," he explained.
- He also ran daily to keep in shape; Jim hated to lift weights and rarely did.
- He quickly learned that during the game it was not the physical fatigue that wore him down, but the mental wear and tear.
- "It takes total concentration to follow the action; you can't let up, not even for a moment," he remarked.
- With 3,000 plays to watch each year, and each taking only seven seconds on average, a blink of the eye could result in a missed call.
- "It is hard to have a good game officiating a bad blowout game," he said.
- During his second year in the league, a rule change allowed defensive men to chuck or bump a potential pass receiver once near the line of scrimmage, and then only when the receiver was within five yards.
- Another rule change allowed offensive linemen to leave their hands open to block when protecting the passer.
- Jim believed the rule changes made the game safer.
- In 1978, a study on the use of instant replay as an officiating aid was made during seven nationally televised pre-season games.
- And the popularity of the game continued to explode.
- Bolstered by the expansion of the regular-season schedule from 14 to 16 weeks, the NFL paid attendance exceeded 12 million for the first time.
- The per-game average of 57,017 was the third-highest in league history and the most since 1973.
- In 1980, Pittsburgh defeated the Los Angeles Rams 31-19 in Super Bowl XIV in a game that was viewed in a record 35,330,000 homes.
- CBS, with a record bid of $12 million, won the national radio rights to 26 NFL regular-season games, including *Monday Night Football,* and all 10 post-season games for the 1980-83 seasons.
- Television ratings in 1980 were the second-best in NFL history, trailing only the combined ratings of the 1976 season.

Jim had only been hit twice during his career.

- All three networks posted gains, and NBC's 15.0 rating was its best ever.
- CBS and ABC had their best ratings since 1977, with 15.3 and 20.8, respectively.
- But the 1982 NFL season, the 63rd regular season of the National Football League, included a 57-day-long players' strike that reduced the season from a 16-game schedule per team to nine games.
- Because of the shortened season, the NFL adopted a special 16-team playoff tournament.
- Division standings were ignored: eight teams from each conference were seeded 1-8 based on their regular season records.
- The season ended with Super Bowl XVII, when the Washington Redskins defeated the Miami Dolphins.
- During the prior six years in the league, Jim had only been hit twice during a game.
- Both were accidental, but painful.
- As the 1983 season got underway, Jim had come to believe that most NFL officials performed for the love of the game.
- "I can't think of anyone who does it for the money, not anyone," he commented.

Life in the Community: Martinsville, Virginia

- The furniture industry, along with textiles, was the lifeblood of Martinsville, located in southern Virginia.
- Founded by American Revolutionary War General, Indian agent and explorer Joseph Martin, Martinsville and its surrounding county boasted a population of 75,000 by the early 1980s and claimed to have more millionaires per capita than any city in the state.
- The city's first major industry in the 1800s was the manufacture of plug chewing tobacco; the area became known as the "Plug Tobacco Capital of the World."
- Thanks to the entrepreneurial efforts of several families, the city's main industry for a century was furniture construction, boasting companies such as Bassett Furniture, American Furniture Company, and Gravely Furniture Company.
- Shortly after World War II, DuPont built a chemical manufacturing plant.
- DuPont later built a large manufacturing plant for producing nylon, a vital war material, which made the city a target for strategic bombing during the Cold War.
- This nylon production jumpstarted the growth of the textiles industry in the area.
- For several years Martinsville was known as the "Sweatshirt Capital of the World."
- Martinsville is also home to the Virginia Museum of Natural History, an affiliate of the Smithsonian Institution and founded by Martinsville native Dr. Noel Boaz, and the Piedmont Arts Association, an affiliate of the Virginia Museum of Fine Arts.
- Martinsville was also present at the birth of NASCAR, possessing a small, half-mile round racetrack that was home for the beginning drivers of the sport like Junior Johnson, Richard Petty, Rex White and Windale Scott.

Furniture making was a major industry in Martinsville, Virginia.

1984: Stephen Hessenfeld, Fine Tuned Hasbro's GI Joe

Stephen Hassenfeld joined his father's company, Hasbro, in 1964, and became president in 1974 when toy sales topped $73 million, spurred by the popularity of the G.I. Joe action figure.

Life at Home

- When Stephen Hassenfeld was a boy, there were toys all over the house.
- That's how it is when your father runs a toy factory.
- The toys not only came from the family factory, but included gifts of salesmen's samples from other companies, such as all the Lionel trains being made.
- Moreover, Stephen was enthralled by Daddy's factory, where everything was interesting: the injection molders, the sewing machines, the assembly line—even the creaky old elevators and the grease-stained floors where Mr. Potato Head had been made.
- By the time Stephen was in his forties and president and chairman of Hasbro Industries, the family company in Pawtucket, Rhode Island, he believed that success would grow out of tradition.
- That's why Hasbro reintroduced its G.I. Joe in 1982 and concentrated on action toys, preschool toys like Mr. Potato Head and action games including Hungry Hungry Hippos—while chasing the video game market.

- The Hassenfeld family fled Poland in 1903 to escape the Jewish pogrom, and settled—like many eastern European Jews—in Manhattan's crowded Lower East Side.
- In 1923, two brothers—Henry and Helal Hassenfeld—founded Hassenfeld Brothers, a textile remnant company in Hasbrouck Heights, New Jersey.
- Over the next two decades, the company expanded to produce pencil cases and school supplies and resettled in Pawtucket, Rhode Island.
- His brothers discovered that filling the empty pencil boxes with rulers, compasses, notebooks, erasers, and things purchased from outside suppliers brought further success.
- Several expansions later, with revenues soaring, Hassenfeld Brothers produced doctor-and-nurse kits—its first toys—in 1940.

Stephen Hassenfeld fine-tuned his family's company, Hasbro, with savvy acquisitions and the help of G.I. Joe.

- Hassenfeld Brothers' first toy hit was Mr. Potato Head, which the company purchased from inventor George Lerner in 1952.
- The concept of attaching plastic noses, ears, eyes, eyeglasses, mustaches and hats to fruit had already been rejected by a slew of other toy manufacturers.
- Stephen's father Merrill thought the funny-looking toy was a good candidate for an advertising campaign on television—a new medium which was being neglected by most toy companies.
- The company paid a $500 advance against a five percent royalty, and in 1952, Mr. Potato Head debuted in newspaper and TV commercials.

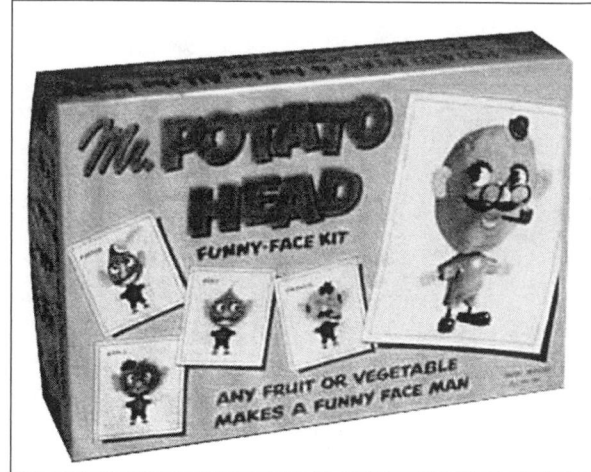

Mr. Potato Head was a long-lasting hit in the world of toys.

- Thanks to its pure silliness, Mr. Potato Head wound up on TV with comedian Jackie Gleason and in favorable newspaper stories nationwide.
- Because the toy was such a success, the company could not keep up with the orders.
- But the toy industry was a difficult place to claim consistency.
- The next big hit came in 1964.
- By then Stephen had graduated from Moses Brown School, a private academy founded by Quakers in 1784 in Providence, Rhode Island, and attended Johns Hopkins University, where he majored in political science, joined a fraternity and was the only student among his peers to have a credit card.
- Early in his senior year, in the fall of 1962, Stephen left Johns Hopkins without graduating.
- At his father's insistence, Stephen worked at a Providence advertising agency before rejoining his father's company, Hasbro, in 1964.
- By then the company had created G.I. Joe, which they termed an "action figure" in order to market the toy to boys who wouldn't want to play with "dolls."
- Toy competitor Mattel had taken the toy world by storm in the late 1950s with its Barbie dolls, and Hasbro wanted to introduce a similar product for boys.
- In 1963, Hasbro began development of a military-themed line of dolls that, like Barbie, could be accessorized with different outfits and equipment.

Hasbro's action figures appealed to children and adults alike.

- The original strategy called for a different figure for each branch of the military, but Hasbro seized on the universality of the kind of soldier depicted in a 1945 film called The Story of G.I. Joe.
- The term "G.I. Joe" itself came from World War II, where it was used as a shorthand symbol for the typical serviceman, or "Government-Issue Joe."
- G.I. Joe was initially a massive success, and Hasbro expanded the line throughout the 1960s, reimagining Joe as an astronaut, a deep-sea diver and a Green Beret.
- What made G.I. Joe unique was its 21 moving parts for interactive play, which helped ignite the imagination of young boys.
- The company's promotional efforts included the catchphrase "Boy Oh Boy! It's A Hasbro Toy!" in television commercials and print ads.
- While orders and cash flowed in, Stephen introduced tighter controls and information systems that helped restore order to the factory.
- Within two years, he restructured Hasbro's national sales force, improved its distribution network, and experimented with the company's marketing profile.
- Stephen was named executive vice president in 1968, the year Hasbro went public, and president in 1974 when toy sales topped $73 million but cash flow was so poor that his father had to use personal collateral to borrow operating capital.

Hassenfeld worked hard to improve the company and the G.I. Joe brand.

- Until then, Hasbro had been run on the philosophy that great products will drive great sales and everything else will resolve itself.
- Stephen focused on inventory control, the collection of receivables, improving cash flow, and the establishment of working capital.
- He often worked 18-hour days, seven days a week to make sure that the company founded by his grandfather was not vulnerable to outside forces, competitors or capricious bankers.
- By the early 1970s, the G.I. Joe brand was doing quite well and Hasbro came up with innovative ways to keep it thriving.
- As the 1970s continued to evolve, so did G.I. Joe: the figure received lifelike hair, moveable eyes and a "kung-fu" grip, enabling him to hold on to objects for the first time.
- But some of the changes proved to be gimmicks, taken even further by Hasbro with the development of a space-traveling "Super Joe" in 1976.
- The reception was lukewarm to "Super Joe," and by 1978, Hasbro gave G.I. Joe an honorable discharge.

Life at Work

- In 1982, G.I. Joe and Stephen Hassenfeld discovered an unlikely savior in *Star Wars*.
- The sci-fi flick and the collectables it spawned had rekindled America's appetite for action figures, so Hasbro reintroduced a line of smallersized G.I. Joes to capitalize on the trend.
- Instead of a single character, there was an entire battalion of G.I. Joes, each given signature weapons, back stories, and code names like Scarlett and Snake Eyes.
- Joe also got a new enemy, Cobra—"a ruthless terrorist organization determined to rule the world," as described in the intro to the 1980s TV cartoon *G.I. Joe: A Real American Hero*.

- Stephen had taken over as the company's president four years earlier when Hasbro posted a loss of $2.5 million on sales of $73 million.
- Hasbro had avoided the fate of some other mid-sized toy companies whose fortunes soured in the late 1970s in the face of rising oil prices and runaway inflation.
- Indeed, Hasbro had increased sales and earnings steadily; it estimated that 1982 revenues would reach $135 million and the company would obtain a net income of $6.5 million.
- It was also in 1982 that G.I. Joe was licensed with Marvel Comics, a

The 1982 film Star Wars *created a renewed interest in collectable action figures.*

partnership critical to selling $51 million worth of the Real American Heroes line that Christmas.
- Television's voluntary guidelines limited extensive information in toy commercials, but there was no rule concerning TV commercials for comics, creating a spectator opportunity to reach children as their Christmas lists were being formed.
- By that time, there were uniforms, weapons, vehicles and comic books rounding out the G.I. Joe brand, along with a marketing plan that included fan clubs, posters for grammar school classrooms, and the outlicensing of G.I. Joe's image on breakfast cereals, lunch boxes, trading cards, sneakers, sleeping bags and swimming fins.
- In 1983, Hasbro produced another successful toy franchise, My Little Pony, a toy for girls.
- But the greatest opportunity in 1984 was not more toy products, but the potential acquisition of competitor Milton Bradley, whose legacy dated back to the Civil War and whose portfolio of products included The Game of Life, Candyland, Twister, Chutes and Ladders and Yahtzee.
- Twenty-three-year-old Milton Bradley was a struggling lithographer looking for new uses for his underutilized press when, in the summer of 1860, he invented The Checkered Game of Life.
- The board game sold 40,000 copies that first winter, launching a new business.
- By the early 1900s, Milton Bradley sold games such as Ring Off, a wireless telephone game; The Auto Game, and Air King Game featuring a zephyr.
- Then, in the early 1980s, Milton Bradley Company, twice the size of Hasbro and still a leader in educational games for children, plunged into video games.

Hassenfeld's partnership with Marvel Comics was well-calculated and netted millions in sales.

- U.S. video hardware sales had reached $950 million annually—more than three times the level just two years earlier—and software sales were growing at a rate of 500 percent a year to $1 billion.
- Mattel and Coleco had already joined Commodore, Atari, and Texas Instruments in a competitive battle for the video game dollar; Milton Bradley did not want to be left behind.
- It was a total disaster.

- Retailers who didn't want ColecoVision or Mattel Intellivision had even less interest in Milton Bradley's Vectrex.
- Collective losses were in the millions.
- Hasbro, which had been tempted to jump into the video game competition that year, had not found the right product and stuck with old-fashioned plastic.
- As a result, Stephen's Hasbro was able to buy the venerable Milton Bradley Company despite competition from Ronald O. Perelman, who was backed by junk bond king Michael Milken.
- Many investors on Wall Street greeted the Bradley deal with derision, but as 1984 came to a close, Stephen found himself chairman of the largest toy company in the world, ahead of archrival Mattel, and owner of the Milton Bradley catalog of games.
- He was even finding some early success with the toy introduction known as transformers.
- And most of it because of sound business practices, good timing, and the popularity of a boy's doll who seemed to have many lives.

Life in the Community: Pawtucket, Rhode Island

- Pawtucket, Rhode Island, was a major contributor of cotton textiles during the Industrial Revolution.
- Slater Mill, built in 1793 by Samuel Slater on the Blackstone River Falls in downtown Pawtucket, was the first commercially successful cotton-spinning mill with a fully mechanized power system in America.
- Other manufacturers followed, transforming Pawtucket into a center for textiles, iron working and other industries.
- The textile business in New England declined during the Great Depression, when manufacturers moved their facilities South where operations and labor were cheaper.

Pawtucket Falls, RI.

- But unlike numerous older mill towns in the region, Pawtucket retained much of its industrial base.
- Goods produced in the city included lace, non-woven and elastic woven materials, jewelry, silverware, metals and textiles.
- Hasbro, one of the world's largest manufacturers of toys and games, was also headquartered in Pawtucket.
- Twenty percent of Pawtucket residents were French or French-Canadian.
- Similar to nearby cities such as Providence and East Providence in Rhode Island, and Fall River and New Bedford in Massachusetts, Pawtucket hosted a significant population from across the Portuguese Empire, as well as an extremely significant Cape Verdean population.
- Pawtucket was also one of the few areas of the United States with a significant Liberian population, mostly refugees from Charles Taylor's regime.

Slater Mill, downtown Pawtucket.

1984: Rigo Garcia, 23-year-old Construction Worker from Costa Rica

Twenty-three-year-old Rigo Garcia came to America to make enough money to build a house for himself and his fiancée in his native Costa Rica.

Life at Home

- Rigo Garcia knew in his heart he always wanted to live in Costa Rica, but to build a house, he needed money.
- The community of San Lorenzo, Costa Rica, was nurturing, warm and secure; he had spent no more than a dozen nights in his entire life away from the community of 312 people.
- His occasional trips to San Jose over Cerro de la Muerte, the Mountain of Death, which often took four to six hours by car, had taught him how treacherous the world can be.
- The activity of a city was overwhelming and exhausting.
- When on his last trip his car broke down, halfway to San Jose in the peak of the mountains, he had never felt so alone.
- At that moment, living in San Lorenzo for the rest of his days offered great appeal.
- But when his trip to San Jose was over, he was reminded once again that any man who wanted to make money must journey into the world and could not live within his mother's womb forever.
- Besides, Rigo was desperately in love with a dark-eyed beauty and broke as a Costa Rican monkey.
- Already three of his friends had journeyed to Paterson, New Jersey, and returned with tales of ready work, eager women and more riches than a Tico farm boy could imagine.
- Rigo had stopped his education at age 14 to work alongside his father on the farm, where a three-acre plot sustained the family's food needs and 10 acres of coffee plants provided ready cash every season.
- Many of the neighbors also grew sugar cane, which could be crushed locally and sold in nearby San Isidro de El General, but Rigo's father never liked farming cane.

Rigo Garcia left Costa Rica when he was 23-years-old.

53

The Catholic Church in San Lorenzo.

- The rough roads of mountainous San Lorenzo caused each car and truck to struggle and strain up every path and down every gully, and thus charge too much to haul away the sugar mash.
- For almost a decade, dependable electricity had energized the community; for nearly twice that time, money earned in America had been used to build the houses that everyone envied.
- Some of the houses took years to construct as local boys living in America sent dribs and drabs of money back to their parents and brothers each month for the construction of the house.
- Sometimes the money would be enough to build a single wall or construct a roof, but rarely was it enough to build the whole house at one time.
- But Rigo knew that Paterson, New Jersey, was no paradise; his best friend Renaldo had admitted that behind all the big talk and ready cash were a lot of lonely and miserable times.
- Some days work was hard to come by; some weeks there was none at all, and the landlords had no sympathy for Spanish-speaking men who did not pay their rent on time.
- Besides, no place, even America, was as friendly as San Lorenzo, where a portion of every Sunday was set aside for visiting each other's homes.
- Up the hill lived his aunts, down the hill his uncles and grandfather; across the valley lived his best friend, and his nine brothers and sisters and grandparents and half a dozen cousins all in one house.
- Even though the Catholic Church, constructed with decorative spaces in the wall shaped like crosses, was just down a hill and served as a vital anchor for the community, Sunday visiting was the buoy that allowed everyone to grow up together.
- Rigo's dream was to earn enough money so he could build an entire house with his own hands with only the help of friends and then present it to his fiancée.
- He had it all planned out: a concrete block house painted green, a red metal roof and walls outfitted with rollout jalousie windows which let in the cool air and kept out the rain.
- His house would have two couches that faced each other so his family could talk to each other every night; too much television was bad for families.
- As a special gift to his new bride, he planned to purchase beautiful green and red tile he had seen in San Isidro to cover the entire floor so the house would always look clean, bright and welcoming.
- On his last day in San Lorenzo before leaving for Mexico, Rigo watched a pair of beautiful green parrots fly across the valley near his parents' home.

- He took it as a symbol he would return soon prepared for marriage.
- To make the journey bearable, more psychologically than anything else, he took time to pick fruit from the mango trees and orange trees and then collected several sweet lemons that grew near his parents' home.
- Then he climbed into the back of his cousin's white Toyota pickup truck and rode for six days to the U.S./Mexican border.
- When they were one hour away, Rigo was instructed to crawl into a space beneath the bed of the truck for the crossing.
- There he stayed for three hours while his cousin and his wife—both U.S. legals—passed through customs and into America.
- By prior agreement, his cousin did not stop to let him go out until they were well within U.S. borders and away from suspicious eyes.
- On his first night in America, Rigo stayed with his cousin and his wife in a small apartment in Paterson, New Jersey.

The beauty of Costa Rica.

- As planned, Rigo and his cousin both rose at six o'clock the next morning and headed toward a labor collection site where men congregated to get construction jobs.
- Rigo was excited by the opportunity but appalled by the smell of the urban landscape; he clearly was not in Costa Rica anymore.

Life at Work

- On that first day, when the man shouted, "I need a roofer," Rigo Garcia put up his hand even though he didn't have a clue what "roofer" meant in English.
- Quickly he was told to join a group Costa Ricans, Guatemalans and Mexicans—all of them standing around chatting separately, waiting for the job to start.

Rigo's cousin smuggled him across the US border.

- Meeting fellow Ticos from Costa Rica helped settle his anxiety.
- In fact, when one of them asked him in Spanish if he really knew anything about roofing, Rigo admitted the truth and everyone laughed.
- "We will teach you," an older man said, " Ticos stick together."
- That was also the day he learned not to stand in front of the gringos who would shout at him in English and expect an answer.
- Standing in the back was always better: don't make eye contact, don't look like you know the answer, and just stand there and watch what the others do.
- Rigo discovered that he had the perfect skills to be a roofer; he was agile, surefooted and strong.
- In the company of other Ticos, work was even fun, even if the foreman spent an enormous amount of energy yelling at everyone in English.

- Rigo quickly learned the construction terms and tools he needed to know by their English names; after all, doing well on the job meant returning to Costa Rica sooner.
- But clearly, some accommodations were being made for Spanish speakers; gringo foremen had learned to identify items they wanted to discard as "trash" and also in Spanish as "basura."
- At a neighborhood grocery store, signs aimed at the Spanish-speaking population read, "Esta Bud es para usted"—"This Bud's for you"—or advertised that a pesticide called Combat would spell the end of "problemas con las cucarachas"—"problems with cockroaches."
- Rigo learned to be cautious around English speakers, especially the police; since most officers in the field only spoke English, Spanish speakers would be taken to the jail to be read their rights in Spanish, and he had no desire to be close to any jail, American or Costa Rican.
- America brought several revelations.
- Never before had he seen toilets in which the waste paper was flushed away; in San Lorenzo where the sewer pipes were gravity fed and flowed into a distant field, toilet paper created too many problems when flushed and thus was placed in a trash can next to the toilet.

Rigo worked as a roofer in New Jersey.

- He also discovered that hot water showers were truly a great invention; all his life he had taken cold showers and never thought of washing any other way.
- Non-political his entire life, Rigo became more interested in reading about American relations with Central America in the Spanish-language newspapers.
- By all appearances President Ronald Reagan was trying to get Costa Rica involved in the latest Central American squabbles even though Costa Rica had long ago dissolved its army to avoid such conflicts.
- The president also became very interested in America's immigration policies.
- Recently, immigration officials had raided job sites throughout the country in an effort to catch illegal aliens who held better-paying jobs.
- The sweeps were designed to apprehend 3,000 to 5,000 aliens, and open up jobs for citizens and legal aliens.
- Rigo was concerned that the arrests would give the impression that undocumented workers were responsible for the nation's high unemployment rate and stir up even more animosity toward Spanish-speaking immigrants.
- He was also concerned about getting caught and losing the $7-an-hour job, which paid more than twice the minimum hourly wage of $3.35.
- In the past, raids had targeted illegal aliens performing low-skilled manual labor—jobs that American citizens did not want.

Life in the Community: Paterson, New Jersey

- Paterson, New Jersey's origins date back to 1791, when Alexander Hamilton helped found the Society for the Establishment of Useful Manufactures.
- The plan was to harness energy from the Great Falls of the Passaic to secure economic independence from British manufacturers.
- French architect, engineer, and city planner Pierre L'Enfant, who developed the plans for Washington, D.C., was the first superintendent for the project.

- The industries developed in Paterson were powered by the 77-foot-high Great Falls and a system of water raceways that harnessed the power of the falls.
- Dozens of mill buildings and other manufacturing structures associated with the textile industry and later, the firearms, silk, and railroad locomotive manufacturing industries, clustered around the raceways.
- In the latter half of the 1800s, silk production became the dominant industry and formed the basis of Paterson's most prosperous period, earning it the nickname "Silk City."
- The city became a Mecca for immigrant laborers who worked in its factories.
- Since its beginnings, Paterson had been a melting pot.
- Irish, Germans, Dutch and Jews settled in the city in the nineteenth century.
- Italian and Eastern European immigrants soon followed.
- As early as 1890, many Syrian and Lebanese immigrants also arrived in Paterson.
- Many second- and third-generation Puerto Ricans had been calling Paterson home since the 1950s, and recently first-generation Dominican, Peruvian, Colombian, Central American, Mexican, Bolivian, and Argentine immigrants arrived.
- Western Market Street, sometimes called Little Lima, was home to many Peruvian and other Latin American businesses.
- The Great Falls Historic District, Cianci Street, Union Avenue and 21st Avenue housed several Italian businesses.
- To the north of the Great Falls was a fast-growing Bengali population.
- Park Avenue and Market Street between Straight Street and Madison Avenue was heavily Dominican and Puerto Rican.
- Main Street was largely populated by Mexicans, with a declining Puerto Rican community.
- Costa Ricans and other Central American immigrant communities were growing in the Riverside and Peoples Park neighborhoods.
- Broadway, or Martin Luther King Jr. Way, was predominantly black, as was the Fourth Ward and parts of Eastside and Northside.

Factories in Paterson NJ were powered by harnessing the energy of the Great Falls.

- Paterson's black community was composed of African Americans of Southern heritage and more recent Caribbean and African immigrants.
- Every summer, Patersonians enjoy an African American Day Parade, a Dominican Day Parade, a Puerto Rican Day Parade, a Peruvian Day Parade, and a Turkish American Day Parade.
- Annually, Paterson's Peruvian community celebrated "El Señor de los Milagros" or "Our Lord of Miracles" on October 18-28.

Immigrant laborers living in Paterson worked for this silk factory, just one of the many manufacturing structures powered by energy from the Great Falls of the Passaic.

1985: James Krenov, Master Woodworker and College Professor

Renowned cabinetmaker James Krenov taught the philosophy of wood and the techniques of building fine furniture at the College of the Redwoods in California.

Life at Work

- At 65 years old, the bearded, long-haired furniture craftsman and teacher Jim Krenov insisted on calling himself "a pre-Kerouac hippie," all the while insisting that he was only an amateur woodworker.
- As the founder of the fine woodworking program at the College of the Redwoods in Fort Bragg, California—one of the most influential programs of its kind in the country—Jim inspired a generation of furniture makers with an aesthetic influenced by organic, subtle details.
- Jim was a philosopher who wrote lyrically about his craft and his reverence for the subtleties of wood.
- Born on October 31, 1920, in the village of Uelen, Siberia, he was the only child of Dimitri and Julia Krenov.
- He and his family left Russia the following year, and after some time in Shanghai, China, they moved to a remote village in Alaska, where Jim's parents worked as teachers.
- They lived in Alaska for seven years.
- Jim vividly remembered airplane drops of goods and supplies onto the snow for the villagers.
- In one of those bundles was a good steel jackknife.
- "From the time I was six, I was making my own toys with the jackknife; It was a joy to me that I could rely on my hands and my eyes to produce things."
- In the mid-1930s, the Krenovs moved to Seattle, where Jim worked at a boatyard, building yachts and sailing on Puget Sound.
- Thanks to his family roots, he later became an interpreter for the Lend-Lease Program to provide supplies to America's allies, dealing with Russian cargo ships throughout World War II.
- His time surrounded by boats influenced his aesthetic; he loved the lines of boats: "There's hardly a straight line on them,

James Krenov founded the fine woodworking program at College of the Redwoods.

but there's harmony. People think right angles produce harmony, but they don't. They produce sleep," Jim said.

- In 1947, he moved to Sweden and found very unsatisfying work at an electrical appliance factory; whenever he could, he roamed Europe.
- He met his future wife in Paris.
- After they were married on March 2, 1951, Jim and Britta traveled together in Italy and France, and spent many summers in the mountains of Sweden where they liked to hike.
- Jim enjoyed trout fishing in the mountain streams.
- Always a writer, Jim published several articles and a novel chronicling these travels.
- Back in Stockholm, Jim enrolled for two years in the school run by Carl Malmsten, considered by many the father of Scandinavian furniture design.

While he worked at a boatyard, Krenov developed a love of boats and their design.

- After graduating, Jim set up shop in the basement of his home.
- Gradually, his work and philosophy gained recognition among peers and buyers.
- One commission, for a box to contain prized ceramics, came from King Gustav VI of Sweden.
- Toiling anonymously for years, he built a reputation for his simple designs; once established as a master woodworker, Jim also began sharing his expertise.
- He taught at Carl Malmsten's in 1967 and 1968; "Carl would look at your table and he would run his hand around it and he would come to the corner, and he'd stand there a while doing this [rubs his hands together] and he wouldn't say another word. He just walked off. And you'd spend the rest of the day wondering what the hell it was about that particular corner that his hand discovered."
- His international engagements began with an invitation from Craig McArt and Wendell Castle to teach at the Rochester Institute of Technology (RIT).
- Subsequent teaching engagements included the establishment of the program in Wood Artisanry for the Franklin Institute of Boston University, and as a Guest Professor in Graz, Austria, in 1978.
- "I traveled all over the world to talk about my work," Jim said. "These weren't high occasions—just people interested in talking with a craftsman. I'm known as the guy who is always interested in the thing that is both beautiful and useful."
- The response of students at RIT led Jim to try his hand at writing again.
- In 1976, Krenov's first book, *A Cabinetmaker's Notebook,* was published and became so successful that he ended up writing four more books, including one that showcased the work of his students, *With Wakened Hands.*
- His publishers of *A Cabinetmaker's Notebook* sent him on a barnstorming author's tour of the U.S. that led, in turn, to an invitation from the University of California, Santa Cruz, to conduct a workshop.
- Three of the students at that workshop were members of the Mendocino Woodworker's Guild who enticed Jim to conduct a workshop at the Mendocino High School in 1978.
- One lecture led to another in 1979, and again in 1980.
- The Woodworker's Guild members then persuaded the College of the Redwoods, a regional community college with a budding branch in Fort Bragg, to establish a cabinetmaking program.

- "They invited Britta and me up for a dinner and a look around, and we fell for the place, and there were people in the community who wanted to start a school and they finally got the College of the Redwoods to promote it and built the building because I promised I would come.
- "So they said, 'We'll build a school if you'll come.' And I said, 'I'll come if you build a school.'"
- The building was finished with the help of the first group of students in the fall of 1981.

Life at Work

- For years, students from across the globe have attended Jim Krenov's classes at the College of the Redwoods.
- The most recent class included two students from New Zealand, two from London, one from Norway, one from Hawaii, two from Alaska, and a smattering from the remainder of the United States.
- The hands-on, intense classes met six days a week for nine months; most of Jim's students stayed one year, while a few stayed two years.
- Few of his students planned to enter high-end cabinetmaking as a full-time profession.
- Instead, most were part of a national trend that emphasized lifelong learning—including classes in cooking, crafts, foreign languages or the fine points of opera.
- "Krenov really helped re-create an interest in fine woodworking that had largely died out by the 1950s," says Frank Ramsay, president of the Bay Area Woodworkers Association.
- "Krenov introduced a dramatic change from the 'make a box, cover it with plywood and paint it' era of the 1960s."

- One of the first lessons College of the Redwoods students tackled was a requirement to fashion their own tools, starting with a wood plane for scraping very thin strips of wood.
- Jim called the plane "the cabinetmaker's violin," and often suggested that it be made from hornbeam wood because of the way it felt in a craftsperson's hands.
- The class then moved on to cabinet construction and design.
- Jim believed machinery had its place in the shop, especially during the rude stages of stock removal, but thought that power tools often erased the "fingerprints" left on the finished piece that only handwork can leave.
- What distinguished a piece of furniture was not the technical skill or even the figure of the wood; Jim's credo was "that the work have life in it."
- It wasn't about showing off technique as much as giving the work personality; it wasn't a matter of conquering the wood, he believed, but letting it breathe.

Krenov's cabinets were known for their simple design.

Krenov called his plane "the cabinetmaker's violin."

- "Early on, we get into the fact that our tools and materials will respond to our sensitivities; it's the first link in a long chain that gradually becomes a natural way of working. You're no longer worrying about the physical aspects of a tool, but about what you're going to do with it. You're thinking of how it's going to feel and how the results will look."
- Over time, the students were trained to develop an instinct for wood combinations, the colors and textures, melding them to make works with an elegant simplicity.
- "Let us know our wood as we do our hands, and work with it in common respect and harmony," he wrote in *The Fine Art of Cabinetmaking*.
- A favorite wood was pear for its tranquility, its color, and its response to planes.
- His cabinets, rarely more than four feet high and 26 inches wide, were recognizable for their long, slim legs.
- On close examination, the legs reveal a variety of delicate shapes, where Jim's knives and planes adhered to the natural contours of the wood and the patterns of its grain.
- He felt that details such as uniformly rounded edges, perfectly flat surfaces, and sharp corners removed the personal touch from a piece of furniture.
- His books extolled the virtues of clean lines, hand-planed surfaces, unfinished or lightly finished wood, and techniques that Jim referred to as "honest."
- He loved curves, and was known for creating door panels with concave, billowing shapes like sails in the wind.
- For that reason, he avoided the word "design," preferring the language of composing, a continual re-evaluation and improvisation open to wherever the wood takes the composer.
- A self-described "wood nut," he often sought out woods that are rare, highly figured, or contain unique coloration; he liked to keep shavings of Lebanon cedar and sandalwood in a box beneath his bed so he could savor their fragrance.

Life in the Community: Fort Bragg, California

- Located in coastal Mendocino County, California, along State Route 1, the major north-south highway along the Pacific Coast, Fort Bragg was founded as a military fort prior to the Civil War.
- Fort Bragg became a popular tourist destination, thanks to its picturesque views of the Pacific Ocean and rugged Northern California coastline.
- The town of 6,500 advertised itself as the official Gateway to the California Coastal National Monument, bragging "We've got bookshops for the bookish, thrift stores for the thrifty, shops for the shoppers, art for the artists, camping supplies for the campers.
- "There are no traffic jams, no rush hour (no rushing of any kind) and no parking meters downtown.
- "The air is some of the purest on earth; the blue-green ocean pristine."
- The Redwoods Community College District was formed in 1964 by an election of the people of Humboldt County; a bond issue of $3.6 million was passed for the initial construction phase of the college.
- Instruction began in 1965 and continued into 1967 at Eureka High School.
- Initially, 45 majors were offered, 15 of which were technical-vocational.
- Over 1,800 students registered at the College in 1965-66.
- The founding President/Superintendent, Dr. Eugene J. Portugal, supervised a full-time faculty and administrative staff of 31, with 85 part-time instructors.

Fort Bragg, California.

"James Krenov, Reflections on the Risks of Pure Craft," Glenn Gordon, *Fine Woodworking Magazine,* November/December, 1985

The air is charged with Krenov, but the mood of the school is actually pretty loose. It isn't a tyranny. The students are generally good humored and relaxed. A certain amount, not all, of student work bears a resemblance to Krenov's, some of it very closely, which makes it tempting to criticize as merely the work of Krenovian clones, but I think this too conveniently misunderstands it. It's plain to see that some of the students regard the imitation of a master as the price of becoming one oneself, but I also saw work being done that looks nothing at all like what one would associate with Krenov. As long as Krenov feels it is done with sensitivity and skill, he doesn't knock it, but it is clear, from the overall look of things, that Krenov isn't running an art school consecrated on the worship of Design. As independent a spirit as Krenov is, he is still the exponent of an essential conservative furniture tradition. He teaches a craft which has definite and settled criteria in his mind. There is room for experiment, but at heart, the school is committed to the classic way of cabinetmaking, not to the search for profound originality, or to the idea of Design as an activity poised on the edge of the breaking wave of innovation.

Welcome Letter to College of the Redwoods, James Krenov

We are a community college accepting students with varying degrees of experience. Our course is organized, but very relaxed. Because the students all have the same beginning point, that is, wanting to be here, we discover that there's a wonderful comradeship and feeling among them; they share a lot.

We try to demystify the process of working wood; we simplify it. We concentrate on the logic and the simple physical and mental relationships in any given process. From the very beginning we work with people, leading them to the realization that wood is a vastly rich material and that different kinds of wood call for different methods of working. Wood also has colors, patterns, and textures that can fit into the work. We help people discover the graphics of wood, and that any shape or proportion can be given additional life through proper use of the wood, whether it's in a cabinet or as something as sculptural as a chair.

We hope that in viewing what we are offering here, you will pay attention to the details, notice the results, and come to realize that if one cares enough, if one pays enough attention to the richness of wood, to the tools, to the marvel of one's own hands and eye, all these things come together so that a person's work becomes that person, that person's message.

In this work, in these details, in these elements, something of a person is included. Their fingerprints or their sense of proportion, line, and detail are there; and what you're experiencing is something very personal from each of these people: something that they've put their heart and soul into.

And we hope some of their enjoyment shows, too.

1985: Paul Howe, Professional Football Player

Paul Howe overcame his lack of stature to fulfill his desire to play professional football for 11 teams spanning three leagues.

Life at Home

- Born in Lexington, Massachusetts, in 1951, Paul Howe grew up with a love for sports that blossomed after his father, Charles, a sales engineer, took him to a Boston Patriots game on Paul's tenth birthday.
- Boston had been awarded the eighth and final franchise in the new American Football League in 1959, and Lou Saban had been named the team's first head coach.
- Paul was giddy with excitement to be going and was ready for the game two hours early.
- He knew all about the team, its players and its plans.
- He had even submitted dozens of entries when the team asked the public to name the team; thousands of entries were submitted and 74 fans suggested the winning name, the Boston Patriots.
- Boston Globe artist Phil Bissell then drew a cartoon of a Minuteman preparing to snap a football; team owners liked the drawing so much "Pat Patriot" was selected as the team logo.
- The team's regular season home opener came on September 9, 1960, when 21,597 fans at Boston University field watched the team lose to the Denver Broncos 13-10.
- Paul's game was a whirlwind of noises, tastes and sounds; his father bought him a souvenir banner, three hot dogs and a drink.
- Paul was deliriously happy, even though his team lost.
- He slept all the way home.
- After that, Paul would rather play football than watch television, unless a game was on.
- As an athlete, Paul developed a team-first attitude that impressed his coaches and teammates, who voted him team captain of both the high school football and hockey teams.

What Paul Howe lacked in size he made up for in perseverance.

When Paul didn't make the NFL draft, he tried out for the World Football League.

- The local newspaper promoted him as a college prospect, but the team's 5 and 5 season didn't draw much attention to a six-foot, 210-pound defensive lineman.
- Paul played his college ball at the University of Pittsburgh while majoring in physical education.
- Most colleges had passed on Paul because he was deemed undersized for both an offensive and defensive lineman, but Pitt used an innovative speed-based defense that allowed undersized linemen to be aggressive.
- Paul set his sights on the pro game; however, he went undrafted in the NFL's 12-round Annual Selection Meeting; most teams were interested in big, space-eating defensive linemen.
- He signed with the Atlanta Falcons, but was cut before the 1974 season began, because he was considered too small to play the run.
- He then tried the rival World Football League.
- He signed with the Chicago Blitz, but again failed to make the final cut.
- It pained him to get the phone call that he was to turn in his playbook.
- Year round, Paul painted houses to make ends meet as he continued to work out and prepare himself for the pros, writing letters to teams hoping to receive an invitation to training camp or to replace an injured player.
- Paul spent two years as a nomad in training camps with the Washington Redskins, the WFL's Charlotte Hornets, and back to the NFL with the New England Patriots.
- His life consisted of sweating in the summer sun of training camp, moving from city to city, learning new playbooks, and finding himself a stranger in every locker room.
- Logic told him to surrender his dream, face facts, and get a job coaching high school sports, but his heart wouldn't let him give up.

- He sharpened his focus and in 1976 his perseverance paid off as he landed on the roster of the Denver Broncos.
- He impressed head coach Robert "Red" Miller with his special team skills and attitude, but the Broncos famous "Orange Crush" defense was talented and deep, so Paul was moved to the offensive line.
- He stayed late, learning every spot on the line, working at all five positions to make himself a more attractive backup.
- Paul made the team and was part of the Denver Broncos 1978 Super Bowl team, a career high for him.

Life at Work

- Paul Howe enjoyed life in the Mile High City with its year-round golfing, skiing and hiking.
- And he had felt financially secure enough to marry Nancy, a sales associate at a sporting goods store he frequented.
- But every season it was a struggle to make the roster as the 12-round draft brought younger, cheaper competition to challenge his roster spot.
- A coaching change in 1981 and a new pass-oriented scheme that didn't fit Paul's abilities left him with only his special team skills to make the team.
- In the NFL, if you are not a starter, you must earn your keep on special teams.
- Special teams were beginning to come to attention in the early 1980s, thanks to players like Bill Bates and Andre Waters, who played with reckless abandon, sacrificing their bodies for the sake of making a tackle.
- Some players did not report concussions for fear of losing playing time or not making the team at all.

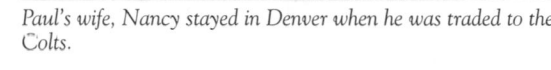

Paul's wife, Nancy stayed in Denver when he was traded to the Colts.

- Paul used his hockey experience to help him play aggressively, but under control, so as not to receive the brain damage that prematurely ended the careers and even the lives of players.
- Undersized for a lineman, but with speed and tenacity, Paul became a hero on special teams.
- Coach Red Miller called his style of play "hell-bent."
- His teammate, the tough, undersized linebacker Tom Jackson, gave him the nickname "Thumper."
- "Whenever I made a hit, Tom said I *thumped* somebody."
- Paul's prowess for special team play was not only appreciated by his coach and teammates, but also the fans.
- The Bronco fans loved and identified with his blue-collar background and rooted for him to make the roster each year.
- Some fans wore T-shirts that had "Howe's Herd" emblazoned on the back, turning Paul into a cult hero.
- Mile High Stadium would shake as fans stomped their feet to a Howe tackle.
- But loyalty was a rare commodity; Paul was traded to the Baltimore Colts in 1982, just as the league went on strike.
- With Nancy in Denver and no locker room fellowship, Paul increased his drinking, going to bars and making bets with customers who wanted to try and outdrink a tough guy pro football player.
- When the season began, the marriage was strained and Paul found himself depressed, which kept his drinking at a dangerous level.

"Thumper" was Paul's nickname.

- His on-field performance suffered and the Colts dumped him, but he signed with the Chicago Fire of a new World Football League.
- But the WFL had financial difficulties, and some teams even had their uniforms confiscated by sheriff's deputies.
- Things grew worse at home as Nancy admitted to having an affair; Paul felt helpless.
- The next football season, Paul jumped at a chance to return to Denver and play for his old Broncos head coach, Red Miller, now in charge of the Denver Gold of the United States Football League (USFL).
- Miller was fired four games into the season due to difficulties with ownership, and new coach Darrell "Mouse" Davis preferred a wide open passing offense.
- After the 1984 spring USFL season ended, Paul was released and no team came calling.
- He was losing his wife, about to lose his home, and knew he was going in the wrong direction.
- His never-give-up attitude aided him in the difficult challenge of turning his life around, as one day he said to himself, "Paul, you're a bum and you weren't raised to be a bum."
- He told Nancy he wanted to get back together; he promised to quit drinking and join a church support group.
- They began attending church regularly and vowed to make a new start.

- Word of getting his act cleaned up got back to the Broncos, who signed him to the biggest contract he had ever received.
- In a job where only 215 out of every 100,000 high school senior football players make it to the NFL and with an average career length of only 3.5 years, Paul felt blessed to celebrate his tenth year in professional football.

Life in the Community: Denver, Colorado

- Like Paul Howe, visitors have long been attracted by Colorado's frontier past, informal living and breathtaking scenery.
- Admitted to the Union in 1876, Colorado holds the title of the highest of the 50 states and has an average of 300 days of sunshine each year.
- Although gold started Colorado's road to statehood, crude oil, natural gas and coal now played a critical role in the economy of the state.
- In addition, Colorado was the major source of steel hardening minerals such as molybdenum and tungsten.
- Originally known as the "Queen City of the Plains," Denver is now recognized as the "Mile High City."
- Denver spreads over nearly 100 square miles, with the city and surrounding areas claiming more than one million people.
- Dominating the Denver skyline is the gold-domed state Capitol building, which is topped with solid 28-carat gold leaf from the mines of the Rockies.
- More than 200 federal bureaus, agencies and regional offices are located in Denver, giving rise to its claim of being the "Western Washington, DC."
- Military facilities in and around Denver house more than 52,000 people, providing an annual federal payroll of more than $700 million.

Paul was drawn to Colorado's natural beauty.

1985: Edwidge Dominique, 23-year-old Artist from Haiti in Miami, Florida

After a lifetime of dreaming, two-and-a-half years of planning, and 18 months in America, Edwidge Dominique was no closer to being a highly recognized artist than he had been when he left Haiti.

Life at Home

- Twenty-three year-old Edwidge Dominique's anger was on the edge of bitterness.
- Since he was a small boy, Edwidge had been fascinated by the vibrant colors of Haiti's landscape and had grown adept at using paint to differentiate shadow from dimness, light from brightness.
- Color subtlety was so fascinating to Edwidge, he spent nearly a month doing six paintings of an acacia tree illuminated by different light cast at various times during the day.
- His older brothers and sisters thought the tree series was an enormous waste of time; "Pretty pictures will not feed you or get you a wife," his older sister Kaiama hissed.
- But his grandmother, the only parent he had ever known, loved his artwork and said over and over, "One day you will be famous."
- That was Edwidge's dream.
- How this fire could be quenched became clear when he met an American couple who were in Les Cayes to visit the Sisters of Charity Orphanage in the middle of the city.
- As was his habit, Edwidge was selling his latest paintings that day in the market alongside fruit vendors, woodworkers and dressmakers when the Americans stopped, admired, and then bought everything he had on display without haggling over the price.
- He trembled at the sight of US$85.00 in his hand.
- Unable as he was to understand English, only later did Edwidge learn from an old fruit dealer that the woman had said, "These will sell for five times more in America. He is very talented and should display his work in New York and Miami."
- Edwidge had never experienced such happiness; her words were burned in his soul.
- In America, he told himself, "I can be an artist who is famous and rich."
- So for the next two and a half years, Edwidge was consumed by the idea of

Edwidge Dominique, shown here with his sisters, left Haiti to become a famous artist.

71

America, particularly Miami, where his second cousin was living and doing well enough so that every month he sent money home.

- Everyone was in agreement that he should go, especially if he planned to send money back; even his doctor, who was trained in Cuba, said, "I think you should go."
- Since the late 1970s thousands had fled Haiti with no money, using makeshift boats and totally lacking any documentation, taking only their fervent prayer "God is good" as a sign that somehow they would be admitted to the United States.
- Most were not.
- Thousands drowned during the journey; more were caught by the Coast Guard or Immigration officials and unceremoniously sent back to Haiti.
- Some made it to America and asked for asylum or at least the same privileges offered Cubans fleeing that neighboring Caribbean island.
- Terrified that an all-volunteer army of unemployed, illiterate Haitians was about to descend on America's privileged Gold Coast, Florida's residents fought back.

Painting by a Haitian artist.

- Cubans should have special privileges because they were fleeing Castro's communism, they said; Haitians, they remarked, were running from poverty and would only bring more crime, AIDS, drugs and additional burdens for the area schools.
- But after a series of battles in American courts, some Haitians were given the status of "Cuban/Haitian entrant," which provided an ambiguous legal position in the United States, but did allow them to stay.
- More Haitians, most of whom could not swim, transformed themselves into "boat people" in hopes of gaining entry into the U.S.; the U.S. Coast Guard was instructed to seek them out and make sure they didn't arrive.
- Those who were captured at sea were rapidly repatriated to Haiti with the cooperation of the Haitian government and the Reagan Administration.
- By 1983, Edwidge knew that unrest was rumbling throughout Haiti and that the Duvalier family might one day be dethroned.
- Now was the time to chase his dream, he decided.
- In all, he had gathered together $480, which he gave to a well-dressed man from Port-au-Prince who promised that Edwidge would land safely in Miami "without even getting your feet wet."
- It was not the first lie Edwidge would be told.

Life at Work

- Edwidge Dominique's boat trip to America began in a rubberized raft loaded to overflowing with desperate people; 14 nervous men were jammed into a raft designed to hold eight.
- Upon hitting the first wave, the raft sagged into the sea and everyone was soaked within minutes.

- Edwidge was able to keep his spare clothing dry but the art supplies he had packed so carefully were ruined.
- The raft was then paddled very slowly into the inky night to a waiting trawler that had seen better days and soon was overwhelmed by the number of rafts that congregated at its side.
- The trawler, operating mostly at night, drifted toward Miami for more than two weeks; Edwidge's many questions went unanswered even when a group of men threatened the captain's life if land was not found soon.
- The final stage of the trip was by a small speedboat, with a faulty motor, that was intended to take the illegal immigrants to an isolated dock south of Miami near Homestead.
- Underpowered and overloaded, the boat accidentally dumped Edwidge into the water when they were just within sight of land.
- Edwidge swam for his life, guided only by lights at the dock.
- Exhausted by the long trip and the arduous swim, he offered no resistance to the police awaiting his arrival.
- Altogether the voyage had taken 18 days; the boat carried supplies for about 10 days and the trip ended in a detention facility, courtesy of the United States Government.
- For 11 months, Edwidge was held at the Krome Center in Miami while politicians and federal agencies considered whether he and nearly 15,000 other Haitian refugees should be allowed to stay in the country.
- His family did not know whether he had arrived or was lost at sea.
- No paints, no privacy and few lawyers who spoke Creole were available.
- Then, he was freed from detention without any explanation he could understand.
- He was given special permission to stay temporarily in America but denied all immigration papers that would allow him to work.
- Housing was provided until his case was settled.
- Edwidge felt listless and unable to paint; without the special light of Haiti his paintings grew dark, less vibrant and apparently unsellable.
- Every day he waited for the knock on the door that said he would be sent back; maybe it was a knock he would embrace, he repeatedly told himself.

Life in the Community: Haiti and Miami, Florida

- Even though Haiti was one of the poorest countries in the Western Hemisphere, Haitians had a rich culture and historical heritage.
- Haiti was the second-oldest republic in the Americas, established by slaves in a revolt against the French, grounded on the "rights of man" in 1804.
- Historians believe that the defeat of Napoleon's forces by the Haitian slave rebellion paved the way for the Louisiana Purchase, which doubled the size of America and dramatically reduced the holdings of the French on the continent.
- The French took possession of Santo Domingo, as colonial Haiti was known, at the end of the seventeenth century.
- By the middle of the eighteenth century, when 400,000 imported African slaves worked at the sugar cane, coffee, cotton and indigo plantations, Haiti was the most profitable colony in the world, far more valuable to the French than 13 North American colonies were to the British.
- But little of that wealth remained after the land was divided into subsistence farms and Western powers, including the United States, established punitive policies against the only country in the Americas to be established through a slave revolt.
- Situated between Spanish-speaking Cuba and the Dominican Republic, mountainous Haiti retained its distinct linguistic and cultural identity; French Creole and French remained the major languages.

- Haiti was at once the most densely populated and the most rural nation in the Caribbean region; peasant agriculture dominated the economy.
- Even in the southern seaport city of Les Cayes, with a population of 36,000, the electricity was unreliable, sometimes only working four hours a day.
- At night the entire city was dark except for a few dozen homes and businesses outfitted with solar power collectors.
- Locally made charcoal was used for heating, and clean water was a luxury; hundreds of children died yearly from waterborne diseases.
- To escape the poverty of Haiti, a growing body of Haitians, including the country's educated elite, gravitated to Miami and created the nucleus of a community that needed Creole-speaking teachers, professionals and entrepreneurs.
- Officially, 50,000 Haitians were said to live in the Miami area; Haitian community leaders put the figure closer to 75,000.
- Educated Haitians found in Miami an agreeable climate and a sense of community that had been denied them in exile elsewhere.
- Haitians who grew up in other parts of the U.S. were often ashamed of their nationality; Miami changed that, especially for professionals.
- However, the people who came by boat encountered a stream of legal and social problems in the United States, principally, the inability to gain asylum as political refugees.
- Twenty-five thousand Haitians in south Florida faced proceedings that could lead to their departure from the United States.
- The Haitian boat people were catapulted into the national spotlight in 1980 when some 15,000 began arriving in south Florida on the heels of the larger Cuban refugee boatlift.
- The United States 1980 Census found 90,000 people who said one or both parents were of Haitian ancestry, and the Immigration and Naturalization Service estimated that there were probably an equal number of Haitians in America illegally.
- A survey published by the Behavioral Science Research Institute of Coral Gables estimated that 22,800 Haitians resided in the Edison-Little River community, which included Little Haiti.
- The survey concluded that half were unemployed, half could not converse in English and two-thirds had a household income of less than $150 a week.
- Despite the high unemployment rate among Haitians, four times that of the U.S., the study noted that there was no greater dependency upon public agencies for assistance among Haitians than other groups.
- The report said this reflected the strong desire among many Haitians to be self-sufficient rather than depend on agencies for help.
- But the Haitian community had found few ways to confront the public reaction to the discovery that some victims of AIDS were Haitian.
- Of the 1,641 AIDS cases reported in the United States, 5 percent were Haitian, yet AIDS was being identified as a disease associated with homosexuals, drug users and Haitians.

1985: Valerie Jaffen, 12-year-old Cellist from Connecticut

Talented, musically gifted 12-year-old Valerie Jaffen was anxiously waiting to celebrate her Bas Mitzvah in a new home in Stamford, Connecticut.

Life at Home

- Valerie Jaffen was only a few weeks away from her twelfth birthday and her long-awaited Bas Mitzvah.
- For the past several months, she had been learning the passage of the Torah assigned to the week of her birthday and working closely with Rabbi Edelman on her speech.
- Each week she and the Rabbi met at the Reformed Temple not far from her home in Stamford, Connecticut.
- The memorization was not difficult—Valerie prided herself on learning passages quickly—but preparing her talk was a challenge because it must be perfect and accurately reflect the impact on her of becoming an adult and being a Jew.
- True to her meticulous nature and depth of religious feeling, she struggled through draft after draft.
- Rabbi Edelman believed that her parents were less devoted than she and that her speech would help guide them into a deeper faith.
- He kept telling her how impressed he is with her effort, which made her work even harder.
- For Valerie, order was important.
- She brought the same dedication to playing the cello, doing her homework, or arranging her complex schedule.
- Over her parents' heated objections, she was currently involved in sailing, horseback riding, tennis and dance.
- Her mother repeatedly said she must give up something, but Valerie insisted that as long as her grades were good, she has earned the right to stay busy.
- She kept a calendar on her bedroom door so everyone in the house knew her daily schedule: Monday, horseback riding and cello; Tuesday, sailing and allergy shot; Wednesday, tennis and

Valerie Jaffen was looking forward to her Bas Mitzvah.

cello; Thursday, dance and orchestra; Friday, Hebrew School and Bas Mitzvah preparation.

- From sundown Friday until sundown Saturday, she kept free for Temple, reflection, and work on her Bas Mitzvah speech.
- Sailing and tennis she found hard and unnatural, but when she was on horseback, especially a quarter horse named Perry, she felt totally alive.
- Her other passion, when she is alone and playing her cello, was talking with her cat Greyboy, who had been her best friend since she was three.
- Her father liked for her to play the Romantics and more modern works on the cello, but she preferred Baroque, particularly Bach, because of its order and precision.
- She had few friends, since her family only moved to Stamford last summer from her childhood home in Mount Kisco, New York, where her grandparents still lived.
- Her sprawling new house had 10,000 square feet, encompassing six bedrooms, six full baths and an artist's studio, which is being used as a music room.

Tennis was one of Valerie's many interests.

- Sitting on two acres, the house was built in 1914 on the tip of a point extending into Long Island Sound.
- The compound included a pool, tennis court and four-car garage.

Her sprawling 10,000 square foot home was built in 1914.

Valerie's busy schedule included sailing.

- Valerie's mother, Ruth, was completely redecorating the interior of the home; this was her dream project.
- For two years she had been lobbying for a new home, ever since her husband Richard took several companies public and earned millions of dollars in bonuses.
- After all, as Ruth has said repeatedly, she quit college to support Richard through the Wharton School of Business; now that their hard work and investments had been paid off, this house was her diploma.
- Valerie's Bas Mitzvah reception will be her mother's first opportunity to unveil the new home, a way of greeting her new community in style.
- She was currently splitting her time between supervising the renovations and planning the reception.
- Valerie wanted to keep the reception simple, but feels no one is listening to her.
- She was saving her excitement for the arrival of both sets of grandparents, who will be coming from Mount Kisco for her birthday, the Bas Mitzvah and the reception.

Life at School
- The move from Mount Kisco to Stamford had been difficult.
- In contrast to her old school, Greenwich Academy, which she then attended, is private, all-female, and has fewer Jewish students.
- The teachers were very nice, the classes hard, and the girls very cliquish; she found it hard to make the kind of friends she enjoyed in her old school.
- Some girls have even made remarks about her hair, which she had considered one of her best features.
- Valerie was self-conscious that she must take an allergy shot once a week; no one at the school knew about her allergy except her friend Amy.

Growing up, she learned to play the Romantics, but preferred Baroque pieces.

- For her birthday, Valerie's mother is getting contact lenses to replace her glasses, and though Valerie was not sure she wanted contacts, her mother insists it will help her fit in better at the new school.
- The one major change she liked at Greenwich Academy is the school uniform of a plaid skirt, white blouse and blazer; it suits her sense of order.
- Since arriving at the school, she had auditioned and been accepted by the Young Artists Philharmonic, which was known throughout the state.
- The audition in front of dozens of people she had never seen scared her to death; to block them out of her mind, she concentrated on playing her audition piece perfectly.
- She had been disappointed by the lack of Baroque music on the orchestra program, but was glad to have found her friend Amy McAdam, who was one year older and played the violin with the orchestra, and loved Bach and cats as much as Valerie did.
- They practice together frequently and have devised plans to invite two other girls to join them so they can form a string quartet.
- But Valerie knew that might mean giving up something, like sailing or horseback riding, or tennis, or dance.
- Naomi, the au pair from Israel, who was a distant cousin of her mother, made meeting the hectic schedule possible.
- Naomi came to America to perfect her English, meet boys and have adventures; getting up at 6:30 a.m. to coddle two children was not her favorite part of the plan.
- Even though she thought keeping up with two kids was a chore, she knew better than to complain out loud.
- Most mornings Valerie got up, feeds Greyboy, changed his litter box and is in the shower by the time Naomi came upstairs to wake up six-year-old David.

- After breakfast, Naomi piled Valerie and David into the family station wagon and drives them to their respective schools.
- After school, she picked them up and began the seemingly endless procession to lessons and appointments.
- Valerie normally sees her mother at dinner and sometimes before bed, but seldom sees her father since their move to Connecticut.
- When they lived in Mount Kisco, he worked hard but always came home at night, no matter how late.
- Now, he had an apartment in the city, coming to Stamford only on Sundays.
- When home, he delighted in hearing Valerie play the cello; sometimes entire Sunday afternoons were spent showing her father all she has done during the past week.
- Recently, she even dressed up for a Sunday concert for one, as though it were a formal orchestra recital, wearing her long black skirt, white blouse and black dress pumps.
- While her father enjoyed her performances, Valerie knew that he liked her brother best.
- David's boisterous recitations and antics have her father roaring with laughter; he never laughs that hard at her stories.
- Late at night, after Valerie went to bed, she sometimes heard her mother and father argue; one night her father called for a driver and left in the middle of the night.
- The next night at dinner, her mother said terrible things and even blurted out that Valerie's music teacher thought that she is very technically competent, but will never be a great artist.
- That night Valerie cried herself to sleep, afraid her father might never come back, and equally afraid her music teacher was right in his assessment of her talent.

Life in the Community: Stamford, Connecticut

- Located in southwestern Connecticut, Stamford is located on Long Island Sound, at the New York border; its population is approximately 103,000.
- Because of its location, the city serves as the headquarters of numerous Fortune 500 corporations.
- Ruth Jaffen felt that living closer to New York City would provide the children with the many advantages they deserve.
- Stamford boasts a branch of the University of Connecticut, a branch of the Whitney Museum of American Art, and the Stamford Museum and Nature Center.

- In music, the city is known for the Stamford Symphony Orchestra, the Young Artists Philharmonic, and the Connecticut Grand Opera.
- The Young Artists Philharmonic was organized in 1960 to give talented young musicians a chance to play challenging music and participate in concerts.
- Through the years, it has been invited to perform for national, state and special events; quartets and quintets from the orchestra often perform at local functions.
- The Stamford Marriott Crossword Puzzle Tournament is an annual event in the city, attracting thousands.
- Since incorporation in 1893, city officials have bestowed a variety of nicknames and mottoes on Stamford: City of Research, City in Step with Tomorrow, and Lock City.

The Young Artists Philharmonic, Admission

Admission to the orchestra is by closed auditions which are held in September and May of each year. Students should come prepared to play any short piece or étude of their choice which best reflects their abilities. Older students will be asked to sight-read. Students are auditioned on an individual basis by the conductors, who have the sole determination as to group placement. Students are placed by ability, not age, although some students find it beneficial to be placed relative to their peer group. Students, with the exception of the flute players, are informed of their placement at the time of their audition.

1985: Alex Behr, Corporate Director of European Operations

Alex and Naomi Behr returned to Switzerland for the second time where Alex headed European operations for Union Carbide. He was in charge of Union Carbide companies in three countries, and during his reign, the full impact of an attempted takeover was becoming clear.

Life at Home

- The Behrs lived in a Swiss section of Geneva, Switzerland, avoiding the section of the city populated by "IAs" or Internationally Assigned foreigners, mostly Americans.
- They believed it is more exotic to live with Swiss neighbors.
- They were renting a home previously occupied by a company executive who recently retired.
- The home was a duplex, and large by European standards at 2,000 square feet.
- They were paying $1,600 a month in rent.
- He traveled extensively in his job, often nine out of 10 weeks, and was rarely home.
- When he traveled to the Middle East or eastern Europe on business, he did not even make it home on weekends.
- His wife Naomi attempted to make friends, but their son, a sophomore in high school, was miserable.
- His son wanted to return to the United States where he could play American football, see his girlfriend, and drive a car.
- Even though he had a driver's license from the United States, the laws of Switzerland do not permit the teenager to drive until he is 18 years old.
- Naomi returned occasionally to the United States to see her two oldest children, both of whom were in college.
- The couple also took several trips together, including an antique-buying spree in London, a cruise in the Mediterranean, and a trip to northern Africa to buy rugs.
- They purchased a vacation home on Cape Cod in Massachusetts.
- Each month, they mailed $2,000 to the United States for mortgage and upkeep of the second home.
- The first of three children and the son of a salesman, Alex was born in the Boston community of Hyde Park in 1940, and was raised in that city.

Alex Behr was in charge of companies in three countries and five businesses.

The Behrs lived in a Swiss section of Geneva, Switzerland, adjacent to farms but not far from the more populated parts of the city.

- His father worked as a salesman at various times for the family lumber business, Bendix, during the Second World War, and for a company that manufactured commercial laundry equipment.
- His mother, who did not work, was active in the Episcopal Church in the altar guild as a Sunday school teacher, and also as a welcome hostess in the community.
- She enjoyed playing bridge and taking part in a "Thought Club" of women that gathered once a month to discuss current books.
- His father took his work seriously, rarely allowing himself time to participate in his children's activities and athletic events.
- His paternal grandparents and his maternal grandmother all lived within a few blocks of his childhood home.
- Because a relative previously worked for Union Carbide, Alex interviewed with the company following his graduation from MIT.
- Until he was six years old, the family rented a home; after the third child was born, his parents bought the first and last home they would own.
- To accommodate the growing family, the house was expanded, adding a two-story addition that provided an additional bedroom upstairs and a breakfast room downstairs.
- After the addition, the house had four bedrooms, one bathroom upstairs, and a half-bathroom downstairs and also included a two-car garage.
- When the home was built, the streets within the city limits of Boston were still unpaved.
- In the 1950s, Alex's sister developed polio and nearly died.
- Only a few years later, the Salk vaccine was introduced, dramatically reducing the occurrence of the illness.

- Growing up, he walked to the area schools, which were often more than a mile away; in the seventh grade, he enrolled in West Roxbury Latin School, after which his father drove him to and from school.
- There he was required to participate in organized athletics and selected baseball, football, and wrestling as his sports.
- Prior to attending Roxbury Latin, he had never played football.
- His education included training in Greek, allowing him to read the Bible in Greek by his junior year; he had considered a career in the ordained clergy, but did not pursue the inclination.
- At MIT, he majored in beer, girls, and engineering, roughly in that order.
- During his sophomore year, he began specializing in chemical engineering because many of his friends were headed in that direction and it required less math.
- At MIT, he participated in the two years of mandatory ROTC training and then elected to participate in it his third and fourth years; his senior year he was a Senior Regional Commander of the Perishing Rifles, a subsidiary activity of ROTC.

Life at Work

- He is at the pinnacle of his career as a vice president at Union Carbide, with authority over five businesses and three country companies—Germany, Turkey, and Dubai.
- His home base is Geneva, Switzerland, although he travels nine weeks out of 10.
- He thinks nothing of making a day trip from Geneva to Dusseldorf, Germany, headquarters of the German operations.
- Chauffeurs drive him to and from the airport, occasionally the company's private plane flies him where he needs to be that day.
- A trip away from home may last a day, but often will take more than a week, especially when he visits customers throughout eastern Europe or the Middle East.
- Business meetings are held with suppliers of the raw materials used by the company, customers, and prospects.
- He often conducts business over dinner, and his days are frequently very long.
- The trips also allow him to review the business performance of the areas he manages, which include films for the food industry, metal coatings, proprietary catalysts, and engineering services.
- Language is rarely an issue; English is spoken well and freely by the people he meets, especially businessmen in developed countries.
- Alex also speaks French, but not well enough, he believes, to negotiate sensitive deals in that language.
- Six times a year, he flies back to the United States for planning sessions and meetings in Connecticut at corporate headquarters.
- Even though Union Carbide's market reach is global, most strategic decision making is still centralized in the United States.
- Union Carbide's current employment worldwide tops 100,000.
- The company describes itself in annual reports as a "global powerhouse."
- It leads the world in polyolefin production, dry-cell batteries, and graphite electrodes for steel making, and is the largest producer of industrial gases in the United States.
- Its portfolio includes an agricultural products business, the world's largest-selling brand of antifreeze, and such specialty businesses as food-processing, silicones, molecular sieves, coating services, specialty chemicals, and specialty polymers.
- A Carbide associate's identity is built around reliability, responsibility, and stability.
- Many Wall Street analysts view Carbide as a dull, underperforming company and are growing more concerned about the impact of the chemical leak at Bhopal and a hostile takeover bid that is now under way.

Union Carbide's employment worldwide topped 100,000.

- The December 3, 1984, tragedy of a chemical leak at Bhopal, India, changed the company.
- The release of the gas methyl isocyanate, used in the preparation of insecticides, resulted in the deaths of more than 3,500 people in India and 150,000 injuries.
- When stockholders met in the spring of 1985, the per-share stock price had fallen from $60 a share to $30.
- Union Carbide is currently attempting to fend off a hostile takeover by GAF Corporation.
- This has been one of the most turbulent years for Carbide, which began its operations in 1917 in the Kanawha Valley of West Virginia.
- Alex joined Union Carbide in 1961 in Charleston, West Virginia, the same year he married Naomi.
- Within a year, he returned to MIT to obtain a master's degree while Union Carbide held his job open; he did not believe himself equipped to handle the demands of the job without more education.
- Their first child was born in 1963 while he was studying at MIT.
- Once his master's degree was completed, he finished his military commitment in the Signal Corps and was assigned to Fort Gordon, Georgia, and Fort Monmonth, New Jersey, where he served on the radio and electrical engineering faculty.
- Their second child, a son, was born during this time.
- He returned to Union Carbide in 1965 in the Chemical and Plastics Division.
- There, Alex spent his time doing "rough appraisals," a new idea—evaluation process that linked engineering, research and development, and marketing; it was heavily layered in the bureaucracy for which Union Carbide is well known.
- Carefully constructed layers of bureaucracy within the company make every decision slow, safe, and often cumbersome.
- Shortly after returning to the company, Alex joined the agricultural chemicals business, known for its popular Sevin insecticide and Temik, a more toxic insecticide used only by professionals.
- For the next two years, he was involved in collaborative projects between the chemical engineering staff and research and development.
- Then he was asked to take a cross-training assignment for a year in production—the actual making of 10 different products at a plant in West Virginia.

- Most of the products were for metal crafting, paints, automotive fluids, or chemical intermediates.
- In 1967, he and Naomi purchased their first home, a split-entry home of 1,144 square feet, for which they paid $25,575; their house payments are $179 per month.
- The next year, he moved into engineering with the hydrocarbon group, where gas concentrates were cracked into chemical products.
- The company also assigned him to a team investigating a multi-million plant explosion in Texas; working with experts in production, research and development, and engineering, the team reconstructed the accident.
- The six-month investigation required frequent trips to the company's room-size IBM 360 computer; computer time was so precious, he was permitted only 20 to 30 minutes, often after midnight, to run his calculations.
- Once a computer run was completed and analyzed, a new set of computer cards was created so another set of calculations could be run—when time was available.
- The writing of software and running of calculations consumed half of the six-month investigation.
- He was then promoted and asked to move to New York, the corporate headquarters.
- There, at 31 years old, he served as a business analyst working for a business vice president.
- He, Naomi, and their three children lived in Norwalk, Connecticut, in a house near the commuter line.
- Each morning at 7:00 a.m., he rode the train to Manhattan, often not returning home until after 9 p.m.
- The workday sometimes included entertaining customers and party time after work—all considered part of the job.
- Union Carbide was in its heyday—a world leader in a variety of products and processes.
- After two years of long hours, frequent weekend projects, and close interaction with the leaders of the company, he was asked in 1973 to move to Geneva, Switzerland, and join the agricultural product marketing.
- It was a time of travel and adventure for his growing family.
- Two years later, he returned to Charleston, West Virginia, where his career had begun, to work in agricultural products, and then accepted a role as director of Engineering, establishing an engineering department in Jacksonville, Florida.
- When he and the family moved back to New York in 1979, he was head of engineering and operations at age 37, supervising half a dozen plants and dozens of engineers.
- In New York, he was named vice president over herbicide and plant growth regulators worldwide; it was an exciting time, but the company was changing, and when he was asked to return to Europe he jumped at the chance.
- He liked being with customers and having direct responsibility for day-to-day results.

Life in the Community: Geneva, Switzerland
- They lived in a small community outside the city of Geneva, Switzerland.
- This scenic, affluent city sits on Lake Geneva, the largest Alpine Lake.
- The city was remarkably international; its non-Swiss population accounts for one third of its 165,000 residents
- Geneva was home to the European headquarters of the United Nations and the central offices of more than 200 international bodies from the Red Cross to the World Council of Churches.
- Natives are more likely to speak English as their second language, in addition to German, Italian, or French.
- Geneva's Old Town is an architectural gem of cathedrals and stately buildings, which attest to the city's wealth in the late Middle Ages and Renaissance periods.
- Crescent-shaped Lake Geneva is 45 miles long and two to nine miles wide.

- The city was known for its elegant cafés, lakeside promenades, and trees; there are at least three trees for every resident within the city limits.
- Characteristic of its opulence, two thirds of the 13,000 hotel beds in the city are in deluxe or first-class hotels.[1]

1985: Carleen Cahill, Classical Music Singer

Carleen Cahill's classical music career began by "playing" a stringless violin, and progressed to successful New York City opera singer before transitioning into voice teacher/performer in a small upstate New York community.

Life at Home

- Carleen Rose Cahill was born in Detroit, Michigan, in 1951.
- She was first exposed to music through her parents, who would play 78 rpm records of swing and big band music.
- Her family would often dance and sing along to the music of Benny Goodman and Glen Miller, and Carleen actually sang before she spoke.
- Carleen sang in the school chorus as early as she could remember, and had her first solo—the third verse of "The Battle Hymn of the Republic"—in the fourth grade.
- Carleen's first instrument was the violin, which she started playing in fifth grade, after seeing her school's orchestra play *The Nutcracker Suite*.
- Carleen used a family violin that belonged to her grandmother, but it did not have any strings.
- She practiced finger positions and "played" on that stringless instrument for almost a year.
- When her teacher saw Carleen practicing finger positions on the edge of her desk, she encouraged Carleen's mother to put strings on her violin.
- As she got older, Carleen became increasingly interested in the rock music of the 1960s—including the Beatles, Chuck Berry, and the Rolling Stones—becoming a lifelong Beatles fan.
- Carleen's brother bought her a guitar for her sixteenth birthday, which she played in local bands, especially Joni Mitchell songs.
- Although she continued to play guitar and violin throughout high school, she discovered that singing brought her the most pleasure.
- Singing had always felt very natural to her, and she sang it all while growing up—pop, rock, church, classic and folk, but not opera.
- In fact, she did not enjoy opera at all during high school.

Classically trained singer Carleen Cahill thrived in New York City's opera scene.

- After high school, Carleen worked in an insurance company as a secretary.
- She also sang in a folk trio after work, performing at coffeehouses and making very little money.
- Her sister persuaded her to go to college to pursue a music career.
- Carleen got her Bachelor's of Music in Voice Performance at Western Michigan University in Kalamazoo, several hours west of Detroit—close enough to her family, but far enough to be on her own.
- Studying music in college in the early 1970s was not terribly common.

Make-up was important in transforming performers into many operatic roles.

- There were fewer career resources, and students had to figure out—by themselves—the practical aspects of how to become professional musicians.
- In college, Carleen discovered her love of opera and her ability to perform.
- Her music department put on three full-scale opera performances per year—a lot for a school of its size—giving Carleen the opportunity to experience a variety of musical styles, and to discover how much she enjoyed working as part of a team with the other cast and crew members.
- She found that she never got nervous when singing with other people in an opera production.
- As a voice performance music major, she was also required to study four languages: Spanish, French, Italian and German.
- During her college years, she sang with the Muskegon Symphony for $200, and with the Detroit Symphony for the experience.
- Upon graduating college, her goal was clear—to train as a classical singer.
- Carleen took the next step and got her Master's of Music in Voice Performance from the University of Michigan in Ann Arbor.
- In graduate school, Carleen performed six fullscale operas, which she added to her professional repertoire, as: the mother in E. Humperdinck's *Hansel and Gretel;* Donna Elvira and Donna Anna in Mozart's *Don Giovanni;* the widow in F. Lehar's *The Merry Widow;* Rosalinda in J. Strauss' *Die Fledermaus; and Musetta in Puccini's La Bohème.*
- Opera required much more than just singing; the best performers needed to act, be physically fit, have a good sense of timing, and the ability to work well with a cast and crew.
- Carleen paid her way through graduate school by singing at local church ceremonies for $50 per event, and by her permanent position as the church soloist.

In college, Carleen performed the leading role in Falstaff *by Verdi.*

Life at Work

- Armed with her Master's of Music in Voice Performance, Carleen Cahill moved to New York City in 1975 to pursue a classical singing career —a necessary career move for a classical singer.
- Upon arriving in New York, Carleen waitressed to support herself and her continued studies with a professional voice teacher—another necessary career decision that cost $50 per lesson.
- Professional voice teachers in New York required students to audition before being accepted to study in their studios.
- Carleen auditioned and was accepted into the studio of a teacher who was recommended by her professors in graduate school.

Carleen with her sister, mother and brother after a graduate school performance.

- The teacher was very strict, and would not let Carleen audition for anything for a year and a half.
- Once Carleen began auditioning for parts, however, she had great success and began performing often in and around New York.
- Her work at this time included three different roles with the Bronx Opera (Donna Anna in Mozart's *Don Giovanni,* Susannah in Carlyle Floyd's *Susannah,* and Violetta in Giuseppe Verdi's *La Traviata*).
- She also sang as the soprano soloist in Handel's *Judas Maccabeus* in the New York City's Choral Festival, and was engaged by Boris Goldovsky to sing for several of his numerous lectures at the Metropolitan Museum of Art lecture series on opera.
- Three years after arriving in New York, Carleen took her career to the next level by engaging a professional management company.
- The management company helped Carleen get high-level performing jobs, such as the soprano soloist in Beethoven's *Ninth Symphony* at the Saratoga Arts Festival, Musetta in Puccini's *La Bohème* with the Houston Grand Opera Festival, and Nedda in Ruggiero Leoncavallo's *I Pagliacci* with the New York City Opera Touring Company.
- Once professionally managed, Carleen was able to support herself exclusively with music, even though the management company typically took 15 percent of her paycheck for opera roles and 20 percent for oratorio and orchestral work.

Conductor Boris Goldovsky engaged Carleen to sing at his opera lecture series at the Metropolitan Museum of Art

- Carleen often got jobs through the international opera circuit that regularly traveled to New York to hold auditions for shows in other cities.
- The representatives of the opera companies in this circuit often cast performers based on very specific—and sometimes non-talent-related criteria.
- For example, if a company had already found an especially tall woman to play the female lead, they would open auditions for the male lead to only tall men.
- Carleen's management company arranged for her to audition for suitable parts, one of her favorite being Violetta in Verdi's *La Traviata.*

- Once she got a role, Carleen would travel to the city of the performance for one to two months of rehearsals and shows.
- This gave her an opportunity to travel around the world and make many new friends and colleagues.
- The opera circuit was also a steady source of income, and compensation per show was $2,000-$8,000, depending on the size of the company.
- Carleen performed all over the country and abroad, including with opera companies in San Francisco, New Orleans, Austin, Phoenix, Seattle, Geneva, and Buenos Aires.
- Her favorite performance was as Mimi in Puccini's *La Bohème*, performed in Maracaibo, Venezuela; the audience sat in the aisles and sang along to all of the opera choruses.

Playing Mimi in La Boheme, *in Venezuela, was one of Carleen's most memorable performances.*

- She also accepted roles with smaller opera companies, depite less pay; this was a way to try out new roles in a smaller and often more forgiving arena before performing them in a larger city.
- It was just such a role that led her to upstate New York, where she fell in love with the area's natural beauty and relaxed pace.
- In 1980, she bought a house in Hillsdale, New York, and began splitting her time between city and country.

Life in the Community: Hillsdale, New York

- While Carleen enjoyed living in New York City and traveling around the world to perform, this lifestyle prevented her from putting down roots.
- In 1980, The Columbia County Opera Company was founded by a wealthy opera lover from New York looking to recreate the country opera experience that was popular in his native England.
- The small opera company offered an intimate performance environment, and produced a series of outdoor concerts set against the scenic backdrop of beautiful upstate New York.
- While the year-round population of the area was small, the community's proximity to the city made it a popular tourist destination, and the Columbia County Opera's audience was accustomed to top-rate performances.
- Despite its beautiful location and proximity to New York City, however, it was difficult for the opera company to attract top-rate performers, mostly because they couldn't meet big city salaries, which could be as much as $2,000-$5,000 higher per show.
- Despite less money, the Columbia County Opera Company was exactly what Carleen was looking for—more time in the country combined with her passion for music.
- In 1981, she performed in their second season, and again in 1982, in Mozart's *L'oca del Cairo* and *La Finta Giardiniera.*
- In 1983, Carleen married Joseph, the Italian repairman who often came to fix her less-than-dependable country phone service, ending her city/country lifestyle.
- In Hillsdale full-time, Carleen had fewer musical opportunities than in New York, but she enjoyed living in one place and being involved in the community.
- She began teaching voice at the local music school.
- She also became an adjunct music professor at a nearby college.
- Some of her students were involved in school plays for which Carleen enjoyed helping them rehearse, and was often in the front row on opening night.

Carleen as Rosalinda in J. Strauss' Die Fledermaus.

1986: Jake Szmanda, Timber Industry Worker and Animal Conservationist

Jake Szmanda worked in the timber industry at a time when environmentalists, on behalf of the northern spotted owl, threatened to destroy his livelihood. He felt there was room enough for both people and animals in the woods.

Life at Home

- Jake Szmanda grew up in the tiny town of Lakeview, located in the southeast corner of Oregon and nestled against the Willamette National Forest—the source of 86 million feet of board lumber a year.
- Jake's father Larry worked in the timber industry, first for a major company and then as an independent contractor running his own crew.
- As a project manager, Larry supervised much of the on-site logging work, while Jake's older sister, Mary, worked as an administrative assistant.
- The family shared a love for nature and respected the wood products that supported them financially.
- Jake's grandfather even built their house from trees he had cut, boarded, dried and nailed.
- The cabin was given to Jake's parents as a wedding present; Jake was always told that the house was part of his legacy and should never leave the family.
- Jake grew up in the woods and loved to track rabbits, identify snakes and recite excited tales about grizzly bears he spotted.
- He was taught that there was room enough for man and animals in the woods if they showed each other some respect.
- Early on, Jake learned that working with timber was demanding, requiring 11- to 12-hour days of hard physical labor.
- As a boy he was taught how to fell a tree to an exact spot using either an axe or a saw.
- Jake's father was proud of his profession; wood from the Willamette forests was shipped across the entire United States and used for homes, businesses, furniture and many other things which were "vital to the American way of life," Larry frequently said.
- But not everyone felt that way.

Jake Szmanda fought for the right to work in the timber industry.

- A new species of human beings who called themselves environmentalists wanted a say in how the national forests were managed.
- Of particular concern were recent studies that determined that the old-growth trees that brought a premium price were also home to northern spotted owls, a rare, nocturnal species uniquely dependent on the Northwest's virgin forests.
- The centuries-old trees were the primary nesting ground for the northern spotted owls, which were declining in population as the old-growth forests were harvested.
- Concentrated for the most part in 12 national forests on the western slope of the Cascades, these giant evergreen stands of spruce, hemlock and Douglas fir—some taller than a 30-story building—once covered an estimated 19 million acres.
- Scientists said that only 2.5 million to 3.5 million acres of oldgrowth timber remained and were disappearing at the rate of 67,000 acres a year.
- About 900,000 acres were permanently protected in parks or wilderness areas.

Jake's grandfather built their house from trees he had cut, boarded, dried and nailed.

- But the weapon that environmentalists wanted to wield against loggers was the Endangered Species Act, which protected birds and animals that were in danger of becoming scarce or extinct.
- Larry said that the definition of an environmentalist was a "city dweller with a new pair of hiking boots in his closet."
- But he secretly knew his industry was in a death struggle over the future of the Northwest's dwindling ancient forests, a mountainous, fog-shrouded realm that stretched from northern California to British Columbia.
- He also knew that the power enjoyed by the wood products industry was changing as Americans got their nature knowledge from the Discovery Channel and Disney.
- When Jake graduated high school in 1984, he planned to attend community college.
- Then, unexpectedly, his girlfriend Holly told him that she was pregnant.
- They married, Jake dropped out of college and joined his father in the Oregon forest, where work was steady and the pay excellent.

Jake's family shared a love for nature.

- But tensions were already building between the logging industry and environmental groups.
- Demonstrations and petitions against logging became more common.
- Logging roads were blockaded and loggers threatened; some radical environmentalists began driving metal railroad spikes into the uncut trees to

make harvesting more dangerous and less profitable.
- Jake's father called them all "tree huggers" and said they were a passing fad.
- One day, Jake's sister came to the work site extremely upset.
- She said that there were news cameras and demonstrators outside her office: city people, every one of them.
- The next day it was all over the papers: the demonstrators wanted to stop logging in the Willamette.
- The northern spotted owls were now more important than the livelihood of loggers.

Life at Work

- Jake Szmanda and his family quickly learned that the northern spotted owl controversy would not go away.
- With another mouth to feed, Jake was haunted by the phantom owl as he tried to sleep.
- He needed to work steadily, not when the government said it was okay.
- Besides, everyone in logging agreed the compromise offered by the United States Forest Service was a giveaway to the eco-freaks who wouldn't know a spotted owl from a mockingbird.
- The plan called for the protection of 314,000 to 690,000 acres of national forest and would cost the timber industry $28 million to $32 million a year.
- The agency considered a number of alternatives, ranging from no formal measures to protect the owl to a complete ban on timber production in existing owl habitats.
- Then, the Reagan Administration declared that America's resources should be used, not hidden away; besides, new fast-growing trees could be planted in their place.
- It was great to have the president on your side, Larry said, but he was concerned about the future.
- After years of saying, "Don't worry," Larry had changed his tune to "We're now the ones who are endangered."
- Larry and Jake agreed that if the spotted owl gained federal protection under the Endangered Species Act, their livelihoods were doomed.
- After a lifetime of ignoring newspapers and magazines, Jake became a reader.
- And he was appalled to see loggers branded as wasteful despoilers of the land; clear cutting was an effective land management tool.
- The environmentalists clearly knew little about the economics or the dangers of harvesting the wood products Americans were eager to buy, but they knew everything about running their mouths and crying to Congress.
- Activists had petitioned Congress to declare the northern spotted owl an endangered species, which would forbid the logging industry to destroy any part of the forest that the owls might inhabit.
- The people in the logging industry were enraged.

The Northern Spotted Owl

- Small towns all over the Pacific Northwest, many of which were dependent on logging, were in turmoil.
- Jake was caught right in the middle of the crossfire.
- Without logging he, his father, and his sister would be out of a job with no qualifications to do anything else.
- Larry's solution was to cut as much timber as he could before the restrictions were put in place; Jake and Holly decided to take on the environmentalists by using the media.
- Jake told Holly, "Our kids are a lot cuter than any spotted owl; someone has to say that timbering is about people's lives."
- "Besides," Holly said, "it isn't an all-or-nothing situation. We may not have as many spotted owls if we keep cutting, but they won't disappear."
- To get his first interview, Jake approached a TV reporter and told him he had something to say.
- The interview, which took place right in front of a bunch of signwaving city kids, lasted three full minutes.
- That night, Holly, Larry and Mary were thrilled to hear him say, "The environmental community would have you believe that the last of the old growth is on a logging truck heading for the mill, and that's not the case. It's time for some truth-telling and a lot less yelling." And then the camera swung over to the demonstrators.
- For the second interview, Holly dressed the two boys in bib overalls and held them on her lap while Jake talked about his love of the woods, including the spotted owl, a bird he had only seen twice.
- After that, TV stations from San Francisco to Boston couldn't wait to interview the cute family who thought there was room enough in the woods for both birds and people.
- But it quickly stopped being fun.
- Wood product executives—whose hands had never held a chainsaw—started telling him what to say, what to do and how to dress the kids.
- Eco-demonstrators hurled a stuffed owl at his oldest son and yelled "bird-killer" in his four-year-old's face.
- And business was drying up.
- With the changing regulations and uncertainty, the little guy was getting squeezed out by the more sophisticated corporations with lobbyists in Washington.
- Owl or no owl, some days there was no wood to cut.
- Small mills were closing up and small towns suffering.
- So Jake started talking about hard times and unemployment checks during the TV interviews, and the requests to speak stopped coming.
- He just wasn't cute anymore.

Life in the Community: Willamette National Forest, Oregon

- Nowhere were competing pressures of environment versus economy more acute than in the 1.7-million-acre Willamette National Forest, which sprawled across Oregon's western Cascades.
- Like many national forests in the Northwest, the Willamette remained largely undisturbed until the postwar building boom.
- About 500,000 acres of old growth remained in the Willamette, and 90,000 of that was permanently protected as designated wilderness.
- But many environmentalists felt that more of the old-growth forests should have been set aside to save the spotted owl.
- Scientists estimated that a single pair of the 15-inch-tall nocturnal birds required about 4,000 acres of old-growth forest to ensure an adequate food supply.
- Biologists said that the bird's population, currently at about 3,000 pairs, was declining at the rate of 1 to 2 percent a year.

- Meanwhile, forest managers in the Willamette were obligated to provide timber at the levels specified by Congress and thus found themselves at odds with their own biologists.
- Spotted owls and environmentalists notwithstanding, timber accounted for 85 percent of the Willamette's management budget.
- Besides, the Reagan Administration was urging the Forest Service to accelerate the liquidation of the old trees in these virgin stands and replace them with faster-growing young stock.
- The approach reflected the goal of the Reagan Administration to greatly increase the production of timber, as well as oil, minerals and other commodities from the national forests.
- Under the plan, more economic activity could be generated from federal lands by turning over their resources to private industry as quickly as possible.
- The National Forest system had been created by the Forest Reserve Act of 1891.
- Based in part on the recommendations of Gifford Pinchot, the nation's first chief forester, the law was intended to prevent the reckless pillaging of the nation's forests.
- Reflecting Pinchot's views, the forests were to first serve the purpose of watershed protection, and then to assure "a continuous supply of timber for the use and necessities of the United States."
- The role of the forests was gradually broadened through such laws as the Multiple Use-Sustained Yield Act of 1960 and the National Forest Management Act of 1976, which required the forests to serve a broad spectrum of purposes, including wildlife protection and recreation.

Willamette National Forest.

WOODWORKING GUIDE

CUT AND DRIED

Working with wood is a joint venture between you
and the material. Learn to get along.

1986: James Kenny Jarrett, Super Accurate Rifle Guru

James Kenny Jarrett's farm machinery know-how helped him build rifles with accuracy never seen before.

Life at Home

- James Kenny Jarrett was obsessed with achieving the kind of pinpoint rifle accuracy most hunters never considered possible.
- Kenny's precision standard revolved around the ability to fire three bullets through the same hole at a distance of 300 yards.
- Or, at the very least, to consistently hit a penny from a distance of three football fields.
- He already personally held six world records for competitive shooting and his rifles had established nine more.
- But since his first love was hunting, Kenny's real passion was for the development of super accurate hunting rifles and hand-loaded cartridges that delivered in the field.
- His inventive dedication to accuracy had already earned the bearded, tobacco-chewing "good ol' boy" from rural South Carolina a local following of Southern hunters eager to take down a big buck at 400 yards.
- Now it was time to expand his market to include a national audience.
- Kenny grew up a soybean farmer on his uncle's 10,000-acre Cowden Plantation, situated on a secondary road near Jackson, South Carolina.
- By the age of 12, he had a farm boy's familiarity with machinery, matched by a natural ability to create and fabricate with his hands what his brain envisioned.
- His days were consumed by farming problems and deer hunting pleasures on the expansive property of Cowden Plantation, bordered by the Savannah River to the west and the government-controlled Savannah River Site to the south, where plutonium had been manufactured since the 1950s.
- But Kenny eventually grew frustrated that off-the-rack hunting rifles rarely delivered the accuracy he needed to

James Kennedy Jarrett's handcrafted precision rifles were a hunter's dream.

bag the shy bucks who warily stayed on the fringes of the soybean fields 400 yards away—and out of range.

- He decided to do something about it: he bought a metal lathe and began building precision big-game rifles as a hobby.
- Like most one-man operations, Kenny started out making rifles using customer-supplied actions which he retuned to fit with an outsourced barrel and stock.
- His results were inconsistent.
- The performance of the rifle, after all, depended on the quality of the components as much as the skill with which they've been put together.

Jarrett was not satisfied with a "good enough for hunting" rifle.

- It was a time of learning, listening, and absorbing the accuracy lessons of the hyper-competitive benchrest shooting crowd.
- He came to hate the phrase "good enough," as in "good enough for hunting," as he formed a vision of inventing a precision rifle that exceeded expectations for accuracy.
- Then, in 1979, after farming most of his life, Kenny turned to gunsmithing full-time.
- For the next seven years, Kenny stayed busy building hunting rifles to his exacting specifications—often exceeding the expectations of his customers, who bragged about their Jarrett rifle at every hunt camp in the South.
- His own field exploits added to the mystique after Kenny fired one memorable shot that took down a gemsbok in Africa at 557 yards.

- At the same time, he continued pursuing another passion—collecting the artifacts left on the river banks of the Savannah River or in the fields by multiple generations of Native Americans.
- The flowing waters of the Savannah River had attracted some of the earliest inhabitants to the region, most of whom left some evidence of their lives: from scrapers, to projectile points, to nutting rocks.
- Nearly every year's plowing exposed new "points" and even delicately carved gorgets, which were worn around the neck.
- Each was appropriately preserved and mounted in glass cases that dominated an entire room in Kenny's home.
- Like most things in his life, there was an exacting artistry to the display.
- In addition, to accommodate the needs of a growing family, Kenny built a swimming pool and fishing ponds, and purchased trampoline sets for the children.
- A fourth-generation soybean farmer, Kenny was determined to keep his kids on the farm.

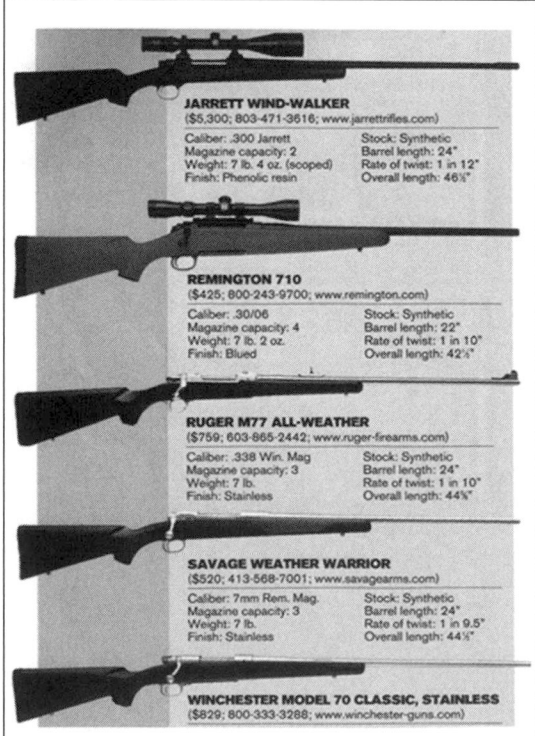

JARRETT WIND-WALKER
($5,300; 803-471-3616; www.jarrettrifles.com)

Caliber: .300 Jarrett	Stock: Synthetic
Magazine capacity: 2	Barrel length: 24"
Weight: 7 lb. 4 oz. (scoped)	Rate of twist: 1 in 12"
Finish: Phenolic resin	Overall length: 46½"

REMINGTON 710
($425; 800-243-9700; www.remington.com)

Caliber: .30/06	Stock: Synthetic
Magazine capacity: 4	Barrel length: 22"
Weight: 7 lb. 2 oz.	Rate of twist: 1 in 10"
Finish: Blued	Overall length: 42⅝"

RUGER M77 ALL-WEATHER
($759; 603-865-2442; www.ruger-firearms.com)

Caliber: .338 Win. Mag	Stock: Synthetic
Magazine capacity: 3	Barrel length: 24"
Weight: 7 lb.	Rate of twist: 1 in 10"
Finish: Stainless	Overall length: 44⅜"

SAVAGE WEATHER WARRIOR
($520; 413-568-7001; www.savagearms.com)

Caliber: 7mm Rem. Mag.	Stock: Synthetic
Magazine capacity: 3	Barrel length: 24"
Weight: 7 lb.	Rate of twist: 1 in 9.5"
Finish: Stainless	Overall length: 44¼"

WINCHESTER MODEL 70 CLASSIC, STAINLESS
($829; 800-333-3288; www.winchester-guns.com)

A Jarrett rifle, although more expensive than most, was well worth the money.

Life at Work

- Kenny Jarrett realized early on there was a niche in the gun market for an accurate game rifle that was built the right way—even when experts predicted that hunters would not pay topdrawer prices for a hunting rifle.
- Traditionally, the highest-priced rifles sported highly carved walnut stocks that added artistry and weight to the rifle, but not dependability.
- Kenny abstained from using walnut stocks—in fact, any wood stocks at all—convinced that wood movement was a handicap to accuracy.
- To attract the elite hunter willing to spend triple the ordinary price for a one-of-a-kind hunting experience, he needed to be the best.
- To be the entrepreneur he envisioned, he also had to capture the title of inventor and find a mentor.
- The most influential accuracy expert was Texas gunmaker and benchrest shooter Harold Broughton, who took the time to set Kenny on the right path to making accurate rifles.
- But it was hundreds of hours in the shop and more than a few sleepless nights that gave Kenny the insights he needed to be a pioneer.
- His first year building rifles he grossed $17,000—enough to encourage expansion.
- By 1985, the sale of Jarrett rifles topped $300,000 and 13 people were working in his 2,200-square-foot shop built of cypress wood milled by Kenny using trees cut from his property.

Crafting a Jarrett rifle took many hours and each customer waited a long time to own one.

- The basic price for a Jarrett rifle was about $2,800; extensive options could hike the price up to as much as $4,500.
- "If your rifle ain't accurate, you might as well have a pocket full of firecrackers, 'cause all you'll have is a noisemaker," he told the nation's top sports writers when they journeyed to remote Jackson, 40 minutes from Aiken, South Carolina.
- There he entertained the nation's most widely read hunting experts with long-range shooting demonstrations, fried catfish dinners and lots of homespun wisdom.
- "There's no magic in what I do. It ties correctly education, trial and error, and beating my head against the wall until it's right."
- He talked his Bubba talk, spat his chewing tobacco, and dazzled the writers with his long-range weapons, soon dubbed the "beanfield rifle"—an ultra-deadly rifle/cartridge combination for taking whitetail deer at long distances, typically 300 to 400 yards.
- In appreciation, the nation's most respected hunting and fishing magazines featured Kenny's country-wise quotes, constant suspenders and expensive rifles on their pages.
- He understood that the number of hunters willing to risk a marital fight to own a Jarrett was small and scattered, and he had to find that market by becoming a national name.

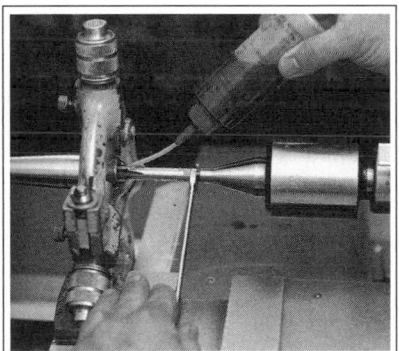

The specifications for a Jarrett rifle were so exact that many supplier parts had to be refitted.

- So he traveled to gun shows and national meetings where he talked, promoted and demonstrated.
- Eventually, the cult of accuracy and the personality of Kenny Jarrett were intertwined.
- Sales increased, his delivery time on a custom gun stretched to one year, and competitors scrambled out of the woodwork—each claiming to be an accuracy guru.
- "I never wanted to be rich; I just wanted to be the best," he explained.
- So he continued to listen, innovate and promote.
- But building a Jarrett rifle was a very labor-intensive process, limiting the number of guns that could be made to his exacting standards.
- He was encouraged to borrow more money and double the size of his shop, so the nine- to 12-month backlog of orders could be reduced.
- He was encouraged to move to a city where he'd have more exposure to customers, and advised to make less expensive rifles, even if it meant compromising quality.
- He listened, but took his own path.

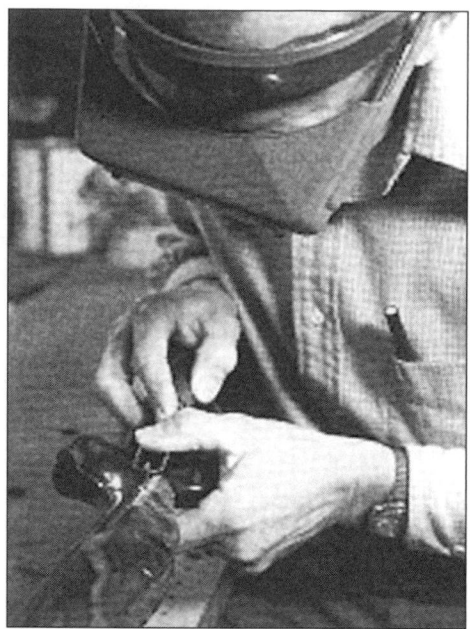

Jarrett's words of wisdom were almost as famous as his standards for accuracy.

- "When you get one of my rifles, the other rifles will gather dust 'cause you won't want to shoot them anymore."
- "It isn't that you need a half minute rifle to shoot deer; you pay the extra because accurate is what a rifle should be, and you can't abide a rifle that doesn't measure up."
- Of the one million-plus rifles sold each year, less than 5,000 were custom-built.
- "We are not everything to everybody and we don't try to be" Kenny said.
- But challenges remained.
- He found that one-third of the barrels he bought from the best supplier in the business would not shoot to his standard of sub one minute.
- These barrels were well built and achieved the benchrest standard of the day with a bore diameter with a consistency of three 10-thousands of an inch from the breech to the muzzle.
- Kenny decided that to get better performance, a barrel must have a deviation of no more than one-tenth of a thousandth.

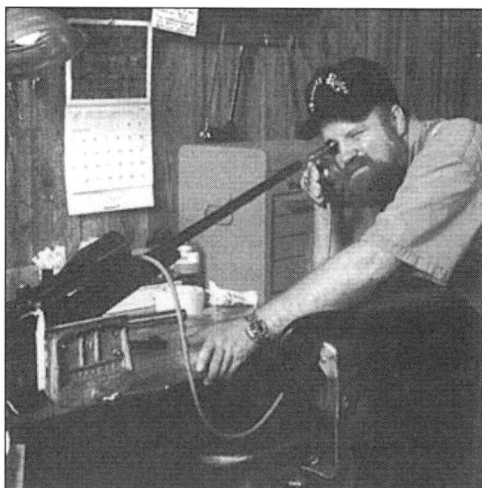

- No one manufactured a barrel with that standard, so Kenny decided he would do it himself.
- Most Jarrett rifles began with a Remington 700 action, but so much time was devoted to refitting; he was moving toward custom actions for all his rifles—a project that could take years.
- For testing his new rifles, Kenny established a state-of-the-art 100-, 200- and even 600-yard firing range; that way he didn't have to guess what his guns and cartridges would do at these distances—he knew.
- And he tested every rifle before it was sent to a customer.
- But most of all, the accuracy guru who loved to promote his inventions listened.
- He asked questions, made adjustments and studied the trends.

Jarrett tested each rifle before it was sent to the customer.

- "You can't get educated in a day," Kenny said, "I learn something everyday."

Life in the Community: Cowden Plantation, Jackson, South Carolina

- Cowden Plantation in tiny Jackson, South Carolina snuggled up to the broad shoulders of the Savannah River for more than a mile.
- For 4,000 years, hunters had roamed the fields, oxbows and cypress swamps.
- Ancient artifacts, left behind thousands of years ago, tell the tale of tribes of hunters who relied on this land for their survival.
- Antebellum days brought King Cotton to Cowden under the ownership of James Henry Hammond, a South Carolina governor whose home, Redcliffe, still proudly stands.
- The sprawling Savannah River Site near Cowden Plantation was constructed during the early 1950s to produce the basic materials used in the fabrication of nuclear weapons, primarily tritium and plutonium-239.
- These materials were used in support of our nation's defense programs, a result of the Cold War.
- The communist Soviet Union had recently tested a nuclear weapon of its own, and America's brief tenure as the lone holder of nuclear weapons in the world was at an end.
- In the immediate aftermath of the American bombing of Nagasaki and Hiroshima, scientists worldwide were horrified by the power that had been unleashed.
- But the emergence of the Soviet Union as a nuclear power happened in the midst of scientific and political debate; retaliation, it was felt, was the only defense, and a remote corner of South Carolina was a necessary tool in that battle.

COWDEN
PLANTATION

**Deer Hunting
    Augusta 15 to Oct 30th.. $250.00
month of Nov. (during the rut)................................ $350.00

**Hog Hunting
    August 15 to March 1st
    (from stands over bait)....................................... $250.00

**Turkey Hunting
    Self guided.. $250.00
    With a guide.. $350.00
    Maximium of 3 gobblers per hunter per season

Non Hunting guest with lodging.................................. $60.00
Fishing only.. $100.00

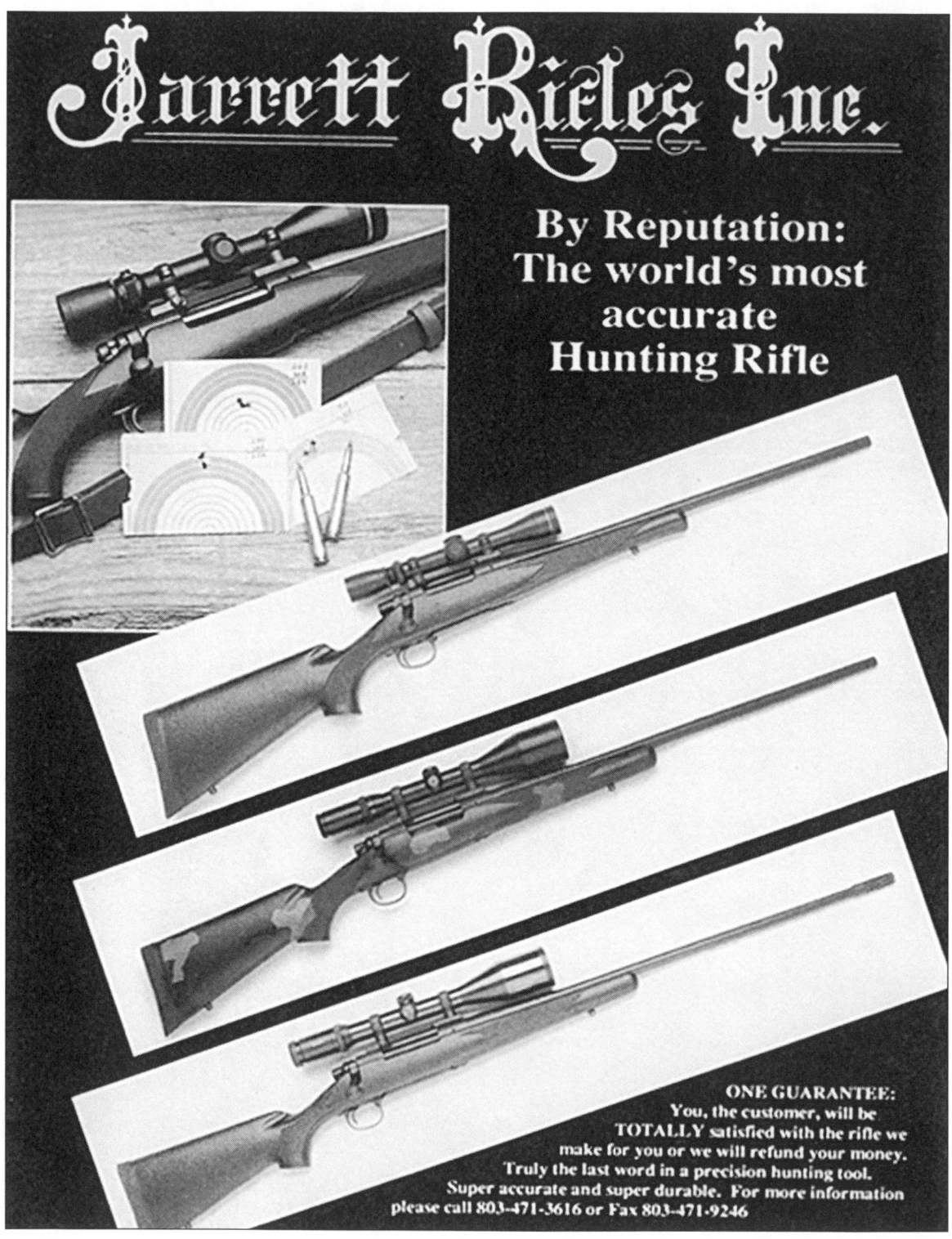

1986: Maria Knapp, Scientist from California

German-born Maria Knapp held the patents for more than a dozen scientific developments derived from a lifetime of molecular research, though the millions she earned interested her little. At 66, her focus remained her first and only love—science.

Life at Home

- At 66, Maria Knapp displayed the Old World manners she learned growing up in Germany; unfailingly gracious, she enjoyed entertaining guests—as long as the topic was science.
- To stay in shape, she ran every day and continued to do push-ups and calisthenics in the privacy of her bedroom, since she found public gymnasiums distracting, disorienting and frivolous.
- Although she bought a car—an Oldsmobile that is "all American"—she was often driven to work by an associate from the lab.
- Lab assistants also helped with her paperwork and chores such as changing the batteries in her hearing aid.
- Her first research paper—published when she was only a 14-year-old child living in Germany—described a series of fruit fly mutations that cast whisker-thin rays of light on the knowledge of embryo development.
- Her parents' home was often populated with eminent scientists from around the world who came to Berlin, the epicenter of brain research in the 1930s.
- She even traveled with her parents to Moscow, where her father was invited to study Lenin's brain, which had been preserved after his death.
- As a university and medical student in Germany, she often skipped classes to putter around the lab, making up the missed lectures by memorizing the textbooks.
- Her work continued throughout the Nazi era, even after her parents were thrown out of a leading institute in Berlin, where her father was director.
- His previous trips to communist Russia, along with the couple's close association with many fellow scientists who were Jewish, made the family untrustworthy; thus, they were banished.

As long as the topic was science, Maria Knapp was unfailingly gracious.

- Thanks to the intervention of a prominent German family who had been her father's patients, Maria's family was not imprisoned.
- Using money provided by their wealthy benefactors, her father established a private institute in the backwoods of Neustadt where their work could continue; there, they were able to offer refuge to many Jewish scientists and their families.
- During this time, Maria avoided every man, refusing to date; "I did not want to end up dating a Nazi, and in Germany at that time, you could never be sure of someone's politics."
- Devoting herself to science, she never married or had children; "Science was my milk," she likes to say.
- Her older sister, a scientist studying the biochemistry of the brain, has also opted against marriage and children.
- Maria wishes to die as her father did—in the laboratory, his last glimpse of life being the view through a microscope.

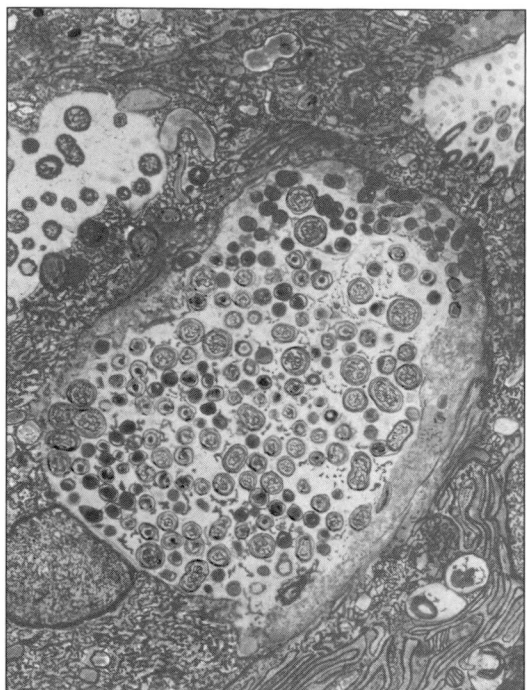

Maria had spent her life studying viruses and telomeres.

- She emigrated to Great Britain before the war broke out, becoming prominent in neuroscience, which has earned her election to the Royal Society of London.
- Repelled by her wartime experiences, she jumped at the opportunity to leave Germany in 1950 and come to the United States, even though it meant abandoning fruit fly genetics; "There was no interest in *Drosophila* research, so I had to take up something new," she recalls.
- She then emigrated to the United States when she was 30 years old, going first to the California Institute of Technology, and afterwards accepting a job at the Salk Institute.
- There, she participated in groundbreaking studies of how the polio virus forms distinctive plaques in tissue culture—an essential discovery in the development of the polio vaccine.
- Her intensity for her work has often superseded her own safety; while studying the polio virus, she did much of the work while laboring alongside a pathogen that other biochemists would not touch.
- Her parents were very angry when they learned that she was working with the polio virus.
- When she emigrated to the U.S., the only possession she brought with her was a grand piano, which she still plays regularly, often on Sundays when fellow musician-scientists hold recitals.
- Otherwise, she left Germany behind; when young German scientists come to the lab to meet the famous researcher and chat with her in their native tongue, she replies, often sternly, in English.
- By contrast, when a visiting Sorbonne student recently met with her and spoke in French, Maria's responses were also in French.
- She is known as a soft touch, often lending money from her own pocket to students in need.

Life at Work

- She had spent a lifetime in her own personal toy store—a scientific laboratory.
- Even at 66, she worked 10 hours a day, seven days a week; "If I were to stay at home, I'd be bored," she says.
- Her credits included groundbreaking studies on the polio virus and how a type of mammalioma virus called the polyoma virus transforms ordinary cells into cancer cells.

- This type of early research helped lift the study of cancer biology from simply cataloging the gross anatomy of a tumor cell to an exploration of the genetic mutations underlying the disease.
- Two of her colleagues were awarded the Nobel Prize for research, but she does not like or seek awards, saying, "When you get too famous, you stop being able to work."
- Fellow scientists say she deserves more recognition.
- She has been awarded patents for 16 of her scientific breakthroughs, earning her millions of dollars, most of which are invested in a trust managed by Bank of America.
- Her Last Will and Testament states that her wealth is to be used to promote science.
- Although some of her fellow female scientists lobbied her to donate her money exclusively to the education of women scientists, she had not responded; money, grants, wills and recipients are not subjects she likes to think about or discuss.

Maria worked with Dr. Barbara McClintock, who won a Nobel Prize in 1983.

- Her research through the years has ranged from oncogenes, the genes that when mutated result in cancer; immunology; and the behavior of telomeres—the distinctive chromosome tips that serve as molecular timepieces in healthy cells, but play a nefarious role in cancer when they fail to shorten as anticipated.
- She worked with some of the finest talent in the world, including Dr. Barbara McClintock, the corn geneticist who won a Nobel Prize for her research.

Life in the Community: San Diego, California

- Maria loves her adopted city of San Diego; now the second-largest city in California, it is not only picturesque, but has learned how to manage its growth well.
- The seventh-largest city in the United States, San Diego boasts a wonderful climate and a wide range of recreational activities.
- Several years ago, Maria began charting the number of times an executive in the building across the way—who often works the same long hours she does—slips out early in the afternoons for a spin in his sailboat; her chart shows he plays hooky 6.4 times a month.
- On a lark, a dozen years ago, she began collecting postcards of her beloved San Diego; today, she has hundreds.
- She especially enjoyed watching downtown transform itself from a seedy city center into a vibrant downtown, housing 120 shops, 30 eating establishments, seven movie screens and two performing arts theaters.
- The showcase is Horton Plaza, painted 49 different pastel colors, bordering the historic Gaslamp Quarter, which was undergoing renovation.
- Seven Amtrak connections ran from Los Angeles to San Diego daily, taking about two and a half hours, including a stop at Del Mar.
- When scientists came to visit, she always put them up at the Horton Grand, a 110-room restored Victorian hotel in the downtown section.
- On Sundays, she sometimes had brunch at the hotel and then rented a horse-drawn carriage for a gentle ride through the city.

Maria loved collecting old postcards featuring her adopted city of San Diego.

1987: Aaron Slayton, Brainy Kid Turned Tutor

Aaron Slayton learned the facts of life for a smart kid in the third grade; he was always picked first for the spelling bee team and last for the kickball team.

Life at Home

- Aaron Slayton was the bespectacled smart kid in the class who always did his homework, always did it right, and was willing to share.
- His parents were both college professors; his mother's specialty was Jacobean plays, while his father was known nationally for his research into tenth-century fighting techniques.
- The elder Slayton's research had explained the critical role that horse stirrups played in the changing face of battle; without the stabilizing power of the stirrup, the emergence of the lance would have been impossible.
- Aaron couldn't care less about Ben Johnson or Thomas Kyd—did his mother really need to discuss her work at the dinner table?—he wanted to write novels whose protagonist was a mathematician capable of solving complex crimes using numbers.
- His friend Michael encouraged Aaron's ambition, but secretly believed the concept to be both flawed and stupid.
- Michael's dad was a motorcycle mechanic, which was way cooler than a college professor.
- Nevertheless, Aaron followed the logical steps to join the family business one day.
- His parents loved their jobs—except for the college politics—so all he had to do was avoid the internal battles so common in education and he would have a nice life.
- After several years of public school, Aaron was shipped off to Hotchkiss, an exclusive school in Lakeville, Connecticut, followed by four years at Dartmouth, a graduate degree from MIT, and then a doctorate from Berkeley.
- At 28, he found himself steeped in knowledge, prepared for the future, and totally burned out.
- After three months of hanging out in Kauai, Hawaii, Aaron returned to California to teach.
- Even as an adjunct professor teaching four freshman-level math classes, he

Aaron Slayton was the smart kid who always did his homework.

was under enormous pressure to publish, participate in college committees, and compete for a tenure track position.

- After four years in academia, he was looking for a change.
- So when a tutor's slot came open at St. John's College in Annapolis, Maryland, he couldn't say "yes" fast enough.
- St. John's College was a four-year liberal arts college with campuses in Annapolis and in Santa Fe, New Mexico.

Aaron traded his traditional teaching position for tutoring at St. John's College.

- Founded in 1696 as King William's School, it received a collegiate charter in 1784, making it one of the oldest institutions of higher learning in the United States.
- Francis Scott Key, author of the "The Star Spangled Banner," was valedictorian of the class of 1796.
- Since 1937, St. John's had followed a distinctive curriculum, known as the Great Books School, based on a four-year discussion of works from the Western canon of philosophical, religious, historical, mathematical, scientific, and literary works.
- "The New Program" was developed at the University of Chicago by Stringfellow Barr, Scott Buchanan, Robert Hutchins, and Mortimer Adler in the mid-1930s as an alternative form of education.
- The college was in dire financial straits, and Barr and Buchanan were given nearly free license to develop a new model for the college.
- This took place amidst a milieu of reevaluation and debate regarding pedagogy in the United States.
- World events—including a recent world war, the rise of European fascism, and the fomenting domestic struggles for women's rights and civil rights for black Americans—precipitated questions about the significance of Western traditions and assumptions.
- The inception of the St. John's New Program drew not only attention for its seemingly radical reversion, but also considerable skepticism.
- Aaron knew that tutors, as faculty were called, were expected to lead discussions in a wide variety of topics.
- Small classes dominated, tests were few, and grades largely invisible.
- To Aaron's way of thinking, a better environment for learning could not have been created.

Life at Work

- Aaron Slayton was mesmerized by the simplistic beauty of St. John's College in the center of historic Annapolis, located one block from the state capitol building.
- The 400-student institution known for its alternative teaching style was located right beside the strait-laced, tall yellow walls of the U.S. Naval Academy.
- The location of the two schools side by side on the Severn River could not have been a finer display of American diversity and attitudes, Aaron thought, and had inspired many a comparison to Athens and Sparta.
- The schools operated on very different schedules, but did carry on a spirited rivalry, seen in the annual croquet match between the two schools on the front lawn of St. John's.
- Aaron was also pleased that—unlike most colleges—St. John's provided a set curriculum for all four years.

- In the campus bookstore, it was clear that St. John's avoided modern textbooks, lectures, and examinations in favor of a series of manuals.
- Every freshman started life as a Johnnie, reading works such as *Nicomachean Ethics* by Aristotle, and every tutor had to be ready every day to accept the challenges of the discussion.
- In a class of eight, in which everyone was expected to participate, there was little room to hide after a night of partying.
- In addition, the discussion format demanded

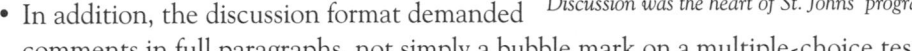

Discussion was the heart of St. Johns' programs.

comments in full paragraphs, not simply a bubble mark on a multiple-choice test.
- Aaron especially liked the comprehensive face-to-face evaluation of every student at the end of the semester.
- It was a time to boost some and remove others.
- Students who failed to understand the proper decorum during discussions could be told not to return.
- St John's was not for everyone.
- One of Aaron's first classes focused on Plato and whether virtue was teachable, which logically moved to what constituted virtue.
- He also led a discussion of Ptolemy's *Almagest*, a treatise on planetary movements and atomic theory.
- Every night, Aaron was deep into the lessons until 2 a.m. trying to stay ahead.
- In lab, he had to keep reminding himself that learning evolved from direct observation, and all knowledge was historically linear at St. John's; students couldn't speculate on how the circulatory system worked unless they could prove it themselves.
- Down the hall, another tutor with a Ph.D. in art history and a master's degree in comparative literature stood at the chalkboard drawing parallelograms, constructing angles, and otherwise dismembering Euclid's Proposition 32.
- Clearly, Aaron was not the only tutor who had traded the traditional three-course academic career—writing journal articles, attending conferences, and teaching a specific subject—for the intellectual buffet at St. John's.
- While traditional (A-F) grades were given, the culture of the school de-emphasized their importance, and grades were based largely on class participation and papers, and released only at the request of the student.
- Compared to mainstream colleges, tutors played a non-directive role in the classroom.
- Conversation was at the heart of the St. John's Program.
- Eva Brann, a St. John's tutor, explained, "We are not writing but a speaking school. Conversation is the public complement to that original dialogue of the soul with itself that is called thinking."
- By necessity, class size was small, with a student-to-tutor ratio of 8:1.
- The seminar was the largest class, with around 20 students led by two tutors.
- The rigid structure of New Program's curriculum, based on its historical and cultural focus, was designed to foster open inquiry.
- Developing the educational policy for the college, Buchanan identified three factors, which were intended "to regulate teaching and learning in every part of the program":
  1. The community of the learning effort
  2. The continuity of the learning process
  3. The spontaneity of the learning itself

- The tracing of Western thoughts and currents provided the students—and Aaron—with an understanding of historical content, which was vital to making an informed critique of social, political, and scientific movements of thought, past and present.
- St. John's was not a school where students studied great books, but a community whose members examined life.
- The St. John's Seminar curriculum was unchanging:
  Freshman year: Greek philosophy, poetry, and history
  Sophomore year: The Bible and theology,

Sophomores studied Dante, Chaucer and Shakespeare.

following some Roman poetry and history, and followed by Dante, Chaucer, and Shakespeare
Junior and Senior year: Modern philosophy from Descartes to Kant, including modern political philosophy
- Seminars always began with a question pertaining to a particular text, and was intended to precipitate discussion, not to direct or confine it.
- Tutorials covered mathematics, language and music.
- Mathematics and language were studied in all four years at St. John's.
- Language was the realm of the St. John's contemplation of and deliberation on the trivium—the study of grammar, logic and rhetoric.
- Greek was the language focus of the freshman and sophomore years, and French that of the junior and senior years.
- Language study began with learning vocabulary and grammar, and progressing to translation.
- The mathematics tutorial was a component of the curriculum in all four years of the St. John's Program, beginning with Euclid's *Elements*, the definitions and propositions of ancient geometry.

Life in the Community: Annapolis, Maryland
- Incorporated as a city in 1708, Annapolis, from the middle of the eighteenth century until the Revolutionary War, was noted for its wealthy and cultivated society.
- Supported by the slave trade and water trades such as oyster packing, boatbuilding and sail making, Annapolis was known for its theater and sophistication.
- The city became the temporary capital of the United States after the signing of the Treaty of Paris in 1783, and it was in Annapolis, on December 23, 1783, that General Washington resigned his commission as commander-in-chief of the Continental Army.
- During the Civil War, a prisoner-of-war Camp Parole was set up in Annapolis; wounded Union soldiers and Confederate prisoners were brought by sea to a major hospital there.
- In 1900, Annapolis had a population of 8,585.
- Anchoring the historic district, near St. John's College, was Saint Anne's Episcopal Church, erected late in the seventeenth century for the House of Delegates.
- Annapolis maintains many of it finest eighteenth-century houses.
- The names of several of the streets—King George's, Prince George's, Hanover, Duke of Gloucester, etc.—date from colonial days.
- The United States Naval Academy was founded there in 1845.
- During World War II, shipyards in Annapolis built a number of PT boats, and military vessels such as minesweepers and patrol boats were built there during the Korean and Vietnam wars.

- The Maryland State House remains the oldest in continuous legislative use in the United States.
- Construction started in 1772, and the Maryland legislature first met there in 1779; it remains the largest wooden dome built without nails in the country.
- The Maryland State House held the workings of the U.S. Government from November 26, 1783, to August 13, 1784, and the Treaty of Paris was ratified there on January 14, 1784, making Annapolis the first peacetime capital of the U.S.
- St. John's College, a non-sectarian private college that was once supported by the state, was opened in 1789 as the successor of King William's School, which was founded by an act of the Maryland legislature in 1696 and opened in 1701.
- Its principal building, McDowell Hall, was originally to be the governor's mansion, and although £4,000 was appropriated to build it in 1742, it was not completed until after the War of Independence.

Annapolis, Maryland.

1987: Adam Quigley, Lawyer from New York

Adam Quigley was a distinguished partner and co-founder of Quigley Ullberg Creswell, a New York-based law firm with 650 lawyers in 12 offices across the country.

Life at Home

- The son and grandson of successful New York lawyers, Adam Quigley had spent two decades building one of the nation's most successful and visible law firms.
- A graduate of Yale and Harvard Law School, Adam married Jennifer during his final year of law school, and they immediately began having children; they now have four girls and two boys.
- One of their sons was in law school at Harvard, following in his father's footsteps; their oldest daughter had also talked about entering law.
- The fabulous growth of Quigley Ullberg Creswell allowed Adam and his family the luxury of a Fifth Avenue home as well as a Vermont farm, where Jennifer raised thoroughbred horses.
- The 80-year-old country house, which contains 33 rooms, was situated on 96 acres of pasture and farmland, and features a wide veranda, now used as an outdoor living room, decorated with upholstered wicker furniture to keep the setting informal.
- To care for the house, the couple employed a gardener year-round who grows fields of fresh flowers that decorate every room when they visit from the city.
- Even though many aspects of the home have been updated and modernized, they had returned to the old-fashioned fixtures in the bathroom and kitchen.
- Jennifer visited often to exercise her horses and supervise the birth of new colts and fillies.
- Adam accepted that his wife controlled the decorating and furnishings in every room of the sprawling house except one—the traditional gunroom, which he used as a study.
- A masculine room paneled in walnut at the turn of the century, it had become his

Adam Quigley co-founded one of the nation's most influential law firms.

Adam's son loved to backpack, particularly in the Florida Everglades.

hideaway, where he could be messy, disorganized and childlike.

- Dozens of books were stacked up on the floor waiting to be read.
- In one corner, he had the parts of a 1953 Cherokee motorcycle he wishes to restore, along with plans for building a dollhouse-sized haunted house—complete with rotating fireplaces and monsters that fly into rooms when electronically triggered.
- It delighted him that his room included a secret passageway, obviously built during Prohibition, leading to the wine cellar; within the walls of this room, he can read, sip wine and lock out the world—on those rare occasions he is able to slip away from the law firm and into the country.
- Their children showed a great love for nature and adventure; their youngest daughter spent much of her time rock climbing in the West, while their son loved to backpack on the Appalachian Trail and through the Florida Everglades.

Life at Work

- Quigley Ullberg Creswell was created in 1968, with eight lawyers whose primary expertise was real-estate law.
- By 1982, the firm had either acquired or merged its way into offices in Los Angeles, Miami and Washington.
- Its clients included Occidental Petroleum Corporation and Giant Food, Inc.; today, these relationships have been expanded to include corporations such as Citicorp and Burlington Industries.
- Recently, Citicorp gained worldwide headlines when it decided to write down more than $2 billion in Third-World debt.

- The law firm relishes its involvement with such high-profile cases; its recruiting focus has always been on acquiring the biggest, richest and fastest-growing corporate clients.
- To help them gain the right kind of clients, they often paid intermediaries such as well-connected politicians and business "rainmakers," including governors, senators and key congressional committee men.
- A decade ago, Adam became active in Republican politics, deciding early to back the presidential aspirations of California Governor Ronald Reagan and personally raising more than $1 million from his friends and clients to fund Reagan's run for the presidency.
- The gamble paid off handsomely through increased business and unparalleled access to key figures in Washington, including several Cabinet members and education czar William Bennett, who became Adam's personal friend and confidant.
- The firm was headed by a 29-person management committee, which was feuding over how the nationally based firm is being run.

Adam's law firm's headquarters were in New York City.

- Many believed that the firm is too much of a one-man show, and were convinced that Adam should no longer be its comanager, even though it now generates more than $165 million in annual revenues.
- Partners were being asked to take sides concerning the future structure of the firm in a battle that has become so intense, some senior partners are no longer speaking to each other.
- One of the key issues was the lack of communication and relationships among all the offices; despite Adam's best intentions, his sprawling, nationally based legal empire has few connections, resulting in many lawyers being loyal only to their own offices.
- They felt that New York has too much power and provides too little help; one office in a major Florida city issued standing orders not to accept or return telephone calls from any New York partner who "called up shouting."
- Daryl Posner, the lawyer engineering the internal coup, is a New York litigator whom Adam helped recruit to the firm three years ago.
- Posner believed that too much time has been spent in honoring the "finders" of business, and too little in rewarding the "minders"; he wants to lead a law firm based on quality, not on high-profile cases that have the potential to blow up in the media at any moment.
- He also felt that Quigley has sacrificed the integrity of the firm with his deal-making and political connections, and prefers to work for a firm that is respected in New York—not in Washington; a showdown is expected early next year.
- Without question, the firm has been in the news recently because of its ever-expanding client list that includes the flamboyantly ultra rich, such as the Sultan of Brunei, one of the most affluent nations in the world thanks to its oil reserves.
- Recently, the firm had been involved in a spate of acquisitions by the Sultan's brother, who has spent more than $1 billion on hotels in Paris, apartments in New York, racecars and dozens of airplanes.

- As a reward for his work, Adam and his family recently visited Brunei, near Malaysia, where the people enjoy free education and amusement parks, as well as high employment in the oil and gas industry—without paying taxes.
- He and Jennifer were fascinated by the culture and its ability to create a utopian society through the wealth of the monarchy.
- The firm has also represented Cabbage Patch doll inventor Xavier Roberts, whose phenomenal success has allowed him to purchase a 30-bedroom mansion, decorated with three paintings by Picasso and complemented by a waterslide from a second-story window directly into an Olympic-sized swimming pool.
- Through the firm's legal and lobbying efforts, page 219 of the 1986 Tax Reform Act includes an oblique reference to a "taxpayer incorporated on September 7, 1978, who is engaged in the business of manufacturing dolls and accessories," in language that allowed Roberts and his company, The Original Appalachian Artworks, a tax break worth $6 million.
- In the same section of the Tax Act, the heirs of the late Samuel A. Horvitz, who control a fortune estimated at $400 million, received a special rule worth $1 million.
- Many at Quigley Ullberg Creswell were embarrassed when these personal tax breaks were widely discussed in newspaper and magazine articles across the country.
- Currently, several members of the firm are handling the sale of Burlington Industries, the nation's number one textile producer.
- An investor group headed by Morgan Stanley Group Inc. has offered $2.74 billion as a counter offer made by an alliance of Asher B. Edelman, a New York investor, and Dominion Textile, Inc., Canada's largest textile concern.
- The Morgan Stanley offer includes a group of top Burlington executives who have been fighting the Canadian takeover for months.
- Adam has made numerous trips to Greensboro, North Carolina, where Burlington is headquartered, to structure a deal.
- The Morgan Stanley deal calls for Bankers Trust Company to head a lending syndicate that would provide $2.1 billion of the cost, about $250 million of which would be in bridge loans or temporary financing; the remainder will be provided by Morgan Stanley.
- Adam's firm will earn a fee exceeding $2.5 million for negotiating this deal and structuring the financing.

Life in the Community: New York City

- The children of Margaret Strong de Larrain, heiress to the Rockefeller oil fortune, have gone to court to overturn their mother's will, which disinherits them in favor of her last husband, whom she married when she was 80 and he was 42; at stake is Exxon Corporation stock worth $76 million.
- Jerry Della Femina, chairman of the New York ad agency Della Femina, Travisan and Partners, resigned the Lifestyle condom account after his client was quoted in *Time* magazine as saying "AIDS is a condom marketer's dream."
- New York Governor Mario Cuomo announced that he would not make a run for the Democratic presidential nomination, setting off a scramble for a qualified candidate.
- "Butt buckets" have begun showing up throughout the city as thousands of firms move to prohibit employee smoking in buildings, sending thousands of smokers into the streets.
- *The New York Times* reported that workers in the city's garment district were often under age, paid less than $3.35 a hour and required to work 11-hour days, six days a week.
- Interstate highway speeds increased from 55 miles per hour to 65, as New York and the nation bury their fears of another fuel crisis, although government officials continue to predict that the United States will start to run out of gas in as little as three decades.

- Civilian complaints against Transit Authority police officers were up 33 percent over the previous year; the 50 officers against whom the most complaints are lodged will be asked to undergo sensitivity training.
- New York City changed the name of 122nd Street to Seminary Row because of the two giant institutions of religious learning located there—Union Theological Seminary on the west side of Broadway, and the Jewish Theological Seminary of America on the east side.
- The City of New York predicted that within five years, the spreading AIDS epidemic in the city will cost more than $1 billion a year in hospital expenses alone.
- New York City accounted for one third of the AIDS cases in the United States.
- Collectors of fishing rods and reels were being lured to an auction in Roscoe, NY, all for the benefit of the Catskill Fly Fishing Center, a nonprofit educational organization devoted to "preserving the heritage and protecting the future of fly fishing in the United States."
- According to a report prepared by the Fund for Renewable Energy and the Environment, New York ranked among the top five states in establishing and enforcing programs to protect the environment.

BASIL · EDE'S
wild birds of america

The price of collectible artwork was rising rapidly at New York Auction galleries.

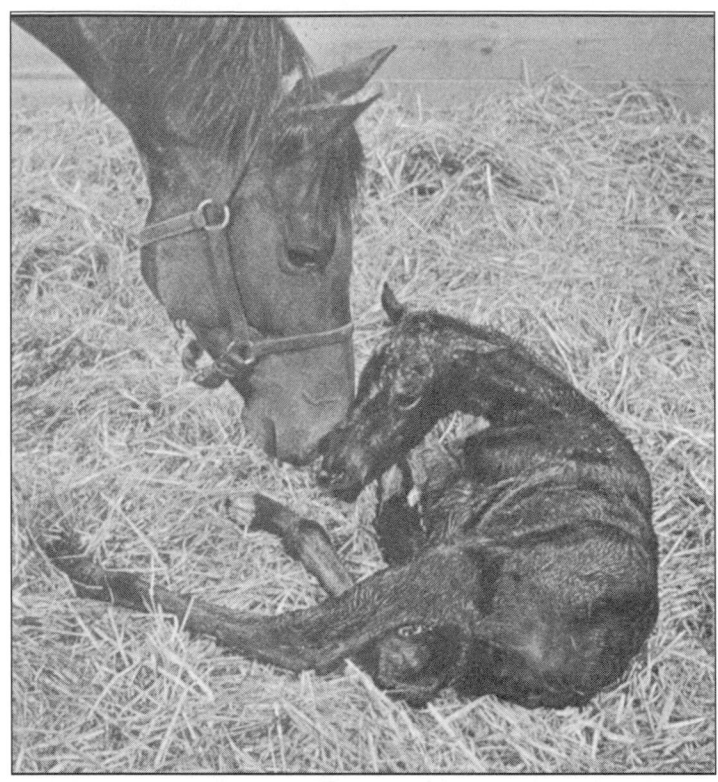

Jennifer Quigley often visited the country house to exercise the horses and supervise the birth of new colts and fillies.

1988: Ahmed Waltari, Cell Phone Magnate from Williamstown, New York, and Monaco

When 54-year-old, Egyptian-born Ahmed Waltari realized that cellular telephones represented "the future," he transformed his multimillion-dollar business to get a piece of the action.

Life at Home

- The Waltari family lived in Williamstown, Massachusetts, near Williams College.
- They moved there because Miki hated raising children in New York City, and loved the fact that the Williamstown community of 9,000 is dominated by Williams College, known for its art and historic collections.
- Ahmed maintained a 2,000-square-foot apartment a dozen blocks from his office in Manhattan.
- Often spending Monday through Thursday in New York or traveling, and Friday through Sunday in Williamstown, he enjoyed hard work, pressure and the freedom and privacy the separate homes provide.
- His New York apartment was decorated with expensive bird prints collected from around the world, including several important Audubon prints and the prized Mark Catsby originals he acquired in England years ago.
- His greatest obsession, however, was the avoidance of alcohol; the son of an alcoholic, he does not allow it to be served in his home or at office parties, but enjoys fine dining.
- His children were told that drinking was the one sin he will not tolerate.
- The family normally spent six weeks each summer in Monaco, where Miki, the daughter of a diamond merchant, vacationed in her youth.
- The most celebrated gaming tables in the world are in Monte Carlo, part of the 468-acre sovereign principality of Monaco, named after a Ligurian tribe called the Monoikos who occupied the land in the sixth century BC.
- The ruling Grimaldi family seized Monaco from the Genoese in 1297.
- In 1865, the reigning Prince Charles III inaugurated gambling on the island, giving the aristocracy a reason to vacation there.

Egyptian-born Ahmed Waltari was at the forefront of the cellular revolution.

- The casino was built on a rock and named Monte Carlo, or Mount Charles, in the prince's honor.
- Soon, with the arrival of the railway, the wealthy, noble, famous and infamous came to gamble.
- In 1878, architect Charles Garnier, who built the Paris Opera, constructed a new casino in his signature gilt-edged, belle époque style, complete with a formal tropical garden and terrace.
- Once near bankruptcy, Monaco became rich overnight, and despite the vagaries of history, wars and fashion, it has continued to be the place where the rich have gathered for more than 120 years.
- As predictable as birds flying south, the international moneyed and titled set descends upon the island.
- There they find the Salle Garnier theater, home of the renowned Opéra de Monte Carlo, Monte Carlo Philharmonic Orchestra and one of Europe's most outstanding ballet companies.

The Waltari family moved to Williamstown, Massachusetts to escape New York City.

- Miki believed that the Princess Grace Classical Dance Academy produces the finest dancers in the world.
- In the opulent casino, Ahmed enjoyed European games such as roulette, trente-et-quarante, baccarat and chemin de fer; his 22-year-old son migrates toward American games such as craps, blackjack and one-armed bandits.
- To keep gambling in perspective, Ahmed insists that losses be limited to $10,000 per trip, and so avoids the private gambling tables where millions can change hands in an evening.
- The teenage girls preferred trips to Monaco for the warm waters of the Mediterranean, with its 300 days of sunshine a year and the chance to lie by the pool and watch some of the world's most eligible-and richest-men walk by.
- The family also loved to plan trips around the automobile rally and Grand Prix each year, where speed, beauty and power are all combined.
- They also loved the safety of Monaco, which is a highly monitored state with a vigilant police force.
- When in Monaco, the Waltari family liked to stay at the S.B.M. Hôtel de Paris, which was built around the same time as the casino to support the incoming tourists; with its ideal location, it has long been *the* place to stay.
- Their favorite rooms overlook the sea and are situated across from the casino and the Café de Paris, the central meeting place since 1968 for everyone who has been anyone.
- In addition, the hotel's majestic foyer provides a splendid backdrop for dramatic entrances and exits; the bar serves as an essential point of rendezvous.

Life at Work

- Twenty-eight years ago, Ahmed founded his first U.S. company, Waltari Imports, to import Japanese goods to the United States.
- Thanks to his connections in Egypt and Monaco, he was able to pull together a wide range of deals using only a small portion of his own capital.
- The inheritance he received from his father exceeded seven figures, but he was determined to use the money only as leverage whenever possible and not expose his own capital to the vagaries of business.
- For five years he imported a wide variety of goods from baseball gloves and fishing reels to porcelain dinnerware.
- In 1965, he opened a carton and, finding a car radio, had a revelation-this was the future!
- Within months, he phased out the other merchandise, changed the name of his company to Waltari Enterprises and began selling Japanese car radios, and afterwards stereo radios and tape decks, to new car dealers.
- He carved out a market by selling car radios for 30 percent less than Detroit was charging the Ford and General Motors dealers.
- By 1983, his company-still private and owned only by members of his family-achieved sales of more than $100 million; today, it has gone public and is three times larger.
- Unfortunately, while the company was growing, revenues were shrinking because of the huge inventory commitments required by rapid growth.
- In 1984, following his instincts as he had during his entire career, he jumped onto the cellular telephone bandwagon with a vengeance.
- To get a major piece of the action, he set up an exclusive U.S. distribution deal with Toshiba, one of Japan's leading mobile phone manufacturers, whose early phones proved to be exceptionally popular and dependable.
- Then in a stroke of luck in 1985, Waltari Enterprises was able to grab a dominant market share when Panasonic and others were hit with huge, government-imposed antidumping penalties on their phones.

- His company sold 15 to 20 percent of all cellular phones nationwide; of its $277 million in sales, half came from cellular phones-where the margins were thin.
- Whereas car stereos sold at wholesale for as little as $55 and earned the company gross margins of 30 percent, the cellular phones sold for $1,200 at wholesale had had margins of less than 20 percent; thus, the phones exhausted more capital while producing smaller gross profits.
- To finance the telephone inventory, Ahmed allowed public ownership of his company, raising $33 million on the sale of 2.2 million shares of its nine million shares of stock, and fueling Waltari Enterprises to expand.
- Unfortunately, earlier this year Toshiba came under scrutiny by Congress for selling military gear to the Russians.

- Fearing that the U.S. Government would restrict the import of Toshiba phones, Ahmed dramatically increased his order by more than 30 percent over sales projections, but the feared cutoff never occurred; wholesale prices of cellular phones are now plunging and his warehouse is overstocked.
- Thus, the company was faced with the prospect that it would see a 45-percent increase in the sales of cellular phones, but a 25-percent decline in profits until the inventory glut is dissolved.
- Despite the prospect that Waltari Enterprises' stock price could be cut by half, Ahmed remained optimistic; telecommunications consultants were estimating that the number of cellular subscribers would increase from 1.1 million to 1.6 million in a year.
- Ahmed believed that with falling prices, he will double the 127,000 phone sales he made last year.
- His biggest concern was whether competition will crowd him out in the future.
- As the cellular phone increasingly becomes regarded as a consumer electronic product rather than a specialty product, retailers such as New York's 47th Street Photo or Crazy Eddie could jump into the game, driving down profit margins and cutting sales.
- Some days, he thought that slowing down might be all right; using his earnings through the years, he acquired a controlling interest in seven major income-producing office buildings, financed in part with interest-free loans from the company.
- Last year alone, he earned more than $1 million in rent; in addition, his 83-year-old mother earned more than $700,000 on investments that he arranged.

Life in the Community: Williamstown; New York; and Monaco

- Williamstown, Massachusetts, was a small, pretty town of 9,000 people, 2,000 of whom were students.
- Because Ahmed's professional life was centered in New York, Williamstown was the wrong place to live, but Miki, a lover of art and museums, insists; both New York and Boston are only three hours away.
- The town, originally called West Hoosuc, was reborn as Williamstown in the late eighteenth century in accordance with the terms of the will of Ephraim Williams, who promised to endow a secondary school if the town agreed to perpetuate his name.
- In 1793, the school, in the shadow of three mountains, became Williams College, which has since become a magnet for art and historical artifacts.
- In 1938, the college museum was given the collection of American muralist Edwin Howland Blashfeld.
- This was followed by the Cluett collection of Spanish pre-Goya paintings, plus a substantial part of the Bloedel collection of twentiethcentury American art.
- Then came the Robert Sterling Clark collection.
- Clark, one of four grandsons of Edward Clark, the business partner of sewing machine developer Isaac Singer, had no connection to Williams College; nevertheless, in the 1950s, he gave the school a building to house his collection of silver and paintings by notables such as Botticelli, Degas, Manet, Monet, Renoir and Pissaro.
- Then in 1983, an expanded museum opened with shows featuring Indian art, work by Edvard Munch, and displays of Greek art, Roman terra cotta and Renaissance woodwork.
- A few years ago, Williams College bought for $412,500 a recently discovered copy of the Declaration of Independence that had belonged to one of its signers, Joseph Hewes of North Carolina.
- The purchase rounded out Williams' remarkable collection of essential documents of the American Revolution: its copy of the Articles of Confederation of 1777, two early versions of the Bill of Rights and one of the 14 surviving copies of the Committee of Style draft of the Constitution, containing on the reverse the handwritten objections of Virginia constitutionalist George Mason.
- In addition, the school's Chapin Library of rare books contains James Madison's copy of Paine's *Common Sense*, General Greene's written order for boats for the crossing of the Delaware, General Knox's letter thanking Martha Washington for a gift of two hair nets, and the ledger used by the executors of George Washington's will.

Williams College had long been a magnet for fine art and historical artifacts.

BREATHE SPRING IN SAPPORO.

CALL JAPAN.
95¢ A MINUTE.
To find out more about calling overseas, call **1 800 874-4000 Ext. 112.** Go ahead. **Reach out and touch someone.®**

JAPAN	Economy 3am–2pm $ .95	Discount 8pm–3am $1.20	Standard 2pm–8pm $1.58

AVERAGE COST PER MINUTE FOR A 10-MINUTE CALL*

*Average cost per minute varies depending on the length of the call. First minute costs more, additional minutes cost less. All prices are for calls dialed direct from anywhere in the continental U.S. during the hours listed. Add 3% federal excise tax and applicable state surcharges. © 1988 AT&T

AT&T
The right choice.

1989: Bill Reindollar, Created Cash Register Repair Service

A heart attack at 34-years-old transformed Bill Reindollar, creator of Cash Register Service, from a caring cop to a moneywise entrepreneur.

Life at Home

- Born in 1939 in Hollidaysburg, Pennsylvania, near Altoona, the middle child of Paul and Isabel Reindollar, Bill was born into world that was economically struggling and politically divided over concerns on how to handle the burgeoning militaristic nation of Germany and its leader, Adolph Hitler.
- Early on, Bill developed a curiosity for how things worked, and at age six took apart his elder sister's talking doll so he could see how it worked, removing the record cylinders in the doll's torso from which emanated songs and nursery rhymes.
- When he attempted to put the doll back together, he was left with extra parts and a doll that no longer worked.
- Over time, as his skills at taking apart and putting them back together again improved, family members came to believe that his interest in tools came from his paternal grandfather, a worker on the Pennsylvania Railroad, whose hobby was woodworking.
- Bill was very close to his grandparents, Mervin and Agnes, and cherished the time spent building furniture in his grandfather's woodshop.
- Bill also worked a paper route to help the family during some lean financial years.
- Kind and trusting, he sometimes went home without money because his customers couldn't pay him on time.
- This angered his father, who once threw a hot iron at him when he learned that Bill didn't collect from a customer who had fallen on hard times.
- Bill preferred to stay with his grandparents, where his grandfather would go into his woodshop after work, smoke his pipe, and work on a project to relax—habits that Bill would use later in his own life.

Bill Reindollar turned a life-threatening event into an opportunity to create Cash Register Service.

- When Bill was 14, his grandfather died.
- He moved in with his grandmother to become the man of the house.
- At the same time, Bill worked at the local hardware store, saving his money to buy a Schwinn bicycle that came with one year of free theft protection.
- Schwinn was quickly becoming the favorite bike of Americans, selling 500,000 a year; one out of every four bicycles in the U.S. was a Schwinn.
- After graduating from high school in 1957, Bill got a job at National Cash Register (NCR).
- He had little choice in the matter.
- His father, once a janitor at NCR, had seen how well the company cared for its service technicians and wanted his son to have that opportunity.
- So, after church one Sunday, his parents drove him to the NCR headquarters in Dayton, Ohio, and dropped him off outside to wait—in his wool suit in the humid summer weather—for the office to open on Monday morning.

Reindollar reluctantly followed in his father's footsteps, taking a position at National Cash Register (NCR).

- Shy by nature, Bill was encouraged by NCR to take a 14-week correspondence course offered by Dale Carnegie, called "How to Win Friends and Influence People."
- The book, first published in 1937, was one of the first bestselling self-help books on the market, selling millions of copies.
- However, despite his talent and the excellent company, NCR was not his dream job, but his father's, though, out of loyalty, Bill worked more than a decade for the company.

Life at Work

- At age 29, Bill Reindollar decided to leave NCR to pursue his dream job and become a state trooper.
- Just coming in under the age limit, Bill trained at the police academy in Hershey, Pennsylvania, where he learned to swim, enhance his observation skills and improve his problem solving.
- The only downside was working in the stables, something every cadet was required to master since the police still relied on horses for patrolling and exhibitions.
- Upon graduation, he was sent "to serve and to protect" in the western part of the state, where he focused on helping people, often giving breaks to youths he believed had simply fallen in with the wrong crowd or had a rough home life.
- He spent time talking with the kids and even fed them, learning sometimes that it was their first meal in days.
- The other officers called him "the Social Worker."
- Life was not only changing professionally, but personally after he met and began dating Sharon Nulph at her parent's family restaurant.
- Having lived a sheltered life, Sharon thought that when Bill suggested eating at McDonald's, he was referring to the home of one of his friends.

Reindollar played an active role in his community.

TANNERY SCHOOL SAFETY PATROL

Shown are members of the safety patrol at Tannery school in Allegheny township, two miles west of Duncansville. They are (left to right): Lynn Johnston, Judy Diehl, Billy Reindollar, Polly Hoover, Betty Yeckley and Ralph Pounds.

Young Reindollar had always wanted to help people and be a state trooper.

- Even though the Big Mac was founded by Pittsburgh McDonald's owner/operator Jim Delligatti one year earlier in 1967, the small towns were devoid of franchises.
- On their first date, they saw *Midnight Cowboy*, the first X-rated motion picture to win the Academy Award for Best Picture.
- They were married within a year and had four children in seven years.
- Bill became a detective and handled homicide cases and a kidnapping.
- Going to the family of a young woman who had drowned was the most difficult thing he had ever had to do.
- Though grieved by the news, the family was grateful for his compassion during this horrific period in their lives, and added him to their Christmas card list.
- The siblings of the girl bought him a children's book called *Sam Sunday and the Strange Disappearance of Chester Cats* that told of a compassionate detective aggressively on the case, and gave it to Bill as a "thank you" gift, addressing him as Sam Sunday.
- The odors of a homicide and difficult moments led him to take up smoking at age 34, initially to help him through dealing with crime scenes; it would later became a crutch for stressful moments.
- Only air traffic controllers and dentists were believed to have more stressful occupations than law enforcement officials, who were also renowned for not seeking help with their stress.
- Officers who committed suicide rarely had a record of discussing the problems they dealt with: continual danger, a difficult boss and public, and shift work that disrupted family life.
- In 1982, Bill began having chest pains and insisted on being admitted to the hospital, where he collapsed in the hall and had to be shocked back to life.

- Having had a heart attack meant he had to retire from police work; for a time his senses and memory were affected.
- Afterwards, Bill coached his son's little league baseball team as he recuperated and relied on his woodworking and electrical skills for several years to help out the family financially.
- The national unemployment rate was more than 10 percent, and the economically depressed small town didn't offer many opportunities.
- Uncertain of what to do, Bill recalled his NCR training.
- In the 18 years he had been away from that line of work, business machines had become more technological; however, he decided to take a risk repairing old machines.
- In 1985, he filled up the gas tank in the car and drove to Butler, the closest city, where he cold-called on businesses that owned old wood and iron NCR cash registers no one was willing to service.

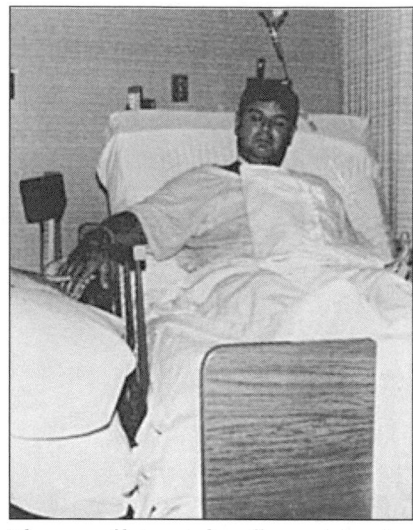

The stress of being a police officer took its toll on Reindollar's health.

- NCR was encouraging the use of smaller, easier to use electronic cash registers, and no longer trained service techs to repair aging machines.
- Bill did several repairs and made $350 that first day.
- With the windfall, Bill and Sharon bought a Zenith VCR, and though cable TV was not an option in the rural areas, they passed on a satellite dish, which would cost $1,995 to receive 100 channels.
- Since the turn of the twentieth century, NCR had been the dominant company for business machines.
- Founded in 1879 as National Manufacturing Company in Dayton, Ohio, to sell the cash register invented by James Ritty, the firm was renamed in 1894.
- A training school was established in 1893, along with a social welfare program for the employees.
- By 1911, the company had sold one million machines and had 6,000 employees.
- NCR controlled 95 percent of the market.
- In 1922, the company went public and issued $55 million in stock; at the time it was the largest public company ever in the United States.
- Since the company treated its employees so well, they were loyal, refusing to do business with restaurants or stores that used a competitor's cash register.
- Another established, but smaller company, also known by its initials, claimed it would compete with NCR; Bill and his coworkers at NCR quipped that the company's initials stood for, Itty Bitty Machines.
- Bill's repair business blossomed as he worked a wider and wider territory comprising, almost exclusively, small towns.
- One day, Bill picked up a register to take back to the office for repair work.

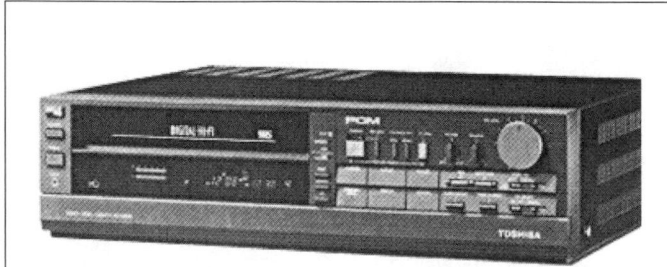

Reindollar bought a VCR with the money he made repairing old cash registers.

- He drove two hours to pick up the machine and two hours to the office, only to discover that the client had left money in the cash drawer of the machine.
- He elected to drive two hours back to give them their money and then back to the office, spending an entire workday essentially traveling for one machine.

- After that, Bill always checked for himself to make sure the money had been removed before taking a cash register.
- After getting his feet wet in the field again, he decided to accept a job with an established company; after working for the company for a month, without pay, he and the other employees realized they needed to go elsewhere.
- The experience helped Bill find suppliers and additional clientele who needed a new service company when the dysfunctional company folded.
- As an entrepreneur, Bill maintained a repair shop in the basement of his family's home.
- Monday through Friday, he would fill up his large thermos of coffee and drive 45 minutes to and from Butler, where he had his business office.
- He called the company Cash Register Service.

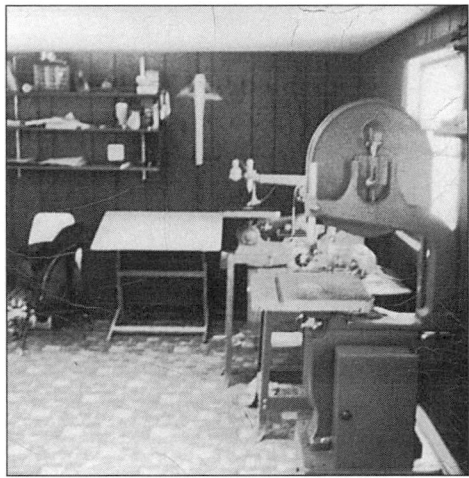

This home office and workshop was soon a thriving and profitable business.

- Like many children of the Depression, Bill distrusted banks and the stock market, and was uncomfortable borrowing money.
- He always believed the money could disappear, so rather than seek loans for his business needs, he saved up the money for purchases.
- He built an office in the basement of the house and purchased an Apple II home computer for $795.00 (he still couldn't bring himself to buy an IBM), a non-rotary telephone that remembered three phone numbers and had a speaker, and a separate answering machine.
- The 5 1/4-inch floppy disks that the computer required sold for $9.95 a box.
- Bill also discovered there was money to be made in antique machines, which he refurbished and sold to stores and collectors.
- He enjoyed being out in the field and working with the machines, but soon grew weary of sitting in the office returning phone calls and handling the paperwork.
- The company grew and its value eventually became $50,000.
- In need of money to support a family of six and wanting to have fewer office details to deal with, Bill decided to sell the company.
- There were not many takers in the small town who could pay that sum, so he offered the company for $30,000, with the condition that he be employed as a service tech, relieving him of office work.
- The company was purchased by a local restaurant owner looking for a business investment, who had relied extensively on get-rich-quick books and was determined to apply those techniques to a small company.
- The new owner placed no emphasis on employee happiness, but considerable focus on fast and high profits.
- Bill believed that if you did your job right and took care of the customer, the money would come; the new owner's approach, plus increased prices, caused many customers to look elsewhere for service.

Reindollar did not want to be tied to a desk or the paperwork.

- As stress built up for Bill, a patch of hair fell out of the back of his head from what he considered execrable business practices.
- Part of each week was consumed with meetings, where Bill would get bored and angry at the direction the company was taking.
- Bill didn't believe in the big-business approach to his once home-based business operation, and made his feelings known; he thought the business had become unnecessarily complicated.
- The owner did not like Bill's questioning him and fired him, adding him to the 5.3 percent unemployed in the U.S.
- The patch of hair grew back shortly thereafter.

Life in the Community: Butler, Pennsylvania

- Butler, Pennsylvania, where Bill Reindollar established his business, was named after American Revolutionary War General Richard Butler in 1800.
- The 2.7-square-mile city of 15,000 was 35 miles north of Pittsburgh and was known for its trolley cars.
- The Army's Jeep prototype was produced in Butler by American Bantam Car Company, and was called the BRC (Bantam Reconnaissance Car) 40.
- The company's 1938 model was the inspiration for Donald Duck's car.
- Butler was also known for Moraine State Park, named for its moraine glaciers, which attracted over a million visitors each year.
- The park covered 16,725 acres; hunting, a popular pastime in the area, was allowed on 13,000 acres.
- The North Country Trail, which goes from Lake Champlain in New York to Lake Sakakawea in North Dakota, passes through Moraine State Park.
- The famous low-budget black-and-white horror movie *Night of the Living Dead* was filmed in Butler County; made for $114,000, the film grossed $30 million internationally.

Butler, Pennsylvania was where the Army's Jeep prototype was produced.

1989: Carlos Piccolo, Cross-Country Runner

Carlos Piccolo, built to be a runner, began running at a very early age, trained hard, and carefully kept track of his progress.

Life at Home

- For Carlos Piccolo there was no high like a runner's high.
- He was first swept away by the runner's sensation at an early age, before he was 12, but did not remember the exact moment.
- Starting when he was 13, Carlos began keeping a runner's journal, logging his times, distances and feelings ("legs sore, hot day, ran 4.5 miles").
- His older brother possessed a massive, powerful chest and legs like tree trunks; even as a small boy everyone expected him to be a football player.
- Carlos, on the other hand, was shaped like a second-grader's hand-drawn crayon stick figure.
- With long pipe cleaner legs attached to a frame that would never conquer 150 pounds, Carlos was a genetic aberration in an aggressive family that once destroyed the living room sofa when it was used as a football blocking dummy.
- Carlos's grandparents brought the family to America when they left Mexico in 1929 seeking better opportunities for their growing family; they settled in Albuquerque, New Mexico, two years later.
- His grandfather tended horses, managed ranch maintenance and dreamed that his children would one day graduate from high school.
- Carlos's father filled that expectation, and while still in his twenties opened his own store that sold fresh fruits and vegetables, quality meats and many, many tobacco products.
- Even the white people of Albuquerque, some of whom spoke very little Spanish, would drive across town to shop for his special hand-rolled cigars and top-grade chewing tobacco.
- The Piccolo family also loved to talk loudly, long and often; shouting over each other was acceptable, even expected, by everyone.
- Everyone, that is, except Carlos.

Carlos Piccolo loved to run.

- He learned early that he could best do his talking with his feet, especially after his football linebacker brother lost a bet and had to train with Carlos for a week.
- His brother said simply, "I'll never bet against you again."
- Training for a cross country meet was not Carlos's biggest problem, though; relaxing was.
- In the final five minutes before a high school race, Carlos's brain was bombarded by his past mistakes-poor pacing, moves made too late, running out of energy, missing a turn or failing to anticipate the late strength of a competitor.
- Besides, cross country meets were unpredictable since they were staged on an open course over rough terrain.
- The high school 5km courses often combined routes that incorporated grass, mud, asphalt, rocks, steep inclines, woodlands, and even water.
- On race days, Carlos normally rose at 5:30 a.m. to be prepared-but Carlos was always prepared.
- He only stopped ironing his underwear because his brother teased him so unmercifully.
- He planned what and when he would eat, the level and pace of his water intake and his sleep patterns.
- He knew from experience that when the pain struck, he would "man up" and run through the agony; he always wanted to be ready.
- The question was whether he could run through his own anxiety and stay focused on winning, not on failing.
- He had become successful enough that his parents actually came to see him run in cross country meets, proud that he once ran the mile in under 4:20 and could consistently maintain 5:35 per mile splits on the 3.2-mile courses.
- They also realized that running could be Carlos's ticket to college, if the college recruiters were to be believed.
- Carlos only went on one college recruiting trip.
- At an altitude of 7,700 feet, Western State College's campus among the Colorado Rocky Mountains in Gunnison, Colorado, was so beautiful and inspiring, it sold itself.
- Carlos knew immediately that this was the perfect place to test his limits within the rugged alpine playground.
- The beauty of the place reminded him of the runner's adage, "If you're not enjoying the journey, you probably won't enjoy the destination," and agreed to attend the 2,000-person campus.
- His first year was good, his second year better.
- As a junior, Carlos was expected to challenge the best that Colorado, Stanford, and the University of Arkansas had to offer and then win his division.

Life at Work

- At Western State College Carlos Piccolo's teammates hailed from seven different states and all had been proclaimed as cross-country heroes in high school, assuming local newspapers even knew the sport existed.
- Cross country was difficult for most reporters to explain, especially when the runners disappeared into the woods near the starting line and often did not re-emerge until they neared the finish line.
- Besides, who in their good senses would voluntarily run 95 miles a week to earn the right to run some more.
- At least in baseball, exhausting fitness work made the players eligible to hit a baseball or in football to hit each other.
- But long-distance running was the niche Carlos had claimed for himself and now he wanted to prove himself at a collegiate level at Western State College.

- During the previous summer, Carlos had trained extensively in high-altitude conditions until he could comfortably run a five-mile aerobic threshold in less than 26 minutes; in addition, he ran 100 miles weekly.
- At the college level, meet distances were usually 8 km (5 miles) for men and for women, 6 km at regional and national competitions.
- Carlos's very first qualifying meet was staged at the University of Colorado and attracted some 250 runners from 16 colleges.
- The University of Colorado had signed a contract with Nike, permitting each runner to receive Terra Humma training shoes, crosscountry racing flats, track flats, shorts, long sleeve and short sleeve T-shirts, sweatpants, sweatshirts, wristbands and headbands.
- Schools the size of Western State rarely received that level of endorsement support and resented the slight; Carlos saw the Nike logo as a personal snub directed against him and his team.
- Cross-country was an intensely individualistic sport whose scoring was entirely dependent on team results.
- Points were awarded to the individual runners, equal to the position in which each crossed the finish line (first place got one point, second place got two points, etc.).
- Only the first five runners in for a team were counted toward that team's score; the points for these runners were summed, and the teams were ranked based on the total, with lowest being best.
- The lowest possible score in a five-to-score match was 15 (1+2+3+4+5), achieved by a team's runners finishing in each of the top five positions.
- In the first invitational meet of Carlos's junior year, his goal was to improve on his personal best time and finish in the top five.
- A hamstring injury was too fresh to take extraordinary risks on the first meet.
- But once the gun sounded and his competitive juices began to cascade, Carlos decided it was crucial that he win the race against the big schools and make a statement.
- His coach tried to slow him down, but Carlos would not listen.

Runners often ran in packs.

- After three miles he was third; on the steep hill on mile four he took second, and after his finishing kick for the final 800 yards he was first.
- Winning was why he ran nearly 20 miles a day in all kinds of weather.
- When the race ended he was first, proud and re-injured.
- The pain was nauseatingly intense.
- He couldn't walk, he couldn't think, and he had another meet in three weeks.
- The coach called for rest; Carlos was convinced he could run through the pain and make a statement to Division II champion South Dakota State.
- For 20 days he stretched carefully, underwent massage therapy daily on his leg and ran through the pain.
- A routine day of jogging always seemed to end in a full bore run.

- On the day of the race, Carlos was unable to get out of bed; his thigh was swollen dramatically, the pain terrific.
- At a distance he could hear the other teams arriving, but he was still unable to stir from his bed.

Life in the Community: Albuquerque, New Mexico

- Albuquerque, New Mexico, which embraced roughly half of the population of the state, bordered on its eastern side by the Sandia Mountains and divided by the Rio Grande, which flows through the city, north to south.
- Albuquerque's enticing charm was born from its deep roots, starting with the Native Americans who lived there for thousands of years before the city's official founding by the Spanish.
- The Rio Grande Valley had been populated and cultivated since as far back as 2000 B.C.

Albuquerque is situated on the Rio Grande.

- The Pueblo people who lived in the area when Europeans arrived had a sophisticated culture and advanced skills in stone masonry, ceramics and a wide range of arts and crafts.
- The first Spanish explorers arrived in Albuquerque in approximately 1540 under General Francisco de Coronado.
- In 1706, a group of colonists were granted permission by King Philip of Spain to establish a new city and chose a spot at the foot of the mountains where the Rio Grande River made a wide curve, provided good irrigation for crops and a source of wood from the cottonwoods, willows and olive trees.
- The early Spanish settlers erected a small adobe chapel where today's San Felipe de Neri Church still stands in Albuquerque's Old Town.

Sandia National Laboratories in Albuquerque was established in 1949.

- Its plaza was surrounded by adobe homes clustered close together for protection.
- Albuquerque's dry climate brought many tuberculosis patients to the city in search of a cure during the early 1900s, and several sanitaria sprang up on the West Mesa to serve them.
- The establishment of Kirtland Air Force Base in 1939, Sandia Base in the early 1940s, and Sandia National Laboratories in 1949, made Albuquerque a key player of the Atomic Age.
- The city continued to expand outward onto the West Mesa, reaching a population of 384,736 in 1989.

1989: Sergeant Luella Sprague, Invasion of Panama

Staff Sergeant Luella Sprague was part of a Military Police Battalion sent to invade Panama, where the presence of women in combat captured headlines across the nation.

Life at Home

- Luella Sprague enlisted in the army right out of high school in order to help pay for college; her childhood dream was to become part of the Tennessee Bureau of Investigation.
- Luella grew up in the community of Alto, Tennessee, at the foot of the Cumberland plateau.
- In high school, her report card reflected more C's than A's, but her prowess as a leadoff-hitting softball shortstop earned her several partial scholarship offers to small colleges in the area.
- Her parents' persistent struggles with debt convinced her that she would not attend college on the "borrow now, pay back later" plan; money worries, she already knew, could be a huge burden.
- Besides, the army's offer to see the world and earn money toward college was appealing.
- Before she joined the army, Luella's longest journey from home had been to Graceland on the anniversary of Elvis Presley's death.
- She knew she had made the right decision almost immediately; the army assigned her to military police training and offered additional courses toward a degree in criminal justice.
- As an MP, she not only received police training, but also was qualified with an M-16 and all other basic combat tactics.
- Luella enjoyed the day-to-day routine of police work in the 503rd Military Police Battalion at Fort Bragg, North Carolina, but she loved the idea that her unit could be assigned in a hostile situation to keep peace.
- Traditionally, women were not allowed in combat units; military police served a support function.
- Luella thought the prohibition against women in combat ridiculous, and though many of her fellow male soldiers agreed, few were willing to speak publicly.
- A quarter of the soldiers in her company were tough and aggressive—and female.
- She could out-arm-wrestle many of the men, and out-drink all of them.
- However, she was just as wary as the men when in the spring of 1989, after

Luella Sprague joined the army to pay for college.

more than a decade in service, her platoon got a new female commanding officer, Second Lieutenant Alice Zayicek, a Chicago native straight out of ROTC.

- Zayicek was a rigid disciplinarian who expected respect, and conducted herself with a quiet confidence not always found in new officers.
- After a few months, Luella decided that Lt. Zayicek was the best officer she had served with in over 11 years of service.

Life at Work

- For much of 1988 and 1989, the country of Panama and its leader General Manuel Noriega had been in the headlines.
- Despite nearly 12,000 American troops in Panama, Noriega and his Panama Defense Force were exercising nearly absolute control over the country.

Traditionally, women were not allowed in combat units, but might see action as members of the 503rd Military Police

- Since the Panama Canal Treaty was signed during the Carter Administration, the influence of the United States in Panama had been declining.
- The treaty, which was derided by many, called for the entire American military presence to be gone by the end of 1999-just a decade away.
- Currently, 12,700 American troops are assigned to Panama; the Central American country serves as the headquarters of the U.S. Southern Command.
- In May, a national election was held, with Noriega claiming victory even though neutral observers said he had lost in a landslide.
- In early October, a failed coup attempt increased tensions and exacerbated anti-American sentiment among Noriega supporters, particularly the Panama Defense Force.
- Word circulated around Fort Bragg that U.S. military involvement was imminent, although President Bush publicly denied any plans to invade Panama.
- In mid-December, Noriega's Panama Defense Force shot an American officer and tortured another while threatening to gang-rape the officer's wife.
- Bush ordered that Noriega be captured and his rogue government taken down.

A failed coup attempt increased tensions and exacerbated anti-American sentiment in Panama.

- Seven thousand troops, including Ranger, airborne and infantry, were airlifted to Panama to join the forces on the ground.
- The operation was designated "Just Cause."
- Early on the morning of December 20, a multipronged attack-the largest force in the field since Vietnam-hit targets in Panama.
- As part of the assault, 3,000 members of the 82nd Airborne Division made the largest parachute drop since World War II.
- Noriega's defense forces provided token resistance before fading into the landscape to conduct guerrilla warfare.
- Luella's company was deployed early in the attack plan.
- Approximately 2,500 troops consisting primarily of MPs landed in Panama behind the air assault.

- Although for Luella, excitement had been building all week, some soldiers were visibly nervous, while others were in a panic about childcare, since both mother and father were deployed at the same time.
- The night before she shipped out, Luella wrote her family the longest letter of her life, describing her pride at being an American, her joy of being a female soldier, and her excitement that she would be allowed to fight for her country.
- Upon landing in Panama, the MPs were immediately immersed in the thick of the fray.
- Luella's squad was assigned to join a perimeter force around the Ministry of Foreign Affairs.
- Almost immediately, she was subjected to fire; as the day progressed, the sounds of war were persistent, but not heavy.
- One soldier in her unit was hit, and although the wound was not life-threatening, he screamed in pain and fear at seeing blood gushing out of his body.
- Luella was embarrassed by his behavior as he was carried off for medical treatment.
- In the second of several firefights during the first day, she was sure she had taken down two of the enemy.
- What a rush!
- Late in the day, an exhausted Lt. Zayicek stopped at Luella's post, offering encouragement with a firm "Carry on, soldier," and moving on.
- Luella marveled at the maturity of the 22-year-old officer.
- Panamanian resistance collapsed quickly in the face of superior strength.
- In the days that followed, the MPs set up a police department, as well as a night court staffed by Panamanian magistrates.
- Luella had performed similar operations on the island of St. Croix after Hurricane Hugo struck the island in September.
- Her other concern was containing the looters trying to take advantage of the chaos; each day, she patrolled with several Panamanian policemen.

Luella's squad was assigned to join a perimeter force around the Ministry of Foreign Affairs.

- A stickler for details, she kept those in her unit alert and aware of the dangers.
- Weapons were cleaned, oiled and on ready at all times, as the MPs were still subject to fire from burned-out buildings and looted storefronts.
- Rumors were bruited of sniper killings in the forbidding streets; every face and building were scanned for potential danger.
- Luella knew that she could die in seconds in these situations.
- She was amused that the stateside media was obsessed with the idea that women like her were in the line of fire, because in Panama, hundreds of women operated in the combat zone and had come under enemy fire.

Luella was concerned with looters trying to take advantage of the chaos; each day, she patrolled with several Panamanian policemen.

- Also, for the first time, women led soldiers into action against an enemy.
- Official army policy still kept women from serving in units designated for combat; since the mid-1970s, women had served in support units such as the Military Police and the Signal Corps.
- The Panama invasion was now proving what military experts had said for years-in today's urban warfare, the line between combat and support is quickly blurred.
- Just as life began to fall into a routine-albeit still harrowing at times-word arrived that one of Noriega's chief lieutenants was hiding in a nearby apartment complex.
- Luella was beside herself with excitement as the entire unit piled in HMMWVs (high mobility multipurpose wheeled vehicles) and roared to the location.
- She leapt from the vehicle, her M-16 ready.
- As the building was quickly surrounded, a group led by Lt. Zayicek was the first inside, with Luella leading a group in right behind her.
- At each door, Lt. Zayicek knocked, producing a search warrant from the newly constituted Panamanian courts, then instructed Luella's team to fan quickly through the apartment from room to room with weapons highly visible.
- The Panamanian policemen watched in awe.
- Little was found until the fifth apartment search, where a soldier discovered a padlocked satchel from which, when slit open, tumbled out wads of U.S. bills.
- The three women occupying the apartment vehemently denied knowledge of the money as they were frisked and cuffed by Luella, who had little patience for their denials.
- She had even less patience with a soldier who began using the barrel of his gun to encourage one of the women to talk.
- "We're pros!" she barked, and the interrogation ended.
- She knew the prisoners would talk in good time.
- For the time being, it was her job to secure the money and wait for the women to be driven to the police station.
- Within weeks, she and her unit shifted from fighting to peacekeeping.
- Through a cash-for-weapons program, the U.S. paid out $60,000 for 75,000 guns collected by the police; one Panamanian received $5,000 for driving an armored personnel carrier up to the doorstep of the U.S. troops.

Luella and her unit found money in a raid on one of Noriega's apartments.

Life in the Community: Washington, DC and Panama

- Critics in Washington were condemning the invasion of Panama as a "throwback to the era of gunboat diplomacy."
- Others were saying it was simply a contrived, glorious moment in the "war against drugs" for a commander-in-chief who was still suspected of being wimpish.
- The United Nations did not approve the invasion, considering it an illegal, unilateral use of force.
- Approximately 23 American and 300 Panamanian soldiers died in the assault.
- Editorial writers generally agree with President Bush that the invasion of Panama was necessary as a crusade for a democratic and drug-free hemisphere.
- The president of the Panamanian Chamber of Commerce calculates that losses from looting and damage caused by the military invasion will top $1 billion.
- Millions more, it was believed, would be needed to refurbish streets, waterworks, public buildings and other facilities long neglected by a government more obsessed with power than governance.
- To help out in the crisis, the United States asked Japan, which extensively uses the Panama Canal, to provide aid.

1989: Charles Coughlin Myers, Anti-Abortion Protestor

Charles Coughlin Myers, an anti-abortion protester, was convinced that America was perched on a new era of greatness that would bring quality values back into the mainstream.

Life at Home

- Charles Coughlin Myers knew in his heart that, thanks to the leadership of President Ronald Reagan, the horrors of the New Deal era were being wiped out, Communism was on the verge of collapse, and AIDS was punishing the homosexuals and drug abusers for their deviant ways.
- The crowning achievement would be the abolishment of abortion in the United States.
- Now, with the election of President Reagan's handpicked successor, George Bush, America was destined to complete the work already begun.
- Charles's greatest disappointment in this quest was the refusal of the United States Senate to confirm Robert H. Bork for the Supreme Court in 1987.

- Judge Bork would have revolutionized the thinking of the court if the liberals had not ambushed him by mailings, fervent lobbying, scare rhetoric and television ads.
- Charles was also convinced the liberal press finally could see the sea change underway and was running scared.
- That's why it had demonized Judge Bork and frightened the voters into thinking that he was a monster who would sterilize women, bring back the poll tax and eliminate condoms.
- The day the Senate refused to recognize the brilliance of Judge Bork was the day Charles understood that America was engaged in a civil war over its future moral framework.
- And he knew it was a wake-up call to stand on the front lines to defend America from decay.
- Born in 1946, Charles Coughlin Myers was proud that his parents had named him after the 1930s crusading Roman Catholic priest Father Charles Coughlin, who had used his radio broadcasts to challenge immorality, the bank cartel that was ruining the country, and America's first elected dictator, Franklin D. Roosevelt.

Charles Myers was an anti-abortion protester.

- It took courage to swim upstream against public opinion then, and the same was true today.
- That's why two years earlier, Charles resigned from his job as a software designer to become a full-time protestor with one goal: to stop government-approved murder of the unborn.
- Easy access to abortions had encouraged sexual relations by the unmarried and a decline in morality, Charles believed.
- He fully understood that the purpose of sex was the propagation of children and had fostered that belief throughout his 18-year marriage.
- During his first year as a professional protester, or as Charles preferred, "Pioneer for God," his wife and four children had traveled with him from march to demonstration to abortion clinic confrontation.
- The palpable tension and boisterous condemnation of women seeking abortions upset the children.
- Now they stayed in the New York apartment overlooking Central Park with their mother and attended school regularly again.
- Charles tried to visit at least once a month, no matter how busy he was.

Life at Work

- Charles Coughlin Myers appreciated that his father had been supportive of his beliefs; in fact, he even died at the right time.
- Just as boredom was setting in at work and his desire to reclaim the goodness of America at its peak, Charles's father had suddenly died of a massive heart attack, leaving behind a multimillion-dollar estate.
- That meant that Charles was unbound from the earthly need to provide for his family and freed to fight the iniquity unleashed in 1973 when the U.S. Supreme Court ruled in *Roe v Wade* that abortions could be performed legally nationwide.
- But Charles believed that, thanks to the Reagan "Era of Righteousness," restrictions on abortions were coming back step by step.
- After years of writing letters and talking to friends, he first decided to act during a protest condemning the opening of a gynecologist's office in Manhattan.
- Charles brought the entire family to the event, part of a week-long effort by a young organization known as Operation Rescue, the members of which believed that direct confrontation was essential for meaningful change.
- Charles's day began at 6 a.m., when the demonstrators assembled in the lobby of the Times Square Hotel on West 43rd Street, where many were staying.
- Groups of people held hands and prayed, and then left for the subway.
- They were told to follow guides who held American flags and were the only ones to know the route or destination.
- Charles was jubilant when he arrived at the protest and joined the others.

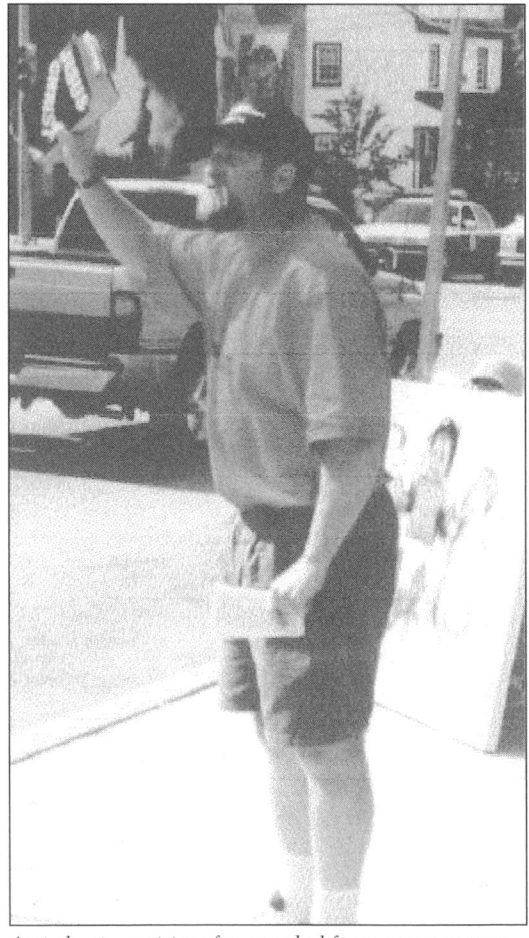

Anti-abortion activists often preached from street corners to get their message out.

The police watched as protests defied an injunction issued by a Manhattan federal judge.

- Boisterously but peacefully, they sat on the sidewalk and street, praying and chanting before the office of the gynecologist at 154 East 85th Street, where they had been told abortions were performed.
- Across the street, supporters of abortion rights, including representatives of the National Organization for Women and the National Abortion Rights Action League, chanted, too.
- No one tried to enter the small residential building that housed the doctor's office because access was blocked.
- A few patients stood on the sidelines and then left, while medical personnel were blocked from going to work.
- That's when the arrests began in an orderly and peaceful manner.
- Charles had never been arrested before and was unsure whether to be proud or ashamed.
- Their leader, Operation Rescue founder Randall A. Terry of Binghamton, New York, told the press, "Our goal is to completely close down abortion facilities for an entire day, and each day we will target another one."
- He told *The New York Times* that he had been planning the events for a year and a half.
- "We are simply producing the social tensions that bring about political change," he said.
- "Everyone here is committed to being arrested."

- During the three-hour protest, 503 demonstrators were taken into custody, bused to the Police Academy on East 20th Street, charged with disorderly conduct and released.
- Charles fully realized that too much energy had been concentrated on changing laws through the courts and legislatures; Operation Rescue wanted to save babies right now in the most direct way possible—by keeping women out of abortion centers.
- Minutes after being released from jail, Charles signed up for the protest in Chicago, where he learned the value of graphic pictures to shock women into keeping their babies.
- Women seeking abortions needed to face the visual consequences of their actions, Charles had come to understand.
- Several abortion-seekers turned away from his sign during the Chicago demonstration, but one woman actually threw up on the sidewalk when he showed her a picture of an aborted baby.
- It may have been his proudest moment in Chicago.

Charles' children watched their father's arrests.

- From there Charles traveled the country at his own expense, fighting for the rights of the unborn.
- Quickly he learned that the press could not be trusted and refused to talk to them.
- In Atlanta, during the Democratic National Convention that year, the various protest groups had to take turns demonstrating in a two-acre area of parking lots that the city had set aside for that purpose.
- But Operation Rescue commanded headlines after 134 hymn-singing opponents of abortion blocked access to a medical clinic by lying across the steps in front of the door.
- Thirty-one of the anti-abortion demonstrators, including Charles, got further publicity for their cause when they refused to disclose their identities to police.
- Operation Rescue wanted to overcrowd the prison system by refusing to give their real names to police, thus making them ineligible for bond.
- For 40 days the protesters from New York, California, Virginia and Illinois sang and prayed behind bars.
- At the same time in Chicago, the police were unable to take two of the protesters into custody because they locked themselves to a bar attached to a concrete block, while in Pennsylvania, 74 activists were found guilty of trespassing outside a women's health clinic in Paoli.
- On New Year's Day, 1989, Charles was more optimistic than ever about the future of the right to life movement.
- The arrest Charles relished the most was the day he was handcuffed as a leader of the movement, while his children watched.
- For months his wife had been saying that he was setting a poor example for the children.
- Now it was his time to shine.
- That day police arrested 685 abortion opponents for demonstrating outside a Manhattan abortion clinic for the second consecutive day.
- Many of the protesters had stopped traffic and blocked sidewalks, but it was Charles's idea to chain 12 people, just like disciples, together in a line.

- Charles then swallowed the key to the locking system securing the chain and dared the police to make them stop blocking the doors of the Margaret Sanger Center, operated by Planned Parenthood.
- The protests defied an injunction issued by a Manhattan federal judge that forbade Operation Rescue from obstructing access to abortion clinics in the city.
- Charles's delight with the blocking maneuver turned to elation when the police shouted, "Take him first; he's their leader."
- And it was all said right in front of his children: a great day indeed.

Life in the Community: New York City

- Until the Supreme Court ruled on *Roe v Wade,* each state had set its own laws concerning abortions and conditions under which they could be performed.
- New York State had the most liberal abortion access laws in the nation.
- So anti-abortion leaders began preparing early for the day when the Supreme Court ruling that legalized abortion was overturned and the issue returned to the states.
- Charles Coughlin Myers expected that some time during George Bush's Administration, the great evil of abortion would be halted.
- He believed that President Bush would shift the Supreme Court away from the 1973 *Roe v. Wade* decision through wise, conservative appointments, now that three of the Justices who had joined in the ruling were in their eighties.
- Sixteen years earlier, the Supreme Court had declared that a woman's right must be weighed against the fetus's growing potential for life.
- Therefore, the court reasoned, the state's interest in protecting life increased as the fetus grew.
- Accordingly, the decision was left up to a woman and her doctor whether to continue a pregnancy, at least during the first trimester.
- States were allowed to impose some limitation on abortion in the second trimester, and allowed stronger limitation in the third.
- Polls indicated that a substantial majority of Americans believed strongly in a woman's right to an abortion, although anti-abortion groups contended that their support was growing rapidly.
- "I think there is a definite movement away from abortion now, as more people come to believe that it is not acceptable for mothers to murder their babies," according to Joseph Scheidler, executive director of the Chicago-based Pro-Life Action League.
- "We have whole groups of ex-abortionists coming and telling us how persuasive we've been.
- "And since the Democratic convention, there have been 10,000 arrests in antiabortion demonstrations. That's a lot of people putting their bodies on the line."
- According to figures provided by Congress, half of all pregnancies in America were unintended and half of these unintended pregnancies ended in abortion.
- Nearly half of the unintended pregnancies were the result of a contraceptive failure.
- Nationwide, doctors performed 1.6 million abortions annually.

Heavily-populated New York had liberal abortion access laws.

1989: An Dung and Nguyet Nguyen, Vietnamese Immigrants who Valued Education

An Dung and Nguyet Nguyen were Vietnamese immigrants who believed that education was the key to being successful in the United States.

Life at Home

- An Dung and Nguyet Nguyen from Vietnam were part of a revolutionary immigrant tidal wave that struck America's shores in the 1980s.
- From Vietnam alone, two million refugees had uprooted themselves; almost one million of them came to the United States.
- As a result, many American cities were experiencing a cultural makeover.
- Unleashed by the Immigrant Act of 1965, legal immigration expanded from 178,000 new residents a year, under the National Origins System, to one million by 1989.
- Illegal immigration added another 300,000 to 500,000 people each year.
- By 1989, immigration accounted for 60 percent of America's population growth, 82 percent of whom came from Latin American and Asian nations, and 13 percent from Europe.
- Global population had expanded from one billion in 1804 to 5.3 billion in 1989.
- The Immigration Act came just as a worldwide population spike was sending a second great wave of human migration searching for relief from overcrowded, economically damaged nations.
- New Americans were being minted from Mexico, the Philippines, China, the Republic Korea, India, the USSR, and Jamaica.
- The Nguyet family had entered the United States legally a decade earlier, shortly after the fall of Saigon, but the new amnesty program brought peace of mind to their cousins who had reached Chicago through Canada.
- The foreign-born population nationwide had reached 8 percent and accounted for one in eight workers, the highest total for foreign-born workers since 1910.
- "Immigration created winners and losers," An Dung told his son Ba.
- Which are we?
- "We don't know yet."

An Dung steered his son toward a vocational education.

147

- An Dung had been successful enough during the previous decade to own one small building and a restaurant; children, parents and cousins alike were the labor force that kept it running.
- But schoolwork came first; education was the ticket to the good life in America, along with a good, hardworking spouse, An Dung had preached.
- So when thousands of Asians—from Cambodia, Laos, Vietnam, and China—arrived in Chicago, many were escorted to Argyle Street, home to addicts, pimps and winos, where the newcomers helped push out the drugs, opened small shops, added a new ethnic character to the gang mix and generally participated in an economic turnaround.
- An Dung's greatest concern was the growing number of Mexican and Central American immigrants who were crowding into the area.
- A substantial number of the Hispanic immigrants were illegally in the country; lacking in green cards and vulnerable to deportation, the workers worked for less, possessed

Chicago was home to a variety of different cultures.

little ability to complain about work conditions, and generally made conditions worse for An Dung and his family.
- He was especially concerned about the immigrants' impact on his children's schools.
- His son Ba attended a number of classes with the Hispanic immigrants, whose lack of English skills made the classes progress slowly; the teenage Ba often complained about being bored.
- An Dung couldn't allow others to ruin the American dream for his family—not after all they had gone through.
- Like many of his fellow Southeast Asian immigrants fearing wage competition, An Dung was eager to close the door on additional immigration.
- America's schools were becoming less a melting pot and more of a salad bowl.
- So to protect his children's future, An Dung devoted a considerable amount of his time to improving conditions within the community and steering his children toward vocational education, where they could always make a living.
- The purpose of education was clear to An Dung: to prepare children for the ever-changing workplace in America.
- The study of dead writers like Shakespeare could wait.

Life at School

- An Dung Nguyen's business background told him that schools should be modeled after corporations so they could be responsive to the workplace.
- Schools should be able to show—through the performance of its children—quality results, or at least measurable progress.
- Every time a school failed to do its job, hundreds of children were impacted—possibly for their entire lives.
- Many high schools with large foreign-born populations already experienced a 50 percent dropout rate—a statistic that was harmful to both the children and the community.
- The reformers who supported "progressive education" and preached the value of allowing children to seek their own interests, avoided an emphasis on grades, and rewarded group efforts had obviously never lived in a world that demanded that their restaurant open at 5:30 a.m. instead of 6:30 to catch one more shift of workers.
- The key was a quality education that prepared people for work.
- For nearly 100 years, business leaders in Chicago and elsewhere had been influencing area schools, their organization, and most importantly, their curricula.
- Business had been demanding that America's schools provide a better-trained workforce.
- As a result, businesses had started schools, helped educators massage their curricula, donated cash and equipment, and persuaded children, parents and teachers of the importance of market economy by subsidizing programs aimed at enhancing teacher knowledge and skill.
- In the public policy arena, business leaders lobbied state and federal officials to guide specific education bills and direct educational funding where it might benefit business.
- An Dung saw his son Ba's future in air conditioning repair and installation—an occupation always in demand, could not be done by cheaper labor in a foreign country, and would not go out of style.
- An Dung, whose Vietnamese upbringing did not include air conditioning, was amazed at how Americans hated sweat or just a little warmth.
- They would never give up air conditioning, even in the worst of times, and Ba would always have a job.
- His thinking meshed with those of American educators since the turn of the twentieth century when schools were struggling to meet the labor force needs of an America shifting from an agrarian to an industrial economic base.
- In his 1907 address to Congress, President Theodore Roosevelt urged major school reform that would provide industrial education in urban centers and agriculture education in rural areas.
- A powerful alliance supporting federal funding for vocational education was formed in 1910, when the American Federation of Labor (AFL), which had long opposed such programs as discriminatory, gave its approval to the National Association of Manufacturers' (NAM) promotion of trade instruction in schools.
- Federal support for vocational education began with the

An Dung's son learned the circuitry necessary to succeed in the air conditioning industry.

Trade schools were popular in the early 1900s and again in the 1980s during a second wave of popularity.

Smith-Hughes Act of 1917, which established vocational education, particularly agricultural education, as a federal program.

- The act reflected the view of reformers who believed that youth should be prepared for entry-level jobs by learning specific occupational skills in separated vocational schools.
- Vocationalism had its critics, including the American philosopher and educator John Dewey, who believed that such specific skill training was unnecessarily narrow and undermined democracy.
- By the 1960s, the vocational education system had been firmly established, and Congress recognized the need for a new focus.
- As a result, the 1963 Vocational Education Act broadened the definition of vocational education to include occupational programs, such as business and commerce, in comprehensive high schools.
- The act also included the improvement of vocational education programs and the provision of programs and services for disadvantaged and disabled students.
- Education reforms focusing on secondary education began in the early 1980s, prompted by concern about the nation's declining competitiveness in the international market, the relatively poor performance of American students on achievement tests, and complaints from the business community about the low level of high school graduates' skills and abilities.
- This reform came in two waves.
- The first wave called for increased effort from the current education system: more academic course requirements for high school graduation, more stringent college entrance requirements, longer school days and years, and an emphasis on standards and testing for both students and teachers.
- Beginning in the mid-1980s, a second wave of school reform arose, based in part on the belief that the first wave did not go far enough.

- The second wave emphasized school-to-work that created closer links between vocational and academic education, secondary and postsecondary institutions, and schools and workplaces.
- The reform movement, particularly its first phase, received major impetus from the publication in 1983 of the National Commission on Excellence in Education's report *A Nation at Risk.*
- This influential report observed that the United States was losing ground in international economic competition, and attributed the decline in large part to the relatively low standards and poor performance of the American educational system.
- The report recommended many of the changes subsequently enacted in first-wave reforms: the strengthening of requirements for high school graduation, including the requirement of a core academic curriculum; the development and use of rigorous educational standards; more time in school or the more efficient use of presently available time; and better preparation of teachers.
- The response to this report and related education reform initiatives was rapid and widespread.
- By the mid-1980s, 43 states had increased course requirements for high school graduation; 17 had developed stronger requirements for admission to state colleges and universities; 37 had created statewide student assessment programs; 29 had developed teacher competency tests; and 28 had increased teacher licensure requirements.
- Between 1984 and 1986, more than 700 state laws affecting some aspect of the teaching profession had been enacted.
- An Dung thought the schools would welcome his son into the heating and air curriculum.
- Instead, they discouraged the notion, saying that an Asian like Ba should be encouraged to explore engineering or software development.
- Jobs in construction, heating, air and auto repair were a loser's path, which confused An Dung even more.
- Every morning his restaurant was crowded with hardworking carpenters, plumbers and factory workers capable of paying with cash and telling delightful stories.

Life in the Community: Chicago, Illinois

- The Windy City, as Chicago was called, loved to refer to itself as America's Second City, reveling in the brashness of its notorious past.
- It was also a city that has always made room for the next wave of immigrants, whether they're coming from Greece, Sweden, Poland, or the American South during the Great Black Migration of the 1920s.
- Architectural giants such as Louis Henri Sullivan, William Le Baron Jenney, and Frank Lloyd Wright left a permanent elegance to Chicago's buildings and boulevards, as well as the world's tallest building.
- In addition to the beaches of Lake Michigan, Chicago boasts 430 parks where visitors find works of art by Picasso, Calder, Miro, and Chagall.
- In 1833, Chicago was a village of 350 residents that grew by 1850 as the world's busiest rail center.
- By the 1980s, the city had the world's busiest airport.
- Chicago's population grew from just under 30,000 in 1850 to about 300,000 by 1870, then to almost 1.1 million by 1890.
- By 1930, the city's population approached 3.4 million.
- In 1930, the "Chicago Industrial Area"—comprising a five-county section—was the second-largest manufacturing area in the U.S., behind only the "New York City Industrial Area," which had over twice as many people.
- Although the electrical machinery industry, iron and steel production, and machineshop and foundry production constituted the three largest components of Chicago's manufacturing economy in 1930, employment in the clothing industry topped 30,000, over 25,000 were employed in printing and publishing, and another 18,000 worked in the furniture industry.

- Chicago remained the leading railroad center in the country, and, as the U.S. automotive industrial complex became increasingly centralized in the Great Lakes Region, the city came to play a leading role in the automobile and trucking industries, too.
- Finally, as the city's population grew wealthier and more sophisticated, Chicago began to invest more in human capital—in education and in healthcare, most notably—and to spend more on sports, entertainment, and the arts.
- As a result, service-related activities—the food, beverage, and lodging industries, for example—grew as well.
- Like most other cities in the industrial Midwest, Chicago suffered terribly during the Great Depression, as the demand for Chicago-made capital goods and consumer durables plummeted.
- Similarly, both the city and the entire metropolitan region were devastated by the decline of jobs in heavy industry as the region lost a staggering 188,000 jobs in this sector during the 1980s alone.

Chicago, Illinois was known for its architecture.

1989: Irby Hipp, Teenage Video-Game Player from West Virginia

Six-foot, six-inch Irby Hipp of Charleston, West Virginia, loved to play video games and listen to Nirvana, and he memorized facts to help him excel at a schoolyard version of Trivial Pursuit.

Life at Home

- Everyone—his father, his brother, the coach and kids at school—wanted Irby to be a basketball player.
- Irby wanted to play video games and one day, like Douglas Smith, become a developer himself.
- After all, Smith wrote Lode Runner on a VAX 11780 computer while he was a student at the University of Washington; who better to develop America's next video-game sensation than a video-head?
- Besides, Nintendo's Game Boy was introduced, the field was expanding, and more competition was opening up—your own skills were your only limitation.
- While others in his hometown spent their time incessantly dribbling a basketball, Irby and his friends had contests to see who can imitate the most video-game sounds: The descending arpeggio that signals "Game Over" for Pitfall Harry, the sounds of dragons crashing into the walls in Adventure, or the sound of Mario jumping over a barrel in Donkey Kong.
- When bored with a lecture at school or at home, he loved to quietly make the "wakka-wakka" dot-eating noise of Pac-Man.
- Irby cut his video teeth on Pac-Man and Defender and stole quarters from his father's dresser top so he could compete at the arcade.
- If his father suspected where his spare change was going, he never said anything.
- Then Zonk, the world's first commercially distributed interactive adventure game, was introduced—and Irby was hooked.
- The key to Zonk was its puzzles, requiring the players to think their way through the Great Underground Empire, past lakes and grottoes and trolls.
- Irby was fascinated by the possibilities, returning to the game week after week to see what lay around the corner the next time.

Irby Hipp's interests included video games, Nirvana and surfing.

- Indifferent to subjects such as who won the basketball game on Friday night or who is going out with whom, Irby and his friends would joust for respect by talking about their progress through various video games.
- It was great to belong to something that didn't require you to strain yourself and ache all the time.
- Recently, his father attempted to get Irby more involved in the city's annual Sternwheel Regatta festival; Irby's father was chairing one of the major committees that year.
- Every five minutes, it seemed, Irby was being asked to drop the controls on his game and look something up on his computer.
- He thought it was a plot to lure him away from his games because his father thinks all this computer/video time serves no purpose.
- Irby was exploring Populous and the ability to rotate and alter the scale of the game's isometric world.
- His room was the universe he controls; on one wall was a huge picture of a surfer high and tight in the inner realm of a wave—cool and powerful.
- Irby never learned to surf and rarely swam, but the poster epitomized all the skills and control he would like to have.
- On his other wall was a picture of Nirvana's Kurt Cobain sprawled on a drum kit in total abandon.
- The rest of his room was cluttered with pictures of people like Clint Eastwood and old dinosaur models he created from wooden kits as a child.
- The only thing that will lure him out of his room is a chance to see another segment of a new cartoon program, *The Simpsons*.

Irby had surfing posters on his bedroom wall.

Life at School

- High school, in a word, sucked.
- When he was a freshman, everyone talked about how he was going to help the basketball team and which college he could attend.
- During his sophomore year, he was caught smoking dope and got kicked out for a semester.
- He was held back and behind the rest of his class.
- The teachers thought he was a slacker and watched him like a hawk, while the popular girls thought he was a dopehead, and the athletes didn't talk to him because he wouldn't go out for the basketball team.
- Who cared?
- The teachers never consulted each other about assigning homework, so they always gave out loads to do on the same day.

- It's not fair—how was anyone supposed to read a chapter in a boring English novel, do chemistry and algebra, and still be in a good mood?
- His mother said he doesn't handle pressure well.
- He was sure he handled it just fine; he just didn't think that all of his time should be consumed by useless, stupid facts.
- After all, no one—but no one—talked about people named Heathcliff when class was over.
- If only they taught real stuff, or let him show everyone his best game moves, everything would be different.
- His school was an amalgamation of three schools brought together in redistricting, creating a huge campus with sparkling new buildings.
- The School Board believed that changing district lines will draw the community together.
- Irby just felt hostile.
- His only school activity, besides organizing video-game tournaments, was playing Trivial Pursuit.

Irby's room was cluttered with pictures of Clint Eastwood and old dinosaur models made of wood.

- At lunchtime, teams formed on each side of a picnic table and call out questions; the other team must answer eight of the 10 questions to gain the right to call out questions in the second round.

Nirvana's Kurt Cobain symbolized the freedom Irby desired.

- Irby especially liked questions such as, "What part of the body gets cut during a bunionectomy?" or "Which of Jean-Paul Sartre's novels has the sickest title?"
- He hated TV trivia questions such as "Which of TV's Cartwright boys wears the biggest hat?"

Life in the Community: Charleston, West Virginia

- Charleston was West Virginia's capital and its second-largest city.
- Started as a frontier fort, the city is now a major center for the chemical industry, as well as glass-fabricated metals and synthetic fabrics.
- Charleston's Italian Renaissance-style Capitol, built on the banks of the Kanawha River, was considered one of the most beautiful buildings in the state.
- The city was experiencing an economic boom, thanks to new industry moving into the area.

SECTION TWO: HISTORICAL SNAPSHOTS

The 1980s was a decade of great social, political, and economic change, including Ronald Reagan's presidential win, concern about the rising national debt, and inventions of the Internet and laptop computers. Americans enjoyed Michael Jackson's "Thriller" album, the Nintendo Entertainment System, and the debut of WrestleMania. These Historical Snapshots highlight hundreds of significant people, places, events, and things that dominated the 1980s.

Early 1980s

- Actress Jennifer Beals established a new fashion trend in the movie *Flashdance* by wearing clothing with holes and tears
- After four years of major losses, the automotive industry rebounded and appeared to be on the road to financial recovery
- Ameritech received the FCC's first cellular phone license
- An eight-year study revealed that Vietnam veterans suffered more emotional, social, educational, and job-related problems than veterans of other recent wars
- An estimated 750 million people watched the marriage of Prince Charles to kindergarten teacher Lady Diana Spencer
- Anti-drunk driver campaigns were credited with a reduction in automobile accident fatalities for the year
- Apple Inc. released the Apple Lisa personal computer
- At the 17th General Conference on Weights and Measures, the metre was defined in terms of the speed of light as the distance light travels in a vacuum in 1/299,792,458 of a second
- Australia won the America's Cup
- Average tuition for four-year private colleges was $7,475; Harvard cost $8,195
- Baltimore Orioles defeated the Philadelphia Phillies 5-0 in game 5 to win the series four games to one for their third World Championship
- Baseball fans suffered through a seven-week strike, the longest in sports history
- Bestselling books included *In Search of Excellence* by Thomas J. Peters and Robert H. Waterman, *Megatrends* by John Naisbitt, *Jane Fonda's Workout Book* by Jane Fonda and *On the Wings of Eagles* by Ken Follet
- Björn Borg retired from tennis after winning five consecutive Wimbledon championships
- Braniff International Airlines and F.W. Woolworth declared bankruptcy
- Cave paintings of sacred Mayan ball games, circa A.D. 800, were found in Guatemala
- Cellular telephones became available to motorists, costing $3,000, plus $150.00 per month for service
- Checker Motors Corporation ceased production of automobiles
- Columbia, the last all-male college in the Ivy League, decided to begin accepting women in 1983
- Combination of First Lady Nancy Reagan's elegance and the wedding of Lady Diana to Prince Charles stimulated a return to opulent styles

- Comedian and Blues Brother John Belushi was found dead of an apparent drug overdose in the Chateau Marmont Hotel in Los Angeles
- Commodore 64 8-bit home computer was introduced by Commodore International at the Winter Consumer Electronics Show
- Compact disk, polyurethane car bumpers, the Honda Accord, and the NCAA major college basketball championship for women all made their first appearances
- Computer "mouse" was introduced by Apple
- Computers reached 1.5 million homes—five times the number in 1980
- Congress released a report critical of the United States' practice of Japanese internment during World War II
- Cordless telephones, front-wheel-drive subcompact cars, 24-hour-a-day news coverage and Discover magazine made their first appearance
- Courts ordered the breakup of AT&T, the U.S. telephone monopoly, into AT&T longdistance lines and regional telephone companies
- *Dallas, M*A*S*H, The Dukes of Hazzard, 60 Minutes, Three's Company, Private Benjamin, Diff'rent Strokes, House Calls, The Jeffersons* and *Too Close for Comfort* were the top-rated television shows
- Degas' painting Waiting sold for $3.7 million—a record price for an Impressionist's work, while Mary Cassatt's Reading Le Figaro sold for $1.1 million
- Divorce rate had grown from one in three marriages in 1970 to one in two a decade later
- Dow experienced a one-day drop of a record 39 points; the high for the year was 1,070, while the low was 776
- Dow Jones Industrial Average closed at 1,065.49, its first all-time high since January 11, 1973, when the average closed at 1,051.70
- Dr. Ruth began her radio sex-talk show
- Dun and Bradstreet reported a total of 20,365 bankruptcies by October, the highest figure since the Great Depression
- Efforts at library censorship tripled; books under fire in New York included *The Adventures of Huckleberry Finn, The Grapes of Wrath,* and *The Catcher in the Rye*
- Ellen Taaffe Zwilich became the first woman to win the Pulitzer Prize for Music
- Equal Rights Amendment fell short of the 38 states needed to pass; Phyllis Schlafly and other leaders of the Christian right took credit for its defeat
- Fads included books about cats (Garfield, 101 Uses for a Dead Cat) and Rubik's Cube; the book, *The Solution to Rubik's Cube,* sold four million copies
- Fifty-fourth Academy Awards presented Chariots of Fire with Best Picture
- Final episode of M*A*S*H set records for the most watched episode in television history
- First artificial heart recipient, Barney Clark, died after 112 days
- First non-American Disney theme park opened in Japan as Tokyo Disneyland
- First successful embryo transfer was performed
- First U.S. execution by lethal injection was carried out in Texas
- First United States cruise missiles arrived at Greenham Common Airbase in
- Firsts for the year included the hatching of a California condor in captivity, fingerprinting of infants, the first black mayor of Chicago, the first woman in space and a female Secretary of Transportation
- *Flashdance* and *Star Wars Episode VI: Return of the Jedi* were box-office hits
- Following the terrorist truck bombing in Beirut that killed 239 Marines, South Carolina Senator Ernest Hollings said, "If they've been put there to fight, then there are far too few. If they've been put there to be killed, there are far too many."

- Four hundred cases of toxic shock syndrome, caused by extended tampon use, were reported
- Global Positioning System (GPS) became available for civilian use
- Hezbollah terrorists bombed the U.S. Embassy in Beirut, killing 63 people
- *Hill Street Blues* won an Emmy for best drama and *Barney Miller* won for best comedy
- Hit records included "Lady," "Starting Over," "9 to 5," "Slow Hand" and "Take It on the Run"
- Hit songs for the year featured "Billie Jean," "Every Breath You Take," "Maniac," "Total Eclipse of the Heart," "Say, Say, Say," and "Islands in the Stream"
- IBM Personal Computer was marketed for the first time
- Immunosuppressant cyclosporine was approved by the FDA, leading to a revolution in the field of transplantation
- In a Gallup Poll, 51 percent of Americans did not accept homosexuality as normal
- In professional football, a strike cut the regular season to nine games
- International Whaling Commission voted to end commercial whaling by 1985-1986
- Italy beat West Germany 3-1 to win the 1982 FIFA World Cup in Spain
- Japanese marketed the wristwatch-sized television with a 1.2 inch screen
- Johnny Ramone suffered a near-fatal head injury during a fight over a woman
- Kellogg's introduced Nutri-Grain wheat cereal
- Lotus 1-2-3 was released for IBM-PC compatible computers
- Magazines reported a new phenomenon: computer widows
- Magazines with the highest circulation were *Reader's Digest, TV Guide, National Geographic, Modern Maturity, Better Homes and Gardens,* and *AARP News Bulletin*
- Maine schoolgirl Samantha Smith was invited to visit the Soviet Union by its leader Yuri Andropov after he read her letter in which she expressed fears about nuclear war
- McDonald's introduced the chicken McNugget
- Members of Kiss showed their faces without their makeup for the first time on MTV
- Michael Jackson unveiled his version of the moonwalk during a performance of "Billie Jean" on the Motown 25 Special aired on NBC
- Michael Jackson's *Thriller* album tracked 37 weeks as #1 on the U.S. charts
- Microsoft Word was first released
- Moments after Ronald Reagan was inaugurated president, Iran released 52 hostages who had been held for 444 days
- More than 100 million people watched The Day After, a made-for-TV film about a nuclear attack on Lawrence, Kansas
- Most successful group of the 1970s, ABBA, released their final original single "Under Attack"
- Movies *Chariots of Fire, Raiders of the Lost Ark, On Golden Pond* and *The French Lieutenant's Woman* premiered
- MTV was received in 17.5 million homes and credited with reviving the record industry
- Musical Annie was performed for the last time after 2,377 shows in New York City
- National Basketball Association contract was the first in sports to include revenue sharing with players
- National unemployment rate topped eight percent for the nation, 16.8 percent for blacks and 40 percent for black teenagers
- Nationwide, 93 percent of homes had a telephone
- New York and Miami increased transit fares from $0.60 to $0.75
- NutraSweet was introduced as a synthetic sugar substitute

- Ocean Spray was introduced in paper bottles
- Over-the-counter drug packaging procedures changed in response to the 1982 cyanide tampering of Tylenol bottles in Chicago
- Ozzy Osbourne bit the head off a live bat thrown at him during a performance in Des Moines, Iowa
- Picasso's self portrait Yo, painted in 1901, sold for $5.3 million, the highest price ever paid for a twentieth-century work
- Pioneer 10 became the first manmade object to leave the solar system
- President Reagan signed a bill creating a federal holiday on the third Monday of every January to honor American civil rights leader Martin Luther King, Jr.
- President Ronald Reagan announced plans to develop technology to intercept enemy missiles, which the media dubbed "Star Wars"
- President Ronald Reagan proclaimed May 6 "National Day of Prayer" and endorsed a constitutional amendment to permit school prayer; it was defeated
- Prices for computers plummeted; Timex sold a personal computer for $99.95, while the
- Proposed equal rights amendment (ERA) ran out of time, receiving only 35 of the 38 state ratifications required
- Psychologists reported increased marital stress due to computer preoccupation, which was creating computer widows and widowers
- Public debt hit $1 trillion
- Quiet Riot's Metal Health album became the first heavy metal album to hit #1 in America
- Red Hot Chili Peppers launched their first, self-titled album
- Researchers at the University of California, San Diego, reported that "passive smoking" can lead to lung cancer
- Reverend Sun Myung Moon was sentenced to 18 months in prison and fined $25,000 for tax fraud and conspiracy to obstruct justice
- Richard Noble set a new land speed record of 633.468 mph, driving Thrust 2 at the Black Rock Desert, Nevada
- Rolling Stones earned a record $25 million from their U.S. tour of 40 American cities
- Rubik's Cube tested the patience of Americans
- Sally Ride was first American woman in space on the space shuttle Challenger
- Sandra Day O'Connor of the Arizona State Court of Appeals was named to the United States Supreme Court
- Sears, Roebuck bought real estate broker Coldwell Banker & Co., and a securities concern, Dean Witter Reynolds
- Simultaneous suicide truck bombings destroyed both the French and the United States Marine Corps barracks in Beirut, killing 241 U.S. servicemen, 58 French paratroopers and six Lebanese civilians
- Sixty-one-year-old retired dentist Barney Clark became the first person to receive a permanent artificial heart; he lived for 112 days with the device
- Soviet military officer Stanislav Petrov averted a worldwide nuclear war by refusing to believe that the United States had launched missiles against the USSR, despite the indications given by his computerized early warning systems
- Space Shuttle Challenger carried Guion S. Bluford, the first African-American astronaut, into space
- Spanish priest Juan María Fernández y Krohn tried to stab Pope John Paul II with a bayonet during a pilgrimage to the shrine at Fatima
- Stern magazine published the "Hitler Diaries," which were later found to be forgeries

- Supply-side economics proposed that government increase incentives, such as tax reform, to stimulate production
- Supreme Court reaffirmed its 1973 *Roe v. Wade* decision affirming a woman's constitutional right to an abortion
- Supreme Court upheld a Florida law denying high school diplomas to students who failed a literacy test
- Surgeons were able to relieve coronary artery obstructions with a stretchable balloon-tipped catheter
- Television premieres included *The A-Team, Wheel of Fortune, Night Court,* and *Webster*
- *Time Magazine's* Man of the Year was given for the first time to a non-human-the computer
- Top albums included Pink Floyd's *The Wall,* Blondie's *Eat to the Beat, Off the Wall* by Michael Jackson and *Glass Houses* by Billy Joel
- U.S Embassy in Beirut was bombed, killing 63 people
- U.S. Government approved the use of aspartame as an artificial sweetener in soft drinks
- U.S. population hit 228 million
- U.S. Steel acquired Marathon Oil
- United Auto Workers agreed to wage concessions with Ford Motor Company
- United Nations Resolution 37 demanded that the Soviet Union withdraw from Afghanistan
- United States invaded Grenada
- United States Supreme Court ruled that radio and television coverage of criminal trials was constitutional
- *USA Today,* the first national general interest daily newspaper, was introduced
- Vanessa Lynn Williams became the first African American to be crowned Miss America
- VCR sales increased; 34 million units were in use
- Vietnam Veterans' Memorial, inscribed with the 57,939 names of American soldiers killed or missing in Vietnam, was dedicated in Washington, DC
- Walter Cronkite retired as the CBS news anchor and was replaced by Dan Rather
- Weather Channel aired on cable television for the first time
- World Health Organization announced that smallpox had been eradicated
- Yellow ribbons were a widely used symbol of American concern for the hostages in Iran

Mid 1980s

- ABC was acquired by Capital Cities Communications for $3.43 billion
- Actor Rock Hudson became the first celebrity to die of AIDS, raising awareness of the disease
- After 35 years on the airwaves and holding the title of longest-running non-news program on network television, the daytime drama *Search for Tomorrow* ended
- After Coca-Cola introduced a new formula known as New Coke, public reaction forced it to reintroduce the Coca-Cola Classic
- After four years of work and a cost of $55 million, the Museum of Modern Art in New York reopened twice its original size
- After losing a patent battle with Polaroid, Kodak left the instant camera business
- After waiting 37 years, the U.S. Senate approved a treaty outlawing genocide
- Agriculture Minister Mikhail Gorbachev, 54, became premier of the Soviet Union
- AMA reported that medical malpractice suits had tripled since 1975; the average award increased from $95,000 to $333,000

- *Amadeus* won Best Picture at the 57th Academy Awards
- American naturalist Dian Fossey was found murdered in Rwanda
- American spy John Walker was turned in by his wife and daughter
- Androgynous rock singers such as Michael Jackson, Boy George, Prince, Duran Duran and Grace Jones captured national attention
- Apple Macintosh was introduced
- Approximately 35 percent of high school graduates entered college
- Approximately five million people formed a human chain from New York City to Long Beach, California, to raise money to fight hunger and homelessness
- *ARTnews* magazine pressured the Austrian government to return 3,900 works seized by the Nazis during World War II
- Astronauts Bruce McCandless II and Robert L. Stewart made the first untethered space walk
- Average salaries in the National Football League reached $163,145, up from $90,102 in 1982
- Average salary of elementary and secondary schoolteachers was $26,700
- Bach, Handel and Scarlatti tercentenaries were celebrated throughout the world; at Yale, 33 recently discovered Bach chorale preludes were performed
- *Back to the Future* opened in American theaters and became the highest grossing film of 1985
- Beverly Lynn Burns became the first woman Boeing 747 captain in the world
- *Bill Cosby Show* premiered on television featuring for the first time a professional upper middle class black family
- Boxer Mike Tyson knocked out Hector Mercedes to win his first professional fight
- Bruce Merrifield won the Nobel Prize in chemistry for developing an automated method to make proteins
- California Wilderness Act was passed which designated 23 new areas in 20 states
- Capital Cities Communications bought television network ABC for $3.5 billion
- Centennial of the Statue of Liberty's dedication was celebrated in New York Harbor
- César Chávez delivered his speech, "What the Future Holds for Farm Workers and Hispanics" at the Commonwealth Club in San Francisco
- Coca-Cola began marketing "New Coke"; three months later, after a consumer uprising, the company reinstated its original product under the name "Coca-Cola Classic"
- Comic strip *Calvin and Hobbes* debuted in 35 newspapers
- Computer game Tetris was released
- Consumers who sought professional assistance with home decorating spent an average of
- Corporate takeovers reached a record high of $120 billion
- Crack, a cheap, smokable form of cocaine, was first introduced into the Los Angeles area and soon spread across the United States in what became known as the Crack Epidemic
- Desmond Tutu became the first black Anglican Church bishop in South Africa
- Discovery of a 4.4 million-year-old anthropoid jawbone in Burma created speculation that our human ancestors may have originated in Asia and migrated to Africa
- DNA was first used in a criminal case
- Dow and six other chemical companies settled with Agent Orange victims for $180 million
- Dow Jones Industrial Average hit 1,955; the prime rate dropped to seven percent
- Dr. John Buster and the research team at Harbor-UCLA Medical Center announced the first embryo transfer, from one woman to another, resulting in a live birth
- Drexel, Burnham, Lambert executive Dennis Levine pled guilty to insider trading, by which he had earned $12.6 million

- Eddie Robinson of Grambling University won his 324th game, giving him more wins than any coach in the history of football
- Eight airlines controlled 90 percent of the domestic market
- Eric Thomas developed LISTSERV, the first e-mail list management software
- Estimates of America's homeless included 40,000 in New York City, 38,000 in Los Angeles and 25,000 in Chicago
- Explosive device sent by the Unabomber injured John Hauser at the University of California, Berkeley
- FBI brought charges against the heads of five Mafia families in New York City
- Federal workers in sensitive jobs were randomly drug-tested after a presidential commission estimated that each month, 20 million Americans smoked marijuana, five million did cocaine and 500,000 used heroin
- Fifty-eight percent of American students failed the basic fitness test (compared to 8 percent in Europe)
- First bio-insecticides, designed to eliminate insects without harming the environment, were introduced
- First genetically engineered microorganisms were licensed for commercial purposes
- First Live-Aid concert was watched on television worldwide by 1.6 billion viewers, raising $70 million for famine relief in Ethiopia
- First PC virus, Brain, spread
- Fitness foods high in fiber and low in sodium, fat, cholesterol, calories and caffeine accounted for 10 percent of the $300 billion retail food market
- Food and Drug Administration approved a blood test for AIDS to screen all blood donations in the U.S.
- Food fads included wafer-thin pizza with toppings like duck and lamb sausage, whole grain pita bread and ice cream substitutes like tofu and yogurt
- For the first time the American Cancer Society made specific dietary food recommendations endorsing whole grains and fruits and vegetables high in vitamin A and C
- Ford Taurus and Mercury Sable went on sale
- General Westmoreland dropped his $120 million 1982 libel suit against CBS for its documentary alleging that he deceived the public concerning Vietcong strength
- Greenpeace vessel Rainbow Warrior was bombed and sunk in Auckland Harbor by French Directorate-General for External Security (DGSE) agents
- Hands Across America chain, stretching from New York City to Long Beach, California, raised $100 million for the poor and homeless
- Harvard University celebrated its 350th birthday
- High for the Dow Jones Industrial Average for the year was 1,553; the low was 1,184
- Hit songs included Madonna's "Material Girl"
- Hollywood movie premieres included *Out of Africa, The Color Purple, Back to the Future, Rambo: First Blood Part II, Desperately Seeking Susan* and *Kiss of the Spider Woman*
- In Hiroshima, tens of thousands marked the fortieth anniversary of the atomic bombing of the city
- In Hollywood, California, the charity single "We Are the World" was recorded by USA *for Africa*
- In New York City, Mafia bosses Paul Castellano and Thomas Bilotti were shot dead in front of Spark's Steak House, making hit organizer John Gotti the leader of the powerful
- In professional baseball, Pete Rose broke Ty Cobb's record with his 4,192nd hit
- Income for video cassette rentals equaled movie box office income for the first time
- Incumbent President Reagan defeated Walter F. Mondale with 59 percent of the popular vote, the highest percentage since Richard Nixon's 61 percent victory in 1972; President Reagan carried 49 states in the electoral college

- John Anthony Walker, Jr., was arrested by the FBI for passing classified Naval communications to the Soviet Union, and Thomas Patrick Cavanaugh was sentenced to life in prison for attempting to sell stealth bomber secrets to the Soviet Union
- John Hendricks launched the Discovery Channel
- Lebanese magazine *Ash-Shiraa* reported that the United States was selling weapons to Iran in secret, in order to secure the release of seven American hostages held by pro-Iranian groups in Lebanon
- Live Aid concert in Philadelphia and London was viewed by 1.6 billion people worldwide on television and grossed $70 million for famine-starved Africa
- *Lonesome Dove* by Larry McMurtry won the Pulitzer Prize for fiction; *The Flying Change* by Henry Taylor captured the prize for poetry
- Major movie openings included *Amadeus, The Killing Fields, Places in the Heart, Beverly Hills Cop, Ghostbusters, The Gods Must Be Crazy, The Karate Kid* and *Terminator*
- Microsoft Corporation released the first version of Windows, Windows 1.0
- Mike Tyson won his first world boxing title by defeating Trevor Berbick
- Milk cartons with photos of missing children, the Ford Taurus, a female Harlem Globetrotter, Wrestlemania and the Rock and Roll Hall of Fame all made their first appearance
- Minolta released the Maxxum 7000, world's first autofocus single-lens reflex camera
- Missing children's photos on milk cartons, the Ford Taurus, a female Harlem Globetrotter, a congressman in space and the Rock and Roll Hall of Fame all made their first appearance
- More than 2,000 people died in plane crashes, the worst year in civilian air travel
- Movie premieres included Out of Africa, The Color Purple, Kiss of the Spider Woman, Back to the Future, Rambo, and The Breakfast Club
- National debt passed $2 trillion—twice the level in 1981
- New York transit fares rose from $0.75 to $1.00
- New Zealand refused to allow a U.S. warship entry into its waters on the grounds that it contained nuclear arms
- News Corporation completed its acquisition of the Metromedia group of companies,
- NeXT was founded by Steve Jobs after he resigned from Apple Computer
- Nintendo Entertainment System, including the Super Mario Bros. pack-in game, was released
- Nobel peace prize went to the International Physicians for the Prevention of Nuclear War, founded by two cardiologists, one at Harvard, the other in Moscow
- Nostalgia was big in the music industry with Bruce Springsteen's "Glory Days" and "My Hometown," Bryan Adams's "Summer of '69," and the Jefferson Starship's "We Built This City"
- Number of Barbie dolls surpassed the American population
- Office Depot, one of the first office supply warehouse-type stores, opened in Lauderdale Lakes, Florida
- Official observance of Martin Luther King, Jr.'s Birthday, the Honda Acura, the onestick Popsicle and the outdoor testing of genetically engineered plants all made their first appearance
- Olympics produced a record $150 million surplus after being run as a private enterprise for the first time
- *Out of Africa* won Best Picture at the 58th Annual Academy Awards
- Parents and local school boards fought over keeping AIDS-afflicted children in public schools
- Pete Rose became the all-time hit leader in Major League Baseball with his 4,192nd hit at Riverfront Stadium in Cincinnati
- Phrase "Where's the Beef?" became a national slogan of exasperation, thanks to a Wendy's Hamburgers television advertisement

- Pixar Animation Studios opened
- President Reagan sold the rights to his autobiography to Random House for a record $3 million
- President Reagan, during a voice check for a radio broadcast, remarked, "My fellow Americans, I'm pleased to tell you today that I've signed legislation that will outlaw Russia forever. We begin bombing in five minutes"
- President Ronald Reagan called for an international ban on chemical weapons
- President Ronald Reagan proclaimed in his State of the Union speech, "America is back standing tall, looking to the eighties with courage, confidence and hope"
- President Ronald Reagan sold the rights to his autobiography to Random House for a record $3 million
- Pulitzer Prize-winning novel, *Lonesome Dove,* by Larry McMurtry, was published
- Reagan administration threatened to withdraw aid from nations that advocated abortion
- Rock Hudson became one of the first public figures to acknowledge his battle with AIDS, raising public awareness of the disease
- Route 66 was officially decommissioned
- Scientists of the British Antarctic Survey announced the discovery of the ozone hole
- Senate allowed its debates to be televised
- Sheep cloning, a woman walking in space, the Apple Macintosh, a state requiring seatbelts use, male bunnies at the Playboy Club and PG-13 ratings all made their first appearance
- Song "We Are the World" raised $50 million for African famine relief
- Soviet Union boycotted the 1984 Summer Olympics in Los Angeles, California
- Space Shuttle Challenger disintegrated 73 seconds after launch, killing the crew of seven astronauts, including schoolteacher Christa McAuliffe
- Space Shuttle Columbia was launched with the first Hispanic-American astronaut, Dr. Franklin Chang-Diaz
- Sperry Rand and Burroughs merged to form Unisys, becoming the second-largest computer company
- Stephen King received a $3 million advance for his novel, *It*
- Steve Jobs resigned as chairman of Apple Computers
- Studies indicated an estimated 27 million American adults were functionally illiterate
- Supreme Court held that the military may enforce a uniform dress code in a case involving three men who were prohibited from wearing yarmulkes indoors
- Supreme Court modified the Miranda ruling to say that illegally obtained evidence was admissible in court if otherwise obtainable
- Supreme Court upheld affirmative-action hiring quotas
- Television premieres included *Miami Vice; The Bill Cosby Show; Murder, She Wrote; Highway to Heaven; Spenser for Hire; The Oprah Winfrey Show;* and *Golden Girls*
- Thirty-eight people died during a riot by soccer fans at the European Cup finals in Brussels
- Thomas Patrick Cavanaugh was sentenced to life in prison for attempting to sell stealth bomber secrets to the Soviet Union
- Tommy Hilfiger brand was established
- Top albums of the year included *Born in the U.S.A.* by Bruce Springsteen, *Like a Virgin* by Madonna, *Private Dancer* by Tina Turner and *No Jacket Required* by Phil Collins
- Trade deficit hit a record $16.5 billion
- Two weeks after it was stolen, the Picasso painting Weeping Woman was found in a locker at the Spencer Street Station in Melbourne, Australia
- U.S. Army ruled that male officers were forbidden to carry umbrellas
- U.S. national debt topped $1.8 trillion

- U.S. Rabbinical Assembly of Conservative Judaism accepted women rabbis
- U.S. Supreme Court upheld Affirmative Action hiring quotas
- Unemployment rate reached 7.5 percent; the high on the Dow Jones Stock exchange was 1,287
- United Kingdom and France announced plans to construct the Channel Tunnel
- United States became a debtor nation for the first time since 1914
- Vanessa Lynn Williams became the first Miss America to resign when she surrendered her crown after nude photos of her appeared in Penthouse magazine
- Vice President George H. W. Bush announced that New Hampshire teacher Christa McAuliffe would become the first schoolteacher to ride aboard the space shuttle Challenger
- Videocassette movie-rental income equaled movie theater receipts
- Virgin Atlantic Airways made its inaugural flight
- Voyager 2 space probe made its first encounter with Uranus
- William J. Schroeder became the first artificial heart patient to leave the hospital where his surgery had been performed
- Words golden parachute, leveraged buyout, and poison pill all entered the corporate Language
- World oil prices collapsed, bottoming out at $7.20 per barrel
- Worldwide, more than 2,000 people died in plane crashes, marking it the worst year in civil air travel
- Wreck of Titanic in the North Atlantic was located by a joint American-French expedition led by Dr. Robert Ballard and Jean-Louis Michel using side-scan sonar from RV Knorr
- WrestleMania debuted at Madison Square Garden
- Young children watched 27 hours and 21 minutes of television a week

Late 1980s

- Across America, 57 percent of households had cable TV, and 66 percent owned a VCR
- Allan Bloom's book, *The Closing of the American Mind*, criticized the U.S. educational system and called for a return to "great books" in its attack on cultural relativism
- American lawyers averaged $914 a week; nurses, $516 and secretaries, $299
- American Motors Corporation was acquired by the Chrysler Corporation
- Americans watched live news coverage of the Chinese and Eastern European revolutions and the San Francisco earthquake
- Andrew Lloyd Webber musical *Phantom of the Opera* opened on Broadway
- Andrew Wyeth, with his Helga Pictures, became the first living American painter to have a one-man show of his work in the West Building of the National Gallery of Art in Washington, DC
- Ansell America became the first condom manufacturer to advertise on television
- Approximately 35 percent of high school graduates entered college
- Aretha Franklin became the first woman inducted into the Rock and Roll Hall of Fame
- At the trial of Oliver North on charges related to the Iran-Contra Affair, the jury found North guilty of three criminal charges and not guilty of nine
- AZT was shown to delay the onset of AIDS
- B-2 Stealth bomber, felony convictions for computer-virus insertions and the Video Walkman all made their first appearance
- Barbara Clementine Harris was consecrated as the first female bishop of the Episcopal Church in the United States

- Baseball Commissioner Bart Giamatti banned ballplayer Pete Rose for life from the game for allegedly betting on games
- Black teenager Tawana Brawley gained national publicity when she claimed she was raped by a group of white men; a grand jury found no evidence for the charges and called her advisors, including the Rev. Al Sharpton, "unethical"
- Books published included *Billy Bathgate* by E.L. Doctrow, *Midnight* by Dean Koontz, *A Time to Kill* by John Grisham, and *A Prayer For Owen Meany* by John Irving
- Bowing to public outrage, Congress voted to kill their scheduled 51 percent pay increase
- Braniff Incorporated filed for bankruptcy for the second time since 1982
- Bush Administration announced a ban on imports of semiautomatic assault rifles
- CBS became the last American network to cease a chime intonation at the beginning of telecasts; satellite feeds had made the tones obsolete
- Chinese military launched a savage assault on the demonstrators in Tiananmen Square, killing an unknown number and crushing dissent in China
- Cocaine and crack cocaine use was up 35 percent over 1985
- Congress overrode President Ronald Reagan's veto of the Civil Rights Restoration Act and restored jurisdiction over Title IX issues in athletic programs to the Office for Civil Rights
- Congress overrode the president's veto of the $20 billion Clean Water Bill
- Congress passed $166 billion legislation to bail out the savings and loan industry
- Congress passed a bill to protect the jobs of whistleblowers who exposed government waste or fraud
- Congress passed legislation to raise the minimum wage from $3.35 to $4.25 an hour by April 1991
- Congress passed the Financial Institutions Reform, Recovery, and Enforcement Act of 1989, which provided a $166 billion bailout to failed savings and loans institutions, and overhauled regulation of the industry
- Controversial movie The Last Temptation of Christ, directed by Martin Scorsese, premiered despite objections by some Christian groups
- Danish parliament allowed legal marriage among homosexuals
- David Dinkins became the first African-American mayor of New York City
- Demonstrators at Tiananmen Square carried a Styrofoam Statue of Liberty as part of the protest against the Chinese government
- Dick Clark's *American Bandstand* aired for the 2,751st and last time on ABC, after 30 years on the network
- Douglas Wilder won the Virginia governor's race, becoming the first elected African-American governor in the United States
- Dow Jones Industrial Average peaked at 2,722 during August 1987, and then fell 508 points in a single day on October 19; the record drop represented $500 billion in lost equity
- During a visit to Berlin, Germany, President Reagan challenged Soviet Premier Mikhail Gorbachev to tear down the Berlin Wall
- Eastern Air Lines machinists and baggage workers walked off the job to protest pay cuts; the airline subsequently filed for bankruptcy protection
- Eight airlines controlled 90 percent of the domestic market
- *Eight-Week Cholesterol Cure, The Bonfire of the Vanities, Trump: The Art of the Deal* and *Swim with the Sharks without Being Eaten Alive* were all bestsellers
- Elementary and secondary schoolteachers earned an average salary of $26,700
- Exxon Valdez hit a reef off the coast of Prince William Sound in Alaska, spilling nearly 10 million gallons of oil

- FBI's promotion system was found to have systematically discriminated against its Hispanic employees in both advancements and assignments
- Federal budget exceeded $1 trillion for the first time
- *Field of Dreams; When Harry Met Sally; Glory; Driving Miss Daisy; Sex, Lies and Videotape;* and *Roger and Me* premiered at movie theaters
- Fifty thousand people gathered at Graceland in Memphis, Tennessee, on the tenth anniversary of Elvis Presley's death
- Fifty-eight-year-old artist Andy Warhol died of a heart attack after routine gallbladder surgery
- First bio-insecticides, designed to eliminate insects without harming the environment, were announced
- First Global Positioning System satellite was placed into orbit
- First increase in the minimum wage since 1980 was announced, from $3.15 to $3.80 per hour
- First National Coming Out Day was held in celebration of the second National March on Washington for Lesbian and Gay Rights
- First of 24 Global Positioning System satellites were placed into orbit
- First open-air use of a genetically engineered bacteria, a frost retardant, was attempted on strawberry plants
- Florida rapist Tommy Lee Andrews was the first person to be convicted as a result of DNA evidence and was sentenced to 22 years in prison
- Former chief aid Donald Regan claimed that Nancy Reagan used astrology to plan her husband's activities
- Former national security aides Oliver L. North and John M. Poindexter and two businessmen were indicted in the Iran-Contra affair
- Forty states restricted smoking in public buildings, restaurants and schools following the Surgeon General's warnings on the negative impact of secondhand smoke
- Fox TV network made its prime-time debut, marking the first time since 1955 that four networks filled the U.S. prime-time television landscape; the network debuted two shows, *Married...with Children* and *The Tracey Ullman Show*
- Fundamentalists picketed *The Last Temptation of Christ;* the film was an unexpected financial success
- George H. W. Bush succeeded Ronald Reagan as the 41st U.S. president
- Harris Trust and Savings Bank of Chicago settled a government enforcement action by agreeing to pay $14 million in back pay to women and minorities, the largest such settlement ever obtained from a single employer
- Harvard scientists obtained the first animal patent for a genetically engineered mouse with immune properties
- HBO's Comedy Channel (soon to be Comedy Central) debuted
- Heidi Chronicles by Wendy Wasserstein won the Pulitzer Prize for drama; the Anchorage Daily News won the public service award for its reports on alcoholism and suicide among native Alaskans
- Hong Kong announced a clampdown on "boat people," saying newly arriving Vietnamese refugees would be incarcerated and returned to Vietnam if they could not prove that they had fled religious or political persecution
- Hungary proclaimed itself a republic and declared an end to Communist rule
- In a meeting off the coast of Malta, President Bush and Soviet leader Mikhail Gorbachev released statements indicating that the Cold War between their nations may have been coming to an end
- In Alaska's Prince William Sound the Exxon Valdez spilled 240,000 barrels of oil after running aground

- In Charlotte, North Carolina, televangelist Jim Bakker, head of PTL Ministries, resigned after admitting having an affair with church secretary Jessica Hahn
- In Chicago, U.S. veterans protested at the Art Institute where the American flag was draped on the floor
- In Edwards v. Aguillard, the Supreme Court ruled that a Louisiana law requiring that creation science be taught in public schools whenever evolution was taught was unconstitutional
- In Super Bowl XXI, the New York Giants defeated the Denver Broncos 39-20
- In *Texas v. Johnson,* the Supreme Court ruled that burning the U.S. flag was protected under the First Amendment
- In women's fashion, Calvin Klein's lean and refined look included soft fabrics with little or no jewelry
- Iran's Ayatollah Khomeini called on Muslims to kill Salman Rushdie, author of The Satanic Verses, a novel Khomeini condemned as blasphemous
- Iranian leader Ayatollah Khomeini died
- Iranian leader Ruhollah Khomeini encouraged Muslims to kill *The Satanic Verses* author Salman Rushdie
- Jerry Jones bought the NFL Dallas Cowboys for $143 million
- July Fourth birthday party for the Statue of Liberty included a 40,000-piece fireworks display; the total cost was $30 million
- Kenya called for a worldwide ban on trading ivory
- Last of the known dusky seaside sparrows died of old age, marking the extinction of the species
- Last Ohrbach's department store closed in New York City after 64 years of operation
- Longest peacetime period of economic expansion reached its eighty-fifth month in December; per capita income was up 19 percent since 1982
- Lt. Col. Oliver North was found guilty of felony in the Iran-Contra affair
- Macintosh II, Kodak Fling, Spuds MacKenzie and Captain Power toys that interacted with the TV show all made their first appearance
- Matt Groening's *The Simpsons* debuted as a series of short, animated segments on *The Tracey Ullman Show*
- Michael Jackson released his third solo album, *Bad*
- Microsoft released Windows 2.0
- Microsoft surpassed Lotus to become the number one computer software vendor
- More than 300,000 demonstrators marched in Washington, DC, in support of legal abortions
- Movie *Batman* grossed $250 million, the fifth-highest in movie history
- Movie *Rain Man* won the Academy Award for best picture
- National debt was $2.684 trillion, more than 26 times the figure in 1980
- New South African President F.W. de Klerk, permitted apartheid marches and released some political prisoners
- New York Mafiosi Anthony "Fat Tony" Salerno and Carmine Peruccia were sentenced to 100 years in prison for racketeering
- Ninety percent of major corporations reported sexual harassment complaints
- Novel Beloved by Toni Morrison was awarded the Pulitzer Prize for fiction, while the Charlotte Observer (NC) won the prize for public service for its coverage of the Praise the Lord scandal
- Office Depot, one of the first office supply warehouse-type stores, opened in Lauderdale Lakes, Florida
- Original script for the movie *Citizen Kane* was sold at auction for $210,000
- Panamanians voted out General Manuel Noriega, but he refused to step down, causing the use of military force to oust him

- Philip Morris bought Kraft for $12.9 billion
- Phrase "couch potato" came into popular usage
- Popular songs included The B-52s' "Love Shack," Billy Joel's "We Didn't Start the
- President Bush and the governors of the 50 states met at the University of Virginia to discuss education policy
- President George H. W. Bush named William Bennett as the first Director of the Office of National Drug Control Policy
- President Reagan signed the Civil Liberties Act, a measure providing $20,000 payments to Japanese-Americans interned by the U.S. government during World War II
- President Ronald Reagan addressed the American people on the Iran-Contra Affair, and acknowledged that his overtures to Iran had "deteriorated" into an arms-for-hostages deal
- Professional baseball player Mark McGwire set a rookie record for hitting home runs, smashing 49
- Professional heavyweight boxer Mike Tyson's fight with Michael Spinks produced a $40 million gate; Spinks was knocked out in one round
- Prozac made its debut in the United States
- Pulitzer Prize for history was awarded to Taylor Branch's *Parting the Waters: America in the King Years 1954-1963*
- Research studies showed that children from smaller families attained a better education than did children from larger families
- Rev. Barbara Harris became the first female bishop of the Episcopal Church
- Reverend Barbara C. Harris became the first woman consecrated as a bishop in the Episcopal Church
- Robots were used for picking fruit
- Romania's hard-line Communist ruler, Nicolae Ceausescu, was ousted in a popular
- Scientific experiments on the Shroud of Turin indicated that it dated from the Middle Ages, not from the time of Christ's death
- Scientists speculated that the New World Peruvian architecture could be as old as the Egyptian pyramids
- Scientists speculated that the New World Peruvian architecture could be as old as the Egyptian pyramids
- Sears celebrated its 100th anniversary
- Sixty percent of American kitchens had microwave ovens; 40 percent of the food dollar was spent eating out
- Some 2,500 veterans and supporters marched at the Art Institute of Chicago to demand the removal of an American flag placed on the floor as part of a student's exhibit
- Sony purchased Columbia Pictures, sparking concerns about a Japanese invasion of Hollywood
- Soviet Union announced that all of its troops had left Afghanistan
- Spending for cultural events topped $3.4 billion, exceeding spectator sports for the first time
- Stanley Pons and Martin Fleischmann announced that they had achieved cold fusion at the University of Utah
- Stock market plunged 508 points in one day (October 19), the largest drop in history
- Supertanker Exxon Valdez ran into Bligh Reef in Alaska's Prince William Sound and spilled 11 million gallons of crude oil
- Supreme Court ruled that public school officials had broad powers to censor school newspapers, school plays and other "school-sponsored expressive activities"
- Supreme Court unanimously upheld a New York City law making it illegal for private clubs to exclude women and minorities

- Supreme Court upheld Affirmative Action hiring quotas
- Surgeon General C. Everett Koop told President Ronald Reagan he would not issue a report on the health risks of abortion
- Television show *Seinfeld* premiered
- Television's top programs included *Roseanne, The Cosby Show, Cheers, A Different World, Dear John, The Wonder Years* and *Golden Girls*
- The Last Emperor won best picture at the 60th Annual Academy Awards ceremony; Cher won best actress for *Moonstruck*, while Michael Douglas won best actor for *Wall Street*
- Thousands of civil rights marchers gathered in Washington, D.C., for the 25th anniversary of Martin Luther King's "I Have a Dream" speech
- Time and Warner Communications announced plans for a merger, forming Time Warner
- Time Inc. and Warner Communications Inc. announced a deal to merge into the world's largest media and entertainment conglomerate
- Toni Morrison's *Beloved* won the Pulitzer Prize for fiction; David Herbert Donald won the biography prize for Look Homeward: The Life of Thomas Wolfe
- TV sitcom *Roseanne* premiered
- U.N. Secretary-General Javier Perez de Cuellar announced a ceasefire between Iran and Iraq
- U.S. auto makers produced 13 million cars and trucks
- U.S. military detonated an atomic weapon at the Nevada Test Site
- U.S. national debt topped $2 billion
- U.S. Patent and Trademark Office issued a patent to Harvard University for a genetically engineered mouse, the first patent granted for an animal life form
- U.S. Protestants numbered 53 million in more than 23,000 churches
- U.S. savings and loan industry lost $13.4 billion
- U.S. Senate rejected a proposed constitutional amendment barring desecration of the American flag
- Under a new law, three Americans became the first foreign lawyers permitted to practice in Japan
- Union Carbide agreed to pay $470 million to the government of India in a court-ordered settlement of the 1984 Bhopal gas leak disaster
- United States sent troops into Panama to topple the government of General Manuel Noriega
- Van Cliburn made a successful comeback after 11 years, playing the Liszt and Tchaikovsky piano concertos in Philadelphia and Dallas
- West German citizens were permitted to visit East Germany without visas
- When sports coverage of the U.S. Tennis Open intruded into the traditional news time, journalist Dan Rather stormed off the set; TV screens were blank for six minutes
- When the board of trustees at Gallaudet University in Washington, D.C., a liberal arts college for the deaf, selected a hearing woman to be school president, outraged students shut down the campus and forced the selection of a deaf president
- Women accounted for nearly half of all graduating accountants, one third of MBAs and one quarter of lawyers
- World Health Organization estimated the number of AIDS cases would increase from 450,000 to five million by the year 2000
- World Wrestling Entertainment presented WrestleMania III in the Pontiac Silverdome in Detroit, Michigan, attended by over 90,000 that set an all-time indoor attendance record

California's Silicon Valley Is Mass-producing Millionaires

IN THE CHIPS

On the roof of a plant in Santa Clara, a phalanx of Silicon Valley executives marches toward an array of the industry's latest desk-top terminals. Armed with umbrellas in anticipation of heavy weather blowing in from Japan, the executives are (left to right): Don Tonn of TeleVideo, Codata's Jim Nakasuji, Harry Garland of Cromemco, Gary Oates of Codata, Bruce MacKay and Chuck Grant of North Star, Exidy's Paul Terrell and Philip Hwang of TeleVideo. At left is a $5,000 wafer of Intel silicon from which 200 computer chips will be made.

SECTION THREE: ECONOMY OF THE TIMES

Despite a steady increase in the annual income of Americans from 1980 to 1989, there was also an increase in the cost of basic utilities and consumer goods due to inflation. Economy of the Times illustrates three economic elements: Consumer Expenditures; Annual Income of Standard Jobs; and Selected Prices. We highlighted three years for each category—1982, 1985, and 1988. The Value of a Dollar chart at the end of the section shows the change in the value of $1.00 yearly, from 1860 to 2015.

Consumer Expenditures

The numbers below are per capita expenditures in the years 1982, 1985, 1988 for all employees nationwide.

Category	1982	1985	1988
Auto Parts	$64.88	$72.34	$79.53
Auto Usage	$1,034.58	$1,153.58	$1,268.29
Clothing	$435.45	$485.54	$533.82
Dentists	$74.94	$83.56	$91.87
Food	$1,662.57	$1,853.81	$2,038.70
Furniture	$90.45	$100.85	$110.88
Gas and Oil	$405.30	$451.92	$496.15
Health Insurance	$77.09	$85.96	$93.70
Housing	$1,339.96	$1,494.09	$1,642.55
Intercity Transport	$77.09	$85.96	$94.32
Local Transport	$23.26	$25.94	$28.13
New Auto Purchase	$229.57	$255.98	$282.16
Personal Business	$525.91	$586.40	$655.71
Personal Care	$127.92	$167.32	$184.05
Physicians	$237.76	$265.11	$292.96
Private Education and Research	$179.61	$200.27	$220.39
Recreation	$603.00	$672.36	$740.22
Religion/Welfare Activities	$206.31	$230.04	$252.88
Telephone and Telegraph	$151.18	$168.57	$185.33
Tobacco	$104.66	$116.70	$128.30
Utilities	$425.55	$474.50	$522.31
Per Capita Consumption	$8,869.32	$9,889.52	$10,872.96

Annual Income of Standard Jobs

The numbers below are annual income for standard jobs across America in the years 1982, 1985, and 1988.

Category	1982	1985	1988
Bituminous Coal Mining	$29,110.00	$34,837.00	$36,660.00
Building Trades	$21,868.00	$23,590.00	$25,872.00
Domestics	$10,260.00	$7,072.00	$11,353.00
Farm Labor	$8,781.00	$7,228.00	$10,472.00
Federal Civilian	$24,452.00	$25,591.00	$29,957.00
Federal Employees, Executive Departments	$20,689.00	$26,598.00	$28,725.00
Finance, Insurance, and Real Estate	$18,966.00	$22,308.00	$27,716.00
Gas, Electricity, and Sanitation Workers	$26,185.00	$31,096.00	$35,308.00
Manufacturing, Durable Goods	$22,256.00	$23,868.00	$29,170.00
Manufacturing, Nondurable Goods	$19,272.00	$20,800.00	$25,407.00
Medical/Health Services Workers	$17,861.00	$18,668.00	$25,665.00
Miscellaneous Manufacturing	$16,680.00	$18,200.00	$20,904.00
Motion Picture Services	$21,452.00	$27,040.00	$27,716.00
Nonprofit Organization Workers	$11,971.00	$11,440.00	$15,635.00
Passenger Transportation Workers, Local and Highway	$15,224.00	$12,589.00	$17,356.00
Personal Services	$11,752.00	$10,088.00	$14,758.00
Private Industries, Including Farm Labor	$15,721.00	$18,534.00	$23,794.00
Public School Teachers	$18,061.00	$20,973.00	$23,992.00
Radio Broadcasting and Television Workers	$22,550.00	$25,064.00	$30,857.00
Railroad Workers	$29,692.00	$23,036.00	$40,862.00
State and Local Government Workers	$17,762.00	$18,363.00	$24,284.00
Telephone and Telegraph Workers	$27,313.00	$29,276.00	$37,210.00

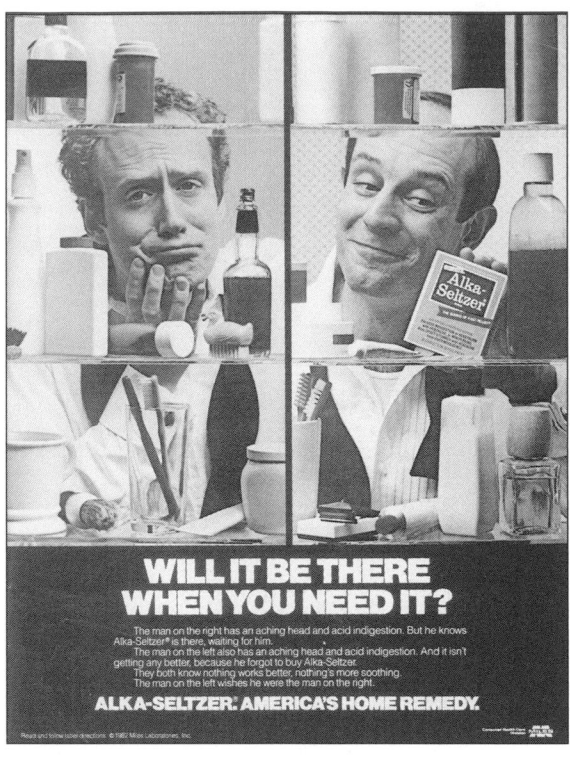

Selected Prices

1982

Air Conditioner $299.00
Automobile, Cadillac Eldorado $19,700.00
Automobile, Honda Civic $7,517.00
Automobile, Pontiac Firebird $6,132.00
Bass Tracker 1 Boat $3,795.00
Beef Jerky $1.99
Beef Roast, Sirloin Top Round, per Pound $1.89
Beer, Pabst 12-Pack $3.19
Beer, 12-Pack $3.19
Bicycle $179.99
Blouse, Polyester $12.00
Boat, Bass Tracker 1 . . . .$3,795.00
Briefcase $89.99
Cabela Camouflage Hunting Suit $74.95
Caftan $22.00
Canvas-Cloth Work Gloves $6.49
Casting Reel $95.00
Cigars, Cuban Sampler $10.90
Circus Ticket $8.50
Computer, IBM, 256RAM $1,795.00
Cranapple Juice, Oceanspray $0.93
Fan $34.99
Fishing Tackle Box $89.95
Footlocker $49.99

Game, FisherPrice $9.97
Gas Grill $179.99
Golf Balls, Spalding Top-Flite $13.99
Golf Clubs, Wilson $219.99
Heater, Kerosene $289.95
Kero-Sun Omni Heater $289.95
Knee Pads $5.99
Knife, Six-Inch Chef's $10.00
L.L.Bean Chamois Cloth Shirt $18.25
Lawn Mower, Craftsman $299.99
Leather Boots $102.95
Macintosh Computer $1,788.00
Milk, Half Gallon $1.01
Pork Loin, per Pound $0.99
Printer, Epson $239.00
Rental Car, Budget, per Day $44.95
Rifle, 177 Caliber $299.50
Rollerblades $24.99
Roller Skates $24.99
Screwdriver, Stanley $14.95
Seiko Ladies' Wristwatch $84.95
Sharp Video Camera $359.50
Shirt, L.L. Bean $18.25
Shotgun, 12-Gauge $1,200.00
Telephone, Cordless $139.95
Truck, Dodge Ram 50 . . . .$5,999.00
Turco Saratoga Gas Grill $179.99

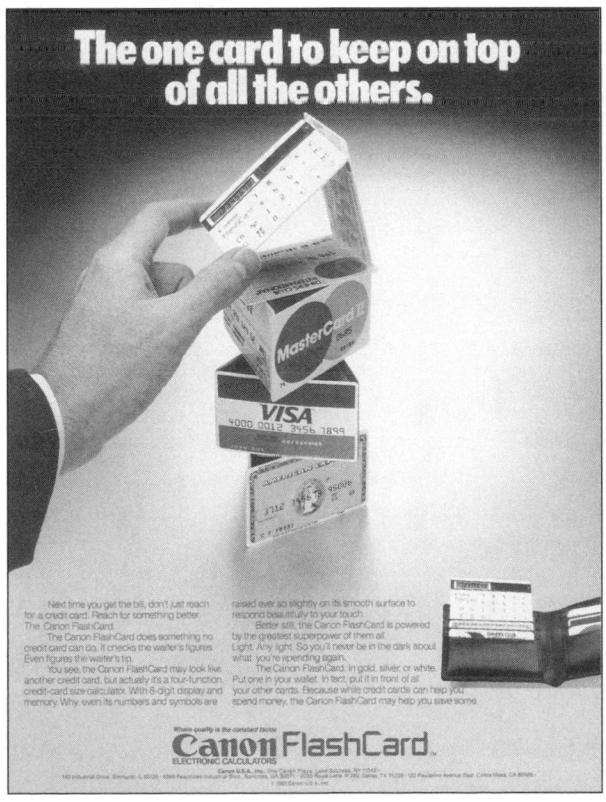

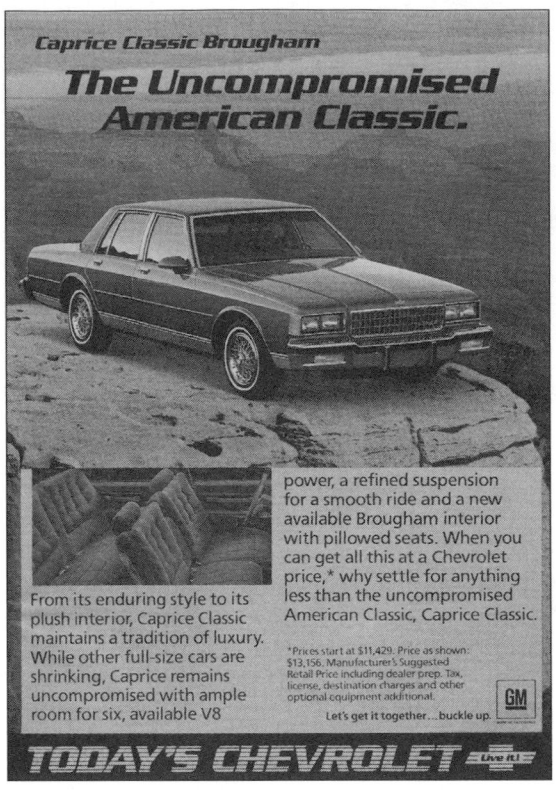

Turntable, Sony $200.00
Vacuum Cleaner, Eureka $39.95
Video Camera, Sharp $359.50
Video Game $54.95
Video Game Home Arcade $299.95
Washing Machine, Kenmore $529.95
Window Fan, Two-Speed $34.99
Wing-Tip, Oxford Men's Shoes $39.99
Work Shirt, Man's $9.95
Wristwatch, Seiko $84.95

1985

Apple IIGS Computer $795.00
Arvin Heater, Fan-Forced Heat $23.88
AT&T Reachout America, Baby's First Shoes, Bronze-Plated $5.99
Ballet Ticket to *The Nutcracker* $18.00
Bicycle, Aero Urban Cowboy $600.00
Briefcase, Leather $565.00
Camcorder $994.00
Car Phone, Metrocom $995.00
Clogs $19.95
Coca-Cola, Two-Liter $1.00
Compact Disc Player $229.95
Computer $895.00
Computer Chess Game $149.00
Disposable Diapers $16.46
Doll, Playskool $24.97

Dove Bar Ice Cream $1.45
Epson Printer. $429.00
Floppy Disks, Fuji $9.95
Fuji Diskettes, 5.5" DS/DD, per Box $9.95
Guitar. $89.99
Ice Cream, Dove Bar. $1.45
Kodak 3440 Camcorder $893.00
Light Bulb $4.00
Liqueur, Kahlua, Bottle. $9.97
Martini for Two $1.08
Metrocom Car Phone, Hands-Free $995.00
Microwave. $199.99
Milk, Two Percent, Plastic Carton $1.59
Modem $119.95
Movie Ticket, *Lady and the Tramp* $2.00
One Hour of Long-Distance Calls $9.45
Pen & Pencil Set, Cross $30.00
Player and Recorder $37.00
Shirt, Man's Velour $14.92
Shirt, Men's $15.88
Silk Spider Plant $54.99
Sweatshirt $19.95

Synthesizer, Yamaha $188.88
Tape Rule. $8.99
Television Satellite Dish $1,995.00
Tuna, 6.5-Ounce Can $0.59
Walkman, Sony $19.95

1988
Adirondack Chair and Ottoman $119.95
Alcohol, Double Martini $1.08
Audiotape, Sony, Three-Pack $7.99
Azalea, Six-inch Pot $3.99
Ballet Ticket $18.00
Bed Pillow, Hermes $75.00
Beer, Michelob, per Case $9.95
Bicycle Child Carrier. $14.99
Bicycle, Aero Urban Cowboy $600.00
Bicycle, Boy's 20-Inch Challenger BMX Bike $59.99
Camcorder, Sharp 8x $1799.99
Car Phone $995.00
Car Radio, Alpine $199.00
Cash Register $179.99

Cereal, Kellogg's Corn Flakes $1.59
Chain, 14-Karat Gold $79.00
Chicken Pot Pies, Three $0.99
Coffee Maker. $25.00
Coffee, per Pound $2.92
Compact Disc $11.99
Compact Disc Player, Technics. $229.95
Computer Game $149.00
Computer Printer, Epson $429.00
Computer, Apple IIGS $795.00
Corn, Five Ears $1.00
Currency Calculator $32.00
Disposable Diaper, Pampers, Each $0.21
Easter Lily $4.99
Exercise Machine, Nordic Track $399.99
Floppy Disks, Fuji, per Box $9.95
Glue Gun, Craftsman $24.99
Grandfather Clock $280.00
Ground Beef, per Pound $1.71
Gun Kit $19.99
Hammer $10.99
Hosiery, Ladies', Three Pairs. $8.07
Ice Cream, Dove Bar. $1.45
Lawn Chair, Adirondack. $129.00
Light Bulb $4.00
Literary Guild $1.00
Luggage Carrier, X-cargo Rooftop $169.99
Microwave, Kenmore $199.99
Olive Oil $8.28
Panty Hose, Three Pairs $8.07
Perfume, Jovan Andron, per Ounce $2,750.00
Pillow, Hermes. $75.00
Scanner $299.99
Set of Four. $675.00
Shoes, Naturalizer. $45.00
Silk Azalea $24.99
Silk Spider Plant $54.99
Socks, Child's, Six-Pack $4.99
Sofa Bed $799.00
Soft Drink, Coke, Two-Liter. $1.00
Sweater, Men's Long Sleeve $29.25
Sweatshirt, Man's $18.95
Synthesizer, Yamaha $188.88
Television Satellite Dish $1,995.00
Television, Sony Watchman $95.00
Vacuum Cleaner, Mini-Vac. $44.88
Water Heater, Kenmore $89.99

The Value of a Dollar, 1860-2015

Composite Consumer Price Index; 1860=1

Year	Amount	Year	Amount	Year	Amount	Year	Amount
1860	$1.00	1899	$1.00	1938	$1.70	1977	$7.30
1861	$1.06	1900	$1.01	1939	$1.67	1978	$7.85
1862	$1.22	1901	$1.02	1940	$1.69	1979	$8.74
1863	$1.52	1902	$1.04	1941	$1.77	1980	$9.97
1864	$1.89	1903	$1.06	1942	$1.96	1981	$10.94
1865	$1.96	1904	$1.07	1943	$2.08	1982	$11.62
1866	$1.92	1905	$1.06	1944	$2.12	1983	$11.99
1867	$1.78	1906	$1.08	1945	$2.17	1984	$12.50
1868	$1.71	1907	$1.13	1946	$2.35	1985	$12.95
1869	$1.64	1908	$1.11	1947	$2.68	1986	$13.20
1870	$1.58	1909	$1.10	1948	$2.90	1987	$13.67
1871	$1.47	1910	$1.14	1949	$2.87	1988	$14.24
1872	$1.47	1911	$1.14	1950	$2.90	1989	$14.92
1873	$1.45	1912	$1.17	1951	$3.13	1990	$15.72
1874	$1.37	1913	$1.19	1952	$3.19	1991	$16.38
1875	$1.32	1914	$1.20	1953	$3.22	1992	$16.88
1876	$1.29	1915	$1.22	1954	$3.24	1993	$17.38
1877	$1.26	1916	$1.31	1955	$3.23	1994	$17.83
1878	$1.20	1917	$1.54	1956	$3.28	1995	$18.33
1879	$1.20	1918	$1.82	1957	$3.39	1996	$18.88
1880	$1.23	1919	$2.08	1958	$3.48	1997	$19.32
1881	$1.23	1920	$2.41	1959	$3.50	1998	$19.63
1882	$1.23	1921	$2.16	1960	$3.56	1999	$20.06
1883	$1.22	1922	$2.02	1961	$3.60	2000	$20.74
1884	$1.18	1923	$2.06	1962	$3.64	2001	$21.32
1885	$1.17	1924	$2.06	1963	$3.68	2002	$21.66
1886	$1.13	1925	$2.11	1964	$3.73	2003	$22.16
1887	$1.14	1926	$2.13	1965	$3.79	2004	$22.76
1888	$1.14	1927	$2.09	1966	$3.90	2005	$23.53
1889	$1.11	1928	$2.06	1967	$4.02	2006	$24.29
1890	$1.09	1929	$2.06	1968	$4.19	2007	$24.97
1891	$1.09	1930	$2.01	1969	$4.42	2008	$25.91
1892	$1.09	1931	$1.83	1970	$4.67	2009	$25.81
1893	$1.08	1932	$1.65	1971	$4.88	2010	$26.22
1894	$1.04	1933	$1.57	1972	$5.03	2011	$27.06
1895	$1.01	1934	$1.61	1973	$5.35	2012	$27.63
1896	$1.01	1935	$1.65	1974	$5.93	2013	$28.05
1897	$1.00	1936	$1.67	1975	$6.47	2014	$28.49
1898	$1.00	1937	$1.73	1976	$6.85	2015	$28.54

SECTION FOUR: ALL AROUND US

This section offers a ringside seat to the issues and attitudes that were 1980s America. These 29 documents, listed in chronological order below, come from newspapers and magazines of the time. They show how America's changing ideas on education, politics, music, sports, immigration, and health were shaped.

~~~~~~~~~~~~~~~

"Homecoming Album for a Hostage, the Year Jimmy Lopez Missed,"
by Anne Fadiman, *Life*, December 1980

On November 4, 1979, Sergeant James Lopez of the U.S. Marine Corps was taken hostage at the U.S. Embassy in Tehran. He was 21. Until 1977, when he joined the Marines, Jimmy Lopez had spent most of his life in Globe, Ariz., a mining town of 7,900 in the foothills of the Pinal Mountains, 80 miles east of Phoenix. He was the starting left guard of the Globe High School football team, played cornet and trumpet in the band and is remembered by his classmates as a distinguished Saturday night carouser. Once named Marine of the Month and twice offered officers' training (he declined, wishing to work his way up in the ranks), Jimmy was posted to Iran in August 1979 as an embassy guard.

Jimmy is the third of six children. His father Jesse Lopez is a timekeeper for Kennecott Copper. His mother Mary works part-time keeping accounts for the *Arizona Republic.* Like many residents of Globe, both are second-generation Mexican-Americans. Jimmy's oldest brother

Rick is an officer with the Globe police force (his wife Velia is a former truck driver). Anna is 27, a training coordinator at Inspiration Copper... Danny, 19, is, like Jimmy, a Marine-a lance corporal working as an avionics technician at the Marine Corps Air Station in El Toro, California. Lori, 17, is a senior at Globe High. Marcie, 10, is in the fifth grade at Holy Angels School...

Mary: I found out when I was driving home from work, just driving around the block here when I turned the radio on and I heard, "Terror in Iran-Tehran embassy has been overrun!" I hadn't even realized I was driving fast, but the children said they heard the car just screech to a halt outside.

Lori: We found out that afternoon that Jimmy was one of the hostages for sure. Mom was on the phone with the

newspaper and she just hit her fist down on the table and got this real blank look. It was real cold, just starting the winter season, and I remember sitting outside, looking up into the mountains, and trying to picture him there in my mind and thinking, "Oh, God, what are they doing to him?"

Velia: The night before, Rick and I had finally decided to get married, and when we came over with the good news everyone was crying. "Jimmy has been taken hostage," said Mary. So we changed our wedding plans. We'd intended to get married at Our Lady of the Blessed Sacrament, a big wedding with a long dress and everything, but instead we ended up just going to the justice of the peace.

Jesse: I started smoking that day. I'd never smoked before and now I've smoked for a year.

Mary: Jesse wouldn't eat. He didn't eat one bite until Danny came home and said, "Old man, you sit down right here and eat that chicken or I'm gonna get it and stuff it down your mouth."

Danny: When I came home I started drinking too much, got in too many fights. A friend of mine and I beat each other up right in front of the Catholic Church. At home Mom was always in tears, and that I could hack, but when I saw my father put his head in his hands and cry, I went in the bathroom and pulled the towel rack right off the wall.

Mary: I don't know what happened to us, we all started sleeping in the living room. We couldn't sleep anyway, and Marcie would keep turning up in my bed or Lori's bed, so we just spread out bedrolls together on the floor and slept that way for a month.

Anna: Two weeks after it happened Lynn and I went to a Marriage Encounter weekend, which is designed to make good marriages even better. I didn't want to go but we had it planned, so we went ahead. And it really helped me. You know, you have so much pent up inside, you have to let it out somehow.

Mary: I stopped cooking, and yet there was always a meal on the table. People would just bring things by. But Thanksgiving Day I made turkey and all the trimmings just like I usually do. There's this special salad I always make. It's got shredded lettuce, shredded carrots, olives, green onions, pickles, all mixed up with mayonnaise, and the kids just love it. But no one really enjoyed it. When we sat down at the table, Danny said he'd say grace. But then he continued to say a prayer for his brother and that just did us all in...

Lori: I used to write Jimmy a lot. I sent a lot of cards because a card has more color in it, to make it brighter-but I ran out of things to say. You feel guilty telling him about the things you're doing.

Mary: At Easter we got a message out through one of the clergymen. It's the last one we've gotten, and we hadn't known if he's gotten our letters. He said he had a terrific craving for a beef tamale. Typical Jimmy. And then we saw him in a film the militants had made. He was taking Holy Communion, and when we saw it we hardly recognized him.

Marcie: It didn't even look like him. The Jimmy I know is nice and bulky. He was so thin.

Danny: When I first heard about the rescue attempt in April, first I thought, "Damn, it didn't work." And then I thought, "Those guys, they died for my brother, trying to save my brother, and that's all that matters to me. They died for him and they didn't even know this man." And that's when I came to be proud. It takes one hell of a man to say, "Hey, I'll do it," because it's the same thing Jimmy did.

187

"Education, A Case of Despair,"
by Ronald L. Goldfarb, *The Iowa State University Press,* 1981

Education is the classic route out of poverty. A painful reality is that the very migrancy of these farm workers often forecloses this route to their children. Inherent in the migrant life is the special problem of educating the young. When always on the move, there can be no stable school life for children; their children are constantly in and out of different schools. When they are attending, they are strangers, often marked by language and cultural differences. They usually are without friends and meaningful associations. Migrant children are hungry and without necessary books and supplies; they usually can be found in the worst facilities, in places not conducive to a good educational experience. They have no assistance at home because their parents are away all day and often are without means and abilities to be helpful when they return. These children are strangers in a hard and puzzling world.

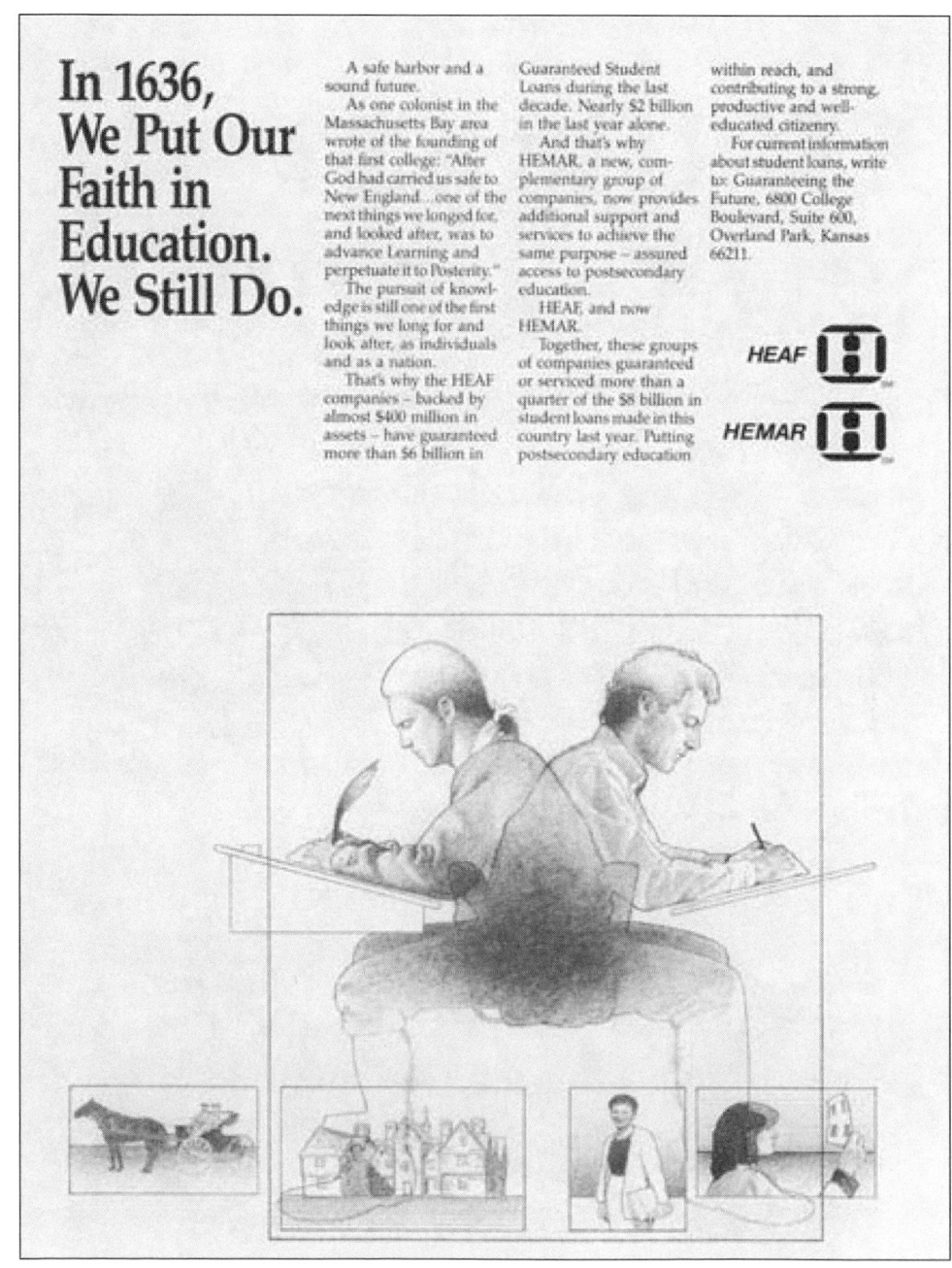

In 1636, We Put Our Faith in Education. We Still Do.

A safe harbor and a sound future.

As one colonist in the Massachusetts Bay area wrote of the founding of that first college: "After God had carried us safe to New England...one of the next things we longed for, and looked after, was to advance Learning and perpetuate it to Posterity."

The pursuit of knowledge is still one of the first things we long for and look after, as individuals and as a nation.

That's why the HEAF companies – backed by almost $400 million in assets – have guaranteed more than $6 billion in

Guaranteed Student Loans during the last decade. Nearly $2 billion in the last year alone.

And that's why HEMAR, a new, complementary group of companies, now provides additional support and services to achieve the same purpose – assured access to postsecondary education.

HEAF, and now HEMAR.

Together, these groups of companies guaranteed or serviced more than a quarter of the $8 billion in student loans made in this country last year. Putting postsecondary education

within reach, and contributing to a strong, productive and well-educated citizenry.

For current information about student loans, write to: Guaranteeing the Future, 6800 College Boulevard, Suite 600, Overland Park, Kansas 66211.

HEAF

HEMAR

"How Software Is Manufactured,"
Inc., January 1982

"It is important to distinguish between software authors and publishers, though they may overlap.

The author writes the program itself, which involves a dogged attention to detail that may require long stretches of 18-hour days until a program is completed.

The author writes step-by-step instructions telling the computer exactly how to execute a task. Computers operate by recognizing either the presence or absence of an electrical impulse, so they can only manipulate long strings of yes or no commands. That means the programmer can't leave anything to the imagination. Each step in a task must be spelled out in excruciating detail. The finished program ends up as a series of encoded lines of computer instructions that, if written out line by line, would fill dozens of pages of text; it's usually stored on a compact 5.5-inch magnetic disk.

'Once a program is completed to the programmer's satisfaction, he typically submits it on a disk to a publisher,' says Harris Landgarten, director of software applications at Lifeboat Associates.

The program, along with the documentation (the manual that describes the program and how to use it), is evaluated for its sales potential, its probable markets, and its user-friendliness.

The author and publisher then negotiate a contract in which the author assigns the publication rights to the publisher for either a flat fee or a royalty of 15 percent to 30 percent of the retail price of the program. If they can come to an agreement, both parties work on perfecting the program (called 'working out the bugs,' in the jargon of the trade). The software is tested, usually by both an in-house staff (called alphatesters) and by outsiders (called beta-testers), and the manual is typeset and printed.

Finally, the program is mass-produced on disks or tapes in formats compatible with the operating systems of different microcomputers.

A software author may opt to self-publish. A number of authors have been successful enough to establish and build companies that specialize in writing programs and have started to publish their own products. And, with sophisticated programming languages like Microsoft BASIC and the increased accessibility of personal computers, many non-technical people have learned how to program computers well enough to create useful software for specialized purposes. Duplicating a diskette is a simple operation: In minutes just about anyone can turn a blank $2 disk into a $50 to $500 program disk."

"Prab Robots Inc. Keeps It Simple,"
Inc., June 1982

"Prab Robots Inc. of Kalamazoo, Michigan, is noteworthy among robot manufacturers. It has been involved from the outset with smaller companies, and 60 to 80 percent of its business is with companies not in the automotive industries. 'I think we have as broad, if not a broader, base than anyone in the game,' says Prab president Jack Wallace. The company owes not only its success to smaller businesses-during 1981 it sold about 180 units, and had revenues of $17.8 million and net earnings of $740,000, a one-year increase of 161 percent-but its existence as well.

In 1961, Wallace was fired from his job as general manager of the Hapman Corp., a small manufacturer of industrial conveyors. His response was to get together with another Hapman employee, Charles Larson, raise some money, and buy a competitor, Prab Conveyors, Inc.

The company, founded in 1959 by Peter Ruppe and Allen Bodycomb (whose initials yielded PRAB), specialized in the production of equipment used to transport and process scrap metal. Attempting to expand his market base, Wallace got involved in the die-casting industry, a fortuitous turn of events, since it exposed him to robotics technology.

'The classic scheme in die casting was to drop the hot parts from the die-casting machine into a water tank and have a conveyor down there to convey them to a trimming machine. We made a lot of conveyors like that,' says Wallace. 'The first robot we saw-it was a Unimate-was in a die-casting plant, and we were told it was going to put us out of the conveyor business.' Wallace was pretty sure that wouldn't happen, and he was also sure that the unit was overkill for the application. 'Our people came back and said, "Let's make something for half the price that will do the job." That's how we got started.'

The principle has remained intact as the company has grown. 'We don't believe in pushing technology,' says Wallace. 'We're pushing results.' The firm's current advertising slogan makes the same point: 'Prab Robots Inc. keeps it simple.'

It was natural that Prab sell to small companies. Its robots were uncomplicated, it had started out with smaller firms, and was a small company itself. 'An order for 200 robots would have killed us back then,' says Wallace.

'The other companies devoted most of their time to going after the automotive spot-welding lines; we've devoted our time to going after the one-here, two-there applications,' says Prab vice president Walt Weisel. 'Our biggest user doesn't have more than 20 machines.' "

Whitney Houston

"A Moon-Made Match, Two of the Reverend's Disciples Embark on a 'Spiritual Blind Date,'" by Anne Fadiman, *Life*, August 1982

"It was a moment for misty eyes: the radiant, young bride-to-be, the homemade wedding dress, the hush of anticipation as she tried on the veil . . . but wait. What was the cloud of tulle on the floor? More veils? To be exact, 2,074 of them-and each one identical to her own. Nina Perry's wedding was going to be, as she says, 'a little different.' Nina is a Moonie, and along with 4,149 other Unification Church members, she would recite her vows at Madison Square Garden in the largest mass marriage in history.

Moonies do not choose their own spouses. They are 'matched' by the Reverend Sun Myung Moon, often to people neither they nor Moon have ever met. A third of the couples were matched only seven days before their wedding. When Nina Perry modeled her gown, she did not yet know who her fiancé would be. When asked his name by an unenlightened relative, she called him Mr. X. 'Do you love him?' asked the relative. 'Yes,' replied Nina, 'I know I will.' 'Reverend Moon is directly guided by the Heavenly Father,' says Nina, 'so I was confident that he would choose better for me than I could choose myself.' Moon made all his decisions on the spur of the moment, allotting about two minutes per couple until 1,306 Moonies were matched. Sometimes he asked direct questions:

How old are you? Where are you from? How many degrees do you have? Would you like to marry someone of a different race? Sometimes he merely looked-'right into your soul' says Nina. Moonies may reject their matches after talking for a few minutes, though few did, since they have been told the most perfect union may be with 'the ugly person, the hard-to-love person, the person you think you hate.' Nina was among the first to be matched. 'When Reverend Moon touched me,' she says, 'I thought, "I'm about to meet my spiritual partner, not just for the rest of my life but for eternity"-and I wasn't even nervous. We walked down a row of brothers and as soon as Father stopped I knew it was my whoever. "What's your name?" I asked. "Gil," he said.' Gilbert Alexander, a 33-year-old engineer from Perth, Australia, who had mentally prepared himself to accept 'a toad,' wrote in his diary that night: 'I felt great joy and excitement beyond anything I had ever experienced. I knew without a doubt that Nina was right for me.'"

"Country Balladeer to Give Acoustic Concert in SF," *Santa Fe New Mexican*, December 24, 1982

Michael Murphey's Christmas gift to New Mexico will be a series of appearances in northern New Mexico over the next few weeks, including stops at the Kachina Lodge in Taos, Club West in Santa Fe, and the Golden Inn in Golden.

The progressive country-western performer recently had the hit song "What's Forever For." His 10th album, *Michael Martin Murphey,* which features the song, has remained in the top 100 albums on popular music charts since its release five months ago.

Murphey, who lives in Taos, has had several hit records over his 10-year career, including "Wildfire," "Geronimo's Cadillac," and "Cherokee Fiddle." He also was the musical supervisor, cowriter, and one of the actors in the film Hard Country....

Thursday night, Murphey will give an acoustic performance without his band at Club West. During a recent telephone interview, Murphey said he's really looking forward to the show.

"The acoustic shows are something I really enjoy doing. And Club West is one of the few places on earth that you can do that kind of thing and people really listen; it's really special for me," Murphey said "It's something I get to do maybe just 20 times a year."

Murphey said he just recently was taped for an Austin City Limits television performance, which will probably air in February.

"When Austin City Limits asked me to play, I asked if it would be all right if I just came down there with my guitar and no band at all, not even a bass player, just play solo 40 minutes on TV with no commercial interruptions. It's a dream I've had my whole career to do one TV show that way. And they were very skeptical at first. They had only done one other acoustic show and it was with Chet Atkins. And no one doubts his ability to pull it off!" Murphey said with a laugh. "It worked out real well."

"There's a myth that sometimes stuck in people's minds that the fewer the instruments, the less the music, which really isn't true. There's a lot present in the guitar alone. People like Leo Kottke have proven it. Being friends with him is what inspired me to try it," Murphey said.

સ્ત્ર૭સ્ત્રૢ૭સ્ત્રૢ૭સ્ત્રૢ૭

"Top 100,"
Inc., 1982

"There is a bright side to the economy of the past year, however, and it can be found in the 1982 *Inc. 100*-fourth annual ranking of the fastest-growing publicly held smaller corporations in the United States.

While the giants posted a 1981 sales gain of about 12 percent, the *Inc. 100* companies chalked up a vigorous 77 percent increase... Sporting nameplates from the exotic, such as HemoTec and Healthdyne, to the simple such as Liz Claiborne and Taco Charley, the ranking represents a diverse range of manufacturing, mining, and service industries. It includes 24 computer and business equipment makers, 11 oil and gas producers, nine manufacturers in the medical field, three restaurant chains, and two airlines. The elite group is headquartered in 28 states:

California is the front-runner with 17 companies, followed by New York and Texas with 15 each and Minnesota with seven. Diverse as they are in industry and location, the *Inc. 100* share four qualities: youth, innovation, high productivity, and a healthy bottom line. Fifty-six have incorporated since 1972, 89 have increased since 1962. On average, the *Inc. 100* firms have been in business less than 12 years."

સ્ત્ર૭સ્ત્રૢ૭સ્ત્રૢ૭સ્ત્રૢ૭

"Reagan's Case Against the Freeze,"
excerpts from a speech by President Ronald Reagan to the
Los Angeles World Affairs Council, March 31, 1983

The freeze concept is dangerous for many reasons. It would preserve today's high, unequal and unstable levels of nuclear forces and, by so doing, reduce Soviet incentives to negotiate for real reductions.

It would pull the rug out from under our negotiators in Geneva, as they have testified. After all, why should the Soviets negotiate if they've already achieved a freeze in a position of advantage to them? Also, some think a freeze would be easy to agree on, but it raises

enormously complicated problems of what is to be frozen, how it is to be achieved, and verified.

Attempting to negotiate these critical details would only divert us from the goal of negotiating reductions for who knows how long.

The freeze proposal would also make a lot more sense if a similar movement against nuclear weapons were putting similar pressures on Soviet leaders in Moscow.

As former Secretary of Defense Harold Brown has pointed out: The effect of the freeze "is to put pressure on the United States, but not on the Soviet Union." Finally, the freeze would reward the Soviets for their 15-year buildup while locking us to our existing equipment, which in many cases is obsolete and badly in need of modernization. Three-quarters of the Soviet strategic warheads are on delivery systems five years old or less. Three-quarters of the American strategic warheads are on delivery systems 15 years old or older. The time comes when everything wears out. The trouble is it comes a lot sooner for us than for them. And, under a freeze, we couldn't do anything about it.

"Cries of Plague for Mysterious AIDS," by Loudon Wainwright, *Life*, July 1983

"Assured and neat in his dark blue suit, the young man testified before a New York State Senate committee about a new and terrifying disease. 'My life has become totally controlled by AIDS and my fight to recover,' he said. 'I am subject to fevers and night sweats and an unendurable fatigue. I live with the fear that every cold or sore throat or skin rash may be a sign of something more serious. At the age of 28, I wake up every morning to face the very real possibility of my own death.'

Michael Callen is one of more than 1,500 people who have been diagnosed since 1981 as having acquired immune deficiency syndrome, a complex disease of unknown origin about which fears of death are appropriate. There is no known treatment for it; only the diseases that come in its wake can be fought directly. According to some calculations, it eventually kills more than 80 percent of its victims, most within two to three years.

Like 70 percent of AIDS victims, Callen is a gay male who has had many sexual partners, which suggests to researchers that the disease is transmitted sexually. But there are other possibilities. The fact that many among the rest of the ill are drug users who use needles, or hemophiliacs, who require frequent blood transfusions, suggests that it is transmitted by blood. That five percent of those with AIDS are natives of Haiti with no clear hemophilic, homosexual, or drug-use background has almost everyone puzzled. And because a very few patients seem to fit into none of the categories, many people are badly frightened.

Their fear, of course, is that the disease, which has already been called an epidemic by authorities and is cropping up at the rate of three to five new cases a day, will be spread uncontrollably by casual, even unknowing, contacts with the general population. The fear, in fact, is quite possibly more dangerous and degrading than the pestilence."

∂∾∂∾∂∾∂∾∂∾∂∾

"6-Month Surge in AIDS Reported,"
UPI, August 5, 1983

The number of cases of acquired immune deficiency syndrome that are reported weekly has more than doubled in the last six months, federal health officials said today.

The national Centers for Disease Control said the number of cases of the disease, known as AIDS, increased to a weekly average of 53 in July, as against 24 a week in January and 11 a week in July 1982.

The daily average of cases reported to the centers increased to nearly eight a day from three or four a year ago. As of Aug. 1, the federal agency said, 1,972 cases had been reported and 331, or 17 percent of the total, occurred over the last six weeks. Of all patients, 759, or 38 percent, have died.

New York City reported most of the cases, with 44 percent; San Francisco had 10 percent and Los Angeles 6 percent, the agency said in its *Morbidity and Mortality Weekly Report.* Better Cooperation Cited Dr. James Allen of the centers' special task force for AIDS traced the increasing number of reported AIDS cases in part to better cooperation by state health departments in reporting the disease. But he added that there was also no doubt about the rising incidence.

Seventy-one percent of the victims have been homosexuals. Other groups considered high risks for the disease are people who take narcotics intravenously, recent Haitian immigrants and hemophiliacs. There have been 117 cases that either did not fit into any of these groups, or the risk factors were not known.

∂∾∂∾∂∾∂∾∂∾∂∾

"107 Immigrants Arrested As Illegal in Jersey Raid,"
Associated Press, August 20, 1983

The Immigration and Nationalization Service has arrested 107 suspected illegal aliens and is holding them in custody awaiting deportation hearings as a result of a raid on a South Plainfield handbag factory, authorities reported today.

Immigration agents spent more than a day processing employees of the factory, all but three of them Haitians.

They were detained as they arrived at the Bag Bazaar factory early Thursday morning, according to the supervisory investigator, Louis Galoppo.

Mr. Galoppo said that of the 167 people detained, 60 were found to be in the country legally and were released. The others are being held at an immigration facility in Brooklyn and in county jails pending deportation hearings before an immigration judge, he said.

Officials said it was the largest round-up of suspected illegal aliens by the Immigration Service in Newark in memory.

Mr. Galoppo said the factory's owners do not face legal action because there is no law preventing employers from hiring illegal aliens.

He said that besides the Haitians, one of the persons detained was Costa Rican and two were from Panama. Officer Green said the investigation was continuing.

"The Battle for Grenada, American Troops Take Charge on the Island but Face Surprisingly Stiff Opposition,"
Newsweek, November 7, 1983

Dawn had just broken over the beaches of Grenada. At True Blue campus of St George's Medical College, an odd droning noise woke firstyear student Ron Emerson from a fitful sleep. Rushing outside, he looked into the sky. Just west of the campus, two planes were circling the southern edge of Point Salines Airport. Minutes later, helicopters roared in off the ocean and flew straight into a hail of antiaircraft fire. Emerson and dozens of other students scrambled for cover. "Get down! Get down!" A. J. Quaranta, 22, screamed at his roommate, Jeff Geller.

Geller dove under his bed. After a few minutes passed, some of the students crawled to the windows. At first they could see only red tracer bullets streaking across the fading darkness. More planes swooped low. Billowing parachutes filled the air. Soldiers rushed up and cut through a chain-link fence surrounding the campus. Terrified, Karen Young, 23, wondered if Grenada's rebel military junta was sending men to take the students hostage. An eerie lull fell over the fighting. Then, at one end of the men's dorm, a menacing figure in combat fatigues, his face streaked with green camouflage paint, burst through the door. "American soldier," he barked in an unmistakable Southern drawl. "We're here to take you home."

Operation Urgent Fury had begun just a few hours earlier on the other side of the tiny island. At Pearl's Airport, 400 Marines from Amphibious Ready Group 1-84 landed aboard armed helicopters from the U.S. aircraft carrier *Guam,* part of a nine-ship task force hovering off Grenada to back up the invasion. The Marines met weak resistance from a ragtag force of Grenadian Army troops, militia and some Cuban defenders. They secured the airfield within two hours. The northern half of Urgent Fury had gone exactly according to plan.

The invasion forces didn't have as much luck in the southern half. At Point Salines, transport planes carrying 500 Army Rangers in and off the ocean flew into a storm of antiaircraft and machine- gun fire. The lead plane managed to drop its load of paratroopers. But the next two planes had to peel off, then circle back under cover from AC-130 gunships. The planes swooped so low that the Rangers had to jump from 500 feet-something U.S. troops haven't done since World War II. As some of the Rangers floated through the air, machine-gun fire punched holes through their parachutes. The Rangers finally landed and fanned out toward

True Blue campus, a compound consisting of five barracks-style dorms, a lecture hall, a cafeteria and a basketball court. As they advanced, they had to dodge through withering AK-47 and machine-gun fire. The barrage came from Cuban forces arrayed in a defensive arc north of the airstrip. By midmorning, the Rangers knew that they were up against more defending troops than expected-as many as 1,000. Most of them were Cubans-not just the airport construction workers known to be on the island, but well-armed, well-trained combat troops. "The Cubans were much tougher than expected," said Maj. James Holt, an 82nd Airborne commander. "They were professionals."

"Grenada Syndrome,"
by Michael T. Klare, *The Nation,* November 12, 1983

Although it took many people by surprise, the U.S. invasion of Grenada was a logical extension of a well-established Reagan Administration defense policy. For three years, officials have suggested that the Cuba-Grenada alliance represented a severe threat to U.S. security and that extraordinary measures would be justified to overcome that threat. Indeed, what is most surprising is that the Administration did not move sooner to carry out its strategic design.

Since Reagan took office, his Administration has enunciated a clear and consistent military doctrine, holding that: (1) America's overseas economic interests are severely threatened by growing rebellion and "terrorism" in the Third World, most of it attributable to Soviet-Cuban adventurism; (2) this disorder was encouraged by the U.S. disinclination to use military force in resisting such threats (the Vietnam syndrome); and (3) it is imperative that America actively combat Soviet-inspired insurgency to restore the "credibility" of American power and thereby discourage future threats to U.S. interests. These three concerns have produced an interventionist sentiment in the Administration which can now be given a name: the Grenada syndrome.

One of the earliest articulations of the Administration's defense policy came in a speech to the American Newspaper Publishers Association by Secretary of Defense Weinberger in May 1981. Said Weinberger, "We and our allies have come to be critically dependent on places in the world which are subject to great instability." These instabilities are a significant threat in their own right, he said, and furthermore, they "present a temptation for various forms of Soviet intervention."

Unless they are firmly resisted, this threat will multiply. Therefore, the United States urgently needs to develop "a better ability to respond to crises far from our shores, and to stay there as long as necessary."

Weinberger expanded on this theme the following April in a speech to the corporate members of the Council on Foreign Relations, in New York City. Contending that the Soviet Union had been "emboldened by America's post-Vietnam paralysis" to push "its traditional policy of global expansion to new dimensions," Weinberger said that the United States must not only resist Soviet incursions in the Third World but also "seek to reverse the geographic expansion of Soviet control and presence, particularly when it threatens a vital interest or further erodes the geostrategic position of the United States and its allies." That reference to the "geostrategic position" of the United States reflects the presumption, long advanced by conservative military analysts, that the Russians seek to cripple the West by gaining control of the world's sea lanes and maritime "choke points." Because the United States and its allies are so dependent on imported raw materials, the argument goes, the Russians can gain a "stranglehold" over the Western economies by "interdicting" these key trade routes.

Clearly, the Reagan Administration views the Grenada operation as a test both of its military doctrine and of domestic political sentiment. If the reaction to the invasion is circumscribed or muted, the Administration will not be persuaded that the Vietnam syndrome has finally been overcome and that Americans will accept a policy of global intervention-the Grenada Doctrine. In the wake of the invasion, the Administration will hold an unofficial plebiscite on U.S. foreign policy. All who oppose it should make sure their votes are counted.

Music Quarterly: Aretha Franklin, Yo-Yo Ma, Hank Williams Jr.
Surfing with the Lord out in Southern California

ESQUIRE

MARCH 1982 · PRICE $2.00

Man At His Best

If You Survive the Coming Nuclear War...

Don't Worry. Our Leaders Have a Swell Plan

Plus: In Praise of the Prose Murray Kempton

"Grenada's Gain, Our Loss,"
Editorial in *Commonweal*, November 18, 1983

Nowhere in the world are people so pleased with the American invasion of Grenada as in Grenada itself. Under the circumstances, some of the Grenadian enthusiasm should be taken with a grain of salt. Still, the reaction has been so widespread that critics of the invasion cannot ignore it.

It sets the Grenada action apart from other recent Great Power interventions. In Afghanistan, for example, and in Nicaragua, the populations have hardly welcomed their "liberators." But the Grenadians' contentment was far from a conclusive answer to the disturbing questions this invasion raises... Invading another country is not a small matter; even invading a small country is not a small matter. America's action has reinforced the pattern of quick military strikes, meant to confront objecting nations with *faits accomplis,* that buys success of putting the world on hair trigger. The invasion twisted international law into a pretzel and undermined the U.S.'s own invocations of the principle of nonintervention. International law, full of loopholes as it is and frequently honored in the breach, is not absolute, nor is the principle of nonintervention...

Grenada was ruled by an increasingly bizarre and fratricidal group of Marxists. Like many Third-World governments, including the one they succeeded, they are a burden on their own people. Their thuggishness, however, was scarcely in the same league with that of some of the thugs Washington has chosen generously to aid and abet for the same reason. If throwing out thugs were our concern, then the Rangers and Marines ought to be heading toward Haiti or Guatemala or perhaps El Salvador, where American Embassy officials have identified the Constituent Assembly's security chief and other ranking government officials as directing and financing death squads that have assassinated thousands of Salvadorans. The evidence that the Grenadian hard-liners were threatening American medical students has never emerged; what has emerged instead is considerable evidence that the Grenadians were assuring the Americans' safety and that obstacles to the students' evacuation came not from Grenada, but from other Caribbean states already involved in the invasion plans. All this was apparently known and conveniently ignored by Washington. It wanted this invasion.

"The Meaning of Grenada,"
National Review, November 25, 1983

Amid the kaleidoscopic onrush of images and events associated with Grenada, two moments of exquisite meaning stand out. One was the emotional outpouring of gratitude and praise from the American medical students rescued from Grenada-a response that all too obviously stunned and embarrassed the establishment media. The other was when Fidel Castro sagged limply backward into an armchair, telling reporters feebly that there is nothing he could do. Grenada, evidently, pierced Fidel to his very paranoic quick.

Full well Fidel might sag, for the action in Grenada represents the first time in history that U.S. military powers have reversed a Communist revolution and liberated a people from Marxist-Leninist rule. (The only other Communist regimes that have been toppled since 1917 have been overthrown by other Communist regimes-a phenomenon akin to inter-gang warfare.) This gives the action in Grenada a historical significance even greater, by a good bit, than the strategic importance of the island. Marx and Lenin preached historical inevitability, and Brezhnev proclaimed a doctrine of the irreversibility of Communist rule. Grenada confounds this Communist pantheon. The Marines did not just take an island; they stopped the march of history dead in its inexorable tracks.

There have been rumors of Cuban retaliation and speculation about a bold Soviet response to Grenada. Almost certainly, we will see neither, for both Havana and Moscow-like anti-American regimes everywhere-partake of a bully spirit that preys on weakness, but shrinks in the face of strength.

The liberation of Grenada will have positive reverberations for U.S. foreign policy around the globe. Surinam's disinvitation of its Cuban advisors is an early case in point. Our action will deter for a time Cuban adventurism in the Caribbean, it will knock a little sense into the Sandinistas (expect temporary sweetness and light from that quarter), and it will dampen "revolutionary ardor" (bully instincts) in El Salvador. Even the Kremlin will likely beat a prudent retreat for a time; Andropov, said to be suffering from a physical ailment, more likely is in a state of acute shock. Viewed from this perspective, the U.S. operation in Grenada represents a powerful blow on behalf of the cause to which Reagan's most passionate critics fervently claim allegiance. Grenada was a blow for peace.

"Defense Key in Playoffs,"
The Capital **(Annapolis, Maryland), December 26, 1984**

Nobody in professional football appreciates defense more than Pittsburgh coach Chuck Noll, who assembled the Steel Curtain that produced four Steelers Super Bowl championships.

So Pittsburgh goes into Sunday's American Football Conference semi-final game with proper respect for the Denver Broncos, who allowed only 241 points all season, second lowest in the National Football League.

Noll was not surprised that the wild-card victories of the New York Giants and Seattle Seahawks were constructed by stifling defense that simply shut down the Los Angeles Rams and Los Angeles Raiders.

"Defense has been important in championship football games as long as I can remember," Noll said. "Before you can win, you have to not lose."

Denver didn't lose very frequently, dropping only three games all season. And the opportunistic Bronco defenders scored eight touchdowns after forcing fumbles and picking up passes. Noll, a connoisseur of defense, was suitably impressed.

Bronco coach Dan Reeves knows the Steelers' reputation for being stingy with yards and points and spent much of the last week drilling Denver on defending against the blitz.

Nobody, however, blitzes more than the Chicago Bears, who led the league in rushing defense, total defense, and set a record with 72 quarterback sacks. The Washington Redskins, hoping for a third straight trip to the Super Bowl, must control the Bear defenders as well as handle Walter Payton, the NFL's all-time rushing leader.

இ~இ~இ~இ~இ~இ~இ~இ

"The Lucrative Little LBO Shops: Who Needs Mega-Mergers?"
by Solveig Jansson, *Institutional Investor*, August 22, 1985

Canny investors have long sought out shares of emerging companies for their potentially dazzling returns, of course. But why just buy the stock of such promising enterprises, reasons a small group of merger and acquisition specialists, when you can reap far greater rewards by buying the companies themselves?

By doing precisely that-acting as principals in leveraged buyouts of small companies with sparkling prospects, nurturing their growth and then taking them public-these little LBO shops have achieved some spectacular payoffs. Small to mid-sized companies-those with sales of less than $100 million-offer higher growth potential, higher return on assets and higher gross margins than 500-list behemoths, points out Theodore Stolberg of the investment counseling firm of Weiss, Peck and Greer.

So enticing is this little LBO business, in fact, that Carl Marks & Co., the maverick market maker of foreign securities, has committed more capital to it-some $150 million-through its CM Capital Corp. subsidiary than it has to its regular trading activities...

In contrast to the headline-grabbing megamergers, small buyouts tend to be conducted in relative obscurity-which suits the dealmakers just fine. "Large transactions add no real value," contends Weiss. "They tend to be overpriced and shopped all over the country." Because little LBO's never appear on the national auction block, they don't get bid up excessively. "When you buy small private companies, you typically get them for discounts of 20 to 40 percent vis-à-vis equivalent public companies."

"High Blood Pressure? It May Be in Your Genes,"
Business Week, April 3, 1985

"Hypertension has long been the scourge of many active, hard-driving people, and no amount of research has been able to pin down its cause or find a cure for the condition once it has developed.

Now, after 15 years of work in this field, Dr. Lewis K. Dahl, of Brookhaven National Laboratory's medical department, has found a cure that may ultimately reduce the incidence of the disease. Dahl, the man who established a correlation between salt and high blood pressure, has laboratory evidence that heredity plays a role in essential hypertension, the most common form of high blood pressure. Estimates vary, but it's believed that hypertension affects more than 10 percent of the U.S. adult population.

People don't inherit hypertension, Dahl thinks, but may inherit a susceptibility that somehow can be triggered by other factors: kidney infection, emotional stress or, more commonly, too much intake of table salt in the diet.

In his lab, Dahl has bred two strains of rats. Under certain conditions, one strain quickly develops hypertension; under identical conditions, the other strain doesn't.

Dr. Dahl, a senior scientist in Brookhaven's medical research center and chief of medical services for its 48-bed hospital, is among the first to admit this genetic research on rats can't be applied directly to human patients. But it sheds new light on possible predisposition of people to hypertension, and perhaps on how people can avoid triggering the disease."

"Broncos, Saints Inspire Opposite in Fans,"
The Capital (Annapolis, Maryland), November 15, 1985

Dan Reeves knows the two sides of Denver Broncos fans. Some of them, after all, wanted his head after the Broncos had the affront to lose again to Seattle last season and fell to 11-2 after 10 straight wins.

But after Reeves' Broncos beat the San Francisco 49ers Monday night, he gave them full credit.

"When they come out in this kind of weather and cheer us on like they did, that's showing terrific support," he said. "They helped us win the game."

More precisely, one snowball-throwing fan helped them win the game.

The missile in question, one of numerous snowballs flung from the stands in Mile High Stadium during the game, landed in front of San Francisco's Matt Cavanaugh as he was about to spot the ball for Ray Wersching's 19-yard yard field-goal attempt. The best Cavanaugh could do was pick up the ball and heave it awkwardly (and unsuccessfully) into the end zone.

The 49ers ended up losing 17-16. The police ended up escorting five people from the stadium on what Detective Ken Chaves said was a charge of "throwing missiles."

And the incident tarnished Denver's image. As Dan Gayer of Commerce City, Colorado, said after the game: "It makes us look bad, especially when it's on national television."

Yesterday, the young man whose snowball may have cost the 49ers the game, called the *San Francisco Examiner* to apologize. He turned down a $500 reward offered for his story...

Denver fans are probably the most blindly loyal in the National Football League: 73,173 of them showed up Monday in 20-degree weather despite a 30-10 defeat in San Diego the previous week. They would have been there had the Broncos entered the game 3-6 instead of 6-3.

The waiting list for season tickets is as long as the waiting list in Washington and New York, where the population base is millions larger. There have been divorce cases in which the battle for custody of Broncos tickets is more bitter than the battle for custody of the kids.

And memories linger. Lou Saban, who hasn't coached the Broncos since 1971, is still known there scornfully as "half a loaf," because he played for a tie against the Dolphins that season and excused his actions by saying: "Half a loaf is better than none."

"Football Fanatics Set Record Straight,"
Salina Journal (Kansas), December 12, 1985

They are football's dedicated detectives, historians who enjoy the sport not only on television, but on microfilm monitors that transport them to the halcyon days of professional football.

They're 150 members of the loosely knit professional Football Researchers Association scattered across the country. Most are mere spectators; some, including former all-pro guard Joe Kopcha of the Chicago Bears, are former players. All are fans.

Bob Carroll, for instance, is a Pittsburgh area researcher and illustrator with an encyclopedic knowledge of football's forgotten heroes. Lido Starelli, a San Francisco plasterer, has missed only one 49ers game in 43 years and has every game program to prove it.

The amateur researchers specialize in debunking the myths and mysteries of the sport's sometimes nomadic and often misunderstood past.

"It's amazing how much of the myth and lore associated with pro football don't stand up under research," said Carroll, 49, the editor of *The Coffin Corner*, the PFRA's semi-monthly newsletter. "Much of what has been written even in encyclopedias isn't always accurate."

For example, it has long been accepted that the National Football League was formed September 17, 1920, as the legendary George Halas and other founding fathers squatted on Hupmobile running boards in a Canton, Ohio, auto dealership. An illustration of the historic meeting hangs in a prominent place in the Pro Football Hall of Fame in Canton.

But, Carroll said, Canton newspaper headlines blared "New League Is Formed" more than a month before, and that the car dealer meeting may have served merely to formalize plans for a league that later would capture the imagination of the nation. Carroll, citing the fruits of research, offered these tidbits:

- Only several years before the historic 1958 Baltimore Colts-New York Giants overtime championship game, "pro football was only about as popular as indoor soccer is today."

- Just six years before that game, "the turning point in NFL history," the Colts were called that Dallas Texans and "were so bad, they wound up finishing the season in Hershey, Pennsylvania."

- Even in the early 1950s, newspaper columnists frequently wrote that an average college football team could beat any pro team.

- Pro football's first great passing quarterback wasn't the revolutionary Sammy Baugh, but a highly underrated former Michigan All-American named Benny Friedman who once threw 18 touchdown passes in a single season with a ball "more like a watermelon than a football..."

"Michael Jackson Inks Multimillion-Dollar Deal With Pepsi," *Rolling Stone*, June 19, 1986

Whether or not it's the choice of a new generation, Pepsi's definitely generating a ton of money for Michael Jackson. Over the next three years, Jackson will make at least three commercials for Pepsi as part of the most lucrative advertising deal ever negotiated between a celebrity and a corporation: the singer will make $10 million.

Jackson and his brothers earned roughly $5.5 million when they appeared in two Pepsi commercials in 1984 and signed a tour-sponsorship deal with the soft drink company. In the new deal, Jackson is committed to producing two pieces of original music for the new ads. The singer's manager, Frank DiLeo, said that a song from Jackson's upcoming LP, due this fall, may also be used for one of the commercials. Jackson will film a minimum of two spots plus a Spanish-language ad. Pepsi plans to show the commercials worldwide and will premiere the first one in early 1987.

Under the terms of the deal, Jackson will be involved in writing the spots, choosing the directors, and designing the visuals. The contract also calls for Jackson to become a "creative consultant" for Pepsi in 1988, at which point he will direct a commercial itself. And while it is not definite Pepsi would be the sponsor of any forthcoming Jackson tour, Pepsi USA President Roger Enrico said that "whatever activities Michael does in support of his new album, we will be involved...."

Enrico estimates that the cost of the Jackson ad campaign, including production cost and airtime, "will be well in excess of $50 million." He has no doubt Michael is worth the price. The 1984 ads are credited with sharply boosting Pepsi sales. "My judgment is that these amounts of money, which seemed to be huge, do in fact payoff," Enrico said.

Jackson reportedly does not drink Pepsi himself and will not even hold the product in his hand for the ads, but, according to Pepsi spokesman, a truckload of the beverage is dropped off at his house every week.

❧❧❧❧❧❧❧❧❧❧

"The Rod Stewart Concert Video, Video News," Rolling Stone, June 19, 1986

Rod Stewart has one of the biggest egos in the music business, and every ounce of it is on display in the Rod Stewart Concert Video. There's not a moment when he's not swaggering, strutting and preening as he dominates the screen.

If he weren't having so much fun, this would be completely repellent. But Stewart seasons his posing with a sense of glee that, combined with the driving precision of his band, produces an unexpectedly entertaining show.

The cassette opens with an audio-visual bio that's just short enough to avoid being boring. Stewart begins the concert footage with a string of his hits starting with "Infatuation" and proceeding to "Tonight's the Night," "Young Turks," and "Passion." Between songs, he shows a reedy, easygoing magnetism that helps this tape escape the tedium that dogs most concert tapes.

"0.5 Percent of Families Found to Hold 35 Percent of Wealth,"
by Michael Wines, *Los Angeles Times*, July 26, 1986

"More than a third of the nation's net worth is held by 0.5 percent of America's households, a concentration of economic clout that has snowballed to levels not seen since the Great Depression, Democrats on Congress' Joint Economic Committee concluded in a study released Friday.

Their report, using 1983 figures compiled for the Federal Reserve Board, stated that the 420,000 richest U.S. families controlled $3.7 trillion in assets after debts. That is 35.1 percent of total wealth.

An earlier Fed study using 1962 data concluded that the same 0.5 percent of the population then controlled 25.4 percent of the national wealth. By comparison, the report stated the share of assets held by the poorest 90 percent of Americans dropped during those 21 years from 34.9 percent to 28 percent.

The committee Democrats' report provided the first public comparison of the two studies, both of which were conducted for the Fed by the University of Michigan's prestigious Survey Research Center. The 1983 study was based on projections from a survey of about 4,000 Americans. The sample included 432 members of the country's wealthiest families...

In the report the 1983 data is divided into four classes of households:

- 420,000 'super rich' families with more than a third of the wealth and comprising 0.5 percent of families. None of these families were worth less than $2.5 million; their average wealth after debts was $8.85 million.

- 420,000 'very rich' with 6.7 percent of all net assets and an average wealth of $1.7 million.

- 7.6 million 'rich' with net wealth ranging from $206,000 to $1.4 million and an average net worth of $419,616. The rich, nine percent of all households, owned 29.9 percent of the wealth.

- 'Everyone else,' the 75.5 million households that make up the remaining 90 percent of the population. Their net worth ranged no higher than $206,000 and averaged $39,584.

The wealthy excelled in another crucial statistical measure as well. The net worth of the super rich rose during the 21-year period by 147 percent, adjusted for inflation. The very rich managed only a 64 percent increase and the rich, a 66 percent gain. Everyone else posted a more modest 45 percent increase...

Nearly half the net assets of the bottom 90 percent were tied up in real estate, most of it in homes. Real estate was among the fastest appreciating assets, more than doubling in value from 1962 to 1983.

The super rich, meanwhile, had less than a fifth of their money in real estate in 1983. But the worth of their property holdings grew sevenfold during the 21 years between surveys."

"Gold Medal Gear,"
Popular Mechanics, March 1988

When it comes to high tech, America can put a man on the moon-but it can't build a respectable bobsled. That, anyway, has long been the rap against American Olympic efforts. Soviet-led Eastern Bloc Olympians have long been rated the leaders in high-tech and medium-tech Olympic sports such as bobsled, biathlon, skating, archery and shooting. American sports technologists have lagged behind in such basic research as aerodynamics, bioengineering and materials science.

But all that is changing, and the first evidence of that change will be seen at the 1988 Winter Olympic Games in Calgary, Canada. Back in 1983 the U.S. Olympic Committee, recognizing a desperate need for better performing and safer equipment for athletes, formed the Sports Equipment and Technology Committee to provide funding and act as a liaison between the individual sports industry and government. Results can be seen in such sports as bobsled, the biathlon and other winter events:

Bobsled

In Livonia, Michigan, Airflow Sciences Corp. (ASC), a consulting engineering firm specializing in fluid dynamics, illustrates the new emphasis on technology with a revolutionary approach to designing two-man and four man sleds for the U.S. Olympic team using automotive modeling clay, wind tunnel testing, and employing the same construction technology for building Indianapolis and Formula 1 race cars. The firm, by late 1987, had achieved a 42 percent reduction in drag in the two-man sled and a 44 percent reduction for the four-man sled compared to 1984 Winter Olympic baseline sleds.

Among the more radical design changes was a replacement of the old welded-steel chassis with a high strength, fiberglass composite of Nomex honeycomb, sandwiched in layers of graphite/Kevlar cloth with epoxy resins. The molded body increases design flexibility while reducing weight...

Nordic Skiing

Whether in biathlon, Nordic combined (cross-country and ski jumping) or Nordic skiing, the major innovation in cross-country skiing in the past six years has been the dramatic introduction of the skating technique in which the skier kicks the skis outward as though ice-skating. The new technique has resulted in changes in ski waxes and in shorter skis (10 cm shorter) with a stiffer camber, or arch. But the greatest changes have occurred in ski poles. They reach the eyes now instead of the armpit. Skating also puts more weight on the poles, causing increased pole deflection, and the poles are more apt to be bent of the skis during skating...

Hockey

American hockey players will be wearing innovative protective equipment consisting of a triple layer of foam laced with very tiny air cells. The impact of a puck or errant stick forces air out of the cells laterally as the foam collapses. The dense outermost layer collapses only on the hardest hits. The pads will be worn over the shoulders, upper arms, sternum, elbows and on the lower back...

Speed Skating

Because of the extremely tight curves of Calgary's new short-track speed skating oval, a Canadian skate maker, Raymond Laberge, has developed a skate with the blade offset from center that can be adjusted for each skater.

The feature allows the skater to adjust the skate to fit the track. Laberge also custom-molds a skating shell of graphite fiber, Kevlar, fiberglass and epoxy resins. The formfitting boot prevents heel sloppiness in the turns, which reduces control and power. A Velcro attached lace cover ensures waterproofing and helps to limit the skates' aerodynamic drag, critical in a game where inches count.

"Great Expectations,"
Forbes, April 18, 1988

"With today's newer portable phones, you can walk down Fifth Avenue in Manhattan while talking to your spouse in Boise, or your partner in Tokyo. Pretty soon the gear will be cheap enough that teenagers can take a phone with them on dates. No more, 'Gee, Mom, I would've called but I didn't have a quarter.' In the U.S., car facsimile machines are just around the corner. So cellular communications is no gadgetry gimmick: it is a service that fills a real need for a society on the go.

But in the real work of business, there's many a slip twixt cup and lip. With little in the way of earnings or cash flow, cellular franchises today sell on the basis of two expectations: 1) the

number of potential customers in the area covered by their franchise, and 2) how much each of these customers is likely to spend. The first expectation is the population that lives in the cellular franchisee's area-the so-called pops figure. If a franchise area has a population of, say, two million, and a company owns 60 percent of the franchise (partners accounting for the rest), then the company would have 1.2 million pops.

What's a pop worth? BellSouth is paying some $80 to $85 a pop for Mobile Communications. McCaw, which about 18 months ago was paying only about $20 per pop for franchises, a few months ago paid $80 a pop for The Washington Post Company's Florida cellular business. McCaw itself is being valued in the stock market at $75 to $80 per pop.

These prices are assuming a great deal. They assume that a significant percentage of the pops will sign up for the services and that, once signed, they will use the expensive service on a big scale.

When the Federal Communications Commission started to divvy up the cellular industry in the early 1980s, it awarded two franchises for each market, to make sure there was competition. The 'wireline' franchise went to the local Bell operating company. The independent or 'nonwireline' franchise was at first chosen by the FCC in some markets. Later markets were awarded by lottery.

Let's crunch a few numbers. What 'per pop' amounts to is an assumption that a given independent company will have about half the cellular market, and the local phone company will have the other half. Let's say cellular's penetration will be four percent five years from now. Then the independent franchise's penetration will likely be two percent.

Let's go on with the numbers. If the franchise covers one million pops and ultimately signs two percent of them, it will have 20,000 customers. Paying $80 a pop is the same as paying $4,000 today for tomorrow's projected customer. By contrast, cable TV systems can currently be purchased for around $2,000 per existing subscriber."

ক্রক্রক্রক্রক্রক্র

"Twins Scott and Stuart Gentling Sell off a High-Priced Audubon and Give Wing to Their Own Bird Book," *People*, June 15, 1988

"Two records were under siege last week when a standing-room-only crowd converged on Sotheby's auction house in New York. Outside, an early heat wave was threatening to push the mercury over 97 degrees, an all-time high for the date. Inside, brisk bidding closed in on, and soon surpassed, the highest price ever paid for a work by the naturalist painter John James Audubon. When the gavel fell, a New York dealer had paid $253,000 for an 1824 watercolor of two boattailed grackles-known to most people simply as blackbirds.

Just two and a half years ago the same painting had been offered in the mail-order catalog of a Philadelphia print dealer for $18,000-and was snapped up by two Audubon fanatics who recognized it as one of the master's long-missing early works. Not long afterward, the new owners, 44-year-old twins Scott and Stuart Gentling of Fort Worth, decided to use their treasure to help bankroll their own Audubon-inspired masterwork, *Of Birds and Texas*. A massive boxed portfolio of 50 paintings of birds and landscapes, it was 10 years and $550,000 in the making, and might never have seen the light of day without the grackle windfall. 'We literally ran out of money,' says Stuart, like his brother a full-time artist since college, 'and we had to use the grackles as collateral.' Most of the $210,000 profit the brothers expect to clear from the sale will go towards clearing up their grackle-backed debts.

Stuart also hopes the publicity surrounding the auction will produce some national recognition for him and his twin. 'It's so difficult to get people to take us seriously,' he says. 'They don't think that something like Of Birds and Texas could be created in the boondocks.'

They may now, however, since the Gentlings' opus has been getting rave reviews. *The Dallas Morning News* described it as 'destined to become a classic of ornithology and fine printing,' and painter Andrew Wyeth declared it 'overwhelming.' It is certainly that: Two feet long and weighing 46 pounds, it could pass for a coffee table without legs. The price is a Texas-size too: $2,500 for one of a limited edition of 500 books."

෪ᚸ෪ᚸ෪ᚸ෪ᚸ෪ᚸ

෪ᚸ෪ᚸ෪ᚸ෪ᚸ෪ᚸ

"Dining on an Ancient Hilltop,"
Bon Appetit, November, 1988

"Just outside Monaco there is the ninth-century hilltop village of Eze, perched 1,300 feet almost sheer above the sea on a rocky outcrop. To reach its center, you park and walk narrow alleys. It is worth the trek to visit the Chateau de la Chevre d'Or, an eleventh-century medieval manor house artistically converted into a glorious 10-room hotel and Chateau Eze, a cluster of medieval houses (formerly the summer home of HRH Prince William of Sweden) that has been open to the public as a small luxury hotel since 1983.

At Chateau de la Chevre d'Or, I've enjoyed many of Chef Elie Mazot's delicacies as much as the panorama. At Chateau Eze, the kitchen has recently been handed over to Dominique Le Stanc, and his culinary genius is unmistakable. Highly recommended among his creations are open-face ravioli with sautéed artichokes, asparagus and langoustines; smoked pigeon and lentil salad; and cream of pea soup with asparagus and morel garnish."

꼬옹ꇙ옹ꇙ옹ꇙ옹

"Looking for Dedication? Cross Country Sets the Pace," by Bob Frisk, *Chicago Daily Herald*, November 11, 1988

There was a time when cross country was a sport designed primarily to get you in shape for a more glamorous activity like basketball. That's certainly the way it was when I was in high school. The rewards really appeared meager in comparison with the time and exertion put into the endeavor.

The changes have been dramatic. A fitness revolution ran across the country. Dedicated coaches worked in developing successful training techniques, and high school cross country programs were, well, off and running.

Today, the cross country runner in this area is a big man or woman on campus. Saturday's hero may not always be a football player. Saturday's real hero may be that young person who is running over the river and through the woods and not just to grandmother's house.

Last weekend, the Mid-Suburban League (MSL) completed another amazing double in state cross country. Schaumburg's boys and Conant's girls just added to an incredible record of accomplishments for this remarkable high school sports conference.

Mid-Suburban boys now have won three state cross country championships in the past four years and five overall. Mid-Suburban girls have won six titles in the past seven seasons and seven overall. Remarkable? Yes. Surprising? Not really. You just have to look at the caliber of coaches down the line throughout the MSL, the important continuity of most staffs and the impressive feeder systems to develop early this talent.

Nevertheless, it still can be difficult telling young people, particularly incoming freshmen, that there is satisfaction in a sport where you run, run, run, run. Run until it hurts and then run some more. I've always admired cross country coaches because they are faced with the daily challenge of keeping their practices interesting.

"Well, athletes, let's see. I think we'll...run." Meets take care of themselves because of their importance, runners jockey for position as they near the chute, but it has to be extremely difficult for a coach to motivate these athletes through their arduous, daily workouts.

There's so much more to this sport than just a crisp fall run, but a cross country coach must be surrounded with believers. So many young people are just waiting for someone to guide them and care about them. No, it doesn't take a great athlete to be cross country runner. You may not need the coordination of the basketball player or the agility and speed of a halfback or the strength of a tackle.

But you definitely need desire and dedication and endurance. You can work on endurance, but you must have desire and dedication to succeed. Do you know what really impresses me at any cross country meet? I watch those young runners, boys and girls, who are laboring far behind the field, struggling with every move, obviously aching.

I stood at the Mid-Suburban League meet and marveled at the tenacity of these young people as the field spread out, dramatically separating the levels of ability. Those runners hundreds of yards behind the leaders were hurting. It showed. Many could barely see the competitors in front of them. The distance was that great.

This was not a glamorous time for a young athlete. You couldn't hide out there when you're so far behind. Everybody lining the course can see you. It's certainly a different kind of spotlight. I just had to stand there that day and applaud this kind of determination. This is truly the dedicated high school athlete in action.

The only real reward may be the personal satisfaction you get from passing another runner in the final few yards to finish 80th instead of 81st, or from knocking a second off your best time. These runners may be in as good or better shape than the athletes who finish well in front, but each individual has his or her own limitations, and that's what makes this sport such a thrilling competition.

Cross country takes a very special kind of desire and dedication, those intangible traits that can be so hard to define. Although this area may be extremely proficient at collecting state trophies in cross country, the biggest rewards for most of our young runners are not to be reaped in high school. Those rewards will come later in life, when that incredible dedication needed in cross country day after day after day in a very lonely sport carries over into the real world and leads to something which others, less dedicated, might miss. I don't know about you, but I certainly would look at a high school cross country background as a big plus in anyone's job application.

"Securing Participants Keeps Coaches on the Run,"
by Ira Josephs, *Doyleston Intelligencer* (Pennsylvania), August 27, 1989

Cross country, a sport that flourished in the Bucks-Mont area as recently as the early 1980s, may have reached a numbers crossroads as the calendar turns toward 1990. For although a handful of area teams and individuals enjoyed success in both the district and state level in recent years, Bucks-Mont area coaches say it has become more and more of an uphill climb to maintain that top-flight level of performance in the long run.

Declining numbers, they say, appear to be taking their toll on specific programs in some cases, and on the sport in general in others. But veteran coaches aware of the cyclical nature of the sport also noticed that the quantity and quality, two key ingredients in a program's success, have tended traditionally to fluctuate from year to year, rising and falling due to a variety of different factors.

It is a sport of peaks and valleys. Not just on the course, either. Said Central Bucks East head coach Paul Wilson:

"It's really hard to predict trends." But it has not been hard for coaches to notice the dwindling cross-country numbers in many area schools. Said William Tennent head coach Andy Warren, the Warminster school is no exception.

"In the late '60s and '70s, we had teams of 35 or 40," Warren said. "The last three years, we've been anywhere from 20 to 25. A big school squad for a public school is 25." The decline of participants is more noticeable at Pennridge where Dick Leight is entering his 29th year as coach this fall.

"In the late '70s and early '80s we had 23 kids on the team," Leight said. "They were kids who ran since they were in 10th grade. "Last year I had 20, but many of them were seniors who were running cross country for the first time. That's not the way to be a successful cross-country runner.

"I'm confident that if I have a kid for three years, by the end of those three years he'll be a respectable runner. It's the kids who come out for three years that make the team."

JARED GOEGELINE: 12-year-old Junior High Student; Hunter; 50,000th Junior Member of the National Rifle Association.

"My first gun was a BB gun I shot at a hay bale in our backyard. I was ten years old when I first shot a firearm. I haven't done much competitive shooting, but once I shot at a target in a turkey shoot and won a seven-pound ham. It's challenging to see how good a shot you are.

"I thought I should be a member of the NRA because everybody in my family is. So my Dad signed me up. I can go to shooting competitions and read interesting stories about hunting in <u>InSights</u> magazine. I like how they teach you to clean your gun and handle it safely. That's real important.

"Young people who like to shoot might want to become NRA Junior Members. It's fun and you can call the people at the NRA to get involved in all kinds of fun things."

I'm the NRA.

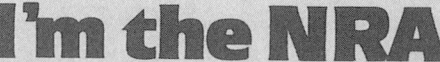

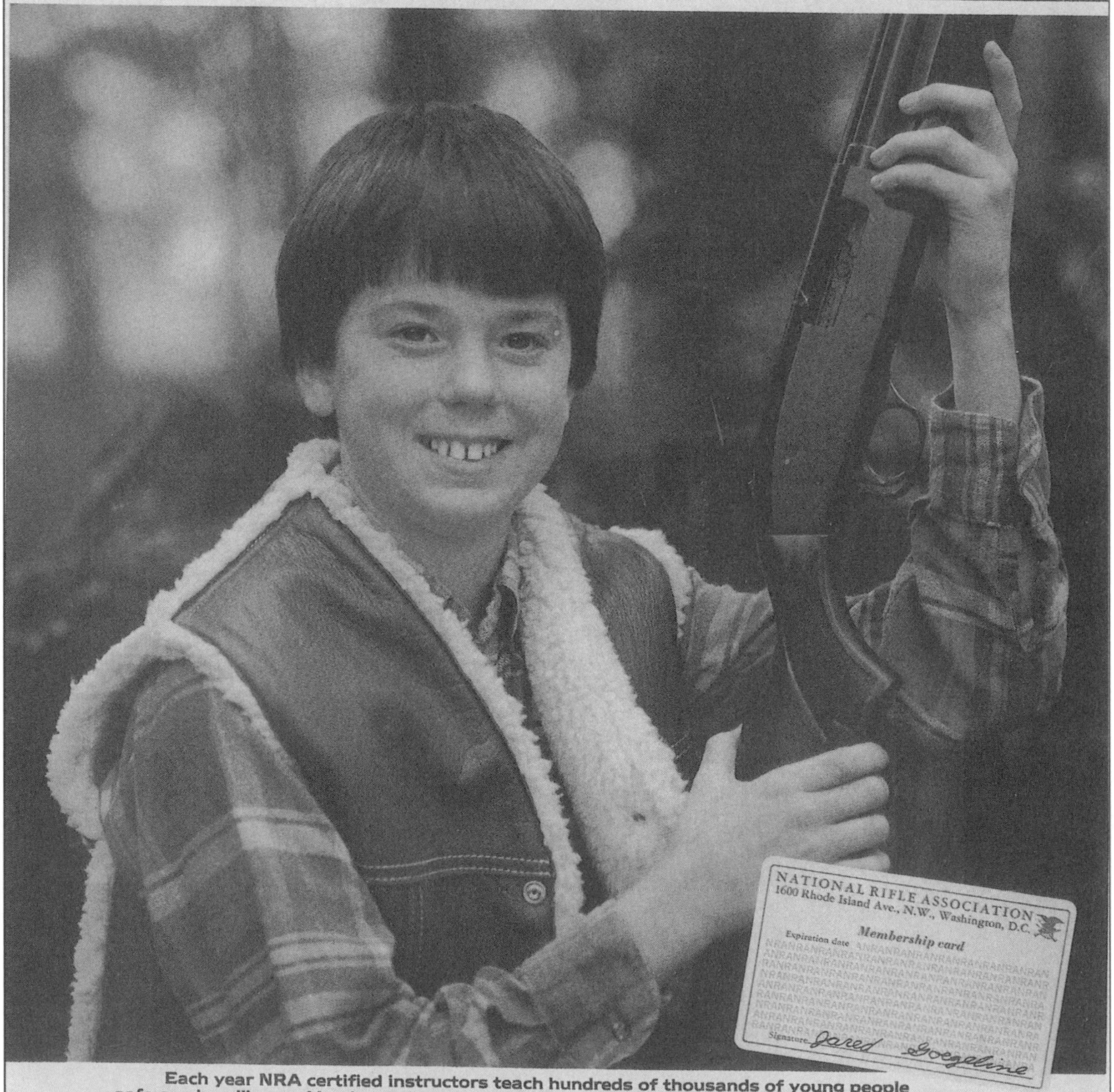

Each year NRA certified instructors teach hundreds of thousands of young people safe gun handling and basic marksmanship skills. If you would like to join the NRA and want more information about our programs and benefits, write G. Ray Arnett, Executive Vice President, P.O. Box 37484, Dept. JG-13, Washington, D.C. 20013.

This section begins with eighteen state-by-state ranking tables from the 1980, 1990, and 2010 Census, designed to help define the times during which the families profiled in Section One lived. Table topics are listed below. Following the state-by-state tables are reprints from the special report series We the Americans published in 1993 by the U.S. Census Bureau. Finally, data portrayed by maps, tables, graphs, charts and narrative from the 1990 Census, help to visualize the environment at that time.

State-by-State Comparative Tables: 1980, 1990 and 2010

Note: When reviewing the ranking columns, be aware that the District of Columbia is included in the list of states.

Twenty-First Decennial Census of the United States

Special Reports

Total Population

Area	Population 1980	Population 1990	Population 2010	1980 Area	Rank	1990 Area	Rank	2010 Area	Rank
Alabama	3,893,888	4,040,587	4,779,736	California	1	California	1	California	1
Alaska	401,851	550,043	710,231	New York	2	New York	2	Texas	2
Arizona	2,718,215	3,665,228	6,392,017	Texas	3	Texas	3	New York	3
Arkansas	2,286,435	2,350,725	2,915,918	Pennsylvania	4	Florida	4	Florida	4
California	23,667,902	29,760,021	37,253,956	Illinois	5	Pennsylvania	5	Illinois	5
Colorado	2,889,964	3,294,394	5,029,196	Ohio	6	Illinois	6	Pennsylvania	6
Connecticut	3,107,576	3,287,116	3,574,097	Florida	7	Ohio	7	Ohio	7
Delaware	594,338	666,168	897,934	Michigan	8	Michigan	8	Michigan	8
D.C.	638,333	606,900	601,723	New Jersey	9	New Jersey	9	Georgia	9
Florida	9,746,324	12,937,926	18,801,310	North Carolina	10	North Carolina	10	North Carolina	10
Georgia	5,463,105	6,478,216	9,687,653	Massachusetts	11	Georgia	11	New Jersey	11
Hawaii	964,691	1,108,229	1,360,301	Indiana	12	Virginia	12	Virginia	12
Idaho	943,935	1,006,749	1,567,582	Georgia	13	Massachusetts	13	Washington	13
Illinois	11,426,518	11,430,602	12,830,632	Virginia	14	Indiana	14	Massachusetts	14
Indiana	5,490,224	5,544,159	6,483,802	Missouri	15	Missouri	15	Indiana	15
Iowa	2,913,808	2,776,755	3,046,355	Wisconsin	16	Wisconsin	16	Arizona	16
Kansas	2,363,679	2,477,574	2,853,118	Tennessee	17	Tennessee	17	Tennessee	17
Kentucky	3,660,777	3,685,296	4,339,367	Maryland	18	Washington	18	Missouri	18
Louisiana	4,205,900	4,219,973	4,533,372	Louisiana	19	Maryland	19	Maryland	19
Maine	1,124,660	1,227,928	1,328,361	Washington	20	Minnesota	20	Wisconsin	20
Maryland	4,216,975	4,781,468	5,773,552	Minnesota	21	Louisiana	21	Minnesota	21
Massachusetts	5,737,037	6,016,425	6,547,629	Alabama	22	Alabama	22	Colorado	22
Michigan	9,262,078	9,295,297	9,883,640	Kentucky	23	Kentucky	23	Alabama	23
Minnesota	4,075,970	4,375,099	5,303,925	South Carolina	24	Arizona	24	South Carolina	24
Mississippi	2,520,638	2,573,216	2,967,297	Connecticut	25	South Carolina	25	Louisiana	25
Missouri	4,916,686	5,117,073	5,988,927	Oklahoma	26	Colorado	26	Kentucky	26
Montana	786,690	799,065	989,415	Iowa	27	Connecticut	27	Oregon	27
Nebraska	1,569,825	1,578,385	1,826,341	Colorado	28	Oklahoma	28	Oklahoma	28
Nevada	800,493	1,201,833	2,700,551	Arizona	29	Oregon	29	Connecticut	29
New Hampshire	920,610	1,109,252	1,316,470	Oregon	30	Iowa	30	Iowa	30
New Jersey	7,364,823	7,730,188	8,791,894	Mississippi	31	Mississippi	31	Mississippi	31
New Mexico	1,302,894	1,515,069	2,059,179	Kansas	32	Kansas	32	Arkansas	32
New York	17,558,072	17,990,455	19,378,102	Arkansas	33	Arkansas	33	Kansas	33
North Carolina	5,881,766	6,628,637	9,535,483	West Virginia	34	West Virginia	34	Utah	34
North Dakota	652,717	638,800	672,591	Nebraska	35	Utah	35	Nevada	35
Ohio	10,797,630	10,847,115	11,536,504	Utah	36	Nebraska	36	New Mexico	36
Oklahoma	3,025,290	3,145,585	3,751,351	New Mexico	37	New Mexico	37	West Virginia	37
Oregon	2,633,105	2,842,321	3,831,074	Maine	38	Maine	38	Nebraska	38
Pennsylvania	11,863,895	11,881,643	12,702,379	Hawaii	39	Nevada	39	Idaho	39
Rhode Island	947,154	1,003,464	1,052,567	Rhode Island	40	New Hampshire	40	Hawaii	40
South Carolina	3,121,820	3,486,703	4,625,364	Idaho	41	Hawaii	41	Maine	41
South Dakota	690,768	696,004	814,180	New Hampshire	42	Idaho	42	New Hampshire	42
Tennessee	4,591,120	4,877,185	6,346,105	Nevada	43	Rhode Island	43	Rhode Island	43
Texas	14,229,191	16,986,510	25,145,561	Montana	44	Montana	44	Montana	44
Utah	1,461,037	1,722,850	2,763,885	South Dakota	45	South Dakota	45	Delaware	45
Vermont	511,456	562,758	625,741	North Dakota	46	Delaware	46	South Dakota	46
Virginia	5,346,818	6,187,358	8,001,024	D.C.	47	North Dakota	47	Alaska	47
Washington	4,132,156	4,866,692	6,724,540	Delaware	48	D.C.	48	North Dakota	48
West Virginia	1,949,644	1,793,477	1,852,994	Vermont	49	Vermont	49	Vermont	49
Wisconsin	4,705,767	4,891,769	5,686,986	Wyoming	50	Alaska	50	D.C.	50
Wyoming	469,557	453,588	563,626	Alaska	51	Wyoming	51	Wyoming	51
United States	226,545,805	248,709,873	308,745,538	United States	–	United States	–	United States	–

Source: U.S. Census Bureau, 1980 Census of Population; U.S. Census Bureau, 1990 Census of Population; U.S. Census Bureau, Census 2010

White Population

Area	Percent of Population			1980		1990		2010	
	1980	1990	2010	Area	Rank	Area	Rank	Area	Rank
Alabama	73.8	73.7	68.5	Vermont	1	Vermont	1	Vermont	1
Alaska	77.1	75.5	66.7	New Hampshire	2	Maine	2	Maine	2
Arizona	82.4	80.9	73.0	Maine	3	New Hampshire	3	West Virginia	3
Arkansas	82.7	82.7	77.0	Iowa	4	Iowa	4	New Hampshire	4
California	76.2	69.0	57.6	Minnesota	5	West Virginia	5	Iowa	5
Colorado	89.0	88.2	81.3	West Virginia	6	North Dakota	6	Wyoming	6
Connecticut	90.1	87.0	77.6	North Dakota	7	Idaho	7	North Dakota	7
Delaware	82.1	80.3	68.9	Idaho	8	Minnesota	7	Montana	8
D.C.	26.9	29.6	38.5	Wyoming	9	Wyoming	9	Idaho	9
Florida	84.0	83.1	75.0	Nebraska	10	Nebraska	10	Kentucky	10
Georgia	72.3	71.0	59.7	Rhode Island	11	Utah	11	Wisconsin	11
Hawaii	33.0	33.4	24.7	Utah	12	Oregon	12	Nebraska	12
Idaho	95.5	94.4	89.1	Oregon	13	Montana	13	Utah	13
Illinois	80.8	78.3	71.5	Wisconsin	14	Wisconsin	14	South Dakota	14
Indiana	91.2	90.6	84.3	Montana	15	Kentucky	15	Minnesota	15
Iowa	97.4	96.6	91.3	Massachusetts	16	South Dakota	16	Indiana	16
Kansas	91.7	90.1	83.8	South Dakota	17	Rhode Island	17	Kansas	17
Kentucky	92.3	92.0	87.8	Kentucky	18	Indiana	18	Oregon	18
Louisiana	69.2	67.3	62.6	Kansas	19	Kansas	19	Missouri	19
Maine	98.7	98.4	95.2	Washington	20	Massachusetts	20	Ohio	20
Maryland	74.9	71.0	58.2	Indiana	21	Washington	21	Pennsylvania	21
Massachusetts	93.5	89.8	80.4	Connecticut	22	Pennsylvania	21	Rhode Island	22
Michigan	85.0	83.4	79.0	Pennsylvania	23	Colorado	23	Colorado	23
Minnesota	96.6	94.4	85.3	Colorado	24	Ohio	24	Massachusetts	24
Mississippi	64.1	63.5	59.1	Ohio	25	Missouri	25	Michigan	25
Missouri	88.4	87.7	82.8	Missouri	26	Connecticut	26	Connecticut	26
Montana	94.1	92.8	89.4	Nevada	27	Nevada	27	Tennessee	27
Nebraska	94.9	93.8	86.1	Oklahoma	28	Michigan	28	Washington	28
Nevada	87.5	84.3	66.2	Michigan	29	Florida	29	Arkansas	29
New Hampshire	98.9	98.0	93.9	Florida	30	Tennessee	30	Florida	30
New Jersey	83.2	79.3	68.6	Tennessee	31	Arkansas	31	Arizona	31
New Mexico	75.0	75.6	68.4	New Jersey	32	Oklahoma	32	Oklahoma	32
New York	79.5	74.4	65.8	Arkansas	33	Arizona	33	Illinois	33
North Carolina	75.8	75.6	68.5	Arizona	34	Delaware	34	Texas	34
North Dakota	95.8	94.6	90.0	Delaware	35	New Jersey	35	Delaware	35
Ohio	88.9	87.8	82.7	Illinois	36	Illinois	36	New Jersey	36
Oklahoma	85.9	82.1	72.2	New York	37	Virginia	37	Virginia	36
Oregon	94.6	92.8	83.7	Virginia	38	New Mexico	38	Alabama	38
Pennsylvania	89.8	88.5	81.9	Texas	39	North Carolina	39	North Carolina	39
Rhode Island	94.7	91.4	81.4	Alaska	40	Alaska	40	New Mexico	40
South Carolina	68.8	69.0	66.2	California	41	Texas	41	Alaska	41
South Dakota	92.6	91.6	85.9	North Carolina	42	New York	42	Nevada	42
Tennessee	83.5	83.0	77.6	New Mexico	43	Alabama	43	South Carolina	42
Texas	78.7	75.2	70.4	Maryland	44	Georgia	44	New York	44
Utah	94.6	93.8	86.1	Alabama	45	Maryland	45	Louisiana	45
Vermont	99.1	98.6	95.3	Georgia	46	South Carolina	46	Georgia	46
Virginia	79.1	77.4	68.6	Louisiana	47	California	47	Mississippi	47
Washington	91.5	88.5	77.3	South Carolina	48	Louisiana	48	Maryland	48
West Virginia	96.2	96.2	93.9	Mississippi	49	Mississippi	49	California	49
Wisconsin	94.4	92.3	86.2	Hawaii	50	Hawaii	50	D.C.	50
Wyoming	95.1	94.2	90.7	D.C.	51	D.C.	51	Hawaii	51
United States	83.2	80.3	72.4	United States	–	United States	–	United States	–

Source: U.S. Census Bureau, 1980 Census of Population; U.S. Census Bureau, 1990 Census of Population; U.S. Census Bureau, Census 2010

Black Population

Area	Percent of Population			1980		1990		2010	
	1980	1990	2010	Area	Rank	Area	Rank	Area	Rank
Alabama	25.6	25.3	26.2	D.C.	1	D.C.	1	D.C.	1
Alaska	3.4	4.1	3.3	Mississippi	2	Mississippi	2	Mississippi	2
Arizona	2.8	3.0	4.1	South Carolina	3	Louisiana	3	Louisiana	3
Arkansas	16.4	15.9	15.4	Louisiana	4	South Carolina	4	Georgia	4
California	7.7	7.4	6.2	Georgia	5	Georgia	5	Maryland	5
Colorado	3.5	4.0	4.0	Alabama	6	Alabama	6	South Carolina	6
Connecticut	7.0	8.3	10.1	Maryland	7	Maryland	7	Alabama	7
Delaware	16.1	16.9	21.4	North Carolina	8	North Carolina	8	North Carolina	8
D.C.	70.3	65.8	50.7	Virginia	9	Virginia	9	Delaware	9
Florida	13.8	13.6	16.0	Arkansas	10	Delaware	10	Virginia	10
Georgia	26.8	27.0	30.5	Delaware	11	Tennessee	11	Tennessee	11
Hawaii	1.8	2.5	1.6	Tennessee	12	Arkansas	12	Florida	12
Idaho	0.3	0.3	0.6	Illinois	13	New York	13	New York	13
Illinois	14.7	14.8	14.6	Florida	14	Illinois	14	Arkansas	14
Indiana	7.6	7.8	9.1	New York	15	Michigan	15	Illinois	15
Iowa	1.4	1.7	2.9	Michigan	16	Florida	16	Michigan	16
Kansas	5.3	5.8	5.9	New Jersey	17	New Jersey	17	New Jersey	17
Kentucky	7.1	7.1	7.8	Texas	18	Texas	18	Ohio	18
Louisiana	29.4	30.8	32.0	Missouri	19	Missouri	19	Texas	19
Maine	0.3	0.4	1.2	Ohio	20	Ohio	20	Missouri	20
Maryland	22.7	24.9	29.5	Pennsylvania	21	Pennsylvania	21	Pennsylvania	21
Massachusetts	3.9	5.0	6.6	California	22	Connecticut	22	Connecticut	22
Michigan	13.0	13.9	14.2	Indiana	23	Indiana	23	Indiana	23
Minnesota	1.3	2.2	5.2	Kentucky	24	Oklahoma	24	Nevada	24
Mississippi	35.2	35.6	37.0	Connecticut	25	California	25	Kentucky	25
Missouri	10.5	10.7	11.6	Oklahoma	26	Kentucky	26	Oklahoma	26
Montana	0.2	0.3	0.4	Nevada	27	Nevada	27	Massachusetts	27
Nebraska	3.1	3.6	4.5	Kansas	28	Kansas	28	Wisconsin	28
Nevada	6.4	6.6	8.1	Wisconsin	29	Wisconsin	29	California	29
New Hampshire	0.4	0.7	1.1	Massachusetts	30	Massachusetts	30	Kansas	30
New Jersey	12.6	13.4	13.7	Colorado	31	Alaska	31	Rhode Island	31
New Mexico	1.8	2.0	2.1	Alaska	32	Colorado	32	Minnesota	32
New York	13.7	15.9	15.9	West Virginia	33	Rhode Island	33	Nebraska	33
North Carolina	22.4	22.0	21.5	Nebraska	34	Nebraska	34	Arizona	34
North Dakota	0.4	0.6	1.2	Rhode Island	35	West Virginia	35	Colorado	35
Ohio	10.0	10.7	12.2	Arizona	36	Washington	36	Washington	36
Oklahoma	6.8	7.4	7.4	Washington	37	Arizona	37	West Virginia	37
Oregon	1.4	1.6	1.8	New Mexico	38	Hawaii	38	Alaska	38
Pennsylvania	8.8	9.2	10.9	Hawaii	39	Minnesota	39	Iowa	39
Rhode Island	2.9	3.9	5.7	Iowa	40	New Mexico	40	New Mexico	40
South Carolina	30.4	29.8	27.9	Oregon	41	Iowa	41	Oregon	41
South Dakota	0.3	0.5	1.3	Minnesota	42	Oregon	42	Hawaii	42
Tennessee	15.8	16.0	16.7	Wyoming	43	Wyoming	43	South Dakota	43
Texas	12.0	11.9	11.9	Utah	44	Utah	44	Maine	44
Utah	0.6	0.7	1.1	New Hampshire	45	New Hampshire	45	North Dakota	44
Vermont	0.2	0.4	1.0	North Dakota	46	North Dakota	46	New Hampshire	46
Virginia	18.9	18.8	19.4	South Dakota	47	South Dakota	47	Utah	47
Washington	2.6	3.1	3.6	Idaho	48	Maine	48	Vermont	48
West Virginia	3.3	3.1	3.4	Maine	49	Vermont	49	Wyoming	49
Wisconsin	3.9	5.0	6.3	Montana	50	Idaho	50	Idaho	50
Wyoming	0.7	0.8	0.8	Vermont	51	Montana	51	Montana	51
United States	11.7	12.1	12.6	United States	–	United States	–	United States	–

Source: U.S. Census Bureau, 1980 Census of Population; U.S. Census Bureau, 1990 Census of Population; U.S. Census Bureau, Census 2010

American Indian/Alaska Native Population

Area	Percent of Population			1980		1990		2010	
	1980	1990	2010	Area	Rank	Area	Rank	Area	Rank
Alabama	0.2	0.4	0.6	Alaska	1	Alaska	1	Alaska	1
Alaska	16.0	15.6	14.8	New Mexico	2	New Mexico	2	New Mexico	2
Arizona	5.6	5.6	4.6	South Dakota	3	Oklahoma	3	South Dakota	3
Arkansas	0.4	0.5	0.8	Arizona	4	South Dakota	4	Oklahoma	4
California	0.9	0.8	1.0	Oklahoma	5	Montana	5	Montana	5
Colorado	0.6	0.8	1.1	Montana	6	Arizona	6	North Dakota	6
Connecticut	0.2	0.2	0.3	North Dakota	7	North Dakota	7	Arizona	7
Delaware	0.2	0.3	0.5	Nevada	8	Wyoming	8	Wyoming	8
D.C.	0.2	0.2	0.4	Wyoming	9	Washington	9	Washington	9
Florida	0.2	0.3	0.4	Washington	10	Nevada	10	Oregon	10
Georgia	0.1	0.2	0.3	Utah	11	Utah	11	Idaho	11
Hawaii	0.3	0.5	0.3	Idaho	12	Idaho	12	North Carolina	12
Idaho	1.1	1.4	1.4	North Carolina	13	Oregon	13	Nevada	13
Illinois	0.1	0.2	0.3	Oregon	14	North Carolina	14	Utah	13
Indiana	0.1	0.2	0.3	Minnesota	15	Minnesota	15	Minnesota	15
Iowa	0.2	0.3	0.4	California	16	Kansas	16	Colorado	16
Kansas	0.7	0.9	1.0	Kansas	17	Colorado	17	Nebraska	17
Kentucky	0.1	0.2	0.2	Colorado	18	California	18	Kansas	18
Louisiana	0.3	0.4	0.7	Wisconsin	18	Wisconsin	18	California	19
Maine	0.4	0.5	0.7	Nebraska	20	Nebraska	20	Wisconsin	20
Maryland	0.2	0.3	0.4	Michigan	21	Michigan	21	Arkansas	21
Massachusetts	0.1	0.2	0.3	Arkansas	22	Arkansas	22	Texas	22
Michigan	0.4	0.6	0.6	Maine	23	Maine	23	Louisiana	23
Minnesota	0.9	1.1	1.2	Rhode Island	24	Hawaii	24	Maine	24
Mississippi	0.3	0.3	0.5	Hawaii	25	Louisiana	25	Michigan	25
Missouri	0.3	0.4	0.5	Louisiana	25	Rhode Island	26	Alabama	26
Montana	4.7	6.0	6.3	Texas	27	Alabama	26	Rhode Island	27
Nebraska	0.6	0.8	1.0	Missouri	28	Texas	28	New York	28
Nevada	1.7	1.6	1.2	Mississippi	28	Missouri	28	Mississippi	29
New Hampshire	0.2	0.2	0.2	New York	30	New York	30	Delaware	30
New Jersey	0.1	0.2	0.3	Delaware	31	Mississippi	31	Missouri	31
New Mexico	8.1	8.9	9.4	Florida	32	Delaware	32	South Carolina	32
New York	0.2	0.4	0.6	Maryland	33	Vermont	32	Florida	33
North Carolina	1.1	1.2	1.3	Iowa	33	Florida	34	Virginia	34
North Dakota	3.1	4.1	5.4	Alabama	33	Maryland	35	Iowa	35
Ohio	0.1	0.2	0.2	Vermont	33	Iowa	36	D.C.	36
Oklahoma	5.6	8.0	8.6	Virginia	37	Virginia	37	Maryland	36
Oregon	1.0	1.4	1.4	South Carolina	37	D.C.	38	Vermont	36
Pennsylvania	0.1	0.1	0.2	D.C.	39	South Carolina	38	Illinois	39
Rhode Island	0.3	0.4	0.6	Connecticut	40	Indiana	40	Georgia	40
South Carolina	0.2	0.2	0.4	New Hampshire	40	Georgia	41	New Jersey	40
South Dakota	6.5	7.3	8.8	Illinois	42	Tennessee	41	Tennessee	42
Tennessee	0.1	0.2	0.3	Indiana	42	Connecticut	43	Connecticut	43
Texas	0.3	0.4	0.7	Georgia	42	Massachusetts	43	Hawaii	43
Utah	1.3	1.4	1.2	Massachusetts	45	New Jersey	45	Massachusetts	45
Vermont	0.2	0.3	0.4	New Jersey	46	Illinois	45	Indiana	46
Virginia	0.2	0.3	0.4	Ohio	46	Ohio	45	New Hampshire	47
Washington	1.5	1.7	1.5	Tennessee	46	New Hampshire	45	Kentucky	48
West Virginia	0.1	0.1	0.2	Kentucky	49	Kentucky	49	Ohio	49
Wisconsin	0.6	0.8	1.0	Pennsylvania	50	West Virginia	50	Pennsylvania	50
Wyoming	1.5	2.1	2.4	West Virginia	50	Pennsylvania	51	West Virginia	51
United States	0.6	0.8	1.0	United States	–	United States	–	United States	–

Source: U.S. Census Bureau, 1980 Census of Population; U.S. Census Bureau, 1990 Census of Population; U.S. Census Bureau, Census 2010

Asian Population

Area	Percent of Population			1980		1990		2010	
	1980	1990	2010	Area	Rank	Area	Rank	Area	Rank
Alabama	0.3	0.5	1.1	Hawaii	1	Hawaii	1	Hawaii	1
Alaska	2.0	3.6	5.4	California	2	California	2	California	2
Arizona	0.8	1.5	2.8	Washington	3	Washington	3	New Jersey	3
Arkansas	0.3	0.5	1.2	Alaska	4	New York	4	New York	4
California	5.3	9.6	13.1	New York	5	Alaska	5	Nevada	5
Colorado	1.0	1.8	2.8	Nevada	5	New Jersey	6	Washington	6
Connecticut	0.6	1.5	3.8	Maryland	7	Nevada	7	Maryland	7
Delaware	0.7	1.4	3.2	New Jersey	8	Maryland	8	Virginia	8
D.C.	1.0	1.9	3.5	Illinois	9	Virginia	9	Alaska	9
Florida	0.6	1.2	2.4	Oregon	10	Illinois	10	Massachusetts	10
Georgia	0.5	1.2	3.3	Virginia	11	Oregon	11	Illinois	11
Hawaii	60.5	61.8	38.6	Colorado	12	Massachusetts	12	Minnesota	12
Idaho	0.6	0.9	1.2	D.C.	12	Utah	13	Texas	13
Illinois	1.4	2.5	4.6	Utah	14	Texas	14	Connecticut	14
Indiana	0.4	0.7	1.6	Massachusetts	15	D.C.	15	Oregon	15
Iowa	0.4	0.9	1.7	Texas	16	Rhode Island	16	D.C.	16
Kansas	0.6	1.3	2.4	Arizona	17	Colorado	17	Georgia	17
Kentucky	0.3	0.5	1.1	Delaware	18	Minnesota	18	Delaware	18
Louisiana	0.6	1.0	1.6	Minnesota	19	Connecticut	19	Rhode Island	19
Maine	0.3	0.5	1.0	Kansas	20	Arizona	20	Arizona	20
Maryland	1.5	2.9	5.5	Idaho	21	Delaware	21	Colorado	20
Massachusetts	0.9	2.4	5.3	Connecticut	22	Kansas	22	Pennsylvania	22
Michigan	0.6	1.1	2.4	Michigan	22	Florida	23	Florida	23
Minnesota	0.7	1.8	4.0	Florida	24	Georgia	24	Michigan	24
Mississippi	0.3	0.5	0.9	Louisiana	25	Pennsylvania	25	Kansas	25
Missouri	0.5	0.8	1.6	Oklahoma	25	Michigan	26	Wisconsin	26
Montana	0.3	0.5	0.6	Rhode Island	27	Wisconsin	27	North Carolina	27
Nebraska	0.5	0.8	1.8	Pennsylvania	28	Oklahoma	28	New Hampshire	28
Nevada	1.8	3.2	7.2	New Mexico	29	Louisiana	29	Utah	29
New Hampshire	0.3	0.8	2.2	Missouri	30	New Mexico	30	Nebraska	30
New Jersey	1.4	3.5	8.3	Nebraska	31	Idaho	30	Iowa	31
New Mexico	0.5	0.9	1.4	Georgia	31	Iowa	32	Oklahoma	32
New York	1.8	3.9	7.3	Ohio	33	Ohio	33	Ohio	33
North Carolina	0.4	0.8	2.2	Wyoming	34	New Hampshire	33	Missouri	34
North Dakota	0.3	0.5	1.0	Iowa	35	Missouri	35	Indiana	35
Ohio	0.4	0.8	1.7	Wisconsin	36	Nebraska	36	Louisiana	36
Oklahoma	0.6	1.1	1.7	South Carolina	37	North Carolina	36	Tennessee	37
Oregon	1.3	2.4	3.7	Indiana	38	Indiana	38	New Mexico	38
Pennsylvania	0.5	1.2	2.8	North Carolina	39	Tennessee	39	South Carolina	39
Rhode Island	0.6	1.8	2.9	Montana	40	South Carolina	40	Vermont	40
South Carolina	0.4	0.6	1.3	New Hampshire	40	Wyoming	41	Arkansas	41
South Dakota	0.3	0.5	0.9	Tennessee	42	Vermont	42	Idaho	42
Tennessee	0.3	0.7	1.4	North Dakota	42	North Dakota	43	Kentucky	43
Texas	0.9	1.9	3.8	Mississippi	44	Alabama	43	Alabama	44
Utah	1.0	1.9	2.0	Arkansas	44	Maine	43	North Dakota	45
Vermont	0.3	0.6	1.3	Kentucky	46	Montana	46	Maine	46
Virginia	1.2	2.6	5.5	West Virginia	46	Arkansas	46	South Dakota	47
Washington	2.5	4.3	7.2	Vermont	48	Mississippi	48	Mississippi	48
West Virginia	0.3	0.4	0.7	Maine	48	Kentucky	49	Wyoming	49
Wisconsin	0.4	1.1	2.3	Alabama	50	South Dakota	50	West Virginia	50
Wyoming	0.4	0.6	0.8	South Dakota	50	West Virginia	51	Montana	51
United States	1.6	2.9	4.8	United States	–	United States	–	United States	–

Note: In the 1980/1990 Census, the Asian category included Native Hawaiian/Other Pacific Islanders.
Source: U.S. Census Bureau, 1980 Census of Population; U.S. Census Bureau, 1990 Census of Population; U.S. Census Bureau, Census 2010

Hispanic Population

Area	Percent of Population			1980		1990		2010	
	1980	1990	2010	Area	Rank	Area	Rank	Area	Rank
Alabama	0.9	0.6	3.9	New Mexico	1	New Mexico	1	New Mexico	1
Alaska	2.3	3.2	5.5	Texas	2	California	2	California	2
Arizona	16.3	18.8	29.7	California	3	Texas	3	Texas	2
Arkansas	0.7	0.9	6.4	Arizona	4	Arizona	4	Arizona	4
California	19.2	25.8	37.6	Colorado	5	Colorado	5	Nevada	5
Colorado	11.8	12.9	20.7	New York	6	New York	6	Florida	6
Connecticut	4.0	6.5	13.4	Florida	7	Florida	7	Colorado	7
Delaware	1.6	2.4	8.2	Hawaii	8	Nevada	8	New Jersey	8
D.C.	2.8	5.4	9.1	Nevada	9	New Jersey	9	New York	9
Florida	8.8	12.2	22.5	New Jersey	10	Illinois	10	Illinois	10
Georgia	1.1	1.7	8.8	Illinois	11	Hawaii	11	Connecticut	11
Hawaii	7.4	7.3	8.9	Wyoming	12	Connecticut	12	Utah	12
Idaho	3.9	5.3	11.2	Utah	13	Wyoming	13	Rhode Island	13
Illinois	5.6	7.9	15.8	Connecticut	14	D.C.	14	Oregon	14
Indiana	1.6	1.8	6.0	Idaho	15	Idaho	15	Washington	15
Iowa	0.9	1.2	5.0	Washington	16	Utah	16	Idaho	16
Kansas	2.7	3.8	10.5	D.C.	17	Massachusetts	17	Kansas	17
Kentucky	0.7	0.6	3.1	Kansas	18	Rhode Island	18	Massachusetts	18
Louisiana	2.4	2.2	4.3	Oregon	19	Washington	19	Nebraska	19
Maine	0.5	0.6	1.3	Massachusetts	20	Oregon	20	D.C.	20
Maryland	1.5	2.6	8.2	Louisiana	21	Kansas	21	Wyoming	21
Massachusetts	2.5	4.8	9.6	Alaska	22	Alaska	22	Hawaii	22
Michigan	1.7	2.2	4.4	Rhode Island	23	Oklahoma	23	Oklahoma	23
Minnesota	0.8	1.2	4.7	Oklahoma	24	Maryland	24	Georgia	24
Mississippi	1.0	0.6	2.8	Nebraska	25	Virginia	25	North Carolina	25
Missouri	1.1	1.2	3.6	Michigan	26	Delaware	26	Delaware	26
Montana	1.3	1.5	2.9	Delaware	27	Nebraska	27	Maryland	26
Nebraska	1.8	2.3	9.2	Indiana	28	Louisiana	28	Virginia	28
Nevada	6.8	10.4	26.5	Maryland	29	Michigan	29	Arkansas	29
New Hampshire	0.6	1.0	2.8	Virginia	30	Pennsylvania	30	Indiana	30
New Jersey	6.7	9.6	17.7	Wisconsin	31	Wisconsin	31	Wisconsin	31
New Mexico	36.6	38.2	46.3	Pennsylvania	32	Indiana	32	Pennsylvania	32
New York	9.5	12.3	17.6	Montana	33	Georgia	33	Alaska	33
North Carolina	1.0	1.2	8.4	Georgia	34	Montana	34	South Carolina	34
North Dakota	0.5	0.7	2.0	Ohio	35	Ohio	35	Iowa	35
Ohio	1.1	1.3	3.1	South Carolina	36	Minnesota	36	Minnesota	36
Oklahoma	1.9	2.7	8.9	Missouri	37	Missouri	37	Tennessee	37
Oregon	2.5	4.0	11.8	Mississippi	38	Iowa	38	Michigan	38
Pennsylvania	1.3	2.0	5.7	North Carolina	39	North Carolina	39	Louisiana	39
Rhode Island	2.0	4.6	12.4	Iowa	40	New Hampshire	40	Alabama	40
South Carolina	1.1	0.9	5.1	Alabama	41	South Carolina	41	Missouri	41
South Dakota	0.6	0.8	2.7	Minnesota	42	Arkansas	42	Ohio	42
Tennessee	0.7	0.7	4.6	Arkansas	43	South Dakota	43	Kentucky	43
Texas	21.0	25.6	37.6	Tennessee	43	North Dakota	44	Montana	44
Utah	4.1	4.9	13.0	Kentucky	43	Tennessee	45	New Hampshire	45
Vermont	0.7	0.7	1.5	West Virginia	46	Vermont	46	Mississippi	46
Virginia	1.5	2.6	7.9	Vermont	47	Mississippi	47	South Dakota	47
Washington	2.9	4.4	11.2	New Hampshire	48	Alabama	48	North Dakota	48
West Virginia	0.7	0.5	1.2	South Dakota	49	Kentucky	49	Vermont	49
Wisconsin	1.3	1.9	5.9	North Dakota	50	Maine	50	Maine	50
Wyoming	5.2	5.7	8.9	Maine	51	West Virginia	51	West Virginia	51
United States	6.5	9.0	16.4	United States	–	United States	–	United States	–

Source: U.S. Census Bureau, 1980 Census of Population; U.S. Census Bureau, 1990 Census of Population; U.S. Census Bureau, Census 2010

Foreign-Born Population

Area	Percent of Population			1980		1990		2010	
	1980	1990	2010	Area	Rank	Area	Rank	Area	Rank
Alabama	1.0	1.1	3.4	California	1	California	1	California	1
Alaska	4.0	4.5	7.2	Hawaii	2	New York	2	New York	2
Arizona	6.0	7.6	14.2	New York	3	Hawaii	3	New Jersey	3
Arkansas	1.0	1.1	4.3	Florida	4	Florida	4	Nevada	4
California	15.1	21.7	27.2	New Jersey	5	New Jersey	5	Florida	5
Colorado	3.9	4.3	9.8	Rhode Island	6	D.C.	6	Hawaii	6
Connecticut	8.6	8.5	13.2	Massachusetts	7	Massachusetts	7	Texas	7
Delaware	3.2	3.3	8.2	Connecticut	8	Rhode Island	7	Massachusetts	8
D.C.	6.4	9.7	13.0	Illinois	9	Texas	9	Arizona	9
Florida	10.9	12.9	19.2	Nevada	10	Nevada	10	Illinois	10
Georgia	1.7	2.7	9.6	D.C.	11	Connecticut	11	Connecticut	11
Hawaii	14.2	14.7	17.7	Texas	12	Illinois	12	Maryland	11
Idaho	2.5	2.9	5.9	Arizona	12	Arizona	13	D.C.	13
Illinois	7.2	8.3	13.6	Washington	14	Washington	14	Washington	14
Indiana	1.9	1.7	4.4	Maryland	15	Maryland	14	Rhode Island	15
Iowa	1.6	1.6	4.1	Michigan	16	New Mexico	16	Virginia	16
Kansas	2.0	2.5	6.3	New Hampshire	17	Virginia	17	Colorado	17
Kentucky	0.9	0.9	3.1	Oregon	18	Oregon	18	New Mexico	18
Louisiana	2.0	2.1	3.6	Vermont	18	Alaska	19	Oregon	18
Maine	3.9	3.0	3.3	New Mexico	20	Colorado	20	Georgia	20
Maryland	4.6	6.6	13.2	Alaska	20	Michigan	21	Delaware	21
Massachusetts	8.7	9.5	14.5	Colorado	22	New Hampshire	22	Utah	21
Michigan	4.5	3.8	5.9	Maine	22	Utah	23	North Carolina	23
Minnesota	2.6	2.6	7.0	Utah	24	Delaware	24	Alaska	24
Mississippi	0.9	0.8	2.2	Pennsylvania	25	Pennsylvania	25	Minnesota	25
Missouri	1.7	1.6	3.7	Virginia	26	Vermont	25	Kansas	26
Montana	2.3	1.7	2.0	Delaware	27	Maine	27	Idaho	27
Nebraska	2.0	1.8	5.9	Ohio	28	Idaho	28	Michigan	27
Nevada	6.7	8.7	19.3	Wisconsin	29	Georgia	29	Nebraska	27
New Hampshire	4.4	3.7	5.3	Minnesota	30	Minnesota	30	Pennsylvania	30
New Jersey	10.3	12.5	20.3	Idaho	31	Kansas	31	New Hampshire	31
New Mexico	4.0	5.3	9.7	Montana	32	Wisconsin	31	Oklahoma	32
New York	13.6	15.9	21.7	North Dakota	32	Ohio	33	South Carolina	33
North Carolina	1.3	1.7	7.4	Wyoming	34	Oklahoma	34	Wisconsin	34
North Dakota	2.3	1.5	2.4	Kansas	34	Louisiana	34	Indiana	35
Ohio	2.8	2.4	3.8	Louisiana	34	Nebraska	36	Tennessee	35
Oklahoma	1.9	2.1	5.2	Nebraska	34	Wyoming	37	Arkansas	37
Oregon	4.1	4.9	9.7	Oklahoma	38	Indiana	37	Iowa	38
Pennsylvania	3.4	3.1	5.6	Indiana	38	Montana	37	Vermont	39
Rhode Island	8.9	9.5	12.6	Georgia	40	North Carolina	37	Ohio	40
South Carolina	1.5	1.4	4.7	Missouri	40	Missouri	41	Missouri	41
South Dakota	1.4	1.1	2.3	Iowa	42	Iowa	41	Louisiana	42
Tennessee	1.1	1.2	4.4	South Carolina	43	North Dakota	43	Alabama	43
Texas	6.0	9.0	16.1	South Dakota	44	South Carolina	44	Maine	44
Utah	3.5	3.4	8.2	North Carolina	45	Tennessee	45	Kentucky	45
Vermont	4.1	3.1	4.0	Tennessee	46	Arkansas	46	Wyoming	45
Virginia	3.3	5.0	10.8	West Virginia	46	South Dakota	46	North Dakota	47
Washington	5.8	6.6	12.7	Alabama	48	Alabama	46	South Dakota	48
West Virginia	1.1	0.9	1.3	Arkansas	48	Kentucky	49	Mississippi	49
Wisconsin	2.7	2.5	4.6	Mississippi	50	West Virginia	49	Montana	50
Wyoming	2.0	1.7	3.1	Kentucky	50	Mississippi	51	West Virginia	51
United States	6.2	7.9	12.7	United States	–	United States	–	United States	–

Source: U.S. Census Bureau, 1980 Census of Population; U.S. Census Bureau, 1990 Census of Population; U.S. Census Bureau, Census 2010

Urban Population

Area	Percent of Population 1980	Percent of Population 1990	Percent of Population 2010	1980 Area	1980 Rank	1990 Area	1990 Rank	2010 Area	2010 Rank
Alabama	60.0	60.4	55.0	D.C.	1	D.C.	1	D.C.	1
Alaska	64.3	67.5	60.5	California	2	California	2	New Jersey	2
Arizona	83.8	87.5	86.7	New Jersey	3	New Jersey	3	California	3
Arkansas	51.6	53.5	52.0	Rhode Island	4	Hawaii	4	Massachusetts	4
California	91.3	92.6	93.2	Hawaii	5	Nevada	5	Rhode Island	5
Colorado	80.6	82.4	82.0	Nevada	6	Arizona	6	Nevada	6
Connecticut	78.8	79.1	87.9	New York	7	Utah	7	Hawaii	7
Delaware	70.6	73.0	80.1	Utah	8	Rhode Island	8	Florida	8
D.C.	100.0	100.0	100.0	Florida	9	Florida	9	Connecticut	9
Florida	84.3	84.8	89.3	Arizona	10	Illinois	10	Illinois	10
Georgia	62.4	63.2	70.7	Massachusetts	10	New York	11	Arizona	11
Hawaii	86.5	89.0	90.0	Illinois	12	Massachusetts	11	Maryland	12
Idaho	54.0	57.4	63.8	Colorado	13	Colorado	13	New York	13
Illinois	83.3	84.6	87.3	Maryland	14	Maryland	14	Utah	14
Indiana	64.2	64.9	72.1	Texas	15	Texas	15	Colorado	15
Iowa	58.6	60.6	61.4	Connecticut	16	Connecticut	16	Washington	16
Kansas	66.7	69.1	71.1	Washington	17	Washington	17	Texas	17
Kentucky	50.9	51.8	55.9	Ohio	18	Ohio	18	Delaware	18
Louisiana	68.6	68.1	72.1	New Mexico	19	New Mexico	19	Ohio	19
Maine	47.5	44.6	36.6	Michigan	20	Delaware	19	Oregon	20
Maryland	80.3	81.3	86.4	Delaware	21	Oregon	21	Pennsylvania	21
Massachusetts	83.8	84.3	91.1	Pennsylvania	22	Michigan	21	New Mexico	22
Michigan	70.7	70.5	72.2	Louisiana	23	Minnesota	23	Michigan	23
Minnesota	66.9	69.9	68.3	Missouri	24	Virginia	24	Indiana	24
Mississippi	47.3	47.1	48.7	Oregon	25	Kansas	25	Louisiana	24
Missouri	68.1	68.7	68.3	Oklahoma	26	Pennsylvania	26	Virginia	26
Montana	52.9	52.5	52.0	Minnesota	27	Missouri	27	Kansas	27
Nebraska	62.9	66.1	68.4	Kansas	28	Louisiana	28	Georgia	28
Nevada	85.3	88.3	90.6	Virginia	29	Oklahoma	29	Nebraska	29
New Hampshire	52.2	51.0	55.6	Alaska	30	Alaska	30	Minnesota	30
New Jersey	89.0	89.4	94.7	Indiana	31	Nebraska	31	Missouri	30
New Mexico	72.1	73.0	73.7	Wisconsin	31	Wisconsin	32	Wisconsin	32
New York	84.6	84.3	85.6	Nebraska	33	Wyoming	33	Oklahoma	33
North Carolina	48.0	50.4	59.1	Wyoming	34	Indiana	34	Idaho	34
North Dakota	48.8	53.3	54.0	Georgia	35	Georgia	35	Tennessee	35
Ohio	73.3	74.1	78.9	Tennessee	36	Tennessee	36	Wyoming	36
Oklahoma	67.3	67.7	65.1	Alabama	37	Iowa	37	Iowa	37
Oregon	67.9	70.5	77.9	Iowa	38	Alabama	38	South Carolina	38
Pennsylvania	69.3	68.9	76.4	South Carolina	39	Idaho	39	Alaska	39
Rhode Island	87.0	86.0	90.9	Idaho	40	South Carolina	40	North Carolina	40
South Carolina	54.1	54.6	61.2	Montana	41	Arkansas	41	Kentucky	41
South Dakota	46.4	50.0	51.6	New Hampshire	42	North Dakota	42	New Hampshire	42
Tennessee	60.4	60.9	63.6	Arkansas	43	Montana	43	Alabama	43
Texas	79.6	80.3	80.7	Kentucky	44	Kentucky	44	North Dakota	44
Utah	84.4	87.0	85.4	North Dakota	45	New Hampshire	45	Arkansas	45
Vermont	33.8	32.2	33.6	North Carolina	46	North Carolina	46	Montana	45
Virginia	66.0	69.4	71.4	Maine	47	South Dakota	47	South Dakota	47
Washington	73.5	76.4	81.3	Mississippi	48	Mississippi	48	Mississippi	48
West Virginia	36.2	36.1	46.4	South Dakota	49	Maine	49	West Virginia	49
Wisconsin	64.2	65.7	65.8	West Virginia	50	West Virginia	50	Maine	50
Wyoming	62.7	65.0	62.4	Vermont	51	Vermont	51	Vermont	51
United States	73.7	75.2	77.6	United States	–	United States	–	United States	–

Source: U.S. Census Bureau, 1980 Census of Population; U.S. Census Bureau, 1990 Census of Population; U.S. Census Bureau, Census 2010

Rural Population

Area	Percent of Population			1980		1990		2010	
	1980	1990	2010	Area	Rank	Area	Rank	Area	Rank
Alabama	40.0	39.6	45.0	Vermont	1	Vermont	1	Vermont	1
Alaska	35.7	32.5	39.5	West Virginia	2	West Virginia	2	Maine	2
Arizona	16.2	12.5	13.3	South Dakota	3	Maine	3	West Virginia	3
Arkansas	48.4	46.5	48.0	Mississippi	4	Mississippi	4	Mississippi	4
California	8.7	7.4	6.8	Maine	5	South Dakota	5	South Dakota	5
Colorado	19.4	17.6	18.0	North Carolina	6	North Carolina	6	Arkansas	6
Connecticut	21.2	20.9	12.1	North Dakota	7	New Hampshire	7	Montana	6
Delaware	29.4	27.0	19.9	Kentucky	8	Kentucky	8	North Dakota	8
D.C.	n/a	n/a	n/a	Arkansas	9	Montana	9	Alabama	9
Florida	15.7	15.2	10.7	New Hampshire	10	North Dakota	10	New Hampshire	10
Georgia	37.6	36.8	29.3	Montana	11	Arkansas	11	Kentucky	11
Hawaii	13.5	11.0	10.0	Idaho	12	South Carolina	12	North Carolina	12
Idaho	46.0	42.6	36.2	South Carolina	13	Idaho	13	Alaska	13
Illinois	16.7	15.4	12.7	Iowa	14	Alabama	14	South Carolina	14
Indiana	35.8	35.1	27.9	Alabama	15	Iowa	15	Iowa	15
Iowa	41.4	39.4	38.6	Tennessee	16	Tennessee	16	Wyoming	16
Kansas	33.3	30.9	28.9	Georgia	17	Georgia	17	Tennessee	17
Kentucky	49.1	48.2	44.1	Wyoming	18	Indiana	18	Idaho	18
Louisiana	31.4	31.9	27.9	Nebraska	19	Wyoming	19	Oklahoma	19
Maine	52.5	55.4	63.4	Indiana	20	Wisconsin	20	Wisconsin	20
Maryland	19.7	18.7	13.6	Wisconsin	20	Nebraska	21	Minnesota	21
Massachusetts	16.2	15.7	8.9	Alaska	22	Alaska	22	Missouri	21
Michigan	29.3	29.5	27.8	Virginia	23	Oklahoma	23	Nebraska	23
Minnesota	33.1	30.1	31.7	Kansas	24	Louisiana	24	Georgia	24
Mississippi	52.7	52.9	51.3	Minnesota	25	Missouri	25	Kansas	25
Missouri	31.9	31.3	31.7	Oklahoma	26	Pennsylvania	26	Virginia	26
Montana	47.1	47.5	48.0	Oregon	27	Kansas	27	Indiana	27
Nebraska	37.1	33.9	31.6	Missouri	28	Virginia	28	Louisiana	27
Nevada	14.7	11.7	9.4	Louisiana	29	Minnesota	29	Michigan	29
New Hampshire	47.8	49.0	44.4	Pennsylvania	30	Oregon	30	New Mexico	30
New Jersey	11.0	10.6	5.3	Delaware	31	Michigan	30	Pennsylvania	31
New Mexico	27.9	27.0	26.3	Michigan	32	New Mexico	32	Oregon	32
New York	15.4	15.7	14.4	New Mexico	33	Delaware	32	Ohio	33
North Carolina	52.0	49.6	40.9	Ohio	34	Ohio	34	Delaware	34
North Dakota	51.2	46.7	46.0	Washington	35	Washington	35	Texas	35
Ohio	26.7	25.9	21.1	Connecticut	36	Connecticut	36	Washington	36
Oklahoma	32.7	32.3	34.9	Texas	37	Texas	37	Colorado	37
Oregon	32.1	29.5	22.1	Maryland	38	Maryland	38	Utah	38
Pennsylvania	30.7	31.1	23.6	Colorado	39	Colorado	39	New York	39
Rhode Island	13.0	14.0	9.1	Illinois	40	New York	40	Maryland	40
South Carolina	45.9	45.4	38.8	Arizona	41	Massachusetts	40	Arizona	41
South Dakota	53.6	50.0	48.4	Massachusetts	41	Illinois	42	Illinois	42
Tennessee	39.6	39.1	36.4	Florida	43	Florida	43	Connecticut	43
Texas	20.4	19.7	19.3	Utah	44	Rhode Island	44	Florida	44
Utah	15.6	13.0	14.6	New York	45	Utah	45	Hawaii	45
Vermont	66.2	67.8	66.4	Nevada	46	Arizona	46	Nevada	46
Virginia	34.0	30.6	28.6	Hawaii	47	Nevada	47	Rhode Island	47
Washington	26.5	23.6	18.7	Rhode Island	48	Hawaii	48	Massachusetts	48
West Virginia	63.8	63.9	53.6	New Jersey	49	New Jersey	49	California	49
Wisconsin	35.8	34.3	34.2	California	50	California	50	New Jersey	50
Wyoming	37.3	35.0	37.6	D.C.	n/a	D.C.	n/a	D.C.	n/a
United States	26.3	24.8	22.4	United States	–	United States	–	United States	–

Source: U.S. Census Bureau, 1980 Census of Population; U.S. Census Bureau, 1990 Census of Population; U.S. Census Bureau, Census 2010

Males per 100 Females

Area	Males per 100 Females 1980	1990	2010	1980 Area	Rank	1990 Area	Rank	2010 Area	Rank
Alabama	92.5	92.0	94.3	Alaska	1	Alaska	1	Alaska	1
Alaska	112.8	111.4	108.5	Hawaii	2	Nevada	2	Wyoming	2
Arizona	96.9	97.6	98.7	Wyoming	3	Hawaii	3	North Dakota	3
Arkansas	93.5	93.1	96.5	Nevada	4	California	4	Nevada	4
California	97.2	100.2	98.8	North Dakota	5	Wyoming	4	Utah	5
Colorado	98.5	98.1	100.5	Idaho	6	North Dakota	6	Montana	6
Connecticut	93.1	94.0	94.8	Montana	7	Idaho	7	Colorado	7
Delaware	93.1	94.1	93.9	Washington	8	Utah	8	Idaho	8
D.C.	86.1	87.4	89.5	Colorado	9	Washington	9	Hawaii	9
Florida	92.2	93.8	95.6	Utah	10	Colorado	10	South Dakota	10
Georgia	93.5	94.3	95.4	South Dakota	11	Montana	10	Washington	11
Hawaii	105.2	103.6	100.3	New Mexico	12	Arizona	12	California	12
Idaho	99.7	99.0	100.4	California	12	Texas	13	Arizona	13
Illinois	94.0	94.5	96.2	Oregon	14	South Dakota	14	Minnesota	14
Indiana	94.4	94.1	96.8	Arizona	15	New Mexico	15	Nebraska	14
Iowa	94.6	93.9	98.1	Texas	16	Oregon	16	Wisconsin	14
Kansas	95.9	96.2	98.4	Minnesota	17	Kansas	17	Kansas	17
Kentucky	95.6	94.0	96.8	Virginia	18	Virginia	17	Texas	17
Louisiana	94.2	92.8	95.9	Wisconsin	18	Minnesota	17	Iowa	19
Maine	94.4	94.9	95.8	Kansas	20	New Hampshire	20	Oklahoma	20
Maryland	94.0	94.1	93.6	Kentucky	21	Vermont	21	Oregon	20
Massachusetts	90.8	92.4	93.7	Oklahoma	22	Wisconsin	22	New Mexico	22
Michigan	95.2	94.4	96.3	Nebraska	23	Nebraska	23	New Hampshire	23
Minnesota	96.1	96.2	98.5	Michigan	24	Maine	24	West Virginia	23
Mississippi	92.9	91.7	94.4	New Hampshire	25	Oklahoma	25	Vermont	25
Missouri	92.7	92.9	96.0	Vermont	26	Illinois	26	Indiana	26
Montana	99.6	98.1	100.8	South Carolina	27	Michigan	27	Kentucky	26
Nebraska	95.3	95.1	98.5	Iowa	28	Georgia	28	Arkansas	28
Nevada	102.4	103.7	102.0	Indiana	29	Maryland	29	Michigan	29
New Hampshire	95.0	96.1	97.3	Maine	29	Delaware	29	Virginia	29
New Jersey	92.2	93.5	94.8	North Carolina	31	Indiana	29	Illinois	31
New Mexico	97.2	96.8	97.7	Louisiana	32	North Carolina	29	Missouri	32
New York	90.5	92.1	93.8	West Virginia	33	Connecticut	33	Louisiana	33
North Carolina	94.3	94.1	95.0	Illinois	34	Kentucky	33	Maine	34
North Dakota	101.3	99.3	102.1	Maryland	34	Iowa	35	Florida	35
Ohio	93.5	93.0	95.4	Georgia	36	South Carolina	35	Georgia	36
Oklahoma	95.4	94.8	98.0	Ohio	36	Florida	37	Ohio	36
Oregon	97.0	96.7	98.0	Arkansas	36	New Jersey	38	Pennsylvania	38
Pennsylvania	91.9	92.0	95.1	Tennessee	39	Arkansas	39	Tennessee	38
Rhode Island	91.0	92.2	93.4	Connecticut	40	Ohio	40	North Carolina	40
South Carolina	94.7	93.9	94.7	Delaware	40	Missouri	41	Connecticut	41
South Dakota	97.3	96.9	100.1	Mississippi	42	Tennessee	41	New Jersey	41
Tennessee	93.3	92.9	95.1	Missouri	43	Louisiana	43	South Carolina	43
Texas	96.8	97.0	98.4	Alabama	44	Massachusetts	44	Mississippi	44
Utah	98.4	98.7	100.9	Florida	45	West Virginia	44	Alabama	45
Vermont	94.9	95.9	97.1	New Jersey	45	Rhode Island	46	Delaware	46
Virginia	96.0	96.2	96.3	Pennsylvania	47	New York	47	New York	47
Washington	98.7	98.4	99.3	Rhode Island	48	Pennsylvania	48	Massachusetts	48
West Virginia	94.1	92.4	97.3	Massachusetts	49	Alabama	48	Maryland	49
Wisconsin	96.0	95.8	98.5	New York	50	Mississippi	50	Rhode Island	50
Wyoming	105.0	100.2	104.1	D.C.	51	D.C.	51	D.C.	51
United States	94.5	95.1	96.7	United States	–	United States	–	United States	–

Source: U.S. Census Bureau, 1980 Census of Population; U.S. Census Bureau, 1990 Census of Population; U.S. Census Bureau, Census 2010

Median Age

Area	Years			1980		1990		2010	
	1980	1990	2010	Area	Rank	Area	Rank	Area	Rank
Alabama	29.2	32.9	37.9	Alaska	1	Alaska	1	Alaska	1
Alaska	26.0	29.3	33.8	Hawaii	2	Nevada	2	Wyoming	2
Arizona	29.2	32.0	35.9	Wyoming	3	Hawaii	3	North Dakota	3
Arkansas	30.6	33.7	37.4	Nevada	4	California	4	Nevada	4
California	29.9	31.3	35.2	North Dakota	5	Wyoming	4	Utah	5
Colorado	28.6	32.4	36.1	Idaho	6	North Dakota	6	Montana	6
Connecticut	32.0	34.3	40.0	Montana	7	Idaho	7	Colorado	7
Delaware	29.7	32.7	38.8	Washington	8	Utah	8	Idaho	8
D.C.	31.0	33.2	33.8	Colorado	9	Washington	9	Hawaii	9
Florida	34.7	36.2	40.7	Utah	10	Colorado	10	South Dakota	10
Georgia	28.6	31.4	35.3	South Dakota	11	Montana	10	Washington	11
Hawaii	28.3	32.5	38.6	New Mexico	12	Arizona	12	California	12
Idaho	27.5	31.5	34.6	California	12	Texas	13	Arizona	13
Illinois	29.9	32.7	36.6	Oregon	14	South Dakota	14	Minnesota	14
Indiana	29.2	32.7	37.0	Arizona	15	New Mexico	15	Nebraska	14
Iowa	30.0	34.0	38.1	Texas	16	Oregon	16	Wisconsin	14
Kansas	30.1	32.8	36.0	Minnesota	17	Kansas	17	Kansas	17
Kentucky	29.1	32.9	38.1	Virginia	18	Virginia	17	Texas	17
Louisiana	27.3	30.9	35.8	Wisconsin	18	Minnesota	17	Iowa	19
Maine	30.4	33.8	42.7	Kansas	20	New Hampshire	20	Oklahoma	20
Maryland	30.3	32.9	38.0	Kentucky	21	Vermont	21	Oregon	20
Massachusetts	31.1	33.4	39.1	Oklahoma	22	Wisconsin	22	New Mexico	22
Michigan	28.8	32.5	38.9	Nebraska	23	Nebraska	23	New Hampshire	23
Minnesota	29.2	32.4	37.4	Michigan	24	Maine	24	West Virginia	23
Mississippi	27.6	31.1	36.0	New Hampshire	25	Oklahoma	25	Vermont	25
Missouri	30.8	33.4	37.9	Vermont	26	Illinois	26	Indiana	26
Montana	29.0	33.8	39.8	South Carolina	27	Michigan	27	Kentucky	26
Nebraska	29.7	32.9	36.2	Iowa	28	Georgia	28	Arkansas	28
Nevada	30.2	33.2	36.3	Indiana	29	Maryland	29	Michigan	29
New Hampshire	30.1	32.7	41.1	Maine	29	Delaware	29	Virginia	29
New Jersey	32.2	34.3	39.0	North Carolina	31	Indiana	29	Illinois	31
New Mexico	27.3	31.1	36.7	Louisiana	32	North Carolina	29	Missouri	32
New York	31.8	33.7	38.0	West Virginia	33	Connecticut	33	Louisiana	33
North Carolina	29.6	33.0	37.4	Illinois	34	Kentucky	33	Maine	34
North Dakota	28.1	32.3	37.0	Maryland	34	Iowa	35	Florida	35
Ohio	29.9	33.3	38.8	Georgia	36	South Carolina	35	Georgia	36
Oklahoma	30.1	33.1	36.2	Ohio	36	Florida	37	Ohio	36
Oregon	30.2	34.5	38.4	Arkansas	36	New Jersey	38	Pennsylvania	38
Pennsylvania	32.1	34.9	40.1	Tennessee	39	Arkansas	39	Tennessee	38
Rhode Island	31.7	33.8	39.4	Connecticut	40	Ohio	40	North Carolina	40
South Carolina	28.0	31.9	37.9	Delaware	40	Missouri	41	Connecticut	41
South Dakota	28.8	32.4	36.9	Mississippi	42	Tennessee	41	New Jersey	41
Tennessee	30.1	33.5	38.0	Missouri	43	Louisiana	43	South Carolina	43
Texas	28.0	30.6	33.6	Alabama	44	Massachusetts	44	Mississippi	44
Utah	24.2	26.2	29.2	Florida	45	West Virginia	44	Alabama	45
Vermont	29.4	32.9	41.5	New Jersey	45	Rhode Island	46	Delaware	46
Virginia	29.8	32.5	37.5	Pennsylvania	47	New York	47	New York	47
Washington	29.8	33.0	37.3	Rhode Island	48	Pennsylvania	48	Massachusetts	48
West Virginia	30.4	35.3	41.3	Massachusetts	49	Alabama	48	Maryland	49
Wisconsin	29.4	32.8	38.5	New York	50	Mississippi	50	Rhode Island	50
Wyoming	27.0	32.0	36.8	D.C.	51	D.C.	51	D.C.	51
United States	30.0	32.8	37.2	United States	–	United States	–	United States	–

Source: U.S. Census Bureau, 1980 Census of Population; U.S. Census Bureau, 1990 Census of Population; U.S. Census Bureau, Census 2010

High School Graduates

Area	Percent of Population			1980		1990		2010	
	1980	1990	2010	Area	Rank	Area	Rank	Area	Rank
Alabama	56.5	66.9	82.1	Alaska	1	Alaska	1	Wyoming	1
Alaska	82.5	86.6	91.0	Utah	2	Utah	2	Minnesota	2
Arizona	72.4	78.7	85.6	Colorado	3	Colorado	3	Montana	3
Arkansas	55.5	66.3	82.9	Wyoming	4	Washington	4	New Hampshire	4
California	73.5	76.2	80.7	Washington	5	Wyoming	5	Alaska	5
Colorado	78.6	84.4	89.7	Oregon	6	Minnesota	6	Vermont	5
Connecticut	70.3	79.2	88.6	Nevada	7	New Hampshire	7	Iowa	7
Delaware	68.6	77.5	87.7	Montana	8	Nebraska	8	Utah	7
D.C.	67.1	73.1	87.4	Hawaii	9	Oregon	9	Nebraska	9
Florida	66.7	74.4	85.5	Idaho	10	Kansas	10	Maine	10
Georgia	56.4	70.9	84.3	California	11	Montana	11	North Dakota	10
Hawaii	73.8	80.1	89.9	Nebraska	12	Vermont	12	Wisconsin	12
Idaho	73.7	79.7	88.3	Kansas	13	Hawaii	13	Hawaii	13
Illinois	66.5	76.2	86.9	Minnesota	14	Iowa	13	Washington	14
Indiana	66.4	75.6	87.0	Arizona	15	Massachusetts	15	Colorado	15
Iowa	71.5	80.1	90.6	New Hampshire	16	Idaho	16	South Dakota	16
Kansas	73.3	81.3	89.2	Massachusetts	17	Connecticut	17	Kansas	17
Kentucky	53.1	64.6	81.9	Iowa	18	Nevada	18	Massachusetts	18
Louisiana	57.7	68.3	81.9	Vermont	19	Maine	18	Oregon	19
Maine	68.7	78.8	90.3	Connecticut	20	Arizona	20	Michigan	20
Maryland	67.4	78.4	88.1	Wisconsin	21	Wisconsin	21	Connecticut	21
Massachusetts	72.2	80.0	89.1	New Mexico	22	Maryland	22	Pennsylvania	22
Michigan	68.0	76.8	88.7	Maine	23	Delaware	23	Idaho	23
Minnesota	73.1	82.4	91.8	Delaware	24	South Dakota	24	Maryland	24
Mississippi	54.8	64.3	81.0	Michigan	25	Michigan	25	Ohio	24
Missouri	63.5	73.9	86.9	South Dakota	26	New Jersey	26	New Jersey	26
Montana	74.4	81.0	91.7	New Jersey	27	North Dakota	26	Delaware	27
Nebraska	73.4	81.8	90.4	Maryland	27	California	28	D.C.	28
Nevada	75.5	78.8	84.7	D.C.	29	Illinois	28	Indiana	29
New Hampshire	72.3	82.2	91.5	Ohio	30	Ohio	30	Illinois	30
New Jersey	67.4	76.7	88.0	Florida	31	Indiana	31	Missouri	30
New Mexico	68.9	75.1	83.3	Illinois	32	Virginia	32	Virginia	32
New York	66.3	74.8	84.9	Indiana	33	New Mexico	33	Oklahoma	33
North Carolina	54.8	70.0	84.7	North Dakota	33	New York	34	Arizona	34
North Dakota	66.4	76.7	90.3	New York	35	Pennsylvania	35	Florida	35
Ohio	67.0	75.7	88.1	Oklahoma	36	Oklahoma	36	New York	36
Oklahoma	66.0	74.6	86.2	Pennsylvania	37	Florida	37	Nevada	37
Oregon	75.6	81.5	88.8	Missouri	38	Missouri	38	North Carolina	37
Pennsylvania	64.7	74.7	88.4	Texas	39	D.C.	39	Georgia	39
Rhode Island	61.1	72.0	83.5	Virginia	40	Texas	40	South Carolina	40
South Carolina	53.7	68.3	84.1	Rhode Island	41	Rhode Island	41	Tennessee	41
South Dakota	67.9	77.1	89.6	Louisiana	42	Georgia	42	Rhode Island	42
Tennessee	56.2	67.1	83.6	Alabama	43	North Carolina	43	New Mexico	43
Texas	62.6	72.1	80.7	Georgia	44	Louisiana	44	West Virginia	44
Utah	80.0	85.1	90.6	Tennessee	45	South Carolina	44	Arkansas	45
Vermont	71.0	80.8	91.0	West Virginia	46	Tennessee	46	Alabama	46
Virginia	62.4	75.2	86.5	Arkansas	47	Alabama	47	Kentucky	47
Washington	77.6	83.8	89.8	Mississippi	48	Arkansas	48	Louisiana	47
West Virginia	56.0	66.0	83.2	North Carolina	48	West Virginia	49	Mississippi	49
Wisconsin	69.6	78.6	90.1	South Carolina	50	Kentucky	50	California	50
Wyoming	77.9	83.0	92.3	Kentucky	51	Mississippi	51	Texas	50
United States	66.5	75.2	85.6	United States	–	United States	–	United States	–

Source: U.S. Census Bureau, 1980 Census of Population; U.S. Census Bureau, 1990 Census of Population; U.S. Census Bureau, Census 2010

College Graduates

Area	Percent of Population			1980		1990		2010	
	1980	1990	2010	Area	Rank	Area	Rank	Area	Rank
Alabama	12.2	15.7	21.9	D.C.	1	D.C.	1	D.C.	1
Alaska	21.1	23.0	27.9	Colorado	2	Connecticut	2	Massachusetts	2
Arizona	17.4	20.3	25.9	Alaska	3	Massachusetts	2	Colorado	3
Arkansas	10.8	13.3	19.5	Connecticut	4	Colorado	4	Maryland	4
California	19.6	23.4	30.1	Maryland	5	Maryland	5	Connecticut	5
Colorado	23.0	27.0	36.4	Hawaii	6	New Jersey	6	New Jersey	6
Connecticut	20.7	27.2	35.5	Massachusetts	7	Virginia	7	Virginia	7
Delaware	17.5	21.4	27.8	Utah	8	New Hampshire	8	Vermont	8
D.C.	27.5	33.3	50.1	California	9	Vermont	9	New Hampshire	9
Florida	14.9	18.3	25.8	Virginia	10	California	10	New York	10
Georgia	14.6	19.3	27.3	Washington	11	New York	11	Minnesota	11
Hawaii	20.3	22.9	29.5	Vermont	11	Alaska	12	Washington	12
Idaho	15.8	17.7	24.4	New Jersey	13	Hawaii	13	Illinois	13
Illinois	16.2	21.0	30.8	New Hampshire	14	Washington	13	Rhode Island	14
Indiana	12.5	15.6	22.7	New York	15	Utah	15	California	15
Iowa	13.9	16.9	24.9	Oregon	15	Minnesota	16	Kansas	16
Kansas	17.0	21.1	29.8	New Mexico	17	Delaware	17	Hawaii	17
Kentucky	11.1	13.6	20.5	Delaware	18	Rhode Island	18	Utah	18
Louisiana	13.9	16.1	21.4	Montana	18	Kansas	19	Montana	19
Maine	14.4	18.8	26.8	Arizona	20	Illinois	20	Oregon	19
Maryland	20.4	26.5	36.1	Minnesota	20	Oregon	21	Nebraska	21
Massachusetts	20.0	27.2	39.0	Wyoming	22	New Mexico	22	Alaska	22
Michigan	14.3	17.4	25.2	Kansas	23	Texas	23	Delaware	23
Minnesota	17.4	21.8	31.8	Texas	24	Arizona	23	North Dakota	24
Mississippi	12.3	14.7	19.5	Illinois	25	Montana	25	Georgia	25
Missouri	13.9	17.8	25.6	Idaho	26	Georgia	26	Pennsylvania	26
Montana	17.5	19.8	28.8	Nebraska	27	Nebraska	27	Maine	27
Nebraska	15.5	18.9	28.6	Rhode Island	28	Wyoming	28	North Carolina	28
Nevada	14.4	15.3	21.7	Oklahoma	29	Maine	28	South Dakota	29
New Hampshire	18.2	24.4	32.8	Florida	30	Florida	30	Wisconsin	29
New Jersey	18.3	24.9	35.4	Wisconsin	31	North Dakota	31	Arizona	31
New Mexico	17.6	20.4	25.0	North Dakota	31	Pennsylvania	32	Texas	31
New York	17.9	23.1	32.5	Georgia	33	Oklahoma	33	Florida	33
North Carolina	13.2	17.4	26.5	Nevada	34	Missouri	33	Missouri	34
North Dakota	14.8	18.1	27.6	Maine	34	Idaho	35	Michigan	35
Ohio	13.7	17.0	24.6	Michigan	36	Wisconsin	35	New Mexico	36
Oklahoma	15.1	17.8	22.9	South Dakota	37	Michigan	37	Iowa	37
Oregon	17.9	20.6	28.8	Louisiana	38	North Carolina	37	Ohio	38
Pennsylvania	13.6	17.9	27.1	Missouri	38	South Dakota	39	South Carolina	39
Rhode Island	15.4	21.3	30.2	Iowa	38	Ohio	40	Idaho	40
South Carolina	13.4	16.6	24.5	Ohio	41	Iowa	41	Wyoming	41
South Dakota	14.0	17.2	26.3	Pennsylvania	42	South Carolina	42	Tennessee	42
Tennessee	12.6	16.0	23.1	South Carolina	43	Louisiana	43	Oklahoma	43
Texas	16.9	20.3	25.9	North Carolina	44	Tennessee	44	Indiana	44
Utah	19.9	22.3	29.3	Tennessee	45	Alabama	45	Alabama	45
Vermont	19.0	24.3	33.6	Indiana	46	Indiana	46	Nevada	46
Virginia	19.1	24.5	34.2	Mississippi	47	Nevada	47	Louisiana	47
Washington	19.0	22.9	31.1	Alabama	48	Mississippi	48	Kentucky	48
West Virginia	10.4	12.3	17.5	Kentucky	49	Kentucky	49	Arkansas	49
Wisconsin	14.8	17.7	26.3	Arkansas	50	Arkansas	50	Mississippi	49
Wyoming	17.2	18.8	24.1	West Virginia	51	West Virginia	51	West Virginia	51
United States	16.2	20.3	28.2	United States	–	United States	–	United States	–

Source: U.S. Census Bureau, 1980 Census of Population; U.S. Census Bureau, 1990 Census of Population; U.S. Census Bureau, Census 2010

231

One-Person Households

Area	Percent of Population			1980		1990		2010	
	1980	1990	2010	Area	Rank	Area	Rank	Area	Rank
Alabama	20.4	23.8	27.4	D.C.	1	D.C.	1	D.C.	1
Alaska	20.1	22.1	25.6	New York	2	New York	2	North Dakota	2
Arizona	20.9	24.7	26.1	California	3	Colorado	3	Montana	3
Arkansas	21.3	24.0	27.1	Nevada	4	Nebraska	4	Rhode Island	4
California	24.7	23.4	23.3	Massachusetts	5	North Dakota	4	South Dakota	5
Colorado	23.5	26.6	27.9	Nebraska	6	South Dakota	6	New York	6
Connecticut	21.6	24.2	27.3	Washington	7	Montana	7	Ohio	7
Delaware	20.9	23.2	25.6	Illinois	8	Rhode Island	8	Massachusetts	8
D.C.	39.5	41.5	44.0	Rhode Island	8	Missouri	9	Nebraska	8
Florida	23.6	25.5	27.2	Kansas	10	Kansas	10	Maine	10
Georgia	20.5	22.7	25.4	Missouri	10	Iowa	10	Pennsylvania	10
Hawaii	17.1	19.4	23.3	Florida	12	Massachusetts	12	Iowa	12
Idaho	19.9	22.4	23.8	Colorado	13	Nevada	13	West Virginia	12
Illinois	24.0	25.7	27.8	Oregon	13	Illinois	13	Missouri	14
Indiana	21.4	24.1	26.9	South Dakota	13	Oklahoma	15	Vermont	15
Iowa	23.4	25.9	28.4	Oklahoma	16	Pennsylvania	15	Wisconsin	15
Kansas	23.8	25.9	27.8	Montana	16	Florida	17	Minnesota	17
Kentucky	20.0	23.3	27.5	Iowa	16	Washington	18	New Mexico	17
Louisiana	21.3	23.7	26.9	Minnesota	19	Oregon	19	Wyoming	17
Maine	21.3	23.3	28.6	North Dakota	20	Minnesota	20	Colorado	20
Maryland	20.8	22.6	26.1	Pennsylvania	21	Ohio	21	Michigan	20
Massachusetts	24.4	25.8	28.7	Wisconsin	22	Arizona	22	Illinois	22
Michigan	21.1	23.7	27.9	Ohio	23	Wyoming	23	Kansas	22
Minnesota	23.2	25.1	28.0	Vermont	24	West Virginia	23	Kentucky	24
Mississippi	20.4	23.4	26.3	Texas	25	Wisconsin	25	Oklahoma	24
Missouri	23.8	26.0	28.3	Connecticut	26	Connecticut	26	Alabama	26
Montana	23.4	26.3	29.7	Indiana	27	Indiana	27	Oregon	26
Nebraska	24.3	26.5	28.7	Wyoming	28	Arkansas	28	Connecticut	28
Nevada	24.6	25.7	25.7	Louisiana	28	Texas	29	Florida	29
New Hampshire	21.2	22.0	25.6	Arkansas	28	Tennessee	29	Washington	29
New Jersey	21.1	23.1	25.2	Maine	28	Alabama	31	Arkansas	31
New Mexico	21.0	23.0	28.0	New Hampshire	32	Louisiana	32	North Carolina	32
New York	26.0	27.2	29.1	New Jersey	33	Michigan	32	Indiana	33
North Carolina	20.0	23.7	27.0	Michigan	33	North Carolina	32	Louisiana	33
North Dakota	22.9	26.5	31.5	New Mexico	35	California	35	Tennessee	33
Ohio	22.4	25.0	28.9	Arizona	36	Vermont	35	South Carolina	36
Oklahoma	23.4	25.6	27.5	Delaware	36	Mississippi	35	Mississippi	37
Oregon	23.5	25.3	27.4	Maryland	38	Kentucky	38	Arizona	38
Pennsylvania	22.7	25.6	28.6	West Virginia	39	Maine	38	Maryland	38
Rhode Island	24.0	26.2	29.6	Virginia	40	Delaware	40	Virginia	40
South Carolina	19.2	22.4	26.5	Georgia	40	New Jersey	41	Nevada	41
South Dakota	23.5	26.4	29.4	Mississippi	42	New Mexico	42	Alaska	42
Tennessee	20.4	23.9	26.9	Alabama	42	Virginia	43	Delaware	42
Texas	21.7	23.9	24.2	Tennessee	42	Georgia	44	New Hampshire	42
Utah	17.2	18.9	18.7	Alaska	45	Maryland	45	Georgia	45
Vermont	22.0	23.4	28.2	North Carolina	46	Idaho	46	New Jersey	46
Virginia	20.5	22.9	26.0	Kentucky	46	South Carolina	46	Texas	47
Washington	24.2	25.4	27.2	Idaho	48	Alaska	48	Idaho	48
West Virginia	20.7	24.5	28.4	South Carolina	49	New Hampshire	49	California	49
Wisconsin	22.5	24.3	28.2	Utah	50	Hawaii	50	Hawaii	49
Wyoming	21.3	24.5	28.0	Hawaii	51	Utah	51	Utah	51
United States	22.7	24.6	26.7	United States	–	United States	–	United States	–

Source: U.S. Census Bureau, 1980 Census of Population; U.S. Census Bureau, 1990 Census of Population; U.S. Census Bureau, Census 2010

Homeownership

Area	Percent of Population			1980		1990		2010	
	1980	1990	2010	Area	Rank	Area	Rank	Area	Rank
Alabama	70.1	70.5	69.7	West Virginia	1	West Virginia	1	West Virginia	1
Alaska	58.3	56.1	63.1	Michigan	2	Minnesota	2	Minnesota	2
Arizona	68.3	64.2	66.0	Idaho	3	Mississippi	3	Iowa	3
Arkansas	70.5	69.6	66.9	Iowa	4	Michigan	4	Michigan	3
California	55.9	55.6	56.0	Indiana	5	Pennsylvania	5	Delaware	5
Colorado	64.5	62.2	65.5	Minnesota	5	Alabama	6	Maine	6
Connecticut	63.9	65.6	67.5	Mississippi	7	Maine	6	New Hampshire	7
Delaware	69.1	70.2	72.0	Maine	8	Delaware	8	Vermont	8
D.C.	35.5	38.9	42.0	Utah	9	Indiana	8	Utah	9
Florida	68.3	67.2	67.3	Oklahoma	9	Idaho	10	Idaho	10
Georgia	65.0	64.9	65.7	Arkansas	11	Iowa	11	Indiana	11
Hawaii	51.7	53.9	57.7	Kansas	12	South Carolina	12	Alabama	12
Idaho	72.0	70.1	69.9	South Carolina	12	Arkansas	13	Mississippi	13
Illinois	62.6	64.2	67.4	Alabama	14	Kentucky	13	Pennsylvania	13
Indiana	71.7	70.2	69.8	Kentucky	15	Vermont	15	South Carolina	15
Iowa	71.8	70.0	72.1	Pennsylvania	16	Missouri	16	Wyoming	15
Kansas	70.2	67.9	67.7	Missouri	17	New Hampshire	17	Missouri	17
Kentucky	70.0	69.6	68.7	South Dakota	18	Utah	18	Kentucky	18
Louisiana	65.5	65.9	67.3	Wyoming	19	Oklahoma	18	New Mexico	19
Maine	70.9	70.5	71.3	Delaware	20	North Carolina	20	Tennessee	20
Maryland	62.0	65.0	67.5	Vermont	21	Tennessee	20	South Dakota	21
Massachusetts	57.5	59.3	62.3	North Dakota	21	Kansas	22	Wisconsin	21
Michigan	72.7	71.0	72.1	Montana	23	Wyoming	23	Montana	23
Minnesota	71.7	71.8	73.1	Tennessee	23	Ohio	24	Kansas	24
Mississippi	71.0	71.5	69.6	Nebraska	25	New Mexico	25	Ohio	25
Missouri	69.6	68.8	68.8	Ohio	25	Montana	26	Connecticut	26
Montana	68.6	67.3	68.0	North Carolina	25	Florida	27	Maryland	26
Nebraska	68.4	66.5	67.2	Arizona	28	Wisconsin	28	Illinois	28
Nevada	59.6	54.8	58.8	Florida	28	Nebraska	29	Florida	29
New Hampshire	67.6	68.2	70.9	Wisconsin	30	Virginia	30	Louisiana	29
New Jersey	62.0	64.9	65.4	New Mexico	31	South Dakota	31	Oklahoma	29
New Mexico	68.1	67.4	68.5	New Hampshire	32	Louisiana	32	Nebraska	32
New York	48.6	52.2	53.3	Washington	33	Connecticut	33	Virginia	32
North Carolina	68.4	68.0	66.7	Virginia	33	North Dakota	33	Arkansas	34
North Dakota	68.7	65.6	65.4	Louisiana	35	Maryland	35	North Carolina	35
Ohio	68.4	67.5	67.6	Oregon	36	New Jersey	36	Arizona	36
Oklahoma	70.7	68.1	67.3	Georgia	37	Georgia	36	Georgia	37
Oregon	65.1	63.1	62.1	Colorado	38	Arizona	38	Colorado	38
Pennsylvania	69.9	70.6	69.6	Texas	39	Illinois	38	New Jersey	39
Rhode Island	58.8	59.5	60.7	Connecticut	40	Oregon	40	North Dakota	39
South Carolina	70.2	69.8	69.3	Illinois	41	Washington	41	Washington	41
South Dakota	69.3	66.1	68.1	New Jersey	42	Colorado	42	Texas	42
Tennessee	68.6	68.0	68.2	Maryland	42	Texas	43	Alaska	43
Texas	64.3	60.9	63.7	Nevada	44	Rhode Island	44	Massachusetts	44
Utah	70.7	68.1	70.5	Rhode Island	45	Massachusetts	45	Oregon	45
Vermont	68.7	69.0	70.7	Alaska	46	Alaska	46	Rhode Island	46
Virginia	65.6	66.3	67.2	Massachusetts	47	California	47	Nevada	47
Washington	65.6	62.6	63.9	California	48	Nevada	48	Hawaii	48
West Virginia	73.6	74.1	73.4	Hawaii	49	Hawaii	49	California	49
Wisconsin	68.2	66.7	68.1	New York	50	New York	50	New York	50
Wyoming	69.2	67.8	69.3	D.C.	51	D.C.	51	D.C.	51
United States	64.4	64.2	65.1	United States	–	United States	–	United States	–

Source: U.S. Census Bureau, 1980 Census of Population; U.S. Census Bureau, 1990 Census of Population; U.S. Census Bureau, Census 2010

Median Home Value

Area	Median Home Value ($)			1980		1990		2010	
	1980	1990	2010	Area	Rank	Area	Rank	Area	Rank
Alabama	33,900	53,700	123,900	Hawaii	1	Hawaii	1	Hawaii	1
Alaska	76,300	94,400	241,400	California	2	California	2	D.C.	2
Arizona	54,800	80,100	168,800	Alaska	3	Connecticut	3	California	3
Arkansas	31,100	46,300	106,300	D.C.	4	Massachusetts	4	New Jersey	4
California	84,500	195,500	370,900	Nevada	5	New Jersey	5	Massachusetts	5
Colorado	64,100	82,700	236,600	Connecticut	6	Rhode Island	6	Maryland	6
Connecticut	65,600	177,800	288,800	Colorado	7	New York	7	New York	7
Delaware	44,400	100,100	243,600	New Jersey	8	New Hampshire	8	Connecticut	8
D.C.	68,800	123,900	426,900	Washington	9	D.C.	9	Washington	9
Florida	45,100	77,100	164,200	Wyoming	10	Maryland	10	Rhode Island	10
Georgia	36,900	71,300	156,200	Maryland	11	Delaware	11	Virginia	11
Hawaii	118,100	245,300	525,400	Utah	12	Nevada	12	Oregon	12
Idaho	45,600	58,200	165,100	Oregon	13	Vermont	13	Delaware	13
Illinois	52,800	80,900	191,800	Arizona	14	Alaska	14	New Hampshire	14
Indiana	37,200	53,900	123,300	Minnesota	15	Washington	15	Alaska	15
Iowa	40,600	45,900	123,400	Illinois	16	Virginia	16	Colorado	16
Kansas	37,800	52,200	127,300	Wisconsin	17	Maine	17	Utah	17
Kentucky	34,200	50,500	121,600	Massachusetts	18	Colorado	18	Vermont	18
Louisiana	43,000	58,500	137,500	Virginia	19	Illinois	19	Minnesota	19
Maine	37,900	87,400	179,100	New Hampshire	19	Arizona	20	Illinois	20
Maryland	58,300	116,500	301,400	Rhode Island	21	Florida	21	Montana	21
Massachusetts	48,400	162,800	334,100	Montana	22	Minnesota	22	Wyoming	22
Michigan	39,000	60,600	123,300	New York	23	Georgia	23	Maine	23
Minnesota	53,100	74,000	194,300	Idaho	23	New Mexico	24	Nevada	24
Mississippi	31,400	45,600	100,100	New Mexico	25	Pennsylvania	25	Wisconsin	25
Missouri	36,700	59,800	139,000	Florida	26	Utah	26	Arizona	26
Montana	46,500	56,600	181,200	Ohio	27	Oregon	27	Pennsylvania	27
Nebraska	38,000	50,400	127,600	Delaware	28	North Carolina	28	Idaho	28
Nevada	68,700	95,700	174,800	North Dakota	29	Ohio	29	Florida	29
New Hampshire	48,000	129,400	243,000	Louisiana	30	Wisconsin	30	New Mexico	30
New Jersey	60,200	162,300	339,200	Vermont	31	Wyoming	31	Georgia	31
New Mexico	45,300	70,100	161,200	Iowa	32	South Carolina	32	North Carolina	32
New York	45,600	131,600	296,500	Texas	33	Michigan	33	Missouri	33
North Carolina	36,000	65,800	154,200	Pennsylvania	33	Missouri	34	Tennessee	33
North Dakota	43,900	50,800	123,000	Michigan	35	Texas	35	South Carolina	35
Ohio	44,900	63,500	134,400	West Virginia	36	Louisiana	36	Louisiana	36
Oklahoma	35,600	48,100	111,400	Nebraska	37	Tennessee	37	Ohio	37
Oregon	56,900	67,100	244,500	Maine	38	Idaho	38	South Dakota	38
Pennsylvania	39,100	69,700	165,500	Kansas	39	Montana	39	Texas	39
Rhode Island	46,800	133,500	254,500	Indiana	40	Indiana	40	Nebraska	40
South Carolina	35,100	61,100	138,100	Georgia	41	Alabama	41	Kansas	41
South Dakota	36,600	45,200	129,700	Missouri	42	Kansas	42	Alabama	42
Tennessee	35,600	58,400	139,000	South Dakota	43	North Dakota	43	Iowa	43
Texas	39,100	59,600	128,100	North Carolina	44	Kentucky	44	Indiana	44
Utah	57,300	68,900	217,200	Oklahoma	45	Nebraska	45	Michigan	44
Vermont	42,200	95,500	216,800	Tennessee	45	Oklahoma	46	North Dakota	46
Virginia	48,000	91,000	249,100	South Carolina	47	West Virginia	47	Kentucky	47
Washington	59,900	93,400	271,800	Kentucky	48	Arkansas	48	Oklahoma	48
West Virginia	38,500	47,900	95,100	Alabama	49	Iowa	49	Arkansas	49
Wisconsin	48,600	62,500	169,400	Mississippi	50	Mississippi	50	Mississippi	50
Wyoming	59,800	61,600	180,100	Arkansas	51	South Dakota	51	West Virginia	51
United States	47,200	79,100	179,900	United States	–	United States	–	United States	–

Source: U.S. Census Bureau, 1980 Census of Population; U.S. Census Bureau, 1990 Census of Population; U.S. Census Bureau, Census 2010.

Median Gross Rent

Area	Median Gross Rent ($/month)			1980		1990		2010	
	1980	1990	2010	Area	Rank	Area	Rank	Area	Rank
Alabama	188	325	667	Alaska	1	Hawaii	1	Hawaii	1
Alaska	368	559	981	Hawaii	2	California	2	D.C.	2
Arizona	264	438	844	Nevada	3	Connecticut	3	California	3
Arkansas	185	328	638	California	4	New Jersey	4	Maryland	4
California	283	620	1,163	New Jersey	5	Massachusetts	5	New Jersey	5
Colorado	252	418	863	Maryland	6	Alaska	6	New York	6
Connecticut	260	598	992	Arizona	7	New Hampshire	7	Virginia	7
Delaware	247	495	952	Connecticut	8	Maryland	8	Massachusetts	8
D.C.	224	479	1,198	Virginia	9	Nevada	9	Connecticut	9
Florida	255	481	947	Oregon	10	Virginia	10	Alaska	10
Georgia	211	433	819	Florida	11	Delaware	10	Delaware	11
Hawaii	311	650	1,291	Massachusetts	11	Rhode Island	12	Nevada	11
Idaho	218	330	683	Washington	13	New York	13	New Hampshire	13
Illinois	246	445	848	Colorado	14	Florida	14	Florida	14
Indiana	218	374	683	Wyoming	14	D.C.	15	Washington	15
Iowa	226	336	629	New Hampshire	16	Vermont	16	Rhode Island	16
Kansas	218	372	682	Michigan	17	Illinois	17	Colorado	17
Kentucky	198	319	613	New York	18	Washington	17	Illinois	18
Louisiana	214	352	736	Delaware	19	Arizona	19	Arizona	19
Maine	216	419	707	Texas	20	Georgia	20	Vermont	20
Maryland	266	548	1,131	Illinois	20	Michigan	21	Georgia	21
Massachusetts	255	580	1,009	Minnesota	22	Minnesota	22	Oregon	22
Michigan	250	423	730	Utah	23	Maine	23	Texas	23
Minnesota	236	422	764	Wisconsin	24	Colorado	24	Utah	24
Mississippi	180	309	672	Iowa	25	Oregon	25	Minnesota	25
Missouri	211	368	682	Ohio	26	Pennsylvania	26	Pennsylvania	26
Montana	200	311	642	D.C.	27	Wisconsin	27	Louisiana	27
Nebraska	213	348	669	Pennsylvania	27	Texas	28	North Carolina	28
Nevada	310	509	952	Vermont	27	North Carolina	29	Michigan	29
New Hampshire	251	549	951	Rhode Island	30	Ohio	30	South Carolina	30
New Jersey	270	592	1,114	Idaho	31	South Carolina	31	Wisconsin	31
New Mexico	215	372	699	Kansas	31	Indiana	32	Maine	32
New York	249	486	1,020	Indiana	31	New Mexico	33	New Mexico	33
North Carolina	205	382	731	Maine	34	Kansas	33	Tennessee	34
North Dakota	206	313	583	New Mexico	35	Utah	35	Wyoming	35
Ohio	225	379	685	Oklahoma	35	Missouri	36	Ohio	36
Oklahoma	215	340	659	Louisiana	37	Tennessee	37	Idaho	37
Oregon	257	408	816	Nebraska	38	Louisiana	38	Indiana	37
Pennsylvania	224	404	763	Georgia	39	Nebraska	39	Kansas	39
Rhode Island	222	489	868	Missouri	39	Oklahoma	40	Missouri	39
South Carolina	206	376	728	South Carolina	41	Iowa	41	Mississippi	41
South Dakota	188	306	591	North Dakota	41	Wyoming	42	Nebraska	42
Tennessee	203	357	697	North Carolina	43	Idaho	43	Alabama	43
Texas	246	395	801	Tennessee	44	Arkansas	44	Oklahoma	44
Utah	235	369	796	Montana	45	Alabama	45	Montana	45
Vermont	224	446	823	Kentucky	46	Kentucky	46	Arkansas	46
Virginia	259	495	1,019	West Virginia	47	North Dakota	47	Iowa	47
Washington	254	445	908	Alabama	48	Montana	48	Kentucky	48
West Virginia	195	303	571	South Dakota	48	Mississippi	49	South Dakota	49
Wisconsin	234	399	715	Arkansas	50	South Dakota	50	North Dakota	50
Wyoming	252	333	693	Mississippi	51	West Virginia	51	West Virginia	51
United States	243	447	855	United States	–	United States	–	United States	–

Source: U.S. Census Bureau, 1980 Census of Population; U.S. Census Bureau, 1990 Census of Population; U.S. Census Bureau, Census 2010

Households Lacking Complete Plumbing Facilities

Area	Percent of Households			1980		1990		2010	
	1980	1990	2010	Area	Rank	Area	Rank	Area	Rank
Alabama	5.2	1.6	3.6	Alaska	1	Alaska	1	Alaska	1
Alaska	12.2	12.5	11.9	Kentucky	2	Maine	2	West Virginia	2
Arizona	2.6	1.9	2.3	Mississippi	3	New Mexico	3	Maine	3
Arkansas	5.3	1.8	4.3	West Virginia	4	West Virginia	3	New Mexico	4
California	1.4	0.6	1.1	Maine	5	Kentucky	5	Arkansas	5
Colorado	1.8	0.8	1.3	Arkansas	6	Vermont	6	Mississippi	5
Connecticut	1.4	0.4	1.1	North Carolina	7	Mississippi	7	Montana	7
Delaware	2.0	0.6	1.6	Alabama	7	South Dakota	8	Louisiana	8
D.C.	2.4	0.8	2.2	Virginia	9	North Dakota	8	Alabama	9
Florida	1.2	0.5	1.4	South Carolina	9	Arizona	10	Kentucky	10
Georgia	3.8	1.1	2.2	New Mexico	11	Montana	10	Oklahoma	11
Hawaii	2.3	1.1	1.5	Tennessee	12	Virginia	12	Indiana	12
Idaho	2.0	1.5	1.6	South Dakota	13	Arkansas	12	Michigan	12
Illinois	2.0	0.7	2.1	North Dakota	14	Wyoming	14	Missouri	12
Indiana	2.1	0.7	3.1	Georgia	15	Tennessee	14	South Dakota	12
Iowa	2.4	0.9	1.7	Montana	16	Alabama	14	Pennsylvania	16
Kansas	2.0	0.8	2.3	Vermont	17	Idaho	17	South Carolina	17
Kentucky	7.5	2.9	3.5	Louisiana	18	North Carolina	17	Texas	17
Louisiana	3.1	1.3	3.9	Missouri	19	Wisconsin	19	Vermont	17
Maine	5.8	3.5	4.7	New York	20	South Carolina	19	North Carolina	20
Maryland	2.1	0.7	1.5	New Hampshire	20	Louisiana	21	North Dakota	21
Massachusetts	1.7	0.5	1.0	Minnesota	22	Minnesota	21	Tennessee	21
Michigan	1.8	0.8	3.1	Texas	23	Texas	23	Arizona	23
Minnesota	2.8	1.3	2.1	Arizona	23	Missouri	23	Kansas	23
Mississippi	7.2	2.2	4.3	Wisconsin	25	New Hampshire	23	Ohio	23
Missouri	3.0	1.2	3.1	Pennsylvania	25	Hawaii	26	D.C.	26
Montana	3.4	1.9	4.1	D.C.	27	Georgia	26	Georgia	26
Nebraska	1.9	0.8	2.2	Iowa	27	Utah	28	Nebraska	26
Nevada	1.4	0.5	1.2	Hawaii	29	Oklahoma	28	Illinois	29
New Hampshire	2.9	1.2	1.6	Wyoming	29	Pennsylvania	28	Minnesota	29
New Jersey	1.7	0.5	1.2	Indiana	31	New York	31	Virginia	31
New Mexico	4.8	3.2	4.6	Maryland	31	Washington	31	Rhode Island	32
New York	2.9	0.9	1.6	Illinois	33	Oregon	31	Wyoming	32
North Carolina	5.2	1.5	2.5	Idaho	33	Iowa	31	Wisconsin	34
North Dakota	4.2	2.0	2.4	Kansas	33	Colorado	35	Iowa	35
Ohio	2.0	0.8	2.3	Oklahoma	33	D.C.	35	Delaware	36
Oklahoma	2.0	1.0	3.2	Delaware	33	Kansas	35	Idaho	36
Oregon	1.8	0.9	1.3	Ohio	33	Nebraska	35	New Hampshire	36
Pennsylvania	2.5	1.0	2.7	Rhode Island	39	Michigan	35	New York	36
Rhode Island	1.9	0.5	1.9	Nebraska	39	Ohio	35	Hawaii	40
South Carolina	5.1	1.4	2.6	Colorado	41	Illinois	41	Maryland	40
South Dakota	4.3	2.0	3.1	Oregon	41	Maryland	41	Washington	40
Tennessee	4.6	1.6	2.4	Michigan	41	Indiana	41	Florida	43
Texas	2.6	1.2	2.6	New Jersey	44	California	44	Colorado	44
Utah	1.1	1.0	1.2	Washington	44	Delaware	44	Oregon	44
Vermont	3.3	2.3	2.6	Massachusetts	44	Florida	46	Nevada	46
Virginia	5.1	1.8	2.0	California	47	Nevada	46	New Jersey	46
Washington	1.7	0.9	1.5	Nevada	47	New Jersey	46	Utah	46
West Virginia	6.9	3.2	5.2	Connecticut	47	Massachusetts	46	California	49
Wisconsin	2.5	1.4	1.8	Florida	50	Rhode Island	46	Connecticut	49
Wyoming	2.3	1.6	1.9	Utah	51	Connecticut	51	Massachusetts	51
United States	2.7	1.1	2.2	United States	–	United States	–	United States	–

Note: The reader is cautioned against comparing values across decades as the definition of plumbing facilities has changed over time.
Source: U.S. Census Bureau, 1980 Census of Population; U.S. Census Bureau, 1990 Census of Population; U.S. Census Bureau, American Community Survey, 2010 1-Year Estimate

We the Americans:

Issued September 1993

U.S. Department of Commerce
Economics and Statistics Administration
BUREAU OF THE CENSUS

Acknowledgments

This report was prepared by **Claudette E. Bennett,** assisted by **Barbara M. Martin** and **Kymberly DeBarros,** under the supervision of **Roderick J. Harrison,** Chief, Racial Statistics Branch.

General direction was provided by **Susan J. Lapham,** Population Division. The contents of the report were reviewed by **Janice Valdisera** and **Michael Levin,** Population Division, and **Paula Coupe** and **Dwight Johnson,** Public Information Office. **Marie Pees,** Population Division, provided computer programming support. **Debra Niner** and **Mary Kennedy,** Population Division, provided review assistance.

Sampling review was provided by **Alfredo Navarro** of Decennial Statistical Studies Division.

The staff of the Administrative and Publications Services Division, **Walter C. Odom,** Chief, performed publication planning, design, composition, editorial review, and printing planning and procurement. **Cynthia G. Brooks** provided publication coordination and editing. **Kim Blackwell** provided design and graphics services. **Diane Oliff-Michael** coordinated printing services.

For sale by the Superintendent of Documents,
U.S. Government Printing Office,
Washington, DC 20402.

e, the American Women

Introduction

We, the American Women, have experienced dramatic changes over the last three decades. We are increasingly delaying marriage and childbirth to attend college and establish careers. College enrollment of women is now near that of men, but we still choose subjects of study that are different from those of men and less likely to lead to higher-paying jobs.

More of us are in the labor force than ever before and we are more likely to have continuous lifetime work experience. There has been a remarkable increase in the proportion of mothers who work. This is partly a result of noneconomic factors such as changes in the attitudes of society toward working mothers and the desires of women themselves, as well as economic factors such as inflation, recession, and unemployment of husbands.

Most of us meet the usual demands of housework and family care in addition to our work in the labor force. The responsibilities of work and home life have changed little for most married men, while for most wives, home responsibilities follow traditional patterns despite the profound change in their lives outside their families.

We remain in a secondary economic status despite unprecedented change. Over the past few years, we have been spending more years prior to marriage supporting ourselves; in marriage, we have been contributing more to the household income, and a greater number of us have been rearing children alone, often with little or no financial help.

The future course of women is uncertain and remains a challenge to the American economic, political, and social system, and to the American women themselves.

Overall, we outnumber men by 6 million.

In 1990, there were 127,470,455 women in the Nation. That is about 11 million more than a decade earlier. By 2050, there would be 383 million people, about 195 million females. The Baby Boom bulge would have disappeared and the population pyramid would look more like a sky scraper.

In 1990, beginning at age 40, women outnumbered men. The most notable difference occurred in the elderly ages (65 years old and over). Elderly women outnumbered elderly men 3 to 2 (18.7 million versus 12.6 million).

In 2050, the number of elderly women would be 43 million, more than double the number in 1990. About 11 million elderly women would be among the oldest-old (85 years old and over).

From age 25 to 34, we are about the same number as men.

The sex ratio (number of males per 100 females) is a summary measure of the sex composition of the population. More males than females are born each year, and during childhood, there are more males than females.

Males have higher death rates at every age than females. Typically during the young adult years the sex ratio begins to even out.

In 1990, for the 25-to-34-year old group, the proportion of males and females was about the same. For those under 14 years old, the sex ratio was about 105, but for those 65 years old and over, the sex ratio was only 67. In general, the sex ratio has remained constant over time.

Figure 1.

Age Distribution of the Population by Sex: 1990 and 2050

(Percent. Middle series projections)

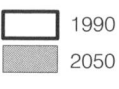
1990
2050

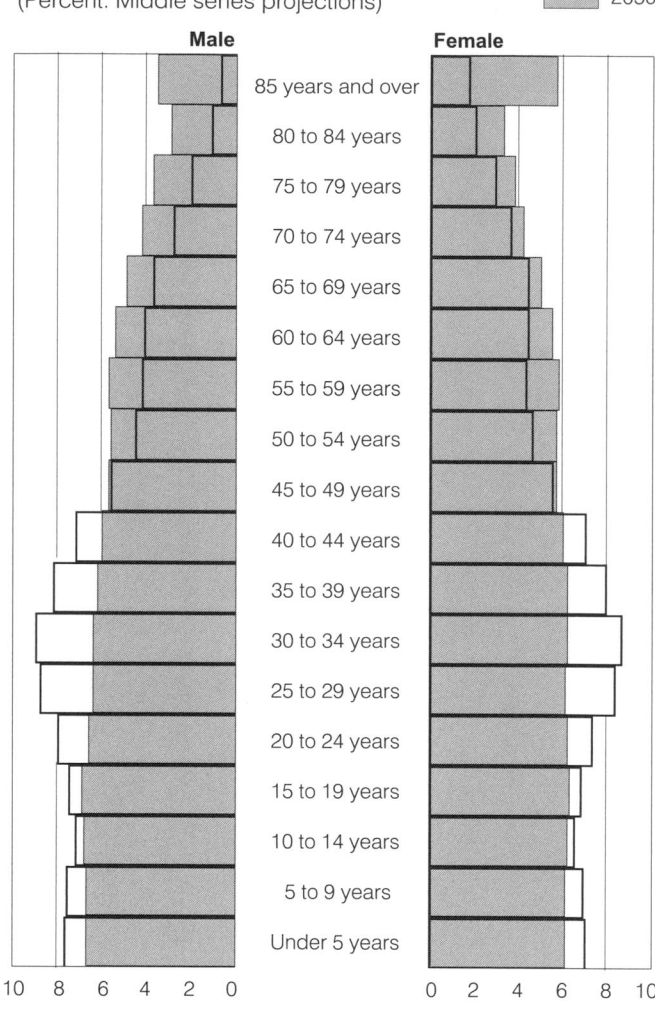

Figure 2.

Sex Ratio of Persons by Age: 1990

(Males per 100 females)

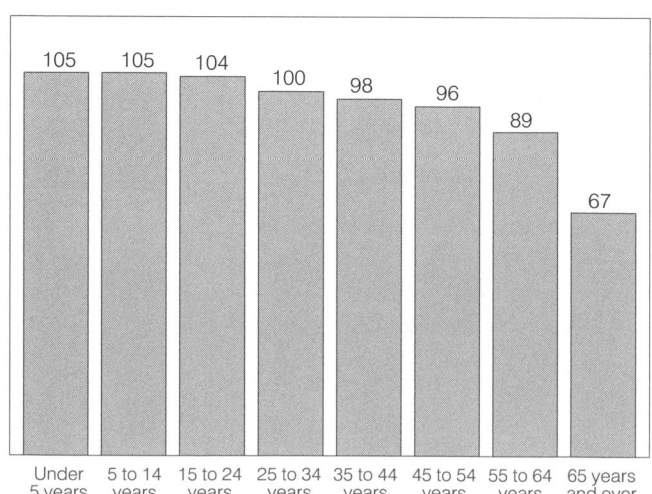

Our life expectancy varies by race, but on average we live longer than men.

As a result of reductions in mortality, there have been impressive increases in life expectancy. Demographers estimate that life expectancy at birth was about 35 years when this Nation was founded and had increased to about 42 years by the mid-1800's.

Life expectancy continued to increase dramatically in the first half of the 20th century, primarily because of decreased mortality among the young.

From 1940 to 1990, life expectancy at birth for men increased from 61 years to 72 years; for women, the increase was from 65 years to nearly 79 years.

Life expectancy at birth increased for Black women from 68 years in 1970 to 74 years in 1990 and for White women from 76 years to 79 years.

In the past few decades, the most recent reductions in mortality have occurred among elderly women.

Figure 3.
Life Expectancy by Sex and Race: 1940 to 1990

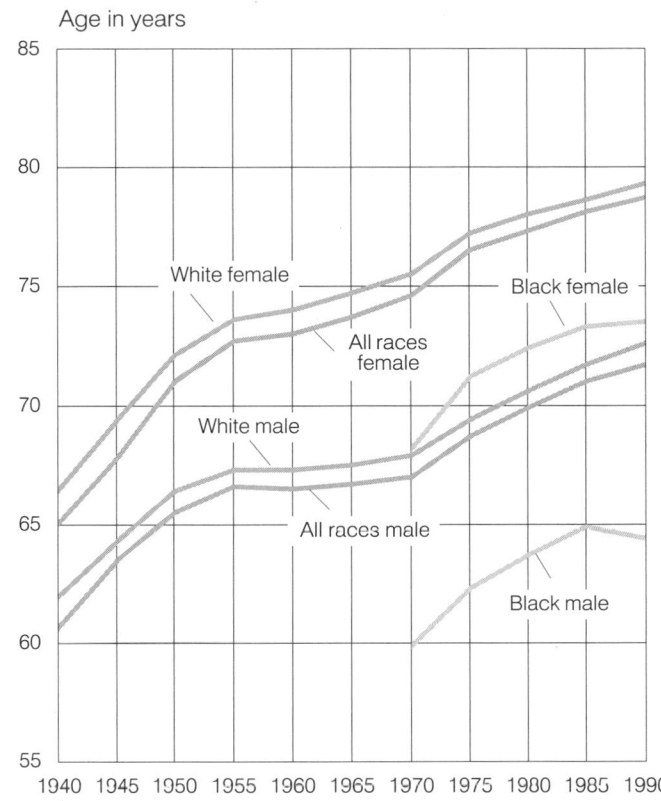

Age in years

We are improving our education, especially at the college level.

As a Nation, a higher proportion of both women and men are earning high school diplomas and college degrees than they did 20 years ago.

In 1990, 75 percent of women and 76 percent of men received a high school diploma. In 1970, about 53 percent of women and 52 percent of men completed high school.

In the last several decades, women have been narrowing the education gap. In 1990, men were more likely to have graduated from college than women (23 percent versus 18 percent). In 1970, 8 percent of women and 14 percent of men completed college.

Figure 4.
Educational Attainment by Sex: 1970, 1980, and 1990

(Percent of persons 25 years old and over)

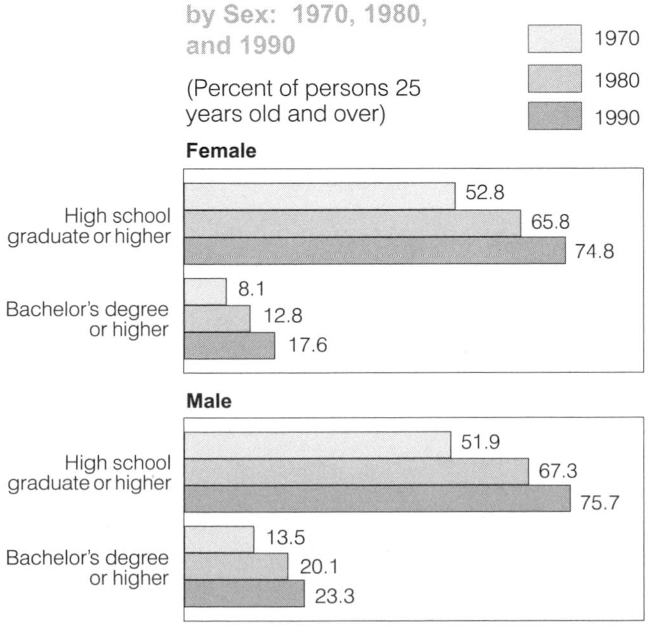

1970
1980
1990

Female

High school graduate or higher
52.8
65.8
74.8

Bachelor's degree or higher
8.1
12.8
17.6

Male

High school graduate or higher
51.9
67.3
75.7

Bachelor's degree or higher
13.5
20.1
23.3

More of us are enrolled in college particularly in our twenties and thirties.

Women have made significant strides in increasing their level of education, making them better qualified for jobs than ever before.

Since 1980, college enrollment of all women 15 to 39 years old has neared that for men, narrowing the significant gap of a decade earlier.

In 1990, about 80 percent of women 15 to 19 years old were enrolled in school compared with about 75 percent in 1980. The most striking difference occurred for women in their thirties. In 1990, 1 of every 5 women were enrolled in school.

Women have been more likely to attend school part time while working or raising families or both.

Figure 5.

School Enrollment for Women by Age: 1980 and 1990

☐ 1980
■ 1990

(Percent enrolled in school)

Age	1980	1990
15 to 19 years	75.3	80.1
20 to 24 years	22.2	33.6
25 to 29 years	9.3	13.6
30 to 34 years	7.0	10.4
35 to 39 years	5.6	10.3

Source: 1990 Census of Population, Public Use Microdata Sample.

We earn over half of all bachelor's degrees.

Women received 53 percent of all the bachelor's degrees awarded in 1990. In 1970, women received 43 percent of all bachelor's degrees conferred.

Women are entering male-dominated fields of study in ever-increasing numbers. For example, in 1970, less than 1 percent of all bachelor's degrees in engineering went to women, but by 1980, 14 percent of all such degrees were awarded to women.

In 1970, relatively few women majored in business and only 9 percent of business degrees went to women. By 1990, almost as many women as men were business majors and fully 47 percent of all business degrees went to women.

Fields such as fine arts and foreign languages continue to be female dominated. However, fewer degrees were awarded in these fields in 1990 than in 1970; women are majoring in fields that offer higher financial remuneration.

Figure 6.

Bachelor's Degrees Conferred to Women: 1969-70 and 1989-90

☐ 1969-70
■ 1989-90

(Percent)

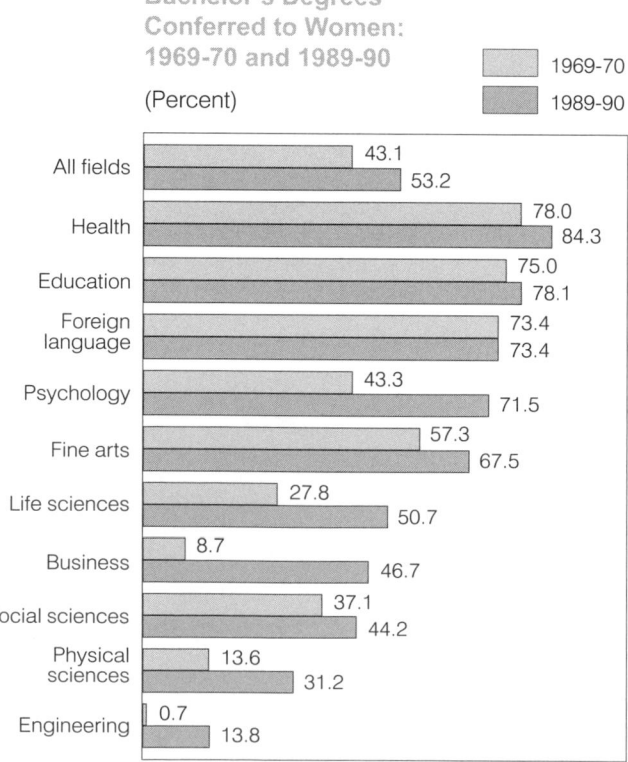

Field	1969-70	1989-90
All fields	43.1	53.2
Health	78.0	84.3
Education	75.0	78.1
Foreign language	73.4	73.4
Psychology	43.3	71.5
Fine arts	57.3	67.5
Life sciences	27.8	50.7
Business	8.7	46.7
Social sciences	37.1	44.2
Physical sciences	13.6	31.2
Engineering	0.7	13.8

Source: U.S. Department of Health and Human Services, National Center for Education Statistics, *Digest of Education Statistics, 1971,* table 117, and *Digest of Education Statistics, 1992,* table 234.

Many of us are delaying marriage.

Marriage and childbirth are being delayed while women go to college or establish themselves in the labor force. In 1990, 63 percent of all women in their early twenties had not yet married compared with only 36 percent in 1970.

The most dramatic increase in the proportion of never-married women occurred among women in their late twenties and early thirties. In 1970, 11 percent of women 25 to 29 years old and only 6 percent of women 30 to 34 years old had not married. By 1990, the proportion nearly tripled to 31 percent for women in their late twenties and 16 percent for women in their early thirties.

Figure 7.
Never-Married Women by
Age: 1970 to 1990

(Percent of never-married females
18 years old and over)

1970
1980
1990

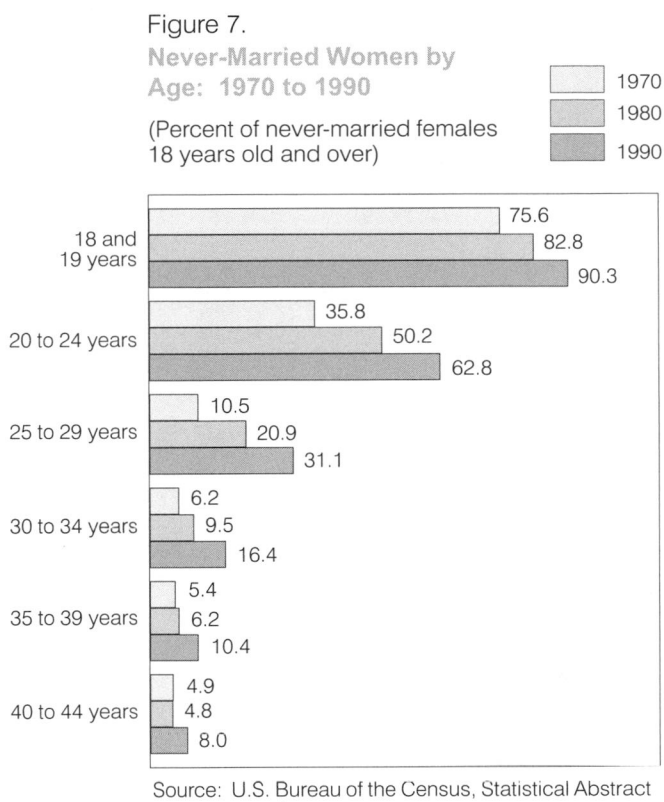

Source: U.S. Bureau of the Census, Statistical Abstract
of the United States: 1992.

**Increasing proportions of us
are divorced.**

Divorce has become much more common in the past 20 years. In 1970, just 4 percent of women and 3 percent of men reported their current marital status as divorced. By 1990, 10 percent of women and 7 percent of men were divorced.

The proportion of women who had never married also increased between 1970 and 1990, from 21 percent to 23 percent. At the same time, the proportion of married women decreased from 63 percent to 55 percent.

Because women live longer than men, it is not surprising that 12 percent of women and only 3 percent of men reported their marital status as widowed.

Figure 8.
Marital Status by Sex: 1970, 1980, and 1990

(Percent of persons 15 years
old and over)

1970
1980
1990

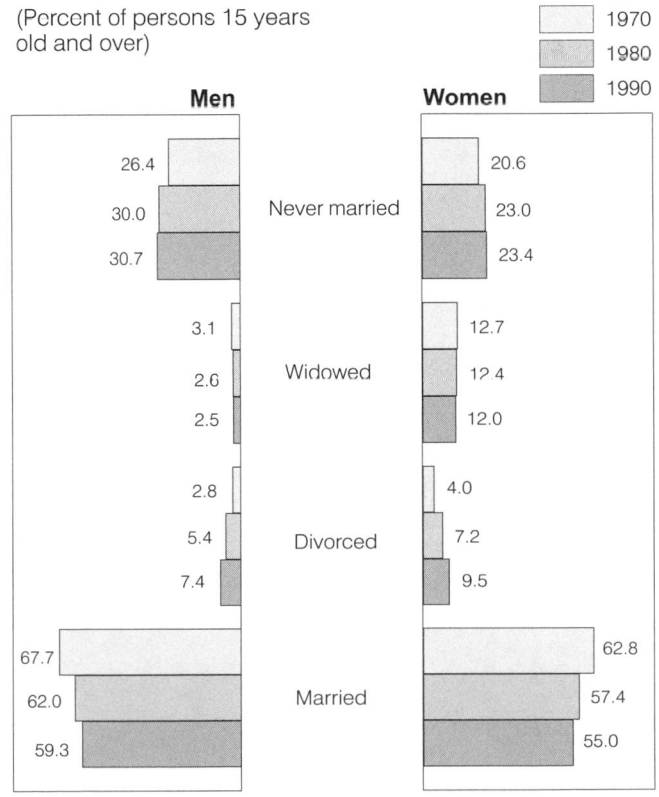

We are having children later in life.

In 1990, there were about 4,158,200 babies born in the United States. This number was the highest reported since 1962 (4,167,362), near the end of the Baby Boom.

In 1990, the birth rate for women 30 to 34 years old was the highest it has been in the past two decades (81 per 1,000 women). During the past decade, birth rates for women in this age group have increased more than any other age group. Women 35 to 39 had the next highest increase. Their birth rate was the highest it has been since 1971.

Between 1980 and 1990, women 20 to 24 years old experienced the smallest increase in birth rates (115.1 to 116.5).

Figure 9.

Birth Rates by Age of Mother: 1970, 1980, and 1990

	1970
	1980
	1990

(Births per 1,000 women)

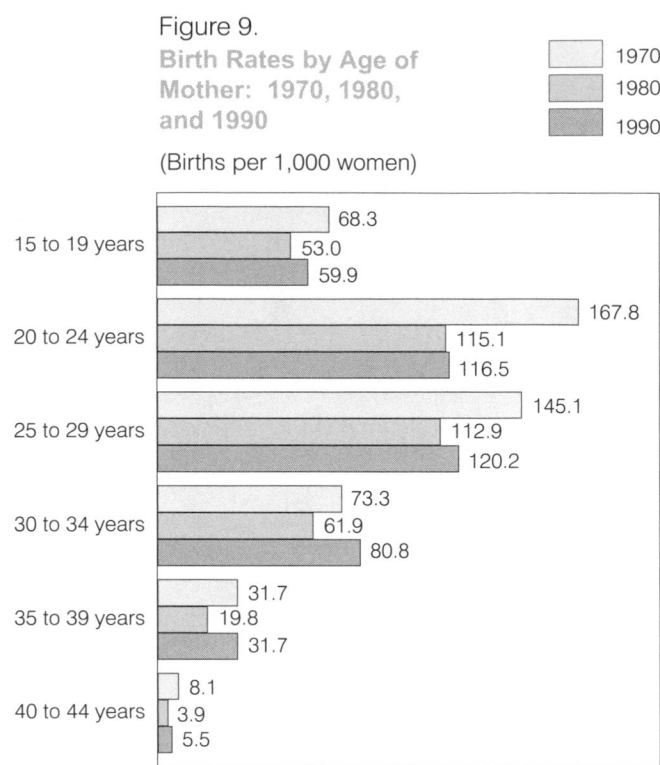

Age	1970	1980	1990
15 to 19 years	68.3	53.0	59.9
20 to 24 years	167.8	115.1	116.5
25 to 29 years	145.1	112.9	120.2
30 to 34 years	73.3	61.9	80.8
35 to 39 years	31.7	19.8	31.7
40 to 44 years	8.1	3.9	5.5

Source: Monthly Vital Statistics Report, Vol. 41, No. 9 Supplement, Advance Report of Final Natality Statistics, 1990 (February 25, 1993).

Many of us are maintaining families without a husband.

The proportion of families maintained by women has increased steadily since 1970, although the increases in the 1980's were at a slower rate.

The proportion of families maintained by women is higher for Blacks than for any other race group or women of Hispanic origin. Between 1970 and 1990, Blacks also had the greatest increase in the proportion of families maintained by women.

In 1990, the racial groups with the smallest proportions of families maintained by women were Whites (13 percent) and Asian and Pacific Islanders (12 percent).

The proportion of families maintained by Hispanic women increased from 14 percent in 1970 to 22 percent in 1990.

Figure 10.

Families Maintained by Women, by Race and Hispanic Origin: 1970, 1980, and 1990

	1970
	1980
	1990

(Percent)

	1970	1980	1990
All races	10.8	14.3	16.5
White	9.0	11.2	12.7
Black	27.4	37.8	43.7
American Indian, Eskimo, and Aleut	NA	23.4	27.3
Asian and Pacific Islander	NA	11.0	12.2
Hispanic origin (of any race)	13.7	19.9	22.2

NA (Not available)

In 1990, 13.4 million of us lived alone.

In 1990, 13.4 million female householders and 9.2 million male householders lived alone. Persons living alone accounted for one-fourth of all households in 1990.

Elderly women were more likely than elderly men to live by themselves. In 1990, 52 percent of all women living alone were elderly, while only 21 percent of men living alone were elderly.

Only 21 percent of women living alone were 25 to 44 years old compared with 48 percent of males living alone. Women in this age group who were not currently married were more likely to have children in their households than their male counterparts.

We continue to increase our participation in the labor force.

The majority of adult women are at work or looking for work. In 1990, the number of women with full time year round jobs was 28.7 million. The proportion of women 16 years old and over in the labor force increased from 50 percent in 1980 to 57 percent in 1990.

The increased employment of women is a central issue in the consideration of the economic status of women in our society. Despite the fact that there has been no discernible reduction in household and family responsibilities, women have joined the labor force in record numbers.

Women of every race group, as well as Hispanic women (who may be of any race), increased their labor force participation rates between 1980 and 1990. In 1980 and 1990, Asian and Pacific Islander women and Black women had the highest labor force participation rates. American Indian, Eskimo, and Aleut women had the lowest. The range of variation among the race groups diminished between 1980 and 1990, however.

Figure 11.

Persons Living Alone by Sex and Age: 1970, 1980, and 1990

(Percent)

Legend:
- 65 years old and over
- 45 to 64 years old
- 25 to 44 years old
- Under 25 years old

Women

Year	65+	45 to 64	25 to 44	Under 25
1970	51.8	33.9	9.7	4.6
1980	50.5	25.9	16.9	6.7
1990	51.8	23.0	21.3	4.0

Men

Year	65+	45 to 64	25 to 44	Under 25
1970	30.9	31.8	28.6	8.7
1980	20.4	23.7	42.4	13.4
1990	20.6	24.2	48.0	7.2

Figure 12.

Labor Force Participation Rates of Women by Race and Hispanic Origin: 1980 and 1990

(Females 16 years old and over)

Legend:
- 1980
- 1990

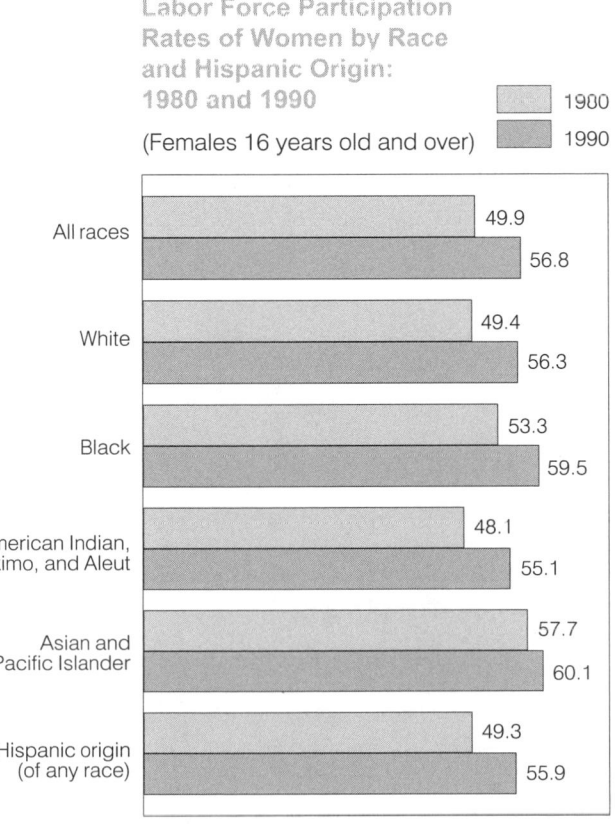

Race	1980	1990
All races	49.9	56.8
White	49.4	56.3
Black	53.3	59.5
American Indian, Eskimo, and Aleut	48.1	55.1
Asian and Pacific Islander	57.7	60.1
Hispanic origin (of any race)	49.3	55.9

245

We are not equally represented in all professions.

The distribution of both women and men across occupations has changed, sometimes dramatically, since 1970. Despite some evidence of female carpenters and male nurses, the overall labor market remains sharply segregated by sex.

Even though women have made progress in entering occupations predominately held by men in the past, especially managerial and professional specialty occupations, the majority of women are still in traditional "female" occupations.

Women continue to be overrepresented in clerical (administrative support) and service occupations and underrepresented in production, craft, repair, and labor occupations.

Figure 13.

Percentage Of Persons in Occupations by Sex: 1990

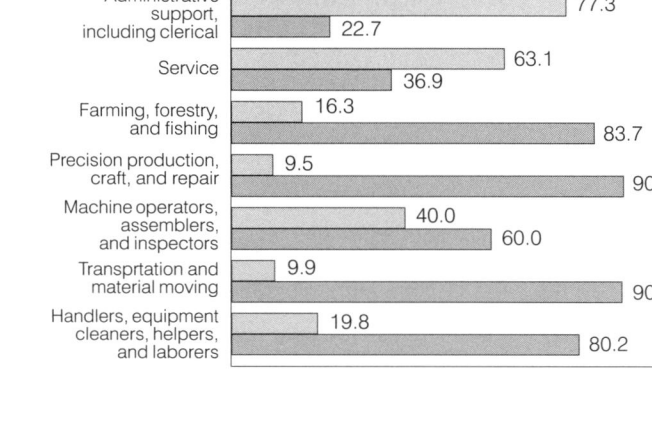

Those of us who maintain families without husbands have significantly lower incomes.

Few statistics about women reveal as much about their place in the economy as income data. The economic position of women is considerably lower than that of men.

In 1989, the median family income for families with a female householder, no husband present was $17,414, significantly less than the median family income for married-couple families ($39,584).

During the 1980's, the median income of married-couple families rose at a faster rate than that of families with a female householder, no husband present.

Figure 14.

Number and Median Income of Families: 1969, 1979, and 1989

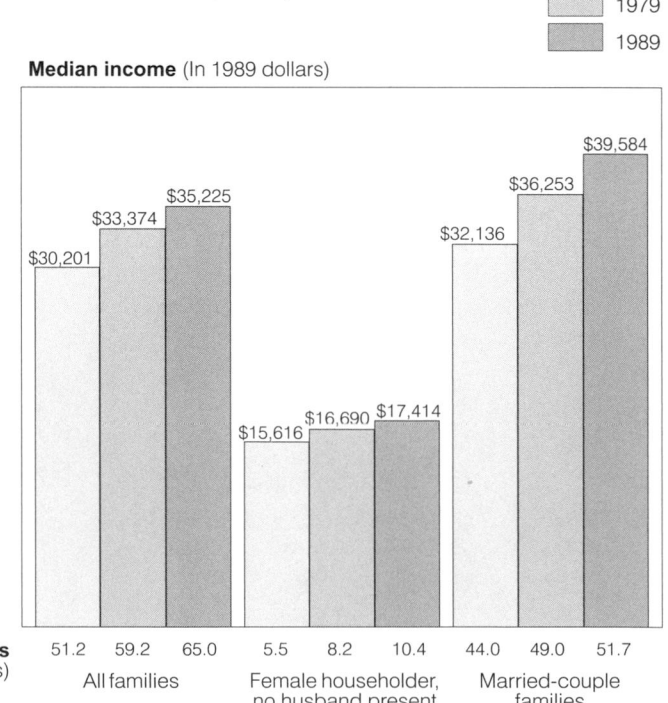

We are nearly six times as likely to be living in poverty than married-couple families.

Women who maintain families with no husband present are more likely to be poor than married-couple families. Families maintained by a women had a poverty rate of 31.1 percent in 1989 and accounted for nearly half of all poor families.

Not only is the poverty rate of families maintained by women much higher than that for other families, but also the rate for Black female householders with no husband present is higher than that of their White counterparts.

Since the mid-1960's, even with major changes in the economy over this period, there has been relatively little fluctuation in the poverty rates for families maintained by women.

Figure 15.

Poverty Rates of Families by Type: 1969, 1979, 1989

(Percent)

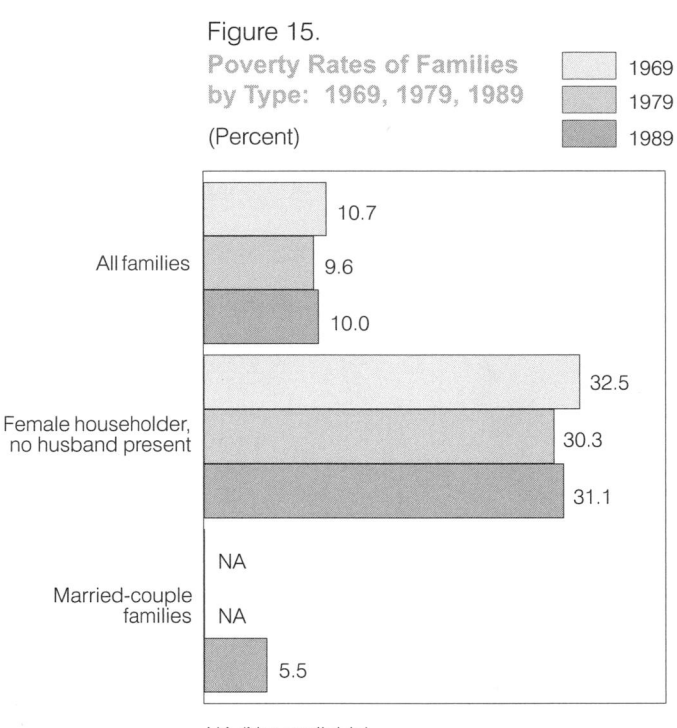

NA (Not available)

At all age groups, we have higher poverty rates than men.

Two-thirds of the poor female population in 1989 were either under 18 years old (37 percent) or 65 years old and over (30 percent). The poverty rate for children continues to be higher than that for any other age group and highest for females under 5 years old.

The largest difference between the poverty rates for females and males occurred for the oldest population shown (75 years old and over). The poverty rate for females 75 years old and over was 17.3 percent compared with 10.1 percent for males.

Figure 16.

Poverty Rates of Persons by Age and Sex: 1989

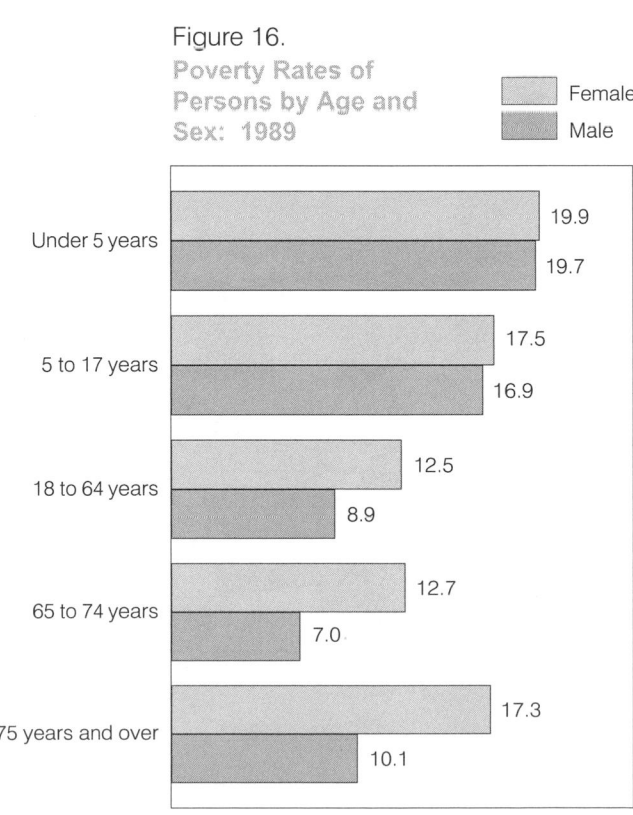

247

e, the American Blacks

Introduction

The 1990 census counted nearly 30 million Blacks, an increase of about 4 million from the 1980 census. Our population grew by 13 percent between 1980 and 1990, to about 12 percent of America's population. Although most of the growth in the Black population is due to natural increase, immigration from Caribbean and African countries also contributed significantly to our growth.

Our life expectancy is increasing and we are growing older, however, our median age continues to be about 6 years lower than that for the White population. Less than one-tenth of our population is 65 years old and over. Black women, like women in most population groups, tend to live longer than Black men.

We are located in all States, ranging from about 2,000 in Vermont to over 2 million in New York. Blacks are largely an urban people; most of us live in cities and in large metropolitan areas. The majority of us live in the 20 largest metropolitan areas of the Nation. More of us are buying our homes, especially in the suburbs.

Between 1980 and 1990, we made significant gains in educational attainment and college enroll-ment. More Black women than Black men have completed college.

The number of Black households, especially female-headed Black households, has increased since 1980, in part because of the increase in divorce and separation rates. As a result, fewer of our children are being reared in two-parent households. Also, consistent with national trends, more of our men and women are choosing not to marry or to live alone.

A higher proportion of Black women than Black men are in the labor force; and there are now more Black females than Black males in the civilian labor force. The number of Blacks employed in professional jobs, such as lawyers, doctors, and engineers has increased.

The median income of Black married-couple families also improved and grew to 83 percent of comparable White families.

In 1989, our per capita income of $8,850 was lower than the national per capita income of $14,140. Poverty levels for Black persons and families were similar at the beginning and end of the decade, in part because of the effect of the recessions during the decade.

In 1790, we numbered about 760,000 and in 1990, we numbered nearly 30 million.

In 1790, when the first census was taken, Blacks numbered about 760,000. In 1860, at the start of the Civil War, the Black population increased to 4.4 million, but the percentage dropped to 14 percent from 19 percent. Most were slaves, with only 488,000 counted as "freemen." By 1900, our population had doubled and reached 8.8 million.

In 1910, about 90 percent of the Black population lived in the South but large numbers began migrating north looking for better job opportunities and living conditions. The Black population reached the 15 million mark in 1950 and was close to 27 million in 1980.

In 1990, the Black population numbered about 30 million and represented 12 percent of the total population, the same proportion as in 1900. The 13-percent population growth between 1980 and 1990 was one-third higher than the national growth of 10 percent.

In 1990, about one-third of the Black population was under 18 years old.

The median age of Blacks in 1990 was 28 years, up from 25 years in 1980. Black males had a lower median age than Black females. A smaller proportion of Black males than Black females were 65 years old and over. This reflects, in part, the higher mortality of Black males.

The Black voting-age population increased to 20.4 million in 1990 from 17.1 million in 1980.

About 47 percent of the Black population were male, and 53 percent were female.

The average life expectancy for a newborn Black baby in 1980 was 68 years, compared with 74 years for a White baby. By 1990, life expectancy for Blacks averaged 69 years, about 6 years less than that for Whites.

Figure 1.
Black Population: 1900 to 1990

(Millions)

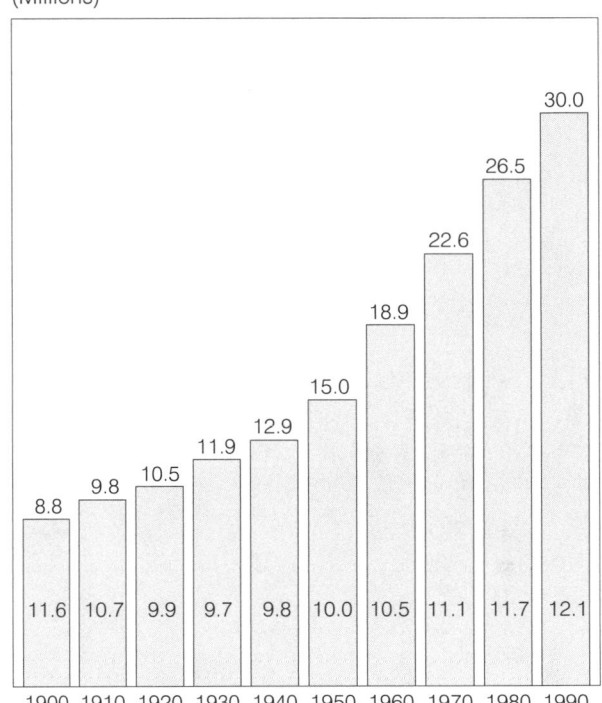

Note: Numbers in bars represent Blacks as a percent of the total population.

Figure 2.
Age and Sex of the Black Population: 1990

(Percent)

	Male			Female	
6.8		65 years and over			9.8
2.9		60 to 64 years		3.5	
3.2		55 to 59 years		3.6	
3.8		50 to 54 years		4.1	
4.5		45 to 49 years		4.8	
6.1		40 to 44 years		6.4	
7.6		35 to 39 years		7.9	
8.8		30 to 34 years		9.0	
9.1		25 to 29 years		9.0	
8.9		20 to 24 years		8.3	
9.5		15 to 19 years		8.3	
9.3		10 to 14 years		8.1	
9.5		5 to 9 years		8.4	
9.9		Under 5 years		8.7	

Median age = 26.6   Median age − 29.5

249

Between 1980 and 1990, the number of Black persons 65 years old and over increased from 2.1 to 2.5 million.

Black women dominated the older age groups. In 1990, 62 percent of Black elderly persons were women, and only 38 percent were men.

The proportion of Blacks who were elderly grew from 7.9 percent in 1980 to 8.4 percent in 1990. In contrast, the elderly were a higher proportion among Whites; they were 14 percent in 1990, up from 12 percent in 1980.

Black elderly persons are located in all States of this country. The regional distribution of Black elderly persons was similar to the distribution of all Blacks in the United States—55 percent of the Black elderly were in the South.

Figure 3.

Black Persons 65 Years Old and Over by Sex for the United States and Regions: 1990

(Percent distribution)

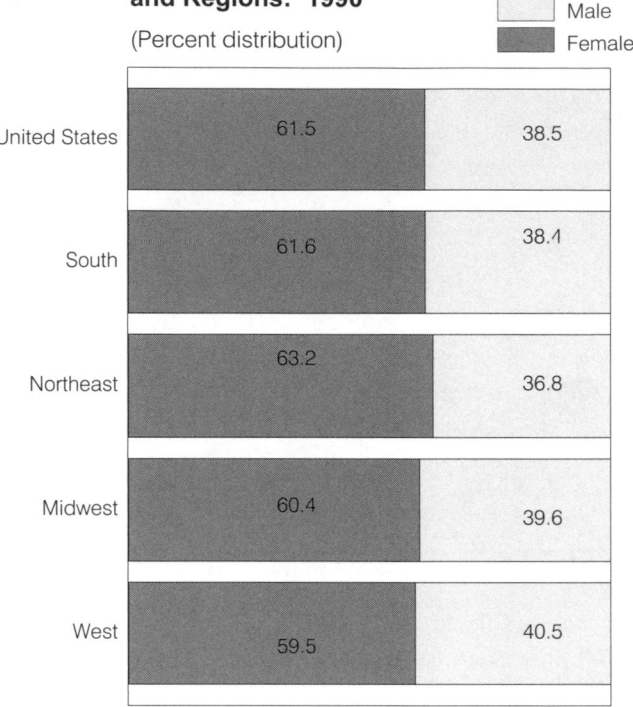

In 1990, most of us live in metropolitan areas.

Nationally, 84 percent of the Black population lived in metropolitan areas in 1990, 57 percent in the central cities, and 27 percent in the suburbs (outside central cities).

In 1990, at least 95 percent of all Blacks in the Northeast, Midwest, and West regions lived in metropolitan areas. In contrast, only 72 percent of those in the South lived in metropolitan areas.

Our suburban population grew by 29 percent between 1980 and 1990, reaching about 7 percent of the Nation's suburban population.

Over one-half of the Black population lived in the South in 1990 — a proportion that has not changed since 1970. The Midwest and Northeast each had 19 percent Black, and 9 percent lived in the West.

Between 1980 and 1990, the Black population growth rate was highest in the West and lowest in the Midwest.

Figure 4.

Black Population in Metropolitan Areas for the United States and Regions: 1990

(Percent distribution)

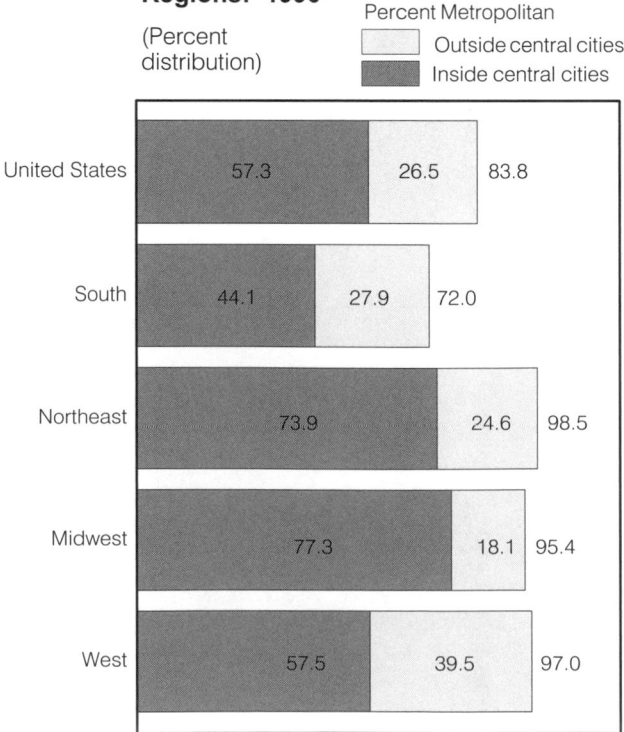

Many of us live in the Nation's largest metropolitan areas.

In 1990, about 40 percent of the Black population resided in just 10 consolidated metropolitan statistical areas (CMSA's) and metropolitan statistical areas (MSA's), nearly the same proportion as in 1980.

Seven of these 10 metropolitan areas were also among the 10 most populous in the Nation.

Blacks represented 20 percent or more of the total population in 4 of these 10 metropolitan areas. For example, Blacks represented 27 percent of all persons residing in the Washington DC, MSA. Although the 10 metropolitan areas were scattered across the country, 5 were located in the South.

Figure 5.
Ten Metropolitan Statistical Areas With the Largest Black Population: 1990

(Thousands)

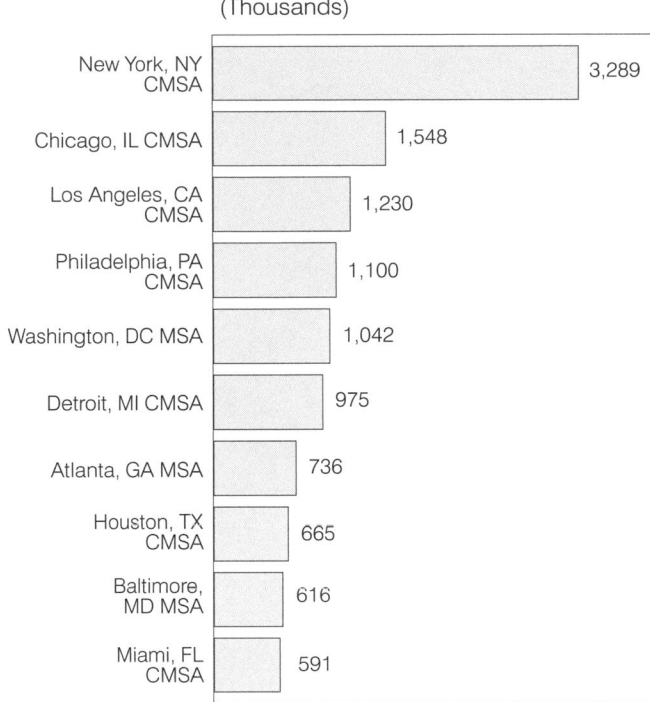

New York, NY CMSA	3,289
Chicago, IL CMSA	1,548
Los Angeles, CA CMSA	1,230
Philadelphia, PA CMSA	1,100
Washington, DC MSA	1,042
Detroit, MI CMSA	975
Atlanta, GA MSA	736
Houston, TX CMSA	665
Baltimore, MD MSA	616
Miami, FL CMSA	591

The cities with the most populous Black populations in both 1990 and 1980 were New York, Chicago, Detroit, and Philadelphia.

Of the 10 cities with the largest Black population, 5 gained population and 5 lost population during the 1980's. New York City had the largest numerical and percentage increase, while Chicago decreased by about 9 percent and Washington, DC lost about 11 percent between 1980 and 1990.

In 5 of these 10 cities, Blacks represented more than 50 percent of the total population. They were Detroit, Washington, DC, New Orleans, Baltimore, and Memphis.

Among the 100 cities with the largest Black populations, the city with the highest proportion of Blacks in both 1980 and 1990 was East St. Louis, Illinois, where 98 percent of its residents were Black.

Figure 6.
Ten Cities With the Largest Black Population: 1990

(Thousands)

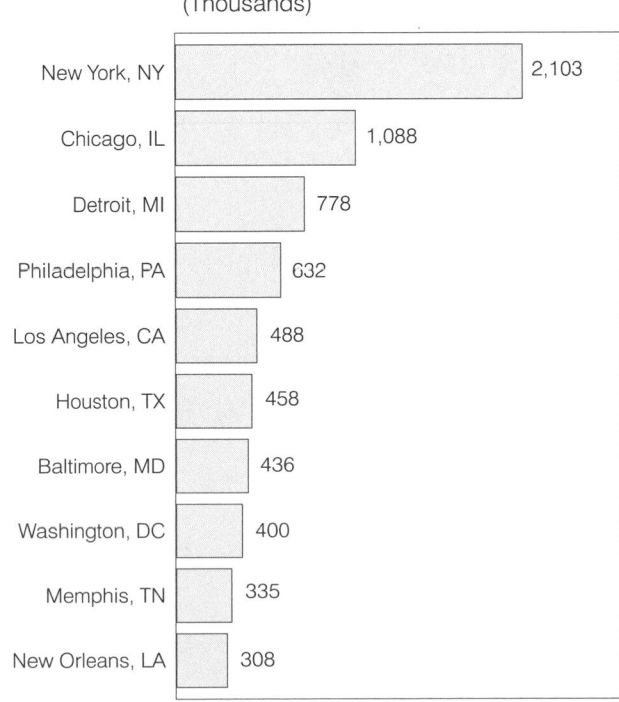

New York, NY	2,103
Chicago, IL	1,088
Detroit, MI	778
Philadelphia, PA	632
Los Angeles, CA	488
Houston, TX	458
Baltimore, MD	436
Washington, DC	400
Memphis, TN	335
New Orleans, LA	308

In 1990, our population was 1 million or more in 16 States.

Blacks were represented in every State in 1990, from about 2,000 in Vermont to 2.9 million in New York, and 16 States had 1 million or more Blacks in 1990. These 16 States were home to 80 percent of the Black population.

Four States, New Jersey, Maryland, South Carolina, and Alabama, reached 1 million between 1980 and 1990. Six of the 10 States with the largest Black populations were in the South.

California and Texas joined New York as the only States with Black populations exceeding 2 million.

Figure 7.
States with a Black Population of 1 Million or More: 1990

(Thousands)

State	Population
New York	2,859
California	2,209
Texas	2,022
Florida	1,760
Georgia	1,747
Illinois	1,694
North Carolina	1,456
Louisiana	1,299
Michigan	1,292
Maryland	1,190
Virginia	1,163
Ohio	1,155
Pennsylvania	1,090
South Carolina	1,040
New Jersey	1,037
Alabama	1,021

In 1990, we were better educated and more of us were staying in school.

The proportion of Blacks 25 years old and over completing high school rose from 51 percent in 1980 to 63 percent in 1990. In 1940, only 7 percent of Blacks 25 years old and over had completed high school. Among the Black population, a slightly higher proportion of females (64 percent) than males (62 percent) had completed high school.

The high school dropout rate for Blacks declined from 16 percent in 1980 to 14 percent in 1990.

In 1990, 2 million Blacks were enrolled in college, 1 1/2 times the number in 1980. Twelve percent of Black females and 11 percent of Black males 25 years old and over had at least a bachelor's degree in 1990.

Eleven percent of Blacks, compared with 22 percent of Whites had earned at least a bachelor's degree in 1990. The corresponding figures for 1980 were 8 percent and 17 percent, respectively.

Figure 8.
Educational Attainment by Sex: 1990

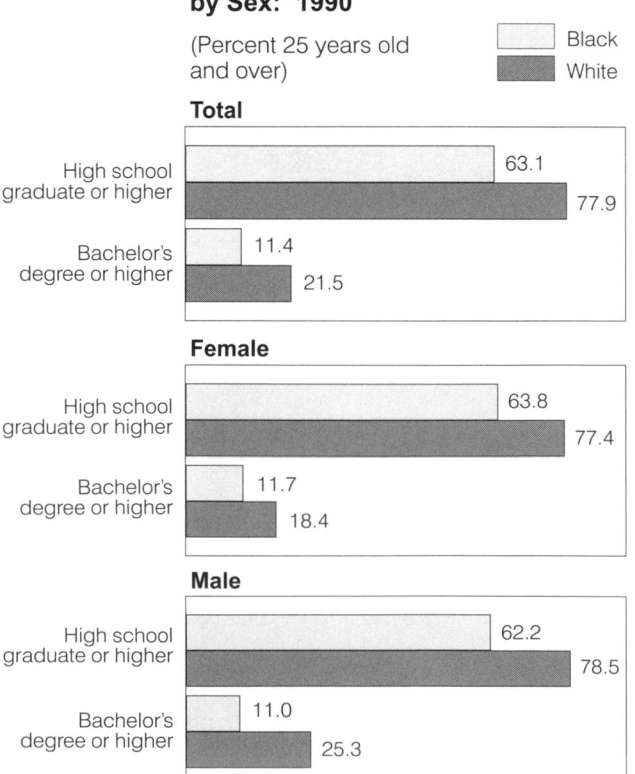

Greater proportions of us are postponing marriage or not marrying at all.

Forty-four percent of Black men were never married in 1990, compared with 41 percent in 1980. For Black women, the figures were 38 percent and 34 percent, respectively.

Since 1980, there has been a 27 percent increase in the number of young Black adults 15 years old and over who never married.

In 1990, a higher proportion of Black men, nearly 4 of every 10, than Black women, about 3 of every 10, were married. In addition, four times as many Black women as Black men were widowed.

The proportion of divorced Black men increased from 6 percent in 1980 to 8 percent in 1990, while the proportion of divorced Black women increased from 9 percent to 11 percent.

A larger proportion of Black women than Black men were separated.

The number of Black families increased from 6 million in 1980 to 7 million in 1990.

Nearly one-half of Black families were married-couple families compared with more than four-fifths of White families.

Our families are not as large as they used to be. The average number of persons per family dropped from 3.7 persons in 1980 to 3.5 persons in 1990.

Since 1980, the number of Black male and Black female nonfamily households (persons living alone or with someone unrelated) increased by 25 percent and 30 percent, respectively.

Single parents have become more common. More than half of Black children under 18 years old lived in one-parent families in 1990, up from 47 percent in 1980.

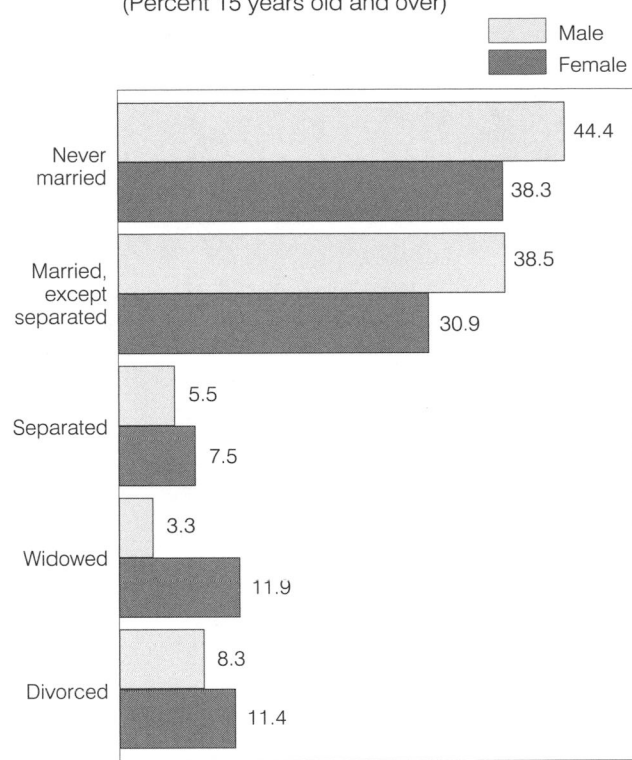

Figure 9.
Marital Status of Blacks by Sex: 1990

(Percent 15 years old and over)

☐ Male
■ Female

Never married — Male 44.4 / Female 38.3
Married, except separated — Male 38.5 / Female 30.9
Separated — Male 5.5 / Female 7.5
Widowed — Male 3.3 / Female 11.9
Divorced — Male 8.3 / Female 11.4

Figuro 10.
Type of Family: 1990

(Percent of families)

☐ Black
■ White

Married-couple families — Black 48.8 / White 83.0
Female householder families, no husband present — Black 43.7 / White 12.7
Male householder families, no wife present — Black 7.5 / White 4.3

We were less likely than Whites to participate in the labor force in 1989.

Of the 21 million Blacks 16 years old and over, 63 percent were in the labor force in 1989, 2 percentage points below the 65 percent rate for both the White and total populations.

Sixty-seven percent of Black males 16 years old and over were in the labor force in 1989 compared with 75 percent of White males.

The proportion of Black women in the labor force increased from 53 percent in 1979 to 60 percent in 1989. Their participation rate was higher than that for White women.

In 1979, the Black unemployment rate was about twice that of Whites. Ten years later, our unemployment rate was more than twice that of Whites, 13 percent and 5 percent, respectively.

In 1990, we numbered 13 million in the labor force.

In 1990, 6.8 million Black women and 6.2 million Black men were in the civilian labor force. More Black men than Black women were in the Armed Forces.

A smaller proportion of Black men than Black Black women were managers and professionals. Larger percentages of Black women also worked in technical, sales, and administrative support and in service occupations than did Black men.

However, a larger proportion of Black men than Black women were employed as operators, fabricators, and laborers; in precision production, craft, and repair jobs; and in farming, forestry, and fishing occupations.

Figure 11.

Labor Force Participation Rates by Sex: 1989

(Percent 16 years old and over)

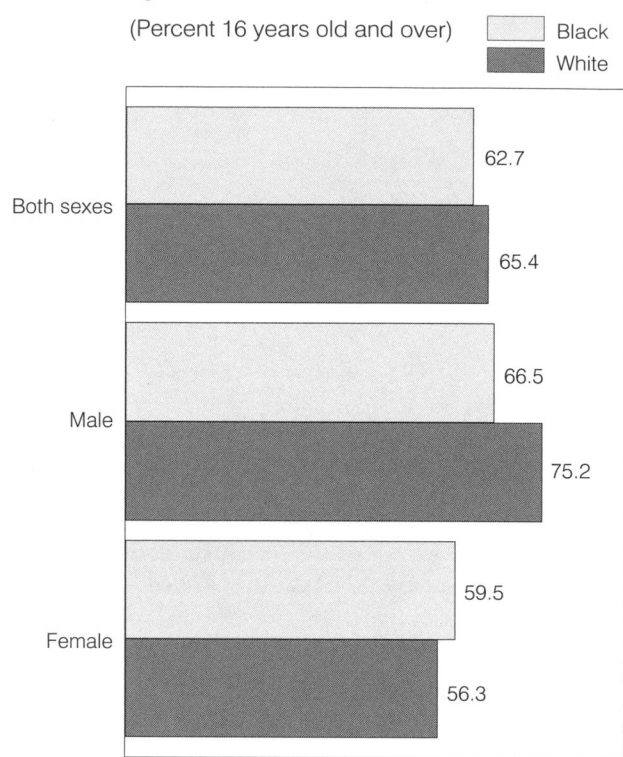

Figure 12.

Major Occupations for Blacks by Sex: 1990

(Percent distribution of employed persons 16 years old and over)

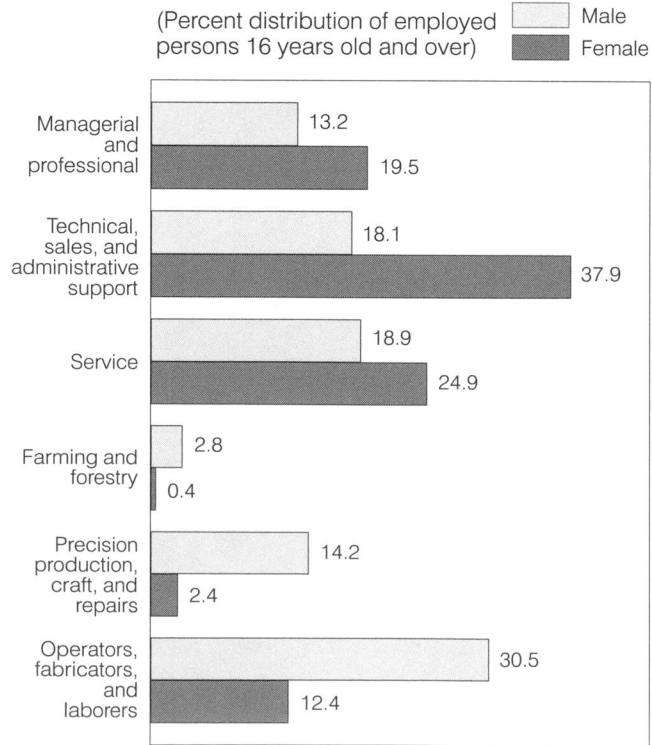

We were heavily concentrated in certain jobs.

In 1990, 22 percent of all Black managers and professionals were teachers. The majority of both Black male and Black female teachers were elementary school teachers.

Nearly 3 out of every 10 Black females employed in technical, sales, and administrative support jobs were cashiers, secretaries, and typists.

Half of Black females employed in service occupations were nursing aides, orderlies and attendants, cooks, janitors, and cleaners.

Thirty-one percent of Black males were operators, fabricators, and laborers. Of these, 30 percent were truckdrivers, assemblers, and stock handlers and baggers. Within service occupations, 45 percent of Black males were employed as janitors and cleaners or as cooks; and 12 percent as guards and police, except public service.

Figure 13.

Selected Occupational Groups for Blacks by Sex: 1990

(Thousands)

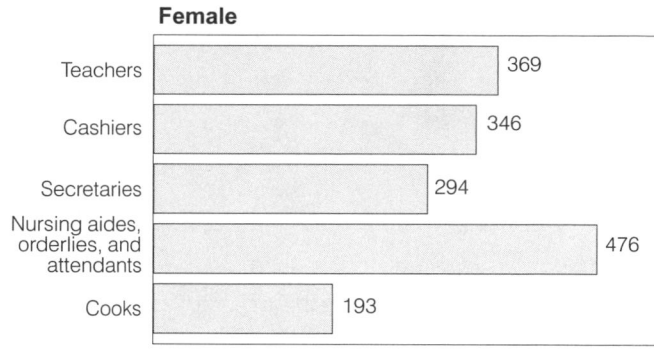

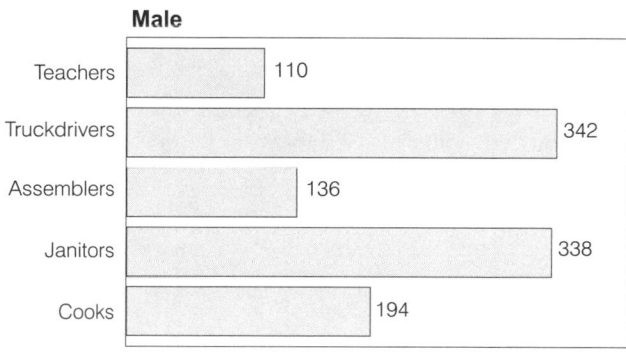

Our income reflects our education, our job opportunities, and our family composition.

In 1989, the median income for all Black families was $22,430 and it was about $21,110 in 1979. Family income reflects several factors, such as family composition, the number of workers in the family, educational attainment, and job opportunities.

The 1989 median income for Black families maintained by women was only $12,520, 37 percent of the $33,540 median income for Black married-couple families.

The large number of Black families maintained by women with no husband present and the often low incomes of these families contributed to the lack of improvement in the median family income of Blacks.

Thirty-three percent of Black families had one worker in 1989, 37 percent had two workers, and 13 percent had three or more workers.

Figure 14.

Median Family Income by Type of Family for Blacks: 1979 and 1989

(In 1989 dollars)

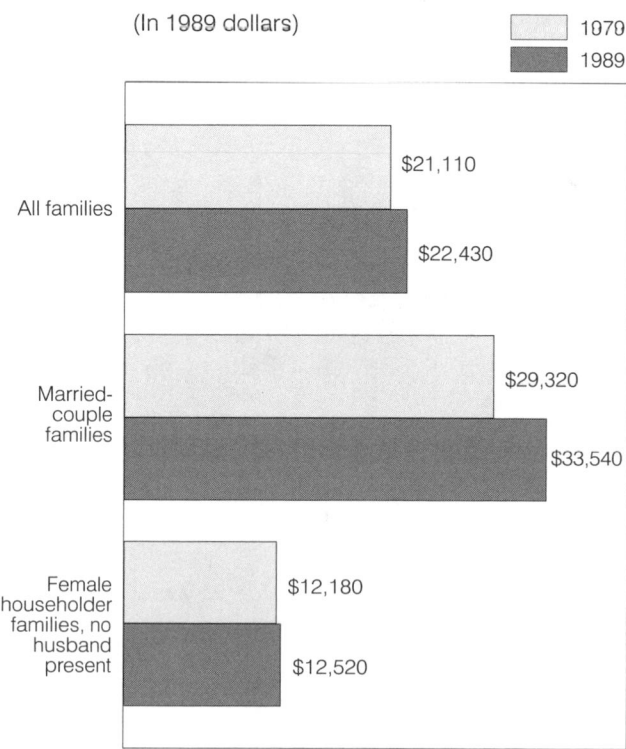

Our poverty rates improved only slightly between 1979 and 1989, from 29.9 percent to 29.5 percent.

We made significant progress in several areas during the past decade, but partially due to recessions, our poverty rates from 1979 to 1989 declined by less than half a percentage point.

In 1989, 8.4 million Black persons were poor, compared with 19.0 million Whites. The poverty rate for Whites was 10 percent in 1989 and 9 percent in 1979.

About 2 million, or 26 percent, of all Black families had money incomes below the poverty level in 1989.

In 1989, 45 percent of Black female householders and 11 percent of married-couple families were poor. These family types accounted for 94 percent of all poor Black families. The corresponding figures for White families were 23 percent and 5 percent.

Note: The Federally defined poverty level does not include noncash benefits such as housing, food, and medical assistance.

Figure 15.
Poverty Rates for Black Persons and Families: 1989

(Percent)

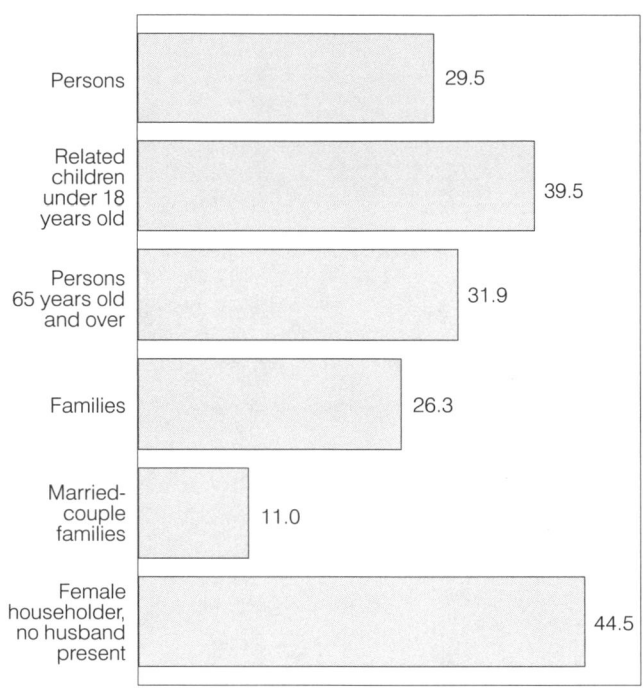

Over 4 million of us owned our own homes in 1990.

The number of homes owned by Blacks increased from 3.7 million in 1980 to 4.3 million in 1990.

By 1990, 43 percent of Blacks lived in homes they either owned or were buying, compared with 68 percent for Whites. The proportion of Black homeowners has remained relatively stable over the past 20 years.

The median value of our homes in 1990 was $50,700, compared with $80,200 for White homeowners. The median value of Black homes was about 56 percent of the White median home value in 1980, but grew to 63 percent in 1990.

Seventy-two percent of Blacks residing in rural areas owned their own homes compared with 40 percent of urban Blacks.

Inside metropolitan areas, 41 percent of Black householders were homeowners, compared with 59 percent of those outside metropolitan areas.

Seventeen percent of Black housing units were occupied by a person 65 years old and over compared with 23 percent of White housing units.

Figure 16.
Tenure: 1990

(Percent)

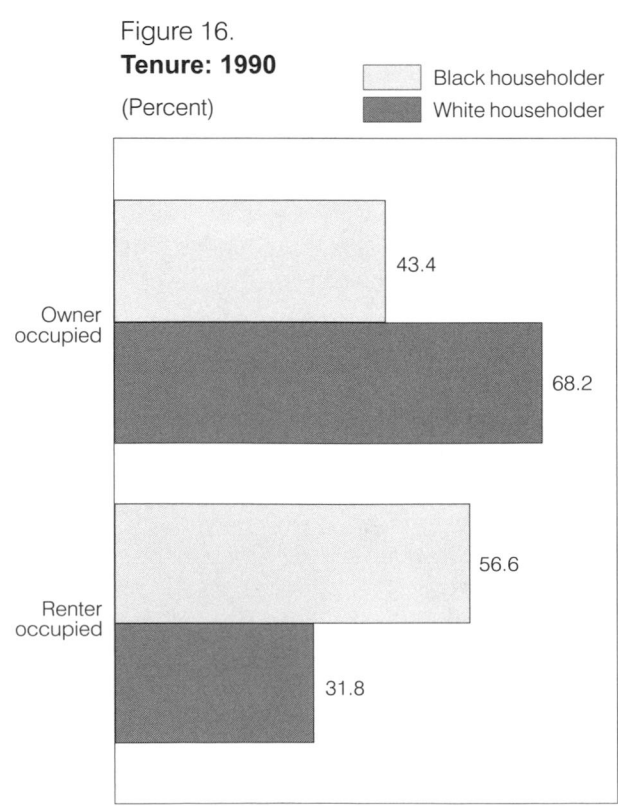

 **e, the American Hispanics**

Introduction

We, the American Hispanics trace our origin or descent to Spain or to Mexico, Puerto Rico, Cuba, and many other Spanish-speaking countries of Latin America. Our ancestors were among the early explorers and settlers of the New World. In 1609, 11 years before the Pilgrims landed at Plymouth Rock, our Mestizo (Indian and Spanish) ancestors settled in what is now Santa Fe, New Mexico.

Several historical events also shaped our presence in America: the Louisiana Purchase, admission of Florida and Texas into the Union, the Treaty of Guadalupe Hidalgo which ended the Mexican-American War, the Spanish-American War, the Mexican Revolution, labor shortages during World War I and World War II, the Cuban Revolution, and political instability in Central and South America in the recent past. Although our common ancestry and language bind us, we are quite diverse.

We have not always appeared in the census as a separate ethnic group. In 1930, "Mexicans" were counted and in 1940, "persons of Spanish mother tongue" were reported. In 1950 and 1960, "persons of Spanish surname" were reported. The 1970 census asked persons about their "origin," and respondents could choose among several Hispanic origins listed on the questionnaire. In 1980 and 1990, persons of "Spanish/Hispanic" origin reported as Mexican, Puerto Rican, Cuban, or "other Hispanic." The 1990 census tabulated information for about 30 additional Hispanic-origin groups.

Because of our increasing diversity, the Census Bureau presents social and economic characteristics for specific Hispanic-origin groups such as Mexican, Puerto Rican, or Cuban. This report represents a fraction of the wealth of information available from the Bureau of the Census on Hispanic Americans.

257

We are a large, fast growing segment of the Nation's population.

Since 1930, some segments of the Hispanic population have been counted in the census. In 1930, 1.3 million "Mexicans" were reported. In 1950, 2.3 million "persons of Spanish surname" were reported, and in 1970, 9.1 million persons of "Spanish" origin were reported.

In 1990, there were 22.4 million Hispanics in the United States, almost 9 percent of the Nation's nearly 250 million people. The Hispanic population in 1990 was slightly less than the entire U.S. population in 1850.

The Census Bureau's 1992 middle series projections suggest rapid growth may continue into the 20th century. The population could rise from 24 million in 1992 to 31 million by the year 2000, 59 million by 2030, and 81 million by 2050.

Our population grew over 7 times as fast as the rest of the Nation between 1980 and 1990.

The Hispanic population grew by 53 percent between 1980 and 1990 and by 61 percent between 1970 and 1980. Several factors contributed to the tremendous increase in the Hispanic population since 1970. Among them are a higher birth rate than the rest of the population and substantial immigration from Mexico, Central America, the Caribbean, and South America.

The Mexican population nearly doubled between 1970 and 1980, and nearly doubled again by 1990.

Both the Cuban and Puerto Rican populations grew at a rate at least four times as fast as the rest of the Nation.

Other Hispanic populations grew dramatically between 1980 and 1990, partly as a result of the large influx of Central and South American immigrants during this time period.

Figure 1.
Hispanic Population: 1930 to 2050
(Millions. Middle series projections)

Census
Projections

1930: 1.3
1940: 1.6
1950: 2.3
1960: 3.5
1970: 9.1
1980: 14.6
1990: 22.4
1992: 24.1
2000: 30.6
2010: 39.3
2020: 49.0
2030: 59.2
2040: 70.0
2050: 80.7

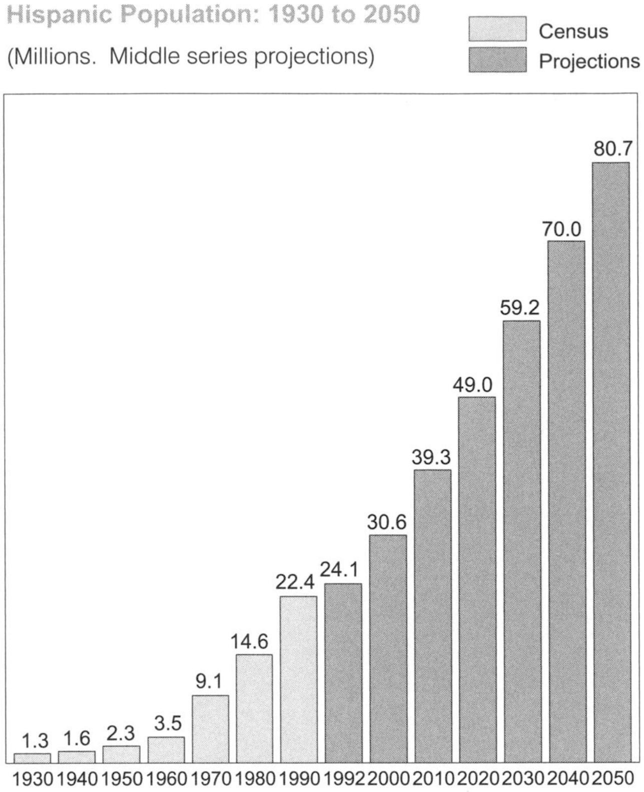

Note: Data for 1930 include only "Mexicans," data for 1940 include persons of "Spanish mother tongue," and data for 1950 and 1960 include persons of "Spanish surname."

Figure 2.
Hispanic Population Growth: 1970 to 1990
(Percent)

1980 to 1990
1970 to 1980

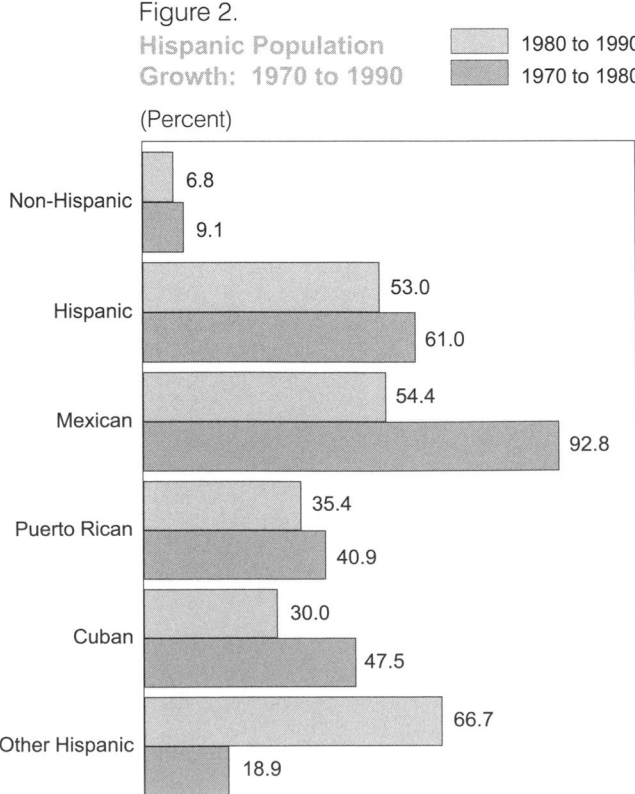

Non-Hispanic: 6.8 / 9.1
Hispanic: 53.0 / 61.0
Mexican: 54.4 / 92.8
Puerto Rican: 35.4 / 40.9
Cuban: 30.0 / 47.5
Other Hispanic: 66.7 / 18.9

We are concentrated in a small number of States, mostly in the South and West.

In 1990, nearly 9 of every 10 Hispanics lived in just 10 States. The four States with the largest proportion of Hispanics were California, Texas, New York, and Florida.

The remaining States with significant proportions of Hispanics were Illinois, New Jersey, Arizona, New Mexico, Colorado, and Massachusetts.

Most Hispanics lived in the Southwestern States of the Nation: New Mexico, California, Texas, and Arizona.

Nearly 40 percent of New Mexican residents were Hispanic, and about 26 percent of California and Texas residents were Hispanic. Nearly 20 percent of Arizona residents were Hispanic.

More than 10 percent of the residents of Colorado, New York, Florida, and Nevada were Hispanic.

Figure 3.
Hispanic Population for Selected States: 1990

(Percent distribution)

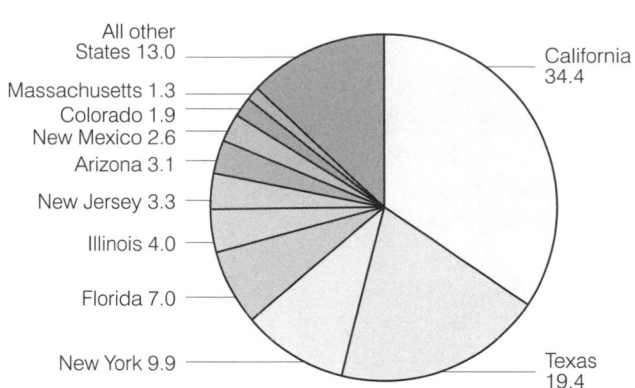

Figure 4.
Hispanic Population: 1990

(Percent of State)

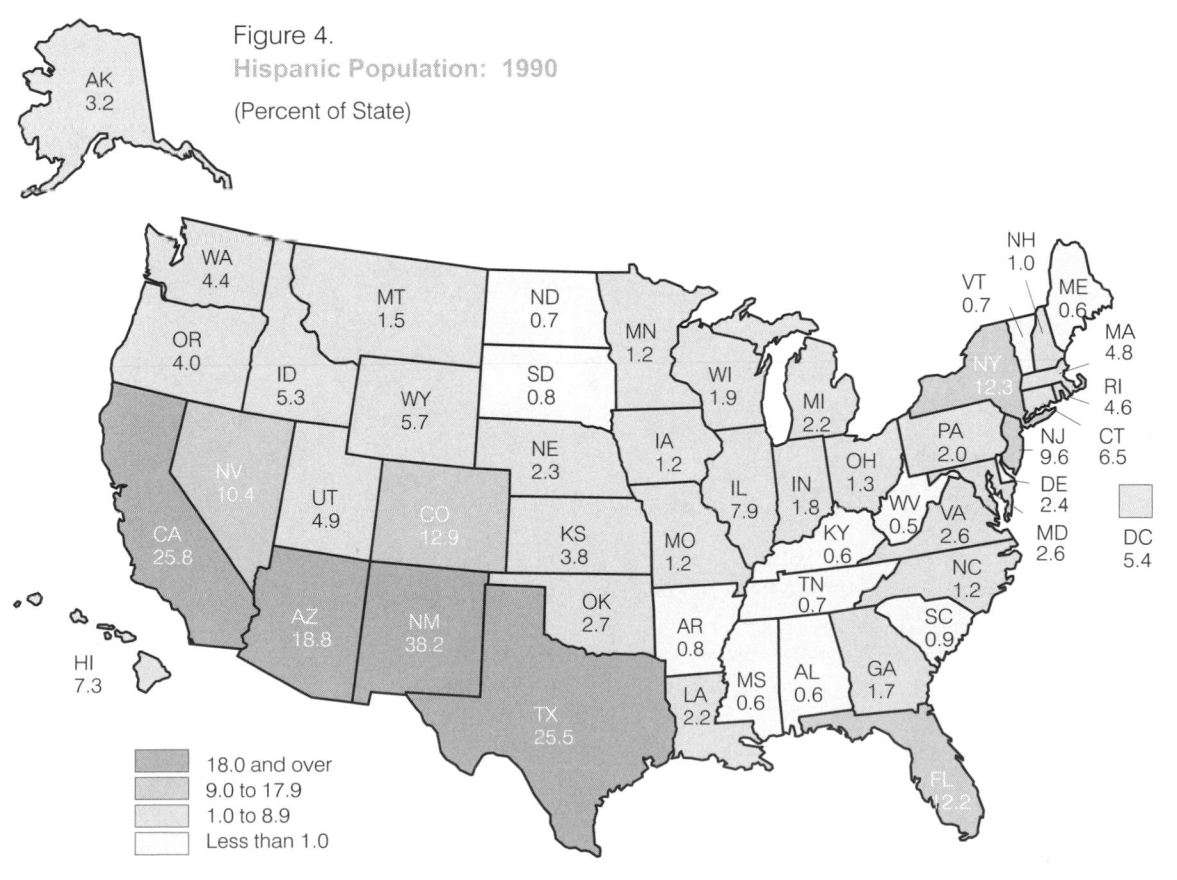

18.0 and over
9.0 to 17.9
1.0 to 8.9
Less than 1.0

**We come from many
different origins.**

In 1990, Mexicans were the
largest Hispanic group, representing about 61 percent of
the 22.3 million Hispanics.

Puerto Ricans were the second largest group, about
12 percent; and Cubans were
about 5 percent of the Hispanic population.

Central Americans repre-
sented about 6 percent of the
total Hispanic population.
However, of the Central Americans, about 43 percent were
Salvadoran, 20 percent were
Guatemalan, and
about 15 percent were Nicaraguan.

South Americans represented nearly 5 percent
of the Hispanic population. Of the South Americans, 37 percent were Colombian, 19 percent
were Ecuadorian, and 17 percent were Peruvian.

Dominicans, Spaniards, and other Hispanics each
were over 2 percent of the Hispanic population.

Figure 5.
Hispanic Population by Type
of Origin: 1990

(Percent)

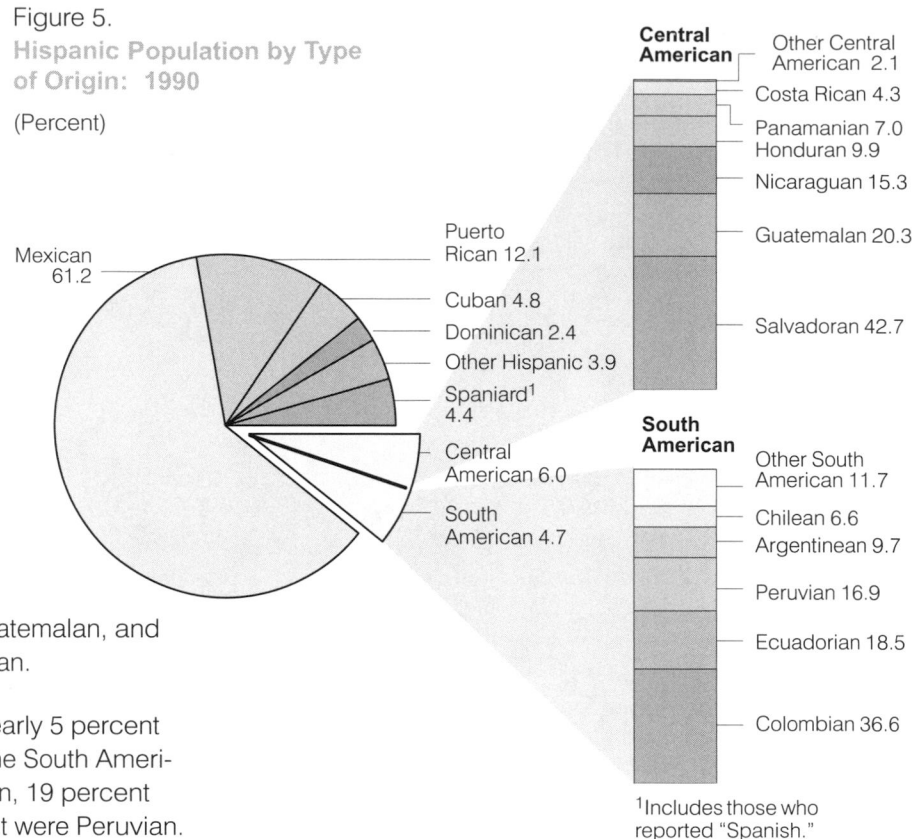

Mexican
61.2

Puerto
Rican 12.1

Cuban 4.8

Dominican 2.4

Other Hispanic 3.9

Spaniard[1]
4.4

Central
American 6.0

South
American 4.7

**Central
American**

Other Central
American 2.1

Costa Rican 4.3

Panamanian 7.0

Honduran 9.9

Nicaraguan 15.3

Guatemalan 20.3

Salvadoran 42.7

**South
American**

Other South
American 11.7

Chilean 6.6

Argentinean 9.7

Peruvian 16.9

Ecuadorian 18.5

Colombian 36.6

[1]Includes those who
reported "Spanish."

**Our population has a higher
proportion of young adults and children
and fewer elderly than the non-
Hispanic population.**

In 1990, nearly 7 out of every 10 Hispanics were
younger than 35 years old compared with just
over 5 out of every 10 non-Hispanics.

Among the elderly, about 5 percent of
Hispanics were 65 years old and over compared
with 13 percent of non-Hispanics.

Nearly 40 percent of the Hispanic population was
under 20 years old, compared with 28 percent
of the non-Hispanic population. This reflects a
relatively high fertility rate among Hispanics who
have recently immigrated.

Figure 6.
Age of the Population: 1990

(Percent)

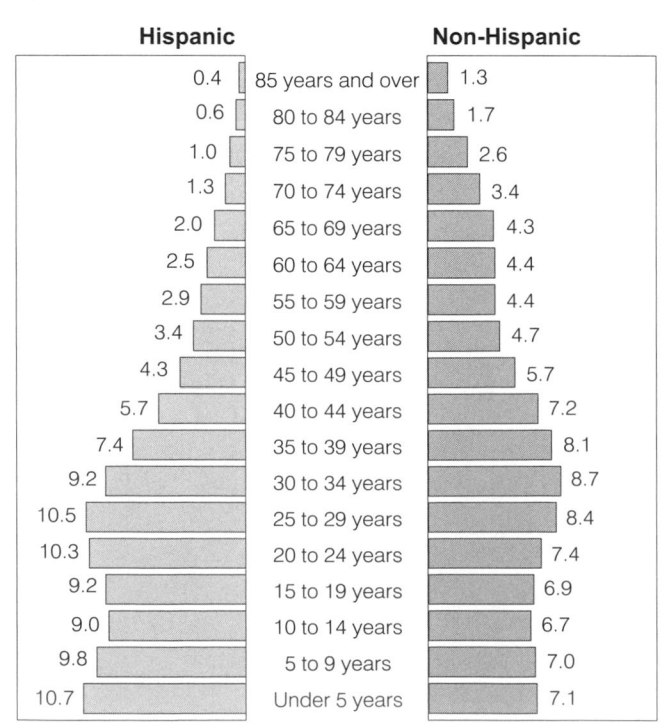

Hispanic		Non-Hispanic
0.4	85 years and over	1.3
0.6	80 to 84 years	1.7
1.0	75 to 79 years	2.6
1.3	70 to 74 years	3.4
2.0	65 to 69 years	4.3
2.5	60 to 64 years	4.4
2.9	55 to 59 years	4.4
3.4	50 to 54 years	4.7
4.3	45 to 49 years	5.7
5.7	40 to 44 years	7.2
7.4	35 to 39 years	8.1
9.2	30 to 34 years	8.7
10.5	25 to 29 years	8.4
10.3	20 to 24 years	7.4
9.2	15 to 19 years	6.9
9.0	10 to 14 years	6.7
9.8	5 to 9 years	7.0
10.7	Under 5 years	7.1

We made great strides in educational attainment since 1970.

In 1990, about half of the Hispanic population had at least a high school diploma and 1 in 11 earned a bachelor's degree or higher. However, Hispanic adults were less likely than non-Hispanic adults to complete high school or college.

In 1980, about 4 of 10 Hispanics completed 4 years or more of high school and 1 of every 13 completed 4 years or more of college.

In 1970, only 3 of 10 Hispanics 25 years old and over completed at least 4 years of high school. Less than 1 in 20 completed 4 years or more of college.

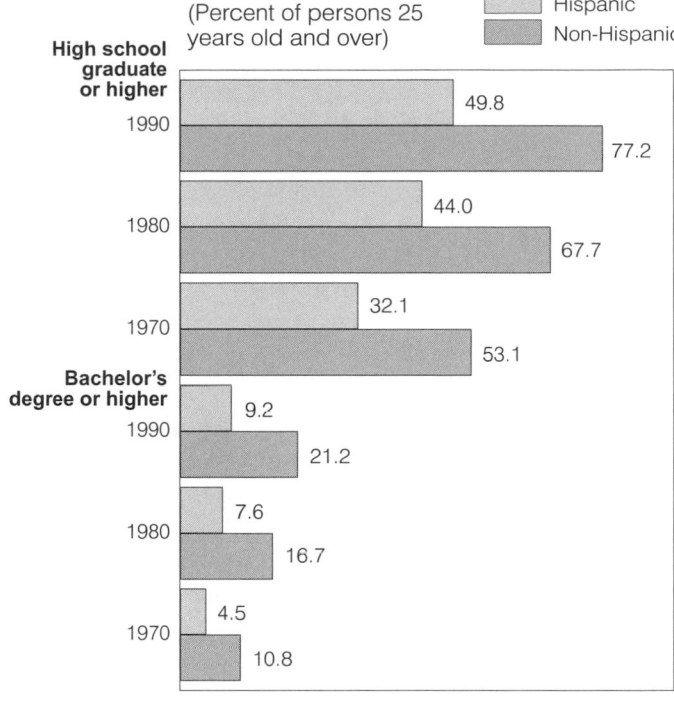

Figure 7.
Educational Attainment: 1970 to 1990

(Percent of persons 25 years old and over)

Legend: Hispanic / Non-Hispanic

High school graduate or higher
1990: 49.8 / 77.2
1980: 44.0 / 67.7
1970: 32.1 / 53.1

Bachelor's degree or higher
1990: 9.2 / 21.2
1980: 7.6 / 16.7
1970: 4.5 / 10.8

Our educational attainment varies among different Hispanic groups.

Although about half of the Hispanic population received a high school diploma or higher in 1990, individual Hispanic groups varied from a high of 77 percent for Spaniards to a low of 43 percent for Dominicans.

About 44 percent of Mexicans, 53 percent of Puerto Ricans, and 57 percent of Cubans had a high school diploma or higher.

About 46 percent of Central Americans and 71 percent of South Americans received a high school diploma or higher in 1990.

Nearly 10 percent of the Hispanic population received a bachelor's degree or higher in 1990. However, about 20 percent of Spaniards and South Americans received a bachelor's degree or higher compared with only 6 percent of Mexicans.

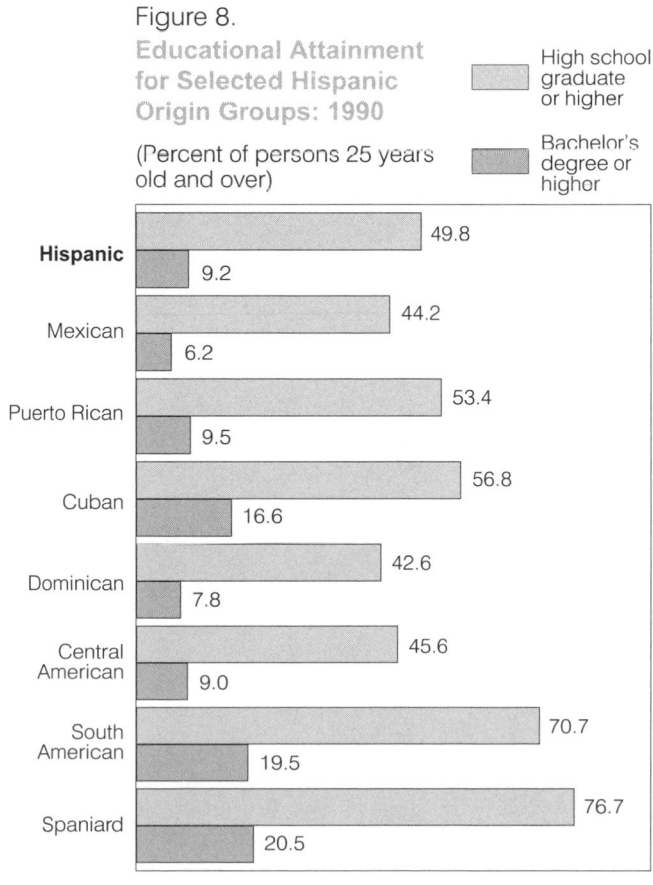

Figure 8.
Educational Attainment for Selected Hispanic Origin Groups: 1990

(Percent of persons 25 years old and over)

Legend: High school graduate or higher / Bachelor's degree or higher

Hispanic: 49.8 / 9.2
Mexican: 44.2 / 6.2
Puerto Rican: 53.4 / 9.5
Cuban: 56.8 / 16.6
Dominican: 42.6 / 7.8
Central American: 45.6 / 9.0
South American: 70.7 / 19.5
Spaniard: 76.7 / 20.5

Although many of us were foreign born, about 64 percent of us were born in the United States.

In 1990, over 7.8 million Hispanics were foreign born. Hispanic foreign born from Mexico, Central America, the Caribbean, and South America represented about 43 percent of all foreign-born persons in the United States.

Nearly three-quarters of the Hispanic population were native-born and naturalized citizens compared with about 97 percent of the non-Hispanic population.

About 83 percent of Spaniards and about 67 percent of Mexicans were born in the United States. About 21 percent of Central Americans and 25 percent of South Americans were born here.

Among foreign-born Hispanics, the proportion who were not citizens in 1990 varied from less than 10 percent for Spaniards to nearly 65 percent for Central Americans. Many Central Americans are relatively recent immigrants to America and have not had time to go through the naturalization process.

Note: All persons born in Puerto Rico are American citizens.

About half of us who were foreign born came to the United States between 1980 and 1990.

Whether pulled by the need to be reunited with families or pushed by political events in the country of birth, many Hispanics moved to the United States between 1980 and 1990.

Just over half of the Hispanic foreign born arrived in America since 1980. About 28 percent arrived between 1970 and 1979, 15 percent between 1960 and 1969, and about 7 percent before 1960.

About 20 percent of the Central American foreign born arrived between 1970 and 1979, and about 70 percent arrived between 1980 and 1990. Central Americans represented the largest proportion of newly arrived Hispanic immigrants during the 1980's.

About 46 percent of the Cuban foreign born arrived between 1960 and 1969. Many Cuban refugees arrived in the United States following the Cuban Missile Crisis in the early part of that decade.

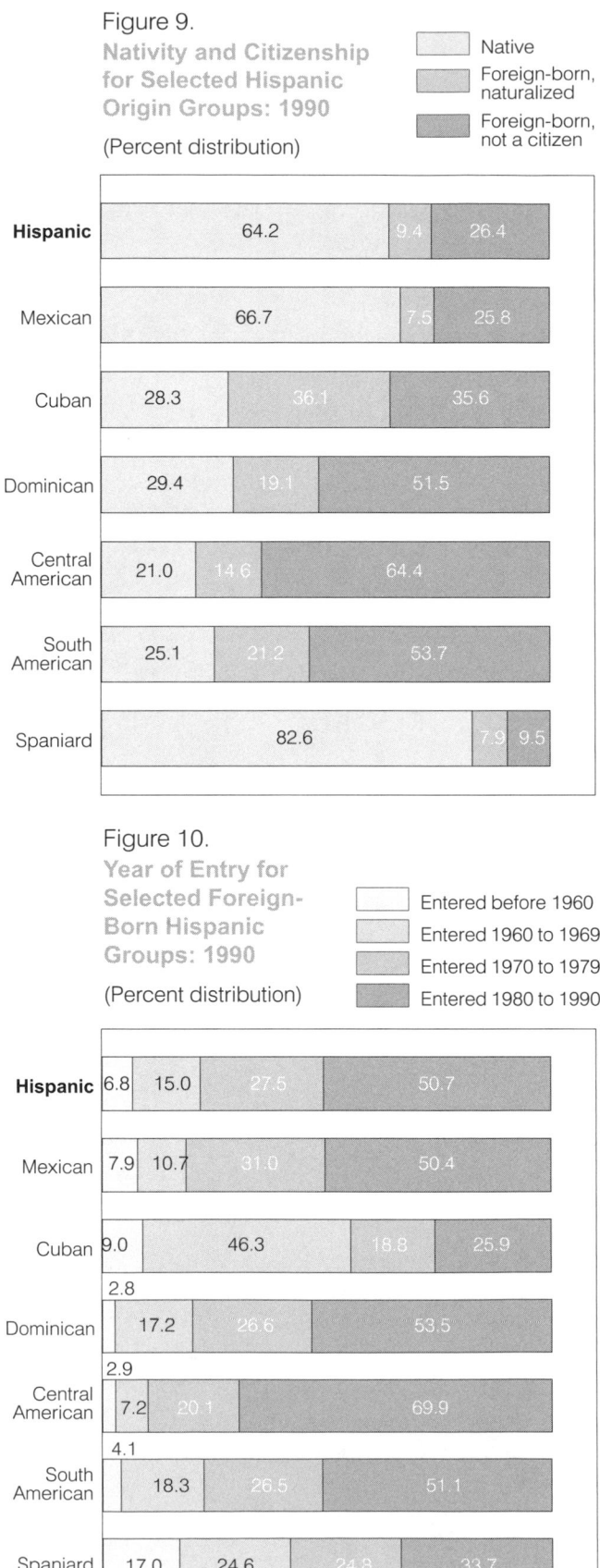

Figure 9.
Nativity and Citizenship for Selected Hispanic Origin Groups: 1990

(Percent distribution)

Native
Foreign-born, naturalized
Foreign-born, not a citizen

Group	Native	Foreign-born, naturalized	Foreign-born, not a citizen
Hispanic	64.2	9.4	26.4
Mexican	66.7	7.5	25.8
Cuban	28.3	36.1	35.6
Dominican	29.4	19.1	51.5
Central American	21.0	14.6	64.4
South American	25.1	21.2	53.7
Spaniard	82.6	7.9	9.5

Figure 10.
Year of Entry for Selected Foreign-Born Hispanic Groups: 1990

(Percent distribution)

Entered before 1960
Entered 1960 to 1969
Entered 1970 to 1979
Entered 1980 to 1990

Group	Entered before 1960	Entered 1960 to 1969	Entered 1970 to 1979	Entered 1980 to 1990
Hispanic	6.8	15.0	27.5	50.7
Mexican	7.9	10.7	31.0	50.4
Cuban	9.0	46.3	18.8	25.9
Dominican	2.8	17.2	26.6	53.5
Central American	2.9	7.2	20.1	69.9
South American	4.1	18.3	26.5	51.1
Spaniard	17.0	24.6	24.8	33.7

Nearly 3 million of us are legal immigrants who arrived between 1980 and 1990.

Prior to 1950, the vast majority of legal immigrants arrived from Europe. From 1950 to 1990, a new wave (nearly 20 million) of legal immigrants arrived, many from Latin America. Between 1951 and 1960, over 2.5 million people entered the country legally. Of those, 1 in 5 came from Latin America.

Between 1961 and 1970, 3.3 million immigrants entered the United States, with 1 in 3 coming from Latin America. During the 1970's, there were nearly 4.5 million immigrants, with about 40 percent coming from Latin America.

By the 1980's, 47 percent of immigrants were from Latin America.

Figure 11.

Legal Immigration by Area of Origin: 1951 to 1990

(Thousands)

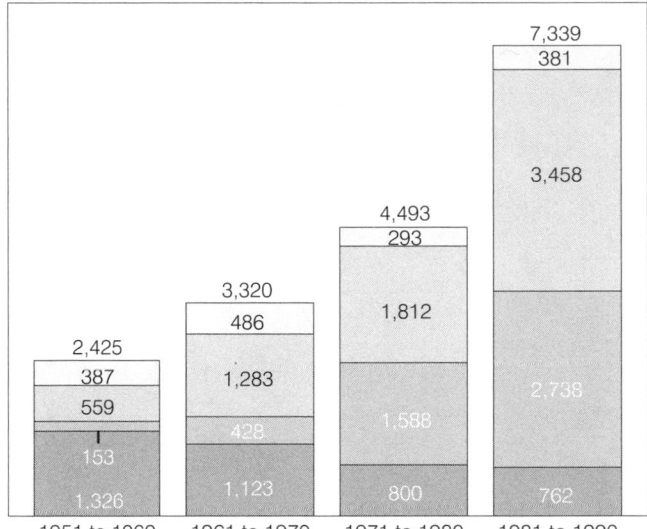

Note: Information for this graph came from the 1991 Statistical Yearbook of Immigration and Naturalization Service, M-367. Latin America includes Mexico, Central America, the Caribbean, and South America.

The Spanish language is a tie that binds us together.

In 1990, about 14 percent of the Nation's population 5 years old and over spoke a language other than English at home. Spanish was spoken by about one-half of all non-English speakers in the United States.

Also in 1990, about 78 percent of Hispanics spoke a language other than English at home. Spanish was spoken by nearly all of the Hispanic non-English speakers.

Of the Hispanics who spoke Spanish at home, about one-half spoke English "very well" and about half did not speak English "very well."

A greater proportion of Dominicans and Central Americans than Puerto Ricans and Spaniards who spoke Spanish at home did not speak English "very well."

Figure 12.

Language Spoken at Home and Ability to Speak English for Selected Hispanic Groups: 1990

(Percent of persons 5 years old and over who speak Spanish at home)

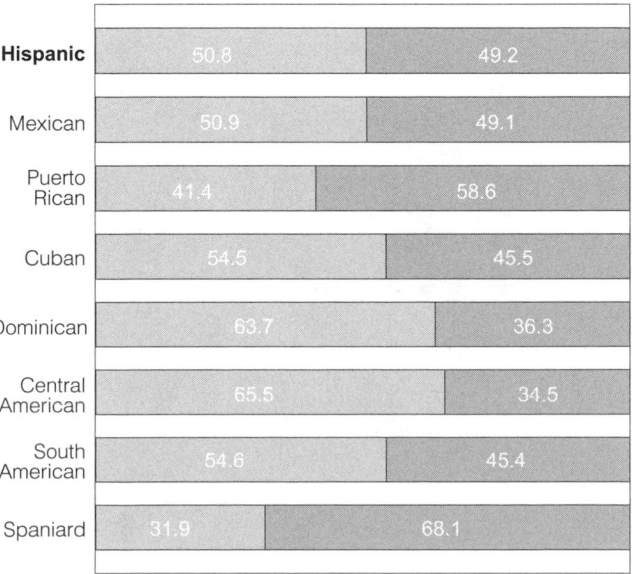

263

Fewer of us held jobs as managers or professionals than non-Hispanics.

In 1990, about 28 percent of Hispanic males 16 years old and over worked as operators, fabricators, and laborers compared with about 19 percent of non-Hispanic males.

Technical, sales, and administrative support positions provided employment for the largest share (about 39 percent) of Hispanic females compared with about 45 percent for non-Hispanic females.

Only about 12 percent of Hispanic males held managerial and professional specialty positions compared with about 27 percent of non-Hispanic males.

Service occupations provided employment for about 17 percent of non-Hispanic females compared with about 24 percent of Hispanic females.

In 1990, most of us lived in family households.

About 70 percent of Hispanic families were maintained by married couples, about 9 percent by a male with no wife present, and 22 percent by a female with no husband present.

The distribution of families by type varied among Hispanic groups. Over three-quarters of Cuban and Spaniard families were maintained by married couples.

Families maintained by a female with no husband present were found primarily among Puerto Rican and Dominican families.

About 14 percent of Central American families were families maintained by a male with no wife present.

Figure 13.
Occupation by Sex: 1990

(Percent 16 years old and over in civilian labor force)

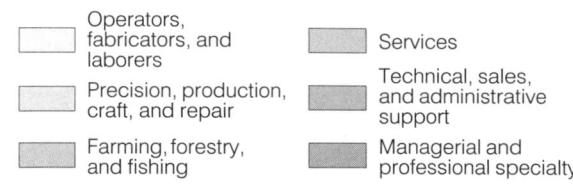

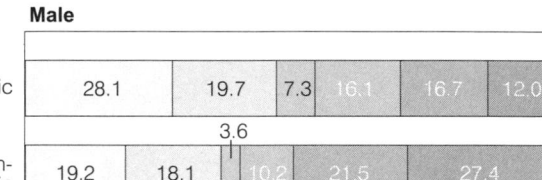

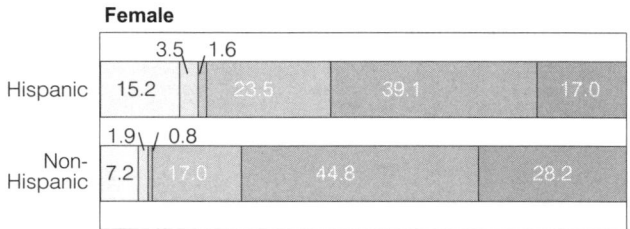

Figure 14.
Families by Type for Selected Hispanic Groups: 1990

(Percent of families)

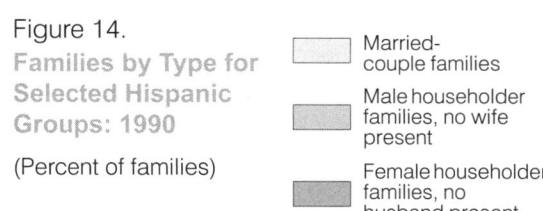

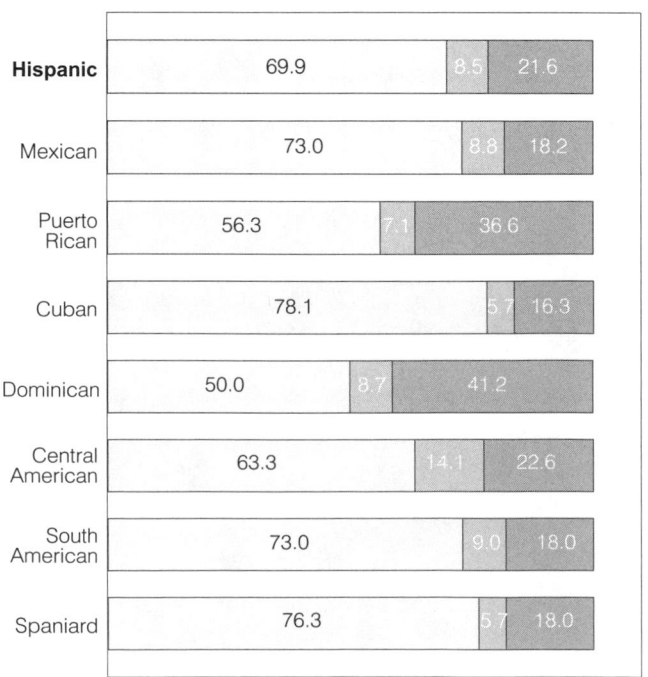

Our median family income was lower than that for all Americans.

In 1990, the median family income for Hispanics was $25,064, lower than the median family income of $35,225 for all Americans.

Hispanic female householders with no husband present had lower median incomes than all female householders with no husband present, $12,406 and $17,414, respectively.

Of the Hispanic groups shown, Dominicans had the lowest median family income ($19,726), and Spaniards had the highest median family income ($36,680).

Puerto Rican female householders with no husband present had the lowest income, $8,912, while Cuban and Spaniard female householders with no husband present had the highest incomes, $19,511 and $20,000, respectively.

Over 1 million of our families lived in poverty in 1990.

Just over 2 of every 10 Hispanic families were living in poverty in 1990 compared with less than 1 of every 10 non-Hispanic families.

About 30 percent of Puerto Rican families, 33 percent of Dominican families, about 10 percent of Spaniard families, 11 percent of Cuban families, 23 percent of Mexican families, and 21 percent of Central American families were below the poverty level in 1990.

Hispanic females, children, and elderly also had higher proportions living in poverty than their non-Hispanic counterparts. About 27 percent of Hispanic females lived in poverty compared with 13 percent of non-Hispanic females.

About 18 percent of Hispanic children under 18 years old lived in poverty compared with 17 percent of non-Hispanic children. Twice as many elderly Hispanics 65 years old and over lived in poverty than non-Hispanic elderly, 24 percent and 12 percent, respectively.

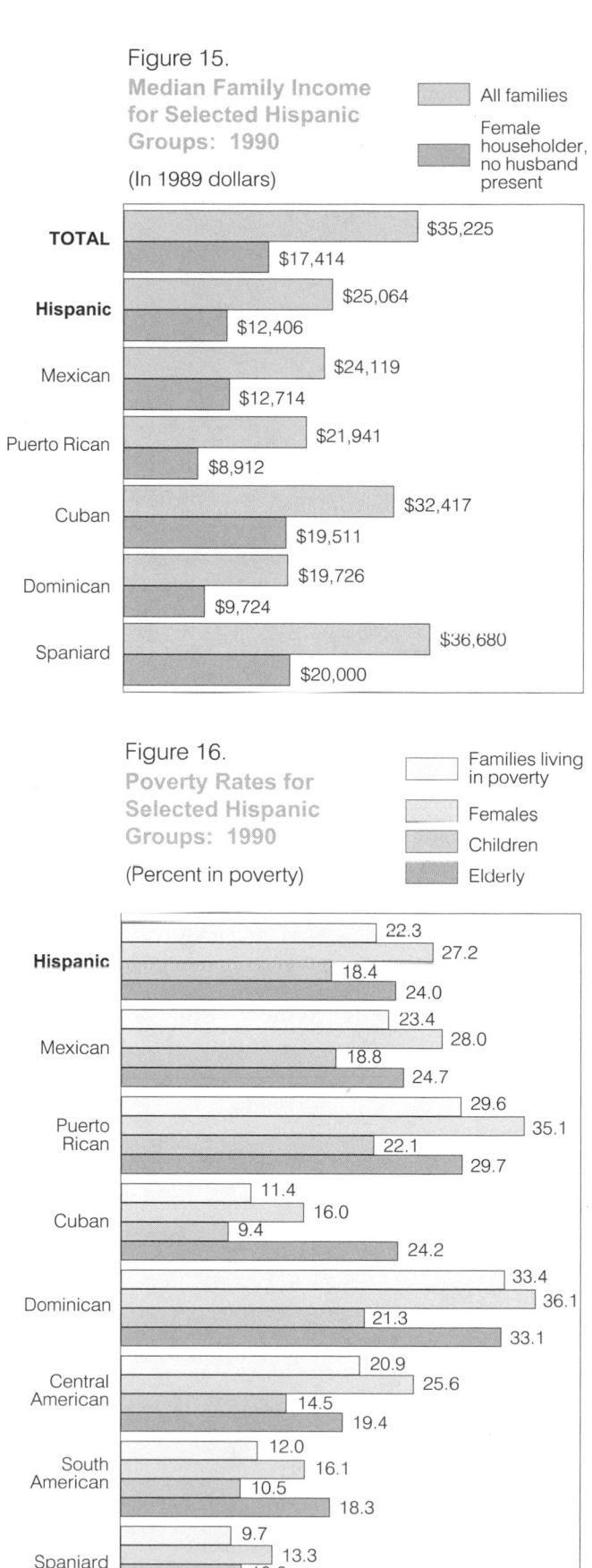

Figure 15.

Median Family Income for Selected Hispanic Groups: 1990

(In 1989 dollars)

All families / Female householder, no husband present

TOTAL: $35,225 / $17,414
Hispanic: $25,064 / $12,406
Mexican: $24,119 / $12,714
Puerto Rican: $21,941 / $8,912
Cuban: $32,417 / $19,511
Dominican: $19,726 / $9,724
Spaniard: $36,680 / $20,000

Figure 16.

Poverty Rates for Selected Hispanic Groups: 1990

(Percent in poverty)

Families living in poverty / Females / Children / Elderly

Hispanic: 22.3 / 27.2 / 18.4 / 24.0
Mexican: 23.4 / 28.0 / 18.8 / 24.7
Puerto Rican: 29.6 / 35.1 / 22.1 / 29.7
Cuban: 11.4 / 16.0 / 9.4 / 24.2
Dominican: 33.4 / 36.1 / 21.3 / 33.1
Central American: 20.9 / 25.6 / 14.5 / 19.4
South American: 12.0 / 16.1 / 10.5 / 18.3
Spaniard: 9.7 / 13.3 / 10.6 / 12.7

e, the American Asians

Introduction

We, the American Asians, number 6.9 million, a 99 percent increase since the 1980 census. This report focuses on Asian Americans — Chinese, Filipinos, Koreans, Asian Indians, Japanese, Vietnamese, Cambodians, Laotians, Hmong, and Thai. Pacific Islanders are profiled in a companion report, "We, The American Pacific Islanders," in this series.

For the last two decades, the number of Asians and Pacific Islanders in the United States doubled, from 1.5 million in 1970 to 3.7 million in 1980 to 7.3 million in 1990. The percentage of Asians and Pacific

Islanders in the total population also nearly doubled during the 1980's, from 1.5 percent to 2.9 percent.

Our dramatic increases are the result of increased immigration from China, India, Korea, the Philippines, and other Asian and Pacific Island areas following the adoption of the Immigration Act of 1965.

In addition to immigration and natural increase, part of the growth of our numbers during the 1970's reflect changes in the census race definition to include more groups, as well as improvements in review procedures in the 1990 census.

We, the American Asians are a rapidly growing, diverse part of America.

The 1990 census counted 6,908,638 Asians, a 99 percent increase over the 1980 census count of 3,466,847.

In 1990, the largest proportions of Asian Americans were Chinese (24 percent) and Filipino (20 percent) followed by Japanese, with 12 percent of the Asian population.

Newer immigrant groups— Laotian, Cambodian, Thai, and Hmong—each accounted for 2 percent or less of the Asians in America.

Note: All Asian groups, regardless of size, are important and make continuing contributions to the diversity of the United States. This discussion focuses on only the 10 largest Asian groups.

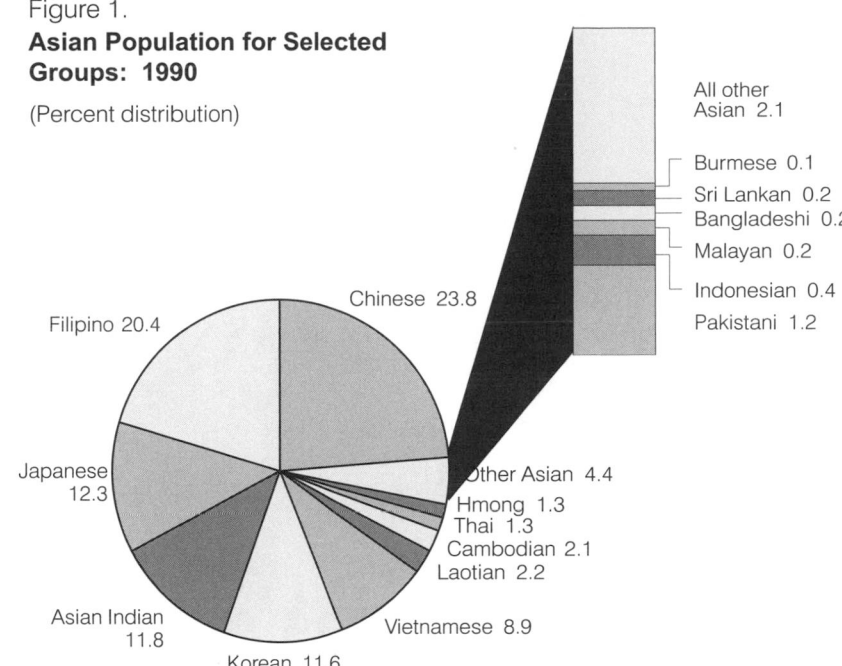

Figure 1.
Asian Population for Selected Groups: 1990

(Percent distribution)

Chinese 23.8
Filipino 20.4
Japanese 12.3
Asian Indian 11.8
Korean 11.6
Vietnamese 8.9
Other Asian 4.4
Hmong 1.3
Thai 1.3
Cambodian 2.1
Laotian 2.2

All other Asian 2.1
Burmese 0.1
Sri Lankan 0.2
Bangladeshi 0.2
Malayan 0.2
Indonesian 0.4
Pakistani 1.2

Most of us make our homes in the West.

Fifty-four percent of the Asian population lived in the West in 1990 compared with 21 percent of the total population.

Approximately 66 percent of Asians lived in just five States — California, New York, Hawaii, Texas, and Illinois. The Asian population was highly concentrated in California, New York, and Hawaii, but the concentration varied by Asian groups.

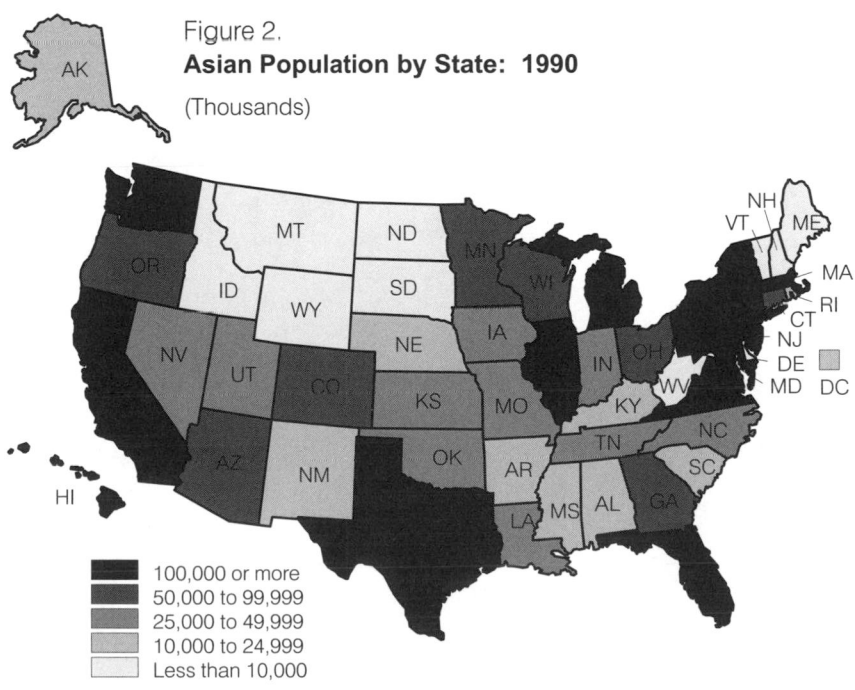

Figure 2.
Asian Population by State: 1990

(Thousands)

100,000 or more
50,000 to 99,999
25,000 to 49,999
10,000 to 24,999
Less than 10,000

Many of us were born in other countries.

Immigration has contributed heavily to the growth of the Asian population in the past two decades, but the percentages who are foreign born differ considerably among groups.

Sixty-six percent of Asians were born in foreign countries. Among Asian groups, Vietnamese, Laotian, and Cambodian groups had the highest proportion of foreign born, while Japanese had the lowest proportion.

Thirty-eight percent of Asians entered the United States from 1980 to 1990. The Cambodians, Laotians, and Hmong had the highest proportion of persons who entered the United States during this period.

The IndoChina Migration and Refugee Assistance Act of 1975 established a program of resettlement for refugees who fled from Cambodia and Vietnam. One year later, the Immigration Act of 1976 made Laotians eligible for the same refugee resettlement programs. Seventy-five percent or more of the Vietnamese, Cambodian, and Laotian born entered the country since 1975.

We are a young population.

Asians had a median age of 30 years in 1990, younger than the national median of 33 years. Only 6 percent of Asians were 65 years old and older compared with 13 percent for the total population.

The Japanese were the eldest of the Asian populations with a median age of 36 years, in part because fewer Japanese were foreign born.

The Hmong and Cambodian, with their large proportions of recent immigrants were the youngest Asians with a median age of 13 years and 19 years, respectively. Immigrant populations tend to have higher fertility than native populations.

In 1990, Asian males were younger than Asian females, with median ages of 29 years and 31 years, respectively, in part because females tend to live longer.

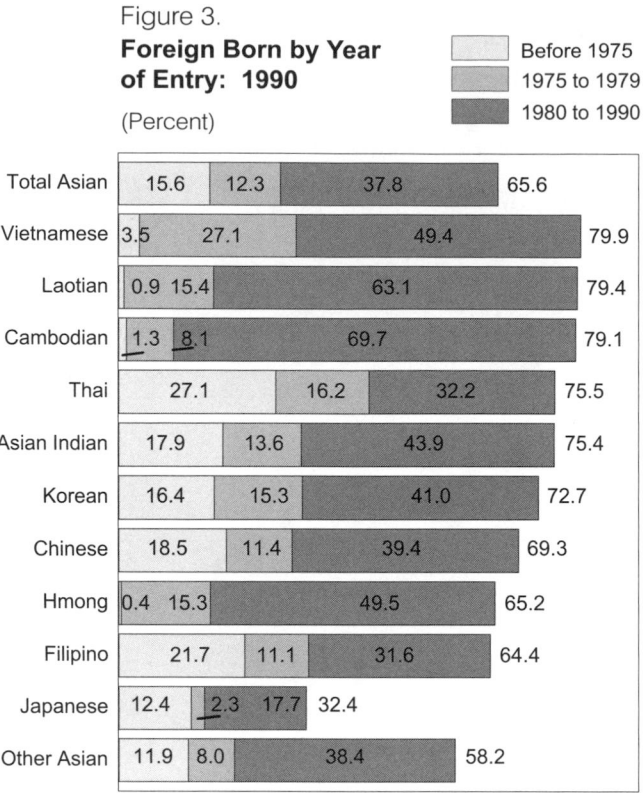

Figure 3.
Foreign Born by Year of Entry: 1990
(Percent)

Before 1975 / 1975 to 1979 / 1980 to 1990

- Total Asian: 15.6 | 12.3 | 37.8 = 65.6
- Vietnamese: 3.5 | 27.1 | 49.4 = 79.9
- Laotian: 0.9 | 15.4 | 63.1 = 79.4
- Cambodian: 1.3 | 8.1 | 69.7 = 79.1
- Thai: 27.1 | 16.2 | 32.2 = 75.5
- Asian Indian: 17.9 | 13.6 | 43.9 = 75.4
- Korean: 16.4 | 15.3 | 41.0 = 72.7
- Chinese: 18.5 | 11.4 | 39.4 = 69.3
- Hmong: 0.4 | 15.3 | 49.5 = 65.2
- Filipino: 21.7 | 11.1 | 31.6 = 64.4
- Japanese: 12.4 | 2.3 | 17.7 = 32.4
- Other Asian: 11.9 | 8.0 | 38.4 = 58.2

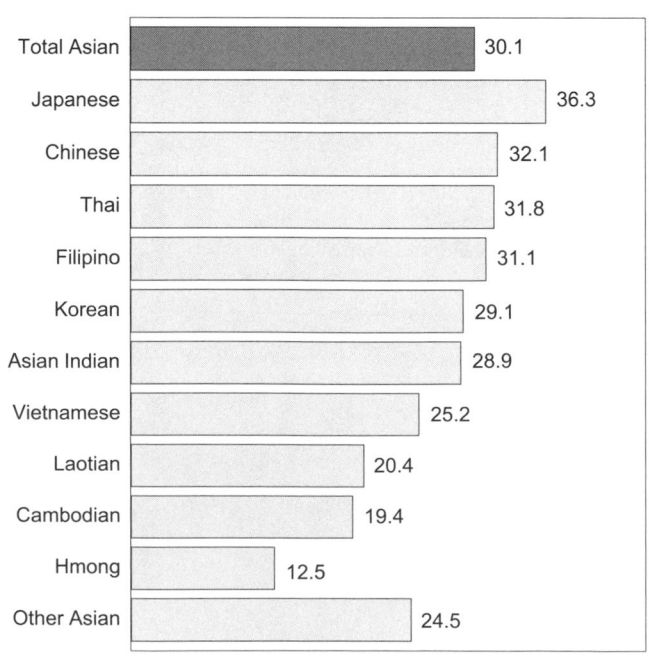

Figure 4.
Median Age: 1990

- Total Asian: 30.1
- Japanese: 36.3
- Chinese: 32.1
- Thai: 31.8
- Filipino: 31.1
- Korean: 29.1
- Asian Indian: 28.9
- Vietnamese: 25.2
- Laotian: 20.4
- Cambodian: 19.4
- Hmong: 12.5
- Other Asian: 24.5

Our families are larger than the average American family.

The average Asian family had 3.8 persons in 1990, larger than the average of 3.2 persons for all U.S. families. Asian families were larger partly because the percentage of children under 18 years old who lived with both parents was higher than the general population, 81 percent versus 70 percent.

Among Asian groups, Hmong had the largest family size with 6.6 persons, and Japanese the smallest family size with 3.1 persons. Other groups with more than four persons per family were Filipino, Vietnamese, Cambodian, and Laotian.

The proportion of Asian families maintained by a husband and wife was 82 percent, slightly higher than the national figure of 79 percent. The proportion of Asian female-headed families with no husband present was significantly less than the national average, 12 percent versus 17 percent. However, two groups had proportions above the national average: Cambodian, 26 percent and Thai, 20 percent.

Our educational attainment varied widely by group.

In 1990, 78 percent of all Asians 25 years old and over were at least high school graduates; the national rate was 75 percent.

Education is highly valued in Asian communities, but the educational attainment of different groups varied widely. The proportion completing high school or higher was 88 percent for Japanese, compared with 31 percent for Hmong.

In general, Asian men had higher rates of high school graduation or higher than Asian women: 82 percent versus 74 percent in 1990. Japanese women had a high school or higher completion rate of 86 percent compared with 19 percent for Hmong women.

At the college level, 38 percent of Asians had graduated with a bachelor's degree or higher by 1990, compared with 20 percent of the total population. Asian Indians had the highest attainment rates, and Cambodians, Laotians, and Hmong had the lowest.

Figure 5.
Persons Per Family: 1990

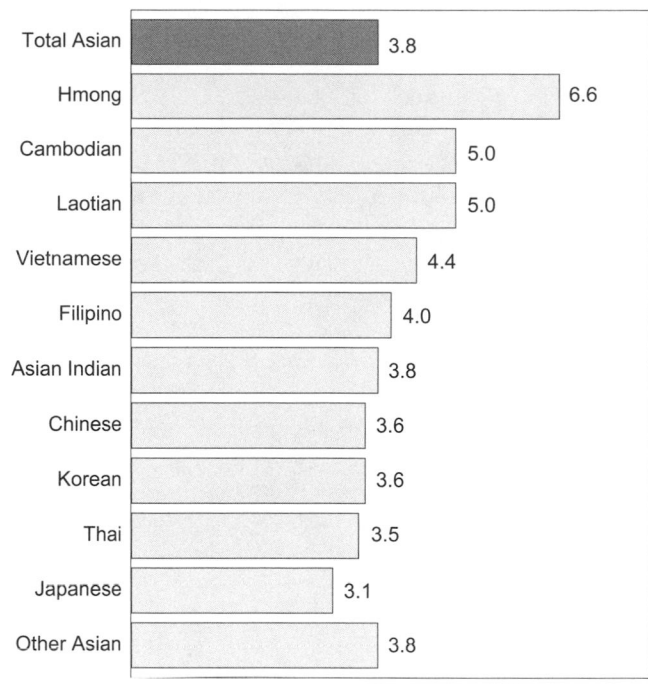

	Persons Per Family
Total Asian	3.8
Hmong	6.6
Cambodian	5.0
Laotian	5.0
Vietnamese	4.4
Filipino	4.0
Asian Indian	3.8
Chinese	3.6
Korean	3.6
Thai	3.5
Japanese	3.1
Other Asian	3.8

Table 1.
Educational Attainment by Sex: 1990

(Percent 25 years old and over)

	High school graduate or higher		Bachelor's degree or higher	
	Male	Female	Male	Female
Total population	**75.7**	**74.8**	**23.3**	**17.6**
Total Asian	81.7	73.9	43.2	32.7
Chinese	77.2	70.2	46.7	35.0
Filipino	84.2	81.4	36.2	41.6
Japanese	89.9	85.6	42.6	28.2
Asian Indian	89.4	79.0	65.7	48.7
Korean	89.1	74.1	46.9	25.9
Vietnamese	68.5	53.3	22.3	12.2
Cambodian	46.2	25.3	8.6	3.2
Hmong	44.1	19.0	7.0	3.0
Laotian	49.4	29.8	7.0	3.5
Thai	88.6	66.2	47.7	24.9
Other Asian	85.9	78.7	47.5	34.2

Nearly two-thirds of us spoke an Asian or Pacific Islander language at home.

Of the 4.1 million Asians 5 years old and over, 56 percent did not speak English "very well," and 35 percent were linguistically isolated.

The Hmong, Laotians, and Cambodians had the highest proportions of persons 5 years old and over speaking an Asian or Pacific Islander (API) language at home. Asian Indians, at 15 percent, had the lowest proportion.

Hmong and Cambodians who spoke an Asian or Pacific Islander language at home had the highest proportion of linguistically isolated, 61 percent and 56 percent, respectively.

Table 2.

Asian or Pacific Islander Language Spoken at Home and Ability to Speak English: 1990

(Percent)

	Speak Asian or Pacific Islander language at home	Do not speak English "very well"	Linguistically isolated
Total Asian ..	**65.2**	**56.0**	**34.9**
Chinese	82.9	60.4	40.3
Filipino	66.0	35.6	13.0
Japanese	42.8	57.7	33.0
Asian Indian . .	14.5	31.0	17.2
Korean	80.8	63.5	41.4
Vietnamese . . .	92.5	65.0	43.9
Cambodian . . .	95.0	73.2	56.1
Hmong	96.9	78.1	60.5
Laotian	95.6	70.2	52.4
Thai	79.1	58.0	31.8
Other Asian . .	21.0	49.9	30.2

Note: Linguistic isolation refers to persons in households in which no one 14 years old or over speaks only English and no one who speaks a language other than English speaks English "very well."

We are more likely to participate in the labor force than the population as a whole.

In 1990, 67 percent of Asian Americans, compared with 65 percent of all Americans, were in the labor force. Filipino, Asian Indian, Thai, and Chinese had participation rates higher than the national average — 75 percent, 72 percent, 71 percent, and 66 percent, respectively.

Asian women had a higher participation rate than all women. Sixty percent of Asian women were in the labor force compared with 57 percent of all women in the United States.

Asian men had about the same participation rate as all men, 75 percent and 74 percent, respectively, and Asian Indian men had the largest participation rate of 84 percent.

Figure 6.

Labor Force Participation Rates: 1990

(Percent 16 years old and over)

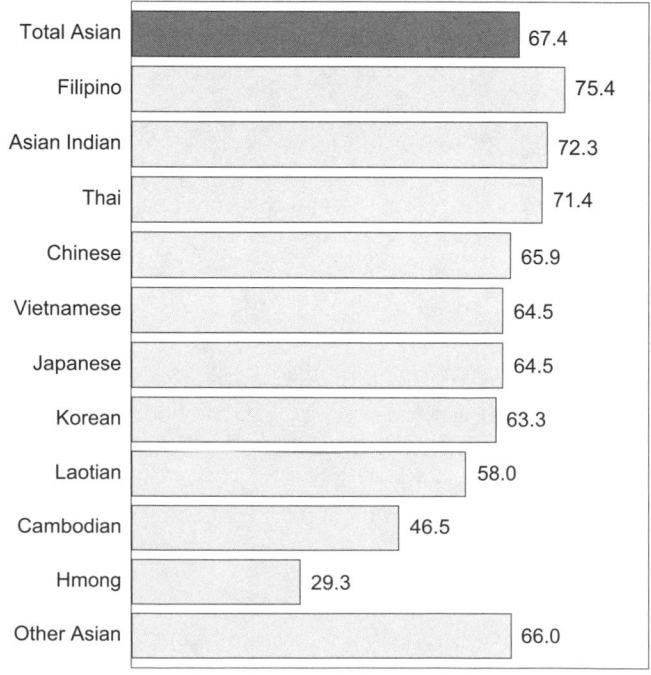

Total Asian	67.4
Filipino	75.4
Asian Indian	72.3
Thai	71.4
Chinese	65.9
Vietnamese	64.5
Japanese	64.5
Korean	63.3
Laotian	58.0
Cambodian	46.5
Hmong	29.3
Other Asian	66.0

More of our family members are in the work force.

The proportion of Asian families with three or more workers was 20 percent compared with the national proportion of 13 percent.

Among Asian families, Filipinos (30 percent) and Vietnamese, (21 percent) had the highest proportions of families with three or more workers.

Hmong families had the lowest proportion with three or more workers.

Figure 7.

Families With Three or More Workers: 1990

(Percent)

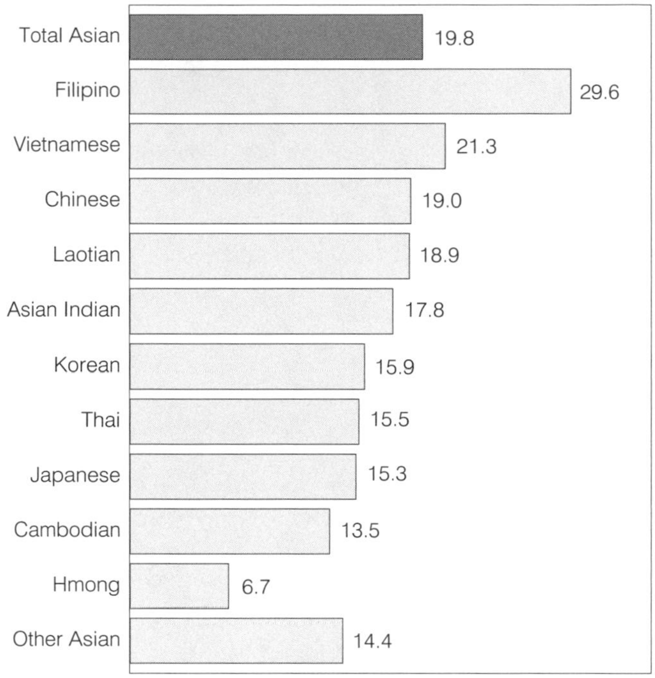

Total Asian	19.8
Filipino	29.6
Vietnamese	21.3
Chinese	19.0
Laotian	18.9
Asian Indian	17.8
Korean	15.9
Thai	15.5
Japanese	15.3
Cambodian	13.5
Hmong	6.7
Other Asian	14.4

Many of us work in higher paying occupations, in part because of higher educational attainment.

Asians were more likely to be in technical, sales, and administrative support, and managerial and professional specialty jobs (33 percent and 31 percent, respectively) than the total population — 32 percent and 26 percent, respectively.

The proportion in technical, sales, and administrative support occupations varies from 37 percent for Korean workers to 5 percent for Laotian workers.

Asians were less likely than the total population to work in precision production, craft, and repair occupations or to work as operators, fabricators, and laborers.

Figure 8.

Occupation: 1990

(Percent employed persons 16 years old and over)

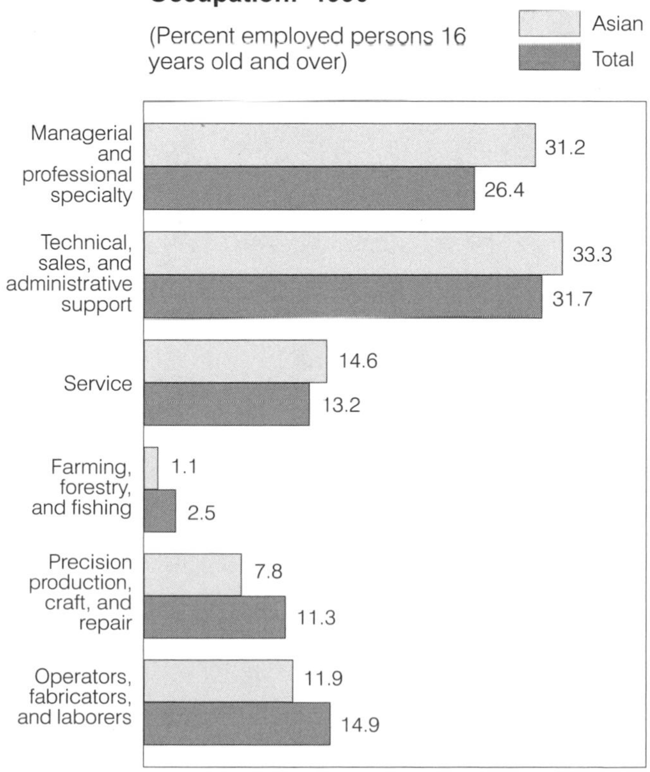

Asian / Total

Occupation	Asian	Total
Managerial and professional specialty	31.2	26.4
Technical, sales, and administrative support	33.3	31.7
Service	14.6	13.2
Farming, forestry, and fishing	1.1	2.5
Precision production, craft, and repair	7.8	11.3
Operators, fabricators, and laborers	11.9	14.9

Japanese had the highest per capita income at $19,373 and Hmong, one of the most recent Asian immigrant groups, had the lowest at $2,692.

In 1989, the Asian per capita income was $13,806 compared with the national per capita income of $14,143.

Asian families had higher median family incomes ($41,583) in 1989 than all families ($35,225), partly because of more family members in the work force and higher educational attainment.

Figure 9.
Per Capita Income: 1990

(In 1989 dollars)

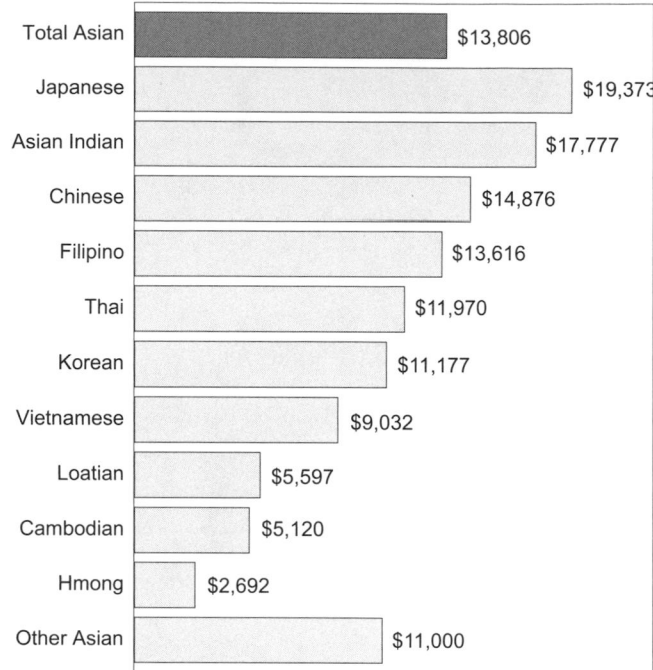

We experience poverty rates slightly higher than all Americans, despite our higher median family income.

About 14 percent of Asian Americans lived in poverty in 1989, a rate slightly higher than the 13 percent for the entire Nation.

The Hmong had one of the highest poverty rates followed by the Cambodians and Laotians. The lowest poverty rates were for the Japanese and Filipinos.

About 11 percent of Asian families were in poverty in 1989, a rate slightly higher than the 10 percent for all American families.

Hmong and Cambodian families had the highest family poverty rates, 62 percent and 42 percent, respectively. The lowest poverty rates were for Filipino (5 percent) and Japanese (3 percent) families.

Figure 10.
Poverty Rates for Asian Persons: 1989

(Percent)

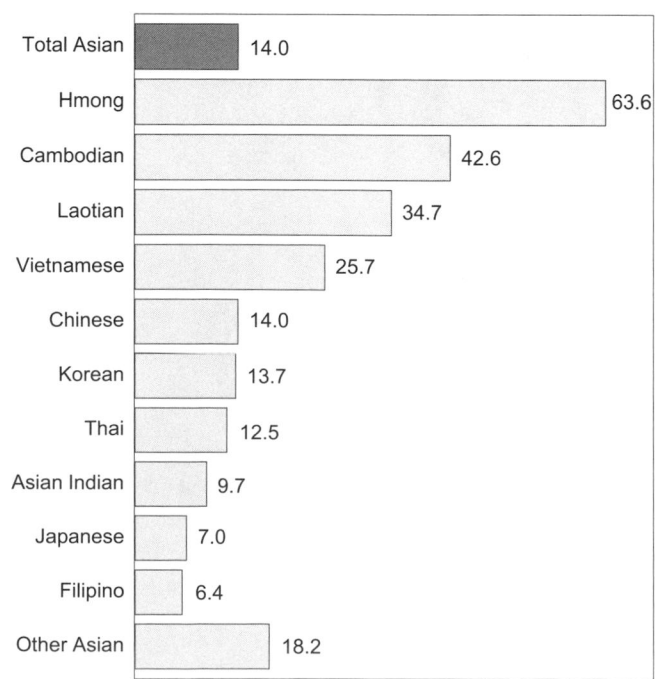

We, the American Pacific Islanders

Introduction

We, the American Pacific Islanders, are a small but distinct and important component of the Asian and Pacific Islander population.

A companion report, "We, the American Asians" provides a statistical portrait of the Asian component of the Asian and Pacific Islander population.

The 1990 census counted 365,024 Pacific Islanders, a 41 percent increase over the 1980 count of 259,566. We were about 5 percent of all Asian and Pacific Islander Americans in 1990. Pacific Islanders include diverse populations who differ in language and culture. They are of Polynesian, Micronesian, and Melanesian backgrounds. The Polynesian group is the largest of the three and includes Hawaiians, Samoans, Tongans, and Tahitians. The Micronesian group, the second largest, is primarily Guamanian (or Chamorros), but also includes other Mariana Islanders, Marshall Islanders, Palauans, and several other groups. The Fijian population is the largest Melanesian group.

Immigration was a major factor in the growth of the Asian and Pacific Islander population as a whole, with large numbers coming to the United States from Asia and the Pacific Islands following the adoption of the Immigration Act of 1965.

Immigration played a much more varied role, however, in the growth of our Pacific Islander population. Only 13 percent of us were foreign born. Hawaiians are, of course, native to this land. Persons born in American Samoa are United States nationals with the right of free entry into the United States, and since 1950 inhabitants of Guam are United States citizens.

In addition to immigration and natural increase, part of our growth between 1970 and 1990 reflects changes in the race question on the census form to include more groups, as well as improvements in collection and processing procedures in the 1990 census.

Although some groups are small, all Pacific Islander groups are important and make continuing contributions to the diversity of the United States. The table at the end of this report shows some characteristics for selected Pacific Islander groups. This report, however, will focus on the five largest Pacific Islander groups.

Our population grew 41 percent between 1980 and 1990, from 259,566 to 365,024.

Hawaiians, the largest Pacific Islander group, were 58 percent of the total Pacific Islander population.

Samoans and Guamanians were the next largest groups, representing 17 percent and 14 percent, respectively, followed by Tongans and Fijians who were 5 percent and 2 percent, respectively, of all Pacific Islanders.

Other Pacific Islanders, including Palauans, Northern Mariana Islanders, and Tahitians each constituted less than one-half of 1 percent of Pacific Islander Americans.

Tongans grew more rapidly (146 percent) during the 1980's than any of the top three groups.

Figure 1.

Distribution of the Pacific Islander Population: 1990

(Percent)

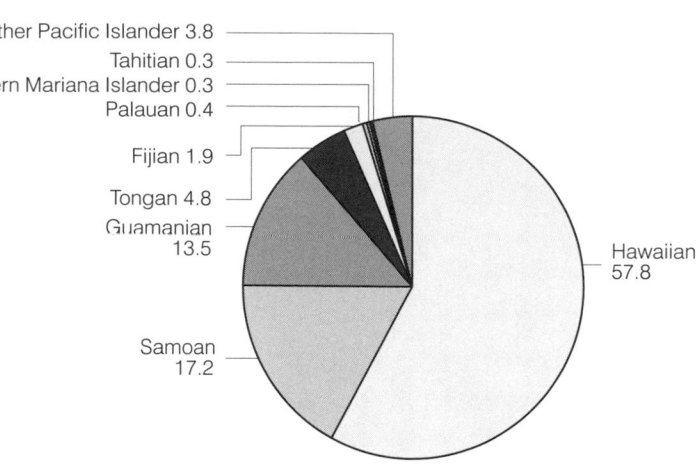

All other Pacific Islander 3.8
Tahitian 0.3
Northern Mariana Islander 0.3
Palauan 0.4
Fijian 1.9
Tongan 4.8
Guamanian 13.5
Samoan 17.2
Hawaiian 57.8

Most of us live in the West.

Eighty-six percent of the Pacific Islander population lived in the West in 1990 compared with 56 percent of the Asian and Pacific Islander group as a whole and 21 percent of the total population.

Approximately 75 percent of Pacific Islanders lived in just two States — California and Hawaii. These two States had more than 100,000 Pacific Islanders.

Washington was the only other State that had 15,000 or more Pacific Islanders.

The number of States with 5,000 or more Pacific Islanders doubled between 1980 and 1990, when Oregon, Texas, and Utah joined California, Hawaii, and Washington.

Figure 2.

Pacific Islander Population: 1990

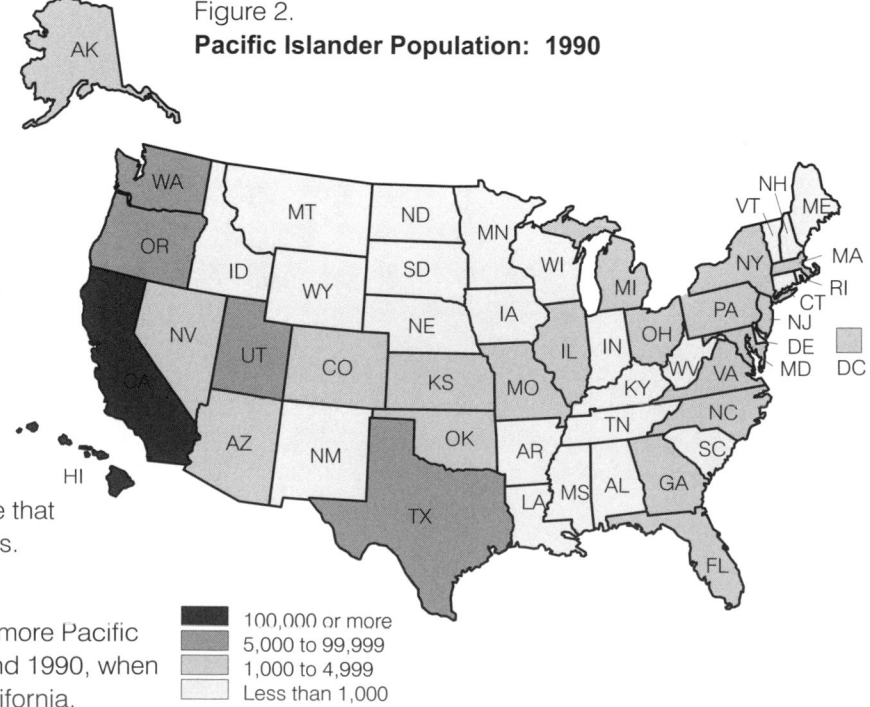

- 100,000 or more
- 5,000 to 99,999
- 1,000 to 4,999
- Less than 1,000

Most of us are native born.

Only 13 percent of Pacific Islanders were foreign born, much lower than the 63 percent for the total Asian and Pacific Islander population.

Among the Pacific Islander groups, Tongans had the highest proportion of foreign born at 61 percent.

Samoans and Guamanians had much lower proportions of foreign born, 23 percent and 11 percent, respectively.

Only 1 percent of Hawaiians, natives to this land, were foreign born.

Figure 3.
Foreign-Born Population: 1990

(Percent)

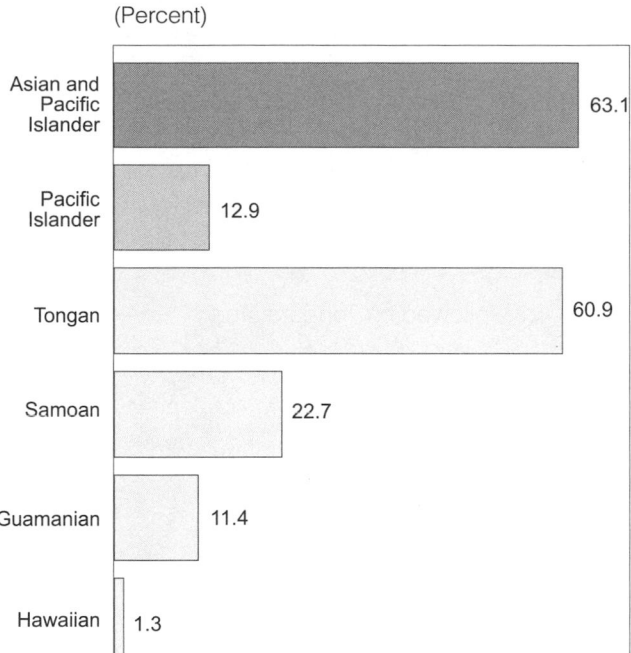

We are a relatively young population.

Pacific Islanders had a median age of 25 years in 1990. The median age was about 30 years for the Asian and Pacific Islander population as a whole and 33 for the total population.

Only 4 percent of Pacific Islanders were 65 years old and over compared with 6 percent of all Asians and Pacific Islanders and 13 percent of the total population.

In 1990, Hawaiians had the oldest median age among Pacific Islanders, 26 years, followed by Guamanians with a median age of 25.

Samoans, at 22 years, had the youngest median age among Pacific Islanders.

Figure 4.
Median Age: 1990

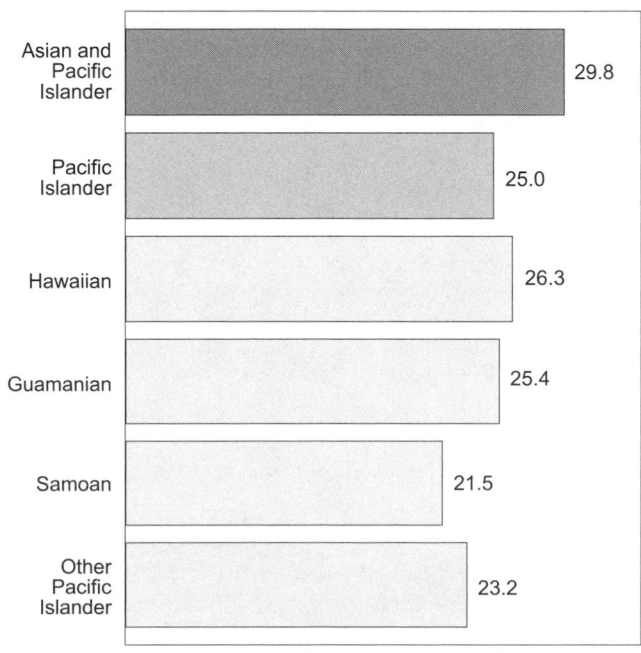

We have larger families than the average for the Nation.

The average Pacific Islander family had 4.1 persons in 1990, larger than the average number of persons per family for Asians and Pacific Islanders (3.8 persons) and all American families (3.2 persons). Pacific Islander families were larger partly because of higher fertility rates, but also because many maintain traditions of strong and cohesive extended families.

Family size ranged from 4.8 persons for Samoans to 3.8 persons for Hawaiians. Among Pacific Islander families, 73 percent were maintained by a husband and wife compared with 81 percent of Asian and Pacific Islander families.

Pacific Islanders were more likely to have a female householder with no spouse present (19 percent) than all Asians and Pacific Islanders (12 percent).

Many of us first come to America to pursue higher education.

In 1990, 76 percent of all Pacific Islanders 25 years old and over were at least high school graduates. The rate for all Asians and Pacific Islanders was 78 percent and the national rate was 75 percent.

Within the Pacific Islander group, the proportion who received a high school diploma or higher ranged from 80 percent for Hawaiians to 64 percent for Tongans.

In general, Pacific Islander men had higher rates of high school completion than women, 77 percent versus 75 percent. Tongan women, however, had higher rates of high school completion than Tongan men.

At the college level, 11 percent of Pacific Islanders were graduates compared with 37 percent of all Asians and Pacific Islanders and 20 percent of the total population.

Hawaiians had the highest college completion rate among Pacific Islanders at 12 percent, followed by Guamanians at 10 percent, Samoans at 8 percent, and Tongans at 6 percent.

Figure 5.
Persons Per Family: 1990

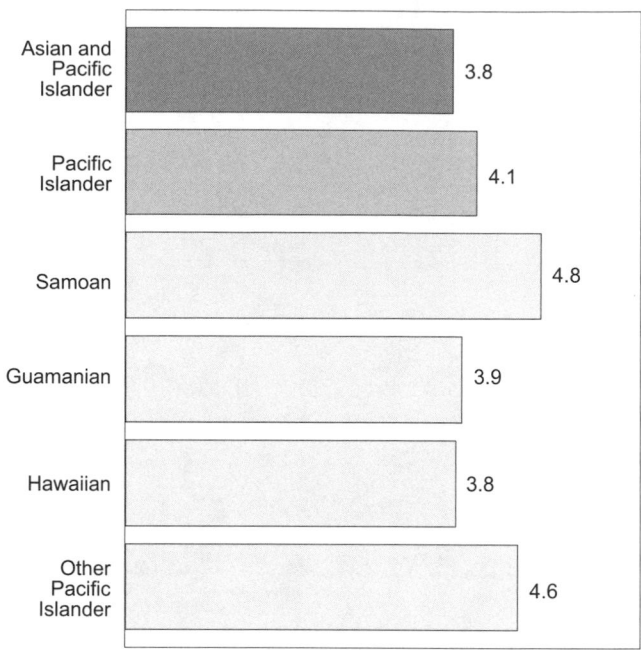

Table 1.
Educational Attainment by Sex: 1990

(Percent 25 years old and over)

	High school graduate or higher		Bachelor's degree or higher	
	Men	Women	Men	Women
Total	**75.7**	**74.8**	**23.3**	**17.6**
Asian and Pacific Islander .	81.5	74.0	41.9	31.8
Pacific Islander ..	77.2	75.0	12.0	9.6
Hawaiian	79.9	79.0	13.0	10.7
Samoan	74.7	66.5	9.8	6.1
Tongan	61.4	66.8	5.6	5.9
Guamanian	73.9	70.6	11.8	8.2

One-fourth of us speak a language other than English at home.

Of the 78,000 Pacific Islander persons 5 years old and over speaking a language other than English at home, 25 percent spoke an Asian or Pacific Islander language at home. Thirty-three percent of these did not speak English "very well," and 11 percent were "linguistically isolated."

Among Pacific Islanders, Tongans and Samoans had the highest proportion of persons 5 years old and over speaking an Asian or Pacific Islander language at home. Hawaiians had the lowest proportion.

Tongans had the highest proportion of persons who were linguistically isolated among Pacific Islander groups.

Table 2.
Language Spoken at Home and Ability to Speak English: 1990

(Percent 5 years old and over)

	Speak Asian or Pacific Islander language at home	Do not speak English "very well"	Linguis- tically isolated
Asian and Pacific Islander ...	63.3	55.6	34.4
Pacific Islander ...	24.9	33.4	11.1
Hawaiian	7.7	26.7	8.1
Samoan	63.9	32.7	9.3
Tongan	72.4	47.4	21.6
Guamanian .	30.2	24.1	7.1

Note: Linguistic isolation refers to persons in households in which no one 14 years old or over speaks only English and no one who speaks a language other than English speaks English "very well."

We are well represented in the labor force.

A larger proportion of Pacific Islanders partici- pated in the labor force than did the Asian and Pacific Islander population as a whole. Only Samoans and Tongans were below the Pacific Islander average.

Guamanians had the highest labor force partici- pation rate at 72 percent.

Sixty-three percent of Pacific Islander women were in the labor force compared with 60 percent of all Asian and Pacific Islander women and 57 percent of all women in the United States.

The percent of Pacific Islander women in the labor force ranged from 55 percent for Samoans to 63 percent for Guamanians.

Figure 6.
Labor Force Participation: 1990

(Percent persons 16 years old and over)

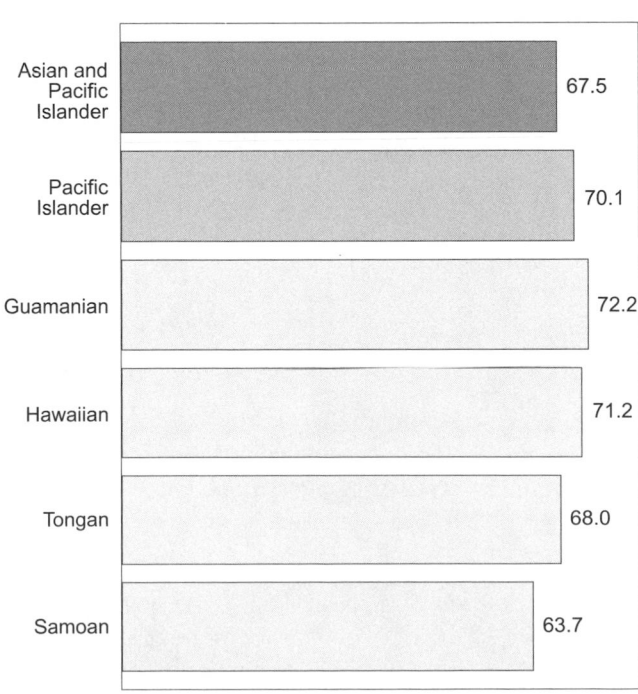

Asian and Pacific Islander	67.5
Pacific Islander	70.1
Guamanian	72.2
Hawaiian	71.2
Tongan	68.0
Samoan	63.7

Nearly one-third of Pacific Islanders are employed in technical, sales, and administrative support jobs.

Pacific Islanders were more likely to be in service occupations than the total Asian and Pacific Islander population, but less likely to be in managerial or professional occupations.

Tongans were more likely than all Pacific Islanders to work in service occupations and less likely to be managers or professionals.

Pacific Islanders were more likely than all Asian and Pacific Islanders to work in precision production, craft, and repair occupations or as operators, fabricators, and laborers.

Although farming, forestry, and fishing are common in many Pacific Island areas, less than 3 percent of Pacific Islanders worked in farming, forestry, and fishing in the United States.

Figure 7.
Occupation: 1990

(Percent employed persons 16 years old and over)

Asian and Pacific Islander

Pacific Islander

Occupation	Asian and Pacific Islander	Pacific Islander
Managerial and professional specialty	30.6	18.1
Technical, sales, and administrative support	33.2	32.1
Service	14.8	19.2
Farming, forestry, and fishing	1.2	2.5
Precision production, craft, and repair	8.0	11.9
Operators, fabricators, and laborers	12.1	16.3

Our families are well represented in the work force.

About 19.7 percent of Pacific Islander families and 19.8 percent of Asian and Pacific Islander families had three or more workers compared with 13.4 percent of the Nation's families.

Pacific Islander families were also less likely than all families to have no workers (9 percent compared with 13 percent). Only 3 percent of Tongan families had no workers.

About 26 percent of Pacific Islander families had one worker and 46 percent had two workers. These percentages were similar to those for all Asian and Pacific Islander families.

Samoans were somewhat more likely than Pacific Islanders as a whole to have one-worker families (30 percent compared with 26 percent) and less likely to have two-worker families (40 percent compared with 46 percent).

Figure 8.
Families With Three or More Workers: 1990

(Percent)

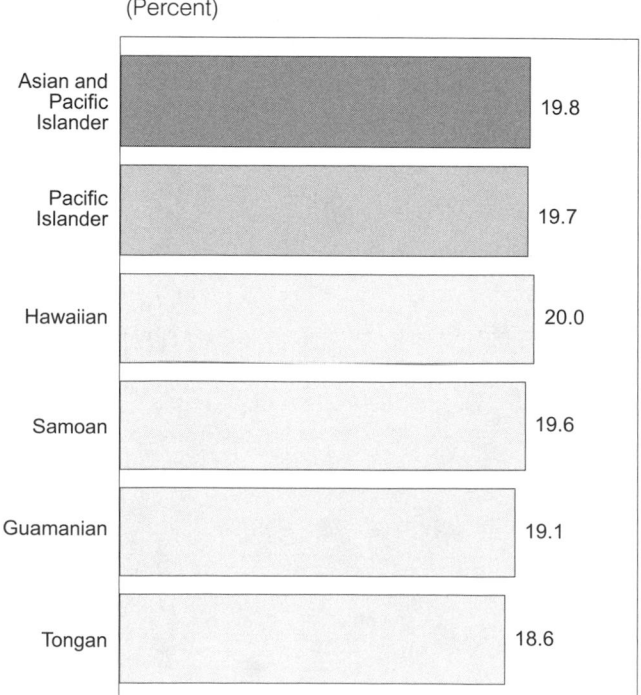

	Percent
Asian and Pacific Islander	19.8
Pacific Islander	19.7
Hawaiian	20.0
Samoan	19.6
Guamanian	19.1
Tongan	18.6

Our per capita income is below the National average.

In 1989, the Pacific Islander per capita income was $10,342, lower than $13,638 for Asians and Pacific Islanders and $14,143 for the Nation.

The lower per capita income of Pacific Islanders in part reflects the larger average size of Pacific Islander families (4.08) compared to all families nationally (3.16).

The median income of Pacific Islander families ($33,955) is slightly lower than that for all families ($35,225). Pacific Islanders' median household income in 1989 ($31,980) was slightly higher than that for all households ($30,056).

Hawaiians had the highest per capita income at $11,446 of all Pacific Islander groups, followed by Guamanians with $10,834.

Tongan and Samoan per capita income was about half the National per capita income, $6,144 and $7,690, respectively.

Figure 9.
Per Capita Income: 1990

(In 1989 dollars)

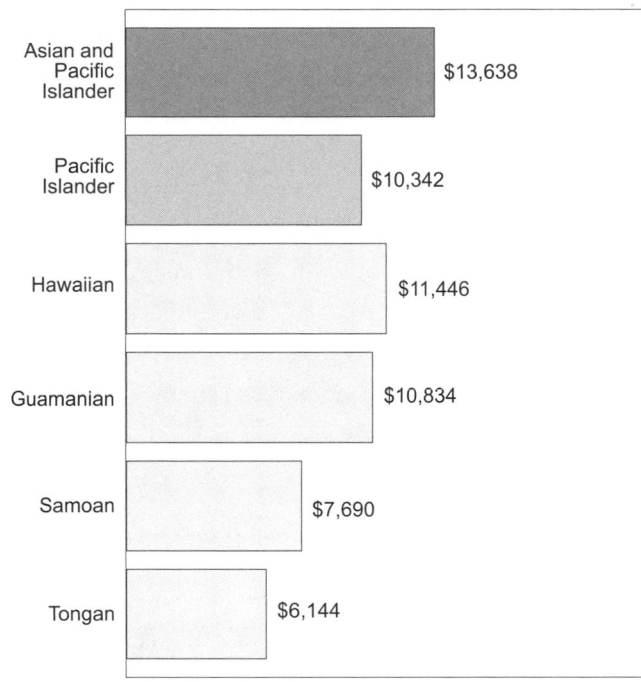

Our poverty rate is higher than that for all Asians and Pacific Islanders.

About 58,000 or 17 percent of Pacific Islanders lived below the poverty level in 1989, higher than the 14 percent poverty rate for all Asians and Pacific Islanders.

Among Pacific Islanders, Samoans had the highest poverty rate at 26 percent. Tongans had the next highest poverty rate in 1989 at 23 percent.

About 1 of every 4 Samoan families and 1 of every 5 Tongan families were below the poverty level in 1989.

Figure 10.
Poverty Rates for Persons: 1989

(Percent In poverty)

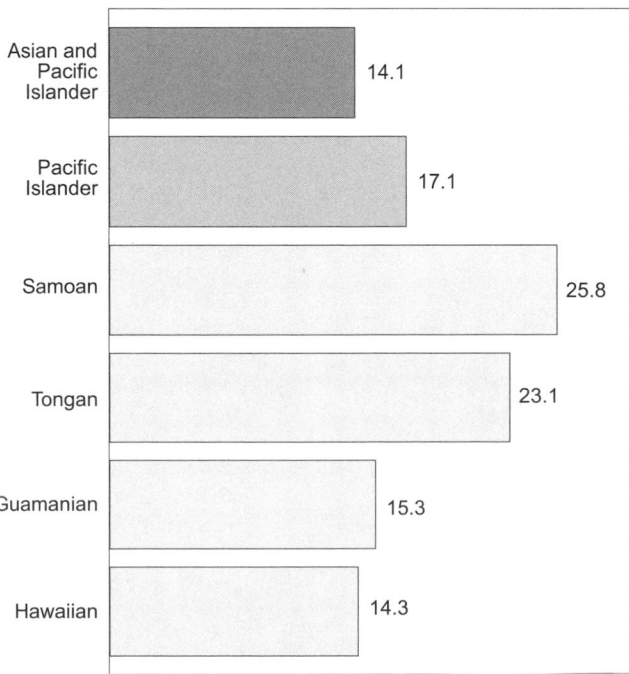

e, the First Americans

Introduction

We, the American Indians and Alaska Natives, are the original inhabitants of America. Our land once was a vast stretch of forest, plains, and mountains extending from the Atlantic to the Pacific Ocean and from the Arctic Circle to the tip of South America. In many American Indian and Alaska Native lands across the country, we still hunt, fish, and gather from the land, rivers, and seas, much as we have for thousands of years.

Our long and proud heritage continues in our many traditional foods, medicines, and names all Americans use. We have survived numerous disruptions of our lives and dislocations from our native habitats. Today, while still maintaining our tribal traditions and languages, we strive to accept new technologies which address our needs.

This is a descriptive profile of the American Indian and Alaska Native populations. Characteristics such as population size, family composition, education, labor force status, occupation, income, and poverty status are presented in three sections.

Section 1 — Figures 1-10.

Characteristics of the American Indian, Eskimo, and Aleut Population

The nearly 2 million American Indians, Eskimos, and Aleuts living in the United States in 1990 represented an increase of 38 percent over the 1980 total. Data are presented for the total American Indian, Eskimo, and Aleut population compared with the total population of the United States.

Section 2 — Figures 11-22.

Characteristics of the American Indian, Eskimo, and Aleut Population on 10 Largest Reservations and Trust Lands

The 1990 census showed that 437,079 American Indians, 182 Eskimos, and 97 Aleuts lived on 314 reservations and trust lands; about 218,290 American Indians, 25 Eskimos, and 5 Aleuts lived on the 10 largest reservations and trust lands.

Data are presented for the American Indian, Eskimo, and Aleut population on all reservations and trust lands, as well as the 10 reservations and trust lands with the largest populations — Navajo, Pine Ridge, Fort Apache, Gila River, Papago, Rosebud, Hopi, San Carlos, Zuni Pueblo, and Blackfeet.

Section 3 — Figures 23-32.

Characteristics of the Alaska Native Population (American Indians, Eskimos, and Aleuts) in Alaska

In 1990, there were 85,698 Alaska Natives living in Alaska. Most were Eskimos, but substantial numbers were American Indians and Aleuts. In 1980, the Alaska Native population numbered 64,103, a 34 percent increase during the 1980's. Data are presented for all Alaska Natives, as well as separately for the three groups— American Indians, Eskimos, and Aleuts.

The increase in the American Indian, Eskimo, and Aleut population cannot be attributed only to natural increase. Other factors may have contributed to the higher count of American Indians, Eskimos, and Aleuts such as: improvements in the way the Census Bureau counted people on reservations, on trust lands, and in Alaska Native villages; continued use of self-identification to obtain information on race; greater propensity in 1990 than in earlier censuses for individuals (especially those of mixed Indian and non-Indian parentage) to report themselves as American Indian; and improved outreach programs and promotion campaigns.

The possible effect of these factors upon the data in this report should be considered in interpreting changes from 1980 to 1990 in the size, distribution, and characteristics of the American Indian, Eskimo, and Aleut population.

Section 1 - **American Indian, Eskimo, and Aleut Population**

Although we are the First Americans, we have only been counted as a population for 100 years.

Estimates of the number of American Indians (including Eskimos and Aleuts) have been made since the founding of the Nation, but it was not until 1860 that the Federal Government counted this group. In 1860, Indians were counted if they had left their reservations and lived among other Americans. The 1890 census was the first to obtain a complete census of American Indians throughout the country.

In the first half of this century, the American Indian population grew slowly in contrast to the period from 1950 to 1990, which was one of rapid growth.

Projections show growth of the American Indian population, reaching 4.6 million by 2050.

Nearly one-half of the American Indian population lived in the West in 1990, 29 percent in the South, 17 percent in the Midwest, and 6 percent in the Northeast. Between 1980 and 1990, the proportion of American Indians increased noticeably only in the South, from 26 percent to 29 percent.

Our 500 tribes vary greatly in size.

In 1990, the only tribes with more than 100,000 persons were the Cherokee, Navajo, Chippewa, and Sioux. Approximately 16 percent of all Indians reported themselves as Cherokee, 12 percent as Navajo, and 6 percent each as Chippewa and Sioux.

The Choctaw, Pueblo, and Apache had populations of at least 50,000 persons. The Choctaw accounted for 4 percent of the American Indian population. The Iroquois Confederacy, Lumbee, and Creek all had 43,000 or more persons.

The 1990 census showed that 14 tribes had a population between 10,000 and 21,000 persons. Most tribes had populations of less than 10,000.

Figure 1.

American Indian, Eskimo, and Aleut Population: 1890 to 1990

(Thousands)

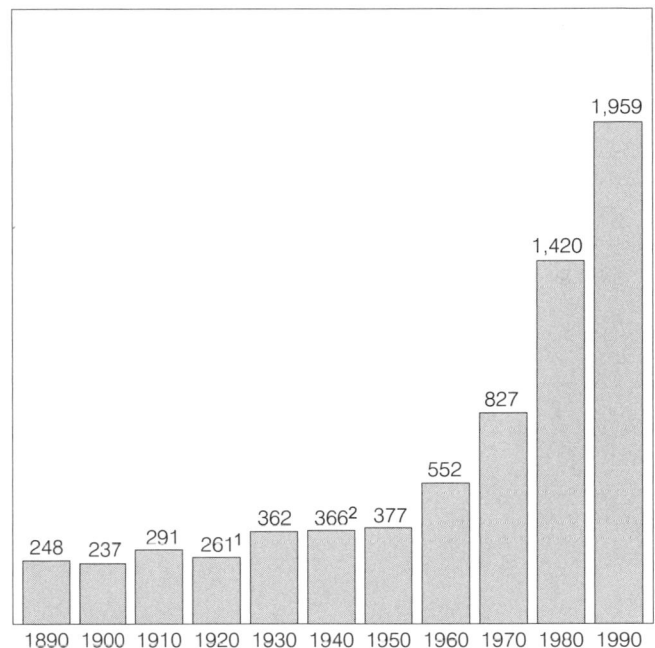

[1] Partially estimated.
[2] Eskimo and Aleut population are based on 1939 counts.

Figure 2.

Ten Largest American Indian Tribes: 1990

(Thousands)

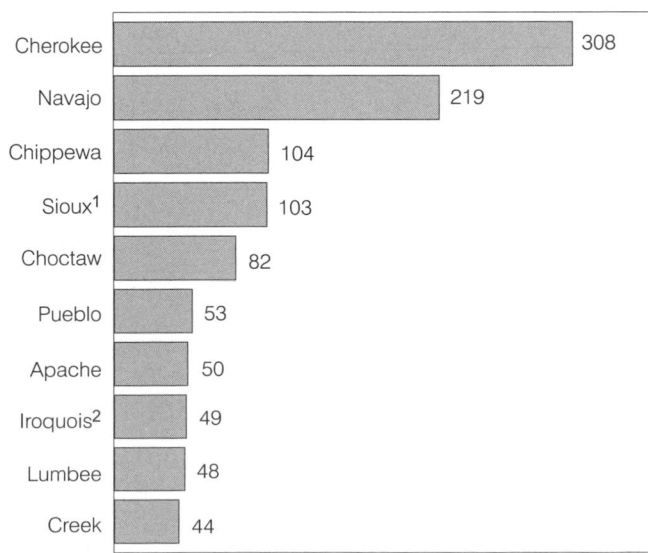

[1] Any entry with the spelling "Siouan" was miscoded to Sioux in North Carolina.
[2] Reporting and/or processing problems have affected the data for this tribe.

281

Section 1 - **American Indian, Eskimo, and Aleut Population**—Con.

Nearly one-half of us live West of the Mississippi River.

Two of every three American Indians (including Eskimos and Aleuts) lived in the 10 States with the largest American Indian populations in 1990. Of these States, only North Carolina, Michigan, and New York are east of the Mississippi River.

In 1990, more than half of the American Indian population lived in just six States: Oklahoma, California, Arizona, New Mexico, Alaska, and Washington.

Oklahoma was the State with the largest American Indian population in 1990, climbing from second position in 1980. Between 1980 and 1990, California dropped from first to second place, and Arizona and New Mexico stayed at third and fourth place, respectively.

Figure 3.
Ten States With the Largest Number of American Indians, Eskimos, and Aleuts: 1990

(Thousands)

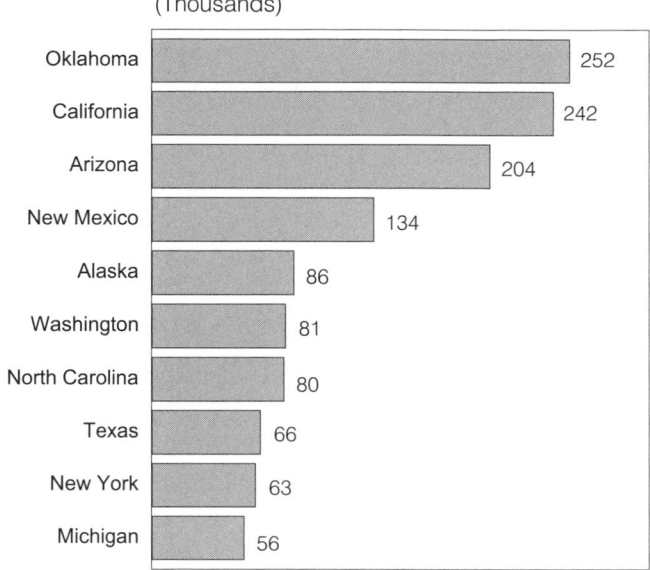

Oklahoma	252
California	242
Arizona	204
New Mexico	134
Alaska	86
Washington	81
North Carolina	80
Texas	66
New York	63
Michigan	56

We have a young and growing population.

Thirty-nine percent of the American Indian (including Eskimo and Aleut) population was under 20 years old in 1990 compared with 29 percent of the Nation's total population.

About 8 percent of all American Indians were 60 years old and over in 1990, about half of the proportion (17 percent) for the total population.

The median age of the American Indian population was 26 years, considerably younger than the U.S. median age of 33 years. The American Indian population is younger in part because of higher fertility rates than the total population.

Figure 4.
Population by Age and Sex: 1990

(Percent distribution)

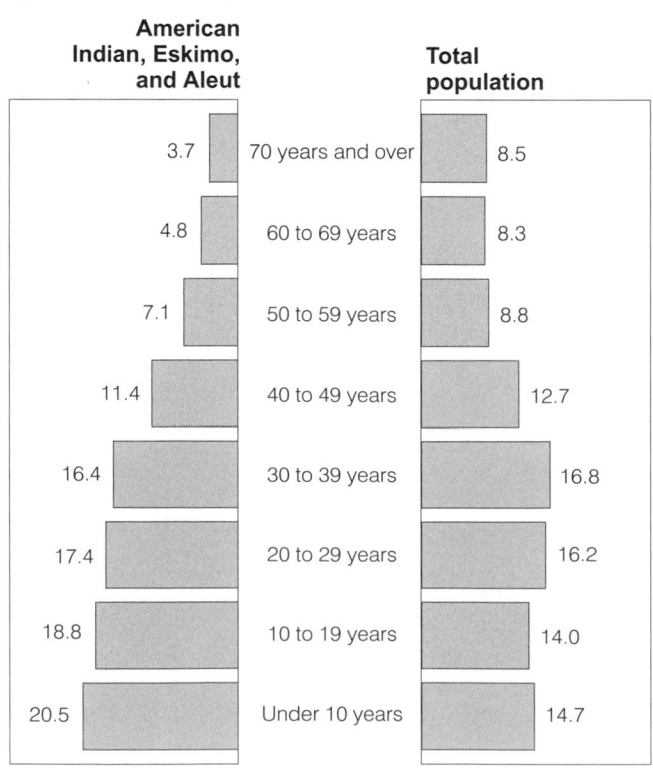

American Indian, Eskimo, and Aleut		Total population
3.7	70 years and over	8.5
4.8	60 to 69 years	8.3
7.1	50 to 59 years	8.8
11.4	40 to 49 years	12.7
16.4	30 to 39 years	16.8
17.4	20 to 29 years	16.2
18.8	10 to 19 years	14.0
20.5	Under 10 years	14.7

Section 1 - **American Indian, Eskimo, and Aleut Population**—Con.

We have more families maintained by a female householder than the total population.

In 1990, the vast majority of American Indian (including Eskimo and Aleut) families had both a husband and wife present. However, the proportion of families maintained by a female householder without a husband present was higher than the national figure.

Among the Nation's 442,000 American Indian families in 1990, 6 in 10 were married-couple families compared with about 8 in 10 of the Nation's 64.5 million families.

Consistent with the national trend, the proportion of American Indian families maintained by a female householder without a husband present increased during the last decade and reached 27 percent in 1990. This proportion was considerably larger than the national figure of 17 percent.

American Indian families were slightly larger than all families—3.6 persons per family versus 3.2 persons per family. In 1990, American Indian married-couple families (54 percent) were less likely to have children under 18 years old compared with all married-couple families (70 percent).

Our educational attainment improved during the 1980's.

The educational attainment levels of American Indians (including Eskimos and Aleuts) improved significantly during the 1980's, but remained considerably below the levels of the total population.

In 1990, 66 percent of the 1,080,000 American Indians 25 years old and over were high school graduates or higher compared with only 56 percent in 1980. Despite the advances, the 1990 proportion was still below the total population (75 percent).

American Indians were not as likely as the entire U.S. population to have completed a bachelor's degree or higher. About 9 percent of American Indians completed a bachelor's degree or higher in 1990 compared with 8 percent in 1980—still lower than the 20 percent for the total population in 1990.

Figure 5.
Families by Type of Family: 1990

(Percent)

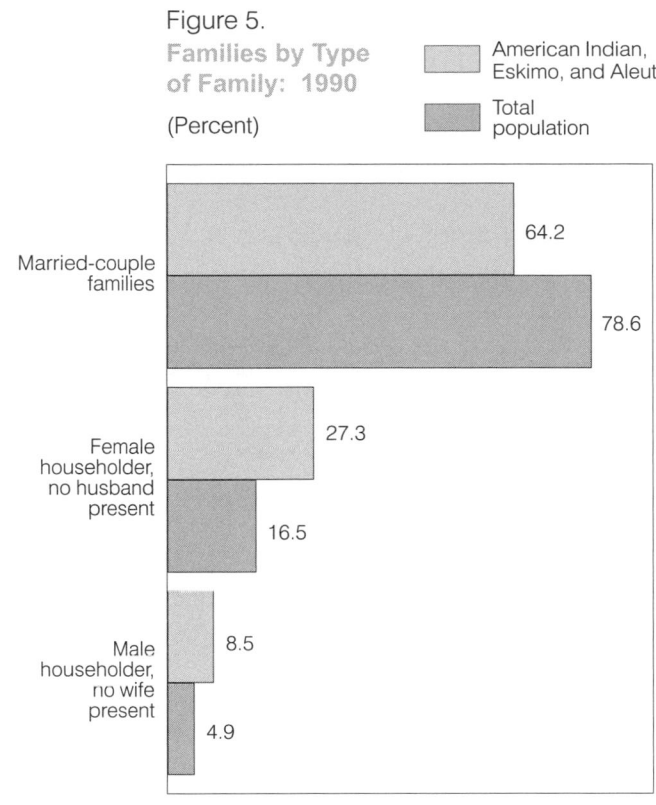

Figure 6.
Educational Attainment: 1990

(Percent of persons 25 years old and over)

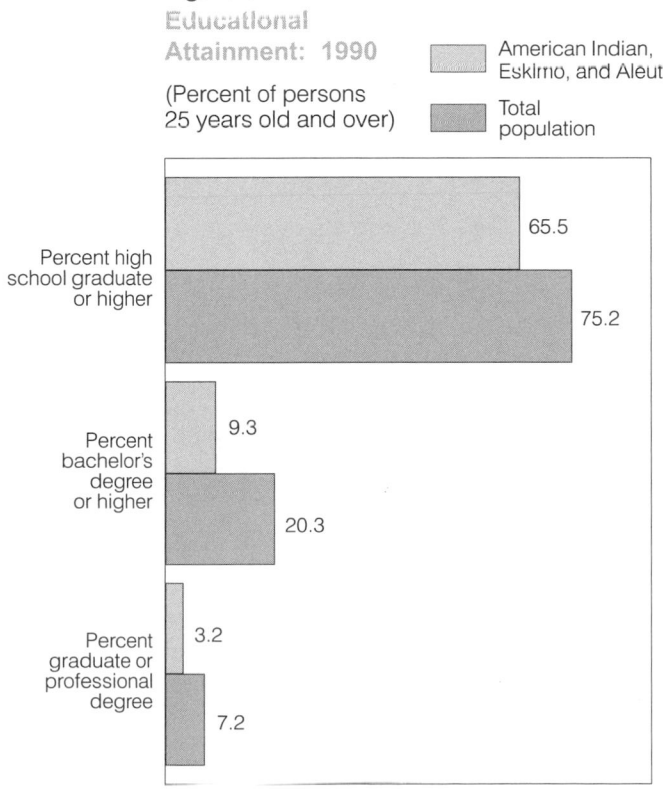

Section 1 - **American Indian, Eskimo, and Aleut Population**—Con.

We have lower labor force participation rates than the total population.

Overall, 62 percent of the 1,395,009 American Indians (including Eskimos and Aleuts) 16 years old and over were in the labor force in 1990, 3 percentage points below the 65 percent for the total population.

Sixty-nine percent of American Indian males 16 years old and over were in the labor force compared with more than 74 percent for all males.

American Indian women have shared in the national trend of increased labor force participation by women. The proportion of American Indian women in the labor force increased from 48 percent in 1980 to 55 percent in 1990. The rate for all women in 1990 was only slightly higher at 57 percent.

Figure 7.

Labor Force Participation Rates by Sex: 1990

(Percent of persons 16 years old and over)

American Indian, Eskimo, and Aleut

Total population

Both sexes: 62.1 / 65.3

Male: 69.4 / 74.4

Female: 55.1 / 56.8

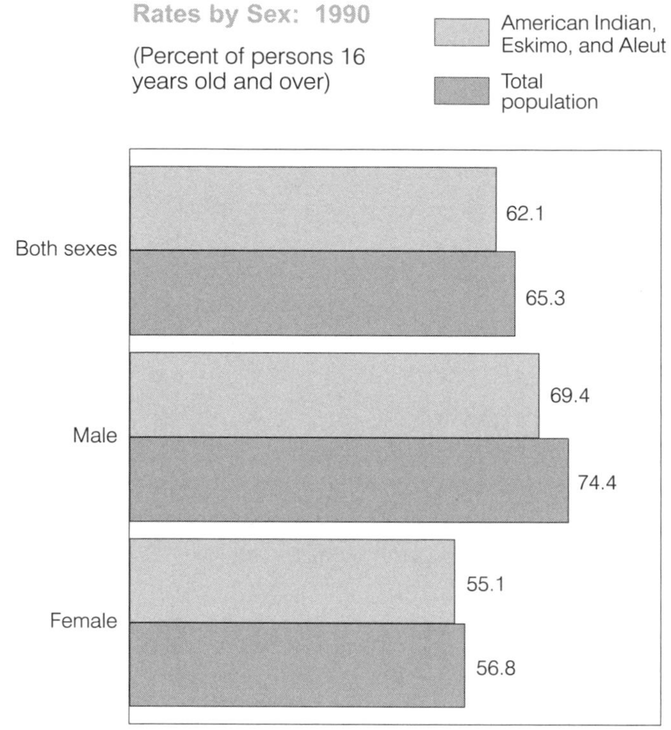

Our choices of occupations differ from those of all Americans.

In 1990, 729,000 American Indians (including Eskimos and Aleuts) were employed in various occupations. The distribution of employed American Indians among the six major occupational categories differed from that of the general population.

A smaller proportion of American Indians than of the total population were employed in managerial and professional specialty occupations. This was also true for technical, sales, and administrative support jobs.

A larger proportion of American Indians than of the total population were employed in service occupations; farming, forestry, and fishing jobs; precision production, craft, and repair occupations; or were employed as operators, fabricators, and laborers.

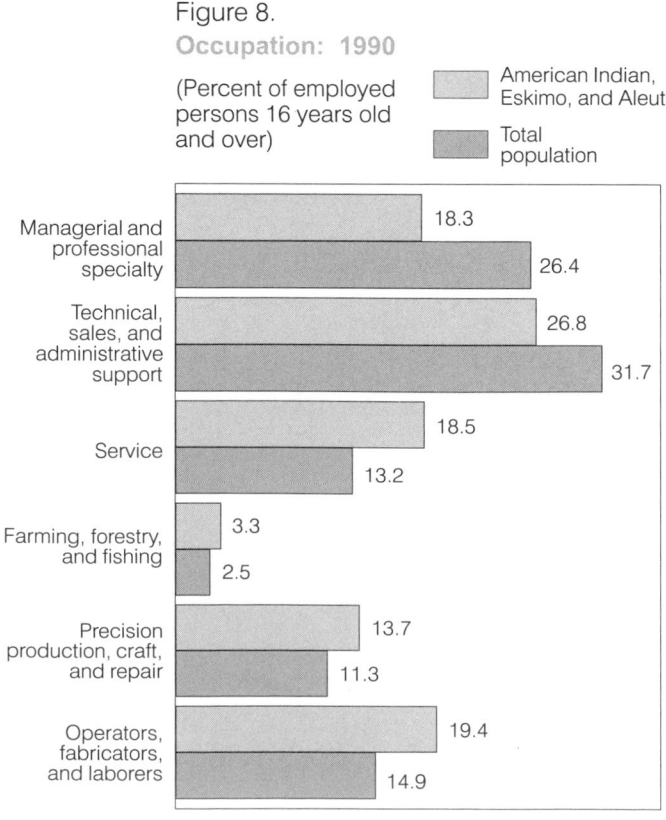

Figure 8.

Occupation: 1990

(Percent of employed persons 16 years old and over)

American Indian, Eskimo, and Aleut

Total population

Managerial and professional specialty: 18.3 / 26.4

Technical, sales, and administrative support: 26.8 / 31.7

Service: 18.5 / 13.2

Farming, forestry, and fishing: 3.3 / 2.5

Precision production, craft, and repair: 13.7 / 11.3

Operators, fabricators, and laborers: 19.4 / 14.9

Section 1 - **American Indian, Eskimo, and Aleut Population**—Con.

Our incomes are well below those of all Americans.

In 1990, the median family income of American Indians (including Eskimos and Aleuts) was $21,750 compared with $35,225 for the total population. Stated another way, for every $100 U.S. families received, American Indian families received $62.

The median income of American Indian married-couple families was $28,287, or 71 percent of the $39,584 median for all married-couple families.

Twenty-seven percent of all American Indian families were maintained by a female householder with no husband present in 1990. The median income for these families was $10,742, about 62 percent of the $17,414 median for all families maintained by women without husbands.

Many of our people live in poverty.

The proportion of American Indian (including Eskimo and Aleut) persons and families living below the official Government poverty level In 1989 was considerably higher than that of the total population.

In 1989, about 603,000, or 31 percent, of American Indians were living below the poverty level. The national poverty rate was about 13 percent (31.7 million persons).

Twenty-seven percent, or 125,000, American Indian families were in poverty in 1989 compared with 10 percent of all families (6.5 million).

Fifty percent of American Indian families maintained by females with no husband present were in poverty compared with 31 percent of all families maintained by women without husbands.

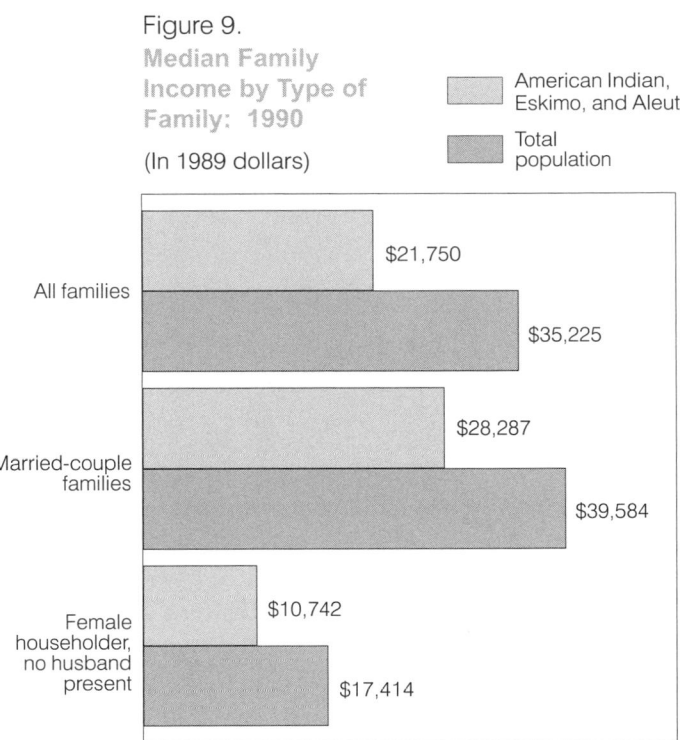

Figure 9.

Median Family Income by Type of Family: 1990

(In 1989 dollars)

American Indian, Eskimo, and Aleut

Total population

- All families: $21,750 / $35,225
- Married-couple families: $28,287 / $39,584
- Female householder, no husband present: $10,742 / $17,414

Figure 10.

Poverty Rates in 1989 by Type of Family

(Percent in poverty)

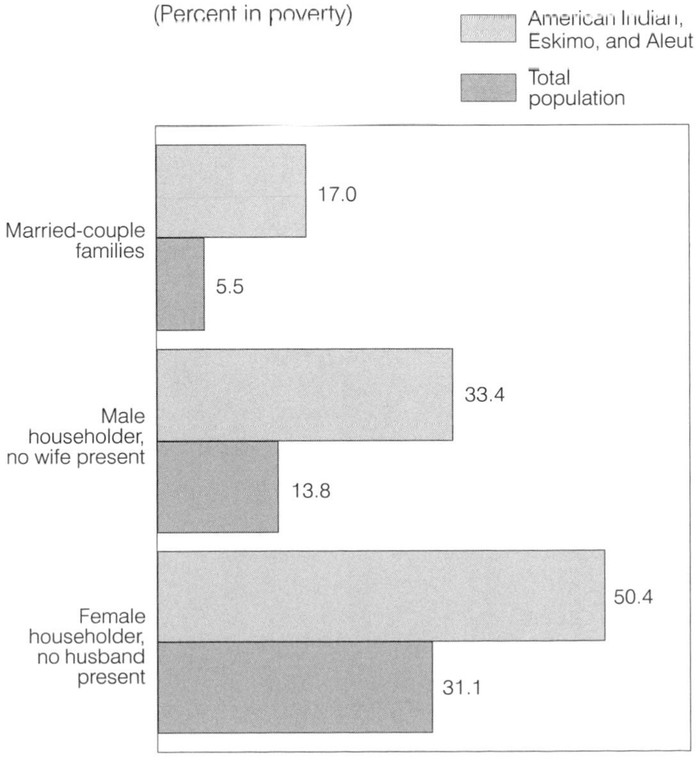

American Indian, Eskimo, and Aleut

Total population

- Married-couple families: 17.0 / 5.5
- Male householder, no wife present: 33.4 / 13.8
- Female householder, no husband present: 50.4 / 31.1

Section 2 - **American Indian, Eskimo, and Aleut Population on Reservations**

One-fifth of us live on reservations and trust lands.

Twenty-two percent, or 437,431, of all American Indians (including Eskimos and Aleuts) lived on reservations and trust lands in 1990. Reservations and trust lands are areas with boundaries established by treaty, statute, and/or executive or court order.

The American Indian population in the Tribal Jurisdiction Statistical Areas in Oklahoma numbered 200,789, and comprised 10 percent of the total American Indian population.

Three percent, or 53,644, of the American Indian population lived in Tribal Designated Statistical Areas and 2 percent, or 47,244, lived in Alaska Native Village Statistical Areas.

Figure 11.

American Indians, Eskimos, and Aleuts by Type of Area: 1990

(Percent distribution)

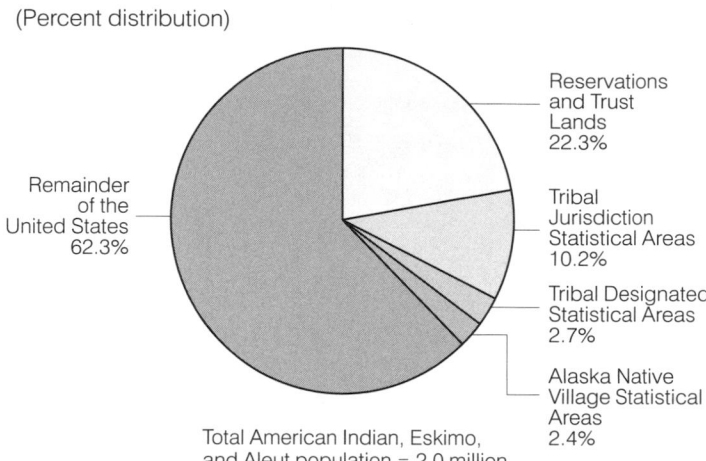

Total American Indian, Eskimo, and Aleut population = 2.0 million.

Our numbers on our 314 reservations and trust lands vary considerably.

The number of American Indians (including 182 Eskimos and 97 Aleuts) living on the 314 reservations and trust lands varied substantially. Only 10 reservations had more than 7,000 American Indians in 1990; most had fewer than 1,000.

Only the Navajo Reservation and trust lands had more than 100,000 American Indians, while the Pine Ridge Reservation and trust lands was the only other reservation with more than 10,000 American Indians in 1990.

An additional eight reservations had more than 7,000 American Indians; Fort Apache, Gila River, Papago, Rosebud, San Carlos, Zuni Pueblo, Hopi, and Blackfeet.

Seven of the 10 reservations and trust lands with the largest American Indian populations were entirely or partially located in Arizona.

The 218,320 American Indians living on the 10 largest reservations and trust lands accounted for about half of all American Indians living on reservations and trust lands.

Figure 12.

Ten Reservations With the Largest Number of American Indians, Eskimos, and Aleuts: 1990

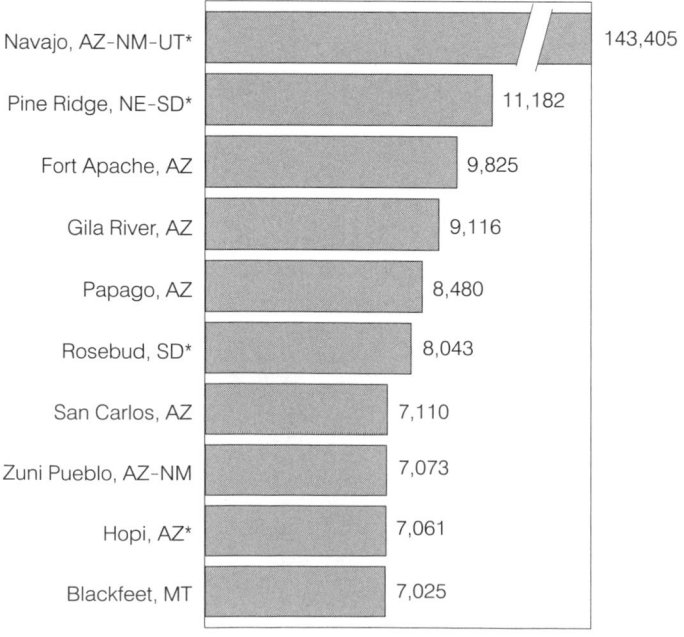

*Includes trust lands.

Section 2 - **American Indian, Eskimo, and Aleut Population on Reservations**—Con.

Our population on reservations is considerably younger because of high fertility rates.

The median age of the American Indian population on all reservations and trust lands was 22 years, considerably younger than the median age of 26 years for the total American Indian population and the U.S. median age of 33 years.

Among the 10 largest reservations and trust lands, Rosebud had the youngest median age followed by Pine Ridge, both approximately 19 years.

Hopi is the only reservation where the median age was about the same as the total American Indian median age of 26.

Figure 13.
Median Age: 1990

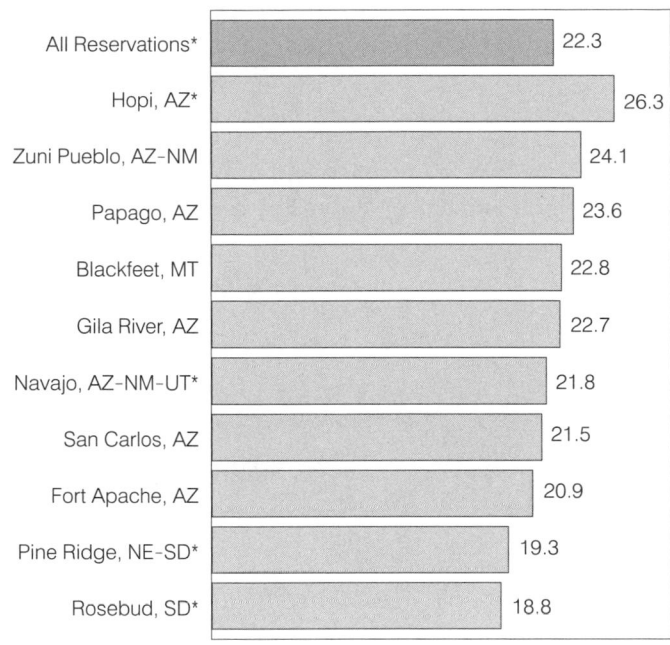

All Reservations*	22.3
Hopi, AZ*	26.3
Zuni Pueblo, AZ-NM	24.1
Papago, AZ	23.6
Blackfeet, MT	22.8
Gila River, AZ	22.7
Navajo, AZ-NM-UT*	21.8
San Carlos, AZ	21.5
Fort Apache, AZ	20.9
Pine Ridge, NE-SD*	19.3
Rosebud, SD*	18.8

*Includes trust lands.

Our school enrollment rates are higher on reservations.

Overall, more than 31 percent of American Indians 3 years old and over living on reservations and trust lands were enrolled in elementary or high school.

The enrollment rates for all American Indians 3 years old and over was 25 percent compared with 18 percent for the total U.S. population.

Of the 10 largest reservations, Rosebud, Pine Ridge, Gila River, and Navajo had the highest proportions enrolled in elementary or high school.

Figure 14.
School Enrollment: 1990

(Percent of persons 3 years old and over enrolled in elementary or high school)

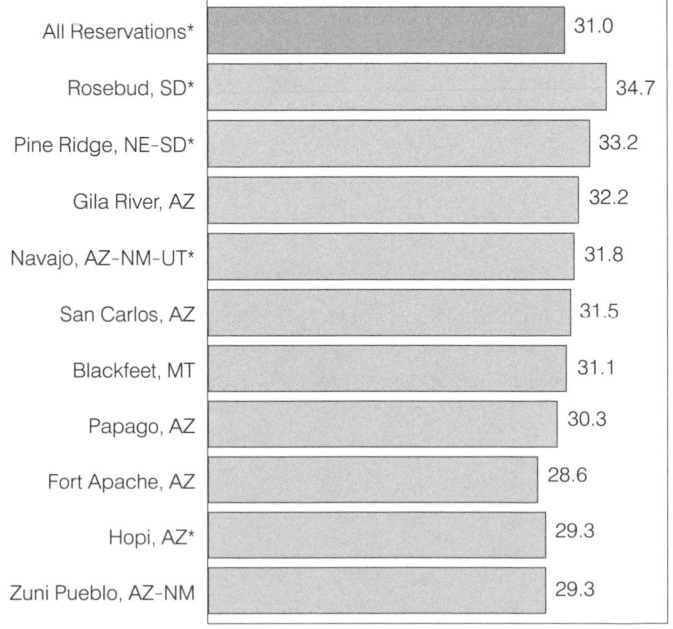

All Reservations*	31.0
Rosebud, SD*	34.7
Pine Ridge, NE-SD*	33.2
Gila River, AZ	32.2
Navajo, AZ-NM-UT*	31.8
San Carlos, AZ	31.5
Blackfeet, MT	31.1
Papago, AZ	30.3
Fort Apache, AZ	28.6
Hopi, AZ*	29.3
Zuni Pueblo, AZ-NM	29.3

*Includes trust lands.

287

Section 2 - **American Indian, Eskimo, and Aleut Population on Reservations**—Con.

Our educational attainment rates differ substantially among reservations.

The proportion of American Indian adults 25 years old and over with high school diplomas or higher on the 10 largest reservations and trust lands ranged from 37 percent to 66 percent.

Overall, 54 percent of American Indian adults living on all reservations and trust lands were high school graduates or higher.

Blackfeet and Hopi had similar proportions (66 percent and 63 percent) of high school graduates or higher.

Gila River, at about 37 percent, had the lowest proportion of high school graduates or higher, followed by Navajo with 41 percent.

Figure 15.
Educational Attainment: 1990

(Percent of persons 25 years old and over with a high school diploma or higher)

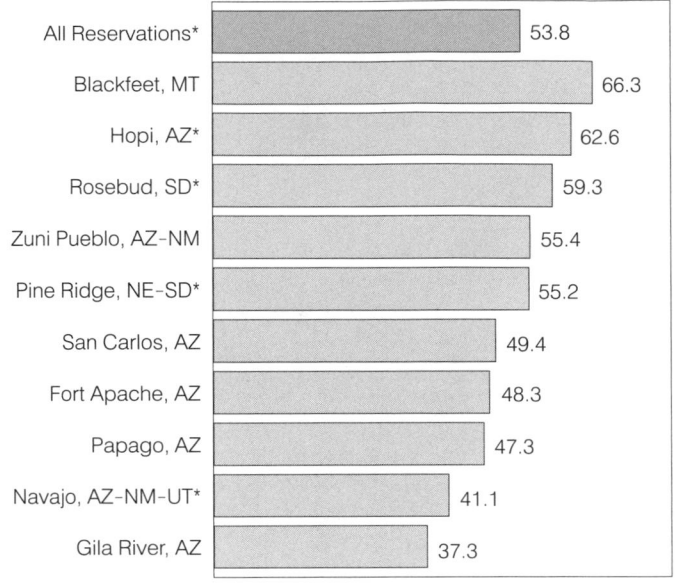

All Reservations*	53.8
Blackfeet, MT	66.3
Hopi, AZ*	62.6
Rosebud, SD*	59.3
Zuni Pueblo, AZ-NM	55.4
Pine Ridge, NE-SD*	55.2
San Carlos, AZ	49.4
Fort Apache, AZ	48.3
Papago, AZ	47.3
Navajo, AZ-NM-UT*	41.1
Gila River, AZ	37.3

*Includes trust lands.

Our labor force participation rates differ substantially among reservations.

There were substantial differences in civilian labor force participation rates for American Indians 16 years old and over on the 10 largest reservations and trust lands.

Zuni Pueblo had the highest proportion of American Indians employed in the civilian labor force in 1990.

About 69 percent or less of the American Indian population was employed in the civilian labor force at Blackfeet, Gila River, San Carlos, Pine Ridge, and Fort Apache.

Figure 16.
Employment Rates: 1990

(Percent of employed persons 16 years old and over in the civilian labor force)

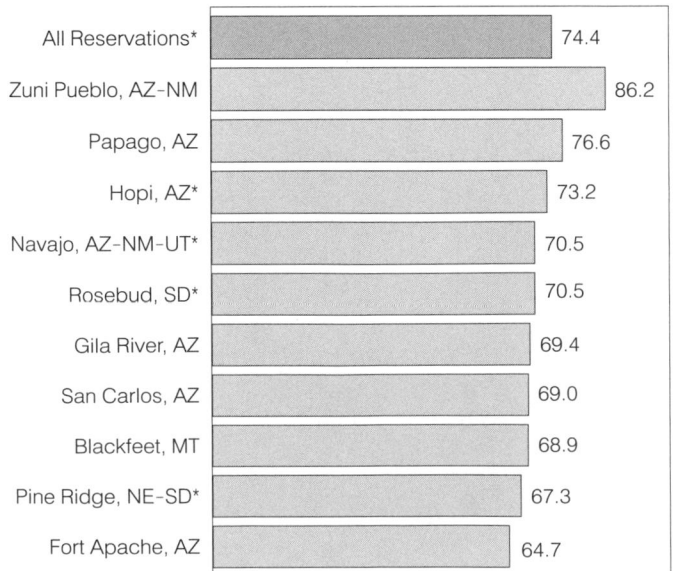

All Reservations*	74.4
Zuni Pueblo, AZ-NM	86.2
Papago, AZ	76.6
Hopi, AZ*	73.2
Navajo, AZ-NM-UT*	70.5
Rosebud, SD*	70.5
Gila River, AZ	69.4
San Carlos, AZ	69.0
Blackfeet, MT	68.9
Pine Ridge, NE-SD*	67.3
Fort Apache, AZ	64.7

*Includes trust lands.

Section 2 - **American Indian, Eskimo, and Aleut Population on Reservations**—Con.

Our per capita income ranged from just over $3,000 per person to nearly $5,000 per person in 1989.

The per capita income in 1989 was about $4,478 for American Indians residing on all reservations and trust lands.

The per capita income of American Indians on the 10 largest reservations ranged from $3,113 to $4,718. Blackfeet and Hopi had the highest per capita incomes.

The remaining eight reservations had per capita incomes of less than $4,000. Papago and Pine Ridge had the lowest per capita incomes of about $3,100.

Figure 17.
Per Capita Income: 1990

(In 1989 dollars)

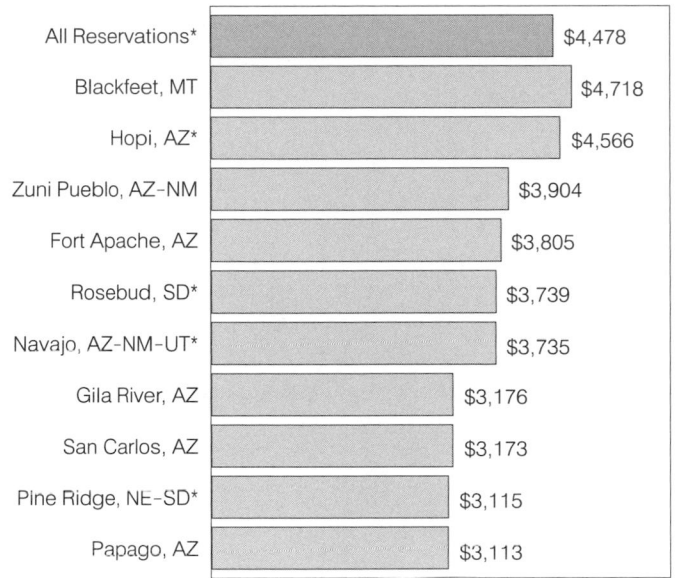

Reservation	Per Capita Income
All Reservations*	$4,478
Blackfeet, MT	$4,718
Hopi, AZ*	$4,566
Zuni Pueblo, AZ-NM	$3,904
Fort Apache, AZ	$3,805
Rosebud, SD*	$3,739
Navajo, AZ-NM-UT*	$3,735
Gila River, AZ	$3,176
San Carlos, AZ	$3,173
Pine Ridge, NE-SD*	$3,115
Papago, AZ	$3,113

*Includes trust lands.

Half of our people on reservations live in poverty.

A very high proportion, 51 percent, of the 437,431 American Indians residing on reservations and trust lands were living below the poverty level in 1989.

There were vast differences in poverty rates in 1989 among the 10 largest reservations and trust lands. About 2 in 3 persons on the Papago, Pine Ridge, Gila River, and San Carlos Reservations and trust lands were in poverty.

The Hopi, Blackfeet, Zuni Pueblo, and Fort Apache Reservations had the lowest percentages of American Indians in poverty, about 50 percent.

Figure 18.
Poverty Rates in 1989

(Percent in poverty in 1989)

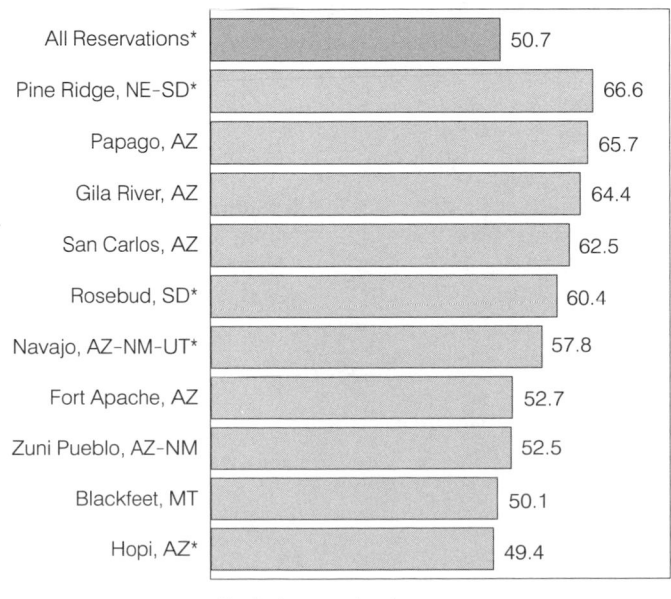

Reservation	Percent in Poverty
All Reservations*	50.7
Pine Ridge, NE-SD*	66.6
Papago, AZ	65.7
Gila River, AZ	64.4
San Carlos, AZ	62.5
Rosebud, SD*	60.4
Navajo, AZ-NM-UT*	57.8
Fort Apache, AZ	52.7
Zuni Pueblo, AZ-NM	52.5
Blackfeet, MT	50.1
Hopi, AZ*	49.4

*Includes trust lands.

Section 2 - **American Indian, Eskimo, and Aleut Population on Reservations**—Con.

Our 10 largest reservations had high proportions of housing units occupied by American Indian householders.

In 1990, only 45 percent of the occupied housing units on all reservations and trust lands had an American Indian householder. Substantially larger percentages of occupied housing units on the 10 largest reservations and trust lands had American Indian householders.

The proportion was as high as 95 percent on the San Carlos, Gila River, and Papago Reservations. Rosebud had the lowest percent of its units occupied by American Indian householders, at 76 percent.

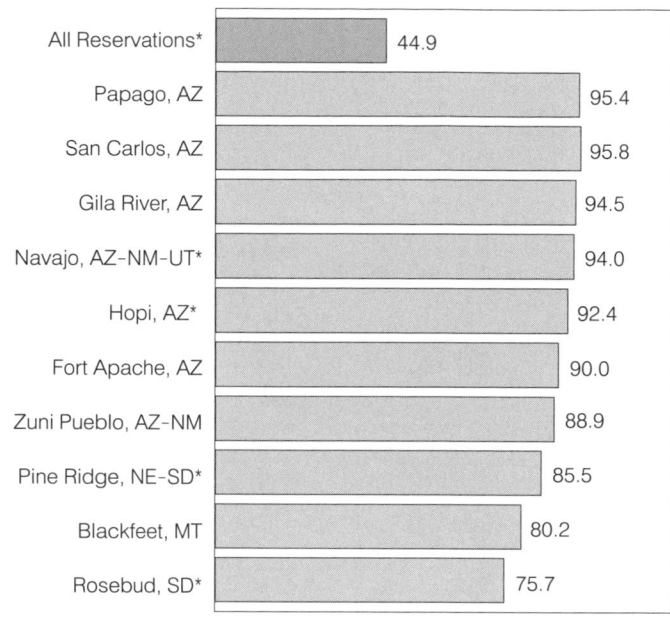

Figure 19.

Occupied Housing Units With an American Indian, Eskimo, or Aleut Householder: 1990

(Percent)

All Reservations*	44.9
Papago, AZ	95.4
San Carlos, AZ	95.8
Gila River, AZ	94.5
Navajo, AZ-NM-UT*	94.0
Hopi, AZ*	92.4
Fort Apache, AZ	90.0
Zuni Pueblo, AZ-NM	88.9
Pine Ridge, NE-SD*	85.5
Blackfeet, MT	80.2
Rosebud, SD*	75.7

*Includes trust lands.

About 67 percent of us on reservations are homeowners.

Two-thirds of the American Indian householders living on reservations and trust lands owned their own homes. In comparison, 54 percent of all American Indian householders were homeowners.

Among the 10 largest reservations and trust lands, at least 3 of every 4 householders were homeowners on the Hopi, Zuni Pueblo, Navajo, and Papago Reservations.

In contrast, Rosebud, Pine Ridge, and Blackfeet had the lowest proportions of owner-occupied housing units.

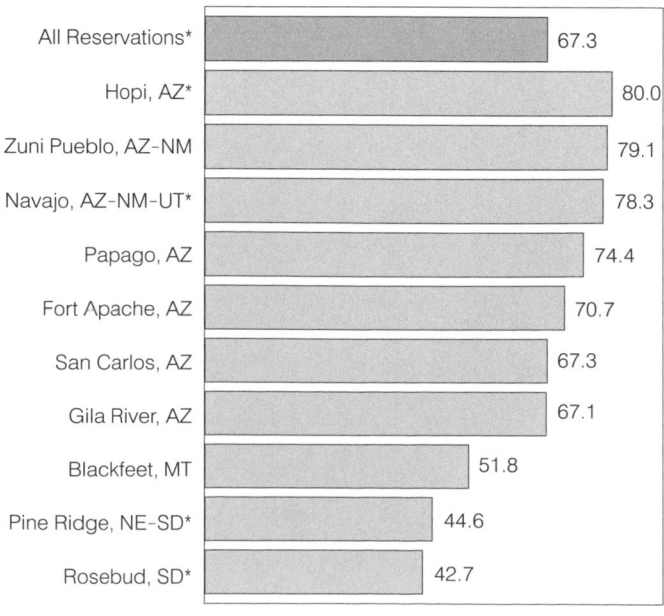

Figure 20.

Owner-Occupied Housing Units With an American Indian, Eskimo, or Aleut Householder: 1990

(Percent)

All Reservations*	67.3
Hopi, AZ*	80.0
Zuni Pueblo, AZ-NM	79.1
Navajo, AZ-NM-UT*	78.3
Papago, AZ	74.4
Fort Apache, AZ	70.7
San Carlos, AZ	67.3
Gila River, AZ	67.1
Blackfeet, MT	51.8
Pine Ridge, NE-SD*	44.6
Rosebud, SD*	42.7

*Includes trust lands.

Section 2 - **American Indian, Eskimo, and Aleut Population on Reservations**—Con.

Our household sizes vary by reservation, from about 3.5 persons to nearly 4.6 persons per household.

The median number of persons in American Indian households on all reservations and trust lands was 3.6.

Among the 10 largest reservations and trust lands, the median persons per unit ranged from 4.6 for Zuni Pueblo to 3.5 for Blackfeet.

Zuni Pueblo, Pine Ridge, San Carlos, and Fort Apache had 4.0 or more persons per unit.

Figure 21.

Median Persons Per Unit for Housing Units With an American Indian, Eskimo, or Aleut Householder: 1990

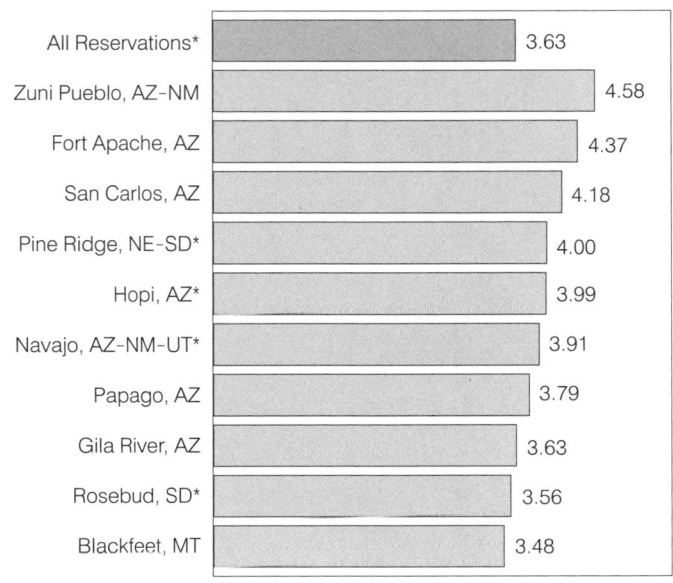

Reservation	Median
All Reservations*	3.63
Zuni Pueblo, AZ-NM	4.58
Fort Apache, AZ	4.37
San Carlos, AZ	4.18
Pine Ridge, NE-SD*	4.00
Hopi, AZ*	3.99
Navajo, AZ-NM-UT*	3.91
Papago, AZ	3.79
Gila River, AZ	3.63
Rosebud, SD*	3.56
Blackfeet, MT	3.48

*Includes trust lands.

One-fifth of our homes on reservations lack complete plumbing facilities.

In 1990, more than 22,793, or 20 percent, of American Indian housing units on reservations and trust lands lacked complete plumbing facilities compared with 6 percent of all American Indian households in the United States.

Navajo and Hopi Reservations had the largest proportion without complete plumbing facilities.

Among the 10 largest reservations, the lowest proportions of housing units without complete plumbing facilities was on the Blackfeet Reservation.

Figure 22.

Plumbing Facilities for Housing Units With an American Indian, Eskimo, or Aleut Householder: 1990

(Percent lacking complete plumbing facilities)

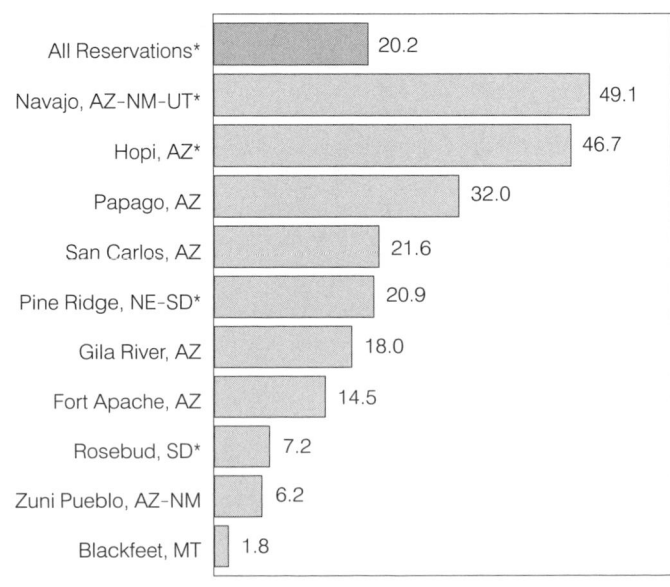

Reservation	Percent
All Reservations*	20.2
Navajo, AZ-NM-UT*	49.1
Hopi, AZ*	46.7
Papago, AZ	32.0
San Carlos, AZ	21.6
Pine Ridge, NE-SD*	20.9
Gila River, AZ	18.0
Fort Apache, AZ	14.5
Rosebud, SD*	7.2
Zuni Pueblo, AZ-NM	6.2
Blackfeet, MT	1.8

*Includes trust lands.

Section 3 - **Alaska Native Population in Alaska**

We, the Alaska Native population, have been counted since 1880.

The Alaska Native population includes Eskimos, American Indians, and Aleuts living in Alaska. The growth of the Alaska Native population was relatively slow from 1880 to 1950.

In contrast, the period from 1950 to 1990 was a time of rapid growth for Alaska Natives. The population rose by more than 50,000 persons (153 percent) and numbered 85,698 in 1990.

Figure 23.
Alaska Native Population in Alaska: 1880 to 1990

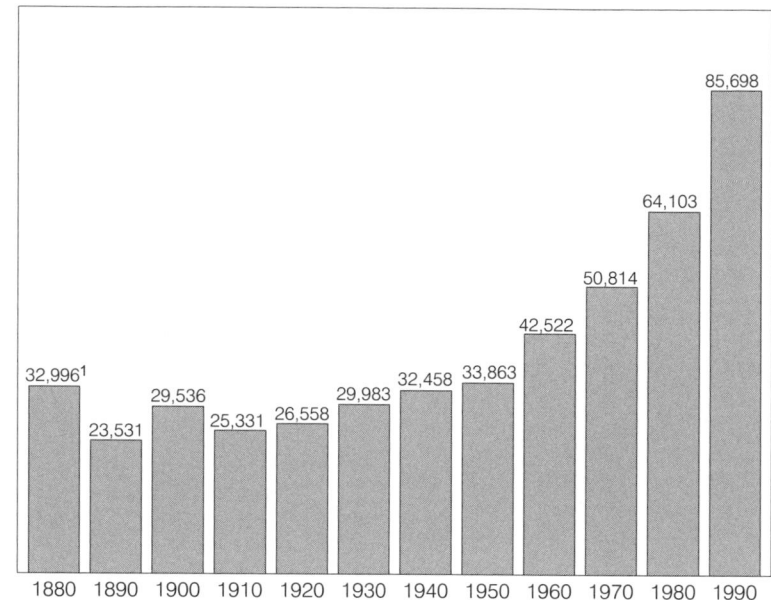

[1] Partially estimated.

Half of our people are Eskimos.

In 1990, more than half of all Alaska Natives were Eskimos, about 36 percent were American Indians, and about 12 percent were Aleuts.

The two main Eskimo groups, Inupiat and Yupik, are distinguished by their language and geography. The former live in the north and northwest parts of Alaska and speak Inupiaq, while the latter live in the south and southwest and speak Yupik.

The American Indian tribes are the Alaskan Athabaskan (11,696) in the central part of the State, and the Tlingit (9,448), Tsimshian (1,653), and Haida (1,083) in the southeast.

The Aleuts (10,052) live mainly in the Aleutian Islands.

Figure 24.
Distribution of Alaska Natives in Alaska: 1990

(Percent)

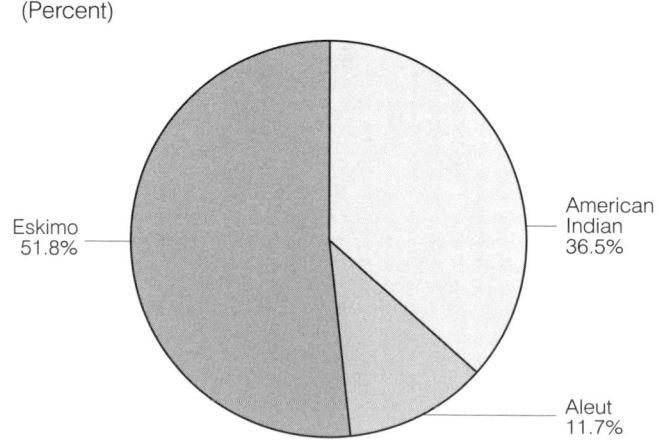

Total Alaska Native population
in Alaska = 85,698.

Section 3 - **Alaska Native Population in Alaska**—Con.

We live and work in Alaska Native Regional Corporations.

After 1971, all of Alaska (except the Annette Islands Reserve) was divided into 12 geographically defined Alaska Native Regional Corporations, a corporate entity organized to conduct business for profit. The boundaries of these regions have been legally established.

In 1990, the largest number of Alaska Natives lived in the Cook Inlet Regional Corporation and the smallest number lived in Ahtna.

Of the 12 Regional Corporations in Alaska, Calista had the highest concentration of Alaska Natives at 86 percent of the total population. Although Cook Inlet had the largest number of Alaska Natives, they comprised only 6 percent of that Corporation's total population.

Figure 25.
Alaska Natives in Alaska Native Regional Corporations: 1990

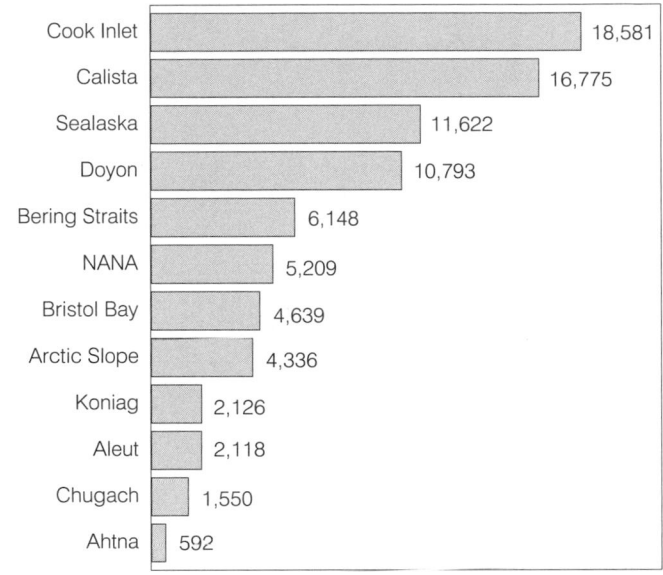

Corporation	Population
Cook Inlet	18,581
Calista	16,775
Sealaska	11,622
Doyon	10,793
Bering Straits	6,148
NANA	5,209
Bristol Bay	4,639
Arctic Slope	4,336
Koniag	2,126
Aleut	2,118
Chugach	1,550
Ahtna	592

Alaska is a young State, and our people are younger still.

The median age of Alaska Natives was 24 years, compared with 29 years for the total State population and 33 years for the total United States.

About 44 percent of Alaska Natives were under 20 years of age compared with 34 percent of Alaska's total population.

However, 49 percent of Alaska Natives and 60 percent of the State's population were 20 to 59 years old.

About the same percentage of Alaska Natives (7 percent) and of Alaska's total population (6 percent) were 60 years old and over.

Figure 26.
Alaska Natives in Alaska by Age: 1990

(Percent distribution)

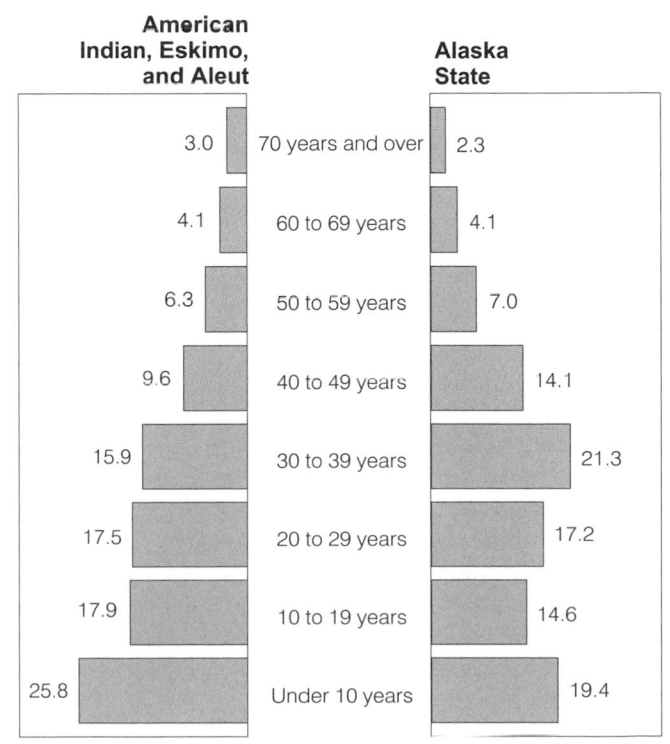

American Indian, Eskimo, and Aleut		Alaska State
3.0	70 years and over	2.3
4.1	60 to 69 years	4.1
6.3	50 to 59 years	7.0
9.6	40 to 49 years	14.1
15.9	30 to 39 years	21.3
17.5	20 to 29 years	17.2
17.9	10 to 19 years	14.6
25.8	Under 10 years	19.4

293

Section 3 - **Alaska Native Population in Alaska**—Con.

Many of our families are maintained by women only.

Alaska Natives had proportionately fewer married-couple families and more families with a female householder and no husband present than the State as a whole.

Only 58 percent of the 16,432 Alaska Native families consisted of a husband and wife compared with 80 percent of all 132,837 families in Alaska.

Among Alaska Natives, Aleuts had the largest percentage of married-couple families.

The proportion of families with a female householder and no husband present was twice as high among Alaska Natives as Alaska's total population.

Thirty-one percent of American Indian families, 28 percent of Eskimo families, and 26 percent of Aleut families were maintained by female house-holders with no husband present compared with 14 percent of all Alaska's families.

Figure 27.
Type of Family: 1990
(Percent)

Married-couple families

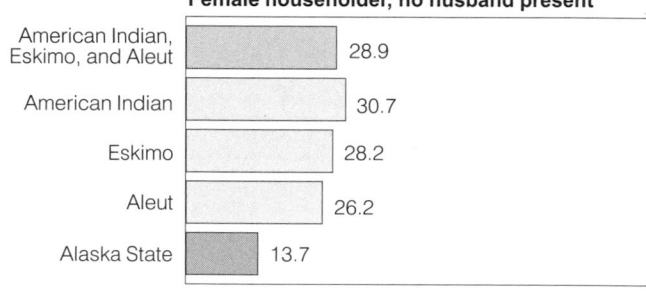

Female householder, no husband present

We are making great strides in educa-tion but still have room to improve.

Although Alaska Natives have made great strides in education during this century, Alaska Natives remain less likely to have high school diplomas and bachelor's degrees or higher than other Alaskans.

Sixty-three percent of the 41,949 Alaska Natives 25 years old and over had completed high school or higher compared with 87 percent statewide.

Four percent of Alaska Natives were college graduates with a bachelor's degree or higher, while the statewide total was 23 percent.

Among Alaska Native groups, American Indians were more likely to have a high school education and a college degree or higher than were Eskimos and Aleuts.

Figure 28.
Educational Attainment: 1990
(Percent of persons 25 years old and over)

High school graduate or higher

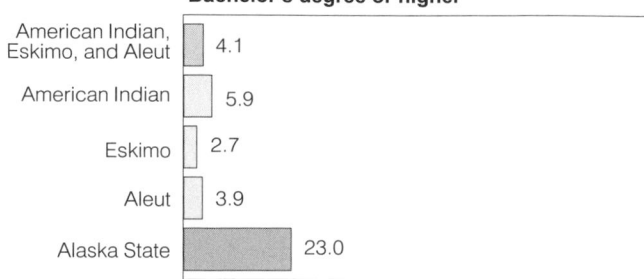

Bachelor's degree or higher

Section 3 - **Alaska Native Population in Alaska**—Con.

Our labor force participation is much lower than that for our State.

Just 56 percent of the 54,614 Alaska Natives 16 years old and over were in the labor force in 1990 compared with 75 percent of Alaska's total population.

Fifty-one percent of all Alaska Native females 16 years old and over compared to 66 percent of all females in Alaska were in the labor force in 1990. Similarly, 61 percent of all Alaska Native males 16 years old and over were in the labor force in 1990 compared with 82 percent of all males in Alaska.

American Indians had the highest labor force participation rate of the three Alaska Native groups; this may be because they were more likely to live in urban areas. Aleuts and Eskimos, who tend to live in rural areas, had lower rates.

We are more likely to work in the service sector than all Alaskans.

Among the 23,506 employed Alaska Natives 16 years old and over, 20 percent were in managerial and professional occupations compared with 30 percent of all workers in the State.

However, Alaska Natives were as likely as the State's total population to work in technical, sales, and administrative jobs. About 3 of every 10 workers in each population held such jobs.

Alaska Natives were more likely than the statewide population to be in service jobs and to be operators, fabricators, or laborers.

Figure 29.
Labor Force Participation Rates: 1990
(Percent of persons 16 years old and over)

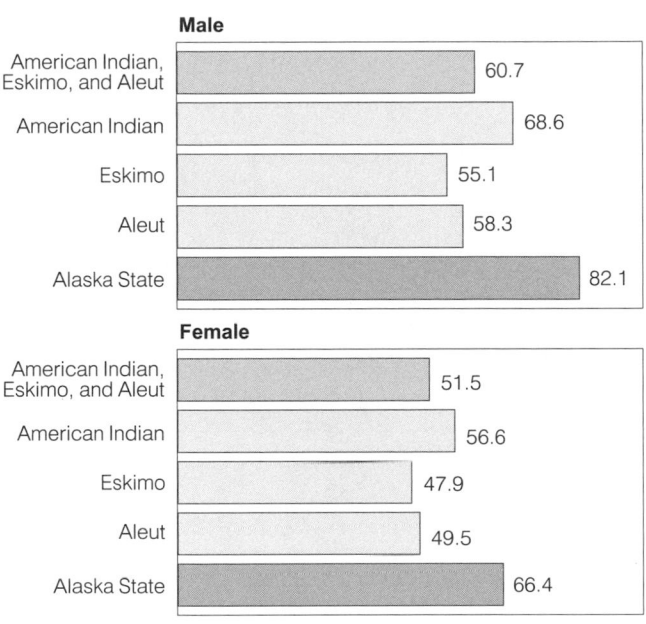

Male

American Indian, Eskimo, and Aleut	60.7
American Indian	68.6
Eskimo	55.1
Aleut	58.3
Alaska State	82.1

Female

American Indian, Eskimo, and Aleut	51.5
American Indian	56.6
Eskimo	47.9
Aleut	49.5
Alaska State	66.4

Figure 30.
Occupation: 1990

(Percent of employed persons 16 years old and over)

American Indian, Eskimo, and Aleut

Alaska State

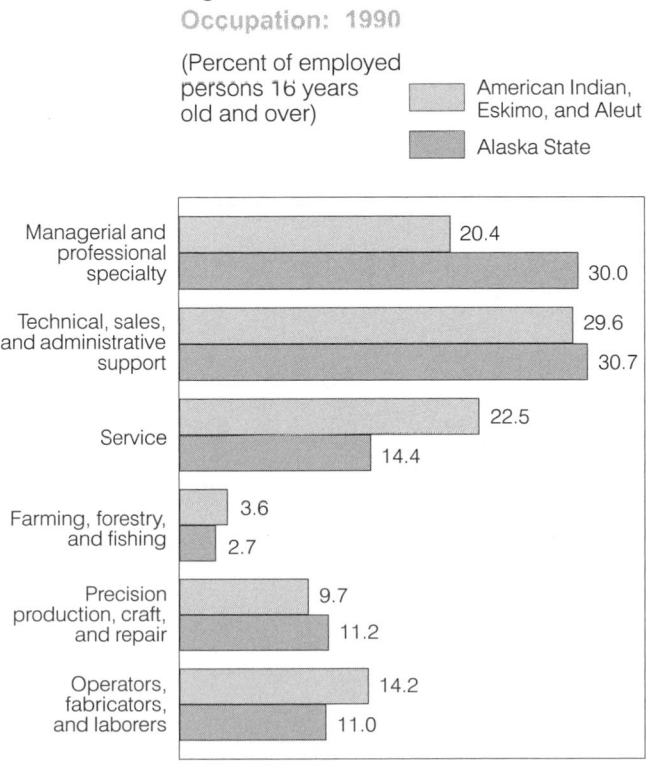

	American Indian, Eskimo, and Aleut	Alaska State
Managerial and professional specialty	20.4	30.0
Technical, sales, and administrative support	29.6	30.7
Service	22.5	14.4
Farming, forestry, and fishing	3.6	2.7
Precision production, craft, and repair	9.7	11.2
Operators, fabricators, and laborers	14.2	11.0

Section 3 - **Alaska Native Population in Alaska**—Con.

Although Alaska has the highest median income of any State, our incomes remain below the average for Alaska.

Alaska, with a median family income of $46,581, had the highest income of any State. However, the median family income for Alaska Natives was $26,695, only 57 percent of the median income for the State.

Aleut families earned an average of $36,472 followed by American Indians ($29,339) and Eskimos ($23,257).

Among married-couple families, median income levels were $52,022 for the State and $37,407, or 72 percent of the State total, for Alaska Natives.

Figure 31.
Median Family Income in 1989 by Type of Family

(In 1989 dollars)

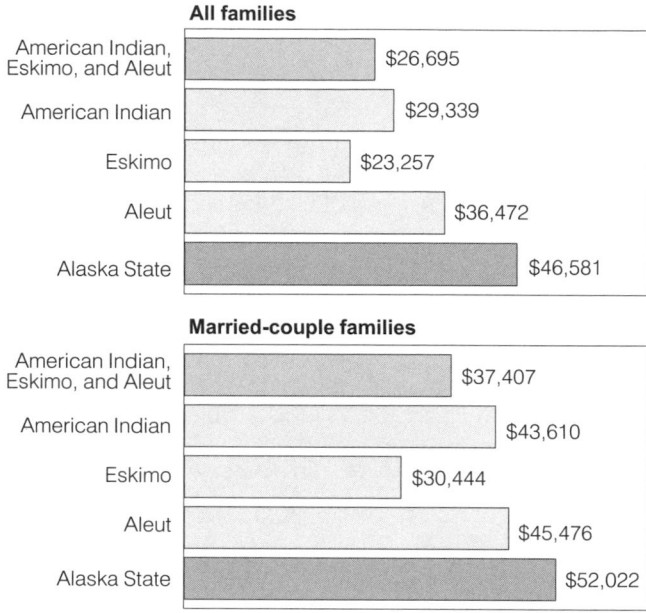

Sizeable proportions of our people and families live in poverty.

In 1989, 23 percent, or 19,250 Alaska Native persons, were poor compared with 9 percent, or 47,906, persons for the State as a whole.

Twenty-eight percent of Eskimos lived in poverty compared with 20 percent of American Indians and 13 percent of Aleuts.

Twenty-one percent of Alaska Native families and 7 percent of families statewide lived below the poverty level.

Figure 32.
Poverty Rates in 1989

(Percent in poverty)

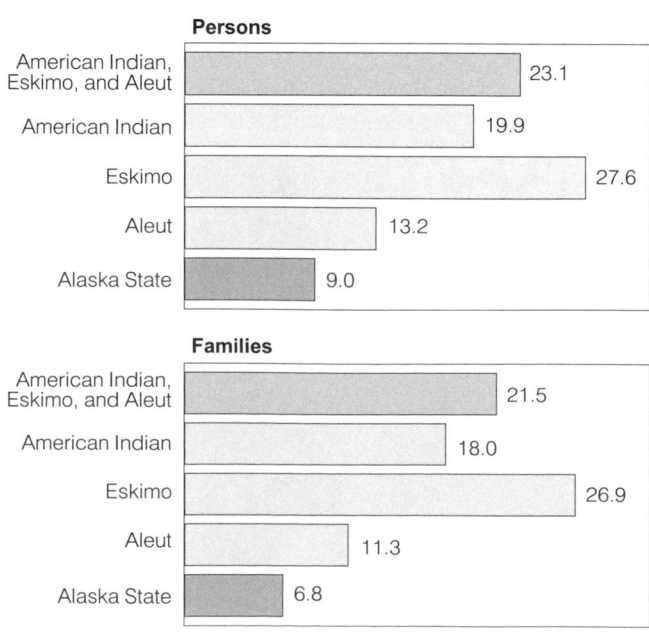

e, the American Foreign Born

Introduction

Most of us are descended from people who were born and reared in the United States. Almost 20 million of us, however, must go back to Mexico, the Philippines, Canada, Cuba, Germany, and many other countries to learn about previous generations. We, who were born in another country of foreign parents and now live in the United States, are America's foreign born.

In colonial days, most of America's immigrants came from Great Britain and Ireland, with a few from Germany, France, the Netherlands, Belgium, and Luxembourg. During the early 19th century, Germans began coming in ever-increasing numbers, while the French, Norwegians, and Swedes, feeling the push of economic pressures at home and the pull of prospective free land and good wages in America, began moving to the United States.

Between 1850 and 1882, the Chinese, fleeing famine in their homeland, immigrated to America, where they worked in mining camps and on the expanding railroad. Immigration stopped for several decades when American labor reacted to the low wages the Chinese accepted

and forced Congress to pass the Chinese Exclusion Act.

For 20 years following the Civil War, a relatively large number of Canadians entered the country. Italians began arriving in 1890, and from 1900 until the start of World War I, about a quarter of all immigrants were Italian. After World War II, many Germans arrived in the United States. The 1970's saw large numbers of Asians and Latin Americans arriving in the United States.

Today, the flow of immigrants to America is regulated by laws, and prospective immigrants are admitted at many ports of entry. In addition, an estimated 200,000 undocumented aliens enter the country annually.

Where do we, the foreign born, come from? Where do we live in the United States? What kind of work do we do? What education do we have? How much do we earn? We are a mosaic of social and cultural characteristics.

The following pages provide a portrait of We, the American foreign born.

In 1990, we the American foreign born reached our greatest number in the history of the United States.

In 1990, the foreign-born population was 19.8 million or 7.9 percent of the total population. This was the largest number of foreign-born persons in U.S. history and the highest proportion of foreign born in the past 40 years.

In 1980, the foreign-born population numbered 14.1 million or 6.2 percent of the total population; 1970 figures were 9.6 million or 4.7 percent; and 1960 figures were 9.7 million or 5.4 percent.

Around the turn of the century, however, the proportions of foreign born were higher than in 1990. For example, in 1900, the foreign-born population was 13.6 percent of the population or 10.4 million; and in 1910, the proportion of foreign born was 14.8 percent or about 13.6 million.

Figure 1.
Foreign-Born Population: 1900 to 1990

(Millions)

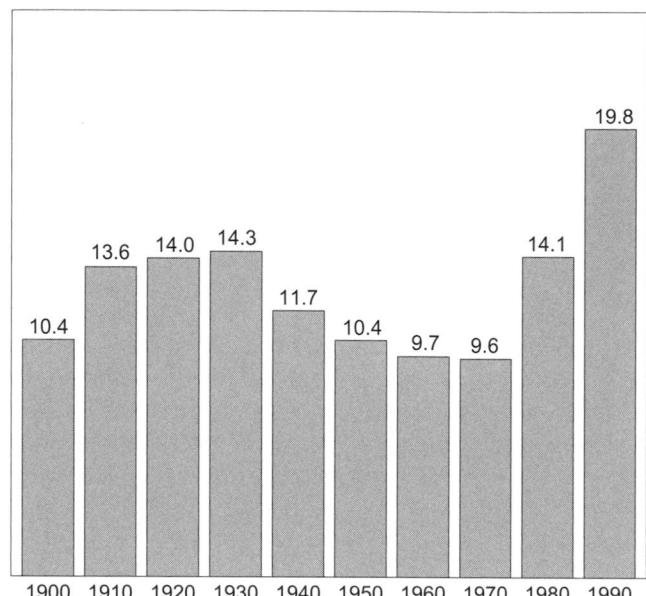

Today, most of us come from Asia or Latin America.

Immigration records, started in 1820, show that until 1970 most of the foreign born came to America from Europe. Of the total of nearly 42 million people who immigrated between 1820 and 1960, 34 million were European. In the 30 years since then, only 2.7 of the 15 million immigrants who came to the United States were European.

The proportion of the total foreign born from European countries declined from 85 percent in 1900 to 22 percent in 1990.

The proportion of the total foreign born from Latin America and Asia increased from less than 1.5 percent each in 1900 to 43 percent and 25 percent, respectively, in 1990.

Figure 2.
Percent Foreign Born by Region of Birth:
1900 and 1990

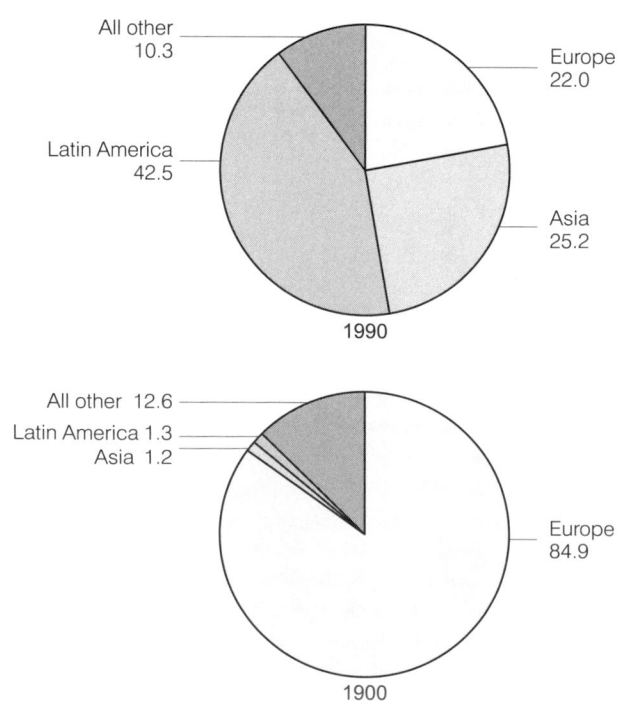

We come from many countries, including Mexico, the Philippines, Canada, and Cuba.

Ten countries contributed at least 500,000 people each to the foreign-born population living in the United States in 1990.

Poor economic conditions in Mexico combined with its proximity to the southern border and demand for unskilled labor in the United States resulted in a very large increase in the number of Mexican foreign born since 1970. More than 1 in 5 of the country's foreign born were born in Mexico, which was the largest foreign-born group in 1990.

Several foreign-born groups lost population between 1980 and 1990. Of the 40 groups with more than 100,000 foreign-born persons in 1990, 14 declined in size. With the exception of Canadians, all of these groups were European. Italians, followed by Scottish, Hungarians, Germans, and Greeks had the largest declines.

One of every four of us came to America between 1985 and 1990.

The largest wave of immigrants occurred between 1985 and 1990. During this period, 1 of every 4 foreign born arrived in the United States. Nearly 44 percent of the total foreign-born population arrived between 1980 and 1990.

Between 1980 and 1990, 3 of every 4 Salvadoran immigrants arrived along with more than half of the immigrants from Korea, Vietnam, and China, and nearly half of the Mexican and Filipino immigrants.

More than 70 percent of Canadian, German, and Italian immigrants arrived prior to 1970. Cubans arrived in large numbers during the 1950's and 1960's.

Figure 3.

Largest Foreign-Born Groups by Country of Birth: 1980 and 1990

(Thousands)   1990 / 1980

Country	1990	1980
Mexico	4,298	2,199
Philippines	913	501
Canada	745	843
Cuba	737	608
Germany	712	849
United Kingdom	640	669
Italy	581	832
Korea	568	290
Vietnam	543	231
China	530	286
El Salvador	465	94

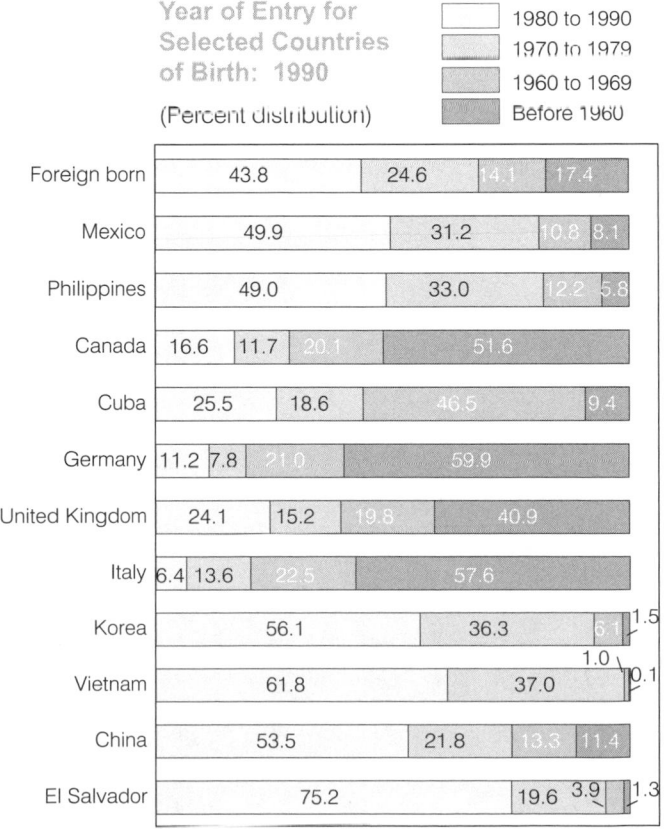

Figure 4.

Year of Entry for Selected Countries of Birth: 1990

(Percent distribution)

1980 to 1990 / 1970 to 1979 / 1960 to 1969 / Before 1960

Country	1980 to 1990	1970 to 1979	1960 to 1969	Before 1960
Foreign born	43.8	24.6	14.1	17.4
Mexico	49.9	31.2	10.8	8.1
Philippines	49.0	33.0	12.2	5.8
Canada	16.6	11.7	20.1	51.6
Cuba	25.5	18.6	46.5	9.4
Germany	11.2	7.8	21.0	59.9
United Kingdom	24.1	15.2	19.8	40.9
Italy	6.4	13.6	22.5	57.6
Korea	56.1	36.3	6.1	1.5
Vietnam	61.8	37.0	1.0	0.1
China	53.5	21.8	13.3	11.4
El Salvador	75.2	19.6	3.9	1.3

299

We settle near our ports of entry.

American immigrants tend to settle near their port of entry. More than two-thirds of those who came from Italy, for example, live in the northeastern part of the country, where they landed. Similarly, more than half of the foreign born who immigrated from China and Japan have remained in the West, and most immigrants from Mexico live in the States that border Mexico.

Throughout this century, both California and New York have had the largest share of immigrant population. As the source of immigration changed from mostly European to mostly Latin American and Asian, California and New York traded places in rank. In 1950, nearly 25 percent of immigrants lived in New York, while only 14 percent lived in California. In 1990, nearly one-third of the immigrants lived in California, while New York's share of immigrants decreased to 14 percent. Nearly half of all the foreign born in America live in California or New York. Eight of every 10 immigrants live in just 10 States. Florida, Texas, New Jersey, and Illinois each have between 5 and 8 percent of the foreign-born population.

In recent decades, most immigrants have settled in big cities and their suburbs. In 10 cities throughout America, foreign born account for half or more of the city's population. In Hialeah city, Florida, 7 out of every 10 people are foreign born.

Figure 5.
Foreign-Born Population for Selected Cities: 1990

(Thousands)

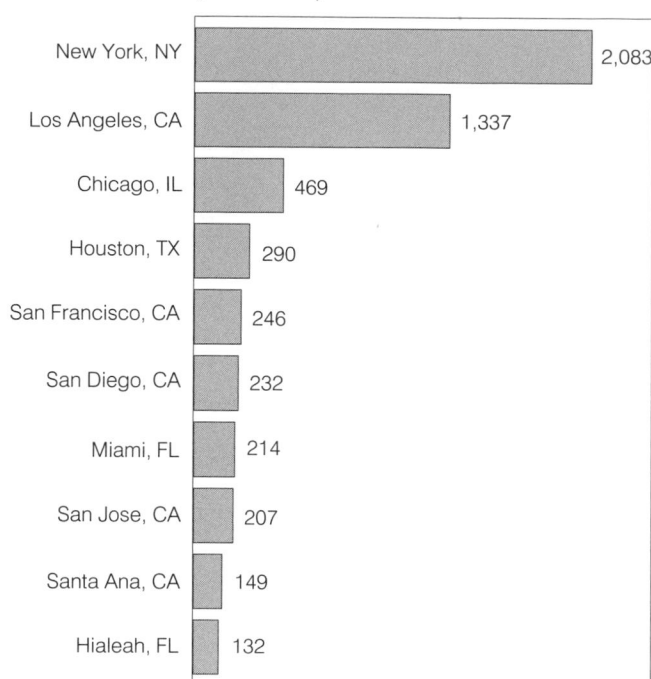

Figure 6.
Percent of Total Foreign Born by State: 1990

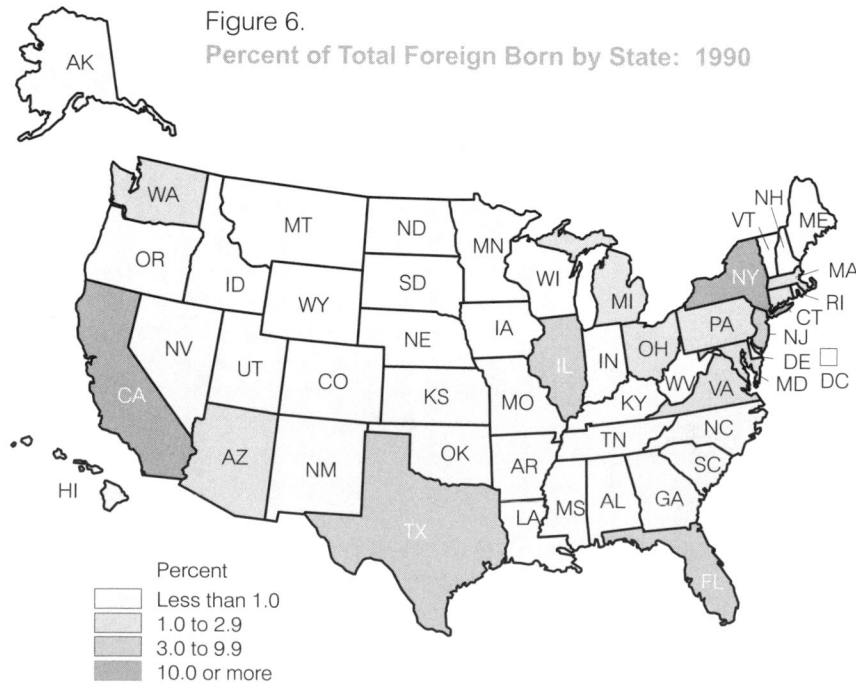

300

We are older than the native-born population.

Compared with the native-born population, a greater proportion of both male and female foreign born were between the ages of 20 and 64. One of every four foreign-born males was between the ages of 25 and 34. In 1990, about 13 percent of the foreign-born population was 65 years old and over, compared with about 12 percent of the native population.

There has been a dramatic shift in the median age of the foreign-born population over the past 20 years. With the large influx of immigrants since 1970, the median age had decreased from 52 years old to 37 years old in 1990.

Among foreign-born groups, Mexicans, Salvadorans, and Vietnamese had the youngest populations with median ages of about 30. Italian immigrants had the highest median age at 59. Canadian and German immigrants had median ages of 53.

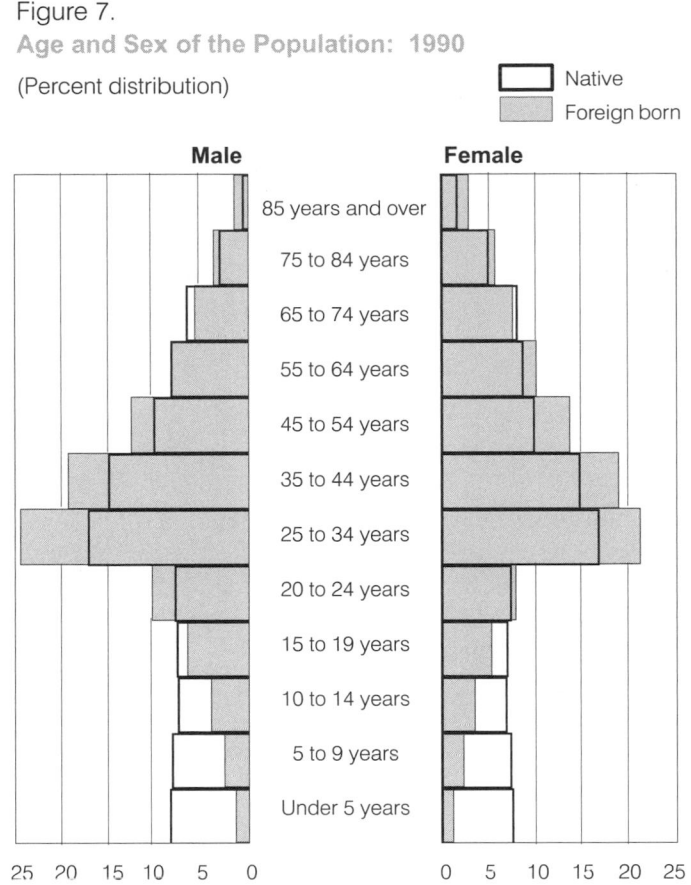

Figure 7.

Age and Sex of the Population: 1990

(Percent distribution)

Native
Foreign born

We represent a larger share of some racial and ethnic population groups.

Among the foreign born, about 23 percent were Asian and Pacific Islander, 7 percent were Black, and nearly 40 percent were Hispanic. Among all Americans, 3 percent were Asian and Pacific Islander, 12 percent were Black, and 9 percent were Hispanic in 1990.

Our racial and ethnic composition has shifted during the past 20 years. In 1970, the foreign-born population was 90 percent White. The share of Whites among the foreign-born population decreased to about 50 percent in 1990.

The share of Hispanics among the foreign-born population increased from 15 percent in 1970 to 40 percent in 1990.

Figure 8.

Race and Hispanic Origin. 1990

(Percent of total population. Persons of Hispanic origin may be of any race)

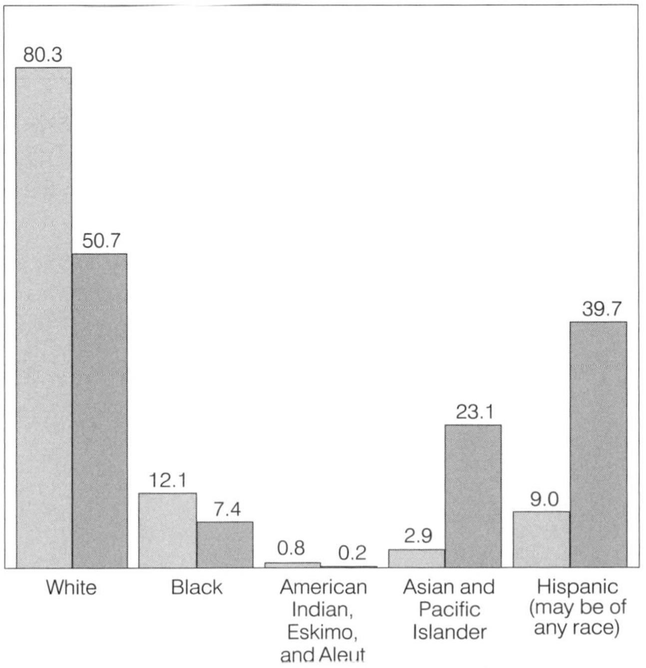

Total
Foreign born

	White	Black	American Indian, Eskimo, and Aleut	Asian and Pacific Islander	Hispanic (may be of any race)
Total	80.3	12.1	0.8	2.9	9.0
Foreign born	50.7	7.4	0.2	23.1	39.7

We have about the same proportion of college graduates but a smaller proportion of high school gradutes than the native-born population.

About 26 percent of the foreign-born population 25 years old and over had less than a 9th grade education compared with 9 percent of native-born Americans. About 59 percent of the foreign born had at least a high school diploma compared with about 77 percent of their native-born counterparts. About 20 percent of both groups have bachelor's degrees or higher.

About 6 percent of both the native and foreign-born populations have an associate's degree, and 13 percent and 12 percent, respectively, have a bachelor's degree. A larger share of foreign born (9 percent) than native Americans (7 percent) have graduate degrees.

About 43 percent of the foreign born from the Philippines had a college degree or higher compared to only 4 percent from Mexico.

Many of us speak a language other than English in our homes.

About 80 percent of the newcomers speak a language other than English at home compared with about 8 percent of the native-born population.

Over 95 percent of Mexicans, Cubans, or Salvadorans spoke Spanish at home. More than 9 of 10 foreign born from the Philippines, Korea, Vietnam, or China spoke an Asian language, and 79 percent of those from Italy and 58 percent of those from Germany spoke a language other than English.

More than half of those who spoke Spanish or an Asian and Pacific Islander language at home did not speak English "very well." In fact, 43 percent of the Mexican and nearly half of the Salvadoran foreign born were "linguistically isolated."

Figure 9.
Educational Attainment for Selected Countries of Birth: 1990
(Percent of persons 25 years old and over)

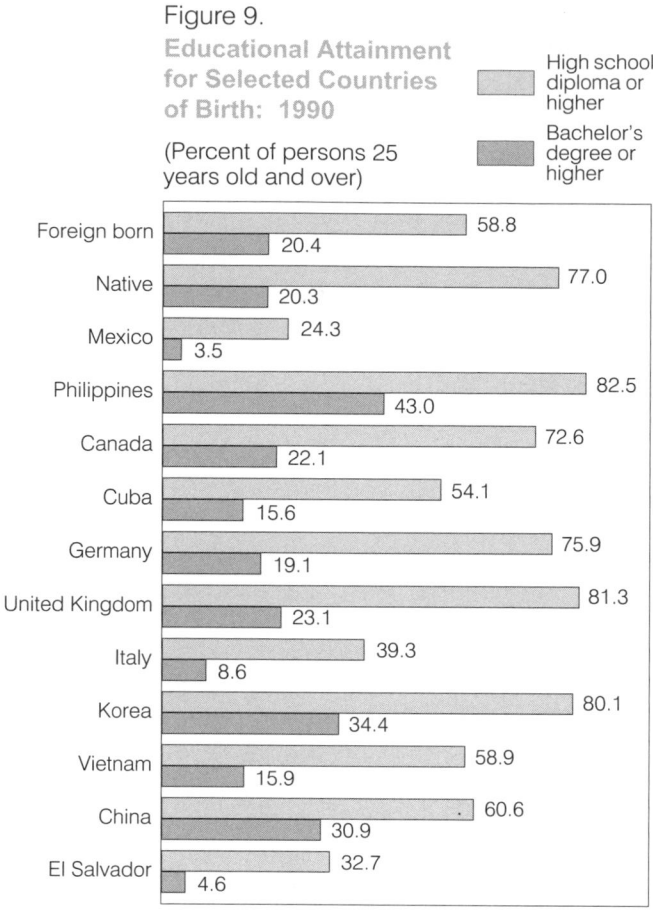

Figure 10.
Language Spoken at Home and Ability to Speak English for Selected Countries of Birth: 1990
(Percent)

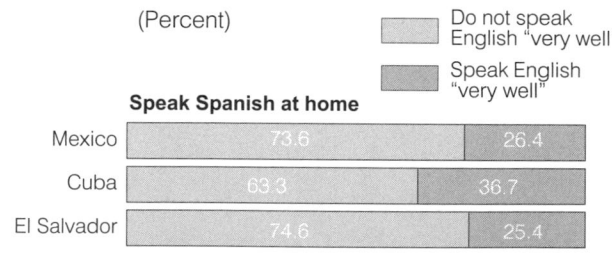
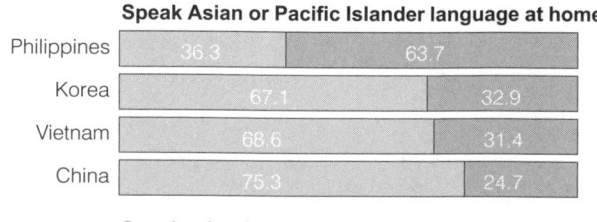
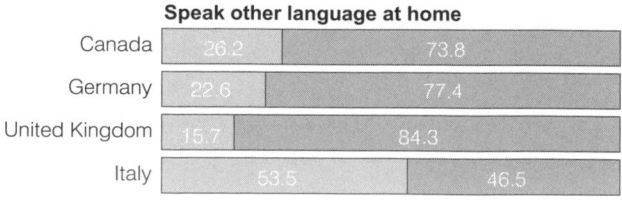

Like native-born Americans, the occupations of foreign-born males differed from foreign-born females.

A greater proportion of foreign-born males than foreign-born females tend to be in farming, fishing, or forestry occupations. However, foreign-born females are as likely as foreign-born males to be managers and professional workers.

In general, foreign-born males were less likely to be in managerial and technical types of occupations and more likely to be in labor, service, and farming type occupations than native-born males.

About 23 percent of foreign-born females were employed as household and service workers compared with about 16 percent of native-born females.

Nearly 8 percent of the foreign born compared to about 6 percent of the native born were unemployed in 1989. About 19 percent of families with a foreign-born householder had three or more workers compared with about 13 percent of families with a native-born householder.

Our occupations differ depending on our country of birth.

The proportion of employed foreign-born workers 16 years old and over in managerial and professional occupations ranged from 6 percent for immigrants from Mexico to more than 40 percent for immigrants from the United Kingdom.

More than one-third of Canadian, German, United Kingdom, and Chinese foreign born worked as managers. One of every five Italians were engaged as craft and repair workers.

Probably reflecting the older median age of the Canadian, German, United Kingdom, and Italian foreign born, higher proportions of these groups were not in the labor force.

Figure 11.

Occupations of Employed Males and Females: 1990
(Percent)

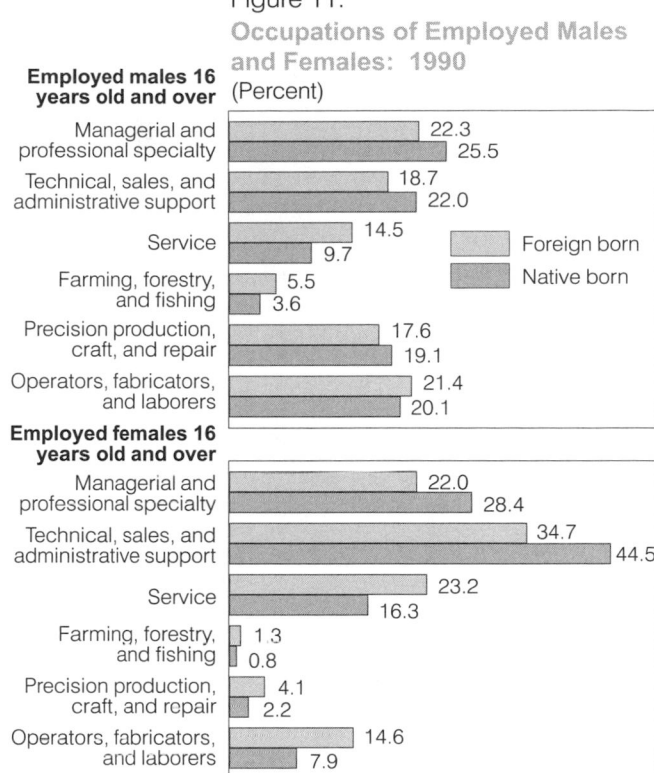

Figure 12.

Occupational Distribution for Selected Countries of Birth: 1990

(Percent of employed persons 16 years old and over)

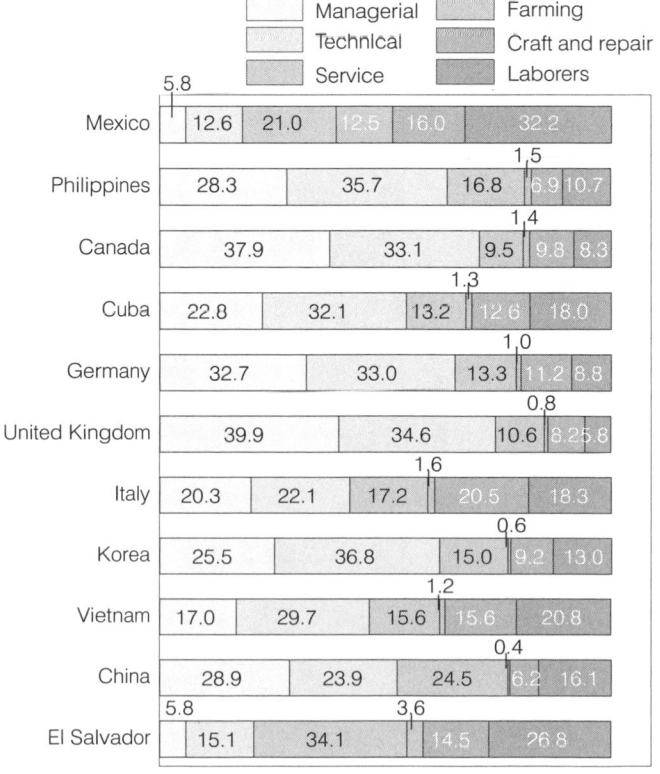

Our incomes vary depending on our country of birth.

Median family income varied widely by country of birth. In 1989, median income of the nearly 6 million families headed by a foreign-born person was $31,785 compared with $35,225 for all American families. However, median income for families with a householder born in the Philippines was $47,794. Medians among householders born in Mexico and El Salvador were the lowest at $21,585 and $21,818, respectively.

About 55 percent of the foreign-born population were living in households with incomes over $25,000, 24 percent had incomes over $50,000, and 5 percent had incomes over $100,000.

In general, families maintained by a female with no husband present had lower median incomes than all families. However, families with a foreign-born female householder had a slightly higher median income than for all families, $18,860 versus $17,414.

More of us fall below the poverty level than the total population.

Children of the foreign born were about twice as likely to be living in poverty than all children. Among both foreign born and the remainder of the population, children were more likely to be living in poverty than adults.

About one-third of the population 65 years old and over born in Cuba, Germany, or the United Kingdom were living below the poverty level. Twenty-five percent of the Canadian elderly and 56 percent of the Italian elderly were living in poverty.

Slightly smaller proportions of households maintained by a foreign-born female with no husband present were living in poverty than households maintained by a native-born counterpart.

Figure 13.

Median Family Income for Selected Countries of Birth: 1990

(In 1989 dollars)

All families
Female householder, no husband present

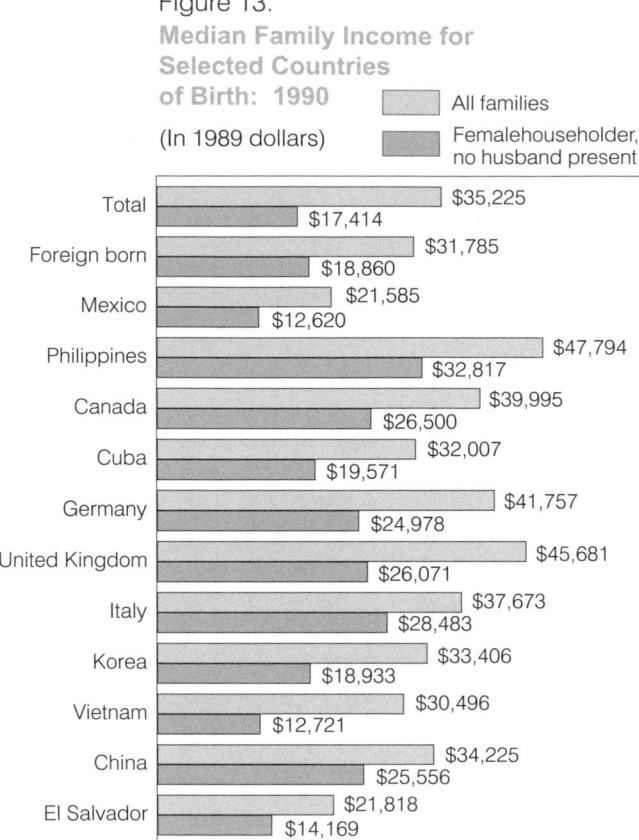

Country	All families	Female householder, no husband present
Total	$35,225	$17,414
Foreign born	$31,785	$18,860
Mexico	$21,585	$12,620
Philippines	$47,794	$32,817
Canada	$39,995	$26,500
Cuba	$32,007	$19,571
Germany	$41,757	$24,978
United Kingdom	$45,681	$26,071
Italy	$37,673	$28,483
Korea	$33,406	$18,933
Vietnam	$30,496	$12,721
China	$34,225	$25,556
El Salvador	$21,818	$14,169

Figure 14.

Poverty Rates for Persons and Families: 1990

(Percent below the poverty level)

Foreign born
Native

Persons

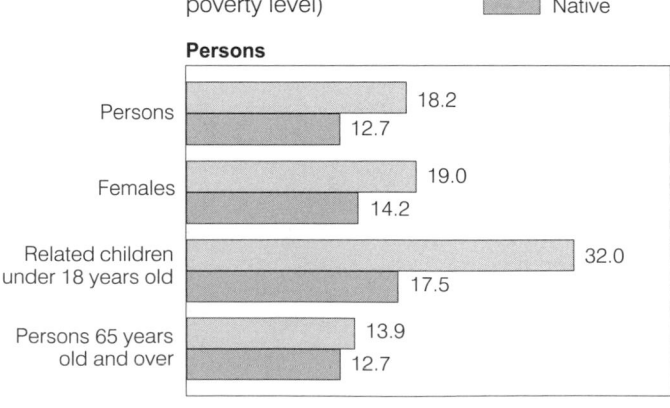

	Foreign born	Native
Persons	18.2	12.7
Females	19.0	14.2
Related children under 18 years old	32.0	17.5
Persons 65 years old and over	13.9	12.7

Families

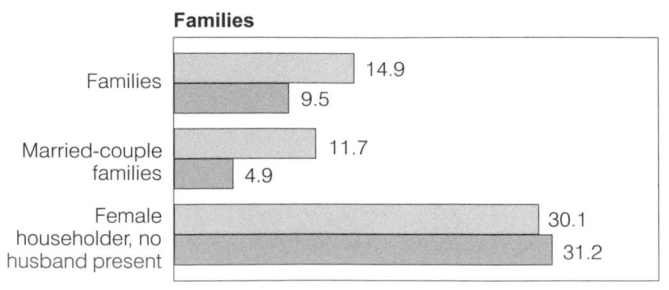

	Foreign born	Native
Families	14.9	9.5
Married-couple families	11.7	4.9
Female householder, no husband present	30.1	31.2

e, the American Elderly

Introduction

Diversity and growth are two terms that describe us, America's elderly population. "The elderly" is a commonly used label for the population 65 years old and over. Yet, we are a heterogeneous population. Our social and economic diversities are too complex to understand based on sweeping generalizations about us.

Our age, gender, race, and ethnic groups have distinctive characteristics, and we have different experiences in aging. Some of us have significant financial and health problems while others of us spend our winters skiing and our summers mountain climbing. Some stay in the paid work force until death while most others have much leisure time which is filled with volunteer work, care of children or the frail elderly, puttering about, or in other activities that are personally satisfying. Others of us are bored or depressed. In short, "the elderly," like other
age groups, are mixed in needs, abilities, and resources.

Growth is another significant aspect of the elderly population, especially the oldest-old. Since the founding of this Nation, the United States has been thought of as a Nation of youth. Eventually, there will be more grandparents than there will be youth.

Because we are increasing in number and living longer into our retirement, the United States has begun to experience the changes in our culture that come with an aging society and affect all of us.

Note: Data in this report differ slightly from the 1990 census counts. The data were modified because some persons reported their age as of a date after April 1, 1990, making them 1 year older than at the time of the census. Adjustments to race classification were also made.

As we entered the 20th century, we were a small segment of the population.

In 1900, there were 3.1 million elderly in the United States. About 1 in 25 Americans were elderly.

There were about 122,000 oldest-old Americans (persons 85 years old and over) in 1900, only a fraction of 1 percent of the population.

Average life expectancy for persons born in 1900 was 47 years.

Source for life expectancy: National Center for Health Statistics, *Health, United States, 1990,* Hyattsville, MD: Public Health Service, 1991, Table 15.

Figure 1.
Population by Age and Sex: 1900

(Millions)

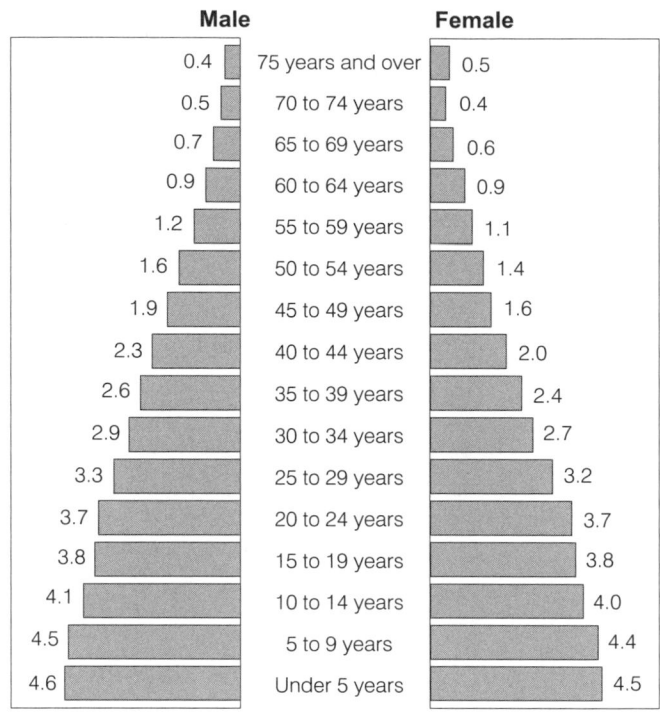

As we near the 21st century, our population is 10 times larger than 1900.

In 1990, there were 31.1 million elderly Americans, 10 times as many as in 1900. About 1 in 8 Americans were elderly in 1990.

In 1990, the oldest-old numbered 3.0 million persons, 1.2 percent of the population.

The post-World War II "Baby Boom" (the 75 million people born from 1946 to 1964) were 26 to 44 years old in 1990. They will contribute to large increases in the elderly population after the year 2010.

In 1990, life expectancy at birth was a little over 75 years old — more than a quarter of a century longer than in 1900.

Source for life expectancy: National Center for Health Statistics, "Advance Report of Final Mortality Statistics, 1990," *Monthly Vital Statistics Report,* Vol.41, no. 7, Supplement, Hyattsville, MD: Public Health Service, 1993, Table 4.

Figure 2.
Population by Age and Sex: 1990

(Millions)

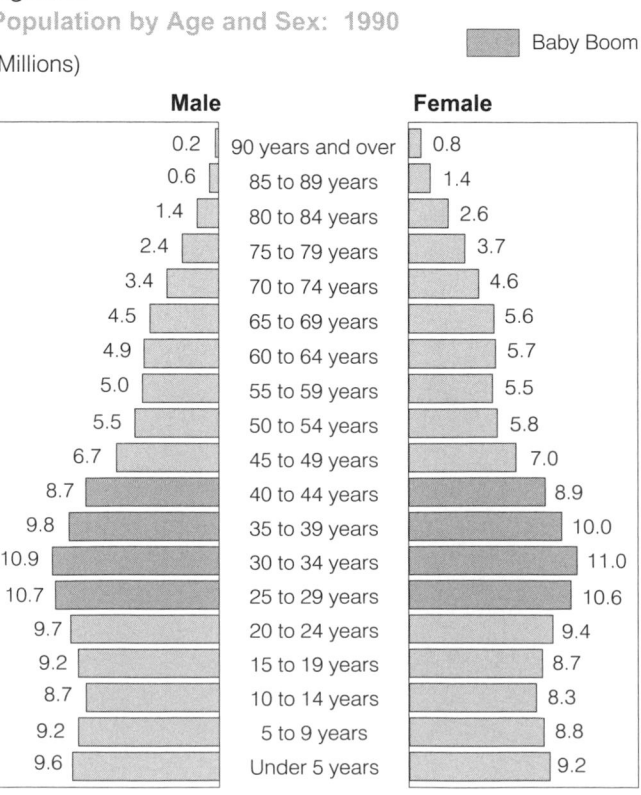

We are projected to grow much faster than the total population from 1990 to 2020.

From 1990 to 2020, the elderly population is projected to increase to 54 million persons. The growth rate of the elderly would be more than double that of the total population during this period. Beginning in 2011, the first members of the Baby Boom will reach age 65.

In 2020, about 1 in 6 Americans would be elderly. More children would know their great grandparents, as the four-generation family would become more common.

About 6.5 million persons would be 85 years old and over in 2020 — more than double the 1990 number. The number of Americans 100 years old and over could increase 8 times from 1990.

Figure 3.
Population by Age and Sex: 2020
(Millions. Middle series projections)

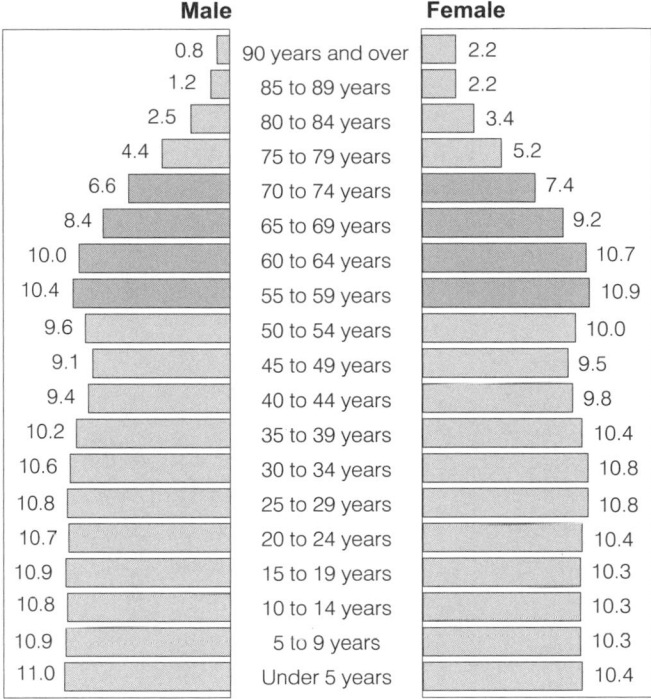

By the middle of the next century, our number could reach 79 million.

In 2050, the final phase of the gerontological explosion would occur. The elderly population as a whole would number about 79 million people, more than double its present size. About 1 in 5 Americans would be elderly.

The population 65 to 74 years old would reach its projected peak of 38 million in 2030 and drop to about 35 million in 2050, still about twice as large as in 1990.

The population 75 to 84 years old would reach a peak of 29 million in 2040, then decrease to 26 million in 2050. This age group would be about 2 1/2 times as large as in 1990.

Figure 4.
Population by Age and Sex: 2050
(Millions. Middle series projections)

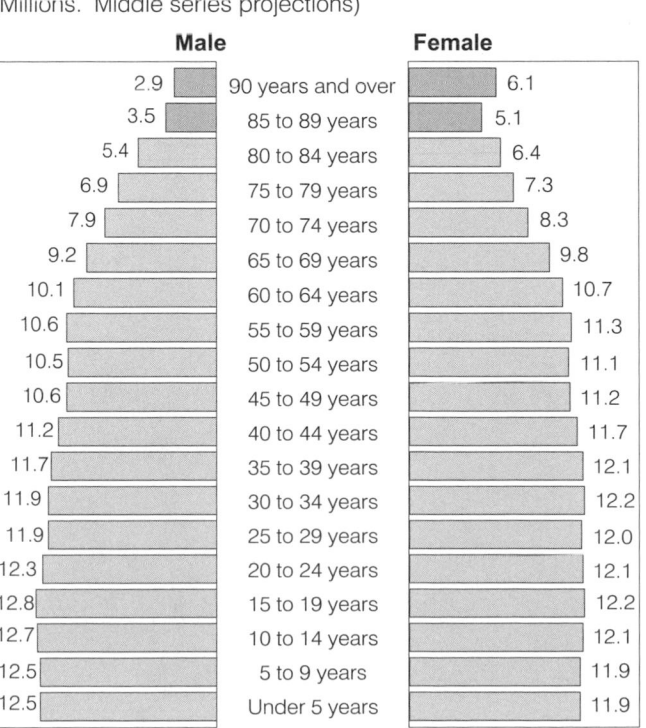

The elderly population is aging.

While the elderly population as a whole grew 22 percent from 1980 to 1990, the number of oldest-old grew 35 percent. In 1990, the oldest-old population had grown to 3.0 million persons, about 1.2 percent of the total population.

In 2050, the survivors of the Baby-Boom generation will be the Great-Grandparent Boom, 85 years old and over. They would number about 18 million persons, nearly 3 times the size of the oldest-old population in 2020, and nearly 6 times as large as this age group was in 1990. The oldest-old would be about 5 percent of the total population in 2050.

These projected population numbers assume that recent trends in fertility, mortality, and im-migration will continue. If mortality decreases, for example, due to better health habits and medical advances, the number of elderly could be even higher than reflected in these projections.

We will be a larger proportion of race groups and Hispanics in 2050.

Compared with other race groups or Hispanics, the White population had the highest proportion of elderly in 1990. This is because Whites have higher survival rates to 65 years old and lower recent fertility rates. Also, the White proportion of immigrants has declined over the past 30 years. In 2050, an even larger proportion of the White population may be elderly.

From 1990 to 2050, the percentage of elderly in the Black population could nearly double from 8 percent to 15 percent.

Among American Indians, Eskimos, and Aleuts, the proportion of elderly could more than double from nearly 6 percent to just over 12 percent.

The elderly constituted 6 percent of the Asian and Pacific Islander population in 1990 and could reach 16 percent of this group in 2050.

Only 5 percent of persons of Hispanic origin were elderly in 1990. This could triple to 15 percent by 2050.

Figure 5.
Population 85 Years Old and Over: 1900 to 2050

(Millions. Middle series projections)

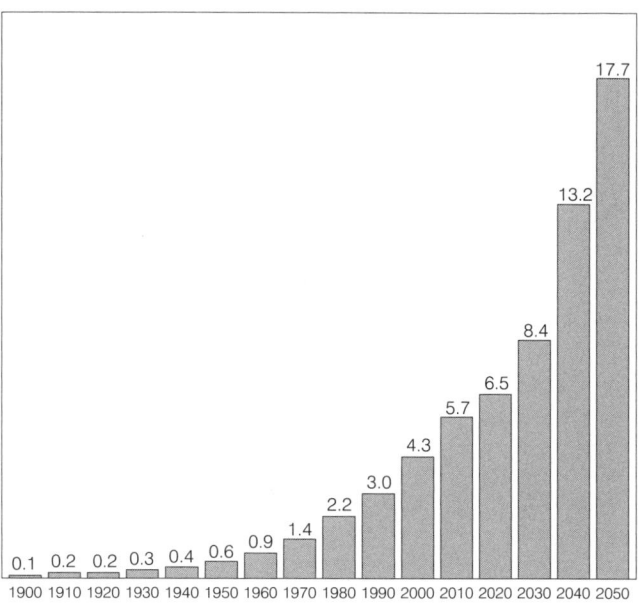

Figure 6.
Persons 65 Years Old and Over by Race and Hispanic Origin: 1990 and 2050

(Percent. Middle series projections)

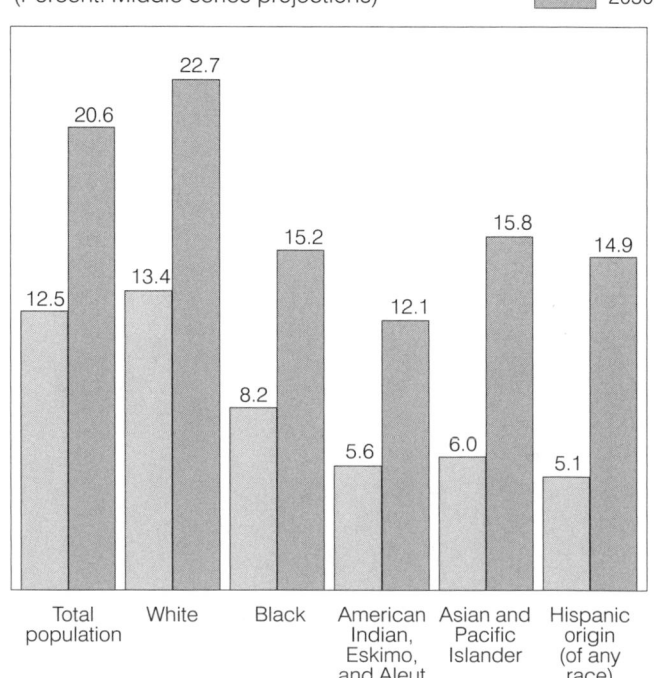

As our population grows in number, we will also grow more diverse.

In 1990, of the 31 million elderly people of all races, 28 million were White; 2.5 million were Black; about 114,000 were American Indian, Eskimo, or Aleut; and about 454,000 were Asian and Pacific Islander. There were 1.1 million elderly persons of Hispanic origin in 1990.

There were more than 600,000 persons of races other than White 80 years old and over in 1990.

In 2050, there would be 79 million elderly Americans. While the number of elderly Whites would more than double to 62 million in 2050, the number of elderly Blacks would nearly quadruple to over 9 million.

The number of American Indian, Eskimo, and Aleut elderly would be 562,000. The number of Asian and Pacific Islander elderly would approach 7 million.

The number of elderly Hispanics in 2050, 12 million, would be 11 times as many as in 1990.

The number of persons 80 years old and over would increase at a faster rate. The number of Hispanics 80 years old and over would increase from about 200,000 in 1990 to more than 4 million in 2050.

Figure 7.

Persons 65 Years Old and Over by Age, Race, and Hispanic Origin: 1990

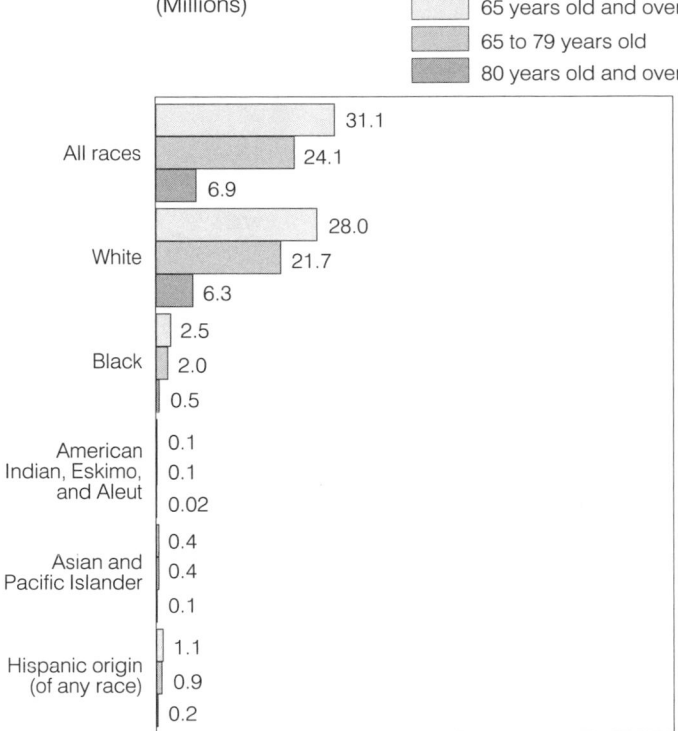

Figure 8.

Persons 65 Years Old and Over by Age, Race, and Hispanic Origin: 2050

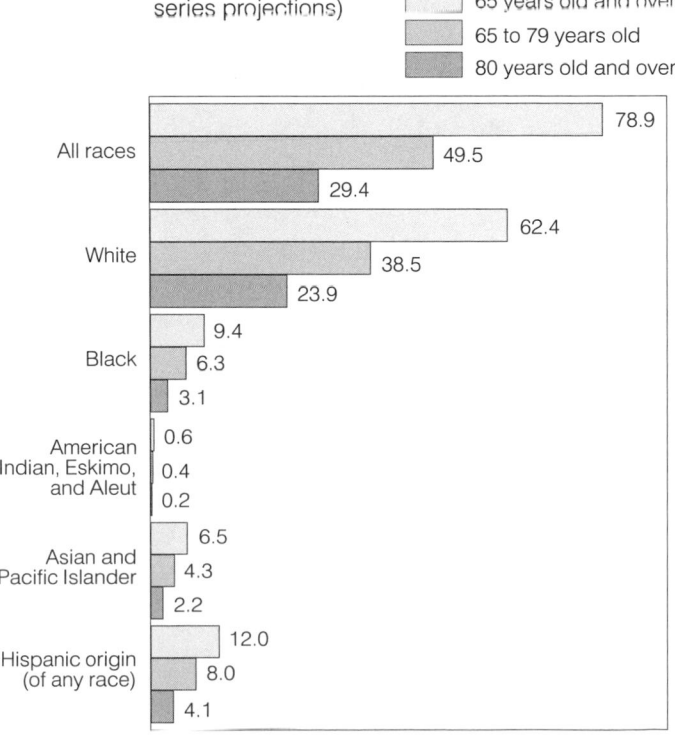

Nine States had more than 1 million elderly in 1990.

America's most populous States are also those with the largest elderly populations. California, Florida, New York, Pennsylvania, Texas, Illinois, Ohio, Michigan, and New Jersey each had more than 1 million elderly.

The number of elderly increased in every State from 1980 to 1990. The greatest increase in the elderly population was in Western and Southeastern coastal States. Although California had the largest number of elderly, Florida had the Nation's highest proportion of elderly, 18 percent. Pennsylvania, Iowa, Rhode Island, West Virginia, Arkansas, South Dakota, North Dakota, Nebraska, and Missouri all had 14 to 15 percent of their population who were elderly.

Some Midwestern States with a high percentage of farmland, such as North Dakota, South Dakota, Nebraska, and Iowa, have a higher proportion of elderly than for the total United States (13 percent in 1990), primarily because of out-migration of the young.

Figure 9.
Population 65 Years Old and Over by State: 1990

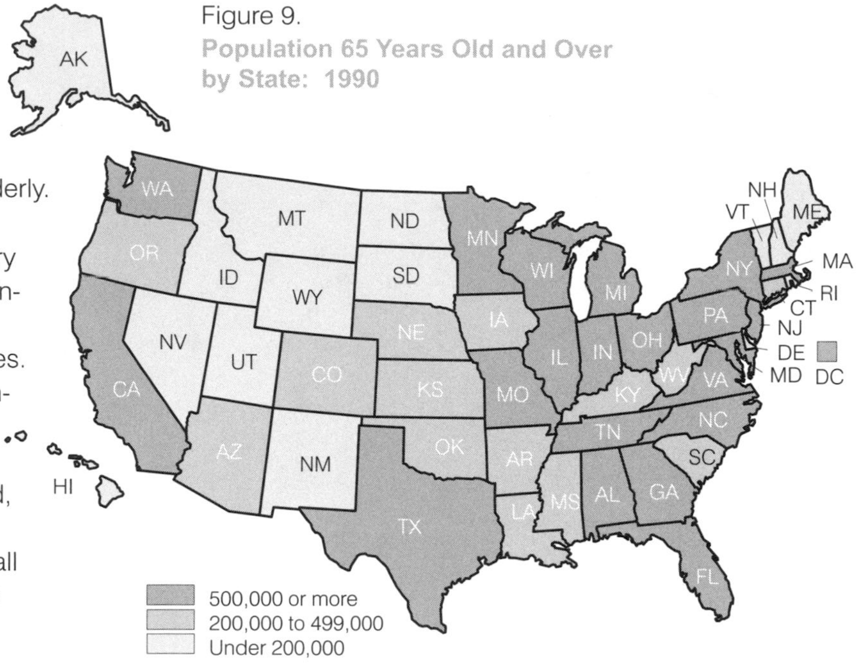

500,000 or more
200,000 to 499,000
Under 200,000

About 1.6 million of us live in nursing homes.

About 1.6 million elderly persons lived in nursing homes in 1990. Nine States had more than 50,000 elderly nursing home residents: California, Florida, Illinois, Massachusetts, Michigan, New York, Ohio, Pennsylvania, and Texas.

About 1.3 million of the 1.6 million elderly were female. Only 1 in 7 elderly living in nursing homes was married in 1990. The great majority, 3 in 5, were widowed.

The likelihood of living in a nursing home increases with age. Only 1.4 percent of the population 65 to 74 years old lived in nursing homes in 1990 compared with 6 percent of those 75 to 84 years old and 25 percent of those 85 years old and over.

Figure 10.
Persons 65 Years Old and Over in Nursing Homes: 1990

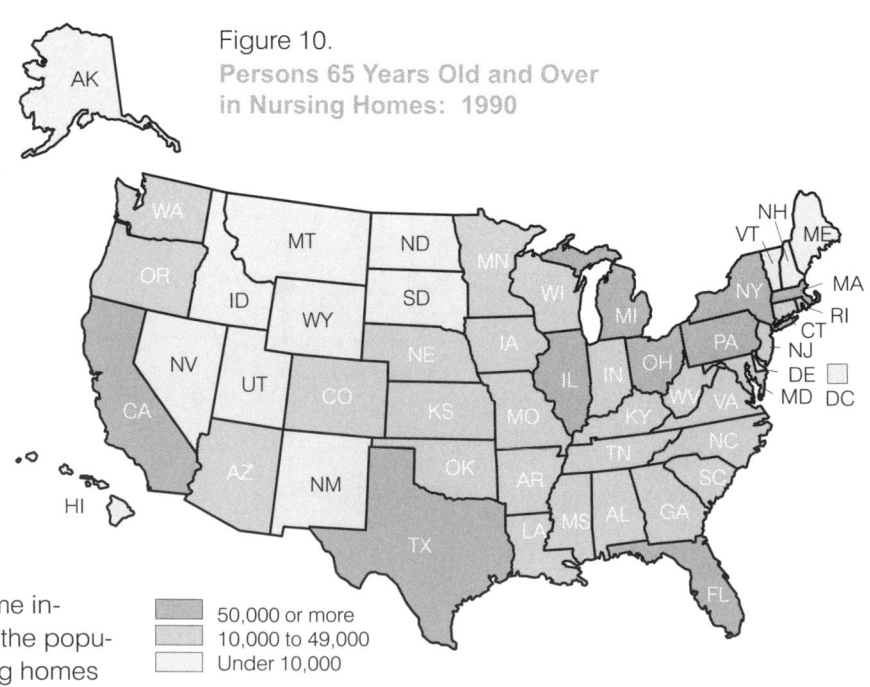

50,000 or more
10,000 to 49,000
Under 10,000

The death of our husbands often marks the starting point of economic reversals for us.

In 1990, elderly women outnumbered elderly men 3 to 2. There were 18.6 million elderly women and 12.5 million elderly men.

The difference between the number of men and women grows with advancing age. At 65 to 69 years old, there were 81 men per 100 women in 1990. This ratio was sharply lower for the oldest-old: 42 men per 100 women for persons 85 to 89 years old, and 27 men per 100 women for persons 95 years old and over.

This decreasing sex ratio is due to the longer life expectancy of women. In the future, mortality differences between men and women may narrow.

The health, social, and economic problems of the oldest-old are primarily the problems of women. Women live alone in higher proportions than men, they tend to move to nursing homes earlier, their income is lower on average, and they tend to experience a disproportionately high level of poverty.

At 85 years old and over, about half of our elderly men are married, while four-fifths of our elderly women are widowed.

Most elderly men are married, while most elderly women are not. Elderly men were nearly twice as likely as elderly women to be married in 1990. Elderly women were more than 3 times as likely as men to be widowed.

One implication of these data is that most elderly men have a spouse for assistance if health fails, while the majority of elderly women do not.

Marital status differs considerably by both age and sex. At 65 to 74 years old, about four-fifths of men and half of women are married. At 85 years old and over, about half of the men are married while four-fifths of women are widowed.

Figure 11.
Number of Elderly Men Per 100
Women by Age: 1990

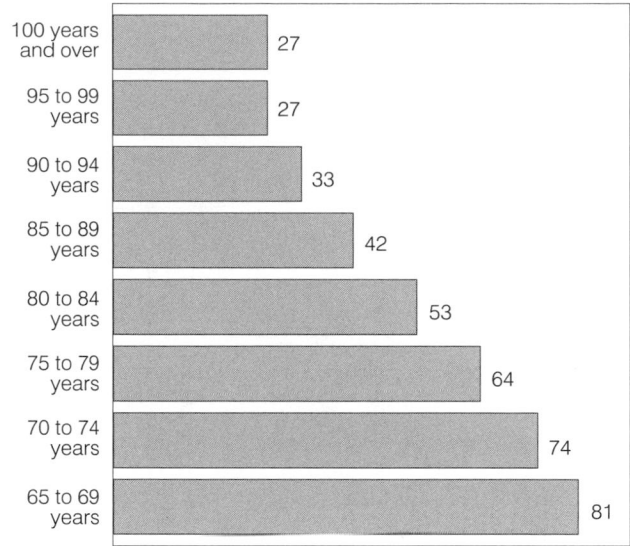

Figure 12.
Marital Status of the Elderly: 1990

(Thousands)

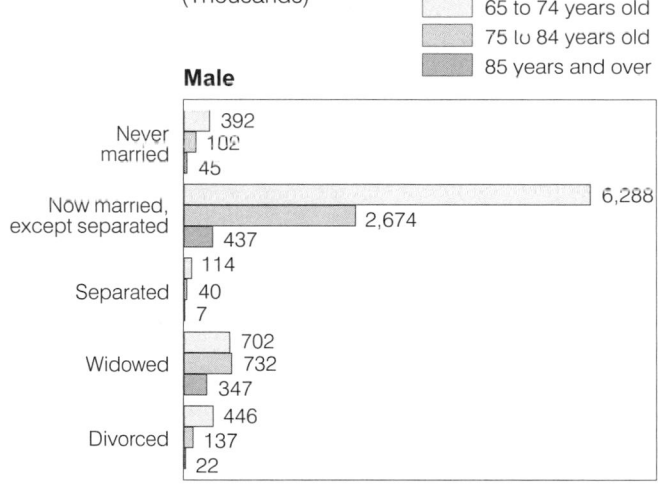

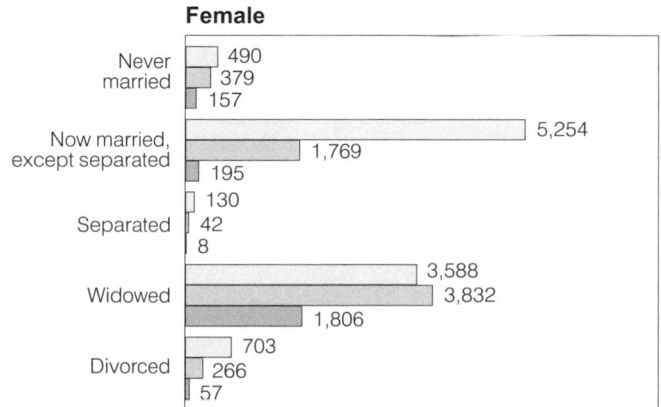

Many of us live alone.

In 1990, 8.8 million elderly persons were living alone. About 8 in 10 were elderly women living alone. Among the oldest-old, 56 percent of women lived alone compared with about 29 percent of men.

Nearly 3 in 4 elderly men in households lived with their wives in 1990 compared with less than 4 in 10 elderly women. Among the oldest-old in households, 51 percent of men and only 9 percent of women lived with a spouse.

As more of us live longer, long-term chronic illness, disability, and dependency become more likely.

With longer life expectancy and more persons 85 years old and over, it is likely that more and more people, especially in their fifties and sixties, will have surviving older relatives. In 1950, there were 3 persons 85 years old and over for every 100 persons age 50 to 64. In 2050, this ratio would increase to 27.

As people live longer, long-term chronic illness, disability, and dependency become more likely. About half of the oldest-old living in their homes are frail and need assistance with everyday activities. Their relatives, in their fifties and sixties, face the difficulties of providing care.

The elderly of the future may be quite different from the elderly of today, however. Emerging data suggest that limitations to activities among the elderly due to disabilities may have decreased during the 1980's, even among the oldest-old. Increased education and the use of mechanical aids may be helping many to overcome their health limitations.

Figure 13.
Living Arrangements of the Elderly: 1990

(Thousands)

- 65 to 74 years old
- 75 to 84 years old
- 85 years and over

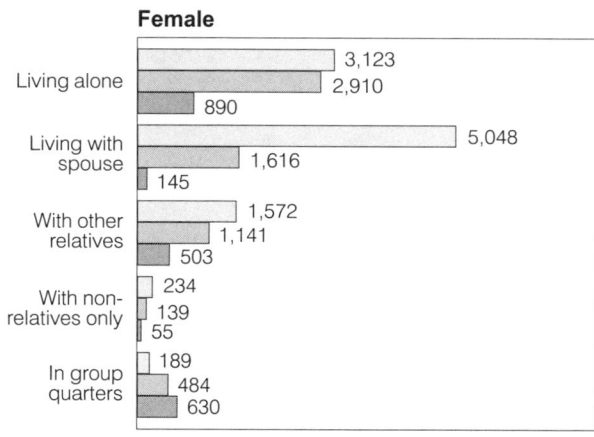

Figure 14.
Parent Support Ratio: 1950 to 2050

(Persons 85 years old and over per 100 persons 50 to 64 years old. Middle series projections)

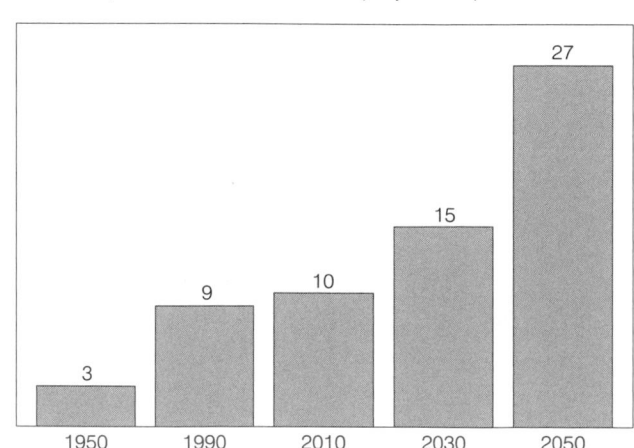

Our educational attainment levels are increasing significantly.

Among persons 75 years old and over, 23 percent had a high school diploma only in 1990 compared with 31 percent of those 70 to 74 years old and 33 percent of persons 65 to 69 years old. The younger elderly (65 to 74 years old) were more likely to have completed some college than those 75 years old and over.

The proportion of the elderly population with at least a high school education is likely to increase significantly. More than 80 percent of the population 25 to 64 years old had at least a high school education in 1990. Better educated people tend to be better off economically and stay healthier longer.

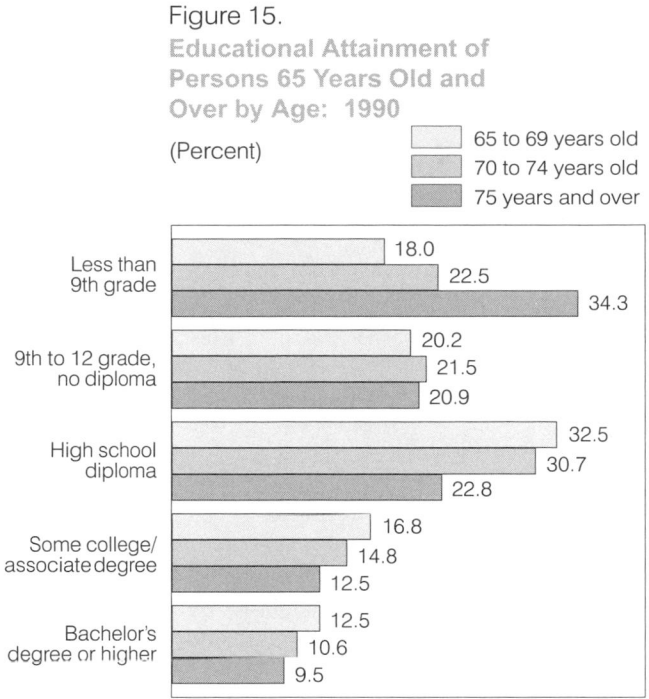

Figure 15.

Educational Attainment of Persons 65 Years Old and Over by Age: 1990

(Percent)

- 65 to 69 years old
- 70 to 74 years old
- 75 years and over

Our economic picture has improved overall, but large differences remain among our groups.

Overall, the economic picture for the elderly has improved since 1970. Large differences remain, however, among subgroups of the elderly. There are differences between men and women and among different types of households, for example.

Nationally, 3.8 million elderly were poor in 1989. In nine States, all in the South, more than 1 in 5 elderly persons were poor.

Elderly women had a higher poverty rate in 1989 than elderly men, 16 percent and 8 percent, respectively.

Elderly female householders not living with a husband (most of whom lived alone) had a poverty rate of 14 percent in 1989. By contrast, the poverty rate for elderly married couples was nearly 6 percent.

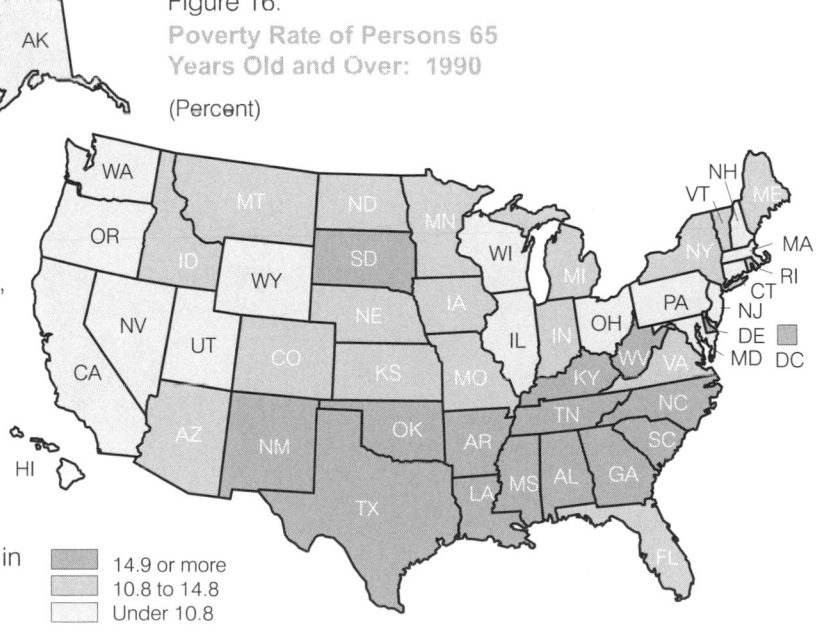

Figure 16.

Poverty Rate of Persons 65 Years Old and Over: 1990

(Percent)

- 14.9 or more
- 10.8 to 14.8
- Under 10.8

e, the American Children

Introduction

We, the American children, numbered 63.6 million in 1990. This report focuses on our family living arrangements and our economic circumstances. Special attention is devoted to similarities and differences between non-Hispanic White children and non-Hispanic Black or Hispanic origin children.

Throughout the past 50 years, fewer than one-half of us have lived in "traditional" families where the father was a full-time worker and the mother a full-time homemaker. A majority of us live with two parents, but an increasing proportion have only one parent in the home. Few of us have grandparents in the home, and most of us live in families with only one, two, or three children.

Nearly all of us who live with a father have a father who is employed, but many of us have fathers who work part-time. Most of us who live with a mother only, have a mother who works for pay. For every child who lives in a "traditional" family where

the father is a full-time worker and the mother a full-time homemaker, four children live in "nontraditional" two-parent families. Even at age 1, only one-sixth of us live in "traditional" two-parent families.

The proportion of us living in families with high incomes increased during the 1980's, and the proportion with low and poverty level incomes also increased during the 1980's. Children living with two parents have high family incomes compared with children living with one parent.

Whether we have high or low family incomes also depends on the amount of time our parents work. Children in "traditional" two-parent families and children living in mother-only families where the mother works full time are similar in their chances of having a low family income and living in poverty. Whether we live with two parents or only our mother, Black and Hispanic children experience much higher poverty rates than White children.

Since 1940, a minority of us have lived in "traditional" families with a full-time working father and a homemaker mother.

In 1940, only 43 percent of children lived in "traditional" families with a father who worked full time year round and a mother who was not in the labor force.

The proportion of children living in "traditional" families rose to 47 percent in 1950, but a majority of children continued to live in "nontraditional" families.

After 1950, "traditional" family living declined, and by 1990 fewer than one-fifth of all children lived in families with fathers as full-time providers and homemaking mothers.

Between 1940 and 1960, only 45 to 50 percent of White children lived in "traditional" families, and this declined to 20 percent in 1990.

Since 1940, fewer than 30 percent of Black children lived with fathers who were full-time workers and mothers who were full-time homemakers, and this declined to only 5 percent in 1990.

Figure 1.
Children Living With a Father Working Full-Time and a Mother Not in the Labor Force: 1940 to 1990

(Percent of children under 18 years old)

All children
White
Black

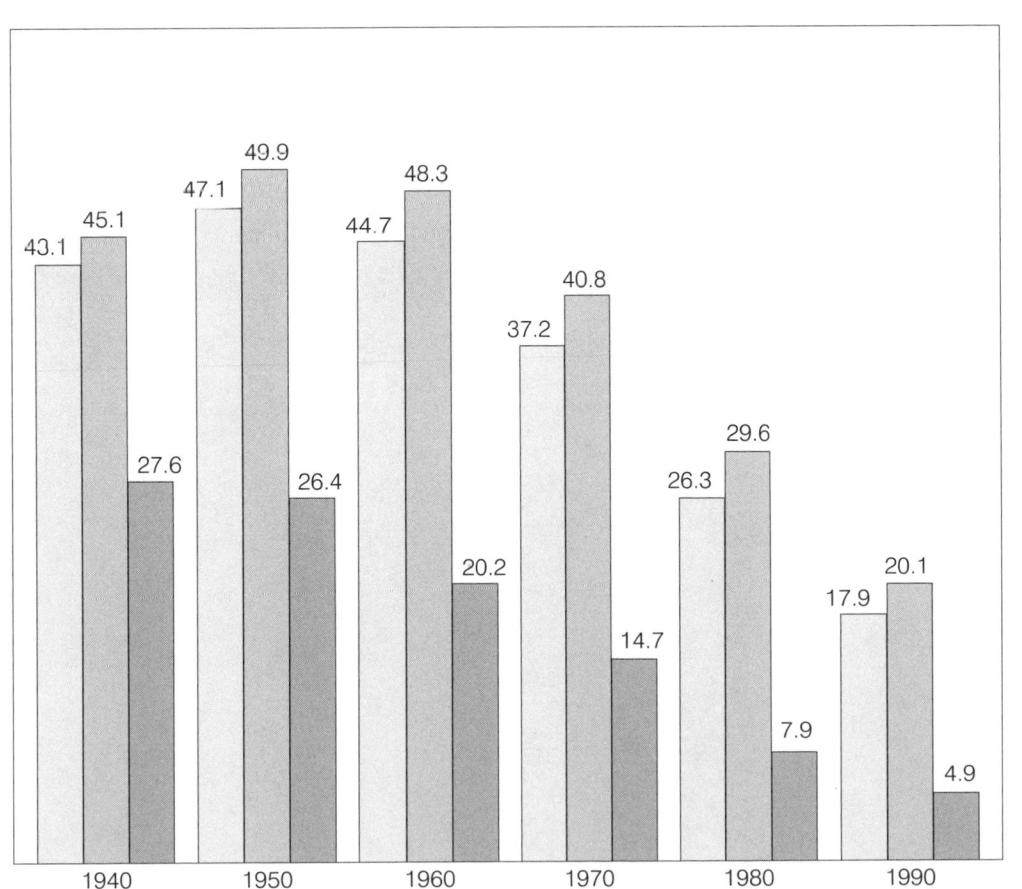

Two-thirds of us are non-Hispanic Whites, while one-third of us belong to racial or ethnic groups.

The 1990 census counted 63,604,432 children under age 18.

About two-thirds of American children were White but not of Hispanic origin, while nearly one-third were non-White or Hispanic.

Non-Hispanic Black children were the largest non-White group (15 percent).

Hispanic children accounted for 12 percent of all children. Two-thirds of Hispanic children were of Mexican origin. But many Hispanic children traced their origins to Puerto Rico, Cuba, El Salvador, Colombia, Guatemala, Nicaragua, Ecuador, Peru, Honduras, or other Central and South American countries.

Three percent of American children belonged to Asian and Pacific Islander groups, including Chinese, Filipino, Japanese, Asian Indian, Korean, Vietnamese, Laotian, Cambodian, Thai, and Hmong.

Figure 2.
Race and Hispanic Origin of Children: 1990

(Percent distribution of children under 18 years old)

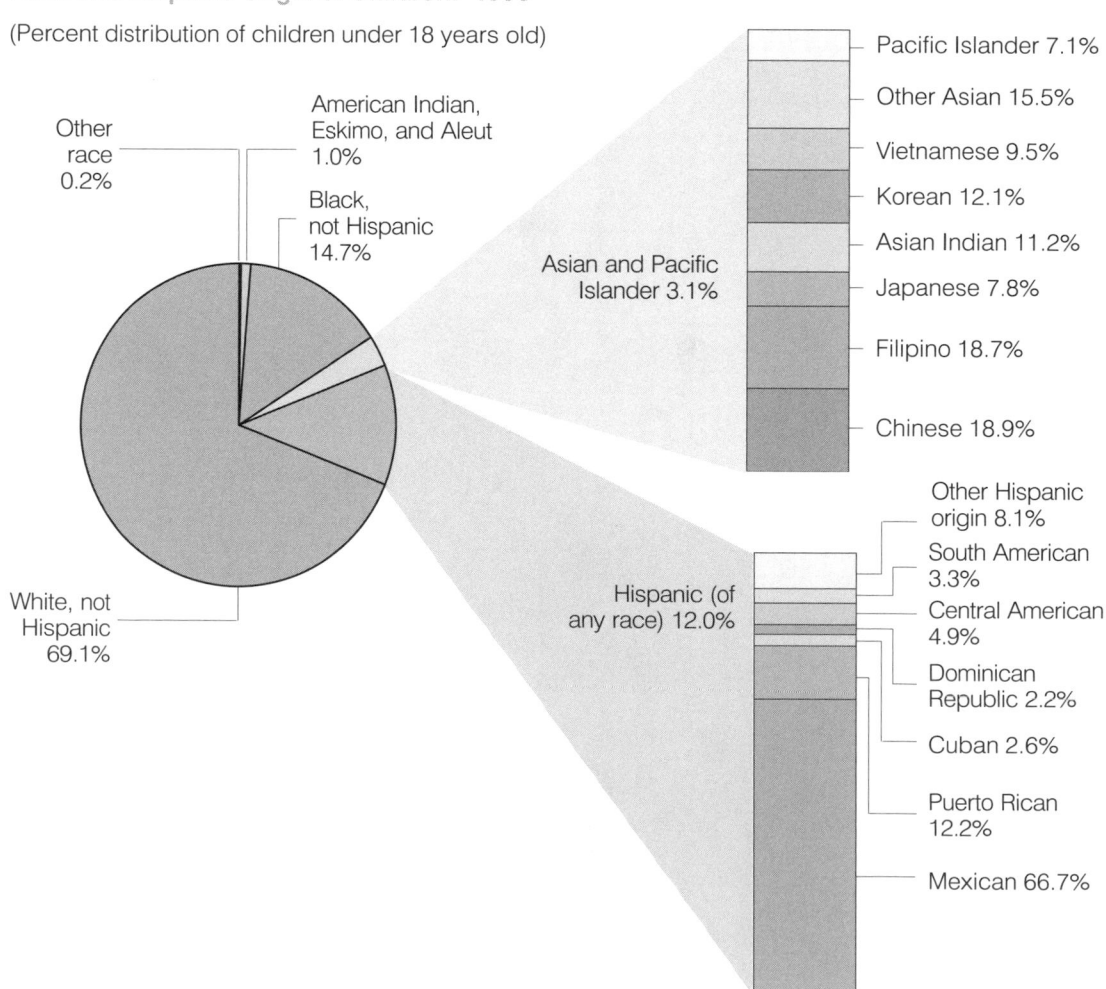

Other race 0.2%

American Indian, Eskimo, and Aleut 1.0%

Black, not Hispanic 14.7%

Asian and Pacific Islander 3.1%

White, not Hispanic 69.1%

Pacific Islander 7.1%

Other Asian 15.5%

Vietnamese 9.5%

Korean 12.1%

Asian Indian 11.2%

Japanese 7.8%

Filipino 18.7%

Chinese 18.9%

Hispanic (of any race) 12.0%

Other Hispanic origin 8.1%

South American 3.3%

Central American 4.9%

Dominican Republic 2.2%

Cuban 2.6%

Puerto Rican 12.2%

Mexican 66.7%

Most of us live with two parents, but our chances of living in a one-parent family rose during the 1980's.

Children living with two parents declined substantially from 77 percent in 1980 to 72 percent in 1990, while those living with one parent increased from 18 percent to 24 percent.

In 1990, the total proportion with one parent or no parent in the home was 20 percent for non-Hispanic Whites, 63 percent for non-Hispanic Blacks, and 36 percent for Hispanics.

During the 1980's, the proportion of children living with one parent rose by 3 percentage points for non-Hispanic Whites, by 13 percentage points for non-Hispanic Blacks, and by 9 percentage points for Hispanics.

More than 4 out of every 5 children living with one parent in 1980 and in 1990 lived with their mother.

Children living with only their father doubled from 2 percent to 4 percent during the 1980's, but the rise in mother-only families accounted for most of the increase in one-parent family living.

Figure 3.
Parental Living Arrangements of Children: 1980 and 1990

(Percent distribution of children under 18 years old)

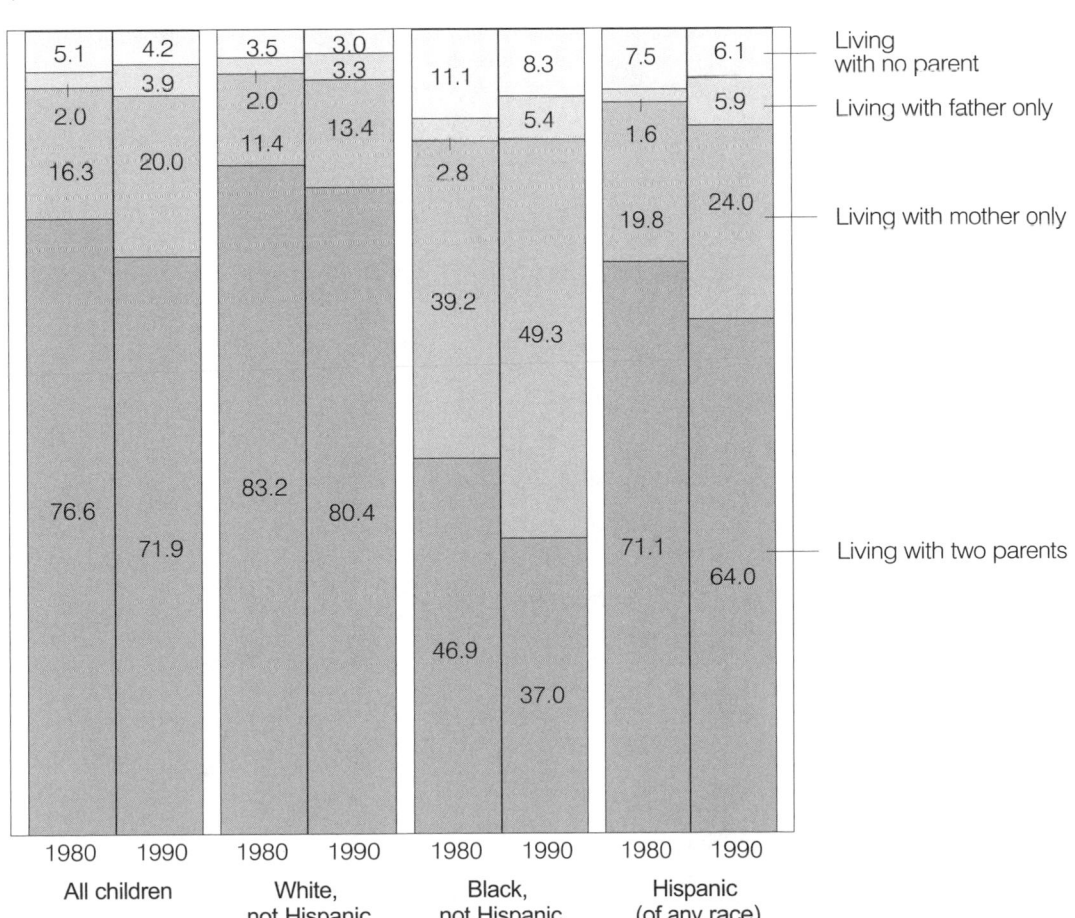

Whether we live with two parents or one, few of us have a grandparent in the home.

Only 3 percent of children in two-parent families in 1990 had a grandparent in the home.

Non-Hispanic White children (2 percent), non-Hispanic Black children (3 percent), and Hispanic children (5 percent) in two-parent families were about equally likely to live with a grandparent.

Children in one-parent families were more likely than those living with two parents to have a grandparent in the home.

About 80 percent of children in one-parent families did not live with a grandparent compared with about 97 percent of children in two-parent families.

Figure 4.

Grandparents in the Homes of Children: 1990

(Percent with grandparent)

☐ Total
☐ Living with two parents
▨ Living with mother only
▨ Living with father only

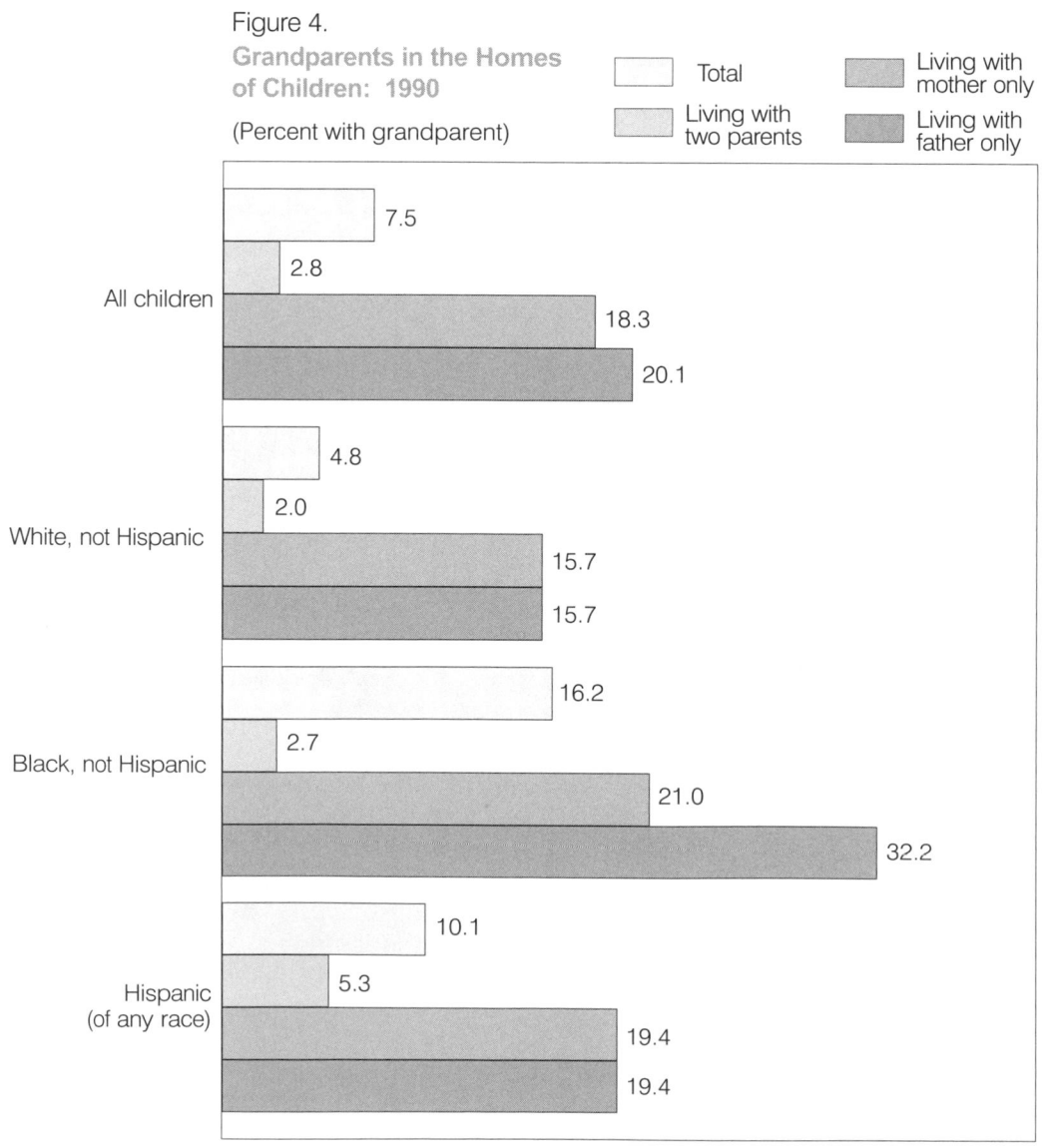

All children
- 7.5
- 2.8
- 18.3
- 20.1

White, not Hispanic
- 4.8
- 2.0
- 15.7
- 15.7

Black, not Hispanic
- 16.2
- 2.7
- 21.0
- 32.2

Hispanic (of any race)
- 10.1
- 5.3
- 19.4
- 19.4

Most of us live in families with one, two, or three children.

The vast majority of pre-school children under 6 years old in 1990 lived in families with one, two, or three children.

About 25 percent of pre-schoolers had no brothers or sisters, about 40 percent had only one sibling, and another 22 percent had two siblings.

Ninety percent of non-Hispanic White preschoolers lived in families with one to

three children, and about 80 percent of non-Hispanic Black and Hispanic pre-schoolers also lived in small families.

Adolescents had more broth-ers and sisters than pre-school children, but most adolescents also lived in families with one, two, or three children.

The proportion of adoles-cents in families with one

to three children was 78 percent for non-Hispanic Whites, 64 percent for non-Hispanic Blacks, and 56 percent for Hispanics.

No more than 15 percent of preschoolers and adoles-cents lived in large families with six or more children, regardless of their racial or ethnic heritage.

Figure 5

Number of Siblings in the Homes of Children 0 to 5 Years Old
and 12 to 17 Years Old, by Race and Hispanic Origin: 1990

(Percent distribution by mother's number of children ever born for children living with mother)

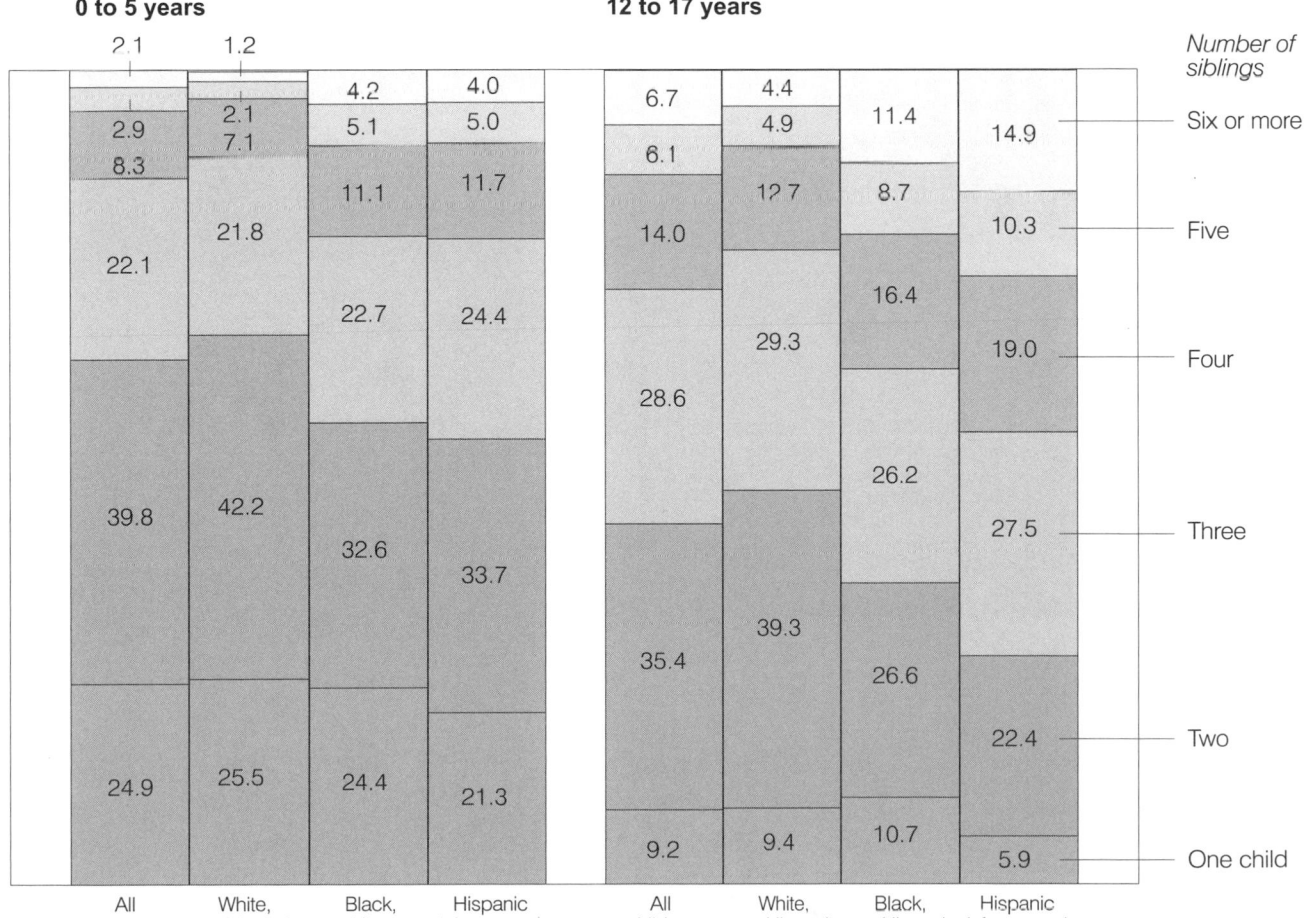

The educational attainments of our parents rose during the past decade.

Children living with mothers who had at least a high school diploma increased from 74 percent in 1980 to 80 percent in 1990.

The proportion with mothers having a bachelor's degree rose from 11 percent to 18 percent.

In 1990, non-Hispanic Black children were one-half as likely as non-Hispanic White children to have a mother with a bachelor's degree, and the proportion for Hispanics was much smaller.

Non-Hispanic Black children also were substantially less likely than non-Hispanic White children to have a mother with a high school diploma, and only 50 percent of Hispanic children had mothers with this much education.

One-fourth of Hispanic children had mothers with less than 9 years of education compared with fewer than 1 in 20 non-Hispanic White children and non-Hispanic Black children.

Figure 6.
Mother's Educational Attainment for Children:
1980 and 1990

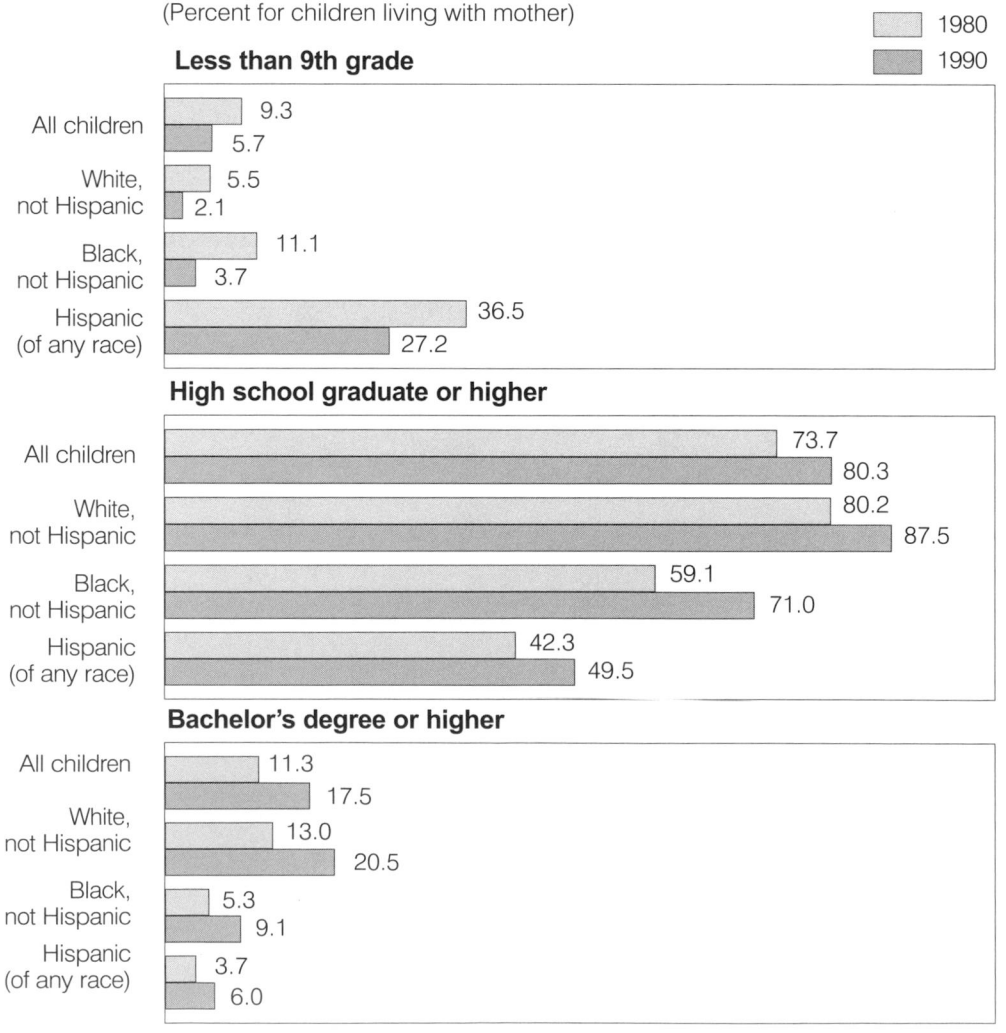

(Percent for children living with mother)

1980
1990

Less than 9th grade

All children — 9.3 / 5.7
White, not Hispanic — 5.5 / 2.1
Black, not Hispanic — 11.1 / 3.7
Hispanic (of any race) — 36.5 / 27.2

High school graduate or higher

All children — 73.7 / 80.3
White, not Hispanic — 80.2 / 87.5
Black, not Hispanic — 59.1 / 71.0
Hispanic (of any race) — 42.3 / 49.5

Bachelor's degree or higher

All children — 11.3 / 17.5
White, not Hispanic — 13.0 / 20.5
Black, not Hispanic — 5.3 / 9.1
Hispanic (of any race) — 3.7 / 6.0

Nearly all of us who live with our fathers have a father who is employed, but many fathers are part-time workers.

In 1990, 96 percent of children living with their fathers (in father-only or two-parent families) had fathers who worked for pay.

Seventy percent of children living with fathers had fathers who were full-time workers, while 26 percent had fathers who worked part time, and

4 percent had fathers who did not work.

Both non-Hispanic Black children and Hispanic children living with fathers were somewhat less likely than non-Hispanic White children living with fathers to have a father who worked.

One-fourth of non-Hispanic White children living with their fathers had fathers who worked part time or not at all, but the proportion was more than 4 in 10 for non-Hispanic Black children and Hispanic children who lived with their fathers.

Figure 7.
Father's Amount of Work and Parental Living
Arrangements for Children: 1980 and 1990

(Percent distribution for children under 18 years old living with father)

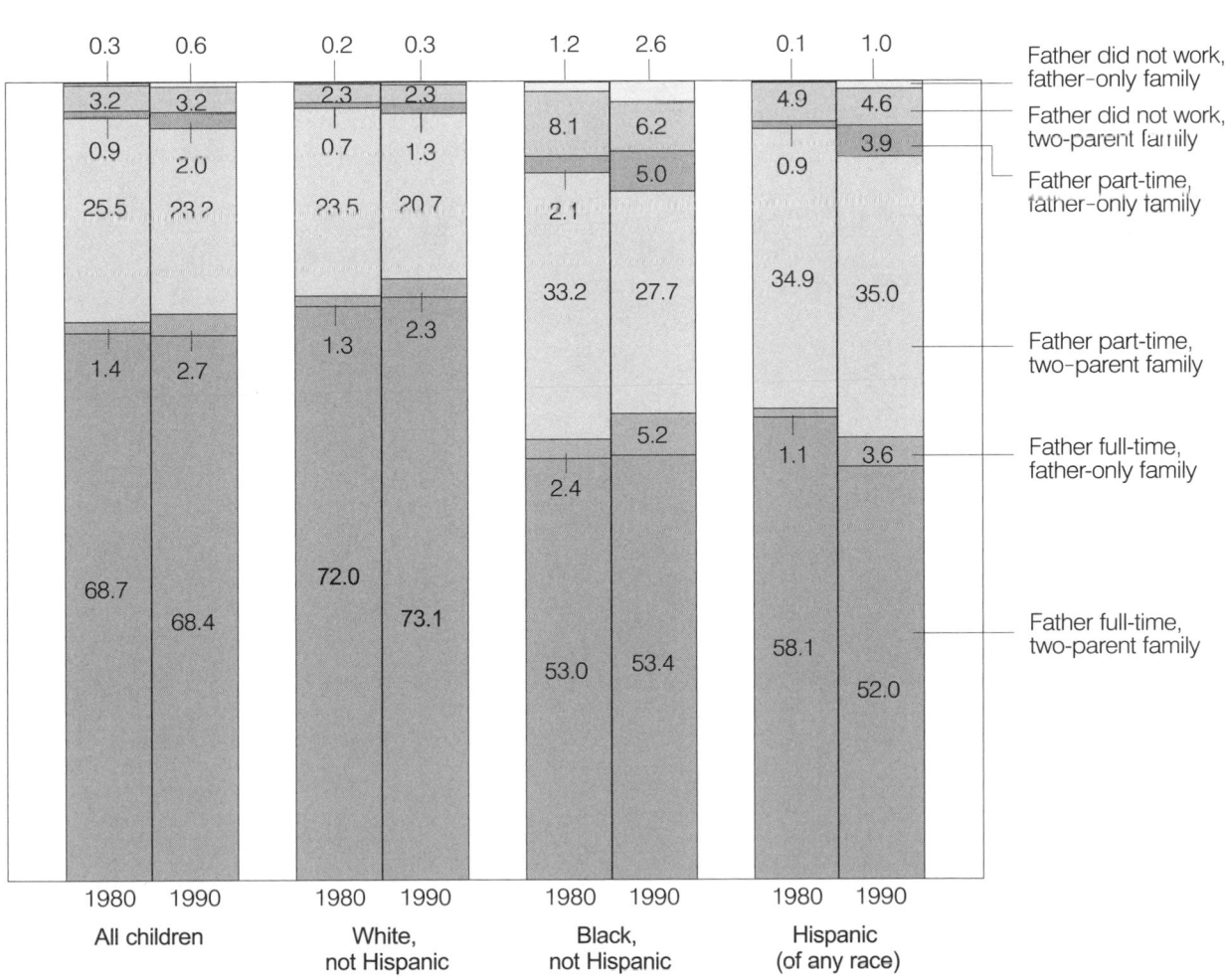

	1980	1990		1980	1990		1980	1990		1980	1990
	All children			White, not Hispanic			Black, not Hispanic			Hispanic (of any race)	

Father did not work, father-only family
Father did not work, two-parent family
Father part-time, father-only family
Father part-time, two-parent family
Father full-time, father-only family
Father full-time, two-parent family

Most of us who live with our mothers have a mother who is employed.

Among children living with their mothers, the proportion with a working mother increased from 60 percent in 1980 to 72 percent in 1990.

Most of the increase in the proportion of children with working mothers occurred because of the rise in mothers who were full-time workers.

By 1990, the proportion of children living with mothers whose mothers were full-time workers was 27 percent for non-Hispanic Whites, 30 percent for non-Hispanic Blacks, and 21 percent for Hispanics.

The proportion living with mothers who were part-time workers was substantially larger, at 47 percent for non-Hispanic Whites and 41 percent for non-Hispanic Blacks and for Hispanics.

Figure 8.
Mother's Amount of Work and Parental Living Arrangements for Children: 1980 and 1990

(Percent distribution for children under 18 years old living with mother)

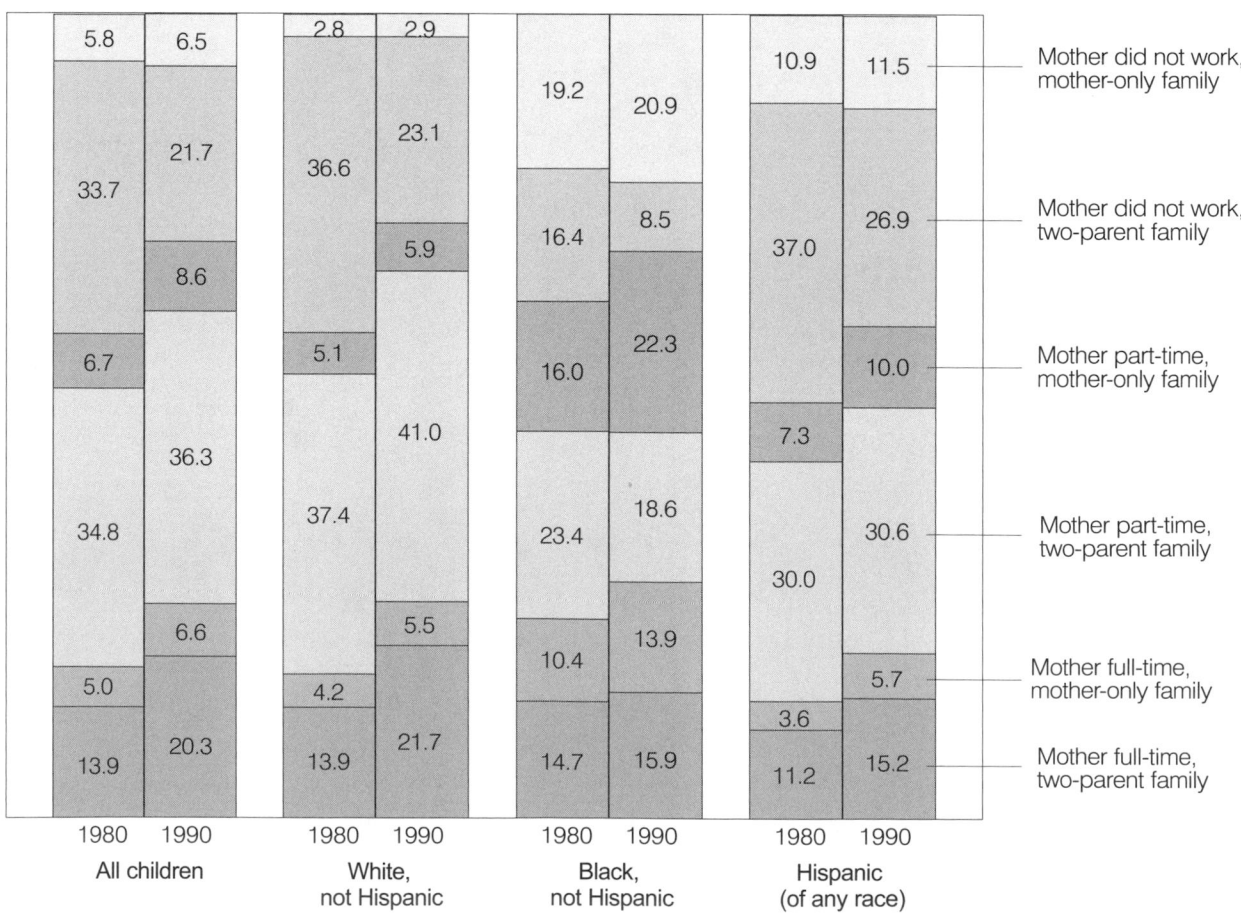

For every one of us who lives in a "traditional" two-parent family, four of us live in "nontraditional" two-parent families.

In 1990, 14 percent of children lived in "traditional" families with fathers who worked full time year round and mothers who did not work during the year.

Four times as many children lived in "nontraditional" two-parent families, where the father was not a full-time worker, or where the mother did work.

Children were about equally likely to live in a "traditional" family with a fully-employed father and homemaking mother or in a "nontraditional" family where both parents were full-time workers.

Children were substantially more likely to live in a "nontraditional" two-parent family where the father was a full-time worker and the mother a part-time worker or where the father was a part-time worker.

Figure 9.
Father's and Mother's Amount of Work and Parental Living Arrangements for Children: 1980 and 1990

(Percent distribution for children under 18 years old)

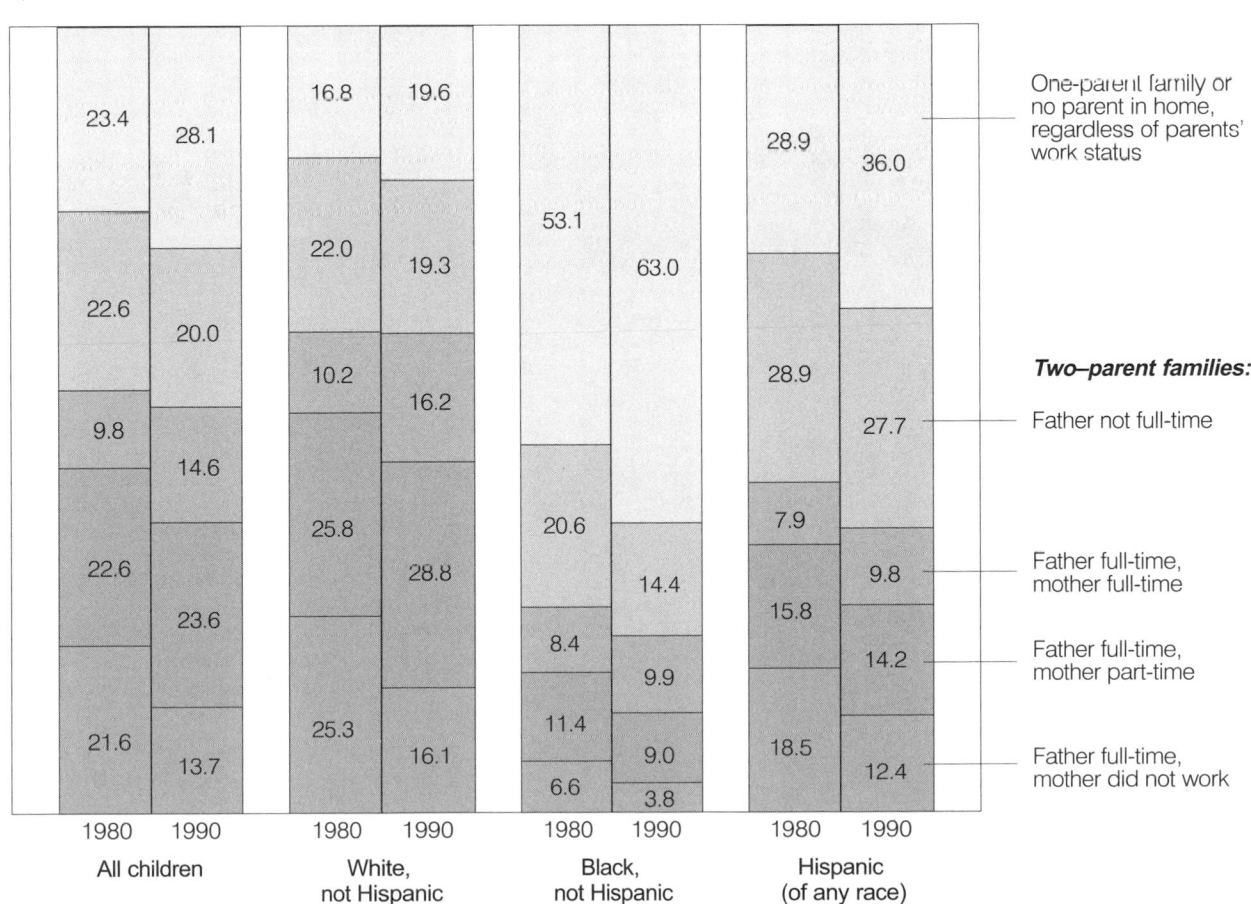

At age 1 year, for every one of us who lives in "traditional" two-parent families, more than three of us live in "non-traditional" two-parent families.

For children age 1, the proportion living with a father who worked full time year round and a mother who was a full-time homemaker declined from 28 percent in 1980 to 17 percent in 1990.

The proportion living in such "traditional" families declined

from 34 percent to 20 percent for non-Hispanic Whites, from 8 percent to 4 percent for non-Hispanic Blacks, and from 21 percent to 15 percent for Hispanics.

In 1990, for every child age 1 living in "traditional" families with a fully-employed father

and homemaking mother, there were more than three children who lived in "non-traditional" two-parent families with a father who was not a full-time worker or a mother who worked.

Figure 10.
Father's and Mother's Amount of Work and Parental Living Arrangements for Children 1 Year Old: 1980 and 1990

(Percent distribution)

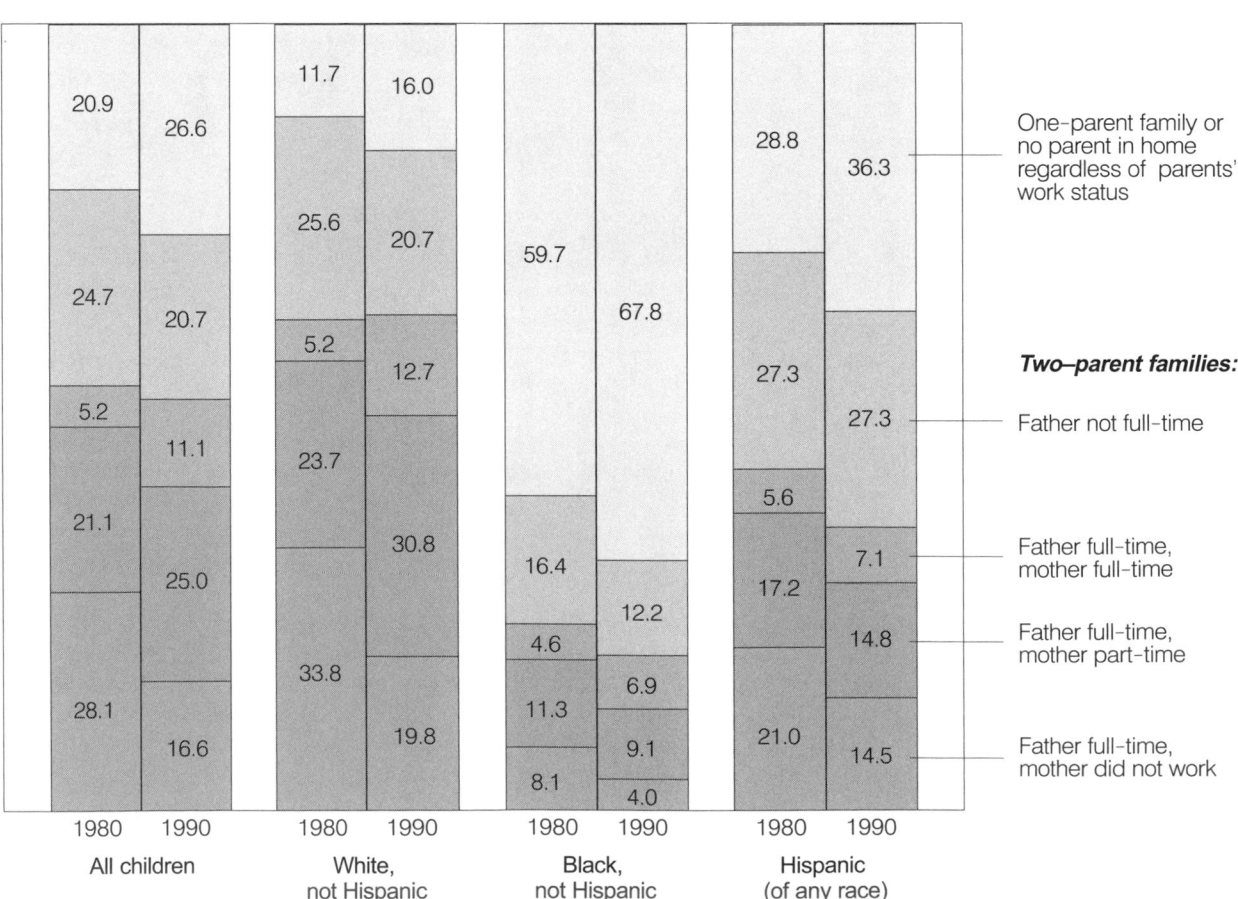

The proportion of us in high and low income families increased during the 1980's.

Children in low income families increased from 24 percent in 1980 to 26 percent in 1990, while the proportion in high income families increased from 18 percent to 21 percent.

Between 1980 and 1990, the proportion of children with comfortable or prosperous family incomes declined from 42 percent to 37 percent.

Non-Hispanic White children in 1990 were about three times more likely than non-Hispanic Black children and Hispanic children to live in families with high incomes.

Comfortable or prosperous family incomes were also more often experienced by non-Hispanic White children than by non-Hispanic Black children or Hispanic children.

The proportion living in a family with low income was more than 2 1/2 times larger for non-Hispanic Blacks and Hispanics than for non-Hispanic Whites.

Figure 11.
Family Income Level for Children: 1980 and 1990

(Percent distribution)

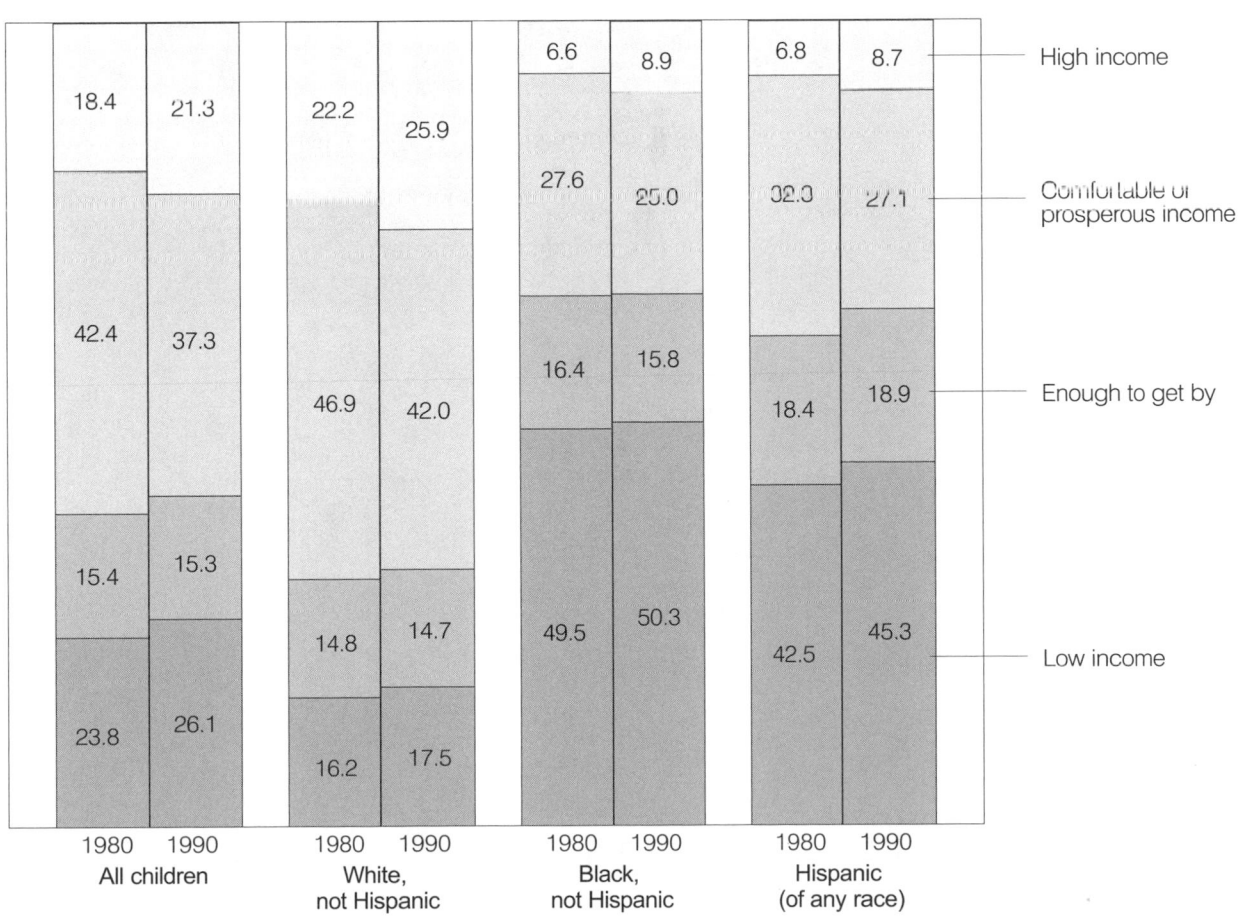

Our family incomes are higher if we live with two parents.

In 1990, 69 percent of children in two-parent families had comfortable or high family incomes compared with 47 percent in father-only families and 27 percent in mother-only families.

About 58 percent of children in mother-only families were low-income families compared with 34 percent of children in father-only families and 16 percent of children in two-parent families.

For children in two-parent families, the chances of living at comfortable or high income levels reached 74 percent for non-Hispanic Whites, but only 57 percent for non-Hispanic Blacks and 44 percent for Hispanics.

Among mother-only families, non-Hispanic Black and Hispanic children were most likely to be in low-income families, at 69 percent for each compared with 46 percent for non-Hispanic White children.

Figure 12.
Family Income Level for Children by Parental Living Arrangements: 1990

(Percent distribution)

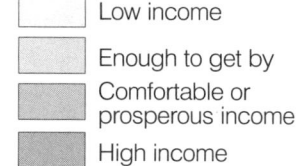

Low income

Enough to get by

Comfortable or prosperous income

High income

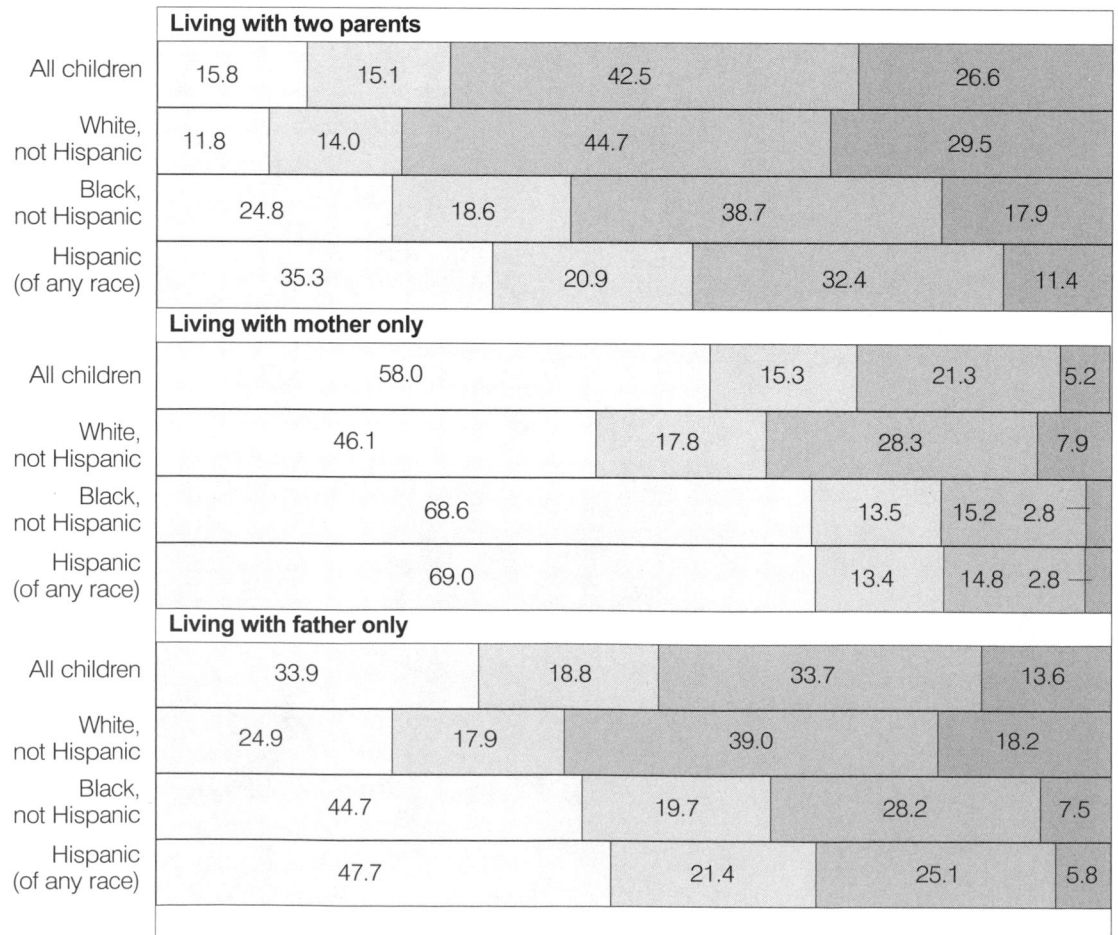

Living with two parents

	Low income	Enough to get by	Comfortable or prosperous	High income
All children	15.8	15.1	42.5	26.6
White, not Hispanic	11.8	14.0	44.7	29.5
Black, not Hispanic	24.8	18.6	38.7	17.9
Hispanic (of any race)	35.3	20.9	32.4	11.4

Living with mother only

	Low income	Enough to get by	Comfortable or prosperous	High income
All children	58.0	15.3	21.3	5.2
White, not Hispanic	46.1	17.8	28.3	7.9
Black, not Hispanic	68.6	13.5	15.2	2.8
Hispanic (of any race)	69.0	13.4	14.8	2.8

Living with father only

	Low income	Enough to get by	Comfortable or prosperous	High income
All children	33.9	18.8	33.7	13.6
White, not Hispanic	24.9	17.9	39.0	18.2
Black, not Hispanic	44.7	19.7	28.2	7.5
Hispanic (of any race)	47.7	21.4	25.1	5.8

Our official poverty rate is higher if we live with one parent.

The poverty rate for children in 1990 was 18 percent, but it was 3 or 4 times larger for non-Hispanic Blacks and Hispanics than for non-Hispanic Whites.

Nine percent of children in two-parent families were poor, but children in father-only families were more than twice as likely to be poor, and children in mother-only families were more than 5 times as likely to be poor.

Among children in two-parent families, the Hispanic poverty rate was more than 3 times greater than for non-Hispanic White children, and the rate for non-Hispanic Blacks was about 2 times the rate for non-Hispanic Whites.

The poverty rate for Hispanic and non-Hispanic Black children in mother-only families was much greater than for non-Hispanic Whites in mother-only families.

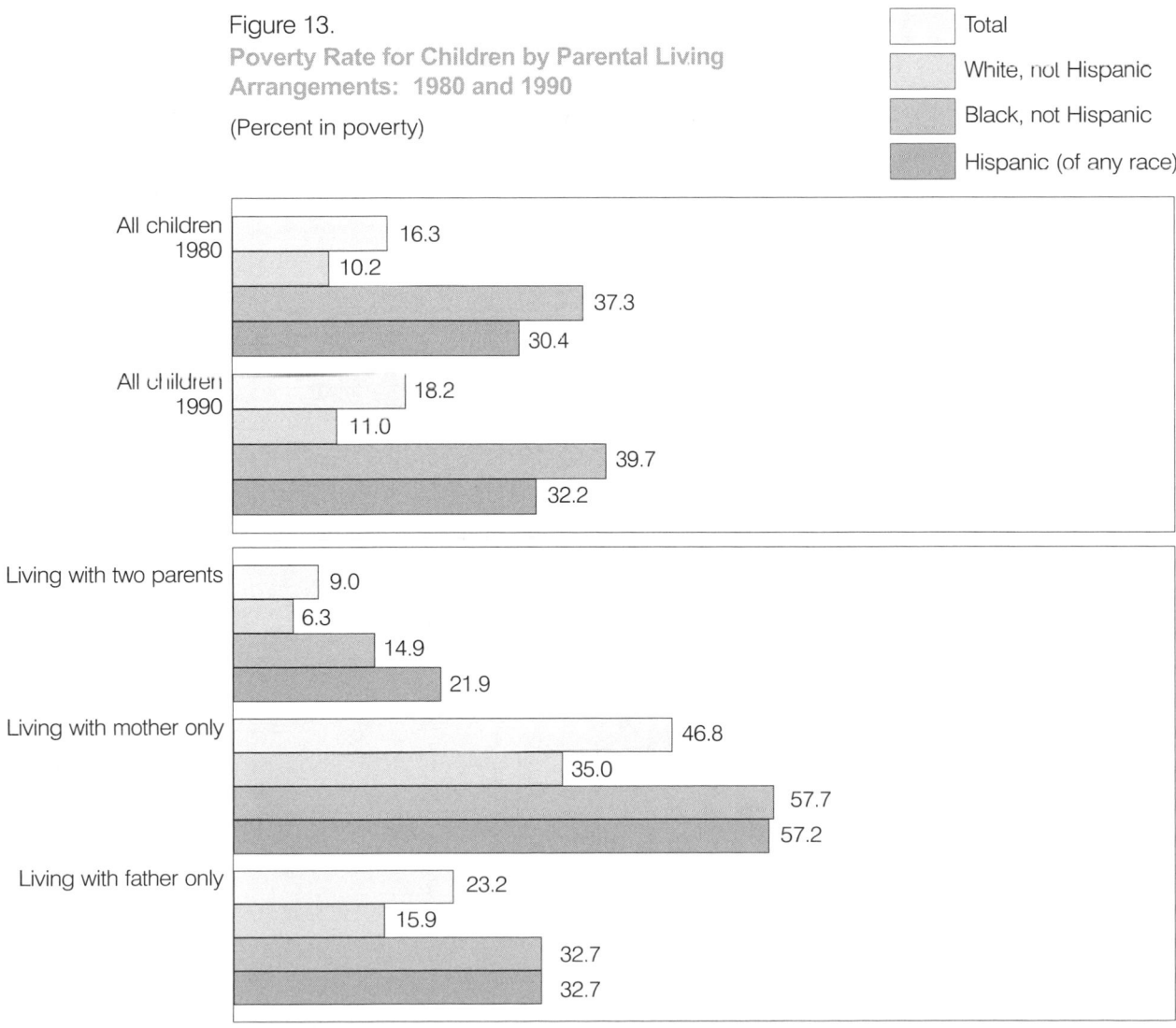

Figure 13.
Poverty Rate for Children by Parental Living Arrangements: 1980 and 1990

(Percent in poverty)

Total
White, not Hispanic
Black, not Hispanic
Hispanic (of any race)

All children 1980
16.3
10.2
37.3
30.4

All children 1990
18.2
11.0
39.7
32.2

Living with two parents
9.0
6.3
14.9
21.9

Living with mother only
46.8
35.0
57.7
57.2

Living with father only
23.2
15.9
32.7
32.7

Our chances of having a comfortable, prosperous, or high family income depend on the amount of time our parents work.

For non-Hispanic White children in families with only one working parent, the proportion experiencing a comfortable, prosperous, or high standard of living was higher if the parent was working full time than if the parent was working part time.

For non-Hispanic Black children and for Hispanic children in families with only one employed parent, the proportions experiencing this standard of living were substantially lower than for non-Hispanic Whites.

For children living with two employed parents, if one worked full time year round and the other worked part time, the proportion experiencing this economic level was higher than in families with parents who worked less.

Figure 14.
Percent With Comfortable, Prosperous, or High Family Income for Children by Parental Amount of Work and Living Arrangements: 1990

(Percent with comfortable, prosperous, or high family income)

Two parents work
One parent works

All children

Father full-time, mother full-time	89.7
Father full-time, mother part-time	77.9
Father part-time, mother full-time	71.6
Father full-time, mother did not work	64.7
Mother full-time, father absent	50.7
Father part-time, mother did not work	32.6
Mother part-time, father absent	22.7

White, not Hispanic

Father full-time, mother full-time	91.6
Father full-time, mother part-time	80.6
Father part-time, mother full-time	75.6
Father full-time, mother did not work	69.7
Mother full-time, father absent	57.0
Father part-time, mother did not work	40.6
Mother part-time, father absent	28.9

Black, not Hispanic

Father full-time, mother full-time	84.2
Father full-time, mother part-time	63.4
Father part-time, mother full-time	63.4
Father full-time, mother did not work	38.0
Mother full-time, father absent	41.0
Father part-time, mother did not work	17.7
Mother part-time, father absent	16.3

Hispanic (of any race)

Father full-time, mother full-time	79.1
Father full-time, mother part-time	58.5
Father part-time, mother full-time	55.7
Father full-time, mother did not work	36.9
Mother full-time, father absent	42.5
Father part-time, mother did not work	15.5
Mother part-time, father absent	17.6

328

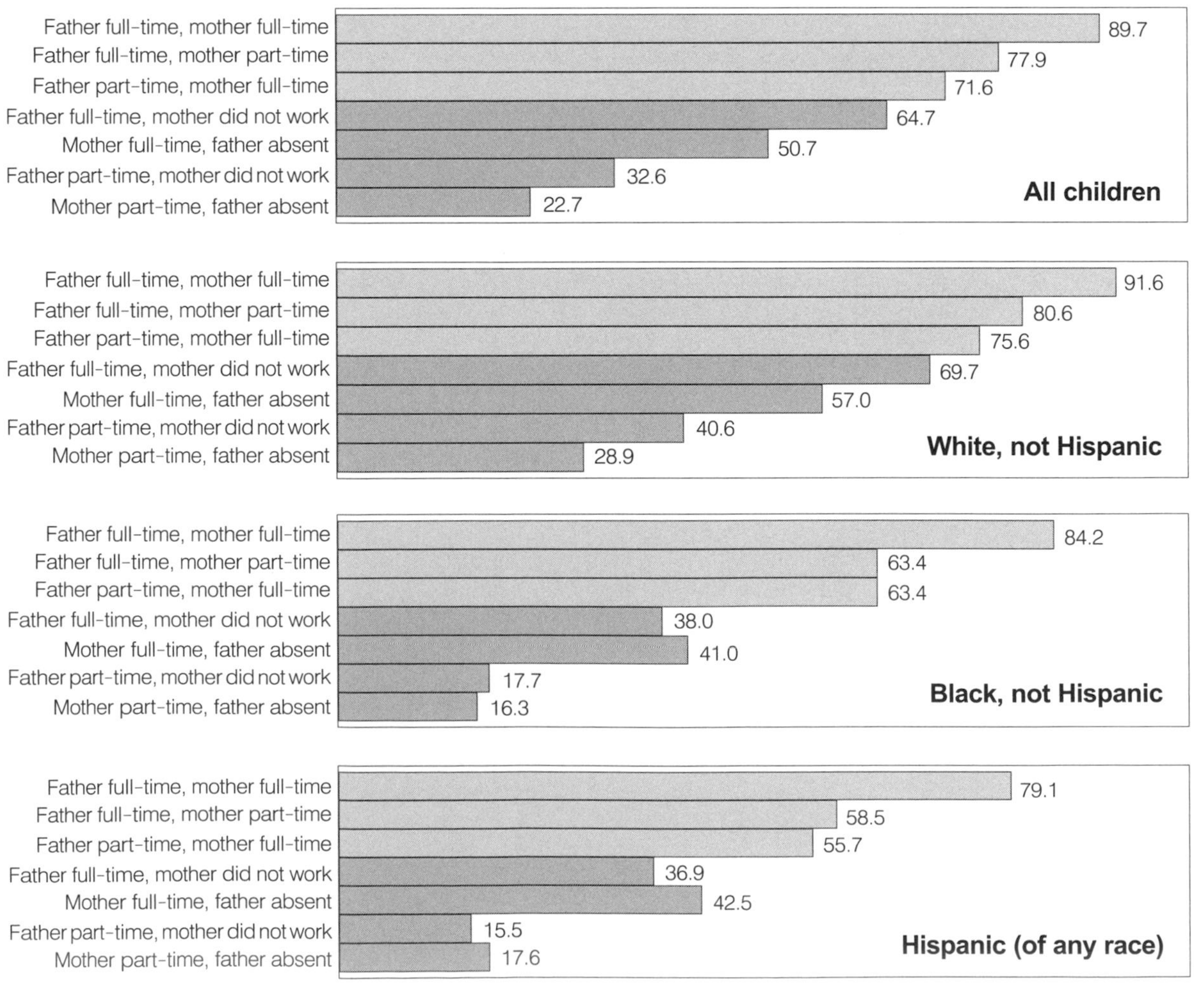

Our chances of having a low family income are similar in "traditional" families and in mother-only families where the mother is a full-time worker.

For non-Hispanic White children in "traditional" families where the father was a full-time worker and the mother a full-time homemaker and in mother-only families where the mother was a full-time worker, the chances of having a low family income were small.

Non-Hispanic White children in families where only one parent worked were 2 times more likely to have a low family income if the parent worked part time than if the parent worked full time.

For non-Hispanic Black and Hispanic children, the

chances of having a low family income were much lower in "traditional" families and mother-only families where one parent worked full time year round than in those with one employed parent who worked part time.

Figure 15.
Percent With Low Family Income for Children by Parental Amount of Work and Living Arrangements: 1990

(Percent with low family income)

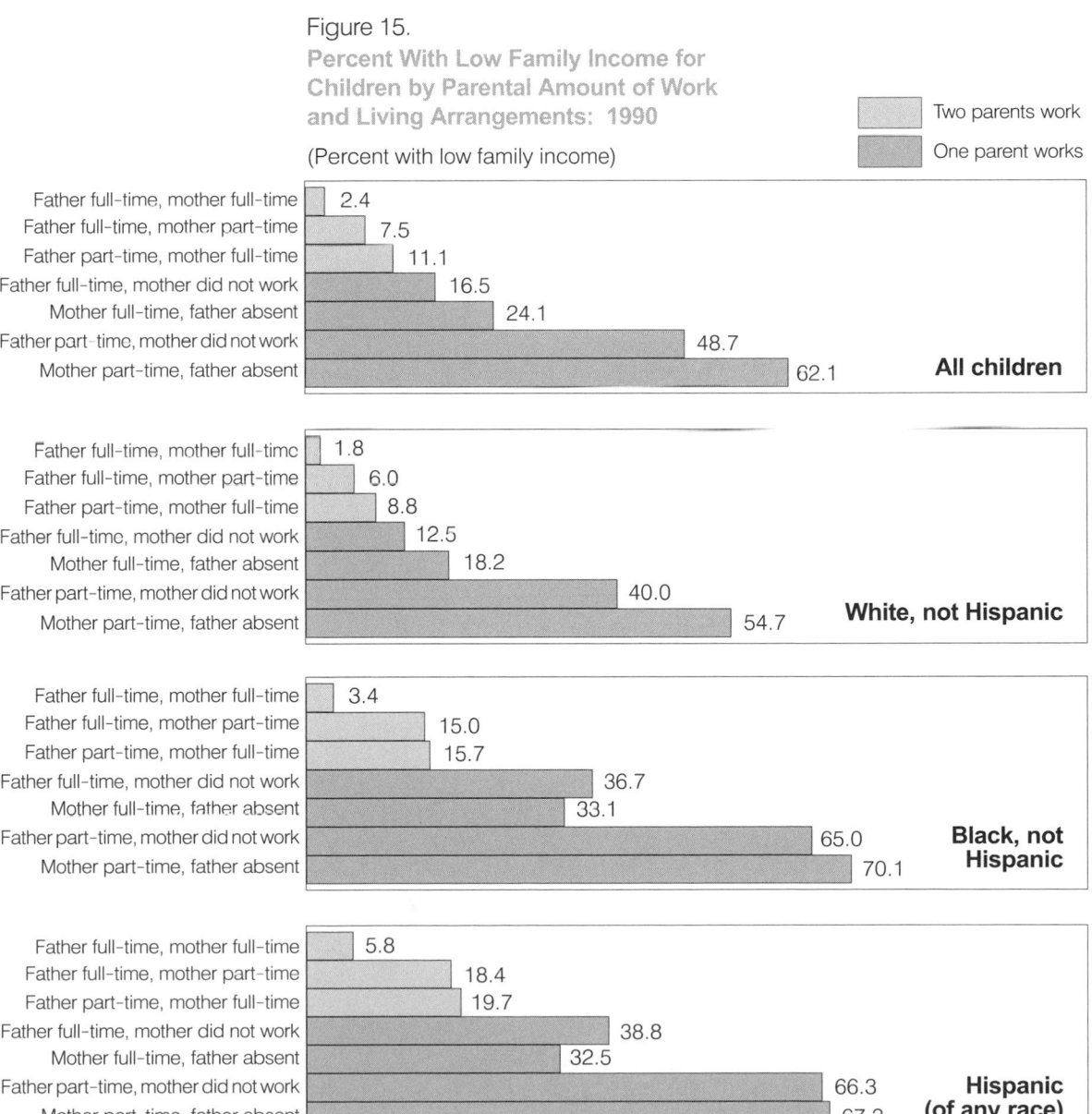

| | Two parents work |
| | One parent works |

All children

Father full-time, mother full-time	2.4
Father full-time, mother part-time	7.5
Father part-time, mother full-time	11.1
Father full-time, mother did not work	16.5
Mother full-time, father absent	24.1
Father part-time, mother did not work	48.7
Mother part-time, father absent	62.1

White, not Hispanic

Father full-time, mother full-time	1.8
Father full-time, mother part-time	6.0
Father part-time, mother full-time	8.8
Father full-time, mother did not work	12.5
Mother full-time, father absent	18.2
Father part-time, mother did not work	40.0
Mother part-time, father absent	54.7

Black, not Hispanic

Father full-time, mother full-time	3.4
Father full-time, mother part-time	15.0
Father part-time, mother full-time	15.7
Father full-time, mother did not work	36.7
Mother full-time, father absent	33.1
Father part-time, mother did not work	65.0
Mother part-time, father absent	70.1

Hispanic (of any race)

Father full-time, mother full-time	5.8
Father full-time, mother part-time	18.4
Father part-time, mother full-time	19.7
Father full-time, mother did not work	38.8
Mother full-time, father absent	32.5
Father part-time, mother did not work	66.3
Mother part-time, father absent	67.3

329

Whether we live with two parents or only our mother, our official poverty rates are higher if we are Black or Hispanic.

Poverty rates were lower for non-Hispanic White, than for non-Hispanic Black, and Hispanic children, if they lived with two working parents.

Whether they lived with two parents or only their mother, if children had only one working parent and the parent was a full-time worker, the poverty rate was 2 to 4 times greater for non-Hispanic

Blacks and Hispanics than it was for non-Hispanic Whites.

The poverty rates were higher still for children in two-parent and mother-only families with one working parent who was a part-time worker.

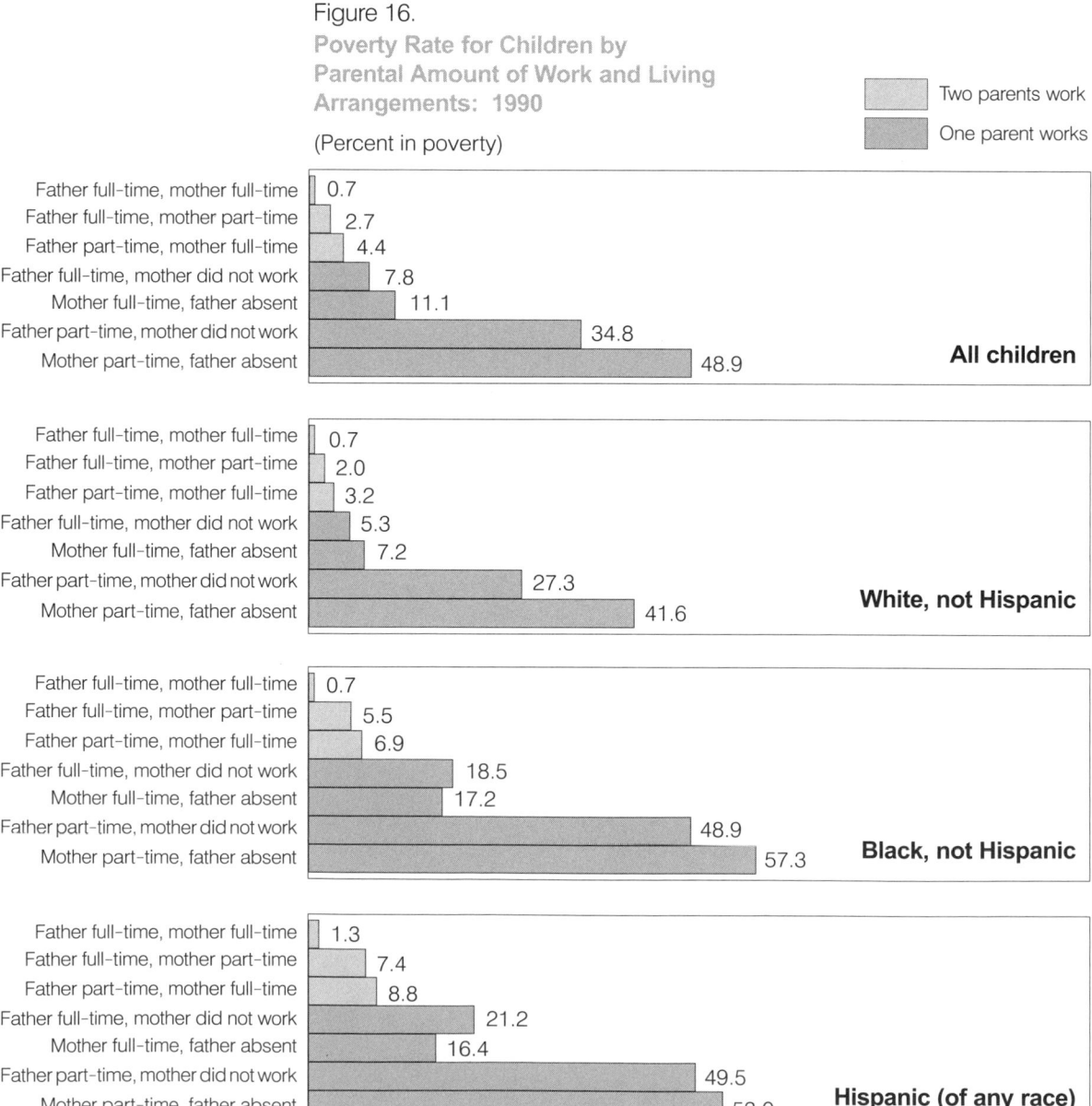

Figure 16.
Poverty Rate for Children by
Parental Amount of Work and Living
Arrangements: 1990

(Percent in poverty)

□ Two parents work
■ One parent works

All children

Father full-time, mother full-time	0.7
Father full-time, mother part-time	2.7
Father part-time, mother full-time	4.4
Father full-time, mother did not work	7.8
Mother full-time, father absent	11.1
Father part-time, mother did not work	34.8
Mother part-time, father absent	48.9

White, not Hispanic

Father full-time, mother full-time	0.7
Father full-time, mother part-time	2.0
Father part-time, mother full-time	3.2
Father full-time, mother did not work	5.3
Mother full-time, father absent	7.2
Father part-time, mother did not work	27.3
Mother part-time, father absent	41.6

Black, not Hispanic

Father full-time, mother full-time	0.7
Father full-time, mother part-time	5.5
Father part-time, mother full-time	6.9
Father full-time, mother did not work	18.5
Mother full-time, father absent	17.2
Father part-time, mother did not work	48.9
Mother part-time, father absent	57.3

Hispanic (of any race)

Father full-time, mother full-time	1.3
Father full-time, mother part-time	7.4
Father part-time, mother full-time	8.8
Father full-time, mother did not work	21.2
Mother full-time, father absent	16.4
Father part-time, mother did not work	49.5
Mother part-time, father absent	53.0

e, the Americans: Our Education

Introduction

We Americans are known for many achievements — our standard of living, our discoveries and inventions, and our ability to organize and overcome problems. We tend to think of these achievements in terms of material things — things like the space shuttle, microwave ovens, and super computers. But as important as these are, they are only byproducts of America's greatest achievement — the ever increasing level of education of its population.

The first question about education — "Can you read and write?" — was asked in the 1840 census. At that time, more than 1 in every 5 persons were illiterate. The general illiteracy rate decreased steadily over the years. Questions on illiteracy were dropped in the 1940 census.

Since the Census Bureau first began measuring educational attainment as completed schooling in the 1940 census, the educational level of the population has risen steadily. In the 50 years since then, the United States has made great strides in education. Not only are more of us going to school, but we are also starting earlier and staying longer. In 1990, about 75 percent of the adult population had received at least a high school diploma compared with about 25 percent in 1940.

In the 1990 census, we measured the completion of specific college degrees (for example, bachelor's, master's and doctoral degrees) for the first time. These data show that over 20 million Americans held a bachelor's degree as their highest level of schooling, and another 11 million have a professional or graduate degree.

The advantages of a good education are many, but they boil down to one main point: having a good education gives a person the opportunity to make the most of his or her talents. The quality of life in America's future is inseparably bound to the quality — and quantity — of education obtained by each of its members.

In 1990, there were nearly 65 million of us enrolled in school.

Because the school-age population of the United States has grown tremendously since 1940, it's not surprising to find that the number of us going to school is greater now than in 1940.

More importantly, the proportion of Americans between the ages of 5 and 24 going to school has grown from 58 percent in 1940 to 70 percent in 1990.

Nearly half of the total 65 million students were enrolled in elementary school; 17 percent were in high school, and over one-fourth were enrolled in colleges across the Nation.

Figure 1a.
School-Age Population and Enrollment: 1940 to 1990

School-age population
Percent enrolled

(Millions. Persons 5 to 24 years old)

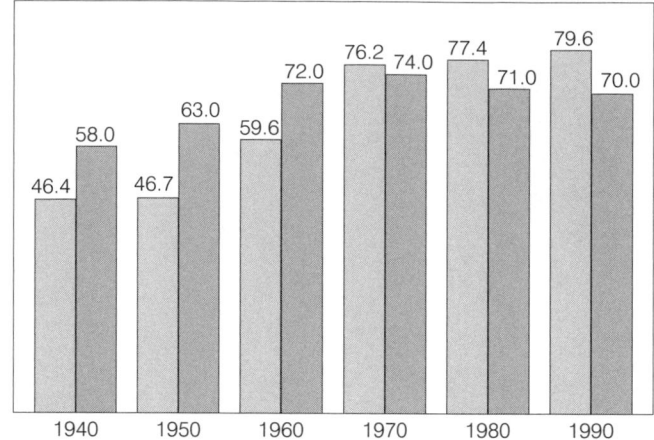

Figure 1b.
Percent Distribution of Students: 1990

(Persons 3 years old and over enrolled in school)

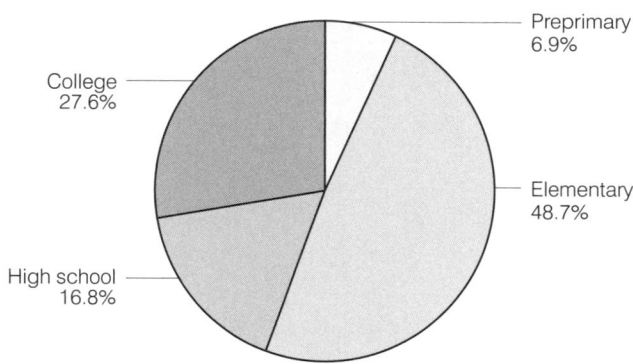

Preprimary 6.9%
College 27.6%
Elementary 48.7%
High school 16.8%

Not only are more of us going to school, but we are starting earlier and staying longer.

Since the turn of the century, it has been compulsory for almost all children between 7 and 15 years old to go to school. About 96 percent of persons 7 to 15 years old were enrolled in school in 1990.

Nearly 30 percent of persons 3 and 4 years old were enrolled in preschool and about 80 percent of persons 5 and 6 years old were enrolled in school.

About 34 percent of persons 20 to 24 years old and 12 percent of persons 25 to 34 years old were enrolled in college.

Figure 2.
School Enrollment by Age: 1990

(Percent of persons 3 to 54 years old enrolled in school)

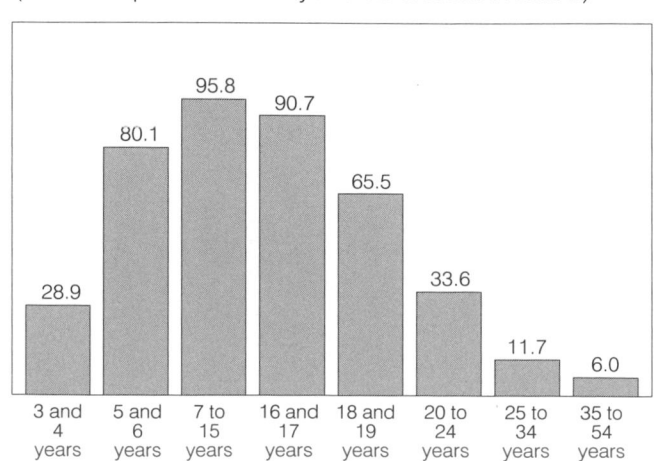

Our educational attainment increased steadily since 1940.

Educational attainment levels for all persons 25 years old and over have increased over the last 50 years. During the period from 1940 to 1990, the proportion of the population completing high school rose substantially.

Three-quarters of the adult population had completed at least a high school diploma in 1990 compared with about 25 percent in 1940, 41 percent in 1960, and 67 percent in 1980.

One-fifth of the adult population had completed a bachelor's degree or more in 1990 compared with about 5 percent in 1940, 8 percent in 1960, and 16 percent in 1980.

In 1990, over 1 million persons held a doctorate degree.

For the first time in our Nation's history more than three-fourths of us graduated from high school.

Part of the rising level of educational attainment is the natural replacement of older generations by younger people who have had better educational opportunities.

In 1990, about 34 percent of persons 75 years old and over did not complete the 9th grade compared with only 4 percent of persons 25 to 34 years old.

About 45 percent of persons 75 years old and over completed a high school diploma or more compared with 84 percent of persons 25 to 34 years old.

The proportion of persons 75 years old and over with a bachelor's degree or more was about 10 percent in 1990 compared with about 23 percent of persons 25 to 34 years old.

Figure 3a.

Educational Attainment of the Adult Population: 1940 to 1990

(Percent 25 years old and over)

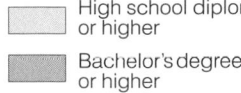

High school diplom or higher

Bachelor's degree or higher

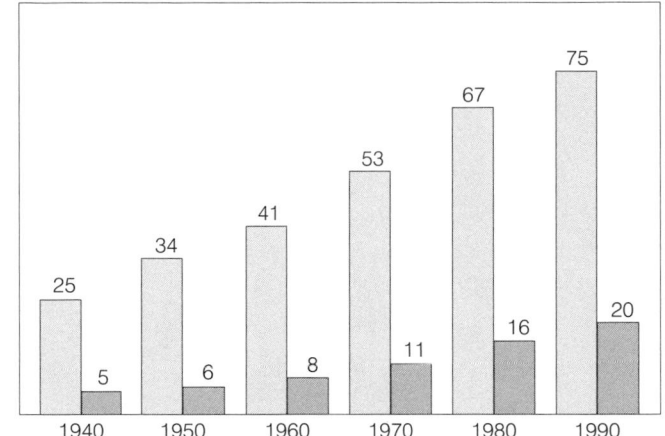

Figure 3b.

Educational Distribution of the Adult Population: 1990

(Percent 25 years old and over)

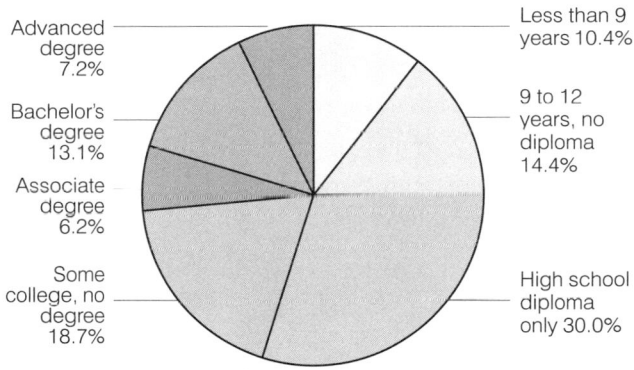

Figure 4.

Educational Attainment for Selected Age Groups: 1990

(Percent 25 years old and over)

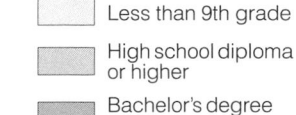

Less than 9th grade

High school diploma or higher

Bachelor's degree or higher

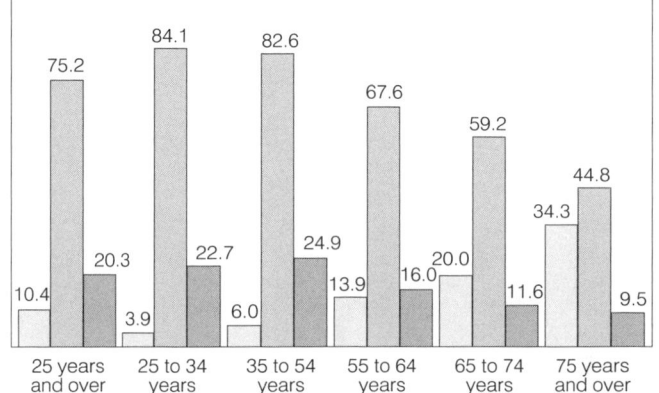

333

Differences in the educational attainment of men and women are relatively small.

A larger proportion of men (27 percent) than women (24 percent) hold a college degree of some kind. Women are more likely than men to have completed only a high school diploma, 32 percent and 28 percent, respectively.

Among women 25 to 34 years old, 32 percent have a college degree compared with 30 percent of men in this age group.

Young women 25 to 39 years old also were slightly more likely than young men in this age group to be enrolled in school, 11 percent and 10 percent, respectively.

Figure 5.

Educational Attainment of Adults by Sex: 1990

(Percent of persons 25 years old and over)

Male
Female

	Less than 9 years	9 to 12 years, no diploma	High school diploma only	Some college, no degree	Associate degree	Bachelor's degree	Advanced degree
Male	10.4	13.9	27.6	19.0	5.8	14.4	9.0
Female	10.4	14.8	32.1	18.6	6.5	12.0	5.7

Our educational attainment differs by racial and ethnic groups, but all groups have improved in the past decade.

In 1990, high school completion levels were highest for Whites, with Asian and Pacific Islanders not far behind.

Substantial improvements in high school completion occurred during the decade for Blacks and American Indians, Eskimos, and Aleuts.

There was also an increase in the proportion of college graduates for each racial group and Hispanics from 1980 to 1990.

In 1990, the highest level of college completion was for Asian and Pacific Islanders at 37 percent.

Figure 6.

Completion Rates by Race and Hispanic Origin: 1980 and 1990

(Percent 25 years old and over)

1980
1990

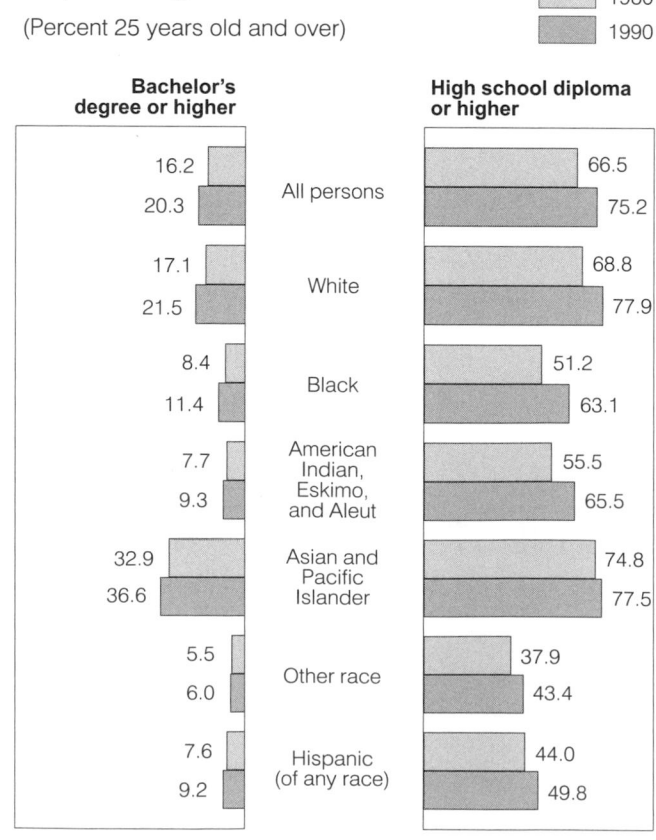

	Bachelor's degree or higher		High school diploma or higher
All persons	16.2 / 20.3		66.5 / 75.2
White	17.1 / 21.5		68.8 / 77.9
Black	8.4 / 11.4		51.2 / 63.1
American Indian, Eskimo, and Aleut	7.7 / 9.3		55.5 / 65.5
Asian and Pacific Islander	32.9 / 36.6		74.8 / 77.5
Other race	5.5 / 6.0		37.9 / 43.4
Hispanic (of any race)	7.6 / 9.2		44.0 / 49.8

Some Asian and Pacific Islander groups have among the highest high school and college completion rates.

In 1990, among Asian and Pacific Islander groups, Japanese persons had the highest proportion of high school graduates, at 88 percent. Other Asian and Pacific Islander groups with proportions greater than 80 percent included Asian Indians, Filipinos, and Koreans.

In general, Asian and Pacific Islanders had a higher proportion of college graduates than all persons 25 years old and over, 37 percent versus 20 percent.

Asians (38 percent) had a higher proportion of college graduates than Pacific Islanders (11 percent).

Among Asian and Pacific Islanders, Asian Indians had the highest level of college graduates at 58 percent.

Figure 7.

High School and Bachelor's Degree Completion Rates for Selected Asian and Pacific Islander Groups: 1990

(Percent 25 years old and over)

High school diploma or higher

Bachelor's degree or higher

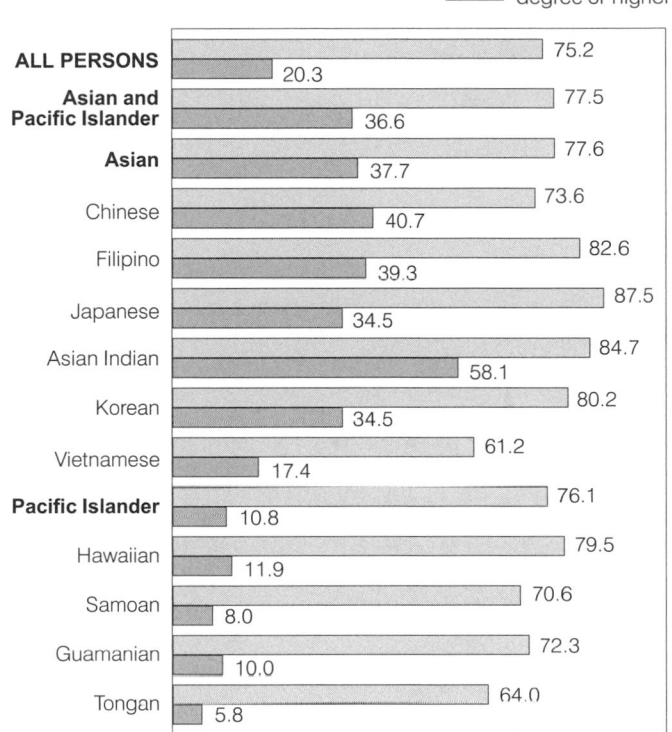

	High school diploma or higher	Bachelor's degree or higher
ALL PERSONS	75.2	20.3
Asian and Pacific Islander	77.5	36.6
Asian	77.6	37.7
Chinese	73.6	40.7
Filipino	82.6	39.3
Japanese	87.5	34.5
Asian Indian	84.7	58.1
Korean	80.2	34.5
Vietnamese	61.2	17.4
Pacific Islander	76.1	10.8
Hawaiian	79.5	11.9
Samoan	70.6	8.0
Guamanian	72.3	10.0
Tongan	64.0	5.8

There is great variability in the educational attainment of Hispanic persons.

Like the rest of the Nation, persons of Hispanic origin (who may be of any race) have made great strides in their educational attainment since 1970. In 1970, about 36 percent of Hispanic adults had finished high school, compared with about half in 1990.

High school completion varied considerably among Hispanic groups, from a high of 77 percent for Spaniards (persons who identified themselves as "Spaniard" in the Hispanic origin question) to a low of 34 percent for Salvadorans.

About 9 percent of all Hispanics held a bachelor's degree or higher in 1990.

As with high school completion, Hispanic groups varied in terms of college completion, ranging from 20 percent for Spaniards to 5 percent for Salvadorans.

Figure 8.

High School and Bachelor's Degree Completion Rates for Selected Hispanic Origin Groups: 1990

(Percent 25 years old and over)

High school diploma or higher

Bachelor's degree or higher

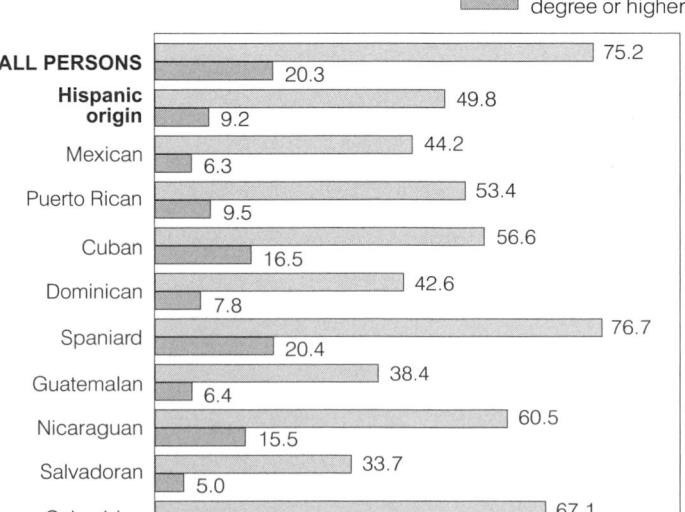

	High school diploma or higher	Bachelor's degree or higher
ALL PERSONS	75.2	20.3
Hispanic origin	49.8	9.2
Mexican	44.2	6.3
Puerto Rican	53.4	9.5
Cuban	56.6	16.5
Dominican	42.6	7.8
Spaniard	76.7	20.4
Guatemalan	38.4	6.4
Nicaraguan	60.5	15.5
Salvadoran	33.7	5.0
Colombian	67.1	16.1

Educational attainment levels vary markedly across the United States. As the following series of maps show, there is great diversity in America in our schooling.

About 11 percent of all persons 16 to 19 years old have dropped out of school.

The proportion of "dropouts," persons 16 to 19 years old who are not enrolled in school and not high school graduates, tells us a lot about how well areas are educating their youth.

With the exception of the District of Columbia and Hawaii, all States had a lower proportion of drop-outs in 1990 than in 1980.

Many of the States with the lowest dropout rates were in the Midwest, for example, North Dakota, Minnesota, and Iowa.

Despite improvements across the Nation, the States with the highest proportions of dropouts were in the South and West in 1990. The highest dropout rate was in Nevada, at 15 percent.

Table 1.

Rank Order by State of Persons Not Enrolled in School and Not a High School Graduate: 1990

(Percent of persons 16 to 19 years old)

United States	**11.2**		
Nevada	15.2	Delaware	10.4
Arizona	14.4	Oklahoma	10.4
Florida	14.3	Michigan	10.0
California	14.2	Virginia	10.0
Georgia	14.1	New York	9.9
DC	13.9	Colorado	9.8
Tennessee	13.4	New Jersey	9.6
Kentucky	13.3	New Hampshire	9.4
Texas	12.9	Pennsylvania	9.1
Alabama	12.6	Connecticut	9.0
Louisiana	12.5	Ohio	8.9
North Carolina	12.5	Kansas	8.7
Mississippi	11.8	Utah	8.7
Oregon	11.8	Massachusetts	8.5
South Carolina	11.7	Maine	8.3
New Mexico	11.7	Montana	8.1
Missouri	11.4	Vermont	8.0
Arkansas	11.4	South Dakota	7.7
Indiana	11.4	Hawaii	7.5
Rhode Island	11.1	Wisconsin	7.1
West Virginia	10.9	Nebraska	7.0
Alaska	10.9	Wyoming	6.9
Maryland	10.9	Iowa	6.6
Illinois	10.6	Minnesota	6.4
Washington	10.6	North Dakota	4.6
Idaho	10.4		

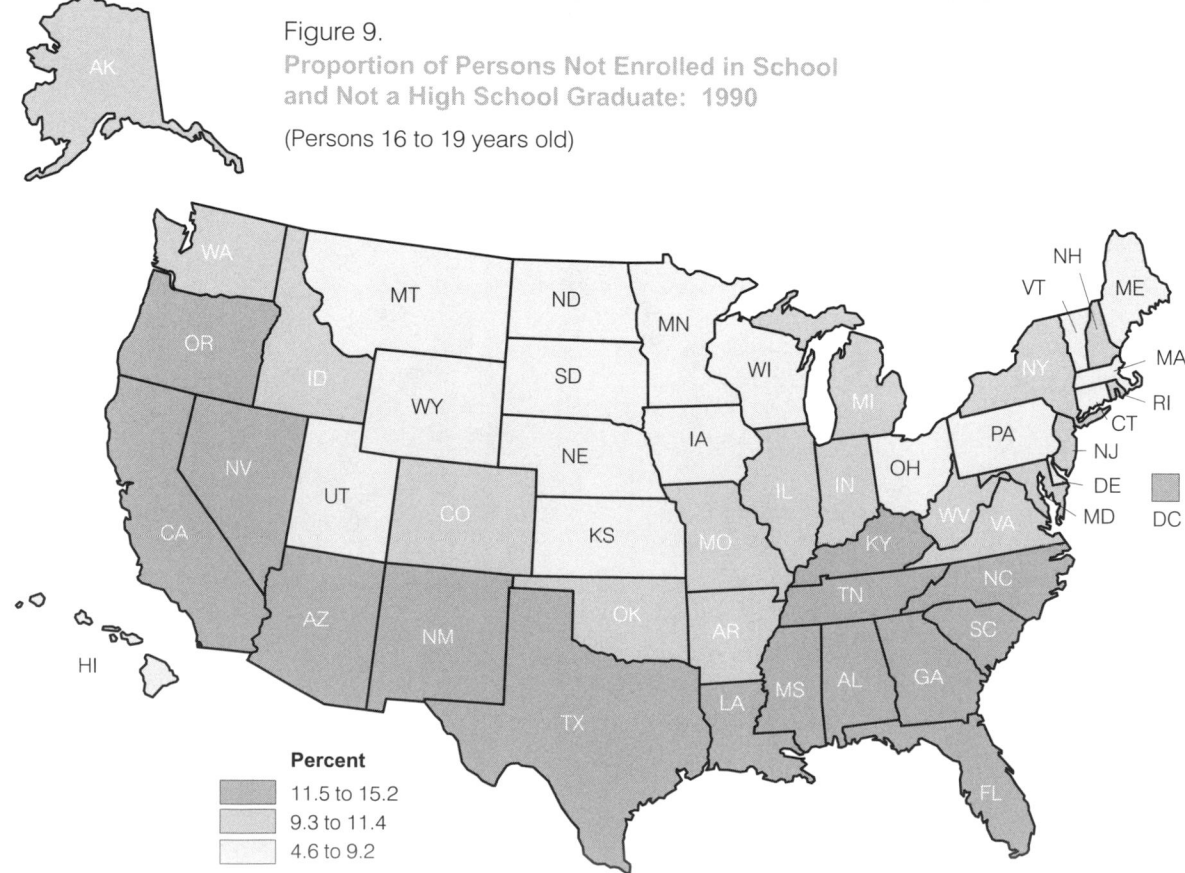

Figure 9.

Proportion of Persons Not Enrolled in School and Not a High School Graduate: 1990

(Persons 16 to 19 years old)

Percent
- 11.5 to 15.2
- 9.3 to 11.4
- 4.6 to 9.2

Nationally, three-quarters of all adults have completed a high school diploma or more.

The fundamental measure of educational status is the proportion of persons who have completed high school. This single measure is the one most often used to portray the educational achievement of the population.

In both 1980 and 1990, Alaska ranked first as the State with the highest proportion of high school graduates.

Every State in the country showed an increase from 1980 in the proportion of persons with a high school diploma.

Many of the States in the South are among those with the lowest high school completion levels, while the States in the Midwest and Northwest tend to be higher than the national average (75 percent).

Table 2.

Rank Order by State of Persons Who Have Completed a High School Diploma or More: 1990

(Percent of persons 25 years old and over)

United States	**75.2**

State	%	State	%
Alaska	86.6	North Dakota	76.7
Utah	85.1	Illinois	76.2
Colorado	84.4	California	76.2
Washington	83.8	Ohio	75.7
Wyoming	83.0	Indiana	75.6
Minnesota	82.4	Virginia	75.2
New Hampshire	82.2	New Mexico	75.1
Nebraska	81.8	New York	74.8
Oregon	81.5	Pennsylvania	74.7
Kansas	81.3	Oklahoma	74.6
Montana	81.0	Florida	74.4
Vermont	80.8	Missouri	73.9
Iowa	80.1	DC	73.1
Hawaii	80.1	Texas	72.1
Massachusetts	80.0	Rhode Island	72.0
Idaho	79.7	Georgia	70.9
Connecticut	79.2	North Carolina	70.0
Nevada	78.8	Louisiana	68.3
Maine	78.8	South Carolina	68.3
Arizona	78.7	Tennessee	67.1
Wisconsin	78.6	Alabama	66.9
Maryland	78.4	Arkansas	66.3
Delaware	77.5	West Virginia	66.0
South Dakota	77.1	Kentucky	64.6
Michigan	76.8	Mississippi	64.3
New Jersey	76.7		

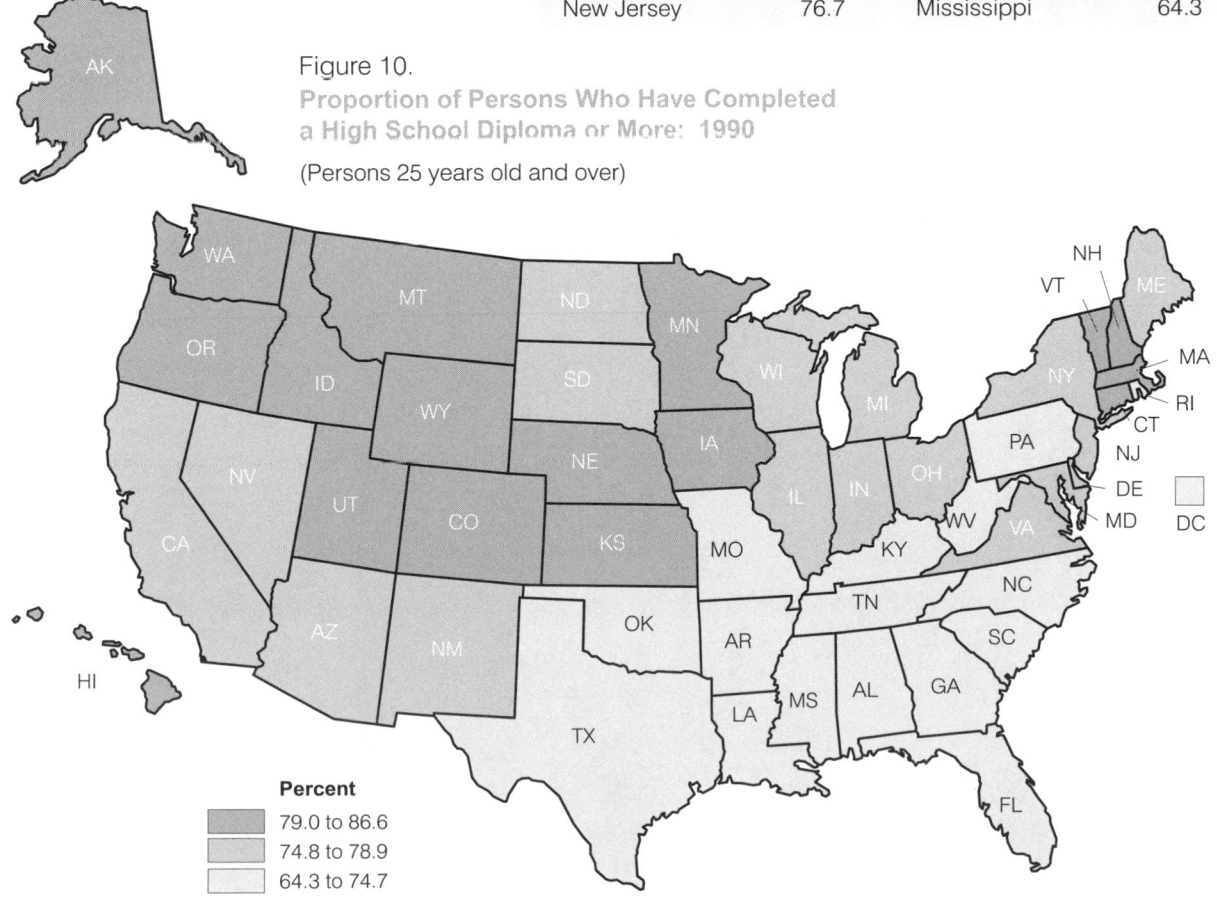

Figure 10.
Proportion of Persons Who Have Completed a High School Diploma or More: 1990

(Persons 25 years old and over)

Percent
79.0 to 86.6
74.8 to 78.9
64.3 to 74.7

About one-fifth of all adults have earned a bachelor's degree or higher.

The proportion of college graduates increased from 1980 for the Nation as a whole, as well as for every State.

Massachusetts, New Jersey, and Rhode Island were among States with the largest increase in the proportion of persons with postsecondary degrees compared to 1980.

The District of Columbia, relatively low in its proportion of high school graduates, had the highest college completion rates in both 1980 (28 percent) and 1990 (33 percent).

The areas with the largest proportion of college graduates are the District of Columbia, the Northeast, and a group of selected "high-tech" States in the West.

Table 3.

Rank Order by State of Persons With a Bachelor's Degree or Higher: 1990

(Percent of persons 25 years old and over)

United States	**13.1**		
DC	33.3	Nebraska	18.9
Massachusetts	27.2	Maine	18.8
Connecticut	27.2	Wyoming	18.8
Colorado	27.0	Florida	18.3
Maryland	26.5	North Dakota	18.1
New Jersey	24.9	Pennsylvania	17.9
Virginia	24.5	Oklahoma	17.8
New Hampshire	24.4	Missouri	17.8
Vermont	24.3	Idaho	17.7
California	23.4	Wisconsin	17.7
New York	23.1	Michigan	17.4
Alaska	23.0	North Carolina	17.4
Washington	22.9	South Dakota	17.2
Hawaii	22.9	Ohio	17.0
Utah	22.3	Iowa	16.9
Minnesota	21.8	South Carolina	16.6
Delaware	21.4	Louisiana	16.1
Rhode Island	21.3	Tennessee	16.0
Kansas	21.1	Alabama	15.7
Illinois	21.0	Indiana	15.6
Oregon	20.6	Nevada	15.3
New Mexico	20.4	Mississippi	14.7
Texas	20.3	Kentucky	13.6
Arizona	20.3	Arkansas	13.3
Montana	19.8	West Virginia	12.3
Georgia	19.3		

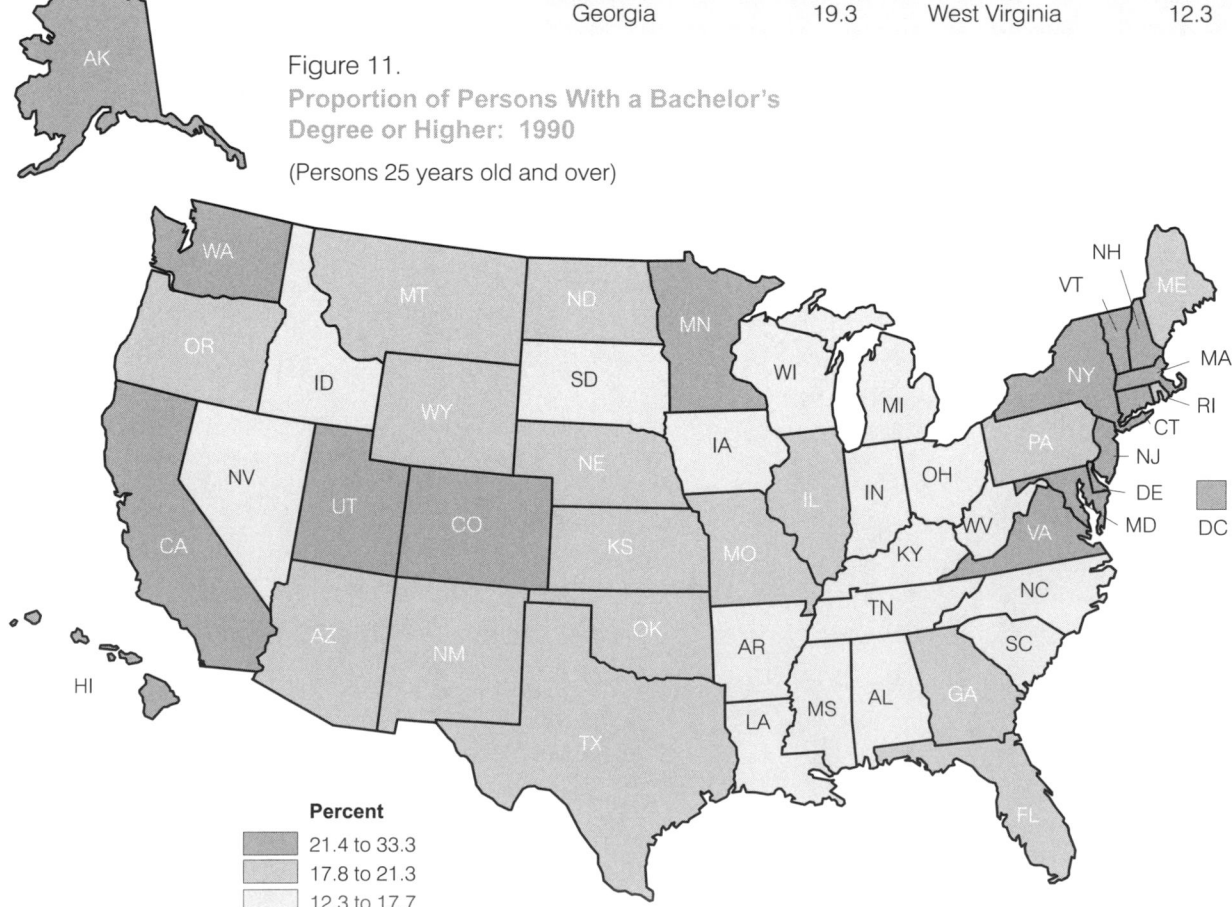

Figure 11.

Proportion of Persons With a Bachelor's Degree or Higher: 1990

(Persons 25 years old and over)

Percent

- 21.4 to 33.3
- 17.8 to 21.3
- 12.3 to 17.7

In 1990, 7 percent of adults reported that they held an advanced degree—master's, doctorate, or professional.

In 1990, the District of Columbia had the highest level of advanced degree holders at 17 percent.

Most States with high proportions of persons with advanced degrees also have a major metropolitan area or have a large concentration of high-technology industries, for example, Massachusetts, New York, and California.

States with relatively low proportions of advanced degree holders tend to be concentrated in the rural South and Northwest.

Table 4.

Rank Order by State of Persons With an Advanced Degree: 1990

(Percent of persons 25 years old and over)

United States	**7.2**		
DC	17.2	Michigan	6.4
Connecticut	11.0	Florida	6.3
Maryland	10.9	Minnesota	6.3
Massachusetts	10.6	Missouri	6.1
New York	9.9	Maine	6.1
Virginia	9.1	Oklahoma	6.0
Colorado	9.0	Nebraska	5.9
Vermont	8.9	Ohio	5.9
New Jersey	8.8	Montana	5.7
New Mexico	8.3	Wyoming	5.7
California	8.1	Wisconsin	5.6
Alaska	8.0	Louisiana	5.6
New Hampshire	7.9	Alabama	5.5
Rhode Island	7.8	Kentucky	5.5
Delaware	7.7	Tennessee	5.4
Illinois	7.5	North Carolina	5.4
Hawaii	7.1	South Carolina	5.4
Washington	7.0	Idaho	5.3
Arizona	7.0	Nevada	5.2
Kansas	7.0	Iowa	5.2
Oregon	7.0	Mississippi	5.1
Utah	6.8	South Dakota	4.9
Pennsylvania	6.6	West Virginia	4.8
Texas	6.5	Arkansas	4.5
Indiana	6.4	North Dakota	4.5
Georgia	6.4		

Figure 12.

Proportion of Persons With an Advanced Degree: 1990

(Persons 25 years old and over)

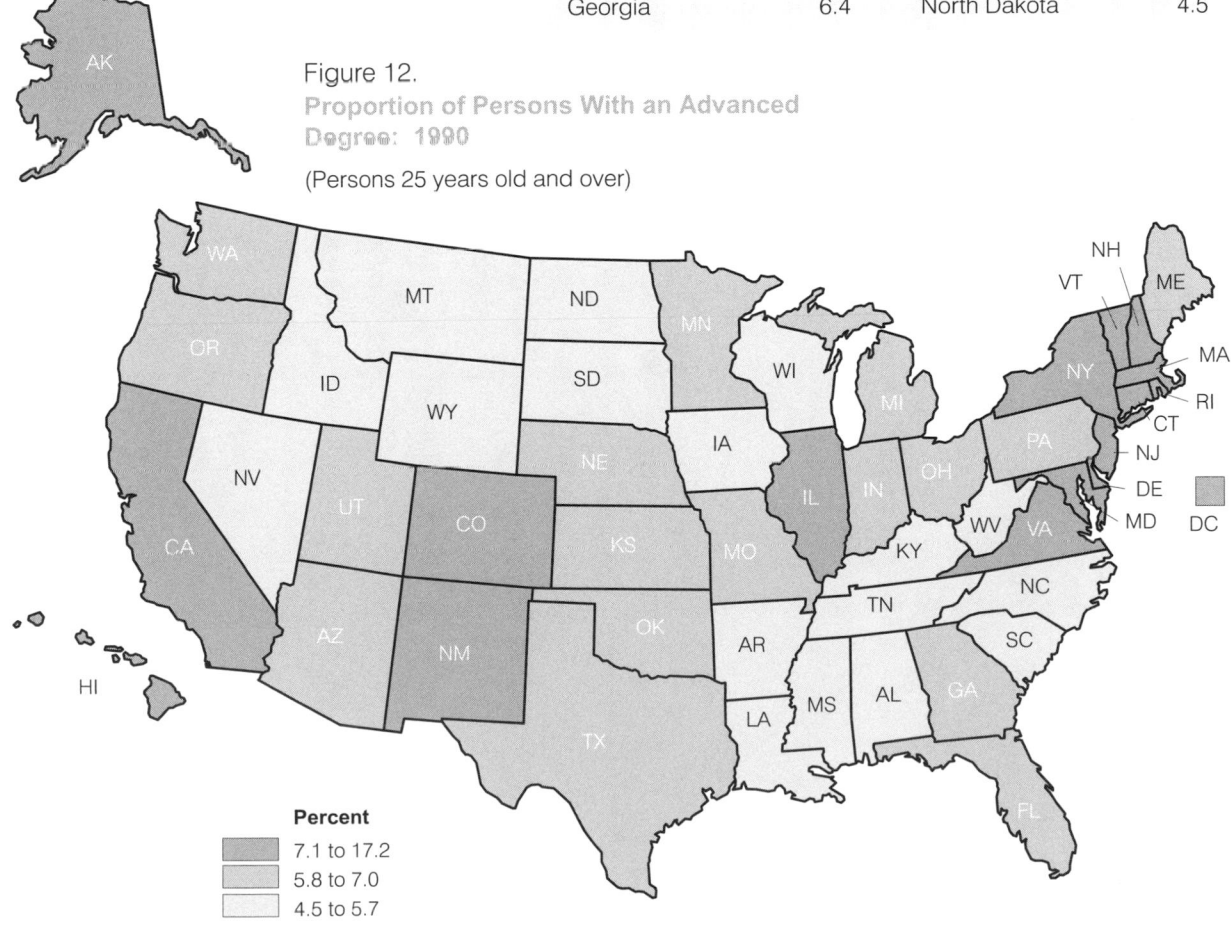

Percent

- 7.1 to 17.2
- 5.8 to 7.0
- 4.5 to 5.7

e, the Americans: Our Homes

Introduction

We still dream of owning our own homes, and for many of us that dream has become a reality. No matter what we earn, how old we are, or what we do, our homes are where our hearts are — and where the heart of the Nation rests.

Since World War II, we have been building homes at a healthy, sometimes astonishing rate, which validates our strength as a people and a Nation. The 1990 census provides a vivid portrait of American housing and the situations in which we live. It helps us see how we have changed and how we are changing and how we can anticipate change in the decades ahead.

In 1990, there were over 102 million housing units in the United States, almost 14 million more than 1980. That is a 16 percent increase in housing units during the decade.

While there was an increase in the number of owner-occupied homes, the homeownership rate between 1980 and 1990 declined slightly for the first time since the depression era. The number of owner-occupied units rose 14 percent while renter-occupied units increased 15 percent.

The percentage of units with more than one person per room rose during the 1980's for the first time since the first census of housing was taken in 1940. The proportion of householders who were elderly increased slightly during the decade.

Single-family homes still made up the majority of the housing inventory. Mobile homes, the fastest growing type of housing, increased by almost 3 million units from 1980 to 1990. Both median value and median contract rent rose faster than inflation.

Our housing "population" is up by nearly 16 percent since 1980.

In 1990, there were 102,263,678 housing units in the United States, up by 16 percent from the 1980 census. There was a net increase of nearly 14 million housing units.

There was an increase in the housing stock every decade since 1940. The 1970's had the largest percentage change, at 29 percent, while the 1980's had the smallest, at 16 percent.

The 1970's had the largest numerical increase in housing units, almost 20 million, while the 1940's had the smallest increase, almost 9 million.

The South (22.6 percent) and the West (22.3 percent) Regions had the greatest increase in housing units, while the Northeast and Midwest regions had more modest gains of 9 percent and 7 percent, respectively.

Housing and population growth almost always go hand in hand.

Since 1890, the percentage increase between decades for the number of occupied housing units was always greater than that for the number of persons. This is related to a decline in household size and an increase in one-person households.

The 1910 census showed the largest percentage increase between decades for occupied units, and 1990 had the smallest increase. The 1910 census also showed the largest increase for number of persons, but the 1940 census had the smallest.

The 1980 census was the first in the 20th century to show a divergence between the growth rates of population and occupied housing units. After years of moving almost in parallel, the growth rate for housing increased between 1970 and 1980, while the growth rate for population declined, so there was a greater supply of housing units in relation to the total population than before.

In 1990, the pattern of the growth rate for population and occupied units returned to the pattern exhibited before 1980, that is, both percentages moved in the same direction when compared to the previous decade.

Figure 1.
Number of Housing Units: 1940 to 1990

(Thousands)

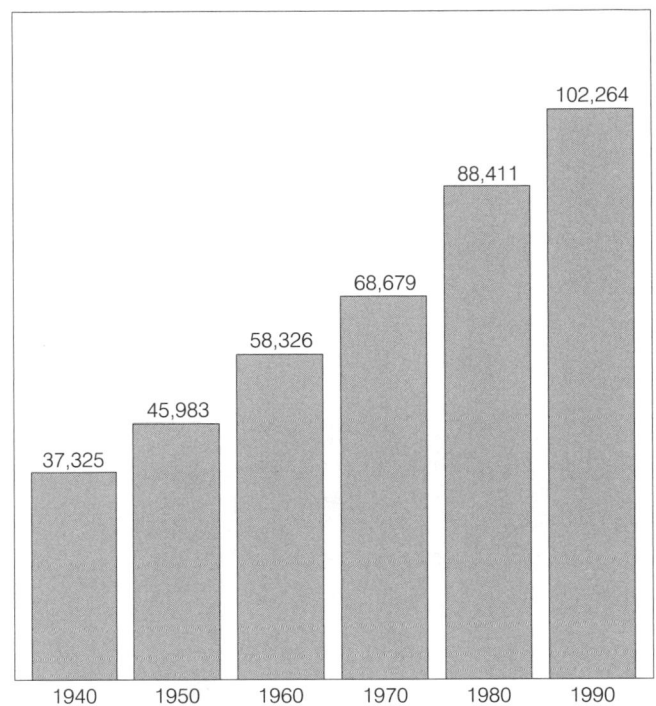

Figure 2.
Population and Number of Occupied Housing Units: 1890 to 1990

(Percent change)

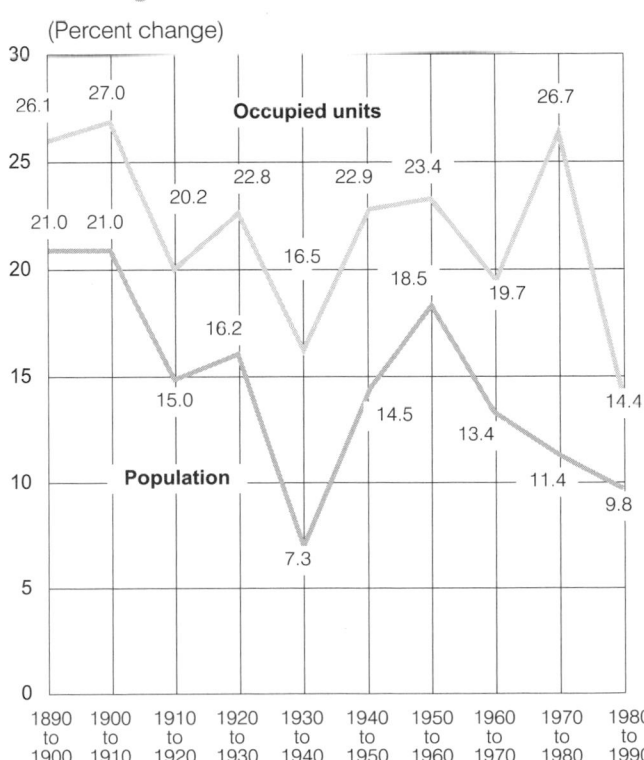

341

Our dream of homeownership is a reality for many of us.

Owner-occupied units increased by 14 percent during the 1980's, while renter-occupied units increased by 15 percent. As a result, the homeownership rate in the United States decreased slightly for the first time since the Great Depression.

The homeownership rate increased dramatically between 1940 and 1960, because of new legislation introducing mortgages which made it easier to afford a home. Since 1960, the homeownership rate has increased at a much slower rate.

The Midwest Region had the highest homeownership rate at 68 percent, while the South Region was not far behind at 66 percent. The Northeast Region was below the average for the United States at 61 percent, and the West had the lowest, at 59 percent.

West Virginia had the highest homeownership rate of all States in the Nation at 74 percent, while Minnesota was the next highest at 72 percent. New York had the lowest homeownership rate of any State at 52 percent.

Most of us live in single family homes.

In 1990, among all housing units, single-family homes increased the most in absolute terms by almost 7.5 million units during the decade.

Almost 30 percent of all housing units were in multiunit structures, with almost 10 percent in buildings with 2 to 4 units and 18 percent in buildings with 5 or more units.

Mobile homes, the fastest growing type of housing, increased nearly 60 percent, but represented only 7 percent of all units.

The South led the Nation with 11 percent of its units being mobile homes, while the Northeast had the smallest percentage at only 3 percent. The South also had the highest number of mobile homes, almost 4 million, while the Northeast had the fewest, with only 640,000.

Figure 3.
Homeownership Rate: 1890 to 1990

(Percent of owner-occupied housing units)

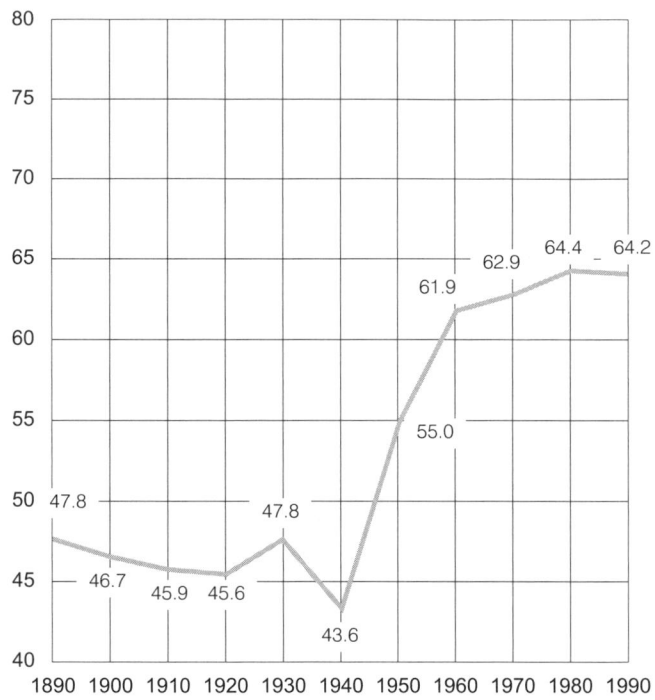

Figure 4.
Units in Structure: 1980 and 1990

(Thousands)

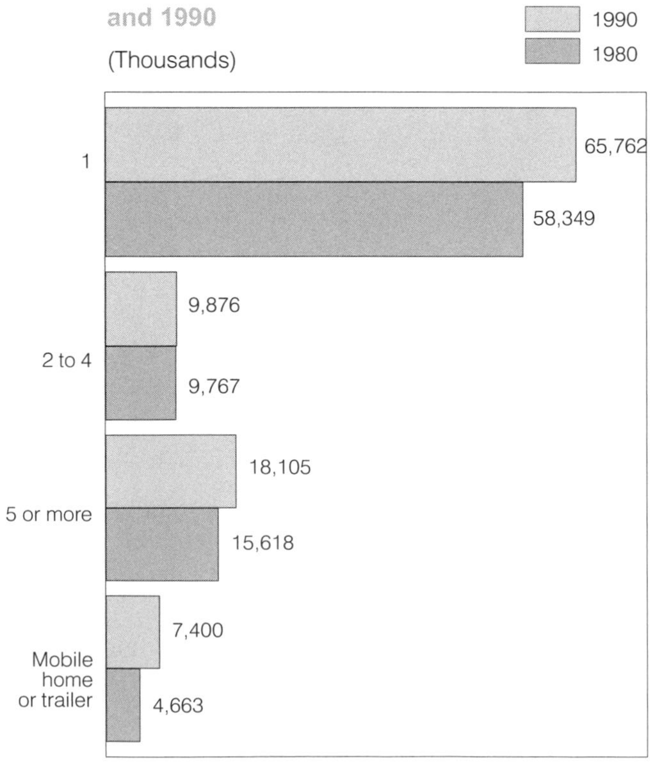

**The value of our homes varies
by the region in which we live.**

During the decade of the 1980's, the median
value of owner-occupied homes in the United
States increased 5.5 percent faster than the
rate of inflation.

The Northeast Region fared the best during the
decade, with an increase of 66 percent in median
home value. The West and South also had increases in median value, while the Midwest fared
the worst, with a decrease relative to inflation.

California and Hawaii were the only two States in
the West to show an increase in median value
between 1980 and 1990, while Missouri was the
only State in the Midwest to show an increase.

Massachusetts had the largest gain, with New
York and Rhode Island close behind. Wyoming
showed the largest loss, with Iowa and North
Dakota not far behind.

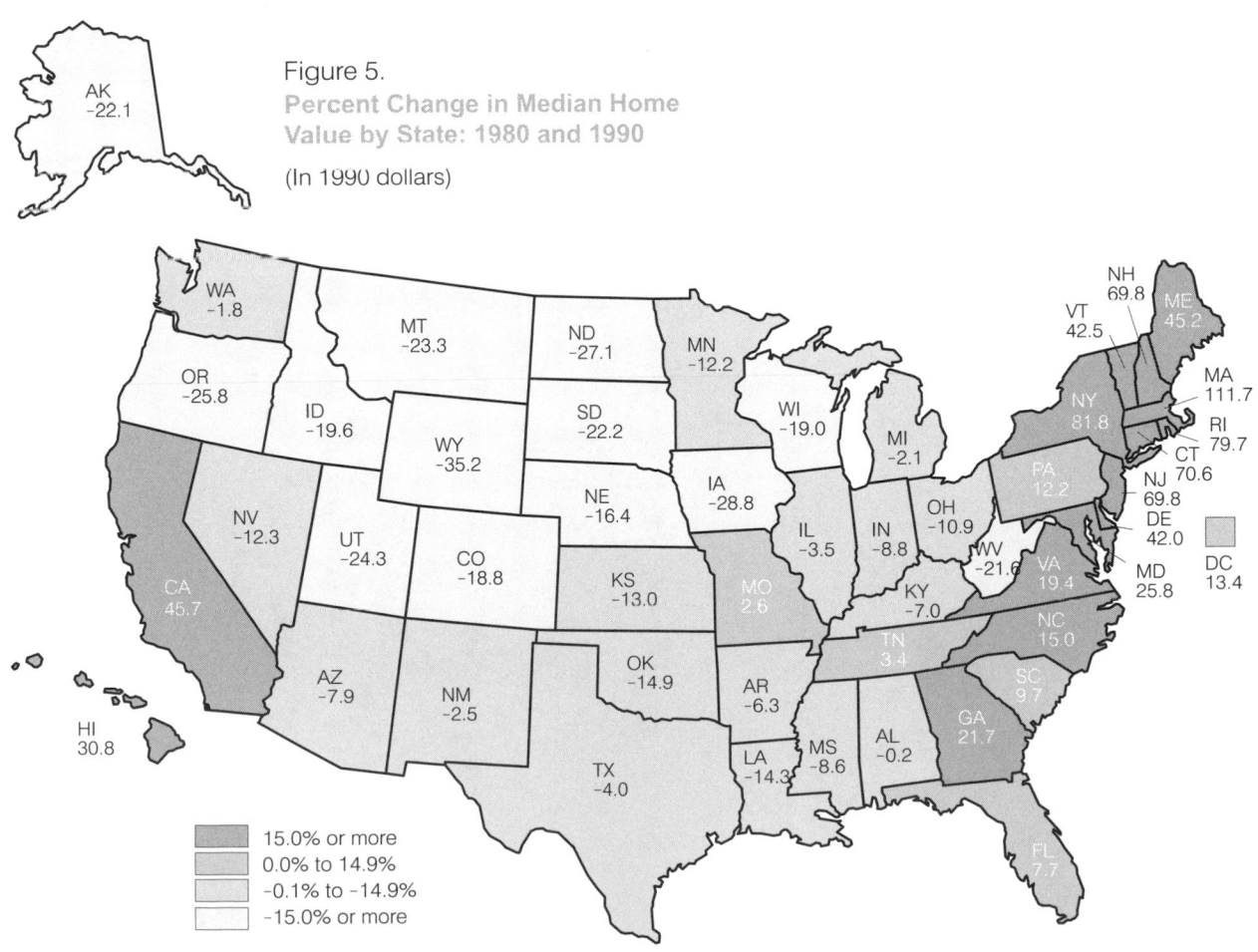

Figure 5.
Percent Change in Median Home
Value by State: 1980 and 1990

(In 1990 dollars)

AK
-22.1

WA -1.8
MT -23.3
ND -27.1
MN -12.2
OR -25.8
ID -19.6
WY -35.2
SD -22.2
WI -19.0
MI -2.1
NE -16.4
IA -28.8
NV -12.3
UT -24.3
CO -18.8
IL -3.5
IN -8.8
OH -10.9
WV -21.6
KS -13.0
MO 2.6
KY -7.0
VA 19.4
CA 45.7
AZ -7.9
NM -2.5
OK -14.9
AR -6.3
TN 3.4
NC 15.0
SC 9.7
HI 30.8
TX -4.0
LA -14.3
MS -8.6
AL -0.2
GA 21.7
FL 7.7
NH 69.8
VT 42.5
ME 45.2
MA 111.7
NY 81.8
RI 79.7
CT 70.6
PA 12.2
NJ 69.8
DE 42.0
MD 25.8
DC 13.4

15.0% or more
0.0% to 14.9%
-0.1% to -14.9%
-15.0% or more

343

Our rents are increasing or staying the same.

Between 1980 and 1990, median gross rent for renter-occupied homes in the Nation increased 16 percent above the rate of inflation.

By regions, the pattern of median gross rent was similar to that for median value, except there were no decreases. The Northeast increased the most, by 27 percent, with the West and the South next, while the Midwest had the smallest increase.

California and Hawaii were the only States in the West to have an increase in median gross rent greater than 20 percent, while the Midwest had none. Also, the Northeast Region was the only one that had no States showing a decline between 1980 and 1990.

Connecticut had the highest increase in median gross rent, and Massachusetts had the second highest. Wyoming had the largest decrease, and Iowa had the second largest decrease.

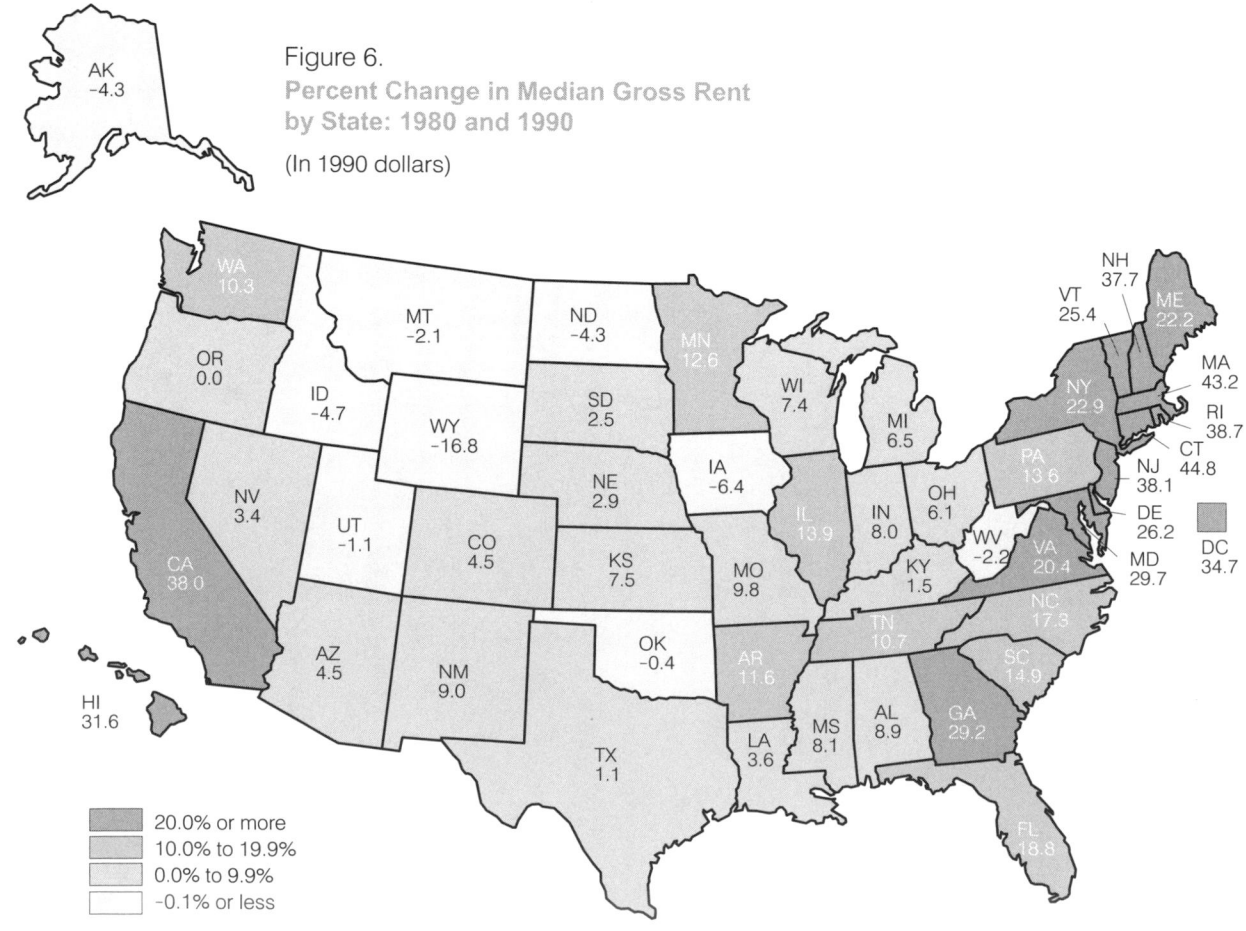

Figure 6.
Percent Change in Median Gross Rent by State: 1980 and 1990

(In 1990 dollars)

AK -4.3

WA 10.3
MT -2.1
ND -4.3
MN 12.6
NH 37.7
VT 25.4
ME 22.2
OR 0.0
ID -4.7
WY -16.8
SD 2.5
WI 7.4
MI 6.5
NY 22.9
MA 43.2
RI 38.7
CT 44.8
NJ 38.1
NV 3.4
UT -1.1
CO 4.5
NE 2.9
IA -6.4
IL 13.9
IN 8.0
OH 6.1
PA 13.6
DE 26.2
DC 34.7
CA 38.0
KS 7.5
MO 9.8
KY 1.5
WV -2.2
VA 20.4
MD 29.7
AZ 4.5
NM 9.0
OK -0.4
AR 11.6
TN 10.7
NC 17.3
SC 14.9
HI 31.6
TX 1.1
LA 3.6
MS 8.1
AL 8.9
GA 29.2
FL 18.8

- 20.0% or more
- 10.0% to 19.9%
- 0.0% to 9.9%
- -0.1% or less

Our houses are larger than they have ever been.

Since 1950, the median number of rooms for all units has increased steadily from 4.6 to 5.2, with the largest increase occurring between 1950 and 1960.

The largest difference in median number of rooms (2 rooms) between owner-occupied units and renter-occupied units was in 1990. The smallest difference (1.5 rooms) occurred in 1940 and 1950.

In 1990, owner-occupied households were the largest they have ever been, on average, with a median number of rooms of 6.0.

The number of rooms in renter-occupied units peaked in 1940 with a median of 4.1 rooms. The number of rooms in both owner and renter units was smallest in 1950, with medians of 5.3 rooms and 3.8 rooms, respectively.

We often have a room of our own.

Units with more than one person per room are often considered crowded. This proportion rose from 4.5 percent of occupied units in 1980 to 4.9 percent in 1990. This was the first increase since 1940 (the first census to include housing data), when the proportion was just over 20 percent.

The steady decline or minimal increase in the percentage of units with more than one person per room and the recent substantial increase of units with 0.5 persons per room or less resulted in an overall decline in persons per room, showing improved living conditions.

From 1980 to 1990, the percentage of units with 1.01 or more persons per room rose in the West and Northeast and fell in the Midwest and South.

The decade of the 1970's showed the greatest increase in units with 0.5 persons per room or less, from 50 percent in 1970 to 61 percent in 1980. The 1940's showed the greatest decrease in units with more than one person per room, from 20 percent in 1940 to 16 percent in 1950.

Figure 7.
Median Number of Rooms Per Housing Unit: 1940 to 1990

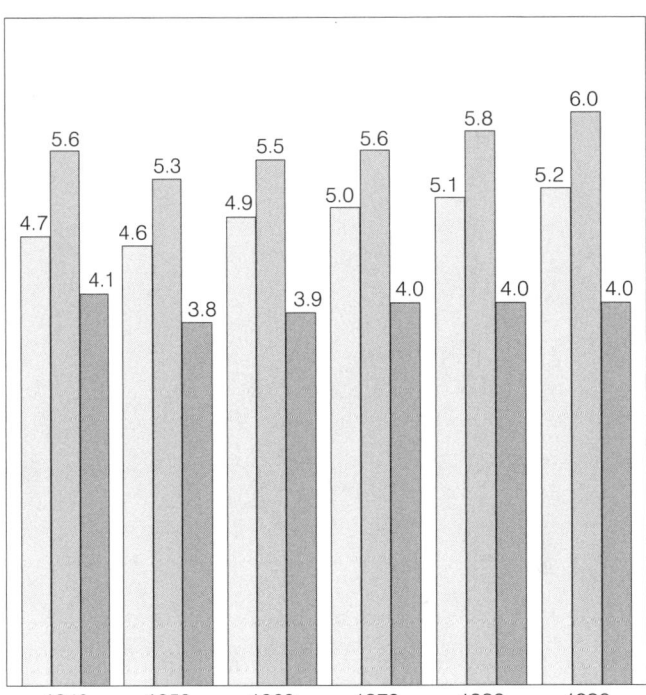

Figure 8.
Persons Per Room: 1940 to 1990

(Percent)

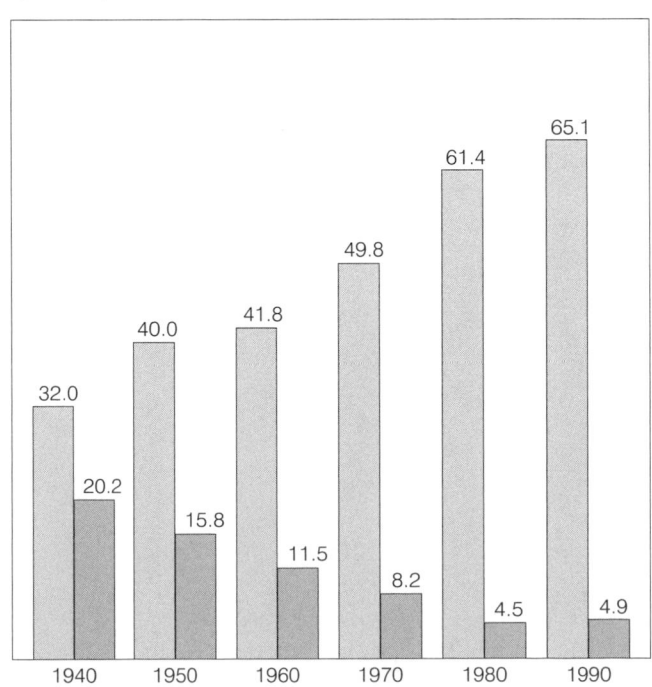

345

Many of our homes are 30 years old or older.

In 1990, a large portion of the Nation's housing units were built before 1960. Despite the large proportion of older homes, about 21 percent of all housing units in the United States were built during the 1980's.

The 1970's saw the most housing units constructed, just over 22 million, while the 1940's had the least, about 8.5 million, primarily because of the lack of homebuilding during World War II.

The South had 44 percent of all new units built in 1990. The Northeast had the lowest percentage of these units, at 14 percent, while the West had 25 percent, and the Midwest had 17 percent.

The median year the structure was built also followed the same pattern, with the Northeast being the oldest with a median of 1954 and the West and South the newest at 1970 and 1971, respectively. The Midwest was in the middle at 1960. The median year structure built for the Nation was 1965.

Figure 9.
Year Structure Built: 1990

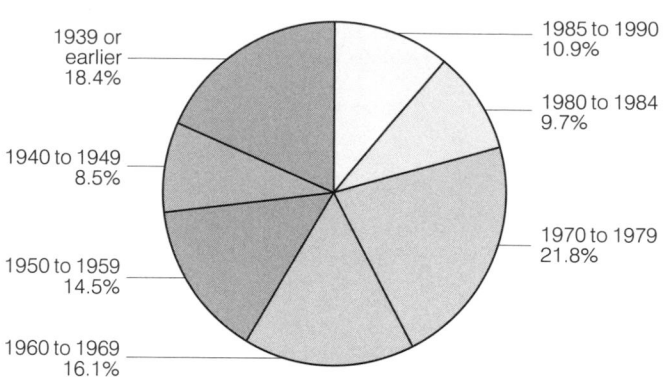

Once we buy a home, we tend to stay in it.

Over 45 million households, or about 49 percent of all households, changed residences between 1985 and 1990. Of these households, over 19 million moved during the 15 months preceding the 1990 census. Still, almost one-tenth of all households lived at their current residence since 1960.

Between 1980 and 1990, 70 percent of all households in the West reported moving into their current residence, while in the Northeast, the figure was only 56 percent.

Renter households were more than four times as likely to have moved between 1989 and 1990 as owner households, 42 percent versus 9 percent. Conversely, only 4 percent of renters lived in the same residence for more than 20 years, compared with 26 percent of owners.

Figure 10.
Year Householder Moved Into Unit: 1990

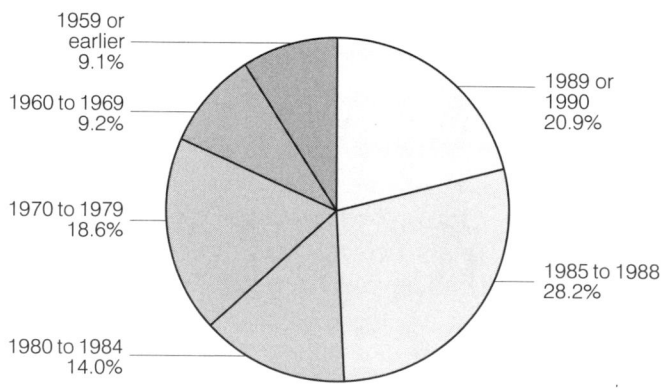

Our monthly ownership costs are lowest in the Midwestern States.

In 1990, median selected monthly owner costs as a percentage of household income in 1989 for mortgaged units was 21 percent. Owner costs include payment for all mortgages, real estate taxes, homeowner insurance, utilities, fuels, and associated homeowner fees.

On average, households in the West spent more for mortgaged homes than any other region, at 23 percent. The Northeast and South followed, and the Midwest had the lowest costs for mortgaged homes at 19 percent.

Florida was the only State in the South to have a median percentage of income spent on owner costs over 22 percent, while the Midwest had no such States.

California had the highest median percentage of income spent at 25 percent, followed closely by New Hampshire at 24 percent. Costs were lowest in Indiana, at 17 percent, and Iowa and West Virginia, at just under 18 percent.

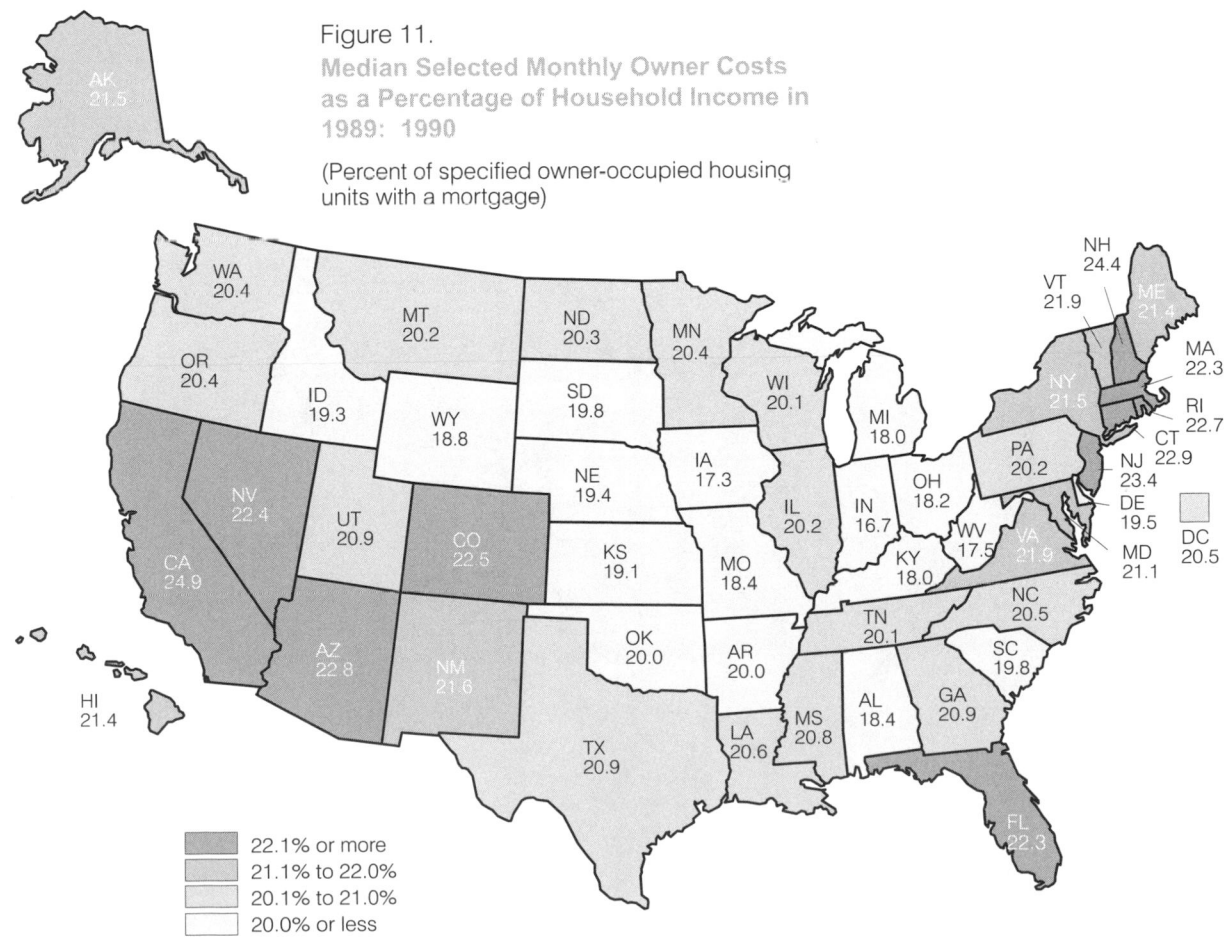

Figure 11.
Median Selected Monthly Owner Costs as a Percentage of Household Income in 1989: 1990

(Percent of specified owner-occupied housing units with a mortgage)

22.1% or more
21.1% to 22.0%
20.1% to 21.0%
20.0% or less

347

Our monthly rental costs are highest in California.

In 1990, median gross rent as a percentage of household income in 1989 was 26.4 percent for the United States. Renter costs include the rental payment plus estimated average monthly costs of utilities and fuels.

Renter costs as a percentage of income showed the same pattern as that for owners. The West had the highest percentage at 28 percent, the Northeast and South following, and the Midwest showing the lowest median percentage at 25 percent.

Michigan was the only State in the Midwest with a median renter percentage over 27 percent. In the Northeast, Rhode Island and Vermont were at 28 percent and 27 percent, respectively.

California had the highest median percentage for renters, at 29 percent, and Florida the next highest at 28 percent. Nebraska and Wyoming had the lowest of all States, at 24 percent.

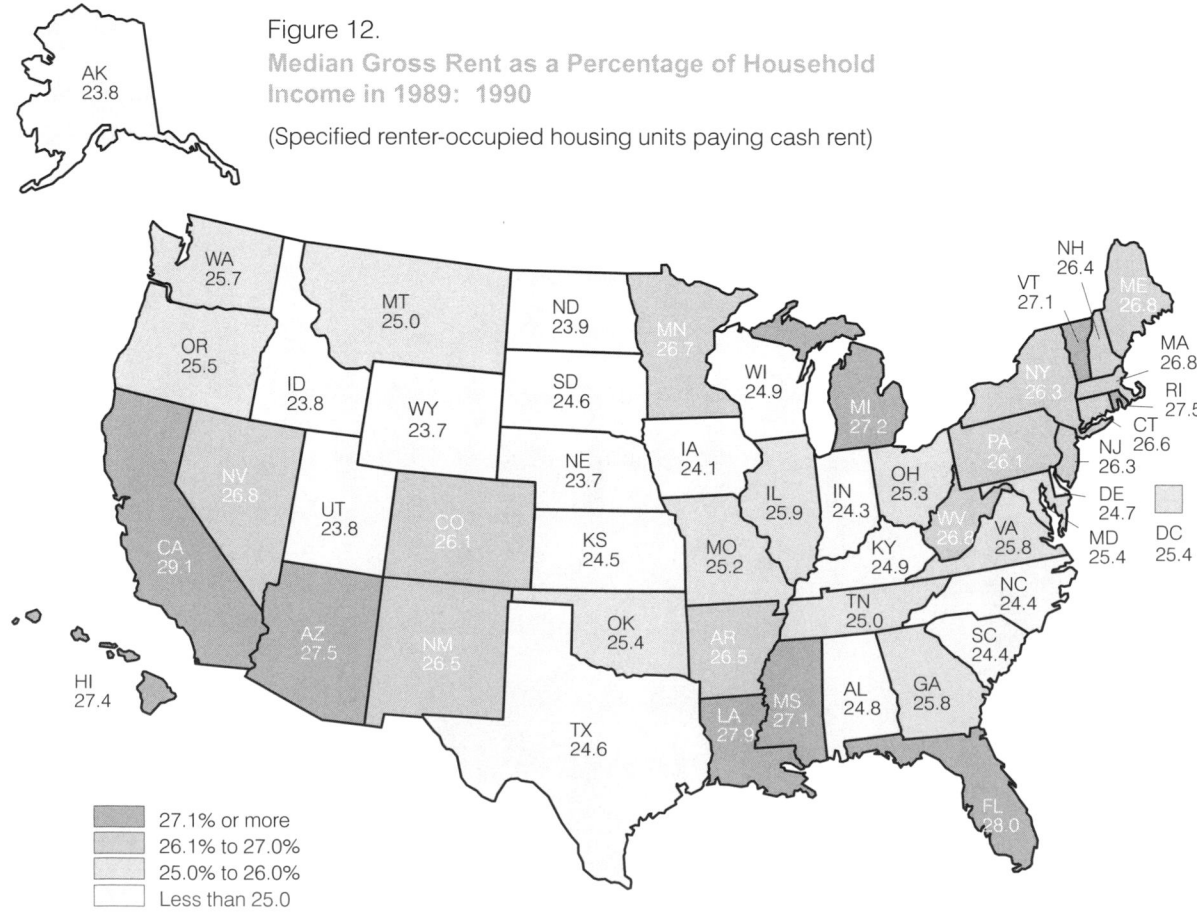

Figure 12.

Median Gross Rent as a Percentage of Household Income in 1989: 1990

(Specified renter-occupied housing units paying cash rent)

27.1% or more
26.1% to 27.0%
25.0% to 26.0%
Less than 25.0

U.S. Department of Commerce
Economics and Statistics Administration
BUREAU OF THE CENSUS

CENSUS '90

1990 CP-1-1

1990 Census of Population

**General Population
Characteristics**

United States

Table 1. Summary of General Characteristics of Persons: 1990

[For definitions of terms and meanings of symbols, see text]

United States / Urban and Rural and Size of Place / Population Size Class of Urbanized Area / Inside and Outside Metropolitan Area / Population Size Class of Metropolitan Area	All persons	Percent of all persons — Under 5 years	Under 18 years	18 to 24 years	25 to 44 years	45 to 64 years	65 years and over	80 years and over	Median age	Persons 18 years and over— Males per 100 females	In households — In families	Non-family householders and non-relatives of householder	In group quarters	Persons in group quarters — Total	Percent institutionalized
United States	248 709 873	7.4	25.6	10.8	32.5	18.6	12.6	2.8	32.9	91.9	82.0	15.3	2.7	6 697 744	49.8
URBAN AND RURAL AND SIZE OF PLACE															
Urban	187 053 487	7.5	25.0	11.4	33.0	18.0	12.6	2.9	32.5	90.1	80.1	17.0	2.9	5 487 334	45.1
Inside urbanized area	158 258 878	7.5	24.8	11.3	33.6	18.2	12.1	2.7	32.5	90.6	80.2	17.2	2.6	4 107 630	44.8
Central place	78 847 406	7.7	24.7	12.6	33.3	17.0	12.4	2.9	31.5	89.4	76.5	20.2	3.3	2 589 435	40.2
Urban fringe	79 411 472	7.3	24.9	10.1	33.9	19.3	11.8	2.5	33.3	91.9	83.8	14.3	1.9	1 518 195	52.7
Outside urbanized area	28 794 609	7.4	26.0	12.0	29.3	17.4	15.4	4.0	32.6	87.4	79.7	15.5	4.8	1 379 704	46.0
Place of 10,000 or more	13 825 022	7.4	25.6	13.7	29.5	16.8	14.5	3.7	31.6	88.2	77.7	16.6	5.7	783 059	38.5
Place of 2,500 to 9,999	14 969 587	7.4	26.5	10.3	29.1	17.9	16.2	4.2	33.6	86.6	81.5	14.5	4.0	596 645	55.8
Rural	61 656 386	7.1	27.3	8.7	31.0	20.5	12.4	2.6	34.1	97.8	87.7	10.4	2.0	1 210 410	70.9
Place of 1,000 to 2,499	7 050 858	7.2	26.6	8.9	28.7	18.9	16.9	4.4	34.8	86.8	83.7	13.7	2.6	182 300	71.5
Place of less than 1,000	3 801 051	7.2	27.3	8.1	27.8	19.1	17.7	4.6	35.0	88.7	85.0	13.6	1.4	53 078	75.4
Other rural	50 804 477	7.1	27.4	8.7	31.6	20.8	11.4	2.1	34.0	100.2	88.4	9.6	1.9	975 032	70.5
POPULATION SIZE CLASS OF URBANIZED AREA															
1,000,000 or more	94 016 294	7.5	24.6	10.8	34.5	18.4	11.7	2.6	32.7	91.1	80.5	17.4	2.1	1 963 186	50.2
Central place	41 010 559	7.6	24.4	11.9	34.3	17.3	12.0	2.8	31.8	90.4	76.2	21.1	2.7	1 110 238	42.2
Urban fringe	53 005 735	7.4	24.7	9.9	34.6	19.3	11.5	2.5	33.3	91.6	83.7	14.6	1.6	852 948	60.7
5,000,000 or more	34 239 045	7.4	24.4	11.1	33.9	18.9	11.7	2.6	32.6	91.3	81.2	16.8	2.0	684 437	52.1
Central place	16 304 119	7.6	24.5	11.8	34.2	17.8	11.7	2.7	31.8	90.1	77.5	20.2	2.3	377 030	45.4
Urban fringe	17 934 926	7.3	24.4	10.4	33.6	19.9	11.6	2.5	33.4	92.5	84.6	13.6	1.7	307 407	60.4
2,500,000 to 4,999,999	23 787 767	7.4	24.3	10.8	35.5	18.4	10.9	2.4	32.6	91.1	79.9	18.0	2.1	508 289	48.1
Central place	9 541 204	7.6	24.0	12.3	35.2	17.1	11.5	2.6	31.6	90.3	74.6	22.4	2.9	279 290	38.5
Urban fringe	14 246 563	7.3	24.5	9.9	35.8	19.4	10.5	2.2	33.2	91.6	83.4	15.0	1.6	228 999	59.8
1,000,000 to 2,499,999	35 989 482	7.6	24.9	10.5	34.3	18.0	12.3	2.8	32.7	90.9	80.1	17.7	2.1	770 460	49.9
Central place	15 165 236	7.8	24.6	11.8	34.0	16.9	12.7	3.1	31.9	90.9	75.9	21.1	3.0	453 918	41.7
Urban fringe	20 824 246	7.5	25.1	9.6	34.5	18.8	12.0	2.6	33.3	90.8	83.2	15.3	1.5	316 542	61.6
Less than 1,000,000	64 242 584	7.5	25.1	12.1	32.4	17.7	12.6	2.8	32.1	89.9	79.8	16.9	3.3	2 144 404	39.9
Central place	37 836 847	7.7	25.0	13.3	32.2	16.7	12.8	3.0	31.3	88.2	76.9	19.2	3.9	1 479 197	38.8
Urban fringe	26 405 737	7.2	25.3	10.4	32.6	19.2	12.5	2.6	33.4	92.3	83.9	13.5	2.5	665 247	42.5
500,000 to 999,999	17 955 916	7.5	25.0	11.3	33.3	18.0	12.4	2.8	32.4	89.4	80.3	17.2	2.5	455 609	46.0
Central place	9 403 669	7.7	24.7	12.7	33.4	16.9	12.4	2.9	31.4	88.0	76.5	20.2	3.3	312 414	41.8
Urban fringe	8 552 247	7.2	25.4	9.7	33.3	19.2	12.5	2.6	33.6	90.8	84.5	13.8	1.7	143 195	55.3
250,000 to 499,999	15 470 005	7.6	25.7	11.3	32.5	17.9	12.6	2.8	32.3	89.2	80.9	16.2	2.9	444 726	42.7
Central place	8 327 127	7.9	25.8	12.3	32.5	16.8	12.7	3.0	31.4	87.4	77.9	18.6	3.4	287 237	40.7
Urban fringe	7 142 878	7.3	25.5	10.2	32.6	19.2	12.5	2.5	33.4	91.3	84.5	13.3	2.2	157 489	46.4
100,000 to 249,999	18 879 599	7.5	25.0	12.9	32.4	17.4	12.3	2.8	31.7	91.0	79.0	17.1	3.9	729 068	36.1
Central place	11 928 889	7.7	25.0	13.7	32.2	16.5	12.5	3.0	31.0	88.9	76.8	19.1	4.1	487 009	38.5
Urban fringe	6 950 710	7.2	25.1	11.5	32.6	19.0	11.9	2.4	32.8	94.8	82.8	13.7	3.5	242 059	31.4
Less than 100,000	11 937 064	7.3	24.8	13.1	30.9	17.6	13.6	3.1	32.1	89.7	78.6	17.0	4.3	515 041	37.4
Central place	8 177 162	7.4	24.6	14.3	30.7	16.8	13.6	3.3	31.3	88.1	76.3	18.9	4.8	392 537	35.3
Urban fringe	3 759 902	7.1	25.2	10.5	31.2	19.3	13.7	2.8	33.8	93.1	83.7	13.1	3.3	122 504	44.2
INSIDE AND OUTSIDE METROPOLITAN AREA															
Inside metropolitan area	192 725 741	7.5	25.3	10.9	33.4	18.5	11.9	2.6	32.6	91.7	81.4	16.0	2.5	4 914 490	47.6
In central city	77 843 533	7.6	24.7	12.5	33.3	17.1	12.4	2.9	31.6	89.2	76.5	20.2	3.3	2 557 779	40.4
Not in central city	114 882 208	7.3	25.7	9.9	33.4	19.4	11.6	2.4	33.3	93.4	84.8	13.2	2.1	2 356 711	55.5
Urban	88 439 928	7.4	25.2	10.2	33.7	19.0	12.0	2.6	33.2	91.7	83.7	14.2	2.1	1 823 634	51.7
Inside urbanized area	79 755 134	7.3	25.0	10.1	33.9	19.2	11.8	2.5	33.3	91.9	83.8	14.3	1.9	1 516 416	53.0
Outside urbanized area	8 684 794	7.9	27.1	11.0	31.1	17.2	13.5	3.3	32.1	90.2	82.8	13.7	3.5	307 218	45.3
Rural	26 442 280	7.2	27.3	8.8	32.7	20.6	10.5	2.0	33.8	99.5	88.4	9.6	2.0	533 077	68.5
Outside metropolitan area	55 984 132	7.1	26.6	10.1	29.3	19.3	14.7	3.4	33.8	92.7	83.8	13.0	3.2	1 783 254	55.7
Urban	20 851 951	7.2	25.4	12.5	28.5	17.4	16.1	4.3	32.8	86.6	78.3	16.4	5.3	1 108 128	45.2
Inside urbanized area	1 520 259	7.1	24.0	14.3	30.6	17.0	14.2	3.1	31.8	92.3	77.0	17.8	5.2	79 438	31.6
Outside urbanized area	19 331 692	7.2	25.6	12.3	28.4	17.5	16.2	4.3	32.9	86.2	78.4	16.3	5.3	1 028 690	46.3
Place of 10,000 or more	9 873 345	7.2	25.1	14.3	28.8	16.9	14.9	3.9	31.7	87.6	76.5	17.3	6.2	612 658	37.0
Place of 2,500 to 9,999	9 458 347	7.2	26.1	10.3	28.0	18.1	17.6	4.8	34.2	84.6	80.3	15.3	4.4	416 032	60.0
Rural	35 132 181	7.0	27.4	8.6	29.7	20.4	13.9	3.0	34.4	96.6	87.2	10.9	1.9	675 126	72.8
POPULATION SIZE CLASS OF METROPOLITAN AREA															
1,000,000 or more	124 775 608	7.5	25.0	10.7	34.2	18.5	11.6	2.6	32.7	91.8	81.3	16.5	2.2	2 761 938	50.9
In central city	48 263 927	7.7	24.5	12.0	34.2	17.2	12.1	2.8	31.7	90.2	76.3	20.9	2.8	1 349 449	42.4
Not in central city	76 511 681	7.4	25.3	9.8	34.1	19.3	11.3	2.4	33.3	92.9	84.4	13.7	1.8	1 412 489	59.1
5,000,000 or more	52 837 069	7.5	24.6	10.8	34.0	18.8	11.7	2.6	32.8	92.3	81.3	16.6	2.2	1 157 609	51.8
In central city	22 256 704	7.6	24.4	11.7	34.3	17.7	11.9	2.8	32.0	90.5	77.2	20.3	2.4	542 725	44.6
Not in central city	30 580 365	7.4	24.8	10.1	33.9	19.6	11.6	2.5	33.4	93.6	84.2	13.8	2.0	614 884	58.2
2,500,000 to 4,999,999	31 701 991	7.6	25.1	10.7	35.2	18.3	10.7	2.4	32.4	91.7	81.3	16.7	2.0	624 490	51.4
In central city	10 347 206	7.7	24.0	12.4	34.7	17.0	11.9	2.8	31.6	90.4	74.7	22.3	3.0	312 254	41.6
Not in central city	21 354 785	7.5	25.6	9.8	35.5	18.9	10.1	2.1	32.8	92.3	84.5	14.0	1.5	312 236	61.2
1,000,000 to 2,499,999	40 236 548	7.5	25.4	10.6	33.6	18.2	12.2	2.7	32.7	91.3	81.3	16.3	2.4	979 839	49.6
In central city	15 660 017	7.8	24.8	12.3	33.9	16.6	12.4	3.0	31.4	89.7	76.0	20.9	3.2	494 470	40.6
Not in central city	24 576 531	7.4	25.8	9.5	33.3	19.3	12.2	2.6	33.5	92.4	84.6	13.4	2.0	485 369	58.7
Less than 1,000,000	67 950 133	7.4	25.7	11.4	32.0	18.4	12.5	2.8	32.5	91.5	81.8	15.1	3.2	2 152 552	43.4
In central city	29 579 606	7.6	25.0	13.4	31.8	16.9	12.9	3.1	31.4	87.7	76.9	19.0	4.1	1 208 330	38.1
Not in central city	38 370 527	7.2	26.3	10.0	32.0	19.5	12.2	2.5	33.4	94.5	85.5	12.0	2.5	944 222	50.3
500,000 to 999,999	24 905 921	7.4	25.4	11.2	32.9	18.4	12.2	2.7	32.6	90.7	81.8	15.4	2.8	699 935	45.1
In central city	10 438 257	7.6	24.6	12.9	32.8	17.0	12.7	3.0	31.6	87.2	76.7	19.5	3.8	394 598	38.4
Not in central city	14 467 664	7.3	26.0	9.9	33.0	19.4	11.8	2.4	33.4	93.5	85.5	12.3	2.1	305 337	53.9
250,000 to 499,999	21 528 297	7.4	26.1	10.9	31.6	18.5	12.9	2.8	32.7	91.6	82.5	14.5	2.9	632 026	47.9
In central city	8 783 875	7.8	25.9	12.4	31.8	16.9	13.1	3.1	31.5	87.8	78.2	18.3	3.5	309 992	43.2
Not in central city	12 744 422	7.2	26.3	9.9	31.4	19.6	12.8	2.6	33.6	94.4	85.5	12.0	2.5	322 034	52.5
100,000 to 249,999	19 403 087	7.3	25.7	12.3	31.3	18.2	12.5	2.8	32.2	92.3	81.0	15.2	3.8	735 533	38.4
In central city	9 054 420	7.4	24.6	14.8	31.0	16.6	12.9	3.2	30.9	88.4	75.9	19.3	4.9	440 815	34.5
Not in central city	10 348 667	7.2	26.7	10.1	31.5	19.6	12.1	2.5	33.3	96.0	85.5	11.6	2.8	294 718	44.2
Less than 100,000	2 112 828	7.2	26.0	12.3	31.0	18.0	12.8	3.1	32.1	90.5	80.6	15.4	4.0	85 058	39.4
In central city	1 303 054	7.3	24.9	13.9	30.4	17.1	13.7	3.5	31.6	86.8	76.8	18.3	4.8	62 925	36.6
Not in central city	809 774	7.2	27.8	9.7	31.9	19.5	11.2	2.4	32.9	96.9	86.5	10.7	2.7	22 133	47.6

Table 2. Summary of General Characteristics of Households and Families: 1990

[For definitions of terms and meanings of symbols, see text]

United States / Urban and Rural and Size of Place / Population Size Class of Urbanized Area / Inside and Outside Metropolitan Area / Population Size Class of Metropolitan Area	All households	Family households Total	Family households With own children under 18 years	Married-couple family Total	Married-couple family With own children under 18 years	Female householder, no husband present Total	Female householder, no husband present With own children under 18 years	Nonfamily households Total	Householder living alone Total	Householder living alone Female	65 years and over Total	65 years and over Female	Householder 65 years and over	Persons per Household	Persons per Family
United States	91 947 410	70.2	33.6	55.1	25.6	11.6	6.6	29.8	24.6	14.5	9.6	7.5	21.7	2.63	3.16
URBAN AND RURAL AND SIZE OF PLACE															
Urban	70 045 167	67.7	32.4	51.5	23.7	12.7	7.2	32.3	26.3	15.8	9.8	7.8	21.5	2.59	3.16
Inside urbanized area	59 251 993	67.5	32.1	51.1	23.5	12.8	7.2	32.5	26.2	15.5	9.3	7.3	20.6	2.60	3.17
Central place	30 147 116	62.8	30.1	43.6	19.7	15.2	8.8	37.2	30.1	17.5	10.2	8.0	21.2	2.53	3.19
Urban fringe	29 104 877	72.4	34.3	58.8	27.4	10.3	5.5	27.6	22.3	13.4	8.2	6.6	20.0	2.68	3.16
Outside urbanized area	10 793 174	68.6	33.6	53.6	24.7	12.0	7.4	31.4	26.9	17.4	13.1	10.7	26.5	2.54	3.10
Place of 10,000 or more	5 169 559	67.2	33.2	52.0	24.1	12.2	7.6	32.8	27.4	17.4	12.4	10.1	25.0	2.52	3.09
Place of 2,500 to 9,999	5 623 615	69.9	34.0	55.1	25.2	11.9	7.3	30.1	26.4	17.4	13.7	11.1	27.8	2.56	3.10
Rural	21 902 243	78.2	37.5	66.9	31.5	8.2	4.4	21.8	18.9	10.6	8.8	6.6	22.5	2.76	3.16
Place of 1,000 to 2,499	2 676 603	71.2	33.9	57.6	26.1	10.7	6.3	28.8	25.8	16.9	14.2	11.4	29.0	2.57	3.10
Place of less than 1,000	1 464 016	71.0	33.5	58.3	26.4	9.7	5.6	29.0	26.6	17.1	15.5	12.3	31.3	2.56	3.11
Other rural	17 761 624	79.8	38.3	69.0	32.8	7.6	4.1	20.2	17.2	9.2	7.5	5.4	20.8	2.81	3.17
POPULATION SIZE CLASS OF URBANIZED AREA															
1,000,000 or more	34 897 543	67.3	31.8	50.3	23.3	13.1	7.0	32.7	26.3	15.4	8.9	7.0	20.0	2.64	3.22
Central place	15 561 630	61.4	29.1	40.7	18.3	16.3	9.0	38.6	31.2	17.7	10.1	7.7	20.7	2.56	3.27
Urban fringe	19 335 913	72.0	34.1	58.0	27.3	10.5	5.5	28.0	22.4	13.4	8.0	6.4	19.4	2.70	3.19
5,000,000 or more	12 213 357	68.2	31.9	49.8	23.3	13.9	7.1	31.8	26.0	15.3	9.2	7.1	20.5	2.75	3.34
Central place	5 980 246	62.5	29.6	40.1	18.5	17.2	9.2	37.5	30.9	17.8	10.2	7.7	20.8	2.66	3.38
Urban fringe	6 233 111	73.7	34.1	59.1	27.8	10.7	5.0	26.3	21.2	12.8	8.2	6.5	20.2	2.83	3.31
2,500,000 to 4,999,999	8 941 231	66.4	31.6	49.6	23.3	13.0	6.9	33.6	26.8	15.4	8.2	6.4	18.5	2.60	3.20
Central place	3 701 940	59.2	27.8	38.0	17.0	16.8	9.2	40.8	32.9	18.2	9.4	7.1	19.6	2.50	3.25
Urban fringe	5 239 291	71.5	34.3	57.8	27.7	10.3	5.3	28.5	22.6	13.4	7.5	6.0	17.7	2.68	3.17
1,000,000 to 2,499,999	13 742 955	67.1	31.9	51.2	23.3	12.4	7.1	32.9	26.3	15.4	9.2	7.3	20.5	2.56	3.13
Central place	5 879 444	61.8	29.3	42.9	19.0	14.9	8.7	38.2	30.4	17.4	10.4	8.1	21.4	2.50	3.17
Urban fringe	7 863 511	71.0	33.9	57.3	26.5	10.5	5.9	29.0	23.3	14.0	8.3	6.7	19.8	2.61	3.10
Less than 1,000,000	24 354 450	67.8	32.6	52.2	23.8	12.4	7.4	32.2	26.1	15.6	9.7	7.7	21.4	2.55	3.11
Central place	14 585 486	64.2	31.2	46.8	21.2	14.0	8.5	35.8	28.9	17.2	10.4	8.3	21.6	2.49	3.11
Urban fringe	9 768 964	73.1	34.7	60.3	27.8	9.9	5.6	26.9	22.0	13.4	8.6	6.9	21.1	2.63	3.10
500,000 to 999,999	6 886 227	67.2	32.0	51.1	23.2	12.9	7.5	32.8	26.7	15.7	9.3	7.4	20.8	2.54	3.12
Central place	3 690 862	62.5	29.9	43.5	19.3	15.5	9.2	37.5	30.4	17.5	10.0	7.8	20.8	2.46	3.12
Urban fringe	3 195 365	72.6	34.5	59.9	27.8	9.8	5.5	27.4	22.5	13.7	8.5	6.8	20.7	2.63	3.12
250,000 to 499,999	5 840 087	68.6	33.0	52.5	24.0	12.9	7.6	31.4	25.9	15.5	9.6	7.6	21.4	2.57	3.13
Central place	3 195 892	64.6	31.6	46.2	21.0	14.9	9.1	35.4	29.0	17.2	10.4	8.3	21.6	2.52	3.14
Urban fringe	2 644 195	73.4	34.8	60.0	27.6	10.4	5.9	26.6	22.0	13.4	8.6	6.9	21.2	2.64	3.11
100,000 to 249,999	7 100 845	67.7	32.8	52.6	24.3	12.0	7.2	32.3	25.0	15.4	9.6	7.7	21.0	2.56	3.10
Central place	4 563 687	64.6	31.6	48.1	22.1	13.2	8.1	35.4	28.2	16.9	10.3	8.3	21.4	2.51	3.11
Urban fringe	2 537 158	73.2	35.0	60.6	28.1	9.7	5.5	26.8	21.6	12.9	8.3	6.6	20.3	2.64	3.10
Less than 100,000	4 527 291	67.7	32.4	53.1	23.8	11.7	7.2	32.3	26.1	16.0	10.6	8.6	23.1	2.52	3.06
Central place	3 135 045	65.0	31.4	49.4	22.2	12.6	7.8	35.0	28.0	17.2	11.1	0.0	23.0	2.48	3.06
Urban fringe	1 392 246	73.9	34.6	61.2	27.4	9.8	5.8	26.1	21.7	13.4	9.4	7.5	23.4	2.61	3.06
INSIDE AND OUTSIDE METROPOLITAN AREA															
Inside metropolitan area	71 265 264	69.3	33.2	53.8	25.0	12.1	6.8	30.7	24.9	14.6	9.0	7.1	20.5	2.64	3.18
In central city	29 793 822	62.7	30.0	43.5	19.6	15.2	8.8	37.3	30.2	17.5	10.3	8.0	21.2	2.53	3.19
Not in central city	41 471 442	74.1	35.6	61.1	28.9	9.8	5.3	25.9	21.1	12.5	8.1	6.4	20.0	2.71	3.17
Urban	32 340 947	72.4	34.6	58.7	27.5	10.4	5.7	27.6	22.3	13.5	8.5	6.8	20.3	2.68	3.16
Inside urbanized area	29 201 839	72.4	34.4	58.8	27.5	10.3	5.5	27.6	22.2	13.4	8.2	6.6	19.9	2.68	3.16
Outside urbanized area	3 139 108	72.4	36.4	58.1	28.0	11.1	6.8	27.6	23.2	14.7	11.0	8.9	23.8	2.67	3.16
Rural	9 130 495	80.2	39.1	69.6	33.7	7.5	4.0	19.8	16.5	9.0	6.9	5.1	19.0	2.84	3.19
Outside metropolitan area	20 682 146	73.0	34.8	59.9	27.4	10.0	5.9	27.0	23.5	14.3	11.5	9.0	25.9	2.62	3.11
Urban	7 938 898	67.1	32.3	51.9	23.3	12.3	7.6	32.9	28.2	18.3	13.7	11.2	27.4	2.49	3.07
Inside urbanized area	575 362	67.2	31.1	53.1	23.0	11.3	6.9	32.8	25.6	15.4	10.1	8.0	23.8	2.50	3.03
Outside urbanized area	7 363 536	67.0	32.4	51.8	23.3	12.4	7.7	33.0	28.4	18.5	14.0	11.4	27.7	2.49	3.07
Place of 10,000 or more	3 735 404	65.9	32.2	50.7	23.0	12.3	7.8	34.1	28.5	18.2	12.9	10.6	25.7	2.48	3.07
Place of 2,500 to 9,999	3 628 132	68.2	32.7	53.0	23.6	12.4	7.6	31.8	28.3	18.9	15.1	12.3	29.7	2.49	3.07
Rural	12 743 248	76.7	36.3	64.9	30.0	8.6	4.8	23.3	20.6	11.8	10.2	7.7	25.0	2.70	3.13
POPULATION SIZE CLASS OF METROPOLITAN AREA															
1,000,000 or more	45 957 542	68.7	32.8	52.6	24.6	12.4	6.8	31.3	25.2	14.7	8.8	6.9	19.9	2.65	3.21
In central city	18 366 553	61.7	29.3	41.4	18.7	16.0	9.0	38.3	30.9	17.6	10.1	7.8	20.7	2.55	3.25
Not in central city	27 590 989	73.4	35.2	60.0	28.5	10.0	5.3	26.6	21.4	12.7	7.9	6.3	19.4	2.72	3.19
5,000,000 or more	18 913 934	68.8	32.4	51.6	24.2	13.0	6.7	31.2	25.1	14.7	9.0	7.0	20.4	2.73	3.30
In central city	8 179 362	62.6	29.6	41.0	18.9	16.7	8.9	37.4	30.3	17.5	10.2	7.8	21.0	2.65	3.36
Not in central city	10 734 572	73.5	34.5	59.6	28.2	10.2	5.0	26.5	21.2	12.6	8.0	6.3	19.9	2.79	3.26
2,500,000 to 4,999,999	11 848 591	68.4	33.3	52.5	25.0	12.3	6.9	31.6	25.3	14.5	8.0	6.3	18.1	2.62	3.18
In central city	4 059 898	59.6	28.1	39.2	17.2	16.2	9.3	40.4	32.6	18.1	9.7	7.4	19.9	2.47	3.19
Not in central city	7 788 693	73.0	35.9	59.5	29.0	10.3	5.6	27.0	21.5	12.6	7.2	5.7	17.2	2.70	3.17
1,000,000 to 2,499,999	15 195 017	68.9	33.0	53.9	24.8	11.8	6.8	31.1	25.2	14.9	9.2	7.2	20.7	2.58	3.12
In central city	6 127 293	61.9	29.8	43.3	19.3	15.0	8.9	38.1	30.4	17.5	10.2	8.0	20.9	2.48	3.13
Not in central city	9 067 724	73.6	35.2	61.0	28.5	9.6	5.4	26.4	21.6	13.1	8.5	6.7	20.6	2.66	3.12
Less than 1,000,000	25 307 722	70.5	34.0	55.9	25.8	11.4	6.7	29.5	24.3	14.5	9.4	7.5	21.6	2.60	3.12
In central city	11 427 269	64.2	31.1	47.0	21.2	14.0	8.5	35.8	29.1	17.3	10.6	8.5	21.9	2.48	3.10
Not in central city	13 880 453	75.6	36.4	63.2	29.6	9.4	5.3	24.4	20.4	12.1	8.5	6.7	21.2	2.70	3.13
500,000 to 999,999	9 345 825	69.9	33.5	54.7	25.2	12.0	6.9	30.1	24.8	14.6	9.1	7.2	20.7	2.59	3.12
In central city	4 069 887	63.2	30.1	44.6	19.7	15.1	8.9	36.8	30.0	17.6	10.2	8.1	21.4	2.47	3.11
Not in central city	5 275 938	75.1	36.2	62.4	29.5	9.6	5.3	24.9	20.8	12.3	8.2	6.5	20.3	2.68	3.13
250,000 to 499,999	7 944 081	71.4	34.3	56.9	26.0	11.4	6.8	28.6	23.6	14.1	9.6	7.5	22.4	2.63	3.13
In central city	3 352 818	65.4	32.1	48.0	21.8	14.1	8.7	34.6	28.3	16.9	10.7	8.6	22.5	2.53	3.13
Not in central city	4 591 263	75.8	35.9	63.4	29.1	9.4	5.3	24.2	20.2	12.1	8.7	6.8	22.3	2.71	3.13
100,000 to 249,999	7 224 474	70.3	34.2	56.5	26.2	10.8	6.6	29.7	24.3	14.5	9.7	7.7	21.7	2.58	3.10
In central city	3 498 653	64.1	31.3	48.4	22.0	12.7	7.9	35.9	28.7	17.3	10.7	8.7	21.9	2.46	3.06
Not in central city	3 725 821	76.1	37.0	64.0	30.2	9.1	5.3	23.9	20.1	11.9	8.7	6.8	21.5	2.70	3.12
Less than 100,000	793 342	69.4	34.6	56.2	26.7	10.5	6.6	30.6	25.3	15.3	10.4	8.3	22.0	2.56	3.09
In central city	505 911	64.9	31.9	50.1	22.9	12.1	7.7	35.1	28.8	17.8	11.6	9.5	23.1	2.45	3.05
Not in central city	287 431	77.4	39.3	66.9	33.3	7.8	4.6	22.6	19.1	10.9	8.2	6.3	20.0	2.74	3.15

Table 3. Race and Hispanic Origin: 1990

[For definitions of terms and meanings of symbols, see text]

United States Urban and Rural and Size of Place	United States	Urban Total	Inside urbanized area Total	Central place	Urban fringe	Outside urbanized area Total	Place of 10,000 or more	Place of 2,500 to 9,999	Rural Total	Place of 1,000 to 2,499	Place of less than 1,000	Other rural
RACE												
All persons	248 709 873	187 053 487	158 258 878	78 847 406	79 411 472	28 794 609	13 825 022	14 969 587	61 656 386	7 050 858	3 801 051	50 804 477
White	199 686 070	143 807 279	119 359 248	52 192 735	67 166 513	24 448 031	11 562 503	12 885 528	55 878 791	6 299 526	3 402 922	46 176 343
Black	29 986 060	26 153 444	23 533 536	17 308 291	6 225 245	2 619 908	1 366 724	1 253 184	3 832 616	447 585	205 368	3 179 663
American Indian, Eskimo, or Aleut	1 959 234	1 100 534	768 135	468 915	299 220	332 399	134 735	197 664	858 700	108 037	140 600	610 063
American Indian	1 878 285	1 057 906	740 310	449 290	291 020	317 596	131 874	185 722	820 379	105 989	110 786	603 604
Eskimo	57 152	26 519	14 647	11 065	3 582	11 872	2 019	9 853	30 633	1 083	25 583	3 967
Aleut	23 797	16 109	13 178	8 560	4 618	2 931	842	2 089	7 688	965	4 231	2 492
Asian or Pacific Islander	7 273 662	6 934 689	6 507 391	3 421 439	3 085 952	427 298	227 888	199 410	338 973	65 784	17 286	255 903
Asian	6 908 638	6 608 042	6 248 838	3 294 837	2 954 001	359 204	206 403	152 801	300 596	53 455	13 650	233 491
Chinese	1 645 472	1 605 768	1 556 372	880 564	675 808	49 396	31 979	17 417	39 704	4 404	1 034	34 266
Filipino	1 406 770	1 336 071	1 240 840	630 593	610 247	95 231	44 581	50 650	70 699	18 728	4 940	47 031
Japanese	847 562	793 189	719 257	346 461	372 796	73 932	42 259	31 673	54 373	13 740	3 340	37 293
Asian Indian	815 447	776 825	738 855	327 210	411 645	37 970	23 526	14 444	38 622	3 855	624	34 143
Korean	798 849	754 574	718 748	332 749	385 999	35 826	21 766	14 060	44 275	4 564	1 741	37 970
Vietnamese	614 547	597 323	578 567	320 820	257 747	18 756	11 939	6 817	17 224	3 166	532	13 526
Cambodian	147 411	145 086	141 335	109 281	32 054	3 751	2 553	1 198	2 325	526	74	1 725
Hmong	90 082	87 433	80 909	70 731	10 178	6 524	4 795	1 729	2 649	269	36	2 344
Laotian	149 014	142 208	129 808	93 323	36 485	12 400	7 368	5 032	6 806	1 501	394	4 911
Thai	91 275	85 132	79 399	38 854	40 545	5 733	3 263	2 470	6 143	685	294	5 164
Other Asian	302 209	284 433	264 748	144 251	120 497	19 685	12 374	7 311	17 776	2 017	641	15 118
Bangladeshi	11 838	11 626	11 223	8 284	2 939	403	309	94	212	17	4	191
Burmese	6 177	5 968	5 750	2 570	3 180	218	138	80	209	10	6	193
Indonesian	29 252	28 201	26 340	12 569	13 771	1 861	1 416	445	1 051	123	25	903
Malayan	12 243	11 873	10 194	7 093	3 101	1 679	1 321	358	370	45	24	301
Okinawan	2 247	2 014	1 797	865	932	217	87	130	233	54	16	163
Pakistani	81 371	78 676	75 431	38 715	36 716	3 245	2 245	1 000	2 695	259	88	2 348
Sri Lankan	10 970	10 507	9 903	4 944	4 959	604	414	190	463	26	3	434
All other Asian	148 111	135 568	124 110	69 211	54 899	11 458	6 444	5 014	12 543	1 483	475	10 585
Pacific Islander	365 024	326 647	258 553	126 602	131 951	68 094	21 485	46 609	38 377	12 329	3 636	22 412
Hawaiian	211 014	181 082	126 569	60 926	65 643	54 513	16 112	38 401	29 932	10 743	3 190	15 999
Samoan	62 964	60 204	54 437	27 217	27 220	5 767	1 718	4 049	2 760	606	145	2 009
Guamanian	49 345	45 871	42 449	21 927	20 522	3 422	1 932	1 490	3 474	450	129	2 895
Other Pacific Islander	41 701	39 490	35 098	16 532	18 566	4 392	1 723	2 669	2 211	530	172	1 509
Tongan	17 606	16 997	15 257	6 545	8 712	1 740	484	1 256	609	245	46	318
Tahitian	944	862	661	330	331	201	30	171	82	27	14	41
Northern Mariana Islander	960	900	796	371	425	104	61	43	60	4	12	44
Palauan	1 439	1 314	1 073	630	443	241	165	76	125	15	4	106
Fijian	7 036	6 796	6 506	2 861	3 645	290	104	186	240	43	12	185
All other Pacific Islander	13 716	12 621	10 805	5 795	5 010	1 816	879	937	1 095	196	84	815
Other race	9 804 847	9 057 541	8 090 568	5 456 026	2 634 542	966 973	533 172	433 801	747 306	129 926	34 875	582 505
HISPANIC ORIGIN												
All persons	248 709 873	187 053 487	158 258 878	78 847 406	79 411 472	28 794 609	13 825 022	14 969 587	61 656 386	7 050 858	3 801 051	50 804 477
Hispanic origin (of any race)	22 354 059	20 426 228	18 355 980	11 671 728	6 684 252	2 070 248	1 102 447	967 801	1 927 831	318 036	89 028	1 520 767
Mexican	13 495 938	12 059 149	10 410 737	6 536 468	3 874 279	1 648 412	892 330	756 082	1 436 789	249 720	65 531	1 121 538
Puerto Rican	2 727 754	2 624 410	2 532 294	1 925 468	606 826	92 116	49 662	42 454	103 344	12 193	2 729	88 422
Cuban	1 043 932	1 013 773	993 592	489 602	503 990	20 181	11 280	8 901	30 159	2 602	489	27 068
Other Hispanic	5 086 435	4 728 896	4 419 357	2 720 200	1 699 157	309 539	149 175	160 364	357 539	53 521	20 279	283 739
Not of Hispanic origin	226 355 814	166 627 259	139 902 898	67 175 678	72 727 220	26 724 361	12 722 575	14 001 786	59 728 555	6 732 822	3 712 023	49 283 710
RACE AND HISPANIC ORIGIN												
All persons	248 709 873	187 053 487	158 258 878	78 847 406	79 411 472	28 794 609	13 825 022	14 969 587	61 656 386	7 050 858	3 801 051	50 804 477
White	199 686 070	143 807 279	119 359 248	52 192 735	67 166 513	24 448 031	11 562 503	12 885 528	55 878 791	6 299 526	3 402 922	46 176 343
Hispanic origin	11 557 774	10 431 881	9 383 738	5 573 158	3 810 580	1 048 143	541 821	506 322	1 125 893	179 840	50 282	895 771
Not of Hispanic origin	188 128 296	133 375 398	109 975 510	46 619 577	63 355 933	23 399 888	11 020 682	12 379 206	54 752 898	6 119 686	3 352 640	45 280 572
Black	29 986 060	26 153 444	23 533 536	17 308 291	6 225 245	2 619 908	1 366 724	1 253 184	3 832 616	447 585	205 368	3 179 663
Hispanic origin	769 767	738 650	709 285	549 256	160 029	29 365	17 128	12 237	31 117	3 083	980	27 054
Not of Hispanic origin	29 216 293	25 414 794	22 824 251	16 759 035	6 065 216	2 590 543	1 349 596	1 240 947	3 801 499	444 502	204 388	3 152 609
American Indian, Eskimo, or Aleut	1 959 234	1 100 534	768 135	468 915	299 220	332 399	134 735	197 664	858 700	108 037	140 600	610 063
Hispanic origin	165 461	137 776	117 612	74 863	42 749	20 164	10 196	9 968	27 685	3 964	2 436	21 285
Not of Hispanic origin	1 793 773	962 758	650 523	394 052	256 471	312 235	124 539	187 696	831 015	104 073	138 164	588 778
Asian or Pacific Islander	7 273 662	6 934 689	6 507 391	3 421 439	3 085 952	427 298	227 888	199 410	338 973	65 784	17 286	255 903
Hispanic origin	305 303	287 147	260 830	152 524	108 306	26 317	11 627	14 690	18 156	4 481	1 336	12 339
Not of Hispanic origin	6 968 359	6 647 542	6 246 561	3 268 915	2 977 646	400 981	216 261	184 720	320 817	61 303	15 950	243 564
Other race	9 804 847	9 057 541	8 090 568	5 456 026	2 634 542	966 973	533 172	433 801	747 306	129 926	34 875	582 505
Hispanic origin	9 555 754	8 830 774	7 884 515	5 321 927	2 562 588	946 259	521 675	424 584	724 980	126 668	33 994	564 318
Not of Hispanic origin	249 093	226 767	206 053	134 099	71 954	20 714	11 497	9 217	22 326	3 258	881	18 187
PERCENT DISTRIBUTION BY RACE												
All persons	100.0	100.0	100.0	100.0	100.0	100.0	100.0	100.0	100.0	100.0	100.0	100.0
White	80.3	76.9	75.4	66.2	84.6	84.9	83.6	86.1	90.6	89.3	89.5	90.9
Black	12.1	14.0	14.9	22.0	7.8	9.1	9.9	8.4	6.2	6.3	5.4	6.3
American Indian, Eskimo, or Aleut	.8	.6	.5	.6	.4	1.2	1.0	1.3	1.4	1.5	3.7	1.2
American Indian	.8	.6	.5	.6	.4	1.1	1.0	1.2	1.3	1.5	2.9	1.2
Asian or Pacific Islander	2.9	3.7	4.1	4.3	3.9	1.5	1.6	1.3	.5	.9	.5	.5
Asian	2.8	3.5	3.9	4.2	3.7	1.2	1.5	1.0	.5	.8	.4	.5
Pacific Islander	.1	.2	.2	.2	.2	.2	.2	.3	.1	.2	.1	—
Other race	3.9	4.8	5.1	6.9	3.3	3.4	3.9	2.9	1.2	1.8	.9	1.1
PERCENT DISTRIBUTION BY HISPANIC ORIGIN												
All persons	100.0	100.0	100.0	100.0	100.0	100.0	100.0	100.0	100.0	100.0	100.0	100.0
Hispanic origin (of any race)	9.0	10.9	11.6	14.8	8.4	7.2	8.0	6.5	3.1	4.5	2.3	3.0
Mexican	5.4	6.4	6.6	8.3	4.9	5.7	6.5	5.1	2.3	3.5	1.7	2.2
Puerto Rican	1.1	1.4	1.6	2.4	.8	.3	.4	.3	.2	.2	.1	.2
Cuban	.4	.5	.6	.6	.6	.1	.1	.1	—	—	—	.1
Other Hispanic	2.0	2.5	2.8	3.4	2.1	1.1	1.1	1.1	.6	.8	.5	.6
Not of Hispanic origin	91.0	89.1	88.4	85.2	91.6	92.8	92.0	93.5	96.9	95.5	97.7	97.0
PERCENT WHITE, NOT OF HISPANIC ORIGIN												
All persons	100.0	100.0	100.0	100.0	100.0	100.0	100.0	100.0	100.0	100.0	100.0	100.0
White	80.3	76.9	75.4	66.2	84.6	84.9	83.6	86.1	90.6	89.3	89.5	90.9
Not of Hispanic origin	75.6	71.3	69.5	59.1	79.8	81.3	79.7	82.7	88.8	86.8	88.2	89.1

Table 4. Race and Hispanic Origin: 1990

[For definitions of terms and meanings of symbols, see text]

United States Population Size Class of Urbanized Area	1,000,000 or more								
	Total			5,000,000 or more			2,500,000 to 4,999,999		
	Total	Central place	Urban fringe	Total	Central place	Urban fringe	Total	Central place	Urban fringe
RACE									
All persons	94 016 294	41 010 559	53 005 735	34 239 045	16 304 119	17 934 926	23 787 767	9 541 204	14 246 563
White	67 356 421	23 700 299	43 656 122	22 461 002	8 468 435	13 992 567	16 834 101	4 983 496	11 850 605
Black	15 387 703	10 879 622	4 508 081	5 705 341	4 293 698	1 411 643	4 536 123	3 267 559	1 268 564
American Indian, Eskimo, or Aleut	389 044	207 148	181 896	113 011	62 270	50 741	79 264	34 199	45 065
American Indian	376 436	200 534	175 902	108 743	59 657	49 086	76 681	33 082	43 599
Eskimo	5 287	2 833	2 454	1 727	1 076	651	1 098	497	601
Aleut	7 321	3 781	3 540	2 541	1 537	1 004	1 485	620	865
Asian or Pacific Islander	4 815 262	2 347 588	2 467 674	2 297 774	1 143 533	1 154 241	1 270 383	548 749	721 634
Asian	4 690 667	2 292 906	2 397 761	2 253 151	1 123 408	1 129 743	1 238 795	538 716	700 079
Chinese	1 291 020	700 925	590 095	643 103	349 528	293 575	411 207	228 582	182 625
Filipino	947 328	464 595	482 733	411 930	205 914	206 016	251 025	92 629	158 396
Japanese	423 399	167 971	255 428	223 087	81 198	141 889	77 316	28 901	48 415
Asian Indian	576 479	234 136	342 343	306 550	147 355	159 195	153 422	43 198	110 224
Korean	559 784	239 195	320 589	332 676	169 550	163 126	112 307	31 646	80 661
Vietnamese	449 998	228 372	221 626	159 201	60 633	98 568	124 816	62 806	62 010
Cambodian	88 905	62 927	25 978	37 535	29 885	7 650	23 858	15 180	8 678
Hmong	32 690	28 460	4 230	1 175	830	345	1 795	1 546	249
Laotian	67 756	41 873	25 883	8 909	5 089	3 820	18 637	9 598	9 039
Thai	57 947	26 305	31 642	32 292	16 857	15 435	11 862	4 176	7 686
Other Asian	195 361	98 147	97 214	96 693	56 569	40 124	52 550	20 454	32 096
Bangladeshi	9 509	7 162	2 347	6 910	6 048	862	1 836	747	1 089
Burmese	4 890	2 024	2 866	2 228	959	1 269	1 907	739	1 168
Indonesian	20 480	8 294	12 186	10 766	4 101	6 665	4 465	1 675	2 790
Malayan	5 430	3 048	2 382	2 116	1 367	749	1 596	799	797
Okinawan	566	242	324	214	100	114	111	37	74
Pakistani	62 260	30 827	31 433	35 455	21 621	13 834	17 113	5 858	11 255
Sri Lankan	7 289	3 229	4 060	3 848	1 980	1 868	1 847	550	1 297
All other Asian	84 937	43 321	41 616	35 156	20 393	14 763	23 675	10 049	13 626
Pacific Islander	124 595	54 682	69 913	44 623	20 125	24 498	31 588	10 033	21 555
Hawaiian	39 373	15 713	23 660	13 284	5 286	7 998	9 364	2 901	6 463
Samoan	34 900	16 234	18 666	15 845	6 819	9 026	7 187	3 000	4 187
Guamanian	28 337	14 486	13 851	9 939	5 981	3 958	6 088	2 390	3 698
Other Pacific Islander	21 985	8 249	13 736	5 555	2 039	3 516	8 949	1 742	7 207
Tongan	9 133	2 936	6 197	2 361	648	1 713	4 335	806	3 529
Tahitian	350	139	211	144	60	84	99	31	68
Northern Mariana Islander	476	216	260	102	51	51	118	26	92
Palauan	502	227	275	91	36	55	121	22	99
Fijian	5 171	1 795	3 376	716	399	317	2 591	243	2 348
All other Pacific Islander	6 353	2 936	3 417	2 141	845	1 296	1 685	614	1 071
Other race	6 067 864	3 875 902	2 191 962	3 661 917	2 336 183	1 325 734	1 067 896	707 201	360 695
HISPANIC ORIGIN									
All persons	94 016 294	41 010 559	53 005 735	34 239 045	16 304 119	17 934 926	23 787 767	9 541 204	14 246 563
Hispanic origin (of any race)	13 600 190	8 108 012	5 492 178	7 469 886	4 558 322	2 911 564	2 189 445	1 286 752	902 693
Mexican	7 225 591	4 062 035	3 163 556	3 719 577	1 824 422	1 895 155	1 295 728	804 860	490 868
Puerto Rican	1 895 981	1 455 320	440 661	1 423 187	1 104 400	238 787	224 203	153 383	70 820
Cuban	904 594	443 160	461 434	219 051	106 754	112 297	37 673	17 363	20 310
Other Hispanic	3 574 024	2 147 497	1 426 527	2 108 071	1 442 746	665 325	631 841	311 146	320 695
Not of Hispanic origin	80 416 104	32 902 547	47 513 557	26 769 159	11 745 797	15 023 362	21 598 322	8 254 452	13 343 870
RACE AND HISPANIC ORIGIN									
All persons	94 016 294	41 010 559	53 005 735	34 239 045	16 304 110	17 934 920	23 787 767	9 541 204	14 246 563
White	67 356 421	23 700 299	43 656 122	22 461 002	8 468 435	13 992 567	16 834 101	4 983 496	11 850 605
Hispanic origin	6 818 818	3 708 498	3 110 320	3 340 900	1 848 823	1 492 077	1 018 506	513 831	504 675
Not of Hispanic origin	60 537 603	19 991 801	40 545 802	19 120 102	6 619 612	12 500 490	15 815 595	4 469 665	11 345 930
Black	15 387 703	10 879 622	4 508 081	5 705 341	4 293 698	1 411 643	4 536 123	3 267 559	1 268 564
Hispanic origin	581 105	450 741	130 364	397 841	332 902	64 939	85 746	60 786	24 960
Not of Hispanic origin	14 806 598	10 428 881	4 377 717	5 307 500	3 960 796	1 346 704	4 450 377	3 206 773	1 243 604
American Indian, Eskimo, or Aleut	389 044	207 148	181 896	113 011	62 270	50 741	79 264	34 199	45 065
Hispanic origin	77 625	45 625	32 000	36 040	21 797	14 243	12 221	6 666	5 555
Not of Hispanic origin	311 419	161 523	149 896	76 971	40 473	36 498	67 043	27 533	39 510
Asian or Pacific Islander	4 815 262	2 347 588	2 467 674	2 297 774	1 143 533	1 154 241	1 270 383	548 749	721 634
Hispanic origin	188 558	107 975	80 583	96 213	59 267	36 946	39 144	18 359	20 785
Not of Hispanic origin	4 626 704	2 239 613	2 387 091	2 201 561	1 084 266	1 117 295	1 231 239	530 390	700 849
Other race	6 067 864	3 875 902	2 191 962	3 661 917	2 336 183	1 325 734	1 067 896	707 201	360 695
Hispanic origin	5 934 084	3 795 173	2 138 911	3 598 892	2 295 533	1 303 359	1 033 828	687 110	346 718
Not of Hispanic origin	133 780	80 729	53 051	63 025	40 650	22 375	34 068	20 091	13 977
PERCENT DISTRIBUTION BY RACE									
All persons	100.0	100.0	100.0	100.0	100.0	100.0	100.0	100.0	100.0
White	71.6	57.8	82.4	65.6	51.9	78.0	70.8	52.2	83.2
Black	16.4	26.5	8.5	16.7	26.3	7.9	19.1	34.2	8.9
American Indian, Eskimo, or Aleut	.4	.5	.3	.3	.4	.3	.3	.4	.3
American Indian	.4	.5	.3	.3	.4	.3	.3	.3	.3
Asian or Pacific Islander	5.1	5.7	4.7	6.7	7.0	6.4	5.3	5.8	5.1
Asian	5.0	5.6	4.5	6.6	6.9	6.3	5.2	5.6	4.9
Pacific Islander	.1	.1	.1	.1	.1	.1	.1	.1	.2
Other race	6.5	9.5	4.1	10.7	14.3	7.4	4.5	7.4	2.5
PERCENT DISTRIBUTION BY HISPANIC ORIGIN									
All persons	100.0	100.0	100.0	100.0	100.0	100.0	100.0	100.0	100.0
Hispanic origin (of any race)	14.5	19.8	10.4	21.8	28.0	16.2	9.2	13.5	6.3
Mexican	7.7	9.9	6.0	10.9	11.2	10.6	5.4	8.4	3.4
Puerto Rican	2.0	3.5	.8	4.2	7.3	1.3	.9	1.6	.5
Cuban	1.0	1.1	.9	.6	.7	.6	.2	.2	.1
Other Hispanic	3.8	5.2	2.7	6.2	8.8	3.7	2.7	3.3	2.3
Not of Hispanic origin	85.5	80.2	89.6	78.2	72.0	83.8	90.8	86.5	93.7
PERCENT WHITE, NOT OF HISPANIC ORIGIN									
All persons	100.0	100.0	100.0	100.0	100.0	100.0	100.0	100.0	100.0
White	71.6	57.8	82.4	65.6	51.9	78.0	70.8	52.2	83.2
Not of Hispanic origin	64.4	48.7	76.5	55.8	40.6	69.7	66.5	46.8	79.6

4 UNITED STATES SUMMARY

GENERAL POPULATION CHARACTERISTICS

Table 4. Race and Hispanic Origin: 1990—Con.

[For definitions of terms and meanings of symbols, see text]

United States Population Size Class of Urbanized Area	1,000,000 or more—Con. 1,000,000 to 2,499,999			Less than 1,000,000 Total			Less than 1,000,000 500,000 to 999,999		
	Total	Central place	Urban fringe	Total	Central place	Urban fringe	Total	Central place	Urban fringe
RACE									
All persons	35 989 482	15 165 236	20 824 246	64 242 584	37 836 847	26 405 737	17 955 916	9 403 669	8 552 247
White	28 061 318	10 248 368	17 812 950	52 002 827	28 492 436	23 510 391	14 060 661	6 435 430	7 625 231
Black	5 146 239	3 318 365	1 827 874	8 145 833	6 428 669	1 717 164	2 594 678	2 108 473	486 205
American Indian, Eskimo, or Aleut	196 769	110 679	86 090	379 091	261 767	117 324	95 114	59 119	35 995
American Indian	191 012	107 795	83 217	363 874	248 756	115 118	93 645	58 196	35 449
Eskimo	2 462	1 260	1 202	9 360	8 232	1 128	698	436	262
Aleut	3 295	1 624	1 671	5 857	4 779	1 078	771	487	284
Asian or Pacific Islander	1 247 105	655 306	591 799	1 692 129	1 073 851	618 278	698 114	410 967	287 147
Asian	1 198 721	630 782	567 939	1 558 171	1 001 931	556 240	622 430	367 313	255 117
Chinese	236 710	122 815	113 895	265 352	179 639	85 713	110 246	74 889	35 357
Filipino	284 373	166 052	118 321	293 512	165 998	127 514	136 589	65 143	71 446
Japanese	122 996	57 872	65 124	295 858	178 490	117 368	189 544	118 719	70 825
Asian Indian	116 507	43 583	72 924	162 376	93 074	69 302	45 113	20 210	24 903
Korean	114 801	37 999	76 802	158 964	93 554	65 410	53 369	31 084	22 285
Vietnamese	165 981	104 933	61 048	128 569	92 448	36 121	35 559	22 623	12 936
Cambodian	27 512	17 862	9 650	52 430	46 354	6 076	11 106	8 491	2 615
Hmong	29 720	26 084	3 636	48 219	42 271	5 948	1 378	1 256	122
Laotian	40 210	27 186	13 024	62 052	51 450	10 602	13 512	10 187	3 325
Thai	13 793	5 272	8 521	21 452	12 549	8 903	6 641	3 283	3 358
Other Asian	46 118	21 124	24 994	69 387	46 104	23 283	19 373	11 428	7 945
Bangladeshi	763	367	396	1 714	1 122	592	615	354	261
Burmese	755	326	429	860	546	314	183	101	82
Indonesian	5 249	2 518	2 731	5 860	4 275	1 585	1 430	1 009	421
Malayan	1 718	882	836	4 764	4 045	719	1 268	1 035	233
Okinawan	241	105	136	1 231	623	608	838	472	366
Pakistani	9 692	3 348	6 344	13 171	7 888	5 283	3 809	1 756	2 053
Sri Lankan	1 594	699	895	2 614	1 715	899	758	437	321
All other Asian	26 106	12 879	13 227	39 173	25 890	13 283	10 472	6 264	4 208
Pacific Islander	48 384	24 524	23 860	133 958	71 920	62 038	75 684	43 654	32 030
Hawaiian	16 725	7 526	9 199	87 196	45 213	41 983	52 814	30 919	21 895
Samoan	11 868	6 415	5 453	19 537	10 983	8 554	12 065	6 759	5 306
Guamanian	12 310	6 115	6 195	14 112	7 441	6 671	3 353	1 711	1 642
Other Pacific Islander	7 481	4 468	3 013	13 113	8 283	4 830	7 452	4 265	3 187
Tongan	2 437	1 482	955	6 124	3 609	2 515	4 591	2 482	2 109
Tahitian	107	48	59	311	191	120	195	129	66
Northern Mariana Islander	256	139	117	320	155	165	115	55	60
Palauan	290	169	121	571	403	168	287	226	61
Fijian	1 864	1 153	711	1 335	1 066	269	161	98	63
All other Pacific Islander	2 527	1 477	1 050	4 452	2 859	1 593	2 103	1 275	828
Other race	1 338 051	832 518	505 533	2 022 704	1 580 124	442 580	507 349	389 680	117 669
HISPANIC ORIGIN									
All persons	35 989 482	15 165 236	20 824 246	64 242 584	37 836 847	26 405 737	17 955 916	9 403 669	8 552 247
Hispanic origin (of any race)	3 940 859	2 262 938	1 677 921	4 755 790	3 563 716	1 192 074	1 284 790	923 451	361 339
Mexican	2 210 286	1 432 753	777 533	3 185 146	2 474 423	710 723	790 503	627 345	163 158
Puerto Rican	248 591	117 537	131 054	636 313	470 148	166 165	229 488	152 780	76 708
Cuban	647 870	319 043	328 827	88 998	46 442	42 556	42 004	17 757	24 247
Other Hispanic	834 112	393 605	440 507	845 333	572 703	272 630	222 795	125 569	97 226
Not of Hispanic origin	32 048 623	12 902 298	19 146 325	59 486 794	34 273 131	25 213 663	16 671 126	8 480 218	8 190 908
RACE AND HISPANIC ORIGIN									
All persons	35 989 482	15 165 236	20 824 246	64 242 584	37 836 847	26 405 737	17 955 916	9 403 669	8 552 247
White	28 061 318	10 248 368	17 812 950	52 002 827	28 492 436	23 510 391	14 060 661	6 435 430	7 625 231
Hispanic origin	2 459 412	1 345 844	1 113 568	2 564 920	1 864 660	700 260	720 186	496 513	223 673
Not of Hispanic origin	25 601 906	8 902 524	16 699 382	49 437 907	26 627 776	22 810 131	13 340 475	5 938 917	7 401 558
Black	5 146 239	3 318 365	1 827 874	8 145 833	6 428 669	1 717 164	2 594 678	2 108 473	486 205
Hispanic origin	97 518	57 053	40 465	128 180	98 515	29 665	40 391	30 060	10 331
Not of Hispanic origin	5 048 721	3 261 312	1 787 409	8 017 653	6 330 154	1 687 499	2 554 287	2 078 413	475 874
American Indian, Eskimo, or Aleut	196 769	110 679	86 090	379 091	261 767	117 324	95 114	59 119	35 995
Hispanic origin	29 364	17 162	12 202	39 987	29 238	10 749	9 915	6 829	3 086
Not of Hispanic origin	167 405	93 517	73 888	339 104	232 529	106 575	85 199	52 290	32 909
Asian or Pacific Islander	1 247 105	655 306	591 799	1 692 129	1 073 851	618 278	698 114	410 967	287 147
Hispanic origin	53 201	30 349	22 852	72 272	44 549	27 723	28 366	14 750	13 616
Not of Hispanic origin	1 193 904	624 957	568 947	1 619 857	1 029 302	590 555	669 748	396 217	273 531
Other race	1 338 051	832 518	505 533	2 022 704	1 580 124	442 580	507 349	389 680	117 669
Hispanic origin	1 301 364	812 530	488 834	1 950 431	1 526 754	423 677	485 932	375 299	110 633
Not of Hispanic origin	36 687	19 988	16 699	72 273	53 370	18 903	21 417	14 381	7 036
PERCENT DISTRIBUTION BY RACE									
All persons	100.0	100.0	100.0	100.0	100.0	100.0	100.0	100.0	100.0
White	78.0	67.6	85.5	80.9	75.3	89.0	78.3	68.4	89.2
Black	14.3	21.9	8.8	12.7	17.0	6.5	14.5	22.4	5.7
American Indian, Eskimo, or Aleut	.5	.7	.4	.6	.7	.4	.5	.6	.4
American Indian	.5	.7	.4	.6	.7	.4	.5	.6	.4
Asian or Pacific Islander	3.5	4.3	2.8	2.6	2.8	2.3	3.9	4.4	3.4
Asian	3.3	4.2	2.7	2.4	2.6	2.1	3.5	3.9	3.0
Pacific Islander	.1	.2	.1	.2	.2	.2	.4	.5	.4
Other race	3.7	5.5	2.4	3.1	4.2	1.7	2.8	4.1	1.4
PERCENT DISTRIBUTION BY HISPANIC ORIGIN									
All persons	100.0	100.0	100.0	100.0	100.0	100.0	100.0	100.0	100.0
Hispanic origin (of any race)	11.0	14.9	8.1	7.4	9.4	4.5	7.2	9.8	4.2
Mexican	6.1	9.4	3.7	5.0	6.5	2.7	4.4	6.7	1.9
Puerto Rican	.7	.8	.6	1.0	1.2	.6	1.3	1.6	.9
Cuban	1.8	2.1	1.6	.1	.1	.2	.2	.2	.3
Other Hispanic	2.3	2.6	2.1	1.3	1.5	1.0	1.2	1.3	1.1
Not of Hispanic origin	89.0	85.1	91.9	92.6	90.6	95.5	92.8	90.2	95.8
PERCENT WHITE, NOT OF HISPANIC ORIGIN									
All persons	100.0	100.0	100.0	100.0	100.0	100.0	100.0	100.0	100.0
White	78.0	67.6	85.5	80.9	75.3	89.0	78.3	68.4	89.2
Not of Hispanic origin	71.1	58.7	80.2	77.0	70.4	86.4	74.3	63.2	86.5

Table 4. Race and Hispanic Origin: 1990—Con.

[For definitions of terms and meanings of symbols, see text]

United States Population Size Class of Urbanized Area	Less than 1,000,000—Con.								
	250,000 to 499,999			100,000 to 249,999			Less than 100,000		
	Total	Central place	Urban fringe	Total	Central place	Urban fringe	Total	Central place	Urban fringe
RACE									
All persons	15 470 005	8 327 127	7 142 878	18 879 599	11 928 889	6 950 710	11 937 064	8 177 162	3 759 902
White	12 264 139	5 969 730	6 294 409	15 534 992	9 346 512	6 188 480	10 143 035	6 740 764	3 402 271
Black	2 166 471	1 614 142	552 329	2 218 683	1 762 876	455 807	1 166 001	943 178	222 823
American Indian, Eskimo, or Aleut	105 896	71 368	34 528	100 675	72 491	28 184	77 406	58 789	18 617
American Indian	104 063	70 253	33 810	90 212	62 623	27 589	75 954	57 684	18 270
Eskimo	970	582	388	7 001	6 693	308	691	521	170
Aleut	863	533	330	3 462	3 175	287	761	584	177
Asian or Pacific Islander	352 353	232 973	119 380	433 880	274 240	159 640	207 782	155 671	52 111
Asian	340 085	226 434	113 651	395 642	257 882	137 760	200 014	150 302	49 712
Chinese	49 783	30 701	19 082	70 330	46 305	24 025	34 993	27 744	7 249
Filipino	56 123	35 122	21 001	70 345	44 137	26 208	30 455	21 596	8 859
Japanese	28 835	16 098	12 737	56 721	27 909	28 812	20 758	15 764	4 994
Asian Indian	41 718	21 932	19 786	48 857	32 411	16 446	26 688	18 521	8 167
Korean	36 214	17 151	19 063	46 966	29 472	17 494	22 415	15 847	6 568
Vietnamese	39 726	30 917	8 809	38 250	27 211	11 039	15 034	11 697	3 337
Cambodian	21 312	20 221	1 091	16 031	14 548	1 483	3 981	3 094	887
Hmong	24 015	22 136	1 879	5 062	4 283	779	17 764	14 596	3 168
Laotian	19 878	18 267	1 611	15 926	12 870	3 056	12 736	10 126	2 610
Thai	4 943	2 808	2 135	6 399	4 065	2 334	3 469	2 393	1 076
Other Asian	17 538	11 081	6 457	20 755	14 671	6 084	11 721	8 924	2 797
Bangladeshi	375	251	124	468	328	140	256	189	67
Burmese	249	156	93	267	183	84	161	106	55
Indonesian	1 403	923	480	2 100	1 599	501	927	744	183
Malayan	1 039	831	208	1 528	1 338	190	929	841	88
Okinawan	83	37	46	251	76	175	59	38	21
Pakistani	3 482	1 953	1 529	3 632	2 474	1 158	2 248	1 705	543
Sri Lankan	531	298	233	840	651	189	485	329	156
All other Asian	10 376	6 632	3 744	11 669	8 022	3 647	6 656	4 972	1 684
Pacific Islander	12 268	6 539	5 729	38 238	16 358	21 880	7 768	5 369	2 399
Hawaiian	4 908	2 602	2 306	26 062	9 199	16 863	3 412	2 493	919
Samoan	2 760	1 597	1 163	3 721	2 040	1 681	991	587	404
Guamanian	3 344	1 553	1 791	4 895	2 501	2 394	2 520	1 676	844
Other Pacific Islander	1 256	787	469	3 560	2 618	942	845	613	232
Tongan	236	131	105	1 183	920	263	114	76	38
Tahitian	23	14	9	82	38	44	11	10	1
Northern Mariana Islander	82	25	57	88	52	36	35	23	12
Palauan	97	64	33	136	75	61	51	38	13
Fijian	153	130	23	917	771	146	104	67	37
All other Pacific Islander	665	423	242	1 154	762	392	530	399	131
Other race	581 146	438 914	142 232	591 369	472 770	118 599	342 840	278 760	64 080
HISPANIC ORIGIN									
All persons	15 470 005	8 327 127	7 142 878	18 879 599	11 928 889	6 950 710	11 937 064	8 177 162	3 759 902
Hispanic origin (of any race)	1 344 597	982 762	361 835	1 348 272	1 049 745	298 527	778 131	607 758	170 373
Mexican	929 689	685 846	243 843	895 683	709 613	186 070	569 271	451 619	117 652
Puerto Rican	155 341	122 740	32 601	185 741	145 144	40 597	65 743	49 404	16 259
Cuban	16 313	9 332	6 981	20 094	13 320	6 774	10 587	6 033	4 554
Other Hispanic	243 254	164 844	78 410	246 754	181 668	65 086	132 530	100 622	31 908
Not of Hispanic origin	14 125 408	7 344 365	6 781 043	17 531 327	10 879 144	6 652 183	11 158 933	7 569 404	3 589 529
RACE AND HISPANIC ORIGIN									
All persons	15 470 005	8 327 127	7 142 878	18 879 599	11 928 889	6 950 710	11 937 064	8 177 162	3 760 002
White	12 264 139	5 969 730	6 294 409	15 534 992	9 346 512	6 188 480	10 143 035	6 740 764	3 402 271
Hispanic origin	719 701	510 439	209 262	713 732	546 968	166 764	411 301	310 740	100 561
Not of Hispanic origin	11 544 438	5 459 291	6 085 147	14 821 260	8 799 544	6 021 716	9 731 734	6 430 024	3 301 710
Black	2 166 471	1 614 142	552 329	2 218 683	1 762 876	455 807	1 166 001	943 178	222 823
Hispanic origin	31 717	24 721	6 996	38 391	30 401	7 990	17 681	13 333	4 348
Not of Hispanic origin	2 134 754	1 589 421	545 333	2 180 292	1 732 475	447 817	1 148 320	929 845	218 475
American Indian, Eskimo, or Aleut	105 896	71 368	34 528	100 675	72 491	28 184	77 406	58 789	18 617
Hispanic origin	11 686	8 550	3 136	10 711	7 718	2 993	7 675	6 141	1 534
Not of Hispanic origin	94 210	62 818	31 392	89 964	64 773	25 191	69 731	52 648	17 083
Asian or Pacific Islander	352 353	232 973	119 380	433 880	274 240	159 640	207 782	155 671	52 111
Hispanic origin	15 657	10 967	4 690	19 058	11 896	7 162	9 191	6 936	2 255
Not of Hispanic origin	336 696	222 006	114 690	414 822	262 344	152 478	198 591	148 735	49 856
Other race	581 146	438 914	142 232	591 369	472 770	118 599	342 840	278 760	64 080
Hispanic origin	565 836	428 085	137 751	566 380	452 762	113 618	332 283	270 608	61 675
Not of Hispanic origin	15 310	10 829	4 481	24 989	20 008	4 981	10 557	8 152	2 405
PERCENT DISTRIBUTION BY RACE									
All persons	100.0	100.0	100.0	100.0	100.0	100.0	100.0	100.0	100.0
White	79.3	71.7	88.1	82.3	78.4	89.0	85.0	82.4	90.5
Black	14.0	19.4	7.7	11.8	14.8	6.6	9.8	11.5	5.9
American Indian, Eskimo, or Aleut	.7	.9	.5	.5	.6	.4	.6	.7	.5
American Indian	.7	.8	.5	.5	.5	.4	.6	.7	.5
Asian or Pacific Islander	2.3	2.8	1.7	2.3	2.3	2.3	1.7	1.9	1.4
Asian	2.2	2.7	1.6	2.1	2.2	2.0	1.7	1.8	1.3
Pacific Islander	.1	.1	.1	.2	.1	.3	.1	.1	.1
Other race	3.8	5.3	2.0	3.1	4.0	1.7	2.9	3.4	1.7
PERCENT DISTRIBUTION BY HISPANIC ORIGIN									
All persons	100.0	100.0	100.0	100.0	100.0	100.0	100.0	100.0	100.0
Hispanic origin (of any race)	8.7	11.8	5.1	7.1	8.8	4.3	6.5	7.4	4.5
Mexican	6.0	8.2	3.4	4.7	5.9	2.7	4.8	5.5	3.1
Puerto Rican	1.0	1.5	.5	1.0	1.2	.6	.6	.6	.4
Cuban	.1	.1	.1	.1	.1	.1	.1	.1	.1
Other Hispanic	1.6	2.0	1.1	1.3	1.5	.9	1.1	1.2	.8
Not of Hispanic origin	91.3	88.2	94.9	92.9	91.2	95.7	93.5	92.6	95.5
PERCENT WHITE, NOT OF HISPANIC ORIGIN									
All persons	100.0	100.0	100.0	100.0	100.0	100.0	100.0	100.0	100.0
White	79.3	71.7	88.1	82.3	78.4	89.0	85.0	82.4	90.5
Not of Hispanic origin	74.6	65.6	85.2	78.5	73.8	86.6	81.5	78.6	87.8

GENERAL POPULATION CHARACTERISTICS

Table 5. Race and Hispanic Origin: 1990

[For definitions of terms and meanings of symbols, see text]

United States Inside and Outside Metropolitan Area	United States	Inside metropolitan area						Outside metropolitan area				
				Not in central city					Urban			
					Urban					Outside urbanized area		
		Total	In central city	Total	Inside urbanized area	Outside urbanized area	Rural	Total	Inside urbanized area	Place of 10,000 or more	Place of 2,500 to 9,999	Rural
RACE												
All persons	248 709 873	192 725 741	77 843 533	114 882 208	79 755 134	8 684 794	26 442 280	55 984 132	1 520 259	9 873 345	9 458 347	35 132 181
White	199 686 070	150 863 170	51 452 071	99 411 099	67 365 275	7 521 124	24 524 700	48 822 900	1 267 155	8 245 260	8 026 268	31 284 217
Black	29 986 060	25 122 054	17 169 430	7 952 624	6 235 478	554 608	1 162 538	4 864 006	201 221	1 052 836	949 100	2 660 849
American Indian, Eskimo, or Aleut	1 959 234	1 002 984	465 364	537 620	302 903	63 229	171 488	956 250	8 925	106 069	155 180	686 076
American Indian	1 878 285	972 439	445 863	526 576	294 610	62 331	169 635	905 846	8 759	103 587	143 849	649 651
Eskimo	57 152	16 103	11 002	5 101	3 618	475	1 008	41 049	103	1 817	9 537	29 592
Aleut	23 797	14 442	8 499	5 943	4 675	423	845	9 355	63	665	1 794	6 833
Asian or Pacific Islander	7 273 662	6 823 859	3 373 675	3 450 184	3 125 833	136 925	187 426	449 803	23 044	165 504	110 414	150 841
Asian	6 908 638	6 523 794	3 253 737	3 270 057	2 987 329	109 365	173 363	384 844	22 153	147 107	88 954	126 630
Chinese	1 645 472	1 594 517	873 056	721 461	679 881	14 019	27 561	50 955	5 689	23 680	9 516	12 070
Filipino	1 406 770	1 310 413	616 438	693 975	623 288	35 378	35 309	96 357	3 169	28 805	29 124	35 259
Japanese	847 562	759 633	337 149	422 484	381 022	15 776	25 686	87 929	2 783	34 752	21 800	28 594
Asian Indian	815 447	778 533	324 536	453 997	413 952	12 766	27 279	36 914	3 009	15 203	7 430	11 272
Korean	798 849	755 219	329 577	425 642	387 749	11 087	26 806	43 630	2 861	16 179	7 230	17 360
Vietnamese	614 547	593 569	318 295	275 274	259 446	5 780	10 048	20 978	1 446	8 596	3 818	7 118
Cambodian	147 411	143 679	108 738	34 941	32 255	1 050	1 636	3 732	521	1 768	754	689
Hmong	90 082	86 060	71 543	14 517	10 126	2 442	1 949	4 022	129	2 362	831	700
Laotian	149 014	137 627	93 854	43 773	36 731	3 444	3 598	11 387	613	4 499	3 076	3 199
Thai	91 275	84 290	38 038	46 252	41 004	1 872	3 376	6 985	586	2 293	1 355	2 751
Other Asian	302 209	280 254	142 513	137 741	121 875	5 751	10 115	21 955	1 347	8 970	4 020	7 618
Bangladeshi	11 838	11 414	8 257	3 157	2 966	68	123	424	23	253	61	87
Burmese	6 177	5 958	2 497	3 461	3 233	78	150	219	23	100	37	59
Indonesian	29 252	27 269	12 298	14 971	13 950	404	617	1 983	144	1 186	220	433
Malayan	12 243	10 603	7 024	3 579	3 101	278	200	1 640	106	1 113	251	170
Okinawan	2 247	1 964	841	1 123	957	43	123	283	4	75	94	110
Pakistani	81 371	78 150	38 580	39 570	36 896	938	1 736	3 221	251	1 530	491	949
Sri Lankan	10 970	10 331	4 792	5 539	5 072	144	323	639	86	280	133	140
All other Asian	148 111	134 565	68 224	66 341	55 700	3 798	6 843	13 546	710	4 433	2 733	5 670
Pacific Islander	365 024	300 065	119 938	180 127	138 504	27 560	14 063	64 959	891	18 397	21 460	24 211
Hawaiian	211 014	156 558	55 371	101 187	71 084	20 685	9 418	54 456	435	14 701	18 833	20 487
Samoan	62 964	59 579	26 882	32 697	27 522	3 596	1 579	3 385	135	1 224	873	1 153
Guamanian	49 345	45 821	21 430	24 391	20 997	1 461	1 933	3 524	178	1 168	684	1 494
Other Pacific Islander	41 701	38 107	16 255	21 852	18 901	1 818	1 133	3 594	143	1 304	1 070	1 077
Tongan	17 606	16 377	6 385	9 992	8 840	729	423	1 229	43	423	577	186
Tahitian	944	839	312	527	340	151	36	105	9	24	26	46
Northern Mariana Islander	960	858	369	489	423	36	30	102	4	49	19	30
Palauan	1 439	1 177	609	568	462	47	59	262	3	139	54	66
Fijian	7 036	6 830	2 777	4 053	3 746	163	144	206	13	46	51	96
All other Pacific Islander	13 716	12 026	5 803	6 223	5 090	692	441	1 690	71	623	343	653
Other race	9 804 847	8 913 674	5 382 993	3 530 681	2 725 645	408 908	396 128	891 173	19 914	303 676	217 385	350 198
HISPANIC ORIGIN												
All persons	248 709 873	192 725 741	77 843 533	114 882 208	79 755 134	8 684 794	26 442 280	55 984 132	1 520 259	9 873 345	9 458 347	35 132 181
Hispanic origin (of any race)	22 354 059	20 204 818	11 514 252	8 690 566	6 854 456	815 181	1 020 929	2 149 241	51 453	655 690	537 526	904 572
Mexican	13 495 938	11 874 570	6 422 658	5 451 912	4 008 050	668 503	775 359	1 621 368	26 984	525 101	409 199	660 084
Puerto Rican	2 727 754	2 639 645	1 914 213	725 432	619 195	42 097	64 140	88 109	6 028	25 819	17 476	38 786
Cuban	1 043 932	1 019 689	487 526	532 163	505 658	6 717	19 788	24 243	1 145	7 311	5 481	10 306
Other Hispanic	5 086 435	4 670 914	2 689 855	1 981 059	1 721 553	97 864	161 642	415 521	17 296	97 459	105 370	195 396
Not of Hispanic origin	226 355 814	172 520 923	66 329 281	106 191 642	72 900 678	7 869 613	25 421 351	53 834 891	1 468 806	9 217 655	8 920 821	34 227 609
RACE AND HISPANIC ORIGIN												
All persons	248 709 873	192 725 741	77 843 533	114 882 208	79 755 134	8 684 794	26 442 280	55 984 132	1 520 259	9 873 345	9 458 347	35 132 181
White	199 686 070	150 863 170	77 843 533	114 882 208	67 365 275	7 521 124	24 524 700	48 822 900	1 267 155	8 245 260	8 026 268	31 284 217
Hispanic origin	11 557 774	10 366 970	5 494 364	4 872 606	3 884 808	386 541	601 257	1 190 804	28 965	334 964	303 436	523 439
Not of Hispanic origin	188 128 296	140 496 200	45 957 707	94 538 493	63 480 467	7 134 583	23 923 443	47 632 096	1 238 190	7 910 296	7 722 832	30 760 778
Black	29 986 060	25 122 054	17 169 430	7 952 624	6 235 478	554 608	1 162 538	4 864 006	201 221	1 052 836	949 100	2 660 849
Hispanic origin	769 767	732 516	545 953	186 563	161 373	10 219	14 971	37 251	3 076	10 443	7 700	16 032
Not of Hispanic origin	29 216 293	24 389 538	16 623 477	7 766 061	6 074 105	544 389	1 147 567	4 826 755	198 145	1 042 393	941 400	2 644 817
American Indian, Eskimo, or Aleut	1 959 234	1 002 984	465 364	537 620	302 903	63 229	171 488	956 250	8 925	106 069	155 180	686 076
Hispanic origin	165 461	135 073	73 369	61 704	44 188	6 295	11 221	30 388	836	6 651	6 479	16 422
Not of Hispanic origin	1 793 773	867 911	391 995	475 916	258 715	56 934	160 267	925 862	8 089	99 418	148 701	669 654
Asian or Pacific Islander	7 273 662	6 823 859	3 373 675	3 450 184	3 125 833	136 925	187 426	449 803	23 044	165 504	110 414	150 841
Hispanic origin	305 303	279 889	149 596	130 293	111 284	10 202	8 807	25 414	716	7 571	7 823	9 304
Not of Hispanic origin	6 968 359	6 543 970	3 224 079	3 319 891	3 014 549	126 723	178 619	424 389	22 328	157 933	102 591	141 537
Other race	9 804 847	8 913 674	5 382 993	3 530 681	2 725 645	408 908	396 128	891 173	19 914	303 676	217 385	350 198
Hispanic origin	9 555 754	8 690 370	5 250 970	3 439 400	2 652 803	401 924	384 673	865 384	17 860	296 061	212 088	339 375
Not of Hispanic origin	249 093	223 304	132 023	91 281	72 842	6 984	11 455	25 789	2 054	7 615	5 297	10 823
PERCENT DISTRIBUTION BY RACE												
All persons	100.0	100.0	100.0	100.0	100.0	100.0	100.0	100.0	100.0	100.0	100.0	100.0
White	80.3	78.3	66.1	86.5	84.5	86.6	92.7	87.2	83.4	83.5	84.9	89.0
Black	12.1	13.0	22.1	6.9	7.8	6.4	4.4	8.7	13.2	10.7	10.0	7.6
American Indian, Eskimo, or Aleut	.8	.5	.6	.5	.4	.7	.6	1.7	.6	1.1	1.6	2.0
American Indian	.8	.5	.6	.5	.4	.7	.6	1.6	.6	1.0	1.5	1.8
Asian or Pacific Islander	2.9	3.5	4.3	3.0	3.9	1.6	.7	.8	1.5	1.7	1.2	.4
Asian	2.8	3.4	4.2	2.8	3.7	1.3	.7	.7	1.5	1.5	.9	.4
Pacific Islander	.1	.2	.2	.2	.2	.3	.1	.1	.1	.2	.2	.1
Other race	3.9	4.6	6.9	3.1	3.4	4.7	1.5	1.6	1.3	3.1	2.3	1.0
PERCENT DISTRIBUTION BY HISPANIC ORIGIN												
All persons	100.0	100.0	100.0	100.0	100.0	100.0	100.0	100.0	100.0	100.0	100.0	100.0
Hispanic origin (of any race)	9.0	10.5	14.8	7.6	8.6	9.4	3.9	3.8	3.4	6.6	5.7	2.6
Mexican	5.4	6.2	8.3	4.7	5.0	7.7	2.9	2.9	1.8	5.3	4.3	1.9
Puerto Rican	1.1	1.4	2.5	.6	.8	.5	.2	.2	.4	.3	.2	.1
Cuban	.4	.5	.6	.5	.6	.1	.1	—	.1	.1	.1	—
Other Hispanic	2.0	2.4	3.5	1.7	2.2	1.1	.6	.7	1.1	1.0	1.1	.6
Not of Hispanic origin	91.0	89.5	85.2	92.4	91.4	90.6	96.1	96.2	96.6	93.4	94.3	97.4
PERCENT WHITE, NOT OF HISPANIC ORIGIN												
All persons	100.0	100.0	100.0	100.0	100.0	100.0	100.0	100.0	100.0	100.0	100.0	100.0
White	80.3	78.3	66.1	86.5	84.5	86.6	92.7	87.2	83.4	83.5	84.9	89.0
Not of Hispanic origin	75.6	72.9	59.0	82.3	79.6	82.2	90.5	85.1	81.4	80.1	81.7	87.6

Table 6. Race and Hispanic Origin: 1990
[For definitions of terms and meanings of symbols, see text]

United States Population Size Class of Metropolitan Area	1,000,000 or more								
	Total			5,000,000 or more			2,500,000 to 4,999,999		
	Total	In central city	Not in central city	Total	In central city	Not in central city	Total	In central city	Not in central city
RACE									
All persons	124 775 608	48 263 927	76 511 681	52 837 069	22 256 704	30 580 365	31 701 991	10 347 206	21 354 785
White	94 402 349	29 171 220	65 231 129	36 734 791	12 050 920	24 683 871	24 218 918	6 113 253	18 105 665
Black	17 638 128	12 140 180	5 497 948	7 705 099	5 585 464	2 119 635	5 368 985	3 202 461	2 166 524
American Indian, Eskimo, or Aleut	530 902	241 540	289 362	201 590	91 201	110 389	114 976	42 873	72 103
American Indian	515 232	234 026	281 206	194 656	87 704	106 952	110 419	40 986	69 433
Eskimo	6 885	3 320	3 565	2 889	1 493	1 396	2 059	880	1 179
Aleut	8 785	4 194	4 591	4 045	2 004	2 041	2 498	1 007	1 491
Asian or Pacific Islander	5 317 229	2 524 580	2 792 649	3 518 730	1 724 860	1 793 870	910 401	322 412	587 989
Asian	5 167 501	2 462 082	2 705 419	3 428 983	1 688 509	1 740 474	890 845	315 103	575 742
Chinese	1 378 468	731 149	647 319	1 021 738	567 494	454 244	208 201	81 341	126 860
Filipino	1 033 128	489 547	543 581	733 190	340 450	392 740	108 733	36 509	72 224
Japanese	478 121	184 121	294 000	324 602	120 075	204 527	67 884	23 596	44 288
Asian Indian	648 976	256 201	392 775	406 467	178 009	228 458	150 787	41 378	109 409
Korean	620 009	255 262	364 747	416 330	198 946	217 384	116 343	26 216	90 127
Vietnamese	486 209	243 497	242 712	269 427	132 416	137 011	115 880	50 596	65 284
Cambodian	111 547	82 040	29 507	55 980	44 955	11 025	33 084	20 035	13 049
Hmong	35 330	29 984	5 346	2 169	1 105	1 064	2 709	1 844	865
Laotian	87 478	54 166	33 312	25 876	15 188	10 688	21 633	10 889	10 744
Thai	65 357	28 203	37 154	40 479	19 685	20 794	13 648	3 997	9 651
Other Asian	222 878	107 912	114 966	132 725	70 186	62 539	51 943	18 702	33 241
Bangladeshi	10 054	7 363	2 691	7 482	6 253	1 229	1 993	833	1 160
Burmese	5 339	2 149	3 190	3 805	1 641	2 164	981	291	690
Indonesian	22 725	9 113	13 612	15 747	5 779	9 968	3 602	1 400	2 202
Malayan	6 503	3 666	2 837	2 996	1 749	1 247	1 832	932	900
Okinawan	693	269	424	352	156	196	148	33	115
Pakistani	68 199	32 792	35 407	42 644	24 140	18 504	18 258	5 764	12 494
Sri Lankan	8 387	3 618	4 769	5 126	2 397	2 729	1 773	496	1 277
All other Asian	100 978	48 942	52 036	54 573	28 071	26 502	23 356	8 953	14 403
Pacific Islander	149 728	62 498	87 230	89 747	36 351	53 396	19 556	7 309	12 247
Hawaiian	40 363	18 073	30 290	27 821	10 099	17 722	7 316	2 304	5 012
Samoan	39 691	17 824	21 867	26 840	12 036	14 804	4 650	2 435	2 215
Guamanian	33 742	16 148	17 594	19 536	9 910	9 626	4 502	1 465	3 037
Other Pacific Islander	27 932	10 453	17 479	15 550	4 306	11 244	3 088	1 105	1 983
Tongan	12 985	4 584	8 401	6 998	1 652	5 346	1 043	313	730
Tahitian	444	172	272	246	95	151	68	16	52
Northern Mariana Islander	560	219	341	239	84	155	130	35	95
Palauan	593	258	335	259	93	166	118	41	77
Fijian	5 587	1 880	3 707	3 899	903	2 996	357	155	202
All other Pacific Islander	7 763	3 340	4 423	3 909	1 479	2 430	1 372	545	827
Other race	6 887 000	4 186 407	2 700 593	4 676 859	2 804 259	1 872 600	1 088 711	666 207	422 504
HISPANIC ORIGIN									
All persons	124 775 608	48 263 927	76 511 681	52 837 069	22 256 704	30 580 365	31 701 991	10 347 206	21 354 785
Hispanic origin (of any race)	15 435 936	8 724 237	6 711 699	9 646 762	5 470 682	4 176 080	3 047 711	1 607 576	1 440 135
Mexican	8 298 418	4 319 325	3 979 093	5 158 631	2 369 611	2 789 020	1 269 166	760 144	509 011
Puerto Rican	2 253 436	1 671 607	581 829	1 694 031	1 364 595	329 436	275 458	144 465	130 993
Cuban	946 418	454 634	491 784	245 200	116 755	128 445	627 824	304 565	323 259
Other Hispanic	3 937 664	2 278 671	1 658 993	2 548 900	1 619 721	929 179	875 274	398 402	476 872
Not of Hispanic origin	109 339 672	39 539 690	69 799 982	43 190 307	16 786 022	26 404 285	28 654 280	8 739 630	19 914 650
RACE AND HISPANIC ORIGIN									
All persons	124 775 608	48 263 927	76 511 681	52 837 069	22 256 704	30 580 365	31 701 991	10 347 206	21 354 785
White	94 402 349	29 171 220	65 231 129	36 734 791	12 050 920	24 683 871	24 218 918	6 113 253	18 105 665
Hispanic origin	7 772 561	3 984 614	3 787 947	4 403 878	2 241 722	2 162 156	1 845 659	875 866	969 793
Not of Hispanic origin	86 629 788	25 186 606	61 443 182	32 330 913	9 809 198	22 521 715	22 373 259	5 237 387	17 135 872
Black	17 638 128	12 140 180	5 497 948	7 705 099	5 585 464	2 119 635	5 368 985	3 202 461	2 166 524
Hispanic origin	638 038	483 969	154 069	454 134	366 370	87 764	112 784	68 250	44 534
Not of Hispanic origin	17 000 090	11 656 211	5 343 879	7 250 965	5 219 094	2 031 871	5 256 201	3 134 211	2 121 990
American Indian, Eskimo, or Aleut	530 902	241 540	289 362	201 590	91 201	110 389	114 976	42 873	72 103
Hispanic origin	94 923	50 211	44 712	54 695	28 400	26 295	12 962	6 974	5 988
Not of Hispanic origin	435 979	191 329	244 650	146 895	62 801	84 094	102 014	35 899	66 115
Asian or Pacific Islander	5 317 229	2 524 580	2 792 649	3 518 730	1 724 860	1 793 870	910 401	322 412	587 989
Hispanic origin	209 260	115 312	93 948	143 781	80 772	63 009	26 926	12 023	14 903
Not of Hispanic origin	5 107 969	2 409 268	2 698 701	3 374 949	1 644 088	1 730 861	883 475	310 389	573 086
Other race	6 887 000	4 186 407	2 700 593	4 676 859	2 804 259	1 872 600	1 088 711	666 207	422 504
Hispanic origin	6 721 154	4 090 131	2 631 023	4 590 274	2 753 418	1 836 856	1 049 380	644 463	404 917
Not of Hispanic origin	165 846	96 276	69 570	86 585	50 841	35 744	39 331	21 744	17 587
PERCENT DISTRIBUTION BY RACE									
All persons	100.0	100.0	100.0	100.0	100.0	100.0	100.0	100.0	100.0
White	75.7	60.4	85.3	69.5	54.1	80.7	76.4	59.1	84.8
Black	14.1	25.2	7.2	14.6	25.1	6.9	16.9	31.0	10.1
American Indian, Eskimo, or Aleut	.4	.5	.4	.4	.4	.4	.4	.4	.3
American Indian	.4	.5	.4	.4	.4	.3	.3	.4	.3
Asian or Pacific Islander	4.3	5.2	3.6	6.7	7.7	5.9	2.9	3.1	2.8
Asian	4.1	5.1	3.5	6.5	7.6	5.7	2.8	3.0	2.7
Pacific Islander	.1	.1	.1	.2	.2	.2	.1	.1	.1
Other race	5.5	8.7	3.5	8.9	12.6	6.1	3.4	6.4	2.0
PERCENT DISTRIBUTION BY HISPANIC ORIGIN									
All persons	100.0	100.0	100.0	100.0	100.0	100.0	100.0	100.0	100.0
Hispanic origin (of any race)	12.4	18.1	8.8	18.3	24.6	13.7	9.6	15.5	6.7
Mexican	6.7	8.9	5.2	9.8	10.6	9.1	4.0	7.3	2.4
Puerto Rican	1.8	3.5	.8	3.2	6.1	1.1	.9	1.4	.6
Cuban	.8	.9	.6	.5	.5	.4	2.0	2.9	1.5
Other Hispanic	3.2	4.7	2.2	4.8	7.3	3.0	2.8	3.9	2.2
Not of Hispanic origin	87.6	81.9	91.2	81.7	75.4	86.3	90.4	84.5	93.3
PERCENT WHITE, NOT OF HISPANIC ORIGIN									
All persons	100.0	100.0	100.0	100.0	100.0	100.0	100.0	100.0	100.0
White	75.7	60.4	85.3	69.5	54.1	80.7	76.4	59.1	84.8
Not of Hispanic origin	69.4	52.2	80.3	61.2	44.1	73.6	70.6	50.6	80.2

Table 6. Race and Hispanic Origin: 1990—Con.

[For definitions of terms and meanings of symbols, see text]

United States Population Size Class of Metropolitan Area	1,000,000 or more—Con.			Less than 1,000,000					
	1,000,000 to 2,499,999			Total			500,000 to 999,999		
	Total	In central city	Not in central city	Total	In central city	Not in central city	Total	In central city	Not in central city
RACE									
All persons	**40 236 548**	**15 660 017**	**24 576 531**	**67 950 133**	**29 579 606**	**38 370 527**	**24 905 921**	**10 438 257**	**14 467 664**
White	33 448 640	11 007 047	22 441 593	56 460 821	22 280 851	34 179 970	19 725 324	7 114 029	12 611 295
Black	4 564 044	3 352 255	1 211 789	7 483 926	5 029 250	2 454 676	3 351 612	2 336 258	1 015 354
American Indian, Eskimo, or Aleut	214 336	107 466	106 870	472 082	223 824	248 258	188 446	82 651	105 795
American Indian	210 157	105 336	104 821	457 207	211 837	245 370	186 498	81 605	104 893
Eskimo	1 937	947	990	9 218	7 682	1 536	895	464	431
Aleut	2 242	1 183	1 059	5 657	4 305	1 352	1 053	582	471
Asian or Pacific Islander	888 098	477 308	410 790	1 506 630	849 095	657 535	875 741	454 580	421 161
Asian	847 673	458 470	389 203	1 356 293	791 655	564 638	753 567	412 319	341 248
Chinese	148 529	82 314	66 215	216 049	141 907	74 142	124 313	80 579	43 734
Filipino	191 205	112 588	78 617	277 285	126 891	150 394	173 047	68 937	104 110
Japanese	85 635	40 450	45 185	281 512	153 028	128 484	224 453	120 754	103 699
Asian Indian	91 722	36 814	54 908	129 557	68 335	61 222	52 017	24 562	27 455
Korean	87 336	30 100	57 236	135 210	74 315	60 895	60 604	33 370	27 234
Vietnamese	100 902	60 485	40 417	107 360	74 798	32 562	40 327	27 219	13 108
Cambodian	22 483	17 050	5 433	32 132	26 698	5 434	10 522	8 106	2 416
Hmong	30 452	27 035	3 417	50 730	41 559	9 171	18 986	17 123	1 863
Laotian	39 969	28 089	11 880	50 149	39 688	10 461	18 155	14 794	3 361
Thai	11 230	4 521	6 709	18 933	9 835	9 098	7 760	3 589	4 171
Other Asian	38 210	19 024	19 186	57 376	34 601	22 775	23 383	13 286	10 097
Bangladeshi	579	277	302	1 360	894	466	606	383	223
Burmese	553	217	336	619	348	271	298	172	126
Indonesian	3 376	1 934	1 442	4 544	3 185	1 359	1 883	1 257	626
Malayan	1 675	985	690	4 100	3 358	742	1 502	1 137	365
Okinawan	193	80	113	1 271	572	699	1 056	468	588
Pakistani	7 297	2 888	4 409	9 951	5 788	4 163	3 955	1 987	1 968
Sri Lankan	1 488	725	763	1 944	1 174	770	850	475	375
All other Asian	23 049	11 918	11 131	33 587	19 282	14 305	13 233	7 407	5 826
Pacific Islander	40 425	18 838	21 587	150 337	57 440	92 897	122 174	42 261	79 913
Hawaiian	13 226	5 670	7 556	108 195	37 298	70 897	96 737	31 142	65 595
Samoan	8 201	3 353	4 848	19 888	9 058	10 830	15 508	6 693	8 815
Guamanian	9 704	4 773	4 931	12 079	5 282	6 797	4 188	1 742	2 446
Other Pacific Islander	9 294	5 042	4 252	10 175	5 802	4 373	5 741	2 684	3 057
Tongan	4 944	2 619	2 325	3 392	1 801	1 591	2 307	912	1 395
Tahitian	130	61	69	395	140	255	328	108	220
Northern Mariana Islander	191	100	91	298	150	148	139	65	74
Palauan	216	124	92	584	351	233	352	238	114
Fijian	1 331	822	509	1 243	897	346	295	113	182
All other Pacific Islander	2 482	1 316	1 166	4 263	2 463	1 800	2 320	1 248	1 072
Other race	1 121 430	715 941	405 489	2 026 674	1 196 586	830 088	764 798	450 739	314 059
HISPANIC ORIGIN									
All persons	**40 236 548**	**15 660 017**	**24 576 531**	**67 950 133**	**29 579 606**	**38 370 527**	**24 905 921**	**10 438 257**	**14 467 664**
Hispanic origin (of any race)	2 741 463	1 645 979	1 095 484	4 768 882	2 790 015	1 978 867	1 696 135	1 020 275	675 860
Mexican	1 870 632	1 189 570	681 062	3 576 152	2 103 333	1 472 819	1 239 532	767 381	472 151
Puerto Rican	283 947	162 547	121 400	386 209	242 606	143 603	178 184	117 994	60 190
Cuban	73 394	33 314	40 080	73 271	32 892	40 379	38 770	16 268	22 502
Other Hispanic	513 490	260 548	252 942	733 250	411 184	322 066	239 649	118 632	121 017
Not of Hispanic origin	37 495 085	14 014 038	23 481 047	63 181 251	26 789 591	36 391 660	23 209 786	9 417 982	13 791 804
RACE AND HISPANIC ORIGIN									
All persons	**40 236 548**	**15 660 017**	**24 576 531**	**67 950 133**	**29 579 606**	**38 370 527**	**24 905 921**	**10 438 257**	**14 467 664**
White	33 448 640	11 007 047	22 441 593	56 460 821	22 280 851	34 179 970	19 725 324	7 114 029	12 611 295
Hispanic origin	1 523 024	867 026	655 998	2 594 409	1 509 750	1 084 659	855 568	529 716	325 852
Not of Hispanic origin	31 925 616	10 140 021	21 785 595	53 866 412	20 771 101	33 095 311	18 869 756	6 584 313	12 285 443
Black	4 564 044	3 352 255	1 211 789	7 483 926	5 029 250	2 454 676	3 351 612	2 336 258	1 015 354
Hispanic origin	71 120	49 349	21 771	94 478	61 984	32 494	38 937	26 077	12 860
Not of Hispanic origin	4 492 924	3 302 906	1 190 018	7 389 448	4 967 266	2 422 182	3 312 675	2 310 181	1 002 494
American Indian, Eskimo, or Aleut	214 336	107 466	106 870	472 082	223 824	248 258	188 446	82 651	105 795
Hispanic origin	27 266	14 837	12 429	40 150	23 158	16 992	15 390	8 504	6 886
Not of Hispanic origin	187 070	92 629	94 441	431 932	200 666	231 266	173 056	74 147	98 909
Asian or Pacific Islander	888 098	477 308	410 790	1 506 630	849 095	657 535	875 741	454 580	421 161
Hispanic origin	38 553	22 517	16 036	70 629	34 284	36 345	41 368	16 608	24 760
Not of Hispanic origin	849 545	454 791	394 754	1 436 001	814 811	621 190	834 373	437 972	396 401
Other race	1 121 430	715 941	405 489	2 026 674	1 196 586	830 088	764 798	450 739	314 059
Hispanic origin	1 081 500	692 250	389 250	1 969 216	1 160 839	808 377	744 872	439 370	305 502
Not of Hispanic origin	39 930	23 691	16 239	57 458	35 747	21 711	19 926	11 369	8 557
PERCENT DISTRIBUTION BY RACE									
All persons	**100.0**	**100.0**	**100.0**	**100.0**	**100.0**	**100.0**	**100.0**	**100.0**	**100.0**
White	83.1	70.3	91.3	83.1	75.3	89.1	79.2	68.2	87.2
Black	11.3	21.4	4.9	11.0	17.0	6.4	13.5	22.4	7.0
American Indian, Eskimo, or Aleut	.5	.7	.4	.7	.8	.6	.8	.8	.7
American Indian	.5	.7	.4	.7	.7	.6	.7	.8	.7
Asian or Pacific Islander	2.2	3.0	1.7	2.2	2.9	1.7	3.5	4.4	2.9
Asian	2.1	2.9	1.6	2.0	2.7	1.5	3.0	4.0	2.4
Pacific Islander	.1	.1	.1	.2	.2	.2	.5	.4	.6
Other race	2.8	4.6	1.6	3.0	4.0	2.2	3.1	4.3	2.2
PERCENT DISTRIBUTION BY HISPANIC ORIGIN									
All persons	**100.0**	**100.0**	**100.0**	**100.0**	**100.0**	**100.0**	**100.0**	**100.0**	**100.0**
Hispanic origin (of any race)	6.8	10.5	4.5	7.0	9.4	5.2	6.8	9.8	4.7
Mexican	4.6	7.6	2.8	5.3	7.1	3.8	5.0	7.4	3.3
Puerto Rican	.7	1.0	.5	.6	.8	.4	.7	1.1	.4
Cuban	.2	.2	.2	.1	.1	.1	.2	.2	.2
Other Hispanic	1.3	1.7	1.0	1.1	1.4	.8	1.0	1.1	.8
Not of Hispanic origin	93.2	89.5	95.5	93.0	90.6	94.8	93.2	90.2	95.3
PERCENT WHITE, NOT OF HISPANIC ORIGIN									
All persons	**100.0**	**100.0**	**100.0**	**100.0**	**100.0**	**100.0**	**100.0**	**100.0**	**100.0**
White	83.1	70.3	91.3	83.1	75.3	89.1	79.2	68.2	87.2
Not of Hispanic origin	79.3	64.8	88.6	79.3	70.2	86.3	75.8	63.1	84.9

Table 6. Race and Hispanic Origin: 1990—Con.

[For definitions of terms and meanings of symbols, see text]

United States Population Size Class of Metropolitan Area	Less than 1,000,000—Con.								
	250,000 to 499,999			100,000 to 249,999			Less than 100,000		
	Total	In central city	Not in central city	Total	In central city	Not in central city	Total	In central city	Not in central city
RACE									
All persons	21 528 297	8 783 875	12 744 422	19 403 087	9 054 420	10 348 667	2 112 828	1 303 054	809 774
White	18 093 596	6 679 010	11 414 586	16 745 333	7 361 451	9 383 882	1 896 568	1 126 361	770 207
Black	2 174 861	1 387 488	787 373	1 819 417	1 191 268	628 149	138 036	114 236	23 800
American Indian, Eskimo, or Aleut	115 866	56 851	59 015	146 185	68 103	78 082	21 585	16 219	5 366
American Indian	113 773	55 713	58 060	135 589	58 444	77 145	21 347	16 075	5 272
Eskimo	1 155	593	562	7 015	6 532	483	153	93	60
Aleut	938	545	393	3 581	3 127	454	85	51	34
Asian or Pacific Islander	358 684	220 522	138 162	251 215	157 629	93 586	20 990	16 364	4 626
Asian	342 229	211 334	130 895	240 215	152 158	88 057	20 282	15 844	4 438
Chinese	49 443	30 238	19 205	37 753	27 194	10 559	4 540	3 896	644
Filipino	69 720	39 839	29 881	32 166	16 652	15 514	2 352	1 463	889
Japanese	32 388	18 024	14 364	22 662	12 699	9 963	2 009	1 551	458
Asian Indian	40 749	21 329	19 420	34 124	20 480	13 644	2 667	1 964	703
Korean	37 696	17 568	20 128	33 939	21 300	12 639	2 971	2 077	894
Vietnamese	41 028	29 761	11 267	24 818	16 839	7 979	1 187	979	208
Cambodian	17 302	15 559	1 743	4 221	2 958	1 263	87	75	12
Hmong	12 353	10 597	1 756	17 450	11 920	5 530	1 941	1 919	22
Laotian	18 413	14 739	3 674	13 215	9 810	3 405	366	345	21
Thai	5 721	3 203	2 518	4 864	2 653	2 211	588	390	198
Other Asian	17 416	10 477	6 939	15 003	9 653	5 350	1 574	1 185	389
Bangladeshi	380	227	153	321	240	81	53	44	9
Burmese	166	84	82	143	82	61	12	10	2
Indonesian	1 382	941	441	1 146	865	281	133	122	11
Malayan	922	790	132	1 500	1 264	236	176	167	9
Okinawan	88	46	42	123	54	69	4	4	–
Pakistani	3 544	2 273	1 271	2 212	1 374	838	240	154	86
Sri Lankan	435	234	201	570	400	170	89	65	24
All other Asian	10 499	5 882	4 617	8 988	5 374	3 614	867	619	248
Pacific Islander	16 455	9 188	7 267	11 000	5 471	5 529	708	520	188
Hawaiian	6 439	3 477	2 962	4 722	2 489	2 233	297	190	107
Samoan	2 429	1 289	1 140	1 880	1 029	851	71	47	24
Guamanian	4 461	2 133	2 328	3 260	1 276	1 984	170	131	39
Other Pacific Islander	3 126	2 289	837	1 138	677	461	170	152	18
Tongan	850	681	169	213	186	27	22	22	
Tahitian	47	23	24	17	8	9	3	1	2
Northern Mariana Islander	67	34	33	89	50	39	3	1	2
Palauan	133	62	71	93	47	46	6	4	2
Fijian	893	755	138	51	29	22	4	–	4
All other Pacific Islander	1 136	734	402	675	357	318	132	124	8
Other race	785 290	440 004	345 286	440 937	275 969	164 968	35 649	29 874	5 775
HISPANIC ORIGIN									
All persons	21 528 297	8 783 875	12 744 422	19 403 087	9 054 420	10 348 667	2 112 828	1 303 054	809 774
Hispanic origin (of any race)	1 941 524	1 065 089	876 435	1 048 036	636 781	411 255	83 187	67 870	15 317
Mexican	1 496 462	807 859	688 603	773 231	472 626	300 605	66 927	55 467	11 460
Puerto Rican	136 042	77 203	59 639	68 334	45 418	22 916	2 849	1 991	858
Cuban	18 717	9 230	9 487	15 131	6 947	8 184	653	447	206
Other Hispanic	289 503	170 797	118 706	191 340	111 790	79 550	12 758	9 965	2 793
Not of Hispanic origin	19 586 773	7 718 786	11 867 987	18 355 051	8 417 639	9 937 412	2 029 641	1 235 184	794 457
RACE AND HISPANIC ORIGIN									
All persons	21 528 297	8 783 875	12 744 422	19 403 087	9 054 420	10 348 667	2 112 828	1 303 054	809 774
White	18 093 596	6 679 010	11 414 586	16 745 333	7 361 451	9 383 882	1 896 568	1 126 361	770 207
Hispanic origin	1 107 804	594 435	513 369	585 821	349 444	236 377	45 216	36 155	9 061
Not of Hispanic origin	16 985 792	6 084 575	10 901 217	16 159 512	7 012 007	9 147 505	1 851 352	1 090 206	761 146
Black	2 174 861	1 387 488	787 373	1 819 417	1 191 268	628 149	138 036	114 236	23 800
Hispanic origin	33 276	21 010	12 266	20 560	13 554	7 006	1 705	1 343	362
Not of Hispanic origin	2 141 585	1 366 478	775 107	1 798 857	1 177 714	621 143	136 331	112 893	23 438
American Indian, Eskimo, or Aleut	115 866	56 851	59 015	146 185	68 103	78 082	21 585	16 219	5 366
Hispanic origin	13 699	8 130	5 569	9 808	5 504	4 304	1 253	1 020	233
Not of Hispanic origin	102 167	48 721	53 446	136 377	62 599	73 778	20 332	15 199	5 133
Asian or Pacific Islander	358 684	220 522	138 162	251 215	157 629	93 586	20 990	16 364	4 626
Hispanic origin	18 835	11 745	7 090	9 681	5 342	4 339	745	589	156
Not of Hispanic origin	339 849	208 777	131 072	241 534	152 287	89 247	20 245	15 775	4 470
Other race	785 290	440 004	345 286	440 937	275 969	164 968	35 649	29 874	5 775
Hispanic origin	767 910	429 769	338 141	422 166	262 937	159 229	34 268	28 763	5 505
Not of Hispanic origin	17 380	10 235	7 145	18 771	13 032	5 739	1 381	1 111	270
PERCENT DISTRIBUTION BY RACE									
All persons	100.0	100.0	100.0	100.0	100.0	100.0	100.0	100.0	100.0
White	84.0	76.0	89.6	86.3	81.3	90.7	89.8	86.4	95.1
Black	10.1	15.8	6.2	9.4	13.2	6.1	6.5	8.8	2.9
American Indian, Eskimo, or Aleut	.5	.6	.5	.8	.8	.8	1.0	1.2	.7
American Indian	.5	.6	.5	.7	.6	.7	1.0	1.2	.7
Asian or Pacific Islander	1.7	2.5	1.1	1.3	1.7	.9	1.0	1.3	.6
Asian	1.6	2.4	1.0	1.2	1.7	.9	1.0	1.2	.5
Pacific Islander	.1	.1	.1	.1	.1	.1	–	–	–
Other race	3.6	5.0	2.7	2.3	3.0	1.6	1.7	2.3	.7
PERCENT DISTRIBUTION BY HISPANIC ORIGIN									
All persons	100.0	100.0	100.0	100.0	100.0	100.0	100.0	100.0	100.0
Hispanic origin (of any race)	9.0	12.1	6.9	5.4	7.0	4.0	3.9	5.2	1.9
Mexican	7.0	9.2	5.4	4.0	5.2	2.9	3.2	4.3	1.4
Puerto Rican	.6	.9	.5	.4	.5	.2	.1	.2	.1
Cuban	.1	.1	.1	.1	.1	.1	–	–	–
Other Hispanic	1.3	1.9	.9	1.0	1.2	.8	.6	.8	.3
Not of Hispanic origin	91.0	87.9	93.1	94.6	93.0	96.0	96.1	94.8	98.1
PERCENT WHITE, NOT OF HISPANIC ORIGIN									
All persons	100.0	100.0	100.0	100.0	100.0	100.0	100.0	100.0	100.0
White	84.0	76.0	89.6	86.3	81.3	90.7	89.8	86.4	95.1
Not of Hispanic origin	78.9	69.3	85.5	83.3	77.4	88.4	87.6	83.7	94.0

Table 7. **Summary of General Characteristics of White Persons and Households: 1990**

[For definitions of terms and meanings of symbols, see text]

United States Urban and Rural and Size of Place Population Size Class of Urbanized Area Inside and Outside Metropolitan Area Population Size Class of Metropolitan Area	All White persons						All households with a White householder									
		Percent of all persons						Family households as a percent of all households							Persons per—	
										Married-couple family		Female householder, no husband present				
	Total	Under 18 years	65 years and over	Median age	Persons 18 years and over—Males per 100 females	Percent in group quarters	Total	Total	With own children under 18 years	Total	With own children under 18 years	Total	With own children under 18 years	Household	Family
United States	**199 686 070**	**23.9**	**13.9**	**34.4**	**92.4**	**2.5**	**76 880 105**	**69.5**	**31.7**	**57.7**	**25.7**	**8.9**	**4.7**	**2.54**	**3.06**
URBAN AND RURAL AND SIZE OF PLACE															
Urban	143 807 279	22.8	14.4	34.2	90.5	2.9	56 613 098	66.4	29.8	54.0	23.6	9.5	5.0	2.47	3.04
Inside urbanized area	119 359 248	22.4	13.9	34.2	91.2	2.5	47 112 854	66.2	29.4	53.7	23.4	9.4	4.8	2.48	3.04
Central place	52 192 735	20.9	15.0	33.8	90.7	3.6	21 600 072	59.7	25.9	46.6	19.5	10.0	5.2	2.34	3.00
Urban fringe	67 166 513	23.6	13.1	34.5	91.6	1.8	25 512 782	71.6	32.3	59.7	26.6	9.0	4.5	2.59	3.08
Outside urbanized area	24 448 031	24.4	16.7	34.1	87.0	4.6	9 500 244	67.8	31.9	55.2	24.6	9.9	6.0	2.46	3.01
Place of 10,000 or more	11 562 503	23.8	15.8	33.1	87.6	5.6	4 486 590	66.3	31.4	53.6	23.9	10.0	6.1	2.44	3.00
Place of 2,500 to 9,999	12 885 528	24.9	17.4	35.0	86.4	3.8	5 013 654	69.2	32.5	56.6	25.2	9.9	6.0	2.48	3.02
Rural	55 878 791	26.7	12.8	34.8	97.5	1.5	20 267 007	78.2	37.0	68.3	31.8	7.0	3.8	2.72	3.11
Place of 1,000 to 2,499	6 299 526	25.5	17.8	35.8	86.8	2.5	2 452 238	70.8	32.9	58.9	26.2	9.2	5.4	2.51	3.03
Place of less than 1,000	3 402 922	26.1	18.6	36.1	88.8	1.4	1 346 368	70.5	32.6	59.6	26.5	8.2	4.7	2.50	3.04
Other rural	46 176 343	26.9	11.7	34.6	99.8	1.4	16 468 401	79.9	37.9	70.4	33.0	6.6	3.5	2.77	3.13
POPULATION SIZE CLASS OF URBANIZED AREA															
1,000,000 or more	67 356 421	21.9	13.8	34.7	92.0	2.0	26 635 557	65.6	28.5	53.1	23.0	9.3	4.4	2.49	3.07
Central place	23 700 299	19.5	15.4	34.7	92.8	2.9	10 039 879	56.6	23.2	43.4	17.5	9.7	4.5	2.30	3.02
Urban fringe	43 656 122	23.2	13.0	34.7	91.5	1.5	16 595 678	71.0	31.7	59.0	26.3	9.0	4.3	2.60	3.09
5,000,000 or more	22 461 002	21.1	14.6	35.4	92.1	1.9	8 715 609	65.6	27.3	52.6	22.3	9.5	3.9	2.53	3.14
Central place	8 468 435	18.9	16.3	35.6	92.4	2.5	3 560 593	56.2	22.0	42.2	16.7	10.0	4.2	2.32	3.08
Urban fringe	13 992 567	22.4	13.6	35.2	92.0	1.6	5 155 016	72.2	30.9	59.8	26.1	9.1	3.7	2.68	3.17
2,500,000 to 4,999,999	16 834 101	21.8	12.5	34.3	92.2	2.0	6 686 811	65.0	28.8	52.9	23.5	9.0	4.2	2.47	3.07
Central place	4 983 496	18.3	14.5	34.3	93.7	3.4	2 181 437	53.2	21.6	41.0	16.4	9.1	4.1	2.22	2.97
Urban fringe	11 850 605	23.3	11.7	34.3	91.5	1.5	4 505 374	70.7	32.3	58.7	26.9	9.0	4.3	2.60	3.10
1,000,000 to 2,499,999	28 061 318	22.6	14.0	34.4	91.6	2.0	11 233 137	65.9	29.4	53.6	23.2	9.3	4.9	2.46	3.02
Central place	10 248 368	20.6	15.2	34.2	92.7	3.1	4 297 849	58.8	25.1	45.7	18.8	9.8	5.0	2.32	2.98
Urban fringe	17 812 950	23.7	13.3	34.5	91.0	1.4	6 935 288	70.4	32.0	58.5	26.0	9.0	4.8	2.54	3.03
Less than 1,000,000	52 002 827	23.1	14.0	33.6	90.3	3.2	20 477 297	66.9	30.4	54.5	23.9	9.6	5.3	2.46	3.01
Central place	28 492 436	22.1	14.6	33.0	89.0	4.1	11 560 193	62.4	28.2	49.4	21.2	10.2	5.8	2.37	2.98
Urban fringe	23 510 391	24.3	13.4	34.3	92.0	2.2	8 917 104	72.7	33.3	61.1	27.3	8.9	4.8	2.58	3.05
500,000 to 999,999	14 060 661	23.0	13.7	33.8	90.5	2.5	5 599 143	66.3	29.9	53.8	23.6	9.6	5.1	2.46	3.03
Central place	6 435 430	21.3	14.2	33.1	90.1	3.6	2 683 850	60.0	26.4	46.6	19.6	10.4	5.6	2.32	2.97
Urban fringe	7 625 231	24.5	13.3	34.4	90.8	1.6	2 915 293	72.0	33.1	60.5	27.3	8.9	4.7	2.58	3.07
250,000 to 499,999	12 264 139	23.2	14.2	34.1	89.8	2.8	4 836 001	67.6	30.5	55.0	24.0	9.8	5.3	2.47	3.02
Central place	5 969 730	22.1	15.0	33.7	88.4	3.6	2 445 935	62.4	27.8	49.1	20.7	10.4	5.8	2.36	2.98
Urban fringe	6 294 409	24.3	13.5	34.4	91.3	1.9	2 390 066	72.9	33.3	61.1	27.3	9.1	4.8	2.59	3.06
100,000 to 249,999	15 534 992	23.1	13.6	33.1	91.2	3.7	6 064 730	66.8	30.7	54.5	24.1	9.5	5.3	2.48	3.02
Central place	9 346 512	22.5	14.2	32.7	89.4	4.1	3 744 783	63.1	28.9	50.3	22.0	10.0	5.7	2.40	3.00
Urban fringe	6 188 480	24.1	12.7	33.8	94.0	3.0	2 319 947	72.8	33.6	61.3	27.6	8.7	4.7	2.59	3.05
Less than 100,000	10 143 035	23.0	14.8	33.5	89.5	4.1	3 977 423	67.0	30.6	54.7	23.6	9.7	5.7	2.45	2.98
Central place	6 740 764	22.4	15.0	32.8	88.1	4.8	2 685 625	63.9	29.2	51.2	22.0	10.0	6.0	2.40	2.97
Urban fringe	3 402 271	24.3	14.6	34.7	92.3	2.8	1 291 798	73.5	33.4	61.9	27.0	8.9	5.1	2.57	3.01
INSIDE AND OUTSIDE METROPOLITAN AREA															
Inside metropolitan area	150 863 170	23.3	13.4	34.2	92.2	2.4	58 333 897	68.5	31.0	56.4	25.1	9.1	4.7	2.53	3.07
In central city	51 452 071	20.9	15.0	33.9	90.6	3.6	21 323 382	59.6	25.8	46.5	19.4	10.0	5.2	2.33	2.99
Not in central city	99 411 099	24.6	12.6	34.4	93.1	1.8	37 010 515	73.6	34.0	62.1	28.4	8.5	4.4	2.64	3.10
Urban	74 886 399	23.8	13.2	34.4	91.4	1.9	28 390 886	71.6	32.6	59.6	26.8	9.1	4.6	2.59	3.08
Inside urbanized area	67 365 275	23.6	13.1	34.5	91.7	1.7	25 573 614	71.6	32.3	59.7	26.7	9.0	4.5	2.60	3.08
Outside urbanized area	7 521 124	25.8	14.6	33.3	89.4	3.3	2 817 272	71.7	34.9	59.1	27.6	9.7	5.8	2.59	3.08
Rural	24 524 700	26.9	10.8	34.3	98.7	1.5	8 619 629	80.2	38.8	70.4	33.7	6.9	3.6	2.81	3.16
Outside metropolitan area	48 822 900	25.5	15.5	35.0	92.7	2.9	18 546 208	72.8	33.8	61.8	27.7	8.2	4.7	2.56	3.04
Urban	17 538 683	23.6	17.5	34.4	86.4	5.2	6 923 987	66.2	30.6	53.7	23.3	9.9	6.0	2.41	2.98
Inside urbanized area	1 267 155	22.3	15.5	33.2	93.0	4.8	495 534	66.5	29.3	55.5	23.1	8.6	5.0	2.44	2.96
Outside urbanized area	16 271 528	23.7	17.6	34.5	85.9	5.2	6 428 453	66.2	30.7	53.6	23.3	10.0	6.1	2.41	2.98
Place of 10,000 or more	8 245 260	23.2	16.3	33.2	87.2	6.1	3 234 124	65.0	30.4	52.4	23.0	10.0	6.1	2.40	2.98
Place of 2,500 to 9,999	8 026 268	24.3	19.1	35.9	84.6	4.3	3 194 329	67.4	31.0	54.8	23.7	10.0	6.1	2.41	2.98
Rural	31 284 217	26.5	14.4	35.3	96.6	1.6	11 622 221	76.7	35.6	66.7	30.3	7.1	3.9	2.65	3.07
POPULATION SIZE CLASS OF METROPOLITAN AREA															
1,000,000 or more	94 402 349	22.9	13.3	34.4	92.5	2.1	36 587 278	67.6	30.3	55.4	24.6	9.1	4.5	2.53	3.09
In central city	29 171 220	19.9	15.2	34.4	92.2	3.0	12 266 573	57.5	24.0	44.2	18.1	9.9	4.8	2.31	3.01
Not in central city	65 231 129	24.2	12.5	34.4	92.6	1.6	24 320 705	72.7	33.4	61.0	27.9	8.7	4.3	2.64	3.12
5,000,000 or more	36 734 791	21.9	14.1	35.1	92.9	2.1	14 132 945	66.9	28.7	54.2	23.5	9.2	4.1	2.55	3.13
In central city	12 050 920	19.3	16.0	35.4	92.6	2.6	5 024 912	57.0	22.9	43.2	17.4	10.0	4.3	2.34	3.07
Not in central city	24 683 871	23.2	13.2	35.0	93.0	1.8	9 108 033	72.3	31.9	60.3	26.8	8.8	3.9	2.67	3.15
2,500,000 to 4,999,999	24 218 918	23.1	12.1	33.9	92.7	1.8	9 420 776	67.7	31.1	55.8	25.4	8.9	4.5	2.53	3.08
In central city	6 113 253	19.0	14.8	34.1	92.7	3.4	2 639 642	55.2	22.8	42.5	16.9	9.5	4.7	2.24	2.96
Not in central city	18 105 665	24.5	11.2	33.8	92.6	1.3	6 781 134	72.6	34.3	61.0	28.7	8.7	4.4	2.64	3.11
1,000,000 to 2,499,999	33 448 640	23.8	13.4	34.0	92.0	2.3	13 033 557	68.4	31.4	56.3	25.2	9.1	4.9	2.52	3.05
In central city	11 007 047	21.2	14.6	33.4	91.5	3.3	4 602 019	59.4	26.1	46.3	19.5	10.0	5.3	2.32	2.98
Not in central city	22 441 593	25.0	12.8	34.2	92.2	1.7	8 431 538	73.3	34.2	61.8	28.3	8.7	4.7	2.62	3.08
Less than 1,000,000	56 460 821	24.1	13.6	33.8	91.8	2.9	21 746 619	70.0	32.3	58.2	26.0	9.0	5.1	2.53	3.03
In central city	22 280 851	22.1	14.7	33.2	88.6	4.3	9 056 809	62.5	28.2	49.6	21.2	10.1	5.8	2.36	2.97
Not in central city	34 179 970	25.4	12.9	34.3	94.1	2.1	12 689 810	75.3	35.3	64.3	29.4	8.2	4.5	2.64	3.07
500,000 to 999,999	19 725 324	23.5	13.3	34.0	91.5	2.6	7 697 165	69.3	31.7	57.5	25.6	9.0	4.8	2.50	3.02
In central city	7 114 029	21.0	14.8	33.6	88.8	4.0	2 959 624	60.8	26.4	47.8	19.9	10.1	5.3	2.31	2.95
Not in central city	12 611 295	24.9	12.5	34.3	93.1	1.8	4 737 541	74.6	35.0	63.5	29.2	8.4	4.5	2.62	3.06
250,000 to 499,999	18 093 596	24.4	14.2	34.2	91.8	2.7	6 910 423	70.9	32.4	58.9	26.0	9.1	5.1	2.55	3.05
In central city	6 679 010	22.9	15.1	33.5	88.3	3.7	2 689 303	63.7	28.9	50.3	21.6	10.5	6.0	2.40	3.00
Not in central city	11 414 586	25.3	13.6	34.6	93.9	2.1	4 221 120	75.5	34.7	64.4	28.8	8.3	4.6	2.65	3.08
100,000 to 249,999	16 745 333	24.3	13.4	33.3	92.3	3.5	6 413 108	69.9	32.8	58.3	26.3	8.9	5.2	2.53	3.03
In central city	7 361 451	22.3	14.3	32.4	88.7	4.9	2 958 245	62.9	29.0	50.4	21.9	9.9	5.9	2.37	2.97
Not in central city	9 383 882	25.9	12.7	34.1	95.4	2.4	3 454 863	75.9	36.1	65.1	30.1	8.0	4.6	2.66	3.08
Less than 100,000	1 896 568	25.0	13.3	33.0	90.5	3.8	725 923	69.3	33.7	57.6	26.9	9.1	5.6	2.52	3.05
In central city	1 126 361	23.3	14.7	32.8	86.8	4.8	449 637	64.3	30.4	51.6	22.9	10.2	6.3	2.39	2.98
Not in central city	770 207	27.5	11.3	33.3	96.4	2.4	276 286	77.4	39.1	67.4	33.3	7.4	4.4	2.73	3.13

Table 8. Summary of General Characteristics of Black Persons and Households: 1990

[For definitions of terms and meanings of symbols, see text]

United States — Urban and Rural and Size of Place — Population Size Class of Urbanized Area — Inside and Outside Metropolitan Area — Population Size Class of Metropolitan Area	All Black persons						All households with a Black householder						Persons per—	
	Total	Percent of all persons Under 18 years	65 years and over	Median age	Persons 18 years and over—Males per 100 females	Percent in group quarters	Total	Family households as a percent of all households Total	Married-couple family Total	Married-couple family With own children under 18 years	Female householder, no husband present Total	Female householder, no husband present With own children under 18 years	House-hold	Family
United States	29 986 060	32.0	8.4	28.1	84.1	4.2	9 976 161	70.0	39.2	34.2	17.8	30.6	19.0	2.87	3.48
URBAN AND RURAL AND SIZE OF PLACE															
Urban	26 153 444	32.0	8.0	28.0	82.1	3.7	8 836 740	69.3	39.1	32.8	17.1	31.2	19.7	2.84	3.45
Inside urbanized area	23 533 536	31.7	7.8	28.2	82.0	3.4	7 996 181	69.1	38.9	32.8	17.0	31.0	19.5	2.84	3.44
Central place	17 308 291	31.7	8.7	28.4	79.9	3.2	5 970 947	67.6	37.2	29.6	14.5	32.7	20.4	2.80	3.44
Urban fringe	6 225 245	31.9	5.4	27.9	88.3	4.0	2 025 234	73.5	43.8	42.2	24.4	26.0	16.8	2.95	3.44
Outside urbanized area	2 619 908	34.3	10.1	26.2	82.9	6.8	840 559	71.3	41.7	33.5	18.2	33.1	21.4	2.91	3.52
Place of 10,000 or more	1 366 724	34.0	9.6	25.9	85.2	7.5	441 625	70.3	41.7	33.3	18.3	32.4	21.3	2.86	3.48
Place of 2,500 to 9,999	1 253 184	34.7	10.8	26.5	80.4	6.0	398 934	72.4	41.6	33.7	18.0	33.9	21.5	2.95	3.56
Rural	3 832 616	31.8	10.7	28.9	99.1	7.5	1 139 421	75.8	39.4	44.7	23.2	25.8	14.0	3.11	3.66
Place of 1,000 to 2,499	447 585	34.6	11.7	27.2	80.1	4.5	143 168	72.3	39.7	34.8	17.9	32.7	19.7	2.98	3.61
Place of less than 1,000	205 368	34.7	13.2	28.3	77.5	2.1	67 033	72.2	37.9	36.1	18.3	30.9	17.5	3.00	3.65
Other rural	3 179 663	31.3	10.3	29.1	103.5	8.2	929 220	76.6	39.5	46.8	24.4	24.4	12.9	3.14	3.67
POPULATION SIZE CLASS OF URBANIZED AREA															
1,000,000 or more	15 387 703	30.8	7.8	28.9	81.5	2.9	5 252 282	68.4	37.5	32.1	16.3	30.8	18.8	2.84	3.45
Central place	10 879 622	30.6	8.9	29.2	79.7	2.8	3 768 376	66.7	35.5	28.4	13.4	32.6	19.7	2.80	3.46
Urban fringe	4 508 081	31.3	5.2	28.4	85.9	3.1	1 483 906	72.8	42.7	41.4	23.6	26.1	16.5	2.93	3.44
5,000,000 or more	5 705 341	29.7	8.0	29.6	79.6	2.9	1 912 046	68.5	36.2	31.6	15.6	31.1	18.2	2.89	3.52
Central place	4 293 698	29.7	8.6	29.6	78.0	2.7	1 463 187	67.0	35.0	28.6	13.7	32.5	19.0	2.05	3.52
Urban fringe	1 411 643	29.6	6.3	29.3	84.4	3.6	448 859	73.5	40.1	41.3	22.0	26.5	15.5	3.02	3.51
2,500 to 4,999,999	4 536 123	29.9	8.2	29.4	82.1	2.8	1 588 712	67.4	36.2	31.8	15.9	30.0	18.0	2.77	3.40
Central place	3 267 559	29.7	9.5	29.7	80.0	2.5	1 158 641	65.7	33.9	28.0	12.8	32.0	18.9	2.74	3.41
Urban fringe	1 268 564	30.4	4.8	28.8	87.7	3.4	430 071	71.7	42.2	42.1	24.2	24.5	15.5	2.84	3.35
1,000,000 to 2,499,999	5 146 239	32.8	7.3	27.8	83.1	3.0	1 751 524	69.4	40.1	32.9	17.4	31.1	20.2	2.84	3.43
Central place	3 318 365	32.5	8.7	28.0	81.6	3.3	1 146 548	67.4	37.6	28.7	13.8	33.4	21.4	2.79	3.43
Urban fringe	1 827 874	33.3	4.7	27.3	85.9	2.5	604 976	73.1	45.0	41.0	24.2	26.8	18.0	2.94	3.44
Less than 1,000,000	8 145 833	33.5	7.7	26.9	83.1	4.3	2 743 899	70.3	41.5	34.0	18.5	31.5	20.8	2.84	3.42
Central place	6 428 669	33.5	8.3	27.0	80.2	3.8	2 202 571	69.0	40.2	31.5	16.5	32.8	21.6	2.80	3.42
Urban fringe	1 717 164	33.4	5.7	26.5	95.0	6.4	541 328	75.3	46.7	44.5	26.7	26.0	17.6	2.97	3.45
500,000 to 999,999	2 594 678	32.9	8.0	27.7	80.9	3.0	903 037	69.1	40.0	32.7	17.2	31.6	20.7	2.78	3.39
Central place	2 108 473	32.7	8.7	27.9	79.2	2.9	743 180	67.9	38.6	30.1	15.1	33.0	21.4	2.75	3.38
Urban fringe	486 205	33.8	5.4	27.2	89.1	3.6	159 857	74.7	46.5	44.5	26.7	25.3	17.3	2.93	3.41
250,000 to 499,999	2 166 471	34.0	7.4	26.7	82.2	3.9	722 006	71.1	42.1	34.3	18.8	31.9	21.1	2.88	3.46
Central place	1 614 142	34.1	7.9	26.8	79.5	3.5	546 266	69.7	40.8	31.3	16.6	33.5	22.0	2.84	3.45
Urban fringe	552 329	33.8	5.8	26.6	90.4	5.1	175 740	75.4	46.2	43.6	25.8	27.1	18.1	2.98	3.47
100,000 to 249,999	2 218 683	33.5	7.5	26.2	85.2	5.4	735 786	70.5	42.1	35.0	19.4	30.9	20.6	2.85	3.43
Central place	1 762 876	33.6	8.0	26.5	81.0	4.4	596 970	69.4	40.9	32.6	17.4	32.1	21.4	2.82	3.42
Urban fringe	455 807	32.9	5.5	25.5	103.6	9.4	138 816	75.1	47.6	45.1	27.7	25.5	17.5	2.98	3.46
Less than 100,000	1 166 001	33.9	8.2	26.4	85.8	5.9	383 070	71.1	42.3	35.1	19.2	31.4	20.9	2.86	3.44
Central place	943 178	34.1	8.6	26.2	82.1	5.1	316 155	69.9	41.4	32.8	17.6	32.5	21.7	2.82	3.43
Urban fringe	222 823	32.9	6.8	26.8	103.0	9.2	66 915	76.6	46.8	45.9	27.1	25.9	17.2	3.03	3.49
INSIDE AND OUTSIDE METROPOLITAN AREA															
Inside metropolitan area	25 122 054	31.7	7.9	28.2	83.4	3.8	8 455 952	69.5	39.0	33.5	17.4	30.7	19.2	2.85	3.45
In central city	17 169 430	31.6	8.7	28.4	79.9	3.2	5 925 383	67.5	37.2	29.5	14.5	32.7	20.4	2.80	3.44
Not in central city	7 952 624	31.7	6.2	28.0	91.4	5.3	2 530 569	74.0	43.2	42.8	24.3	26.0	16.3	2.97	3.47
Urban	6 790 086	32.0	5.6	27.7	88.2	4.3	2 201 473	73.5	43.7	41.9	24.1	26.4	17.0	2.95	3.45
Inside urbanized area	6 235 478	31.9	5.4	27.8	88.3	4.0	2 028 435	73.5	43.8	42.2	24.4	26.1	16.8	2.95	3.44
Outside urbanized area	554 608	33.6	8.8	26.4	87.1	7.1	173 038	73.5	43.0	37.9	21.0	30.5	19.4	2.98	3.52
Rural	1 162 538	29.7	9.5	29.6	111.7	11.3	329 096	77.3	39.4	49.0	25.4	22.9	11.9	3.13	3.62
Outside metropolitan area	4 864 006	33.5	10.8	27.4	88.2	6.1	1 520 209	73.2	40.3	38.0	20.1	30.1	18.1	3.00	3.60
Urban	2 203 157	34.3	10.4	26.2	81.7	6.6	712 516	70.8	41.3	32.6	17.6	33.6	21.7	2.89	3.51
Inside urbanized area	201 221	32.9	8.6	26.8	83.4	6.8	65 249	71.7	41.7	35.5	19.5	31.7	20.2	2.87	3.44
Outside urbanized area	2 001 936	34.5	10.5	26.1	81.5	6.6	647 267	70.7	41.3	32.4	17.4	33.8	21.9	2.89	3.52
Place of 10,000 or more	1 052 836	34.1	9.8	25.7	84.3	7.5	341 554	69.9	41.5	32.5	17.9	32.9	21.6	2.85	3.49
Place of 2,500 to 9,999	949 100	34.9	11.3	26.6	78.6	5.5	305 713	71.7	41.0	32.1	16.9	34.9	22.1	2.93	3.56
Rural	2 660 849	32.8	11.2	28.5	93.8	5.8	807 693	75.2	39.4	42.8	22.3	27.0	14.9	3.10	3.68
POPULATION SIZE CLASS OF METROPOLITAN AREA															
1,000,000 or more	17 638 128	31.0	7.8	28.7	82.7	3.4	5 981 262	68.8	37.9	32.6	16.7	30.6	18.9	2.84	3.45
In central city	12 140 180	30.8	8.7	29.0	79.9	2.9	4 204 163	66.9	35.9	28.6	13.7	32.7	19.9	2.80	3.45
Not in central city	5 497 948	31.3	5.6	28.3	89.2	4.4	1 777 099	73.3	42.7	42.0	23.8	25.8	16.3	2.95	3.45
5,000,000 or more	7 705 099	29.8	8.2	29.5	81.6	3.5	2 580 861	68.6	36.2	32.0	15.8	30.8	18.0	2.87	3.49
In central city	5 585 464	29.8	8.8	29.7	78.8	2.8	1 909 758	66.9	34.7	28.5	13.5	32.5	18.8	2.84	3.50
Not in central city	2 119 635	29.9	6.4	29.0	89.4	5.3	671 103	73.4	40.5	41.9	22.3	26.0	15.5	2.98	3.47
2,500 to 4,999,999	5 368 985	31.1	7.2	28.6	83.0	2.8	1 844 955	68.7	38.7	33.6	17.8	29.5	18.4	2.82	3.43
In central city	3 202 461	30.6	8.9	29.1	80.8	2.7	1 129 432	66.1	35.4	28.3	13.2	32.1	19.8	2.75	3.42
Not in central city	2 166 524	31.8	4.6	28.0	86.5	2.9	715 523	72.7	44.0	42.0	25.0	25.4	16.3	2.94	3.45
1,000,000 to 2,499,999	4 564 044	32.8	7.8	27.6	84.1	3.8	1 555 446	69.3	39.9	32.5	16.8	31.7	20.8	2.81	3.41
In central city	3 352 255	32.9	8.4	27.7	80.8	3.1	1 164 973	67.7	38.4	29.2	14.3	33.5	21.9	2.78	3.41
Not in central city	1 211 789	32.7	6.1	27.6	94.1	5.8	390 473	74.0	44.2	42.5	24.0	26.5	17.7	2.92	3.41
Less than 1,000,000	7 483 926	33.3	8.2	27.0	85.1	5.0	2 474 690	71.1	41.4	35.6	19.3	30.8	19.9	2.87	3.46
In central city	5 029 250	33.6	8.5	26.9	79.9	3.9	1 721 220	69.1	40.2	31.7	16.6	32.7	21.5	2.80	3.42
Not in central city	2 454 676	32.7	7.6	27.3	96.6	7.2	753 470	75.7	44.2	44.6	25.5	26.2	16.4	3.02	3.53
500,000 to 999,999	3 351 612	32.5	8.3	27.6	82.7	4.1	1 136 147	70.2	40.1	34.7	18.5	30.7	19.5	2.83	3.42
In central city	2 336 258	32.5	8.7	27.6	78.6	3.5	814 418	68.2	38.7	30.8	15.7	32.7	21.0	2.77	3.39
Not in central city	1 015 354	32.4	7.4	27.7	92.9	5.6	321 729	75.2	43.7	44.5	25.4	25.6	16.0	2.98	3.48
250,000 to 499,999	2 174 861	34.3	7.8	26.7	86.2	5.2	704 863	72.2	42.7	36.3	20.0	31.1	20.6	2.92	3.49
In central city	1 387 488	34.9	8.2	26.5	80.3	3.6	468 127	70.2	41.6	32.2	17.1	33.3	22.4	2.85	3.45
Not in central city	787 373	33.2	7.1	26.8	97.4	8.0	236 736	76.0	44.9	44.5	25.7	26.8	17.0	3.06	3.56
100,000 to 249,999	1 819 417	33.6	8.4	26.4	88.1	6.3	588 034	71.7	42.2	36.6	20.1	30.5	20.0	2.90	3.48
In central city	1 191 268	34.2	8.4	26.0	81.6	5.0	400 177	69.6	41.3	32.8	17.7	32.3	21.6	2.82	3.43
Not in central city	628 149	32.6	8.3	27.1	101.3	8.6	187 857	76.2	44.2	44.6	25.3	26.7	16.6	3.06	3.56
Less than 100,000	138 036	33.9	9.9	26.2	87.7	6.1	45 646	69.6	41.1	35.5	19.6	29.4	19.4	2.83	3.47
In central city	114 236	34.5	9.4	25.8	82.5	4.9	38 498	69.0	41.7	33.1	18.4	31.2	21.1	2.81	3.46
Not in central city	23 800	31.2	12.1	28.2	115.9	11.5	7 148	72.9	38.1	48.5	25.9	19.7	10.4	2.95	3.54

Table 9. Summary of General Characteristics of American Indian, Eskimo, or Aleut Persons and Households: 1990

[For definitions of terms and meanings of symbols, see text]

United States / Urban and Rural and Size of Place / Population Size Class of Urbanized Area / Inside and Outside Metropolitan Area / Population Size Class of Metropolitan Area	All American Indian, Eskimo, or Aleut persons						All households with an American Indian, Eskimo, or Aleut householder								
		Percent of all persons			Persons 18 years and over—			Family households as a percent of all households						Persons per—	
										Married-couple family		Female householder, no husband present			
	Total	Under 18 years	65 years and over	Median age	Males per 100 females	Percent in group quarters	Total	Total	With own children under 18 years	Total	With own children under 18 years	Total	With own children under 18 years	House-hold	Family
United States	1 959 234	35.6	5.8	26.2	94.2	2.9	591 372	74.8	45.1	48.0	28.1	20.4	13.3	3.12	3.60
URBAN AND RURAL AND SIZE OF PLACE															
Urban	1 100 534	33.1	5.4	26.8	92.5	3.7	349 899	70.9	42.7	44.3	25.3	20.9	14.1	2.93	3.44
Inside urbanized area	768 135	31.1	5.1	27.7	93.6	3.6	252 845	69.3	40.6	43.2	23.9	20.4	13.6	2.86	3.37
Central place	468 915	31.6	5.3	27.1	92.3	4.2	155 508	66.3	39.6	37.8	21.0	22.6	15.4	2.81	3.38
Urban fringe	299 220	30.2	4.9	28.7	95.4	2.6	97 337	74.1	42.4	51.8	28.7	16.8	10.8	2.94	3.36
Outside urbanized area	332 399	37.8	6.1	24.7	89.8	4.1	97 054	75.1	48.1	47.1	28.9	22.2	15.5	3.13	3.61
Place of 10,000 or more	134 735	35.4	6.3	25.2	89.7	5.4	42 111	71.5	45.0	45.0	26.4	21.3	15.3	2.87	3.38
Place of 2,500 to 9,999	197 664	39.5	6.0	24.2	89.9	3.3	54 943	77.9	50.5	48.7	30.9	23.0	15.7	3.32	3.78
Rural	858 700	38.7	6.4	25.3	96.7	1.8	241 473	80.3	48.5	53.4	32.0	19.8	12.2	3.39	3.80
Place of 1,000 to 2,499	108 037	40.0	6.4	24.3	90.1	2.0	31 067	78.5	50.1	47.0	29.4	24.3	16.2	3.32	3.76
Place of less than 1,000	140 600	42.2	6.2	23.1	97.1	.9	37 317	80.3	51.2	47.5	30.7	23.8	15.1	3.63	4.07
Other rural	610 063	37.7	6.4	26.0	97.8	1.9	173 089	80.7	47.6	55.8	32.8	18.2	10.8	3.35	3.75
POPULATION SIZE CLASS OF URBANIZED AREA															
1,000,000 or more	389 044	29.7	5.1	28.4	93.9	3.0	128 575	68.6	39.1	42.0	23.0	20.4	13.0	2.89	3.41
Central place	207 148	30.2	5.3	27.7	93.6	3.8	68 687	64.6	37.5	34.6	19.1	23.3	15.1	2.85	3.45
Urban fringe	181 896	29.0	4.9	29.3	94.3	2.0	59 888	73.1	40.9	50.4	27.4	17.0	10.6	2.94	3.37
5,000,000 or more	113 011	28.0	6.0	29.4	93.9	2.5	36 625	69.0	37.4	41.6	22.8	20.3	11.6	2.99	3.53
Central place	62 270	28.0	6.1	29.2	94.0	3.0	20 455	65.5	35.7	35.8	20.2	22.2	12.6	2.94	3.56
Urban fringe	50 741	27.9	5.8	29.6	93.7	2.0	16 170	73.4	39.5	49.0	26.1	18.1	10.4	3.06	3.50
2,500,000 to 4,999,999	79 264	26.2	5.6	30.3	94.1	2.9	28 181	66.5	35.3	43.5	22.6	17.8	10.3	2.74	3.30
Central place	34 199	25.4	6.7	30.2	94.3	4.2	12 718	59.7	31.0	34.1	16.8	20.5	12.0	2.62	3.32
Urban fringe	45 065	26.8	4.9	30.4	94.0	1.9	15 463	72.1	38.9	51.3	27.4	15.6	9.0	2.83	3.28
1,000,000 to 2,499,999	196 769	32.1	4.4	27.1	93.9	3.2	63 769	69.2	41.8	41.5	23.3	21.5	15.0	2.91	3.39
Central place	110 679	33.0	4.4	26.2	93.1	4.2	35 514	65.9	40.9	34.1	19.3	25.0	17.7	2.88	3.44
Urban fringe	86 090	30.9	4.3	28.4	94.9	2.0	28 255	73.4	42.9	50.7	28.3	17.2	11.6	2.93	3.35
Less than 1,000,000	379 091	32.5	5.2	26.8	93.1	4.2	124 270	70.1	42.2	44.4	24.9	20.3	14.2	2.83	3.32
Central place	261 767	32.7	5.3	26.5	91.3	4.5	86 821	67.7	41.2	40.3	22.4	22.1	15.6	2.78	3.32
Urban fringe	117 324	32.1	5.0	27.7	97.3	3.5	37 449	75.7	44.7	54.1	30.6	16.4	11.0	2.94	3.34
500,000 to 999,999	95 114	32.1	5.5	27.4	92.8	3.1	31 920	69.1	40.3	44.3	24.4	19.5	13.0	2.79	3.33
Central place	59 119	31.4	5.8	27.5	92.3	3.8	20 534	65.7	38.1	39.1	20.9	21.2	14.3	2.71	3.31
Urban fringe	35 995	33.2	5.1	27.3	93.7	2.0	11 386	75.3	44.2	53.7	30.7	16.4	10.6	2.94	3.37
250,000 to 499,999	105 896	32.4	5.6	27.1	90.7	3.3	35 206	70.4	41.6	45.2	24.9	19.8	13.5	2.81	3.31
Central place	71 368	32.6	5.7	26.7	88.1	3.3	24 057	67.7	40.1	40.6	22.1	21.6	14.8	2.76	3.30
Urban fringe	34 528	32.2	5.2	28.1	96.3	3.2	11 149	76.3	44.9	55.0	31.0	15.8	10.7	2.93	3.32
100,000 to 249,999	100 675	32.0	4.6	26.8	95.2	5.2	32 531	69.7	43.0	44.0	25.0	20.5	14.9	2.84	3.32
Central place	72 491	32.8	4.6	26.4	92.6	5.3	23 458	67.8	42.6	40.1	23.0	22.4	16.5	2.81	3.32
Urban fringe	28 184	29.8	4.6	28.1	101.9	4.9	9 073	74.7	43.9	54.0	30.2	15.7	10.8	2.91	3.31
Less than 100,000	77 406	33.7	5.1	25.7	94.2	5.5	24 613	71.5	44.7	44.1	25.2	22.1	16.1	2.89	3.35
Central place	58 789	33.9	5.1	25.4	92.8	5.8	18 772	69.9	44.2	41.2	23.6	23.2	17.1	2.86	3.35
Urban fringe	18 617	33.2	5.1	26.8	98.9	4.5	5 841	76.8	46.5	53.2	30.3	18.4	13.0	2.99	3.34
INSIDE AND OUTSIDE METROPOLITAN AREA															
Inside metropolitan area	1 002 984	31.9	5.4	27.7	94.8	3.4	323 542	71.5	41.8	46.2	25.7	19.5	12.9	2.92	3.40
In central city	465 364	31.6	5.3	27.1	92.2	4.2	154 315	66.3	39.5	37.7	20.9	22.7	15.4	2.81	3.38
Not in central city	537 620	32.2	5.4	28.3	97.0	2.7	169 227	76.3	43.8	54.0	30.0	16.6	10.6	3.02	3.42
Urban	366 132	31.1	5.2	28.3	95.0	2.6	118 225	74.6	43.1	52.0	28.9	17.1	11.2	2.96	3.37
Inside urbanized area	302 903	30.2	4.9	28.7	95.5	2.5	98 568	74.2	42.4	51.9	28.7	16.7	10.7	2.94	3.36
Outside urbanized area	63 229	35.3	6.4	26.7	92.6	2.8	19 657	77.0	46.6	52.4	30.1	19.1	13.3	3.05	3.44
Rural	171 488	34.5	5.9	28.3	101.7	2.9	51 002	80.0	45.4	58.5	32.5	15.4	9.4	3.17	3.52
Outside metropolitan area	956 250	39.4	6.3	24.4	93.6	2.3	267 830	78.7	49.0	50.1	30.9	21.6	13.8	3.36	3.82
Urban	270 174	38.3	6.0	24.2	89.3	4.5	77 696	74.5	48.4	45.6	28.5	23.0	16.1	3.14	3.65
Inside urbanized area	8 925	33.4	4.9	25.4	96.6	5.0	2 815	69.8	44.2	44.3	25.9	19.6	14.6	2.86	3.34
Outside urbanized area	261 249	38.5	6.0	24.1	89.0	4.5	74 881	74.7	48.6	45.7	28.6	23.1	16.2	3.15	3.67
Place of 10,000 or more	106 069	35.8	6.3	24.8	88.3	5.8	32 868	70.4	44.9	43.1	25.5	22.1	16.1	2.85	3.38
Place of 2,500 to 9,999	155 180	40.3	5.8	23.6	89.6	3.6	42 013	78.0	51.5	47.7	31.1	23.9	16.3	3.39	3.87
Rural	686 076	39.8	6.5	24.6	95.3	1.5	190 134	80.4	49.3	52.0	31.9	21.0	12.9	3.45	3.88
POPULATION SIZE CLASS OF METROPOLITAN AREA															
1,000,000 or more	530 902	30.3	5.1	28.4	95.4	3.2	173 535	70.1	40.4	44.1	24.4	19.8	12.8	2.93	3.42
In central city	241 540	30.4	5.3	27.7	93.6	3.8	80 394	64.9	38.0	35.1	19.4	23.3	15.3	2.85	3.44
Not in central city	289 362	30.2	5.0	29.0	97.0	2.7	93 141	74.6	42.4	52.0	28.6	16.8	10.6	3.00	3.41
5,000,000 or more	201 590	28.3	5.9	29.5	94.7	2.9	65 905	70.0	38.4	44.2	23.9	19.3	11.4	2.97	3.47
In central city	91 201	27.9	6.1	29.2	94.1	3.4	30 249	65.5	36.0	36.6	20.3	21.8	12.7	2.91	3.51
Not in central city	110 389	28.7	5.7	29.7	95.3	2.4	35 656	73.8	40.4	50.6	27.0	17.1	10.2	3.02	3.44
2,500,000 to 4,999,999	114 976	29.0	4.9	29.3	95.8	2.9	39 230	69.4	39.0	46.2	25.1	17.9	11.3	2.82	3.32
In central city	42 873	28.0	5.8	29.0	94.2	4.2	15 312	60.9	33.3	34.0	17.1	21.6	13.6	2.64	3.30
Not in central city	72 103	29.5	4.3	29.4	96.8	2.2	23 918	74.8	42.7	54.1	30.1	15.5	9.8	2.93	3.32
1,000,000 to 2,499,999	214 336	32.9	4.6	26.8	95.8	3.7	68 400	70.7	43.0	42.9	24.4	21.5	15.1	2.95	3.43
In central city	107 466	33.5	4.3	25.9	92.8	4.1	34 833	66.2	41.8	34.2	19.7	25.4	18.3	2.88	3.43
Not in central city	106 870	32.4	4.8	27.8	98.9	3.4	33 567	75.3	44.3	51.9	29.3	17.5	11.7	3.02	3.42
Less than 1,000,000	472 082	33.8	5.7	26.9	94.0	3.6	150 007	73.1	43.4	48.6	27.2	19.1	13.1	2.92	3.38
In central city	223 824	33.0	5.4	26.4	90.8	4.6	73 921	67.8	41.2	40.6	22.6	21.9	15.5	2.77	3.31
Not in central city	248 258	34.5	5.9	27.5	97.1	2.6	76 086	78.3	45.6	56.4	31.7	16.3	10.7	3.06	3.44
500,000 to 999,999	188 446	33.4	6.3	27.5	93.0	2.6	61 285	72.8	41.4	49.9	27.1	17.6	11.4	2.86	3.35
In central city	82 651	31.7	6.3	27.6	90.5	3.2	28 664	67.0	38.0	42.4	22.3	19.7	13.0	2.70	3.27
Not in central city	105 795	34.8	6.3	27.5	95.0	2.0	32 621	77.8	44.3	56.6	31.3	15.9	10.0	3.01	3.40
250,000 to 499,999	115 866	31.9	5.4	27.4	95.3	3.8	37 521	72.7	43.2	47.9	26.9	19.1	13.1	2.93	3.37
In central city	56 851	32.0	5.2	26.4	91.8	4.5	18 844	67.8	41.6	40.4	22.8	21.6	15.3	2.82	3.34
Not in central city	59 015	31.9	5.7	28.6	98.8	3.1	18 677	77.6	44.9	55.6	30.9	16.6	10.8	3.03	3.40
100,000 to 249,999	146 185	35.0	5.2	26.2	95.0	4.1	44 976	73.8	45.4	48.3	27.8	19.9	14.2	2.97	3.42
In central city	68 103	34.1	4.7	25.8	91.1	5.6	21 739	67.8	43.0	39.2	22.4	23.3	17.3	2.78	3.31
Not in central city	78 082	35.9	5.6	26.7	98.7	2.8	23 237	79.5	47.6	56.8	32.8	16.8	11.3	3.14	3.50
Less than 100,000	21 585	38.0	4.7	23.3	88.9	7.3	6 225	74.6	50.5	42.3	26.2	27.0	20.8	3.02	3.49
In central city	16 219	38.2	4.7	22.8	86.5	7.9	4 674	73.0	50.8	37.4	23.8	30.3	23.4	3.00	3.50
Not in central city	5 366	37.2	4.7	25.3	96.6	5.4	1 551	79.2	49.6	57.1	33.7	17.0	12.7	3.08	3.45

Table 10. Summary of General Characteristics of Asian or Pacific Islander Persons and Households: 1990

[For definitions of terms and meanings of symbols, see text]

United States / Urban and Rural and Size of Place / Population Size Class of Urbanized Area / Inside and Outside Metropolitan Area / Population Size Class of Metropolitan Area	All Asian or Pacific Islander persons						All households with an Asian or Pacific Islander householder								
		Percent of all persons			Persons 18 years and over—			Family households as a percent of all households		Married-couple family		Female householder, no husband present		Persons per—	
	Total	Under 18 years	65 years and over	Median age	Males per 100 females	Percent in group quarters	Total	Total	With own children under 18 years	Total	With own children under 18 years	Total	With own children under 18 years	House-hold	Family
United States	7 273 662	28.6	6.2	29.8	92.6	2.1	2 013 735	77.4	45.5	62.8	39.2	9.5	4.8	3.34	3.80
URBAN AND RURAL AND SIZE OF PLACE															
Urban	6 934 689	28.4	6.2	29.8	93.2	2.0	1 934 866	77.2	45.4	62.6	39.1	9.5	4.8	3.34	3.81
Inside urbanized area	6 507 391	28.2	6.2	30.0	93.2	1.8	1 823 436	77.4	45.4	62.7	39.2	9.5	4.7	3.35	3.81
Central place	3 421 439	26.8	7.2	29.6	95.6	2.5	995 571	72.4	40.1	56.5	33.5	10.3	5.0	3.23	3.80
Urban fringe	3 085 952	29.7	5.1	30.3	90.6	1.1	827 865	83.4	51.8	70.1	46.1	8.5	4.3	3.49	3.82
Outside urbanized area	427 298	31.1	6.6	27.4	91.8	5.2	111 430	75.3	45.5	60.8	37.5	10.0	6.0	3.27	3.77
Place of 10,000 or more	227 888	29.0	6.6	27.4	94.3	6.0	62 955	71.3	42.5	58.1	35.5	9.0	5.4	3.08	3.64
Place of 2,500 to 9,999	199 410	33.5	6.8	27.4	88.8	4.3	48 475	80.4	49.2	64.3	40.2	11.2	6.8	3.52	3.92
Rural	338 973	34.1	6.8	29.6	80.1	3.4	78 869	81.6	48.8	68.9	42.2	8.4	4.7	3.33	3.71
Place of 1,000 to 2,499	65 784	32.8	10.9	30.4	86.7	1.9	17 569	79.1	42.9	63.5	35.0	10.5	5.8	3.28	3.72
Place of less than 1,000	17 286	32.5	10.3	30.4	81.8	4.1	4 208	77.6	39.1	61.1	31.4	10.6	5.4	3.21	3.69
Other rural	255 903	34.5	5.5	29.3	78.3	3.7	57 092	82.7	51.3	71.1	45.2	7.5	4.4	3.36	3.71
POPULATION SIZE CLASS OF URBANIZED AREA															
1,000,000 or more	4 815 262	27.7	6.1	30.4	94.1	1.4	1 355 163	78.2	46.0	63.6	40.1	9.3	4.4	3.38	3.82
Central place	2 347 588	25.9	7.2	30.2	96.4	2.0	686 728	73.1	40.0	57.0	33.8	10.1	4.7	3.26	3.82
Urban fringe	2 467 674	29.5	5.0	30.5	91.9	.9	668 435	83.5	52.2	70.4	46.7	8.3	4.1	3.50	3.83
5,000,000 or more	2 297 774	26.5	6.3	31.1	95.7	1.2	655 466	79.1	45.5	64.4	40.1	9.1	4.0	3.39	3.81
Central place	1 143 533	24.0	7.3	31.2	97.4	1.5	344 618	73.7	38.9	57.5	33.2	9.0	4.2	3.21	3.74
Urban fringe	1 154 241	28.9	5.4	30.9	93.9	.9	310 848	85.1	52.9	72.1	47.8	8.1	3.7	3.59	3.87
2,500,000 to 4,999,999	1 270 383	27.3	6.5	30.6	92.9	1.7	362 354	77.3	45.1	63.2	39.5	9.0	4.2	3.33	3.80
Central place	548 749	24.6	8.5	30.5	95.5	3.1	166 311	69.6	36.5	54.1	30.6	9.9	4.4	3.12	3.78
Urban fringe	721 634	29.4	4.9	30.7	90.8	.7	196 043	83.8	52.5	70.9	47.1	8.2	4.0	3.50	3.82
1,000,000 to 2,499,999	1 247 105	30.5	5.3	28.6	92.4	1.6	337 343	77.6	48.1	62.4	40.8	9.9	5.6	3.41	3.87
Central place	655 306	30.4	6.0	28.0	95.3	1.9	175 799	75.3	45.7	58.8	37.9	10.7	6.1	3.47	4.00
Urban fringe	591 799	30.6	4.5	29.4	89.3	1.2	161 544	80.1	50.6	66.3	43.9	9.0	5.1	3.34	3.75
Less than 1,000,000	1 692 129	29.5	6.5	28.6	90.7	3.0	468 273	74.8	43.5	60.2	36.6	10.2	5.5	3.26	3.77
Central place	1 073 851	28.8	7.1	28.0	93.7	3.6	308 843	70.8	40.2	55.5	33.0	10.6	5.7	3.16	3.76
Urban fringe	618 278	30.7	5.5	29.6	85.7	2.0	159 430	82.7	50.0	69.2	43.5	9.4	5.1	3.45	3.79
500,000 to 999,999	698 114	25.4	9.6	31.6	91.3	2.3	208 783	74.4	37.3	58.8	31.1	10.9	4.9	3.12	3.63
Central place	410 967	22.6	11.7	32.2	92.5	3.3	132 387	68.8	31.0	52.4	24.9	11.7	4.8	2.89	3.50
Urban fringe	287 147	29.6	6.6	30.7	89.5	.9	76 396	84.1	48.3	69.9	41.8	9.7	5.0	3.51	3.81
250,000 to 499,999	352 353	35.2	4.4	26.1	89.1	2.1	89 710	77.5	51.9	62.5	43.4	10.4	6.8	3.53	4.05
Central place	232 973	36.6	4.6	24.8	95.1	2.3	59 159	75.9	51.1	59.7	41.8	11.3	7.5	3.64	4.22
Urban fringe	119 380	32.7	4.1	29.2	78.9	1.8	30 551	80.5	53.5	68.0	46.7	8.8	5.4	3.32	3.73
100,000 to 249,999	433 880	30.1	4.4	27.5	91.2	3.7	116 100	75.3	46.7	61.5	39.6	9.5	5.6	3.28	3.76
Central place	274 240	30.1	4.0	26.8	95.2	4.1	75 703	71.7	45.4	57.8	37.9	9.5	5.9	3.20	3.76
Urban fringe	159 640	30.2	5.1	29.1	84.7	3.0	40 397	81.9	49.0	68.4	42.6	9.5	6.0	3.42	3.77
Less than 100,000	207 782	32.1	3.6	25.0	90.4	5.5	53 680	71.2	47.1	58.8	40.1	8.5	5.5	3.28	3.88
Central place	155 671	31.3	3.6	24.8	92.7	5.5	41 594	68.0	44.5	55.4	37.5	8.6	5.5	3.22	3.87
Urban fringe	52 111	34.6	3.6	26.0	83.5	5.5	12 086	82.1	55.8	70.2	48.9	8.2	5.4	3.51	3.91
INSIDE AND OUTSIDE METROPOLITAN AREA															
Inside metropolitan area	6 823 859	28.5	6.2	29.9	92.7	1.9	1 896 281	77.7	45.7	63.1	39.5	9.5	4.7	3.36	3.81
In central city	3 373 675	26.8	7.2	29.6	95.6	2.5	982 551	72.3	40.1	56.5	33.5	10.3	5.0	3.23	3.80
Not in central city	3 450 184	30.1	5.2	30.2	89.9	1.3	913 730	83.4	51.8	70.1	45.9	8.6	4.4	3.50	3.83
Urban	3 262 758	29.9	5.2	30.2	90.4	1.2	870 648	83.4	51.8	70.0	45.9	8.7	4.4	3.50	3.83
Inside urbanized area	3 125 833	29.7	5.2	30.3	90.6	1.1	838 502	83.4	51.8	70.2	46.0	8.6	4.3	3.50	3.82
Outside urbanized area	136 925	33.6	5.9	26.9	86.2	4.2	32 146	81.8	51.6	66.2	42.9	10.9	6.7	3.64	4.03
Rural	187 426	34.2	5.7	29.7	81.3	2.9	43 082	83.9	52.4	72.8	46.8	7.2	4.0	3.44	3.77
Outside metropolitan area	449 803	30.8	7.3	27.9	89.7	5.4	117 454	73.6	42.7	59.6	35.2	9.5	5.6	3.11	3.62
Urban	298 962	29.2	6.8	27.3	95.3	6.2	81 811	71.3	42.0	57.6	34.5	9.4	5.7	3.08	3.62
Inside urbanized area	23 044	23.7	2.9	24.9	101.9	10.5	6 234	59.2	36.1	49.4	30.9	6.6	3.9	2.81	3.43
Outside urbanized area	275 918	29.6	7.1	27.6	94.8	5.8	75 577	72.3	42.5	58.3	34.8	9.6	5.8	3.10	3.63
Place of 10,000 or more	165 504	27.6	6.9	27.3	96.5	6.8	47 167	69.1	39.8	55.6	32.7	9.3	5.5	2.97	3.55
Place of 2,500 to 9,999	110 414	32.7	7.4	28.2	92.0	4.4	28 410	77.8	46.9	62.6	38.3	10.3	6.3	3.32	3.76
Rural	150 841	33.9	8.2	29.4	78.7	3.9	35 643	78.9	44.4	64.2	36.6	9.7	5.6	3.20	3.64
POPULATION SIZE CLASS OF METROPOLITAN AREA															
1,000,000 or more	5 317 229	28.1	5.9	30.2	93.6	1.6	1 485 853	78.2	46.5	63.8	40.5	9.2	4.5	3.38	3.82
In central city	2 524 580	26.2	7.0	30.0	96.4	2.1	735 860	73.0	40.4	56.9	34.0	10.2	4.9	3.26	3.82
Not in central city	2 792 649	29.8	5.0	30.3	91.1	1.1	749 993	83.4	52.4	70.4	46.8	8.2	4.2	3.49	3.82
5,000,000 or more	3 518 730	26.9	6.6	30.9	94.4	1.4	992 516	78.9	45.5	64.2	39.9	9.2	4.2	3.40	3.82
In central city	1 724 860	24.7	7.8	31.0	96.2	1.7	507 210	74.0	39.4	57.8	33.5	10.2	4.4	3.28	3.80
Not in central city	1 793 870	29.0	5.4	30.8	92.6	1.0	485 306	84.1	51.9	71.0	46.6	8.3	3.9	3.53	3.84
2,500,000 to 4,999,999	910 401	29.2	4.4	29.3	94.0	1.8	258 229	77.1	48.4	63.6	42.3	8.5	4.7	3.28	3.75
In central city	322 412	26.6	5.3	28.3	100.2	3.5	99 951	67.7	39.1	52.1	31.9	9.9	5.6	3.00	3.65
Not in central city	587 989	30.6	3.9	29.9	90.6	.8	158 278	83.1	54.3	70.8	48.8	7.7	4.1	3.45	3.80
1,000,000 to 2,499,999	888 098	31.9	4.8	27.5	89.9	2.1	235 108	76.5	48.5	61.8	41.0	9.8	5.9	3.37	3.88
In central city	477 308	31.4	5.2	26.8	94.2	2.4	128 699	73.0	45.7	57.3	37.6	10.5	6.4	3.39	3.99
Not in central city	410 790	32.4	4.3	28.6	85.1	1.8	106 409	80.7	52.0	67.3	45.1	9.1	5.3	3.36	3.76
Less than 1,000,000	1 506 630	29.9	7.1	28.8	89.6	3.0	410 428	75.5	43.0	60.5	36.0	10.5	5.5	3.29	3.80
In central city	849 095	28.7	7.8	28.4	93.1	3.6	246 691	70.3	39.0	55.0	32.0	10.7	5.5	3.13	3.76
Not in central city	657 535	31.4	6.3	29.5	85.2	2.2	163 737	83.3	49.0	68.8	41.9	10.2	5.5	3.53	3.86
500,000 to 999,999	875 741	27.5	9.3	30.8	91.3	2.3	250 038	76.3	39.2	60.5	32.7	11.1	5.1	3.25	3.74
In central city	454 580	24.9	11.0	31.2	93.0	3.1	141 894	69.7	33.1	53.5	26.9	11.5	4.9	2.99	3.61
Not in central city	421 161	30.3	7.4	30.5	89.3	1.4	108 144	85.0	47.3	69.7	40.3	10.7	5.3	3.59	3.88
250,000 to 499,999	358 684	33.5	4.9	26.6	86.9	3.1	91 094	76.7	49.9	62.1	41.8	10.1	6.4	3.44	3.95
In central city	220 522	34.7	5.0	25.7	91.8	3.0	57 307	74.6	49.0	59.2	40.4	10.7	6.9	3.49	4.07
Not in central city	138 162	31.6	4.9	28.5	79.9	3.4	33 787	80.2	51.3	66.9	44.2	9.1	5.5	3.36	3.76
100,000 to 249,999	251 215	33.1	3.2	25.5	87.3	5.0	63 758	71.7	47.8	58.9	40.3	8.8	6.0	3.23	3.84
In central city	157 629	31.6	2.8	25.2	94.8	5.5	42 912	67.6	44.9	55.0	37.6	8.6	5.8	3.12	3.80
Not in central city	93 586	35.5	3.9	26.2	75.4	4.2	20 846	80.2	53.8	67.0	45.7	9.3	6.4	3.46	3.92
Less than 100,000	20 990	30.1	2.2	25.1	89.6	7.6	5 538	65.3	42.8	54.3	36.8	7.5	5.0	2.92	3.60
In central city	16 364	28.9	2.4	24.9	95.6	8.2	4 578	62.4	40.4	51.4	34.5	7.6	4.9	2.90	3.64
Not in central city	4 626	34.2	1.8	25.9	69.6	5.4	960	79.1	54.4	68.3	47.8	7.2	5.4	3.04	3.45

Table 11. Summary of General Characteristics of Hispanic Origin Persons and Households: 1990

[Persons of Hispanic origin may be of any race. For definitions of terms and meanings of symbols, see text]

United States Urban and Rural and Size of Place Population Size Class of Urbanized Area Inside and Outside Metropolitan Area Population Size Class of Metropolitan Area	All Hispanic origin persons						All households with an Hispanic origin householder								
		Percent of all persons			Persons 18 years and over—			Family households as a percent of all households						Persons per—	
										Married-couple family		Female householder, no husband present			
	Total	Under 18 years	65 years and over	Median age	Males per 100 females	Percent in group quarters	Total	Total	With own children under 18 years	Total	With own children under 18 years	Total	With own children under 18 years	Household	Family
United States	22 354 059	34.7	5.2	25.5	103.3	2.3	6 001 718	79.8	50.5	54.9	35.5	17.7	11.6	3.53	3.88
URBAN AND RURAL AND SIZE OF PLACE															
Urban	20 426 228	34.4	5.2	25.5	101.6	2.0	5 530 932	79.5	50.2	53.9	34.8	18.4	12.1	3.53	3.88
Inside urbanized area	18 355 980	33.9	5.2	25.7	101.1	1.8	4 988 301	79.2	49.7	53.3	34.2	18.6	12.2	3.52	3.87
Central place	11 671 728	34.2	5.4	25.5	100.1	1.8	3 235 169	77.5	48.8	49.2	31.5	20.8	13.8	3.47	3.87
Urban fringe	6 684 252	33.6	4.8	26.0	102.9	1.9	1 753 132	82.3	51.5	60.8	39.1	14.6	9.2	3.62	3.88
Outside urbanized area	2 070 248	38.6	5.7	23.7	106.2	3.1	542 631	82.0	54.4	59.7	40.0	16.1	11.1	3.56	3.91
Place of 10,000 or more	1 102 447	38.2	5.5	23.7	105.2	3.2	291 255	81.4	54.0	58.3	38.9	16.8	11.7	3.53	3.88
Place of 2,500 to 9,999	967 801	39.1	5.8	23.8	107.3	3.0	251 376	82.7	54.9	61.3	41.2	15.3	10.5	3.59	3.94
Rural	1 927 831	37.8	4.9	24.8	124.8	6.1	470 786	83.5	54.3	67.3	44.6	10.0	6.5	3.62	3.95
Place of 1,000 to 2,499	318 036	39.8	5.9	23.8	107.1	2.0	82 639	83.3	54.7	63.9	42.7	13.3	8.8	3.60	3.95
Place of less than 1,000	89 028	40.2	7.0	24.0	106.9	1.8	23 929	80.0	50.2	61.7	39.0	12.5	8.1	3.36	3.79
Other rural	1 520 767	37.2	4.6	25.0	129.8	7.2	364 218	83.8	54.5	68.4	45.5	9.1	5.9	3.64	3.96
POPULATION SIZE CLASS OF URBANIZED AREA															
1,000,000 or more	13 600 190	33.0	5.2	26.0	101.6	1.6	3 683 627	79.2	49.1	52.8	33.7	18.6	11.9	3.56	3.90
Central place	8 108 012	33.0	5.4	25.9	101.2	1.6	2 245 865	77.2	47.7	47.9	30.5	21.0	13.6	3.51	3.89
Urban fringe	5 492 178	33.0	4.9	26.2	102.2	1.6	1 437 762	82.4	51.1	60.4	38.7	14.8	9.2	3.65	3.90
5,000,000 or more	7 469 886	33.3	4.5	25.7	102.1	1.5	1 938 047	80.7	51.1	51.1	33.8	20.8	13.4	3.74	4.02
Central place	4 558 322	33.1	4.5	25.7	100.6	1.5	1 224 019	78.7	49.9	45.8	30.2	23.9	15.6	3.64	3.96
Urban fringe	2 911 564	33.6	4.4	25.5	104.7	1.5	714 028	84.2	53.3	60.3	39.9	15.6	9.6	3.92	4.11
2,500,000 to 4,999,999	2 189 445	34.1	4.0	25.4	108.6	1.5	596 053	77.2	49.7	53.8	36.2	15.6	10.2	3.50	3.89
Central place	1 286 752	34.5	4.0	24.9	111.2	1.6	353 545	75.0	48.7	49.5	33.8	17.2	11.4	3.51	3.97
Urban fringe	902 693	33.4	3.9	26.0	104.9	1.5	242 508	80.3	51.2	60.1	39.7	13.2	8.5	3.49	3.78
1,000,000 to 2,499,999	3 940 859	31.9	7.3	27.4	97.1	1.7	1 149 527	77.7	45.3	55.1	32.3	16.4	10.1	3.29	3.68
Central place	2 262 938	32.1	8.0	27.2	97.2	1.7	668 301	75.5	43.3	51.0	29.3	17.9	11.0	3.26	3.71
Urban fringe	1 677 921	31.7	6.2	27.6	97.0	1.6	481 226	80.9	47.9	60.8	36.4	14.3	8.9	3.33	3.64
Less than 1,000,000	4 755 790	36.6	5.1	24.5	99.6	2.6	1 304 674	79.2	51.6	54.6	35.5	18.6	13.1	3.42	3.81
Central place	3 563 716	36.7	5.2	24.4	97.5	2.3	989 304	78.3	51.1	52.1	33.8	20.1	14.2	3.40	3.82
Urban fringe	1 192 074	36.2	4.7	25.0	106.1	3.4	315 370	81.9	53.1	62.4	40.8	13.8	9.4	3.47	3.80
500,000 to 999,999	1 284 790	35.5	5.4	25.3	93.3	1.9	368 088	77.8	49.7	52.4	33.2	19.9	13.8	3.29	3.73
Central place	923 451	35.7	5.6	25.0	90.7	1.9	266 781	76.9	49.3	49.0	31.0	22.4	15.6	3.28	3.75
Urban fringe	361 339	34.8	4.8	26.0	100.3	2.0	101 307	80.3	51.0	61.3	39.1	13.6	9.1	3.33	3.68
250,000 to 499,999	1 344 597	36.8	5.3	24.8	97.7	2.1	370 419	79.6	51.3	54.1	34.7	19.4	13.4	3.42	3.81
Central place	982 762	36.7	5.4	24.8	96.2	2.0	275 064	78.4	50.7	51.4	32.8	20.8	14.6	3.39	3.80
Urban fringe	361 835	37.1	5.2	24.9	101.8	2.5	95 355	82.9	53.3	62.1	40.1	15.1	10.2	3.53	3.85
100,000 to 249,999	1 348 272	37.2	4.6	23.9	104.4	3.1	356 836	80.0	53.4	56.2	37.7	17.7	12.6	3.52	3.89
Central place	1 049 745	37.5	4.8	23.8	101.3	2.5	281 217	79.6	53.1	54.2	36.3	19.1	13.7	3.52	3.90
Urban fringe	298 527	36.3	3.8	24.1	115.6	5.0	75 619	81.7	54.4	63.5	42.8	12.2	8.6	3.54	3.85
Less than 100,000	778 131	36.9	5.0	24.1	106.2	3.5	209 331	79.4	52.3	56.6	37.3	16.6	11.7	3.44	3.82
Central place	607 758	36.9	5.0	24.0	104.7	3.0	166 242	78.3	51.5	54.8	36.0	17.2	12.2	3.41	3.81
Urban fringe	170 373	36.8	4.9	24.5	112.1	5.5	43 089	83.4	55.3	63.5	42.4	14.1	9.8	3.56	3.86
INSIDE AND OUTSIDE METROPOLITAN AREA															
Inside metropolitan area	20 204 818	34.4	5.1	25.6	102.5	2.1	5 427 548	79.7	50.4	54.3	35.1	18.1	11.9	3.55	3.89
In central city	11 514 252	34.1	5.4	25.5	99.9	1.8	3 196 572	77.5	48.7	49.0	31.4	20.9	13.8	3.47	3.87
Not in central city	8 690 566	34.7	4.7	25.6	106.0	2.5	2 230 976	83.0	52.7	61.9	40.4	14.2	9.1	3.66	3.93
Urban	7 669 637	34.3	4.8	25.7	103.7	1.9	1 994 710	82.7	52.3	61.0	39.6	14.7	9.4	3.65	3.91
Inside urbanized area	6 854 456	33.7	4.8	25.9	103.0	1.9	1 794 407	82.4	51.6	60.8	39.2	14.6	9.2	3.62	3.89
Outside urbanized area	815 181	39.2	4.6	23.3	110.5	2.4	200 303	84.9	57.7	62.3	43.2	15.5	10.8	3.83	4.09
Rural	1 020 929	37.6	4.1	24.7	125.6	6.7	236 266	85.8	56.9	69.9	47.5	9.6	6.3	3.81	4.07
Outside metropolitan area	2 149 241	37.9	6.1	24.4	112.0	4.5	574 170	80.4	51.8	60.8	39.4	13.9	9.4	3.39	3.80
Urban	1 244 669	37.9	6.4	24.1	104.2	3.9	340 214	79.8	52.0	58.1	37.8	16.3	11.1	3.37	3.78
Inside urbanized area	51 453	32.3	4.9	25.2	128.0	10.9	14 034	72.1	45.9	52.7	32.8	14.2	10.4	2.98	3.41
Outside urbanized area	1 193 216	38.2	6.4	24.1	103.2	3.6	326 180	80.2	52.2	58.3	38.0	16.3	11.2	3.38	3.80
Place of 10,000 or more	655 690	37.9	6.0	23.8	102.5	3.8	177 936	80.0	52.5	57.5	37.8	16.9	11.6	3.40	3.81
Place of 2,500 to 9,999	537 526	38.4	6.9	24.5	104.0	3.3	148 244	80.4	51.9	59.3	38.4	15.7	10.6	3.37	3.78
Rural	904 572	37.9	5.8	24.8	123.8	5.4	233 956	81.2	51.6	64.7	41.8	10.4	6.8	3.43	3.81
POPULATION SIZE CLASS OF METROPOLITAN AREA															
1,000,000 or more	15 435 936	33.5	5.1	25.9	102.7	1.8	4 154 630	79.5	49.7	53.4	34.3	18.4	11.9	3.56	3.89
In central city	8 724 237	33.3	5.3	25.8	101.3	1.6	2 414 004	77.2	48.1	47.8	30.5	21.3	13.9	3.50	3.89
Not in central city	6 711 699	33.6	4.7	26.0	104.6	2.1	1 740 626	82.6	51.8	61.2	39.5	14.3	9.0	3.65	3.90
5,000,000 or more	9 646 762	33.7	4.5	25.5	103.9	1.8	2 489 327	80.7	51.2	52.3	34.6	19.9	12.8	3.73	4.01
In central city	5 470 682	33.4	4.6	25.6	101.7	1.6	1 458 170	78.7	49.9	46.4	30.6	23.3	15.3	3.65	3.97
Not in central city	4 176 080	34.2	4.4	25.4	106.8	2.0	1 031 157	83.6	53.1	60.7	40.1	15.0	9.4	3.84	4.06
2,500,000 to 4,999,999	3 047 711	30.9	6.6	27.5	101.7	1.3	893 130	77.7	46.0	56.3	34.3	14.6	9.0	3.33	3.71
In central city	1 607 576	31.0	7.3	27.2	104.0	1.2	480 869	74.4	43.4	50.6	30.3	16.2	10.1	3.28	3.74
Not in central city	1 440 135	30.9	5.8	28.0	99.3	1.3	412 261	81.6	49.1	62.9	38.9	12.7	7.7	3.38	3.67
1,000,000 to 2,499,999	2 741 463	35.4	5.5	25.3	99.4	2.6	772 173	77.5	48.7	53.6	33.4	18.0	12.3	3.30	3.72
In central city	1 645 979	35.5	6.0	25.2	97.2	2.1	474 965	75.6	47.4	49.2	30.5	20.3	13.8	3.28	3.76
Not in central city	1 095 484	35.2	4.8	25.6	104.1	3.5	297 208	80.6	50.8	60.5	38.1	14.3	9.8	3.34	3.67
Less than 1,000,000	4 768 882	37.3	5.2	24.4	101.6	2.9	1 272 918	80.5	52.7	57.4	37.8	17.2	11.8	3.50	3.89
In central city	2 790 015	36.6	5.5	24.5	95.5	2.2	782 568	78.1	50.5	52.9	34.1	19.5	13.5	3.36	3.80
Not in central city	1 978 867	38.2	4.7	24.1	110.9	3.8	490 350	84.3	56.1	64.5	43.7	13.6	9.1	3.72	4.02
500,000 to 999,999	1 696 135	36.7	5.0	24.7	99.7	2.6	460 666	79.5	51.6	55.0	35.8	18.4	12.7	3.44	3.84
In central city	1 020 275	36.3	5.4	24.7	92.5	2.0	289 670	77.5	49.9	50.6	32.4	21.2	14.7	3.33	3.78
Not in central city	675 860	37.2	4.4	24.6	111.8	3.6	170 996	82.8	54.5	62.2	41.6	13.8	9.4	3.63	3.93
250,000 to 499,999	1 941 524	37.5	5.4	24.4	101.5	2.7	506 839	82.0	53.6	59.0	39.0	17.1	11.5	3.60	3.97
In central city	1 065 089	36.7	5.7	24.8	96.5	2.0	293 970	79.1	51.0	53.9	34.9	19.2	13.1	3.43	3.85
Not in central city	876 435	38.4	5.1	24.0	108.2	3.7	212 869	86.0	57.1	66.0	44.8	14.1	9.2	3.84	4.12
100,000 to 249,999	1 048 036	37.8	4.9	23.7	104.9	3.5	281 793	79.8	52.9	58.4	39.0	15.7	10.9	3.44	3.85
In central city	636 781	37.0	5.4	23.9	98.7	2.9	179 215	77.6	50.7	54.5	35.6	17.7	12.3	3.32	3.79
Not in central city	411 255	39.0	4.2	23.4	115.6	4.4	102 578	83.6	56.9	65.2	44.8	12.1	8.6	3.64	3.96
Less than 100,000	83 187	37.5	5.6	24.3	100.0	3.4	23 620	78.3	50.4	58.0	37.0	15.6	10.7	3.21	3.66
In central city	67 870	37.1	5.9	24.4	97.6	3.1	19 713	77.2	49.2	55.6	35.0	16.9	11.5	3.18	3.65
Not in central city	15 317	39.1	4.3	24.0	111.7	4.4	3 907	84.3	56.2	70.1	47.0	9.2	6.6	3.40	3.72

Table 12. **Summary of General Characteristics of White, Not of Hispanic Origin Persons and Households: 1990**

[For definitions of terms and meanings of symbols, see text]

United States Urban and Rural and Size of Place Population Size Class of Urbanized Area Inside and Outside Metropolitan Area Population Size Class of Metropolitan Area	All White, not of Hispanic origin persons						All households with a White, not of Hispanic origin householder								
		Percent of all persons						Family households as a percent of all households						Persons per—	
										Married-couple family		Female householder, no husband present			
	Total	Under 18 years	65 years and over	Median age	Persons 18 years and over—Males per 100 females	Percent in group quarters	Total	Total	With own children under 18 years	Total	With own children under 18 years	Total	With own children under 18 years	Household	Family
United States	**188 128 296**	**23.3**	**14.4**	**34.9**	**92.0**	**2.5**	**73 633 749**	**69.2**	**31.1**	**57.8**	**25.4**	**8.6**	**4.5**	**2.51**	**3.03**
URBAN AND RURAL AND SIZE OF PLACE															
Urban	133 375 398	22.0	15.0	34.8	90.0	3.0	53 651 540	65.9	29.0	53.9	23.1	9.2	4.8	2.43	3.00
Inside urbanized area	109 975 510	21.6	14.5	34.9	90.8	2.6	44 437 315	65.5	28.5	53.6	22.8	9.0	4.5	2.43	3.00
Central place	46 619 577	19.6	15.9	34.7	90.1	3.8	19 974 619	58.5	24.5	46.3	18.7	9.4	4.7	2.27	2.92
Urban fringe	63 355 933	23.1	13.5	35.0	91.3	1.8	24 462 696	71.2	31.7	59.6	26.2	8.8	4.4	2.56	3.05
Outside urbanized area	23 399 888	23.8	17.1	34.5	86.5	4.7	9 214 225	67.5	31.4	55.1	24.2	9.8	5.9	2.43	2.98
Place of 10,000 or more	11 020 682	23.1	16.2	33.5	87.2	5.7	4 338 311	65.9	30.8	53.5	23.5	9.8	5.9	2.41	2.97
Place of 2,500 to 9,999	12 379 206	24.4	17.8	35.4	85.9	3.9	4 875 914	68.9	32.0	56.5	24.8	9.8	5.9	2.45	2.99
Rural	54 752 898	26.4	13.0	35.0	97.2	1.4	19 982 209	78.1	36.8	68.3	31.6	7.0	3.8	2.71	3.10
Place of 1,000 to 2,499	6 119 686	25.1	18.1	36.2	86.5	2.5	2 404 005	70.6	32.6	58.8	25.9	9.1	5.3	2.49	3.02
Place of less than 1,000	3 352 640	25.9	18.7	36.3	88.7	1.4	1 332 309	70.5	32.4	59.6	26.4	8.1	4.6	2.49	3.04
Other rural	45 280 572	26.7	11.8	34.8	99.5	1.3	16 245 895	79.9	37.8	70.4	32.9	6.5	3.4	2.76	3.12
POPULATION SIZE CLASS OF URBANIZED AREA															
1,000,000 or more	60 537 603	20.9	14.6	35.5	91.3	2.1	24 680 136	64.7	27.4	53.0	22.3	8.8	4.0	2.42	3.01
Central place	19 991 801	17.5	16.9	36.0	91.8	3.2	8 944 618	54.6	21.0	42.8	16.2	8.8	3.9	2.18	2.90
Urban fringe	40 545 802	22.6	13.5	35.2	91.0	1.5	15 735 518	70.5	31.0	58.9	25.8	8.8	4.1	2.56	3.06
5,000,000 or more	19 120 102	19.3	16.1	37.0	90.9	2.1	7 803 290	64.2	25.2	52.6	21.1	8.6	3.2	2.42	3.04
Central place	6 619 612	15.5	19.1	38.4	90.5	2.9	3 037 073	52.9	18.2	41.3	14.6	8.4	2.9	2.14	2.91
Urban fringe	12 500 490	21.3	14.5	36.3	91.1	1.6	4 766 217	71.4	29.6	59.8	25.3	8.7	3.4	2.60	3.10
2,500,000 to 4,999,999	15 815 595	21.1	13.0	34.9	91.6	2.1	6 395 313	64.6	28.1	52.9	23.0	8.8	4.1	2.44	3.03
Central place	4 469 665	16.8	15.5	35.3	92.3	3.6	2 030 143	52.0	20.1	40.4	15.4	8.7	3.8	2.14	2.89
Urban fringe	11 345 930	22.9	12.0	34.7	91.3	1.5	4 365 170	70.4	31.8	58.6	26.5	8.9	4.2	2.58	3.08
1,000,000 to 2,499,999	25 601 906	22.0	14.4	34.9	91.4	2.1	10 481 533	65.2	28.6	53.5	22.8	8.9	4.6	2.41	2.97
Central place	8 902 524	19.4	15.9	34.9	92.5	3.3	3 877 402	57.2	23.7	45.1	18.0	9.1	4.6	2.24	2.90
Urban fringe	16 699 382	23.4	13.7	34.9	90.8	1.4	6 604 131	69.9	31.4	58.4	25.6	8.7	4.6	2.51	3.01
Less than 1,000,000	49 437 907	22.5	14.4	34.0	90.1	3.3	19 757 179	66.5	29.8	54.4	23.5	9.4	5.2	2.44	2.99
Central place	26 627 776	21.2	15.1	33.6	88.8	4.2	11 030 001	61.8	27.3	49.2	20.6	9.8	5.5	2.33	2.94
Urban fringe	22 810 131	24.0	13.6	34.6	91.8	2.2	8 727 178	72.5	33.0	61.0	27.1	8.8	4.7	2.57	3.04
500,000 to 999,999	13 340 475	22.4	14.1	34.2	90.4	2.5	5 390 389	65.9	29.3	53.8	23.3	9.3	4.9	2.43	3.00
Central place	5 938 917	20.2	14.8	33.6	90.2	3.7	2 538 831	59.1	25.3	46.3	19.0	9.9	5.2	2.27	2.92
Urban fringe	7 401 558	24.2	13.5	34.6	90.6	1.6	2 851 558	71.9	32.8	60.4	27.0	8.8	4.7	2.57	3.06
250,000 to 499,999	11 544 438	22.5	14.7	34.6	89.6	2.8	4 634 179	67.2	29.8	55.0	23.6	9.4	5.1	2.44	2.99
Central place	5 459 291	20.9	15.8	34.4	88.0	3.8	2 300 188	61.5	26.6	48.8	20.1	9.9	5.4	2.31	2.92
Urban fringe	6 085 147	23.9	13.7	34.7	91.1	1.9	2 333 991	72.7	32.9	61.1	27.0	9.0	4.7	2.57	3.04
100,000 to 249,999	14 821 260	22.5	14.0	33.5	90.9	3.7	5 870 252	66.4	30.1	54.4	23.8	9.3	5.2	2.45	2.99
Central place	8 799 544	21.6	14.7	33.2	89.0	4.2	3 594 039	62.5	28.1	50.1	21.5	9.7	5.5	2.36	2.96
Urban fringe	6 021 716	23.8	13.0	34.1	93.7	3.0	2 276 213	72.7	33.3	61.3	27.4	8.6	4.7	2.58	3.04
Less than 100,000	9 731 734	22.5	15.2	33.9	89.1	4.2	3 862 359	66.7	30.1	54.6	23.3	9.5	5.5	2.43	2.96
Central place	6 430 024	21.8	15.4	33.2	87.7	4.9	2 596 943	63.5	28.6	51.1	21.7	9.8	5.8	2.37	2.94
Urban fringe	3 301 710	23.0	14.8	35.0	92.1	2.7	1 265 416	73.4	33.0	61.9	26.7	8.8	5.0	2.55	2.99
INSIDE AND OUTSIDE METROPOLITAN AREA															
Inside metropolitan area	140 406 200	22.0	13.9	34.8	91.8	2.4	55 416 863	68.0	30.3	56.5	24.7	8.7	4.4	2.49	3.03
In central city	45 957 707	19.6	15.9	34.7	89.9	3.8	19 718 548	58.4	24.4	46.2	18.6	9.4	4.7	2.26	2.92
Not in central city	94 538 493	24.2	13.0	34.8	92.8	1.8	35 698 315	73.4	33.5	62.1	28.1	8.4	4.3	2.62	3.07
Urban	70 615 050	23.3	13.7	34.9	91.1	1.9	27 223 089	71.2	32.0	59.6	26.3	8.9	4.5	2.56	3.05
Inside urbanized area	63 480 467	23.1	13.5	35.0	91.3	1.7	24 504 557	71.2	31.7	59.6	26.3	8.8	4.4	2.56	3.05
Outside urbanized area	7 134 583	25.1	15.1	33.8	88.8	3.4	2 718 532	71.3	34.2	59.0	27.1	9.5	5.7	2.55	3.04
Rural	23 923 443	26.6	10.9	34.5	98.3	1.4	8 475 226	80.2	38.5	70.4	33.5	6.8	3.6	2.79	3.14
Outside metropolitan area	47 632 096	25.2	15.7	35.2	92.5	2.8	18 216 886	72.7	33.5	61.9	27.5	8.1	4.6	2.55	3.03
Urban	16 871 318	23.1	17.9	34.8	86.1	5.3	6 734 755	65.9	30.1	53.6	23.0	9.8	5.9	2.39	2.96
Inside urbanized area	1 238 190	22.1	15.7	33.4	92.5	4.7	487 340	66.5	29.1	55.5	23.0	8.5	5.0	2.44	2.95
Outside urbanized area	15 633 128	23.2	18.0	34.9	85.6	5.3	6 247 415	65.8	30.2	53.5	23.0	9.9	6.0	2.38	2.96
Place of 10,000 or more	7 910 296	22.6	16.6	33.6	86.9	6.2	3 140 028	64.6	29.8	52.3	22.6	9.8	6.0	2.38	2.96
Place of 2,500 to 9,999	7 722 832	23.8	19.5	36.3	84.2	4.4	3 107 387	67.1	30.6	54.7	23.3	9.9	6.0	2.39	2.96
Rural	30 760 778	26.3	14.6	35.4	96.4	1.5	11 482 131	76.6	35.5	66.7	30.2	7.1	3.9	2.65	3.07
POPULATION SIZE CLASS OF METROPOLITAN AREA															
1,000,000 or more	86 629 788	22.1	13.9	35.1	91.9	2.1	34 380 434	67.1	29.4	55.4	24.1	8.7	4.2	2.48	3.04
In central city	25 186 606	18.2	16.4	35.5	91.2	3.3	11 093 261	55.8	22.2	43.7	17.0	9.1	4.2	2.22	2.92
Not in central city	61 443 182	23.7	12.9	34.9	92.2	1.6	23 287 173	72.4	32.8	61.0	27.5	8.5	4.2	2.61	3.09
5,000,000 or more	32 330 913	20.6	15.2	36.3	91.8	2.1	12 941 717	65.9	27.2	54.3	22.6	8.6	3.5	2.47	3.05
In central city	9 809 198	16.6	18.2	37.6	90.9	2.9	4 396 322	54.5	19.9	42.6	15.7	8.7	3.3	2.19	2.93
Not in central city	22 521 715	22.3	13.9	35.8	92.2	1.8	8 545 395	71.7	30.9	60.3	26.2	8.5	3.7	2.61	3.10
2,500,000 to 4,999,999	22 373 259	22.7	12.3	34.3	92.4	1.9	8 847 994	67.2	30.4	55.8	25.0	8.6	4.3	2.49	3.05
In central city	5 237 387	17.7	15.5	34.8	91.9	3.7	2 355 334	53.3	21.1	41.5	15.9	8.9	4.3	2.15	2.87
Not in central city	17 135 872	24.2	11.4	34.1	92.6	1.3	6 492 660	72.3	33.8	60.9	28.4	8.5	4.3	2.62	3.09
1,000,000 to 2,499,999	31 925 616	23.3	13.7	34.3	91.7	2.2	12 590 723	68.2	30.9	56.4	25.0	8.9	4.8	2.50	3.03
In central city	10 140 021	20.1	15.1	34.0	91.2	3.4	4 341 605	58.6	25.1	46.1	18.9	9.6	5.0	2.28	2.93
Not in central city	21 785 595	24.8	13.0	34.5	92.0	1.7	8 249 118	73.2	34.0	61.9	28.1	8.6	4.6	2.61	3.07
Less than 1,000,000	53 866 412	23.5	13.9	34.3	91.6	3.0	21 036 429	69.7	31.8	58.2	25.6	8.8	4.9	2.50	3.01
In central city	20 771 101	21.2	15.3	33.7	88.4	4.4	8 625 287	61.8	27.3	49.4	20.6	9.8	5.5	2.32	2.93
Not in central city	33 095 311	25.0	13.1	34.6	93.8	2.0	12 411 142	75.2	34.9	64.3	29.1	8.1	4.5	2.62	3.05
500,000 to 999,999	18 869 756	23.0	13.6	34.4	91.4	2.6	7 456 900	69.0	31.2	57.5	25.4	8.8	4.6	2.48	3.00
In central city	6 584 313	19.9	15.4	34.3	88.8	4.2	2 806 395	59.9	25.3	47.6	19.2	9.6	5.0	2.27	2.90
Not in central city	12 285 443	24.6	12.7	34.5	92.9	1.8	4 650 505	74.5	34.7	63.5	29.0	8.3	4.4	2.61	3.05
250,000 to 499,999	16 985 792	23.6	14.6	34.8	91.5	2.7	6 615 723	70.5	31.7	58.9	25.5	8.8	4.9	2.51	3.01
In central city	6 084 575	21.6	15.9	34.3	88.0	3.8	2 522 528	62.8	27.7	50.0	20.8	10.0	5.7	2.34	2.93
Not in central city	10 901 217	24.7	13.9	35.0	93.6	2.0	4 093 195	75.2	34.1	64.3	28.4	8.1	4.4	2.62	3.04
100,000 to 249,999	16 159 512	23.9	13.6	33.7	92.1	3.5	6 250 874	69.7	32.4	58.3	26.1	8.7	5.1	2.51	3.01
In central city	7 012 007	21.6	14.6	32.8	88.5	5.0	2 857 399	62.4	28.4	50.2	21.5	9.6	5.7	2.35	2.94
Not in central city	9 147 505	25.6	12.9	34.3	95.2	2.4	3 393 475	75.8	35.8	65.1	29.9	8.0	4.6	2.64	3.06
Less than 100,000	1 851 352	24.7	13.5	33.2	90.4	3.8	712 932	69.1	33.5	57.6	26.7	9.0	5.5	2.51	3.04
In central city	1 090 206	22.9	15.0	33.1	86.7	4.8	438 965	64.0	30.0	51.5	22.6	10.1	6.2	2.38	2.97
Not in central city	761 146	27.3	11.4	33.4	96.4	2.4	273 967	77.4	39.0	67.4	33.2	7.4	4.4	2.72	3.13

Table 13. **Single Years of Age by Sex, Race, and Hispanic Origin: 1990**

[For definitions of terms and meanings of symbols, see text]

United States	All persons			Race								
				White			Black			American Indian, Eskimo, or Aleut		
	Total	Male	Female	Total	Male	Female	Total	Male	Female	Total	Male	Female
All persons	**248 709 873**	**121 239 418**	**127 470 455**	**199 686 070**	**97 475 880**	**102 210 190**	**29 986 060**	**14 170 151**	**15 815 909**	**1 959 234**	**967 186**	**992 048**
Under 1 year	3 217 312	1 644 801	1 572 511	2 404 258	1 232 872	1 171 386	480 022	242 400	237 622	36 089	18 303	17 786
1 year	3 949 107	2 022 292	1 926 815	2 924 714	1 501 743	1 422 971	606 682	306 688	299 994	43 077	21 932	21 145
2 years	3 815 040	1 952 242	1 862 798	2 814 615	1 443 588	1 371 027	594 379	300 974	293 405	42 157	21 375	20 782
3 years	3 683 177	1 884 023	1 799 154	2 740 124	1 405 927	1 334 197	557 295	281 772	275 523	40 519	20 656	19 863
4 years	3 689 807	1 889 051	1 800 756	2 765 779	1 420 351	1 345 428	547 524	276 661	270 863	40 108	20 362	19 746
5 years	3 689 533	1 889 177	1 800 356	2 768 212	1 421 766	1 346 446	545 555	275 929	269 626	40 657	20 636	20 021
6 years	3 577 632	1 829 832	1 747 800	2 695 163	1 383 042	1 312 121	522 290	263 945	258 345	39 454	19 985	19 469
7 years	3 645 761	1 865 700	1 780 061	2 744 498	1 408 754	1 335 744	536 416	271 512	264 904	40 875	20 751	20 124
8 years	3 508 668	1 794 355	1 714 313	2 638 590	1 353 997	1 284 593	518 764	261 738	257 026	38 295	19 346	18 949
9 years	3 677 585	1 883 463	1 794 122	2 769 805	1 422 972	1 346 833	548 084	277 141	270 943	40 165	20 470	19 695
10 years	3 653 177	1 874 172	1 779 005	2 739 524	1 409 578	1 329 946	560 039	283 915	276 124	40 017	20 316	19 701
11 years	3 455 515	1 771 334	1 684 181	2 596 959	1 335 768	1 261 191	528 407	266 494	261 913	37 788	19 307	18 481
12 years	3 423 450	1 752 999	1 670 451	2 576 523	1 324 022	1 252 501	519 424	262 327	257 097	37 420	19 055	18 365
13 years	3 339 000	1 706 417	1 632 583	2 507 044	1 286 049	1 220 995	505 268	254 519	250 749	37 047	18 977	18 070
14 years	3 243 107	1 662 245	1 580 862	2 433 508	1 251 309	1 182 199	488 452	247 153	241 299	35 728	18 092	17 636
15 years	3 321 609	1 705 780	1 615 829	2 493 892	1 283 835	1 210 057	499 514	253 591	245 923	35 740	18 348	17 392
16 years	3 304 890	1 697 995	1 606 895	2 469 848	1 271 496	1 198 352	504 009	256 012	247 997	35 886	18 320	17 566
17 years	3 410 062	1 758 400	1 651 662	2 545 173	1 313 056	1 232 117	522 291	266 726	255 565	35 945	18 644	17 301
18 years	3 641 238	1 862 377	1 778 861	2 731 047	1 395 825	1 335 222	545 985	274 060	271 925	35 798	18 618	17 180
19 years	4 076 216	2 078 146	1 998 070	3 102 743	1 581 359	1 521 384	586 694	291 874	294 820	37 147	19 128	18 019
20 years	4 009 414	2 044 082	1 965 332	3 059 999	1 557 979	1 502 020	553 265	273 585	279 680	35 124	18 159	16 965
21 years	3 817 220	1 947 811	1 869 409	2 921 434	1 487 818	1 433 616	513 252	253 358	259 894	33 401	17 422	15 979
22 years	3 655 792	1 865 082	1 790 710	2 779 790	1 418 886	1 360 904	498 096	243 120	254 976	31 599	16 185	15 414
23 years	3 742 903	1 900 305	1 842 598	2 859 839	1 453 571	1 406 268	503 428	243 460	259 968	32 490	16 503	15 987
24 years	3 794 983	1 918 316	1 876 667	2 902 850	1 470 126	1 432 724	510 912	245 103	265 809	32 935	16 774	16 161
25 years	4 212 100	2 128 319	2 083 781	3 240 404	1 641 478	1 598 926	558 774	267 761	291 013	35 524	17 911	17 613
26 years	4 168 508	2 089 771	2 078 737	3 243 473	1 632 096	1 611 377	534 323	254 485	279 838	34 771	17 450	17 321
27 years	4 256 124	2 135 488	2 120 636	3 321 556	1 673 294	1 648 262	540 113	256 753	283 360	35 247	17 683	17 564
28 years	4 253 634	2 133 374	2 120 260	3 340 638	1 683 482	1 657 156	528 966	250 062	278 904	34 456	16 979	17 477
29 years	4 422 679	2 208 984	2 213 695	3 492 473	1 754 465	1 738 008	545 589	256 699	288 890	35 579	17 451	18 128
30 years	4 734 587	2 370 937	2 363 650	3 702 218	1 866 200	1 836 018	605 296	284 517	320 779	37 895	18 657	19 238
31 years	4 151 337	2 060 115	2 091 222	3 306 890	1 652 992	1 653 898	505 052	235 681	269 371	32 340	15 725	16 615
32 years	4 448 958	2 214 154	2 234 804	3 534 538	1 772 048	1 762 490	541 982	253 043	288 939	34 584	16 685	17 899
33 years	4 307 844	2 138 926	2 168 918	3 437 230	1 720 974	1 716 256	519 382	241 027	278 355	33 236	16 072	17 164
34 years	4 220 161	2 092 801	2 127 360	3 370 637	1 687 331	1 683 306	510 012	236 342	273 670	32 613	15 605	17 008
35 years	4 381 379	2 190 853	2 190 526	3 484 921	1 756 882	1 728 039	538 509	253 149	285 360	33 282	16 196	17 086
36 years	4 039 788	1 994 887	2 044 901	3 253 450	1 621 568	1 631 882	470 838	217 318	253 520	30 710	14 720	15 990
37 years	3 960 965	1 962 032	1 998 933	3 209 740	1 605 113	1 604 627	451 752	208 997	242 755	29 634	14 289	15 345
38 years	3 784 903	1 872 696	1 912 207	3 060 493	1 530 429	1 530 064	436 952	201 122	235 830	28 043	13 433	14 610
39 years	3 796 082	1 881 775	1 914 307	3 073 002	1 540 137	1 532 865	438 715	202 465	236 250	28 513	13 956	14 557
40 years	3 956 970	1 960 986	1 995 984	3 176 114	1 589 424	1 586 690	473 601	221 124	252 477	29 212	14 214	14 998
41 years	3 430 115	1 683 874	1 746 241	2 817 410	1 396 969	1 420 441	373 607	171 333	202 274	24 684	12 001	12 683
42 years	3 792 198	1 874 883	1 917 315	3 138 792	1 566 685	1 572 107	392 633	181 110	211 523	26 776	12 948	13 828
43 years	3 686 510	1 820 999	1 865 511	3 099 315	1 545 444	1 553 871	352 453	162 218	190 235	25 880	12 656	13 224
44 years	2 749 993	1 351 242	1 398 751	2 274 759	1 128 709	1 146 050	283 768	129 875	153 893	19 602	9 375	10 227
45 years	3 033 291	1 500 522	1 532 769	2 491 644	1 242 530	1 249 114	325 982	151 719	174 263	21 876	10 587	11 289
46 years	2 843 408	1 391 830	1 451 578	2 387 067	1 179 147	1 207 920	278 713	126 640	152 073	19 723	9 435	10 288
47 years	2 940 252	1 445 216	1 495 036	2 483 253	1 231 155	1 252 098	285 800	130 607	155 193	19 724	9 608	10 116
48 years	2 546 830	1 242 348	1 304 482	2 127 894	1 046 954	1 080 940	259 123	117 278	141 845	17 610	8 621	8 989
49 years	2 508 792	1 230 681	1 278 111	2 095 845	1 036 797	1 059 048	256 148	116 197	139 951	17 884	8 742	9 142
50 years	2 537 983	1 240 132	1 297 851	2 091 940	1 030 254	1 061 686	281 092	128 615	152 477	18 028	8 624	9 404
51 years	2 191 015	1 064 572	1 126 443	1 847 208	904 768	942 440	219 448	99 031	120 417	14 719	7 065	7 654
52 years	2 294 122	1 117 210	1 176 912	1 925 058	945 634	979 424	235 032	105 810	129 222	15 312	7 396	7 916
53 years	2 170 359	1 051 596	1 118 763	1 825 937	892 477	933 460	220 802	99 093	121 709	14 415	6 928	7 487
54 years	2 157 034	1 041 228	1 115 806	1 814 728	884 251	930 477	222 637	99 427	123 210	14 240	6 875	7 365
55 years	2 205 152	1 061 296	1 143 856	1 857 550	902 359	955 191	226 271	101 314	124 957	13 978	6 653	7 325
56 years	2 024 012	970 951	1 053 061	1 710 171	829 015	881 156	206 974	91 791	115 183	12 541	6 035	6 506
57 years	2 089 901	998 969	1 090 932	1 775 429	857 958	917 471	210 474	93 110	117 364	12 358	5 768	6 590
58 years	2 043 408	969 949	1 073 459	1 751 788	840 172	911 616	193 288	84 653	108 635	11 361	5 443	5 918
59 years	2 169 283	1 033 205	1 136 078	1 873 478	901 307	972 171	195 742	86 051	109 691	11 581	5 455	6 126
60 years	2 209 589	1 039 557	1 170 032	1 893 442	900 121	993 321	211 459	92 222	119 237	11 651	5 511	6 140
61 years	2 018 714	948 483	1 070 231	1 756 346	833 876	922 470	178 873	77 099	101 774	9 794	4 697	5 097
62 years	2 209 518	1 031 185	1 178 333	1 915 259	902 702	1 012 557	201 718	87 161	114 557	10 759	5 121	5 638
63 years	2 093 966	970 712	1 123 254	1 826 325	854 890	971 435	184 894	79 261	105 633	9 778	4 544	5 234
64 years	2 084 380	957 110	1 127 270	1 819 751	843 195	976 556	184 675	78 502	106 173	9 407	4 319	5 088
65 years	2 201 718	996 570	1 205 148	1 912 348	872 415	1 039 933	204 209	86 700	117 509	10 146	4 695	5 451
66 years	1 999 363	901 946	1 097 417	1 761 324	799 494	961 830	168 440	71 137	97 303	8 483	3 802	4 681
67 years	2 010 737	904 098	1 106 639	1 765 187	798 071	967 116	174 985	73 950	101 035	8 372	3 878	4 494
68 years	1 985 205	882 016	1 103 189	1 758 524	785 611	972 913	162 607	67 722	94 885	8 118	3 601	4 517
69 years	1 914 712	847 677	1 067 035	1 702 254	757 638	944 616	152 804	63 433	89 371	7 591	3 322	4 269
70 years	1 817 009	787 423	1 029 586	1 597 219	695 933	901 286	160 421	65 575	94 846	7 033	3 064	3 969
71 years	1 611 869	697 537	914 332	1 440 543	626 614	813 929	127 295	51 487	75 808	5 854	2 552	3 302
72 years	1 622 781	693 843	928 938	1 449 728	623 453	826 275	127 086	50 542	76 544	6 020	2 578	3 442
73 years	1 506 979	632 968	874 011	1 349 924	570 382	779 542	116 707	45 169	71 538	5 242	2 214	3 028
74 years	1 436 185	597 535	838 650	1 289 150	539 347	749 803	108 906	41 926	66 980	5 121	2 092	3 029
75 years	1 420 300	576 084	844 216	1 269 901	516 976	752 925	112 823	43 057	69 766	4 819	1 971	2 848
76 years	1 288 590	515 320	773 270	1 154 838	463 613	691 225	100 529	37 654	62 875	4 538	1 795	2 743
77 years	1 214 654	475 918	738 736	1 089 921	428 095	661 826	94 911	34 959	59 952	4 333	1 758	2 575
78 years	1 134 677	434 529	700 148	1 018 092	389 933	628 159	87 885	32 185	55 700	3 910	1 561	2 349
79 years	1 063 148	397 917	665 231	952 273	355 782	596 491	85 122	30 685	54 437	3 552	1 375	2 177
80 years	977 849	353 349	624 500	873 193	314 454	558 739	80 549	28 487	52 062	3 290	1 262	2 028
81 years	829 584	296 518	533 066	753 333	268 134	485 199	58 635	20 586	38 049	2 395	894	1 501
82 years	800 448	277 509	522 939	726 294	250 424	475 870	57 015	19 500	37 515	2 375	882	1 493
83 years	704 073	236 260	467 813	638 306	212 772	425 534	50 815	16 852	33 963	2 115	800	1 315
84 years	621 785	202 458	419 327	561 569	181 318	380 251	46 624	15 234	31 390	1 941	719	1 222
85 years	560 545	175 581	384 964	505 217	156 359	348 858	43 222	14 035	29 187	1 750	655	1 095
86 years	469 208	143 684	325 524	426 623	129 174	297 449	32 952	10 405	22 547	1 358	484	874
87 years	398 712	117 746	280 966	361 740	105 419	256 321	28 920	8 978	19 942	1 216	436	780
88 years	325 721	93 513	232 208	296 887	83 958	212 929	22 424	6 902	15 522	952	329	623
89 years	306 061	83 512	222 549	274 086	73 460	200 626	25 456	7 522	17 934	967	326	641
90 to 94 years	769 481	190 089	579 392	702 256	170 311	531 945	53 391	14 698	38 693	2 039	732	1 307
95 to 99 years	213 131	45 672	167 459	191 138	39 970	151 168	17 944	4 465	13 479	659	213	446
100 to 104 years	30 947	5 944	25 003	25 881	4 616	21 265	4 208	1 025	3 183	180	68	112
105 years and over	6 359	1 957	4 402	4 224	1 183	3 041	1 666	562	1 104	84	31	53
Median age	32.9	31.7	34.1	34.4	33.1	35.6	28.1	26.6	29.5	26.2	25.3	27.2

GENERAL POPULATION CHARACTERISTICS UNITED STATES SUMMARY 17

366

Table 13. Single Years of Age by Sex, Race, and Hispanic Origin: 1990—Con.

[For definitions of terms and meanings of symbols, see text]

United States	Race—Con.						Hispanic origin (of any race)			White, not of Hispanic origin		
	Asian or Pacific Islander			Other race								
	Total	Male	Female	Total	Male	Female	Total	Male	Female	Total	Male	Female
All persons	7 273 662	3 558 038	3 715 624	9 804 847	5 068 163	4 736 684	22 354 059	11 388 059	10 966 000	188 128 296	91 656 591	96 471 705
Under 1 year	93 460	47 604	45 856	203 483	103 622	99 861	427 454	217 883	209 571	2 197 217	1 127 357	1 069 860
1 year	130 536	67 255	63 281	244 098	124 674	119 424	518 131	264 614	253 517	2 672 461	1 372 916	1 299 545
2 years	126 175	64 635	61 540	237 714	121 670	116 044	502 284	256 941	245 343	2 571 497	1 319 430	1 252 067
3 years	120 256	61 133	59 123	224 983	114 535	110 448	477 574	243 056	234 518	2 507 627	1 287 610	1 220 017
4 years	119 418	60 719	58 699	216 978	110 958	106 020	462 081	235 700	226 381	2 539 917	1 305 210	1 234 707
5 years	121 788	61 701	60 087	213 321	109 145	104 176	457 089	233 523	223 566	2 543 243	1 306 800	1 236 443
6 years	119 463	60 486	58 977	201 262	102 374	98 888	434 252	221 089	213 163	2 480 472	1 273 657	1 206 815
7 years	119 740	60 576	59 164	204 232	104 107	100 125	441 276	224 818	216 458	2 525 976	1 297 437	1 228 539
8 years	116 064	58 736	57 328	196 955	100 538	96 417	426 113	217 191	208 922	2 427 541	1 246 539	1 181 002
9 years	119 078	60 334	58 744	200 453	102 546	97 907	435 122	222 112	213 010	2 552 859	1 312 446	1 240 413
10 years	117 357	59 764	57 593	196 240	100 599	95 641	427 686	218 916	208 770	2 526 043	1 300 460	1 225 583
11 years	109 049	55 652	53 397	183 312	94 113	89 199	400 840	205 488	195 352	2 396 621	1 233 211	1 163 410
12 years	108 190	54 938	53 252	181 893	92 657	89 236	397 566	203 316	194 250	2 377 773	1 222 081	1 155 692
13 years	109 012	55 361	53 651	180 629	91 511	89 118	393 120	199 836	193 284	2 311 109	1 186 188	1 124 921
14 years	107 944	55 410	52 534	177 475	90 281	87 194	382 405	195 827	186 578	2 244 557	1 154 031	1 090 526
15 years	112 663	58 385	54 278	179 800	91 621	88 179	387 038	198 402	188 636	2 303 102	1 185 489	1 117 613
16 years	115 477	59 630	55 847	179 670	92 537	87 133	385 257	199 659	185 598	2 280 559	1 172 833	1 107 726
17 years	117 717	60 945	56 772	188 936	99 029	89 907	402 212	212 793	189 419	2 348 737	1 208 299	1 140 438
18 years	125 310	64 788	60 522	203 098	109 086	94 012	426 930	229 367	197 563	2 525 629	1 285 390	1 240 239
19 years	132 594	68 669	63 925	217 038	117 116	99 922	452 520	243 672	208 848	2 886 674	1 465 437	1 421 237
20 years	134 694	70 127	64 567	226 332	124 232	102 100	469 015	256 052	212 963	2 837 680	1 437 359	1 400 321
21 years	129 179	67 260	61 919	219 954	121 953	98 001	451 608	248 677	202 931	2 709 305	1 371 815	1 337 490
22 years	123 721	63 644	60 077	222 586	123 247	99 339	454 901	250 382	204 519	2 566 968	1 302 325	1 264 643
23 years	120 703	61 967	58 736	226 443	124 804	101 639	465 373	254 368	211 005	2 640 455	1 334 513	1 305 942
24 years	123 961	62 984	60 977	224 325	123 329	100 996	463 544	252 021	211 523	2 683 516	1 351 963	1 331 553
25 years	137 384	69 268	68 116	240 014	131 901	108 113	500 168	271 894	228 274	3 001 634	1 512 911	1 488 723
26 years	134 707	66 796	67 911	221 234	118 944	102 290	468 087	249 071	219 016	3 016 904	1 512 777	1 504 127
27 years	139 470	69 288	70 182	219 738	118 470	101 268	468 756	249 945	218 811	3 093 304	1 552 831	1 540 473
28 years	138 490	68 281	70 209	211 084	114 570	96 514	454 001	242 129	211 872	3 117 625	1 566 396	1 551 229
29 years	141 018	68 995	72 023	208 020	111 374	96 646	450 227	237 319	212 908	3 270 682	1 639 143	1 631 539
30 years	163 757	80 005	83 752	225 421	121 558	103 863	489 375	259 604	229 771	3 460 911	1 739 983	1 720 928
31 years	133 594	64 159	69 435	173 461	91 558	81 903	382 881	198 732	184 149	3 115 382	1 555 170	1 560 212
32 years	148 142	71 939	76 203	189 712	100 439	89 273	419 088	217 743	201 345	3 325 175	1 664 923	1 660 252
33 years	140 777	67 633	73 144	177 219	93 220	83 999	395 515	204 988	190 527	3 237 780	1 618 884	1 618 896
34 years	139 913	66 071	73 842	166 986	87 452	79 534	375 444	193 390	182 054	3 180 783	1 590 861	1 589 922
35 years	151 770	73 145	78 625	172 897	91 481	81 416	388 775	201 192	187 583	3 288 370	1 656 975	1 631 395
36 years	135 092	63 843	71 249	149 698	77 438	72 260	341 228	173 416	167 812	3 079 028	1 534 156	1 544 872
37 years	130 621	61 699	68 922	139 218	71 934	67 284	321 456	163 121	158 335	3 043 358	1 521 852	1 521 506
38 years	126 147	58 931	67 216	133 268	68 781	64 487	307 984	156 421	151 563	2 901 153	1 450 543	1 450 610
39 years	126 188	58 904	67 284	129 664	66 313	63 351	301 283	152 011	149 272	2 916 492	1 461 948	1 454 544
40 years	142 627	66 545	76 082	135 416	69 679	65 737	316 316	159 775	156 541	3 011 535	1 507 407	1 504 128
41 years	113 125	52 300	60 825	101 289	51 271	50 018	244 989	122 108	122 881	2 685 780	1 332 127	1 353 653
42 years	121 207	56 923	64 284	112 790	57 217	55 573	270 991	135 290	135 701	2 993 865	1 495 178	1 498 687
43 years	107 547	49 789	57 758	101 315	50 892	50 423	247 481	122 425	125 056	2 965 075	1 479 653	1 485 422
44 years	87 688	41 235	46 453	84 176	42 048	42 128	204 491	100 570	103 921	2 164 215	1 074 893	1 089 322
45 years	98 728	47 340	51 388	95 061	48 346	46 715	231 000	115 545	115 455	2 366 707	1 180 715	1 185 992
46 years	82 035	38 933	43 102	75 870	37 675	38 195	192 060	93 912	98 148	2 279 851	1 127 103	1 162 668
47 years	77 811	37 438	40 373	73 664	36 408	37 256	187 645	90 930	96 715	2 378 326	1 180 874	1 197 452
48 years	74 146	35 742	38 404	68 057	33 753	34 304	172 593	84 258	88 335	2 031 650	1 000 433	1 031 217
49 years	72 870	35 953	36 917	66 045	32 992	33 053	170 612	83 612	87 000	1 999 428	990 050	1 009 378
50 years	77 926	38 388	39 538	68 997	34 251	34 746	180 217	87 818	92 399	1 989 990	981 194	1 008 796
51 years	58 333	28 557	29 776	51 307	25 151	26 156	140 870	67 861	73 009	1 764 403	865 264	899 139
52 years	62 292	30 608	31 684	56 428	27 762	28 666	152 708	73 683	79 025	1 835 955	903 190	932 765
53 years	57 683	28 004	29 679	51 522	25 094	26 428	142 667	68 402	74 265	1 741 365	852 203	889 102
54 years	55 417	26 528	28 889	50 012	24 147	25 865	139 527	66 455	73 072	1 731 791	844 954	886 837
55 years	56 870	26 597	30 273	50 483	24 373	26 110	142 122	67 749	74 373	1 772 492	862 070	910 422
56 years	50 381	23 185	27 196	43 945	20 925	23 020	126 620	60 143	66 477	1 633 286	792 482	840 804
57 years	49 771	22 273	27 498	41 869	19 860	22 009	123 871	58 087	65 784	1 699 282	822 386	876 896
58 years	46 300	20 533	25 767	40 671	19 148	21 523	120 886	56 848	64 038	1 676 844	804 876	871 968
59 years	47 311	20 921	26 390	41 171	19 471	21 700	125 809	59 544	66 265	1 794 431	863 875	930 556
60 years	50 992	22 118	28 874	42 045	19 585	22 460	127 442	59 148	68 294	1 813 723	863 109	950 614
61 years	40 644	17 442	23 202	33 057	15 369	17 688	106 407	49 697	56 710	1 687 510	801 556	885 954
62 years	45 206	19 447	25 759	36 576	16 754	19 822	116 034	53 486	62 548	1 840 838	868 206	972 632
63 years	41 413	17 762	23 651	31 556	14 255	17 301	103 321	47 131	56 190	1 759 024	823 920	935 104
64 years	40 262	17 370	22 892	30 285	13 724	16 561	100 438	45 494	54 944	1 753 992	813 323	940 669
65 years	42 772	18 552	24 220	32 243	14 208	18 035	104 919	47 021	57 898	1 844 322	841 537	1 002 785
66 years	35 232	15 585	19 647	25 884	11 928	13 956	87 638	39 889	47 749	1 703 223	773 092	930 131
67 years	36 375	16 331	20 044	25 818	11 868	13 950	87 452	39 754	47 698	1 707 386	771 745	935 641
68 years	33 254	15 090	18 164	22 702	9 992	12 710	80 384	35 544	44 840	1 704 068	761 397	942 671
69 years	30 864	13 960	16 904	21 199	9 324	11 875	75 864	33 370	42 494	1 650 793	734 930	915 863
70 years	31 971	14 137	17 834	20 365	8 714	11 651	72 465	30 890	41 575	1 548 277	675 049	873 228
71 years	23 812	10 759	13 053	14 365	6 125	8 240	55 455	23 540	31 915	1 401 918	610 152	791 766
72 years	24 334	10 756	13 578	15 613	6 514	9 099	58 146	24 221	33 925	1 409 700	606 748	802 952
73 years	21 754	9 680	12 074	13 352	5 523	7 829	51 575	21 140	30 435	1 313 894	555 630	758 264
74 years	20 363	8 968	11 395	12 645	5 202	7 443	49 131	20 014	29 117	1 254 699	525 290	729 409
75 years	20 005	8 903	11 102	12 752	5 177	7 575	49 386	19 825	29 561	1 235 223	503 128	732 095
76 years	17 369	7 731	9 638	11 316	4 527	6 789	45 091	17 823	27 268	1 122 904	451 068	671 836
77 years	15 048	6 972	8 076	10 441	4 134	6 307	41 929	16 184	25 745	1 060 182	416 760	643 422
78 years	14 772	6 817	7 955	10 018	4 033	5 985	39 602	15 235	24 367	990 162	379 403	610 759
79 years	12 945	6 378	6 567	9 256	3 697	5 559	37 257	14 288	22 969	925 742	345 769	579 973
80 years	12 421	5 954	6 467	8 396	3 192	5 204	33 568	12 712	20 856	849 385	305 518	543 867
81 years	8 875	4 396	4 479	6 346	2 508	3 838	26 768	10 182	16 586	733 906	260 879	473 027
82 years	8 587	4 273	4 314	6 177	2 430	3 747	26 314	9 835	16 479	707 190	243 482	463 708
83 years	7 333	3 603	3 730	5 504	2 233	3 271	23 074	8 748	14 326	621 514	206 587	414 927
84 years	6 634	3 203	3 431	5 017	1 984	3 033	20 701	7 697	13 004	546 581	175 904	370 677
85 years	5 875	2 743	3 132	4 481	1 789	2 692	18 916	6 870	12 046	491 458	151 556	339 902
86 years	4 648	2 153	2 495	3 627	1 468	2 159	15 004	5 550	9 454	415 744	125 291	290 453
87 years	3 817	1 713	2 104	3 019	1 200	1 819	12 635	4 652	7 983	352 549	102 136	250 413
88 years	3 106	1 363	1 743	2 352	961	1 391	10 010	3 674	6 336	289 578	81 375	208 203
89 years	3 003	1 247	1 756	2 549	957	1 592	10 058	3 525	6 533	266 909	71 011	195 898
90 to 94 years	6 944	2 518	4 426	4 851	1 830	3 021	20 383	6 807	13 576	687 416	165 602	521 814
95 to 99 years	1 853	487	1 366	1 537	537	1 000	5 916	1 838	4 078	186 966	38 722	148 244
100 to 104 years	357	122	235	321	113	208	1 051	317	734	25 186	4 421	20 765
105 years and over	135	53	82	250	128	122	591	264	327	3 944	1 069	2 875
Median age	29.8	28.7	30.7	23.9	23.7	24.1	25.5	25.0	26.1	34.9	33.6	36.1

Table 14. **Age and Sex: 1990**

[For definitions of terms and meanings of symbols, see text]

United States Urban and Rural and Size of Place	United States	Urban								Rural			
			Inside urbanized area			Outside urbanized area						
		Total	Total	Central place	Urban fringe	Total	Place of 10,000 or more	Place of 2,500 to 9,999	Total	Place of 1,000 to 2,499	Place of less than 1,000	Other rural
AGE												
All persons	**248 709 873**	**187 053 487**	**158 258 878**	**78 847 406**	**79 411 472**	**28 794 609**	**13 825 022**	**14 969 587**	**61 656 386**	**7 050 858**	**3 801 051**	**50 804 477**
Under 5 years	18 354 443	13 989 160	11 852 403	6 039 978	5 812 425	2 136 757	1 025 480	1 111 277	4 365 283	504 385	271 872	3 589 026
Under 1 year	3 217 312	2 476 749	2 101 480	1 078 124	1 023 356	375 269	180 874	194 395	740 563	86 935	47 256	606 372
1 year	3 949 107	3 036 683	2 583 162	1 323 146	1 260 016	453 521	218 329	235 192	912 424	105 852	56 645	749 927
2 years	3 815 040	2 916 981	2 476 053	1 267 929	1 208 124	440 928	211 865	229 063	898 059	103 847	55 589	738 623
3 years	3 683 177	2 789 250	2 358 883	1 198 794	1 160 089	430 367	206 158	224 209	893 927	102 662	55 117	736 148
4 years	3 689 807	2 769 497	2 332 825	1 171 985	1 160 840	436 672	208 254	228 418	920 310	105 089	57 265	757 956
5 to 9 years	18 099 179	13 288 047	11 121 462	5 500 842	5 620 620	2 166 585	1 023 431	1 143 154	4 811 132	539 794	299 267	3 972 071
5 years	3 689 533	2 746 250	2 307 876	1 153 758	1 154 118	438 374	208 279	230 095	943 283	106 830	58 700	777 753
6 years	3 577 632	2 640 914	2 212 610	1 096 219	1 116 391	428 304	202 760	225 544	936 718	105 953	58 567	772 198
7 years	3 645 761	2 676 137	2 239 905	1 104 839	1 135 066	436 232	206 110	230 122	969 624	109 044	60 638	799 942
8 years	3 508 668	2 560 679	2 139 986	1 055 560	1 084 426	420 693	198 428	222 265	947 989	105 546	58 607	783 836
9 years	3 677 585	2 664 067	2 221 085	1 090 466	1 130 619	442 982	207 854	235 128	1 013 518	112 421	62 755	838 342
10 to 14 years	17 114 249	12 273 417	10 243 848	4 992 277	5 251 571	2 029 569	946 015	1 083 554	4 840 832	526 971	295 792	4 018 069
10 years	3 653 177	2 637 707	2 200 936	1 083 221	1 117 715	436 771	204 235	232 536	1 015 470	111 428	62 730	841 312
11 years	3 455 515	2 480 334	2 068 155	1 011 218	1 056 937	412 179	192 705	219 474	975 181	106 875	59 824	808 482
12 years	3 423 450	2 448 745	2 042 859	992 430	1 050 429	405 886	189 531	216 355	974 705	105 948	59 294	809 463
13 years	3 339 000	2 386 778	1 992 796	966 382	1 026 414	393 982	183 217	210 765	952 222	103 127	58 057	791 038
14 years	3 243 107	2 319 853	1 939 102	939 026	1 000 076	380 751	176 327	204 424	923 254	99 593	55 887	767 774
15 to 19 years	17 754 015	13 188 758	10 947 774	5 620 093	5 327 681	2 240 984	1 129 350	1 111 634	4 565 257	502 183	268 186	3 794 888
15 years	3 321 609	2 374 518	1 987 022	961 246	1 025 776	387 496	180 263	207 233	947 091	102 124	57 087	787 880
16 years	3 304 890	2 366 450	1 984 422	963 675	1 020 747	382 028	177 417	204 611	938 440	100 310	56 126	782 004
17 years	3 410 062	2 458 583	2 065 156	1 009 124	1 056 032	393 427	183 064	210 363	951 479	102 521	57 167	791 791
18 years	3 641 238	2 755 482	2 271 127	1 204 852	1 066 275	484 355	253 206	231 149	885 756	98 924	51 619	735 213
19 years	4 076 216	3 233 725	2 640 047	1 481 196	1 158 851	593 678	335 400	258 278	842 491	98 304	46 187	698 000
20 to 24 years	19 020 312	15 371 060	13 006 162	7 217 767	5 788 395	2 364 898	1 305 053	1 059 845	3 649 252	426 794	210 861	3 011 597
20 years	4 009 414	3 230 815	2 673 647	1 512 655	1 160 992	557 168	318 059	239 109	778 599	91 093	42 842	644 664
21 years	3 817 220	3 093 570	2 576 929	1 457 779	1 119 150	516 641	295 249	221 392	723 650	84 897	40 799	597 954
25 to 29 years	21 313 045	16 898 657	14 652 774	7 654 100	6 998 674	2 245 883	1 113 484	1 132 399	4 414 388	501 725	264 190	3 648 473
30 to 34 years	21 862 887	16 779 795	14 502 886	7 230 660	7 272 226	2 276 909	1 100 615	1 176 294	5 083 092	544 341	287 612	4 251 139
35 to 39 years	19 963 117	14 944 849	12 853 531	6 209 742	6 643 789	2 091 318	1 002 298	1 089 020	5 018 268	516 320	268 121	4 233 827
40 to 44 years	17 615 786	13 013 170	11 202 038	5 189 570	6 012 468	1 811 132	858 953	952 179	4 602 616	460 083	235 921	3 906 612
45 to 49 years	13 872 573	10 070 112	8 655 362	3 938 395	4 716 967	1 414 750	660 574	754 176	3 802 461	371 819	198 330	3 232 312
50 to 54 years	11 350 513	8 208 772	7 018 648	3 266 976	3 751 672	1 190 124	552 130	637 994	3 141 741	320 269	174 831	2 646 641
55 to 59 years	10 531 756	7 657 284	6 500 855	3 071 278	3 429 577	1 156 429	535 443	620 986	2 874 472	310 550	171 658	2 392 264
60 to 64 years	10 616 167	7 801 852	6 556 094	3 160 980	3 395 114	1 245 758	572 094	673 664	2 814 315	332 943	183 076	2 298 296
65 to 69 years	10 111 735	7 520 892	6 245 185	3 068 094	3 177 091	1 275 707	582 794	692 913	2 590 843	338 924	187 504	2 064 415
70 to 74 years	7 994 823	5 981 647	4 887 495	2 446 409	2 441 086	1 094 152	494 758	599 394	2 013 176	295 553	167 143	1 550 480
75 to 79 years	6 121 369	4 625 077	3 722 553	1 928 668	1 793 885	902 524	405 718	496 806	1 496 292	246 104	142 129	1 108 059
80 to 84 years	3 933 739	3 021 594	2 397 973	1 277 137	1 120 836	623 621	280 568	343 053	912 145	168 306	97 722	646 117
85 years and over	3 080 165	2 419 344	1 891 835	1 034 440	857 395	527 509	236 264	291 245	660 821	143 794	76 836	440 191
18 years and over	185 105 441	140 303 312	119 004 565	59 380 264	59 624 301	21 298 747	10 289 352	11 009 395	44 802 129	5 174 753	2 763 740	36 863 636
62 years and over	37 629 695	28 265 910	23 080 028	11 657 083	11 422 945	5 185 882	2 348 972	2 836 910	9 363 785	1 396 525	783 604	7 183 656
65 years and over	31 241 831	23 568 554	19 145 041	9 754 748	9 390 293	4 423 513	2 000 102	2 423 411	7 673 277	1 192 681	671 334	5 809 262
Median age	32.9	32.5	32.5	31.5	33.3	32.6	31.6	33.6	34.1	34.8	35.0	34.0
Male	**121 239 418**	**90 386 114**	**76 628 073**	**37 947 570**	**38 680 503**	**13 758 041**	**6 626 550**	**7 131 491**	**30 853 304**	**3 365 091**	**1 830 081**	**25 658 132**
Under 5 years	9 392 409	7 153 760	6 062 403	3 083 819	2 978 584	1 091 357	523 653	567 704	2 238 649	258 288	138 968	1 841 393
Under 1 year	1 644 801	1 265 656	1 074 026	550 158	523 868	191 630	92 372	99 258	379 145	44 514	24 163	310 468
1 year	2 022 292	1 554 714	1 323 178	676 453	646 725	231 536	111 467	120 069	467 578	54 132	28 959	384 487
2 years	1 952 242	1 492 205	1 267 042	647 656	619 386	225 163	108 108	117 055	460 037	53 151	28 469	378 417
3 years	1 884 023	1 424 950	1 205 100	611 554	593 546	219 850	105 326	114 524	459 073	52 579	28 233	378 261
4 years	1 889 051	1 416 235	1 193 057	597 998	595 059	223 178	106 380	116 798	472 816	53 912	29 144	389 760
5 to 9 years	9 262 527	6 786 574	5 679 795	2 803 808	2 875 987	1 106 779	523 559	583 220	2 475 953	275 964	152 928	2 047 061
5 years	1 889 177	1 403 231	1 179 097	588 528	590 569	224 134	106 463	117 671	485 946	54 752	30 084	401 110
6 years	1 829 832	1 349 226	1 130 985	559 044	571 941	218 241	103 535	114 706	480 606	53 929	29 976	396 701
7 years	1 865 700	1 366 677	1 144 358	562 876	581 482	222 319	105 098	117 221	499 023	55 812	30 930	412 281
8 years	1 794 355	1 306 521	1 091 133	537 505	553 628	215 388	101 720	113 668	487 834	53 905	29 961	403 968
9 years	1 883 463	1 360 919	1 134 222	555 855	578 367	226 697	106 743	119 954	522 544	57 566	31 977	433 001
10 to 14 years	8 767 167	6 266 694	5 231 500	2 543 119	2 688 381	1 035 194	481 471	553 723	2 500 473	269 936	151 575	2 078 962
10 years	1 874 172	1 349 600	1 126 271	553 262	573 009	223 329	104 605	118 724	524 572	57 273	32 223	435 076
11 years	1 771 334	1 267 730	1 057 197	515 819	541 378	210 533	98 122	112 411	503 604	54 885	30 716	418 003
12 years	1 752 999	1 249 894	1 042 785	504 954	537 831	207 109	96 463	110 646	503 105	54 074	30 342	418 689
13 years	1 706 417	1 215 618	1 015 129	491 458	523 671	200 489	92 965	107 524	490 799	52 581	29 716	408 502
14 years	1 662 245	1 183 852	990 118	477 626	512 492	193 734	89 316	104 418	478 393	51 123	28 578	398 692
15 to 19 years	9 102 698	6 703 124	5 572 777	2 833 597	2 739 180	1 130 347	565 191	565 156	2 399 574	257 033	138 438	2 004 103
15 years	1 705 780	1 212 777	1 015 569	489 841	525 728	197 208	91 457	105 751	493 003	52 211	29 424	411 368
16 years	1 697 995	1 207 996	1 013 050	490 248	522 802	194 946	90 449	104 497	489 999	51 281	28 825	409 893
17 years	1 758 400	1 260 036	1 059 058	516 136	542 922	200 978	93 389	107 589	498 364	52 432	29 602	416 330
18 years	1 862 377	1 392 211	1 151 950	601 227	550 723	240 261	123 729	116 532	470 166	50 733	26 788	392 645
19 years	2 078 146	1 630 104	1 333 150	736 145	597 005	296 954	166 167	130 787	448 042	50 376	23 799	373 867
20 to 24 years	9 675 596	7 773 590	6 569 259	3 624 185	2 945 074	1 204 331	668 055	536 276	1 902 006	212 760	104 886	1 584 360
20 years	2 044 082	1 632 679	1 352 727	754 284	598 443	279 952	158 741	121 211	411 403	45 973	21 639	343 791
21 years	1 947 811	1 566 575	1 305 655	730 953	574 702	260 920	148 772	112 148	381 236	42 822	20 431	317 983
25 to 29 years	10 695 936	8 475 923	7 352 411	3 852 987	3 499 424	1 123 512	562 598	560 914	2 220 013	246 214	130 436	1 843 363
30 to 34 years	10 876 933	8 333 244	7 208 602	3 606 765	3 601 837	1 124 642	546 470	578 172	2 543 689	266 080	142 677	2 134 932
35 to 39 years	9 902 243	7 368 671	6 335 379	3 075 502	3 259 877	1 033 292	496 438	536 854	2 533 572	254 572	134 295	2 144 705
40 to 44 years	8 691 984	6 358 595	5 465 510	2 533 134	2 932 376	893 085	424 352	468 733	2 333 389	227 372	117 831	1 988 186
45 to 49 years	6 810 597	4 883 234	4 196 477	1 891 365	2 305 112	686 757	320 481	366 276	1 927 363	181 520	97 741	1 648 102
50 to 54 years	5 514 738	3 929 356	3 363 133	1 539 427	1 823 706	566 223	262 203	304 020	1 585 382	153 470	85 289	1 346 623
55 to 59 years	5 034 370	3 608 813	3 075 513	1 422 991	1 652 522	533 300	246 639	286 661	1 425 557	145 849	81 309	1 198 399
60 to 64 years	4 947 047	3 564 943	3 006 968	1 418 628	1 588 340	557 975	255 294	302 681	1 382 104	152 571	85 080	1 144 453
65 to 69 years	4 532 307	3 295 344	2 745 225	1 321 200	1 424 025	550 119	250 065	300 054	1 236 963	148 747	83 572	1 004 644
70 to 74 years	3 409 306	2 483 734	2 039 011	994 045	1 044 966	444 723	199 915	244 808	925 572	122 401	70 266	732 905
75 to 79 years	2 399 768	1 750 709	1 416 266	713 498	702 768	334 443	148 888	185 555	649 059	94 545	56 231	498 283
80 to 84 years	1 366 094	1 006 221	801 456	416 119	385 337	204 765	90 862	113 903	359 873	57 777	35 221	266 875
85 years and over	857 698	643 585	506 388	273 381	233 007	137 197	60 416	76 781	214 113	39 992	23 338	150 783
18 years and over	88 655 140	66 498 277	56 566 698	28 020 599	28 546 099	9 931 579	4 822 572	5 109 007	22 156 863	2 404 979	1 298 759	18 453 125
62 years and over	15 524 180	11 307 841	9 296 350	4 564 118	4 732 232	2 011 491	904 813	1 106 678	4 216 339	556 937	320 872	3 338 530
65 years and over	12 565 173	9 179 593	7 508 346	3 718 243	3 790 103	1 671 247	750 146	921 101	3 385 580	463 462	268 628	2 653 490
Median age	31.7	31.1	31.2	30.3	32.2	30.8	29.9	31.7	33.3	33.0	33.4	33.4

Table 14. **Age and Sex: 1990**—Con.

[For definitions of terms and meanings of symbols, see text]

United States Urban and Rural and Size of Place	United States	Urban							Rural			
		Total	Inside urbanized area			Outside urbanized area			Total	Place of 1,000 to 2,499	Place of less than 1,000	Other rural
			Total	Central place	Urban fringe	Total	Place of 10,000 or more	Place of 2,500 to 9,999				
AGE—Con.												
Female	127 470 455	96 667 373	81 630 805	40 899 836	40 730 969	15 036 568	7 198 472	7 838 096	30 803 082	3 685 767	1 970 970	25 146 345
Under 5 years	8 962 034	6 835 400	5 790 000	2 956 159	2 833 841	1 045 400	501 827	543 573	2 126 634	246 097	132 904	1 747 633
Under 1 year	1 572 511	1 211 093	1 027 454	527 966	499 488	183 639	88 502	95 137	361 418	42 421	23 093	295 904
1 year	1 926 815	1 481 969	1 259 984	646 693	613 291	221 985	106 862	115 123	444 846	51 720	27 686	365 440
2 years	1 862 798	1 424 776	1 209 011	620 273	588 738	215 765	103 757	112 008	438 022	50 696	27 120	360 206
3 years	1 799 154	1 364 300	1 153 783	587 240	566 543	210 517	100 832	109 685	434 854	50 083	26 884	357 887
4 years	1 800 756	1 353 262	1 139 768	573 987	565 781	213 494	101 874	111 620	447 494	51 177	28 121	368 196
5 to 9 years	8 836 652	6 501 473	5 441 667	2 697 034	2 744 633	1 059 806	499 872	559 934	2 335 179	263 830	146 339	1 925 010
5 years	1 800 356	1 343 019	1 128 779	565 230	563 549	214 240	101 816	112 424	457 337	52 078	28 616	376 643
6 years	1 747 800	1 291 688	1 081 625	537 175	544 450	210 063	99 225	110 838	456 112	52 024	28 591	375 497
7 years	1 780 061	1 309 460	1 095 547	541 963	553 584	213 913	101 012	112 901	470 601	53 232	29 708	387 661
8 years	1 714 313	1 254 158	1 048 853	518 055	530 798	205 305	96 708	108 597	460 155	51 641	28 646	379 868
9 years	1 794 122	1 303 148	1 086 863	534 611	552 252	216 285	101 111	115 174	490 974	54 855	30 778	405 341
10 to 14 years	8 347 082	6 006 723	5 012 348	2 449 158	2 563 190	994 375	464 544	529 831	2 340 359	257 035	144 217	1 939 107
10 years	1 779 005	1 288 107	1 074 665	529 959	544 706	213 442	99 630	113 812	490 898	54 155	30 507	406 236
11 years	1 684 181	1 212 604	1 010 958	495 399	515 559	201 646	94 583	107 063	471 577	51 990	29 108	390 479
12 years	1 670 451	1 198 851	1 000 074	487 476	512 598	198 777	93 068	105 709	471 600	51 874	28 952	390 774
13 years	1 632 583	1 171 160	977 667	474 924	502 743	193 493	90 252	103 241	461 423	50 546	28 341	382 536
14 years	1 580 862	1 136 001	948 984	461 400	487 584	187 017	87 011	100 006	444 861	48 470	27 309	369 082
15 to 19 years	8 651 317	6 485 634	5 374 997	2 786 496	2 588 501	1 110 637	564 159	546 478	2 165 683	245 150	129 748	1 790 785
15 years	1 615 829	1 161 741	971 453	471 405	500 048	190 288	88 806	101 482	454 088	49 913	27 663	376 512
16 years	1 606 895	1 158 454	971 372	473 427	497 945	187 082	86 968	100 114	448 441	49 029	27 301	372 111
17 years	1 651 662	1 198 547	1 006 098	492 988	513 110	192 449	89 675	102 774	453 115	50 089	27 565	375 461
18 years	1 778 861	1 363 271	1 119 177	603 625	515 552	244 094	129 477	114 617	415 590	48 191	24 831	342 568
19 years	1 998 070	1 603 621	1 306 897	745 051	561 846	296 724	169 233	127 491	394 449	47 928	22 388	324 133
20 to 24 years	9 344 716	7 597 470	6 436 903	3 593 582	2 843 321	1 160 567	636 998	523 569	1 747 246	214 034	105 975	1 427 237
20 years	1 965 332	1 598 136	1 320 920	758 371	562 549	277 216	159 318	117 898	367 196	45 120	21 203	300 873
21 years	1 869 409	1 526 995	1 271 274	726 826	544 448	255 721	146 477	109 244	342 414	42 075	20 368	279 971
25 to 29 years	10 617 109	8 422 734	7 300 363	3 801 113	3 499 250	1 122 371	550 886	571 485	2 194 375	255 511	133 754	1 805 110
30 to 34 years	10 985 954	8 446 551	7 294 284	3 623 895	3 670 389	1 152 267	554 145	598 122	2 539 403	278 261	144 935	2 116 207
35 to 39 years	10 060 874	7 576 178	6 518 152	3 134 240	3 383 912	1 058 026	505 860	552 166	2 484 696	261 748	133 826	2 089 122
40 to 44 years	8 923 802	6 654 575	5 736 528	2 656 436	3 080 092	918 047	434 601	483 446	2 269 227	232 711	118 090	1 918 426
45 to 49 years	7 061 976	5 186 878	4 458 885	2 047 030	2 411 855	727 993	340 093	387 900	1 875 098	190 299	100 589	1 584 210
50 to 54 years	5 835 775	4 279 416	3 655 515	1 727 549	1 927 966	623 901	289 927	333 974	1 556 359	166 799	89 542	1 300 018
55 to 59 years	5 497 386	4 048 471	3 425 342	1 648 287	1 777 055	623 129	288 804	334 325	1 448 915	164 701	90 349	1 193 865
60 to 64 years	5 669 120	4 236 909	3 549 126	1 742 352	1 806 774	687 783	316 800	370 983	1 432 211	180 372	97 996	1 153 843
65 to 69 years	5 579 428	4 225 548	3 499 960	1 746 894	1 753 066	725 588	332 729	392 859	1 353 880	190 177	103 932	1 059 771
70 to 74 years	4 585 517	3 497 913	2 848 484	1 452 364	1 396 120	649 429	294 843	354 586	1 087 604	173 152	96 877	817 575
75 to 79 years	3 721 601	2 874 368	2 306 287	1 215 170	1 091 117	568 081	256 830	311 251	847 233	151 559	85 898	609 776
80 to 84 years	2 567 645	2 015 373	1 596 517	861 018	735 499	418 856	189 706	229 150	552 272	110 529	62 501	379 242
85 years and over	2 222 467	1 775 759	1 385 447	761 059	624 388	390 312	175 848	214 464	446 708	103 802	53 498	289 408
18 years and over	96 450 301	73 805 035	62 437 867	31 359 665	31 078 202	11 367 168	5 466 780	5 900 388	22 645 266	2 769 774	1 464 981	18 410 511
62 years and over	22 105 515	16 958 069	13 783 678	7 092 965	6 690 713	3 174 391	1 444 159	1 730 232	5 147 446	839 588	462 732	3 845 126
65 years and over	18 676 658	14 388 961	11 636 695	6 036 505	5 600 190	2 752 266	1 249 956	1 502 310	4 287 697	729 219	402 706	3 155 772
Median age	34.1	33.8	33.7	32.9	34.5	34.4	33.4	35.4	34.9	36.5	36.7	34.6
PERCENT DISTRIBUTION												
All persons	100.0	100.0	100.0	100.0	100.0	100.0	100.0	100.0	100.0	100.0	100.0	100.0
Under 18 years	25.6	25.0	24.8	24.7	24.9	26.0	25.6	26.5	27.3	26.6	27.3	27.4
Under 5 years	7.4	7.5	7.5	7.7	7.3	7.4	7.4	7.4	7.1	7.2	7.2	7.1
5 to 17 years	18.2	17.5	17.3	17.0	17.6	18.6	18.2	19.0	20.3	19.5	20.1	20.4
18 to 64 years	61.9	62.4	63.1	62.9	63.3	58.6	60.0	57.4	60.2	56.5	55.0	61.1
18 to 24 years	10.8	11.4	11.3	12.6	10.1	12.0	13.7	10.3	8.7	8.9	8.1	8.7
25 to 44 years	32.5	33.0	33.6	33.3	33.9	29.3	29.5	29.1	31.0	28.7	27.8	31.6
45 to 64 years	18.6	18.0	18.2	17.0	19.3	17.4	16.8	17.9	20.5	18.9	19.1	20.8
65 years and over	12.6	12.6	12.1	12.4	11.8	15.4	14.5	16.2	12.4	16.9	17.7	11.4
65 to 79 years	9.7	9.7	9.4	9.4	9.3	11.4	10.7	12.0	9.9	12.5	13.1	9.3
80 years and over	2.8	2.9	2.7	2.9	2.5	4.0	3.7	4.2	2.6	4.4	4.6	2.1
Male	100.0	100.0	100.0	100.0	100.0	100.0	100.0	100.0	100.0	100.0	100.0	100.0
Under 18 years	26.9	26.4	26.2	26.2	26.2	27.8	27.2	28.4	28.2	28.5	29.0	28.1
Under 5 years	7.7	7.9	7.9	8.1	7.7	7.9	7.9	8.0	7.3	7.7	7.6	7.2
5 to 17 years	19.1	18.5	18.3	18.0	18.5	19.9	19.3	20.4	20.9	20.9	21.4	20.9
18 to 64 years	62.8	63.4	64.0	64.0	64.0	60.0	61.5	58.7	60.8	57.7	56.3	61.6
18 to 24 years	11.2	11.9	11.8	13.1	10.6	12.7	14.5	11.0	9.1	9.3	8.5	9.2
25 to 44 years	33.1	33.8	34.4	34.4	34.4	30.3	30.6	30.1	31.2	29.5	28.7	31.6
45 to 64 years	18.4	17.7	17.8	16.5	19.1	17.0	16.4	17.7	20.5	18.8	19.1	20.8
65 years and over	10.4	10.2	9.8	9.8	9.8	12.1	11.3	12.9	11.0	13.8	14.7	10.3
65 to 79 years	8.5	8.3	8.1	8.0	8.2	9.7	9.0	10.2	9.1	10.9	11.5	8.7
80 years and over	1.8	1.8	1.7	1.8	1.6	2.5	2.3	2.7	1.9	2.9	3.2	1.6
Female	100.0	100.0	100.0	100.0	100.0	100.0	100.0	100.0	100.0	100.0	100.0	100.0
Under 18 years	24.3	23.7	23.5	23.3	23.7	24.4	24.1	24.7	26.5	24.9	25.7	26.8
Under 5 years	7.0	7.1	7.1	7.2	7.0	7.0	7.0	6.9	6.9	6.7	6.7	6.9
5 to 17 years	17.3	16.6	16.4	16.1	16.7	17.5	17.1	17.8	19.6	18.2	10.9	19.8
18 to 64 years	61.0	61.5	62.2	61.9	62.6	57.3	58.6	56.1	59.6	55.4	53.9	60.7
18 to 24 years	10.3	10.9	10.9	12.1	9.6	11.3	13.0	9.8	8.3	8.4	7.8	8.3
25 to 44 years	31.8	32.2	32.9	32.3	33.5	28.3	28.4	28.1	30.8	27.9	26.9	31.5
45 to 64 years	18.9	18.4	18.5	17.5	19.5	17.7	17.2	18.2	20.5	19.1	19.2	20.8
65 years and over	14.7	14.9	14.3	14.8	13.7	18.3	17.4	19.2	13.9	19.8	20.4	12.5
65 to 79 years	10.9	11.0	10.6	10.8	10.4	12.9	12.3	13.5	10.7	14.0	14.5	9.9
80 years and over	3.8	3.9	3.7	4.0	3.3	5.4	5.1	5.7	3.2	5.8	5.9	2.7
MALES PER 100 FEMALES												
All persons	95.1	93.5	93.9	92.8	95.0	91.5	92.1	91.0	100.2	91.3	92.9	102.0
Under 18 years	105.0	104.5	104.5	104.1	105.0	104.3	104.2	104.4	106.6	104.8	105.0	107.0
Under 5 years	104.8	104.7	104.7	104.3	105.1	104.4	104.3	104.4	105.3	105.0	104.6	105.4
5 to 17 years	105.1	104.4	104.4	103.9	104.9	104.2	104.1	104.4	107.1	104.8	105.2	107.5
18 to 64 years	97.8	96.5	96.6	96.0	97.2	95.9	96.6	95.2	102.3	95.1	97.0	103.6
18 to 24 years	103.8	102.2	102.2	100.4	104.4	102.4	102.4	102.3	110.3	101.2	101.5	112.3
25 to 44 years	99.0	98.2	98.2	98.9	97.5	98.2	99.2	97.3	101.5	96.7	99.0	102.3
45 to 64 years	92.7	90.1	90.4	87.5	93.0	88.0	87.8	88.3	100.1	90.2	92.3	102.0
65 years and over	67.3	63.8	64.5	61.6	67.7	60.7	60.0	61.3	79.0	63.6	66.7	84.1
65 to 79 years	74.5	71.1	71.6	68.6	74.8	68.4	67.7	69.0	85.5	71.0	73.3	89.9
80 years and over	46.4	43.5	43.9	42.5	45.5	42.3	41.4	43.0	57.5	45.6	50.5	62.5

Table 15. **Age and Sex: 1990**

[For definitions of terms and meanings of symbols, see text]

United States Inside and Outside Metropolitan Area	United States	Inside metropolitan area						Outside metropolitan area				
				Not in central city					Urban			
					Urban					Outside urbanized area		
		Total	In central city	Total	Inside urbanized area	Outside urbanized area	Rural	Total	Inside urbanized area	Place of 10,000 or more	Place of 2,500 to 9,999	Rural
AGE												
All persons	**248 709 873**	**192 725 741**	**77 843 533**	**114 882 208**	**79 755 134**	**8 684 794**	**26 442 280**	**55 984 132**	**1 520 259**	**9 873 345**	**9 458 347**	**35 132 181**
Under 5 years	18 354 443	14 393 769	5 951 667	8 442 102	5 856 830	684 979	1 900 293	3 960 674	107 991	710 011	683 664	2 459 008
Under 1 year	3 217 312	2 532 944	1 062 184	1 470 760	1 031 344	119 267	320 149	684 368	19 188	125 531	120 217	419 432
1 year	3 949 107	3 117 923	1 303 338	1 814 585	1 270 196	145 654	398 735	831 184	23 197	151 189	144 369	512 429
2 years	3 815 040	3 000 947	1 249 487	1 751 460	1 217 416	141 958	392 086	814 093	22 478	146 085	140 812	504 718
3 years	3 683 177	2 878 691	1 181 562	1 697 129	1 168 851	138 336	389 942	804 486	21 423	142 776	137 596	502 691
4 years	3 689 807	2 863 264	1 155 096	1 708 168	1 169 023	139 764	399 381	826 543	21 705	144 430	140 670	519 738
5 to 9 years	18 099 179	13 831 349	5 423 701	8 407 648	5 657 479	685 136	2 065 033	4 267 830	104 773	714 324	708 897	2 739 836
5 years	3 689 533	2 847 068	1 137 388	1 709 680	1 162 176	139 697	407 807	842 465	21 459	144 998	141 845	534 163
6 years	3 577 632	2 743 174	1 080 609	1 662 565	1 123 780	135 772	403 013	834 458	20 884	141 652	139 447	532 475
7 years	3 645 761	2 785 475	1 089 230	1 696 245	1 142 439	137 771	416 035	860 286	21 159	143 740	143 007	552 380
8 years	3 508 668	2 671 435	1 040 937	1 630 498	1 091 426	133 084	405 988	837 233	20 315	138 277	137 905	540 736
9 years	3 677 585	2 784 197	1 075 537	1 708 660	1 137 658	138 812	432 190	893 388	20 956	145 657	146 693	580 082
10 to 14 years	17 114 249	12 884 093	4 925 473	7 958 620	5 279 826	629 392	2 049 402	4 230 156	97 274	666 847	680 470	2 785 565
10 years	3 653 177	2 760 366	1 068 568	1 691 798	1 124 110	136 644	431 044	892 811	20 934	143 528	145 156	583 193
11 years	3 455 515	2 601 304	997 487	1 603 817	1 062 808	127 687	413 322	854 211	19 841	135 822	137 869	560 679
12 years	3 423 450	2 573 348	979 156	1 594 192	1 056 070	125 659	412 463	850 102	19 465	133 610	136 008	561 019
13 years	3 339 000	2 509 068	953 651	1 555 417	1 031 807	121 758	401 852	829 932	18 748	129 341	132 610	549 233
14 years	3 243 107	2 440 007	926 611	1 513 396	1 005 031	117 644	390 721	803 100	18 286	124 546	128 827	531 441
15 to 19 years	17 754 015	13 501 631	5 546 375	7 955 256	5 349 362	650 613	1 955 281	4 252 384	116 640	827 261	704 141	2 604 342
15 years	3 321 609	2 502 071	949 036	1 553 035	1 030 762	119 293	402 980	819 538	18 182	127 716	130 642	542 998
16 years	3 304 890	2 492 575	951 957	1 540 618	1 025 516	117 034	398 068	812 315	17 921	125 581	129 566	539 247
17 years	3 410 062	2 582 674	996 982	1 585 692	1 060 950	120 200	404 542	827 388	18 355	129 782	133 452	545 799
18 years	3 641 238	2 775 502	1 188 847	1 586 655	1 069 862	136 779	380 014	865 736	26 363	188 173	146 590	504 610
19 years	4 076 216	3 148 809	1 459 553	1 689 256	1 162 272	157 307	369 677	927 407	35 819	256 009	163 891	471 688
20 to 24 years	19 020 312	15 178 845	7 108 880	8 069 965	5 816 958	662 752	1 590 255	3 841 467	154 809	972 256	660 460	2 053 942
20 years	4 009 414	3 148 716	1 489 573	1 659 143	1 165 474	149 499	344 170	860 698	35 746	241 468	150 104	433 380
21 years	3 817 220	3 015 226	1 433 828	1 581 398	1 123 911	139 644	317 843	801 994	35 122	223 797	138 222	404 853
25 to 29 years	21 313 045	17 229 958	7 549 946	9 680 012	7 042 497	712 811	1 924 704	4 083 087	131 233	780 150	688 717	2 482 987
30 to 34 years	21 862 887	17 481 441	7 134 855	10 346 586	7 314 573	739 600	2 292 413	4 381 446	125 371	762 009	711 002	2 783 064
35 to 39 years	19 963 117	15 773 452	6 133 762	9 639 690	6 673 937	668 068	2 297 685	4 189 665	112 758	698 507	665 043	2 713 357
40 to 44 years	17 615 786	13 883 004	5 127 178	8 755 826	6 036 215	580 818	2 138 793	3 732 782	95 694	598 926	580 828	2 457 334
45 to 49 years	13 872 573	10 823 997	3 894 063	6 929 934	4 732 899	449 328	1 747 707	3 048 576	72 717	463 771	463 040	2 049 048
50 to 54 years	11 350 513	8 729 415	3 233 364	5 496 051	3 761 388	360 048	1 374 615	2 621 098	59 936	395 300	403 213	1 762 649
55 to 59 years	10 531 756	8 012 739	3 039 800	4 972 939	3 435 566	336 706	1 200 667	2 519 017	59 804	388 485	400 851	1 669 877
60 to 64 years	10 616 167	7 997 871	3 127 576	4 870 295	3 398 304	351 627	1 120 364	2 618 296	65 615	419 559	442 770	1 690 352
65 to 69 years	10 111 735	7 558 466	3 031 136	4 527 330	3 179 927	356 533	990 870	2 553 269	69 309	427 402	459 453	1 597 105
70 to 74 years	7 994 823	5 892 987	2 416 741	3 476 246	2 442 561	296 871	736 814	2 101 836	57 073	364 254	406 133	1 274 376
75 to 79 years	6 121 369	4 463 816	1 907 706	2 556 110	1 796 155	236 508	523 447	1 657 553	42 150	299 626	344 262	971 515
80 to 84 years	3 933 739	2 855 256	1 265 128	1 590 128	1 121 864	156 349	311 915	1 078 483	27 147	208 416	243 449	599 471
85 years and over	3 080 165	2 233 652	1 026 182	1 207 470	858 793	126 655	222 022	846 513	19 965	176 241	211 954	438 353
18 years and over	185 105 441	144 039 210	58 644 717	85 394 493	59 843 771	6 328 760	19 221 962	41 066 231	1 155 763	7 399 084	6 991 656	25 519 728
62 years and over	37 629 695	27 800 318	11 528 617	16 271 701	11 433 483	1 387 192	3 451 026	9 829 377	256 059	1 732 233	1 937 798	5 903 287
65 years and over	31 241 831	23 004 177	9 646 893	13 357 284	9 399 300	1 172 916	2 785 068	8 237 654	215 644	1 475 939	1 665 251	4 880 820
Median age	32.9	32.6	31.6	33.3	33.3	32.1	33.8	33.8	31.8	31.7	34.2	34.4
Male	**121 239 418**	**93 823 988**	**37 445 427**	**56 378 561**	**38 856 067**	**4 205 832**	**13 316 662**	**27 415 430**	**740 907**	**4 717 395**	**4 462 453**	**17 494 675**
Under 5 years	9 392 409	7 365 699	3 038 559	4 327 140	3 001 457	350 463	975 220	2 026 710	55 182	362 584	348 624	1 260 320
Under 1 year	1 644 801	1 294 785	541 855	752 930	528 023	60 978	163 929	350 016	9 872	64 251	61 182	214 711
1 year	2 022 292	1 597 281	666 247	931 034	652 051	74 423	204 560	425 011	11 836	77 298	73 512	262 365
2 years	1 952 242	1 536 195	638 114	898 081	624 256	72 758	201 067	416 047	11 476	74 447	71 816	258 308
3 years	1 884 023	1 471 794	602 872	868 922	597 990	70 769	200 163	412 229	10 927	72 771	70 303	258 228
4 years	1 889 051	1 465 644	589 471	876 173	599 137	71 535	205 501	423 407	11 071	73 817	71 811	266 708
5 to 9 years	9 262 527	7 073 730	2 764 319	4 309 411	2 895 042	350 680	1 063 689	2 188 797	53 486	365 371	360 958	1 408 982
5 years	1 889 177	1 456 747	580 160	876 587	594 828	71 693	210 066	432 430	10 914	73 876	72 471	275 169
6 years	1 829 832	1 402 967	550 984	851 983	575 739	69 166	207 078	426 865	10 686	72 531	70 777	272 871
7 years	1 865 700	1 424 335	554 869	869 466	585 289	70 341	213 836	441 365	10 785	73 381	72 632	284 567
8 years	1 794 355	1 364 820	530 061	834 759	557 235	68 256	209 268	429 535	10 348	70 836	70 427	277 924
9 years	1 883 463	1 424 861	548 245	876 616	581 951	71 224	223 441	458 602	10 753	74 747	74 651	298 451
10 to 14 years	8 767 167	6 592 853	2 508 850	4 084 003	2 702 909	321 742	1 059 352	2 174 314	49 704	339 527	347 002	1 438 081
10 years	1 874 172	1 414 409	545 817	868 592	576 297	69 666	222 629	459 763	10 714	73 585	74 151	301 313
11 years	1 771 334	1 332 040	508 645	823 395	544 480	65 334	213 581	439 294	10 155	69 215	70 494	289 430
12 years	1 752 999	1 316 424	498 153	818 271	540 690	64 370	213 211	436 575	9 934	68 139	69 265	289 237
13 years	1 706 417	1 280 808	484 989	795 819	526 441	61 902	207 476	425 609	9 538	65 665	67 676	282 730
14 years	1 662 245	1 249 172	471 246	777 926	515 001	60 470	202 455	413 073	9 363	62 923	65 416	275 371
15 to 19 years	9 102 698	6 909 143	2 795 864	4 113 279	2 750 923	331 974	1 030 382	2 193 555	57 926	411 885	357 596	1 366 148
15 years	1 705 780	1 282 625	483 495	799 130	528 339	60 734	210 057	423 155	9 293	64 961	66 561	282 340
16 years	1 697 995	1 278 052	484 202	793 850	525 367	59 946	208 537	419 943	9 189	63 931	65 948	280 875
17 years	1 758 400	1 329 317	509 782	819 535	545 555	61 657	212 323	429 083	9 406	66 116	68 176	285 385
18 years	1 862 377	1 417 583	593 117	824 466	552 790	69 650	202 026	444 794	12 760	90 761	73 724	267 549
19 years	2 078 146	1 601 566	725 268	876 298	598 872	79 987	197 439	476 580	17 278	126 116	83 187	249 999
20 to 24 years	9 675 596	7 699 732	3 566 691	4 133 041	2 959 483	336 969	836 589	1 975 864	79 789	499 759	333 459	1 062 857
20 years	2 044 082	1 602 382	742 532	859 850	600 681	76 007	183 162	441 700	17 679	120 165	76 143	227 713
21 years	1 947 811	1 535 331	718 596	816 735	576 963	70 794	168 978	412 480	17 725	113 127	69 843	211 785
25 to 29 years	10 695 936	8 641 906	3 798 005	4 843 901	3 521 723	354 280	967 898	2 054 030	68 630	395 511	341 209	1 248 680
30 to 34 years	10 876 933	8 691 841	3 557 223	5 134 618	3 623 838	365 881	1 144 899	2 185 092	63 422	377 945	348 771	1 394 954
35 to 39 years	9 902 243	7 798 591	3 037 196	4 761 395	3 275 521	331 039	1 154 835	2 103 652	56 516	345 076	327 033	1 375 027
40 to 44 years	8 691 984	6 818 042	2 501 297	4 316 745	2 944 912	288 193	1 083 640	1 873 942	47 815	295 187	284 507	1 246 433
45 to 49 years	6 810 597	5 297 733	1 869 318	3 428 415	2 313 714	221 711	892 990	1 512 864	35 276	223 544	222 620	1 031 424
50 to 54 years	5 514 738	4 231 012	1 523 394	2 707 618	1 828 958	174 870	703 790	1 283 726	28 257	186 590	189 656	879 223
55 to 59 years	5 034 370	3 831 757	1 408 143	2 423 614	1 655 969	159 809	607 836	1 202 613	27 535	177 353	182 042	815 683
60 to 64 years	4 947 047	3 711 061	1 403 879	2 307 182	1 589 663	160 510	557 009	1 235 986	29 470	186 553	196 723	823 240
65 to 69 years	4 532 307	3 362 778	1 304 867	2 057 911	1 424 665	156 383	476 863	1 169 529	30 966	183 034	196 857	758 672
70 to 74 years	3 409 306	2 490 975	980 994	1 509 981	1 044 947	123 686	341 348	918 331	24 891	146 350	163 836	583 254
75 to 79 years	2 399 768	1 726 348	704 730	1 021 618	703 358	90 675	227 585	673 420	16 845	109 186	126 504	420 885
80 to 84 years	1 366 094	971 978	411 442	560 536	385 467	53 034	122 035	394 116	9 647	67 143	79 774	237 552
85 years and over	857 698	608 809	270 656	338 153	233 518	33 933	70 702	248 889	5 550	44 797	55 282	143 260
18 years and over	88 655 140	68 901 712	27 656 220	41 245 492	28 657 398	3 000 610	9 587 484	19 753 428	554 647	3 454 905	3 205 184	12 538 692
62 years and over	15 524 180	11 367 579	4 509 518	6 858 061	4 734 601	554 809	1 568 651	4 156 601	106 003	663 964	743 441	2 643 193
65 years and over	12 565 173	9 160 888	3 672 689	5 488 199	3 791 955	457 711	1 238 533	3 404 285	87 899	550 510	622 253	2 143 623
Median age	31.7	31.4	30.3	32.3	32.2	30.7	33.2	32.5	30.4	29.8	32.0	33.5

Table 15. Age and Sex: 1990—Con.

[For definitions of terms and meanings of symbols, see text]

United States Inside and Outside Metropolitan Area	United States	Inside metropolitan area Total	In central city	Not in central city Total	Urban Inside urbanized area	Urban Outside urbanized area	Rural	Outside metropolitan area Total	Urban Inside urbanized area	Outside urbanized area Place of 10,000 or more	Place of 2,500 to 9,999	Rural
AGE—Con.												
Female	127 470 455	98 901 753	40 398 106	58 503 647	40 899 067	4 478 962	13 125 618	28 568 702	779 352	5 155 950	4 995 894	17 637 506
Under 5 years	8 962 034	7 028 070	2 913 108	4 114 962	2 855 373	334 516	925 073	1 933 964	52 809	347 427	335 040	1 198 688
Under 1 year	1 572 511	1 238 159	520 329	717 830	503 321	58 289	156 220	334 352	9 316	61 280	59 035	204 721
1 year	1 926 815	1 520 642	637 091	883 551	618 145	71 231	194 175	406 173	11 361	73 891	70 857	250 064
2 years	1 862 798	1 464 752	611 373	853 379	593 160	69 200	191 019	398 046	11 002	71 638	68 996	246 410
3 years	1 799 154	1 406 897	578 690	828 207	570 861	67 567	189 779	392 257	10 496	70 005	67 293	244 463
4 years	1 800 756	1 397 620	565 625	831 995	569 886	68 229	193 880	403 136	10 634	70 613	68 859	253 030
5 to 9 years	8 836 652	6 757 619	2 659 382	4 098 237	2 762 437	334 456	1 001 344	2 079 033	51 287	348 953	347 939	1 330 854
5 years	1 800 356	1 390 321	557 228	833 093	567 348	68 004	197 741	410 035	10 545	71 122	69 374	258 994
6 years	1 747 800	1 340 207	529 625	810 582	548 041	66 606	195 935	407 593	10 198	69 121	68 670	259 604
7 years	1 780 061	1 361 140	534 361	826 779	557 150	67 430	202 199	418 921	10 374	70 359	70 375	267 813
8 years	1 714 313	1 306 615	510 876	795 739	534 191	64 828	196 720	407 698	9 967	67 441	67 478	262 812
9 years	1 794 122	1 359 336	527 292	832 044	555 707	67 588	208 749	434 786	10 203	70 910	72 042	281 631
10 to 14 years	8 347 082	6 291 240	2 416 623	3 874 617	2 576 917	307 650	990 050	2 055 842	47 570	327 320	333 468	1 347 484
10 years	1 779 005	1 345 957	522 751	823 206	547 813	66 978	208 415	433 048	10 220	69 943	71 005	281 880
11 years	1 684 181	1 269 264	488 842	780 422	518 328	62 353	199 741	414 917	9 686	66 607	67 375	271 249
12 years	1 670 451	1 256 924	481 003	775 921	515 380	61 289	199 252	413 527	9 531	65 471	66 743	271 782
13 years	1 632 583	1 228 260	468 662	759 598	505 366	59 856	194 376	404 323	9 210	63 676	64 934	266 503
14 years	1 580 862	1 190 835	455 365	735 470	490 030	57 174	188 266	390 027	8 923	61 623	63 411	256 070
15 to 19 years	8 651 317	6 592 488	2 750 511	3 841 977	2 598 439	318 639	924 899	2 058 829	58 714	415 376	346 545	1 238 194
15 years	1 615 829	1 219 446	465 541	753 905	502 423	58 559	192 923	396 383	8 889	62 755	64 081	260 658
16 years	1 606 895	1 214 523	467 755	746 768	500 149	57 088	189 531	392 372	8 732	61 650	63 618	258 372
17 years	1 651 662	1 253 357	487 200	766 157	515 395	58 543	192 219	398 305	8 949	63 666	65 276	260 414
18 years	1 778 861	1 357 919	595 730	762 189	517 072	67 129	177 988	420 942	13 603	97 412	72 866	237 061
19 years	1 998 070	1 547 243	734 285	812 958	563 400	77 320	172 238	450 827	18 541	129 893	80 704	221 689
20 to 24 years	9 344 716	7 479 113	3 542 189	3 936 924	2 857 475	325 783	753 666	1 865 603	75 020	472 497	327 001	991 085
20 years	1 965 332	1 546 334	747 041	799 293	564 793	73 492	161 008	418 998	18 067	121 303	73 961	205 667
21 years	1 869 409	1 479 895	715 232	764 663	546 948	68 850	148 865	389 514	17 397	110 670	68 379	193 068
25 to 29 years	10 617 109	8 588 052	3 751 941	4 836 111	3 520 774	358 531	956 806	2 029 057	62 603	384 639	347 508	1 234 307
30 to 34 years	10 985 954	8 789 600	3 577 632	5 211 968	3 690 735	373 719	1 147 514	2 196 354	61 949	384 064	362 231	1 388 110
35 to 39 years	10 060 874	7 974 861	3 096 566	4 878 295	3 398 416	337 029	1 142 850	2 086 013	56 242	353 431	338 010	1 338 330
40 to 44 years	8 923 802	7 064 962	2 625 881	4 439 081	3 091 303	292 625	1 055 153	1 858 840	47 879	303 739	296 321	1 210 901
45 to 49 years	7 061 976	5 526 264	2 024 745	3 501 519	2 419 185	227 617	854 717	1 535 712	37 441	240 227	240 420	1 017 624
50 to 54 years	5 835 775	4 498 403	1 709 970	2 788 433	1 932 430	185 178	670 825	1 337 372	31 679	208 710	213 557	883 426
55 to 59 years	5 497 386	4 180 982	1 631 657	2 549 325	1 779 597	176 897	592 831	1 316 404	32 269	211 132	218 809	854 194
60 to 64 years	5 669 120	4 286 810	1 723 697	2 563 113	1 808 641	191 117	563 355	1 382 310	36 145	233 006	246 047	867 112
65 to 69 years	5 579 428	4 195 688	1 726 269	2 469 419	1 755 262	200 150	514 007	1 383 740	38 343	244 368	262 596	838 433
70 to 74 years	4 585 517	3 402 012	1 435 747	1 966 265	1 397 614	173 185	395 466	1 183 505	32 182	217 904	242 297	691 122
75 to 79 years	3 721 601	2 737 468	1 202 976	1 534 492	1 092 797	145 833	295 862	984 133	25 305	190 440	217 758	550 630
80 to 84 years	2 567 645	1 883 278	853 686	1 029 592	736 397	103 315	189 880	684 367	17 500	141 273	163 675	361 919
85 years and over	2 222 467	1 624 843	755 526	869 317	625 275	92 722	151 320	597 624	14 415	131 444	156 672	295 093
18 years and over	96 450 301	75 137 498	30 988 497	44 149 001	31 186 373	3 328 150	9 634 478	21 312 803	601 116	3 944 179	3 786 472	12 981 036
62 years and over	22 105 515	16 432 739	7 019 099	9 413 640	6 698 882	832 383	1 882 375	5 672 776	150 056	1 068 269	1 194 357	3 260 094
65 years and over	18 676 658	13 843 289	5 974 204	7 869 085	5 607 345	715 205	1 546 535	4 833 369	127 745	925 429	1 042 998	2 737 197
Median age	34.1	33.8	32.9	34.3	34.4	33.4	34.4	35.1	33.3	33.6	36.4	35.3
PERCENT DISTRIBUTION												
All persons	100.0	100.0	100.0	100.0	100.0	100.0	100.0	100.0	100.0	100.0	100.0	100.0
Under 18 years	25.6	25.3	24.7	25.7	25.0	27.1	27.3	26.6	24.0	25.1	26.1	27.4
Under 5 years	7.4	7.5	7.6	7.3	7.3	7.9	7.2	7.1	7.1	7.2	7.2	7.0
5 to 17 years	18.2	17.8	17.0	18.3	17.6	19.2	20.1	19.6	16.9	17.9	18.9	20.4
18 to 64 years	61.9	62.8	62.9	62.7	63.2	59.4	62.2	58.6	61.8	60.0	56.3	58.7
18 to 24 years	10.8	10.9	12.5	9.9	10.1	11.0	8.8	10.1	14.3	14.3	10.3	8.6
25 to 44 years	32.5	33.4	33.3	33.4	33.9	31.1	32.7	29.3	30.6	28.8	28.0	29.7
45 to 64 years	18.6	18.5	17.1	19.4	19.2	17.2	20.6	19.3	17.0	16.9	18.1	20.4
65 years and over	12.6	11.9	12.4	11.6	11.8	13.5	10.5	14.7	14.2	14.9	17.6	13.9
65 to 79 years	9.7	9.3	9.4	9.2	9.3	10.2	8.5	11.3	11.1	11.1	12.8	10.9
80 years and over	2.8	2.6	2.9	2.4	2.5	3.3	2.0	3.4	3.1	3.9	4.8	3.0
Male	100.0	100.0	100.0	100.0	100.0	100.0	100.0	100.0	100.0	100.0	100.0	100.0
Under 18 years	26.9	26.6	26.1	26.8	26.2	28.7	28.0	27.9	25.1	26.8	28.2	28.3
Under 5 years	7.7	7.9	8.1	7.7	7.7	8.3	7.3	7.4	7.4	7.7	7.8	7.2
5 to 17 years	19.1	18.7	18.0	19.2	18.5	20.3	20.7	20.6	17.7	19.1	20.4	21.1
18 to 64 years	62.8	63.7	64.0	63.4	64.0	60.5	62.7	59.6	63.0	61.6	57.9	59.4
18 to 24 years	11.2	11.4	13.0	10.3	10.6	11.6	9.3	10.6	14.8	15.2	11.0	9.0
25 to 44 years	33.1	34.1	34.4	33.8	34.4	31.8	32.7	30.0	31.9	30.0	29.2	30.1
45 to 64 years	18.4	18.2	16.6	19.3	19.0	17.0	20.7	19.1	16.3	16.4	17.7	20.3
65 years and over	10.4	9.8	9.8	9.7	9.8	10.9	9.3	12.4	11.9	11.7	13.9	12.3
65 to 79 years	8.5	8.1	8.0	8.1	8.2	8.8	7.9	10.1	9.8	9.3	10.9	10.1
80 years and over	1.8	1.7	1.8	1.6	1.6	2.1	1.4	2.3	2.1	2.4	3.0	2.2
Female	100.0	100.0	100.0	100.0	100.0	100.0	100.0	100.0	100.0	100.0	100.0	100.0
Under 18 years	24.3	24.0	23.3	24.5	23.7	25.7	26.6	25.4	22.9	23.5	24.2	26.4
Under 5 years	7.0	7.1	7.2	7.0	7.0	7.5	7.0	6.8	6.8	6.7	6.7	6.8
5 to 17 years	17.3	16.9	16.1	17.5	16.8	18.2	19.6	18.6	16.1	16.8	17.5	19.6
18 to 64 years	61.0	62.0	61.9	62.0	62.5	58.3	61.6	57.7	60.7	58.5	54.9	58.1
18 to 24 years	10.3	10.5	12.1	9.4	9.6	10.5	8.4	9.6	13.8	13.6	9.6	8.2
25 to 44 years	31.8	32.8	32.3	33.1	33.5	30.4	32.8	28.6	29.3	27.7	26.9	29.3
45 to 64 years	18.9	18.7	17.6	19.5	19.4	17.4	20.4	19.5	17.6	17.3	18.4	20.5
65 years and over	14.7	14.0	14.8	13.5	13.7	16.0	11.8	16.9	16.4	17.9	20.9	15.5
65 to 79 years	10.9	10.4	10.8	10.2	10.4	11.6	9.2	12.4	12.3	12.7	14.5	11.8
80 years and over	3.8	3.5	4.0	3.2	3.3	4.4	2.6	4.5	4.1	5.3	6.4	3.7
MALES PER 100 FEMALES												
All persons	95.1	94.9	92.7	96.4	95.0	93.9	101.5	96.0	95.1	91.5	89.3	99.2
Under 18 years	105.0	104.9	104.0	105.4	105.0	104.7	106.8	105.6	104.5	104.2	104.0	106.4
Under 5 years	104.8	104.8	104.3	105.2	105.1	104.8	105.4	104.8	104.5	104.4	104.1	105.1
5 to 17 years	105.1	104.9	103.9	105.5	105.0	104.7	107.3	105.9	104.5	104.1	103.9	106.9
18 to 64 years	97.8	97.5	95.9	98.6	97.2	97.3	103.2	99.2	98.6	96.2	94.1	101.5
18 to 24 years	103.8	103.2	100.3	105.8	104.4	103.5	112.0	105.8	102.5	102.4	102.0	109.0
25 to 44 years	99.0	98.6	98.8	98.4	97.6	98.3	101.1	100.6	103.4	99.1	96.8	101.8
45 to 64 years	92.7	92.3	87.5	95.3	93.1	91.8	103.0	94.0	87.6	86.7	86.1	98.0
65 years and over	67.3	66.2	61.5	69.7	67.6	64.0	80.1	70.4	68.8	59.5	59.7	78.3
65 to 79 years	74.5	73.3	68.5	76.9	74.7	71.4	86.8	77.8	75.9	67.2	67.4	84.7
80 years and over	46.4	45.1	42.4	47.3	45.5	44.4	56.5	50.2	47.6	41.0	42.2	58.0

Table 16. Age and Sex by Race and Hispanic Origin: 1990

[For definitions of terms and meanings of symbols, see text]

United States	All persons	Race					Hispanic origin (of any race)	White, not of Hispanic origin
		White	Black	American Indian, Eskimo, or Aleut	Asian or Pacific Islander	Other race		
AGE								
All persons	**248 709 873**	**199 686 070**	**29 986 060**	**1 959 234**	**7 273 662**	**9 804 847**	**22 354 059**	**188 128 296**
Under 5 years	18 354 443	13 649 490	2 785 902	201 950	589 845	1 127 256	2 387 524	12 488 719
Under 1 year	3 217 312	2 404 258	480 022	36 089	93 460	203 483	427 454	2 197 217
1 year	3 949 107	2 924 714	606 682	43 077	130 536	244 098	518 131	2 672 461
2 years	3 815 040	2 814 615	594 379	42 157	126 175	237 714	502 284	2 571 497
3 years	3 683 177	2 740 124	557 295	40 519	120 256	224 983	477 574	2 507 627
4 years	3 689 807	2 765 779	547 524	40 108	119 418	216 978	462 081	2 539 917
5 to 9 years	18 099 179	13 616 268	2 671 109	199 446	596 133	1 016 223	2 193 852	12 530 091
5 years	3 689 533	2 768 212	545 555	40 657	121 788	213 321	457 089	2 543 243
6 years	3 577 632	2 695 163	522 290	39 454	119 463	201 262	434 252	2 480 472
7 years	3 645 761	2 744 498	536 416	40 875	119 740	204 232	441 276	2 525 976
8 years	3 508 668	2 638 590	518 764	38 295	116 064	196 955	426 113	2 427 541
9 years	3 677 585	2 769 805	548 084	40 165	119 078	200 453	435 122	2 552 859
10 to 14 years	17 114 249	12 853 558	2 601 590	188 000	551 552	919 549	2 001 617	11 856 103
10 years	3 653 177	2 739 524	560 039	40 017	117 357	196 240	427 686	2 526 043
11 years	3 455 515	2 596 959	528 407	37 788	109 049	183 312	400 840	2 396 621
12 years	3 423 450	2 576 523	519 424	37 420	108 190	181 893	397 566	2 377 773
13 years	3 339 000	2 507 044	505 268	37 047	109 012	180 629	393 120	2 311 109
14 years	3 243 107	2 433 508	488 452	35 728	107 944	177 475	382 405	2 244 557
15 to 19 years	17 754 015	13 342 703	2 658 493	180 516	603 761	968 542	2 053 957	12 344 701
15 years	3 321 609	2 493 892	499 514	35 740	112 663	179 800	387 038	2 303 102
16 years	3 304 890	2 469 848	504 009	35 886	115 477	179 670	385 257	2 280 559
17 years	3 410 062	2 545 173	522 291	35 945	117 717	188 936	402 212	2 348 737
18 years	3 641 238	2 731 047	545 985	35 798	125 310	203 098	426 930	2 525 629
19 years	4 076 216	3 102 743	586 694	37 147	132 594	217 038	452 520	2 886 674
20 to 24 years	19 020 312	14 523 912	2 578 953	165 549	632 258	1 119 640	2 304 441	13 437 924
20 years	4 009 414	3 059 999	553 265	35 124	134 694	226 332	469 015	2 837 680
21 years	3 817 220	2 921 434	513 252	33 401	129 179	219 954	451 608	2 709 305
25 to 29 years	21 313 045	16 638 544	2 707 765	175 577	691 069	1 100 090	2 341 239	15 500 149
30 to 34 years	21 862 887	17 351 513	2 681 724	170 668	726 183	932 799	2 062 303	16 320 031
35 to 39 years	19 963 117	16 081 606	2 336 766	150 182	669 818	724 745	1 660 726	15 228 401
40 to 44 years	17 615 786	14 506 390	1 876 062	126 154	572 194	534 986	1 284 268	13 820 470
45 to 49 years	13 872 573	11 585 703	1 405 766	96 817	405 590	378 697	953 910	11 055 962
50 to 54 years	11 350 513	9 504 871	1 179 011	76 714	311 651	278 266	755 989	9 063 504
55 to 59 years	10 531 756	8 968 416	1 032 749	61 819	250 633	218 139	639 308	8 576 335
60 to 64 years	10 616 167	9 211 123	961 619	51 389	218 517	173 519	553 642	8 855 087
65 to 69 years	10 111 735	8 899 637	863 045	42 710	178 497	127 846	436 257	8 609 792
70 to 74 years	7 994 823	7 126 564	640 415	29 270	122 234	76 340	286 772	6 928 488
75 to 79 years	6 121 369	5 485 025	481 270	21 152	80 139	53 783	213 265	5 334 213
80 to 84 years	3 933 739	3 552 695	293 638	12 116	43 863	31 440	130 425	3 458 576
85 years and over	3 080 165	2 788 052	230 183	9 205	29 738	22 987	94 564	2 719 750
18 years and over	185 105 441	152 057 841	20 401 645	1 262 267	5 190 275	6 193 413	14 596 559	144 320 985
62 years and over	37 629 695	33 413 308	3 079 838	144 397	581 339	410 813	1 481 076	32 404 673
65 years and over	31 241 831	27 851 973	2 508 551	114 453	454 458	312 396	1 161 283	27 050 819
Median age	32.9	34.4	28.1	26.2	29.8	23.9	25.5	34.9
Male	**121 239 418**	**97 475 880**	**14 170 151**	**967 186**	**3 558 038**	**5 068 163**	**11 388 059**	**91 656 591**
Under 5 years	9 392 409	7 004 481	1 408 495	102 628	301 346	575 459	1 218 194	6 412 523
Under 1 year	1 644 801	1 232 872	242 400	18 303	47 604	103 622	217 883	1 127 357
1 year	2 022 292	1 501 743	306 688	21 932	67 255	124 674	264 614	1 372 916
2 years	1 952 242	1 443 588	300 974	21 375	64 635	121 670	256 941	1 319 430
3 years	1 884 023	1 405 927	281 772	20 656	61 133	114 535	243 056	1 287 610
4 years	1 889 051	1 420 351	276 661	20 362	60 719	110 958	235 700	1 305 210
5 to 9 years	9 262 527	6 990 531	1 350 265	101 188	301 833	518 710	1 118 733	6 436 879
5 years	1 889 177	1 421 766	275 929	20 636	61 701	109 145	233 523	1 306 800
6 years	1 829 832	1 383 042	263 945	19 985	60 486	102 374	221 089	1 273 657
7 years	1 865 700	1 408 754	271 512	20 751	60 576	104 107	224 818	1 297 437
8 years	1 794 355	1 353 997	261 738	19 346	58 736	100 538	217 191	1 246 539
9 years	1 883 463	1 422 972	277 141	20 470	60 334	102 546	222 112	1 312 446
10 to 14 years	8 767 167	6 606 726	1 314 408	95 747	281 125	469 161	1 023 383	6 095 971
10 years	1 874 172	1 409 578	283 915	20 316	59 764	100 599	218 916	1 300 460
11 years	1 771 334	1 335 768	266 494	19 307	55 652	94 113	205 488	1 233 211
12 years	1 752 999	1 324 022	262 327	19 055	54 938	92 657	203 316	1 222 081
13 years	1 706 417	1 286 049	254 519	18 977	55 361	91 511	199 836	1 186 188
14 years	1 662 245	1 251 309	247 153	18 092	55 410	90 281	195 827	1 154 031
15 to 19 years	9 102 698	6 845 571	1 342 263	93 058	312 417	509 389	1 083 893	6 317 448
15 years	1 705 780	1 283 835	253 591	18 348	58 385	91 621	198 402	1 185 489
16 years	1 697 995	1 271 496	256 012	18 320	59 630	92 537	199 659	1 172 833
17 years	1 758 400	1 313 056	266 726	18 644	60 945	99 029	212 793	1 208 299
18 years	1 862 377	1 395 825	274 060	18 618	64 788	109 086	229 367	1 285 390
19 years	2 078 146	1 581 359	291 874	19 128	68 669	117 116	243 672	1 465 437
20 to 24 years	9 675 596	7 388 380	1 258 626	85 043	325 982	617 565	1 261 500	6 797 975
20 years	2 044 082	1 557 979	273 585	18 159	70 127	124 232	256 052	1 437 359
21 years	1 947 811	1 487 818	253 358	17 422	67 260	121 953	248 677	1 371 815
25 to 29 years	10 695 936	8 384 815	1 285 760	87 474	342 628	595 259	1 250 358	7 784 058
30 to 34 years	10 876 933	8 699 545	1 250 610	82 744	349 807	494 227	1 074 457	8 169 821
35 to 39 years	9 902 243	8 054 129	1 083 051	72 594	316 522	375 947	846 161	7 625 474
40 to 44 years	8 691 984	7 227 231	865 660	61 194	266 792	271 107	640 168	6 889 258
45 to 49 years	6 810 597	5 736 583	642 441	46 993	195 406	189 174	468 257	5 479 265
50 to 54 years	5 514 738	4 657 384	531 976	36 888	152 085	136 405	364 219	4 446 865
55 to 59 years	5 034 370	4 330 811	456 919	29 354	113 509	103 777	302 371	4 145 689
60 to 64 years	4 947 047	4 334 784	414 245	24 192	94 139	79 687	254 956	4 170 114
65 to 69 years	4 532 307	4 013 229	362 942	19 298	79 518	57 320	195 578	3 882 701
70 to 74 years	3 409 306	3 055 729	254 699	12 500	54 300	32 078	119 805	2 972 869
75 to 79 years	2 399 768	2 154 399	178 540	8 460	36 801	21 568	83 355	2 096 128
80 to 84 years	1 366 094	1 227 102	100 659	4 557	21 429	12 347	49 174	1 192 370
85 years and over	857 698	764 450	68 592	3 274	12 399	8 983	33 497	741 183
18 years and over	88 655 140	73 005 755	9 320 654	612 311	2 494 774	3 221 646	7 416 895	69 144 597
62 years and over	15 524 180	13 815 696	1 210 356	62 073	259 026	177 029	627 520	13 390 700
65 years and over	12 565 173	11 214 909	965 432	48 089	204 447	132 296	481 409	10 885 251
Median age	31.7	33.1	26.6	25.3	28.7	23.7	25.0	33.6

Table 16. Age and Sex by Race and Hispanic Origin: 1990—Con.

[For definitions of terms and meanings of symbols, see text]

United States

AGE—Con.	All persons	Race — White	Race — Black	Race — American Indian, Eskimo, or Aleut	Race — Asian or Pacific Islander	Race — Other race	Hispanic origin (of any race)	White, not of Hispanic origin
Female	127 470 455	102 210 190	15 815 909	992 048	3 715 624	4 736 684	10 966 000	96 471 705
Under 5 years	8 962 034	6 645 009	1 377 407	99 322	288 499	551 797	1 169 330	6 076 196
Under 1 year	1 572 511	1 171 386	237 622	17 786	45 856	99 861	209 571	1 069 860
1 year	1 926 815	1 422 971	299 994	21 145	63 281	119 424	253 517	1 299 545
2 years	1 862 798	1 371 027	293 405	20 782	61 540	116 044	245 343	1 252 067
3 years	1 799 154	1 334 197	275 523	19 863	59 123	110 448	234 518	1 220 017
4 years	1 800 756	1 345 428	270 863	19 746	58 699	106 020	226 381	1 234 707
5 to 9 years	8 836 652	6 625 737	1 320 844	98 258	294 300	497 513	1 075 119	6 093 212
5 years	1 800 356	1 346 446	269 626	20 021	60 087	104 176	223 566	1 236 443
6 years	1 747 800	1 312 121	258 345	19 469	58 977	98 888	213 163	1 206 815
7 years	1 780 061	1 335 744	264 904	20 124	59 164	100 125	216 458	1 228 539
8 years	1 714 313	1 284 593	257 026	18 949	57 328	96 417	208 922	1 181 002
9 years	1 794 122	1 346 833	270 943	19 695	58 744	97 907	213 010	1 240 413
10 to 14 years	8 347 082	6 246 832	1 287 182	92 253	270 427	450 388	978 234	5 760 132
10 years	1 779 005	1 329 946	276 124	19 701	57 593	95 641	208 770	1 225 583
11 years	1 684 181	1 261 191	261 913	18 481	53 397	89 199	195 352	1 163 410
12 years	1 670 451	1 252 501	257 097	18 365	53 252	89 236	194 250	1 155 692
13 years	1 632 583	1 220 995	250 749	18 070	53 651	89 118	193 284	1 124 921
14 years	1 580 862	1 182 199	241 299	17 636	52 534	87 194	186 578	1 090 526
15 to 19 years	8 651 317	6 497 132	1 316 230	87 458	291 344	459 153	970 064	6 027 253
15 years	1 615 829	1 210 057	245 923	17 392	54 278	88 179	188 636	1 117 613
16 years	1 606 895	1 198 352	247 997	17 566	55 847	87 133	185 598	1 107 726
17 years	1 651 662	1 232 117	255 565	17 301	56 772	89 907	189 419	1 140 438
18 years	1 778 861	1 335 222	271 925	17 180	60 522	94 012	197 563	1 240 239
19 years	1 998 070	1 521 384	294 820	18 019	63 925	99 922	208 848	1 421 237
20 to 24 years	9 344 716	7 135 532	1 320 327	80 506	306 276	502 075	1 042 941	6 639 949
20 years	1 965 332	1 502 020	279 680	16 965	64 567	102 100	212 963	1 400 321
21 years	1 869 409	1 433 616	259 894	15 979	61 919	98 001	202 931	1 337 490
25 to 29 years	10 617 109	8 253 729	1 422 005	88 103	348 441	504 831	1 090 881	7 716 091
30 to 34 years	10 985 954	8 651 968	1 431 114	87 924	376 376	438 572	987 846	8 150 210
35 to 39 years	10 060 874	8 027 477	1 253 715	77 588	353 296	348 798	814 565	7 602 927
40 to 44 years	8 923 802	7 279 159	1 010 402	64 960	305 402	263 879	644 100	6 931 212
45 to 49 years	7 061 976	5 849 120	763 325	49 824	210 184	189 523	485 653	5 576 697
50 to 54 years	5 835 775	4 847 487	647 035	39 826	159 566	141 861	391 770	4 616 639
55 to 59 years	5 497 386	4 637 605	575 830	32 465	137 124	114 362	336 937	4 430 646
60 to 64 years	5 669 120	4 876 339	547 374	27 197	124 378	93 832	298 686	4 684 973
65 to 69 years	5 579 428	4 886 408	500 103	23 412	98 979	70 526	240 679	4 727 091
70 to 74 years	4 585 517	4 070 835	385 716	16 770	67 934	44 262	166 967	3 955 619
75 to 79 years	3 721 601	3 330 626	302 730	12 692	43 338	32 215	129 910	3 238 085
80 to 84 years	2 567 645	2 325 593	192 979	7 559	22 421	19 093	81 251	2 266 206
85 years and over	2 222 467	2 023 602	161 591	5 931	17 339	14 004	61 067	1 978 567
18 years and over	96 450 301	79 052 086	11 080 991	649 956	2 695 501	2 971 767	7 179 664	75 176 388
62 years and over	22 105 515	19 597 812	1 869 482	82 324	322 313	233 784	853 556	19 013 973
65 years and over	18 676 658	16 637 064	1 543 119	66 364	250 011	180 100	679 874	16 165 568
Median age	34.1	35.6	29.5	27.2	30.7	24.1	26.1	36.1

PERCENT DISTRIBUTION

	All persons	White	Black	Amer. Indian, Eskimo, Aleut	Asian or Pacific Islander	Other race	Hispanic origin (of any race)	White, not of Hispanic origin
All persons	100.0	100.0	100.0	100.0	100.0	100.0	100.0	100.0
Under 18 years	25.6	23.9	32.0	35.6	28.6	36.8	34.7	23.3
Under 5 years	7.4	6.8	9.3	10.3	8.1	11.5	10.7	6.6
5 to 17 years	18.2	17.0	22.7	26.3	20.6	26.3	24.0	16.6
18 to 64 years	61.9	62.2	59.7	58.6	65.1	60.0	60.1	62.3
18 to 24 years	10.8	10.2	12.4	12.2	12.2	15.7	14.2	10.0
25 to 44 years	32.5	32.3	32.0	31.8	36.6	33.6	32.9	32.4
45 to 64 years	18.6	19.7	15.3	14.6	16.3	10.7	13.0	20.0
65 years and over	12.6	13.9	8.4	5.8	6.2	3.2	5.2	14.4
65 to 79 years	9.7	10.8	6.6	4.8	5.2	2.6	4.2	11.1
80 years and over	2.8	3.2	1.7	1.1	1.0	.6	1.0	3.3
Male	100.0	100.0	100.0	100.0	100.0	100.0	100.0	100.0
Under 18 years	26.9	25.1	34.2	36.7	29.9	36.4	34.9	24.6
Under 5 years	7.7	7.2	9.9	10.6	8.5	11.4	10.7	7.0
5 to 17 years	19.1	17.9	24.3	26.1	21.4	25.1	24.2	17.6
18 to 64 years	62.8	63.4	59.0	58.3	64.4	61.0	60.9	63.6
18 to 24 years	11.2	10.6	12.9	12.7	12.9	16.6	15.2	10.4
25 to 44 years	33.1	33.2	31.7	31.4	35.9	34.3	33.5	33.2
45 to 64 years	18.4	19.6	14.4	14.2	15.6	10.0	12.2	19.9
65 years and over	10.4	11.5	6.8	5.0	5.7	2.6	4.2	11.9
65 to 79 years	8.5	9.5	5.6	4.2	4.8	2.2	3.5	9.8
80 years and over	1.8	2.0	1.2	.8	1.0	.4	.7	2.1
Female	100.0	100.0	100.0	100.0	100.0	100.0	100.0	100.0
Under 18 years	24.3	22.7	29.9	34.5	27.5	37.3	34.5	22.1
Under 5 years	7.0	6.5	8.7	10.0	7.8	11.6	10.7	6.3
5 to 17 years	17.3	16.2	21.2	24.5	19.7	25.6	23.9	15.8
18 to 64 years	61.0	61.1	60.3	58.8	65.8	58.9	59.3	61.2
18 to 24 years	10.3	9.8	11.9	11.7	11.6	14.7	13.2	9.6
25 to 44 years	31.8	31.5	32.4	32.1	37.2	32.9	32.3	31.5
45 to 64 years	18.9	19.8	16.0	15.1	17.0	11.4	13.8	20.0
65 years and over	14.7	16.3	9.8	6.7	6.7	3.8	6.2	16.8
65 to 79 years	10.9	12.0	7.5	5.3	5.7	3.1	4.9	12.4
80 years and over	3.8	4.3	2.2	1.4	1.1	.7	1.3	4.4

MALES PER 100 FEMALES

	All persons	White	Black	Amer. Indian, Eskimo, Aleut	Asian or Pacific Islander	Other race	Hispanic origin (of any race)	White, not of Hispanic origin
All persons	95.1	95.4	89.6	97.5	95.8	107.0	103.8	95.0
Under 18 years	105.0	105.7	102.4	103.7	104.2	104.6	104.9	105.7
Under 5 years	104.8	105.4	102.3	103.3	104.5	104.3	104.2	105.5
5 to 17 years	105.1	105.8	102.5	103.9	93.7	110.7	106.7	98.7
18 to 64 years	97.8	99.0	87.6	96.7	96.7	121.2	119.7	102.7
18 to 24 years	103.8	103.7	96.7	106.1	106.7	111.6	107.7	100.2
25 to 44 years	99.0	100.5	87.6	95.4	92.2	94.3	91.9	94.5
45 to 64 years	92.7	94.3	80.7	92.0	87.9	73.5	70.8	67.3
65 years and over	67.3	67.4	62.6	72.5	81.8	75.5	74.2	75.1
65 to 79 years	74.5	75.1	67.0	76.1	81.2	64.4	58.1	45.6
80 years and over	46.4	45.8	47.7	58.1	85.1			

Table 17. **Age and Sex of White Persons: 1990**

[For definitions of terms and meanings of symbols, see text]

United States Urban and Rural Inside and Outside Metropolitan Area	Urban and rural						Inside and outside metropolitan area					
	Urban						Inside metropolitan area			Outside metropolitan area		
		Inside urbanized area										
	Total	Total	Central place	Urban fringe	Outside urbanized area	Rural	Total	In central city	Not in central city	Total	Urban	Rural
AGE												
All persons	**143 807 279**	**119 359 248**	**52 192 735**	**67 166 513**	**24 448 031**	**55 878 791**	**150 863 170**	**51 452 071**	**99 411 099**	**48 822 900**	**17 538 683**	**31 284 217**
Under 5 years	9 793 036	8 104 939	3 447 154	4 657 785	1 688 097	3 856 454	10 373 627	3 385 726	6 987 901	3 275 863	1 165 202	2 110 661
5 to 9 years	9 351 265	7 623 867	3 110 382	4 513 485	1 727 398	4 265 003	10 049 829	3 057 257	6 992 572	3 566 439	1 199 286	2 367 153
10 to 14 years	8 571 734	6 955 416	2 756 656	4 198 760	1 616 318	4 281 824	9 317 486	2 712 461	6 605 025	3 536 072	1 131 789	2 404 283
15 to 19 years	9 339 015	7 529 265	3 275 891	4 253 374	1 809 750	4 003 688	9 791 955	3 226 031	6 565 924	3 550 748	1 320 008	2 230 740
20 to 24 years	11 340 524	9 389 229	4 716 948	4 672 281	1 951 295	3 183 388	11 302 321	4 636 549	6 665 772	3 221 591	1 470 474	1 751 117
25 to 29 years	12 702 568	10 842 624	5 073 672	5 768 952	1 859 944	3 935 976	13 157 035	4 996 551	8 160 484	3 481 509	1 308 931	2 172 578
30 to 34 years	12 753 384	10 840 990	4 787 763	6 053 227	1 912 394	4 598 129	13 558 193	4 716 957	8 841 236	3 793 320	1 322 968	2 470 352
35 to 39 years	11 501 197	9 718 710	4 147 794	5 570 916	1 782 487	4 580 409	12 407 188	4 092 686	8 314 502	3 674 418	1 242 283	2 432 135
40 to 44 years	10 258 030	8 680 582	3 552 806	5 127 776	1 577 448	4 248 360	11 175 027	3 506 363	7 668 664	3 331 363	1 099 077	2 232 286
45 to 49 years	8 050 615	6 805 992	2 723 157	4 082 835	1 244 623	3 535 088	8 835 278	2 689 871	6 145 407	2 750 425	871 620	1 878 805
50 to 54 years	6 585 434	5 534 601	2 255 006	3 279 595	1 050 833	2 919 437	7 134 496	2 229 824	4 904 672	2 370 375	752 743	1 617 632
55 to 59 years	6 289 986	5 258 844	2 189 300	3 069 544	1 031 142	2 678 430	6 677 203	2 165 182	4 512 021	2 291 213	752 600	1 538 613
60 to 64 years	6 580 603	5 455 201	2 347 825	3 107 376	1 125 402	2 630 520	6 813 447	2 320 824	4 492 623	2 397 676	833 436	1 564 240
65 to 69 years	6 476 032	5 311 681	2 361 610	2 950 071	1 164 351	2 423 605	6 552 823	2 330 400	4 222 423	2 346 814	867 022	1 479 792
70 to 74 years	5 242 547	4 235 046	1 944 380	2 290 666	1 007 501	1 884 017	5 188 426	1 918 710	3 269 716	1 938 138	756 296	1 181 842
75 to 79 years	4 091 207	3 258 747	1 566 971	1 691 776	832 460	1 393 818	3 960 211	1 548 934	2 411 277	1 524 814	628 047	896 767
80 to 84 years	2 703 743	2 126 627	1 063 239	1 063 388	577 116	848 952	2 559 144	1 052 733	1 506 411	993 551	440 557	552 994
85 years and over	2 176 359	1 686 887	872 181	814 706	489 472	611 693	2 009 481	865 012	1 144 469	778 571	376 344	402 227
16 years and over	114 433 150	95 325 561	42 348 978	52 976 583	19 107 589	42 639 712	119 313 319	41 775 072	77 538 247	37 759 543	13 825 504	23 934 039
18 years and over	111 078 601	92 587 021	41 266 716	51 320 305	18 491 580	40 979 240	115 664 035	40 708 100	74 955 935	36 393 806	13 391 621	23 002 185
21 years and over	104 370 102	87 227 798	38 616 003	48 611 795	17 142 304	38 793 950	108 994 125	38 100 990	70 893 135	34 169 927	12 366 529	21 803 398
62 years and over	24 670 612	19 909 375	9 231 580	10 677 795	4 761 237	8 742 696	24 372 571	9 122 158	15 250 413	9 040 737	3 580 531	5 460 206
65 years and over	20 689 888	16 618 988	7 808 381	8 810 607	4 070 900	7 162 085	20 270 085	7 715 789	12 554 296	7 581 888	3 068 266	4 513 622
Median age	34.2	34.2	33.8	34.5	34.1	34.8	34.2	33.9	34.4	35.0	34.4	35.3
Male	**69 549 285**	**57 900 997**	**25 230 721**	**32 670 276**	**11 648 288**	**27 926 595**	**73 568 535**	**24 858 112**	**48 710 423**	**23 907 345**	**8 328 139**	**15 579 206**
Under 5 years	5 023 332	4 159 277	1 767 740	2 391 537	864 055	1 981 149	5 323 826	1 736 181	3 587 645	1 680 655	596 195	1 084 460
5 to 9 years	4 791 268	3 906 965	1 593 027	2 313 938	884 303	2 199 263	5 156 643	1 565 681	3 590 962	1 833 888	613 722	1 220 166
10 to 14 years	4 391 353	3 565 288	1 411 696	2 153 592	826 065	2 215 373	4 784 626	1 388 880	3 395 746	1 822 100	578 343	1 243 757
15 to 19 years	4 745 489	3 834 877	1 652 436	2 182 441	910 612	2 100 082	5 014 289	1 626 955	3 387 334	1 831 282	661 185	1 170 097
20 to 24 years	5 744 159	4 753 574	2 386 904	2 366 670	990 585	1 644 221	5 736 564	2 344 551	3 392 013	1 651 816	750 756	901 060
25 to 29 years	6 423 903	5 492 989	2 602 167	2 890 822	930 914	1 960 912	6 637 912	2 561 070	4 076 842	1 746 903	660 996	1 085 907
30 to 34 years	6 409 812	5 463 001	2 446 695	3 016 306	946 811	2 289 733	6 807 035	2 409 432	4 397 603	1 892 510	656 964	1 235 546
35 to 39 years	5 745 143	4 860 989	2 108 535	2 752 454	884 154	2 308 986	6 204 158	2 080 305	4 123 853	1 849 971	616 615	1 233 356
40 to 44 years	5 072 652	4 291 357	1 776 453	2 514 904	781 295	2 154 579	5 549 135	1 752 362	3 796 773	1 678 096	543 644	1 134 452
45 to 49 years	3 942 198	3 335 534	1 335 672	1 999 862	606 664	1 794 385	4 365 991	1 318 984	3 047 007	1 370 592	422 170	948 422
50 to 54 years	3 179 620	2 676 869	1 083 370	1 593 499	502 751	1 477 764	3 489 494	1 071 225	2 418 269	1 167 890	357 220	810 670
55 to 59 years	2 996 413	2 517 695	1 034 524	1 483 171	478 718	1 334 398	3 229 021	1 022 929	2 206 092	1 101 790	345 955	755 835
60 to 64 years	3 036 706	2 529 843	1 070 899	1 458 944	506 863	1 298 078	3 194 894	1 058 760	2 136 134	1 139 890	373 410	766 480
65 to 69 years	2 851 107	2 347 410	1 022 927	1 324 483	503 697	1 162 122	2 932 036	1 008 920	1 923 116	1 081 193	374 214	706 979
70 to 74 years	2 186 233	1 776 139	794 180	981 959	410 094	869 496	2 205 054	782 626	1 422 428	850 675	307 065	543 610
75 to 79 years	1 548 652	1 240 888	578 233	662 655	307 764	605 747	1 533 836	570 514	963 322	620 563	230 954	389 609
80 to 84 years	892 980	705 232	341 426	363 806	187 748	334 122	865 502	337 262	528 240	361 600	142 937	218 663
85 years and over	568 265	443 070	223 837	219 233	125 195	196 185	538 519	221 475	317 044	225 931	95 794	130 137
16 years and over	54 494 478	45 577 914	20 187 027	25 390 887	8 916 564	21 095 829	57 373 959	19 900 343	37 473 616	18 216 348	6 429 217	11 787 131
18 years and over	52 776 638	44 174 685	19 632 770	24 541 915	8 601 953	20 229 117	55 497 212	19 354 105	36 143 107	17 508 543	6 207 793	11 300 750
21 years and over	49 395 799	41 464 333	18 312 798	23 151 535	7 931 466	19 074 793	52 101 334	18 056 034	34 045 300	16 369 258	5 701 202	10 668 056
62 years and over	9 867 436	8 023 101	3 602 757	4 420 344	1 844 335	3 948 260	9 981 196	3 555 394	6 425 802	3 834 500	1 380 098	2 454 402
65 years and over	8 047 237	6 512 739	2 960 603	3 552 136	1 534 498	3 167 672	8 074 947	2 920 797	5 154 150	3 139 962	1 150 964	1 988 998
Median age	32.8	32.9	32.4	33.3	32.2	34.1	33.0	32.4	33.3	33.7	32.3	34.4
Female	**74 257 994**	**61 458 251**	**26 962 014**	**34 496 237**	**12 799 743**	**27 952 196**	**77 294 635**	**26 593 959**	**50 700 676**	**24 915 555**	**9 210 544**	**15 705 011**
Under 5 years	4 769 704	3 945 662	1 679 414	2 266 248	824 042	1 875 305	5 049 801	1 649 545	3 400 256	1 595 208	569 007	1 026 201
5 to 9 years	4 559 997	3 716 902	1 517 355	2 199 547	843 095	2 065 740	4 893 186	1 491 576	3 401 610	1 732 551	585 564	1 146 987
10 to 14 years	4 180 381	3 390 128	1 344 960	2 045 168	790 253	2 066 451	4 532 860	1 323 581	3 209 279	1 713 972	553 446	1 160 526
15 to 19 years	4 593 526	3 694 388	1 623 455	2 070 933	899 138	1 903 606	4 777 666	1 599 076	3 178 590	1 719 466	658 823	1 060 643
20 to 24 years	5 596 365	4 635 655	2 330 044	2 305 611	960 710	1 539 167	5 565 757	2 291 998	3 273 759	1 569 775	719 718	850 057
25 to 29 years	6 278 665	5 349 635	2 471 505	2 878 130	929 030	1 975 064	6 519 123	2 435 481	4 083 642	1 734 606	647 935	1 086 671
30 to 34 years	6 343 572	5 377 989	2 341 068	3 036 921	965 583	2 308 396	6 751 158	2 307 525	4 443 633	1 900 810	666 004	1 234 806
35 to 39 years	5 756 054	4 857 721	2 039 259	2 818 462	898 333	2 271 423	6 203 030	2 012 381	4 190 649	1 824 447	625 668	1 198 779
40 to 44 years	5 185 378	4 389 225	1 776 353	2 612 872	796 153	2 093 781	5 625 892	1 754 001	3 871 891	1 653 267	555 433	1 097 834
45 to 49 years	4 108 417	3 470 458	1 387 485	2 082 973	637 959	1 740 703	4 469 287	1 370 887	3 098 400	1 379 833	449 450	930 383
50 to 54 years	3 405 814	2 857 732	1 171 636	1 686 096	548 082	1 441 673	3 645 002	1 158 599	2 486 403	1 202 485	395 523	806 962
55 to 59 years	3 293 573	2 741 149	1 154 776	1 586 373	552 424	1 344 032	3 448 182	1 142 253	2 305 929	1 189 423	406 645	782 778
60 to 64 years	3 543 897	2 925 358	1 276 926	1 648 432	618 539	1 332 442	3 618 553	1 262 064	2 356 489	1 257 786	460 026	797 760
65 to 69 years	3 624 925	2 964 271	1 338 683	1 625 588	660 654	1 261 483	3 620 787	1 321 480	2 299 307	1 265 621	492 808	772 813
70 to 74 years	3 056 314	2 458 907	1 150 200	1 308 707	597 407	1 014 521	2 983 372	1 136 084	1 847 288	1 087 463	449 231	638 232
75 to 79 years	2 542 555	2 017 859	988 738	1 029 121	524 696	788 071	2 426 375	978 420	1 447 955	904 251	397 093	507 158
80 to 84 years	1 810 763	1 421 395	721 813	699 582	389 368	514 830	1 693 642	715 471	978 171	631 951	297 620	334 331
85 years and over	1 608 094	1 243 817	648 344	595 473	364 277	415 508	1 470 962	643 537	827 425	552 640	280 550	272 090
16 years and over	59 938 672	49 747 647	22 161 951	27 585 696	10 191 025	21 543 883	61 939 360	21 874 729	40 064 631	19 543 195	7 396 287	12 146 908
18 years and over	58 301 963	48 412 336	21 633 946	26 778 390	9 889 627	20 750 123	60 166 823	21 353 995	38 812 828	18 885 263	7 183 828	11 701 435
21 years and over	54 974 303	45 763 465	20 303 205	25 460 260	9 210 838	19 719 157	56 892 791	20 044 956	36 847 835	17 800 669	6 665 327	11 135 342
62 years and over	14 803 176	11 886 274	5 628 823	6 257 451	2 916 902	4 794 436	14 391 375	5 566 764	8 824 611	5 206 237	2 200 433	3 005 804
65 years and over	12 642 651	10 106 249	4 847 778	5 258 471	2 536 402	3 994 413	12 195 138	4 794 992	7 400 146	4 441 926	1 917 302	2 524 624
Median age	35.6	35.6	35.4	35.7	36.0	35.5	35.4	35.4	35.4	36.3	36.6	36.1
PERCENT DISTRIBUTION												
All persons	**100.0**	**100.0**	**100.0**	**100.0**	**100.0**	**100.0**	**100.0**	**100.0**	**100.0**	**100.0**	**100.0**	**100.0**
Under 18 years	22.8	22.4	20.9	23.6	24.4	26.7	23.3	20.9	24.6	25.5	23.6	26.5
18 to 64 years	62.9	63.6	64.1	63.3	59.0	60.5	63.2	64.1	62.8	59.0	58.9	59.1
65 years and over	14.4	13.9	15.0	13.1	16.7	12.8	13.4	15.0	12.6	15.5	17.5	14.4
MALES PER 100 FEMALES												
All persons	**93.7**	**94.2**	**93.6**	**94.7**	**91.0**	**99.9**	**95.2**	**93.5**	**96.1**	**96.0**	**90.4**	**99.2**
Under 18 years	105.1	105.2	105.1	105.3	104.7	106.9	105.5	105.0	105.7	106.1	104.6	106.9
18 to 64 years	98.0	98.3	99.3	97.5	96.1	101.8	98.9	99.2	98.7	99.5	96.0	101.5
65 years and over	63.7	64.4	61.1	67.6	60.5	79.3	66.2	60.9	69.6	70.7	60.0	78.8

Table 18. **Age and Sex of Black Persons: 1990**

[For definitions of terms and meanings of symbols, see text]

United States Urban and Rural Inside and Outside Metropolitan Area	Urban and rural						Inside and outside metropolitan area					
	Urban						Inside metropolitan area			Outside metropolitan area		
		Inside urbanized area										
	Total	Total	Central place	Urban fringe	Outside urbanized area	Rural	Total	In central city	Not in central city	Total	Urban	Rural
AGE												
All persons	**26 153 444**	**23 533 536**	**17 308 291**	**6 225 245**	**2 619 908**	**3 832 616**	**25 122 054**	**17 169 430**	**7 952 624**	**4 864 006**	**2 203 157**	**2 660 849**
Under 5 years	2 480 445	2 222 461	1 641 764	580 697	257 984	305 457	2 351 019	1 627 388	723 631	434 883	216 312	218 571
5 to 9 years	2 335 964	2 082 272	1 526 284	555 988	253 692	335 145	2 217 213	1 513 618	703 595	453 896	212 842	241 054
10 to 14 years	2 243 741	1 998 642	1 461 149	537 493	245 099	357 849	2 137 122	1 448 658	688 464	464 468	207 673	256 795
15 to 19 years	2 288 376	2 028 406	1 492 239	536 167	259 970	370 117	2 182 708	1 479 898	702 810	475 785	218 152	257 633
20 to 24 years	2 272 074	2 033 018	1 484 070	548 948	239 056	306 879	2 169 646	1 470 666	698 980	409 307	201 204	208 103
25 to 29 years	2 395 307	2 174 305	1 556 750	617 555	221 002	312 458	2 312 495	1 543 808	768 687	395 270	184 801	210 469
30 to 34 years	2 362 500	2 149 007	1 533 196	615 811	213 493	319 224	2 288 309	1 520 457	767 852	393 415	178 594	214 821
35 to 39 years	2 046 406	1 865 322	1 324 496	540 826	181 084	290 360	1 988 940	1 313 749	675 191	347 826	151 903	195 923
40 to 44 years	1 644 224	1 509 087	1 064 258	444 829	135 137	231 838	1 607 949	1 055 834	552 115	268 113	113 006	155 107
45 to 49 years	1 230 985	1 130 817	809 070	321 747	100 168	174 781	1 206 282	803 238	403 044	199 484	83 031	116 453
50 to 54 years	1 029 086	943 052	696 748	246 304	86 034	149 925	1 006 300	691 953	314 347	172 711	71 462	101 249
55 to 59 years	896 366	815 692	624 550	191 142	80 674	136 383	871 289	620 376	250 913	161 460	67 529	93 931
60 to 64 years	827 743	746 626	593 527	153 099	81 117	133 876	799 042	589 774	209 268	162 577	68 524	94 053
65 to 69 years	735 330	656 441	531 203	125 238	78 889	127 715	704 538	527 541	176 997	158 507	67 342	91 165
70 to 74 years	537 139	472 009	386 491	85 518	65 130	103 276	509 664	383 838	125 826	130 751	56 050	74 701
75 to 79 years	397 608	343 478	282 821	60 657	54 130	83 662	372 955	280 846	92 109	108 315	46 770	61 545
80 to 84 years	241 092	204 428	169 336	35 092	36 664	52 546	223 160	168 246	54 914	70 478	31 579	38 899
85 years and over	189 058	158 473	130 339	28 134	30 585	41 125	173 423	129 542	43 881	56 760	26 383	30 377
16 years and over	18 665 607	16 849 037	12 400 479	4 448 558	1 816 570	2 762 338	18 007 536	12 303 419	5 704 117	3 420 409	1 526 861	1 893 548
18 years and over	17 789 409	16 067 908	11 827 900	4 240 008	1 721 501	2 612 236	17 166 640	11 735 453	5 431 187	3 235 005	1 446 382	1 788 623
21 years and over	16 318 630	14 770 879	10 869 486	3 901 393	1 547 751	2 397 071	15 772 423	10 785 407	4 987 016	2 943 278	1 301 950	1 641 328
62 years and over	2 590 606	2 275 963	1 852 758	423 205	314 643	489 232	2 456 046	1 840 292	615 754	623 792	269 913	353 879
65 years and over	2 100 227	1 834 829	1 500 190	334 639	265 398	408 324	1 983 740	1 490 013	493 727	524 811	228 124	296 687
Median age	28.0	28.2	28.4	27.9	26.2	28.9	28.2	28.4	28.0	27.4	26.2	28.5
Male	**12 246 371**	**11 012 916**	**8 017 149**	**2 995 767**	**1 233 455**	**1 923 780**	**11 828 868**	**7 952 393**	**3 876 475**	**2 341 283**	**1 031 990**	**1 309 293**
Under 5 years	1 254 215	1 124 115	830 458	293 657	130 100	154 280	1 189 131	823 073	366 058	219 364	109 251	110 113
5 to 9 years	1 180 658	1 052 586	770 748	281 838	128 072	169 607	1 120 981	764 387	356 594	229 284	107 360	121 924
10 to 14 years	1 132 114	1 008 731	736 220	272 511	123 383	182 294	1 079 469	729 918	349 551	234 939	104 351	130 588
15 to 19 years	1 145 133	1 014 187	739 056	275 131	130 946	197 130	1 098 047	733 116	364 931	244 216	109 450	134 766
20 to 24 years	1 090 766	972 330	697 737	274 593	118 436	167 860	1 049 924	691 344	358 580	208 702	99 166	109 536
25 to 29 years	1 116 759	1 011 174	716 302	294 872	105 585	169 001	1 088 057	710 275	377 782	197 703	88 208	109 495
30 to 34 years	1 083 286	982 750	695 772	286 978	100 536	167 324	1 058 078	689 924	368 154	192 532	83 808	108 724
35 to 39 years	933 445	848 223	598 986	249 237	85 222	149 606	913 632	594 042	319 590	169 419	71 162	98 257
40 to 44 years	748 262	684 941	478 929	206 012	63 321	117 398	735 881	474 951	260 930	129 779	52 730	77 049
45 to 49 years	556 307	510 690	359 525	151 165	45 617	86 134	548 804	356 842	191 962	93 637	37 421	56 216
50 to 54 years	460 720	423 026	305 531	117 495	37 694	71 256	454 013	303 401	150 612	77 963	30 888	47 075
55 to 59 years	394 264	360 353	270 057	90 296	33 911	62 655	386 848	268 256	118 592	70 071	27 725	42 346
60 to 64 years	354 281	321 008	251 426	69 582	33 273	59 964	345 112	249 954	95 158	69 133	27 631	41 502
65 to 69 years	307 156	275 682	221 107	54 575	31 474	55 786	297 024	219 662	77 362	65 918	26 671	39 247
70 to 74 years	210 753	185 720	160 574	35 155	25 024	43 948	201 922	149 669	52 253	52 777	21 353	31 424
75 to 79 years	144 063	124 477	101 837	22 640	19 586	34 477	136 754	101 206	35 548	41 786	16 670	25 116
80 to 84 years	79 991	67 607	55 690	11 917	12 384	20 668	74 877	55 390	19 487	25 782	10 507	15 275
85 years and over	54 198	45 307	37 194	8 113	8 891	14 394	50 314	36 983	13 331	18 278	7 638	10 640
16 years and over	8 463 278	7 634 881	5 539 560	2 095 321	828 397	1 380 114	8 231 815	5 495 958	2 735 857	1 611 577	691 122	920 455
18 years and over	8 020 402	7 240 219	5 252 013	1 988 206	780 183	1 300 252	7 804 419	5 210 659	2 593 760	1 516 235	650 429	865 806
21 years and over	7 297 141	6 604 032	4 789 613	1 814 419	693 109	1 183 994	7 114 647	4 752 192	2 362 455	1 366 488	578 628	787 860
62 years and over	1 004 932	887 539	715 045	172 494	117 393	205 424	963 834	710 686	253 148	246 522	99 592	146 930
65 years and over	796 161	698 802	566 402	132 400	97 359	169 271	760 891	562 910	197 981	204 541	82 839	121 702
Median age	26.4	26.6	26.6	26.7	24.3	27.7	26.7	26.6	26.9	25.8	24.2	27.2
Female	**13 907 073**	**12 520 620**	**9 291 142**	**3 229 478**	**1 386 453**	**1 908 836**	**13 293 186**	**9 217 037**	**4 076 149**	**2 522 723**	**1 171 167**	**1 351 556**
Under 5 years	1 226 230	1 098 346	811 306	287 040	127 884	151 177	1 161 888	804 315	357 573	215 519	107 061	108 458
5 to 9 years	1 155 306	1 029 686	755 536	274 150	125 620	165 538	1 096 232	749 231	347 001	224 612	105 482	119 130
10 to 14 years	1 111 627	989 911	724 929	264 982	121 716	175 555	1 057 653	718 740	338 913	229 529	103 322	126 207
15 to 19 years	1 143 243	1 014 219	753 183	261 036	129 024	172 987	1 084 661	746 782	337 879	231 569	108 702	122 867
20 to 24 years	1 181 308	1 060 688	786 333	274 355	120 620	139 019	1 119 722	779 322	340 400	200 605	102 038	98 567
25 to 29 years	1 278 548	1 163 131	840 448	322 683	115 417	143 457	1 224 438	833 533	390 905	197 567	96 593	100 974
30 to 34 years	1 279 214	1 166 257	837 424	328 833	112 957	151 900	1 230 231	830 533	399 698	200 883	94 786	106 097
35 to 39 years	1 112 961	1 017 099	725 510	291 589	95 862	140 754	1 075 308	719 707	355 601	178 407	80 741	97 666
40 to 44 years	895 962	824 146	585 329	238 817	71 816	114 440	872 068	580 883	291 185	138 334	60 276	78 058
45 to 49 years	674 678	620 127	449 545	170 582	54 551	88 647	657 478	446 396	211 082	105 847	45 610	60 237
50 to 54 years	568 366	520 026	391 217	128 809	48 340	78 669	552 287	388 552	163 735	94 748	40 574	54 174
55 to 59 years	502 102	455 339	354 493	100 846	46 763	73 728	484 441	352 120	132 321	91 389	39 804	51 585
60 to 64 years	473 462	425 618	342 101	83 517	47 844	73 912	453 930	339 820	114 110	93 444	40 893	52 551
65 to 69 years	428 174	380 759	310 096	70 663	47 415	71 929	407 514	307 879	99 635	92 589	40 671	51 918
70 to 74 years	326 386	286 280	235 917	50 363	40 106	59 330	307 742	234 169	73 573	77 974	34 697	43 277
75 to 79 years	253 545	219 001	180 984	38 017	34 544	49 185	236 201	179 640	56 561	66 529	30 100	36 429
80 to 84 years	161 101	136 821	113 646	23 175	24 280	31 878	148 283	112 856	35 427	44 696	21 072	23 624
85 years and over	134 860	113 166	93 145	20 021	21 694	26 731	123 109	92 559	30 550	38 482	18 745	19 737
16 years and over	10 202 329	9 214 156	6 860 919	2 353 237	988 173	1 382 224	9 775 721	6 807 461	2 968 260	1 808 832	835 739	973 093
18 years and over	9 769 007	8 827 689	6 575 887	2 251 802	941 318	1 311 984	9 362 221	6 524 794	2 837 427	1 718 770	795 953	922 817
21 years and over	9 021 489	8 166 847	6 079 873	2 086 974	854 642	1 213 077	8 657 776	6 033 215	2 624 561	1 576 790	723 322	853 468
62 years and over	1 585 674	1 388 424	1 137 713	250 711	197 250	283 808	1 492 212	1 129 606	362 606	377 270	170 321	206 949
65 years and over	1 304 066	1 136 027	933 788	202 239	168 039	239 053	1 222 849	927 103	295 746	320 270	145 285	174 985
Median age	29.4	29.6	29.8	28.9	27.9	30.2	29.6	29.9	29.1	29.0	28.0	30.0
PERCENT DISTRIBUTION												
All persons	**100.0**	**100.0**	**100.0**	**100.0**	**100.0**	**100.0**	**100.0**	**100.0**	**100.0**	**100.0**	**100.0**	**100.0**
Under 18 years	32.0	31.7	31.7	31.9	34.3	31.8	31.7	31.6	31.7	33.5	34.3	32.8
18 to 64 years	60.0	60.5	59.7	62.7	55.6	57.5	60.4	59.7	62.1	55.7	55.3	56.1
65 years and over	8.0	7.8	8.7	5.4	10.1	10.7	7.9	8.7	6.2	10.8	10.4	11.2
MALES PER 100 FEMALES												
All persons	**88.1**	**88.0**	**86.3**	**92.8**	**89.0**	**100.8**	**89.0**	**86.3**	**95.1**	**92.8**	**88.1**	**96.9**
Under 18 years	102.1	102.2	101.8	103.1	101.8	104.5	102.4	101.8	103.6	102.6	101.7	103.4
18 to 64 years	85.3	85.0	83.0	90.5	88.3	105.4	86.5	83.0	94.3	93.8	87.2	99.5
65 years and over	61.1	61.5	60.7	65.5	57.9	70.8	62.2	60.7	66.9	63.9	57.0	69.5

Table 19. Age and Sex of American Indian, Eskimo, or Aleut Persons: 1990

[For definitions of terms and meanings of symbols, see text]

Column grouping: "Urban and rural" covers *Total* through *Rural*; "Inside and outside metropolitan area" covers *Inside metro* through *Outside metro Rural*. The Total column is the grand total; within Urban, "Inside urbanized area" (Total, Central place, Urban fringe) and "Outside urbanized area" together make up Urban.

United States — Urban and Rural, Inside and Outside Metropolitan Area	Total	Urban Total	Inside urbanized area Total	Central place	Urban fringe	Outside urbanized area	Rural	Inside metro Total	In central city	Not in central city	Outside metro Total	Outside metro Urban	Outside metro Rural
AGE													
All persons	1 959 234	1 100 534	768 135	468 915	299 220	332 399	858 700	1 002 984	465 364	537 620	956 250	270 174	686 076
Under 5 years	201 950	108 746	70 710	45 663	25 047	38 036	93 204	91 959	45 300	46 659	109 991	31 942	78 049
5 to 9 years	199 446	103 971	67 930	42 420	25 510	36 041	95 475	91 469	42 147	49 322	107 977	29 630	78 347
10 to 14 years	188 000	96 336	63 172	38 243	24 929	33 164	91 664	86 472	38 026	48 446	101 528	27 035	74 493
15 to 19 years	180 516	97 954	66 009	40 124	25 885	31 945	82 562	87 839	39 838	48 001	92 677	26 230	66 447
20 to 24 years	165 549	103 382	74 456	47 474	26 982	28 926	62 167	91 315	46 951	44 364	74 234	24 180	50 054
25 to 29 years	175 577	108 033	78 169	48 909	29 260	29 864	67 544	97 157	48 421	48 736	78 420	24 395	54 025
30 to 34 years	170 668	102 627	74 590	45 325	29 265	28 037	68 041	94 803	44 885	49 918	75 865	22 641	53 224
35 to 39 years	150 182	88 933	64 656	38 394	26 262	24 277	61 249	83 441	38 083	45 358	66 741	19 508	47 233
40 to 44 years	126 154	73 922	54 311	31 458	22 853	19 611	52 232	70 994	31 217	39 777	55 160	15 488	39 672
45 to 49 years	96 817	55 112	40 805	23 240	17 565	14 307	41 705	54 218	23 018	31 200	42 599	11 188	31 411
50 to 54 years	76 714	41 997	30 864	17 613	13 251	11 133	34 717	41 407	17 479	23 928	35 307	8 655	26 652
55 to 59 years	61 819	32 784	23 757	13 770	9 987	9 027	29 035	32 084	13 693	18 391	29 735	7 020	22 715
60 to 64 years	51 389	26 912	19 198	11 511	7 687	7 714	24 477	25 917	11 493	14 424	25 472	6 115	19 357
65 to 69 years	42 710	22 423	15 560	9 576	5 984	6 863	20 287	21 030	9 583	11 447	21 680	5 348	16 332
70 to 74 years	29 270	15 304	10 249	6 441	3 808	5 055	13 966	13 900	6 437	7 463	15 370	4 022	11 348
75 to 79 years	21 152	10 890	6 922	4 362	2 560	3 968	10 262	9 567	4 357	5 210	11 585	3 151	8 434
80 to 84 years	12 116	6 372	3 906	2 508	1 398	2 466	5 744	5 495	2 539	2 956	6 621	1 977	4 644
85 years and over	9 205	4 836	2 871	1 884	987	1 965	4 369	3 917	1 897	2 020	5 288	1 649	3 639
16 years and over	1 334 098	773 302	554 253	335 439	218 814	219 049	560 796	716 518	332 781	383 737	617 580	176 575	441 005
18 years and over	1 262 267	736 173	529 472	320 706	208 766	206 701	526 094	682 630	318 089	364 541	579 637	166 579	413 058
21 years and over	1 154 198	671 657	484 516	292 409	192 107	187 141	482 541	625 696	290 090	335 606	528 502	150 307	378 195
62 years and over	144 397	75 449	50 577	31 414	19 163	24 872	68 948	68 928	31 455	37 473	75 469	19 730	55 739
65 years and over	114 453	59 825	39 508	24 771	14 737	20 317	54 628	53 909	24 813	29 096	60 544	16 147	44 397
Median age	—	26.8	27.7	27.1	28.7	24.7	25.3	27.7	27.1	28.3	24.4	24.2	24.6
Male	967 186	538 646	376 795	228 777	148 018	161 851	428 540	495 301	227 002	268 299	471 885	131 217	340 668
Under 5 years	102 628	55 327	35 981	23 102	12 879	19 346	47 301	46 934	22 954	23 980	55 694	16 174	39 520
5 to 9 years	101 188	52 698	34 351	21 358	12 993	18 347	48 490	46 371	21 206	25 165	54 817	15 028	39 789
10 to 14 years	95 747	48 740	31 844	19 222	12 622	16 896	47 007	43 919	19 123	24 796	51 828	13 755	38 073
15 to 19 years	93 058	50 117	33 752	20 406	13 346	16 365	42 941	45 476	20 238	25 238	47 582	13 396	34 186
20 to 24 years	85 043	52 987	38 501	24 105	14 396	14 486	32 056	47 444	23 822	23 622	37 599	12 061	25 538
25 to 29 years	87 474	53 776	39 066	24 526	14 540	14 710	33 698	48 699	24 297	24 402	38 775	12 006	26 769
30 to 34 years	82 744	49 654	36 300	22 165	14 135	13 354	33 090	46 212	21 968	24 244	36 532	10 715	25 817
35 to 39 years	72 594	42 557	31 096	18 584	12 512	11 461	30 037	40 306	18 431	21 875	32 288	9 139	23 149
40 to 44 years	61 194	35 173	25 848	14 872	10 976	9 325	26 021	34 137	14 761	19 376	27 057	7 360	19 697
45 to 49 years	46 993	26 235	19 480	10 956	8 524	6 755	20 758	26 244	10 841	15 403	20 749	5 272	15 477
50 to 54 years	36 888	19 867	14 693	8 178	6 515	5 174	17 021	19 960	8 102	11 858	16 928	3 975	12 953
55 to 59 years	29 354	15 369	11 192	6 393	4 799	4 177	13 985	15 360	6 355	9 005	13 994	3 209	10 785
60 to 64 years	24 192	12 422	8 954	5 267	3 687	3 468	11 770	12 296	5 262	7 034	11 896	2 735	9 161
65 to 69 years	19 298	9 774	6 816	4 104	2 712	2 958	9 524	9 349	4 100	5 249	9 949	2 324	7 625
70 to 74 years	12 500	6 231	4 207	2 594	1 613	2 024	6 269	5 846	2 595	3 251	6 654	1 613	5 041
75 to 79 years	8 460	4 021	2 540	1 561	979	1 481	4 439	3 628	1 555	2 073	4 832	1 172	3 660
80 to 84 years	4 557	2 159	1 270	797	473	889	2 398	1 858	807	1 051	2 699	734	1 965
85 years and over	3 274	1 539	904	587	317	635	1 735	1 262	585	677	2 012	549	1 463
16 years and over	649 275	372 649	268 530	161 530	107 000	104 119	276 626	349 606	160 189	189 417	299 669	83 690	215 979
18 years and over	612 311	353 705	255 915	153 964	101 951	97 790	258 606	332 141	152 632	179 509	280 170	78 580	201 590
21 years and over	556 406	320 476	232 624	139 594	93 030	87 852	235 930	302 383	138 442	163 941	254 023	70 338	183 685
62 years and over	62 073	30 833	20 790	12 590	8 200	10 043	31 240	28 943	12 599	16 344	33 130	8 004	25 126
65 years and over	48 089	23 724	15 737	9 643	6 094	7 987	24 365	21 943	9 643	12 301	26 146	6 392	19 754
Median age	—	25.9	26.8	26.2	27.7	23.4	24.5	26.8	26.2	27.3	23.4	23.0	23.7
Female	992 048	561 888	391 340	240 138	151 202	170 548	430 160	507 683	238 362	269 321	484 365	138 957	345 408
Under 5 years	99 322	53 419	34 729	22 561	12 168	18 690	45 903	45 025	22 346	22 679	54 297	15 768	38 529
5 to 9 years	98 258	51 273	33 579	21 062	12 517	17 694	46 985	45 098	20 941	24 157	53 160	14 602	38 558
10 to 14 years	92 253	47 596	31 328	19 021	12 307	16 268	44 657	42 553	18 903	23 650	49 700	13 280	36 420
15 to 19 years	87 458	47 837	32 257	19 718	12 539	15 580	39 621	42 363	19 600	22 763	45 095	12 834	32 261
20 to 24 years	80 506	50 395	35 955	23 369	12 586	14 440	30 111	43 871	23 129	20 742	36 635	12 119	24 516
25 to 29 years	88 103	54 257	39 103	24 383	14 720	15 154	33 846	48 458	24 124	24 334	39 645	12 389	27 256
30 to 34 years	87 924	52 973	38 290	23 160	15 130	14 683	34 951	48 591	22 917	25 674	39 333	11 926	27 407
35 to 39 years	77 588	46 376	33 560	19 810	13 750	12 816	31 212	43 135	19 652	23 483	34 453	10 369	24 084
40 to 44 years	64 960	38 749	28 463	16 586	11 877	10 286	26 211	36 857	16 456	20 401	28 103	8 128	19 975
45 to 49 years	49 824	28 877	21 325	12 284	9 041	7 552	20 947	27 974	12 177	15 797	21 850	5 916	15 934
50 to 54 years	39 826	22 130	16 171	9 435	6 736	5 959	17 696	21 447	9 377	12 070	18 379	4 680	13 699
55 to 59 years	32 465	17 415	12 565	7 377	5 188	4 850	15 050	16 724	7 338	9 386	15 741	3 811	11 930
60 to 64 years	27 197	14 490	10 244	6 244	4 000	4 246	12 707	13 621	6 231	7 390	13 576	3 380	10 196
65 to 69 years	23 412	12 649	8 744	5 472	3 272	3 905	10 763	11 681	5 483	6 198	11 731	3 024	8 707
70 to 74 years	16 770	9 073	6 042	3 847	2 195	3 031	7 697	8 054	3 842	4 212	8 716	2 409	6 307
75 to 79 years	12 692	6 869	4 382	2 801	1 581	2 487	5 823	5 939	2 802	3 137	6 753	1 979	4 774
80 to 84 years	7 559	4 213	2 636	1 711	925	1 577	3 346	3 637	1 732	1 905	3 922	1 243	2 679
85 years and over	5 931	3 297	1 967	1 297	670	1 330	2 634	2 655	1 312	1 343	3 276	1 100	2 176
16 years and over	684 823	400 653	285 723	173 909	111 814	114 930	284 170	366 912	172 592	194 320	317 911	92 885	225 026
18 years and over	649 956	382 468	273 557	166 742	106 815	108 911	267 488	350 489	165 457	185 032	299 467	87 999	211 468
21 years and over	597 792	351 181	251 892	152 815	99 077	99 289	246 611	323 313	151 648	171 665	274 479	79 969	194 510
62 years and over	82 324	44 616	29 787	18 824	10 963	14 829	37 708	39 985	18 856	21 129	42 339	11 726	30 613
65 years and over	66 364	36 101	23 771	15 128	8 643	12 330	30 263	31 966	15 171	16 795	34 398	9 755	24 643
Median age	—	27.8	28.6	27.9	29.6	25.9	26.2	28.6	28.0	29.3	25.4	25.3	25.4
PERCENT DISTRIBUTION													
All persons	100.0	100.0	100.0	100.0	100.0	100.0	100.0	100.0	100.0	100.0	100.0	100.0	100.0
Under 18 years	—	33.1	31.1	31.6	30.2	37.8	38.7	31.9	31.6	32.2	39.4	38.3	39.8
18 to 64 years	—	61.5	63.8	63.1	64.8	56.1	54.9	62.7	63.0	62.4	54.3	55.7	53.7
65 years and over	—	5.4	5.1	5.3	4.9	6.1	6.4	5.4	5.3	5.4	6.3	6.0	6.5
MALES PER 100 FEMALES													
All persons	—	95.9	96.3	95.3	97.9	94.9	99.6	97.6	95.2	99.6	97.4	94.4	98.6
Under 18 years	—	103.1	102.6	101.9	103.8	103.9	104.5	103.8	102.0	105.3	103.7	103.3	103.8
18 to 64 years	—	95.3	96.2	95.2	97.6	93.0	98.7	97.4	95.1	99.4	95.8	92.3	97.3
65 years and over	—	65.7	66.2	63.7	70.5	64.8	80.5	68.6	63.6	73.2	76.0	65.5	80.2

Table 20. Age and Sex of Asian or Pacific Islander Persons: 1990

[For definitions of terms and meanings of symbols, see text]

United States Urban and Rural Inside and Outside Metropolitan Area	Urban and rural						Inside and outside metropolitan area					
		Urban					Inside metropolitan area			Outside metropolitan area		
			Inside urbanized area			Outside urbanized area						
	Total	Total	Central place	Urban fringe		Rural	Total	In central city	Not in central city	Total	Urban	Rural
AGE												
All persons	6 934 689	6 507 391	3 421 439	3 085 952	427 298	338 973	6 823 859	3 373 675	3 450 184	449 803	298 962	150 841
Under 5 years	560 450	523 474	272 270	251 204	36 976	29 395	551 986	268 643	283 343	37 859	24 543	13 316
5 to 9 years	563 060	524 247	262 949	261 298	38 813	33 073	556 142	259 559	296 583	39 991	25 465	14 526
10 to 14 years	519 430	483 804	233 339	250 465	35 626	32 122	514 272	230 013	284 259	37 280	23 153	14 127
15 to 19 years	571 479	531 378	277 111	254 267	40 101	32 282	561 367	272 922	288 445	42 394	28 132	14 262
20 to 24 years	610 465	567 057	335 927	231 130	43 408	21 793	587 939	330 432	257 507	44 319	34 383	9 936
25 to 29 years	668 162	630 009	356 965	273 044	38 153	22 907	652 045	352 408	299 637	39 024	28 530	10 494
30 to 34 years	698 614	660 285	349 424	310 861	38 329	27 569	686 812	344 998	341 814	39 371	27 213	12 158
35 to 39 years	640 225	604 610	300 396	304 214	35 615	29 593	632 893	296 211	336 682	36 925	24 607	12 318
40 to 44 years	544 127	514 869	244 799	270 070	29 258	28 067	541 321	241 112	300 209	30 873	19 751	11 122
45 to 49 years	385 039	364 089	172 057	192 032	20 950	20 551	382 910	169 504	213 406	22 680	14 327	8 353
50 to 54 years	296 467	280 719	141 060	139 659	15 748	15 184	294 575	139 288	155 287	17 076	10 584	6 492
55 to 59 years	238 110	224 769	120 536	104 233	13 341	12 523	235 524	118 792	116 732	15 109	9 183	5 926
60 to 64 years	207 568	194 997	109 830	85 167	12 571	10 949	204 267	108 245	96 022	14 250	8 764	5 486
65 to 69 years	169 704	159 158	93 259	65 899	10 546	8 793	166 601	91 987	74 614	11 896	7 398	4 498
70 to 74 years	116 355	109 160	65 568	43 592	7 195	5 879	113 880	64 687	49 193	8 354	5 237	3 117
75 to 79 years	76 071	71 005	44 120	26 885	5 066	4 068	74 272	43 507	30 765	5 867	3 643	2 224
80 to 84 years	41 480	38 303	24 591	13 712	3 177	2 370	40 233	24 320	15 913	3 617	2 201	1 416
85 years and over	27 883	25 458	17 238	8 220	2 425	1 855	26 820	17 047	9 773	2 918	1 848	1 070
16 years and over	5 186 019	4 877 238	2 604 913	2 272 325	308 781	237 450	5 096 446	2 568 108	2 528 338	327 023	221 167	105 856
18 years and over	4 966 898	4 672 426	2 504 058	2 168 368	294 472	223 377	4 878 883	2 468 576	2 410 307	311 392	211 732	99 660
21 years and over	4 590 620	4 324 886	2 304 861	2 020 025	265 734	207 057	4 515 660	2 272 884	2 242 776	282 017	189 709	92 308
62 years and over	551 889	516 054	308 792	207 262	35 835	29 450	540 210	304 658	235 552	41 129	25 523	15 606
65 years and over	431 493	403 084	244 776	158 308	28 409	22 965	421 806	241 548	180 258	32 652	20 327	12 325
Median age	29.8	30.0	29.6	30.3	27.4	29.6	29.9	29.6	30.2	27.9	27.3	29.4
Male	3 401 739	3 193 650	1 694 582	1 499 068	208 089	156 299	3 341 360	1 670 871	1 670 489	216 678	147 402	69 276
Under 5 years	286 826	268 121	139 450	128 671	18 705	14 520	282 386	137 594	144 792	18 960	12 388	6 572
5 to 9 years	285 770	266 198	133 979	132 219	19 572	16 063	281 888	132 246	149 642	19 945	12 772	7 173
10 to 14 years	265 302	247 199	119 625	127 574	18 103	15 823	262 336	117 895	144 441	18 789	11 816	6 973
15 to 19 years	295 943	275 469	144 018	131 451	20 474	16 474	290 585	141 721	148 864	21 832	14 484	7 348
20 to 24 years	314 532	291 049	174 545	116 504	23 483	11 450	301 635	171 450	130 185	24 347	19 126	5 221
25 to 29 years	331 992	313 235	181 926	131 309	18 757	10 636	323 282	179 515	143 767	19 346	14 504	4 842
30 to 34 years	338 041	320 204	174 765	145 439	17 837	11 766	331 525	172 656	158 869	18 282	12 994	5 288
35 to 39 years	304 548	288 431	147 335	141 096	16 117	11 974	300 214	145 407	154 807	16 308	11 277	5 031
40 to 44 years	255 520	242 293	116 611	125 682	13 227	11 272	253 449	114 910	138 539	13 343	9 102	4 241
45 to 49 years	186 448	176 711	82 671	94 040	9 737	8 958	185 324	81 480	103 844	10 082	6 654	3 428
50 to 54 years	145 268	137 898	67 717	70 181	7 370	6 817	144 477	66 929	77 548	7 608	4 961	2 647
55 to 59 years	108 729	103 090	54 872	48 218	5 639	4 780	107 469	54 126	53 343	6 040	3 927	2 113
60 to 64 years	89 756	84 451	47 562	36 889	5 305	4 383	88 221	46 900	41 321	5 918	3 728	2 190
65 to 69 years	75 504	70 690	41 719	28 971	4 814	4 014	74 014	41 197	32 817	5 504	3 402	2 102
70 to 74 years	51 468	48 124	29 091	19 033	3 344	2 832	50 385	28 692	21 693	3 915	2 413	1 502
75 to 79 years	34 617	31 994	20 025	11 969	2 623	2 184	33 731	19 736	13 995	3 070	1 849	1 221
80 to 84 years	19 977	18 138	11 695	6 443	1 839	1 452	19 363	11 537	7 826	2 066	1 190	876
85 years and over	11 498	10 355	6 976	3 379	1 143	901	11 076	6 880	4 196	1 323	815	508
16 years and over	2 508 956	2 360 814	1 276 402	1 084 412	148 142	106 393	2 460 212	1 258 356	1 201 856	155 137	108 105	47 032
18 years and over	2 395 437	2 254 490	1 223 606	1 030 884	140 947	99 337	2 347 530	1 206 274	1 141 256	147 244	103 344	43 900
21 years and over	2 200 455	2 074 642	1 120 709	953 933	125 813	90 735	2 159 671	1 105 303	1 054 368	131 610	91 508	39 921
62 years and over	244 948	227 998	137 148	90 850	16 950	14 078	239 554	135 310	104 244	19 472	11 902	7 570
65 years and over	193 064	179 301	109 506	69 795	13 763	11 383	188 569	108 042	80 527	15 878	9 669	6 209
Median age	28.8	29.0	28.7	29.3	25.9	26.8	28.9	28.7	29.1	26.1	26.0	26.4
Female	3 532 950	3 313 741	1 726 857	1 586 884	219 209	182 674	3 482 499	1 702 804	1 779 695	233 125	151 560	81 565
Under 5 years	273 624	255 353	132 820	122 533	18 271	14 875	269 600	131 049	138 551	18 899	12 155	6 744
5 to 9 years	277 290	258 049	128 970	129 079	19 241	17 010	274 254	127 313	146 941	20 046	12 693	7 353
10 to 14 years	254 128	236 605	113 714	122 891	17 523	16 299	251 936	112 118	139 818	18 491	11 337	7 154
15 to 19 years	275 536	255 909	133 093	122 816	19 627	15 808	270 782	131 201	139 581	20 562	13 648	6 914
20 to 24 years	295 933	276 008	161 382	114 626	19 925	10 343	286 304	158 982	127 322	19 972	15 257	4 715
25 to 29 years	336 170	316 774	175 039	141 735	19 396	12 271	328 763	172 893	155 870	19 678	14 026	5 652
30 to 34 years	360 573	340 081	174 659	165 422	20 492	15 803	355 287	172 342	182 945	21 089	14 219	6 870
35 to 39 years	335 677	316 179	153 061	163 118	19 498	17 619	332 679	150 804	181 875	20 617	13 330	7 287
40 to 44 years	288 607	272 576	128 188	144 388	16 031	16 795	287 872	126 202	161 670	17 530	10 649	6 881
45 to 49 years	198 591	187 378	89 386	97 992	11 213	11 593	197 586	88 024	109 562	12 598	7 673	4 925
50 to 54 years	151 199	142 821	73 343	69 478	8 378	8 367	150 098	72 359	77 739	9 468	5 623	3 845
55 to 59 years	129 381	121 679	65 664	56 015	7 702	7 743	128 055	64 666	63 389	9 069	5 256	3 813
60 to 64 years	117 812	110 546	62 268	48 278	7 266	6 566	116 046	61 345	54 701	8 332	5 036	3 296
65 to 69 years	94 200	88 468	51 540	36 928	5 732	4 779	92 587	50 790	41 797	6 392	3 996	2 396
70 to 74 years	64 887	61 036	36 477	24 559	3 851	3 047	63 495	35 995	27 500	4 439	2 824	1 615
75 to 79 years	41 454	39 011	24 095	14 916	2 443	1 884	40 541	23 771	16 770	2 797	1 794	1 003
80 to 84 years	21 503	20 165	12 896	7 269	1 338	918	20 870	12 783	8 087	1 551	1 011	540
85 years and over	16 385	15 103	10 262	4 841	1 282	954	15 744	10 167	5 577	1 595	1 033	662
16 years and over	2 677 063	2 516 424	1 328 511	1 187 913	160 639	131 057	2 636 234	1 309 752	1 326 482	171 886	113 062	58 824
18 years and over	2 571 461	2 417 936	1 280 452	1 137 484	153 525	124 040	2 531 353	1 262 302	1 269 051	164 148	108 388	55 760
21 years and over	2 390 165	2 250 244	1 184 152	1 066 092	139 921	116 322	2 355 989	1 167 581	1 188 408	150 498	98 111	52 387
62 years and over	306 941	288 056	171 644	116 412	18 885	15 372	300 656	169 348	131 308	21 657	13 621	8 036
65 years and over	238 429	223 783	135 270	88 513	14 646	11 582	233 237	133 506	99 731	16 774	10 658	6 116
Median age	30.7	30.8	30.5	31.1	28.9	31.5	30.8	30.4	31.1	29.7	28.8	31.7
PERCENT DISTRIBUTION												
All persons	100.0	100.0	100.0	100.0	100.0	100.0	100.0	100.0	100.0	100.0	100.0	100.0
Under 18 years	28.4	28.2	26.8	29.7	31.1	34.1	28.5	26.8	30.1	30.8	29.2	33.9
18 to 64 years	65.4	65.6	66.0	65.1	62.3	59.1	65.3	66.0	64.6	62.0	64.0	57.9
65 years and over	6.2	6.2	7.2	5.1	6.6	6.8	6.2	7.2	5.2	7.3	6.8	8.2
MALES PER 100 FEMALES												
All persons	96.3	96.4	98.1	94.5	94.9	85.6	95.9	98.1	93.9	92.9	97.3	84.9
Under 18 years	104.7	104.8	105.5	104.2	102.2	97.1	104.5	105.5	103.6	100.7	102.1	98.3
18 to 64 years	94.4	94.6	97.3	91.6	91.6	78.2	93.9	97.3	90.7	89.1	95.9	75.9
65 years and over	81.0	80.1	81.0	78.9	94.0	98.3	80.8	80.9	80.7	94.7	90.7	101.5

Table 21. Age and Sex of Hispanic Origin Persons: 1990

[Persons of Hispanic origin may be of any race. For definitions of terms and meanings of symbols, see text]

United States Urban and Rural Inside and Outside Metropolitan Area	Total	Urban Total	Central place	Urban fringe	Outside urbanized area	Rural	Inside metro Total	In central city	Not in central city	Outside metro Total	Outside metro Urban	Outside metro Rural
AGE												
All persons	20 426 228	18 355 980	11 671 728	6 684 252	2 070 248	1 927 831	20 204 818	11 514 252	8 690 566	2 149 241	1 244 669	904 572
Under 5 years	2 183 384	1 944 974	1 252 586	692 388	238 410	204 140	2 151 256	1 234 008	917 248	236 268	139 711	96 557
5 to 9 years	1 982 993	1 751 293	1 122 842	628 451	231 700	210 859	1 957 848	1 106 164	851 684	236 004	136 208	99 796
10 to 14 years	1 802 973	1 592 280	1 013 952	578 328	210 693	198 644	1 783 276	999 692	783 584	218 341	125 121	93 220
15 to 19 years	1 865 617	1 660 943	1 060 662	600 281	204 674	188 340	1 843 538	1 046 166	797 372	210 419	122 822	87 597
20 to 24 years	2 134 098	1 935 550	1 244 417	691 133	198 548	170 343	2 108 758	1 226 664	882 094	195 683	118 009	77 674
25 to 29 years	2 163 986	1 972 541	1 249 844	722 697	191 445	177 253	2 147 563	1 232 167	915 396	193 676	112 369	81 307
30 to 34 years	1 890 729	1 717 760	1 078 207	639 553	172 969	171 574	1 882 838	1 063 230	819 608	179 465	101 955	77 510
35 to 39 years	1 516 305	1 372 691	857 412	515 279	143 614	144 421	1 510 316	845 931	664 385	150 410	85 728	64 682
40 to 44 years	1 170 835	1 060 502	659 602	400 900	110 333	113 433	1 165 921	651 505	514 416	118 347	66 934	51 413
45 to 49 years	869 172	789 352	488 813	300 539	79 820	84 738	866 371	482 999	383 372	87 539	48 504	39 035
50 to 54 years	690 244	626 529	390 883	235 646	63 715	65 745	685 029	386 694	298 335	70 960	39 664	31 296
55 to 59 years	583 492	527 044	334 368	192 676	56 448	55 816	576 109	330 818	245 291	63 199	35 884	27 315
60 to 64 years	505 953	455 275	292 314	162 961	50 678	47 689	496 748	289 085	207 663	56 894	32 520	24 374
65 to 69 years	399 066	356 238	232 160	124 078	42 828	37 191	388 641	229 461	159 180	47 616	28 062	19 554
70 to 74 years	263 496	234 947	154 417	80 530	28 549	23 276	254 220	152 762	101 458	32 552	19 438	13 114
75 to 79 years	196 056	174 179	116 608	57 571	21 877	17 209	188 280	115 406	72 874	24 985	15 067	9 918
80 to 84 years	120 303	106 445	70 879	35 566	13 858	10 122	114 726	70 214	44 512	15 699	9 650	6 049
85 years and over	87 526	77 437	51 762	25 675	10 089	7 038	83 380	51 286	32 094	11 184	7 023	4 161
16 years and over	14 108 093	12 758 448	8 086 489	4 671 959	1 349 645	1 275 935	13 966 896	7 981 175	5 985 721	1 417 132	819 924	597 208
18 years and over	13 397 222	12 126 479	7 685 063	4 441 416	1 270 743	1 199 337	13 262 443	7 585 140	5 677 303	1 334 116	772 820	561 296
21 years and over	12 158 025	11 015 645	6 969 821	4 045 824	1 142 380	1 090 069	12 041 695	6 879 882	5 161 813	1 206 399	695 160	511 239
62 years and over	1 358 750	1 211 932	795 050	416 882	146 818	122 326	1 315 737	786 446	529 291	165 339	98 446	66 893
65 years and over	1 066 447	949 246	625 826	323 420	117 201	94 836	1 029 247	619 129	410 118	132 036	79 240	52 796
Median age	25.5	25.7	25.5	26.0	23.7	24.8	25.6	25.5	25.6	24.4	24.1	24.8
Male	10 345 978	9 283 090	5 881 696	3 401 394	1 062 888	1 042 081	10 265 924	5 798 996	4 466 928	1 122 135	634 670	487 465
Under 5 years	1 114 049	992 577	639 071	353 506	121 472	104 145	1 098 170	629 737	468 433	120 024	70 832	49 192
5 to 9 years	1 010 596	892 510	571 587	320 923	118 086	108 137	998 442	563 098	435 344	120 291	69 348	50 943
10 to 14 years	921 102	813 540	517 730	295 810	107 562	102 281	911 689	510 401	401 288	111 694	63 691	48 003
15 to 19 years	979 959	872 667	554 297	318 370	107 292	103 934	971 855	546 425	425 430	112 038	63 807	48 231
20 to 24 years	1 159 762	1 050 241	669 083	381 158	109 521	101 738	1 150 803	658 728	492 075	110 697	64 397	46 300
25 to 29 years	1 147 564	1 044 128	660 436	383 692	103 436	102 794	1 142 208	650 577	491 631	108 502	60 693	47 457
30 to 34 years	977 150	885 735	555 383	330 352	91 415	97 307	976 111	547 225	428 886	98 346	54 090	44 256
35 to 39 years	766 284	691 553	431 992	259 561	74 731	79 877	765 519	425 961	339 558	80 642	44 562	36 080
40 to 44 years	578 435	522 265	324 376	197 889	56 170	61 733	578 321	320 201	258 120	61 847	33 952	27 895
45 to 49 years	422 864	382 804	236 115	146 689	40 060	45 393	423 467	233 072	190 395	44 790	24 019	20 771
50 to 54 years	329 389	298 168	184 315	113 853	31 221	34 830	328 696	182 322	146 374	35 523	19 088	16 435
55 to 59 years	273 327	246 395	154 892	91 503	26 932	29 044	271 600	153 146	118 454	30 771	16 847	13 924
60 to 64 years	230 265	206 543	130 906	75 637	23 722	24 691	227 321	129 450	97 871	27 635	15 137	12 498
65 to 69 years	176 505	156 738	101 297	55 441	19 767	19 073	172 993	100 112	72 881	22 585	12 809	9 776
70 to 74 years	108 556	95 903	62 499	33 404	12 653	11 249	104 961	61 788	43 173	14 844	8 523	6 321
75 to 79 years	75 297	66 170	44 227	21 943	9 127	8 058	72 498	43 742	28 756	10 857	6 195	4 662
80 to 84 years	44 461	38 697	25 730	12 967	5 764	4 713	42 328	25 454	16 874	6 846	3 956	2 890
85 years and over	30 413	26 456	17 760	8 696	3 957	3 084	28 942	17 557	11 385	4 555	2 724	1 831
16 years and over	7 121 825	6 426 291	4 052 960	2 373 331	695 534	707 522	7 080 578	3 996 775	3 083 803	748 769	418 789	329 980
18 years and over	6 751 125	6 096 739	3 844 474	2 252 265	654 386	665 770	6 712 075	3 791 187	2 920 888	704 820	394 326	310 494
21 years and over	6 085 365	5 499 945	3 464 118	2 035 827	585 420	602 439	6 052 939	3 416 408	2 636 531	680 465	353 255	281 610
62 years and over	567 125	502 074	326 679	175 395	65 051	60 395	551 668	322 946	228 722	75 852	43 095	32 757
65 years and over	435 232	383 964	251 513	132 451	51 268	46 177	421 722	248 653	173 069	59 687	34 207	25 480
Median age	24.9	25.1	24.9	25.4	23.5	25.0	25.0	24.9	25.1	24.4	23.8	25.1
Female	10 080 250	9 072 890	5 790 032	3 282 858	1 007 360	885 750	9 938 894	5 715 256	4 223 638	1 027 106	609 999	417 107
Under 5 years	1 069 335	952 397	613 515	338 882	116 938	99 995	1 053 086	604 271	448 815	116 244	68 879	47 365
5 to 9 years	972 397	858 783	551 255	307 528	113 614	102 722	959 406	543 066	416 340	115 713	66 860	48 853
10 to 14 years	881 871	778 740	496 222	282 518	103 131	96 363	871 587	489 291	382 296	106 647	61 430	45 217
15 to 19 years	885 658	788 276	506 365	281 911	97 382	84 406	871 683	499 741	371 942	98 381	59 015	39 366
20 to 24 years	974 336	885 309	575 334	309 975	89 027	68 605	957 955	567 936	390 019	84 986	53 612	31 374
25 to 29 years	1 016 422	928 413	589 408	339 005	88 009	74 459	1 005 355	581 590	423 765	85 526	51 676	33 850
30 to 34 years	913 579	832 025	522 824	309 201	81 554	74 267	906 727	516 005	390 722	81 119	47 865	33 254
35 to 39 years	750 021	681 138	425 420	255 718	68 883	64 544	744 797	419 970	324 827	69 768	41 166	28 602
40 to 44 years	592 400	538 237	335 226	203 011	54 163	51 700	587 600	331 304	256 296	56 500	32 982	23 518
45 to 49 years	446 308	406 548	252 698	153 850	39 760	39 345	442 904	249 927	192 977	42 749	24 485	18 264
50 to 54 years	360 855	328 361	206 568	121 793	32 494	30 915	356 333	204 372	151 961	35 437	20 576	14 861
55 to 59 years	310 165	280 649	179 476	101 173	29 516	26 772	304 509	177 672	126 837	32 428	19 037	13 391
60 to 64 years	275 688	248 732	161 408	87 324	26 956	22 998	269 427	159 635	109 792	29 259	17 383	11 876
65 to 69 years	222 561	199 500	130 863	68 637	23 061	18 118	215 648	129 349	86 299	25 031	15 253	9 778
70 to 74 years	154 940	139 044	91 918	47 126	15 896	12 027	149 259	90 974	58 285	17 708	10 915	6 793
75 to 79 years	120 759	108 009	72 381	35 628	12 750	9 151	115 782	71 664	44 118	14 128	8 872	5 256
80 to 84 years	75 842	67 748	45 149	22 599	8 094	5 409	72 398	44 760	27 638	8 853	5 694	3 159
85 years and over	57 113	50 981	34 002	16 979	6 132	3 954	54 438	33 729	20 709	6 629	4 299	2 330
16 years and over	6 986 268	6 332 157	4 033 529	2 298 628	654 111	568 413	6 886 318	3 984 400	2 901 918	668 363	401 135	267 228
18 years and over	6 646 097	6 029 740	3 840 589	2 189 151	616 357	533 567	6 550 368	3 793 953	2 756 415	629 296	378 494	250 802
21 years and over	6 072 660	5 515 700	3 505 703	2 009 997	556 960	487 630	5 988 756	3 463 474	2 525 282	571 534	341 905	229 629
62 years and over	791 625	709 858	468 371	241 487	81 767	61 931	764 069	463 500	300 569	89 487	55 351	34 136
65 years and over	631 215	565 282	374 313	190 969	65 933	48 659	607 525	370 476	237 049	72 349	45 033	27 316
Median age	26.2	26.4	26.2	26.7	24.0	24.3	26.2	26.2	26.2	24.5	24.5	24.4
PERCENT DISTRIBUTION												
All persons	100.0	100.0	100.0	100.0	100.0	100.0	100.0	100.0	100.0	100.0	100.0	100.0
Under 18 years	34.4	33.9	34.2	33.6	38.6	37.8	34.4	34.1	34.7	37.9	37.9	37.9
18 to 64 years	60.4	60.9	60.5	61.6	55.7	57.3	60.5	60.5	60.6	55.9	55.7	56.2
65 years and over	5.2	5.2	5.4	4.8	5.7	4.9	5.1	5.4	4.7	6.1	6.4	5.8
MALES PER 100 FEMALES												
All persons	102.6	102.3	101.6	103.6	105.5	117.6	103.3	101.5	105.8	109.3	104.0	116.9
Under 18 years	104.7	104.7	104.5	105.1	104.5	106.9	104.9	104.5	105.4	104.9	103.8	106.4
18 to 64 years	105.0	104.5	103.7	106.1	109.6	127.8	105.8	103.5	109.1	115.8	108.0	127.5
65 years and over	69.0	67.9	67.2	69.4	77.8	94.9	69.4	67.1	73.0	82.5	76.0	93.3

Table 22. **Age and Sex of White, Not of Hispanic Origin Persons: 1990**

[For definitions of terms and meanings of symbols, see text]

United States Urban and Rural Inside and Outside Metropolitan Area	Urban and rural						Inside and outside metropolitan area					
	Urban						Inside metropolitan area			Outside metropolitan area		
		Inside urbanized area										
	Total	Total	Central place	Urban fringe	Outside urbanized area	Rural	Total	In central city	Not in central city	Total	Urban	Rural
AGE												
All persons	**133 375 398**	**109 975 510**	**46 619 577**	**63 355 933**	**23 399 888**	**54 752 898**	**140 496 200**	**45 957 707**	**94 538 493**	**47 632 096**	**16 871 318**	**30 760 778**
Under 5 years	8 750 234	7 178 041	2 892 737	4 285 304	1 572 193	3 738 485	9 339 311	2 840 667	6 498 644	3 149 408	1 093 504	2 055 904
5 to 9 years	8 387 897	6 775 200	2 604 769	4 170 431	1 612 697	4 142 194	9 092 571	2 560 077	6 532 494	3 437 520	1 127 799	2 309 721
10 to 14 years	7 690 260	6 179 497	2 299 171	3 880 326	1 510 763	4 165 843	8 440 516	2 262 089	6 178 427	3 415 587	1 065 237	2 350 350
15 to 19 years	8 447 277	6 737 619	2 805 127	3 932 492	1 709 658	3 897 424	8 907 005	2 762 232	6 144 773	3 437 690	1 256 125	2 181 571
20 to 24 years	10 344 616	8 484 512	4 169 561	4 314 951	1 860 104	3 093 308	10 313 508	4 097 174	6 216 334	3 124 416	1 413 507	1 710 909
25 to 29 years	11 660 067	9 889 470	4 507 464	5 382 006	1 770 597	3 840 082	12 116 869	4 438 377	7 678 492	3 383 280	1 253 681	2 129 599
30 to 34 years	11 817 750	9 988 502	4 287 439	5 701 063	1 829 248	4 502 281	12 620 248	4 223 632	8 396 616	3 699 783	1 271 634	2 428 149
35 to 39 years	10 731 482	9 020 641	3 742 471	5 278 170	1 710 841	4 496 919	11 635 656	3 692 817	7 942 839	3 592 745	1 197 343	2 395 402
40 to 44 years	9 640 105	8 120 325	3 230 153	4 890 172	1 519 780	4 180 365	10 556 404	3 187 912	7 368 492	3 264 066	1 062 210	2 201 856
45 to 49 years	7 573 044	6 371 553	2 474 954	3 896 599	1 201 491	3 482 918	8 357 311	2 444 796	5 912 515	2 698 651	843 692	1 854 959
50 to 54 years	6 185 595	5 170 581	2 044 617	3 125 964	1 015 014	2 877 909	6 736 537	2 021 790	4 714 747	2 326 967	729 008	1 597 959
55 to 59 years	5 934 354	4 936 160	1 997 747	2 938 413	998 194	2 641 981	6 325 337	1 975 683	4 349 654	2 250 998	730 321	1 520 677
60 to 64 years	6 256 677	5 161 905	2 170 461	2 991 444	1 094 772	2 598 410	6 494 648	2 145 559	4 349 089	2 360 439	812 695	1 547 744
65 to 69 years	6 212 115	5 074 706	2 214 989	2 859 717	1 137 409	2 397 677	6 295 230	2 185 583	4 109 647	2 314 562	848 509	1 466 053
70 to 74 years	5 061 148	4 072 321	1 842 220	2 230 101	988 827	1 867 340	5 012 916	1 817 678	3 195 238	1 915 572	743 136	1 172 436
75 to 79 years	3 952 710	3 134 854	1 486 996	1 647 858	817 856	1 381 503	3 826 895	1 469 788	2 357 107	1 507 318	617 664	889 654
80 to 84 years	2 616 956	2 049 201	1 013 222	1 035 979	567 755	841 620	2 476 173	1 003 192	1 472 981	982 403	433 801	548 602
85 years and over	2 113 111	1 630 422	835 479	794 943	482 689	606 639	1 949 065	828 661	1 120 404	770 685	371 452	399 233
16 years and over	107 057 488	88 642 194	38 380 849	50 261 345	18 415 294	41 892 793	111 982 833	37 859 553	74 123 280	36 967 448	13 380 407	23 587 041
18 years and over	104 044 881	86 206 402	37 476 926	48 729 476	17 838 479	40 276 104	108 673 875	36 968 310	71 705 565	35 647 110	12 971 484	22 675 626
21 years and over	97 920 728	81 370 503	35 142 277	46 228 226	16 550 225	38 150 274	102 581 810	34 672 559	67 909 251	33 489 192	11 985 423	21 503 769
62 years and over	23 747 989	19 081 299	8 712 452	10 368 847	4 666 690	8 656 684	23 477 355	8 608 900	14 868 455	8 927 318	3 514 413	5 412 905
65 years and over	19 956 040	15 961 504	7 392 906	8 568 598	3 994 536	7 094 779	19 560 279	7 304 902	12 255 377	7 490 540	3 014 562	4 475 978
Median age	348	349	347	350	345	350	348	347	348	352	348	354
Male	**64 323 194**	**53 202 903**	**22 443 986**	**30 758 917**	**11 120 291**	**27 333 397**	**68 356 936**	**22 111 733**	**46 245 203**	**23 299 655**	**7 994 807**	**15 304 848**
Under 5 years	4 491 343	3 686 194	1 484 805	2 201 389	805 149	1 921 180	4 795 968	1 457 955	3 338 013	1 616 555	559 864	1 056 691
5 to 9 years	4 300 382	3 474 435	1 335 585	2 138 850	825 947	2 136 497	4 668 535	1 312 557	3 355 978	1 768 344	577 381	1 190 963
10 to 14 years	3 940 196	3 167 952	1 177 835	1 990 117	772 244	2 155 775	4 335 337	1 158 724	3 176 613	1 760 634	544 478	1 216 156
15 to 19 years	4 275 244	3 417 144	1 404 663	2 012 481	858 100	2 042 204	4 546 082	1 382 958	3 163 124	1 771 366	628 034	1 143 332
20 to 24 years	5 205 711	4 264 510	2 092 226	2 172 284	941 201	1 592 264	5 199 628	2 054 439	3 145 189	1 598 347	720 414	877 933
25 to 29 years	5 876 426	4 992 605	2 303 604	2 689 001	883 821	1 907 632	6 090 034	2 266 790	3 823 244	1 694 024	632 117	1 061 907
30 to 34 years	5 932 149	5 027 868	2 190 379	2 837 489	904 281	2 237 672	6 326 592	2 156 775	4 169 817	1 843 229	630 662	1 212 567
35 to 39 years	5 360 964	4 513 017	1 905 037	2 607 980	847 947	2 264 510	5 817 700	1 879 554	3 938 146	1 807 774	594 047	1 213 727
40 to 44 years	4 770 418	4 017 838	1 617 897	2 399 941	752 580	2 118 840	5 245 306	1 595 885	3 649 421	1 643 952	525 391	1 118 561
45 to 49 years	3 711 899	3 126 325	1 216 159	1 910 166	585 574	1 767 366	4 134 411	1 200 999	2 933 412	1 344 854	408 693	936 161
50 to 54 years	2 990 499	2 504 997	984 953	1 520 044	485 502	1 456 366	3 300 233	973 871	2 326 362	1 146 632	346 022	800 610
55 to 59 years	2 829 950	2 366 690	945 713	1 420 977	463 260	1 315 739	3 063 240	935 131	2 128 109	1 082 449	335 605	746 844
60 to 64 years	2 888 262	2 395 554	990 617	1 404 937	492 708	1 281 852	3 048 071	979 426	2 068 645	1 122 043	363 821	758 222
65 to 69 years	2 733 742	2 242 274	958 355	1 283 919	491 468	1 148 959	2 816 677	945 148	1 871 529	1 066 024	365 854	700 170
70 to 74 years	2 111 349	1 709 398	752 675	956 723	401 951	861 620	2 132 375	741 005	1 390 770	840 494	301 376	539 118
75 to 79 years	1 496 019	1 194 190	548 269	645 921	301 829	600 109	1 482 979	540 889	942 090	613 149	226 787	386 362
80 to 84 years	861 560	677 509	323 562	353 947	184 051	330 810	835 453	319 594	515 859	356 917	140 278	216 639
85 years and over	547 081	424 403	211 652	212 751	122 678	194 102	518 315	209 433	308 882	222 868	93 983	128 885
16 years and over	50 829 272	42 259 604	18 219 807	24 039 797	8 569 668	20 696 457	53 714 229	17 960 079	35 754 150	17 811 500	6 208 745	11 602 755
18 years and over	49 291 074	41 015 496	17 759 121	23 256 375	8 275 578	19 853 523	52 016 812	17 506 026	34 510 786	17 127 785	6 000 370	11 127 415
21 years and over	46 223 623	38 585 960	16 607 710	21 978 250	7 637 663	18 732 788	48 932 340	16 373 899	32 558 441	16 024 071	5 514 199	10 509 872
62 years and over	9 481 070	7 680 635	3 390 093	4 290 542	1 803 444	3 906 621	9 607 291	3 345 291	6 262 000	3 783 409	1 351 707	2 431 702
65 years and over	7 749 751	6 247 774	2 794 513	3 453 261	1 501 977	3 135 500	7 785 799	2 756 669	5 029 130	3 099 452	1 128 278	1 971 174
Median age	334	335	332	338	326	343	335	332	337	339	326	346
Female	**69 052 204**	**56 772 607**	**24 175 591**	**32 597 016**	**12 279 597**	**27 419 501**	**72 139 264**	**23 845 974**	**48 293 290**	**24 332 441**	**8 876 511**	**15 455 930**
Under 5 years	4 258 891	3 491 847	1 407 932	2 083 915	767 044	1 817 305	4 543 343	1 382 712	3 160 631	1 532 853	533 640	999 213
5 to 9 years	4 087 515	3 300 765	1 269 184	2 031 581	786 750	2 005 697	4 424 036	1 247 520	3 176 516	1 669 176	550 418	1 118 758
10 to 14 years	3 750 064	3 011 545	1 121 336	1 890 209	738 519	2 010 068	4 105 179	1 103 365	3 001 814	1 654 953	520 759	1 134 194
15 to 19 years	4 172 033	3 320 475	1 400 464	1 920 011	851 558	1 855 220	4 360 923	1 379 274	2 981 649	1 666 330	628 091	1 038 239
20 to 24 years	5 138 905	4 220 002	2 077 335	2 142 667	918 903	1 501 044	5 113 880	2 042 735	3 071 145	1 526 069	693 093	832 976
25 to 29 years	5 783 641	4 896 865	2 203 860	2 693 005	886 776	1 932 450	6 026 835	2 171 587	3 855 248	1 689 256	621 564	1 067 692
30 to 34 years	5 885 601	4 960 634	2 097 060	2 863 574	924 967	2 264 609	6 293 656	2 066 857	4 226 799	1 856 554	640 972	1 215 582
35 to 39 years	5 370 518	4 507 624	1 837 434	2 670 190	862 894	2 232 409	5 817 956	1 813 263	4 004 693	1 784 971	603 296	1 181 675
40 to 44 years	4 869 687	4 102 487	1 612 256	2 490 231	767 200	2 061 525	5 311 098	1 592 027	3 719 071	1 620 114	536 819	1 083 295
45 to 49 years	3 861 145	3 245 228	1 258 795	1 986 433	615 917	1 715 552	4 222 900	1 243 797	2 979 103	1 353 797	434 999	918 798
50 to 54 years	3 195 096	2 665 584	1 059 664	1 605 920	529 512	1 421 543	3 436 304	1 047 919	2 388 385	1 180 335	382 986	797 349
55 to 59 years	3 104 404	2 569 470	1 052 034	1 517 436	534 934	1 326 242	3 262 097	1 040 552	2 221 545	1 168 549	394 716	773 833
60 to 64 years	3 368 415	2 766 351	1 179 844	1 586 507	602 064	1 316 558	3 446 577	1 166 133	2 280 444	1 238 396	448 874	789 522
65 to 69 years	3 478 373	2 832 432	1 256 634	1 575 798	645 941	1 248 718	3 478 553	1 240 435	2 238 118	1 248 538	482 655	765 883
70 to 74 years	2 949 799	2 362 923	1 089 545	1 273 378	586 876	1 005 820	2 880 541	1 076 073	1 804 468	1 075 078	441 760	633 318
75 to 79 years	2 456 691	1 940 664	938 727	1 001 937	516 027	781 394	2 343 916	928 899	1 415 017	894 169	390 877	503 292
80 to 84 years	1 755 396	1 371 692	689 660	682 032	383 704	510 810	1 640 720	683 598	957 122	625 486	293 523	331 963
85 years and over	1 566 030	1 206 019	623 827	582 192	360 011	412 537	1 430 750	619 228	811 522	547 817	277 469	270 348
16 years and over	56 228 216	46 382 590	20 161 042	26 221 548	9 845 626	21 196 336	58 268 604	19 899 474	38 369 130	19 155 948	7 171 662	11 984 286
18 years and over	54 753 807	45 190 906	19 717 805	25 473 101	9 562 901	20 422 581	56 657 063	19 462 284	37 194 779	18 519 325	6 971 114	11 548 211
21 years and over	51 697 105	42 784 543	18 534 567	24 249 976	8 912 562	19 417 486	53 649 470	18 298 660	35 350 810	17 465 121	6 471 224	10 993 897
62 years and over	14 263 910	11 400 664	5 322 359	6 078 305	2 863 246	4 750 063	13 870 064	5 263 609	8 606 455	5 143 909	2 162 706	2 981 203
65 years and over	1 220 628.9	971 373.0	459 839.3	511 533.7	249 255.9	395 927.9	1 177 448.0	454 823.3	722 624.7	439 108.8	188 628.4	250 480.4
Median age	36.3	36.2	36.3	36.2	36.5	35.7	36.0	36.3	35.8	36.5	37.0	36.3
PERCENT DISTRIBUTION												
All persons	**100.0**	**100.0**	**100.0**	**100.0**	**100.0**	**100.0**	**100.0**	**100.0**	**100.0**	**100.0**	**100.0**	**100.0**
Under 18 years	22.0	21.6	19.6	23.1	23.8	26.4	22.6	19.6	24.2	25.2	23.1	26.3
18 to 64 years	63.0	63.9	64.5	63.4	59.2	60.6	63.4	64.5	62.9	59.1	59.0	59.2
65 years and over	15.0	14.5	15.9	13.5	17.1	13.0	13.9	15.9	13.0	15.7	17.9	14.6
MALES PER 100 FEMALES												
All persons	**93.2**	**93.7**	**92.8**	**94.4**	**90.6**	**99.7**	**94.8**	**92.7**	**95.8**	**95.8**	**90.1**	**99.0**
Under 18 years	105.1	105.2	105.1	105.3	104.7	106.9	105.5	105.1	105.7	106.2	104.7	106.9
18 to 64 years	97.6	98.0	99.0	97.3	95.8	101.5	98.5	98.9	98.4	99.3	95.8	101.2
65 years and over	63.5	64.3	60.8	67.5	60.3	79.2	66.1	60.6	69.6	70.6	59.8	78.7

Table 23. Age and Sex for Selected Racial Groups: 1990

[For definitions of terms and meanings of symbols, see text]

United States	American Indian, Eskimo, or Aleut				Asian or Pacific Islander	Asian					
	Total	American Indian	Eskimo	Aleut	Total	Total	Chinese	Filipino	Japanese	Asian Indian	Korean
All persons	1 959 234	1 878 285	57 152	23 797	7 273 662	6 908 638	1 645 472	1 406 770	847 562	815 447	798 849
Under 5 years	201 950	191 566	7 925	2 459	589 845	551 148	110 487	103 058	47 424	69 579	70 601
Under 1 year	36 089	34 225	1 429	435	93 460	86 647	16 972	17 346	8 099	11 113	9 440
1 year	43 077	40 743	1 796	538	130 536	122 242	26 857	21 853	10 218	15 264	15 268
2 years	42 157	39 989	1 651	517	126 175	118 189	23 669	21 850	9 957	15 001	15 462
3 years	40 519	38 487	1 564	468	120 256	112 558	21 598	21 120	9 718	14 195	15 327
4 years	40 108	38 122	1 485	501	119 418	111 512	21 391	20 889	9 432	14 006	15 104
5 to 9 years	199 446	190 532	6 542	2 372	596 133	557 657	103 942	107 077	45 194	71 698	70 499
5 years	40 657	38 742	1 438	477	121 788	114 018	21 431	21 408	9 506	14 406	14 689
6 years	39 454	37 570	1 386	498	119 463	111 555	21 036	21 095	9 161	14 135	14 841
7 years	40 875	39 031	1 353	491	119 740	111 885	20 737	21 549	9 188	14 397	14 506
8 years	38 295	36 719	1 158	418	116 064	108 553	19 866	21 157	8 486	14 357	13 133
9 years	40 165	38 470	1 207	488	119 078	111 646	20 872	21 868	8 853	14 403	13 330
10 to 14 years	188 000	180 689	5 270	2 041	551 552	516 333	104 336	108 214	40 095	67 230	62 909
10 years	40 017	38 426	1 135	456	117 357	109 734	21 064	22 057	8 596	14 603	13 444
11 years	37 788	36 249	1 126	413	109 049	101 996	20 640	21 428	8 128	13 817	11 945
12 years	37 420	35 947	1 054	419	108 190	101 123	20 359	21 796	8 080	13 368	12 100
13 years	37 047	35 713	948	386	109 012	102 140	21 601	21 850	7 769	12 954	12 524
14 years	35 728	34 354	1 007	367	107 944	101 340	20 672	21 083	7 522	12 488	12 896
15 to 19 years	180 516	173 472	5 056	1 988	603 761	569 378	121 639	117 323	45 945	61 027	74 694
15 years	35 740	34 417	964	359	112 663	106 113	21 683	21 512	7 470	12 387	13 769
16 years	35 886	34 422	1 057	407	115 477	108 879	22 652	22 778	8 001	12 096	14 091
17 years	35 945	34 576	969	400	117 717	111 262	23 190	23 042	8 743	11 364	14 670
18 years	35 798	34 475	958	365	125 310	118 301	25 807	24 679	9 571	12 319	15 685
19 years	37 147	35 582	1 108	457	132 594	124 823	28 307	25 312	12 160	12 861	16 479
20 to 24 years	165 549	157 990	5 371	2 188	632 258	596 283	137 855	118 693	61 441	70 863	65 643
20 years	35 124	33 567	1 095	462	134 694	126 859	29 240	25 271	12 915	13 258	15 731
21 years	33 401	31 947	1 028	426	129 179	121 964	28 672	24 377	12 649	13 484	14 184
25 to 29 years	175 577	167 437	5 680	2 460	691 069	654 163	170 047	119 023	74 696	85 732	70 389
30 to 34 years	170 668	163 502	4 891	2 275	726 183	693 240	174 944	131 691	86 379	85 939	83 593
35 to 39 years	150 182	144 342	3 901	1 939	669 818	642 269	165 244	129 848	78 087	81 729	67 112
40 to 44 years	126 154	121 704	2 847	1 603	572 194	550 098	138 915	118 036	67 380	74 162	60 978
45 to 49 years	96 817	93 430	2 243	1 144	405 590	388 908	85 123	88 339	49 158	53 935	51 905
50 to 54 years	76 714	74 153	1 667	894	311 651	298 961	74 592	67 567	40 767	35 355	40 738
55 to 59 years	61 819	59 441	1 601	777	250 633	240 276	64 466	49 374	51 796	20 951	26 231
60 to 64 years	51 389	49 601	1 249	539	218 517	210 201	59 905	44 321	53 268	14 243	18 310
65 to 69 years	42 710	41 197	1 048	465	178 497	172 517	50 996	37 782	44 246	10 285	14 181
70 to 74 years	29 270	28 376	656	238	122 234	118 302	36 396	25 644	29 212	6 281	10 187
75 to 79 years	21 152	20 360	594	198	80 139	77 647	24 289	21 054	15 736	3 683	6 295
80 to 84 years	12 116	11 668	332	116	43 850	42 529	13 230	13 358	7 704	1 780	3 214
85 years and over	9 205	8 825	279	101	29 738	28 728	9 066	6 368	9 034	975	1 370
18 years and over	1 262 267	1 212 083	34 425	15 759	5 190 275	4 957 246	1 259 182	1 021 089	690 635	571 093	552 310
62 years and over	144 397	139 363	3 629	1 405	581 339	561 840	168 944	131 243	137 266	30 810	45 371
65 years and over	114 453	110 426	2 909	1 118	454 458	439 723	133 977	104 206	105 932	23 004	35 247
Median age	26.2	26.3	23.6	26.8	29.8	30.1	32.1	31.1	36.3	28.9	29.1
Female	992 048	952 229	28 197	11 622	3 715 624	3 534 649	824 348	756 334	458 078	377 604	445 139
Under 5 years	99 322	94 301	3 851	1 170	288 499	269 760	53 496	49 963	23 345	33 992	35 819
Under 1 year	17 786	16 878	686	222	45 856	42 564	8 307	8 504	3 969	5 472	4 676
1 year	21 145	20 012	887	246	63 281	59 336	12 944	10 455	5 024	7 508	7 514
2 years	20 782	19 701	824	257	61 540	57 657	11 406	10 594	4 964	7 295	7 758
3 years	19 863	18 894	751	218	59 123	55 412	10 593	10 228	4 735	6 932	7 985
4 years	19 746	18 816	703	227	58 699	54 791	10 246	10 182	4 653	6 785	7 886
5 to 9 years	98 258	93 882	3 257	1 119	294 300	275 412	50 445	51 822	22 350	35 466	37 676
5 years	20 021	19 048	738	235	60 087	56 279	10 368	10 394	4 721	7 113	7 722
6 years	19 469	18 530	696	243	58 977	55 106	10 265	10 144	4 448	7 018	7 897
7 years	20 124	19 192	694	238	59 164	55 340	10 079	10 079	4 559	7 141	7 841
8 years	18 949	18 207	562	180	57 328	53 592	9 589	10 259	4 258	7 053	6 987
9 years	19 695	18 905	567	223	58 744	55 095	10 144	10 611	4 364	7 141	7 229
10 to 14 years	92 253	88 705	2 562	986	270 427	253 026	50 116	52 532	19 722	33 049	33 365
10 years	19 701	18 940	546	215	57 593	53 829	10 092	10 700	4 255	7 188	7 181
11 years	18 481	17 739	542	200	53 397	49 891	9 941	10 372	3 894	6 820	6 308
12 years	18 365	17 643	513	209	53 252	49 750	9 833	10 568	3 955	6 636	6 398
13 years	18 070	17 410	479	181	53 651	50 283	10 388	10 721	3 850	6 381	6 740
14 years	17 636	16 973	482	181	52 534	49 273	9 862	10 171	3 768	6 024	6 738
15 to 19 years	87 458	84 049	2 474	935	291 344	274 718	57 772	57 063	23 666	29 245	38 194
15 years	17 392	16 725	478	189	54 278	51 121	10 157	10 427	3 769	5 931	7 117
16 years	17 566	16 850	517	199	55 847	52 596	10 745	10 979	4 112	5 906	7 182
17 years	17 301	16 649	472	180	56 772	53 680	10 937	11 253	4 544	5 493	7 644
18 years	17 180	16 553	471	156	60 522	57 136	12 414	11 998	4 924	5 816	8 023
19 years	18 019	17 272	536	211	63 925	60 185	13 519	12 406	6 317	6 099	8 228
20 to 24 years	80 506	76 941	2 551	1 014	306 276	288 843	67 137	60 739	31 012	32 486	33 597
20 years	16 965	16 213	539	213	64 567	60 748	13 907	12 482	6 445	6 180	7 845
21 years	15 979	15 328	474	177	61 919	58 418	13 670	12 127	6 412	6 285	7 114
25 to 29 years	88 103	84 197	2 712	1 194	348 441	330 198	85 334	65 774	39 020	39 300	40 308
30 to 34 years	87 924	84 352	2 484	1 088	376 376	360 018	88 640	77 797	43 788	38 959	48 968
35 to 39 years	77 588	74 700	1 917	971	353 296	339 563	85 143	75 591	39 607	38 193	41 181
40 to 44 years	64 960	62 773	1 377	810	305 402	294 468	71 958	69 075	35 245	33 424	37 446
45 to 49 years	49 824	48 145	1 130	549	210 184	201 974	42 860	50 521	26 652	21 656	29 819
50 to 54 years	39 826	38 539	815	472	159 566	153 189	36 649	37 542	24 568	13 515	21 325
55 to 59 years	32 465	31 236	829	400	137 124	131 888	31 782	27 747	35 595	8 816	14 388
60 to 64 years	27 197	26 296	640	261	124 378	119 946	31 634	25 760	34 273	7 082	10 690
65 to 69 years	23 412	22 620	531	261	98 979	95 822	25 894	22 400	24 883	5 595	8 568
70 to 74 years	16 770	16 289	352	129	67 934	65 687	19 132	15 013	15 464	3 444	6 431
75 to 79 years	12 692	12 209	358	125	43 338	41 891	13 103	10 185	8 443	1 957	4 249
80 to 84 years	7 559	7 278	199	82	22 421	21 585	7 565	4 714	4 312	901	2 141
85 years and over	5 931	5 717	158	56	17 339	16 661	5 688	2 096	6 133	524	974
18 years and over	649 956	625 117	17 060	7 779	2 695 501	2 579 054	638 452	569 358	380 236	257 767	316 336
62 years and over	82 324	79 549	1 984	791	322 313	311 378	90 125	70 016	78 792	16 426	28 437
65 years and over	66 364	64 113	1 598	653	250 011	241 646	71 382	54 408	59 235	12 421	22 363
Median age	27.2	27.3	23.7	27.6	30.7	30.9	32.7	32.6	38.2	28.1	30.3
Male	967 186	926 056	28 955	12 175	3 558 038	3 373 989	821 124	650 436	389 484	437 843	353 710
Median age	25.3	25.4	23.3	26.1	28.7	29.0	31.5	29.0	34.6	29.6	26.9
Males per 100 females	97.5	97.3	102.7	104.8	95.8	95.5	99.6	86.0	85.0	116.0	79.5

Table 23. Age and Sex for Selected Racial Groups: 1990—Con.

[For definitions of terms and meanings of symbols, see text]

United States

| | \multicolumn{11}{c}{Asian or Pacific Islander—Con.} |||||||||||
| | \multicolumn{6}{c}{Asian—Con.} |||||| \multicolumn{5}{c}{Pacific Islander} |||||
	Vietnamese	Cambodian	Hmong	Laotian	Thai	Other Asian	Total	Hawaiian	Samoan	Guamanian	Other Pacific Islander
All persons	**614 547**	**147 411**	**90 082**	**149 014**	**91 275**	**302 209**	**365 024**	**211 014**	**62 964**	**49 345**	**41 701**
Under 5 years	53 095	19 727	19 526	17 210	4 828	35 613	38 697	20 638	8 271	4 643	5 145
Under 1 year	7 819	2 713	3 207	2 798	785	6 355	6 813	3 786	1 417	772	838
1 year	12 281	3 888	4 159	3 633	1 043	7 778	8 294	4 404	1 762	996	1 132
2 years	11 714	4 222	4 052	3 679	1 006	7 577	7 986	4 164	1 782	958	1 082
3 years	10 596	4 408	3 986	3 504	980	7 126	7 698	4 100	1 639	954	1 005
4 years	10 685	4 496	4 122	3 596	1 014	6 777	7 906	4 184	1 671	963	1 088
5 to 9 years	56 310	26 000	19 280	20 577	5 625	31 455	38 476	21 350	7 768	4 598	4 760
5 years	11 659	5 033	4 118	3 916	1 040	6 812	7 770	4 191	1 644	926	1 009
6 years	11 353	4 861	3 907	3 673	1 076	6 417	7 908	4 326	1 628	966	988
7 years	11 356	4 873	3 859	4 015	1 169	6 236	7 855	4 394	1 542	944	975
8 years	11 116	5 231	3 721	4 402	1 100	5 984	7 511	4 223	1 516	880	892
9 years	10 826	6 002	3 675	4 571	1 240	6 006	7 432	4 216	1 438	882	896
10 to 14 years	55 616	15 340	10 991	18 497	7 342	25 763	35 219	19 972	6 851	4 373	4 023
10 years	10 886	5 006	2 782	4 003	1 420	5 873	7 623	4 383	1 469	895	876
11 years	10 502	3 076	2 353	3 579	1 355	5 173	7 053	4 055	1 337	831	830
12 years	10 794	2 388	2 111	3 669	1 429	5 029	7 067	4 026	1 384	902	755
13 years	10 944	2 405	1 903	3 648	1 583	4 959	6 872	3 791	1 394	887	800
14 years	12 490	2 465	1 842	3 598	1 555	4 729	6 604	3 717	1 267	858	762
15 to 19 years	74 012	14 312	8 355	17 100	8 561	26 410	34 383	18 978	6 516	4 968	3 921
15 years	14 218	2 929	1 917	3 821	1 682	4 725	6 550	3 680	1 286	879	705
16 years	14 562	2 758	1 829	3 652	1 632	4 828	6 598	3 726	1 281	849	742
17 years	15 456	3 030	1 708	3 443	1 696	4 920	6 455	3 616	1 179	943	717
18 years	15 171	2 977	1 579	3 271	1 763	5 479	7 009	3 744	1 346	1 113	806
19 years	14 605	2 618	1 322	2 913	1 788	6 458	7 771	4 212	1 424	1 184	951
20 to 24 years	66 186	12 558	6 544	13 367	8 214	34 919	35 975	19 313	6 586	5 566	4 510
20 years	14 541	2 935	1 381	2 823	1 823	6 941	7 835	4 162	1 472	1 220	981
21 years	13 361	2 435	1 264	2 793	1 587	7 158	7 215	3 878	1 296	1 082	959
25 to 29 years	63 236	10 362	5 829	13 592	8 137	33 120	36 906	20 657	6 061	5 832	4 356
30 to 34 years	61 999	11 433	4 510	12 751	8 518	31 483	32 943	18 774	5 053	5 031	4 085
35 to 39 years	57 019	11 052	4 038	10 618	11 702	25 820	27 549	16 231	4 084	4 019	3 215
40 to 44 years	40 568	7 971	2 849	7 507	13 009	18 723	22 096	13 199	3 247	3 261	2 389
45 to 49 years	26 759	5 902	2 087	5 807	8 114	11 779	16 682	10 795	2 384	1 785	1 718
50 to 54 years	18 477	4 046	1 496	3 918	3 455	8 550	12 690	8 113	1 755	1 637	1 185
55 to 59 years	13 218	3 001	1 126	2 572	1 447	6 094	10 357	6 931	1 286	1 272	868
60 to 64 years	9 968	1 983	916	1 801	907	4 579	8 316	5 830	1 055	837	594
65 to 69 years	7 013	1 603	927	1 552	662	3 270	5 980	4 190	770	608	412
70 to 74 years	5 030	1 115	850	1 143	430	2 014	3 932	2 786	505	392	249
75 to 79 years	3 319	593	503	632	217	1 326	2 492	1 789	314	249	140
80 to 84 years	1 737	254	167	231	69	785	1 321	909	200	130	82
85 years and over	985	159	88	139	38	506	1 010	559	258	144	49
18 years and over	405 290	77 627	34 831	81 814	68 470	194 905	233 029	138 032	36 328	33 060	25 609
62 years and over	23 472	4 740	3 010	4 649	1 922	10 413	19 499	13 590	2 652	1 993	1 264
65 years and over	18 084	3 724	2 535	3 697	1 416	7 901	14 735	10 233	2 047	1 523	932
Median age	25.2	19.4	12.5	20.4	31.8	24.5	25.0	26.3	21.5	25.4	23.2
Female	**289 303**	**75 724**	**44 192**	**71 984**	**53 696**	**138 247**	**180 975**	**105 212**	**30 978**	**24 140**	**20 645**
Under 5 years	25 739	9 732	9 485	8 402	2 358	17 429	18 739	10 033	3 941	2 248	2 517
Under 1 year	3 819	1 369	1 575	1 398	372	3 103	3 292	1 814	703	371	404
1 year	5 906	1 934	1 992	1 767	508	3 784	3 945	2 110	822	456	557
2 years	5 715	2 081	1 959	1 713	484	3 688	3 883	2 019	876	462	526
3 years	5 109	2 152	1 063	1 722	494	3 509	3 711	1 987	759	488	477
4 years	5 190	2 196	2 006	1 802	500	3 345	3 908	2 103	781	471	553
5 to 9 years	27 163	12 729	9 505	10 055	2 738	15 463	18 888	10 529	3 821	2 264	2 274
5 years	5 630	2 497	2 048	1 903	532	3 351	3 808	2 027	822	471	488
6 years	5 514	2 391	1 937	1 790	511	3 191	3 871	2 122	808	473	468
7 years	5 460	2 338	1 899	1 995	552	3 062	3 824	2 184	746	448	446
8 years	5 389	2 597	1 830	2 146	544	2 940	3 736	2 097	762	438	439
9 years	5 170	2 906	1 791	2 221	599	2 919	3 649	2 099	683	434	433
10 to 14 years	26 111	7 474	5 272	8 966	3 627	12 792	17 401	9 764	3 436	2 171	2 030
10 years	5 138	2 438	1 323	1 970	659	2 885	3 764	2 164	732	430	438
11 years	4 958	1 502	1 133	1 689	676	2 598	3 506	2 000	671	419	416
12 years	5 143	1 166	1 038	1 776	693	2 544	3 502	1 985	703	445	369
13 years	5 132	1 138	895	1 792	790	2 456	3 368	1 828	700	429	411
14 years	5 740	1 230	883	1 739	809	2 309	3 261	1 787	630	448	396
15 to 19 years	33 098	6 757	3 775	8 246	4 281	12 621	16 626	9 157	3 093	2 388	1 988
15 years	6 427	1 377	894	1 859	834	2 329	3 157	1 754	611	428	364
16 years	6 619	1 277	818	1 799	814	2 345	3 251	1 841	593	425	392
17 years	6 835	1 411	731	1 616	888	2 328	3 092	1 712	551	450	379
18 years	6 790	1 408	714	1 543	889	2 617	3 386	1 805	679	509	393
19 years	6 427	1 284	618	1 429	856	3 002	3 740	2 045	659	576	460
20 to 24 years	28 717	6 492	3 142	6 553	4 164	14 804	17 433	9 362	3 203	2 590	2 278
20 years	6 393	1 492	663	1 405	907	3 029	3 819	1 981	721	594	523
21 years	5 814	1 211	617	1 350	794	3 024	3 501	1 879	650	489	483
25 to 29 years	26 714	5 819	2 689	6 700	4 406	14 134	18 243	10 302	2 981	2 773	2 187
30 to 34 years	27 843	6 622	2 290	6 228	5 234	13 649	16 358	9 467	2 504	2 404	1 983
35 to 39 years	28 248	5 818	1 931	4 959	7 912	10 980	13 733	8 134	1 995	2 001	1 603
40 to 44 years	21 308	4 165	1 393	3 464	8 968	8 022	10 934	6 546	1 565	1 661	1 162
45 to 49 years	13 560	3 032	1 082	2 599	5 245	4 948	8 210	5 317	1 156	900	837
50 to 54 years	9 035	2 144	788	1 672	2 220	3 731	6 377	4 152	861	799	565
55 to 59 years	6 415	1 562	641	1 114	938	2 890	5 236	3 553	672	589	422
60 to 64 years	4 941	1 130	548	905	617	2 366	4 432	3 104	552	472	304
65 to 69 years	3 830	946	614	851	473	1 768	3 157	2 225	408	325	199
70 to 74 years	2 880	686	555	661	303	1 118	2 247	1 592	294	215	146
75 to 79 years	2 000	352	316	382	143	761	1 447	1 042	177	145	83
80 to 84 years	1 028	160	105	140	47	472	836	575	129	90	42
85 years and over	673	104	61	87	22	299	678	358	190	105	25
18 years and over	190 409	41 724	17 487	39 287	42 437	85 561	116 444	69 579	18 025	16 154	12 689
62 years and over	13 136	2 819	1 937	2 605	1 339	5 746	10 935	7 593	1 528	1 155	659
65 years and over	10 411	2 248	1 651	2 121	988	4 418	8 365	5 792	1 198	880	495
Median age	25.7	20.8	12.6	20.2	35.0	23.6	25.4	26.8	21.7	25.7	23.2
Male	**325 244**	**71 687**	**45 890**	**77 030**	**37 579**	**163 962**	**184 049**	**105 802**	**31 986**	**25 205**	**21 056**
Median age	24.8	18.0	12.4	20.6	26.7	25.2	24.5	25.7	21.2	25.2	23.3
Males per 100 females	112.4	94.7	103.8	107.0	70.0	118.6	101.7	100.6	103.3	104.4	102.0

Table 24. Age and Sex by Type of Hispanic Origin: 1990

[For definitions of terms and meanings of symbols, see text]

United States	All persons	Hispanic origin (of any race) Total	Mexican	Puerto Rican	Cuban	Other Hispanic	Not of Hispanic origin
All persons	**248 709 873**	**22 354 059**	**13 495 938**	**2 727 754**	**1 043 932**	**5 086 435**	**226 355 814**
Under 5 years	18 354 443	2 387 524	1 578 141	286 856	56 239	466 288	15 966 919
Under 1 year	3 217 312	427 454	284 194	49 181	9 807	84 272	2 789 858
1 year	3 949 107	518 131	340 985	62 810	12 104	102 232	3 430 976
2 years	3 815 040	502 284	330 489	61 185	11 830	98 780	3 312 756
3 years	3 683 177	477 574	316 077	57 566	11 332	92 599	3 205 603
4 years	3 689 807	462 081	306 396	56 114	11 166	88 405	3 227 726
5 to 9 years	18 099 179	2 193 852	1 455 722	268 850	50 200	419 080	15 905 327
5 years	3 689 533	457 089	303 788	55 228	10 771	87 302	3 232 444
6 years	3 577 632	434 252	288 208	52 720	10 537	82 787	3 143 380
7 years	3 645 761	441 276	293 726	53 857	10 481	83 212	3 204 485
8 years	3 508 668	426 113	282 345	52 798	9 360	81 610	3 082 555
9 years	3 677 585	435 122	287 655	54 247	9 051	84 169	3 242 463
10 to 14 years	17 114 249	2 001 617	1 290 338	261 102	47 375	402 802	15 112 632
10 years	3 653 177	427 686	279 868	55 194	9 078	83 546	3 225 491
11 years	3 455 515	400 840	258 336	53 187	9 056	80 261	3 054 675
12 years	3 423 450	397 566	254 058	52 654	9 607	81 247	3 025 884
13 years	3 339 000	393 120	252 503	50 989	9 820	79 808	2 945 880
14 years	3 243 107	382 405	245 573	49 078	9 814	77 940	2 860 702
15 to 19 years	17 754 015	2 053 957	1 314 657	248 535	58 336	432 429	15 700 058
15 years	3 321 609	387 038	248 504	48 459	10 514	79 561	2 934 571
16 years	3 304 890	385 257	247 021	47 245	10 870	80 121	2 919 633
17 years	3 410 062	402 212	259 054	47 273	11 625	84 260	3 007 850
18 years	3 641 238	426 930	273 263	50 334	12 329	91 004	3 214 308
19 years	4 076 216	452 520	286 815	55 224	12 998	97 483	3 623 696
20 to 24 years	19 020 312	2 304 441	1 457 815	260 858	69 015	516 753	16 715 871
20 years	4 009 414	469 015	298 887	54 396	13 085	102 647	3 540 399
21 years	3 817 220	451 608	287 973	51 237	12 508	99 890	3 365 612
25 to 29 years	21 313 045	2 341 239	1 413 224	268 713	95 790	563 512	18 971 806
30 to 34 years	21 862 887	2 062 303	1 214 778	243 983	85 705	517 837	19 800 584
35 to 39 years	19 963 117	1 660 726	961 559	200 915	74 956	423 296	18 302 391
40 to 44 years	17 615 786	1 284 268	717 158	170 916	63 634	332 560	16 331 518
45 to 49 years	13 872 573	953 910	510 954	129 824	64 306	248 826	12 918 663
50 to 54 years	11 350 513	755 989	389 874	101 632	72 234	192 249	10 594 524
55 to 59 years	10 531 756	639 308	330 853	84 809	69 241	154 405	9 892 448
60 to 64 years	10 616 167	553 642	288 307	66 459	68 511	130 365	10 062 525
65 to 69 years	10 111 735	436 257	225 218	51 191	56 214	103 634	9 675 478
70 to 74 years	7 994 823	286 772	138 007	34 449	41 913	72 403	7 708 051
75 to 79 years	6 121 369	213 265	100 960	25 099	33 858	53 348	5 908 104
80 to 84 years	3 933 739	130 425	62 307	13 961	21 791	32 366	3 803 314
85 years and over	3 080 165	94 564	46 066	9 602	14 614	24 282	2 985 601
18 years and over	185 105 441	14 596 559	8 417 158	1 767 969	857 109	3 554 323	170 508 882
62 years and over	37 629 695	1 481 076	738 568	172 717	208 704	361 087	36 148 619
65 years and over	31 241 831	1 161 283	572 558	134 302	168 390	286 033	30 080 548
Median age	32.9	25.5	23.8	25.7	38.9	27.7	33.7
Female	**127 470 455**	**10 966 000**	**6 474 754**	**1 395 653**	**530 784**	**2 564 809**	**116 504 455**
Under 5 years	8 962 034	1 169 330	772 763	140 587	27 398	228 582	7 792 704
Under 1 year	1 572 511	209 571	139 433	24 042	4 800	41 296	1 362 940
1 year	1 926 815	253 517	166 793	30 885	5 929	49 910	1 673 298
2 years	1 862 798	245 343	161 441	29 762	5 655	48 485	1 617 455
3 years	1 799 154	234 518	154 774	28 478	5 576	45 690	1 564 636
4 years	1 800 756	226 381	150 322	27 420	5 438	43 201	1 574 375
5 to 9 years	8 836 652	1 075 119	712 972	131 670	24 394	206 083	7 761 533
5 years	1 800 356	223 566	148 054	27 167	5 215	43 130	1 576 790
6 years	1 747 800	213 163	141 598	25 809	5 057	40 699	1 534 637
7 years	1 780 061	216 458	144 058	26 431	5 165	40 804	1 563 603
8 years	1 714 313	208 922	138 510	25 872	4 522	40 018	1 505 391
9 years	1 794 122	213 010	140 752	26 391	4 435	41 432	1 581 112
10 to 14 years	8 347 082	978 234	630 841	127 045	22 948	197 400	7 368 848
10 years	1 779 005	208 770	136 369	26 938	4 446	41 017	1 570 235
11 years	1 684 181	195 352	126 094	25 823	4 391	39 044	1 488 829
12 years	1 670 451	194 250	124 115	25 494	4 676	39 965	1 476 201
13 years	1 632 583	193 284	124 233	25 012	4 784	39 255	1 439 299
14 years	1 580 862	186 578	120 030	23 778	4 651	38 119	1 394 284
15 to 19 years	8 651 317	970 064	614 609	121 857	27 975	205 623	7 681 253
15 years	1 615 829	188 636	121 085	23 695	4 989	38 867	1 427 193
16 years	1 606 895	185 598	118 677	23 067	5 297	38 557	1 421 297
17 years	1 651 662	189 419	120 977	23 032	5 500	39 910	1 462 243
18 years	1 778 861	197 563	124 425	24 688	5 890	42 560	1 581 298
19 years	1 998 070	208 848	129 445	27 375	6 299	45 729	1 789 222
20 to 24 years	9 344 716	1 042 941	638 294	131 325	33 569	239 753	8 301 775
20 years	1 965 332	212 963	131 880	26 998	6 389	47 696	1 752 369
21 years	1 869 409	202 931	125 288	25 650	6 086	45 907	1 666 478
25 to 29 years	10 617 109	1 090 881	637 555	137 371	46 106	269 849	9 526 228
30 to 34 years	10 985 954	987 846	566 047	125 785	39 882	256 132	9 998 108
35 to 39 years	10 060 874	814 565	457 844	104 801	35 822	216 098	9 246 309
40 to 44 years	8 923 802	644 100	348 376	90 182	31 636	173 906	8 279 702
45 to 49 years	7 061 976	485 653	252 526	68 455	32 833	131 839	6 576 323
50 to 54 years	5 835 775	391 770	196 941	53 607	37 095	104 127	5 444 005
55 to 59 years	5 497 386	336 937	170 245	45 420	35 783	85 489	5 160 449
60 to 64 years	5 669 120	298 686	152 485	36 208	35 682	74 311	5 370 434
65 to 69 years	5 579 428	240 679	120 065	29 394	30 454	60 766	5 338 749
70 to 74 years	4 585 517	166 967	77 349	20 735	24 337	44 546	4 418 550
75 to 79 years	3 721 601	129 910	59 499	15 717	21 023	33 671	3 591 691
80 to 84 years	2 567 645	81 251	37 486	8 925	14 015	20 825	2 486 394
85 years and over	2 222 467	61 067	28 857	6 569	9 832	15 809	2 161 400
18 years and over	96 450 301	7 179 664	3 997 439	926 557	440 258	1 815 410	89 270 637
62 years and over	22 105 515	853 556	411 706	102 449	120 687	218 714	21 251 959
65 years and over	18 676 658	679 874	323 256	81 340	99 661	175 617	17 996 784
Median age	34.1	26.1	24.0	26.6	41.0	28.8	34.9
Male	**121 239 418**	**11 388 059**	**7 021 184**	**1 332 101**	**513 148**	**2 521 626**	**109 851 359**
Median age	31.7	25.0	23.7	24.7	36.9	26.7	32.5
Males per 100 females	95.1	103.8	108.4	95.4	96.7	98.3	94.3

Table 25. Age and Sex for Race by Hispanic Origin: 1990

[For definitions of terms and meanings of symbols, see text]

United States	All persons	White Hispanic origin	White Not of Hispanic origin	Black Hispanic origin	Black Not of Hispanic origin	American Indian, Eskimo, or Aleut Hispanic origin	American Indian, Eskimo, or Aleut Not of Hispanic origin	Asian or Pacific Islander Hispanic origin	Asian or Pacific Islander Not of Hispanic origin	Other race Hispanic origin	Other race Not of Hispanic origin
All persons	248 709 873	11 557 774	188 128 296	769 767	29 216 293	165 461	1 793 773	305 303	6 968 359	9 555 754	249 093
Under 5 years	18 354 443	1 160 771	12 488 719	87 974	2 697 928	22 062	179 888	32 936	556 909	1 083 781	43 475
Under 1 year	3 217 312	207 041	2 197 217	15 465	464 557	4 034	32 055	5 933	87 527	194 981	8 502
1 year	3 949 107	252 253	2 672 461	19 503	587 179	4 792	38 285	7 247	123 289	234 336	9 762
2 years	3 815 040	243 118	2 571 497	18 991	575 388	4 649	37 508	6 914	119 261	228 612	9 102
3 years	3 683 177	232 497	2 507 627	17 468	539 827	4 412	36 107	6 508	113 748	216 689	8 294
4 years	3 689 807	225 862	2 539 917	16 547	530 977	4 175	35 933	6 334	113 084	209 163	7 815
5 to 9 years	18 099 179	1 086 177	12 530 091	74 197	2 596 912	20 178	179 268	30 705	565 428	982 595	33 628
5 years	3 689 533	224 969	2 543 243	15 758	529 797	4 145	36 512	6 236	115 552	205 981	7 340
6 years	3 577 632	214 691	2 480 472	14 836	507 454	3 981	35 473	6 145	113 318	194 599	6 663
7 years	3 645 761	218 522	2 525 976	14 895	521 521	4 162	36 713	6 169	113 571	197 528	6 704
8 years	3 508 668	211 049	2 427 541	14 328	504 436	4 028	34 267	6 102	109 962	190 606	6 349
9 years	3 677 585	216 946	2 552 859	14 380	533 704	3 862	36 303	6 053	113 025	193 881	6 572
10 to 14 years	17 114 249	997 455	11 856 103	66 643	2 534 947	17 595	170 405	28 100	523 452	891 824	27 725
10 years	3 653 177	213 481	2 526 043	14 418	545 621	3 887	36 130	6 002	111 355	189 898	6 342
11 years	3 455 515	200 338	2 396 621	13 497	514 910	3 619	34 169	5 810	103 239	177 576	5 736
12 years	3 423 450	198 750	2 377 773	13 474	505 950	3 407	34 013	5 607	102 583	176 328	5 565
13 years	3 339 000	195 935	2 311 109	12 846	492 422	3 461	33 586	5 381	103 631	175 497	5 132
14 years	3 243 107	188 951	2 244 557	12 408	476 044	3 221	32 507	5 300	102 644	172 525	4 950
15 to 19 years	17 754 015	998 002	12 344 701	66 120	2 592 373	16 007	164 509	28 326	575 435	945 502	23 040
15 years	3 321 609	190 790	2 303 102	12 364	487 150	3 226	32 514	5 507	107 156	175 151	4 649
16 years	3 304 890	189 289	2 280 559	12 255	491 754	3 164	32 722	5 426	110 051	175 123	4 547
17 years	3 410 062	196 436	2 348 737	12 582	509 709	3 134	32 811	5 480	112 237	184 580	4 356
18 years	3 641 238	205 418	2 525 629	13 789	532 196	3 245	32 553	5 800	119 510	198 678	4 420
19 years	4 076 216	216 069	2 886 674	15 130	571 564	3 238	33 909	6 113	126 481	211 970	5 068
20 to 24 years	19 020 312	1 085 988	13 437 924	75 429	2 503 524	15 706	149 843	29 354	602 904	1 097 964	21 676
20 years	4 009 414	222 319	2 837 680	15 528	537 737	3 326	31 798	6 219	128 475	221 623	4 709
21 years	3 817 220	212 129	2 709 305	14 700	498 552	3 182	30 219	6 022	123 157	215 575	4 379
25 to 29 years	21 313 045	1 138 395	15 500 149	79 110	2 628 655	15 473	160 104	29 231	661 838	1 079 030	21 060
30 to 34 years	21 862 887	1 031 482	16 320 031	74 695	2 607 029	14 614	156 054	27 621	698 562	913 891	18 908
35 to 39 years	19 963 117	853 205	15 228 401	61 112	2 275 654	11 826	138 356	24 522	645 296	710 061	14 684
40 to 44 years	17 615 786	685 920	13 820 470	46 144	1 829 918	9 045	117 109	19 631	552 563	523 528	11 458
45 to 49 years	13 872 573	529 741	11 055 962	33 214	1 372 552	6 215	90 602	14 098	391 492	370 642	8 055
50 to 54 years	11 350 513	441 367	9 063 504	26 997	1 152 014	4 601	72 113	10 819	300 832	272 205	6 061
55 to 59 years	10 531 756	392 081	8 576 335	21 795	1 010 954	3 591	58 228	8 586	242 047	213 255	4 884
60 to 64 years	10 616 167	356 036	8 855 087	18 499	943 120	2 879	48 510	7 125	211 392	169 103	4 416
65 to 69 years	10 111 735	289 845	8 609 792	14 602	848 443	2 281	40 429	5 389	173 108	124 140	3 706
70 to 74 years	7 994 823	198 076	6 928 488	9 870	630 545	1 438	27 832	3 642	118 592	73 746	2 594
75 to 79 years	6 121 369	150 812	5 334 213	6 909	474 361	989	20 163	2 561	77 578	51 994	1 789
80 to 84 years	3 933 739	94 119	3 458 576	3 759	289 879	508	11 608	1 680	42 170	30 359	1 081
85 years and over	3 080 165	68 302	2 719 750	2 698	227 485	453	8 752	977	28 761	22 134	853
18 years and over	185 105 441	7 736 856	144 320 985	503 752	19 897 893	96 102	1 166 165	197 149	4 993 126	6 062 700	130 713
62 years and over	37 629 695	1 008 635	32 404 673	48 517	3 031 321	7 289	137 108	18 392	562 947	398 243	12 570
65 years and over	31 241 831	801 154	27 050 819	37 838	2 470 713	5 669	108 784	14 249	440 209	302 373	10 023
Median age	32.9	34.9	34.9	28.2	28.2	26.7	26.7	30.0	30.0	19.3	19.3
Female	127 470 455	5 738 485	96 471 705	378 743	15 437 166	81 517	910 531	154 392	3 561 232	4 612 863	123 821
Under 5 years	8 962 034	568 813	6 076 196	43 058	1 334 349	10 929	88 393	16 147	272 352	530 383	21 414
Under 1 year	1 572 511	101 526	1 069 860	7 554	230 068	1 968	15 818	2 897	42 959	95 026	4 235
1 year	1 926 815	123 426	1 299 545	9 566	290 428	2 351	18 794	3 532	59 749	114 642	4 782
2 years	1 862 798	118 960	1 252 067	9 120	284 285	2 374	18 408	3 313	58 227	111 576	4 468
3 years	1 799 154	114 180	1 220 017	8 605	266 918	2 169	17 694	3 214	55 909	106 350	4 098
4 years	1 800 756	110 721	1 234 707	8 213	262 650	2 067	17 670	3 191	55 508	102 789	3 831
5 to 9 years	8 836 652	532 525	6 093 212	36 558	1 284 286	10 057	88 201	15 044	279 256	480 935	16 678
5 years	1 800 356	110 003	1 236 443	7 857	261 769	2 119	17 902	3 007	57 080	100 580	3 596
6 years	1 747 800	105 306	1 206 815	7 295	251 050	1 929	17 540	3 003	55 974	95 630	3 258
7 years	1 780 061	107 206	1 228 630	7 330	257 508	2 047	18 077	3 054	56 110	96 816	3 309
8 years	1 714 313	103 591	1 181 002	7 069	249 957	2 046	16 903	2 992	54 336	93 224	3 193
9 years	1 794 122	106 420	1 240 413	7 001	263 942	1 916	17 779	2 988	55 756	94 685	3 222
10 to 14 years	8 347 082	486 700	5 760 132	32 575	1 254 607	8 651	83 602	13 722	256 705	436 586	13 802
10 years	1 779 005	104 363	1 225 583	7 033	269 091	1 903	17 798	2 995	54 598	92 476	3 165
11 years	1 684 181	97 781	1 163 410	6 583	255 330	1 774	16 707	2 789	50 608	86 425	2 774
12 years	1 670 451	96 809	1 155 692	6 595	250 502	1 660	16 705	2 744	50 508	86 442	2 794
13 years	1 632 583	96 074	1 124 921	6 329	244 420	1 735	16 335	2 639	51 012	86 507	2 611
14 years	1 580 862	91 673	1 090 526	6 035	235 264	1 579	16 057	2 555	49 979	84 736	2 458
15 to 19 years	8 651 317	469 879	6 027 253	31 241	1 284 989	7 502	79 956	13 630	277 714	447 812	11 341
15 years	1 615 829	92 444	1 117 613	6 122	239 801	1 550	15 842	2 655	51 623	85 865	2 314
16 years	1 606 895	90 626	1 107 726	5 928	242 069	1 496	16 070	2 631	53 216	84 917	2 216
17 years	1 651 662	91 679	1 140 438	5 918	249 647	1 510	15 791	2 608	54 164	87 704	2 203
18 years	1 778 861	94 983	1 240 239	6 421	265 504	1 500	15 680	2 799	57 723	91 860	2 152
19 years	1 998 070	100 147	1 421 237	6 852	287 968	1 446	16 573	2 937	60 988	97 466	2 456
20 to 24 years	9 344 716	495 583	6 639 949	34 363	1 285 964	7 072	73 434	14 106	292 170	491 817	10 258
20 years	1 965 332	101 699	1 400 321	6 945	272 735	1 511	15 454	2 994	61 573	99 814	2 286
21 years	1 869 409	96 126	1 337 490	6 613	253 281	1 397	14 582	2 843	59 076	95 952	2 049
25 to 29 years	10 617 109	537 638	7 716 091	36 659	1 385 346	7 374	80 729	14 547	333 894	494 663	10 168
30 to 34 years	10 985 954	501 758	8 150 210	35 327	1 395 787	7 231	80 693	14 305	362 071	429 225	9 347
35 to 39 years	10 060 874	424 550	7 602 927	29 433	1 224 282	5 948	71 640	12 895	340 401	341 739	7 059
40 to 44 years	8 923 802	347 947	6 931 212	23 018	987 384	4 537	60 423	10 505	294 897	258 093	5 786
45 to 49 years	7 061 976	272 423	5 576 697	16 958	746 367	3 247	46 577	7 509	202 675	185 516	4 007
50 to 54 years	5 835 775	230 848	4 616 639	14 079	632 956	2 371	37 455	5 725	153 841	138 747	3 114
55 to 59 years	5 497 386	206 959	4 430 646	11 746	564 084	1 857	30 608	4 632	132 492	111 743	2 619
60 to 64 years	5 669 120	191 366	4 684 973	10 388	536 986	1 522	25 675	3 995	120 383	91 415	2 417
65 to 69 years	5 579 428	159 317	4 727 091	8 588	491 515	1 237	22 175	3 090	95 889	68 447	2 079
70 to 74 years	4 585 517	115 216	3 955 619	6 061	379 655	810	15 960	2 122	65 812	42 758	1 504
75 to 79 years	3 721 601	92 541	3 238 085	4 378	298 352	597	12 095	1 307	42 031	31 087	1 128
80 to 84 years	2 567 645	59 387	2 266 206	2 484	190 495	290	7 269	687	21 734	18 403	690
85 years and over	2 222 467	45 035	1 978 567	1 829	159 762	285	5 646	424	16 915	13 494	510
18 years and over	96 450 301	3 875 698	75 176 388	248 584	10 832 407	47 324	602 632	101 585	2 593 916	2 906 473	65 294
62 years and over	22 105 515	583 639	19 013 973	29 382	1 840 100	4 078	78 240	9 952	312 361	226 505	7 279
65 years and over	18 676 658	471 496	16 165 568	23 340	1 519 779	3 219	63 145	7 630	242 381	174 189	5 911
Median age	34.1	36.1	36.1	29.6	29.6	27.6	27.6	30.9	30.9	19.5	19.5
Male	121 239 418	5 819 289	91 656 591	391 024	13 779 127	83 944	883 242	150 911	3 407 127	4 942 891	125 272
Median age	31.7	33.6	33.6	26.6	26.6	25.7	25.7	28.9	28.9	19.2	19.2
Males per 100 females	95.1	101.4	95.0	103.2	89.3	103.0	97.0	97.7	95.7	107.2	101.2

Table 26. Persons in Households and in Group Quarters by Age, Sex, Race, and Hispanic Origin: 1990

[For definitions of terms and meanings of symbols, see text]

United States	All persons Total	In households	In group quarters Institutionalized persons	In group quarters Other persons	Male Total	In households	In group quarters Institutionalized persons	In group quarters Other persons	Female Total	In households	In group quarters Institutionalized persons	In group quarters Other persons
TOTAL												
Age												
All persons	248 709 873	242 012 129	3 334 018	3 363 726	121 239 418	117 450 800	1 801 352	1 987 266	127 470 455	124 561 329	1 532 666	1 376 460
Under 18 years	63 604 432	63 339 241	142 403	122 788	32 584 278	32 412 265	104 243	67 770	31 020 154	30 926 976	38 160	55 018
Under 6 years	22 043 976	22 005 760	5 798	32 418	11 281 586	11 261 739	3 247	16 600	10 762 390	10 744 021	2 551	15 818
6 to 14 years	31 523 895	31 433 727	48 083	42 085	16 140 517	16 084 736	32 521	23 260	15 383 378	15 348 991	15 562	18 825
15 to 17 years	10 036 561	9 899 754	88 522	48 285	5 162 175	5 065 790	68 475	27 910	4 874 386	4 833 964	20 047	20 375
18 and 19 years	7 717 454	6 507 428	71 308	1 138 718	3 940 523	3 303 963	63 760	572 800	3 776 931	3 203 465	7 548	565 918
20 to 24 years	19 020 312	17 483 243	255 075	1 281 994	9 675 596	8 663 806	229 904	781 886	9 344 716	8 819 437	25 171	500 108
25 to 29 years	21 313 045	20 783 703	302 482	226 860	10 695 936	10 256 475	266 016	173 445	10 617 109	10 527 228	36 466	53 415
30 to 34 years	21 862 887	21 450 845	269 299	142 743	10 876 933	10 535 426	233 345	108 162	10 985 954	10 915 419	35 954	34 581
35 to 44 years	37 578 903	37 071 167	325 784	181 952	18 594 227	18 183 076	273 815	137 336	18 984 676	18 888 091	51 969	44 616
45 to 54 years	25 223 086	24 985 352	145 242	92 492	12 325 335	12 155 427	106 629	63 279	12 897 751	12 829 925	38 613	29 213
55 to 59 years	10 531 756	10 432 847	63 136	35 773	5 034 370	4 972 511	39 414	22 445	5 497 386	5 460 336	23 722	13 328
60 to 64 years	10 616 167	10 497 337	83 227	35 603	4 947 047	4 880 377	45 685	20 985	5 669 120	5 616 960	37 542	14 618
65 years and over	31 241 831	29 460 966	1 676 062	104 803	12 565 173	12 087 474	438 541	39 158	18 676 658	17 373 492	1 237 521	65 645
65 to 74 years	18 106 558	17 770 393	284 107	52 058	7 941 613	7 794 360	121 615	25 638	10 164 945	9 976 033	162 492	26 420
75 to 84 years	10 055 108	9 384 175	636 138	34 795	3 765 862	3 579 040	176 775	10 047	6 289 246	5 805 135	459 363	24 748
85 years and over	3 080 165	2 306 398	755 817	17 950	857 698	714 074	140 151	3 473	2 222 467	1 592 324	615 666	14 477
Percent Distribution												
All persons	100.0	97.3	1.3	1.4	100.0	96.9	1.5	1.6	100.0	97.7	1.2	1.1
Under 18 years	100.0	99.6	.2	.2	100.0	99.5	.3	.2	100.0	99.7	.1	.2
Under 6 years	100.0	99.8	–	.1	100.0	99.8	–	.1	100.0	99.8	–	.1
6 to 14 years	100.0	99.7	.2	.1	100.0	99.7	.2	.1	100.0	99.8	.1	.1
15 to 17 years	100.0	98.6	.9	.5	100.0	98.1	1.3	.5	100.0	99.2	.4	.4
18 and 19 years	100.0	84.3	.9	14.8	100.0	83.8	1.6	14.5	100.0	84.8	.2	15.0
20 to 24 years	100.0	91.9	1.3	6.7	100.0	89.5	2.4	8.1	100.0	94.4	.3	5.4
25 to 29 years	100.0	97.5	1.4	1.1	100.0	95.9	2.5	1.6	100.0	99.2	.3	.5
30 to 34 years	100.0	98.1	1.2	.7	100.0	96.9	2.1	1.0	100.0	99.4	.3	.3
35 to 44 years	100.0	98.6	.9	.5	100.0	97.8	1.5	.7	100.0	99.5	.3	.2
45 to 54 years	100.0	99.1	.6	.4	100.0	98.6	.9	.5	100.0	99.5	.3	.2
55 to 59 years	100.0	99.1	.6	.3	100.0	98.8	.8	.4	100.0	99.3	.4	.2
60 to 64 years	100.0	98.9	.8	.3	100.0	98.7	.9	.4	100.0	99.1	.7	.3
65 years and over	100.0	94.3	5.4	.3	100.0	96.2	3.5	.3	100.0	93.0	6.6	.4
65 to 74 years	100.0	98.1	1.6	.3	100.0	98.1	1.5	.3	100.0	98.1	1.6	.3
75 to 84 years	100.0	93.3	6.3	.3	100.0	95.0	4.7	.3	100.0	92.3	7.3	.4
85 years and over	100.0	74.9	24.5	.6	100.0	83.3	16.3	.4	100.0	71.6	27.7	.7
WHITE												
Age												
All persons	199 686 070	194 671 440	2 442 062	2 572 568	97 475 880	94 894 328	1 090 356	1 491 196	102 210 190	99 777 112	1 351 706	1 081 372
Under 18 years	47 628 229	47 476 649	83 827	67 753	24 470 125	24 374 359	57 687	38 079	23 158 104	23 102 290	26 140	29 674
Under 6 years	16 417 702	16 398 462	3 661	15 579	8 426 247	8 416 089	2 074	8 084	7 991 455	7 982 373	1 587	7 495
6 to 14 years	23 701 614	23 647 021	31 256	23 337	12 175 491	12 141 762	20 516	13 213	11 526 123	11 505 259	10 740	10 124
15 to 17 years	7 508 913	7 431 166	48 910	28 837	3 868 387	3 816 508	35 097	16 782	3 640 526	3 614 658	13 813	12 055
18 and 19 years	5 833 790	4 873 059	33 617	927 114	2 977 184	2 484 140	28 716	464 328	2 856 606	2 388 919	4 901	462 786
20 to 24 years	14 523 912	13 406 449	117 250	1 000 213	7 388 380	6 679 944	102 925	605 511	7 135 532	6 726 505	14 325	394 702
25 to 29 years	16 638 544	16 349 729	142 194	146 621	8 384 815	8 148 724	121 876	114 215	8 253 729	8 201 005	20 318	32 406
30 to 34 years	17 351 513	17 131 407	131 675	88 431	8 699 545	8 521 768	110 639	67 138	8 651 968	8 609 639	21 036	21 293
35 to 44 years	30 587 996	30 286 814	180 798	120 384	15 281 360	15 046 955	145 134	89 271	15 306 636	15 239 859	35 664	31 113
45 to 54 years	21 090 574	20 920 515	101 333	68 726	10 393 967	10 278 486	70 627	44 854	10 696 607	10 642 029	30 706	23 872
55 to 59 years	8 968 416	8 890 962	48 737	28 717	4 330 811	4 284 424	29 136	17 251	4 637 605	4 606 538	19 601	11 466
60 to 64 years	9 211 123	9 114 060	67 258	29 805	4 334 784	4 282 239	35 732	16 813	4 876 339	4 831 821	31 526	12 992
65 years and over	27 851 973	26 221 796	1 535 373	94 804	11 214 909	10 793 289	387 884	33 736	16 637 064	15 428 507	1 147 489	61 068
65 to 74 years	16 026 201	15 736 070	244 183	45 948	7 068 958	6 945 349	101 770	21 839	8 957 243	8 790 721	142 413	24 109
75 to 84 years	9 037 720	8 424 492	581 117	32 111	3 381 501	3 215 439	157 250	8 812	5 656 219	5 209 053	423 867	23 299
85 years and over	2 788 052	2 061 234	710 073	16 745	764 450	632 501	128 864	3 085	2 023 602	1 428 733	581 209	13 660
Percent Distribution												
All persons	100.0	97.5	1.2	1.3	100.0	97.4	1.1	1.5	100.0	97.6	1.3	1.1
Under 18 years	100.0	99.7	.2	.1	100.0	99.6	.2	.2	100.0	99.8	.1	.1
Under 6 years	100.0	99.9	–	.1	100.0	99.9	–	.1	100.0	99.9	–	.1
6 to 14 years	100.0	99.8	.1	.1	100.0	99.7	.2	.1	100.0	99.8	.1	.1
15 to 17 years	100.0	99.0	.7	.4	100.0	98.7	.9	.4	100.0	99.3	.4	.3
18 and 19 years	100.0	83.5	.6	15.9	100.0	83.4	1.0	15.6	100.0	83.6	.2	16.2
20 to 24 years	100.0	92.3	.8	6.9	100.0	90.4	1.4	8.2	100.0	94.3	.2	5.5
25 to 29 years	100.0	98.3	.9	.9	100.0	97.2	1.5	1.4	100.0	99.4	.2	.4
30 to 34 years	100.0	98.7	.8	.5	100.0	98.0	1.3	.8	100.0	99.5	.2	.2
35 to 44 years	100.0	99.0	.6	.4	100.0	98.5	.9	.6	100.0	99.6	.2	.2
45 to 54 years	100.0	99.2	.5	.3	100.0	98.9	.7	.4	100.0	99.5	.3	.2
55 to 59 years	100.0	99.1	.5	.3	100.0	98.9	.7	.4	100.0	99.3	.4	.2
60 to 64 years	100.0	98.9	.7	.3	100.0	98.8	.8	.4	100.0	99.1	.6	.3
65 years and over	100.0	94.1	5.5	.3	100.0	96.2	3.5	.3	100.0	92.7	6.9	.4
65 to 74 years	100.0	98.2	1.5	.3	100.0	98.3	1.4	.3	100.0	98.1	1.6	.3
75 to 84 years	100.0	93.2	6.4	.4	100.0	95.1	4.7	.3	100.0	92.1	7.5	.4
85 years and over	100.0	73.9	25.5	.6	100.0	82.7	16.9	.4	100.0	70.6	28.7	.7
BLACK												
Age												
All persons	29 986 060	28 722 227	744 500	519 333	14 170 151	13 255 525	591 372	323 254	15 815 909	15 466 702	153 128	196 079
Under 18 years	9 584 415	9 504 188	45 818	34 409	4 849 497	4 793 992	36 785	18 720	4 734 918	4 710 196	9 033	15 689
Under 6 years	3 331 457	3 319 428	1 628	10 401	1 684 424	1 678 218	886	5 320	1 647 033	1 641 210	742	5 081
6 to 14 years	4 727 144	4 702 290	13 160	11 694	2 388 744	2 372 831	9 571	6 342	2 338 400	2 329 459	3 589	5 352
15 to 17 years	1 525 814	1 482 470	31 030	12 314	776 329	742 943	26 328	7 058	749 485	739 527	4 702	5 256
18 and 19 years	1 132 679	963 656	30 561	138 462	565 934	468 824	28 414	68 696	566 745	494 832	2 147	69 766
20 to 24 years	2 578 953	2 283 910	113 009	182 034	1 258 626	1 042 717	104 045	111 864	1 320 327	1 241 193	8 964	70 170
25 to 29 years	2 707 765	2 522 824	133 718	51 223	1 285 760	1 128 059	120 015	37 686	1 422 005	1 394 765	13 703	13 537
30 to 34 years	2 681 724	2 527 366	116 295	38 063	1 250 610	1 118 131	103 637	28 842	1 431 114	1 409 235	12 658	9 221
35 to 44 years	4 212 828	4 046 266	122 725	43 837	1 948 711	1 805 001	109 009	34 701	2 264 117	2 241 265	13 716	9 136
45 to 54 years	2 584 777	2 532 238	36 342	16 197	1 174 417	1 131 842	29 796	12 779	1 410 360	1 400 396	6 546	3 418
55 to 59 years	1 032 749	1 015 789	12 210	4 750	456 919	444 634	8 694	3 591	575 830	571 155	3 516	1 159
60 to 64 years	961 619	944 023	13 726	3 870	414 245	402 806	8 576	2 863	547 374	541 217	5 150	1 007
65 years and over	2 508 551	2 381 967	120 096	6 488	965 432	919 519	42 401	3 512	1 543 119	1 462 448	77 695	2 976
65 to 74 years	1 503 460	1 464 987	34 477	3 996	617 641	598 060	17 054	2 527	885 819	866 927	17 423	1 469
75 to 84 years	774 908	725 948	47 283	1 677	279 199	262 096	16 362	741	495 709	463 852	30 921	936
85 years and over	230 183	191 032	38 336	815	68 592	59 363	8 985	244	161 591	131 669	29 351	571

Table 26. **Persons in Households and in Group Quarters by Age, Sex, Race, and Hispanic Origin: 1990**—Con.

[For definitions of terms and meanings of symbols, see text]

United States	All persons				Male				Female			
			In group quarters				In group quarters				In group quarters	
	Total	In households	Institutionalized persons	Other persons	Total	In households	Institutionalized persons	Other persons	Total	In households	Institutionalized persons	Other persons
BLACK—Con.												
Percent Distribution												
All persons	100.0	95.8	2.5	1.7	100.0	93.5	4.2	2.3	100.0	97.8	1.0	1.2
Under 18 years	100.0	99.2	.5	.4	100.0	98.9	.8	.4	100.0	99.5	.2	.3
Under 6 years	100.0	99.6	–	.3	100.0	99.6	.1	.3	100.0	99.6	–	.3
6 to 14 years	100.0	99.5	.3	.2	100.0	99.3	.4	.3	100.0	99.6	.2	.2
15 to 17 years	100.0	97.2	2.0	.8	100.0	95.7	3.4	.9	100.0	98.7	.6	.7
18 and 19 years	100.0	85.1	2.7	12.2	100.0	82.8	5.0	12.1	100.0	87.3	.4	12.3
20 to 24 years	100.0	88.6	4.4	7.1	100.0	82.8	8.3	8.9	100.0	94.0	.7	5.3
25 to 29 years	100.0	93.2	4.9	1.9	100.0	87.7	9.3	2.9	100.0	98.1	1.0	1.0
30 to 34 years	100.0	94.2	4.3	1.4	100.0	89.4	8.3	2.3	100.0	98.5	.9	.6
35 to 44 years	100.0	96.0	2.9	1.0	100.0	92.6	5.6	1.8	100.0	99.0	.6	.4
45 to 54 years	100.0	98.0	1.4	.6	100.0	96.4	2.5	1.1	100.0	99.3	.5	.2
55 to 59 years	100.0	98.4	1.2	.5	100.0	97.3	1.9	.8	100.0	99.2	.6	.2
60 to 64 years	100.0	98.2	1.4	.4	100.0	97.2	2.1	.7	100.0	98.9	.9	.2
65 years and over	100.0	95.0	4.8	.3	100.0	95.2	4.4	.4	100.0	94.8	5.0	.2
65 to 74 years	100.0	97.4	2.3	.3	100.0	96.8	2.8	.4	100.0	97.9	2.0	.2
75 to 84 years	100.0	93.7	6.1	.2	100.0	93.9	5.9	.3	100.0	93.6	6.2	.2
85 years and over	100.0	83.0	16.7	.4	100.0	86.5	13.1	.4	100.0	81.5	18.2	.4
AMERICAN INDIAN, ESKIMO, OR ALEUT												
Age												
All persons	1 959 234	1 902 958	28 050	28 226	967 186	926 952	21 888	18 346	992 048	976 006	6 162	9 880
Under 18 years	696 967	690 562	3 329	3 076	354 875	351 006	2 299	1 570	342 092	339 556	1 030	1 506
Under 6 years	242 607	241 858	131	618	123 264	122 898	75	291	119 343	118 960	56	327
6 to 14 years	346 789	344 376	1 254	1 159	176 299	174 941	770	588	170 490	169 435	484	571
15 to 17 years	107 571	104 328	1 944	1 299	55 312	53 167	1 454	691	52 259	51 161	490	608
18 and 19 years	72 945	65 375	1 191	6 379	37 746	33 083	1 075	3 588	35 199	32 292	116	2 791
20 to 24 years	165 549	152 775	4 094	8 680	85 043	75 446	3 647	5 950	80 506	77 329	447	2 730
25 to 29 years	175 577	168 379	4 415	2 783	87 474	81 636	3 863	1 975	88 103	86 743	552	808
30 to 34 years	170 668	164 772	3 861	2 035	82 744	77 924	3 377	1 443	87 924	86 848	484	592
35 to 44 years	276 336	269 200	4 367	2 769	133 788	128 017	3 751	2 020	142 548	141 183	616	749
45 to 54 years	173 531	170 290	1 846	1 395	83 881	81 358	1 507	1 016	89 650	88 932	339	379
55 to 59 years	61 819	60 919	507	393	29 354	28 685	385	284	32 465	32 234	122	109
60 to 64 years	51 389	50 549	518	322	24 192	23 609	332	251	27 197	26 940	186	71
65 years and over	114 453	110 137	3 922	394	48 089	46 188	1 652	249	66 364	63 949	2 270	145
65 to 74 years	71 980	70 522	1 180	278	31 798	30 972	639	187	40 182	39 550	541	91
75 to 84 years	33 268	31 653	1 544	71	13 017	12 349	629	39	20 251	19 304	915	32
85 years and over	9 205	7 962	1 198	45	3 274	2 867	384	23	5 931	5 095	814	22
Percent Distribution												
All persons	100.0	97.1	1.4	1.4	100.0	95.8	2.3	1.9	100.0	98.4	.6	1.0
Under 18 years	100.0	99.1	.5	.4	100.0	98.9	.6	.4	100.0	99.3	.3	.4
Under 6 years	100.0	99.7	.1	.3	100.0	99.7	.1	.2	100.0	99.7	–	.3
6 to 14 years	100.0	99.3	.4	.3	100.0	99.2	.4	.3	100.0	99.4	.3	.3
15 to 17 years	100.0	97.0	1.8	1.2	100.0	96.1	2.6	1.2	100.0	97.9	.9	1.2
18 and 19 years	100.0	89.6	1.6	8.7	100.0	87.6	2.8	9.5	100.0	91.7	.3	7.9
20 to 24 years	100.0	92.3	2.5	5.2	100.0	88.7	4.3	7.0	100.0	96.1	.6	3.4
25 to 29 years	100.0	95.9	2.5	1.6	100.0	93.3	4.4	2.3	100.0	98.5	.6	.9
30 to 34 years	100.0	96.5	2.3	1.2	100.0	94.2	4.1	1.7	100.0	98.8	.6	.7
35 to 44 years	100.0	97.4	1.6	1.0	100.0	95.7	2.8	1.5	100.0	99.0	.4	.5
45 to 54 years	100.0	98.1	1.1	.8	100.0	97.0	1.8	1.2	100.0	99.2	.4	.4
55 to 59 years	100.0	98.5	.8	.6	100.0	97.7	1.3	1.0	100.0	99.3	.4	.3
60 to 64 years	100.0	98.4	1.0	.6	100.0	97.6	1.4	1.0	100.0	99.1	.7	.3
65 years and over	100.0	96.2	3.4	.3	100.0	96.0	3.4	.5	100.0	96.4	3.4	.2
65 to 74 years	100.0	98.0	1.6	.4	100.0	97.4	2.0	.6	100.0	98.4	1.3	.2
75 to 84 years	100.0	95.1	4.6	.2	100.0	94.9	4.8	.3	100.0	95.3	4.5	.2
85 years and over	100.0	86.5	13.0	.5	100.0	87.6	11.7	.7	100.0	85.9	13.7	.4
ASIAN OR PACIFIC ISLANDER												
Age												
All persons	7 273 662	7 120 735	22 992	129 935	3 558 038	3 469 336	14 178	74 524	3 715 624	3 651 399	8 814	55 411
Under 18 years	2 083 387	2 076 684	2 181	4 522	1 063 264	1 059 379	1 608	2 277	1 020 123	1 017 305	573	2 245
Under 6 years	711 633	710 447	181	1 005	363 047	362 448	98	501	348 586	347 999	83	504
6 to 14 years	1 025 897	1 024 182	523	1 192	521 257	520 317	339	601	504 640	503 865	184	591
15 to 17 years	345 857	342 055	1 477	2 325	178 960	176 614	1 171	1 175	166 897	165 441	306	1 150
18 and 19 years	257 904	214 936	869	42 099	133 457	111 222	773	21 462	124 447	103 714	96	20 637
20 to 24 years	632 258	576 822	2 097	53 339	325 982	293 157	1 847	30 978	306 276	283 665	250	22 361
25 to 29 years	691 069	676 159	2 175	12 735	342 628	332 080	1 838	8 710	348 441	344 079	337	4 025
30 to 34 years	726 183	718 547	2 012	5 624	349 807	344 387	1 567	3 853	376 376	374 160	445	1 771
35 to 44 years	1 242 012	1 234 115	2 359	5 538	583 314	577 700	1 804	3 810	658 698	656 415	555	1 728
45 to 54 years	717 241	713 888	1 195	2 158	347 491	345 335	765	1 391	369 750	368 553	430	767
55 to 59 years	250 633	249 266	547	820	113 509	112 740	315	454	137 124	136 526	232	366
60 to 64 years	218 517	217 015	665	837	94 139	93 329	331	479	124 378	123 686	334	358
65 years and over	454 458	443 303	8 892	2 263	204 447	200 007	3 330	1 110	250 011	243 296	5 562	1 153
65 to 74 years	300 731	297 408	2 074	1 249	133 818	132 159	975	684	166 913	165 249	1 099	565
75 to 84 years	123 989	120 008	3 225	756	58 230	56 545	1 341	344	65 759	63 463	1 884	412
85 years and over	29 738	25 887	3 593	258	12 399	11 303	1 014	82	17 339	14 584	2 579	176
Percent Distribution												
All persons	100.0	97.9	.3	1.8	100.0	97.5	.4	2.1	100.0	98.3	.2	1.5
Under 18 years	100.0	99.7	.1	.2	100.0	99.6	.2	.2	100.0	99.7	.1	.2
Under 6 years	100.0	99.8	–	.1	100.0	99.8	–	.1	100.0	99.8	–	.1
6 to 14 years	100.0	99.8	.1	.1	100.0	99.8	.1	.1	100.0	99.8	–	.1
15 to 17 years	100.0	98.9	.4	.7	100.0	98.7	.7	.7	100.0	99.1	.2	.7
18 and 19 years	100.0	83.3	.3	16.3	100.0	83.3	.6	16.1	100.0	83.3	.1	16.6
20 to 24 years	100.0	91.2	.3	8.4	100.0	89.9	.6	9.5	100.0	92.6	.1	7.3
25 to 29 years	100.0	97.8	.3	1.8	100.0	96.9	.5	2.5	100.0	98.7	.1	1.2
30 to 34 years	100.0	98.9	.3	.8	100.0	98.5	.4	1.1	100.0	99.4	.1	.5
35 to 44 years	100.0	99.4	.2	.4	100.0	99.0	.3	.7	100.0	99.7	.1	.3
45 to 54 years	100.0	99.5	.2	.3	100.0	99.4	.2	.4	100.0	99.7	.1	.2
55 to 59 years	100.0	99.5	.2	.3	100.0	99.3	.3	.4	100.0	99.6	.2	.3
60 to 64 years	100.0	99.3	.3	.4	100.0	99.1	.4	.5	100.0	99.4	.3	.3
65 years and over	100.0	97.5	2.0	.5	100.0	97.8	1.6	.5	100.0	97.3	2.2	.5
65 to 74 years	100.0	98.9	.7	.4	100.0	98.8	.7	.5	100.0	99.0	.7	.3
75 to 84 years	100.0	96.8	2.6	.6	100.0	97.1	2.3	.6	100.0	96.5	2.9	.6
85 years and over	100.0	87.1	12.1	.9	100.0	91.2	8.2	.7	100.0	84.1	14.9	1.0

Table 26. Persons in Households and in Group Quarters by Age, Sex, Race, and Hispanic Origin: 1990—Con.

[For definitions of terms and meanings of symbols, see text]

United States	All persons				Male				Female			
			In group quarters				In group quarters				In group quarters	
	Total	In households	Institu- tionalized persons	Other per- sons	Total	In households	Institu- tionalized persons	Other per- sons	Total	In households	Institu- tionalized persons	Other per- sons
HISPANIC ORIGIN (OF ANY RACE)												
Age												
All persons	22 354 059	21 836 827	261 693	255 539	11 388 059	10 990 595	219 893	177 571	10 966 000	10 846 232	41 800	77 968
Under 18 years	7 757 500	7 713 003	17 557	26 940	3 971 164	3 942 338	13 829	14 997	3 786 336	3 770 665	3 728	11 943
Under 6 years	2 844 613	2 834 408	717	9 488	1 451 717	1 446 512	407	4 798	1 392 896	1 387 896	310	4 690
6 to 14 years	3 738 380	3 724 171	4 767	9 442	1 908 593	1 900 261	3 231	5 101	1 829 787	1 823 910	1 536	4 341
15 to 17 years	1 174 507	1 154 474	12 073	8 010	610 854	595 565	10 191	5 098	563 653	558 859	1 882	2 912
18 and 19 years	879 450	815 096	11 729	52 625	473 039	431 348	10 960	30 731	406 411	383 748	769	21 894
20 to 24 years	2 304 441	2 180 413	44 804	79 224	1 261 500	1 163 561	41 617	56 322	1 042 941	1 016 852	3 187	22 902
25 to 29 years	2 341 239	2 259 585	50 880	30 774	1 250 358	1 179 433	46 594	24 331	1 090 881	1 080 152	4 286	6 443
30 to 34 years	2 062 303	1 999 989	41 760	20 554	1 074 457	1 020 238	37 895	16 324	987 846	979 751	3 865	4 230
35 to 44 years	2 944 994	2 877 058	44 013	23 923	1 486 329	1 427 576	39 801	18 952	1 458 665	1 449 482	4 212	4 971
45 to 54 years	1 709 899	1 684 308	14 271	11 320	832 476	811 002	12 437	9 037	877 423	873 306	1 834	2 283
55 to 59 years	639 308	631 926	3 864	3 518	302 371	296 624	3 036	2 711	336 937	335 302	828	807
60 to 64 years	553 642	547 285	3 638	2 719	254 956	250 467	2 480	2 009	298 686	296 818	1 158	710
65 years and over	1 161 283	1 128 164	29 177	3 942	481 409	468 008	11 244	2 157	679 874	660 156	17 933	1 785
65 to 74 years	723 029	713 079	7 477	2 473	315 383	309 814	3 955	1 614	407 646	403 265	3 522	859
75 to 84 years	343 690	331 430	11 279	981	132 529	127 905	4 225	399	211 161	203 525	7 054	582
85 years and over	94 564	83 655	10 421	488	33 497	30 289	3 064	144	61 067	53 366	7 357	344
Percent Distribution												
All persons	100.0	97.7	1.2	1.1	100.0	96.5	1.9	1.6	100.0	98.9	.4	.7
Under 18 years	100.0	99.4	.2	.3	100.0	99.3	.3	.4	100.0	99.6	.1	.3
Under 6 years	100.0	99.6	−	.3	100.0	99.6	−	.3	100.0	99.6	−	.3
6 to 14 years	100.0	99.6	.1	.3	100.0	99.6	.2	.3	100.0	99.7	.1	.2
15 to 17 years	100.0	98.3	1.0	.7	100.0	97.5	1.7	.8	100.0	99.1	.3	.5
18 and 19 years	100.0	92.7	1.3	6.0	100.0	91.2	2.3	6.5	100.0	94.4	.2	5.4
20 to 24 years	100.0	94.6	1.9	3.4	100.0	92.2	3.3	4.5	100.0	97.5	.3	2.2
25 to 29 years	100.0	96.5	2.2	1.3	100.0	94.3	3.7	1.9	100.0	99.0	.4	.6
30 to 34 years	100.0	97.0	2.0	1.0	100.0	95.0	3.5	1.5	100.0	99.2	.4	.4
35 to 44 years	100.0	97.7	1.5	.8	100.0	96.0	2.7	1.3	100.0	99.4	.3	.3
45 to 54 years	100.0	98.5	.8	.7	100.0	97.4	1.5	1.1	100.0	99.5	.2	.3
55 to 59 years	100.0	98.8	.6	.6	100.0	98.1	1.0	.9	100.0	99.5	.2	.2
60 to 64 years	100.0	98.9	.7	.5	100.0	98.2	1.0	.8	100.0	99.4	.4	.2
65 years and over	100.0	97.1	2.5	.3	100.0	97.2	2.3	.4	100.0	97.1	2.6	.3
65 to 74 years	100.0	98.6	1.0	.3	100.0	98.2	1.3	.5	100.0	98.9	.9	.2
75 to 84 years	100.0	96.4	3.3	.3	100.0	96.5	3.2	.3	100.0	96.4	3.3	.3
85 years and over	100.0	88.5	11.0	.5	100.0	90.4	9.1	.4	100.0	87.4	12.0	.6
WHITE, NOT OF HISPANIC ORIGIN												
Age												
All persons	188 128 296	183 362 643	2 313 717	2 451 936	91 656 591	89 261 010	987 464	1 408 117	96 471 705	94 101 633	1 326 253	1 043 819
Under 18 years	43 807 311	43 675 672	75 570	56 069	22 511 994	22 429 290	51 328	31 376	21 295 317	21 246 382	24 242	24 693
Under 6 years	15 031 962	15 017 036	3 200	11 726	7 719 323	7 711 429	1 807	6 087	7 312 639	7 305 607	1 393	5 639
6 to 14 years	21 842 951	21 794 668	28 916	19 367	11 226 050	11 196 052	18 965	11 033	10 616 901	10 598 616	9 951	8 334
15 to 17 years	6 932 398	6 863 968	43 454	24 976	3 566 621	3 521 809	30 556	14 256	3 365 777	3 342 159	12 898	10 720
18 and 19 years	5 412 303	4 481 163	28 738	902 402	2 750 827	2 276 466	24 229	450 132	2 661 476	2 204 697	4 509	452 270
20 to 24 years	13 437 924	12 376 111	97 908	963 905	6 797 975	6 132 597	85 156	580 222	6 639 949	6 243 514	12 752	383 683
25 to 29 years	15 500 149	15 248 487	119 470	132 192	7 784 058	7 579 864	101 317	102 877	7 716 091	7 668 623	18 153	29 315
30 to 34 years	16 320 031	16 128 604	112 504	78 923	8 169 821	8 016 795	93 473	59 553	8 150 210	8 111 809	19 031	19 370
35 to 44 years	29 048 871	28 780 489	159 469	108 913	14 514 732	14 308 394	126 108	80 230	14 534 139	14 472 095	33 361	28 683
45 to 54 years	20 119 466	19 963 321	93 461	62 684	9 926 130	9 822 217	63 827	40 086	10 193 336	10 141 104	29 634	22 598
55 to 59 years	8 576 335	8 503 245	46 418	26 672	4 145 689	4 102 660	27 331	15 698	4 430 646	4 400 585	19 087	10 974
60 to 64 years	8 855 087	8 761 965	64 968	28 154	4 170 114	4 120 300	34 188	15 626	4 684 973	4 641 665	30 780	12 528
65 years and over	27 050 819	25 443 586	1 515 211	92 022	10 885 251	10 472 427	380 507	32 317	16 165 568	14 971 159	1 134 704	59 705
65 to 74 years	15 538 280	15 254 619	239 374	44 287	6 855 570	6 735 522	99 274	20 774	8 682 710	8 519 097	140 100	23 513
75 to 84 years	8 792 789	8 188 178	573 239	31 372	3 288 498	3 125 521	154 417	8 560	5 504 291	5 062 657	418 822	22 812
85 years and over	2 719 750	2 000 789	702 598	16 363	741 183	611 384	126 816	2 983	1 978 567	1 389 405	575 782	13 380
Percent Distribution												
All persons	100.0	97.5	1.2	1.3	100.0	97.4	1.1	1.5	100.0	97.5	1.4	1.1
Under 18 years	100.0	99.7	.2	.1	100.0	99.6	.2	.1	100.0	99.8	.1	.1
Under 6 years	100.0	99.9	−	.1	100.0	99.9	−	.1	100.0	99.9	−	.1
6 to 14 years	100.0	99.8	.1	.1	100.0	99.7	.2	.1	100.0	99.8	.1	.1
15 to 17 years	100.0	99.0	.6	.4	100.0	98.7	.9	.4	100.0	99.3	.4	.3
18 and 19 years	100.0	82.8	.5	16.7	100.0	82.8	.9	16.4	100.0	82.8	.2	17.0
20 to 24 years	100.0	92.1	.7	7.2	100.0	90.2	1.3	8.5	100.0	94.0	.2	5.8
25 to 29 years	100.0	98.4	.8	.9	100.0	97.4	1.3	1.3	100.0	99.4	.2	.4
30 to 34 years	100.0	98.8	.7	.5	100.0	98.1	1.1	.7	100.0	99.5	.2	.2
35 to 44 years	100.0	99.1	.5	.4	100.0	98.6	.9	.6	100.0	99.6	.2	.2
45 to 54 years	100.0	99.2	.5	.3	100.0	99.0	.6	.4	100.0	99.5	.3	.2
55 to 59 years	100.0	99.1	.5	.3	100.0	99.0	.7	.4	100.0	99.3	.4	.2
60 to 64 years	100.0	98.9	.7	.3	100.0	98.8	.8	.4	100.0	99.1	.7	.3
65 years and over	100.0	94.1	5.6	.3	100.0	96.2	3.5	.3	100.0	92.6	7.0	.4
65 to 74 years	100.0	98.2	1.5	.3	100.0	98.2	1.4	.3	100.0	98.1	1.6	.3
75 to 84 years	100.0	93.1	6.5	.4	100.0	95.0	4.7	.3	100.0	92.0	7.6	.4
85 years and over	100.0	73.6	25.8	.6	100.0	82.5	17.1	.4	100.0	70.2	29.1	.7

Table 27. Persons in Households by Relationship to Householder, Age, and Sex: 1990

[For definitions of terms and meanings of symbols, see text]

United States

		Householder					Relatives of householder				Nonrelatives of householder	
			Family householder		Nonfamily householder							
	All persons	Total	Total	Married, spouse present	Total	Living alone	Total	Spouse	Child	Other relatives	In family households	In nonfamily households
AGE												
All persons	**242 012 129**	**91 947 410**	**64 517 947**	**50 708 322**	**27 429 463**	**22 580 420**	**139 387 342**	**50 708 322**	**76 728 438**	**11 950 582**	**4 195 531**	**6 481 846**
Under 18 years	63 339 241	51 775	32 672	12 535	19 103	11 194	62 166 144	39 072	57 534 750	4 592 322	628 395	492 927
Under 6 years	22 005 760	–	–	–	–	–	21 649 613	–	19 526 799	2 122 814	206 827	149 320
6 to 14 years	31 433 727	–	–	–	–	–	30 913 591	–	29 043 546	1 870 045	274 011	246 125
15 to 17 years	9 899 754	51 775	32 672	12 535	19 103	11 194	9 602 940	39 072	8 964 405	599 463	147 557	97 482
18 and 19 years	6 507 428	444 538	202 033	81 618	242 505	102 642	5 528 993	217 410	4 805 229	506 354	221 903	311 994
20 to 24 years	17 483 243	4 553 045	2 395 709	1 490 019	2 157 336	1 082 377	10 460 910	2 348 779	6 904 696	1 207 435	724 203	1 745 085
25 to 29 years	20 783 703	9 018 446	6 002 083	4 479 878	3 016 363	1 988 913	9 729 010	5 493 456	3 294 016	941 538	721 472	1 314 775
30 to 34 years	21 450 845	10 831 205	8 150 602	6 309 810	2 680 603	2 002 145	9 267 795	6 892 636	1 749 975	625 184	575 859	775 986
35 to 44 years	37 071 167	20 393 073	16 299 818	12 655 731	4 093 255	3 272 158	15 104 883	12 737 273	1 633 738	733 872	702 112	871 099
45 to 54 years	24 985 352	14 303 214	11 415 583	9 183 817	2 887 631	2 427 627	9 938 180	8 833 054	547 511	557 615	308 426	435 532
55 to 59 years	10 432 847	6 079 086	4 670 236	3 886 302	1 408 850	1 254 332	4 128 275	3 684 411	128 074	315 790	85 736	139 750
60 to 64 years	10 497 337	6 300 327	4 547 773	3 812 559	1 752 554	1 614 187	4 003 648	3 534 867	79 843	388 938	69 454	123 908
65 years and over	29 460 966	19 972 701	10 801 438	8 796 053	9 171 263	8 824 845	9 059 504	6 927 364	50 606	2 081 534	157 971	270 790
65 to 74 years	17 770 393	11 516 582	7 180 147	6 009 758	4 336 435	4 131 233	5 998 273	5 094 657	47 161	856 455	87 602	167 936
75 to 84 years	9 384 175	6 786 873	3 084 715	2 440 996	3 702 158	3 595 301	2 469 928	1 669 485	3 367	797 076	47 666	79 708
85 years and over	2 306 398	1 669 246	536 576	345 299	1 132 670	1 098 311	591 303	163 222	78	428 003	22 703	23 146
Male	**117 450 800**	**62 274 741**	**50 133 040**	**46 989 458**	**12 141 701**	**9 206 811**	**49 690 675**	**3 718 884**	**40 350 873**	**5 620 918**	**2 255 699**	**3 229 685**
Under 18 years	32 412 265	24 301	15 404	8 826	8 897	5 261	31 837 174	1 419	29 500 917	2 334 838	308 143	242 647
Under 6 years	11 261 739	–	–	–	–	–	11 082 016	–	10 003 849	1 078 167	104 887	74 836
6 to 14 years	16 084 736	–	–	–	–	–	15 825 199	–	14 878 246	946 953	137 269	122 268
15 to 17 years	5 065 790	24 301	15 404	8 826	8 897	5 261	4 929 959	1 419	4 618 822	309 718	65 987	45 543
18 and 19 years	3 303 963	211 837	92 574	59 559	119 263	51 786	2 860 439	8 407	2 578 372	273 660	98 357	133 330
20 to 24 years	8 663 806	2 731 116	1 510 693	1 259 664	1 220 423	606 020	4 706 978	152 387	3 866 608	687 983	363 103	862 609
25 to 29 years	10 256 475	6 222 370	4 359 285	3 974 892	1 863 085	1 196 723	2 952 714	437 193	1 959 182	556 339	393 170	688 221
30 to 34 years	10 535 426	7 836 354	6 135 604	5 735 502	1 700 750	1 244 248	1 975 072	548 303	1 052 168	374 601	324 253	399 747
35 to 44 years	18 183 076	15 024 229	12 511 288	11 725 725	2 512 941	1 974 598	2 311 414	929 431	970 026	411 957	412 721	434 712
45 to 54 years	12 155 427	10 605 737	9 139 731	8 606 936	1 466 006	1 193 467	1 147 960	598 197	304 492	245 271	189 719	212 011
55 to 59 years	4 972 511	4 426 096	3 841 705	3 664 358	584 391	496 348	422 634	243 378	64 187	115 069	52 074	71 707
60 to 64 years	4 880 377	4 378 111	3 767 182	3 605 918	610 929	535 746	398 561	233 156	36 500	128 905	40 449	63 256
65 years and over	12 087 474	10 814 590	8 759 574	8 348 078	2 055 016	1 902 614	1 077 729	567 013	18 421	492 295	73 710	121 445
65 to 74 years	7 794 360	7 043 104	5 935 417	5 691 856	1 107 687	1 008 447	623 743	364 868	17 586	241 289	46 936	80 577
75 to 84 years	3 579 040	3 180 847	2 452 506	2 322 944	728 341	685 775	345 137	171 594	818	172 725	19 945	33 111
85 years and over	714 074	590 639	371 651	333 278	218 988	208 392	108 849	30 551	17	78 281	6 829	7 757
Female	**124 561 329**	**29 672 669**	**14 384 907**	**3 718 864**	**15 287 762**	**13 373 609**	**89 696 667**	**46 989 438**	**36 377 565**	**6 329 664**	**1 939 832**	**3 252 161**
Under 18 years	30 926 976	27 474	17 268	3 709	10 206	5 933	30 328 970	37 653	28 033 833	2 257 484	320 252	250 280
Under 6 years	10 744 021	–	–	–	–	–	10 567 597	–	9 522 950	1 044 647	101 940	74 484
6 to 14 years	15 348 991	–	–	–	–	–	15 088 392	–	14 165 300	923 092	136 742	123 857
15 to 17 years	4 833 964	27 474	17 268	3 709	10 206	5 933	4 672 981	37 653	4 345 583	289 745	81 570	51 939
18 and 19 years	3 203 465	232 701	109 459	22 059	123 242	50 856	2 668 554	209 003	2 226 857	232 694	123 546	178 664
20 to 24 years	8 819 437	1 821 929	885 016	230 355	936 913	476 357	5 753 932	2 196 392	3 038 088	519 452	361 100	882 476
25 to 29 years	10 527 228	2 796 076	1 642 798	504 986	1 153 278	792 190	6 776 296	5 056 263	1 334 834	385 199	328 302	626 554
30 to 34 years	10 915 419	2 994 851	2 014 998	574 308	979 853	757 897	7 292 723	6 344 333	697 807	250 583	251 606	376 239
35 to 44 years	18 888 091	5 368 844	3 788 530	930 006	1 580 314	1 297 560	12 793 469	11 807 842	663 712	321 915	289 391	436 387
45 to 54 years	12 829 925	3 697 477	2 275 852	576 881	1 421 625	1 234 160	8 790 220	8 234 857	243 019	312 344	118 707	223 521
55 to 59 years	5 460 336	1 652 990	828 531	221 944	824 459	757 984	3 705 641	3 441 033	63 887	200 721	33 662	68 043
60 to 64 years	5 616 960	1 922 216	780 591	206 641	1 141 625	1 078 441	3 605 087	3 301 711	43 343	260 033	29 005	60 652
65 years and over	17 373 492	9 158 111	2 041 864	447 975	7 116 247	6 922 231	7 981 775	6 360 351	32 185	1 589 239	84 261	149 345
65 to 74 years	9 976 033	4 473 478	1 244 730	317 902	3 228 748	3 122 786	5 374 530	4 729 789	29 575	615 166	40 666	87 360
75 to 84 years	5 805 135	3 606 026	632 209	118 052	2 973 817	2 909 526	2 124 791	1 497 891	2 549	624 351	27 721	46 607
85 years and over	1 592 324	1 078 607	164 925	12 021	913 682	889 919	482 454	132 671	61	349 722	15 874	15 389
PERCENT DISTRIBUTION												
All persons	**100.0**	**38.0**	**26.7**	**21.0**	**11.3**	**9.3**	**57.6**	**21.0**	**31.7**	**4.9**	**1.7**	**2.7**
Under 18 years	100.0	.1	.1	–	–	–	98.1	.1	90.8	7.3	1.0	.8
18 and 19 years	100.0	6.8	3.1	1.3	3.7	1.6	85.0	3.3	73.8	7.8	3.4	4.8
20 to 24 years	100.0	26.0	13.7	8.5	12.3	6.2	59.8	13.4	39.5	6.9	4.1	10.0
25 to 29 years	100.0	43.4	28.9	21.6	14.5	9.6	46.8	26.4	15.8	4.5	3.5	6.3
30 to 34 years	100.0	50.5	38.0	29.4	12.5	9.3	43.2	32.1	8.2	2.9	2.7	3.6
35 to 44 years	100.0	55.0	44.0	34.1	11.0	8.8	40.7	34.4	4.4	2.0	1.9	2.3
45 to 54 years	100.0	57.2	45.7	36.8	11.6	9.7	39.8	35.4	2.2	2.2	1.2	1.7
55 to 59 years	100.0	58.3	44.8	37.3	13.5	12.0	39.6	35.3	1.2	3.0	.8	1.3
60 to 64 years	100.0	60.0	43.3	36.3	16.7	15.4	38.1	33.7	.8	3.7	.7	1.2
65 years and over	100.0	67.8	36.7	29.9	31.1	30.0	30.8	23.5	.2	7.1	.5	.9
65 to 74 years	100.0	64.8	40.4	33.8	24.4	23.2	33.8	28.7	.3	4.8	.5	.9
75 to 84 years	100.0	72.3	32.9	26.0	39.5	38.3	26.3	17.8	–	8.5	.5	.8
85 years and over	100.0	72.4	23.3	15.0	49.1	47.6	25.6	7.1	–	18.6	1.0	1.0
Male	**100.0**	**53.0**	**42.7**	**40.0**	**10.3**	**7.8**	**42.3**	**3.2**	**34.4**	**4.8**	**1.9**	**2.7**
Under 18 years	100.0	.1	–	–	–	–	98.2	–	91.0	7.2	1.0	.7
18 and 19 years	100.0	6.4	2.8	1.8	3.6	1.6	86.6	.3	78.0	8.3	3.0	4.0
20 to 24 years	100.0	31.5	17.4	14.5	14.1	7.0	54.3	1.8	44.6	7.9	4.2	10.0
25 to 29 years	100.0	60.7	42.5	38.8	18.2	11.7	28.8	4.3	19.1	5.4	3.8	6.7
30 to 34 years	100.0	74.4	58.2	54.4	16.1	11.8	18.7	5.2	10.0	3.6	3.1	3.8
35 to 44 years	100.0	82.6	68.8	64.5	13.8	10.9	12.7	5.1	5.3	2.3	2.3	2.4
45 to 54 years	100.0	87.3	75.2	70.8	12.1	9.8	9.4	4.9	2.5	2.0	1.6	1.7
55 to 59 years	100.0	89.0	77.3	73.7	11.8	10.0	8.5	4.9	1.3	2.3	1.0	1.4
60 to 64 years	100.0	89.7	77.2	73.9	12.5	11.0	8.2	4.8	.7	2.6	.8	1.3
65 years and over	100.0	89.5	72.5	69.1	17.0	15.7	8.9	4.7	.2	4.1	.6	1.0
65 to 74 years	100.0	90.4	76.2	73.0	14.2	12.9	8.0	4.7	.2	3.1	.6	1.0
75 to 84 years	100.0	88.9	68.5	64.9	20.4	19.2	9.6	4.8	–	4.8	.6	.9
85 years and over	100.0	82.7	52.0	46.7	30.7	29.2	15.2	4.3	–	11.0	1.0	1.1
Female	**100.0**	**23.8**	**11.5**	**3.0**	**12.3**	**10.7**	**72.0**	**37.7**	**29.2**	**5.1**	**1.6**	**2.6**
Under 18 years	100.0	.1	.1	–	–	–	98.1	.1	90.6	7.3	1.0	.8
18 and 19 years	100.0	7.3	3.4	.7	3.8	1.6	83.3	6.5	69.5	7.3	3.9	5.6
20 to 24 years	100.0	20.7	10.0	2.6	10.6	5.4	65.2	24.9	34.4	5.9	4.1	10.0
25 to 29 years	100.0	26.6	15.6	4.8	11.0	7.5	64.4	48.0	12.7	3.7	3.1	6.0
30 to 34 years	100.0	27.4	18.5	5.3	9.0	6.9	66.8	58.1	6.4	2.3	2.3	3.4
35 to 44 years	100.0	28.4	20.1	4.9	8.4	6.9	67.7	62.5	3.5	1.7	1.5	2.3
45 to 54 years	100.0	28.8	17.7	4.5	11.1	9.6	68.5	64.2	1.9	2.4	.9	1.7
55 to 59 years	100.0	30.3	15.2	4.1	15.1	13.9	67.9	63.0	1.2	3.7	.6	1.2
60 to 64 years	100.0	34.2	13.9	3.7	20.3	19.2	64.2	58.8	.8	4.6	.5	1.1
65 years and over	100.0	52.7	11.8	2.6	41.0	39.8	45.9	36.6	.2	9.1	.5	.9
65 to 74 years	100.0	44.8	12.5	3.2	32.4	31.3	53.9	47.4	.3	6.2	.4	.9
75 to 84 years	100.0	62.1	10.9	2.0	51.2	50.1	36.6	25.8	–	10.8	.5	.8
85 years and over	100.0	67.7	10.4	.8	57.4	55.9	30.3	8.3	–	22.0	1.0	1.0

Table 28. White Persons in Households by Relationship to Householder, Age, and Sex: 1990

[For definitions of terms and meanings of symbols, see text]

United States

United States	All persons	Householder: Total	Householder: Family householder: Total	Householder: Family householder: Married, spouse present	Householder: Nonfamily householder: Total	Householder: Nonfamily householder: Living alone	Relatives of householder: Total	Relatives of householder: Spouse	Relatives of householder: Child	Relatives of householder: Other relatives	Nonrelatives of householder: In family households	Nonrelatives of householder: In nonfamily households
AGE												
All persons	**194 671 440**	**76 880 105**	**53 461 645**	**44 383 489**	**23 418 460**	**19 314 376**	**109 780 405**	**44 282 151**	**58 590 587**	**6 907 667**	**2 678 107**	**5 332 823**
Under 18 years	47 476 649	34 374	20 468	10 184	13 906	8 014	46 680 923	31 788	44 340 746	2 308 389	385 876	375 476
Under 6 years	16 398 462	–	–	–	–	–	16 169 196	–	15 092 950	1 076 246	118 036	111 230
6 to 14 years	23 647 021	–	–	–	–	–	23 285 224	–	22 353 328	931 896	171 192	190 605
15 to 17 years	7 431 166	34 374	20 468	10 184	13 906	8 014	7 226 503	31 788	6 894 468	300 247	96 648	73 641
18 and 19 years	4 873 059	340 194	136 241	68 888	203 953	83 590	4 118 490	185 379	3 654 811	278 300	153 876	260 499
20 to 24 years	13 406 449	3 584 250	1 763 245	1 252 408	1 821 005	889 435	7 853 789	1 987 613	5 186 577	679 599	479 727	1 488 683
25 to 29 years	16 349 729	7 236 083	4 712 595	3 816 007	2 523 488	1 643 796	7 555 444	4 665 720	2 360 063	529 661	464 240	1 093 962
30 to 34 years	17 131 407	8 720 642	6 493 846	5 376 727	2 226 796	1 653 700	7 421 785	5 854 562	1 227 155	340 068	361 040	627 940
35 to 44 years	30 286 814	16 650 515	13 261 300	10 860 789	3 389 215	2 701 379	12 497 772	10 908 211	1 190 795	398 766	438 372	700 155
45 to 54 years	20 920 515	11 894 419	9 521 982	8 006 431	2 372 437	1 991 175	8 484 510	7 730 869	424 098	329 543	191 438	350 148
55 to 59 years	8 890 962	5 144 351	3 977 713	3 451 385	1 166 638	1 040 581	3 582 859	3 286 448	101 487	194 924	52 117	111 635
60 to 64 years	9 114 060	5 446 098	3 961 998	3 449 349	1 484 100	1 371 472	3 525 582	3 210 638	64 342	250 602	42 723	99 657
65 years and over	26 221 796	17 829 179	9 612 257	8 091 321	8 216 922	7 931 234	8 059 251	6 420 923	40 513	1 597 815	108 698	224 668
65 to 74 years	15 736 070	10 185 437	6 378 604	5 517 614	3 806 833	3 639 809	5 356 391	4 713 804	37 810	604 777	56 295	137 947
75 to 84 years	8 424 492	6 129 342	2 762 635	2 257 877	3 366 707	3 277 955	2 193 584	1 556 849	2 646	634 089	34 486	67 080
85 years and over	2 061 234	1 514 400	471 018	315 830	1 043 382	1 013 470	509 276	150 270	57	358 949	17 917	19 641
Male	**94 894 328**	**53 761 843**	**43 615 704**	**41 344 294**	**10 146 139**	**7 673 442**	**37 142 838**	**3 025 177**	**30 994 867**	**3 122 794**	**1 393 917**	**2 595 730**
Under 18 years	24 374 359	16 840	10 736	7 371	6 104	3 544	23 987 254	1 006	22 806 928	1 179 320	186 914	183 351
Under 6 years	8 416 089	–	–	–	–	–	8 300 903	–	7 752 178	548 725	59 608	55 578
6 to 14 years	12 141 762	–	–	–	–	–	11 961 841	–	11 486 694	475 147	85 401	94 520
15 to 17 years	3 816 508	16 840	10 736	7 371	6 104	3 544	3 724 510	1 006	3 568 056	155 448	41 905	33 253
18 and 19 years	2 484 140	171 653	72 356	51 377	99 297	42 011	2 140 283	6 573	1 983 561	150 149	65 189	107 015
20 to 24 years	6 679 944	2 262 048	1 233 824	1 071 466	1 028 224	500 420	3 465 363	117 524	2 958 625	389 214	231 192	721 341
25 to 29 years	8 148 724	5 232 406	3 669 435	3 412 221	1 562 971	995 193	2 107 493	345 158	1 444 865	317 470	246 557	562 268
30 to 34 years	8 521 768	6 611 410	5 196 138	4 919 415	1 415 272	1 031 053	1 396 206	432 584	756 670	206 952	198 101	316 051
35 to 44 years	15 046 955	12 776 488	10 693 660	10 114 747	2 082 828	1 633 538	1 681 189	740 157	714 969	226 063	249 559	339 719
45 to 54 years	10 278 486	9 137 008	7 938 873	7 535 016	1 198 135	972 929	863 417	483 861	235 127	144 429	113 883	164 178
55 to 59 years	4 284 424	3 873 654	3 397 421	3 265 742	476 233	404 599	324 510	202 547	50 585	71 378	30 857	55 403
60 to 64 years	4 282 239	3 897 423	3 393 138	3 272 286	504 285	442 894	311 108	198 791	29 114	83 203	24 346	49 362
65 years and over	10 793 289	9 782 913	8 010 123	7 694 653	1 772 790	1 647 261	866 015	496 976	14 423	354 616	47 319	97 042
65 to 74 years	6 945 349	6 356 824	5 421 504	5 237 408	935 320	854 207	495 239	318 673	13 822	162 744	29 186	64 100
75 to 84 years	3 215 439	2 893 881	2 252 966	2 152 080	640 915	605 505	281 465	151 780	591	129 094	13 351	26 742
85 years and over	632 501	532 208	335 653	305 165	196 555	187 549	89 311	26 523	10	62 778	4 782	6 200
Female	**99 777 112**	**23 118 262**	**9 845 941**	**3 039 195**	**13 272 321**	**11 640 934**	**72 637 567**	**41 256 974**	**27 595 720**	**3 784 873**	**1 284 190**	**2 737 093**
Under 18 years	23 102 290	17 534	9 732	2 813	7 802	4 470	22 693 669	30 782	21 533 818	1 129 069	198 962	192 125
Under 6 years	7 982 373	–	–	–	–	–	7 868 293	–	7 340 772	527 521	58 428	55 652
6 to 14 years	11 505 259	–	–	–	–	–	11 323 383	–	10 866 634	456 749	85 791	96 085
15 to 17 years	3 614 658	17 534	9 732	2 813	7 802	4 470	3 501 993	30 782	3 326 412	144 799	54 743	40 388
18 and 19 years	2 388 919	168 541	63 885	17 511	104 656	41 579	1 978 207	178 806	1 671 250	128 151	88 687	153 484
20 to 24 years	6 726 505	1 322 202	529 421	180 942	792 781	389 015	4 388 426	1 870 089	2 227 952	290 385	248 535	767 342
25 to 29 years	8 201 005	2 003 677	1 043 160	403 786	960 517	648 603	5 447 951	4 320 562	915 198	212 191	217 683	531 694
30 to 34 years	8 609 639	2 109 232	1 297 708	457 312	811 524	622 647	6 025 579	5 421 978	470 485	133 116	162 939	311 889
35 to 44 years	15 239 859	3 874 027	2 567 640	746 042	1 306 387	1 067 841	10 816 583	10 168 054	475 826	172 703	188 813	360 436
45 to 54 years	10 642 029	2 757 411	1 583 109	471 415	1 174 302	1 018 246	7 621 093	7 247 008	188 971	185 114	77 555	185 970
55 to 59 years	4 606 538	1 270 697	580 292	185 643	690 405	635 982	3 258 349	3 083 901	50 902	123 546	21 260	56 232
60 to 64 years	4 831 821	1 548 675	568 860	177 063	979 815	928 578	3 214 474	3 011 847	35 228	167 399	18 377	50 295
65 years and over	15 428 507	8 046 266	1 602 134	396 668	6 444 132	6 283 973	7 193 236	5 923 947	26 090	1 243 199	61 379	127 626
65 to 74 years	8 790 721	3 828 613	957 100	280 206	2 871 513	2 785 602	4 861 152	4 395 131	23 988	442 033	27 109	73 847
75 to 84 years	5 209 053	3 235 461	509 669	105 797	2 725 792	2 672 450	1 912 119	1 405 069	2 055	504 995	21 135	40 338
85 years and over	1 428 733	982 192	135 365	10 665	846 827	825 921	419 965	123 747	47	296 171	13 135	13 441
PERCENT DISTRIBUTION												
All persons	**100.0**	**39.5**	**27.5**	**22.8**	**12.0**	**9.9**	**56.4**	**22.7**	**30.1**	**3.5**	**1.4**	**2.7**
Under 18 years	100.0	.1	–	–	–	–	98.3	.1	93.4	4.9	.8	.8
18 and 19 years	100.0	7.0	2.8	1.4	4.2	1.7	84.5	3.8	75.0	5.7	3.2	5.3
20 to 24 years	100.0	26.7	13.2	9.3	13.6	6.6	58.6	14.8	38.7	5.1	3.6	11.1
25 to 29 years	100.0	44.3	28.8	23.3	15.4	10.1	46.2	28.5	14.4	3.2	2.8	6.7
30 to 34 years	100.0	50.9	37.9	31.4	13.0	9.7	43.3	34.2	7.2	2.0	2.1	3.7
35 to 44 years	100.0	55.0	43.8	35.9	11.2	8.9	41.3	36.0	3.9	1.3	1.4	2.3
45 to 54 years	100.0	56.9	45.5	38.3	11.3	9.5	40.6	37.0	2.0	1.6	.9	1.7
55 to 59 years	100.0	57.9	44.7	38.8	13.1	11.7	40.3	37.0	1.1	2.2	.6	1.3
60 to 64 years	100.0	59.8	43.5	37.8	16.3	15.0	38.7	35.2	.7	2.7	.5	1.1
65 years and over	100.0	68.0	36.7	30.9	31.3	30.2	30.7	24.5	.2	6.1	.4	.9
65 to 74 years	100.0	64.7	40.5	35.1	24.2	23.1	34.0	30.0	.2	3.8	.4	.9
75 to 84 years	100.0	72.8	32.8	26.8	40.0	38.9	26.0	18.5	–	7.5	.4	.8
85 years and over	100.0	73.5	22.9	15.3	50.6	49.2	24.7	7.3	–	17.4	.9	1.0
Male	**100.0**	**56.7**	**46.0**	**43.6**	**10.7**	**8.1**	**39.1**	**3.2**	**32.7**	**3.3**	**1.5**	**2.7**
Under 18 years	100.0	.1	–	–	–	–	98.4	–	93.6	4.8	.8	.8
18 and 19 years	100.0	6.9	2.9	2.1	4.0	1.7	86.2	.3	79.8	6.0	2.6	4.3
20 to 24 years	100.0	33.9	18.5	16.0	15.4	7.5	51.9	1.8	44.3	5.8	3.5	10.8
25 to 29 years	100.0	64.2	45.0	41.9	19.2	12.2	25.9	4.2	17.7	3.9	3.0	6.9
30 to 34 years	100.0	77.6	61.0	57.7	16.6	12.1	16.4	5.1	8.9	2.4	2.3	3.7
35 to 44 years	100.0	84.9	71.1	67.2	13.8	10.9	11.2	4.9	4.8	1.5	1.7	2.3
45 to 54 years	100.0	88.9	77.2	73.3	11.7	9.5	8.4	4.7	2.3	1.4	1.1	1.6
55 to 59 years	100.0	90.4	79.3	76.2	11.1	9.4	7.6	4.7	1.2	1.7	.7	1.3
60 to 64 years	100.0	91.0	79.2	76.4	11.8	10.3	7.3	4.6	.7	1.9	.6	1.2
65 years and over	100.0	90.6	74.2	71.3	16.4	15.3	8.0	4.6	.1	3.3	.4	.9
65 to 74 years	100.0	91.5	78.1	75.4	13.5	12.3	7.1	4.6	.2	2.3	.4	.9
75 to 84 years	100.0	90.0	70.1	66.9	19.9	18.8	8.8	4.7	–	4.0	.4	.8
85 years and over	100.0	84.1	53.1	48.2	31.1	29.7	14.1	4.2	–	9.9	.8	1.0
Female	**100.0**	**23.2**	**9.9**	**3.0**	**13.3**	**11.7**	**72.8**	**41.3**	**27.7**	**3.8**	**1.3**	**2.7**
Under 18 years	100.0	.1	–	–	–	–	98.2	.1	93.2	4.9	.9	.8
18 and 19 years	100.0	7.1	2.7	.7	4.4	1.7	82.8	7.5	70.0	5.4	3.7	6.4
20 to 24 years	100.0	19.7	7.9	2.7	11.8	5.8	65.2	27.8	33.1	4.3	3.7	11.4
25 to 29 years	100.0	24.4	12.7	4.9	11.7	7.9	66.4	52.7	11.2	2.6	2.7	6.5
30 to 34 years	100.0	24.5	15.1	5.3	9.4	7.2	70.0	63.0	5.5	1.5	1.9	3.6
35 to 44 years	100.0	25.4	16.8	4.9	8.6	7.0	71.0	66.7	3.1	1.1	1.2	2.4
45 to 54 years	100.0	25.9	14.9	4.4	11.0	9.6	71.6	68.1	1.8	1.7	.7	1.7
55 to 59 years	100.0	27.6	12.6	4.0	15.0	13.8	70.7	66.9	1.1	2.7	.5	1.2
60 to 64 years	100.0	32.1	11.8	3.7	20.3	19.2	66.5	62.3	.7	3.5	.4	1.0
65 years and over	100.0	52.2	10.4	2.6	41.8	40.7	46.6	38.4	.2	8.1	.4	.8
65 to 74 years	100.0	43.6	10.9	3.2	32.7	31.7	55.3	50.0	.3	5.0	.3	.8
75 to 84 years	100.0	62.1	9.8	2.0	52.3	51.3	36.7	27.0	–	9.7	.4	.8
85 years and over	100.0	68.7	9.5	.7	59.3	57.8	29.4	8.7	–	20.7	.9	.9

Table 29. Black Persons in Households by Relationship to Householder, Age, and Sex: 1990

[For definitions of terms and meanings of symbols, see text]

United States	All persons	Householder Total	Family householder Total	Family householder Married, spouse present	Nonfamily householder Total	Nonfamily householder Living alone	Relatives of householder Total	Relatives Spouse	Relatives Child	Relatives Other relatives	Nonrelatives In family households	Nonrelatives In nonfamily households
AGE												
All persons	28 722 227	9 976 161	6 986 624	3 410 345	2 989 537	2 536 353	17 298 711	3 319 653	10 906 346	3 072 712	816 710	630 645
Under 18 years	9 504 188	10 892	7 554	1 076	3 338	2 275	9 280 037	2 032	7 608 181	1 669 824	139 617	73 642
Under 6 years	3 319 428	–	–	–	–	–	3 242 309	–	2 472 538	769 771	52 824	24 295
6 to 14 years	4 702 290	–	–	–	–	–	4 603 153	–	3 901 926	701 227	63 109	36 028
15 to 17 years	1 482 470	10 892	7 554	1 076	3 338	2 275	1 434 575	2 032	1 233 717	198 826	23 684	13 319
18 and 19 years	963 656	63 199	41 749	4 898	21 450	12 064	850 932	10 193	712 370	128 369	26 603	22 922
20 to 24 years	2 283 910	586 512	385 665	107 981	200 847	129 310	1 482 595	147 644	1 082 021	252 930	102 082	112 721
25 to 29 years	2 522 824	1 087 209	769 576	314 460	317 633	239 962	1 203 157	368 522	637 499	197 136	125 956	106 502
30 to 34 years	2 527 366	1 308 535	996 691	449 486	311 844	251 496	1 019 311	485 504	385 976	147 831	119 071	80 449
35 to 44 years	4 046 266	2 363 511	1 846 501	907 737	517 010	432 411	1 422 483	895 656	339 873	186 954	157 374	102 898
45 to 54 years	2 532 238	1 581 500	1 179 191	641 504	402 309	346 795	820 943	601 732	97 139	122 072	73 318	56 477
55 to 59 years	1 015 789	655 644	462 235	262 638	193 409	171 950	318 408	239 947	21 710	56 751	21 672	20 065
60 to 64 years	944 023	627 174	408 667	231 834	218 507	198 140	281 165	206 934	12 942	61 289	17 491	18 193
65 years and over	2 381 967	1 691 985	888 795	488 731	803 190	751 950	619 680	361 489	8 635	249 556	33 526	36 776
65 to 74 years	1 464 987	1 033 694	591 345	337 671	442 349	410 354	386 627	265 919	7 992	112 716	9 033	10 262
75 to 84 years	725 948	531 038	246 172	130 135	284 866	269 375	175 615	85 484	627	89 504	3 458	2 883
85 years and over	191 032	127 253	51 278	20 925	75 975	72 221	57 438	10 086	16	47 336		
Male	13 255 525	4 899 584	3 491 868	2 967 268	1 407 716	1 140 836	7 542 419	459 663	5 590 763	1 491 993	476 766	336 756
Under 18 years	4 793 992	4 395	2 704	775	1 691	1 170	4 683 053	248	3 844 071	838 734	69 926	36 618
Under 6 years	1 678 218	–	–	–	–	–	1 638 986	–	1 250 694	388 292	27 020	12 212
6 to 14 years	2 372 831	–	–	–	–	–	2 323 117	–	1 972 537	350 580	31 830	17 884
15 to 17 years	742 943	4 395	2 704	775	1 691	1 170	720 950	248	620 840	99 862	11 076	6 522
18 and 19 years	468 824	18 671	8 595	2 949	10 076	5 731	428 112	815	362 409	64 888	11 662	10 379
20 to 24 years	1 042 717	226 780	120 388	80 724	106 392	66 401	707 895	18 969	557 894	131 032	71 767	57 041
25 to 29 years	1 128 059	496 688	316 044	254 563	180 644	131 960	502 563	54 302	341 013	107 248	72 408	43 992
30 to 34 years	1 118 131	632 624	444 637	376 949	187 987	148 015	369 107	70 913	214 345	83 849	72 408	45 966
35 to 44 years	1 805 001	1 224 578	917 233	790 027	307 345	252 129	420 211	122 499	195 180	102 532	103 246	56 966
45 to 54 years	1 131 842	858 345	653 302	569 106	205 043	172 280	190 354	79 102	55 040	56 212	50 919	32 224
55 to 59 years	444 634	353 976	267 895	236 075	86 081	73 784	63 596	30 023	11 159	22 414	14 928	12 134
60 to 64 years	402 806	326 158	239 137	209 322	87 021	76 154	54 198	26 197	6 224	21 777	11 555	10 895
65 years and over	919 519	757 369	521 933	446 778	235 436	213 212	123 330	56 595	3 428	63 307	18 931	19 889
65 to 74 years	598 060	497 590	353 658	307 223	143 932	128 885	74 145	37 194	3 237	33 714	12 904	13 421
75 to 84 years	262 096	215 476	142 353	119 776	73 123	67 227	36 787	16 198	186	20 403	4 629	5 204
85 years and over	59 363	44 303	25 922	19 779	18 381	17 100	12 398	3 203	5	9 190	1 398	1 264
Female	15 466 702	5 076 577	3 494 756	443 077	1 581 821	1 395 517	9 756 292	2 859 990	5 315 583	1 580 719	339 944	293 889
Under 18 years	4 710 196	6 497	4 850	301	1 647	1 105	4 596 984	1 784	3 764 110	831 090	69 691	37 024
Under 6 years	1 641 210	–	–	–	–	–	1 603 323	–	1 221 844	381 479	25 804	12 083
6 to 14 years	2 329 459	–	–	–	–	–	2 280 036	–	1 929 389	350 647	31 279	18 144
15 to 17 years	739 527	6 497	4 850	301	1 647	1 105	713 625	1 784	612 877	98 964	12 608	6 797
18 and 19 years	494 832	44 528	33 154	1 949	11 374	6 333	422 820	9 378	349 961	63 481	14 941	12 543
20 to 24 years	1 241 193	359 732	265 277	27 257	94 455	62 909	774 700	128 675	524 127	121 898	50 658	56 103
25 to 29 years	1 394 765	590 521	453 532	59 897	136 989	108 002	700 594	314 220	296 486	89 888	54 189	49 461
30 to 34 years	1 409 235	675 911	552 054	72 537	123 857	103 481	650 204	414 591	171 631	63 982	46 663	36 457
35 to 44 years	2 241 265	1 138 933	929 268	117 710	209 665	180 282	1 002 272	773 157	144 693	84 422	54 128	45 932
45 to 54 years	1 400 396	723 155	525 889	72 398	197 266	174 515	630 589	522 630	42 099	65 860	22 399	24 253
55 to 59 years	571 155	301 668	194 340	26 563	107 328	98 166	254 812	209 924	10 551	34 337	6 744	7 931
60 to 64 years	541 217	301 016	169 530	22 512	131 486	121 986	226 967	180 737	6 718	39 512	5 936	7 298
65 years and over	1 462 448	934 616	366 862	41 953	567 754	538 738	496 350	304 894	5 207	186 249	14 595	16 887
65 to 74 years	866 927	536 104	237 687	30 448	298 417	281 469	312 482	228 725	4 755	79 002	8 131	10 210
75 to 84 years	463 852	315 562	103 819	10 359	211 743	202 148	138 828	69 286	441	69 101	4 404	5 058
85 years and over	131 669	82 950	25 356	1 146	57 594	55 121	45 040	6 883	11	38 146	2 060	1 619
PERCENT DISTRIBUTION												
All persons	100.0	34.7	24.3	11.9	10.4	8.8	60.2	11.6	38.0	10.7	2.8	2.2
Under 18 years	100.0	.1	.1	–	–	–	97.6	–	80.1	17.6	1.5	.8
18 and 19 years	100.0	6.6	4.3	.5	2.2	1.3	88.3	1.1	73.9	13.3	2.8	2.4
20 to 24 years	100.0	25.7	16.9	4.7	8.8	5.7	64.9	6.5	47.4	11.1	4.5	4.9
25 to 29 years	100.0	43.1	30.5	12.5	12.6	9.5	47.7	14.6	25.3	7.8	5.0	4.2
30 to 34 years	100.0	51.8	39.4	17.8	12.3	10.0	40.3	19.2	15.3	5.8	4.7	3.2
35 to 44 years	100.0	58.4	45.6	22.4	12.8	10.7	35.2	22.1	8.4	4.6	3.9	2.5
45 to 54 years	100.0	62.5	46.6	25.3	15.9	13.7	32.4	23.8	3.8	4.8	2.9	2.2
55 to 59 years	100.0	64.5	45.5	25.9	19.0	16.9	31.3	23.6	2.1	5.6	2.1	2.0
60 to 64 years	100.0	66.4	43.3	24.6	23.1	21.0	29.8	21.9	1.4	6.5	1.9	1.9
65 years and over	100.0	71.0	37.3	20.5	33.7	31.6	26.0	15.2	.4	10.5	1.4	1.5
65 to 74 years	100.0	70.6	40.4	23.0	30.2	28.0	26.4	18.2	.5	7.7	1.4	1.6
75 to 84 years	100.0	73.2	33.9	17.9	39.2	37.1	24.2	11.8	.1	12.3	1.2	1.4
85 years and over	100.0	66.6	26.8	11.0	39.8	37.8	30.1	5.3	–	24.8	1.8	1.5
Male	100.0	37.0	26.3	22.4	10.6	8.6	56.9	3.5	42.2	11.3	3.6	2.5
Under 18 years	100.0	.1	.1	–	–	–	97.7	–	80.2	17.5	1.5	.8
18 and 19 years	100.0	4.0	1.8	.6	2.1	1.2	91.3	.2	77.3	13.8	2.5	2.2
20 to 24 years	100.0	21.7	11.5	7.7	10.2	6.4	67.9	1.8	53.5	12.6	4.9	5.4
25 to 29 years	100.0	44.0	28.0	22.6	16.0	11.7	44.6	4.8	30.2	9.5	6.4	5.1
30 to 34 years	100.0	56.6	39.8	33.7	16.8	13.2	33.0	6.3	19.2	7.5	6.5	3.9
35 to 44 years	100.0	67.8	50.8	43.8	17.0	14.0	23.3	6.8	10.8	5.7	5.7	3.2
45 to 54 years	100.0	75.8	57.7	50.3	18.1	15.2	16.8	7.0	4.9	5.0	4.5	2.8
55 to 59 years	100.0	79.6	60.3	53.1	19.4	16.6	14.3	6.8	2.5	5.0	3.4	2.7
60 to 64 years	100.0	81.0	59.4	52.0	21.6	18.9	13.5	6.5	1.5	5.4	2.9	2.7
65 years and over	100.0	82.4	56.8	48.6	25.6	23.2	13.4	6.2	.4	6.9	2.1	2.2
65 to 74 years	100.0	83.2	59.1	51.4	24.1	21.6	12.4	6.2	.5	5.6	2.2	2.2
75 to 84 years	100.0	82.2	54.3	45.7	27.9	25.6	14.0	6.2	.1	7.8	1.8	2.0
85 years and over	100.0	74.6	43.7	33.3	31.0	28.8	20.9	5.4	–	15.5	2.4	2.1
Female	100.0	32.8	22.6	2.9	10.2	9.0	63.1	18.5	34.4	10.2	2.2	1.9
Under 18 years	100.0	.1	.1	–	–	–	97.6	–	79.9	17.6	1.5	.8
18 and 19 years	100.0	9.0	6.7	.4	2.3	1.3	85.4	1.9	70.7	12.8	3.0	2.5
20 to 24 years	100.0	29.0	21.4	2.2	7.6	5.1	62.4	10.4	42.2	9.8	4.1	4.5
25 to 29 years	100.0	42.3	32.5	4.3	9.8	7.7	50.2	22.5	21.3	6.4	3.9	3.5
30 to 34 years	100.0	48.0	39.2	5.1	8.8	7.3	46.1	29.4	12.2	4.5	3.3	2.6
35 to 44 years	100.0	50.8	41.5	5.3	9.4	8.0	44.7	34.5	6.5	3.8	2.4	2.0
45 to 54 years	100.0	51.6	37.6	5.2	14.1	12.5	45.0	37.3	3.0	4.7	1.6	1.7
55 to 59 years	100.0	52.8	34.0	4.7	18.8	17.2	44.6	36.8	1.8	6.0	1.2	1.4
60 to 64 years	100.0	55.6	31.3	4.2	24.3	22.5	41.9	33.4	1.2	7.3	1.1	1.3
65 years and over	100.0	63.9	25.1	2.9	38.8	36.8	33.9	20.8	.4	12.7	1.0	1.2
65 to 74 years	100.0	61.8	27.4	3.5	34.4	32.5	36.0	26.4	.5	9.1	.9	1.2
75 to 84 years	100.0	68.0	22.4	2.2	45.6	43.6	29.9	14.9	.1	14.9	.9	1.1
85 years and over	100.0	63.0	19.3	.9	43.7	41.9	34.2	5.2	–	29.0	1.6	1.2

Table 30. **American Indian, Eskimo, or Aleut Persons in Households by Relationship to Householder, Age, and Sex: 1990**

[For definitions of terms and meanings of symbols, see text]

United States	All persons	Householder Total	Family householder Total	Family householder Married, spouse present	Nonfamily householder Total	Nonfamily householder Living alone	Relatives of householder Total	Relatives of householder Spouse	Relatives of householder Child	Relatives of householder Other relatives	Nonrelatives of householder In family households	Nonrelatives of householder In nonfamily households
AGE												
All persons	1 902 958	591 372	442 161	283 818	149 211	115 992	1 196 631	284 695	758 135	153 801	64 524	50 431
Under 18 years	690 562	742	431	98	311	167	670 557	362	585 433	84 762	12 623	6 640
Under 6 years	241 858	–	–	–	–	–	236 076	–	197 069	39 007	3 903	1 879
6 to 14 years	344 376	–	–	–	–	–	335 364	–	299 973	35 391	5 674	3 338
15 to 17 years	104 328	742	431	98	311	167	99 117	362	88 391	10 364	3 046	1 423
18 and 19 years	65 375	5 264	2 948	938	2 316	1 061	53 714	2 226	44 441	7 047	3 711	2 686
20 to 24 years	152 775	39 367	26 312	12 912	13 055	6 746	92 371	18 837	59 120	14 414	10 973	10 064
25 to 29 years	168 379	69 033	52 518	30 921	16 515	10 267	79 255	37 453	31 091	10 711	11 428	8 663
30 to 34 years	164 772	80 520	64 790	40 645	15 730	10 970	68 699	44 887	16 741	7 071	9 160	6 393
35 to 44 years	269 200	148 317	120 965	79 159	27 352	20 577	102 278	79 054	14 898	8 326	10 161	8 444
45 to 54 years	170 290	100 356	78 401	54 734	21 955	17 869	61 761	50 862	4 744	6 155	3 882	4 291
55 to 59 years	60 919	37 548	28 085	19 814	9 463	8 308	21 337	17 659	911	2 767	938	1 096
60 to 64 years	50 549	32 803	23 077	16 174	9 726	8 819	16 278	13 156	473	2 649	627	841
65 years and over	110 137	77 422	44 634	28 423	32 788	31 208	30 381	20 199	283	9 899	1 021	1 313
65 to 74 years	70 522	48 640	30 387	20 364	18 253	17 172	20 308	15 374	265	4 669	670	904
75 to 84 years	31 653	23 236	11 828	6 970	11 408	11 005	7 834	4 337	18	3 479	257	326
85 years and over	7 962	5 546	2 419	1 089	3 127	3 031	2 239	488	–	1 751	94	83
Male	926 952	366 438	288 587	251 145	77 851	57 519	503 365	27 105	397 262	78 998	33 435	23 714
Under 18 years	351 006	305	148	50	157	89	341 360	16	297 984	43 360	6 136	3 205
Under 6 years	122 898	–	–	–	–	–	120 052	–	100 201	19 851	1 964	882
6 to 14 years	174 941	–	–	–	–	–	170 453	–	152 326	18 127	2 806	1 682
15 to 17 years	53 167	305	148	50	157	89	50 855	16	45 457	5 382	1 366	641
18 and 19 years	33 083	2 299	1 132	643	1 167	549	28 075	132	24 111	3 832	1 597	1 112
20 to 24 years	75 446	21 822	13 889	10 421	7 933	4 092	43 742	1 577	33 928	8 237	5 152	4 730
25 to 29 years	81 636	42 829	32 025	26 386	10 804	6 712	28 675	3 617	18 640	6 418	5 841	4 291
30 to 34 years	77 924	51 377	40 924	35 260	10 453	7 321	18 692	4 356	10 126	4 210	4 857	2 998
35 to 44 years	128 017	97 315	79 882	70 076	17 433	13 095	21 021	7 307	8 977	4 737	5 822	3 859
45 to 54 years	81 358	66 520	54 928	49 313	11 592	9 272	10 522	4 848	2 690	2 984	2 441	1 875
55 to 59 years	28 685	24 233	19 823	18 026	4 410	3 743	3 295	1 678	477	1 140	600	557
60 to 64 years	23 609	20 257	16 210	14 760	4 047	3 559	2 511	1 274	227	1 010	391	450
65 years and over	46 188	39 481	29 626	26 210	9 855	9 087	5 472	2 300	102	3 070	598	637
65 to 74 years	30 972	26 872	20 751	18 721	6 121	5 570	3 230	1 544	94	1 592	425	445
75 to 84 years	12 349	10 438	7 507	6 457	2 931	2 755	1 627	614	8	1 005	132	152
85 years and over	2 867	2 171	1 368	1 032	803	762	615	142	–	473	41	40
Female	976 006	224 934	153 574	32 673	71 360	58 473	693 266	257 590	360 873	74 803	31 089	26 717
Under 18 years	339 556	437	283	48	154	78	329 197	346	287 449	41 402	6 487	3 435
Under 6 years	118 960	–	–	–	–	–	116 024	–	96 868	19 156	1 939	997
6 to 14 years	169 435	–	–	–	–	–	164 911	–	147 647	17 264	2 868	1 656
15 to 17 years	51 161	437	283	48	154	78	48 262	346	42 934	4 982	1 680	782
18 and 19 years	32 292	2 965	1 816	295	1 149	512	25 639	2 094	20 330	3 215	2 114	1 574
20 to 24 years	77 329	17 545	12 423	2 491	5 122	2 654	48 629	17 260	25 192	6 177	5 821	5 334
25 to 29 years	86 743	26 204	20 493	4 535	5 711	3 555	50 580	33 836	12 451	4 293	5 587	4 372
30 to 34 years	86 848	29 143	23 866	5 385	5 277	3 649	50 007	40 531	6 615	2 861	4 303	3 395
35 to 44 years	141 183	51 002	41 083	9 083	9 919	7 482	81 257	71 747	5 921	3 589	4 339	4 585
45 to 54 years	88 932	33 836	23 473	5 421	10 363	8 597	51 239	46 014	2 054	3 171	1 441	2 416
55 to 59 years	32 234	13 315	8 262	1 788	5 053	4 565	18 042	15 981	434	1 627	338	539
60 to 64 years	26 940	12 546	6 867	1 414	5 679	5 260	13 767	11 882	246	1 639	236	391
65 years and over	63 949	37 941	15 008	2 213	22 933	22 121	24 909	17 899	181	6 829	423	676
65 to 74 years	39 550	21 768	9 636	1 643	12 132	11 602	17 078	13 830	171	3 077	245	459
75 to 84 years	19 304	12 798	4 321	513	8 477	8 250	6 207	3 723	10	2 474	125	174
85 years and over	5 095	3 375	1 051	57	2 324	2 269	1 624	346	–	1 278	53	43
PERCENT DISTRIBUTION												
All persons	100.0	31.1	23.2	14.9	7.8	6.1	62.9	15.0	39.8	8.1	3.4	2.7
Under 18 years	100.0	.1	.1	–	–	–	97.1	.1	84.8	12.3	1.8	1.0
18 and 19 years	100.0	8.1	4.5	1.4	3.5	1.6	82.2	3.4	68.0	10.8	5.7	4.1
20 to 24 years	100.0	25.8	17.2	8.5	8.5	4.4	60.5	12.3	38.7	9.4	7.2	6.6
25 to 29 years	100.0	41.0	31.2	18.4	9.8	6.1	47.1	22.2	18.5	6.4	6.8	5.1
30 to 34 years	100.0	48.9	39.3	24.7	9.5	6.7	41.7	27.2	10.2	4.3	5.6	3.9
35 to 44 years	100.0	55.1	44.9	29.4	10.2	7.6	38.0	29.4	5.5	3.1	3.8	3.1
45 to 54 years	100.0	58.9	46.0	32.1	12.9	10.5	36.3	29.9	2.8	3.6	2.3	2.5
55 to 59 years	100.0	61.6	46.1	32.5	15.5	13.6	35.0	29.0	1.5	4.5	1.5	1.8
60 to 64 years	100.0	64.9	45.7	32.0	19.2	17.4	32.2	26.0	.9	5.2	1.2	1.7
65 years and over	100.0	70.3	40.5	25.8	29.8	28.3	27.6	18.3	.3	9.0	.9	1.2
65 to 74 years	100.0	69.0	43.1	28.9	25.9	24.3	28.8	21.8	.4	6.6	1.0	1.3
75 to 84 years	100.0	73.4	37.4	22.0	36.0	34.8	24.7	13.7	.1	11.0	.8	1.0
85 years and over	100.0	69.7	30.4	13.7	39.3	38.1	28.1	6.1	–	22.0	1.2	1.0
Male	100.0	39.5	31.1	27.1	8.4	6.2	54.3	2.9	42.9	8.5	3.6	2.6
Under 18 years	100.0	.1	–	–	–	–	97.3	–	84.9	12.4	1.7	.9
18 and 19 years	100.0	6.9	3.4	1.9	3.5	1.7	84.9	.4	72.9	11.6	4.8	3.4
20 to 24 years	100.0	28.9	18.4	13.8	10.5	5.4	58.0	2.1	45.0	10.9	6.8	6.3
25 to 29 years	100.0	52.5	39.2	32.3	13.2	8.2	35.1	4.4	22.8	7.9	7.2	5.3
30 to 34 years	100.0	65.9	52.5	45.2	13.4	9.4	24.0	5.6	13.0	5.4	6.2	3.8
35 to 44 years	100.0	76.0	62.4	54.7	13.6	10.2	16.4	5.7	7.0	3.7	4.5	3.0
45 to 54 years	100.0	81.8	67.5	60.6	14.2	11.4	12.9	6.0	3.3	3.7	3.0	2.3
55 to 59 years	100.0	84.5	69.1	62.8	15.4	13.0	11.5	5.8	1.7	4.0	2.1	1.9
60 to 64 years	100.0	85.8	68.7	62.5	17.1	15.1	10.6	5.4	1.0	4.3	1.7	1.9
65 years and over	100.0	85.5	64.1	56.7	21.3	19.7	11.8	5.0	.2	6.6	1.3	1.4
65 to 74 years	100.0	86.8	67.0	60.4	19.8	18.0	10.4	5.0	.3	5.1	1.4	1.4
75 to 84 years	100.0	84.5	60.8	52.3	23.7	22.3	13.2	5.0	.1	8.1	1.1	1.2
85 years and over	100.0	75.7	47.7	36.0	28.0	26.6	21.5	5.0	–	16.5	1.4	1.4
Female	100.0	23.0	15.7	3.3	7.3	6.0	71.0	26.4	37.0	7.7	3.2	2.7
Under 18 years	100.0	.1	.1	–	–	–	96.9	.1	84.7	12.2	1.9	1.0
18 and 19 years	100.0	9.2	5.6	.9	3.6	1.6	79.4	6.5	63.0	10.0	6.5	4.9
20 to 24 years	100.0	22.7	16.1	3.2	6.6	3.4	62.9	22.3	32.6	8.0	7.5	6.9
25 to 29 years	100.0	30.2	23.6	5.2	6.6	4.1	58.3	39.0	14.4	4.9	6.4	5.0
30 to 34 years	100.0	33.6	27.5	6.2	6.1	4.2	57.6	46.7	7.6	3.3	5.0	3.9
35 to 44 years	100.0	36.1	29.1	6.4	7.0	5.3	57.6	50.8	4.2	2.5	3.1	3.2
45 to 54 years	100.0	38.0	26.4	6.1	11.7	9.7	57.6	51.7	2.3	3.6	1.6	2.7
55 to 59 years	100.0	41.3	25.6	5.5	15.7	14.2	56.0	49.6	1.3	5.0	1.0	1.7
60 to 64 years	100.0	46.6	25.5	5.2	21.1	19.5	51.1	44.1	.9	6.1	.9	1.5
65 years and over	100.0	59.3	23.5	3.5	35.9	34.6	39.0	28.0	.3	10.7	.7	1.1
65 to 74 years	100.0	55.0	24.4	4.2	30.7	29.3	43.2	35.0	.4	7.8	.6	1.2
75 to 84 years	100.0	66.3	22.4	2.7	43.9	42.7	32.2	19.3	.1	12.8	.6	.9
85 years and over	100.0	66.2	20.6	1.1	45.6	44.5	31.9	6.8	–	25.1	1.0	.8

Table 31. Asian or Pacific Islander Persons in Households by Relationship to Householder, Age, and Sex: 1990

[For definitions of terms and meanings of symbols, see text]

United States	All persons	Householder Total	Family householder Total	Family householder Married, spouse present	Nonfamily householder Total	Nonfamily householder Living alone	Relatives of householder Total	Relatives Spouse	Relatives Child	Relatives Other relatives	Nonrelatives In family households	Nonrelatives In nonfamily households
AGE												
All persons	7 120 735	2 013 735	1 559 043	1 265 598	454 692	328 330	4 715 174	1 462 478	2 538 730	713 966	168 994	222 832
Under 18 years	2 076 684	1 348	865	183	483	295	2 042 405	694	1 896 175	145 536	22 725	10 206
Under 6 years	710 447	–	–	–	–	–	700 480	–	639 465	61 015	6 871	3 096
6 to 14 years	1 024 182	–	–	–	–	–	1 010 637	–	952 558	58 079	8 994	4 551
15 to 17 years	342 055	1 348	865	183	483	295	331 288	694	304 152	26 442	6 860	2 559
18 and 19 years	214 936	10 737	4 040	862	6 697	2 723	185 794	2 990	158 915	23 889	8 091	10 314
20 to 24 years	576 822	108 375	42 769	19 559	65 606	31 331	374 593	50 131	250 717	73 745	25 994	67 860
25 to 29 years	676 159	218 301	130 431	96 339	87 870	54 623	373 231	173 359	123 594	76 278	29 100	55 527
30 to 34 years	718 547	297 021	228 373	190 842	68 648	49 223	367 759	256 560	55 844	55 355	23 689	30 078
35 to 44 years	1 234 115	584 616	500 029	420 778	84 587	65 463	592 370	491 795	40 697	59 878	29 398	27 731
45 to 54 years	713 888	371 877	327 700	272 809	44 177	36 125	317 532	264 331	9 469	43 732	13 482	10 997
55 to 59 years	249 266	122 189	103 492	85 084	18 697	16 241	119 357	83 461	1 778	34 118	4 475	3 245
60 to 64 years	217 015	98 555	79 338	64 438	19 217	17 252	111 777	63 061	995	47 721	4 065	2 618
65 years and over	443 303	200 716	142 006	114 704	58 710	55 054	230 356	76 096	546	153 714	7 975	4 256
65 to 74 years	297 408	132 878	99 018	80 677	33 860	31 586	156 525	61 591	510	94 424	5 191	2 814
75 to 84 years	120 008	56 008	36 590	29 438	19 418	18 321	60 721	13 238	33	47 450	2 133	1 146
85 years and over	25 887	11 830	6 398	4 589	5 432	5 147	13 110	1 267	3	11 840	651	296
Male	3 469 336	1 534 921	1 279 456	1 176 909	255 465	174 915	1 727 321	83 655	1 319 472	324 194	85 579	121 515
Under 18 years	1 059 379	763	465	117	298	187	1 042 036	25	966 368	75 643	11 363	5 217
Under 6 years	362 448	–	–	–	–	–	357 420	–	326 195	31 225	3 422	1 606
6 to 14 years	520 317	–	–	–	–	–	513 458	–	483 452	30 006	4 557	2 302
15 to 17 years	176 614	763	465	117	298	187	171 158	25	156 721	14 412	3 384	1 309
18 and 19 years	111 222	5 857	2 158	568	3 699	1 586	96 402	108	83 372	12 922	3 769	5 194
20 to 24 years	293 157	65 837	26 489	14 790	39 348	18 677	177 203	2 338	135 199	39 666	12 945	37 172
25 to 29 years	332 080	158 743	99 991	82 251	58 752	35 763	124 939	10 009	72 176	42 754	16 041	32 357
30 to 34 years	344 387	233 921	188 448	172 871	45 473	32 201	80 670	16 159	33 176	31 335	12 854	16 942
35 to 44 years	577 700	467 930	416 018	392 619	51 912	39 430	80 357	27 279	22 836	30 242	14 843	14 570
45 to 54 years	345 335	298 515	274 984	259 672	23 531	18 700	34 813	14 210	4 805	15 798	6 517	5 490
55 to 59 years	112 740	93 868	86 206	81 237	7 662	6 371	15 446	4 260	869	10 317	1 960	1 466
60 to 64 years	93 329	72 231	65 485	61 655	6 746	5 778	18 255	3 284	442	14 529	1 701	1 142
65 years and over	200 007	137 256	119 212	111 129	18 044	16 222	57 200	5 983	229	50 988	3 586	1 965
65 to 74 years	132 159	93 333	82 810	77 841	10 523	9 450	35 393	3 831	214	31 348	2 189	1 244
75 to 84 years	56 545	37 022	31 226	28 768	5 796	5 197	17 885	1 734	14	16 137	1 061	577
85 years and over	11 303	6 901	5 176	4 520	1 725	1 575	3 922	418	1	3 503	336	144
Female	3 651 399	478 814	279 587	88 689	199 227	153 415	2 987 853	1 378 823	1 219 258	389 772	83 415	101 317
Under 18 years	1 017 305	585	400	66	185	108	1 000 369	669	929 807	69 893	11 362	4 989
Under 6 years	347 999	–	–	–	–	–	343 060	–	313 270	29 790	3 449	1 490
6 to 14 years	503 865	–	–	–	–	–	497 179	–	469 106	28 073	4 437	2 249
15 to 17 years	165 441	585	400	66	185	108	160 130	669	147 431	12 030	3 476	1 250
18 and 19 years	103 714	4 880	1 882	294	2 998	1 137	89 392	2 882	75 543	10 967	4 322	5 120
20 to 24 years	283 665	42 538	16 280	4 769	26 258	12 654	197 390	47 793	115 518	34 079	13 049	30 688
25 to 29 years	344 079	59 558	30 440	14 088	29 118	18 860	248 292	163 350	51 418	33 524	13 059	23 170
30 to 34 years	374 160	63 100	39 925	17 971	23 175	17 022	287 089	240 401	22 668	24 020	10 835	13 136
35 to 44 years	656 415	116 686	84 011	28 159	32 675	26 033	512 013	464 516	17 861	29 636	14 555	13 161
45 to 54 years	368 553	73 362	52 716	13 137	20 646	17 425	282 719	250 121	4 664	27 934	6 965	5 507
55 to 59 years	136 526	28 321	17 286	3 847	11 035	9 870	103 911	79 201	909	23 801	2 515	1 779
60 to 64 years	123 686	26 324	13 853	2 783	12 471	11 474	93 522	59 777	553	33 192	2 364	1 476
65 years and over	243 296	63 460	22 794	3 575	40 666	38 832	173 156	70 113	317	102 726	4 389	2 291
65 to 74 years	165 249	39 545	16 208	2 836	23 337	22 136	121 132	57 760	296	63 076	3 002	1 570
75 to 84 years	63 463	18 986	6 364	670	13 022	13 124	42 836	11 504	19	31 313	1 072	569
85 years and over	14 584	4 929	1 222	60	3 707	3 572	9 188	849	2	8 337	315	152
PERCENT DISTRIBUTION												
All persons	100.0	28.3	21.9	17.8	6.4	4.6	66.2	20.5	35.7	10.0	2.4	3.1
Under 18 years	100.0	.1	–	–	–	–	98.3		91.3	7.0	1.1	.5
18 and 19 years	100.0	5.0	1.9	.4	3.1	1.3	86.4	1.4	73.9	11.1	3.8	4.8
20 to 24 years	100.0	18.8	7.4	3.4	11.4	5.4	64.9	8.7	43.5	12.8	4.5	11.8
25 to 29 years	100.0	32.3	19.3	14.2	13.0	8.1	55.2	25.6	18.3	11.3	4.3	8.2
30 to 34 years	100.0	41.3	31.8	26.6	9.6	6.9	51.2	35.7	7.8	7.7	3.3	4.2
35 to 44 years	100.0	47.4	40.5	34.1	6.9	5.3	48.0	39.9	3.3	4.9	2.4	2.2
45 to 54 years	100.0	52.1	45.9	38.2	6.2	5.1	44.5	37.0	1.3	6.1	1.9	1.5
55 to 59 years	100.0	49.0	41.5	34.1	7.5	6.5	47.9	33.5	.7	13.7	1.8	1.3
60 to 64 years	100.0	45.4	36.6	29.7	8.9	7.9	51.5	29.1	.5	22.0	1.9	1.2
65 years and over	100.0	45.3	32.0	25.9	13.2	12.4	52.0	17.2	.1	34.7	1.8	1.0
65 to 74 years	100.0	44.7	33.3	27.1	11.4	10.6	52.6	20.7	.2	31.7	1.7	.9
75 to 84 years	100.0	46.7	30.5	24.5	16.2	15.3	50.6	11.0	–	39.5	1.8	1.0
85 years and over	100.0	45.7	24.7	17.7	21.0	19.9	50.6	4.9	–	45.7	2.5	1.1
Male	100.0	44.2	36.9	33.9	7.4	5.0	49.8	2.4	38.0	9.3	2.5	3.5
Under 18 years	100.0	.1	–	–	–	–	98.4	–	91.2	7.1	1.1	.5
18 and 19 years	100.0	5.3	1.9	.5	3.3	1.4	86.7	.1	75.0	11.6	3.4	4.7
20 to 24 years	100.0	22.5	9.0	5.0	13.4	6.4	60.4	.8	46.1	13.5	4.4	12.7
25 to 29 years	100.0	47.8	30.1	24.8	17.7	10.8	37.6	3.0	21.7	12.9	4.8	9.7
30 to 34 years	100.0	67.9	54.7	50.2	13.2	9.4	23.4	4.7	9.6	9.1	3.7	4.9
35 to 44 years	100.0	81.0	72.0	68.0	9.0	6.8	13.9	4.7	4.0	5.2	2.6	2.5
45 to 54 years	100.0	86.4	79.6	75.2	6.8	5.4	10.1	4.1	1.4	4.6	1.9	1.6
55 to 59 years	100.0	83.3	76.5	72.1	6.8	5.7	13.7	3.8	.8	9.2	1.7	1.3
60 to 64 years	100.0	77.4	70.2	66.1	7.2	6.2	19.6	3.5	.5	15.6	1.8	1.2
65 years and over	100.0	68.6	59.6	55.6	9.0	8.1	28.6	3.0	.1	25.5	1.8	1.0
65 to 74 years	100.0	70.6	62.7	58.9	8.0	7.2	26.8	2.9	.2	23.7	1.7	.9
75 to 84 years	100.0	65.5	55.2	50.9	10.3	9.2	31.6	3.1	–	28.5	1.9	1.0
85 years and over	100.0	61.1	45.8	40.0	15.3	13.9	34.7	3.7	–	31.0	3.0	1.3
Female	100.0	13.1	7.7	2.4	5.5	4.2	81.8	37.8	33.4	10.7	2.3	2.8
Under 18 years	100.0	.1	–	–	–	–	98.3	.1	91.4	6.9	1.1	.5
18 and 19 years	100.0	4.7	1.8	.3	2.9	1.1	86.2	2.8	72.8	10.6	4.2	4.9
20 to 24 years	100.0	15.0	5.7	1.7	9.3	4.5	69.6	16.8	40.7	12.0	4.6	10.8
25 to 29 years	100.0	17.3	8.8	4.1	8.5	5.5	72.2	47.5	14.9	9.7	3.8	6.7
30 to 34 years	100.0	16.9	10.7	4.8	6.2	4.5	76.7	64.3	6.1	6.4	2.9	3.5
35 to 44 years	100.0	17.8	12.8	4.3	5.0	4.0	78.0	70.8	2.7	4.5	2.2	2.0
45 to 54 years	100.0	19.9	14.3	3.6	5.6	4.7	76.7	67.9	1.3	7.6	1.9	1.5
55 to 59 years	100.0	20.7	12.7	2.8	8.1	7.2	76.1	58.0	.7	17.4	1.8	1.3
60 to 64 years	100.0	21.3	11.2	2.3	10.1	9.3	75.6	48.3	.4	26.8	1.9	1.2
65 years and over	100.0	26.1	9.4	1.5	16.7	16.0	71.2	28.8	.1	42.2	1.8	.9
65 to 74 years	100.0	23.9	9.8	1.7	14.1	13.4	73.3	35.0	.2	38.2	1.8	1.0
75 to 84 years	100.0	29.9	8.5	1.1	21.5	20.7	67.5	18.1	–	49.3	1.7	.9
85 years and over	100.0	33.8	8.4	.5	25.4	24.5	63.0	5.8	–	57.2	2.2	1.0

Table 32. Hispanic Origin Persons in Households by Relationship to Householder, Age, and Sex: 1990

[Persons of Hispanic origin may be of any race. For definitions of terms and meanings of symbols, see text]

United States	All persons	Householder — Total	Family householder — Total	Family householder — Married, spouse present	Nonfamily householder — Total	Nonfamily householder — Living alone	Relatives of householder — Total	Relatives — Spouse	Relatives — Child	Relatives — Other relatives	Nonrelatives — In family households	Nonrelatives — In nonfamily households
AGE												
All persons	21 836 827	6 001 718	4 789 261	3 297 572	1 212 457	888 648	14 323 345	3 390 585	8 647 554	2 285 206	940 449	571 315
Under 18 years	7 713 003	8 743	6 402	2 052	2 341	1 069	7 508 444	7 938	6 699 831	800 675	136 056	59 760
Under 6 years	2 834 408	—	—	—	—	—	2 765 145	—	2 394 875	370 270	49 897	19 366
6 to 14 years	3 724 171	—	—	—	—	—	3 646 131	—	3 340 203	305 928	51 565	26 475
15 to 17 years	1 154 424	8 743	6 402	2 052	2 341	1 069	1 097 168	7 938	964 753	124 477	34 594	13 919
18 and 19 years	815 096	49 558	31 874	11 507	17 684	7 081	675 727	31 621	515 354	128 752	57 080	32 731
20 to 24 years	2 180 413	461 729	332 975	185 349	128 754	59 521	1 374 159	286 404	738 462	349 293	201 391	143 134
25 to 29 years	2 259 585	840 549	669 663	450 728	170 886	100 124	1 127 018	533 628	347 087	246 303	176 841	115 177
30 to 34 years	1 999 989	914 409	770 619	540 792	143 790	95 257	887 214	572 841	165 370	149 003	125 848	72 518
35 to 44 years	2 877 058	1 480 178	1 279 415	890 781	200 763	144 500	1 180 355	887 868	130 642	161 845	139 102	77 423
45 to 54 years	1 684 308	912 068	771 916	545 960	140 152	109 466	677 730	523 086	37 020	117 624	57 760	36 750
55 to 59 years	631 926	349 700	281 511	206 145	68 189	57 538	255 536	188 026	7 408	60 102	15 653	11 037
60 to 64 years	547 285	309 509	234 732	173 082	74 777	66 145	217 780	150 445	4 043	63 292	11 418	8 578
65 years and over	1 128 164	675 275	410 154	291 176	265 121	247 947	419 382	208 728	2 337	208 317	19 300	14 207
65 to 74 years	713 079	424 711	281 898	206 289	142 813	132 160	266 852	159 008	2 177	105 667	12 114	9 402
75 to 84 years	331 430	204 060	106 906	72 698	97 154	92 174	118 266	44 986	156	73 124	5 352	3 752
85 years and over	83 655	46 504	21 350	12 189	25 154	23 613	34 264	4 734	4	29 526	1 834	1 053
Male	10 990 595	4 132 072	3 465 108	3 035 883	666 964	445 710	5 997 297	273 253	4 515 571	1 208 473	522 525	338 701
Under 18 years	3 942 338	4 193	2 832	1 168	1 361	609	3 839 136	259	3 427 167	411 710	67 864	31 145
Under 6 years	1 446 512	—	—	—	—	—	1 411 256	—	1 222 981	188 275	25 397	9 859
6 to 14 years	1 900 261	—	—	—	—	—	1 860 889	—	1 705 011	155 878	25 994	13 378
15 to 17 years	595 565	4 193	2 832	1 168	1 361	609	566 991	259	499 175	67 557	16 473	7 908
18 and 19 years	431 348	26 507	15 900	7 389	10 607	4 113	354 880	1 444	275 711	77 725	30 472	19 489
20 to 24 years	1 163 561	303 050	218 404	156 260	84 646	37 507	654 904	22 608	411 241	221 055	116 648	88 959
25 to 29 years	1 179 433	599 722	482 663	402 993	117 059	65 705	407 133	48 229	202 069	156 835	101 051	71 527
30 to 34 years	1 020 238	662 600	561 887	494 387	100 713	64 651	242 595	50 826	96 973	94 796	70 726	44 317
35 to 44 years	1 427 576	1 058 946	921 726	824 694	137 220	96 658	243 589	71 172	75 789	96 628	79 332	45 709
45 to 54 years	811 002	644 855	565 454	510 360	79 401	59 708	112 039	38 406	20 329	53 304	33 412	20 696
55 to 59 years	296 624	244 210	212 611	195 090	31 599	25 208	37 871	12 890	3 615	21 366	8 563	5 980
60 to 64 years	250 467	208 548	178 505	164 559	30 043	25 151	31 678	10 313	1 821	19 544	5 819	4 422
65 years and over	468 008	379 441	305 126	278 533	74 315	66 400	73 472	17 106	856	55 510	8 638	6 457
65 to 74 years	309 814	257 502	213 370	196 864	44 132	38 848	42 086	11 501	798	29 787	5 749	4 477
75 to 84 years	127 905	101 197	77 551	69 820	23 646	21 536	22 955	4 609	56	18 290	2 154	1 599
85 years and over	30 289	20 742	14 205	11 849	6 537	6 016	8 431	996	2	7 433	735	381
Female	10 846 232	1 869 646	1 324 153	261 689	545 493	442 938	8 326 048	3 117 332	4 131 983	1 076 733	417 924	232 614
Under 18 years	3 770 665	4 550	3 570	884	980	460	3 669 308	7 679	3 272 664	388 965	68 192	28 615
Under 6 years	1 387 896	—	—	—	—	—	1 353 889	—	1 171 894	181 995	24 500	9 507
6 to 14 years	1 823 910	—	—	—	—	—	1 785 242	—	1 635 192	150 050	25 571	13 097
15 to 17 years	558 859	4 550	3 570	884	980	460	530 177	7 679	465 578	56 920	18 121	6 011
18 and 19 years	383 748	23 051	15 974	3 668	7 077	2 968	320 847	30 177	239 643	51 027	26 608	13 242
20 to 24 years	1 016 852	158 679	114 571	29 089	44 108	22 014	719 255	263 796	327 221	128 238	84 743	54 175
25 to 29 years	1 080 152	240 827	187 000	47 735	53 827	34 419	719 885	485 399	145 018	89 468	75 790	43 650
30 to 34 years	979 751	251 809	208 732	46 405	43 077	30 606	644 619	522 015	68 397	54 207	55 122	28 201
35 to 44 years	1 449 482	421 232	357 689	66 087	63 543	47 842	936 766	816 696	54 853	65 217	59 770	31 714
45 to 54 years	873 306	267 213	206 462	35 600	60 751	49 758	565 691	484 680	16 691	64 320	24 348	16 054
55 to 59 years	335 302	105 490	68 900	11 055	36 590	32 330	217 665	175 136	3 793	38 736	7 090	5 057
60 to 64 years	296 818	100 961	56 227	8 523	44 734	40 994	186 102	140 132	2 222	43 748	5 599	4 156
65 years and over	660 156	295 834	105 028	12 643	190 806	181 547	345 910	191 622	1 481	152 807	10 662	7 750
65 to 74 years	403 265	167 209	68 528	9 425	98 681	93 312	224 766	147 507	1 379	75 880	6 365	4 925
75 to 84 years	203 525	102 863	29 355	2 878	73 508	70 638	95 311	40 377	100	54 834	3 198	2 153
85 years and over	53 366	25 762	7 145	340	18 617	17 597	25 833	3 738	2	22 093	1 099	672
PERCENT DISTRIBUTION												
All persons	100.0	27.5	21.9	15.1	5.6	4.1	65.6	15.5	39.6	10.5	4.3	2.6
Under 18 years	100.0	.1	.1	—	—	—	97.3	.1	86.9	10.4	1.8	.8
18 and 19 years	100.0	6.1	3.9	1.4	2.2	.9	82.9	3.9	63.2	15.8	7.0	4.0
20 to 24 years	100.0	21.2	15.3	8.5	5.9	2.7	63.0	13.1	33.9	16.0	9.2	6.6
25 to 29 years	100.0	37.2	29.6	19.9	7.6	4.4	49.9	23.6	15.4	10.9	7.8	5.1
30 to 34 years	100.0	45.7	38.5	27.0	7.2	4.8	44.4	28.6	8.3	7.5	6.3	3.6
35 to 44 years	100.0	51.4	44.5	31.0	7.0	5.0	41.0	30.9	4.5	5.6	4.8	2.7
45 to 54 years	100.0	54.2	45.8	32.4	8.3	6.5	40.2	31.1	2.2	7.0	3.4	2.2
55 to 59 years	100.0	55.3	44.5	32.6	10.8	9.1	40.4	29.8	1.2	9.5	2.5	1.7
60 to 64 years	100.0	56.6	42.9	31.6	13.7	12.1	39.8	27.5	.7	11.6	2.1	1.6
65 years and over	100.0	59.9	36.4	25.8	23.5	22.0	37.2	18.5	.2	18.5	1.7	1.3
65 to 74 years	100.0	59.6	39.5	28.9	20.0	18.5	37.4	22.3	.3	14.8	1.7	1.3
75 to 84 years	100.0	61.6	32.3	21.9	29.3	27.8	35.7	13.6	—	22.1	1.6	1.1
85 years and over	100.0	55.6	25.5	14.6	30.1	28.2	41.0	5.7	—	35.3	2.2	1.3
Male	100.0	37.6	31.5	27.6	6.1	4.1	54.6	2.5	41.1	11.0	4.8	3.1
Under 18 years	100.0	.1	.1	—	—	—	97.4	—	86.9	10.4	1.7	.8
18 and 19 years	100.0	6.1	3.7	1.8	2.5	1.0	82.3	.3	63.9	18.0	7.1	4.5
20 to 24 years	100.0	26.0	18.8	13.4	7.3	3.2	56.3	1.9	35.3	19.0	10.0	7.6
25 to 29 years	100.0	50.8	40.9	34.2	9.9	5.6	34.5	4.1	17.1	13.3	8.6	6.1
30 to 34 years	100.0	64.9	55.1	48.5	9.9	6.3	23.8	5.0	9.5	9.3	6.9	4.3
35 to 44 years	100.0	74.2	64.6	57.8	9.6	6.8	17.1	5.0	5.3	6.8	5.6	3.2
45 to 54 years	100.0	79.5	69.7	62.9	9.8	7.4	13.8	4.7	2.5	6.6	4.1	2.6
55 to 59 years	100.0	82.3	71.7	65.8	10.7	8.5	12.8	4.3	1.2	7.2	2.9	2.0
60 to 64 years	100.0	83.3	71.3	65.7	12.0	10.0	12.6	4.1	.7	7.8	2.3	1.8
65 years and over	100.0	81.1	65.2	59.5	15.9	14.2	15.7	3.7	.2	11.9	1.8	1.4
65 to 74 years	100.0	83.1	68.9	63.5	14.2	12.5	13.6	3.7	.3	9.6	1.9	1.4
75 to 84 years	100.0	79.1	60.6	54.6	18.5	16.8	17.9	3.6	—	14.3	1.7	1.3
85 years and over	100.0	68.5	46.9	39.1	21.6	19.9	27.8	3.3	—	24.5	2.4	1.3
Female	100.0	17.2	12.2	2.4	5.0	4.1	76.8	28.7	38.1	9.9	3.9	2.1
Under 18 years	100.0	.1	.1	—	—	—	97.3	.2	86.8	10.3	1.8	.8
18 and 19 years	100.0	6.0	4.2	1.0	1.8	.8	83.6	7.9	62.4	13.3	6.9	3.5
20 to 24 years	100.0	15.6	11.3	2.9	4.3	2.2	70.7	25.9	32.2	12.6	8.3	5.3
25 to 29 years	100.0	22.3	17.3	4.4	5.0	3.2	66.6	44.9	13.4	8.3	7.0	4.0
30 to 34 years	100.0	25.7	21.3	4.7	4.4	3.1	65.8	53.3	7.0	5.5	5.6	2.9
35 to 44 years	100.0	29.1	24.7	4.6	4.4	3.3	64.6	56.3	3.8	4.5	4.1	2.2
45 to 54 years	100.0	30.6	23.6	4.1	7.0	5.7	64.8	55.5	1.9	7.4	2.8	1.8
55 to 59 years	100.0	31.5	20.5	3.3	10.9	9.6	64.9	52.2	1.1	11.6	2.1	1.5
60 to 64 years	100.0	34.0	18.9	2.9	15.1	13.8	62.7	47.2	.7	14.7	1.9	1.4
65 years and over	100.0	44.8	15.9	1.9	28.9	27.5	52.4	29.0	.2	23.1	1.6	1.2
65 to 74 years	100.0	41.5	17.0	2.3	24.5	23.1	55.7	36.6	.3	18.8	1.6	1.2
75 to 84 years	100.0	50.5	14.4	1.4	36.1	34.7	46.8	19.8	—	26.9	1.6	1.1
85 years and over	100.0	48.3	13.4	.6	34.9	33.0	48.4	7.0	—	41.4	2.1	1.3

Table 33. White, Not of Hispanic Origin Persons in Households by Relationship to Householder, Age, and Sex: 1990

[For definitions of terms and meanings of symbols, see text]

United States	All persons	Householder					Relatives of householder				Nonrelatives of householder	
		Total	Family householder		Nonfamily householder		Total	Spouse	Child	Other relatives	In family households	In nonfamily households
			Total	Married, spouse present	Total	Living alone						
AGE												
All persons	183 362 643	73 633 749	50 946 609	42 563 582	22 687 140	18 758 544	102 441 742	42 369 862	54 236 497	5 835 383	2 253 096	5 034 056
Under 18 years	43 675 672	30 467	17 698	9 179	12 769	7 459	42 975 325	28 219	41 012 684	1 934 422	324 365	345 515
Under 6 years	15 017 036	–	–	–	–	–	14 819 529	–	13 916 227	903 302	95 833	101 674
6 to 14 years	21 794 668	–	–	–	–	–	21 470 052	–	20 683 707	786 345	147 659	176 957
15 to 17 years	6 863 968	30 467	17 698	9 179	12 769	7 459	6 685 744	28 219	6 412 750	244 775	80 873	66 884
18 and 19 years	4 481 163	317 907	122 820	63 719	195 087	79 997	3 790 146	171 109	3 396 045	222 992	128 481	244 629
20 to 24 years	12 376 111	3 375 665	1 621 078	1 169 470	1 754 587	858 177	7 191 972	1 854 056	4 808 243	529 673	391 585	1 416 889
25 to 29 years	15 248 487	6 837 242	4 406 148	3 600 763	2 431 094	1 588 577	6 990 839	4 397 403	2 171 965	421 471	386 468	1 033 938
30 to 34 years	16 128 604	8 270 904	6 122 958	5 105 681	2 147 946	1 600 233	6 962 175	5 553 844	1 134 893	273 438	305 216	590 309
35 to 44 years	28 780 489	15 887 702	12 612 142	10 390 396	3 275 560	2 617 898	11 858 782	10 417 585	1 114 693	326 504	374 853	659 152
45 to 54 years	19 963 321	11 382 028	9 093 773	7 689 500	2 288 255	1 924 717	8 088 130	7 412 761	400 947	274 422	163 926	329 237
55 to 59 years	8 503 245	4 930 580	3 807 047	3 319 998	1 123 533	1 004 026	3 423 557	3 161 809	96 590	165 158	44 113	104 995
60 to 64 years	8 761 965	5 246 183	3 811 390	3 332 619	1 434 793	1 327 749	3 384 900	3 106 052	61 525	217 323	36 631	94 251
65 years and over	25 443 586	17 355 071	9 331 555	7 882 257	8 023 516	7 749 711	7 775 916	6 267 024	38 912	1 469 980	97 458	215 141
65 to 74 years	15 254 619	9 894 863	6 188 263	5 371 050	3 706 600	3 546 694	5 178 552	4 597 586	36 318	544 648	49 449	131 755
75 to 84 years	8 188 178	5 980 518	2 687 392	2 204 287	3 293 126	3 207 950	2 111 922	1 522 620	2 539	586 763	31 244	64 494
85 years and over	2 000 789	1 479 690	455 900	306 920	1 023 790	995 067	485 442	146 818	55	338 569	16 765	18 892
Male	89 261 010	51 493 891	41 726 664	39 655 915	9 767 227	7 411 319	34 178 756	2 890 623	28 715 256	2 572 877	1 164 340	2 424 023
Under 18 years	22 429 290	14 850	9 380	6 747	5 470	3 244	22 090 147	879	21 102 269	986 999	156 416	167 877
Under 6 years	7 711 429	–	–	–	–	–	7 612 250	–	7 151 341	460 909	48 407	50 772
6 to 14 years	11 196 052	–	–	–	–	–	11 034 789	–	10 633 982	400 807	73 632	87 631
15 to 17 years	3 521 809	14 850	9 380	6 747	5 470	3 244	3 443 108	879	3 316 946	125 283	34 377	29 474
18 and 19 years	2 276 466	159 439	65 295	47 747	94 144	39 982	1 967 313	5 960	1 844 396	116 957	51 886	97 828
20 to 24 years	6 132 597	2 123 142	1 137 830	1 001 467	985 312	480 885	3 150 093	107 831	2 746 824	295 438	181 188	678 174
25 to 29 years	7 579 864	4 943 279	3 442 733	3 219 618	1 500 546	959 307	1 907 489	323 201	1 335 067	249 221	203 149	525 947
30 to 34 years	8 016 795	6 278 966	4 918 033	4 671 014	1 360 933	995 312	1 276 705	408 875	702 792	165 038	167 513	293 611
35 to 44 years	14 308 394	12 217 336	10 210 612	9 677 071	2 006 724	1 578 785	1 560 221	705 684	671 351	183 186	214 687	316 150
45 to 54 years	9 822 217	8 763 836	7 612 546	7 236 866	1 151 290	937 261	806 645	464 156	222 636	119 853	98 815	152 921
55 to 59 years	4 102 660	3 719 519	3 262 834	3 140 628	456 685	388 866	304 494	195 320	48 219	60 949	26 691	51 956
60 to 64 years	4 120 300	3 758 677	3 273 743	3 160 732	484 934	426 658	293 598	192 699	27 854	73 045	21 392	46 633
65 years and over	10 472 427	9 514 847	7 793 668	7 494 025	1 721 189	1 601 019	822 051	486 012	13 848	322 191	42 603	92 926
65 to 74 years	6 735 522	6 176 979	5 271 506	5 097 007	905 473	827 824	471 202	311 464	13 283	146 455	26 091	61 250
75 to 84 years	3 125 521	2 820 627	2 196 676	2 100 526	623 951	590 050	267 026	148 697	556	117 773	12 144	25 724
85 years and over	611 384	517 241	325 476	296 492	191 765	183 145	83 823	25 851	9	57 963	4 368	5 952
Female	94 101 633	22 139 858	9 219 945	2 907 667	12 919 913	11 347 225	68 262 986	39 479 239	25 521 241	3 262 506	1 088 756	2 610 033
Under 18 years	21 246 382	15 617	8 318	2 432	7 299	4 215	20 885 178	27 340	19 910 415	947 423	167 949	177 638
Under 6 years	7 305 607	–	–	–	–	–	7 207 279	–	6 764 886	442 393	47 426	50 902
6 to 14 years	10 598 616	–	–	–	–	–	10 435 263	–	10 049 725	385 538	74 027	89 326
15 to 17 years	3 342 159	15 617	8 318	2 432	7 299	4 215	3 242 636	27 340	3 095 804	119 492	46 496	37 410
18 and 19 years	2 204 697	158 468	57 525	15 972	100 943	40 015	1 822 833	165 149	1 551 649	106 035	76 595	146 801
20 to 24 years	6 243 514	1 252 523	483 248	168 003	769 275	377 292	4 041 879	1 746 225	2 061 419	234 235	210 397	738 715
25 to 29 years	7 668 623	1 893 963	963 415	381 145	930 548	629 270	5 083 350	4 074 202	836 898	172 250	183 319	507 991
30 to 34 years	8 111 809	1 991 938	1 204 925	434 067	787 013	604 921	5 685 470	5 144 969	432 101	108 400	137 703	296 698
35 to 44 years	14 472 095	3 670 366	2 401 530	713 325	1 268 836	1 039 113	10 298 561	9 711 901	443 342	143 318	160 166	343 002
45 to 54 years	10 141 104	2 618 192	1 481 227	452 634	1 136 965	987 456	7 281 485	6 948 605	178 311	154 569	65 111	176 316
55 to 59 years	4 400 585	1 211 061	544 213	179 370	666 848	615 160	3 119 063	2 966 483	48 371	104 209	17 422	53 039
60 to 64 years	4 641 665	1 487 506	537 647	171 887	949 859	901 091	3 091 302	2 913 353	33 671	144 278	15 239	47 618
65 years and over	14 971 159	7 840 224	1 537 897	388 232	6 302 327	6 148 692	6 953 865	5 781 012	25 064	1 147 789	54 855	122 215
65 to 74 years	8 519 097	3 717 884	916 757	274 043	2 801 127	2 718 870	4 707 350	4 286 122	23 035	398 193	23 358	70 505
75 to 84 years	5 062 657	3 159 891	490 716	103 761	2 669 175	2 617 000	1 844 090	1 373 923	1 983	468 990	19 100	38 770
85 years and over	1 389 405	962 449	130 424	10 428	832 026	811 022	401 619	120 967	46	280 606	12 397	12 940
PERCENT DISTRIBUTION												
All persons	100.0	40.2	27.8	23.2	12.4	10.2	55.9	23.1	29.6	3.2	1.2	2.7
Under 18 years	100.0	.1	–	–	–	–	98.4	.1	93.9	4.4	.7	.8
18 and 19 years	100.0	7.1	2.7	1.4	4.4	1.8	84.6	3.8	75.8	5.0	2.9	5.5
20 to 24 years	100.0	27.3	13.1	9.4	14.2	6.9	58.1	15.0	38.9	4.3	3.2	11.4
25 to 29 years	100.0	44.8	28.9	23.6	15.9	10.4	45.8	28.8	14.2	2.8	2.5	6.8
30 to 34 years	100.0	51.3	38.0	31.7	13.3	9.9	43.2	34.4	7.0	1.7	1.9	3.7
35 to 44 years	100.0	55.2	43.8	36.1	11.4	9.1	41.2	36.2	3.9	1.1	1.3	2.3
45 to 54 years	100.0	57.0	45.6	38.5	11.5	9.6	40.5	37.1	2.0	1.4	.8	1.6
55 to 59 years	100.0	58.0	44.8	39.0	13.2	11.8	40.3	37.2	1.1	1.9	.5	1.2
60 to 64 years	100.0	59.9	43.5	38.0	16.4	15.2	38.6	35.4	.7	2.5	.4	1.1
65 years and over	100.0	68.2	36.7	31.0	31.5	30.5	30.6	24.6	.2	5.8	.4	.8
65 to 74 years	100.0	64.9	40.6	35.2	24.3	23.2	33.9	30.1	.2	3.6	.3	.9
75 to 84 years	100.0	73.0	32.8	26.9	40.2	39.2	25.8	18.6	–	7.2	.4	.8
85 years and over	100.0	74.0	22.8	15.3	51.2	49.7	24.3	7.3	–	16.9	.8	.9
Male	100.0	57.7	46.7	44.4	10.9	8.3	38.3	3.2	32.2	2.9	1.3	2.7
Under 18 years	100.0	.1	–	–	–	–	98.5	–	94.1	4.4	.7	.7
18 and 19 years	100.0	7.0	2.9	2.1	4.1	1.8	86.4	.3	81.0	5.1	2.3	4.3
20 to 24 years	100.0	34.6	18.6	16.3	16.1	7.8	51.4	1.8	44.8	4.8	3.0	11.1
25 to 29 years	100.0	65.2	45.4	42.5	19.8	12.7	25.2	4.3	17.6	3.3	2.7	6.9
30 to 34 years	100.0	78.3	61.3	58.3	17.0	12.4	15.9	5.1	8.8	2.1	2.1	3.7
35 to 44 years	100.0	85.4	71.4	67.6	14.0	11.0	10.9	4.9	4.7	1.3	1.5	2.2
45 to 54 years	100.0	89.2	77.5	73.7	11.7	9.5	8.2	4.7	2.3	1.2	1.0	1.6
55 to 59 years	100.0	90.7	79.5	76.6	11.1	9.5	7.4	4.8	1.2	1.5	.7	1.3
60 to 64 years	100.0	91.2	79.5	76.7	11.8	10.4	7.1	4.7	.7	1.8	.5	1.1
65 years and over	100.0	90.9	74.4	71.6	16.4	15.3	7.8	4.6	.1	3.1	.4	.9
65 to 74 years	100.0	91.7	78.3	75.7	13.4	12.3	7.0	4.6	.2	2.2	.4	.9
75 to 84 years	100.0	90.2	70.3	67.2	20.0	18.9	8.5	4.8	–	3.8	.4	.8
85 years and over	100.0	84.6	53.2	48.5	31.4	30.0	13.7	4.2	–	9.5	.7	1.0
Female	100.0	23.5	9.8	3.1	13.7	12.1	72.5	42.0	27.1	3.5	1.2	2.8
Under 18 years	100.0	.1	–	–	–	–	98.3	.1	93.7	4.5	.8	.8
18 and 19 years	100.0	7.2	2.6	.7	4.6	1.8	82.7	7.5	70.4	4.8	3.5	6.7
20 to 24 years	100.0	20.1	7.7	2.7	12.3	6.0	64.7	28.0	33.0	3.8	3.4	11.8
25 to 29 years	100.0	24.7	12.6	5.0	12.1	8.2	66.3	53.1	10.9	2.2	2.4	6.6
30 to 34 years	100.0	24.6	14.9	5.4	9.7	7.5	70.1	63.4	5.3	1.3	1.7	3.7
35 to 44 years	100.0	25.4	16.6	4.9	8.8	7.2	71.2	67.1	3.1	1.0	1.1	2.4
45 to 54 years	100.0	25.8	14.6	4.5	11.2	9.7	71.8	68.5	1.8	1.5	.6	1.7
55 to 59 years	100.0	27.5	12.4	4.1	15.2	14.0	70.9	67.4	1.1	2.4	.4	1.2
60 to 64 years	100.0	32.0	11.6	3.7	20.5	19.4	66.6	62.8	.7	3.1	.3	1.0
65 years and over	100.0	52.4	10.3	2.6	42.1	41.1	46.4	38.6	.2	7.7	.4	.8
65 to 74 years	100.0	43.6	10.8	3.2	32.9	31.9	55.3	50.3	.3	4.7	.3	.8
75 to 84 years	100.0	62.4	9.7	2.0	52.7	51.7	36.4	27.1	–	9.3	.4	.8
85 years and over	100.0	69.3	9.4	.8	59.9	58.4	28.9	8.7	–	20.2	.9	.9

Table 34. Persons 15 Years and Over by Marital Status, Age, Sex, Race, and Hispanic Origin: 1990

[For definitions of terms and meanings of symbols, see text]

United States

	Males 15 years and over						Females 15 years and over					
	Total	Never married	Now married, except separated	Separated	Widowed	Divorced	Total	Never married	Now married, except separated	Separated	Widowed	Divorced
TOTAL												
Age												
15 years and over	93 817 315	28 804 618	53 781 245	1 896 397	2 377 589	6 957 466	101 324 687	23 755 235	53 144 096	2 676 840	12 121 939	9 626 577
15 to 17 years	5 162 175	5 108 499	42 319	4 983	1 584	4 790	4 874 386	4 762 086	92 808	8 485	4 439	6 568
18 and 19 years	3 940 523	3 786 268	135 388	9 567	2 098	7 202	3 776 931	3 399 406	328 272	24 784	5 619	18 850
20 to 24 years	9 675 596	7 622 622	1 794 993	104 121	6 471	147 389	9 344 716	6 032 648	2 792 767	209 254	18 346	291 701
25 to 29 years	10 695 936	4 924 494	4 923 920	241 725	12 167	593 630	10 617 109	3 400 696	5 936 405	385 669	42 091	852 248
30 to 34 years	10 876 933	2 855 846	6 719 234	300 180	20 250	981 423	10 985 954	2 002 228	7 206 307	442 850	78 946	1 255 623
35 to 44 years	18 594 227	2 493 033	13 228 554	542 942	71 894	2 257 804	18 984 676	1 904 185	13 110 582	747 333	304 050	2 918 526
45 to 54 years	12 325 335	838 551	9 533 674	330 459	134 155	1 488 496	12 897 751	719 994	9 060 712	428 274	665 565	2 023 206
55 to 59 years	5 034 370	280 511	4 037 127	109 312	126 670	480 750	5 497 386	251 599	3 774 291	139 383	658 724	673 389
60 to 64 years	4 947 047	275 901	3 967 364	92 372	220 798	390 612	5 669 120	256 449	3 623 934	110 965	1 118 169	559 603
65 years and over	12 565 173	618 893	9 398 672	160 736	1 781 502	605 370	18 676 658	1 025 944	7 218 018	179 843	9 225 990	1 026 863
65 to 74 years	7 941 613	392 314	6 287 518	113 819	701 651	446 311	10 164 945	489 966	5 253 888	129 986	3 587 808	703 297
75 to 84 years	3 765 862	181 886	2 674 385	39 825	732 438	137 328	6 289 246	379 334	1 768 765	42 309	3 832 368	266 470
85 years and over	857 698	44 693	436 769	7 092	347 413	21 731	2 222 467	156 644	195 365	7 548	1 805 814	57 096
Percent Distribution												
15 years and over	100.0	30.7	57.3	2.0	2.5	7.4	100.0	23.4	52.4	2.6	12.0	9.5
15 to 17 years	100.0	99.0	.8	.1	–	.1	100.0	97.7	1.9	.2	.1	.1
18 and 19 years	100.0	96.1	3.4	.2	.1	.2	100.0	90.0	8.7	.7	.1	.5
20 to 24 years	100.0	78.8	18.6	1.1	.1	1.5	100.0	64.6	29.9	2.2	.2	3.1
25 to 29 years	100.0	46.0	46.0	2.3	.1	5.6	100.0	32.0	55.9	3.6	.4	8.0
30 to 34 years	100.0	26.3	61.8	2.8	.2	9.0	100.0	18.2	65.6	4.0	.7	11.4
35 to 44 years	100.0	13.4	71.1	2.9	.4	12.1	100.0	10.0	69.1	3.9	1.6	15.4
45 to 54 years	100.0	6.8	77.4	2.7	1.1	12.1	100.0	5.6	70.3	3.3	5.2	15.7
55 to 59 years	100.0	5.6	80.2	2.2	2.5	9.5	100.0	4.6	68.7	2.5	12.0	12.2
60 to 64 years	100.0	5.6	80.2	1.9	4.5	7.9	100.0	4.5	63.9	2.0	19.7	9.9
65 years and over	100.0	4.9	74.8	1.3	14.2	4.8	100.0	5.5	38.6	1.0	49.4	5.5
65 to 74 years	100.0	4.9	79.2	1.4	8.8	5.6	100.0	4.8	51.7	1.3	35.3	6.9
75 to 84 years	100.0	4.8	71.0	1.1	19.4	3.6	100.0	6.0	28.1	.7	60.9	4.2
85 years and over	100.0	5.2	50.9	.8	40.5	2.5	100.0	7.0	8.8	.3	81.3	2.6
WHITE												
Age												
15 years and over	76 874 142	21 578 604	46 372 679	1 181 969	1 955 833	5 785 057	82 692 612	17 175 748	45 931 802	1 525 724	10 279 559	7 779 779
15 to 17 years	3 868 387	3 832 943	29 067	2 380	818	3 179	3 640 526	3 559 361	68 430	5 081	2 952	4 702
18 and 19 years	2 977 184	2 859 815	104 653	6 081	1 224	5 411	2 856 606	2 553 819	264 840	18 152	3 954	15 841
20 to 24 years	7 388 380	5 747 631	1 438 387	72 608	3 741	126 013	7 135 532	4 436 391	2 291 653	145 084	12 528	249 876
25 to 29 years	8 384 815	3 639 210	4 071 386	161 981	7 750	504 488	8 253 729	2 312 627	4 959 343	242 970	29 387	709 402
30 to 34 years	8 699 545	2 066 357	5 607 311	189 860	13 797	822 220	8 651 968	1 287 398	6 054 992	254 194	53 180	1 002 204
35 to 44 years	15 281 360	1 834 420	11 201 537	334 083	49 114	1 862 206	15 306 636	1 249 773	11 149 892	410 486	199 355	2 297 130
45 to 54 years	10 393 967	629 879	8 232 405	201 181	95 284	1 235 218	10 696 607	491 672	7 883 200	225 157	472 731	1 623 847
55 to 59 years	4 330 811	218 498	3 555 575	64 033	95 158	397 547	4 637 605	183 834	3 341 688	69 450	500 692	541 941
60 to 64 years	4 334 784	223 469	3 559 405	53 986	172 817	325 107	4 876 339	201 123	3 265 523	56 031	894 137	459 525
65 years and over	11 214 909	526 382	8 572 953	95 776	1 516 130	503 668	16 637 064	899 750	6 652 241	99 119	8 110 643	875 311
65 to 74 years	7 068 958	329 574	5 723 507	66 627	577 846	371 404	8 957 243	413 371	4 828 504	69 667	3 052 569	593 132
75 to 84 years	3 381 501	158 520	2 452 577	24 785	631 144	114 475	5 656 219	341 597	1 643 216	24 802	3 415 057	231 547
85 years and over	764 450	38 288	396 869	4 364	307 140	17 789	2 023 602	144 782	180 521	4 650	1 643 017	50 632
Percent Distribution												
15 years and over	100.0	28.1	60.3	1.5	2.5	7.5	100.0	20.8	55.5	1.8	12.4	9.4
15 to 17 years	100.0	99.1	.8	.1	–	.1	100.0	97.8	1.9	.1	.1	.1
18 and 19 years	100.0	96.1	3.5	.2	–	.2	100.0	89.4	9.3	.6	.1	.6
20 to 24 years	100.0	77.8	19.5	1.0	.1	1.7	100.0	62.2	32.1	2.0	.2	3.5
25 to 29 years	100.0	43.4	48.6	1.9	.1	6.0	100.0	28.0	60.1	2.9	.4	8.6
30 to 34 years	100.0	23.8	64.5	2.2	.2	9.5	100.0	14.9	70.0	2.9	.6	11.6
35 to 44 years	100.0	12.0	73.3	2.2	.3	12.2	100.0	8.2	72.8	2.7	1.3	15.0
45 to 54 years	100.0	6.1	79.2	1.9	.9	11.9	100.0	4.6	73.7	2.1	4.4	15.2
55 to 59 years	100.0	5.0	82.1	1.5	2.2	9.2	100.0	4.0	72.1	1.5	10.8	11.7
60 to 64 years	100.0	5.2	82.1	1.2	4.0	7.5	100.0	4.1	67.0	1.1	18.3	9.4
65 years and over	100.0	4.7	76.4	.9	13.5	4.5	100.0	5.4	40.0	.6	48.8	5.3
65 to 74 years	100.0	4.7	81.0	.9	8.2	5.3	100.0	4.6	53.9	.8	34.1	6.6
75 to 84 years	100.0	4.7	72.5	.7	18.7	3.4	100.0	6.0	29.1	.4	60.4	4.1
85 years and over	100.0	5.0	51.9	.6	40.2	2.3	100.0	7.2	8.9	.2	81.2	2.5
BLACK												
Age												
15 years and over	10 096 983	4 481 750	3 888 986	553 921	332 048	840 278	11 830 476	4 526 232	3 660 332	883 141	1 407 003	1 353 768
15 to 17 years	776 329	764 704	8 258	1 793	454	1 120	749 485	735 098	10 110	2 038	1 018	1 221
18 and 19 years	565 934	548 532	13 674	2 087	531	1 110	566 745	537 576	22 786	3 617	1 172	1 594
20 to 24 years	1 258 626	1 070 532	155 366	19 727	1 486	11 515	1 320 327	1 045 513	207 374	40 935	3 371	23 134
25 to 29 years	1 285 760	782 537	391 721	55 769	2 679	53 054	1 422 005	784 413	436 333	103 036	7 774	90 449
30 to 34 years	1 250 610	533 207	526 924	82 615	4 218	103 646	1 431 114	551 216	542 049	144 551	16 873	176 425
35 to 44 years	1 948 711	470 018	1 016 826	163 421	16 529	281 117	2 264 117	507 203	960 598	262 541	74 165	459 610
45 to 54 years	1 174 417	154 171	697 340	103 707	29 657	189 542	1 410 360	172 931	633 620	160 387	141 987	301 435
55 to 59 years	456 919	46 798	283 186	37 469	24 686	64 780	575 830	50 873	251 198	55 791	117 630	100 338
60 to 64 years	414 245	40 155	250 944	32 406	38 571	52 169	547 374	41 726	216 589	44 228	167 767	77 064
65 years and over	965 432	70 296	544 747	54 927	213 237	82 225	1 543 119	99 683	379 675	66 017	875 246	122 498
65 to 74 years	617 641	48 103	367 806	40 257	100 531	60 944	885 819	59 133	278 488	49 076	410 926	88 196
75 to 84 years	279 199	17 609	149 660	12 481	81 178	18 271	495 709	30 555	90 091	14 435	331 773	28 855
85 years and over	68 592	4 584	27 281	2 189	31 528	3 010	161 591	9 995	11 096	2 506	132 547	5 447

Table 34. Persons 15 Years and Over by Marital Status, Age, Sex, Race, and Hispanic Origin: 1990—Con.

[For definitions of terms and meanings of symbols, see text]

United States

	Males 15 years and over						Females 15 years and over					
	Total	Never married	Now married, except separated	Separated	Widowed	Divorced	Total	Never married	Now married, except separated	Separated	Widowed	Divorced

BLACK—Con.

Percent Distribution

	Total	Never married	Now married, except separated	Separated	Widowed	Divorced	Total	Never married	Now married, except separated	Separated	Widowed	Divorced
15 years and over	100.0	44.4	38.5	5.5	3.3	8.3	100.0	38.3	30.9	7.5	11.9	11.4
15 to 17 years	100.0	98.5	1.1	.2	.1	.1	100.0	98.1	1.3	.3	.1	.2
18 and 19 years	100.0	96.9	2.4	.4	.1	.2	100.0	94.9	4.0	.6	.2	.3
20 to 24 years	100.0	85.1	12.3	1.6	.1	.9	100.0	79.2	15.7	3.1	.3	1.8
25 to 29 years	100.0	60.9	30.5	4.3	.2	4.1	100.0	55.2	30.7	7.2	.5	6.4
30 to 34 years	100.0	42.6	42.1	6.6	.3	8.3	100.0	38.5	37.9	10.1	1.2	12.3
35 to 44 years	100.0	24.2	52.2	8.4	.8	14.4	100.0	22.4	42.4	11.6	3.3	20.3
45 to 54 years	100.0	13.1	59.4	8.8	2.5	16.1	100.0	12.3	44.9	11.4	10.1	21.4
55 to 59 years	100.0	10.2	62.0	8.2	5.4	14.2	100.0	8.8	43.6	9.7	20.4	17.4
60 to 64 years	100.0	9.7	60.6	7.8	9.3	12.6	100.0	7.6	39.6	8.1	30.6	14.1
65 years and over	100.0	7.3	56.4	5.7	22.1	8.5	100.0	6.5	24.6	4.3	56.7	7.9
65 to 74 years	100.0	7.8	59.6	6.5	16.3	9.9	100.0	6.7	31.4	5.5	46.4	10.0
75 to 84 years	100.0	6.3	53.6	4.5	29.1	6.5	100.0	6.2	18.2	2.9	66.9	5.8
85 years and over	100.0	6.7	39.8	3.2	46.0	4.4	100.0	6.2	6.9	1.6	82.0	3.4

AMERICAN INDIAN, ESKIMO, OR ALEUT

Age

	Total	Never married	Now married, except separated	Separated	Widowed	Divorced	Total	Never married	Now married, except separated	Separated	Widowed	Divorced
15 years and over	667 623	258 558	305 865	19 694	15 279	68 227	702 215	208 846	313 686	29 119	60 835	89 729
15 to 17 years	55 312	54 699	415	88	27	83	52 259	50 998	1 009	128	33	91
18 and 19 years	37 746	35 841	1 613	147	37	108	35 199	30 902	3 668	324	47	258
20 to 24 years	85 043	65 054	16 403	1 467	146	1 973	80 506	49 847	24 192	2 591	272	3 604
25 to 29 years	87 474	42 424	35 314	2 905	235	6 596	88 103	30 828	42 544	4 764	613	9 354
30 to 34 years	82 744	24 753	43 734	3 257	340	10 660	87 924	18 885	49 073	5 129	1 189	13 648
35 to 44 years	133 788	21 218	82 864	5 630	1 006	23 070	142 548	16 289	84 898	8 061	4 148	29 152
45 to 54 years	83 881	7 528	57 318	3 125	1 646	14 264	89 650	5 574	53 914	4 413	7 103	18 646
55 to 59 years	29 354	2 200	20 727	1 042	1 261	4 124	32 465	1 622	18 653	1 359	5 411	5 420
60 to 64 years	24 192	1 805	16 856	774	1 695	3 062	27 197	1 212	13 992	954	7 134	3 905
65 years and over	48 089	3 036	30 621	1 259	8 886	4 287	66 364	2 689	21 743	1 396	34 885	5 651
65 to 74 years	31 798	2 063	21 490	898	4 116	3 231	40 182	1 620	16 471	1 026	16 901	4 164
75 to 84 years	13 017	760	7 726	294	3 337	900	20 251	845	4 736	320	13 089	1 261
85 years and over	3 274	213	1 405	67	1 433	156	5 931	224	536	50	4 895	226

Percent Distribution

	Total	Never married	Now married, except separated	Separated	Widowed	Divorced	Total	Never married	Now married, except separated	Separated	Widowed	Divorced
15 years and over	100.0	38.7	45.8	2.9	2.3	10.2	100.0	29.7	44.7	4.1	8.7	12.8
15 to 17 years	100.0	98.9	.8	.2	–	.2	100.0	97.6	1.9	.2	.1	.2
18 and 19 years	100.0	95.0	4.3	.4	.1	.3	100.0	87.8	10.4	.9	.1	.7
20 to 24 years	100.0	76.5	19.3	1.7	.2	2.3	100.0	61.9	30.0	3.2	.3	4.5
25 to 29 years	100.0	48.5	40.4	3.3	.3	7.5	100.0	35.0	48.3	5.4	.7	10.6
30 to 34 years	100.0	29.9	52.9	3.9	.4	12.9	100.0	21.5	55.8	5.8	1.4	15.5
35 to 44 years	100.0	15.9	61.9	4.2	.8	17.2	100.0	11.4	59.6	6.7	2.9	20.5
45 to 54 years	100.0	9.0	68.3	3.7	2.0	17.0	100.0	6.2	60.1	4.9	7.9	20.8
55 to 59 years	100.0	7.5	70.6	3.5	4.3	14.0	100.0	5.0	57.5	4.2	16.7	16.7
60 to 64 years	100.0	7.5	69.7	3.2	7.0	12.7	100.0	4.5	51.4	3.5	26.2	14.4
65 years and over	100.0	6.3	63.7	2.6	18.5	8.9	100.0	4.1	32.8	2.1	52.6	8.5
65 to 74 years	100.0	6.5	67.6	2.8	12.9	10.2	100.0	4.0	41.0	2.6	42.1	10.4
75 to 84 years	100.0	5.8	59.4	2.3	25.6	6.9	100.0	4.2	23.4	1.6	64.6	6.2
85 years and over	100.0	6.5	42.9	2.0	43.8	4.8	100.0	3.8	9.0	.8	82.5	3.8

ASIAN OR PACIFIC ISLANDER

Age

	Total	Never married	Now married, except separated	Separated	Widowed	Divorced	Total	Never married	Now married, except separated	Separated	Widowed	Divorced
15 years and over	2 673 734	1 021 395	1 499 565	35 914	35 088	81 772	2 862 398	789 782	1 680 315	51 857	205 178	135 266
15 to 17 years	178 960	177 522	1 075	200	58	105	166 897	164 309	2 121	209	134	124
18 and 19 years	133 457	130 754	2 304	228	62	109	124 447	117 746	5 989	348	141	223
20 to 24 years	325 982	292 649	30 404	1 442	189	1 298	306 276	227 305	72 584	2 779	592	3 016
25 to 29 years	342 628	205 708	126 756	3 586	304	6 274	348 441	120 520	210 228	5 832	1 122	10 739
30 to 34 years	349 807	103 388	228 529	5 368	513	12 009	376 376	60 568	286 343	7 902	2 536	19 027
35 to 44 years	583 314	72 402	468 743	10 882	1 882	29 405	658 698	56 666	526 942	15 521	11 496	48 073
45 to 54 years	347 491	18 767	301 171	7 013	3 116	17 424	369 750	21 711	288 575	8 996	21 308	29 160
55 to 59 years	113 509	5 614	98 447	2 003	2 316	5 129	137 124	6 496	99 322	3 135	18 673	9 498
60 to 64 years	94 139	4 872	80 436	1 670	3 430	3 731	124 378	5 200	81 111	2 766	28 054	7 247
65 years and over	204 447	9 719	161 700	3 522	23 218	6 288	250 011	9 261	107 100	4 369	121 122	8 159
65 to 74 years	133 818	6 169	111 194	2 289	10 010	4 156	166 913	6 587	86 151	3 360	64 493	6 322
75 to 84 years	58 230	2 705	43 365	1 029	9 390	1 741	65 759	2 190	19 160	908	41 935	1 566
85 years and over	12 399	845	7 141	204	3 818	391	17 339	484	1 789	101	14 694	271

Percent Distribution

	Total	Never married	Now married, except separated	Separated	Widowed	Divorced	Total	Never married	Now married, except separated	Separated	Widowed	Divorced
15 years and over	100.0	38.2	56.1	1.3	1.3	3.1	100.0	27.6	58.7	1.8	7.2	4.7
15 to 17 years	100.0	99.2	.6	.1	–	.1	100.0	98.4	1.3	.1	.1	.1
18 and 19 years	100.0	98.0	1.7	.2	–	.1	100.0	94.6	4.8	.3	.1	.2
20 to 24 years	100.0	89.8	9.3	.4	.1	.4	100.0	74.2	23.7	.9	.2	1.0
25 to 29 years	100.0	60.0	37.0	1.0	.1	1.8	100.0	34.6	60.3	1.7	.3	3.1
30 to 34 years	100.0	29.6	65.3	1.5	.1	3.4	100.0	16.1	76.1	2.1	.7	5.1
35 to 44 years	100.0	12.4	80.4	1.9	.3	5.0	100.0	8.6	80.0	2.4	1.7	7.3
45 to 54 years	100.0	5.4	86.7	2.0	.9	5.0	100.0	5.9	78.0	2.4	5.8	7.9
55 to 59 years	100.0	4.9	86.7	1.8	2.0	4.5	100.0	4.7	72.4	2.3	13.6	6.9
60 to 64 years	100.0	5.2	85.4	1.8	3.6	4.0	100.0	4.2	65.2	2.2	22.6	5.8
65 years and over	100.0	4.8	79.1	1.7	11.4	3.1	100.0	3.7	42.8	1.7	48.4	3.3
65 to 74 years	100.0	4.6	83.1	1.7	7.5	3.1	100.0	3.9	51.6	2.0	38.6	3.8
75 to 84 years	100.0	4.6	74.5	1.8	16.1	3.0	100.0	3.3	29.1	1.4	63.8	2.4
85 years and over	100.0	6.8	57.6	1.6	30.8	3.2	100.0	2.8	10.3	.6	84.7	1.6

Table 34. Persons 15 Years and Over by Marital Status, Age, Sex, Race, and Hispanic Origin: 1990 — Con.

[For definitions of terms and meanings of symbols, see text]

United States	Males 15 years and over						Females 15 years and over					
	Total	Never married	Now married, except separated	Separated	Widowed	Divorced	Total	Never married	Now married, except separated	Separated	Widowed	Divorced
HISPANIC ORIGIN (OF ANY RACE)												
Age												
15 years and over	8 027 749	3 182 556	4 019 205	234 293	115 417	476 278	7 743 317	2 314 256	3 823 012	387 012	526 640	692 397
15 to 17 years	610 854	601 128	7 485	1 052	488	701	563 653	538 443	21 531	1 976	748	955
18 and 19 years	473 039	443 782	25 641	2 019	534	1 063	406 411	339 791	59 079	4 677	764	2 100
20 to 24 years	1 261 500	931 841	295 311	17 686	1 853	14 809	1 042 941	586 722	390 520	34 900	3 337	27 462
25 to 29 years	1 250 358	554 953	602 495	36 330	2 540	54 040	1 090 881	331 945	618 511	58 400	6 591	75 434
30 to 34 years	1 074 457	289 482	663 151	40 396	3 057	78 371	987 846	185 048	624 303	63 493	11 092	103 910
35 to 44 years	1 486 329	221 137	1 038 302	64 230	7 647	155 013	1 450 665	168 246	946 316	103 524	32 893	207 686
45 to 54 years	832 476	71 543	623 845	36 375	10 705	90 008	877 423	68 580	560 527	60 525	53 139	134 652
55 to 59 years	302 371	20 942	232 590	11 952	8 274	28 613	336 937	23 510	203 255	20 877	42 594	46 701
60 to 64 years	254 956	17 145	194 330	9 403	11 975	22 103	298 686	20 853	164 326	16 032	60 286	37 189
65 years and over	481 409	30 603	336 055	14 850	68 344	31 557	679 874	51 118	234 644	22 608	315 196	56 308
65 to 74 years	315 383	20 381	232 733	10 486	28 802	22 981	407 646	30 179	176 810	16 973	143 355	40 329
75 to 84 years	132 529	8 069	86 848	3 687	26 717	7 208	211 161	16 230	51 936	4 960	124 367	13 668
85 years and over	33 497	2 153	16 474	677	12 825	1 368	61 067	4 709	5 898	675	47 474	2 311
Percent Distribution												
15 years and over	**100.0**	**39.6**	**50.1**	**2.9**	**1.4**	**5.9**	**100.0**	**29.9**	**49.4**	**5.0**	**6.8**	**8.9**
15 to 17 years	100.0	98.4	1.2	.2	.1	.1	100.0	95.5	3.8	.4	.1	.2
18 and 19 years	100.0	93.8	5.4	.4	.1	.2	100.0	83.6	14.5	1.2	.2	.5
20 to 24 years	100.0	73.9	23.4	1.4	.1	1.2	100.0	56.3	37.4	3.3	.3	2.6
25 to 29 years	100.0	44.4	48.2	2.9	.2	4.3	100.0	30.4	56.7	5.4	.6	6.9
30 to 34 years	100.0	26.9	61.7	3.8	.3	7.3	100.0	18.7	63.2	6.4	1.1	10.5
35 to 44 years	100.0	14.9	69.9	4.3	.5	10.4	100.0	11.5	64.9	7.1	2.3	14.2
45 to 54 years	100.0	8.6	74.9	4.4	1.3	10.8	100.0	7.8	63.9	6.9	6.1	15.3
55 to 59 years	100.0	6.9	76.9	4.0	2.7	9.5	100.0	7.0	60.3	6.2	12.6	13.9
60 to 64 years	100.0	6.7	76.2	3.7	4.7	8.7	100.0	7.0	55.0	5.4	20.2	12.5
65 years and over	100.0	6.4	69.8	3.1	14.2	6.6	100.0	7.5	34.5	3.3	46.4	8.3
65 to 74 years	100.0	6.5	73.8	3.3	9.1	7.3	100.0	7.4	43.4	4.2	35.2	9.9
75 to 84 years	100.0	6.1	65.5	2.8	20.2	5.4	100.0	7.7	24.6	2.3	58.9	6.5
85 years and over	100.0	6.4	49.2	2.0	38.3	4.1	100.0	7.7	9.7	1.1	77.7	3.8
WHITE, NOT OF HISPANIC ORIGIN												
Age												
15 years and over	72 711 218	20 020 480	44 216 737	1 071 108	1 886 226	5 516 667	78 542 165	16 040 666	43 808 428	1 353 273	9 947 279	7 392 519
15 to 17 years	3 566 621	3 535 789	25 430	1 970	601	2 831	3 365 777	3 296 135	58 635	4 232	2 552	4 223
18 and 19 years	2 750 827	2 646 699	93 009	5 245	984	4 890	2 661 476	2 388 851	238 270	16 036	3 563	14 756
20 to 24 years	6 797 975	5 304 867	1 306 841	64 810	2 986	118 471	6 639 949	4 153 122	2 110 395	129 873	10 995	235 564
25 to 29 years	7 784 058	3 368 061	3 787 747	145 435	6 642	476 173	7 716 091	2 152 666	4 650 047	217 315	26 346	669 717
30 to 34 years	8 169 821	1 923 812	5 281 256	171 636	12 341	780 776	8 150 210	1 199 200	5 728 718	226 371	47 876	948 045
35 to 44 years	14 514 732	1 723 343	10 663 609	304 378	45 453	1 777 949	14 534 139	1 168 188	10 630 823	365 673	183 387	2 186 068
45 to 54 years	9 926 130	591 599	7 878 916	183 439	90 679	1 182 383	10 193 336	456 368	7 546 211	198 581	445 152	1 547 024
55 to 59 years	4 145 689	206 412	3 410 954	57 873	90 679	379 771	4 430 646	170 865	3 209 272	59 766	476 739	514 004
60 to 64 years	4 170 114	212 970	3 431 645	48 920	165 809	310 770	4 684 973	188 857	3 153 575	48 183	858 114	436 244
65 years and over	10 885 251	506 928	8 337 330	87 402	1 470 938	482 653	16 165 568	866 414	6 482 482	87 243	7 892 555	836 874
65 to 74 years	6 855 570	316 727	5 562 207	60 784	559 697	356 155	8 682 710	394 460	4 701 931	60 907	2 959 142	566 270
75 to 84 years	3 288 498	153 195	2 390 065	22 615	613 008	109 615	5 504 291	330 498	1 604 300	22 071	3 325 757	221 665
85 years and over	741 183	37 006	385 058	4 003	298 233	16 883	1 978 567	141 456	176 251	4 265	1 607 656	48 939
Percent Distribution												
15 years and over	**100.0**	**27.5**	**60.8**	**1.5**	**2.6**	**7.6**	**100.0**	**20.4**	**55.8**	**1.7**	**12.7**	**9.4**
15 to 17 years	100.0	99.1	.7	.1	−	.1	100.0	97.9	1.7	.1	.1	.1
18 and 19 years	100.0	96.2	3.4	.2	−	.2	100.0	89.8	9.0	.6	.1	.6
20 to 24 years	100.0	78.0	19.2	1.0	−	1.7	100.0	62.5	31.8	2.0	.2	3.5
25 to 29 years	100.0	43.3	48.7	1.9	.1	6.1	100.0	27.9	60.3	2.8	.3	8.7
30 to 34 years	100.0	23.5	64.6	2.1	.2	9.6	100.0	14.7	70.3	2.8	.6	11.6
35 to 44 years	100.0	11.9	73.5	2.1	.3	12.2	100.0	8.0	73.1	2.5	1.3	15.0
45 to 54 years	100.0	6.0	79.4	1.8	.9	11.9	100.0	4.5	74.0	1.9	4.4	15.2
55 to 59 years	100.0	5.0	82.3	1.4	2.2	9.2	100.0	3.9	72.4	1.3	10.8	11.6
60 to 64 years	100.0	5.1	82.3	1.2	4.0	7.5	100.0	4.0	67.3	1.0	18.3	9.3
65 years and over	100.0	4.7	76.6	.8	13.5	4.4	100.0	5.4	40.1	.5	48.8	5.2
65 to 74 years	100.0	4.6	81.1	.9	8.2	5.2	100.0	4.5	54.2	.7	34.1	6.5
75 to 84 years	100.0	4.7	72.7	.7	18.6	3.3	100.0	6.0	29.1	.4	60.4	4.0
85 years and over	100.0	5.0	52.0	.5	40.2	2.3	100.0	7.1	8.9	.2	81.3	2.5

Table 35. Persons in Group Quarters by Type of Group Quarters, Sex, Race, and Hispanic Origin: 1990

[For definitions of terms and meanings of symbols, see text]

United States	All persons in group quarters	Race					Hispanic origin (of any race)	White, not of Hispanic origin
		White	Black	American Indian, Eskimo, or Aleut	Asian or Pacific Islander	Other race		
All persons	6 697 744	5 014 630	1 263 833	56 276	152 927	210 078	517 232	4 765 653
Institutionalized persons	3 334 018	2 442 062	744 500	28 050	22 992	96 414	261 693	2 313 717
Correctional institutions	1 115 111	506 131	508 084	17 791	7 518	75 587	197 400	417 003
Nursing homes	1 772 032	1 612 292	135 837	4 997	9 723	9 183	32 568	1 590 191
Mental (Psychiatric) hospitals	128 530	94 885	29 279	888	1 259	2 219	6 435	91 489
Hospitals or wards for chronically ill	40 980	31 752	7 574	255	872	527	2 432	30 060
Hospitals or wards for drug/alcohol abuse	20 129	14 782	4 237	474	284	352	1 069	14 187
Schools, hospitals, or wards for the mentally retarded	103 713	84 903	15 996	608	701	1 505	5 004	81 558
Schools, hospitals, or wards for the physically handicapped	20 654	16 488	3 284	210	307	365	1 216	15 677
Wards in general and military hospitals with patients who have no usual home elsewhere	28 669	21 508	5 458	293	776	634	1 725	20 618
Juvenile institutions	104 200	59 321	34 751	2 534	1 552	6 042	13 844	52 934
Other persons in group quarters	3 363 726	2 572 568	519 333	28 226	129 935	113 664	255 539	2 451 936
College dormitories	1 953 558	1 609 977	208 021	9 420	96 025	30 115	70 964	1 572 872
Military quarters	589 700	415 366	129 889	5 592	13 766	25 087	43 754	400 320
Emergency shelters for homeless persons	178 638	87 871	73 385	4 522	2 270	10 590	27 634	76 433
Visible in street locations	49 734	23 955	19 647	1 146	1 110	3 876	16 663	15 042
Shelters for abused women	11 768	6 848	3 469	468	199	784	1 770	6 060
Rooming and boarding houses	127 244	85 650	16 008	1 147	8 311	16 128	32 583	69 975
Group homes	211 675	149 129	50 088	3 738	2 410	6 310	14 436	142 513
Homes or halfway houses for drug/alcohol abuse	52 038	32 281	15 768	1 470	363	2 156	4 812	30 190
Homes for the mentally ill, mentally retarded, and physically handicapped	107 522	87 940	15 941	694	1 062	1 885	5 148	85 066
Maternity homes for unwed mothers	1 682	896	617	40	20	109	250	795
Other group homes	50 433	28 012	17 762	1 534	965	2 160	4 226	26 462
Religious group quarters	61 473	58 674	1 015	87	1 202	495	2 579	56 702
Agriculture workers' dormitories	35 280	18 317	1 693	220	324	14 726	31 587	2 210
Other workers' dormitories	22 920	15 769	3 748	597	1 507	1 299	3 041	14 250
Dormitories for nurses and interns in general and military hospitals	15 068	10 130	3 222	81	1 176	459	970	9 772
Crews of maritime vessels	5 658	4 113	759	104	380	302	655	3 845
Other nonhousehold living situations	97 723	84 360	7 759	1 064	1 138	3 402	8 652	79 679
Staff residents of institutions	2 976	2 239	497	35	116	89	248	2 093
Living quarters for victims of natural disasters	311	170	133	5	1	2	3	170
Male	3 788 618	2 581 552	914 626	40 234	88 702	163 504	397 464	2 395 581
Institutionalized persons	1 801 352	1 090 356	591 372	21 888	14 178	83 558	219 893	987 464
Correctional institutions	1 030 207	466 831	469 451	16 157	6 954	70 814	184 309	384 066
Nursing homes	493 609	431 346	52 171	2 263	3 702	4 127	13 361	422 738
Mental (Psychiatric) hospitals	76 067	54 397	18 856	575	747	1 492	4 203	52 231
Hospitals or wards for chronically ill	24 038	18 254	4 856	155	445	328	1 481	17 230
Hospitals or wards for drug/alcohol abuse	13 187	9 559	2 949	317	102	260	736	9 172
Schools, hospitals, or wards for the mentally retarded	60 118	48 598	9 809	355	400	956	2 980	46 674
Schools, hospitals, or wards for the physically handicapped	10 579	8 262	1 831	111	169	206	715	7 777
Wards in general and military hospitals with patients who have no usual home elsewhere	14 892	10 806	3 179	155	425	327	963	10 287
Juvenile institutions	78 655	42 303	28 270	1 800	1 234	5 048	11 145	37 289
Other persons in group quarters	1 987 266	1 491 196	323 254	18 346	74 524	79 946	177 571	1 408 117
College dormitories	946 117	785 228	90 393	4 806	50 095	14 595	35 238	766 188
Military quarters	532 758	381 330	111 058	4 883	12 645	22 842	39 671	367 682
Emergency shelters for homeless persons	123 358	62 953	48 863	3 088	1 382	7 072	18 879	54 855
Visible in street locations	30 255	19 205	15 222	874	766	3 128	13 999	11 377
Shelters for abused women	2 533	1 372	826	85	38	212	453	1 181
Rooming and boarding houses	79 318	51 606	10 727	671	4 693	11 621	23 039	40 719
Group homes	131 603	90 120	33 048	2 482	1 540	4 413	9 958	85 612
Homes or halfway houses for drug/alcohol abuse	40 041	25 031	11 814	1 131	286	1 779	3 922	23 321
Homes for the mentally ill, mentally retarded, and physically handicapped	61 310	49 547	9 565	419	594	1 185	3 264	47 734
Maternity homes for unwed mothers	149	58	76	1	1	13	25	47
Other group homes	30 103	15 484	11 593	931	659	1 436	2 747	14 510
Religious group quarters	14 298	13 190	372	27	506	203	809	12 629
Agriculture workers' dormitories	28 127	14 697	1 378	181	261	11 610	25 455	1 503
Other workers' dormitories	17 218	11 896	2 746	399	1 078	1 099	2 470	10 693
Dormitories for nurses and interns in general and military hospitals	6 787	4 362	1 652	48	440	285	583	4 151
Crews of maritime vessels	4 865	3 542	638	89	332	264	580	3 301
Other nonhousehold living situations	60 155	50 289	5 927	692	689	2 558	6 309	46 957
Staff residents of institutions	1 614	1 205	291	17	59	42	126	1 128
Living quarters for victims of natural disasters	260	141	113	4	–	2	2	141
Female	2 909 126	2 433 078	349 207	16 042	64 225	46 574	119 768	2 370 072
Institutionalized persons	1 532 666	1 351 706	153 128	6 162	8 814	12 856	41 800	1 326 253
Correctional institutions	84 904	39 300	38 633	1 634	564	4 773	13 091	32 937
Nursing homes	1 278 423	1 180 946	83 666	2 734	6 021	5 056	19 207	1 167 453
Mental (Psychiatric) hospitals	52 463	40 488	10 423	313	512	727	2 232	39 258
Hospitals or wards for chronically ill	16 942	13 498	2 718	100	427	199	951	12 830
Hospitals or wards for drug/alcohol abuse	6 942	5 223	1 288	157	182	92	333	5 015
Schools, hospitals, or wards for the mentally retarded	43 595	36 305	6 187	253	301	549	2 024	34 884
Schools, hospitals, or wards for the physically handicapped	10 075	8 226	1 453	99	138	159	501	7 900
Wards in general and military hospitals with patients who have no usual home elsewhere	13 777	10 702	2 279	138	351	307	762	10 331
Juvenile institutions	25 545	17 018	6 481	734	318	994	2 699	15 645
Other persons in group quarters	1 376 460	1 081 372	196 079	9 880	55 411	33 718	77 968	1 043 819
College dormitories	1 008 441	824 749	117 628	4 614	45 930	15 520	35 726	806 684
Military quarters	56 942	34 036	18 831	709	1 121	2 245	4 083	32 638
Emergency shelters for homeless persons	55 280	24 918	24 522	1 434	888	3 518	8 755	21 578
Visible in street locations	10 479	4 690	4 425	272	344	748	2 664	3 665
Shelters for abused women	9 235	5 476	2 643	383	161	572	1 317	4 879
Rooming and boarding houses	47 926	34 044	5 281	476	3 618	4 507	9 544	29 256
Group homes	80 072	59 009	17 040	1 256	870	1 897	4 478	56 901
Homes or halfway houses for drug/alcohol abuse	11 997	7 250	3 954	339	77	377	890	6 869
Homes for the mentally ill, mentally retarded, and physically handicapped	46 212	38 393	6 376	275	468	700	1 884	37 332
Maternity homes for unwed mothers	1 533	838	541	39	19	96	225	748
Other group homes	20 330	12 528	6 169	603	306	724	1 479	11 952
Religious group quarters	47 175	45 484	643	60	696	292	1 770	44 073
Agriculture workers' dormitories	7 153	3 620	315	39	63	3 116	6 132	707
Other workers' dormitories	5 702	3 873	1 002	198	429	200	571	3 557
Dormitories for nurses and interns in general and military hospitals	8 281	5 768	1 570	33	736	174	387	5 621
Crews of maritime vessels	793	571	121	15	48	38	75	544
Other nonhousehold living situations	37 568	34 071	1 832	372	449	844	2 343	32 722
Staff residents of institutions	1 362	1 034	206	18	57	47	122	965
Living quarters for victims of natural disasters	51	29	20	1	1	–	1	29

Table 36. **Household and Family Characteristics: 1990**

[For definitions of terms and meanings of symbols, see text]

United States Urban and Rural and Size of Place		Urban							Rural			
			Inside urbanized area			Outside urbanized area						
	United States	Total	Total	Central place	Urban fringe	Total	Place of 10,000 or more	Place of 2,500 to 9,999	Total	Place of 1,000 to 2,499	Place of less than 1,000	Other rural
HOUSEHOLD TYPE AND RELATIONSHIP												
All persons	**248 709 873**	**187 053 487**	**158 258 878**	**78 847 406**	**79 411 472**	**28 794 609**	**13 825 022**	**14 969 587**	**61 656 386**	**7 050 858**	**3 801 051**	**50 804 477**
In households	242 012 129	181 566 153	154 151 248	76 257 971	77 893 277	27 414 905	13 041 963	14 372 942	60 445 976	6 868 558	3 747 973	49 829 445
Householder	91 947 410	70 045 167	59 251 993	30 147 116	29 104 877	10 793 174	5 169 559	5 623 615	21 902 243	2 676 603	1 464 016	17 761 624
15 to 24 years	5 049 358	4 232 889	3 501 060	2 208 303	1 292 757	731 829	420 260	311 569	816 469	121 260	61 038	634 171
25 to 34 years	19 849 651	15 709 544	13 527 997	7 126 205	6 401 792	2 181 547	1 084 230	1 097 317	4 140 107	491 783	260 134	3 388 190
35 to 44 years	20 393 073	15 403 569	13 258 729	6 428 703	6 830 026	2 144 840	1 030 766	1 114 074	4 989 504	528 346	271 930	4 189 228
45 to 54 years	14 303 214	10 521 708	9 049 493	4 240 133	4 809 360	1 472 215	689 795	782 420	3 781 506	384 521	205 993	3 190 992
55 to 64 years	12 379 413	9 130 910	7 724 760	3 762 102	3 962 658	1 406 150	651 166	754 984	3 248 503	373 984	206 335	2 668 184
65 to 74 years	11 516 582	8 614 596	7 079 250	3 592 066	3 487 184	1 535 346	698 575	836 771	2 901 986	410 960	232 637	2 258 389
75 to 84 years	6 786 873	5 140 724	4 094 725	2 201 087	1 893 638	1 045 999	470 546	575 453	1 646 149	287 910	175 327	1 182 912
85 years and over	1 669 246	1 291 227	1 015 979	588 517	427 462	275 248	124 221	151 027	378 019	77 839	50 622	249 558
Family householder	64 517 947	47 397 503	39 990 065	18 921 071	21 068 994	7 407 438	3 474 392	3 933 046	17 120 444	1 905 216	1 038 745	14 176 483
Male	50 133 040	35 610 723	29 874 838	13 097 588	16 777 250	5 735 885	2 668 398	3 067 487	14 522 317	1 525 527	852 557	12 144 233
Female	14 384 907	11 786 780	10 115 227	5 823 483	4 291 744	1 671 553	805 994	865 559	2 598 127	379 689	186 188	2 032 250
Nonfamily householder	27 429 463	22 647 664	19 261 928	11 226 045	8 035 883	3 385 736	1 695 167	1 690 569	4 781 799	771 387	425 271	3 585 141
Male	12 141 701	9 905 635	8 587 619	5 077 696	3 509 923	1 318 016	684 030	633 986	2 236 066	288 180	162 617	1 785 269
Living alone	9 206 811	7 407 851	6 384 877	3 804 647	2 580 230	1 022 974	516 368	506 606	1 798 960	236 199	138 735	1 424 026
Female	15 287 762	12 742 029	10 674 309	6 148 349	4 525 960	2 067 720	1 011 137	1 056 583	2 545 733	483 207	262 654	1 799 872
Living alone	13 373 609	11 041 738	9 165 465	5 261 711	3 903 754	1 876 273	898 163	978 110	2 331 871	453 374	250 699	1 627 798
Spouse	50 708 322	36 058 946	30 269 091	13 158 569	17 110 522	5 789 855	2 689 703	3 100 152	14 649 376	1 540 881	852 810	12 255 685
Child	76 728 438	56 706 856	48 072 210	23 278 780	24 793 430	8 634 646	4 055 022	4 579 624	20 021 582	2 194 727	1 200 888	16 625 967
Grandchild	4 189 274	3 218 172	2 758 603	1 715 930	1 042 673	459 569	211 763	247 806	971 102	113 830	64 604	792 668
Brother or sister	2 628 549	2 257 912	2 043 821	1 234 710	809 111	214 091	105 813	108 278	370 637	45 108	23 804	301 725
Parent	1 747 569	1 430 712	1 287 973	654 408	633 565	142 739	67 430	75 309	316 857	34 207	16 335	266 315
Other relatives	3 385 190	2 770 995	2 476 864	1 379 926	1 096 938	294 131	139 279	154 852	614 195	66 680	33 715	513 800
Roomer, boarder, or foster child	1 595 204	1 339 060	1 196 460	692 569	503 891	142 600	73 382	69 218	256 144	29 148	13 798	213 198
Housemate or roommate	4 110 674	3 756 445	3 342 409	2 067 151	1 275 258	414 036	270 187	143 849	354 229	47 311	18 012	288 906
Other nonrelatives	4 971 499	3 981 888	3 451 824	1 928 812	1 523 012	530 064	259 825	270 239	989 611	120 063	59 991	809 557
In group quarters	6 697 744	5 487 334	4 107 630	2 589 435	1 518 195	1 379 704	783 059	596 645	1 210 410	182 300	53 078	975 032
Institutionalized persons	3 334 018	2 475 910	1 841 455	1 041 633	799 822	634 455	301 685	332 770	858 108	130 314	40 042	687 752
Correctional institutions	1 115 111	678 772	508 371	312 653	195 718	170 401	90 439	79 962	436 339	21 829	4 938	409 572
Nursing homes	1 772 032	1 453 231	1 052 003	565 888	486 115	401 228	177 274	223 954	318 801	100 827	32 850	185 124
Other institutions	446 875	343 907	281 081	163 092	117 989	62 826	33 972	28 854	102 968	7 658	2 254	93 056
Other persons in group quarters	3 363 726	3 011 424	2 266 175	1 547 802	718 373	745 249	481 374	263 875	352 302	51 986	13 036	287 280
College dormitories	1 953 558	1 825 151	1 274 657	936 996	337 661	550 494	377 894	172 600	128 407	32 619	4 528	91 260
Military quarters	589 700	535 952	426 761	198 532	228 229	109 191	57 505	51 686	53 748	3 329	1 007	49 412
Emergency shelters for homeless persons	178 638	171 542	159 720	136 572	23 148	11 822	7 929	3 893	7 096	794	210	6 092
Visible in street locations	49 734	46 018	43 796	35 025	8 771	2 222	1 186	1 036	3 716	392	79	3 245
Shelters for abused women	11 768	11 131	8 906	7 251	1 655	2 225	1 559	666	637	141	37	459
Drug/ alcohol abuse group homes	52 038	43 504	39 788	32 083	7 705	3 716	2 178	1 538	8 534	528	198	7 808
Other noninstitutional group quarters	528 290	378 126	312 547	201 343	111 204	65 579	33 123	32 456	150 164	14 183	6 977	129 004
Persons per household	2.63	2.59	2.60	2.53	2.68	2.54	2.52	2.56	2.76	2.57	2.56	2.81
Persons per family	3.16	3.16	3.17	3.19	3.16	3.10	3.09	3.10	3.16	3.10	3.11	3.17
HOUSEHOLD SIZE												
Households	**91 947 410**	**70 045 167**	**59 251 993**	**30 147 116**	**29 104 877**	**10 793 174**	**5 169 559**	**5 623 615**	**21 902 243**	**2 676 603**	**1 464 016**	**17 761 624**
1 person	22 580 420	18 449 589	15 550 342	9 066 358	6 483 984	2 899 247	1 414 531	1 484 716	4 130 831	689 573	389 434	3 051 824
2 persons	29 453 593	22 088 040	18 589 643	9 125 028	9 464 615	3 498 397	1 668 247	1 830 150	7 365 553	880 266	478 176	6 007 111
3 persons	15 970 269	11 912 644	10 130 658	4 855 177	5 275 481	1 781 986	855 713	926 273	4 057 625	440 907	230 581	3 386 137
4 persons	13 860 094	10 073 127	8 529 342	3 824 603	4 704 739	1 543 785	731 373	812 412	3 786 967	392 118	209 913	3 184 936
5 persons	6 188 938	4 523 956	3 844 025	1 824 765	2 019 260	679 931	318 614	361 317	1 664 982	176 666	99 469	1 388 847
6 persons	2 300 520	1 731 069	1 490 151	783 772	706 379	240 918	112 032	128 886	569 451	61 327	35 792	472 332
7 or more persons	1 593 576	1 266 742	1 117 832	667 413	450 419	148 910	69 049	79 861	326 834	35 746	20 651	270 437
FAMILY TYPE BY PRESENCE OF OWN CHILDREN												
Families	**64 517 947**	**47 397 503**	**39 990 065**	**18 921 071**	**21 068 994**	**7 407 438**	**3 474 392**	**3 933 046**	**17 120 444**	**1 905 216**	**1 038 745**	**14 176 483**
With own children under 18 years	30 877 675	22 674 636	19 044 735	9 066 693	9 978 042	3 629 901	1 718 774	1 911 127	8 203 039	907 111	489 801	6 806 127
With own children under 6 years only	7 884 751	6 061 489	5 144 296	2 501 711	2 642 585	917 193	446 390	470 803	1 823 262	210 773	108 104	1 504 385
With own children under 6 and 6 to 17 years	6 403 526	4 720 067	3 953 159	1 955 454	1 997 705	766 908	361 581	405 327	1 683 459	190 809	106 522	1 386 128
Married-couple families	**50 708 322**	**36 058 946**	**30 269 091**	**13 158 569**	**17 110 522**	**5 789 855**	**2 689 703**	**3 100 152**	**14 649 376**	**1 540 881**	**852 810**	**12 255 685**
With own children under 18 years	23 494 726	16 592 716	13 926 651	5 942 303	7 984 348	2 666 065	1 246 865	1 419 200	6 902 010	698 084	386 120	5 817 806
With own children under 6 years only	6 226 406	4 661 007	3 972 585	1 747 978	2 224 607	688 422	331 043	357 379	1 565 399	165 079	86 425	1 313 895
With own children under 6 and 6 to 17 years	5 141 106	3 661 427	3 061 669	1 349 151	1 712 518	599 758	279 278	320 480	1 479 679	156 047	88 669	1 234 963
Female householder, no husband present	**10 666 043**	**8 880 751**	**7 584 008**	**4 577 357**	**3 006 651**	**1 296 743**	**630 280**	**666 463**	**1 785 292**	**286 330**	**141 426**	**1 357 536**
With own children under 18 years	6 028 409	5 056 609	4 253 616	2 648 812	1 604 804	802 993	394 743	408 250	971 800	169 808	81 360	720 632
With own children under 6 years only	1 272 224	1 097 205	915 391	603 628	311 763	181 814	92 262	89 552	175 019	34 967	15 731	124 321
With own children under 6 and 6 to 17 years	1 086 510	923 656	777 249	538 099	239 150	146 407	72 488	73 919	162 854	29 848	14 804	118 202
MARITAL STATUS												
Males 15 years and over	**93 817 315**	**70 179 086**	**59 654 375**	**29 516 824**	**30 137 551**	**10 524 711**	**5 097 867**	**5 426 844**	**23 638 229**	**2 560 903**	**1 386 610**	**19 690 716**
Never married	28 804 618	23 016 034	19 923 942	11 083 053	8 840 889	3 092 092	1 613 920	1 478 172	5 788 584	643 468	336 304	4 808 812
Now married, except separated	53 781 245	38 502 603	32 386 530	14 349 124	18 037 406	6 116 073	2 850 097	3 265 976	15 278 642	1 606 832	882 293	12 789 517
15 to 24 years	1 972 700	1 458 593	1 170 484	634 160	536 324	288 109	145 300	142 809	514 107	60 699	32 864	420 544
25 to 34 years	11 643 154	8 604 834	7 283 867	3 364 390	3 919 477	1 320 967	631 795	689 172	3 038 320	320 259	174 495	2 543 566
35 to 44 years	13 228 554	9 405 642	8 005 998	3 396 755	4 609 243	1 399 644	658 951	740 693	3 822 912	364 745	191 645	3 266 522
45 to 54 years	9 533 674	6 614 441	5 638 160	2 319 744	3 318 416	976 281	449 689	526 592	2 919 233	269 319	147 207	2 502 707
55 to 64 years	8 004 491	5 637 115	4 754 817	2 053 210	2 701 607	882 298	403 579	478 719	2 367 376	244 919	135 461	1 986 996
65 to 74 years	6 287 518	4 514 646	3 719 762	1 691 384	2 028 378	794 884	358 743	436 141	1 772 872	218 164	122 884	1 431 824
75 years and over	3 111 154	2 267 332	1 813 442	889 481	923 961	453 890	202 040	251 850	843 822	128 727	77 737	637 358
Separated	1 896 397	1 518 780	1 326 670	818 204	508 466	192 110	94 143	97 967	377 617	41 799	20 208	315 610
Widowed	2 377 589	1 793 789	1 482 866	802 743	680 123	310 923	139 669	171 254	583 800	84 607	47 853	451 340
Divorced	6 957 466	5 347 880	4 534 367	2 463 700	2 070 667	813 513	400 038	413 475	1 609 586	184 197	99 952	1 325 437
Females 15 years and over	**101 324 687**	**77 323 777**	**65 386 790**	**32 797 485**	**32 589 305**	**11 936 987**	**5 732 229**	**6 204 758**	**24 000 910**	**2 918 805**	**1 547 510**	**19 534 595**
Never married	23 755 235	19 623 461	17 043 417	9 697 233	7 346 184	2 580 044	1 361 038	1 219 006	4 131 774	519 889	253 892	3 357 993
Now married, except separated	53 144 096	38 022 014	31 981 381	14 103 272	17 878 109	6 040 633	2 808 698	3 231 935	15 122 082	1 599 209	880 378	12 642 495
15 to 24 years	3 213 847	2 338 224	1 889 558	996 232	893 326	448 666	219 992	228 674	875 623	102 958	57 396	715 269
25 to 34 years	13 142 712	9 629 455	8 185 408	3 689 160	4 496 248	1 444 047	684 388	759 659	3 513 257	362 158	197 585	2 953 514
35 to 44 years	13 110 582	9 281 386	7 914 967	3 296 001	4 618 966	1 366 419	639 780	726 639	3 829 196	362 485	191 027	3 275 684
45 to 54 years	9 060 712	6 281 384	5 337 080	2 206 768	3 130 312	944 304	433 043	511 261	2 779 328	264 141	145 618	2 369 569
55 to 64 years	7 398 225	5 224 845	4 368 067	1 914 947	2 453 120	856 778	390 089	466 689	2 173 380	236 829	132 710	1 803 841
65 to 74 years	5 253 888	3 811 126	3 125 057	1 428 763	1 696 294	686 069	309 616	376 453	1 442 762	188 588	107 147	1 147 027
75 years and over	1 964 130	1 455 594	1 161 244	571 401	589 843	294 350	131 790	162 560	508 536	82 050	48 895	377 591
Separated	2 676 840	2 258 429	1 964 291	1 242 609	721 682	294 138	143 325	150 813	418 411	62 439	28 154	327 818
Widowed	12 121 939	9 452 550	7 622 534	4 095 593	3 526 941	1 830 016	828 133	1 001 883	2 669 389	483 424	265 756	1 920 209
Divorced	9 626 577	7 967 323	6 775 167	3 658 778	3 116 389	1 192 156	591 035	601 121	1 659 254	253 844	119 330	1 286 080

Table 37. **Household and Family Characteristics for Selected Age Groups: 1990**

[For definitions of terms and meanings of symbols, see text]

United States Urban and Rural and Size of Place		Urban							Rural			
			Inside urbanized area			Outside urbanized area						
	United States	Total	Total	Central place	Urban fringe	Total	Place of 10,000 or more	Place of 2,500 to 9,999	Total	Place of 1,000 to 2,499	Place of less than 1,000	Other rural
Persons under 6 years	**22 043 976**	**16 735 410**	**14 160 279**	**7 193 736**	**6 966 543**	**2 575 131**	**1 233 759**	**1 341 372**	**5 308 566**	**611 215**	**330 572**	**4 366 779**
Own child	19 526 799	14 745 596	12 433 618	6 135 082	6 298 536	2 311 978	1 109 451	1 202 527	4 781 203	550 104	297 031	3 934 068
In married-couple family	15 624 526	11 450 566	9 670 372	4 270 035	5 400 337	1 780 194	842 951	937 243	4 173 960	443 011	243 846	3 487 103
Percent of persons under 6 years	70.9	68.4	68.3	59.4	77.5	69.1	68.3	69.9	78.6	72.5	73.8	79.9
With female householder, no husband present	3 177 757	2 730 832	2 287 405	1 580 447	706 958	443 427	223 551	219 876	446 925	86 679	41 253	318 993
Grandchild	1 772 503	1 381 241	1 193 806	732 988	460 818	187 435	87 200	100 235	391 262	45 181	25 085	320 996
Other relatives	350 311	293 714	260 798	164 270	96 528	32 916	15 980	16 936	56 597	6 915	3 626	46 056
Nonrelatives	356 147	282 676	243 731	140 737	102 994	38 945	18 986	19 959	73 471	8 484	4 714	60 273
Institutionalized persons	5 798	5 206	4 665	3 366	1 299	541	282	259	592	84	12	496
Other persons in group quarters	32 418	26 977	23 661	17 293	6 368	3 316	1 860	1 456	5 441	447	104	4 890
Persons under 18 years	**63 604 432**	**46 750 175**	**39 254 313**	**19 467 142**	**19 787 171**	**7 495 862**	**3 535 670**	**3 960 192**	**16 854 257**	**1 876 105**	**1 037 311**	**13 940 841**
Householder or spouse	90 847	69 374	55 537	35 645	19 892	13 837	6 673	7 164	21 473	3 063	1 556	16 854
Own child	57 461 020	41 992 787	35 164 135	16 969 578	18 194 557	6 828 652	3 219 980	3 608 672	15 468 233	1 718 821	949 803	12 799 609
In married-couple family	44 642 569	31 418 260	26 283 765	11 342 913	14 940 852	5 134 495	2 390 103	2 744 392	13 224 309	1 353 830	764 547	11 105 932
Percent of persons under 18 years	70.2	67.2	67.0	58.3	75.5	68.5	67.6	69.3	78.5	72.2	73.7	79.7
With female householder, no husband present	10 674 900	8 956 970	7 520 120	4 862 384	2 657 736	1 436 850	706 899	729 951	1 717 930	302 114	148 409	1 267 407
Grandchild	3 493 999	2 683 279	2 303 012	1 426 787	876 225	380 267	174 862	205 405	810 720	93 850	53 515	663 355
Other relatives	1 172 053	958 297	843 849	522 987	320 862	114 448	54 779	59 669	213 756	25 008	13 744	175 004
Nonrelatives	1 121 322	853 633	724 382	405 871	318 511	129 251	62 016	67 235	267 689	30 316	16 738	220 635
Institutionalized persons	142 403	99 737	85 132	51 381	33 751	14 605	8 601	6 004	42 666	2 307	921	39 438
Other persons in group quarters	122 788	93 068	78 266	54 893	23 373	14 802	8 759	6 043	29 720	2 740	1 034	25 946
Persons 60 to 64 years	**10 616 167**	**7 801 852**	**6 556 094**	**3 160 980**	**3 395 114**	**1 245 758**	**572 094**	**673 664**	**2 814 315**	**332 943**	**183 076**	**2 298 296**
Family householder	4 547 773	3 276 207	2 761 762	1 268 009	1 493 753	514 445	235 012	279 433	1 271 566	140 960	77 885	1 052 721
Male	3 767 182	2 651 954	2 221 666	967 715	1 253 951	430 288	195 756	234 532	1 115 228	119 972	67 007	928 249
Female	780 591	624 253	540 096	300 294	239 802	84 157	39 256	44 901	156 338	20 988	10 878	124 472
Spouse	3 534 867	2 510 126	2 086 428	919 481	1 166 947	423 698	192 420	231 278	1 024 741	116 746	65 154	842 841
Parent	191 144	162 614	149 038	78 629	70 409	13 576	6 559	7 017	28 530	3 091	1 369	24 070
Other relatives	277 637	219 102	191 166	106 698	84 468	27 936	12 762	15 174	58 535	7 240	3 863	47 432
Nonrelatives	193 362	158 246	140 258	82 294	57 964	17 988	8 722	9 266	35 116	4 217	2 097	28 802
Nonfamily householder	1 752 554	1 382 465	1 154 399	659 873	494 526	228 066	107 035	121 031	370 089	56 613	31 272	282 204
Male	610 929	467 783	399 954	239 978	159 976	67 829	31 629	36 200	143 146	17 881	10 864	114 401
Living alone	535 746	409 040	348 222	210 231	137 991	60 818	28 436	32 382	126 706	16 128	9 967	100 611
Female	1 141 625	914 682	754 445	419 895	334 550	160 237	75 406	84 831	226 943	38 732	20 408	167 803
Living alone	1 078 441	862 259	708 513	394 347	314 166	153 746	72 215	81 531	216 182	37 268	19 777	159 137
Institutionalized persons	83 227	65 780	49 946	30 071	19 875	15 834	7 472	8 362	17 447	3 319	1 076	13 052
Other persons in group quarters	35 603	27 312	23 097	15 925	7 172	4 215	2 112	2 103	8 291	757	360	7 174
Persons 65 years and over	**31 241 831**	**23 568 554**	**19 145 041**	**9 754 748**	**9 390 293**	**4 423 513**	**2 000 102**	**2 423 411**	**7 673 277**	**1 192 681**	**671 334**	**5 809 262**
Family householder	10 801 438	7 874 193	6 466 179	3 152 500	3 313 679	1 408 014	634 382	773 632	2 927 245	388 215	226 571	2 312 459
Male	8 759 574	6 279 369	5 127 147	2 394 363	2 732 784	1 152 222	517 187	635 035	2 480 205	322 329	190 044	1 967 832
Female	2 041 864	1 594 824	1 339 032	758 137	580 895	255 792	117 195	138 597	447 040	65 886	36 527	344 627
Spouse	6 927 364	5 031 101	4 098 308	1 902 251	2 196 057	932 793	420 050	512 743	1 896 263	258 642	150 557	1 487 064
Parent	1 156 730	924 803	826 239	395 041	431 198	98 564	45 829	52 735	231 927	24 702	11 935	195 290
Other relatives	975 410	761 745	663 348	330 592	332 756	98 397	44 755	53 642	213 665	24 868	13 104	175 693
Nonrelatives	428 761	344 614	299 247	171 958	127 289	45 367	21 455	23 912	84 147	11 057	5 255	67 835
Nonfamily householder	9 171 263	7 172 354	5 723 775	3 229 170	2 494 605	1 448 579	658 960	789 619	1 998 909	388 494	232 015	1 378 400
Male	2 055 016	1 533 739	1 258 136	732 123	526 013	275 603	123 977	151 626	521 277	78 084	49 818	393 375
Living alone	1 902 614	1 416 092	1 157 328	674 106	483 222	258 764	116 214	142 550	486 522	73 791	47 671	365 060
Female	7 116 247	5 638 615	4 465 639	2 497 047	1 968 592	1 172 976	534 983	637 993	1 477 632	310 410	182 197	985 025
Living alone	6 922 231	5 476 374	4 326 103	2 415 493	1 910 610	1 150 271	523 807	626 464	1 445 857	305 446	179 923	960 488
Institutionalized persons	1 676 062	1 377 623	998 768	532 360	466 408	378 855	168 121	210 734	298 439	94 111	30 577	173 751
Other persons in group quarters	104 803	82 121	69 177	40 876	28 301	12 944	6 550	6 394	22 682	2 592	1 320	18 770
Persons 65 to 74 years	**18 106 558**	**13 502 539**	**11 132 680**	**5 514 503**	**5 618 177**	**2 369 859**	**1 077 552**	**1 292 307**	**4 604 019**	**634 477**	**354 647**	**3 614 895**
Family householder	7 180 147	5 220 993	4 323 218	2 051 469	2 271 749	897 775	406 027	491 748	1 959 154	244 645	138 439	1 576 070
Male	5 935 417	4 242 061	3 492 467	1 588 983	1 903 484	749 594	337 869	411 725	1 693 356	207 002	118 082	1 368 272
Female	1 244 730	978 932	830 751	462 486	368 265	148 181	68 158	80 023	265 798	37 643	20 357	207 798
Spouse	5 094 657	3 682 064	3 017 023	1 371 861	1 645 162	665 041	300 010	365 031	1 412 593	183 550	104 428	1 124 615
Parent	444 833	366 143	332 731	162 167	170 564	33 412	15 804	17 608	78 690	7 922	3 693	67 075
Other relatives	458 783	362 314	317 189	164 768	152 421	45 125	20 671	24 454	96 469	11 317	5 986	79 166
Nonrelatives	255 538	206 824	180 977	104 845	76 132	25 847	12 127	13 720	48 714	6 304	2 916	39 494
Nonfamily householder	4 336 435	3 393 603	2 756 032	1 540 597	1 215 435	637 571	292 548	345 023	942 832	166 315	94 198	682 319
Male	1 107 687	835 282	696 853	410 354	286 499	138 429	63 236	75 193	272 405	37 768	22 917	211 720
Living alone	1 008 447	758 919	630 962	372 409	258 553	127 957	58 485	69 472	249 528	35 036	21 557	192 935
Female	3 228 748	2 558 321	2 059 179	1 130 243	928 936	499 142	229 312	269 830	670 427	128 547	71 281	470 599
Living alone	3 122 786	2 470 368	1 982 986	1 086 594	896 392	487 382	223 639	263 743	652 418	125 854	70 090	456 474
Institutionalized persons	284 107	231 150	172 544	98 373	74 171	58 606	27 138	31 468	52 957	13 223	4 431	35 303
Other persons in group quarters	52 058	39 448	32 966	20 423	12 543	6 482	3 227	3 255	12 610	1 201	556	10 853
Persons 75 to 84 years	**10 055 108**	**7 646 671**	**6 120 526**	**3 205 805**	**2 914 721**	**1 526 145**	**686 286**	**839 859**	**2 408 437**	**414 410**	**239 851**	**1 754 176**
Family householder	3 084 715	2 253 542	1 821 889	922 890	898 999	431 653	193 127	238 526	831 173	121 079	73 831	636 263
Male	2 452 506	1 764 516	1 417 052	689 851	727 201	347 464	154 689	192 775	687 990	99 158	61 367	527 465
Female	632 209	489 026	404 837	233 039	171 798	84 189	38 438	45 751	143 183	21 921	12 464	108 798
Spouse	1 669 485	1 225 667	982 527	478 424	504 103	243 140	108 983	134 157	443 818	68 151	41 798	333 869
Parent	445 654	351 854	313 217	146 320	166 897	38 637	17 701	20 936	93 800	9 801	4 691	79 308
Other relatives	354 789	275 616	239 737	115 741	123 996	35 879	16 163	19 716	79 173	9 038	4 724	65 411
Nonrelatives	127 374	101 706	87 569	49 921	37 648	14 137	6 714	7 423	25 668	3 373	1 679	20 616
Nonfamily householder	3 702 158	2 887 182	2 272 836	1 278 197	994 639	614 346	277 419	336 927	814 976	166 831	101 496	546 649
Male	728 341	536 313	432 173	247 019	185 154	104 140	46 142	57 998	192 028	30 325	19 834	141 869
Living alone	685 775	503 496	404 430	231 117	173 313	99 066	43 756	55 310	182 279	29 055	19 205	134 019
Female	2 973 817	2 350 869	1 840 663	1 031 178	809 485	510 206	231 277	278 929	622 948	136 506	81 662	404 780
Living alone	2 909 526	2 296 740	1 794 477	1 003 720	790 757	502 263	227 313	274 950	612 786	134 897	80 889	397 000
Institutionalized persons	636 138	523 137	378 903	200 751	178 152	144 234	64 110	80 124	113 001	35 273	11 173	66 555
Other persons in group quarters	34 795	27 967	23 848	13 561	10 287	4 119	2 069	2 050	6 828	864	459	5 505
Persons 85 years and over	**3 080 165**	**2 419 344**	**1 891 835**	**1 034 440**	**857 395**	**527 509**	**236 264**	**291 245**	**660 821**	**143 794**	**76 836**	**440 191**
Family householder	536 576	399 658	321 072	178 141	142 931	78 586	35 228	43 358	136 918	22 491	14 301	100 126
Male	371 651	272 792	217 628	115 529	102 099	55 164	24 629	30 535	98 859	16 169	10 595	72 095
Female	164 925	126 866	103 444	62 612	40 832	23 422	10 599	12 823	38 059	6 322	3 706	28 031
Spouse	163 222	123 370	98 758	51 966	46 792	24 612	11 057	13 555	39 852	6 941	4 331	28 580
Parent	266 243	206 806	180 291	86 554	93 737	26 515	12 324	14 191	59 437	6 979	3 551	48 907
Other relatives	161 838	123 815	106 422	50 083	56 339	17 393	7 921	9 472	38 023	4 513	2 394	31 116
Nonrelatives	45 849	36 084	30 701	17 192	13 509	5 383	2 614	2 769	9 765	1 380	660	7 725
Nonfamily householder	1 132 670	891 569	694 907	410 376	284 531	196 662	88 993	107 669	241 101	55 348	36 321	149 432
Male	218 988	162 144	129 110	74 750	54 360	33 034	14 599	18 435	56 844	9 991	7 067	39 786
Living alone	208 392	153 677	121 936	70 580	51 356	31 741	13 973	17 768	54 715	9 700	6 909	38 106
Female	913 682	729 425	565 797	335 626	230 171	163 628	74 394	89 234	184 257	45 357	29 254	109 646
Living alone	889 919	709 266	548 640	325 179	223 461	160 626	72 855	87 771	180 653	44 695	28 944	107 014
Institutionalized persons	755 817	623 336	447 321	233 236	214 085	176 015	76 873	99 142	132 481	45 615	14 973	71 893
Other persons in group quarters	17 950	14 706	12 363	6 892	5 471	2 343	1 254	1 089	3 244	527	305	2 412

Table 38. **Household and Family Characteristics: 1990**

[For definitions of terms and meanings of symbols, see text]

United States Inside and Outside Metropolitan Area	United States	Inside metropolitan area						Outside metropolitan area				
		Total	In central city	Not in central city				Total	Urban			Rural
				Total	Urban		Rural		Inside urbanized area	Outside urbanized area		
					Inside urbanized area	Outside urbanized area				Place of 10,000 or more	Place of 2,500 to 9,999	
HOUSEHOLD TYPE AND RELATIONSHIP												
All persons	**248 709 873**	**192 725 741**	**77 843 533**	**114 882 208**	**79 755 134**	**8 684 794**	**26 442 280**	**55 984 132**	**1 520 259**	**9 873 345**	**9 458 347**	**35 132 181**
In households	242 012 129	187 811 251	75 285 754	112 525 497	78 238 718	8 377 576	25 909 203	54 200 878	1 440 821	9 260 687	9 042 315	34 457 055
Householder	91 947 410	71 265 264	29 793 822	41 471 442	29 201 839	3 139 108	9 130 495	20 682 146	575 362	3 735 404	3 628 132	12 743 248
15 to 24 years	5 049 358	3 950 710	2 171 190	1 779 520	1 299 884	180 365	299 271	1 098 648	53 114	321 561	207 879	516 094
25 to 34 years	19 849 651	15 941 345	7 034 476	8 906 869	6 438 393	680 349	1 788 127	3 908 306	122 872	764 503	675 034	2 345 897
35 to 44 years	20 393 073	16 171 052	6 353 077	9 817 975	6 857 902	678 457	2 281 616	4 222 021	114 453	722 703	683 846	2 701 019
45 to 54 years	14 303 214	11 180 972	4 195 419	6 985 553	4 824 152	455 457	1 705 944	3 122 242	75 463	489 018	487 753	2 070 008
55 to 64 years	12 379 413	9 413 776	3 724 861	5 688 915	3 968 253	398 579	1 322 083	2 965 637	72 352	476 672	494 456	1 922 157
65 to 74 years	11 516 582	8 522 040	3 551 080	4 970 960	3 489 459	414 435	1 067 066	2 994 542	80 014	516 752	565 862	1 831 914
75 to 84 years	6 786 873	4 889 097	2 179 811	2 709 286	1 895 397	265 559	548 330	1 897 776	46 541	350 746	404 022	1 096 467
85 years and over	1 669 246	1 196 272	583 908	612 364	428 399	65 907	118 058	472 974	10 553	93 449	109 280	259 692
Family householder	64 517 947	49 421 069	18 677 817	30 743 252	21 145 259	2 274 206	7 323 787	15 096 878	386 370	2 461 444	2 475 242	9 773 822
Male	50 133 040	37 806 137	12 910 089	24 896 048	16 835 868	1 804 411	6 255 769	12 326 903	298 214	1 876 987	1 904 840	8 246 862
Female	14 384 907	11 614 932	5 767 728	5 847 204	4 309 391	469 795	1 068 018	2 769 975	88 156	584 457	570 402	1 526 960
Nonfamily householder	27 429 463	21 844 195	11 116 005	10 728 190	8 056 580	864 902	1 806 708	5 585 268	188 992	1 273 960	1 152 890	2 969 426
Male	12 141 701	9 779 628	5 022 267	4 757 361	3 522 391	352 211	882 759	2 362 073	83 573	510 836	417 492	1 350 172
Living alone	9 206 811	7 308 073	3 769 856	3 538 217	2 587 096	267 783	683 338	1 898 738	58 958	386 613	340 030	1 113 137
Female	15 287 762	12 064 567	6 093 738	5 970 829	4 534 189	512 691	923 949	3 223 195	105 419	763 124	735 398	1 619 254
Living alone	13 373 609	10 413 453	5 219 504	5 193 949	3 909 847	461 059	823 043	2 960 156	88 410	678 126	687 004	1 506 616
Spouse	50 708 322	38 312 722	12 969 640	25 343 082	17 165 240	1 823 278	6 354 564	12 395 600	305 271	1 893 519	1 922 133	8 274 677
Child	76 728 438	59 384 924	22 977 553	36 407 371	24 926 995	2 741 372	8 739 004	17 343 514	423 056	2 832 942	2 830 255	11 257 261
Grandchild	4 189 274	3 257 212	1 698 171	1 559 041	1 050 723	131 886	376 432	932 062	21 844	151 319	165 542	593 357
Brother or sister	2 628 549	2 259 629	1 222 724	1 036 905	816 560	68 494	151 851	368 920	11 239	72 122	67 287	218 272
Parent	1 747 569	1 482 217	646 682	835 535	637 921	47 997	149 617	265 352	8 043	45 646	44 960	166 703
Other relatives	3 385 190	2 851 872	1 363 058	1 488 814	1 108 793	101 258	278 763	533 318	14 294	91 903	92 764	334 357
Roomer, boarder, or foster child	1 595 204	1 361 849	682 097	679 752	509 995	47 020	122 737	233 355	8 972	50 626	40 747	133 010
Housemate or roommate	4 110 674	3 590 599	2 027 443	1 563 156	1 283 876	107 330	171 950	520 075	45 339	207 328	85 803	181 605
Other nonrelatives	4 971 499	4 044 963	1 904 564	2 140 399	1 536 776	169 833	433 790	926 536	27 401	179 878	164 692	554 565
In group quarters	6 697 744	4 914 490	2 557 779	2 356 711	1 516 416	307 218	533 077	1 783 254	79 438	612 658	416 032	675 126
Institutionalized persons	3 334 018	2 341 126	1 032 509	1 308 617	804 236	139 302	365 079	992 892	25 067	226 743	249 482	491 600
Correctional institutions	1 115 111	747 571	305 339	442 232	199 965	35 409	206 858	367 540	9 532	69 032	60 609	228 367
Nursing homes	1 772 032	1 243 879	563 594	680 285	485 942	89 406	104 937	528 153	12 423	132 704	169 189	213 837
Other institutions	446 875	349 676	163 576	186 100	118 329	14 487	53 284	97 199	3 112	25 007	19 684	49 396
Other persons in group quarters	3 363 726	2 573 364	1 525 270	1 048 094	712 180	167 916	167 998	790 362	54 371	385 915	166 550	183 526
College dormitories	1 953 558	1 414 084	926 583	487 501	332 145	101 221	54 135	539 474	33 956	315 157	116 123	74 238
Military quarters	589 700	487 197	189 249	297 948	226 444	40 774	30 730	102 503	16 404	36 781	26 820	22 498
Emergency shelters for homeless persons	178 638	166 892	135 632	31 260	23 779	2 843	4 638	11 746	990	6 031	2 271	2 454
Visible in street locations	49 734	47 198	34 760	12 438	8 973	946	2 519	2 536	120	926	299	1 191
Shelters for abused women	11 768	9 566	7 272	2 294	1 635	380	279	2 202	95	1 239	510	358
Drug/ alcohol abuse group homes	52 038	45 116	31 933	13 183	7 813	800	4 570	6 922	230	1 728	1 052	3 912
Other noninstitutional group quarters	528 290	403 311	199 841	203 470	111 391	20 952	71 127	124 979	2 576	24 053	19 475	78 875
Persons per household	2.63	2.64	2.53	2.71	2.68	2.67	2.84	2.62	2.50	2.48	2.49	2.70
Persons per family	3.16	3.18	3.19	3.17	3.16	3.16	3.19	3.11	3.03	3.07	3.07	3.13
HOUSEHOLD SIZE												
Households	**91 947 410**	**71 265 264**	**29 793 822**	**41 471 442**	**29 201 839**	**3 139 108**	**9 130 495**	**20 682 146**	**575 362**	**3 735 404**	**3 628 132**	**12 743 248**
1 person	22 580 420	17 721 526	8 989 360	8 732 166	6 496 943	728 842	1 506 381	4 858 894	147 368	1 064 739	1 027 034	2 619 753
2 persons	29 453 593	22 515 408	9 009 226	13 506 182	9 481 235	1 009 504	3 015 443	6 938 185	202 442	1 211 945	1 183 441	4 340 357
3 persons	15 970 269	12 421 869	4 794 091	7 627 778	5 295 174	550 226	1 782 378	3 548 400	95 822	606 407	576 522	2 269 649
4 persons	13 860 094	10 711 052	3 771 592	6 939 460	4 726 835	497 954	1 714 671	3 149 042	78 204	508 930	494 884	2 067 024
5 persons	6 188 938	4 786 300	1 798 739	2 987 561	2 032 673	221 374	733 514	1 402 638	32 480	220 682	220 164	929 312
6 persons	2 300 520	1 807 520	772 171	1 035 349	712 724	79 495	243 130	493 000	11 934	76 971	78 413	325 682
7 or more persons	1 593 576	1 301 589	658 643	642 946	456 255	51 713	134 978	291 987	7 112	45 730	47 674	191 471
FAMILY TYPE BY PRESENCE OF OWN CHILDREN												
Families	**64 517 947**	**49 421 069**	**18 677 817**	**30 743 252**	**21 145 259**	**2 274 206**	**7 323 787**	**15 096 878**	**386 370**	**2 461 444**	**2 475 242**	**9 773 822**
With own children under 18 years	30 877 675	23 690 098	8 942 878	14 747 220	10 031 359	1 143 561	3 572 300	7 187 577	178 948	1 203 546	1 185 191	4 619 892
With own children under 6 years only	7 884 751	6 233 747	2 464 860	3 768 887	2 659 357	295 000	814 530	1 651 004	48 474	309 637	286 917	1 005 976
With own children under 6 and 6 to 17 years	6 403 526	4 905 043	1 926 362	2 978 681	2 012 483	244 881	721 317	1 498 483	36 971	251 156	250 368	959 988
Married-couple families	**50 708 322**	**38 312 722**	**12 969 640**	**25 343 082**	**17 165 240**	**1 823 278**	**6 354 564**	**12 395 600**	**305 271**	**1 893 519**	**1 922 133**	**8 274 677**
With own children under 18 years	23 494 726	17 826 575	5 850 250	11 976 325	8 024 274	878 431	3 073 620	5 668 151	132 108	860 588	856 616	3 818 839
With own children under 6 years only	6 226 406	4 910 955	1 719 271	3 191 684	2 237 508	234 393	719 783	1 315 451	37 313	225 036	209 968	843 134
With own children under 6 and 6 to 17 years	5 141 106	3 899 750	1 325 877	2 573 873	1 724 131	200 270	649 472	1 241 356	29 357	191 215	192 562	828 222
Female householder, no husband present	**10 666 043**	**8 593 820**	**4 536 147**	**4 057 673**	**3 020 908**	**349 423**	**687 342**	**2 072 223**	**65 158**	**461 284**	**449 636**	**1 096 145**
With own children under 18 years	6 028 409	4 816 841	2 623 371	2 193 470	1 614 205	213 749	365 516	1 211 568	39 481	290 028	276 646	605 413
With own children under 6 years only	1 272 224	1 019 419	597 500	421 919	314 190	45 721	62 008	252 805	9 075	68 816	62 069	112 845
With own children under 6 and 6 to 17 years	1 086 510	868 595	533 188	335 407	241 622	37 694	56 091	217 915	6 745	53 451	51 087	106 632
MARITAL STATUS												
Males 15 years and over	**93 817 315**	**72 791 706**	**29 133 699**	**43 658 007**	**30 256 659**	**3 182 947**	**10 218 401**	**21 025 609**	**582 535**	**3 649 913**	**3 405 869**	**13 387 292**
Never married	28 804 618	23 247 761	10 949 816	12 297 945	8 882 775	884 796	2 530 374	5 556 857	185 824	1 189 149	931 131	3 250 753
Now married, except separated	53 781 245	40 809 868	14 141 120	26 668 748	18 099 762	1 926 640	6 642 346	12 971 377	329 625	2 001 815	2 025 025	8 614 912
15 to 24 years	1 972 700	1 444 334	622 444	821 890	540 335	85 226	196 329	528 366	16 056	104 008	91 383	316 919
25 to 34 years	11 643 154	9 045 366	3 306 188	5 739 178	3 945 083	446 162	1 347 933	2 597 788	73 881	430 533	407 634	1 685 740
35 to 44 years	13 228 554	10 230 238	3 347 704	6 882 534	4 629 172	466 336	1 787 026	2 998 316	74 374	452 024	441 497	2 030 421
45 to 54 years	9 533 674	7 282 877	2 291 167	4 991 710	3 328 328	316 391	1 346 991	2 250 797	49 091	314 120	319 765	1 567 821
55 to 64 years	8 004 491	5 992 690	2 029 114	3 963 576	2 704 578	263 325	995 673	2 011 801	46 874	291 571	304 962	1 368 394
65 to 74 years	6 287 518	4 599 906	1 667 088	2 932 818	2 028 014	227 293	677 511	1 687 612	46 148	261 593	286 495	1 093 376
75 years and over	3 111 154	2 214 457	877 415	1 337 042	924 252	121 907	290 883	896 697	23 201	147 966	173 289	552 241
Separated	1 896 397	1 536 840	810 042	726 798	511 795	57 417	157 586	359 557	10 949	65 894	63 349	219 365
Widowed	2 377 589	1 775 996	795 474	980 522	681 493	82 639	216 390	601 593	14 201	102 916	117 653	366 823
Divorced	6 957 466	5 421 241	2 437 247	2 983 994	2 080 834	231 455	671 705	1 536 225	41 936	290 139	268 711	935 439
Females 15 years and over	**101 324 687**	**78 824 824**	**32 408 993**	**46 415 831**	**32 704 340**	**3 502 340**	**10 209 151**	**22 499 863**	**627 686**	**4 132 250**	**3 979 447**	**13 760 480**
Never married	23 755 235	19 507 237	9 597 476	9 909 761	7 372 241	718 860	1 818 660	4 247 998	155 732	1 009 265	774 987	2 308 014
Now married, except separated	53 144 096	40 309 513	13 903 105	26 406 408	17 938 899	1 902 004	6 565 505	12 834 583	318 154	1 976 110	2 004 787	8 535 532
15 to 24 years	3 213 847	2 348 286	979 309	1 368 977	900 537	135 395	333 045	865 561	22 919	156 110	145 315	541 217
25 to 34 years	13 142 712	10 222 892	3 630 031	6 592 861	4 523 901	491 808	1 577 152	2 919 820	75 986	466 317	446 740	1 930 777
35 to 44 years	13 110 582	10 139 003	3 250 309	6 888 694	4 636 810	453 477	1 798 407	2 971 579	70 283	441 288	434 773	2 025 235
45 to 54 years	9 060 712	6 866 512	2 180 296	4 686 216	3 137 541	297 769	1 250 906	2 194 200	47 744	306 393	315 683	1 524 380
55 to 64 years	7 398 225	5 477 902	1 891 851	3 586 051	2 453 933	248 696	883 422	1 920 323	46 660	284 417	302 142	1 287 104
65 to 74 years	5 253 888	3 845 459	1 407 714	2 437 745	1 696 204	195 902	545 639	1 408 429	39 372	225 452	247 950	895 655
75 years and over	1 964 130	1 409 459	563 595	845 864	589 973	78 957	176 934	554 671	15 190	96 133	112 184	331 164
Separated	2 676 840	2 211 070	1 229 566	981 504	727 581	85 442	168 481	465 770	16 086	100 837	99 460	249 387
Widowed	12 121 939	9 003 019	4 058 865	4 944 154	3 534 368	460 294	949 492	3 118 920	77 024	617 358	707 112	1 717 426
Divorced	9 626 577	7 793 985	3 619 981	4 174 004	3 131 251	335 740	707 013	1 832 592	60 690	428 680	393 101	950 121

Table 39. **Household and Family Characteristics for Selected Age Groups: 1990**

[For definitions of terms and meanings of symbols, see text]

United States Inside and Outside Metropolitan Area		Inside metropolitan area						Outside metropolitan area				
				Not in central city					Urban			
					Urban					Outside urbanized area		
	United States	Total	In central city	Total	Inside urbanized area	Outside urbanized area	Rural	Total	Inside urbanized area	Place of 10,000 or more	Place of 2,500 to 9,999	Rural
Persons under 6 years	**22 043 976**	**17 240 837**	**7 089 055**	**10 151 782**	**7 019 006**	**824 676**	**2 308 100**	**4 803 139**	**129 450**	**855 009**	**825 509**	**2 993 171**
Own child	19 526 799	15 222 435	6 042 806	9 179 629	6 343 832	744 147	2 091 650	4 304 364	116 784	768 272	736 361	2 682 947
In married-couple family	15 624 526	12 113 150	4 196 786	7 916 364	5 435 688	603 866	1 876 810	3 511 376	91 794	573 326	555 158	2 291 098
Percent of persons under 6 years	70.9	70.3	59.2	78.0	77.4	73.2	81.3	73.1	70.9	67.1	67.3	76.5
With female householder, no husband present	3 177 757	2 543 814	1 565 191	978 623	713 992	111 654	152 977	633 943	21 292	166 044	153 038	293 569
Grandchild	1 772 503	1 404 365	724 813	679 552	464 947	56 038	158 567	368 138	9 019	61 599	65 329	232 191
Other relatives	350 311	293 542	162 432	131 110	97 831	10 510	22 769	56 769	1 524	10 692	10 783	33 770
Nonrelatives	356 147	287 867	138 441	149 426	104 602	12 774	32 050	68 280	1 892	12 951	12 129	41 308
Institutionalized persons	5 798	5 067	3 371	1 696	1 288	81	327	731	33	218	215	265
Other persons in group quarters	32 418	27 561	17 192	10 369	6 506	1 126	2 737	4 857	198	1 277	692	2 690
Persons under 18 years	**63 604 432**	**48 686 531**	**19 198 816**	**29 487 715**	**19 911 363**	**2 356 034**	**7 220 318**	**14 917 901**	**364 496**	**2 474 261**	**2 466 691**	**9 612 453**
Householder or spouse	90 847	65 590	35 277	30 313	20 032	3 416	6 865	25 257	591	4 882	5 191	14 593
Own child	57 461 020	43 851 711	16 730 004	27 121 707	18 302 350	2 156 336	6 663 021	13 609 309	333 277	2 252 067	2 238 294	8 785 671
In married-couple family	44 642 569	33 705 198	11 159 396	22 545 802	15 023 091	1 696 133	5 826 578	10 937 371	252 938	1 647 847	1 656 346	7 380 240
Percent of persons under 18 years	70.2	69.2	58.1	76.5	75.4	72.0	80.7	73.3	69.4	66.6	67.1	76.8
With female householder, no husband present	10 674 900	8 497 699	4 816 382	3 681 317	2 676 427	377 314	627 576	2 177 201	69 127	520 387	498 771	1 088 916
Grandchild	3 493 999	2 721 326	1 411 489	1 309 837	883 481	110 229	316 127	772 673	17 985	124 678	136 505	493 505
Other relatives	1 172 053	962 700	517 103	445 597	325 039	36 207	84 351	209 353	5 103	37 116	37 985	129 149
Nonrelatives	1 121 322	877 819	399 271	478 548	322 887	42 045	113 616	243 503	6 286	42 331	41 154	153 732
Institutionalized persons	142 403	110 936	51 170	59 766	34 033	3 404	22 329	31 467	476	6 626	4 238	20 127
Other persons in group quarters	122 788	96 449	54 502	41 947	23 541	4 397	14 009	26 339	778	6 561	3 324	15 676
Persons 60 to 64 years	**10 616 167**	**7 997 871**	**3 127 576**	**4 870 295**	**3 398 304**	**351 627**	**1 120 364**	**2 618 296**	**65 615**	**419 559**	**442 770**	**1 690 352**
Family householder	4 547 773	3 412 284	1 254 088	2 158 196	1 494 769	148 649	514 778	1 135 489	27 567	171 464	181 345	755 113
Male	3 767 182	2 788 684	956 413	1 832 271	1 254 474	125 387	452 410	978 498	23 045	142 666	151 467	661 320
Female	780 591	623 600	297 675	325 925	240 295	23 262	62 368	156 991	4 522	28 798	29 878	93 793
Spouse	3 534 867	2 603 874	907 791	1 696 083	1 166 824	121 561	407 698	930 993	23 665	140 699	150 867	615 762
Parent	191 144	167 874	77 711	90 163	71 091	4 936	14 136	23 270	733	4 230	3 967	14 340
Other relatives	277 637	222 325	105 809	116 516	84 083	8 129	23 504	55 312	1 329	9 077	9 969	34 937
Nonrelatives	193 362	161 015	81 467	79 548	58 372	5 718	15 458	32 347	951	6 127	5 656	19 613
Nonfamily householder	1 752 554	1 341 688	654 791	686 897	495 283	57 692	133 922	410 866	10 664	80 715	83 730	235 757
Male	610 929	468 148	238 342	229 806	160 295	17 762	51 749	142 781	3 276	23 697	24 586	91 222
Living alone	535 746	407 486	208 847	198 639	138 231	15 608	44 800	128 260	2 890	21 423	22 190	81 757
Female	1 141 625	873 540	416 449	457 091	334 988	39 930	82 173	268 085	7 388	57 018	59 144	144 535
Living alone	1 078 441	821 168	391 148	430 020	314 549	38 029	77 442	257 273	7 003	54 708	57 040	138 522
Institutionalized persons	83 227	60 183	30 051	30 132	19 865	3 534	6 733	23 044	601	5 680	6 074	10 689
Other persons in group quarters	35 603	28 628	15 868	12 760	7 217	1 408	4 135	6 975	105	1 567	1 162	4 141
Persons 65 years and over	**31 241 831**	**23 004 177**	**9 646 893**	**13 357 284**	**9 399 300**	**1 172 916**	**2 785 068**	**8 237 654**	**215 644**	**1 475 939**	**1 665 251**	**4 880 820**
Family householder	10 801 438	7 893 741	3 112 373	4 781 368	3 314 461	390 552	1 076 355	2 907 697	76 920	463 987	518 941	1 847 849
Male	8 759 574	6 328 702	2 360 558	3 968 144	2 732 795	323 400	911 949	2 430 872	64 174	377 432	423 528	1 565 738
Female	2 041 864	1 565 039	751 815	813 224	581 666	67 152	164 406	476 825	12 746	86 555	95 413	282 111
Spouse	6 927 364	5 033 966	1 874 392	3 159 574	2 195 518	262 884	701 172	1 893 398	52 889	305 928	341 356	1 193 225
Parent	1 156 730	965 575	390 288	575 287	433 507	32 431	109 349	191 155	5 590	31 522	31 848	122 195
Other relatives	975 410	784 296	326 862	457 434	334 107	29 635	93 692	191 114	5 318	31 535	34 623	119 638
Nonrelatives	428 761	347 443	170 030	177 413	128 083	13 737	35 593	81 318	2 437	15 278	15 161	48 442
Nonfamily householder	9 171 263	6 713 668	3 202 426	3 511 242	2 400 794	355 349	657 099	2 457 595	60 188	496 960	560 223	1 340 224
Male	2 055 016	1 497 026	725 749	771 277	526 832	70 325	174 120	557 990	12 776	93 033	105 504	346 677
Living alone	1 902 614	1 378 007	668 388	709 619	483 900	65 314	160 405	524 607	11 796	87 488	99 638	325 685
Female	7 116 247	5 216 642	2 476 677	2 739 965	1 971 962	285 024	482 979	1 899 605	47 412	403 927	454 719	993 547
Living alone	6 922 231	5 058 287	2 396 008	2 662 279	1 913 722	278 740	460 817	1 863 944	40 114	395 736	447 126	974 968
Institutionalized persons	1 676 062	1 181 286	529 821	651 465	466 424	84 499	100 542	494 776	11 953	125 682	159 297	197 844
Other persons in group quarters	104 803	84 202	40 701	43 501	28 406	3 829	11 266	20 601	349	5 047	3 802	11 403
Persons 65 to 74 years	**18 106 558**	**13 451 453**	**5 447 877**	**8 003 576**	**5 622 488**	**653 404**	**1 727 684**	**4 655 105**	**126 382**	**791 666**	**866 586**	**2 071 401**
Family householder	7 180 147	5 294 509	2 024 568	3 269 941	2 272 086	254 094	743 761	1 885 638	50 957	296 533	324 918	1 213 230
Male	5 935 417	4 326 520	1 566 211	2 760 309	1 903 188	214 142	642 979	1 608 897	43 334	246 297	270 742	1 048 524
Female	1 244 730	967 989	458 357	509 632	368 898	39 952	100 782	276 741	7 623	50 236	54 176	164 706
Spouse	5 094 657	3 719 803	1 351 557	2 368 246	1 644 623	190 194	533 429	1 374 854	38 505	218 471	240 160	877 718
Parent	444 833	383 226	160 151	223 075	171 834	11 869	39 372	61 607	1 873	10 479	10 072	39 183
Other relatives	458 783	371 440	163 039	208 401	153 168	13 673	41 560	87 343	2 361	14 435	15 777	54 770
Nonrelatives	255 538	209 082	103 732	105 350	76 581	7 963	20 806	46 456	1 449	8 592	8 582	27 833
Nonfamily householder	4 336 435	3 227 531	1 526 512	1 701 019	1 217 373	160 341	323 305	1 108 904	29 057	220 219	240 944	618 684
Male	1 107 687	822 984	406 666	416 318	286 882	35 736	93 700	284 703	6 987	47 497	51 796	178 423
Living alone	1 008 447	745 145	369 163	375 982	258 861	32 584	84 537	263 302	6 319	44 097	48 137	164 749
Female	3 228 748	2 404 547	1 119 846	1 284 701	930 491	124 605	229 605	824 201	22 070	172 722	189 148	440 261
Living alone	3 122 786	2 317 707	1 076 694	1 241 013	897 767	121 201	222 045	805 079	21 399	168 578	185 272	429 830
Institutionalized persons	284 107	204 561	97 999	106 562	74 216	13 149	19 197	79 546	1 996	20 494	23 339	33 717
Other persons in group quarters	52 058	41 301	20 319	20 982	12 607	2 121	6 254	10 757	184	2 433	1 794	6 346
Persons 75 to 84 years	**10 055 108**	**7 319 072**	**3 172 834**	**4 146 238**	**2 918 019**	**392 857**	**835 362**	**2 736 036**	**69 297**	**508 042**	**587 711**	**1 570 986**
Family householder	3 084 715	2 214 910	911 524	1 303 386	899 103	116 359	287 924	869 805	22 440	141 560	163 310	542 495
Male	2 452 506	1 739 368	680 286	1 059 082	727 251	94 807	237 024	713 138	18 307	113 121	131 335	450 375
Female	632 209	475 542	231 238	244 304	171 852	21 552	50 900	156 667	4 133	28 439	31 975	92 120
Spouse	1 669 485	1 196 210	471 588	724 622	504 033	66 164	154 425	473 275	13 151	79 379	91 743	289 002
Parent	445 654	369 391	144 582	224 809	167 663	12 687	44 459	76 263	2 198	12 221	12 679	49 165
Other relatives	354 789	285 214	114 357	170 857	124 479	10 884	35 494	69 575	1 937	11 402	12 690	43 546
Nonrelatives	127 374	102 161	49 347	52 814	37 887	4 210	10 717	25 213	723	4 793	4 771	14 926
Nonfamily householder	3 702 158	2 674 187	1 268 287	1 405 900	996 294	149 200	260 406	1 027 971	24 101	209 186	240 712	553 972
Male	728 341	519 481	244 916	274 565	185 501	26 526	62 538	208 860	4 468	34 543	40 517	129 332
Living alone	685 775	486 630	229 179	257 451	173 594	25 033	58 824	199 145	4 232	32 856	38 753	123 304
Female	2 973 817	2 154 706	1 023 371	1 131 335	810 793	122 674	197 868	819 111	19 633	174 643	200 195	424 640
Living alone	2 909 526	2 102 531	996 204	1 106 327	792 013	120 601	193 713	806 995	19 171	171 715	197 464	418 645
Institutionalized persons	636 138	448 590	199 630	248 960	178 252	32 187	38 521	187 548	4 645	47 913	60 520	74 470
Other persons in group quarters	34 795	28 409	13 519	14 890	10 308	1 166	3 416	6 386	102	1 588	1 286	3 410
Persons 85 years and over	**3 080 165**	**2 233 652**	**1 026 182**	**1 207 470**	**858 793**	**126 655**	**222 022**	**846 513**	**19 965**	**176 241**	**211 954**	**438 353**
Family householder	536 576	384 322	176 281	208 041	143 272	20 099	44 670	152 254	3 523	25 894	30 713	92 124
Male	371 651	262 814	114 061	148 753	102 356	14 451	31 946	108 837	2 533	18 014	21 451	66 839
Female	164 925	121 508	62 220	59 288	40 916	5 648	12 724	43 417	990	7 880	9 262	25 285
Spouse	163 222	117 953	51 247	66 706	46 862	6 526	13 318	45 269	1 233	8 078	9 453	26 505
Parent	266 243	212 958	85 555	127 403	94 010	7 875	25 518	53 285	1 519	8 822	9 097	33 847
Other relatives	161 838	127 642	49 466	78 176	56 460	5 078	16 638	34 196	1 020	5 698	6 156	21 322
Nonrelatives	45 849	36 200	16 951	19 249	13 615	1 564	4 070	9 649	265	1 893	1 808	5 683
Nonfamily householder	1 132 670	811 950	407 627	404 323	285 127	45 808	73 388	320 720	7 030	67 555	78 567	167 568
Male	218 988	154 561	74 167	80 394	54 449	8 063	17 882	64 427	1 321	10 993	13 191	38 922
Living alone	208 392	146 232	70 046	76 186	51 445	7 697	17 044	62 160	1 245	10 535	12 748	37 632
Female	913 682	657 389	333 460	323 929	230 678	37 745	55 506	256 293	5 709	56 562	65 376	128 646
Living alone	889 919	638 049	323 110	314 939	223 942	36 938	54 059	251 870	5 544	55 443	64 390	126 493
Institutionalized persons	755 817	528 135	232 192	295 943	213 956	39 163	42 824	227 682	5 312	57 275	75 438	89 657
Other persons in group quarters	17 950	14 492	6 863	7 629	5 491	542	1 596	3 458	63	1 026	722	1 647

Table 40. Household and Family Characteristics by Race and Hispanic Origin: 1990

[For definitions of terms and meanings of symbols, see text]

United States	All persons	Race					Hispanic origin (of any race)	White, not of Hispanic origin
		White	Black	American Indian, Eskimo, or Aleut	Asian or Pacific Islander	Other race		
HOUSEHOLD TYPE AND RELATIONSHIP								
All persons	248 709 873	199 686 070	29 986 060	1 959 234	7 273 662	9 804 847	22 354 059	188 128 296
In households	242 012 129	194 671 440	28 722 227	1 902 958	7 120 735	9 594 769	21 836 827	183 362 643
Householder	91 947 410	76 880 105	9 976 161	591 372	2 013 735	2 486 037	6 001 718	73 633 749
15 to 24 years	5 049 358	3 958 818	660 603	45 373	120 460	264 104	520 030	3 724 039
25 to 34 years	19 849 651	15 956 725	2 395 744	149 553	515 322	832 307	1 754 958	15 108 146
35 to 44 years	20 393 073	16 650 515	2 363 511	148 317	584 616	646 114	1 480 178	15 887 702
45 to 54 years	14 303 214	11 894 419	1 581 500	100 356	371 877	355 062	912 068	11 382 028
55 to 64 years	12 379 413	10 590 449	1 282 818	70 351	220 744	215 051	659 209	10 176 763
65 to 74 years	11 516 582	10 185 437	1 033 694	48 640	132 878	115 933	424 711	9 894 863
75 to 84 years	6 786 873	6 129 342	531 038	23 236	56 008	47 249	204 060	5 980 518
85 years and over	1 669 246	1 514 400	127 253	5 546	11 830	10 217	46 504	1 479 690
Family householder	64 517 947	53 461 645	6 986 624	442 161	1 559 043	2 068 474	4 789 261	50 946 609
Male	50 133 040	43 615 704	3 491 868	288 587	1 279 456	1 457 425	3 465 108	41 726 664
Female	14 384 907	9 845 941	3 494 756	153 574	279 587	611 049	1 324 153	9 219 945
Nonfamily householder	27 429 463	23 418 460	2 989 537	149 211	454 692	417 563	1 212 457	22 687 140
Male	12 141 701	10 146 139	1 407 716	77 851	255 465	254 530	666 964	9 767 227
Living alone	9 206 811	7 673 442	1 140 836	57 519	174 915	160 099	445 710	7 411 319
Female	15 287 762	13 272 321	1 581 821	71 360	199 227	163 033	545 493	12 919 913
Living alone	13 373 609	11 640 934	1 395 517	58 473	153 415	125 270	442 938	11 347 225
Spouse	50 708 322	44 282 151	3 319 653	284 695	1 462 478	1 359 345	3 390 585	42 369 862
Child	76 728 438	58 590 587	10 906 346	758 135	2 538 730	3 934 640	8 647 554	54 236 497
Grandchild	4 189 274	2 208 617	1 576 812	74 998	91 660	237 187	546 787	1 932 774
Brother or sister	2 628 549	1 522 367	565 426	25 951	188 499	326 306	638 238	1 239 968
Parent	1 747 569	1 209 720	244 216	11 064	178 580	103 989	248 313	1 077 947
Other relatives	3 385 190	1 966 963	686 258	41 788	255 227	434 954	851 868	1 584 694
Roomer, boarder, or foster child	1 595 204	1 079 655	310 473	18 548	67 844	118 684	257 711	956 543
Housemate or roommate	4 110 674	3 223 980	382 238	28 936	205 371	270 149	571 286	2 946 700
Other nonrelatives	4 971 499	3 707 295	754 644	67 471	118 611	323 478	682 767	3 383 909
In group quarters	6 697 744	5 014 630	1 263 833	56 276	152 927	210 078	517 232	4 765 653
Institutionalized persons	3 334 018	2 442 062	744 500	28 050	22 992	96 414	261 693	2 313 717
Correctional institutions	1 115 111	506 131	508 084	17 791	7 518	75 587	197 400	417 003
Nursing homes	1 772 032	1 612 292	135 837	4 997	9 723	9 183	32 568	1 590 191
Other institutions	446 875	323 639	100 579	5 262	5 751	11 644	31 725	306 523
Other persons in group quarters	3 363 726	2 572 568	519 333	28 226	129 935	113 664	255 539	2 451 936
College dormitories	1 953 558	1 609 977	208 021	9 420	96 025	30 115	70 964	1 572 872
Military quarters	589 700	415 366	129 889	5 592	13 766	25 087	43 754	400 320
Emergency shelters for homeless persons	178 638	87 871	73 385	4 522	2 270	10 590	27 634	76 433
Visible in street locations	49 734	23 955	19 647	1 146	1 110	3 876	16 663	15 042
Shelters for abused women	11 768	6 848	3 469	468	199	784	1 770	6 060
Drug/alcohol abuse group homes	52 038	32 281	15 768	1 470	363	2 156	4 812	30 190
Other noninstitutional group quarters	528 290	396 270	69 154	5 608	16 202	41 056	89 942	351 019
Persons per household	2.63	2.54	2.87	3.12	3.34	3.85	3.53	2.51
Persons per family	3.16	3.06	3.48	3.60	3.80	4.10	3.88	3.03
HOUSEHOLD SIZE								
Households	91 947 410	76 880 105	9 976 161	591 372	2 013 735	2 486 037	6 001 718	73 633 749
1 person	22 580 420	19 314 376	2 536 353	115 992	328 330	285 369	888 648	18 758 544
2 persons	29 453 593	26 017 821	2 412 716	147 234	445 293	430 529	1 241 704	25 261 316
3 persons	15 970 269	13 146 638	1 888 927	109 371	368 676	456 657	1 105 289	12 549 531
4 persons	13 860 094	11 339 607	1 514 272	99 796	411 524	494 895	1 128 662	10 754 986
5 persons	6 188 938	4 704 211	844 022	59 786	227 069	353 850	754 298	4 336 778
6 persons	2 300 520	1 534 767	408 860	30 877	116 659	209 357	419 758	1 342 808
7 or more persons	1 593 576	822 685	371 011	28 316	116 184	255 380	463 359	629 786
FAMILY TYPE BY PRESENCE OF OWN CHILDREN								
Families	64 517 947	53 461 645	6 986 624	442 161	1 559 043	2 068 474	4 789 261	50 946 609
With own children under 18 years	30 877 675	24 355 935	3 906 750	266 497	916 967	1 431 526	3 031 070	22 887 074
With own children under 6 years only	7 884 751	6 339 932	863 609	62 305	241 935	376 970	779 248	5 970 672
With own children under 6 and 6 to 17 years	6 403 526	4 814 910	906 717	68 514	196 525	416 860	835 326	4 430 159
Married-couple families	50 708 322	44 383 489	3 410 345	283 818	1 265 598	1 365 072	3 297 572	42 563 582
With own children under 18 years	23 494 726	19 777 362	1 779 772	165 951	790 212	981 429	2 132 498	18 698 437
With own children under 6 years only	6 226 406	5 322 689	387 805	36 796	215 773	263 343	561 236	5 043 535
With own children under 6 and 6 to 17 years	5 141 106	4 183 673	431 421	45 468	177 051	303 493	621 907	3 884 802
Female householder, no husband present	10 666 043	6 806 746	3 051 679	120 901	190 898	495 819	1 062 464	6 312 278
With own children under 18 years	6 028 409	3 607 568	1 897 145	78 879	96 429	348 388	697 964	3 306 284
With own children under 6 years only	1 272 224	755 093	404 562	18 436	18 515	75 618	146 494	694 886
With own children under 6 and 6 to 17 years	1 086 510	522 760	438 499	18 683	15 628	90 940	171 533	454 363
MARITAL STATUS								
Males 15 years and over	93 817 315	76 874 142	10 096 983	667 623	2 673 734	3 504 833	8 027 749	72 711 218
Never married	28 804 618	21 578 604	4 481 750	258 558	1 021 395	1 464 311	3 182 556	20 020 480
Now married, except separated	53 781 245	46 372 679	3 888 986	305 865	1 499 565	1 714 150	4 019 205	44 216 737
15 to 24 years	1 972 700	1 572 107	177 298	18 431	33 783	171 081	328 437	1 425 280
25 to 34 years	11 643 154	9 678 697	918 645	79 048	355 285	611 479	1 265 646	9 069 003
35 to 44 years	13 228 554	11 201 537	1 016 826	82 864	468 743	458 584	1 038 302	10 663 609
45 to 54 years	9 533 674	8 232 405	697 340	57 318	301 171	245 440	623 845	7 878 916
55 to 64 years	8 004 491	7 114 980	534 130	37 583	178 883	138 915	426 920	6 842 599
65 to 74 years	6 287 518	5 723 507	367 806	21 490	111 194	63 521	232 733	5 562 207
75 years and over	3 111 154	2 849 446	176 941	9 131	50 506	25 130	103 322	2 775 123
Separated	1 896 397	1 181 969	553 921	19 694	35 914	104 899	234 293	1 071 108
Widowed	2 377 589	1 955 833	332 048	15 279	35 088	39 341	115 417	1 886 226
Divorced	6 957 466	5 785 057	840 278	68 227	81 772	182 132	476 278	5 516 667
Females 15 years and over	101 324 687	82 692 612	11 830 476	702 215	2 862 398	3 236 986	7 743 317	78 542 165
Never married	23 755 235	17 175 748	4 526 232	208 846	789 782	1 054 627	2 314 256	16 040 666
Now married, except separated	53 144 096	45 931 802	3 660 332	313 686	1 680 315	1 557 961	3 823 012	43 808 428
15 to 24 years	3 213 847	2 624 923	240 270	28 869	80 694	239 091	471 130	2 407 300
25 to 34 years	13 142 712	11 014 335	978 382	91 617	496 571	561 807	1 242 814	10 378 765
35 to 44 years	13 110 582	11 149 892	960 598	84 898	526 942	388 252	946 316	10 630 823
45 to 54 years	9 060 712	7 883 200	633 620	53 914	288 575	201 403	560 527	7 546 211
55 to 64 years	7 398 225	6 607 211	467 787	32 645	180 433	110 149	367 581	6 362 847
65 to 74 years	5 253 888	4 828 504	278 488	16 471	86 151	44 274	176 810	4 701 931
75 years and over	1 964 130	1 823 737	101 187	5 272	20 949	12 985	57 834	1 780 551
Separated	2 676 840	1 525 724	883 141	29 119	51 857	186 999	387 012	1 353 273
Widowed	12 121 939	10 279 559	1 407 003	60 835	205 178	169 364	526 640	9 947 279
Divorced	9 626 577	7 779 779	1 353 768	89 729	135 266	268 035	692 397	7 392 519

Table 41. Household and Family Characteristics for Selected Age Groups by Race and Hispanic Origin: 1990

[For definitions of terms and meanings of symbols, see text]

United States	All persons	Race					Hispanic origin (of any race)	White, not of Hispanic origin
		White	Black	American Indian, Eskimo, or Aleut	Asian or Pacific Islander	Other race		
Persons under 6 years	**22 043 976**	**16 417 702**	**3 331 457**	**242 607**	**711 633**	**1 340 577**	**2 844 613**	**15 031 962**
Own child	19 526 799	15 092 950	2 472 538	197 069	639 465	1 124 777	2 394 875	13 916 227
In married-couple family	15 624 526	13 029 756	1 100 527	124 432	576 388	793 423	1 746 172	12 128 431
Percent of persons under 6 years	70.9	79.4	33.0	51.3	81.0	59.2	61.4	80.7
With female householder, no husband present	3 177 757	1 594 586	1 232 057	54 587	47 565	248 962	488 906	1 389 132
Grandchild	1 772 503	919 905	653 637	32 982	43 419	122 560	270 577	788 299
Other relatives	350 311	156 341	116 134	6 025	17 596	54 215	99 693	115 003
Nonrelatives	356 147	229 266	77 119	5 782	9 967	34 013	69 263	197 507
Institutionalized persons	5 798	3 661	1 628	131	181	197	717	3 200
Other persons in group quarters	32 418	15 579	10 401	618	1 005	4 815	9 488	11 726
Persons under 18 years	**63 604 432**	**47 628 229**	**9 584 415**	**696 967**	**2 083 387**	**3 611 434**	**7 757 500**	**43 807 311**
Householder or spouse	90 847	66 162	12 924	1 104	2 042	8 615	16 681	58 686
Own child	57 461 020	44 291 517	7 592 854	584 587	1 894 076	3 097 986	6 686 817	40 969 625
In married-couple family	44 642 569	36 979 207	3 450 352	379 714	1 666 429	2 166 867	4 805 660	34 489 085
Percent of persons under 18 years	70.2	77.6	36.0	54.5	80.0	60.0	61.9	78.7
With female householder, no husband present	10 674 900	5 834 754	3 763 245	160 515	172 769	743 617	1 504 305	5 173 796
Grandchild	3 493 999	1 806 232	1 327 588	65 720	79 874	214 585	488 361	1 562 189
Other relatives	1 172 053	551 386	357 563	19 888	67 761	175 455	325 328	415 292
Nonrelatives	1 121 322	761 352	213 259	19 263	32 931	94 517	195 816	669 880
Institutionalized persons	142 403	83 827	45 818	3 329	2 181	7 248	17 557	75 570
Other persons in group quarters	122 788	67 753	34 409	3 076	4 522	13 028	26 940	56 069
Persons 60 to 64 years	**10 616 167**	**9 211 123**	**961 619**	**51 389**	**218 517**	**173 519**	**553 642**	**8 855 087**
Family householder	4 547 773	3 961 998	408 667	23 077	79 338	74 693	234 732	3 811 390
Male	3 767 182	3 393 138	239 137	16 210	65 485	53 212	178 505	3 273 743
Female	780 591	568 860	169 530	6 867	13 853	21 481	56 227	537 647
Spouse	3 534 867	3 210 638	206 934	13 156	63 061	41 078	150 445	3 106 052
Parent	191 144	113 833	28 331	1 385	31 553	16 042	35 578	96 190
Other relatives	277 637	201 111	45 900	1 737	17 163	11 726	31 757	182 658
Nonrelatives	193 362	142 380	35 684	1 468	6 683	7 147	19 996	130 882
Nonfamily householder	1 752 554	1 484 100	218 507	9 726	19 217	21 004	74 777	1 434 793
Male	610 929	504 285	87 021	4 047	6 746	8 830	30 043	484 934
Living alone	535 746	442 894	76 154	3 559	5 778	7 361	25 151	426 658
Female	1 141 625	979 815	131 486	5 679	12 471	12 174	44 734	949 859
Living alone	1 078 441	928 578	121 986	5 260	11 474	11 143	40 994	901 091
Institutionalized persons	83 227	67 258	13 726	518	665	1 060	3 638	64 968
Other persons in group quarters	35 603	29 805	3 870	322	837	769	2 719	28 154
Persons 65 years and over	**31 241 831**	**27 851 973**	**2 508 551**	**114 453**	**454 458**	**312 396**	**1 161 283**	**27 050 819**
Family householder	10 801 438	9 612 257	888 795	44 634	142 006	113 746	410 154	9 331 555
Male	8 759 574	8 010 123	521 933	29 626	119 212	78 680	305 126	7 793 658
Female	2 041 864	1 602 134	366 862	15 008	22 794	35 066	105 028	1 537 897
Spouse	6 927 364	6 420 923	361 489	20 199	76 096	48 657	208 728	6 267 024
Parent	1 156 730	866 052	135 771	5 753	106 808	42 346	121 631	793 035
Other relatives	975 410	772 276	122 420	4 429	47 452	28 833	89 023	715 857
Nonrelatives	428 761	333 366	70 302	2 334	12 231	10 528	33 507	312 599
Nonfamily householder	9 171 263	8 216 922	803 190	32 788	58 710	59 653	265 121	8 023 516
Male	2 055 016	1 772 790	235 436	9 855	18 044	18 891	74 315	1 721 189
Living alone	1 902 614	1 647 261	213 212	9 087	16 222	16 832	66 400	1 601 019
Female	7 116 247	6 444 132	567 754	22 933	40 666	40 762	190 806	6 302 327
Living alone	6 922 231	6 283 973	538 738	22 121	30 032	38 567	181 547	6 148 692
Institutionalized persons	1 676 062	1 535 373	120 096	3 922	8 892	7 779	29 177	1 515 211
Other persons in group quarters	104 803	94 804	6 488	394	2 263	854	3 942	92 022
Persons 65 to 74 years	**18 106 558**	**16 026 201**	**1 503 460**	**71 980**	**300 731**	**204 186**	**723 029**	**15 628 390**
Family householder	7 100 147	6 378 604	591 345	30 387	99 018	80 793	281 898	6 188 263
Male	5 935 417	5 421 504	353 658	20 751	82 810	56 694	213 370	5 271 506
Female	1 244 730	957 100	237 687	9 636	16 208	24 099	68 528	916 757
Spouse	5 094 657	4 713 804	265 919	15 374	61 591	37 060	159 008	4 597 566
Parent	444 833	295 682	56 769	2 608	65 621	24 153	60 691	262 649
Other relatives	458 783	346 905	63 939	2 326	29 313	16 300	47 153	318 317
Nonrelatives	255 538	194 242	44 666	1 574	8 005	7 051	21 516	181 204
Nonfamily householder	4 336 435	3 806 833	442 349	18 253	33 860	35 140	142 813	3 706 600
Male	1 107 687	935 320	143 932	6 121	10 523	11 791	44 132	905 473
Living alone	1 008 447	854 207	128 885	5 570	9 450	10 335	38 848	827 824
Female	3 228 748	2 871 513	298 417	12 132	23 337	23 349	98 681	2 801 127
Living alone	3 122 786	2 785 602	281 469	11 602	22 136	21 977	93 312	2 718 870
Institutionalized persons	284 107	244 183	34 477	1 180	2 074	2 193	7 477	239 374
Other persons in group quarters	52 058	45 948	3 996	278	1 249	587	2 473	44 287
Persons 75 to 84 years	**10 055 108**	**9 037 720**	**774 908**	**33 268**	**123 989**	**85 223**	**343 690**	**8 792 789**
Family householder	3 084 715	2 762 635	246 172	11 828	36 590	27 490	106 906	2 687 392
Male	2 452 506	2 252 966	142 353	7 507	31 226	18 454	77 551	2 196 676
Female	632 209	509 669	103 819	4 321	5 364	9 036	29 355	490 716
Spouse	1 669 485	1 556 849	85 484	4 337	13 238	9 577	44 986	1 522 620
Parent	445 654	347 209	50 039	2 045	32 980	13 381	42 810	319 867
Other relatives	354 789	289 526	40 092	1 452	14 503	9 216	30 470	269 435
Nonrelatives	127 374	101 566	19 295	583	3 279	2 651	9 104	95 738
Nonfamily householder	3 702 158	3 366 707	284 866	11 408	19 418	19 759	97 154	3 293 126
Male	728 341	640 915	73 123	2 931	5 796	5 576	23 646	623 951
Living alone	685 775	605 505	67 227	2 755	5 197	5 091	21 536	590 050
Female	2 973 817	2 725 792	211 743	8 477	13 622	14 183	73 508	2 669 175
Living alone	2 909 526	2 672 450	202 148	8 250	13 124	13 554	70 638	2 617 900
Institutionalized persons	636 138	581 117	47 283	1 544	3 225	2 969	11 279	573 239
Other persons in group quarters	34 795	32 111	1 677	71	756	180	981	31 372
Persons 85 years and over	**3 080 165**	**2 788 052**	**230 183**	**9 205**	**29 738**	**22 987**	**94 564**	**2 719 750**
Family householder	536 576	471 018	51 278	2 419	6 398	5 463	21 350	455 900
Male	371 651	335 653	25 922	1 368	5 176	3 532	14 205	325 476
Female	164 925	135 365	25 356	1 051	1 222	1 931	7 145	130 424
Spouse	163 222	150 270	10 086	488	1 267	1 111	4 734	146 818
Parent	266 243	223 161	28 963	1 100	8 207	4 812	18 130	210 519
Other relatives	161 838	135 845	18 389	651	3 636	3 317	11 400	128 105
Nonrelatives	45 849	37 558	6 341	177	947	826	2 887	35 657
Nonfamily householder	1 132 670	1 043 382	75 975	3 127	5 432	4 754	25 154	1 023 790
Male	218 988	196 555	18 381	803	1 725	1 524	6 537	191 765
Living alone	208 392	187 549	17 100	762	1 575	1 406	6 016	183 145
Female	913 682	846 827	57 594	2 324	3 707	3 230	18 617	832 025
Living alone	889 919	825 921	55 121	2 269	3 572	3 036	17 597	811 922
Institutionalized persons	755 817	710 073	38 336	1 198	3 593	2 617	10 421	702 598
Other persons in group quarters	17 950	16 745	815	45	258	87	488	16 363

Table 42. **Household and Family Characteristics of White Persons: 1990**

[For definitions of terms and meanings of symbols, see text]

United States Urban and Rural Inside and Outside Metropolitan Area	Urban and rural						Inside and outside metropolitan area					
	Urban						Inside metropolitan area			Outside metropolitan area		
		Inside urbanized area										
	Total	Total	Central place	Urban fringe	Outside urbanized area	Rural	Total	In central city	Not in central city	Total	Urban	Rural
HOUSEHOLD TYPE AND RELATIONSHIP												
All persons	**143 807 279**	**119 359 248**	**52 192 735**	**67 166 513**	**24 448 031**	**55 878 791**	**150 863 170**	**51 452 071**	**99 411 099**	**48 822 900**	**17 538 683**	**31 284 217**
In households	139 640 840	116 328 310	50 339 302	65 989 008	23 312 530	55 030 600	147 243 638	49 617 586	97 626 052	47 427 802	16 628 600	30 799 202
Householder	56 613 098	47 112 854	21 600 072	25 512 782	9 500 244	20 267 007	58 333 897	21 323 382	37 010 515	18 546 208	6 923 987	11 622 221
15 to 24 years	3 218 367	2 595 853	1 539 241	1 056 612	622 514	740 451	3 002 601	1 509 665	1 492 936	956 217	494 225	461 992
25 to 34 years	12 156 768	10 304 848	4 923 502	5 381 346	1 851 920	3 799 957	12 534 169	4 853 397	7 680 772	3 422 556	1 308 621	2 113 935
35 to 44 years	12 043 113	10 188 453	4 391 037	5 797 416	1 854 660	4 607 402	12 903 709	4 334 477	8 569 232	3 746 806	1 298 201	2 448 605
45 to 54 years	8 381 128	7 087 404	2 911 411	4 175 993	1 293 724	3 513 291	9 084 814	2 877 737	6 207 077	2 809 605	915 443	1 894 162
55 to 64 years	7 567 524	6 312 297	2 713 361	3 598 936	1 255 227	3 022 925	7 899 843	2 684 067	5 215 776	2 690 606	924 193	1 766 413
65 to 74 years	7 480 345	6 078 809	2 797 905	3 280 904	1 401 536	2 705 092	7 442 793	2 763 014	4 679 779	2 742 644	1 052 764	1 689 880
75 to 84 years	4 598 902	3 632 928	1 821 835	1 811 093	965 974	1 530 440	4 384 344	1 803 299	2 581 045	1 744 998	734 546	1 010 452
85 years and over	1 166 951	912 262	501 780	410 482	254 689	347 449	1 081 624	497 726	583 898	432 776	195 994	236 782
Family householder	37 613 553	31 169 718	12 901 484	18 268 234	6 443 835	15 848 092	39 965 601	12 716 096	27 249 505	13 496 044	4 583 631	8 912 413
Male	29 926 867	24 751 217	9 887 680	14 863 537	5 175 650	13 688 837	32 240 547	9 736 477	22 504 070	11 375 157	3 669 450	7 705 707
Female	7 686 686	6 418 501	3 013 804	3 404 697	1 268 185	2 159 255	7 725 054	2 979 619	4 745 435	2 120 887	914 181	1 206 706
Nonfamily householder	18 999 545	15 943 136	8 698 588	7 244 548	3 056 409	4 418 915	18 368 296	8 607 286	9 761 010	5 050 164	2 340 356	2 709 808
Male	8 100 268	6 940 327	3 840 449	3 099 878	1 159 941	2 045 871	8 048 069	3 794 789	4 253 280	2 098 070	881 976	1 216 094
Living alone	6 032 762	5 133 292	2 846 470	2 286 822	899 470	1 640 680	5 990 875	2 818 200	3 172 675	1 682 567	683 051	999 516
Female	10 899 277	9 002 809	4 858 139	4 144 670	1 896 468	2 373 044	10 320 227	4 812 497	5 507 730	2 952 094	1 458 380	1 493 714
Living alone	9 466 657	7 742 955	4 151 687	3 591 268	1 723 702	2 174 277	8 926 385	4 116 735	4 809 650	2 714 549	1 323 525	1 391 024
Spouse	30 459 625	25 221 100	10 040 827	15 180 273	5 238 525	13 822 526	32 824 677	9 888 443	22 936 234	11 457 474	3 715 037	7 742 437
Child	40 739 951	33 776 465	13 500 500	20 275 965	6 963 486	17 850 636	43 974 748	13 292 913	30 681 835	14 615 839	4 831 049	9 784 790
Other relatives	5 215 634	4 503 367	2 100 456	2 402 911	712 267	1 692 033	5 512 702	2 072 390	3 440 312	1 394 965	487 136	907 829
Nonrelatives	6 612 532	5 714 524	3 097 447	2 617 077	898 008	1 398 398	6 597 614	3 040 458	3 557 156	1 413 316	671 391	741 925
In group quarters	4 166 439	3 030 938	1 853 433	1 177 505	1 135 501	848 191	3 619 532	1 834 485	1 785 047	1 395 098	910 083	485 015
Institutionalized persons	1 865 715	1 350 514	724 378	626 136	515 201	576 347	1 697 829	721 162	976 667	744 233	401 465	342 768
Correctional institutions	306 447	214 422	129 395	85 027	92 025	199 684	327 925	127 404	200 521	178 206	73 801	104 405
Nursing homes	1 312 157	938 752	482 180	456 572	373 405	300 135	1 121 501	480 083	641 418	490 791	290 785	200 006
Other institutions	247 111	197 340	112 803	84 537	49 771	76 528	248 403	113 675	134 728	75 236	36 879	38 357
Other persons in group quarters	2 300 724	1 680 424	1 129 055	551 369	620 300	271 844	1 921 703	1 113 323	808 380	650 865	508 618	142 247
College dormitories	1 506 728	1 032 698	752 372	280 326	474 030	103 249	1 150 191	745 662	404 529	459 786	400 760	59 026
Military quarters	377 505	298 391	141 842	156 549	79 114	37 861	341 952	134 671	207 281	73 414	57 628	15 786
Emergency shelters for homeless persons	82 969	74 035	61 033	13 002	8 934	4 902	78 869	60 602	18 267	9 002	7 053	1 949
Visible in street locations	21 579	20 330	14 024	6 306	1 249	2 376	22 285	13 846	8 439	1 670	883	787
Shelters for abused women	6 398	4 812	3 843	969	1 586	450	5 258	3 861	1 397	1 590	1 298	292
Drug/ alcohol abuse group homes	26 168	23 144	17 865	5 279	3 024	6 113	27 160	17 749	9 411	5 121	2 445	2 676
Other noninstitutional group quarters	279 377	227 014	138 076	88 938	52 363	116 893	295 988	136 932	159 056	100 282	38 551	61 731
Persons per household	2.47	2.48	2.34	2.59	2.46	2.72	2.53	2.33	2.64	2.56	2.41	2.65
Persons per family	3.04	3.04	3.00	3.08	3.01	3.11	3.07	2.99	3.10	3.04	2.98	3.07
Persons under 18 years	**32 728 678**	**26 772 227**	**10 926 019**	**15 846 208**	**5 956 451**	**14 899 551**	**35 199 135**	**10 743 971**	**24 455 164**	**12 429 094**	**4 147 062**	**8 282 032**
Householder or spouse	46 912	35 564	20 140	15 424	11 348	19 250	44 322	19 890	24 432	21 840	8 807	13 033
Own child	30 372 378	24 822 555	10 000 469	14 822 086	5 549 823	13 919 139	32 688 327	9 832 363	22 855 964	11 603 190	3 866 066	7 737 124
In married-couple family	24 786 040	20 375 425	7 793 217	12 582 208	4 410 615	12 193 167	27 216 967	7 654 145	19 562 822	9 762 240	3 044 980	6 717 260
Percent of persons under 18 years	75.7	76.1	71.3	79.4	74.0	81.8	77.3	71.2	80.0	78.5	73.4	81.1
With female householder, no husband present	4 550 636	3 607 673	1 807 844	1 799 829	942 963	1 284 118	4 385 688	1 785 274	2 600 414	1 449 066	686 386	762 680
Grandchild	1 264 066	1 051 022	472 458	578 564	213 044	542 166	1 362 089	465 740	896 349	444 143	146 327	297 816
Other relatives	405 379	342 936	171 457	171 479	62 443	146 007	427 284	168 947	258 337	124 102	41 955	82 147
Nonrelatives	534 526	434 371	207 784	226 587	100 155	226 826	564 550	203 576	360 974	196 802	68 917	127 885
Institutionalized persons	58 160	48 267	29 380	18 887	9 893	25 667	63 275	29 280	33 995	20 552	7 529	13 023
Other persons in group quarters	47 257	37 512	24 331	13 181	9 745	20 496	49 288	24 175	25 113	18 465	7 461	11 004
Persons 65 years and over	**20 689 888**	**16 618 988**	**7 808 381**	**8 810 607**	**4 070 900**	**7 162 085**	**20 270 085**	**7 715 789**	**12 554 296**	**7 581 888**	**3 068 266**	**4 513 622**
Family householder	6 891 410	5 606 418	2 486 353	3 120 065	1 284 992	2 720 847	6 952 739	2 451 721	4 501 018	2 659 518	960 269	1 699 249
Male	5 661 878	4 584 498	1 987 356	2 597 142	1 077 380	2 348 245	5 731 755	1 956 938	3 774 817	2 278 368	805 901	1 472 467
Female	1 229 532	1 021 920	498 997	522 923	207 612	372 602	1 220 984	494 783	726 201	381 150	154 368	226 782
Spouse	4 614 652	3 733 156	1 625 523	2 107 633	881 496	1 806 271	4 632 386	1 600 001	3 032 385	1 788 537	659 252	1 129 285
Parent	659 314	578 479	237 920	340 559	80 835	206 738	704 581	234 730	469 851	161 471	55 560	105 911
Other relatives	584 369	502 772	220 269	282 503	81 597	187 907	612 043	217 747	394 296	160 233	58 118	102 115
Nonrelatives	258 581	220 076	110 228	109 848	38 505	74 785	263 430	108 724	154 706	69 936	27 558	42 378
Nonfamily householder	6 354 788	5 017 581	2 635 167	2 382 414	1 337 207	1 862 134	5 956 022	2 612 318	3 343 704	2 260 900	1 023 035	1 237 865
Male	1 297 372	1 052 931	559 359	493 572	244 441	475 418	1 274 759	553 954	720 805	498 031	185 381	312 650
Living alone	1 203 492	973 575	519 031	454 544	229 917	443 769	1 178 677	514 178	664 499	468 584	174 830	293 754
Female	5 057 416	3 964 650	2 075 808	1 888 842	1 092 766	1 386 716	4 681 263	2 058 364	2 622 899	1 762 869	837 654	925 215
Living alone	4 925 948	3 853 110	2 017 709	1 835 401	1 072 838	1 358 025	4 552 382	2 001 011	2 551 371	1 731 591	822 840	908 751
Institutionalized persons	1 253 629	899 645	459 208	440 437	353 984	281 744	1 073 790	456 998	616 792	461 583	275 706	185 877
Other persons in group quarters	73 145	60 861	33 713	27 148	12 284	21 659	75 094	33 550	41 544	19 710	8 768	10 942
FAMILY TYPE BY PRESENCE OF OWN CHILDREN												
Families	**37 613 553**	**31 169 718**	**12 901 484**	**18 268 234**	**6 443 835**	**15 848 092**	**39 965 601**	**12 716 096**	**27 249 505**	**13 496 044**	**4 583 631**	**8 912 413**
With own children under 18 years	16 863 126	13 828 054	5 588 974	8 239 080	3 035 072	7 492 809	18 096 560	5 500 834	12 595 726	6 259 375	2 117 983	4 141 392
With own children under 6 years only	4 649 052	3 869 506	1 656 801	2 212 705	779 546	1 690 880	4 880 632	1 629 337	3 251 295	1 459 300	541 514	917 786
With own children under 6 and 6 to 17 years	3 312 199	2 700 038	1 104 347	1 595 691	612 161	1 502 711	3 553 151	1 084 182	2 468 969	1 261 759	424 512	837 247
Married-couple families	**30 545 729**	**25 300 067**	**10 067 751**	**15 232 316**	**5 245 662**	**13 837 760**	**32 913 731**	**9 914 000**	**22 999 731**	**11 469 758**	**3 720 268**	**7 749 490**
With own children under 18 years	13 337 472	11 002 198	4 206 081	6 796 117	2 335 274	6 440 890	14 640 893	4 135 832	10 505 061	5 136 469	1 612 603	3 523 866
With own children under 6 years only	3 842 266	3 230 412	1 310 966	1 919 446	611 854	1 480 423	4 114 451	1 288 039	2 826 412	1 208 238	417 827	790 411
With own children under 6 and 6 to 17 years	2 827 440	2 319 235	899 805	1 419 430	508 205	1 356 233	3 085 630	882 464	2 203 166	1 098 043	349 415	748 628
Female householder, no husband present	**5 386 905**	**4 442 230**	**2 154 147**	**2 288 083**	**944 675**	**1 419 841**	**5 294 188**	**2 131 285**	**3 162 903**	**1 512 558**	**686 799**	**825 759**
With own children under 18 years	2 840 514	2 268 415	1 121 264	1 147 151	572 099	767 054	2 738 328	1 107 567	1 630 761	869 240	417 094	452 146
With own children under 6 years only	615 085	483 188	266 038	217 150	131 897	140 008	569 990	262 741	307 249	185 103	98 919	86 184
With own children under 6 and 6 to 17 years	408 654	319 260	173 552	145 708	89 394	114 106	388 003	171 269	216 734	134 757	65 241	69 516
MARITAL STATUS												
Males 15 years and over	**55 343 332**	**46 269 467**	**20 458 258**	**25 811 209**	**9 073 865**	**21 530 810**	**58 303 440**	**20 167 370**	**38 136 070**	**18 570 702**	**6 539 879**	**12 030 823**
Never married	16 654 406	14 177 238	7 036 503	7 140 735	2 477 168	4 924 198	17 053 713	6 943 132	10 110 581	4 524 891	1 831 490	2 693 401
Now married, except separated	32 041 768	26 559 352	10 690 315	15 869 037	5 482 416	14 330 911	34 464 239	10 524 640	23 939 599	11 908 440	3 893 982	8 014 458
Separated	892 200	757 321	384 059	373 262	134 879	289 769	927 613	379 281	548 332	254 356	94 066	160 290
Widowed	1 441 075	1 175 037	560 995	614 042	266 038	514 758	1 440 318	555 422	884 896	515 515	198 147	317 368
Divorced	4 313 883	3 600 519	1 786 386	1 814 133	713 364	1 471 174	4 417 557	1 764 895	2 652 662	1 367 500	522 194	845 306
Females 15 years and over	**60 747 912**	**50 405 559**	**22 420 285**	**27 985 274**	**10 342 353**	**21 944 700**	**62 818 788**	**22 129 257**	**40 689 531**	**19 873 824**	**7 502 527**	**12 371 297**
Never married	13 692 299	11 657 413	5 795 005	5 862 408	2 034 886	3 483 449	13 806 466	5 728 284	8 078 182	3 369 282	1 508 817	1 860 465
Now married, except separated	31 706 860	26 272 386	10 543 567	15 728 819	5 434 474	14 224 942	34 118 009	10 384 065	23 733 944	11 813 793	3 854 844	7 958 949
Separated	1 210 137	1 012 586	511 938	500 648	197 551	315 587	1 212 706	505 235	707 471	313 018	137 974	175 044
Widowed	7 867 941	6 234 140	3 025 895	3 208 245	1 633 801	2 411 618	7 512 302	2 998 135	4 514 167	2 767 257	1 238 145	1 529 112
Divorced	6 270 675	5 229 034	2 543 880	2 685 154	1 041 641	1 509 104	6 169 305	2 513 538	3 655 767	1 610 474	762 747	847 727

Table 43. **Household and Family Characteristics of Black Persons: 1990**

[For definitions of terms and meanings of symbols, see text]

United States Urban and Rural Inside and Outside Metropolitan Area	Urban and rural						Inside and outside metropolitan area					
	Urban						Inside metropolitan area			Outside metropolitan area		
		Inside urbanized area			Outside urbanized area							
	Total	Total	Central place	Urban fringe		Rural	Total	In central city	Not in central city	Total	Urban	Rural
HOUSEHOLD TYPE AND RELATIONSHIP												
All persons	**26 153 444**	**23 533 536**	**17 308 291**	**6 225 245**	**2 619 908**	**3 832 616**	**25 122 054**	**17 169 430**	**7 952 624**	**4 864 006**	**2 203 157**	**2 660 849**
In households	25 175 299	22 732 611	16 756 887	5 975 724	2 442 688	3 546 928	24 156 861	16 625 760	7 531 101	4 565 366	2 057 655	2 507 711
Householder	8 836 740	7 996 181	5 970 947	2 025 234	840 559	1 139 421	8 455 952	5 925 383	2 530 569	1 520 209	712 516	807 693
15 to 24 years	615 716	551 248	418 185	133 063	64 468	44 887	571 478	414 129	157 349	89 125	55 821	33 304
25 to 34 years	2 179 614	1 980 586	1 417 449	563 137	199 028	216 130	2 072 978	1 405 543	667 435	322 766	167 958	154 808
35 to 44 years	2 110 067	1 933 003	1 372 908	560 095	177 064	253 444	2 038 423	1 362 090	676 333	325 088	149 152	175 936
45 to 54 years	1 399 888	1 287 093	939 398	347 695	112 795	181 612	1 364 044	932 819	431 225	217 456	94 017	123 439
55 to 64 years	1 118 137	1 013 175	797 316	215 859	104 962	164 681	1 078 571	792 113	286 458	204 247	88 554	115 693
65 to 74 years	877 264	775 872	640 355	135 517	101 392	156 430	833 058	635 915	197 143	200 636	87 141	113 495
75 to 84 years	434 714	370 809	313 078	57 731	63 905	96 324	404 243	310 964	93 279	126 795	55 202	71 593
85 years and over	101 340	84 395	72 258	12 137	16 945	25 913	93 157	71 810	21 347	34 096	14 671	19 425
Family householder	6 122 468	5 523 221	4 034 852	1 488 369	599 247	864 156	5 874 349	4 002 278	1 872 071	1 112 275	504 586	607 689
Male	2 971 353	2 683 820	1 821 538	862 282	287 533	520 515	2 900 195	1 805 798	1 094 397	591 673	236 771	354 902
Female	3 151 115	2 839 401	2 213 314	626 087	311 714	343 641	2 974 154	2 196 480	777 674	520 602	267 815	252 787
Nonfamily householder	2 714 272	2 472 960	1 936 095	536 865	241 312	275 265	2 581 603	1 923 105	658 498	407 934	207 930	200 004
Male	1 271 069	1 163 175	902 109	261 066	107 894	136 647	1 217 809	896 043	321 766	189 907	91 654	98 253
Living alone	1 022 461	932 833	734 700	198 133	89 628	118 375	978 370	730 141	248 229	162 466	76 390	86 076
Female	1 443 203	1 309 785	1 033 986	275 799	133 418	138 618	1 363 794	1 027 062	336 732	218 027	116 276	101 751
Living alone	1 267 136	1 145 700	912 080	233 620	121 436	128 381	1 194 697	906 098	288 599	200 820	106 046	94 774
Spouse	2 819 811	2 548 344	1 725 220	823 124	271 467	499 842	2 752 614	1 710 300	1 042 314	567 039	225 444	341 595
Child	9 530 902	8 553 485	6 290 714	2 262 771	977 417	1 375 444	9 104 541	6 241 064	2 863 477	1 801 805	822 325	979 480
Other relatives	2 650 815	2 392 875	1 855 641	537 234	257 940	421 897	2 548 903	1 841 981	706 922	523 809	218 800	305 009
Nonrelatives	1 337 031	1 241 726	914 365	327 361	95 305	110 324	1 294 851	907 032	387 819	152 504	78 570	73 934
In group quarters	978 145	800 925	551 404	249 521	177 220	285 688	965 193	543 670	421 523	298 640	145 502	153 138
Institutionalized persons	506 111	410 013	267 214	142 799	96 098	238 389	537 462	264 262	273 200	207 038	80 003	127 035
Correctional institutions	307 450	244 703	153 850	90 853	62 747	200 634	349 357	151 459	197 898	158 727	51 739	106 988
Nursing homes	119 576	96 358	72 152	24 206	23 218	16 261	104 087	71 959	32 128	31 750	19 757	11 993
Other institutions	79 085	68 952	41 212	27 740	10 133	21 494	84 018	40 844	43 174	16 561	8 507	8 054
Other persons in group quarters	472 034	390 912	284 190	106 722	81 122	47 299	427 731	279 408	148 323	91 602	65 499	26 103
College dormitories	189 151	138 421	108 825	29 596	50 730	18 870	154 681	106 816	47 865	53 340	41 872	11 468
Military quarters	118 642	96 401	42 373	54 028	22 241	11 247	107 196	40 159	67 037	22 693	17 468	5 225
Emergency shelters for homeless persons	71 747	70 410	62 285	8 125	1 337	1 638	72 092	61 953	10 139	1 293	1 027	266
Visible in street locations	19 505	19 151	17 658	1 493	354	142	19 297	17 590	1 707	350	269	81
Shelters for abused women	3 350	3 038	2 553	485	312	119	3 184	2 547	637	285	261	24
Drug/alcohol abuse group homes	13 996	13 517	11 563	1 954	479	1 772	14 534	11 527	3 007	1 234	393	841
Other noninstitutional group quarters	55 643	49 974	38 933	11 041	5 669	13 511	56 747	38 816	17 931	12 407	4 209	8 198
Persons per household	2.84	2.84	2.80	2.95	2.91	3.11	2.85	2.80	2.97	3.00	2.89	3.10
Persons per family	3.45	3.44	3.44	3.44	3.52	3.66	3.45	3.44	3.47	3.60	3.51	3.68
Persons under 18 years	**8 364 035**	**7 465 628**	**5 480 391**	**1 985 237**	**898 407**	**1 220 380**	**7 955 414**	**5 433 977**	**2 521 437**	**1 629 001**	**756 775**	**872 226**
Householder or spouse	11 877	10 827	8 782	2 045	1 050	1 047	11 263	8 728	2 535	1 661	889	772
Own child	6 671 015	5 951 533	4 313 627	1 637 906	719 482	921 839	6 324 838	4 276 646	2 048 192	1 268 016	606 072	661 944
In married-couple family	2 908 054	2 599 140	1 676 330	922 810	308 914	542 298	2 820 899	1 660 191	1 160 708	629 453	254 580	374 873
Percent of persons under 18 years	34.8	34.8	30.6	46.5	34.4	44.4	35.5	30.6	46.0	38.6	33.6	43.0
With female householder, no husband present	3 429 311	3 049 778	2 417 582	632 196	379 533	333 934	3 182 726	2 398 511	784 215	580 519	326 576	253 943
Grandchild	1 118 011	992 354	781 131	211 223	125 657	209 577	1 068 469	774 852	293 617	259 119	106 503	152 616
Other relatives	311 085	279 715	212 222	67 493	31 370	46 478	296 950	210 475	86 475	60 613	26 651	33 962
Nonrelatives	189 456	174 026	125 370	48 656	15 430	23 803	185 127	124 155	60 972	28 132	12 466	15 666
Institutionalized persons	32 422	29 154	17 421	11 733	3 268	13 396	38 030	17 353	20 677	7 788	2 662	5 126
Other persons in group quarters	30 160	28 019	21 838	6 181	2 150	4 240	30 737	21 768	8 969	3 672	1 532	2 140
Persons 65 years and over	**2 100 227**	**1 834 829**	**1 500 190**	**334 639**	**265 398**	**408 324**	**1 983 740**	**1 490 013**	**493 727**	**524 811**	**228 124**	**296 687**
Family householder	725 164	635 294	515 675	119 619	89 870	163 631	693 728	512 022	181 706	195 067	76 786	118 281
Male	421 495	371 730	295 501	76 229	49 765	100 438	408 184	293 619	114 565	113 749	42 081	71 668
Female	303 669	263 564	220 174	43 390	40 105	63 193	285 544	218 403	67 141	81 318	34 705	46 613
Spouse	291 751	256 624	205 334	51 290	35 127	69 738	281 799	204 020	77 779	79 690	29 715	49 975
Parent	118 250	107 918	81 844	26 074	10 332	17 521	114 434	81 201	33 233	21 337	8 938	12 399
Other relatives	102 496	91 003	71 881	19 122	11 493	19 924	98 027	71 261	26 766	24 393	10 079	14 314
Nonrelatives	63 022	58 078	47 847	10 231	4 944	7 280	61 265	47 560	13 705	9 037	4 178	4 859
Nonfamily householder	688 154	595 782	510 016	85 766	92 372	115 036	636 730	506 667	130 063	166 460	80 228	86 232
Male	197 694	172 334	147 472	24 862	25 360	37 742	185 633	146 671	38 962	49 803	21 730	28 073
Living alone	177 925	154 388	132 359	22 029	23 537	35 287	166 633	131 639	34 994	46 579	20 189	26 390
Female	490 460	423 448	362 544	60 904	67 012	77 294	451 097	359 996	91 101	116 657	58 498	58 159
Living alone	464 072	399 436	342 034	57 402	64 636	74 666	425 909	339 585	86 324	112 829	56 486	56 343
Institutionalized persons	105 504	84 665	62 915	21 750	20 839	14 592	91 788	62 613	29 175	28 308	17 919	10 389
Other persons in group quarters	5 886	5 465	4 678	787	421	602	5 969	4 669	1 300	519	281	238
FAMILY TYPE BY PRESENCE OF OWN CHILDREN												
Families	**6 122 468**	**5 523 221**	**4 034 852**	**1 488 369**	**599 247**	**864 156**	**5 874 349**	**4 002 278**	**1 872 071**	**1 112 275**	**504 586**	**607 689**
With own children under 18 years	3 457 336	3 107 229	2 220 709	886 520	350 107	449 414	3 293 709	2 201 568	1 092 141	613 041	294 453	318 588
With own children under 6 years only	786 859	710 071	502 409	207 662	76 788	76 750	745 569	497 641	247 928	118 040	64 143	53 897
With own children under 6 and 6 to 17 years	800 297	714 418	519 409	195 009	85 879	106 420	758 226	515 047	243 179	148 491	71 932	76 559
Married-couple families	**2 901 586**	**2 619 935**	**1 764 539**	**855 396**	**281 651**	**508 759**	**2 831 929**	**1 748 975**	**1 082 954**	**578 416**	**232 587**	**345 829**
With own children under 18 years	1 515 492	1 362 881	868 580	494 301	152 611	264 280	1 474 583	860 063	614 520	305 189	125 319	179 870
With own children under 6 years only	344 018	311 537	192 355	119 182	32 481	43 787	332 363	190 321	142 042	55 442	26 355	29 087
With own children under 6 and 6 to 17 years	366 825	328 019	210 167	117 852	38 806	64 596	355 149	208 138	147 011	76 272	31 735	44 537
Female householder, no husband present	**2 757 829**	**2 479 560**	**1 952 002**	**527 558**	**278 269**	**293 850**	**2 593 853**	**1 937 162**	**656 691**	**457 826**	**239 682**	**218 144**
With own children under 18 years	1 737 190	1 557 696	1 217 686	340 010	179 494	159 955	1 621 718	1 208 129	413 589	275 427	154 704	120 723
With own children under 6 years only	378 376	339 829	267 950	71 879	38 547	26 186	351 478	265 584	85 894	53 084	33 164	19 920
With own children under 6 and 6 to 17 years	401 087	357 054	287 838	69 216	44 033	37 412	371 921	285 672	86 249	66 578	37 781	28 797
MARITAL STATUS												
Males 15 years and over	**8 679 384**	**7 827 484**	**5 679 723**	**2 147 761**	**851 900**	**1 417 599**	**8 439 287**	**5 635 015**	**2 804 272**	**1 657 696**	**711 028**	**946 668**
Never married	3 874 378	3 490 852	2 607 913	882 939	383 526	607 372	3 758 560	2 587 827	1 170 733	723 190	321 446	401 744
Now married, except separated	3 300 792	2 977 417	2 019 438	957 979	323 375	588 194	3 227 805	2 001 442	1 226 363	661 181	267 590	393 591
Separated	482 100	437 856	342 298	95 558	44 244	71 821	466 772	339 851	126 921	87 149	37 865	49 284
Widowed	276 229	241 103	197 475	43 628	35 126	55 819	261 732	196 263	65 469	70 316	29 963	40 353
Divorced	745 885	680 256	512 599	167 657	65 629	94 393	724 418	509 632	214 786	115 860	54 164	61 696
Females 15 years and over	**10 413 910**	**9 402 677**	**6 999 371**	**2 403 306**	**1 011 233**	**1 416 566**	**9 977 413**	**6 944 751**	**3 032 662**	**1 853 063**	**855 302**	**997 761**
Never married	4 048 907	3 668 471	2 796 502	871 969	380 436	477 325	3 865 198	2 775 599	1 089 599	661 034	321 750	339 284
Now married, except separated	3 121 850	2 824 805	1 934 158	890 647	297 045	538 482	3 045 715	1 917 818	1 127 897	614 617	246 484	368 133
Separated	798 232	722 850	566 848	156 002	75 382	84 909	754 855	561 819	193 036	128 286	65 413	62 873
Widowed	1 195 832	1 040 507	847 400	193 107	155 325	211 171	1 116 217	840 694	275 523	290 786	135 037	155 749
Divorced	1 249 089	1 146 044	854 463	291 581	103 045	104 679	1 195 428	848 821	346 607	158 340	86 618	71 722

Table 44. Household and Family Characteristics of American Indian, Eskimo, or Aleut Persons: 1990

[For definitions of terms and meanings of symbols, see text]

United States Urban and Rural Inside and Outside Metropolitan Area	Urban and rural: Total	Urban: Total	Central place	Urban fringe	Outside urbanized area	Rural	Inside metro: Total	In central city	Not in central city	Outside metro: Total	Outside metro: Urban	Outside metro: Rural
HOUSEHOLD TYPE AND RELATIONSHIP												
All persons	1 100 534	768 135	468 915	299 220	332 399	858 700	1 002 984	465 364	537 620	956 250	270 174	686 076
In households	1 059 365	740 758	449 169	291 589	318 607	843 593	969 057	445 748	523 309	933 901	258 022	675 879
Householder	349 899	252 845	155 508	97 337	97 054	241 473	323 542	154 315	169 227	267 830	77 696	190 134
15 to 24 years	31 976	23 023	16 094	6 929	8 953	13 397	26 742	15 879	10 863	18 631	7 612	11 019
25 to 34 years	94 983	69 263	43 717	25 546	25 720	54 570	85 477	43 271	42 206	64 076	20 821	43 255
35 to 44 years	89 034	65 354	38 724	26 630	23 680	59 283	83 715	38 412	45 303	64 602	18 916	45 686
45 to 54 years	56 979	42 297	24 258	18 039	14 682	43 377	55 885	24 050	31 835	44 471	11 451	33 020
55 to 64 years	37 190	26 717	15 950	10 767	10 473	33 161	35 906	15 907	19 999	34 445	8 189	26 256
65 to 74 years	25 291	17 141	10 849	6 292	8 150	23 349	23 233	10 860	12 373	25 407	6 396	19 011
75 to 84 years	11 747	7 382	4 792	2 590	4 365	11 489	10 253	4 800	5 453	12 983	3 477	9 506
85 years and over	2 699	1 668	1 124	544	1 031	2 847	2 331	1 136	1 195	3 215	834	2 381
Family householder	248 185	175 265	103 152	72 113	72 920	193 976	231 412	102 355	129 057	210 749	57 868	152 881
Male	156 697	110 470	60 166	50 304	46 227	131 890	150 768	59 582	91 186	137 819	35 997	101 822
Female	91 488	64 795	42 986	21 809	26 693	62 086	80 644	42 773	37 871	72 930	21 871	51 059
Nonfamily householder	101 714	77 580	52 356	25 224	24 134	47 497	92 130	51 960	40 170	57 081	19 828	37 253
Male	51 530	40 102	27 059	13 043	11 428	26 321	47 725	26 787	20 938	30 126	9 481	20 645
Living alone	36 242	27 706	19 018	8 688	8 536	21 277	33 475	18 864	14 611	24 044	7 095	16 949
Female	50 184	37 478	25 297	12 181	12 706	21 176	44 405	25 173	19 232	26 955	10 347	16 608
Living alone	40 020	29 181	19 701	9 480	10 839	18 453	35 038	19 642	15 396	23 435	8 804	14 631
Spouse	156 824	110 584	59 901	50 683	46 240	127 871	150 386	59 300	91 086	134 309	36 244	98 065
Child	396 795	263 800	160 634	103 166	132 995	361 340	353 996	159 708	194 288	404 139	108 885	295 254
Other relatives	77 245	52 671	33 650	19 021	24 574	76 556	68 874	33 525	35 349	84 927	20 500	64 427
Nonrelatives	78 602	60 858	39 476	21 382	17 744	36 353	72 259	38 900	33 359	42 696	14 697	27 999
In group quarters	41 169	27 377	19 746	7 631	13 792	15 107	33 927	19 616	14 311	22 349	12 152	10 197
Institutionalized persons	17 820	10 166	7 319	2 847	7 654	10 230	14 753	7 319	7 434	13 297	6 657	6 640
Correctional institutions	10 723	6 528	4 744	1 784	4 195	7 068	10 115	4 727	5 388	7 676	3 500	4 176
Nursing homes	3 526	1 469	1 043	426	2 057	1 471	1 914	1 064	850	3 083	1 862	1 221
Other institutions	3 571	2 169	1 532	637	1 402	1 691	2 724	1 528	1 196	2 538	1 295	1 243
Other persons in group quarters	23 349	17 211	12 427	4 784	6 138	4 877	19 174	12 297	6 877	9 052	5 495	3 557
College dormitories	8 274	5 162	4 119	1 043	3 112	1 146	5 520	4 048	1 472	3 900	2 938	962
Military quarters	4 955	4 080	1 786	2 294	875	637	4 795	1 758	3 037	797	595	202
Emergency shelters for homeless persons	4 321	3 651	3 252	399	670	201	3 797	3 222	575	725	604	121
Visible in street locations	932	827	729	98	105	214	892	725	167	254	100	154
Shelters for abused women	443	245	208	37	198	25	255	211	44	213	192	21
Drug/alcohol abuse group homes	1 139	994	798	196	145	331	1 091	802	289	379	128	251
Other noninstitutional group quarters	3 285	2 252	1 535	717	1 033	2 323	2 824	1 531	1 293	2 784	938	1 846
Persons per household	2.93	2.86	2.81	2.94	3.13	3.39	2.92	2.81	3.02	3.36	3.14	3.45
Persons per family	3.44	3.37	3.38	3.36	3.61	3.81	3.40	3.38	3.42	3.82	3.65	3.88
Persons under 18 years	364 361	238 663	148 209	90 454	125 698	332 606	320 354	147 275	173 079	376 613	103 595	273 018
Householder or spouse	721	499	359	140	222	383	590	351	239	514	187	327
Own child	309 916	203 413	125 557	77 856	106 503	274 671	272 852	124 730	148 122	311 735	87 428	224 307
In married-couple family	190 570	123 286	69 641	53 645	67 284	189 144	172 589	69 137	103 452	207 125	54 647	152 478
Percent of persons under 18 years	52.3	51.7	47.0	59.3	53.5	56.9	53.9	46.9	59.8	55.0	52.8	55.8
With female householder, no husband present	97 282	65 530	46 207	19 323	31 752	63 233	80 828	45 967	34 861	79 687	26 514	53 173
Grandchild	27 403	16 888	10 673	6 215	10 515	38 317	23 921	10 684	13 237	41 799	8 773	33 026
Other relatives	10 434	6 909	4 574	2 335	3 525	9 454	9 049	4 553	4 496	10 839	2 974	7 865
Nonrelatives	11 723	8 366	5 143	3 223	3 357	7 540	10 691	5 064	5 627	8 572	2 770	5 802
Institutionalized persons	2 139	1 390	1 002	388	749	1 190	1 828	1 004	824	1 501	698	803
Other persons in group quarters	2 025	1 198	901	297	827	1 051	1 423	889	534	1 653	765	888
Persons 65 years and over	59 825	39 508	24 771	14 737	20 317	54 628	53 909	24 813	29 096	60 544	16 147	44 397
Family householder	20 813	13 739	8 338	5 401	7 074	23 821	19 367	8 361	11 006	25 267	5 591	19 676
Male	13 931	9 299	5 338	3 961	4 632	15 695	13 256	5 340	7 916	16 370	3 599	12 771
Female	6 882	4 440	3 000	1 440	2 442	8 126	6 111	3 021	3 090	8 897	1 992	6 905
Spouse	9 946	6 669	3 870	2 799	3 277	10 253	9 444	3 857	5 587	10 755	2 507	8 248
Parent	3 343	2 559	1 511	1 048	784	2 410	3 216	1 508	1 708	2 537	616	1 921
Other relatives	2 317	1 673	992	681	644	2 112	2 296	998	1 298	2 133	502	1 631
Nonrelatives	1 450	1 111	704	407	339	884	1 422	710	712	912	263	649
Nonfamily householder	18 924	12 452	8 427	4 025	6 472	13 864	16 450	8 435	8 015	16 338	5 116	11 222
Male	5 018	3 409	2 359	1 050	1 609	4 837	4 597	2 351	2 246	5 258	1 307	3 951
Living alone	4 572	3 060	2 128	932	1 512	4 515	4 121	2 121	2 032	4 934	1 230	3 704
Female	13 906	9 043	6 068	2 975	4 863	9 027	11 853	6 084	5 769	11 080	3 809	7 271
Living alone	13 374	8 627	5 770	2 857	4 747	8 747	11 331	5 795	5 536	10 790	3 718	7 072
Institutionalized persons	2 785	1 106	765	341	1 679	1 137	1 483	781	702	2 439	1 510	929
Other persons in group quarters	247	199	164	35	48	147	231	163	68	163	42	121
FAMILY TYPE BY PRESENCE OF OWN CHILDREN												
Families	248 185	175 265	103 152	72 113	72 920	193 976	231 412	102 355	129 057	210 749	57 868	152 881
With own children under 18 years	149 475	102 768	61 516	41 252	46 707	117 022	135 162	61 012	74 150	131 335	37 635	93 700
With own children under 6 years only	38 899	27 333	17 089	10 244	11 566	23 406	33 996	16 894	17 102	28 309	9 452	18 857
With own children under 6 and 6 to 17 years	35 894	23 437	14 487	8 950	12 457	32 620	31 131	14 386	16 745	37 383	10 244	27 139
Married-couple families	154 871	109 158	58 716	50 442	45 713	128 947	149 525	58 203	91 322	134 293	35 433	98 860
With own children under 18 years	88 582	60 499	32 609	27 890	28 083	77 369	83 087	32 322	50 765	82 864	22 176	60 688
With own children under 6 years only	22 676	16 097	9 019	7 078	6 579	14 120	20 666	8 924	11 742	16 130	5 174	10 956
With own children under 6 and 6 to 17 years	22 834	14 703	8 177	6 526	8 131	22 634	20 159	8 096	12 063	25 309	6 650	18 659
Female householder, no husband present	73 055	51 473	35 151	16 322	21 582	47 846	63 053	34 963	28 090	57 848	17 851	39 997
With own children under 18 years	49 500	34 420	23 936	10 484	15 080	29 379	41 802	23 783	18 019	37 077	12 523	24 554
With own children under 6 years only	12 285	8 551	6 256	2 295	3 734	6 151	9 997	6 189	3 808	8 439	3 202	5 237
With own children under 6 and 6 to 17 years	11 112	7 539	5 520	2 019	3 573	7 571	9 289	5 508	3 781	9 394	2 959	6 435
MARITAL STATUS												
Males 15 years and over	381 881	274 619	165 095	109 524	107 262	285 742	358 077	163 719	194 358	309 546	86 260	223 286
Never married	149 798	108 390	69 983	38 407	41 408	108 760	136 402	69 434	66 968	122 156	34 524	87 632
Now married, except separated	168 908	119 356	65 152	54 204	49 552	136 957	162 176	64 534	97 642	143 689	38 668	105 021
Separated	12 227	9 359	6 181	3 178	2 868	7 467	11 548	6 126	5 422	8 146	2 309	5 837
Widowed	7 667	5 156	3 343	1 813	2 511	7 612	7 095	3 336	3 759	8 184	2 068	6 116
Divorced	43 281	32 358	20 436	11 922	10 923	24 946	40 856	20 289	20 567	27 371	8 691	18 680
Females 15 years and over	409 600	291 704	177 494	114 210	117 896	292 615	375 007	176 172	198 835	327 208	95 307	231 901
Never married	122 943	88 347	58 167	30 180	34 596	85 903	108 920	57 699	51 221	99 926	29 155	70 771
Now married, except separated	172 735	121 740	66 792	54 948	50 995	140 951	164 964	66 196	98 768	148 722	40 150	108 572
Separated	19 431	14 545	9 841	4 704	4 886	9 688	17 416	9 767	7 649	11 703	3 930	7 773
Widowed	33 210	21 848	14 091	7 757	11 362	27 625	28 948	14 137	14 811	31 887	9 166	22 721
Divorced	61 281	45 224	28 603	16 621	16 057	28 448	54 759	28 373	26 386	34 970	12 906	22 064

Table 45. Household and Family Characteristics of Asian or Pacific Islander Persons: 1990

[For definitions of terms and meanings of symbols, see text]

United States Urban and Rural Inside and Outside Metropolitan Area	Urban and rural						Inside and outside metropolitan area					
	Urban				Outside urbanized area	Rural	Inside metropolitan area			Outside metropolitan area		
		Inside urbanized area						In central city	Not in central city			
	Total	Total	Central place	Urban fringe			Total			Total	Urban	Rural
HOUSEHOLD TYPE AND RELATIONSHIP												
All persons	6 934 689	6 507 391	3 421 439	3 085 952	427 298	338 973	6 823 859	3 373 675	3 450 184	449 803	298 962	150 841
In households	6 793 124	6 388 075	3 336 407	3 051 668	405 049	327 611	6 695 242	3 290 327	3 404 915	425 493	280 493	145 000
Householder	1 934 866	1 823 436	995 571	827 865	111 430	78 869	1 896 281	982 551	913 730	117 454	81 811	35 643
15 to 24 years	117 635	108 348	74 927	33 421	9 287	2 825	110 511	73 655	36 856	9 949	8 451	1 498
25 to 34 years	499 974	472 549	266 845	205 704	27 425	15 348	487 540	263 725	223 815	27 782	20 789	6 993
35 to 44 years	561 985	532 815	262 314	270 501	29 170	22 631	555 440	258 763	296 677	29 176	20 241	8 935
45 to 54 years	355 414	337 106	162 386	174 720	18 308	16 463	352 867	160 294	192 573	19 010	12 530	6 480
55 to 64 years	210 717	198 382	111 260	87 122	12 335	10 027	207 102	109 732	97 370	13 642	8 754	4 888
65 to 74 years	125 666	116 534	75 832	40 702	9 132	7 212	121 989	74 864	47 125	10 889	6 783	4 106
75 to 84 years	52 468	47 759	34 410	13 349	4 709	3 540	50 311	33 999	16 312	5 697	3 457	2 240
85 years and over	11 007	9 943	7 597	2 346	1 064	823	10 521	7 519	3 002	1 309	806	503
Family householder	1 494 650	1 410 771	720 589	690 182	83 879	64 393	1 472 558	710 629	761 929	86 485	58 368	28 117
Male	1 225 596	1 157 592	573 795	583 797	68 004	53 860	1 209 216	565 577	643 639	70 240	47 409	22 831
Female	269 054	253 179	146 794	106 385	15 875	10 533	263 342	145 052	118 290	16 245	10 959	5 286
Nonfamily householder	440 216	412 665	274 982	137 683	27 551	14 476	423 723	271 922	151 801	30 969	23 443	7 526
Male	247 142	230 822	151 714	79 108	16 320	8 323	237 103	149 805	87 298	18 362	14 145	4 217
Living alone	168 691	157 829	103 568	54 261	10 862	6 224	162 529	102 461	60 068	12 386	9 116	3 270
Female	193 074	181 843	123 268	58 575	11 231	6 153	186 620	122 117	64 503	12 607	9 298	3 309
Living alone	148 308	139 570	95 299	44 271	8 738	5 107	143 522	94 566	48 956	9 893	7 069	2 824
Spouse	1 381 035	1 293 842	629 280	664 562	87 193	81 443	1 366 015	619 168	746 847	96 463	60 384	36 079
Child	2 409 900	2 260 597	1 139 964	1 120 633	149 303	128 830	2 384 962	1 124 948	1 260 014	153 768	97 787	55 981
Other relatives	689 541	656 542	351 164	305 378	32 999	24 425	682 682	346 912	335 770	31 284	20 357	10 927
Nonrelatives	377 782	353 658	220 428	133 230	24 124	14 044	365 302	216 748	148 554	26 524	20 154	6 370
In group quarters	141 565	119 316	85 032	34 284	22 249	11 362	128 617	83 348	45 269	24 310	18 469	5 841
Institutionalized persons	18 777	16 620	10 778	5 842	2 157	4 215	19 436	10 777	8 659	3 556	1 620	1 936
Correctional institutions	4 634	3 843	2 317	1 526	791	2 884	5 718	2 317	3 401	1 800	613	1 187
Nursing homes	9 309	8 357	5 647	2 710	952	414	8 760	5 634	3 126	963	729	234
Other institutions	4 834	4 420	2 814	1 606	414	917	4 958	2 826	2 132	793	278	515
Other persons in group quarters	122 788	102 696	74 254	28 442	20 092	7 147	109 181	72 571	36 610	20 754	16 849	3 905
College dormitories	92 509	76 541	55 953	20 588	15 968	3 516	79 991	54 563	25 428	16 034	14 041	1 993
Military quarters	12 550	10 334	5 337	4 997	2 216	1 216	11 942	5 192	6 750	1 824	1 367	457
Emergency shelters for homeless persons	2 208	1 966	1 649	317	242	62	2 093	1 627	466	177	146	31
Visible in street locations	892	778	673	105	114	218	948	667	281	162	49	113
Shelters for abused women	183	165	131	34	18	16	166	132	34	33	17	16
Drug/alcohol abuse group homes	315	302	227	75	13	48	337	227	110	26	10	16
Other noninstitutional group quarters	14 131	12 610	10 284	2 326	1 521	2 071	13 704	10 163	3 541	2 498	1 219	1 279
Persons per household	3.34	3.35	3.23	3.49	3.27	3.33	3.36	3.23	3.50	3.11	3.08	3.20
Persons per family	3.81	3.81	3.80	3.82	3.77	3.71	3.81	3.80	3.83	3.62	3.62	3.64
Persons under 18 years	1 967 791	1 834 965	917 381	917 584	132 826	115 596	1 944 976	905 099	1 039 877	138 411	87 230	51 181
Householder or spouse	1 960	1 826	1 244	582	134	82	1 896	1 239	657	146	100	46
Own child	1 790 218	1 672 277	825 431	846 846	117 941	103 858	1 770 912	814 691	956 221	123 164	78 138	45 026
In married-couple family	1 573 534	1 473 266	706 252	767 014	100 268	92 895	1 561 127	696 963	864 164	105 302	66 332	38 970
Percent of persons under 18 years	80.0	80.3	77.0	83.6	75.5	80.4	80.3	77.0	83.1	76.1	76.0	76.1
With female householder, no husband present	165 199	151 804	92 415	59 389	13 395	7 570	159 620	91 379	68 241	13 149	8 942	4 207
Grandchild	74 585	66 432	37 665	28 767	8 153	5 289	72 162	36 760	35 402	7 712	4 682	3 030
Other relatives	65 177	61 735	33 982	27 753	3 442	2 584	64 432	33 668	30 764	3 329	2 119	1 210
Nonrelatives	30 322	27 805	15 892	11 913	2 517	2 609	30 057	15 645	14 412	2 874	1 656	1 218
Institutionalized persons	1 708	1 585	898	687	123	473	1 886	981	905	295	76	219
Other persons in group quarters	3 821	3 305	2 269	1 036	516	701	3 631	2 195	1 436	891	459	432
Persons 65 years and over	431 493	403 084	244 776	158 308	28 409	22 965	421 806	241 548	180 258	32 652	20 327	12 325
Family householder	133 618	123 198	79 052	44 146	10 420	8 388	129 560	77 883	51 677	12 446	7 570	4 876
Male	111 906	103 008	65 249	37 750	8 898	7 300	108 527	64 272	44 255	10 685	6 484	4 201
Female	21 712	20 190	13 803	6 387	1 522	1 082	21 033	13 611	7 422	1 761	1 086	675
Spouse	71 151	65 324	41 823	23 501	5 827	4 945	68 852	41 128	27 724	7 244	4 337	2 907
Parent	103 513	99 900	49 340	50 560	3 613	3 295	103 362	48 732	54 630	3 446	2 289	1 157
Other relatives	45 445	43 106	21 598	21 508	2 339	2 007	45 184	21 239	23 945	2 268	1 473	795
Nonrelatives	11 693	10 961	6 856	4 105	732	538	11 556	6 769	4 787	675	431	244
Nonfamily householder	55 523	51 038	38 787	12 251	4 485	3 187	53 261	38 499	14 762	5 449	3 476	1 973
Male	16 757	15 215	11 613	3 602	1 542	1 287	16 130	11 521	4 609	1 914	1 131	783
Living alone	15 048	13 670	10 470	3 200	1 378	1 174	14 473	10 388	4 085	1 749	1 026	723
Female	38 766	35 823	27 174	8 649	2 943	1 900	37 131	26 978	10 153	3 535	2 345	1 190
Living alone	37 012	34 164	25 977	8 187	2 848	1 820	35 394	25 792	9 602	3 438	2 292	1 146
Institutionalized persons	8 408	7 502	5 425	2 077	906	484	7 856	5 404	2 452	1 036	711	325
Other persons in group quarters	2 142	2 055	1 895	160	87	121	2 175	1 894	281	88	40	48
FAMILY TYPE BY PRESENCE OF OWN CHILDREN												
Families	1 494 650	1 410 771	720 589	690 182	83 879	64 393	1 472 558	710 629	761 929	86 485	58 368	28 117
With own children under 18 years	878 510	827 859	399 163	428 696	50 651	38 457	866 820	393 615	473 205	50 147	34 338	15 809
With own children under 6 years only	233 823	221 610	111 386	110 224	12 213	8 112	229 931	109 827	120 104	12 004	8 672	3 332
With own children under 6 and 6 to 17 years	187 836	176 026	89 008	87 018	11 810	8 689	185 192	87 841	97 351	11 333	7 627	3 706
Married-couple families	1 211 272	1 143 540	562 858	580 682	67 732	54 326	1 195 617	554 714	640 903	69 981	47 116	22 865
With own children under 18 years	756 933	715 116	333 821	381 295	41 817	33 279	748 920	329 107	419 813	41 292	28 244	13 048
With own children under 6 years only	208 655	198 328	96 742	101 586	10 327	7 118	205 687	95 372	110 315	10 086	7 343	2 743
With own children under 6 and 6 to 17 years	169 218	158 939	78 019	80 920	10 279	7 833	167 170	76 977	90 193	9 881	6 645	3 236
Female householder, no husband present	184 298	173 179	102 485	70 694	11 119	6 600	179 731	101 274	78 457	11 167	7 700	3 467
With own children under 18 years	92 703	85 968	50 179	35 789	6 735	3 726	89 807	49 588	40 219	6 622	4 639	1 983
With own children under 6 years only	17 891	16 579	10 631	5 948	1 312	624	17 217	10 524	6 693	1 298	931	367
With own children under 6 and 6 to 17 years	14 998	13 747	8 988	4 759	1 251	630	14 493	8 903	5 590	1 135	791	344
MARITAL STATUS												
Males 15 years and over	2 563 841	2 412 132	1 301 528	1 110 604	151 709	109 893	2 514 750	1 283 136	1 231 614	158 984	110 426	48 558
Never married	981 712	919 781	534 528	385 253	61 931	39 683	955 213	526 722	428 491	66 182	47 941	18 241
Now married, except separated	1 436 877	1 357 115	687 211	669 904	79 762	62 688	1 417 653	677 811	739 842	81 912	55 430	26 482
Separated	34 516	32 714	20 417	12 297	1 802	1 398	34 023	20 169	13 854	1 891	1 216	675
Widowed	33 207	30 786	18 848	11 938	2 421	1 881	32 452	18 623	13 829	2 636	1 630	1 006
Divorced	77 529	71 736	40 524	31 212	5 793	4 243	75 409	39 811	35 598	6 363	4 209	2 154
Females 15 years and over	2 727 908	2 563 734	1 351 353	1 212 381	164 174	134 490	2 686 709	1 332 324	1 354 385	175 689	115 375	60 314
Never married	760 884	716 570	408 924	307 646	44 314	28 898	744 410	403 801	340 609	45 372	32 688	12 684
Now married, except separated	1 590 753	1 493 053	738 315	754 738	97 700	89 562	1 573 387	726 993	846 394	106 928	67 313	39 615
Separated	50 101	47 601	28 387	19 214	2 500	1 756	49 451	28 078	21 373	2 406	1 593	813
Widowed	196 555	185 351	108 991	76 360	11 204	8 623	192 998	107 758	85 240	12 180	7 856	4 324
Divorced	129 615	121 159	66 736	54 423	8 456	5 651	126 463	65 694	60 769	8 803	5 925	2 878

Table 46. **Household and Family Characteristics of Hispanic Origin Persons: 1990**

[Persons of Hispanic origin may be of any race. For definitions of terms and meanings of symbols, see text]

United States Urban and Rural Inside and Outside Metropolitan Area	Urban and rural						Inside and outside metropolitan area					
	Urban						Inside metropolitan area			Outside metropolitan area		
		Inside urbanized area			Outside urbanized area							
	Total	Total	Central place	Urban fringe		Rural	Total	In central city	Not in central city	Total	Urban	Rural
HOUSEHOLD TYPE AND RELATIONSHIP												
All persons	**20 426 228**	**18 355 980**	**11 671 728**	**6 684 252**	**2 070 248**	**1 927 831**	**20 204 818**	**11 514 252**	**8 690 566**	**2 149 241**	**1 244 669**	**904 572**
In households	20 026 596	18 020 838	11 462 786	6 558 052	2 005 758	1 810 231	19 784 591	11 310 361	8 474 230	2 052 236	1 196 295	855 941
Householder	5 530 932	4 988 301	3 235 169	1 753 132	542 631	470 786	5 427 548	3 196 572	2 230 976	574 170	340 214	233 956
15 to 24 years	487 340	436 152	301 226	134 926	51 188	32 690	469 257	297 093	172 164	50 773	33 071	17 702
25 to 34 years	1 627 540	1 475 244	950 375	524 869	152 296	127 418	1 601 636	937 820	663 816	153 322	91 710	61 612
35 to 44 years	1 359 997	1 231 676	779 259	452 417	128 321	120 181	1 346 734	769 776	576 958	133 444	77 893	55 551
45 to 54 years	836 577	760 676	478 793	281 883	75 901	75 491	828 721	473 606	355 115	83 347	47 228	36 119
55 to 64 years	602 841	542 438	353 047	189 391	60 403	56 368	591 187	349 556	241 631	68 022	39 192	28 830
65 to 74 years	387 842	342 741	232 007	110 734	45 101	36 869	373 486	229 560	143 926	51 225	30 545	20 680
75 to 84 years	186 305	162 458	114 008	48 450	23 847	17 755	176 437	112 973	63 464	27 623	16 692	10 931
85 years and over	42 490	36 916	26 454	10 462	5 574	4 014	40 090	26 188	13 902	6 414	3 883	2 531
Family householder	4 396 077	3 951 354	2 508 000	1 443 354	444 723	393 184	4 327 720	2 476 015	1 851 705	461 541	271 641	189 900
Male	3 135 030	2 795 880	1 684 987	1 110 893	339 150	330 078	3 100 184	1 659 646	1 440 538	364 924	206 159	158 765
Female	1 261 047	1 155 474	823 013	332 461	105 573	63 106	1 227 536	816 369	411 167	96 617	65 482	31 135
Nonfamily householder	1 134 855	1 036 947	727 169	309 778	97 908	77 602	1 099 828	720 557	379 271	112 629	68 573	44 056
Male	616 740	563 590	393 013	170 577	53 150	50 224	602 461	389 112	213 349	64 503	36 349	28 154
Living alone	410 292	373 630	267 740	105 890	36 662	35 418	399 319	265 696	133 623	46 391	26 012	20 379
Female	518 115	473 357	334 156	139 201	44 758	27 378	497 367	331 445	165 922	48 126	32 224	15 902
Living alone	419 277	380 713	271 599	109 114	38 564	23 661	400 816	269 582	131 234	42 122	27 980	14 142
Spouse	3 062 937	2 733 651	1 626 710	1 106 941	329 286	327 648	3 032 868	1 601 836	1 431 032	357 717	201 532	156 185
Child	7 860 750	6 990 947	4 462 301	2 528 646	869 803	786 804	7 767 373	4 401 055	3 366 318	880 181	512 909	367 272
Other relatives	2 149 974	1 986 575	1 283 483	703 092	163 399	135 232	2 139 902	1 267 762	872 140	145 304	87 075	58 229
Nonrelatives	1 422 003	1 321 364	855 123	466 241	100 639	89 761	1 416 900	843 136	573 764	94 864	54 565	40 299
In group quarters	399 632	335 142	208 942	126 200	64 490	117 600	420 227	203 891	216 336	97 005	48 374	48 631
Institutionalized persons	189 158	158 073	93 988	64 085	31 085	72 535	202 306	89 950	112 356	59 387	27 174	32 213
Correctional institutions	133 087	109 173	61 925	47 248	23 914	64 313	147 763	58 001	89 762	49 637	21 823	27 814
Nursing homes	30 784	26 065	17 491	8 574	4 719	1 784	27 733	17 407	10 326	4 835	3 654	1 181
Other institutions	25 287	22 835	14 572	8 263	2 452	6 438	26 810	14 542	12 268	4 915	1 697	3 218
Other persons in group quarters	210 474	177 069	114 954	62 115	33 405	45 065	217 921	113 941	103 980	37 618	21 200	16 418
College dormitories	66 921	53 004	37 065	15 939	13 917	4 043	57 131	36 487	20 644	13 833	11 877	1 956
Military quarters	39 379	31 428	13 751	17 677	7 951	4 375	37 490	13 817	23 673	6 264	4 908	1 356
Emergency shelters for homeless persons	26 589	24 724	21 279	3 445	1 865	1 045	26 132	21 075	5 057	1 502	1 284	218
Visible in street locations	15 048	14 421	9 509	4 912	627	1 615	16 369	9 471	6 898	294	170	124
Shelters for abused women	1 701	1 522	1 217	305	179	69	1 610	1 227	383	160	125	35
Drug/ alcohol abuse group homes	4 011	3 870	3 288	582	141	801	4 352	3 280	1 072	460	89	371
Other noninstitutional group quarters	56 825	48 100	28 845	19 255	8 725	33 117	74 837	28 584	46 253	15 105	2 747	12 358
Persons per household	3.53	3.52	3.47	3.62	3.56	3.62	3.55	3.47	3.66	3.39	3.37	3.43
Persons per family	3.88	3.87	3.87	3.88	3.91	3.95	3.89	3.87	3.93	3.80	3.78	3.81
Persons under 18 years	**7 029 006**	**6 229 501**	**3 986 665**	**2 242 836**	**799 505**	**728 494**	**6 942 375**	**3 929 112**	**3 013 263**	**815 125**	**471 849**	**343 276**
Householder or spouse	15 153	13 180	9 546	3 634	1 973	1 528	14 541	9 452	5 089	2 140	1 278	862
Own child	6 049 754	5 347 616	3 407 555	1 940 061	702 138	637 063	5 969 188	3 357 682	2 611 506	717 629	416 398	301 231
In married-couple family	4 278 208	3 757 575	2 256 421	1 501 154	520 633	527 452	4 254 321	2 217 070	2 037 251	551 339	305 852	245 487
Percent of persons under 18 years	60.9	60.3	56.6	66.9	65.1	72.4	61.3	56.4	67.6	67.6	64.8	71.5
With female householder, no husband present	1 425 447	1 279 952	943 641	336 311	145 495	78 858	1 372 621	935 815	436 806	131 684	90 536	41 148
Grandchild	445 489	394 243	265 759	128 484	51 246	42 872	436 824	262 545	174 279	51 537	30 966	20 571
Other relatives	305 452	280 797	181 845	98 952	24 655	19 876	304 044	179 547	124 497	21 284	12 704	8 580
Nonrelatives	179 556	163 837	102 490	61 347	15 719	16 260	179 760	100 735	79 025	16 056	8 599	7 457
Institutionalized persons	13 093	11 985	7 463	4 522	1 108	4 464	14 644	7 307	7 337	2 913	738	2 175
Other persons in group quarters	20 509	17 843	12 007	5 836	2 666	6 431	23 374	11 844	11 530	3 566	1 166	2 400
Persons 65 years and over	**1 066 447**	**949 246**	**625 826**	**323 420**	**117 201**	**94 836**	**1 029 247**	**619 129**	**410 118**	**132 036**	**79 240**	**52 796**
Family householder	371 407	326 106	215 914	110 192	45 301	38 747	358 246	213 452	144 794	51 908	30 240	21 668
Male	273 324	238 776	152 393	86 383	34 548	31 802	264 396	150 403	113 993	40 730	23 012	17 718
Female	98 083	87 330	63 521	23 809	10 753	6 945	93 850	63 049	30 801	11 178	7 228	3 950
Spouse	187 807	164 857	104 856	60 001	22 950	20 921	181 453	103 418	78 035	27 275	15 537	11 738
Parent	115 681	108 704	64 938	43 766	6 977	5 950	115 172	64 191	50 981	6 459	4 004	2 455
Other relatives	83 832	77 877	46 438	31 439	5 955	5 191	82 955	45 936	37 019	6 068	3 702	2 366
Nonrelatives	31 619	29 450	19 476	9 974	2 169	1 888	31 348	19 300	12 048	2 159	1 286	873
Nonfamily householder	245 230	216 009	156 555	59 454	29 221	19 891	231 767	155 269	76 498	33 354	20 880	12 474
Male	67 066	58 849	43 772	15 077	8 217	7 249	64 053	43 438	20 615	10 262	5 777	4 485
Living alone	59 844	52 312	39 224	13 088	7 532	6 556	56 911	38 943	17 968	9 489	5 373	4 116
Female	178 164	157 160	112 783	44 377	21 004	12 642	167 714	111 831	55 883	23 092	15 103	7 989
Living alone	169 330	149 020	107 039	41 981	20 310	12 217	159 098	106 137	52 961	22 449	14 666	7 783
Institutionalized persons	27 456	23 109	15 492	7 617	4 347	1 721	24 696	15 406	9 290	4 481	3 432	1 049
Other persons in group quarters	3 415	3 134	2 157	977	281	527	3 610	2 157	1 453	332	159	173
FAMILY TYPE BY PRESENCE OF OWN CHILDREN												
Families	**4 396 077**	**3 951 354**	**2 508 000**	**1 443 354**	**444 723**	**393 184**	**4 327 720**	**2 476 015**	**1 851 705**	**461 541**	**271 641**	**189 900**
With own children under 18 years	2 775 482	2 480 307	1 577 980	902 327	295 175	255 588	2 733 462	1 556 765	1 176 697	297 608	176 800	120 808
With own children under 6 years only	721 655	650 065	414 887	235 178	71 590	57 593	708 442	409 213	299 229	70 806	42 987	27 819
With own children under 6 and 6 to 17 years	759 926	674 510	433 929	240 581	85 416	75 400	751 495	427 457	324 038	83 831	49 136	34 695
Married-couple families	**2 980 794**	**2 656 872**	**1 591 692**	**1 065 180**	**323 922**	**316 778**	**2 948 653**	**1 567 560**	**1 381 093**	**348 919**	**197 629**	**151 290**
With own children under 18 years	1 922 312	1 705 459	1 020 532	684 927	216 853	210 186	1 906 061	1 004 100	901 961	226 437	128 676	97 761
With own children under 6 years only	513 758	461 200	277 602	183 598	52 558	47 478	507 608	273 180	234 428	53 628	31 190	22 438
With own children under 6 and 6 to 17 years	557 186	491 286	297 680	193 606	65 900	64 721	554 651	292 342	262 309	67 256	37 782	29 474
Female householder, no husband present	**1 015 328**	**927 941**	**672 038**	**255 903**	**87 387**	**47 136**	**982 785**	**667 042**	**315 743**	**79 679**	**55 290**	**24 389**
With own children under 18 years	667 252	606 866	445 192	161 674	60 386	30 712	644 144	441 834	202 310	53 820	37 902	15 918
With own children under 6 years only	141 088	128 402	96 621	31 781	12 686	5 406	135 259	95 892	39 367	11 235	8 200	3 035
With own children under 6 and 6 to 17 years	163 961	148 214	112 598	35 616	15 747	7 572	158 235	111 772	46 463	13 298	9 460	3 838
MARITAL STATUS												
Males 15 years and over	**7 300 231**	**6 584 463**	**4 153 308**	**2 431 155**	**715 768**	**727 518**	**7 257 623**	**4 095 760**	**3 161 863**	**770 126**	**430 799**	**339 327**
Never married	2 924 089	2 663 783	1 731 831	931 952	260 306	258 467	2 910 012	1 708 726	1 201 286	272 544	154 508	118 036
Now married, except separated	3 618 669	3 235 319	1 960 185	1 275 134	383 350	400 536	3 603 052	1 930 201	1 672 851	416 153	229 028	187 125
Separated	217 179	199 657	140 534	59 123	17 522	17 114	215 921	139 278	76 643	18 372	10 469	7 903
Widowed	104 320	91 876	62 433	29 443	12 444	11 097	101 136	61 844	39 292	14 281	8 253	6 028
Divorced	435 974	393 828	258 325	135 503	42 146	40 304	427 502	255 711	171 791	48 776	28 541	20 235
Females 15 years and over	**7 156 647**	**6 482 970**	**4 129 040**	**2 353 930**	**673 677**	**586 670**	**7 054 815**	**4 078 628**	**2 976 187**	**688 502**	**412 830**	**275 672**
Never married	2 168 733	1 987 082	1 321 287	665 795	181 651	145 523	2 139 156	1 307 473	831 683	175 100	109 865	65 235
Now married, except separated	3 468 840	3 110 769	1 869 941	1 240 828	358 071	354 172	3 440 509	1 842 118	1 598 391	382 503	216 500	166 003
Separated	370 956	343 298	248 656	94 642	27 658	16 056	363 736	246 658	117 078	23 276	15 931	7 345
Widowed	490 705	439 161	291 772	147 389	51 544	35 935	472 441	288 928	183 513	54 199	34 446	19 753
Divorced	657 413	602 660	397 384	205 276	54 753	34 984	638 973	393 451	245 522	53 424	36 088	17 336

Table 47. Household and Family Characteristics of White, Not of Hispanic Origin Persons: 1990

[For definitions of terms and meanings of symbols, see text]

United States Urban and Rural Inside and Outside Metropolitan Area	Urban and rural							Inside and outside metropolitan area					
	Urban							Inside metropolitan area			Outside metropolitan area		
		Inside urbanized area				Outside urbanized area							
	Total	Total	Total	Central place	Urban fringe		Rural	Total	In central city	Not in central city	Total	Urban	Rural
HOUSEHOLD TYPE AND RELATIONSHIP													
All persons	**133 375 398**	**109 975 510**	**46 619 577**	**63 355 933**		**23 399 888**	**54 752 898**	**140 496 200**	**45 957 707**	**94 538 493**	**47 632 096**	**16 871 318**	**30 760 778**
In households	129 400 845	107 107 450	44 865 635	62 241 815		22 293 395	53 961 798	137 080 437	44 221 587	92 858 850	46 282 206	15 982 857	30 299 349
Householder	53 651 540	44 437 315	19 974 619	24 462 696		9 214 225	19 982 209	55 416 863	19 718 548	35 698 315	18 216 886	6 734 755	11 482 131
15 to 24 years	3 000 621	2 401 465	1 412 459	989 006		599 156	723 418	2 792 513	1 384 867	1 407 646	931 526	478 492	453 034
25 to 34 years	11 378 821	9 597 947	4 497 952	5 099 995		1 780 874	3 729 325	11 763 800	4 433 913	7 329 887	3 344 346	1 263 537	2 080 809
35 to 44 years	11 351 102	9 561 335	4 023 214	5 538 121		1 789 767	4 536 600	12 214 485	3 971 438	8 243 047	3 673 217	1 256 768	2 416 449
45 to 54 years	7 915 645	6 663 332	2 665 548	3 997 784		1 252 313	3 466 383	8 621 965	2 634 756	5 987 209	2 760 063	888 050	1 872 013
55 to 64 years	7 191 230	5 971 959	2 506 008	3 465 951		1 219 271	2 985 533	7 529 922	2 478 927	5 050 995	2 646 841	899 579	1 747 262
65 to 74 years	7 215 920	5 843 470	2 646 500	3 196 970		1 372 450	2 678 943	7 187 341	2 613 301	4 574 040	2 707 522	1 032 342	1 675 180
75 to 84 years	4 463 038	3 513 427	1 740 740	1 772 687		949 611	1 517 480	4 255 261	1 722 986	2 532 275	1 725 257	722 790	1 002 467
85 years and over	1 135 163	884 380	482 198	402 182		250 783	344 527	1 051 576	478 360	573 216	428 114	193 197	234 917
Family householder	35 333 416	29 116 787	11 692 123	17 424 664		6 216 629	15 613 193	37 709 561	11 523 256	26 186 305	13 237 048	4 436 752	8 800 296
Male	28 235 012	23 233 572	9 029 437	14 204 135		5 001 440	13 491 652	30 557 249	8 891 171	21 666 078	11 169 415	3 557 537	7 611 878
Female	7 098 404	5 883 215	2 662 686	3 220 529		1 215 189	2 121 541	7 152 312	2 632 085	4 520 227	2 067 633	879 215	1 188 418
Nonfamily householder	18 318 124	15 320 528	8 282 496	7 038 032		2 997 596	4 369 016	17 707 302	8 195 292	9 512 010	4 979 838	2 298 003	2 681 835
Male	7 751 448	6 620 702	3 628 218	2 992 484		1 130 746	2 015 779	7 706 344	3 584 820	4 121 524	2 060 883	861 266	1 199 617
Living alone	5 792 789	4 914 459	2 697 232	2 217 227		878 330	1 618 530	5 756 628	2 670 259	3 086 369	1 654 691	667 701	986 990
Female	10 566 676	8 699 826	4 654 278	4 045 548		1 866 850	2 353 237	10 000 958	4 610 472	5 390 486	2 918 955	1 436 737	1 482 218
Living alone	9 190 294	7 492 672	3 981 407	3 511 265		1 697 622	2 156 931	8 662 190	3 947 922	4 714 268	2 685 035	1 304 352	1 380 683
Spouse	28 750 819	23 688 309	9 188 030	14 500 279		5 062 510	13 619 043	31 121 884	9 048 928	22 072 956	11 247 978	3 601 549	7 646 429
Child	36 847 928	30 320 188	11 457 842	18 862 346		6 527 740	17 388 569	40 106 574	11 281 357	28 825 217	14 129 923	4 558 450	9 571 473
Other relatives	4 215 490	3 578 703	1 534 949	2 043 754		636 787	1 619 893	4 514 702	1 513 806	3 000 896	1 320 681	443 341	877 340
Nonrelatives	5 935 068	5 082 935	2 710 195	2 372 740		852 133	1 352 084	5 920 414	2 658 948	3 261 466	1 366 738	644 762	721 976
In group quarters	3 974 553	2 868 060	1 753 942	1 114 118		1 106 493	791 100	3 415 763	1 736 120	1 679 643	1 349 890	888 461	461 429
Institutionalized persons	1 772 388	1 272 115	678 196	593 919		500 273	541 329	1 597 253	675 420	921 833	716 464	389 333	327 131
Correctional institutions	247 576	166 144	103 118	63 026		81 432	169 427	260 866	101 504	159 362	156 137	64 863	91 274
Nursing homes	1 291 257	920 933	470 515	450 418		370 324	298 934	1 102 581	468 481	634 100	487 610	288 369	199 241
Other institutions	233 555	185 038	104 563	80 475		48 517	72 968	233 806	105 435	128 371	72 717	36 101	36 616
Other persons in group quarters	2 202 165	1 595 945	1 075 746	520 199		606 220	249 771	1 818 510	1 060 700	757 810	633 426	499 128	134 298
College dormitories	1 471 779	1 004 318	732 764	271 554		467 461	101 093	1 119 783	726 360	393 423	453 089	395 111	57 978
Military quarters	363 779	287 349	136 669	150 680		76 430	36 541	328 940	129 661	199 279	71 380	56 031	15 349
Emergency shelters for homeless persons	72 142	64 348	53 027	11 321		7 794	4 291	68 303	52 641	15 662	8 130	6 299	1 831
Visible in street locations	13 434	12 390	10 054	2 336		1 044	1 608	13 545	9 900	3 645	1 497	767	730
Shelters for abused women	5 648	4 109	3 287	822		1 539	412	4 536	3 305	1 231	1 524	1 258	266
Drug/alcohol abuse group homes	24 499	21 541	16 558	4 983		2 958	5 691	25 301	16 449	8 852	4 889	2 407	2 482
Other noninstitutional group quarters	250 884	201 890	123 387	78 503		48 994	100 135	258 102	122 384	135 718	92 917	37 255	55 662
Persons per household	2.43	2.43	2.27	2.56		2.43	2.71	2.49	2.26	2.62	2.55	2.39	2.65
Persons per family	3.00	3.00	2.92	3.05		2.98	3.10	3.03	2.92	3.07	3.03	2.96	3.07
Persons under 18 years	**29 330 517**	**23 769 108**	**9 142 651**	**14 626 457**		**5 561 409**	**14 476 794**	**31 822 325**	**8 989 397**	**22 832 928**	**11 984 986**	**3 899 834**	**8 085 152**
Householder or spouse	40 243	29 751	16 171	13 580		10 492	18 443	37 856	15 954	21 902	20 830	8 237	12 593
Own child	27 423 560	22 222 647	8 468 217	13 754 430		5 200 913	13 546 065	29 759 634	8 325 381	21 434 253	11 209 991	3 647 136	7 562 855
In married-couple family	22 606 347	18 457 291	6 718 452	11 738 839		4 149 056	11 882 738	25 031 503	6 599 100	18 432 403	9 457 582	2 882 026	6 574 756
Percent of persons under 18 years	77.1	77.7	73.5	80.3		74.6	82.1	78.7	73.4	80.7	78.9	73.9	81.3
With female householder, no husband present	3 935 527	3 063 417	1 437 246	1 626 171		872 110	1 238 269	3 795 353	1 418 919	2 376 434	1 378 443	639 361	739 082
Grandchild	1 045 085	858 240	350 508	507 732		186 845	517 104	1 146 715	345 357	801 358	415 474	129 582	285 892
Other relatives	279 190	226 987	99 422	127 565		52 203	136 102	301 071	97 841	203 230	114 221	36 217	78 004
Nonrelatives	451 900	359 097	163 281	195 816		92 803	217 980	481 364	159 898	321 466	188 516	64 635	123 881
Institutionalized persons	51 994	42 561	25 606	16 955		9 433	23 576	56 332	25 605	30 727	19 238	7 237	12 001
Other persons in group quarters	38 545	29 825	19 446	10 379		8 720	17 524	39 353	19 361	19 992	16 716	6 790	9 926
Persons 65 years and over	**19 956 040**	**15 961 504**	**7 392 906**	**8 568 598**		**3 994 536**	**7 094 779**	**19 560 279**	**7 304 902**	**12 255 377**	**7 490 540**	**3 014 562**	**4 475 978**
Family householder	6 638 005	5 381 752	2 344 419	3 037 333		1 256 253	2 693 550	6 707 376	2 311 482	4 395 894	2 624 179	940 248	1 683 931
Male	5 468 067	4 413 029	1 882 380	2 530 649		1 055 038	2 325 591	5 543 495	1 853 363	3 690 132	2 250 163	790 375	1 459 788
Female	1 169 938	968 723	462 039	506 684		201 215	367 959	1 163 881	458 119	705 762	374 016	149 873	224 143
Spouse	4 476 241	3 610 254	1 550 497	2 059 757		865 987	1 790 783	4 498 142	1 526 062	2 972 080	1 768 882	648 302	1 120 580
Parent	590 096	513 060	201 448	311 612		77 036	202 939	635 464	198 672	436 792	157 571	53 219	104 352
Other relatives	531 275	453 121	192 019	261 102		78 154	184 582	559 410	189 736	369 674	156 447	55 834	100 613
Nonrelatives	238 964	201 694	98 594	103 100		37 270	73 635	243 972	97 193	146 779	68 627	26 776	41 851
Nonfamily householder	6 176 116	4 859 525	2 525 019	2 334 506		1 316 591	1 847 400	5 786 802	2 503 165	3 283 637	2 236 714	1 008 081	1 228 633
Male	1 250 833	1 011 778	529 940	481 838		239 055	470 356	1 230 183	524 794	705 389	491 006	181 489	309 517
Living alone	1 161 851	936 884	492 581	444 303		224 967	439 168	1 138 933	487 949	650 984	462 086	171 218	290 868
Female	4 925 283	3 847 747	1 995 079	1 852 668		1 077 536	1 377 044	4 556 619	1 978 371	2 578 248	1 745 708	826 592	919 116
Living alone	4 800 023	3 741 934	1 940 837	1 801 097		1 058 089	1 348 669	4 433 803	1 924 846	2 508 957	1 714 889	812 092	902 797
Institutionalized persons	1 234 629	883 495	448 694	434 801		351 134	280 582	1 056 597	446 539	610 058	458 614	273 425	185 189
Other persons in group quarters	70 714	58 603	32 216	26 387		12 111	21 308	72 516	32 053	40 463	19 506	8 677	10 829
FAMILY TYPE BY PRESENCE OF OWN CHILDREN													
Families	**35 333 416**	**29 116 787**	**11 692 123**	**17 424 664**		**6 216 629**	**15 613 193**	**37 709 561**	**11 523 256**	**26 186 305**	**13 237 048**	**4 436 752**	**8 800 296**
With own children under 18 years	15 539 150	12 645 122	4 893 692	7 751 430		2 894 028	7 347 924	16 784 277	4 815 660	11 968 617	6 102 797	2 028 642	4 074 155
With own children under 6 years only	4 312 050	3 565 329	1 477 954	2 087 375		746 721	1 658 622	4 547 021	1 453 102	3 093 919	1 423 651	520 859	902 792
With own children under 6 and 6 to 17 years	2 968 381	2 395 153	921 231	1 473 922		573 228	1 461 778	3 210 758	904 049	2 306 709	1 219 401	400 683	818 718
Married-couple families	**28 917 552**	**23 840 498**	**9 249 104**	**14 591 394**		**5 077 054**	**13 646 030**	**31 292 742**	**9 107 903**	**22 184 839**	**11 270 840**	**3 611 829**	**7 659 011**
With own children under 18 years	12 378 067	10 147 185	3 729 545	6 417 640		2 230 882	6 320 370	13 681 635	3 667 034	10 014 601	5 016 802	1 547 363	3 469 439
With own children under 6 years only	3 589 897	3 002 400	1 183 692	1 818 708		587 497	1 453 638	3 862 339	1 162 790	2 699 549	1 181 196	402 874	778 322
With own children under 6 and 6 to 17 years	2 563 914	2 086 035	766 755	1 319 280		477 879	1 320 888	2 820 874	751 844	2 069 030	1 063 928	331 063	732 865
Female householder, no husband present	**4 920 252**	**4 018 972**	**1 870 428**	**2 148 544**		**901 280**	**1 392 026**	**4 843 256**	**1 850 230**	**2 993 026**	**1 469 022**	**657 508**	**811 514**
With own children under 18 years	2 556 836	2 013 455	948 483	1 064 972		543 381	749 448	2 465 345	936 528	1 528 817	840 939	397 796	443 143
With own children under 6 years only	557 924	431 908	230 319	201 589		126 016	136 962	515 588	227 399	288 189	179 298	94 814	84 484
With own children under 6 and 6 to 17 years	344 320	261 957	132 748	129 209		82 363	110 043	326 283	130 875	195 408	128 080	60 630	67 450
MARITAL STATUS													
Males 15 years and over	**51 591 273**	**42 874 322**	**18 445 761**	**24 428 561**		**8 716 951**	**21 119 945**	**54 557 096**	**18 182 497**	**36 374 599**	**18 154 122**	**6 313 084**	**11 841 038**
Never married	15 235 708	12 882 919	6 243 003	6 639 916		2 352 789	4 784 772	15 636 746	6 160 132	9 476 614	4 383 734	1 753 296	2 630 438
Now married, except separated	30 117 589	24 829 195	9 707 274	15 121 921		5 288 394	14 099 148	32 537 912	9 556 430	22 981 482	11 678 825	3 771 413	7 907 412
Separated	790 190	663 670	321 898	341 772		126 520	280 918	825 955	317 690	508 265	245 153	88 958	156 195
Widowed	1 378 367	1 119 561	525 049	594 512		258 806	507 859	1 379 528	519 792	859 736	506 698	193 123	313 575
Divorced	4 069 419	3 378 977	1 648 537	1 730 440		690 442	1 447 248	4 176 955	1 628 453	2 548 502	1 339 712	506 294	833 418
Females 15 years and over	**56 955 734**	**46 968 450**	**20 377 139**	**26 591 311**		**9 987 284**	**21 586 431**	**59 066 706**	**20 112 377**	**38 954 329**	**19 475 459**	**7 271 694**	**12 203 765**
Never married	12 641 208	10 696 380	5 198 567	5 497 813		1 944 828	3 399 458	12 767 326	5 138 612	7 628 714	3 273 340	1 450 394	1 822 946
Now married, except separated	29 802 111	24 557 494	9 580 025	14 977 469		5 244 617	14 006 317	32 217 662	9 435 131	22 782 531	11 590 766	3 733 428	7 857 338
Separated	1 046 529	861 988	410 325	451 663		184 541	306 744	1 052 238	404 601	647 637	301 035	130 025	171 010
Widowed	7 560 027	5 958 213	2 851 018	3 107 195		1 601 814	2 387 252	7 215 809	2 824 938	4 390 871	2 731 470	1 215 824	1 515 646
Divorced	5 905 859	4 894 375	2 337 204	2 557 171		1 011 484	1 486 660	5 813 671	2 309 095	3 504 576	1 578 848	742 023	836 825

Table 48. Household and Family Characteristics for Selected Racial Groups: 1990

[For definitions of terms and meanings of symbols, see text]

United States	American Indian, Eskimo, or Aleut Total	American Indian	Eskimo	Aleut	Asian or Pacific Islander Total	Asian Total	Chinese	Filipino	Japanese	Asian Indian	Korean
HOUSEHOLD TYPE AND RELATIONSHIP											
All persons	1 959 234	1 878 285	57 152	23 797	7 273 662	6 908 638	1 645 472	1 406 770	847 562	815 447	798 849
In households	1 902 958	1 825 128	54 698	23 132	7 120 735	6 766 801	1 606 258	1 382 730	825 977	799 896	781 245
Householder	591 372	570 332	13 877	7 163	2 013 735	1 922 097	504 048	348 847	310 945	237 800	202 556
15 to 24 years	45 373	43 584	1 152	637	120 460	112 746	26 188	17 177	15 362	13 993	12 135
25 to 34 years	149 553	143 680	3 830	2 043	515 322	488 941	125 618	76 728	66 843	68 076	52 971
35 to 44 years	148 317	143 090	3 333	1 894	584 616	560 495	145 784	103 633	73 250	80 480	55 055
45 to 54 years	100 356	97 199	2 050	1 107	371 877	356 389	83 535	74 219	44 912	53 357	46 796
55 to 64 years	70 351	67 887	1 677	787	220 744	210 600	60 648	40 477	48 873	16 604	21 024
65 to 74 years	48 640	47 081	1 119	440	132 878	127 376	40 501	20 467	43 071	3 962	10 229
75 to 84 years	23 236	22 447	583	206	56 008	54 062	17 871	13 618	14 705	1 118	3 895
85 years and over	5 546	5 364	133	49	11 830	11 488	3 903	2 528	3 929	210	451
Family householder	442 161	426 933	10 195	5 033	1 559 043	1 486 349	381 403	287 539	202 954	193 379	161 645
Male	288 587	278 457	6 623	3 507	1 279 456	1 225 991	321 727	223 238	167 916	174 493	135 112
Female	153 574	148 476	3 572	1 526	279 587	260 358	59 676	64 301	35 038	18 886	26 533
Nonfamily householder	149 211	143 399	3 682	2 130	454 692	435 748	122 645	61 308	107 991	44 421	40 911
Male	77 851	74 226	2 382	1 243	255 465	244 233	68 378	28 250	55 063	34 146	18 356
Living alone	57 519	54 762	1 863	894	174 915	167 763	47 113	18 651	43 252	22 328	12 649
Female	71 360	69 173	1 300	887	199 227	191 515	54 267	33 058	52 928	10 275	22 555
Living alone	58 473	56 784	1 010	679	153 415	147 871	42 138	22 708	44 276	7 799	18 142
Spouse	284 695	273 552	7 352	3 791	1 462 478	1 407 617	335 720	286 220	219 083	165 223	186 921
Child	758 135	724 828	24 528	8 779	2 538 730	2 395 894	512 531	486 575	215 907	285 306	304 019
Other relatives	153 801	146 999	5 167	1 635	713 966	673 606	163 731	183 547	36 254	76 341	57 555
Nonrelatives	114 955	109 417	3 774	1 764	391 826	367 587	90 228	77 541	43 788	35 226	30 194
In group quarters	56 276	53 157	2 454	665	152 927	141 837	39 214	24 040	21 585	15 551	17 604
Institutionalized persons	28 050	26 613	1 147	290	22 992	19 635	4 108	3 821	4 318	1 355	1 388
Correctional institutions	17 791	16 927	675	189	7 518	5 960	895	991	457	582	260
Nursing homes	4 997	4 657	287	53	9 723	8 767	2 406	1 873	2 828	421	626
Other institutions	5 262	5 029	185	48	5 751	4 908	807	957	1 033	352	502
Other persons in group quarters	28 226	26 544	1 307	375	129 935	122 202	35 106	20 219	17 267	14 196	16 216
College dormitories	9 420	8 755	481	184	96 025	92 656	28 349	8 708	14 924	12 307	14 095
Military quarters	5 592	5 291	244	57	13 766	11 712	840	6 918	745	438	1 094
Emergency shelters for homeless persons	4 522	4 307	171	44	2 270	1 822	365	370	171	434	136
Visible in street locations	1 146	1 106	32	8	1 110	644	167	163	103	74	46
Shelters for abused women	468	436	24	8	199	145	23	31	19	21	17
Drug/alcohol abuse group homes	1 470	1 371	86	13	363	279	46	75	47	27	37
Other noninstitutional group quarters	5 608	5 278	269	61	16 202	14 944	5 316	3 954	1 258	895	791
Persons per household	3.12	3.11	3.53	3.04	3.34	3.33	3.15	3.70	2.47	3.44	3.19
Persons per family	3.60	3.58	4.18	3.60	3.80	3.79	3.62	4.02	3.09	3.83	3.60
Persons under 18 years	696 967	666 202	22 727	8 038	2 083 387	1 951 392	386 290	385 681	156 927	244 354	246 539
Householder or spouse	1 104	1 061	29	14	2 042	1 906	345	247	127	165	193
Own child	584 587	558 847	18 688	7 052	1 894 076	1 785 910	355 251	341 242	145 103	231 320	233 784
In married-couple family	379 714	361 258	13 281	5 175	1 666 429	1 584 007	325 435	296 467	130 588	216 398	213 616
Percent of persons under 18 years	54.5	54.2	58.4	64.4	80.0	81.2	84.2	76.9	83.2	88.6	86.6
With female householder, no husband present	160 515	155 540	3 538	1 437	172 769	152 286	21 850	33 708	11 104	10 859	14 711
Grandchild	65 720	62 952	2 383	385	79 874	65 542	12 734	23 265	6 882	4 272	5 391
Other relatives	19 888	18 945	697	246	67 761	62 440	12 211	13 793	1 605	6 173	4 257
Nonrelatives	19 263	18 211	751	301	32 931	29 779	4 529	6 229	2 670	1 768	2 241
Institutionalized persons	3 329	3 196	109	24	2 181	1 821	177	310	121	145	239
Other persons in group quarters	3 076	2 990	70	16	4 522	3 994	1 043	595	419	511	434
Persons 65 years and over	114 453	110 426	2 909	1 118	454 458	439 723	133 977	104 206	105 932	23 004	35 247
Family householder	44 634	42 998	1 290	346	142 006	136 582	42 761	29 578	42 248	3 864	8 856
Male	29 626	28 571	819	236	119 212	115 384	36 809	24 629	35 969	3 360	7 572
Female	15 008	14 427	471	110	22 794	21 198	5 952	4 949	6 279	504	1 284
Spouse	20 199	19 521	489	189	76 096	73 455	22 146	13 227	28 082	1 643	4 355
Parent	5 753	5 495	163	95	106 802	105 217	32 108	29 371	6 905	12 230	11 379
Other relatives	4 429	4 273	102	54	47 452	46 272	10 780	18 787	4 660	2 982	3 672
Nonrelatives	2 334	2 261	44	29	12 231	11 743	2 914	4 464	1 470	449	736
Nonfamily householder	32 788	31 894	545	349	58 710	56 344	19 514	7 035	19 457	1 426	5 719
Male	9 855	9 509	231	115	18 044	17 202	6 006	3 117	5 330	663	985
Living alone	9 087	8 763	219	105	16 222	15 462	5 452	2 642	4 980	586	865
Female	22 933	22 385	314	234	40 666	39 142	13 508	3 918	14 127	763	4 734
Living alone	22 121	21 601	299	221	38 832	37 405	12 925	3 441	13 725	727	4 609
Institutionalized persons	3 922	3 627	245	50	8 892	7 932	2 294	1 331	2 969	354	504
Other persons in group quarters	394	357	31	6	2 263	2 178	1 460	413	141	56	26
FAMILY TYPE BY PRESENCE OF OWN CHILDREN											
Families	442 161	426 933	10 195	5 033	1 559 043	1 486 349	381 403	287 539	202 954	193 379	161 645
With own children under 18 years	266 497	256 524	6 783	3 190	916 967	870 922	201 076	171 119	84 261	131 111	99 397
With own children under 6 years only	62 305	59 626	1 787	892	241 935	230 469	57 862	40 136	24 864	35 465	28 340
With own children under 6 and 6 to 17 years	68 514	65 436	2 263	815	196 525	184 086	35 124	35 570	15 408	27 586	15 078
Married-couple families	283 818	274 180	6 176	3 462	1 265 598	1 212 538	320 147	225 127	168 651	172 455	134 760
With own children under 18 years	165 951	159 473	4 256	2 222	790 212	755 637	181 441	143 300	73 516	122 806	86 927
With own children under 6 years only	36 796	35 199	981	616	215 773	207 269	54 321	33 888	22 989	33 718	26 386
With own children under 6 and 6 to 17 years	45 468	43 194	1 648	626	177 051	167 122	33 281	31 822	14 348	26 368	13 969
Female householder, no husband present	120 901	117 047	2 743	1 111	190 898	176 829	37 711	44 412	24 934	10 020	18 689
With own children under 18 years	78 879	76 296	1 821	762	96 429	87 689	14 461	21 634	8 408	5 621	9 963
With own children under 6 years only	18 436	17 697	525	214	18 515	16 409	2 400	4 579	1 328	1 048	1 462
With own children under 6 and 6 to 17 years	18 683	18 056	469	158	15 628	13 561	1 370	2 965	824	843	911
MARITAL STATUS											
Males 15 years and over	667 623	640 157	18 888	8 578	2 673 734	2 547 049	656 416	486 404	322 188	331 843	256 561
Never married	258 558	245 149	9 818	3 591	1 021 395	970 413	240 565	172 197	118 513	110 006	93 774
Now married, except separated	305 865	295 274	6 805	3 786	1 499 565	1 436 831	384 194	280 524	180 080	208 549	151 658
Separated	19 694	18 941	522	231	35 914	33 373	6 261	7 462	3 593	3 371	3 280
Widowed	15 279	14 538	511	230	35 088	33 111	9 569	7 913	5 742	2 895	1 968
Divorced	68 227	66 255	1 232	740	81 772	73 321	15 827	18 308	14 260	7 022	5 881
Females 15 years and over	702 215	675 341	18 527	8 347	2 862 398	2 736 451	670 291	602 017	392 661	275 097	338 279
Never married	208 846	199 944	6 637	2 265	789 782	748 816	191 085	165 527	96 531	62 697	82 556
Now married, except separated	313 686	301 363	8 150	4 173	1 680 315	1 617 381	396 592	348 774	231 049	188 601	207 367
Separated	29 119	28 203	649	267	51 857	48 090	8 246	13 513	4 904	3 176	5 631
Widowed	60 835	58 617	1 571	647	205 178	197 308	51 135	43 275	34 337	14 110	24 511
Divorced	89 729	87 214	1 520	995	135 266	124 856	23 233	30 928	25 840	6 513	18 214

Table 48. Household and Family Characteristics for Selected Racial Groups: 1990—Con.

[For definitions of terms and meanings of symbols, see text]

| | \multicolumn{11}{c}{Asian or Pacific Islander—Con.} |
| --- | | | | | | | | | | | |

United States	\multicolumn{6}{c}{Asian—Con.}	\multicolumn{5}{c}{Pacific Islander}
	Vietnamese	Cambodian	Hmong	Laotian	Thai	Other Asian	Total	Hawaiian	Samoan	Guamanian	Other Pacific Islander

HOUSEHOLD TYPE AND RELATIONSHIP

All persons	614 547	147 411	90 082	149 014	91 275	302 209	365 024	211 014	62 964	49 345	41 701
In households	604 814	146 657	89 709	148 193	89 363	291 959	353 934	205 738	60 347	47 742	40 107
Householder	143 095	28 957	13 742	30 188	23 021	78 898	91 638	56 839	12 933	12 875	8 991
15 to 24 years	10 831	2 089	1 656	2 252	2 107	8 956	7 714	4 310	1 143	1 352	909
25 to 34 years	44 987	7 890	4 748	9 941	5 386	25 753	26 381	14 959	4 017	4 300	3 105
35 to 44 years	46 565	9 899	3 757	9 485	9 147	23 440	24 121	14 367	3 554	3 545	2 655
45 to 54 years	23 846	5 544	1 923	5 438	5 148	11 671	15 488	10 120	2 190	1 787	1 391
55 to 64 years	11 097	2 385	950	2 101	913	5 528	10 144	7 143	1 227	1 154	620
65 to 74 years	4 241	931	545	792	256	2 381	5 502	4 132	604	536	230
75 to 84 years	1 332	192	151	158	56	966	1 946	1 563	160	156	67
85 years and over	196	27	12	21	8	203	342	245	38	45	14
Family householder	119 466	27 104	13 352	27 973	16 451	55 083	72 694	43 586	11 253	10 273	7 582
Male	93 903	18 021	10 909	23 155	11 836	45 681	53 465	31 169	8 235	8 052	6 009
Female	25 563	9 083	2 443	4 818	4 615	9 402	19 229	12 417	3 018	2 221	1 573
Nonfamily householder	23 629	1 853	390	2 215	6 570	23 815	18 944	13 253	1 680	2 602	1 409
Male	17 204	1 214	225	1 746	3 333	16 318	11 232	7 629	1 045	1 662	896
Living alone	10 248	727	157	965	2 040	9 633	7 152	4 944	667	993	548
Female	6 425	639	165	469	3 237	7 497	7 712	5 624	635	940	513
Living alone	4 437	441	148	315	2 215	5 252	5 544	4 082	471	654	337
Spouse	93 404	18 676	11 146	22 825	24 224	44 175	54 861	31 625	8 117	8 358	6 761
Child	243 625	72 941	55 503	72 766	26 191	120 530	142 836	80 628	27 608	17 942	16 658
Other relatives	80 195	17 501	8 103	16 846	8 227	25 306	40 360	22 078	8 572	4 488	5 222
Nonrelatives	44 495	8 582	1 215	5 568	7 700	23 050	24 239	14 568	3 117	4 079	2 475
In group quarters	9 733	754	373	821	1 912	10 250	11 090	5 276	2 617	1 603	1 594
Institutionalized persons	1 807	138	35	204	181	2 280	3 357	1 790	1 000	383	184
Correctional institutions	860	56	13	85	89	1 672	1 558	881	431	146	100
Nursing homes	336	24	3	19	22	209	956	405	357	169	25
Other institutions	611	58	19	100	70	399	843	504	212	68	59
Other persons in group quarters	7 926	616	338	617	1 731	7 970	7 733	3 486	1 617	1 220	1 410
College dormitories	5 121	389	309	368	1 250	6 836	3 369	1 450	711	465	743
Military quarters	791	53	15	92	302	424	2 054	839	502	554	159
Emergency shelters for homeless persons	152	37	2	13	15	127	448	277	87	47	37
Visible in street locations	44	3	–	3	12	29	466	375	58	13	20
Shelters for abused women	13	–	5	4	3	9	54	37	10	1	6
Drug/alcohol abuse group homes	19	1	–	2	1	24	84	62	14	3	5
Other noninstitutional group quarters	1 786	133	7	135	148	521	1 258	446	235	137	440
Persons per household	4.08	5.04	6.51	4.88	3.01	3.18	3.65	3.39	4.51	3.57	4.20
Persons per family	4.36	5.03	6.58	5.01	3.48	3.75	4.08	3.84	4.84	3.91	4.57
Persons under 18 years	209 257	69 784	55 251	67 200	22 805	107 304	131 995	72 982	26 636	16 285	16 092
Householder or spouse	246	87	211	110	41	134	136	60	26	29	21
Own child	185 492	61 273	51 312	60 791	20 648	99 694	108 166	58 589	21 767	14 002	13 808
In married-couple family	153 003	45 641	46 065	52 258	17 377	87 159	82 422	42 838	16 789	10 956	11 839
Percent of persons under 18 years	73.1	65.4	83.4	77.8	76.2	81.2	62.4	58.7	63.0	67.3	73.6
With female householder, no husband present	24 335	13 627	4 372	6 377	2 318	9 025	20 483	12 591	4 184	2 193	1 515
Grandchild	4 397	2 308	1 016	1 909	565	2 803	14 332	9 715	2 680	1 020	917
Other relatives	11 717	3 010	2 179	3 142	891	2 862	5 321	2 251	1 464	671	935
Nonrelatives	6 374	2 376	504	1 127	567	1 394	3 152	1 900	466	496	290
Institutionalized persons	439	52	21	76	54	187	360	173	130	26	31
Other persons in group quarters	592	78	8	45	39	230	528	294	103	41	90
Persons 65 years and over	18 084	3 724	2 535	3 697	1 416	7 901	14 735	10 233	2 047	1 523	932
Family householder	4 418	1 004	624	874	202	2 153	5 424	4 033	627	515	249
Male	3 391	665	435	704	140	1 710	3 828	2 770	445	403	210
Female	1 027	330	180	170	62	443	1 596	1 263	182	112	39
Spouse	1 926	328	248	354	114	1 032	2 641	2 035	236	256	114
Parent	6 600	1 287	1 189	1 498	584	2 066	1 591	789	361	168	273
Other relatives	2 566	632	336	724	317	816	1 180	657	222	139	162
Nonrelatives	928	308	50	130	67	227	488	336	60	50	42
Nonfamily householder	1 351	146	84	97	118	1 397	2 366	1 907	175	222	62
Male	547	64	15	34	29	412	842	685	58	78	21
Living alone	474	36	11	27	20	369	760	618	52	70	20
Female	804	82	69	63	89	985	1 524	1 222	117	144	41
Living alone	755	76	67	60	76	944	1 427	1 142	113	133	39
Institutionalized persons	238	16	3	17	13	193	960	427	346	160	27
Other persons in group quarters	57	3	1	3	1	17	85	49	20	13	3

FAMILY TYPE BY PRESENCE OF OWN CHILDREN

Families	119 466	27 104	13 352	27 973	16 451	55 083	72 694	43 586	11 253	10 273	7 582
With own children under 18 years	81 676	22 439	12 063	23 048	10 419	34 313	46 045	25 529	8 323	6 771	5 422
With own children under 6 years only	19 576	3 969	2 540	4 608	2 468	10 641	11 466	5 957	2 171	1 734	1 604
With own children under 6 and 6 to 17 years	21 836	9 231	6 623	7 143	1 671	8 816	12 439	6 454	2 610	1 735	1 640
Married-couple families	84 317	18 213	11 140	22 513	11 949	43 266	53 060	31 022	8 297	7 656	6 085
With own children under 18 years	64 679	15 865	10 375	19 329	8 128	29 271	34 575	18 363	6 403	5 214	4 595
With own children under 6 years only	16 184	2 415	2 216	3 620	2 083	9 449	8 504	4 200	1 633	1 316	1 355
With own children under 6 and 6 to 17 years	18 597	7 105	5 990	6 253	1 472	7 917	9 929	4 907	2 110	1 426	1 486
Female householder, no husband present	19 401	7 094	1 707	3 375	3 239	6 247	14 069	9 274	2 200	1 668	927
With own children under 18 years	12 296	5 689	1 425	2 656	1 900	3 636	8 740	5 545	1 528	1 088	579
With own children under 6 years only	2 344	1 323	242	637	279	767	2 106	1 289	399	270	148
With own children under 6 and 6 to 17 years	2 648	1 884	540	708	163	705	2 067	1 300	418	227	122

MARITAL STATUS

Males 15 years and over	239 236	40 555	20 355	48 169	28 507	116 815	126 685	74 168	20 294	18 274	13 949
Never married	124 401	16 991	7 154	19 997	13 003	53 812	50 982	29 879	8 375	7 552	5 176
Now married, except separated	102 066	21 467	12 718	26 007	13 673	55 895	62 734	35 526	10 442	8 988	7 778
Separated	5 458	730	203	662	482	1 871	2 541	1 464	397	419	261
Widowed	2 473	730	148	570	136	967	1 977	1 315	287	213	162
Divorced	4 838	637	132	933	1 213	4 270	8 451	5 984	793	1 102	572
Females 15 years and over	210 290	45 789	19 930	44 561	44 973	92 563	125 947	74 886	19 780	17 457	13 824
Never married	75 505	13 832	4 092	13 213	11 857	31 921	40 966	24 008	7 035	5 514	4 409
Now married, except separated	107 740	22 139	12 650	26 006	26 938	49 525	62 934	36 200	9 619	9 234	7 881
Separated	5 795	2 236	441	1 088	1 131	1 929	3 767	2 128	772	556	311
Widowed	12 749	6 120	2 233	2 939	1 426	4 473	7 870	5 107	1 314	843	606
Divorced	8 501	1 462	514	1 315	3 621	4 715	10 410	7 443	1 040	1 310	617

Table 49. Household and Family Characteristics by Type of Hispanic Origin: 1990

[For definitions of terms and meanings of symbols, see text]

United States	All persons	Hispanic origin (of any race)					Not of Hispanic origin
		Total	Mexican	Puerto Rican	Cuban	Other Hispanic	
HOUSEHOLD TYPE AND RELATIONSHIP							
All persons	248 709 873	22 354 059	13 495 938	2 727 754	1 043 932	5 086 435	226 355 814
In households	242 012 129	21 836 827	13 212 981	2 640 308	1 019 602	4 963 936	220 175 302
Householder	91 947 410	6 001 718	3 342 524	825 933	391 261	1 442 000	85 945 692
15 to 24 years	5 049 358	520 030	321 427	75 428	13 628	109 547	4 529 328
25 to 34 years	19 849 651	1 754 958	1 035 122	234 194	71 875	413 767	18 094 693
35 to 44 years	20 393 073	1 480 178	836 262	205 220	68 109	370 587	18 912 895
45 to 54 years	14 303 214	912 068	470 942	134 931	71 667	234 528	13 391 146
55 to 64 years	12 379 413	659 209	338 783	91 782	76 049	152 595	11 720 204
65 to 74 years	11 516 582	424 711	216 251	54 757	55 261	98 442	11 091 871
75 to 84 years	6 786 873	204 060	100 365	24 701	28 824	50 170	6 582 813
85 years and over	1 669 246	46 504	23 372	4 920	5 848	12 364	1 622 742
Family householder	64 517 947	4 789 261	2 751 262	636 273	289 826	1 111 900	59 728 686
Male	50 133 040	3 465 108	2 102 401	355 436	227 839	779 432	46 667 932
Female	14 384 907	1 324 153	648 861	280 837	61 987	332 468	13 060 754
Nonfamily householder	27 429 463	1 212 457	591 262	189 660	101 435	330 100	26 217 006
Male	12 141 701	666 964	348 178	97 003	48 645	173 138	11 474 737
Living alone	9 206 811	445 710	224 303	71 884	36 183	113 340	8 761 101
Female	15 287 762	545 493	243 084	92 657	52 790	156 962	14 742 269
Living alone	13 373 609	442 938	194 628	76 658	45 887	125 765	12 930 671
Spouse	50 708 322	3 390 585	2 021 038	352 132	217 061	800 354	47 317 737
Child	76 728 438	8 647 554	5 530 654	1 087 499	267 016	1 762 385	68 080 884
Other relatives	11 950 582	2 285 206	1 426 048	216 966	95 914	546 278	9 665 376
Nonrelatives	10 677 377	1 511 764	892 717	157 778	48 350	412 919	9 165 613
In group quarters	6 697 744	517 232	282 957	87 446	24 330	122 499	6 180 512
Institutionalized persons	3 334 018	261 693	137 989	44 822	16 018	62 864	3 072 325
Correctional institutions	1 115 111	197 400	101 572	33 911	11 851	50 066	917 711
Nursing homes	1 772 032	32 568	18 827	4 056	3 259	6 426	1 739 464
Other institutions	446 875	31 725	17 590	6 855	908	6 372	415 150
Other persons in group quarters	3 363 726	255 539	144 968	42 624	8 312	59 635	3 108 187
College dormitories	1 953 558	70 964	28 375	11 551	3 559	27 479	1 882 594
Military quarters	589 700	43 754	22 385	9 459	1 220	10 690	545 946
Emergency shelters for homeless persons	178 638	27 634	11 633	9 130	996	5 875	151 004
Visible in street locations	49 734	16 663	10 819	2 832	418	2 594	33 071
Shelters for abused women	11 768	1 770	1 017	408	35	310	9 998
Drug/alcohol abuse group homes	52 038	4 812	2 170	1 716	192	734	47 226
Other noninstitutional group quarters	528 290	89 942	68 569	7 528	1 892	11 953	438 348
Persons per household	2.63	3.53	3.80	3.15	2.78	3.33	2.57
Persons per family	3.16	3.88	4.11	3.56	3.22	3.69	3.10
Persons under 18 years	63 604 432	7 757 500	5 078 780	959 785	186 823	1 532 112	55 846 932
Householder or spouse	90 847	16 681	10 984	2 296	500	2 901	74 166
Own child	57 461 020	6 686 817	4 366 013	830 753	163 441	1 326 610	50 774 203
In married-couple family	44 642 569	4 805 660	3 324 291	422 974	125 475	932 920	39 836 909
Percent of persons under 18 years	70.2	61.9	65.5	44.1	67.2	60.9	71.3
With female householder, no husband present	10 674 900	1 504 305	802 712	360 463	31 133	309 997	9 170 595
Grandchild	3 493 999	488 361	320 703	69 511	14 695	83 452	3 005 638
Other relatives	1 172 053	325 328	224 753	27 833	4 178	68 564	846 725
Nonrelatives	1 121 322	195 816	127 996	21 385	3 349	43 086	925 506
Institutionalized persons	142 403	17 557	10 617	3 482	337	3 121	124 846
Other persons in group quarters	122 788	26 940	17 714	4 525	323	4 378	95 848
Persons 65 years and over	31 241 831	1 161 283	572 558	134 302	168 390	286 033	30 080 548
Family householder	10 801 438	410 154	219 468	45 175	54 121	91 390	10 391 284
Male	8 759 574	305 126	163 721	29 828	44 162	67 415	8 454 448
Female	2 041 864	105 028	55 747	15 347	9 959	23 975	1 936 836
Spouse	6 927 364	208 728	107 512	21 713	30 628	48 875	6 718 636
Parent	1 156 730	121 631	52 358	12 368	20 432	36 473	1 035 099
Other relatives	975 410	89 023	39 370	7 711	18 091	23 851	886 387
Nonrelatives	428 761	33 507	14 700	3 925	5 724	9 158	395 254
Nonfamily householder	9 171 263	265 121	120 520	39 203	35 812	69 586	8 906 142
Male	2 055 016	74 315	35 646	11 315	9 784	17 570	1 980 701
Living alone	1 902 614	66 400	31 846	10 180	8 675	15 699	1 836 214
Female	7 116 247	190 806	84 874	27 888	26 028	52 016	6 925 441
Living alone	6 922 231	181 547	80 568	26 655	24 858	49 466	6 740 684
Institutionalized persons	1 676 062	29 177	16 579	3 663	3 028	5 907	1 646 885
Other persons in group quarters	104 803	3 942	2 051	544	554	793	100 861
FAMILY TYPE BY PRESENCE OF OWN CHILDREN							
Families	64 517 947	4 789 261	2 751 262	636 273	289 826	1 111 900	59 728 686
With own children under 18 years	30 877 675	3 031 070	1 828 910	406 273	119 853	676 034	27 846 605
With own children under 6 years only	7 884 751	779 248	459 794	102 175	32 086	185 193	7 105 503
With own children under 6 and 6 to 17 years	6 403 526	835 326	551 560	97 947	22 888	162 931	5 568 200
Married-couple families	50 708 322	3 297 572	1 978 989	353 609	223 263	741 711	47 410 750
With own children under 18 years	23 494 726	2 132 498	1 366 062	212 608	93 116	460 712	21 362 228
With own children under 6 years only	6 226 406	561 236	347 286	56 763	26 499	130 688	5 665 170
With own children under 6 and 6 to 17 years	5 141 106	621 907	435 276	50 365	18 589	117 677	4 519 199
Female householder, no husband present	10 666 043	1 062 464	518 235	234 328	48 630	261 271	9 603 579
With own children under 18 years	6 028 409	697 964	344 312	167 806	20 813	165 033	5 330 445
With own children under 6 years only	1 272 224	146 494	69 807	36 917	3 822	35 948	1 125 730
With own children under 6 and 6 to 17 years	1 086 510	171 533	89 705	42 784	3 352	35 692	914 977
MARITAL STATUS							
Males 15 years and over	93 817 315	8 027 749	4 813 559	914 595	434 074	1 865 521	85 789 566
Never married	28 804 618	3 182 556	1 921 992	388 538	119 094	752 932	25 622 062
Now married, except separated	53 781 245	4 019 205	2 449 682	403 256	253 575	912 692	49 762 040
Separated	1 896 397	234 293	117 956	42 985	13 296	60 056	1 662 104
Widowed	2 377 589	115 417	64 754	14 546	10 476	25 641	2 262 172
Divorced	6 957 466	476 278	259 175	65 270	37 633	114 200	6 481 188
Females 15 years and over	101 324 687	7 743 317	4 358 178	996 351	456 044	1 932 744	93 581 370
Never married	23 755 235	2 314 256	1 294 882	345 115	88 711	585 548	21 440 979
Now married, except separated	53 144 096	3 823 012	2 272 119	391 235	238 731	920 927	49 321 084
Separated	2 676 840	387 012	183 410	83 549	14 656	105 397	2 289 828
Widowed	12 121 939	526 640	266 272	65 534	57 634	137 200	11 595 299
Divorced	9 626 577	692 397	341 495	110 918	56 312	183 672	8 934 180

Table 50. **Household and Family Characteristics for Race by Hispanic Origin: 1990**

[For definitions of terms and meanings of symbols, see text]

United States	All persons	White		Black		American Indian, Eskimo, or Aleut		Asian or Pacific Islander		Other race	
		Hispanic origin	Not of Hispanic origin	Hispanic origin	Not of Hispanic origin	Hispanic origin	Not of Hispanic origin	Hispanic origin	Not of Hispanic origin	Hispanic origin	Not of Hispanic origin
HOUSEHOLD TYPE AND RELATIONSHIP											
All persons	**248 709 873**	**11 557 774**	**188 128 296**	**769 767**	**29 216 293**	**165 461**	**1 793 773**	**305 303**	**6 968 359**	**9 555 754**	**249 093**
In households	242 012 129	11 308 797	183 362 643	715 612	28 006 615	159 259	1 743 699	299 244	6 821 491	9 353 915	240 854
Householder	91 947 410	3 246 356	73 633 749	209 390	9 766 771	39 978	551 394	75 147	1 938 588	2 430 847	55 190
15 to 24 years	5 049 358	234 779	3 724 039	16 774	643 829	3 938	41 435	5 832	114 628	258 707	5 397
25 to 34 years	19 849 651	848 579	15 108 146	57 814	2 337 930	12 090	137 463	20 673	494 649	815 802	16 505
35 to 44 years	20 393 073	762 813	15 887 702	53 286	2 310 225	10 667	137 650	21 048	563 568	632 364	13 750
45 to 54 years	14 303 214	512 391	11 382 028	33 919	1 547 581	5 897	94 459	12 877	359 000	346 984	8 078
55 to 64 years	12 379 413	413 686	10 176 763	24 060	1 258 758	3 817	66 534	7 888	212 856	209 758	5 293
65 to 74 years	11 516 582	290 574	9 894 863	15 505	1 018 189	2 353	46 287	4 225	128 653	112 054	3 879
75 to 84 years	6 786 873	148 824	5 980 518	6 700	524 338	956	22 280	2 156	53 852	45 424	1 825
85 years and over	1 669 246	34 710	1 479 690	1 332	125 921	260	5 286	448	11 382	9 754	463
Family householder	64 517 947	2 515 036	50 946 609	154 230	6 832 394	30 498	411 663	59 569	1 499 474	2 029 928	38 546
Male	50 133 040	1 889 040	41 726 664	80 649	3 411 219	19 456	269 131	43 901	1 235 555	1 432 062	25 363
Female	14 384 907	625 996	9 219 945	73 581	3 421 175	11 042	142 532	15 668	263 919	597 866	13 183
Nonfamily householder	27 429 463	731 320	22 687 140	55 160	2 934 377	9 480	139 731	15 578	439 114	400 919	16 644
Male	12 141 701	378 912	9 767 227	28 654	1 379 062	5 324	72 527	8 699	246 766	245 375	9 155
Living alone	9 206 811	262 123	7 411 319	21 000	1 119 836	3 479	54 040	5 591	169 324	153 517	6 582
Female	15 287 762	352 408	12 919 913	26 506	1 555 315	4 156	67 204	6 879	192 348	155 544	7 489
Living alone	13 373 609	293 709	11 347 225	21 943	1 373 574	3 117	55 356	4 967	148 448	119 202	6 068
Spouse	50 708 322	1 912 289	42 369 862	77 916	3 241 737	19 601	265 094	48 509	1 413 969	1 332 270	27 075
Child	76 728 438	4 354 090	54 236 497	287 614	10 618 732	71 675	686 460	121 986	2 416 744	3 812 189	122 451
Other relatives	11 950 582	1 072 284	5 835 383	82 972	2 989 740	15 616	138 185	32 772	681 194	1 081 562	20 874
Nonrelatives	10 677 377	723 778	7 287 152	57 720	1 389 635	12 389	102 566	20 830	370 996	697 047	15 264
In group quarters	6 697 744	248 977	4 765 653	54 155	1 209 678	6 202	50 074	6 059	146 868	201 839	8 239
Institutionalized persons	3 334 018	128 345	2 313 717	35 950	708 550	3 087	24 963	1 514	21 478	92 797	3 617
Correctional institutions	1 115 111	89 128	417 003	31 766	476 318	2 505	15 286	1 014	6 504	72 987	2 600
Nursing homes	1 772 032	22 101	1 590 191	1 304	134 533	115	4 882	209	9 514	8 839	344
Other institutions	446 875	17 116	306 523	2 880	97 699	467	4 795	291	5 460	10 971	673
Other persons in group quarters	3 363 726	120 632	2 451 936	18 205	501 128	3 115	25 111	4 545	125 390	109 042	4 622
College dormitories	1 953 558	37 105	1 572 872	3 713	204 308	611	8 809	2 052	93 973	27 483	2 632
Military quarters	589 700	15 046	400 320	2 602	127 287	689	4 903	1 200	12 566	24 217	870
Emergency shelters for homeless persons	178 638	11 438	76 433	5 035	68 350	635	3 887	291	1 979	10 235	355
Visible in street locations	49 734	8 913	15 042	3 344	16 303	359	787	191	919	3 856	20
Shelters for abused women	11 768	788	6 060	150	3 319	51	417	32	167	749	35
Drug/ alcohol abuse group homes	52 038	2 091	30 190	463	15 305	127	1 343	55	308	2 076	80
Other noninstitutional group quarters	528 290	45 251	351 019	2 898	66 256	643	4 965	724	15 478	40 426	630
Persons per household	2.63	3.31	2.51	3.19	2.87	3.35	3.11	3.53	3.34	3.87	3.01
Persons per family	3.16	3.71	3.03	3.66	3.47	3.72	3.59	3.88	3.80	4.11	3.59
Persons under 18 years	**63 604 432**	**3 820 918**	**43 807 311**	**266 015**	**9 318 400**	**69 359**	**627 608**	**108 154**	**1 975 233**	**3 493 054**	**118 380**
Householder or spouse	90 847	7 476	58 686	496	12 428	124	980	156	1 886	8 429	186
Own child	57 461 020	3 321 892	40 969 625	218 723	7 374 131	58 327	526 260	93 759	1 800 317	2 994 116	103 870
In married-couple family	44 642 569	2 490 122	34 489 085	108 624	3 341 728	36 229	343 485	72 088	1 594 341	2 098 597	68 270
Percent of persons under 18 years	70.2	65.2	78.7	40.8	35.9	52.2	54.7	66.7	80.7	60.1	57.7
With female householder, no husband present	10 674 900	660 958	5 173 796	95 418	3 667 827	17 694	142 821	16 742	156 027	713 493	30 124
Grandchild	3 493 999	244 043	1 562 189	23 899	1 303 689	5 617	60 103	7 284	72 590	207 518	7 067
Other relatives	1 172 053	136 094	415 292	10 804	346 759	2 403	17 485	3 920	63 841	172 107	3 348
Nonrelatives	1 121 322	91 472	669 880	8 104	205 155	2 183	17 080	2 600	30 331	91 457	3 060
Institutionalized persons	142 403	8 257	75 570	1 912	43 906	379	2 950	202	1 979	6 807	441
Other persons in group quarters	122 788	11 684	56 069	2 077	32 332	326	2 750	233	4 289	12 620	408
Persons 65 years and over	**31 241 831**	**801 154**	**27 050 819**	**37 838**	**2 470 713**	**5 669**	**108 784**	**14 749**	**440 209**	**302 373**	**10 023**
Family householder	10 801 438	280 702	9 331 555	12 129	876 666	2 089	42 545	4 751	137 255	110 483	3 263
Male	8 759 574	216 465	7 793 658	7 011	514 922	1 428	28 198	3 821	115 391	76 401	2 279
Female	2 041 864	64 237	1 537 897	5 118	361 744	661	14 347	930	21 864	34 082	984
Spouse	6 927 361	163 800	6 267 024	4 004	350 805	870	19 329	2 252	73 844	47 023	1 634
Parent	1 156 730	73 017	793 035	3 912	131 859	543	5 210	2 778	104 030	41 381	965
Other relatives	975 410	56 419	715 857	2 503	119 917	327	4 102	1 558	45 894	28 216	617
Nonrelatives	428 761	20 767	312 599	1 692	68 610	238	2 096	595	11 636	10 215	313
Nonfamily householder	9 171 263	193 406	8 023 516	11 408	791 782	1 480	31 308	2 078	56 632	56 749	2 904
Male	2 055 016	51 601	1 721 189	3 488	231 948	466	9 389	730	17 314	18 030	861
Living alone	1 902 614	46 242	1 601 019	3 073	210 139	406	8 681	632	15 590	16 047	785
Female	7 116 247	141 805	6 302 327	7 920	559 834	1 014	21 919	1 348	39 318	38 719	2 043
Living alone	6 922 231	135 281	6 148 692	7 433	531 305	954	21 167	1 259	37 573	36 620	1 947
Institutionalized persons	1 676 062	20 162	1 515 211	1 249	118 847	97	3 825	188	8 704	7 481	298
Other persons in group quarters	104 803	2 782	92 022	261	6 227	25	369	49	2 214	825	29
FAMILY TYPE BY PRESENCE OF OWN CHILDREN											
Families	**64 517 947**	**2 515 036**	**50 946 609**	**154 230**	**6 832 394**	**30 498**	**411 663**	**59 569**	**1 499 474**	**2 029 928**	**38 546**
With own children under 18 years	30 877 675	1 468 861	22 887 074	97 166	3 809 584	19 972	246 525	37 254	879 713	1 407 817	23 709
With own children under 6 years only	7 884 751	369 260	5 970 672	25 245	838 364	5 094	57 211	9 310	232 625	370 339	6 631
With own children under 6 and 6 to 17 years	6 403 526	384 751	4 430 159	24 947	881 770	5 365	63 149	9 139	187 386	411 124	5 736
Married-couple families	**50 708 322**	**1 819 907**	**42 563 582**	**76 779**	**3 333 566**	**18 233**	**265 585**	**42 381**	**1 223 217**	**1 340 272**	**24 800**
With own children under 18 years	23 494 726	1 078 925	18 698 437	47 983	1 731 789	11 799	154 152	27 507	762 705	966 284	15 145
With own children under 6 years only	6 226 406	279 154	5 043 535	13 079	374 726	2 972	33 824	6 975	208 798	259 056	4 287
With own children under 6 and 6 to 17 years	5 141 106	298 871	3 884 802	12 923	418 498	3 445	42 023	7 127	169 924	299 541	3 952
Female householder, no husband present	**10 666 043**	**494 468**	**6 312 278**	**61 673**	**2 990 006**	**8 965**	**111 936**	**11 821**	**179 077**	**485 537**	**10 282**
With own children under 18 years	6 028 409	301 284	3 306 284	41 515	1 855 630	6 357	72 522	7 410	89 019	341 398	6 990
With own children under 6 years only	1 272 224	60 207	694 886	9 387	395 175	1 491	16 945	1 603	16 912	73 806	1 812
With own children under 6 and 6 to 17 years	1 086 510	68 397	454 363	10 477	428 022	1 592	17 091	1 628	14 000	89 439	1 501
MARITAL STATUS											
Males 15 years and over	**93 817 315**	**4 162 924**	**72 711 218**	**274 401**	**9 822 582**	**53 746**	**613 877**	**104 083**	**2 569 651**	**3 432 595**	**72 238**
Never married	28 804 618	1 558 124	20 020 480	127 697	4 354 053	23 462	235 096	42 859	978 536	1 430 414	33 897
Now married, except separated	53 781 245	2 155 942	44 216 737	105 661	3 783 325	22 278	283 587	51 704	1 447 861	1 683 620	30 530
Separated	1 896 397	110 861	1 071 108	15 928	537 993	2 079	17 615	2 591	33 323	102 834	2 065
Widowed	2 377 589	69 607	1 886 226	5 186	326 862	928	14 351	1 465	33 623	38 231	1 110
Divorced	6 957 466	268 390	5 516 667	19 929	820 349	4 999	63 228	5 464	76 308	177 496	4 636
Females 15 years and over	**101 324 687**	**4 150 447**	**78 542 165**	**266 552**	**11 563 924**	**51 880**	**650 335**	**109 479**	**2 752 919**	**3 164 959**	**72 027**
Never married	23 755 235	1 135 082	16 040 666	100 059	4 426 173	17 335	191 511	33 895	755 887	1 027 885	26 742
Now married, except separated	53 144 096	2 123 374	43 808 428	93 705	3 566 627	22 098	291 588	56 403	1 623 912	1 527 432	30 529
Separated	2 676 840	172 451	1 353 273	23 711	859 430	3 093	26 026	4 099	47 758	183 658	3 341
Widowed	12 121 939	332 280	9 947 279	19 908	1 387 095	3 100	57 735	6 756	198 422	164 596	4 768
Divorced	9 626 577	387 260	7 392 519	29 169	1 324 599	6 254	83 475	8 326	126 940	261 388	6 647

Table 251. Summary of General Characteristics of Persons: 1990

[For definitions of terms and meanings of symbols, see text]

United States Region and Division State	All persons	Percent of all persons — Under 5 years	Under 18 years	18 to 24 years	25 to 44 years	45 to 64 years	65 years and over	80 years and over	Median age	Persons 18 years and over— Males per 100 females	In households — In families	Non-family house-holders and non-relatives of house-holder	In group quarters	Persons in group quarters — Total	Percent institutionalized
United States	248 709 873	7.4	25.6	10.8	32.5	18.6	12.6	2.8	32.9	91.9	82.0	15.3	2.7	6 697 744	49.8
REGION AND DIVISION															
Northeast	50 809 229	6.9	23.4	10.7	32.4	19.6	13.8	3.1	34.2	89.2	81.4	15.7	3.0	1 510 088	47.2
New England	13 206 943	7.0	23.2	11.2	33.4	18.8	13.4	3.2	33.7	90.2	80.2	16.4	3.4	445 031	40.3
Middle Atlantic	37 602 286	6.9	23.5	10.5	32.1	19.9	13.9	3.1	34.3	88.8	81.8	15.4	2.8	1 065 057	50.1
Midwest	59 668 632	7.4	26.2	10.5	31.6	18.7	13.0	3.1	32.9	90.8	82.5	14.8	2.7	1 598 620	53.3
East North Central	42 008 942	7.4	26.1	10.6	31.8	18.9	12.6	2.9	32.9	90.6	82.8	14.7	2.5	1 055 689	53.8
West North Central	17 659 690	7.4	26.4	10.1	31.2	18.3	13.9	3.6	33.1	91.5	81.7	15.2	3.1	542 931	52.4
South	85 445 930	7.3	25.8	10.9	32.1	18.7	12.6	2.7	32.7	91.0	83.0	14.3	2.7	2 294 420	49.9
South Atlantic	43 566 853	7.0	24.1	10.8	32.5	19.2	13.4	2.8	33.6	91.0	81.7	15.4	2.9	1 243 962	46.4
East South Central	15 176 284	7.0	26.2	11.0	30.9	19.2	12.7	2.9	32.9	88.7	85.0	12.5	2.6	392 424	49.5
West South Central	26 702 793	7.9	28.2	10.9	32.1	17.7	11.1	2.5	31.2	92.4	84.1	13.5	2.5	658 034	56.8
West	52 786 082	8.0	26.7	10.9	34.0	17.5	10.9	2.3	31.8	97.6	80.3	17.2	2.5	1 294 616	48.1
Mountain	13 658 776	8.1	28.4	10.3	32.5	17.6	11.2	2.3	31.6	96.0	82.0	15.8	2.2	297 687	48.7
Pacific	39 127 306	7.9	26.0	11.1	34.5	17.5	10.9	2.3	31.8	98.1	79.8	17.7	2.5	996 929	47.9
STATE															
New England	13 206 943	7.0	23.2	11.2	33.4	18.8	13.4	3.2	33.7	90.2	80.2	16.4	3.4	445 031	40.3
Maine	1 227 928	7.0	25.2	10.1	32.5	19.0	13.3	3.3	33.9	91.6	81.2	15.8	3.0	37 169	38.0
New Hampshire	1 109 252	7.6	25.1	10.6	34.9	18.1	11.3	2.7	32.8	93.4	81.5	15.6	2.9	32 151	35.7
Vermont	562 758	7.3	25.4	11.2	33.4	18.2	11.8	2.9	33.0	92.8	78.8	17.4	3.8	21 642	28.5
Massachusetts	6 016 425	6.9	22.5	11.8	33.6	18.5	13.6	3.3	33.5	88.9	79.3	17.2	3.6	214 307	39.4
Rhode Island	1 003 464	6.7	22.5	12.0	32.0	18.5	15.0	3.5	33.9	88.7	80.2	15.9	3.8	38 595	38.3
Connecticut	3 287 116	6.9	22.8	10.5	33.3	19.8	13.6	3.1	34.4	91.0	81.5	15.4	3.1	101 167	47.9
Middle Atlantic	37 602 286	6.9	23.5	10.5	32.1	19.9	13.9	3.1	34.3	88.8	81.8	15.4	2.8	1 065 057	50.1
New York	17 990 455	7.0	23.7	10.9	32.6	19.7	13.1	3.1	33.8	88.5	80.4	16.5	3.0	545 265	49.0
New Jersey	7 730 188	6.9	23.3	10.1	33.1	20.2	13.4	2.9	34.4	90.3	83.9	13.9	2.2	171 368	54.1
Pennsylvania	11 881 643	6.7	23.5	10.3	30.8	20.0	15.4	3.3	35.0	88.3	82.4	14.7	2.9	348 424	50.0
East North Central	42 008 942	7.4	26.1	10.6	31.8	18.9	12.6	2.9	32.9	90.6	82.8	14.7	2.5	1 055 689	53.8
Ohio	10 847 115	7.2	25.8	10.5	31.4	19.3	13.0	2.9	33.3	89.1	83.2	14.3	2.4	261 451	58.3
Indiana	5 544 159	7.2	26.3	10.9	31.3	19.0	12.6	2.9	32.8	90.4	83.1	14.0	2.9	161 992	50.4
Illinois	11 430 602	7.4	25.8	10.6	32.3	18.7	12.6	2.9	32.8	91.0	82.5	15.0	2.5	286 956	52.2
Michigan	9 295 297	7.6	26.5	10.8	32.1	18.7	11.9	2.6	32.6	90.9	83.0	14.7	2.3	211 692	53.3
Wisconsin	4 891 769	7.4	26.4	10.5	31.6	18.2	13.3	3.3	32.9	92.5	81.8	15.4	2.7	133 598	53.4
West North Central	17 659 690	7.4	26.4	10.1	31.2	18.3	13.9	3.6	33.1	91.5	81.7	15.2	3.1	542 931	52.4
Minnesota	4 375 099	7.7	26.7	10.1	33.0	17.7	12.5	3.3	32.4	93.2	80.9	16.4	2.7	117 621	53.8
Iowa	2 776 755	7.0	25.9	10.2	29.7	18.9	15.3	4.1	34.0	90.3	81.4	15.0	3.6	99 520	48.1
Missouri	5 117 073	7.2	25.7	10.1	31.0	19.2	14.0	3.5	33.5	89.0	82.3	14.9	2.8	145 397	55.6
North Dakota	638 800	7.5	27.5	10.6	30.4	17.3	14.3	3.8	32.4	97.0	81.5	14.7	3.8	24 234	43.6
South Dakota	696 004	7.8	28.5	9.8	29.4	17.6	14.7	4.0	32.5	94.0	81.9	14.4	3.7	25 841	51.5
Nebraska	1 578 385	7.6	27.2	9.9	30.8	18.0	14.1	3.9	33.0	91.5	81.9	15.1	3.0	47 553	53.9
Kansas	2 477 574	7.6	26.7	10.3	31.3	17.9	13.8	3.6	32.9	92.9	81.9	14.8	3.3	82 765	51.8
South Atlantic	43 566 853	7.0	24.1	10.8	32.5	19.2	13.4	2.8	33.6	91.0	81.7	15.4	2.9	1 243 962	46.4
Delaware	666 168	7.3	24.5	11.4	32.7	19.2	12.1	2.5	32.8	90.9	81.6	15.3	3.0	20 071	43.2
Maryland	4 781 468	7.5	24.3	10.6	35.1	19.2	10.8	2.2	33.0	91.1	81.9	15.7	2.4	113 856	55.1
District of Columbia	606 900	6.2	19.3	13.6	35.7	18.6	12.8	2.9	33.4	84.0	63.3	29.8	6.9	41 717	33.7
Virginia	6 187 358	7.2	24.3	11.6	34.5	18.8	10.7	2.2	32.6	93.6	81.3	15.3	3.4	209 300	40.3
West Virginia	1 793 477	5.9	24.7	10.0	29.7	20.5	15.0	3.3	35.4	88.4	85.0	13.0	2.1	36 911	52.7
North Carolina	6 628 637	6.9	24.2	11.8	32.5	19.4	12.1	2.5	33.1	91.1	82.7	13.9	3.4	224 470	37.2
South Carolina	3 486 703	7.4	26.4	11.7	32.0	18.6	11.4	2.2	32.0	90.5	84.2	12.4	3.3	116 543	37.9
Georgia	6 478 216	7.6	26.7	11.4	33.8	18.0	10.1	2.1	31.5	90.8	83.5	13.8	2.7	173 633	50.3
Florida	12 937 926	6.6	22.2	9.4	30.4	19.8	18.3	4.0	36.3	90.8	80.2	17.4	2.4	307 461	56.5
East South Central	15 176 284	7.0	26.2	11.0	30.9	19.2	12.7	2.9	32.9	88.7	85.0	12.5	2.6	392 424	49.5
Kentucky	3 685 296	6.8	25.9	10.9	31.5	19.1	12.7	2.9	33.0	90.2	84.9	12.4	2.7	101 176	47.1
Tennessee	4 877 185	6.8	24.9	10.8	31.8	19.7	12.7	2.8	33.5	89.1	84.3	13.1	2.6	129 129	50.6
Alabama	4 040 587	7.0	26.2	11.0	30.5	19.4	12.9	2.9	33.0	87.8	85.4	12.3	2.3	92 402	55.8
Mississippi	2 573 216	7.6	29.0	11.4	29.1	18.0	12.5	2.9	31.1	86.9	85.7	11.6	2.7	69 717	42.6
West South Central	26 702 793	7.9	28.2	10.9	32.1	17.7	11.1	2.5	31.2	92.4	84.1	13.5	2.5	658 034	56.8
Arkansas	2 350 725	7.0	26.4	10.1	29.2	19.4	14.9	3.5	33.8	88.9	84.9	12.6	2.5	58 332	58.7
Louisiana	4 219 973	7.9	29.1	11.0	31.0	17.8	11.1	2.4	31.0	88.6	84.7	12.6	2.7	112 578	59.8
Oklahoma	3 145 585	7.2	26.6	10.2	30.6	19.1	13.5	3.3	33.1	91.2	83.1	13.9	3.0	93 677	54.7
Texas	16 986 510	8.2	28.5	11.1	33.1	17.2	10.1	2.3	30.7	94.1	84.0	13.7	2.3	393 447	56.2
Mountain	13 658 776	8.1	28.4	10.3	32.5	17.6	11.2	2.3	31.6	96.0	82.0	15.8	2.2	297 687	48.7
Montana	799 065	7.4	27.8	8.8	31.3	18.9	13.3	3.0	33.8	95.3	81.6	15.4	3.0	23 747	46.8
Idaho	1 006 749	8.0	30.6	9.8	30.0	17.6	12.0	2.7	31.5	96.3	84.5	13.3	2.1	21 490	48.8
Wyoming	453 588	7.7	29.9	9.1	32.7	17.9	10.4	2.3	32.1	98.0	83.5	14.2	2.3	10 240	53.1
Colorado	3 294 394	7.7	26.1	10.2	35.8	17.9	10.0	2.2	32.5	95.7	79.7	17.9	2.4	79 472	45.3
New Mexico	1 515 069	8.3	29.5	10.0	32.0	17.8	10.8	2.2	31.2	93.9	84.2	13.9	1.9	28 807	48.7
Arizona	3 665 228	8.0	26.8	10.7	31.7	17.7	13.1	2.6	32.2	95.1	81.0	16.8	2.2	80 683	51.4
Utah	1 722 850	9.8	36.4	11.6	29.0	14.3	8.7	1.9	26.3	95.0	87.5	10.8	1.7	29 048	43.9
Nevada	1 201 833	7.7	24.7	9.9	34.5	20.3	10.6	1.6	33.3	103.1	78.2	19.8	2.0	24 200	56.0
Pacific	39 127 306	7.9	26.0	11.1	34.5	17.5	10.9	2.3	31.8	98.1	79.8	17.7	2.5	996 929	47.9
Washington	4 866 692	7.5	25.9	10.0	34.1	18.1	11.8	2.6	33.1	96.1	79.6	17.9	2.5	120 531	45.9
Oregon	2 842 321	7.1	25.5	9.4	32.6	18.3	13.8	3.1	34.6	93.9	79.8	17.9	2.3	66 205	50.4
California	29 760 021	8.1	26.0	11.5	34.7	17.3	10.5	2.3	31.4	98.5	79.7	17.8	2.5	751 860	50.1
Alaska	550 043	10.0	31.3	10.2	39.3	15.2	4.1	.6	29.4	113.6	80.4	15.8	3.8	20 701	22.1
Hawaii	1 108 229	7.5	25.3	10.9	34.2	18.3	11.3	2.1	32.6	102.7	82.6	14.0	3.4	37 632	20.7

Table 252. Summary of General Characteristics of Households and Families: 1990

[For definitions of terms and meanings of symbols, see text]

United States Region and Division State	All households	Family households Total	Family households With own children under 18	Married-couple family Total	Married-couple family With own children under 18	Female householder, no husband present Total	Female householder, no husband present With own children under 18	Nonfamily households Total	Householder living alone Total	Householder living alone Female	65 years and over Total	65 years and over Female	Householder 65 years and over	Persons per Household	Persons per Family
United States	91 947 410	70.2	33.6	55.1	25.6	11.6	6.6	29.8	24.6	14.5	9.6	7.5	21.7	2.63	3.16
REGION AND DIVISION															
Northeast	18 872 713	69.3	31.4	53.5	23.9	12.3	6.3	30.7	25.6	15.7	10.7	8.3	23.4	2.61	3.16
New England	4 942 714	68.9	31.8	54.5	24.6	11.2	6.1	31.1	24.8	15.2	10.4	8.2	22.5	2.58	3.11
Middle Atlantic	13 929 999	69.4	31.3	53.1	23.6	12.7	6.3	30.6	25.9	15.9	10.8	8.4	23.8	2.62	3.18
Midwest	22 316 975	70.2	34.1	56.3	26.3	10.9	6.4	29.8	25.0	15.1	10.4	8.2	22.4	2.60	3.14
East North Central	15 596 590	70.6	34.2	55.8	26.0	11.7	6.8	29.4	24.7	14.8	10.0	7.9	21.9	2.63	3.16
West North Central	6 720 385	69.3	34.0	57.7	27.1	9.0	5.6	30.7	25.8	15.7	11.2	8.9	23.6	2.55	3.09
South	31 822 254	71.4	34.0	55.9	25.7	12.3	6.9	28.6	24.0	14.3	9.4	7.4	21.7	2.61	3.12
South Atlantic	16 503 063	70.5	32.0	55.1	24.0	12.1	6.6	29.5	24.1	14.4	9.4	7.4	22.5	2.56	3.06
East South Central	5 651 671	73.3	35.2	57.2	26.6	13.1	7.3	26.7	23.6	14.5	10.1	8.1	22.7	2.62	3.11
West South Central	9 667 520	71.8	36.8	56.5	28.1	12.0	7.2	28.2	24.1	13.8	8.7	6.9	19.9	2.69	3.23
West	18 935 468	68.9	34.4	54.2	26.1	10.7	6.4	31.1	23.9	13.2	8.1	6.2	19.1	2.72	3.25
Mountain	5 033 336	69.5	35.4	56.2	27.2	9.9	6.3	30.5	24.4	13.3	8.1	6.2	19.4	2.65	3.20
Pacific	13 902 132	68.7	34.0	53.4	25.6	11.0	6.4	31.3	23.7	13.2	8.0	6.2	19.0	2.74	3.27
STATE															
New England	4 942 714	68.9	31.8	54.5	24.6	11.2	6.1	31.1	24.8	15.2	10.4	8.2	22.5	2.58	3.11
Maine	465 312	70.6	34.6	58.1	27.1	9.5	5.9	29.4	23.3	14.3	10.4	8.2	22.3	2.56	3.03
New Hampshire	411 186	71.2	35.5	59.7	29.0	8.5	5.0	28.8	22.0	12.7	8.4	6.6	18.8	2.62	3.09
Vermont	210 650	68.8	35.1	56.4	27.4	9.2	5.9	31.2	23.4	13.9	9.3	7.3	20.1	2.57	3.06
Massachusetts	2 247 110	67.4	30.7	52.1	23.3	12.1	6.3	32.6	25.8	16.1	10.8	8.6	23.0	2.58	3.15
Rhode Island	377 977	68.5	30.9	53.5	23.6	11.7	6.2	31.5	26.2	16.3	11.8	9.3	25.0	2.55	3.11
Connecticut	1 230 479	70.3	31.3	55.6	24.3	11.4	6.0	29.7	24.2	14.6	9.9	7.7	22.4	2.59	3.10
Middle Atlantic	13 929 999	69.4	31.3	53.1	23.6	12.7	6.3	30.6	25.9	15.9	10.8	8.4	23.8	2.62	3.18
New York	6 639 322	67.6	31.1	49.9	22.5	13.8	7.2	32.4	27.2	16.5	10.5	8.2	22.6	2.63	3.22
New Jersey	2 794 711	72.3	32.3	56.5	25.3	12.1	5.7	27.7	23.1	14.1	9.8	7.6	22.9	2.70	3.21
Pennsylvania	4 495 966	70.2	30.9	55.7	24.1	11.3	5.5	29.8	25.6	16.0	11.7	9.2	26.1	2.57	3.10
East North Central	15 596 590	70.6	34.2	55.8	26.0	11.7	6.8	29.4	24.7	14.8	10.0	7.9	21.9	2.63	3.16
Ohio	4 087 546	70.8	33.8	56.1	25.8	11.7	6.7	29.2	25.0	15.2	10.2	8.1	22.3	2.59	3.12
Indiana	2 065 355	71.7	35.0	58.2	27.3	10.5	6.3	28.3	24.1	14.7	10.1	8.1	21.9	2.61	3.11
Illinois	4 202 240	69.6	33.4	54.1	25.4	12.0	6.6	30.4	25.7	15.3	10.1	7.9	21.9	2.65	3.23
Michigan	3 419 331	71.3	34.9	55.1	25.6	12.9	7.8	28.7	23.7	13.9	9.3	7.3	21.0	2.66	3.16
Wisconsin	1 822 118	70.0	34.3	57.5	27.1	9.6	6.0	30.0	24.3	14.6	10.5	8.3	22.8	2.61	3.14
West North Central	6 720 385	69.3	34.0	57.7	27.1	9.0	5.6	30.7	25.8	15.7	11.2	8.9	23.6	2.55	3.09
Minnesota	1 647 853	68.6	34.7	57.2	27.9	8.6	5.5	31.4	25.1	15.0	10.1	8.0	21.3	2.58	3.13
Iowa	1 064 325	69.6	33.2	59.2	26.0	8.0	5.1	30.4	25.9	10.2	12.3	10.0	25.8	2.52	3.05
Missouri	1 961 206	69.8	33.2	56.3	25.6	10.6	6.3	30.2	26.0	16.1	11.3	9.0	23.9	2.54	3.08
North Dakota	240 878	69.0	35.4	59.1	29.4	7.3	4.8	31.0	26.5	15.2	11.6	8.9	24.5	2.55	3.13
South Dakota	259 034	69.6	35.4	58.9	28.6	8.0	5.4	30.4	26.4	15.7	12.2	9.5	25.7	2.59	3.16
Nebraska	602 363	69.0	34.4	58.2	27.9	8.3	5.3	31.0	26.5	15.9	11.6	9.2	24.0	2.54	3.11
Kansas	944 726	69.7	34.3	58.5	27.5	8.6	5.5	30.3	25.9	15.6	11.0	8.9	23.4	2.53	3.08
South Atlantic	16 503 063	70.5	32.0	55.1	24.0	12.1	6.6	29.5	24.1	14.4	9.4	7.4	22.5	2.56	3.06
Delaware	247 497	71.1	33.0	55.8	25.0	11.8	6.5	28.9	23.2	13.7	8.7	6.7	20.6	2.61	3.09
Maryland	1 748 991	71.2	33.5	54.2	25.0	13.3	7.0	28.8	22.6	13.4	7.7	6.1	18.5	2.67	3.14
District of Columbia	249 634	48.9	19.8	25.3	9.0	19.5	9.5	51.1	41.5	24.1	10.9	8.2	21.0	2.26	3.15
Virginia	2 291 830	71.1	34.0	56.8	26.7	11.1	6.0	28.9	22.9	13.4	7.8	6.2	18.4	2.61	3.09
West Virginia	688 557	72.7	34.0	59.0	27.1	10.7	5.5	27.3	24.5	15.8	12.3	9.7	26.6	2.55	3.05
North Carolina	2 517 026	72.0	33.2	56.6	25.2	12.3	6.7	28.0	23.7	14.3	9.0	7.2	20.8	2.54	3.03
South Carolina	1 258 044	73.8	35.5	56.4	26.5	14.0	7.6	26.2	22.4	13.2	8.7	6.9	20.6	2.68	3.16
Georgia	2 366 615	72.4	36.1	55.2	26.8	13.9	8.0	27.6	22.7	13.4	7.8	6.3	17.8	2.66	3.16
Florida	5 134 869	68.4	27.6	54.4	20.3	10.7	5.8	31.6	25.5	15.4	11.5	8.9	28.8	2.46	2.95
East South Central	5 651 671	73.3	35.2	57.2	26.6	13.1	7.3	26.7	23.6	14.5	10.1	8.1	22.7	2.62	3.11
Kentucky	1 379 782	73.6	36.1	59.2	28.3	11.6	6.5	26.4	23.3	14.5	10.3	8.2	22.6	2.60	3.08
Tennessee	1 853 725	72.7	33.9	57.2	25.7	12.6	6.9	27.3	23.9	14.6	9.6	7.7	21.8	2.56	3.05
Alabama	1 506 790	73.3	34.7	57.0	26.3	13.4	7.2	26.7	23.8	14.6	10.2	8.2	23.1	2.62	3.13
Mississippi	911 374	74.0	37.4	54.7	26.5	15.9	9.3	26.0	23.4	14.2	10.8	8.5	23.8	2.75	3.27
West South Central	9 667 520	71.8	36.8	56.5	28.1	12.0	7.2	28.2	24.1	13.8	8.7	6.9	19.9	2.69	3.23
Arkansas	891 179	73.1	34.3	59.2	26.5	11.1	6.5	26.9	24.0	15.0	11.6	9.2	25.9	2.57	3.06
Louisiana	1 499 269	72.7	37.7	53.6	26.9	15.6	9.2	27.3	23.7	13.7	9.2	7.1	20.7	2.74	3.28
Oklahoma	1 206 135	70.9	34.5	57.7	26.6	10.4	6.4	29.1	25.6	15.6	10.9	8.7	23.2	2.53	3.06
Texas	6 070 937	71.6	37.3	56.6	28.9	11.6	6.9	28.4	23.9	13.3	7.8	6.1	18.2	2.73	3.28
Mountain	5 033 336	69.5	35.4	56.2	27.2	9.9	6.3	30.5	24.4	13.3	8.1	6.2	19.4	2.65	3.20
Montana	306 163	69.1	34.8	57.7	27.3	8.6	5.9	30.9	26.3	14.5	10.5	7.8	22.7	2.53	3.08
Idaho	360 723	73.0	37.9	62.2	30.9	8.0	5.5	27.0	22.4	12.6	9.1	7.1	21.8	2.73	3.23
Wyoming	168 839	71.0	38.4	59.7	30.7	8.3	5.9	29.0	24.5	12.8	8.5	6.5	18.5	2.63	3.16
Colorado	1 282 489	66.6	33.9	53.8	25.9	9.7	6.4	33.4	26.6	14.5	7.5	5.8	16.6	2.51	3.07
New Mexico	542 709	72.1	38.1	56.0	28.2	11.9	7.4	27.9	23.0	12.6	7.9	5.9	19.6	2.74	3.26
Arizona	1 368 843	68.7	32.6	54.6	24.2	10.4	6.4	31.3	24.7	13.8	8.7	6.7	22.1	2.62	3.16
Utah	537 273	76.5	45.2	64.8	37.6	9.1	6.2	23.5	18.9	10.9	7.1	5.7	18.0	3.15	3.67
Nevada	466 297	65.9	30.8	51.4	22.6	10.2	6.1	34.1	25.7	11.9	7.1	4.7	17.3	2.53	3.06
Pacific	13 902 132	68.7	34.0	53.4	25.6	11.0	6.4	31.3	23.7	13.2	8.0	6.2	19.0	2.74	3.27
Washington	1 872 431	67.6	33.3	55.0	25.4	9.4	6.2	32.4	25.4	14.1	8.7	6.7	19.7	2.53	3.06
Oregon	1 103 313	68.1	32.0	55.6	24.4	9.2	5.9	31.9	25.3	14.7	9.8	7.7	22.8	2.52	3.02
California	10 381 206	68.8	34.1	52.7	25.6	11.5	6.5	31.2	23.4	13.1	7.9	6.0	18.7	2.79	3.32
Alaska	188 915	70.3	43.2	56.2	33.3	9.6	7.1	29.7	22.1	8.6	3.0	1.9	7.5	2.80	3.33
Hawaii	356 267	73.9	35.2	59.1	28.4	10.5	5.1	26.1	19.4	9.7	5.9	4.0	20.2	3.01	3.48

Table 253. Race and Hispanic Origin: 1990

[For definitions of terms and meanings of symbols, see text]

United States Region and Division State	United States	Northeast Region Total	New England Division	Middle Atlantic Division	Midwest Region Total	East North Central Division	West North Central Division	South Region Total	South Atlantic Division
RACE									
All persons	**248 709 873**	**50 809 229**	**13 206 943**	**37 602 286**	**59 668 632**	**42 008 942**	**17 659 690**	**85 445 930**	**43 566 853**
White	199 686 070	42 068 904	12 032 983	30 035 921	52 017 957	35 764 043	16 253 914	65 582 199	33 390 885
Black	29 986 060	5 613 222	627 547	4 985 675	5 715 940	4 817 436	898 504	15 828 888	8 923 558
American Indian, Eskimo, or Aleut	1 959 234	125 148	32 794	92 354	337 899	149 939	187 960	562 731	172 281
American Indian	1 878 285	121 551	31 986	89 565	333 998	147 399	186 599	557 214	169 554
Eskimo	57 152	1 665	446	1 219	1 975	1 248	727	2 778	1 350
Aleut	23 797	1 932	362	1 570	1 926	1 292	634	2 739	1 377
Asian or Pacific Islander	7 273 662	1 335 375	231 656	1 103 719	768 069	572 673	195 396	1 122 248	631 133
Asian	6 908 638	1 324 865	228 939	1 095 926	755 403	565 235	190 168	1 094 179	616 267
Chinese	1 645 472	445 089	72 299	372 790	133 336	103 253	30 083	204 430	114 013
Filipino	1 406 770	142 958	15 393	127 565	113 354	96 722	16 632	159 378	108 098
Japanese	847 562	74 202	15 055	59 147	63 210	50 477	12 733	67 193	38 849
Asian Indian	815 447	285 103	36 282	248 821	146 211	122 902	23 309	195 525	113 719
Korean	798 849	182 061	21 086	160 975	109 087	80 152	28 935	153 163	100 827
Vietnamese	614 547	60 509	21 737	38 772	51 932	26 351	25 581	168 501	61 944
Cambodian	147 411	30 176	20 560	9 616	12 921	7 046	5 875	19 279	11 125
Hmong	90 082	1 731	1 183	548	37 166	19 373	17 793	1 621	1 119
Laotian	149 014	15 928	10 149	5 779	27 775	14 049	13 726	29 262	12 132
Thai	91 275	11 801	2 520	9 281	12 981	9 135	3 846	23 747	14 283
Other Asian	302 209	75 307	12 675	62 632	47 430	35 775	11 655	72 080	40 158
Bangladeshi	11 838	6 854	437	6 417	1 142	895	247	2 405	1 338
Burmese	6 177	1 100	133	967	622	502	120	1 160	921
Indonesian	29 252	3 724	843	2 881	3 056	2 135	921	4 716	2 563
Malayan	12 243	2 320	660	1 660	3 007	1 994	1 013	3 614	1 252
Okinawan	2 247	78	25	53	150	114	36	267	149
Pakistani	81 371	27 876	2 558	25 318	15 351	13 501	1 850	21 541	12 071
Sri Lankan	10 970	2 761	594	2 167	1 639	1 047	592	2 365	1 569
All other Asian	148 111	30 594	7 425	23 169	22 463	15 587	6 876	36 012	20 295
Pacific Islander	365 024	10 510	2 717	7 793	12 666	7 438	5 228	28 069	14 866
Hawaiian	211 014	4 135	1 142	2 993	5 534	3 471	2 063	12 240	6 562
Samoan	62 964	1 503	389	1 114	2 243	995	1 248	4 055	2 243
Guamanian	49 345	3 603	849	2 754	3 150	2 167	983	8 296	4 504
Other Pacific Islander	41 701	1 269	337	932	1 739	805	934	3 478	1 557
Tongan	17 606	90	21	69	183	58	125	813	169
Tahitian	944	36	8	28	39	21	18	101	75
Northern Mariana Islander	960	23	11	12	85	42	43	183	113
Palauan	1 439	57	14	43	123	54	69	197	102
Fijian	7 036	138	62	76	79	40	39	168	99
All other Pacific Islander	13 716	925	221	704	1 230	590	640	2 016	999
Other race	9 804 847	1 666 580	281 963	1 384 617	828 767	704 851	123 916	2 349 864	448 996
HISPANIC ORIGIN									
All persons	**248 709 873**	**50 809 229**	**13 206 943**	**37 602 286**	**59 668 632**	**42 008 942**	**17 659 690**	**85 445 930**	**43 566 853**
Hispanic origin (of any race)	22 354 059	3 754 389	568 240	3 186 149	1 726 509	1 437 720	288 789	6 767 021	2 132 751
Mexican	13 495 938	174 996	28 773	146 223	1 153 296	944 166	209 130	4 343 523	314 731
Puerto Rican	2 727 754	1 871 981	316 259	1 555 722	257 594	243 587	14 007	405 941	338 080
Cuban	1 043 932	183 636	16 428	167 208	36 577	30 452	6 125	735 458	702 110
Other Hispanic	5 086 435	1 523 776	206 780	1 316 996	279 042	219 515	59 527	1 282 099	777 830
Not of Hispanic origin	226 355 814	47 054 840	12 638 703	34 416 137	57 942 123	40 571 222	17 370 901	78 678 909	41 434 102
RACE AND HISPANIC ORIGIN									
All persons	**248 709 873**	**50 809 229**	**13 206 943**	**37 602 286**	**59 668 632**	**42 008 942**	**17 659 690**	**85 445 930**	**43 566 853**
White	199 686 070	42 068 904	12 032 983	30 035 921	52 017 957	35 764 043	16 253 914	65 582 199	33 390 885
Hispanic origin	11 557 774	1 702 081	267 373	1 434 708	842 687	689 343	153 344	4 222 997	1 570 073
Not of Hispanic origin	188 128 296	40 366 823	11 765 610	28 601 213	51 175 270	35 074 700	16 100 570	61 359 202	31 820 812
Black	29 986 060	5 613 222	627 547	4 985 675	5 715 940	4 817 436	898 504	15 828 888	8 923 558
Hispanic origin	769 767	403 651	44 406	359 245	51 585	43 240	8 345	174 422	107 035
Not of Hispanic origin	29 216 293	5 209 571	583 141	4 626 430	5 664 355	4 774 196	890 159	15 654 466	8 816 523
American Indian, Eskimo, or Aleut	1 959 234	125 148	32 794	92 354	337 899	149 939	187 960	562 731	172 281
Hispanic origin	165 461	18 898	3 079	15 819	17 001	10 250	6 751	29 117	7 773
Not of Hispanic origin	1 793 773	106 250	29 715	76 535	320 898	139 689	181 209	533 614	164 508
Asian or Pacific Islander	7 273 662	1 335 375	231 656	1 103 719	768 069	572 673	195 396	1 122 248	631 133
Hispanic origin	305 303	44 238	5 759	38 479	21 458	16 502	4 956	43 289	21 710
Not of Hispanic origin	6 968 359	1 291 137	225 897	1 065 240	746 611	556 171	190 440	1 078 959	609 423
Other race	9 804 847	1 666 580	281 963	1 384 617	828 767	704 851	123 916	2 349 864	448 996
Hispanic origin	9 555 754	1 585 521	247 623	1 337 898	793 778	678 385	115 393	2 297 196	426 160
Not of Hispanic origin	249 093	81 059	34 340	46 719	34 989	26 466	8 523	52 668	22 836
PERCENT DISTRIBUTION BY RACE									
All persons	**100.0**	**100.0**	**100.0**	**100.0**	**100.0**	**100.0**	**100.0**	**100.0**	**100.0**
White	80.3	82.8	91.1	79.9	87.2	85.1	92.0	76.8	76.6
Black	12.1	11.0	4.8	13.3	9.6	11.5	5.1	18.5	20.5
American Indian, Eskimo, or Aleut	.8	.2	.2	.2	.6	.4	1.1	.7	.4
American Indian	.8	.2	.2	.2	.6	.4	1.1	.7	.4
Asian or Pacific Islander	2.9	2.6	1.8	2.9	1.3	1.4	1.1	1.3	1.4
Asian	2.8	2.6	1.7	2.9	1.3	1.3	1.1	1.3	1.4
Pacific Islander	.1	—	—	—	—	—	—	—	—
Other race	3.9	3.3	2.1	3.7	1.4	1.7	.7	2.8	1.0
PERCENT DISTRIBUTION BY HISPANIC ORIGIN									
All persons	**100.0**	**100.0**	**100.0**	**100.0**	**100.0**	**100.0**	**100.0**	**100.0**	**100.0**
Hispanic origin (of any race)	9.0	7.4	4.3	8.5	2.9	3.4	1.6	7.9	4.9
Mexican	5.4	.3	.2	.4	1.9	2.2	1.2	5.1	.7
Puerto Rican	1.1	3.7	2.4	4.1	.4	.6	.1	.5	.8
Cuban	.4	.4	.1	.4	.1	.1	—	.9	1.6
Other Hispanic	2.0	3.0	1.6	3.5	.5	.5	.3	1.5	1.8
Not of Hispanic origin	91.0	92.6	95.7	91.5	97.1	96.6	98.4	92.1	95.1
PERCENT WHITE, NOT OF HISPANIC ORIGIN									
All persons	**100.0**	**100.0**	**100.0**	**100.0**	**100.0**	**100.0**	**100.0**	**100.0**	**100.0**
White	80.3	82.8	91.1	79.9	87.2	85.1	92.0	76.8	76.6
Not of Hispanic origin	75.6	79.4	89.1	76.1	85.8	83.5	91.2	71.8	73.0

Table 253. **Race and Hispanic Origin: 1990**—Con.

[For definitions of terms and meanings of symbols, see text]

United States Region and Division State	South Region—Con.		West Region			New England Division			
	East South Central Division	West South Central Division	Total	Mountain Division	Pacific Division	Maine	New Hampshire	Vermont	Massachusetts
RACE									
All persons	15 176 284	26 702 793	52 786 082	13 658 776	39 127 306	1 227 928	1 109 252	562 758	6 016 425
White	12 049 158	20 142 156	40 017 010	11 761 851	28 255 159	1 208 360	1 087 433	555 088	5 405 374
Black	2 976 704	3 928 626	2 828 010	373 584	2 454 426	5 138	7 198	1 951	300 130
American Indian, Eskimo, or Aleut	40 839	349 611	933 456	480 516	452 940	5 998	2 134	1 696	12 241
American Indian	40 220	347 440	865 522	478 391	387 131	5 945	2 075	1 650	11 857
Eskimo	333	1 095	50 734	1 290	49 444	34	45	32	210
Aleut	286	1 076	17 200	835	16 365	19	14	14	174
Asian or Pacific Islander	84 464	406 651	4 047 970	217 120	3 830 850	6 683	9 343	3 215	143 392
Asian	81 694	396 218	3 734 191	198 200	3 535 991	6 450	9 121	3 134	142 137
Chinese	14 836	75 581	862 617	40 007	822 610	1 262	2 314	679	53 792
Filipino	8 606	42 674	991 080	31 527	959 553	1 058	874	253	6 212
Japanese	8 681	19 663	642 957	34 254	608 703	590	747	373	8 784
Asian Indian	15 053	66 753	188 608	15 435	173 173	607	1 697	529	19 719
Korean	12 057	40 279	354 538	27 615	326 923	858	1 501	563	11 744
Vietnamese	9 657	96 900	333 605	19 548	314 057	642	553	236	15 449
Cambodian	1 624	6 530	85 035	3 479	81 556	767	276	58	14 050
Hmong	95	407	49 564	1 486	48 078	–	2	3	248
Laotian	3 890	13 240	76 049	6 635	69 414	101	380	115	3 985
Thai	1 754	7 710	42 746	5 831	36 915	113	233	80	1 424
Other Asian	5 441	26 481	107 392	12 383	95 009	452	544	245	6 730
Bangladeshi	232	835	1 437	198	1 239	2	23	8	256
Burmese	38	201	3 295	133	3 162	6	5	2	93
Indonesian	463	1 690	17 756	1 114	16 642	19	45	27	498
Malayan	501	1 861	3 302	530	2 772	15	34	23	220
Okinawan	26	92	1 752	83	1 669	9	2	–	12
Pakistani	872	8 598	16 603	1 651	14 952	25	109	19	1 282
Sri Lankan	113	683	4 205	420	3 785	23	16	8	333
All other Asian	3 196	12 521	59 042	8 254	50 788	353	310	158	4 036
Pacific Islander	2 770	10 433	313 779	18 920	294 859	233	222	81	1 255
Hawaiian	1 350	4 328	189 105	7 144	181 961	115	116	25	505
Samoan	469	1 343	55 163	2 995	52 160	39	23	18	204
Guamanian	746	3 046	34 296	2 429	31 867	58	67	24	364
Other Pacific Islander	205	1 716	35 215	6 352	28 863	21	16	14	182
Tongan	5	639	16 520	4 738	11 782	2	1	–	15
Tahitian	4	22	768	101	667	2	–	–	5
Northern Mariana Islander	18	52	669	81	588	1	3	3	3
Palauan	18	77	1 062	94	968	–	1	4	3
Fijian	8	61	6 651	112	6 539	2	–	3	25
All other Pacific Islander	152	865	9 545	1 226	8 319	14	11	4	131
Other race	25 119	1 875 749	4 959 636	825 705	4 133 931	1 749	3 144	808	155 288
HISPANIC ORIGIN									
All persons	15 176 284	26 702 793	52 786 082	13 658 776	39 127 306	1 227 928	1 109 252	562 758	6 016 425
Hispanic origin (of any race)	95 285	4 530 985	10 106 140	1 991 732	8 114 408	6 829	11 333	3 661	287 549
Mexican	38 798	3 989 994	7 824 123	1 439 943	6 384 180	2 153	2 362	725	12 703
Puerto Rican	12 831	55 030	192 238	25 996	166 242	1 250	3 299	659	151 193
Cuban	5 047	28 301	88 261	11 835	76 426	350	578	168	8 106
Other Hispanic	38 609	465 660	2 001 518	513 958	1 487 560	3 076	5 094	2 109	115 547
Not of Hispanic origin	15 080 999	22 163 808	42 679 942	11 667 044	31 012 898	1 221 099	1 097 919	559 097	5 728 876
RACE AND HISPANIC ORIGIN									
All persons	15 176 284	26 702 793	52 786 082	13 658 776	39 127 306	1 227 928	1 109 252	562 758	6 016 425
White	12 049 158	20 142 156	40 017 010	11 761 851	28 255 159	1 208 360	1 087 433	555 088	5 405 374
Hispanic origin	59 140	2 593 784	4 790 009	1 119 696	3 670 313	5 003	7 949	2 904	125 082
Not of Hispanic origin	11 990 018	17 548 372	35 227 001	10 642 155	24 584 846	1 203 357	1 079 484	552 184	5 280 292
Black	2 976 704	3 928 626	2 828 010	373 584	2 454 426	5 138	7 198	1 951	300 130
Hispanic origin	10 815	56 572	140 109	16 826	123 283	201	449	83	25 666
Not of Hispanic origin	2 965 889	3 872 054	2 687 901	356 758	2 331 143	4 937	6 749	1 868	274 464
American Indian, Eskimo, or Aleut	40 839	349 611	933 456	480 516	452 940	5 998	2 134	1 696	12 241
Hispanic origin	1 099	20 245	100 445	32 311	68 134	100	92	45	1 696
Not of Hispanic origin	39 740	329 366	833 011	448 205	384 806	5 898	2 042	1 651	10 545
Asian or Pacific Islander	84 464	406 651	4 047 970	217 120	3 830 850	6 683	9 343	3 215	143 392
Hispanic origin	2 565	19 014	196 318	12 045	184 273	178	146	56	3 054
Not of Hispanic origin	81 899	387 637	3 851 652	205 075	3 646 577	6 505	9 197	3 159	140 338
Other race	25 119	1 875 749	4 959 636	825 705	4 133 931	1 749	3 144	808	155 288
Hispanic origin	21 666	1 849 370	4 879 259	810 854	4 068 405	1 347	2 697	573	132 051
Not of Hispanic origin	3 453	26 379	80 377	14 851	65 526	402	447	235	23 237
PERCENT DISTRIBUTION BY RACE									
All persons	100.0	100.0	100.0	100.0	100.0	100.0	100.0	100.0	100.0
White	79.4	75.4	75.8	86.1	72.2	98.4	98.0	98.6	89.8
Black	19.6	14.7	5.4	2.7	6.3	.4	.6	.3	5.0
American Indian, Eskimo, or Aleut	.3	1.3	1.8	3.5	1.2	.5	.2	.3	.2
American Indian	.3	1.3	1.6	3.5	1.0	.5	.2	.3	.2
Asian or Pacific Islander	.6	1.5	7.7	1.6	9.8	.5	.8	.6	2.4
Asian	.5	1.5	7.1	1.5	9.0	.5	.8	.6	2.4
Pacific Islander	–	–	.6	.1	.8	–	–	–	
Other race	.2	7.0	9.4	6.0	10.6	.1	.3	.1	2.6
PERCENT DISTRIBUTION BY HISPANIC ORIGIN									
All persons	100.0	100.0	100.0	100.0	100.0	100.0	100.0	100.0	100.0
Hispanic origin (of any race)	.6	17.0	19.1	14.6	20.7	.6	1.0	.7	4.8
Mexican	.3	14.9	14.8	10.5	16.3	.2	.2	.1	.2
Puerto Rican	.1	.2	.4	.2	.4	.1	.3	.1	2.5
Cuban	–	.1	.2	.1	.2	–	.1	–	.1
Other Hispanic	.3	1.7	3.8	3.8	3.8	.3	.5	.4	1.9
Not of Hispanic origin	99.4	83.0	80.9	85.4	79.3	99.4	99.0	99.3	95.2
PERCENT WHITE, NOT OF HISPANIC ORIGIN									
All persons	100.0	100.0	100.0	100.0	100.0	100.0	100.0	100.0	100.0
White	79.4	75.4	75.8	86.1	72.2	98.4	98.0	98.6	89.8
Not of Hispanic origin	79.0	65.7	66.7	77.9	62.8	98.0	97.3	98.1	87.8

Table 253. Race and Hispanic Origin: 1990—Con.

[For definitions of terms and meanings of symbols, see text]

United States Region and Division State	New England Division—Con.		Middle Atlantic Division			East North Central Division				
	Rhode Island	Connecticut	New York	New Jersey	Pennsylvania	Ohio	Indiana	Illinois	Michigan	Wisconsin
RACE										
All persons	1 003 464	3 287 116	17 990 455	7 730 188	11 881 643	10 847 115	5 544 159	11 430 602	9 295 297	4 891 769
White	917 375	2 859 353	13 385 255	6 130 465	10 520 201	9 521 756	5 020 700	8 952 978	7 756 086	4 512 523
Black	38 861	274 269	2 859 055	1 036 825	1 089 795	1 154 826	432 092	1 694 273	1 291 706	244 539
American Indian, Eskimo, or Aleut	4 071	6 654	62 651	14 970	14 733	20 358	12 720	21 836	55 638	39 387
American Indian	3 987	6 472	60 855	14 500	14 210	19 859	12 453	20 970	55 131	38 986
Eskimo	42	83	754	201	264	230	170	414	253	181
Aleut	42	99	1 042	269	259	269	97	452	254	220
Asian or Pacific Islander	18 325	50 698	693 760	272 521	137 438	91 179	37 617	285 311	104 983	53 583
Asian	18 019	50 078	689 303	270 839	135 784	89 723	36 660	282 569	103 501	52 782
Chinese	3 170	11 082	284 144	59 084	29 562	19 447	7 371	49 936	19 145	7 354
Filipino	1 836	5 160	62 259	53 146	12 160	10 268	4 754	64 224	13 786	3 690
Japanese	750	3 811	35 281	17 253	6 613	10 485	4 715	21 831	10 681	2 765
Asian Indian	1 975	11 755	140 985	79 440	28 396	20 848	7 095	64 200	23 845	6 914
Korean	1 294	5 126	95 648	38 540	26 787	11 237	5 475	41 506	16 316	5 618
Vietnamese	772	4 085	15 555	7 330	15 887	4 964	2 467	10 309	6 117	2 494
Cambodian	3 655	1 754	3 646	475	5 495	2 213	412	3 026	874	521
Hmong	884	46	165	25	358	253	57	433	2 257	16 373
Laotian	2 579	2 989	3 253	478	2 048	2 578	674	4 985	2 190	3 622
Thai	141	529	6 230	1 758	1 293	1 515	654	5 180	1 284	502
Other Asian	963	3 741	42 137	13 310	7 185	5 915	2 986	16 939	7 006	2 929
Bangladeshi	14	134	5 406	791	220	162	84	263	342	44
Burmese	8	19	669	129	169	82	32	299	72	17
Indonesian	37	217	2 023	423	435	521	235	506	525	348
Malayan	26	342	1 202	178	280	434	364	571	382	243
Okinawan	–	2	26	6	21	23	12	48	23	8
Pakistani	111	1 012	17 778	5 797	1 743	1 382	624	9 035	1 976	484
Sri Lankan	41	173	1 271	533	363	289	169	311	179	99
All other Asian	726	1 842	13 762	5 453	3 954	3 022	1 466	5 906	3 507	1 686
Pacific Islander	306	620	4 457	1 682	1 654	1 456	957	2 742	1 482	801
Hawaiian	112	269	1 496	638	859	785	528	1 000	787	371
Samoan	20	85	586	217	311	180	151	367	191	106
Guamanian	134	202	1 803	644	307	333	217	1 105	283	229
Other Pacific Islander	40	64	572	183	177	158	61	270	221	95
Tongan	–	3	30	9	30	14	15	15	12	2
Tahitian	–	1	9	12	7	5	1	7	6	2
Northern Mariana Islander	1	–	4	2	6	9	7	8	16	2
Palauan	1	5	22	13	8	13	2	21	16	2
Fijian	25	7	58	14	4	6	1	16	15	2
All other Pacific Islander	13	48	449	133	122	111	35	203	156	85
Other race	24 832	96 142	989 734	275 407	119 476	58 996	41 030	476 204	86 884	41 737
HISPANIC ORIGIN										
All persons	1 003 464	3 287 116	17 990 455	7 730 188	11 881 643	10 847 115	5 544 159	11 430 602	9 295 297	4 891 769
Hispanic origin (of any race)	45 752	213 116	2 214 026	739 861	232 262	139 696	98 788	904 446	201 596	93 194
Mexican	2 437	8 393	93 244	28 759	24 220	57 815	66 736	623 688	138 312	57 615
Puerto Rican	13 016	146 842	1 086 601	320 133	148 988	45 853	14 021	146 059	18 538	19 116
Cuban	840	6 386	74 345	85 378	7 485	3 559	1 853	18 204	5 157	1 679
Other Hispanic	29 459	51 495	959 836	305 591	51 569	32 469	16 178	116 495	39 589	14 784
Not of Hispanic origin	957 712	3 074 000	15 776 429	6 990 327	11 649 381	10 707 419	5 445 371	10 526 156	9 093 701	4 798 575
RACE AND HISPANIC ORIGIN										
All persons	1 003 464	3 287 116	17 990 455	7 730 188	11 881 643	10 847 115	5 544 159	11 430 602	9 295 297	4 891 769
White	917 375	2 859 353	13 385 255	6 130 465	10 520 201	9 521 756	5 020 700	8 952 978	7 756 086	4 512 523
Hispanic origin	21 266	105 169	925 066	411 499	98 143	77 134	55 458	402 770	106 135	47 846
Not of Hispanic origin	896 109	2 754 184	12 460 189	5 718 966	10 422 058	9 444 622	4 965 242	8 550 208	7 649 951	4 464 677
Black	38 861	274 269	2 859 055	1 036 825	1 089 795	1 154 826	432 092	1 694 273	1 291 706	244 539
Hispanic origin	4 578	13 429	289 929	51 980	17 336	7 386	3 480	20 570	8 962	2 842
Not of Hispanic origin	34 283	260 840	2 569 126	984 845	1 072 459	1 147 440	428 612	1 673 703	1 282 744	241 697
American Indian, Eskimo, or Aleut	4 071	6 654	62 651	14 970	14 733	20 358	12 720	21 836	55 638	39 387
Hispanic origin	442	704	12 111	2 480	1 228	1 221	721	3 623	3 067	1 618
Not of Hispanic origin	3 629	5 950	50 540	12 490	13 505	19 137	11 999	18 213	52 571	37 769
Asian or Pacific Islander	18 325	50 698	693 760	272 521	137 438	91 179	37 617	285 311	104 983	53 583
Hispanic origin	741	1 584	26 917	8 180	3 382	1 984	999	9 743	2 477	1 299
Not of Hispanic origin	17 584	49 114	666 843	264 341	134 056	89 195	36 618	275 568	102 506	52 284
Other race	24 832	96 142	989 734	275 407	119 476	58 996	41 030	476 204	86 884	41 737
Hispanic origin	18 725	92 230	960 003	265 722	112 173	51 971	38 130	467 740	80 955	39 589
Not of Hispanic origin	6 107	3 912	29 731	9 685	7 303	7 025	2 900	8 464	5 929	2 148
PERCENT DISTRIBUTION BY RACE										
All persons	100.0	100.0	100.0	100.0	100.0	100.0	100.0	100.0	100.0	100.0
White	91.4	87.0	74.4	79.3	88.5	87.8	90.6	78.3	83.4	92.2
Black	3.9	8.3	15.9	13.4	9.2	10.6	7.8	14.8	13.9	5.0
American Indian, Eskimo, or Aleut	.4	.2	.3	.2	.1	.2	.2	.2	.6	.8
American Indian	.4	.2	.3	.2	.1	.2	.2	.2	.6	.8
Asian or Pacific Islander	1.8	1.5	3.9	3.5	1.2	.8	.7	2.5	1.1	1.1
Asian	1.8	1.5	3.8	3.5	1.1	.8	.7	2.5	1.1	1.1
Pacific Islander	–	–	–	–	–	–	–	–	–	–
Other race	2.5	2.9	5.5	3.6	1.0	.5	.7	4.2	.9	.9
PERCENT DISTRIBUTION BY HISPANIC ORIGIN										
All persons	100.0	100.0	100.0	100.0	100.0	100.0	100.0	100.0	100.0	100.0
Hispanic origin (of any race)	4.6	6.5	12.3	9.6	2.0	1.3	1.8	7.9	2.2	1.9
Mexican	.2	.3	.5	.4	.2	.5	1.2	5.5	1.5	1.2
Puerto Rican	1.3	4.5	6.0	4.1	1.3	.4	.3	1.3	.2	.4
Cuban	.1	.2	.4	1.1	.1	–	–	.2	.1	–
Other Hispanic	2.9	1.6	5.3	4.0	.4	.3	.3	1.0	.4	.3
Not of Hispanic origin	95.4	93.5	87.7	90.4	98.0	98.7	98.2	92.1	97.8	98.1
PERCENT WHITE, NOT OF HISPANIC ORIGIN										
All persons	100.0	100.0	100.0	100.0	100.0	100.0	100.0	100.0	100.0	100.0
White	91.4	87.0	74.4	79.3	88.5	87.8	90.6	78.3	83.4	92.2
Not of Hispanic origin	89.3	83.8	69.3	74.0	87.7	87.1	89.6	74.8	82.3	91.3

Table 253. Race and Hispanic Origin: 1990—Con.

[For definitions of terms and meanings of symbols, see text]

United States Region and Division State	West North Central Division							South Atlantic Division		
	Minnesota	Iowa	Missouri	North Dakota	South Dakota	Nebraska	Kansas	Delaware	Maryland	District of Columbia
RACE										
All persons	4 375 099	2 776 755	5 117 073	638 800	696 004	1 578 385	2 477 574	666 168	4 781 468	606 900
White	4 130 395	2 683 090	4 486 228	604 142	637 515	1 480 558	2 231 986	535 094	3 393 964	179 667
Black	94 944	48 090	548 208	3 524	3 258	57 404	143 076	112 460	1 189 899	399 604
American Indian, Eskimo, or Aleut	49 909	7 349	19 835	25 917	50 575	12 410	21 965	2 019	12 972	1 466
American Indian	49 392	7 217	19 508	25 870	50 501	12 344	21 767	1 982	12 601	1 432
Eskimo	235	67	173	38	62	38	114	19	169	14
Aleut	282	65	154	9	12	28	84	18	202	20
Asian or Pacific Islander	77 886	25 476	41 277	3 462	3 123	12 422	31 750	9 057	139 719	11 214
Asian	76 952	25 037	39 271	3 317	2 938	11 945	30 708	8 888	138 148	10 923
Chinese	8 980	4 442	8 614	557	385	1 775	5 330	2 301	30 868	3 144
Filipino	4 237	1 607	5 624	708	531	1 377	2 548	1 321	19 376	2 082
Japanese	3 581	1 619	3 391	245	286	1 574	2 037	690	6 617	1 029
Asian Indian	8 234	3 021	6 111	482	287	1 218	3 956	2 183	28 330	1 601
Korean	11 576	4 618	5 731	526	525	1 943	4 016	1 229	30 320	814
Vietnamese	9 387	2 882	4 380	281	268	1 806	6 577	348	8 862	747
Cambodian	3 858	611	628	54	76	98	550	23	1 768	55
Hmong	16 833	227	13	2	27	78	613	–	1	–
Laotian	6 381	3 374	654	54	138	810	2 315	107	767	51
Thai	576	921	1 088	114	129	343	675	142	2 578	212
Other Asian	3 309	1 715	3 037	294	286	923	2 091	544	8 661	1 188
Bangladeshi	41	30	52	6	8	19	91	10	360	43
Burmese	47	27	25	1	7	–	13	9	404	71
Indonesian	134	252	275	8	15	64	173	60	693	125
Malayan	128	212	329	17	60	112	155	6	187	112
Okinawan	2	3	21	2	–	3	5	–	19	1
Pakistani	377	298	593	39	19	88	436	163	2 564	169
Sri Lankan	271	49	111	20	9	29	103	29	584	89
All other Asian	2 309	844	1 631	201	168	608	1 115	267	3 850	578
Pacific Islander	934	439	2 006	145	185	477	1 042	169	1 571	291
Hawaiian	383	244	621	76	74	243	422	65	636	101
Samoan	120	59	775	9	13	54	218	23	154	34
Guamanian	165	81	272	30	50	117	268	63	581	108
Other Pacific Islander	266	55	338	30	48	63	134	18	200	48
Tongan	33	10	45	1	22	5	9	1	2	1
Tahitian	1	3	6	1	1	–	6	–	3	1
Northern Mariana Islander	13	–	9	–	5	6	10	–	–	–
Palauan	15	3	25	8	1	11	6	–	28	2
Fijian	9	–	23	2	2	2	1	–	19	7
All other Pacific Islander	195	39	230	18	17	39	102	17	148	37
Other race	21 965	12 750	21 525	1 755	1 533	15 591	48 797	7 538	44 914	14 949
HISPANIC ORIGIN										
All persons	4 375 099	2 776 755	5 117 073	638 800	696 004	1 578 385	2 477 574	666 168	4 781 468	606 900
Hispanic origin (of any race)	53 884	32 647	61 702	4 665	5 252	36 969	93 670	15 820	125 102	32 710
Mexican	34 691	24 386	38 274	2 878	3 438	29 665	75 798	3 083	18 434	2 981
Puerto Rican	3 286	1 270	3 959	386	377	1 159	3 570	8 257	17 528	2 204
Cuban	1 539	488	2 108	63	44	480	1 403	728	6 367	1 241
Other Hispanic	14 368	6 503	17 361	1 338	1 393	5 665	12 899	3 752	82 773	26 284
Not of Hispanic origin	4 321 215	2 744 108	5 055 371	634 135	690 752	1 541 416	2 383 904	650 348	4 656 366	574 190
RACE AND HISPANIC ORIGIN										
All persons	4 375 099	2 776 755	5 117 073	638 800	696 004	1 578 385	2 477 574	666 168	4 781 468	606 900
White	4 130 395	2 683 090	4 486 228	604 142	637 515	1 480 558	2 231 986	535 094	3 393 964	179 667
Hispanic origin	29 129	19 250	37 763	2 550	2 727	20 463	41 462	7 002	67 855	13 536
Not of Hispanic origin	4 101 266	2 663 840	4 448 465	601 592	634 788	1 460 095	2 190 524	528 092	3 326 109	166 131
Black	94 944	48 090	548 208	3 524	3 258	57 404	143 076	112 460	1 189 899	399 604
Hispanic origin	1 904	597	2 681	73	82	693	2 315	1 449	12 076	4 391
Not of Hispanic origin	93 040	47 493	545 527	3 451	3 176	56 711	140 761	111 011	1 177 823	395 213
American Indian, Eskimo, or Aleut	49 909	7 349	19 835	25 917	50 575	12 410	21 965	2 019	12 972	1 466
Hispanic origin	1 658	584	962	327	927	691	1 602	81	829	214
Not of Hispanic origin	48 251	6 765	18 873	25 590	49 648	11 719	20 363	1 938	12 143	1 252
Asian or Pacific Islander	77 886	25 476	41 277	3 462	3 123	12 422	31 750	9 057	139 719	11 214
Hispanic origin	1 657	550	1 190	117	110	396	936	203	3 100	480
Not of Hispanic origin	76 229	24 926	40 087	3 345	3 013	12 026	30 814	8 854	136 619	10 734
Other race	21 965	12 750	21 525	1 755	1 533	15 591	48 797	7 538	44 914	14 949
Hispanic origin	19 536	11 666	19 106	1 598	1 406	14 726	47 355	7 085	41 242	14 089
Not of Hispanic origin	2 429	1 084	2 419	157	127	865	1 442	453	3 672	860
PERCENT DISTRIBUTION BY RACE										
All persons	100.0	100.0	100.0	100.0	100.0	100.0	100.0	100.0	100.0	100.0
White	94.4	96.6	87.7	94.6	91.6	93.8	90.1	80.3	71.0	29.6
Black	2.2	1.7	10.7	.6	.5	3.6	5.8	16.9	24.9	65.8
American Indian, Eskimo, or Aleut	1.1	.3	.4	4.1	7.3	.8	.9	.3	.3	.2
American Indian	1.1	.3	.4	4.0	7.3	.8	.9	.3	.3	.2
Asian or Pacific Islander	1.8	.9	.8	.5	.4	.8	1.3	1.4	2.9	1.8
Asian	1.8	.9	.8	.5	.4	.8	1.2	1.3	2.9	1.8
Pacific Islander	–	–	–	–	–	–	–	–	–	–
Other race	.5	.5	.4	.3	.2	1.0	2.0	1.1	.9	2.5
PERCENT DISTRIBUTION BY HISPANIC ORIGIN										
All persons	100.0	100.0	100.0	100.0	100.0	100.0	100.0	100.0	100.0	100.0
Hispanic origin (of any race)	1.2	1.2	1.2	.7	.8	2.3	3.8	2.4	2.6	5.4
Mexican	.8	.9	.7	.5	.5	1.9	3.1	.5	.4	.5
Puerto Rican	.1	–	.1	.1	.1	.1	.1	1.2	.4	.4
Cuban	–	–	–	–	–	–	.1	.1	.1	.2
Other Hispanic	.3	.2	.3	.2	.2	.4	.5	.6	1.7	4.3
Not of Hispanic origin	98.8	98.8	98.8	99.3	99.2	97.7	96.2	97.6	97.4	94.6
PERCENT WHITE, NOT OF HISPANIC ORIGIN										
All persons	100.0	100.0	100.0	100.0	100.0	100.0	100.0	100.0	100.0	100.0
White	94.4	96.6	87.7	94.6	91.6	93.8	90.1	80.3	71.0	29.6
Not of Hispanic origin	93.7	95.9	86.9	94.2	91.2	92.5	88.4	79.3	69.6	27.4

Table 253. **Race and Hispanic Origin: 1990**—Con.

[For definitions of terms and meanings of symbols, see text]

United States Region and Division State	South Atlantic Division—Con.						East South Central Division			
	Virginia	West Virginia	North Carolina	South Carolina	Georgia	Florida	Kentucky	Tennessee	Alabama	Mississippi
RACE										
All persons	6 187 358	1 793 477	6 628 637	3 486 703	6 478 216	12 937 926	3 685 296	4 877 185	4 040 587	2 573 216
White	4 791 739	1 725 523	5 008 491	2 406 974	4 600 148	10 749 285	3 391 832	4 048 068	2 975 797	1 633 461
Black	1 162 994	56 295	1 456 323	1 039 884	1 746 565	1 759 534	262 907	778 035	1 020 705	915 057
American Indian, Eskimo, or Aleut	15 282	2 458	80 155	8 246	13 348	36 335	5 769	10 039	16 506	8 525
American Indian	14 893	2 385	79 825	8 049	12 926	35 461	5 614	9 859	16 312	8 435
Eskimo	200	36	152	106	223	431	82	96	105	50
Aleut	189	37	178	91	199	443	73	84	89	40
Asian or Pacific Islander	159 053	7 459	52 166	22 382	75 781	154 302	17 812	31 839	21 797	13 016
Asian	156 036	7 283	49 970	21 399	73 764	149 856	16 983	30 944	21 088	12 679
Chinese	21 238	1 170	8 859	3 039	12 657	30 737	2 736	5 653	3 929	2 518
Filipino	35 067	1 606	5 332	5 521	5 848	31 945	2 193	3 032	1 816	1 565
Japanese	7 931	780	5 040	1 885	6 372	8 505	2 513	3 440	2 028	700
Asian Indian	20 494	1 981	9 847	3 900	13 926	31 457	2 922	5 911	4 348	1 872
Korean	30 164	777	7 267	2 577	15 275	12 404	2 972	4 508	3 454	1 123
Vietnamese	20 693	184	5 211	1 752	7 801	16 346	1 506	2 062	2 274	3 815
Cambodian	3 889	27	1 367	239	2 140	1 617	231	942	427	24
Hmong	7	–	708	76	320	7	1	79	8	7
Laotian	2 589	38	2 048	598	3 511	2 423	260	2 772	799	59
Thai	3 312	226	1 183	565	1 608	4 457	403	586	526	239
Other Asian	10 652	494	3 108	1 247	4 306	9 958	1 246	1 959	1 479	757
Bangladeshi	477	26	24	17	135	246	46	91	56	39
Burmese	214	2	50	4	24	143	3	19	8	8
Indonesian	622	24	175	35	206	623	196	120	88	59
Malayan	399	18	112	39	110	269	90	145	172	94
Okinawan	28	3	40	2	13	43	5	8	8	5
Pakistani	4 263	125	539	198	1 250	2 800	130	377	255	110
Sri Lankan	288	32	130	37	112	268	26	45	37	5
All other Asian	4 361	264	2 038	915	2 456	5 566	750	1 154	855	437
Pacific Islander	3 017	176	2 196	983	2 017	4 446	829	895	709	337
Hawaiian	1 384	91	963	426	847	2 049	338	503	343	166
Samoan	440	28	416	159	412	577	194	120	77	78
Guamanian	923	41	636	317	594	1 241	220	209	247	70
Other Pacific Islander	270	16	181	81	164	579	77	63	42	23
Tongan	6	5	12	15	5	122	2	1	2	–
Tahitian	9	–	3	2	8	49	2	1	–	1
Northern Mariana Islander	51	–	11	7	19	25	6	8	3	1
Palauan	15	–	12	9	11	25	6	6	3	3
Fijian	7	2	6	–	26	32	1	2	5	–
All other Pacific Islander	182	9	137	48	95	326	60	45	29	18
Other race	58 290	1 742	31 502	9 217	42 374	238 470	6 976	9 204	5 782	3 157
HISPANIC ORIGIN										
All persons	6 187 358	1 793 477	6 628 637	3 486 703	6 478 216	12 937 926	3 685 296	4 877 185	4 040 587	2 573 216
Hispanic origin (of any race)	160 288	8 489	76 726	30 551	108 922	1 574 143	21 984	32 741	24 629	15 931
Mexican	33 044	2 810	32 670	11 028	49 182	161 499	8 692	13 879	9 509	6 718
Puerto Rican	23 698	897	14 620	6 423	17 443	247 010	3 682	4 292	3 553	1 304
Cuban	6 268	261	3 723	1 652	7 818	674 052	1 075	2 012	1 463	497
Other Hispanic	97 278	4 521	25 713	11 448	34 479	491 582	8 535	12 558	10 104	7 412
Not of Hispanic origin	6 027 070	1 784 988	6 551 911	3 456 152	6 369 294	11 363 783	3 663 312	4 844 444	4 015 958	2 557 285
RACE AND HISPANIC ORIGIN										
All persons	6 187 358	1 793 477	6 628 637	3 486 703	6 478 216	12 937 926	3 685 296	4 877 185	4 040 587	2 573 216
White	4 791 739	1 725 523	5 008 491	2 406 974	4 600 148	10 749 285	3 391 832	4 048 068	2 975 797	1 633 461
Hispanic origin	90 089	6 627	37 364	16 918	56 723	1 273 959	13 810	20 437	15 630	9 263
Not of Hispanic origin	4 701 650	1 718 896	4 971 127	2 390 056	4 543 425	9 475 326	3 378 022	4 027 631	2 960 167	1 624 198
Black	1 162 994	56 295	1 456 323	1 039 884	1 746 565	1 759 534	262 907	778 035	1 020 705	915 057
Hispanic origin	9 861	309	7 181	3 937	9 400	58 431	1 547	3 110	2 992	3 166
Not of Hispanic origin	1 153 133	55 986	1 449 142	1 035 947	1 737 165	1 701 103	261 360	774 925	1 017 713	911 891
American Indian, Eskimo, or Aleut	15 282	2 458	80 155	8 246	13 348	36 335	5 769	10 039	16 506	8 525
Hispanic origin	935	95	1 225	242	727	3 425	251	354	285	209
Not of Hispanic origin	14 347	2 363	78 930	8 004	12 621	32 910	5 518	9 685	16 221	8 316
Asian or Pacific Islander	159 053	7 459	52 166	22 382	75 781	154 302	17 812	31 839	21 797	13 016
Hispanic origin	4 870	207	1 573	1 078	2 056	8 143	611	901	580	473
Not of Hispanic origin	154 183	7 252	50 593	21 304	73 725	146 159	17 201	30 938	21 217	12 543
Other race	58 290	1 742	31 502	9 217	42 374	238 470	6 976	9 204	5 782	3 157
Hispanic origin	54 533	1 251	29 383	8 376	40 016	230 185	5 765	7 939	5 142	2 820
Not of Hispanic origin	3 757	491	2 119	841	2 358	8 285	1 211	1 265	640	337
PERCENT DISTRIBUTION BY RACE										
All persons	100.0	100.0	100.0	100.0	100.0	100.0	100.0	100.0	100.0	100.0
White	77.4	96.2	75.6	69.0	71.0	83.1	92.0	83.0	73.6	63.5
Black	18.8	3.1	22.0	29.8	27.0	13.6	7.1	16.0	25.3	35.6
American Indian, Eskimo, or Aleut	.2	.1	1.2	.2	.2	.3	.2	.2	.4	.3
American Indian	.2	.1	1.2	.2	.2	.3	.2	.2	.4	.3
Asian or Pacific Islander	2.6	.4	.8	.6	1.2	1.2	.5	.7	.5	.5
Asian	2.5	.4	.8	.6	1.1	1.2	.5	.6	.5	.5
Pacific Islander	–	–	–	–	–	–	–	–	–	–
Other race	.9	.1	.5	.3	.7	1.8	.2	.2	.1	.1
PERCENT DISTRIBUTION BY HISPANIC ORIGIN										
All persons	100.0	100.0	100.0	100.0	100.0	100.0	100.0	100.0	100.0	100.0
Hispanic origin (of any race)	2.6	.5	1.2	.9	1.7	12.2	.6	.7	.6	.6
Mexican	.5	.2	.5	.3	.8	1.2	.2	.3	.2	.3
Puerto Rican	.4	.1	.2	.2	.3	1.9	.1	.1	.1	.1
Cuban	.1	–	.1	–	.1	5.2	–	–	–	–
Other Hispanic	1.6	.3	.4	.3	.5	3.8	.2	.3	.3	.3
Not of Hispanic origin	97.4	99.5	98.8	99.1	98.3	87.8	99.4	99.3	99.4	99.4
PERCENT WHITE, NOT OF HISPANIC ORIGIN										
All persons	100.0	100.0	100.0	100.0	100.0	100.0	100.0	100.0	100.0	100.0
White	77.4	96.2	75.6	69.0	71.0	83.1	92.0	83.0	73.6	63.5
Not of Hispanic origin	76.0	95.8	75.0	68.5	70.1	73.2	91.7	82.6	73.3	63.1

Table 253. Race and Hispanic Origin: 1990—Con.

[For definitions of terms and meanings of symbols, see text]

United States Region and Division State	West South Central Division				Mountain Division					
	Arkansas	Louisiana	Oklahoma	Texas	Montana	Idaho	Wyoming	Colorado	New Mexico	Arizona
RACE										
All persons	2 350 725	4 219 973	3 145 585	16 986 510	799 065	1 006 749	453 588	3 294 394	1 515 069	3 665 228
White	1 944 744	2 839 138	2 583 512	12 774 762	741 111	950 451	427 061	2 905 474	1 146 028	2 963 186
Black	373 912	1 299 281	233 801	2 021 632	2 381	3 370	3 606	133 146	30 210	110 524
American Indian, Eskimo, or Aleut	12 773	18 541	252 420	65 877	47 679	13 780	9 479	27 776	134 355	203 527
American Indian	12 641	18 361	252 089	64 349	47 524	13 594	9 426	27 271	134 097	203 009
Eskimo	80	92	202	721	106	132	37	297	162	284
Aleut	52	88	129	807	49	54	16	208	96	234
Asian or Pacific Islander	12 530	41 099	33 563	319 459	4 259	9 365	2 806	59 862	14 124	55 206
Asian	12 125	40 173	32 002	311 918	3 958	8 492	2 638	57 122	13 363	51 699
Chinese	1 726	5 430	5 193	63 232	655	1 420	554	8 695	2 607	14 136
Filipino	1 569	3 731	3 024	34 350	735	1 083	408	5 426	2 018	7 904
Japanese	957	1 526	2 385	14 795	829	2 719	583	11 402	1 895	6 302
Asian Indian	1 329	5 083	4 546	55 795	248	473	240	3 836	1 593	5 663
Korean	1 037	2 750	4 717	31 775	668	935	402	11 339	1 464	5 863
Vietnamese	2 348	17 598	7 320	69 634	159	600	124	7 210	1 485	5 239
Cambodian	28	308	307	5 887	4	66	6	1 320	55	787
Hmong	23	1	207	176	146	–	–	1 202	–	9
Laotian	1 982	1 024	902	9 332	185	482	17	1 996	522	855
Thai	248	704	942	5 816	107	188	91	1 184	440	1 381
Other Asian	878	2 018	2 459	21 126	222	526	213	3 512	1 284	3 560
Bangladeshi	28	56	123	628	1	1	4	42	17	89
Burmese	–	22	7	172	1	7	2	10	10	71
Indonesian	25	140	261	1 264	20	34	3	375	86	356
Malayan	115	175	347	1 224	33	7	22	122	42	189
Okinawan	9	4	16	63	–	8	1	24	9	21
Pakistani	108	352	511	7 627	10	90	44	478	107	465
Sri Lankan	13	89	50	531	15	17	10	106	42	140
All other Asian	580	1 180	1 144	9 617	142	362	127	2 355	971	2 229
Pacific Islander	405	926	1 561	7 541	301	873	168	2 740	761	3 507
Hawaiian	226	411	712	2 979	179	476	93	1 368	408	1 690
Samoan	55	169	203	916	49	145	25	345	119	416
Guamanian	95	291	451	2 209	43	95	35	778	149	709
Other Pacific Islander	29	55	195	1 437	30	157	15	249	85	692
Tongan	1	2	6	630	4	51	2	45	13	388
Tahitian	2	–	1	19	3	1	1	16	12	7
Northern Mariana Islander	–	5	19	28	1	19	–	21	13	6
Palauan	1	3	–	73	1	10	2	18	9	22
Fijian	–	2	3	56	6	6	–	6	3	20
All other Pacific Islander	25	43	166	631	15	70	10	143	35	249
Other race	6 766	21 914	42 289	1 804 780	3 635	29 783	10 636	168 136	190 352	332 785
HISPANIC ORIGIN										
All persons	2 350 725	4 219 973	3 145 585	16 986 510	799 065	1 006 749	453 588	3 294 394	1 515 069	3 665 228
Hispanic origin (of any race)	19 876	93 044	86 160	4 339 905	12 174	52 927	25 751	424 302	579 224	688 338
Mexican	12 496	23 452	63 226	3 890 820	8 362	43 213	18 730	282 478	328 836	616 195
Puerto Rican	1 176	6 180	4 693	42 981	437	665	325	7 225	2 635	8 256
Cuban	494	8 569	1 043	18 195	124	164	63	2 058	903	2 079
Other Hispanic	5 710	54 843	17 198	387 909	3 251	8 885	6 633	132 541	246 850	61 808
Not of Hispanic origin	2 330 849	4 126 929	3 059 425	12 646 605	786 891	953 822	427 837	2 870 092	935 845	2 976 890
RACE AND HISPANIC ORIGIN										
All persons	2 350 725	4 219 973	3 145 585	16 986 510	799 065	1 006 749	453 588	3 294 394	1 515 069	3 665 228
White	1 944 744	2 830 138	2 583 512	12 774 702	741 111	950 451	427 061	2 905 474	1 146 028	2 963 186
Hispanic origin	11 662	63 116	35 924	2 483 082	7 233	21 790	14 350	246 529	381 864	337 001
Not of Hispanic origin	1 933 082	2 776 022	2 547 588	10 291 680	733 878	928 661	412 711	2 658 945	764 164	2 626 185
Black	373 912	1 299 281	233 801	2 021 632	2 381	3 370	3 606	133 146	30 210	110 524
Hispanic origin	1 150	7 811	2 339	45 272	139	159	180	5 089	2 568	5 715
Not of Hispanic origin	372 762	1 291 470	231 462	1 976 360	2 242	3 211	3 426	128 057	27 642	104 809
American Indian, Eskimo, or Aleut	12 773	18 541	252 420	65 877	47 679	13 780	9 479	27 776	134 355	203 527
Hispanic origin	380	1 002	5 789	13 074	1 204	1 362	622	5 708	6 287	13 436
Not of Hispanic origin	12 393	17 539	246 631	52 803	46 475	12 418	8 857	22 068	128 068	190 091
Asian or Pacific Islander	12 530	41 099	33 563	319 459	4 259	9 365	2 806	59 862	14 124	55 206
Hispanic origin	386	1 797	1 197	15 634	136	312	184	3 089	1 537	3 676
Not of Hispanic origin	12 144	39 302	32 366	303 825	4 123	9 053	2 622	56 773	12 587	51 530
Other race	6 766	21 914	42 289	1 804 780	3 635	29 783	10 636	168 136	190 352	332 785
Hispanic origin	6 298	19 318	40 911	1 782 843	3 462	29 304	10 415	163 887	186 968	328 510
Not of Hispanic origin	468	2 596	1 378	21 937	173	479	221	4 249	3 384	4 275
PERCENT DISTRIBUTION BY RACE										
All persons	100.0	100.0	100.0	100.0	100.0	100.0	100.0	100.0	100.0	100.0
White	82.7	67.3	82.1	75.2	92.7	94.4	94.2	88.2	75.6	80.8
Black	15.9	30.8	7.4	11.9	.3	.3	.8	4.0	2.0	3.0
American Indian, Eskimo, or Aleut	.5	.4	8.0	.4	6.0	1.4	2.1	.8	8.9	5.6
American Indian	.5	.4	8.0	.4	5.9	1.4	2.1	.8	8.9	5.5
Asian or Pacific Islander	.5	1.0	1.1	1.9	.5	.9	.6	1.8	.9	1.5
Asian	.5	1.0	1.0	1.8	.5	.8	.6	1.7	.9	1.4
Pacific Islander	–	–	–	–	–	.1	–	.1	.1	.1
Other race	.3	.5	1.3	10.6	.5	3.0	2.3	5.1	12.6	9.1
PERCENT DISTRIBUTION BY HISPANIC ORIGIN										
All persons	100.0	100.0	100.0	100.0	100.0	100.0	100.0	100.0	100.0	100.0
Hispanic origin (of any race)	.8	2.2	2.7	25.5	1.5	5.3	5.7	12.9	38.2	18.8
Mexican	.5	.6	2.0	22.9	1.0	4.3	4.1	8.6	21.7	16.8
Puerto Rican	.1	.1	.1	.3	.1	.1	.1	.2	.2	.2
Cuban	–	.2	–	.1	–	–	–	.1	.1	.1
Other Hispanic	.2	1.3	.5	2.3	.4	.9	1.5	4.0	16.3	1.7
Not of Hispanic origin	99.2	97.8	97.3	74.5	98.5	94.7	94.3	87.1	61.8	81.2
PERCENT WHITE, NOT OF HISPANIC ORIGIN										
All persons	100.0	100.0	100.0	100.0	100.0	100.0	100.0	100.0	100.0	100.0
White	82.7	67.3	82.1	75.2	92.7	94.4	94.2	88.2	75.6	80.8
Not of Hispanic origin	82.2	65.8	81.0	60.6	91.8	92.2	91.0	80.7	50.4	71.7

Table 253. Race and Hispanic Origin: 1990—Con.

[For definitions of terms and meanings of symbols, see text]

United States Region and Division State	Mountain Division—Con.		Pacific Division				
	Utah	Nevada	Washington	Oregon	California	Alaska	Hawaii
RACE							
All persons	**1 722 850**	**1 201 833**	**4 866 692**	**2 842 321**	**29 760 021**	**550 043**	**1 108 229**
White	1 615 845	1 012 695	4 308 937	2 636 787	20 524 327	415 492	369 616
Black	11 576	78 771	149 801	46 178	2 208 801	22 451	27 195
American Indian, Eskimo, or Aleut	24 283	19 637	81 483	38 496	242 164	85 698	5 099
American Indian	24 093	19 377	77 627	37 443	236 078	31 245	4 738
Eskimo	116	156	1 791	545	2 552	44 401	155
Aleut	74	104	2 065	508	3 534	10 052	206
Asian or Pacific Islander	33 371	38 127	210 958	69 269	2 845 659	19 728	685 236
Asian	25 696	35 232	195 918	64 232	2 735 060	17 814	522 967
Chinese	5 322	6 618	33 962	13 652	704 850	1 342	68 004
Filipino	1 905	12 048	43 799	7 411	731 685	7 976	168 682
Japanese	6 500	4 024	34 366	11 796	312 989	2 066	247 486
Asian Indian	1 557	1 825	8 205	3 508	159 973	472	1 015
Korean	2 629	4 315	29 697	8 668	259 941	4 163	24 454
Vietnamese	2 797	1 934	18 696	9 088	280 223	582	5 468
Cambodian	997	244	11 096	2 101	68 190	50	119
Hmong	105	24	741	438	46 892	1	6
Laotian	1 774	804	6 191	3 262	58 058	226	1 677
Thai	617	1 823	2 386	876	32 064	369	1 220
Other Asian	1 493	1 573	6 779	3 432	80 195	567	4 036
Bangladeshi	24	20	48	32	1 134	3	22
Burmese	17	15	112	34	2 947	2	67
Indonesian	121	119	653	803	14 785	39	362
Malayan	68	47	241	145	2 204	6	176
Okinawan	2	18	90	25	411	5	1 138
Pakistani	244	213	579	270	13 965	43	95
Sri Lankan	34	56	131	171	3 385	7	91
All other Asian	983	1 085	4 925	1 952	41 364	462	2 085
Pacific Islander	7 675	2 895	15 040	5 037	110 599	1 914	162 269
Hawaiian	1 396	1 534	5 423	2 415	34 447	934	138 742
Samoan	1 570	326	4 130	565	31 917	522	15 034
Guamanian	148	472	3 779	701	25 059	208	2 120
Other Pacific Islander	4 561	563	1 708	1 356	19 176	250	6 373
Tongan	3 904	331	448	169	7 919	158	3 088
Tahitian	49	12	24	16	267	2	358
Northern Mariana Islander	3	18	130	70	321	4	63
Palauan	5	27	113	90	397	10	358
Fijian	51	20	293	239	5 744	2	261
All other Pacific Islander	549	155	700	772	4 528	74	2 245
Other race	37 775	52 603	115 513	51 591	3 939 070	6 674	21 083
HISPANIC ORIGIN							
All persons	**1 722 850**	**1 201 833**	**4 866 692**	**2 842 321**	**29 760 021**	**550 043**	**1 108 229**
Hispanic origin (of any race)	84 597	124 419	214 570	112 707	7 687 938	17 803	81 390
Mexican	56 842	85 287	155 864	85 632	6 118 996	9 321	14 367
Puerto Rican	2 181	4 272	9 345	2 764	126 417	1 938	25 778
Cuban	456	5 988	2 281	1 333	71 977	277	558
Other Hispanic	25 118	28 872	47 080	22 978	1 370 548	6 267	40 687
Not of Hispanic origin	1 638 253	1 077 414	4 652 122	2 729 614	22 072 083	532 240	1 026 839
RACE AND HISPANIC ORIGIN							
All persons	**1 722 850**	**1 201 833**	**4 866 692**	**2 842 321**	**29 760 021**	**550 043**	**1 108 229**
White	1 615 845	1 012 695	4 308 937	2 636 787	20 524 327	415 492	369 616
Hispanic origin	44 591	66 338	87 315	57 055	3 495 201	8 770	21 972
Not of Hispanic origin	1 571 254	946 357	4 221 622	2 579 732	17 029 126	406 722	347 644
Black	11 576	78 771	149 801	46 178	2 208 801	22 451	27 195
Hispanic origin	708	2 268	3 801	1 196	116 355	652	1 279
Not of Hispanic origin	10 868	76 503	146 000	44 982	2 092 446	21 799	25 916
American Indian, Eskimo, or Aleut	24 283	19 637	81 483	38 496	242 164	85 698	5 099
Hispanic origin	1 535	2 157	5 086	2 747	58 099	1 104	1 098
Not of Hispanic origin	22 748	17 480	76 397	35 749	184 065	84 594	4 001
Asian or Pacific Islander	33 371	38 127	210 958	69 269	2 845 659	19 728	685 236
Hispanic origin	881	2 230	7 290	1 847	135 306	998	38 832
Not of Hispanic origin	32 490	35 897	203 668	67 422	2 710 353	18 730	646 404
Other race	37 775	52 603	115 513	51 591	3 939 070	6 674	21 083
Hispanic origin	36 882	51 426	111 078	49 862	3 882 977	6 279	18 209
Not of Hispanic origin	893	1 177	4 435	1 729	56 093	395	2 874
PERCENT DISTRIBUTION BY RACE							
All persons	**100.0**	**100.0**	**100.0**	**100.0**	**100.0**	**100.0**	**100.0**
White	93.8	84.3	88.5	92.8	69.0	75.5	33.4
Black	.7	6.6	3.1	1.6	7.4	4.1	2.5
American Indian, Eskimo, or Aleut	1.4	1.6	1.7	1.4	.8	15.6	.5
American Indian	1.4	1.6	1.6	1.3	.8	5.7	.4
Asian or Pacific Islander	1.9	3.2	4.3	2.4	9.6	3.6	61.8
Asian	1.5	2.9	4.0	2.3	9.2	3.2	47.2
Pacific Islander	.4	.2	.3	.2	.4	.3	14.6
Other race	2.2	4.4	2.4	1.8	13.2	1.2	1.9
PERCENT DISTRIBUTION BY HISPANIC ORIGIN							
All persons	**100.0**	**100.0**	**100.0**	**100.0**	**100.0**	**100.0**	**100.0**
Hispanic origin (of any race)	4.9	10.4	4.4	4.0	25.8	3.2	7.3
Mexican	3.3	7.1	3.2	3.0	20.6	1.7	1.3
Puerto Rican	.1	.4	.2	.1	.4	.4	2.3
Cuban	—	.5	—	—	.2	.1	.1
Other Hispanic	1.5	2.4	1.0	.8	4.6	1.1	3.7
Not of Hispanic origin	95.1	89.6	95.6	96.0	74.2	96.8	92.7
PERCENT WHITE, NOT OF HISPANIC ORIGIN							
All persons	**100.0**	**100.0**	**100.0**	**100.0**	**100.0**	**100.0**	**100.0**
White	93.8	84.3	88.5	92.8	69.0	75.5	33.4
Not of Hispanic origin	91.2	78.7	86.7	90.8	57.2	73.9	31.4

Table 254. Summary of General Characteristics of White Persons and Households: 1990

[For definitions of terms and meanings of symbols, see text]

United States Region and Division State	All White persons Total	Percent of all persons Under 18 years	Percent of all persons 65 years and over	Median age	Persons 18 years and over— Males per 100 females	Percent in group quarters	All households with a White householder Total	Family households as a percent of all households Total	Family households With own children under 18 years	Married-couple family Total	Married-couple family With own children under 18 years	Female householder, no husband present Total	Female householder, no husband present With own children under 18 years	Persons per— House-hold	Persons per— Family
United States	199 686 070	23.9	13.9	34.4	92.4	2.5	76 880 105	69.5	31.7	57.7	25.7	8.9	4.7	2.54	3.06
REGION AND DIVISION															
Northeast	42 068 904	22.0	15.2	35.5	89.7	2.8	16 123 125	68.8	29.8	56.2	24.4	9.5	4.4	2.54	3.09
New England	12 032 983	22.2	14.2	34.6	90.0	3.2	4 585 058	68.6	30.7	55.7	24.7	9.8	4.9	2.55	3.08
Middle Atlantic	30 035 921	22.0	15.6	35.8	89.5	2.6	11 538 067	68.9	29.4	56.4	24.2	9.4	4.1	2.54	3.10
Midwest	52 017 957	25.0	13.9	33.9	91.3	2.6	19 858 420	70.2	33.1	58.9	27.1	8.6	4.8	2.56	3.09
East North Central	35 764 043	24.8	13.6	33.9	91.3	2.4	13 578 920	70.6	33.0	58.8	26.9	9.0	4.9	2.58	3.10
West North Central	16 253 914	25.6	14.5	33.8	91.5	3.0	6 279 500	69.3	33.3	59.1	27.4	7.7	4.7	2.52	3.06
South	65 582 199	23.6	14.0	34.5	92.3	2.4	25 502 553	71.0	32.0	59.7	26.3	8.5	4.4	2.51	3.01
South Atlantic	33 390 885	22.0	15.1	35.5	92.6	2.5	13 206 025	70.1	29.9	59.1	24.7	8.2	4.1	2.47	2.95
East South Central	12 049 158	24.2	13.5	34.4	90.8	2.3	4 637 700	73.5	33.9	61.8	28.1	9.1	4.6	2.54	3.01
West South Central	20 142 156	25.9	12.5	33.1	92.8	2.3	7 658 828	71.0	34.3	59.5	28.1	8.7	4.9	2.57	3.10
West	40 017 010	24.6	12.7	33.6	96.7	2.3	15 396 007	67.0	31.3	54.6	24.4	9.0	5.3	2.55	3.08
Mountain	11 761 851	27.1	12.2	32.8	95.5	2.1	4 480 798	68.7	33.6	57.1	26.6	8.7	5.5	2.58	3.12
Pacific	28 255 159	23.6	12.8	34.0	97.2	2.5	10 915 209	66.3	30.4	53.6	23.5	9.2	5.2	2.54	3.07
STATE															
New England	12 032 983	22.2	14.2	34.6	90.0	3.2	4 585 058	68.6	30.7	55.7	24.7	9.8	4.9	2.55	3.08
Maine	1 208 360	25.0	13.5	34.0	91.3	2.9	460 110	70.6	34.5	58.2	27.1	9.5	5.9	2.55	3.03
New Hampshire	1 087 433	25.0	11.4	32.9	93.1	2.8	404 832	71.2	35.3	59.7	28.9	8.4	4.9	2.61	3.08
Vermont	555 088	25.3	11.9	33.2	92.7	3.7	208 607	68.8	35.0	56.6	27.4	9.1	5.9	2.57	3.06
Massachusetts	5 405 374	21.3	14.6	34.5	88.6	3.4	2 061 948	67.0	29.3	53.4	23.4	10.6	5.1	2.54	3.11
Rhode Island	917 375	21.4	16.0	34.9	88.1	3.7	352 749	68.0	29.5	54.5	23.4	10.6	5.2	2.51	3.06
Connecticut	2 859 353	21.3	14.8	35.7	91.3	2.9	1 096 812	69.9	29.6	57.9	24.6	9.1	4.1	2.54	3.05
Middle Atlantic	30 035 921	22.0	15.6	35.8	89.5	2.6	11 538 067	68.9	29.4	56.4	24.2	9.4	4.1	2.54	3.10
New York	13 385 255	21.7	15.4	35.7	89.7	2.8	5 184 827	66.5	28.5	53.7	23.1	9.6	4.3	2.52	3.12
New Jersey	6 130 465	21.5	15.2	36.1	90.7	1.9	2 307 810	71.8	30.0	59.2	25.4	9.3	3.7	2.61	3.12
Pennsylvania	10 520 201	22.6	16.2	35.8	88.8	2.7	4 045 430	70.4	30.2	58.2	25.0	9.2	4.1	2.53	3.06
East North Central	35 764 043	24.8	13.6	33.9	91.3	2.4	13 578 920	70.6	33.0	58.8	26.9	9.0	4.9	2.58	3.10
Ohio	9 521 756	24.9	13.6	34.0	89.9	2.2	3 621 244	71.2	33.2	59.0	26.9	9.4	5.1	2.57	3.09
Indiana	5 020 700	25.5	13.0	33.4	90.9	2.0	1 809 053	71.9	34.5	60.2	28.0	0.9	5.1	2.59	3.08
Illinois	8 952 978	23.7	14.2	34.4	91.5	2.4	3 447 865	68.8	31.2	57.4	26.0	8.5	4.2	2.54	3.10
Michigan	7 756 086	25.2	12.7	33.5	92.1	2.1	2 907 741	71.6	33.8	59.1	27.1	9.6	5.4	2.62	3.11
Wisconsin	4 512 523	25.1	14.1	33.7	92.0	2.7	1 712 217	69.7	33.3	59.0	27.4	0.0	4.7	2.57	3.10
West North Central	16 253 914	25.6	14.5	33.8	91.5	3.0	6 279 500	69.3	33.3	59.1	27.4	7.7	4.7	2.52	3.06
Minnesota	4 130 395	25.8	13.0	33.0	92.8	2.6	1 579 722	68.5	34.0	58.0	28.0	7.8	4.8	2.56	3.11
Iowa	2 683 090	25.5	15.7	34.5	90.0	3.5	1 036 774	69.6	32.9	59.6	27.0	7.6	4.8	2.50	3.04
Missouri	4 486 228	24.7	14.8	34.3	89.8	2.7	1 747 422	70.0	32.5	59.1	26.6	8.3	4.7	2.50	3.03
North Dakota	604 142	26.6	14.9	33.1	97.1	3.7	231 488	68.7	34.5	59.7	29.3	6.5	4.2	2.52	3.10
South Dakota	637 515	27.0	15.6	33.6	93.8	3.6	244 847	69.1	34.3	60.0	28.7	6.7	4.4	2.52	3.09
Nebraska	1 480 668	26.5	14.7	33.6	91.4	2.9	571 603	68.9	33.8	59.3	28.1	7.3	4.6	2.52	3.09
Kansas	2 231 986	25.8	14.7	33.8	92.1	3.1	867 644	69.6	33.4	59.7	27.5	7.5	4.7	2.50	3.04
South Atlantic	33 390 885	22.0	15.1	35.5	92.6	2.5	13 206 025	70.1	29.9	59.1	24.7	8.2	4.1	2.47	2.95
Delaware	535 094	22.8	13.3	34.1	91.8	2.7	204 968	70.8	31.3	59.3	25.8	8.5	4.2	2.54	3.02
Maryland	3 393 964	22.6	12.7	34.6	93.1	2.1	1 293 894	70.9	31.5	59.2	26.2	8.6	4.0	2.58	3.04
District of Columbia	179 667	9.7	13.5	34.6	93.9	10.9	88 295	32.6	11.4	26.8	9.4	4.1	1.5	1.84	2.70
Virginia	4 791 739	22.9	11.5	33.7	94.8	2.9	1 839 325	70.7	32.5	60.1	27.4	7.9	3.9	2.54	3.01
West Virginia	1 725 523	24.6	15.0	35.6	88.6	1.9	664 100	72.9	34.0	59.8	27.4	10.2	5.2	2.55	3.04
North Carolina	5 008 491	22.1	13.2	34.7	93.1	3.1	1 977 594	71.9	31.4	61.2	26.3	8.1	4.0	2.46	2.92
South Carolina	2 406 974	23.2	12.5	34.1	94.2	3.2	923 440	73.2	33.1	62.1	27.7	8.3	4.1	2.53	2.98
Georgia	4 600 148	24.1	11.2	33.4	93.7	2.3	1 756 916	72.4	34.0	61.5	28.7	8.3	4.2	2.56	3.03
Florida	10 749 285	19.8	20.6	38.6	91.3	2.1	4 497 493	67.6	25.2	56.6	19.9	8.1	4.0	2.36	2.85
East South Central	12 049 158	24.2	13.5	34.4	90.8	2.3	4 637 700	73.5	33.9	61.8	28.1	9.1	4.6	2.54	3.01
Kentucky	3 391 832	25.4	12.9	33.5	90.5	2.4	1 278 806	74.0	35.8	61.1	29.1	10.1	5.5	2.59	3.06
Tennessee	4 048 068	23.4	13.4	34.8	90.7	2.4	1 576 161	73.0	32.8	61.1	27.0	9.2	4.6	2.51	2.98
Alabama	2 975 797	23.6	13.8	34.9	91.0	2.0	1 159 263	73.4	33.0	62.8	28.0	8.2	3.9	2.52	2.99
Mississippi	1 633 461	24.5	14.0	34.6	91.3	2.6	623 470	73.8	34.3	63.0	29.1	8.3	4.1	2.56	3.03
West South Central	20 142 156	25.9	12.5	33.1	92.8	2.3	7 658 828	71.0	34.3	59.5	28.1	8.7	4.9	2.57	3.10
Arkansas	1 944 744	24.4	15.7	35.4	90.5	2.3	760 287	73.4	33.0	62.9	27.4	8.0	4.4	2.50	2.97
Louisiana	2 839 138	25.9	12.5	33.2	92.0	2.3	1 069 650	72.0	35.2	60.4	29.4	8.8	4.6	2.60	3.12
Oklahoma	2 583 512	24.6	14.7	34.8	90.9	2.8	1 027 966	70.6	33.0	59.6	26.6	8.6	5.1	2.47	2.99
Texas	12 774 762	26.4	11.6	32.5	93.7	2.2	4 800 925	70.5	34.6	58.7	28.2	8.9	5.1	2.60	3.15
Mountain	11 761 851	27.1	12.2	32.8	95.5	2.1	4 480 798	68.7	33.6	57.1	26.6	8.7	5.5	2.58	3.12
Montana	741 111	26.8	14.0	34.7	95.2	2.9	290 030	68.7	33.8	58.3	27.0	7.8	5.3	2.49	3.04
Idaho	950 451	30.2	12.5	32.2	95.1	2.0	345 484	72.8	37.3	62.3	30.4	7.8	5.3	2.70	3.21
Wyoming	427 061	29.4	10.7	32.5	97.8	2.2	160 879	70.7	37.8	60.1	30.6	7.8	5.6	2.60	3.14
Colorado	2 905 474	25.1	10.7	33.3	95.3	2.3	1 154 983	66.2	32.6	54.7	25.6	8.6	5.5	2.46	3.03
New Mexico	1 146 028	27.0	12.5	33.4	93.8	1.8	435 810	70.5	34.8	56.9	26.6	10.0	6.2	2.59	3.11
Arizona	2 963 186	24.0	15.1	34.4	94.4	2.1	1 177 349	67.1	29.4	55.3	22.7	8.7	5.2	2.47	3.00
Utah	1 615 845	36.2	9.0	26.5	94.4	1.6	508 404	76.5	44.8	65.3	37.6	8.8	5.9	3.14	3.66
Nevada	1 012 695	23.3	11.8	34.6	103.1	1.8	407 859	65.1	28.9	52.4	22.0	8.8	5.1	2.45	2.98
Pacific	28 255 159	23.6	12.8	34.0	97.2	2.5	10 915 209	66.3	30.4	53.6	23.5	9.2	5.2	2.54	3.07
Washington	4 308 937	24.8	12.7	34.0	95.5	2.3	1 708 223	67.1	32.1	55.6	24.9	8.6	5.6	2.48	3.01
Oregon	2 636 787	24.8	14.5	35.3	92.9	2.2	1 043 711	67.9	31.4	56.1	24.1	8.8	5.6	2.48	2.98
California	20 524 327	23.2	12.9	33.9	97.4	2.5	7 871 635	65.9	29.6	52.8	22.9	9.4	5.0	2.56	3.09
Alaska	415 492	29.2	4.0	30.7	116.6	3.3	153 215	69.3	41.3	58.0	33.3	7.6	5.7	2.69	3.21
Hawaii	369 616	23.0	9.3	32.3	117.4	5.4	138 425	67.0	33.0	55.6	26.6	7.9	4.8	2.63	3.11

Table 255. Summary of General Characteristics of Black Persons and Households: 1990

[For definitions of terms and meanings of symbols, see text]

United States Region and Division State	All Black persons						All households with a Black householder								
	Percent of all persons				Persons 18 years and over—			Family households as a percent of all households						Persons per—	
										Married-couple family		Female householder, no husband present			
	Total	Under 18 years	65 years and over	Median age	Males per 100 females	Percent in group quarters	Total	Total	With own children under 18 years	Total	With own children under 18 years	Total	With own children under 18 years	Household	Family
United States	29 986 060	32.0	8.4	28.1	84.1	4.2	9 976 161	70.0	39.2	34.2	17.8	30.6	19.0	2.87	3.48
REGION AND DIVISION															
Northeast	5 613 222	29.5	8.1	29.3	82.2	4.7	1 864 479	68.4	36.5	31.3	15.6	31.5	18.6	2.86	3.47
New England	627 547	31.3	6.1	27.3	89.3	5.4	207 066	68.8	40.9	31.9	17.4	31.4	21.1	2.84	3.41
Middle Atlantic	4 985 675	29.3	8.4	29.6	81.3	4.6	1 657 413	68.4	36.0	31.2	15.3	31.5	18.2	2.86	3.48
Midwest	5 715 940	33.0	8.3	27.9	82.4	3.7	1 938 405	68.6	39.3	30.5	15.1	33.0	21.9	2.83	3.46
East North Central	4 817 436	32.9	8.4	28.1	81.5	3.5	1 632 461	68.8	39.1	30.2	14.8	33.4	22.1	2.84	3.47
West North Central	898 504	34.0	8.0	27.0	87.4	4.9	305 944	67.8	40.2	32.1	16.9	30.8	21.0	2.77	3.42
South	15 828 888	32.6	8.8	27.8	82.8	3.9	5 209 880	71.6	40.2	36.4	19.5	30.2	18.6	2.92	3.51
South Atlantic	8 923 558	31.5	8.5	28.3	83.3	4.1	2 947 032	71.5	39.4	36.6	19.3	29.6	17.8	2.90	3.47
East South Central	2 976 704	34.1	10.1	27.1	78.9	3.5	971 172	72.4	41.1	35.3	19.1	32.2	20.0	2.96	3.58
West South Central	3 928 626	34.1	8.4	27.0	84.6	3.9	1 291 676	71.5	41.6	36.5	20.2	30.0	19.2	2.93	3.54
West	2 828 010	30.9	6.8	28.1	99.9	5.9	963 397	67.2	38.3	35.4	18.9	26.0	16.5	2.76	3.34
Mountain	373 584	33.4	5.6	26.8	109.5	5.8	130 090	66.2	40.6	37.8	21.3	23.2	16.2	2.71	3.35
Pacific	2 454 426	30.5	7.0	28.3	98.6	5.9	833 307	67.4	37.9	35.1	18.5	26.5	16.6	2.76	3.34
STATE															
New England	627 547	31.3	6.1	27.3	89.3	5.4	207 066	68.8	40.9	31.9	17.4	31.4	21.1	2.84	3.41
Maine	5 138	33.2	3.3	23.8	179.3	16.0	1 458	65.2	42.2	50.5	32.2	11.2	8.3	2.65	3.26
New Hampshire	7 198	31.7	3.3	25.7	135.5	9.5	2 322	67.7	43.8	48.8	30.8	13.4	9.8	2.74	3.31
Vermont	1 951	35.4	3.7	22.0	147.3	12.9	557	57.1	38.2	41.3	25.5	12.9	10.6	2.56	3.25
Massachusetts	300 130	31.1	6.2	27.3	89.5	5.3	99 402	67.8	40.6	30.6	16.9	31.5	21.2	2.82	3.41
Rhode Island	38 861	33.8	5.7	25.9	98.0	7.1	12 445	69.1	44.1	32.1	18.5	31.0	22.6	2.88	3.46
Connecticut	274 269	31.2	6.2	27.5	85.5	4.8	90 882	70.1	40.7	32.5	17.1	32.3	21.4	2.85	3.41
Middle Atlantic	4 985 675	29.3	8.4	29.6	81.3	4.6	1 657 413	68.4	36.0	31.2	15.3	31.5	18.2	2.86	3.48
New York	2 859 055	29.2	7.9	29.5	80.0	4.6	947 597	68.1	36.6	30.7	15.6	31.8	18.6	2.87	3.50
New Jersey	1 036 825	29.3	7.5	29.1	84.8	4.4	333 782	70.8	37.4	35.3	17.5	29.7	17.5	2.97	3.53
Pennsylvania	1 089 795	29.4	10.4	30.1	81.6	4.7	376 034	66.8	33.2	28.9	12.7	32.3	18.1	2.75	3.38
East North Central	4 817 436	32.9	8.4	28.1	81.5	3.5	1 632 461	68.8	39.1	30.2	14.8	33.4	22.1	2.84	3.47
Ohio	1 154 826	31.9	9.3	29.1	81.0	3.9	415 670	67.0	37.3	31.2	14.6	31.3	20.6	2.67	3.31
Indiana	432 092	33.3	8.8	28.0	82.8	4.0	149 055	68.9	39.8	32.9	16.4	31.2	21.1	2.77	3.39
Illinois	1 694 273	32.6	7.9	28.1	81.4	3.2	550 311	69.8	38.8	30.5	15.1	33.8	21.3	2.97	3.61
Michigan	1 291 706	32.5	8.7	28.2	81.5	3.3	441 984	68.5	39.2	28.7	13.9	34.5	23.1	2.81	3.43
Wisconsin	244 539	40.1	4.4	23.4	82.4	4.0	75 441	72.9	49.0	26.6	15.0	41.5	31.5	3.06	3.59
West North Central	898 504	34.0	8.0	27.0	87.4	4.9	305 944	67.8	40.2	32.1	16.9	30.8	21.0	2.77	3.42
Minnesota	94 944	39.1	3.9	24.0	107.9	5.2	31 201	64.9	45.5	27.7	16.8	31.9	25.6	2.74	3.37
Iowa	48 090	36.7	6.7	24.4	99.1	7.1	15 741	67.0	42.1	33.0	17.4	29.4	21.9	2.73	3.35
Missouri	548 208	32.6	9.2	28.2	80.1	4.0	188 853	67.9	38.3	31.1	15.5	31.8	20.6	2.78	3.45
North Dakota	3 524	37.3	.8	22.7	177.7	11.6	1 077	73.0	56.0	62.9	47.0	7.1	6.6	2.91	3.49
South Dakota	3 258	38.0	2.5	22.9	204.1	11.7	987	69.4	51.3	56.4	40.6	8.9	7.2	2.86	3.46
Nebraska	57 404	36.5	6.4	25.6	89.9	4.6	19 720	67.9	42.7	31.5	17.2	32.1	23.5	2.75	3.39
Kansas	143 076	34.0	7.8	26.5	98.7	7.0	48 365	69.1	42.1	37.5	20.9	27.0	18.8	2.76	3.37
South Atlantic	8 923 558	31.5	8.5	28.3	83.3	4.1	2 947 032	71.5	39.4	36.6	19.3	29.6	17.8	2.90	3.47
Delaware	112 460	31.6	7.8	27.9	84.3	4.4	37 229	71.4	39.5	35.6	18.0	30.0	18.6	2.89	3.41
Maryland	1 189 899	28.7	6.7	29.5	84.2	3.3	401 460	71.0	37.9	36.5	18.5	28.8	16.8	2.86	3.37
District of Columbia	399 604	23.5	13.1	33.2	78.3	5.1	152 356	58.0	24.2	23.9	8.2	28.7	14.3	2.48	3.28
Virginia	1 162 994	29.2	9.2	29.2	87.7	5.3	391 280	71.5	38.1	40.3	20.5	26.5	15.7	2.81	3.35
West Virginia	56 295	29.0	15.6	31.6	81.7	5.8	20 941	64.5	32.9	33.8	16.2	26.2	14.7	2.53	3.22
North Carolina	1 456 323	30.8	9.5	28.5	82.3	4.2	492 214	72.0	38.8	38.1	19.7	29.1	17.2	2.84	3.39
South Carolina	1 039 884	33.5	9.0	27.3	81.2	3.6	323 878	75.4	42.0	40.1	22.4	30.4	17.7	3.10	3.65
Georgia	1 746 565	33.1	7.7	27.3	81.1	3.6	574 113	72.0	41.6	35.7	19.9	31.4	19.6	2.93	3.50
Florida	1 759 534	34.6	7.4	27.0	85.6	4.1	553 561	72.4	42.4	35.5	19.5	30.9	19.8	3.04	3.59
East South Central	2 976 704	34.1	10.1	27.1	78.9	3.5	971 172	72.4	41.1	35.3	19.1	32.2	20.0	2.96	3.58
Kentucky	262 907	31.6	10.2	28.3	85.1	6.0	92 639	68.7	39.3	33.2	16.7	31.2	20.7	2.67	3.29
Tennessee	778 035	32.4	9.5	27.9	79.2	3.8	262 505	71.3	39.9	33.6	17.5	32.8	20.5	2.85	3.45
Alabama	1 020 705	33.6	10.7	27.7	77.7	3.1	334 513	72.7	40.1	36.6	19.6	31.5	18.7	2.96	3.58
Mississippi	915 057	36.9	9.9	25.3	78.1	2.9	281 515	74.2	43.8	36.2	20.6	32.9	20.9	3.16	3.78
West South Central	3 928 626	34.1	8.4	27.0	84.6	3.9	1 291 676	71.5	41.6	36.5	20.2	30.0	19.2	2.93	3.54
Arkansas	373 912	36.5	11.3	26.2	78.4	3.5	121 338	71.5	41.9	36.1	19.9	30.7	19.9	2.97	3.63
Louisiana	1 299 281	35.8	8.6	26.2	79.9	3.5	406 880	74.2	43.5	35.3	19.6	33.8	21.6	3.08	3.67
Oklahoma	233 801	34.3	8.6	26.4	90.8	6.2	79 203	68.8	41.9	35.7	20.0	28.6	19.6	2.78	3.42
Texas	2 021 632	32.5	7.8	27.6	88.1	4.0	684 255	70.2	40.4	37.4	20.6	27.9	17.5	2.84	3.46
Mountain	373 584	33.4	5.6	26.8	109.5	5.8	130 090	66.2	40.6	37.8	21.3	23.2	16.2	2.71	3.35
Montana	2 381	37.0	4.2	23.3	173.7	11.2	760	65.1	44.2	48.3	30.7	11.4	9.5	2.57	3.23
Idaho	3 370	36.7	4.1	23.5	178.0	7.9	1 095	65.5	43.1	51.1	32.9	9.9	7.2	2.72	3.39
Wyoming	3 606	35.2	5.9	25.2	128.6	8.6	1 208	66.5	44.2	43.9	27.0	18.5	15.0	2.63	3.27
Colorado	133 146	32.0	5.3	27.6	105.8	5.4	49 255	63.8	38.8	36.5	20.1	22.8	16.1	2.56	3.24
New Mexico	30 210	34.4	7.0	26.6	114.6	5.8	10 377	69.4	42.5	44.0	25.7	19.8	13.2	2.77	3.35
Arizona	110 524	34.3	6.2	26.5	110.6	6.2	37 140	67.5	41.5	38.7	22.2	23.3	16.1	2.80	3.43
Utah	11 576	35.8	5.4	24.1	162.2	10.2	3 770	65.3	42.6	43.3	26.9	16.4	12.2	2.72	3.36
Nevada	78 771	33.7	4.9	26.9	102.5	5.1	26 485	67.9	41.0	34.7	18.8	27.1	18.9	2.83	3.42
Pacific	2 454 426	30.5	7.0	28.3	98.6	5.9	833 307	67.4	37.9	35.1	18.5	26.5	16.6	2.76	3.34
Washington	149 801	33.6	5.5	26.4	119.9	6.7	51 645	65.8	41.1	38.0	22.0	22.5	16.0	2.67	3.28
Oregon	46 178	35.2	6.9	26.5	111.6	5.6	15 385	63.2	37.6	30.9	16.9	26.2	17.7	2.68	3.33
California	2 208 801	30.1	7.2	28.6	96.2	5.7	751 563	67.4	37.3	34.5	17.8	27.0	16.7	2.77	3.35
Alaska	22 451	35.2	2.2	24.7	131.7	10.0	6 927	74.9	54.6	53.8	37.9	16.3	13.3	2.96	3.43
Hawaii	27 195	30.7	1.4	24.2	187.4	17.1	7 787	78.3	56.2	67.6	48.3	7.4	5.9	3.02	3.41

Table 256. Summary of General Characteristics of American Indian, Eskimo, or Aleut Persons and Households: 1990

[For definitions of terms and meanings of symbols, see text]

United States Region and Division State	All American Indian, Eskimo, or Aleut persons						All households with an American Indian, Eskimo, or Aleut householder							Persons per—	
		Percent of all persons			Persons 18 years and over—			Family households as a percent of all households							
		Under 18 years	65 years and over	Median age	Males per 100 females	Percent in group quarters	Total	Total	Married-couple family		Female householder, no husband present		House-hold	Family
	Total								Total	With own children under 18 years	Total	With own children under 18 years		
United States	1 959 234	35.6	5.8	26.2	94.2	2.9	591 372	74.8	45.1	48.0	28.1	20.4	13.3	3.12	3.60
REGION AND DIVISION															
Northeast	125 148	29.3	6.9	29.3	93.9	3.8	41 978	69.4	39.7	41.4	23.1	21.8	13.6	2.89	3.43
New England	32 794	30.2	6.4	28.6	97.0	4.5	11 145	68.7	40.3	41.3	22.8	22.0	14.6	2.81	3.34
Middle Atlantic	92 354	28.9	7.0	29.5	92.9	3.6	30 833	69.7	39.5	41.4	23.2	21.8	13.2	2.91	3.46
Midwest	337 899	37.3	5.2	25.1	94.2	3.5	101 859	74.0	47.1	43.5	25.8	24.1	17.3	3.10	3.57
East North Central	149 939	32.9	5.5	27.5	95.8	2.9	48 869	72.5	44.0	46.4	26.4	20.6	14.4	2.93	3.41
West North Central	187 960	40.7	4.9	23.2	92.8	4.0	52 990	75.5	50.0	40.8	25.2	27.4	20.1	3.26	3.72
South	562 731	33.1	7.2	28.0	95.2	2.7	183 485	74.9	42.0	54.3	29.9	15.9	9.6	2.88	3.35
South Atlantic	172 281	29.1	6.3	29.3	99.5	3.6	58 436	74.5	42.4	52.1	29.1	17.0	10.4	2.90	3.35
East South Central	40 839	31.7	6.0	29.3	97.6	3.4	13 496	76.0	44.1	55.6	32.3	15.4	9.2	2.96	3.41
West South Central	349 611	35.2	7.7	27.1	92.7	2.1	111 553	75.0	41.6	55.4	30.0	15.3	9.3	2.86	3.35
West	933 456	37.3	5.1	25.3	93.6	2.6	264 050	75.8	47.2	46.4	28.5	22.0	14.3	3.33	3.80
Mountain	480 516	40.6	5.0	23.3	91.4	2.3	124 689	80.0	52.3	47.7	31.8	24.4	15.5	3.66	4.10
Pacific	452 940	33.8	5.3	27.2	95.7	2.9	139 361	72.0	42.7	45.2	25.5	19.9	13.3	3.04	3.50
STATE															
New England	32 794	30.2	6.4	28.6	97.0	4.5	11 145	68.7	40.3	41.3	22.8	22.0	14.6	2.81	3.34
Maine	5 998	35.4	4.2	25.9	95.7	3.8	1 860	72.5	47.0	44.8	27.5	21.0	15.2	2.93	3.36
New Hampshire	2 134	26.0	4.8	30.3	107.9	5.7	764	67.8	38.6	49.3	27.2	13.1	8.2	2.70	3.18
Vermont	1 696	32.0	4.5	28.1	105.0	4.8	591	70.7	45.2	44.5	27.1	21.3	15.4	2.88	3.28
Massachusetts	12 241	29.2	6.9	28.9	95.0	4.8	4 208	67.0	38.9	38.5	20.7	23.5	15.9	2.77	3.35
Rhode Island	4 071	33.4	8.5	27.1	88.5	2.7	1 339	69.5	39.3	35.6	19.3	28.8	17.6	2.92	3.51
Connecticut	6 654	26.1	7.2	30.6	101.6	5.4	2 383	68.1	37.6	43.3	22.5	19.4	12.0	2.73	3.27
Middle Atlantic	92 354	28.9	7.0	29.5	92.9	3.6	30 833	69.7	39.5	41.4	23.2	21.8	13.2	2.91	3.46
New York	62 651	30.3	6.6	28.6	91.2	3.0	20 375	69.8	40.7	39.6	23.0	23.3	14.5	2.95	3.50
New Jersey	14 970	26.0	7.5	30.9	94.7	3.8	5 105	72.2	38.5	46.3	24.4	19.4	11.0	2.96	3.46
Pennsylvania	14 733	25.9	8.2	31.6	97.9	5.6	5 353	67.1	35.8	43.5	22.5	18.3	10.6	2.72	3.31
East North Central	149 939	32.9	5.5	27.5	95.8	2.9	48 869	72.5	44.0	46.4	26.4	20.6	14.4	2.93	3.41
Ohio	20 358	26.5	6.6	31.6	99.3	3.0	7 688	71.3	41.0	49.4	27.2	17.1	11.1	2.80	3.33
Indiana	12 720	28.8	6.7	30.3	98.4	4.0	4 519	70.8	39.5	51.3	27.0	15.0	10.0	2.75	3.25
Illinois	21 836	28.3	5.6	29.4	100.4	3.6	7 438	68.9	39.4	45.8	25.2	17.4	11.3	2.85	3.41
Michigan	55 638	34.2	5.1	26.6	93.0	2.3	17 709	73.4	44.8	47.3	27.2	20.8	14.7	2.93	3.38
Wisconsin	39 387	38.4	5.1	24.4	93.9	3.0	11 515	75.0	49.6	41.4	26.6		10.7	3.14	3.55
West North Central	187 960	40.7	4.9	23.2	92.8	4.0	52 990	75.5	50.0	40.8	25.2	27.4	20.1	3.26	3.72
Minnesota	49 909	41.1	3.9	23.0	93.5	3.8	14 168	74.3	51.8	32.8	20.8	33.1	25.4	3.20	3.59
Iowa	7 349	37.8	4.6	24.4	93.5	4.3	2 157	73.5	47.8	45.1	26.8	22.4	17.1	3.09	3.57
Missouri	19 035	20.5	7.4	30.8	100.0	3.2	7 298	70.3	38.4	53.6	27.7	13.0	8.6	2.68	3.21
North Dakota	25 917	44.9	4.2	20.7	86.2	3.7	6 998	79.3	57.5	38.8	26.8	32.4	24.9	3.44	3.84
South Dakota	50 575	46.4	4.8	19.8	92.1	4.0	12 053	80.3	55.5	36.7	25.7	34.1	23.7	3.86	4.29
Nebraska	12 410	42.2	4.8	22.3	86.9	4.6	3 342	75.3	50.3	37.9	24.1	30.0	21.7	3.30	3.80
Kansas	21 965	33.1	6.3	26.3	95.4	5.3	6 974	71.7	41.8	52.5	29.1	14.8	10.3	2.80	3.31
South Atlantic	172 281	29.1	6.3	29.3	99.5	3.6	58 436	74.5	42.4	52.1	29.1	17.0	10.4	2.90	3.35
Delaware	2 019	24.7	8.9	32.9	100.7	2.4	773	71.7	37.8	50.6	25.4	15.7	9.6	2.65	3.08
Maryland	12 972	26.3	5.0	30.4	99.2	3.8	4 406	73.8	40.0	50.2	26.3	18.0	11.1	2.91	3.31
District of Columbia	1 466	16.4	12.6	35.0	88.2	8.7	612	48.2	17.6	20.8	8.2	21.9	8.2	2.22	3.02
Virginia	15 282	23.6	5.5	30.7	107.9	5.4	5 505	70.7	38.1	52.8	28.1	13.3	7.8	2.75	3.22
West Virginia	2 458	24.0	10.6	34.6	95.3	3.9	965	69.4	37.2	50.7	25.8	14.6	9.0	2.66	3.23
North Carolina	80 155	33.1	6.5	27.3	93.6	2.5	25 528	78.5	47.2	52.6	31.6	20.1	12.3	3.06	3.47
South Carolina	8 246	28.3	5.0	28.3	109.6	6.9	2 747	75.1	43.8	55.4	32.2	14.9	9.1	2.95	3.42
Georgia	13 348	25.8	5.1	30.4	109.1	5.4	4 812	73.0	41.9	55.5	31.3	12.7	8.1	2.82	3.28
Florida	36 335	26.3	6.7	31.3	103.8	3.7	13 088	70.5	37.2	51.1	25.6	14.2	8.9	2.75	3.20
East South Central	40 839	31.7	6.0	29.3	97.6	3.4	13 496	76.0	44.1	55.6	32.3	15.4	9.2	2.96	3.41
Kentucky	5 769	24.8	7.2	31.5	106.4	6.4	2 108	71.7	39.6	50.7	27.0	16.4	10.5	2.71	3.20
Tennessee	10 039	24.8	7.1	32.6	100.5	4.1	3 771	71.2	37.4	52.1	26.9	14.1	8.1	2.71	3.20
Alabama	16 506	34.5	5.3	28.5	94.9	2.0	5 288	78.8	48.5	62.4	38.6	12.7	7.8	2.98	3.41
Mississippi	8 525	38.9	4.9	24.5	92.4	3.1	2 329	81.1	49.1	50.0	31.4	22.9	13.1	3.57	3.89
West South Central	349 611	35.2	7.7	27.1	92.7	2.1	111 553	75.0	41.6	55.4	30.0	15.3	9.3	2.86	3.35
Arkansas	12 773	28.9	8.0	30.6	93.6	2.3	4 539	73.0	38.8	58.0	29.3	11.2	7.3	2.67	3.16
Louisiana	18 541	35.3	5.8	26.3	100.4	2.2	5 686	78.4	47.0	58.5	35.2	14.2	8.4	3.15	3.59
Oklahoma	252 420	37.3	8.3	26.0	89.4	1.9	77 846	75.9	41.9	55.3	29.8	16.3	9.8	2.87	3.34
Texas	65 877	28.3	6.0	30.2	102.5	3.0	23 482	71.7	39.7	54.3	29.4	13.0	7.9	2.81	3.33
Mountain	480 516	40.6	5.0	23.3	91.4	2.3	124 689	80.0	52.3	47.7	31.8	24.4	15.5	3.66	4.10
Montana	47 679	41.7	4.7	23.0	93.8	2.9	13 230	79.0	54.2	45.6	31.0	26.2	18.6	3.42	3.85
Idaho	13 780	37.2	4.8	25.1	99.0	3.3	4 082	77.6	47.9	51.9	31.6	19.1	12.7	3.19	3.61
Wyoming	9 479	41.2	4.3	23.5	93.9	2.5	2 630	78.4	52.5	49.2	32.9	23.2	15.7	3.41	3.86
Colorado	27 776	33.2	4.4	26.9	97.1	3.9	8 959	70.1	43.7	45.0	26.1	19.2	14.0	2.84	3.36
New Mexico	134 355	40.5	5.4	23.4	88.6	1.9	33 489	82.2	53.7	49.2	33.7	24.3	14.4	3.83	4.26
Arizona	203 527	42.0	5.0	22.4	90.8	2.0	49 894	81.8	53.5	47.6	32.4	25.8	16.0	3.90	4.31
Utah	24 283	44.7	3.1	20.4	90.1	3.2	5 841	81.4	59.3	50.3	36.8	23.8	17.8	3.76	4.15
Nevada	19 637	32.1	5.8	28.0	97.5	2.9	6 564	71.5	40.6	43.2	23.0	20.8	13.2	2.87	3.32
Pacific	452 940	33.8	5.3	27.2	95.7	2.9	139 361	72.0	42.7	45.2	25.5	19.9	13.3	3.04	3.50
Washington	81 483	36.1	4.7	26.0	93.7	3.0	24 699	72.4	44.9	42.9	24.3	22.4	16.2	3.03	3.45
Oregon	38 496	34.7	5.3	27.1	94.0	3.3	11 923	72.3	43.4	46.7	25.6	19.4	13.8	2.95	3.36
California	242 164	30.6	5.8	28.7	95.3	2.8	78 848	71.5	40.0	46.3	24.7	18.8	11.9	2.97	3.41
Alaska	85 698	40.6	4.8	24.1	99.2	2.9	22 305	73.7	49.3	43.0	29.1	21.3	14.8	3.37	3.95
Hawaii	5 099	30.9	2.9	27.3	109.5	7.1	1 586	68.5	44.6	49.1	30.5	15.6	11.8	2.90	3.41

Table 257. Summary of General Characteristics of Asian or Pacific Islander Persons and Households: 1990

[For definitions of terms and meanings of symbols, see text]

United States Region and Division State	All Asian or Pacific Islander persons						All households with an Asian or Pacific Islander householder								
		Percent of all persons			Persons 18 years and over—			Family households as a percent of all households						Persons per—	
										Married-couple family		Female householder, no husband present			
	Total	Under 18 years	65 years and over	Median age	Males per 100 females	Percent in group quarters	Total	Total	With own children under 18 years	Total	With own children under 18 years	Total	With own children under 18 years	Household	Family
United States	7 273 662	28.6	6.2	29.8	92.6	2.1	2 013 735	77.4	45.5	62.8	39.2	9.5	4.8	3.34	3.80
REGION AND DIVISION															
Northeast	1 335 375	27.2	4.9	30.0	98.5	2.8	374 245	77.7	46.7	64.6	41.5	8.0	3.8	3.33	3.76
New England	231 656	29.5	3.7	26.9	97.3	5.8	61 399	75.1	47.5	60.8	40.1	9.3	5.8	3.31	3.77
Middle Atlantic	1 103 719	26.8	5.1	30.6	98.8	2.1	312 846	78.3	46.5	65.4	41.8	7.8	3.5	3.33	3.76
Midwest	768 069	32.2	4.0	27.0	94.5	3.3	207 117	75.3	48.9	63.5	43.2	7.9	4.5	3.26	3.82
East North Central	572 673	30.6	4.3	28.2	94.8	3.1	158 836	76.0	48.7	65.0	43.8	7.3	3.9	3.25	3.79
West North Central	195 396	36.9	2.8	23.9	93.7	3.9	48 281	72.9	49.5	58.6	41.4	9.6	6.5	3.31	3.93
South	1 122 248	29.2	3.5	28.9	89.1	2.3	307 418	76.4	49.5	63.5	43.3	8.1	4.7	3.25	3.74
South Atlantic	631 133	28.2	3.8	29.6	86.3	2.3	170 495	78.0	49.2	65.1	43.2	8.3	4.5	3.27	3.71
East South Central	84 464	30.2	2.9	27.9	85.7	4.7	22 711	72.7	48.2	60.9	41.7	8.4	5.2	3.06	3.64
West South Central	406 651	30.6	3.2	28.1	94.5	1.9	114 212	74.8	50.1	61.6	43.8	7.9	4.7	3.25	3.81
West	4 047 970	28.3	7.9	30.5	91.2	1.6	1 124 955	78.0	43.5	62.0	36.6	10.6	5.2	3.39	3.83
Mountain	217 120	29.9	4.9	28.4	84.2	2.3	60 637	70.8	42.6	56.4	35.1	9.6	5.7	3.00	3.59
Pacific	3 830 850	28.2	8.1	30.6	91.6	1.5	1 064 318	78.4	43.5	62.3	36.7	10.7	5.2	3.41	3.85
STATE															
New England	231 656	29.5	3.7	26.9	97.3	5.8	61 399	75.1	47.5	60.8	40.1	9.3	5.8	3.31	3.77
Maine	6 683	33.6	3.1	25.8	84.5	5.9	1 503	75.9	53.0	58.3	41.1	12.6	9.4	3.24	3.68
New Hampshire	9 343	29.4	2.8	27.4	90.9	5.9	2 421	72.0	45.7	62.6	40.9	5.0	3.2	3.00	3.48
Vermont	3 215	32.3	2.2	22.6	87.3	11.7	718	62.7	41.4	49.3	33.1	9.7	7.2	2.81	3.38
Massachusetts	143 392	28.8	4.1	27.0	97.2	5.9	38 728	74.0	45.6	59.1	38.1	9.8	6.0	3.30	3.76
Rhode Island	18 325	34.4	3.3	24.0	99.2	5.6	4 471	79.5	55.8	60.9	43.3	13.5	10.5	3.69	4.12
Connecticut	50 698	29.2	3.2	28.1	100.8	4.9	13 558	77.9	50.1	66.2	44.8	6.8	3.9	3.30	3.72
Middle Atlantic	1 103 719	26.8	5.1	30.6	98.8	2.1	312 846	78.3	46.5	65.4	41.8	7.8	3.5	3.33	3.76
New York	693 760	24.9	5.7	31.0	100.8	2.0	201 644	76.4	42.7	62.4	38.0	8.3	3.5	3.28	3.73
New Jersey	272 521	29.5	4.2	30.7	94.6	1.5	73 840	85.0	55.5	74.7	51.6	6.2	2.8	3.51	3.79
Pennsylvania	137 438	30.6	3.9	27.6	96.7	3.9	37 362	75.4	49.0	63.1	43.0	7.9	4.6	3.27	3.81
East North Central	572 673	30.6	4.3	28.2	94.8	3.1	158 836	76.0	48.7	65.0	43.8	7.3	3.9	3.25	3.79
Ohio	91 179	28.9	3.6	28.4	95.1	3.3	26 824	72.1	46.1	62.0	41.1	6.8	4.0	3.02	3.58
Indiana	37 617	27.1	3.0	27.7	93.3	6.4	10 853	68.9	42.6	59.2	37.5	6.7	4.0	2.85	3.45
Illinois	285 311	28.5	5.3	30.0	94.9	2.6	80 671	78.5	49.0	66.7	44.4	7.5	3.5	3.31	3.81
Michigan	104 983	33.0	3.6	27.0	95.0	3.2	28 204	75.9	50.0	65.6	45.0	7.1	4.0	3.22	3.73
Wisconsin	53 583	42.9	2.9	21.3	94.3	3.5	12 284	75.1	55.0	63.6	48.0	8.4	5.9	3.79	4.50
West North Central	195 396	36.9	2.8	23.9	93.7	3.9	48 281	72.9	49.5	58.6	41.4	9.6	6.5	3.31	3.93
Minnesota	77 886	45.1	2.8	20.4	95.0	2.0	17 198	79.2	56.5	61.9	46.2	11.9	8.5	3.78	4.32
Iowa	25 476	34.2	2.3	23.6	101.8	7.0	6 287	69.0	45.9	56.9	39.0	7.6	5.0	3.10	3.73
Missouri	41 277	28.8	3.3	27.5	90.7	4.6	11 584	69.7	44.6	57.0	38.0	8.6	5.1	2.97	3.59
North Dakota	3 462	31.0	2.0	25.7	83.0	6.0	879	64.3	42.4	52.4	34.7	8.6	6.7	2.70	3.37
South Dakota	3 123	36.0	2.0	24.1	78.2	4.8	712	65.9	44.7	54.5	36.8	9.3	7.0	2.92	3.62
Nebraska	12 422	32.4	3.1	25.9	86.3	4.5	3 264	67.0	43.1	53.8	35.7	8.5	5.6	2.91	3.57
Kansas	31 750	32.0	2.8	25.5	94.8	4.5	8 357	71.0	48.4	58.2	41.4	8.2	5.4	3.20	3.83
South Atlantic	631 133	28.2	3.8	29.6	86.3	2.3	170 495	78.0	49.2	65.1	43.2	8.3	4.5	3.27	3.71
Delaware	9 057	28.9	3.4	29.8	89.6	1.8	2 538	77.2	46.7	65.7	46.3	5.9	3.4	3.13	3.56
Maryland	139 719	27.5	4.6	30.5	91.0	1.4	38 062	82.2	49.9	70.4	45.2	7.6	3.6	3.39	3.73
District of Columbia	11 214	14.0	7.0	31.3	83.6	9.3	4 070	43.3	17.4	32.5	14.2	7.0	2.3	2.18	3.08
Virginia	159 053	28.4	3.7	29.5	86.8	2.2	41 199	80.3	51.0	66.8	45.0	8.6	4.6	3.42	3.80
West Virginia	7 459	29.3	2.8	27.8	87.1	5.0	2 147	69.3	44.7	59.8	39.7	6.5	3.8	2.86	3.50
North Carolina	52 166	29.4	2.5	27.9	83.0	4.2	13 706	75.2	50.4	63.3	44.0	7.9	5.0	3.13	3.64
South Carolina	22 382	29.5	2.9	28.4	75.3	4.2	5 599	75.9	51.1	64.2	44.4	8.4	5.4	3.16	3.66
Georgia	75 781	29.8	2.7	28.7	89.9	2.5	20 279	78.6	52.3	66.3	46.3	7.4	4.4	3.31	3.75
Florida	154 302	28.1	4.1	30.1	82.9	1.6	42 895	76.5	47.9	61.9	40.8	9.4	5.4	3.19	3.65
East South Central	84 464	30.2	2.9	27.9	85.7	4.7	22 711	72.7	48.2	60.9	41.7	8.4	5.2	3.06	3.64
Kentucky	17 812	30.1	2.7	27.9	81.6	6.2	4 634	73.0	48.8	61.0	42.2	9.1	5.3	2.99	3.58
Tennessee	31 839	30.1	2.7	28.0	89.9	4.2	8 797	74.3	49.1	63.4	43.4	7.5	4.6	3.09	3.64
Alabama	21 797	28.8	2.6	28.3	84.0	3.8	6 077	68.6	45.0	57.0	38.6	8.4	5.2	2.93	3.56
Mississippi	13 016	32.9	3.9	26.6	84.3	5.7	3 203	75.3	50.7	61.4	42.4	10.2	6.9	3.31	3.86
West South Central	406 651	30.6	3.2	28.1	94.5	1.9	114 212	74.8	50.1	61.6	43.8	7.9	4.7	3.25	3.81
Arkansas	12 530	32.0	3.0	26.7	83.3	2.4	3 228	73.0	49.8	59.5	42.3	8.2	5.2	3.21	3.81
Louisiana	41 099	34.6	3.4	26.3	95.9	2.7	10 404	76.7	53.1	62.2	45.5	8.5	5.4	3.54	4.12
Oklahoma	33 563	29.0	2.7	26.6	93.0	3.1	9 439	66.7	44.6	54.2	38.1	8.4	5.4	2.98	3.67
Texas	319 459	30.1	3.3	28.6	95.0	1.7	91 141	75.5	50.4	62.4	44.2	7.7	4.6	3.24	3.79
Mountain	217 120	29.9	4.9	28.4	84.2	2.3	60 637	70.8	42.6	56.4	35.1	9.6	5.7	3.00	3.59
Montana	4 259	34.3	4.5	25.7	71.9	4.8	1 040	64.3	40.5	51.3	32.1	8.8	6.6	2.71	3.40
Idaho	9 365	32.1	6.6	27.1	89.0	3.7	2 602	69.6	41.6	57.0	34.2	8.2	5.3	2.83	3.39
Wyoming	2 806	29.3	4.9	28.9	72.0	3.6	772	65.3	39.6	53.6	31.9	8.8	6.1	2.65	3.33
Colorado	59 862	30.3	5.4	28.4	84.2	2.5	17 099	69.7	41.7	55.4	34.1	9.9	6.0	2.93	3.58
New Mexico	14 124	31.3	3.4	28.8	75.0	2.2	3 733	72.6	46.1	58.6	38.0	9.4	5.9	2.97	3.53
Arizona	55 206	28.0	4.4	28.6	87.2	2.1	15 934	69.2	41.7	55.6	34.9	8.9	5.1	2.95	3.54
Utah	33 371	35.2	4.7	25.0	94.5	2.7	8 582	75.2	47.6	63.4	41.6	7.7	4.7	3.38	3.95
Nevada	38 127	25.9	5.1	31.6	77.2	1.2	10 875	71.8	40.9	53.4	31.6	12.3	6.9	2.99	3.50
Pacific	3 830 850	28.2	8.1	30.6	91.6	1.5	1 064 318	78.4	43.5	62.3	36.7	10.7	5.2	3.41	3.85
Washington	210 958	30.6	6.1	28.7	82.9	2.0	59 205	73.4	44.2	56.8	35.2	11.7	7.2	3.10	3.66
Oregon	69 269	29.8	5.3	27.1	91.2	3.8	20 008	69.0	41.0	54.0	33.5	9.8	5.7	2.96	3.58
California	2 845 659	28.5	7.1	30.2	92.1	1.4	777 913	79.0	45.6	63.2	39.0	10.2	5.0	3.49	3.91
Alaska	19 728	31.6	4.3	29.6	85.0	7.0	4 674	77.6	52.0	60.8	42.1	11.5	7.5	3.33	3.77
Hawaii	685 236	26.0	13.0	33.7	92.8	1.7	202 518	78.5	35.3	61.2	28.6	12.3	5.1	3.26	3.69

Table 258. Summary of General Characteristics of Hispanic Origin Persons and Households: 1990

[Persons of Hispanic origin may be of any race. For definitions of terms and meanings of symbols, see text]

United States Region and Division State	All Hispanic origin persons						All households with an Hispanic origin householder								
		Percent of all persons			Persons 18 years and over—			Family households as a percent of all households		Married-couple family		Female householder, no husband present		Persons per—	
	Total	Under 18 years	65 years and over	Median age	Males per 100 females	Percent in group quarters	Total	Total	With own children under 18 years	Total	With own children under 18 years	Total	With own children under 18 years	House-hold	Family
United States	22 354 059	34.7	5.2	25.5	103.3	2.3	6 001 718	79.8	50.5	54.9	35.5	17.7	11.6	3.53	3.88
REGION AND DIVISION															
Northeast	3 754 389	31.8	5.3	27.1	93.2	3.1	1 108 546	77.0	47.1	42.7	25.3	27.3	18.6	3.23	3.61
New England	568 240	36.6	3.9	24.2	94.7	3.7	162 603	77.3	52.9	40.2	25.3	30.7	24.5	3.26	3.61
Middle Atlantic	3 186 149	30.9	5.6	27.7	93.0	3.0	945 943	76.9	46.1	43.1	25.3	26.7	17.6	3.23	3.61
Midwest	1 726 509	37.6	4.1	24.0	110.5	2.2	458 637	78.6	51.8	55.5	37.2	15.9	11.2	3.46	3.87
East North Central	1 437 720	37.3	4.0	24.1	110.9	2.0	378 646	79.7	52.7	55.7	37.8	16.4	11.5	3.54	3.93
West North Central	288 789	38.9	4.8	23.5	108.2	3.4	79 991	73.5	47.3	54.3	34.6	13.7	9.8	3.07	3.58
South	6 767 021	33.7	6.6	26.5	99.6	2.0	1 911 556	79.9	48.8	59.4	37.4	14.7	8.9	3.41	3.81
South Atlantic	2 132 751	26.2	9.3	30.2	99.7	2.9	666 738	76.4	40.4	56.9	30.6	13.3	7.3	3.09	3.46
East South Central	95 285	32.1	6.1	26.3	108.7	7.9	27 987	72.4	42.0	56.1	32.6	12.2	7.6	2.81	3.32
West South Central	4 538 985	37.2	5.4	24.6	99.3	1.5	1 216 831	81.9	53.6	60.8	41.3	15.6	9.8	3.59	3.99
West	10 106 140	36.0	4.4	24.5	109.1	2.2	2 522 979	81.2	53.0	56.9	38.3	16.1	10.7	3.78	4.06
Mountain	1 991 732	37.0	5.7	25.2	100.6	2.0	577 233	77.6	49.4	54.8	34.5	16.4	11.3	3.23	3.67
Pacific	8 114 408	35.7	4.1	24.4	111.3	2.3	1 945 746	82.3	54.1	57.5	39.4	16.0	10.5	3.94	4.17
STATE															
New England	568 240	36.6	3.9	24.2	94.7	3.7	162 603	77.3	52.9	40.2	25.3	30.7	24.5	3.26	3.61
Maine	6 829	36.9	4.5	24.2	99.7	6.5	1 880	69.1	43.4	54.8	32.6	10.5	8.0	2.78	3.28
New Hampshire	11 333	34.8	3.7	25.3	107.9	4.6	3 255	73.7	46.9	56.3	35.5	12.0	8.8	2.98	3.40
Vermont	3 661	30.1	6.9	26.0	97.1	10.7	1 147	65.3	37.1	50.6	27.4	11.1	7.8	2.55	3.07
Massachusetts	287 549	37.3	3.6	23.7	94.5	3.9	81 649	76.7	53.5	37.4	23.9	32.9	26.5	3.29	3.64
Rhode Island	45 752	35.2	4.1	24.5	97.6	2.8	13 092	78.6	54.4	42.1	27.9	28.8	22.8	3.38	3.69
Connecticut	213 116	36.3	4.1	24.6	93.4	3.3	61 580	78.6	52.8	42.0	25.8	30.2	23.7	3.25	3.59
Middle Atlantic	3 186 149	30.9	5.6	27.7	93.0	3.0	945 943	76.9	46.1	43.1	25.3	26.7	17.6	3.23	3.61
New York	2 214 026	30.5	5.8	27.9	90.5	3.1	665 079	75.8	44.9	40.1	23.3	28.7	18.7	3.20	3.60
New Jersey	739 861	30.1	5.2	27.9	98.6	2.1	215 526	80.4	48.6	52.3	31.1	20.4	13.8	3.33	3.63
Pennsylvania	232 262	37.1	4.8	24.3	100.2	5.0	65 338	76.3	50.1	43.4	26.7	26.0	19.5	3.21	3.63
East North Central	1 437 720	37.3	4.0	24.1	110.9	2.0	378 646	79.7	52.7	55.7	37.8	16.4	11.5	3.54	3.93
Ohio	139 696	37.6	5.3	24.7	96.7	2.4	41 119	75.1	47.2	52.2	31.4	17.8	13.0	3.04	3.53
Indiana	98 788	37.1	5.3	24.6	103.5	2.9	27 571	77.6	48.7	67.7	36.0	14.5	10.0	3.22	3.68
Illinois	904 446	36.6	3.5	24.1	116.5	1.6	229 993	81.9	55.2	57.4	40.8	15.6	10.6	3.77	4.10
Michigan	201 596	38.3	5.0	24.0	101.2	2.6	55 798	76.1	48.0	52.5	32.1	18.1	13.1	3.16	3.61
Wisconsin	93 194	42.2	3.6	21.9	110.0	2.8	24 165	76.9	63.6	61.3	34.7	19.0	15.0	3.37	3.82
West North Central	288 789	38.9	4.8	23.5	108.2	3.4	79 991	73.5	47.3	54.3	34.6	13.7	9.8	3.07	3.58
Minnesota	53 884	41.8	3.6	22.2	107.7	3.5	14 039	71.4	48.0	49.0	32.1	16.7	12.8	3.06	3.58
Iowa	32 647	39.4	5.3	22.8	106.6	3.4	8 926	72.4	46.2	52.8	32.6	14.0	10.6	3.03	3.52
Missouri	61 702	34.5	6.2	26.0	101.8	3.7	10 444	70.8	41.4	53.8	31.2	12.4	7.9	2.86	3.42
North Dakota	4 665	44.8	2.9	20.4	101.2	5.4	1 138	74.3	52.0	59.4	40.9	12.2	9.4	3.08	3.60
South Dakota	5 252	44.1	4.9	20.7	98.8	4.7	1 321	71.8	49.3	52.4	35.0	14.3	11.1	2.96	3.52
Nebraska	36 969	39.8	4.8	23.2	109.8	2.4	10 517	73.6	47.8	53.6	34.0	13.8	10.2	3.10	3.61
Kansas	93 670	39.2	4.5	23.1	114.1	3.3	25 606	77.1	50.9	58.3	38.8	12.9	9.0	3.25	3.69
South Atlantic	2 132 751	26.2	9.3	30.2	99.7	2.9	666 738	76.4	40.4	56.9	30.6	13.3	7.3	3.09	3.46
Delaware	15 820	35.3	3.8	24.6	113.3	2.8	4 497	76.1	49.2	51.9	33.4	16.1	11.8	3.28	3.65
Maryland	125 102	29.0	4.4	27.4	101.3	2.5	34 404	77.6	46.5	56.7	35.5	13.3	8.0	3.35	3.61
District of Columbia	32 710	22.2	4.8	28.1	105.0	4.9	10 455	57.7	30.8	32.8	19.1	15.4	8.2	2.86	3.48
Virginia	160 288	29.3	3.3	26.3	112.5	3.8	43 756	76.1	47.0	56.8	36.9	11.8	7.4	3.32	3.58
West Virginia	8 489	30.5	9.8	29.2	97.6	5.9	2 785	69.4	36.0	55.4	28.4	10.9	6.0	2.62	3.19
North Carolina	76 726	31.2	3.7	24.5	142.6	9.0	21 533	74.2	46.3	57.3	36.1	10.6	7.5	3.04	3.40
South Carolina	30 551	31.9	4.1	25.1	118.0	9.3	8 586	74.2	45.8	57.5	35.6	11.9	7.9	2.96	3.40
Georgia	108 922	30.0	3.6	25.5	138.6	7.6	29 873	73.9	45.1	56.5	36.0	10.6	6.8	3.22	3.57
Florida	1 574 143	24.9	11.2	32.1	94.4	2.0	510 849	77.0	38.9	57.5	29.3	13.7	7.3	3.06	3.44
East South Central	95 285	32.1	6.1	26.3	108.7	7.9	27 987	72.4	42.0	56.1	32.6	12.2	7.6	2.81	3.32
Kentucky	21 984	32.3	5.7	25.8	113.6	11.9	6 220	72.5	43.9	58.0	35.0	10.8	7.1	2.78	3.31
Tennessee	32 741	31.4	5.4	26.2	112.7	7.4	9 649	71.9	41.3	56.0	32.3	11.8	7.4	2.80	3.29
Alabama	24 629	32.2	6.4	26.8	107.9	6.4	7 373	72.5	42.2	56.8	33.5	11.7	6.8	2.83	3.35
Mississippi	15 931	33.1	7.9	26.4	95.9	5.7	4 745	73.2	40.6	52.8	28.8	15.4	9.7	2.85	3.36
West South Central	4 538 985	37.2	5.4	24.6	99.3	1.5	1 216 831	81.9	53.6	60.8	41.3	15.6	9.8	3.59	3.99
Arkansas	19 876	37.5	4.7	23.7	112.5	4.2	5 350	74.4	46.6	57.6	36.7	11.5	7.7	3.09	3.57
Louisiana	93 044	28.8	8.5	29.5	96.2	4.1	29 990	72.7	40.2	54.7	30.8	13.3	7.3	2.89	3.44
Oklahoma	86 160	40.2	3.8	22.8	113.6	3.3	23 481	76.4	51.8	58.2	39.6	12.6	9.2	3.19	3.68
Texas	4 339 905	37.3	5.3	24.6	99.1	1.4	1 158 010	82.3	54.1	61.1	41.6	15.7	9.9	3.62	4.01
Mountain	1 991 732	37.0	5.7	25.2	100.6	2.0	577 233	77.6	49.4	54.8	34.5	16.4	11.3	3.23	3.67
Montana	12 174	42.0	4.7	22.6	102.0	3.7	3 374	71.2	46.5	51.0	31.1	15.4	12.2	2.85	3.39
Idaho	52 927	42.5	3.0	21.7	130.6	3.3	13 464	79.3	56.0	60.7	43.7	11.7	9.0	3.53	3.93
Wyoming	25 751	40.3	5.5	24.1	101.8	2.0	7 662	75.1	49.0	55.3	35.0	14.3	10.7	2.98	3.48
Colorado	424 302	36.0	5.7	25.9	99.4	2.2	130 704	75.0	47.0	51.5	31.1	17.9	12.8	3.02	3.50
New Mexico	579 224	35.1	7.3	26.9	95.0	1.5	178 709	77.9	47.9	55.9	33.9	15.9	10.4	3.10	3.53
Arizona	688 338	38.6	5.1	24.0	100.6	2.0	184 942	79.8	52.3	55.8	36.5	17.1	11.8	3.49	3.89
Utah	84 597	41.5	4.0	22.3	105.7	2.9	22 720	77.7	52.9	55.6	37.1	16.4	12.6	3.27	3.70
Nevada	124 419	34.0	4.3	25.6	119.4	1.5	35 658	74.3	46.0	54.2	34.5	11.8	7.8	3.26	3.67
Pacific	8 114 408	35.7	4.1	24.4	111.3	2.3	1 945 746	82.3	54.1	57.5	39.4	16.0	10.5	3.94	4.17
Washington	214 570	40.2	2.9	22.6	120.4	3.5	55 706	75.5	51.9	54.2	37.2	13.8	10.7	3.38	3.82
Oregon	112 707	38.8	3.5	23.0	134.5	4.8	28 204	74.7	50.4	53.5	36.4	12.6	9.5	3.41	3.79
California	7 687 938	35.6	4.1	24.5	110.8	2.2	1 836 989	82.7	54.3	57.6	39.6	16.1	10.5	3.97	4.19
Alaska	17 803	37.9	1.5	24.0	121.8	7.9	4 671	72.7	51.4	54.8	38.6	11.6	9.2	3.05	3.52
Hawaii	81 390	38.3	5.2	24.4	103.9	3.5	20 176	78.6	47.9	57.2	34.7	15.8	10.6	3.39	3.76

Table 259. Summary of General Characteristics of White, Not of Hispanic Origin Persons and Households: 1990

[For definitions of terms and meanings of symbols, see text]

United States Region and Division State	All White, not of Hispanic origin persons						All households with a White, not of Hispanic origin householder								
		Percent of all persons			Persons 18 years and over—			Family households as a percent of all households		Married-couple family		Female householder, no husband present		Persons per—	
	Total	Under 18 years	65 years and over	Median age	Males per 100 females	Percent in group quarters	Total	Total	With own children under 18	Total	With own children under 18	Total	With own children under 18	Household	Family
United States	188 128 296	23.3	14.4	34.9	92.0	2.5	73 633 749	69.2	31.1	57.8	25.4	8.6	4.5	2.51	3.03
REGION AND DIVISION															
Northeast	40 366 823	21.7	15.6	35.8	89.5	2.8	15 596 132	68.7	29.4	56.5	24.3	9.2	4.1	2.53	3.08
New England	11 765 610	22.0	14.4	34.8	89.9	3.2	4 505 486	68.5	30.4	55.9	24.7	9.6	4.7	2.54	3.07
Middle Atlantic	28 601 213	21.7	16.0	36.2	89.3	2.6	11 090 646	68.7	29.0	56.7	24.2	9.0	3.8	2.52	3.08
Midwest	51 175 270	24.9	14.0	34.0	91.2	2.6	19 628 689	70.1	33.0	58.9	27.0	8.5	4.8	2.55	3.08
East North Central	35 074 700	24.6	13.7	34.1	91.1	2.4	13 391 969	70.5	32.9	58.8	26.8	8.9	4.8	2.57	3.09
West North Central	16 100 570	25.5	14.6	33.9	91.4	3.0	6 236 720	69.3	33.3	59.1	27.4	7.7	4.7	2.52	3.06
South	61 359 202	23.0	14.4	35.0	92.2	2.5	24 265 967	70.6	31.3	59.7	25.9	8.3	4.3	2.48	2.97
South Atlantic	31 820 812	21.8	15.3	35.6	92.6	2.5	12 695 448	69.9	29.6	59.1	24.5	8.1	4.0	2.45	2.93
East South Central	11 990 018	24.1	13.5	34.4	90.8	2.3	4 619 625	73.5	33.8	61.8	28.1	9.1	4.6	2.54	3.01
West South Central	17 548 372	24.3	13.4	34.2	92.5	2.4	6 950 894	70.0	32.6	59.4	26.9	8.1	4.5	2.48	3.01
West	35 227 001	23.3	13.6	34.8	95.7	2.4	14 142 961	66.1	29.9	54.5	23.5	8.5	4.9	2.47	3.00
Mountain	10 642 155	26.1	12.7	33.5	95.4	2.1	4 150 892	68.2	32.7	57.2	26.2	8.2	5.1	2.54	3.09
Pacific	24 584 846	22.1	13.9	35.3	95.9	2.5	9 992 069	65.2	28.8	53.3	22.4	8.7	4.9	2.44	2.97
STATE															
New England	11 765 610	22.0	14.4	34.8	89.9	3.2	4 505 486	68.5	30.4	55.9	24.7	9.6	4.7	2.54	3.07
Maine	1 203 357	25.0	13.5	34.1	91.3	2.9	458 677	70.6	34.5	58.2	27.1	9.5	5.9	2.55	3.03
New Hampshire	1 079 484	24.9	11.5	33.0	93.1	2.8	402 540	71.2	35.3	59.7	28.9	8.4	4.9	2.61	3.08
Vermont	552 184	25.3	11.9	33.2	92.6	3.7	207 630	68.9	35.0	56.6	27.4	9.1	5.8	2.57	3.06
Massachusetts	5 280 292	21.0	14.8	34.8	88.5	3.4	2 024 735	66.9	29.0	53.6	23.3	10.3	4.8	2.53	3.10
Rhode Island	896 109	21.1	16.2	35.2	87.9	3.7	346 438	67.9	29.2	54.6	23.3	10.3	5.0	2.49	3.05
Connecticut	2 754 184	20.9	15.2	36.1	91.2	2.9	1 065 466	69.7	29.1	58.2	24.5	8.7	3.7	2.52	3.03
Middle Atlantic	28 601 213	21.7	16.0	36.2	89.3	2.6	11 090 646	68.7	29.0	56.7	24.2	9.0	3.8	2.52	3.08
New York	12 460 189	21.2	15.9	36.2	89.5	2.8	4 892 998	66.2	27.9	54.2	23.1	8.9	3.8	2.49	3.09
New Jersey	5 718 966	21.1	15.8	36.7	90.2	1.9	2 181 225	71.4	29.2	59.5	25.1	8.9	3.3	2.58	3.09
Pennsylvania	10 422 058	22.5	16.3	35.9	88.7	2.7	4 016 423	70.4	30.2	58.3	25.0	9.1	4.1	2.53	3.06
East North Central	35 074 700	24.6	13.7	34.1	91.1	2.4	13 391 969	70.5	32.9	58.8	26.8	8.9	4.8	2.57	3.09
Ohio	9 444 622	24.8	13.6	34.0	89.9	2.2	3 598 377	71.2	33.2	59.0	26.9	9.4	5.1	2.57	3.09
Indiana	4 965 242	25.4	13.1	33.5	90.8	2.4	1 874 351	71.8	34.4	60.2	28.0	8.9	5.1	2.58	3.08
Illinois	8 550 208	23.2	14.7	35.0	90.7	2.5	3 340 992	68.5	30.7	57.4	25.6	8.3	4.0	2.51	3.07
Michigan	7 649 951	25.0	12.8	33.6	92.1	2.1	2 878 531	71.6	33.8	59.1	27.1	9.6	5.4	2.62	3.11
Wisconsin	4 464 677	25.0	14.2	33.9	92.7	2.7	1 699 718	69.7	33.2	59.0	27.3	7.9	4.6	2.57	3.09
West North Central	16 100 570	25.5	14.6	33.9	91.4	3.0	6 236 720	69.3	33.3	59.1	27.4	7.7	4.7	2.52	3.06
Minnesota	4 101 266	25.7	13.1	33.1	92.8	2.6	1 572 087	68.5	34.0	58.0	28.0	7.8	4.8	2.56	3.10
Iowa	2 663 840	25.4	15.8	34.5	89.9	3.5	1 031 485	69.6	32.9	59.7	27.0	7.6	4.8	2.50	3.04
Missouri	4 448 465	24.7	14.9	34.4	89.8	2.7	1 735 995	70.0	32.5	59.1	26.6	8.3	4.7	2.50	3.03
North Dakota	601 592	26.5	14.9	33.2	97.1	3.7	230 846	68.7	34.5	59.7	29.3	6.5	4.2	2.52	3.10
South Dakota	634 788	26.9	15.7	33.7	93.8	3.6	244 158	69.1	34.3	60.0	28.7	6.7	4.4	2.52	3.09
Nebraska	1 460 095	26.3	14.8	33.7	91.3	2.9	565 851	68.9	33.7	59.3	28.1	7.3	4.5	2.52	3.09
Kansas	2 190 524	25.6	14.8	34.0	91.9	3.1	856 298	69.5	33.2	59.7	27.4	7.4	4.6	2.49	3.03
South Atlantic	31 820 812	21.8	15.3	35.6	92.6	2.5	12 695 448	69.9	29.6	59.1	24.5	8.1	4.0	2.45	2.93
Delaware	528 092	22.6	13.4	34.2	91.6	2.7	202 842	70.8	31.2	59.4	25.8	8.5	4.2	2.54	3.02
Maryland	3 326 109	22.4	12.8	34.8	93.0	2.1	1 274 425	70.8	31.3	59.2	26.1	8.5	4.0	2.57	3.04
District of Columbia	166 131	9.0	14.0	35.1	93.6	11.3	83 580	31.7	10.7	26.6	9.0	3.7	1.3	1.80	2.65
Virginia	4 701 650	22.8	11.6	33.9	94.7	2.9	1 813 597	70.7	32.4	60.2	27.3	7.9	3.9	2.53	3.00
West Virginia	1 718 896	24.5	15.1	35.6	88.5	1.9	661 849	72.9	34.0	59.8	27.4	10.2	5.2	2.55	3.04
North Carolina	4 971 127	22.0	13.2	34.8	93.0	3.1	1 966 277	71.9	31.4	61.2	26.2	8.1	4.0	2.46	2.92
South Carolina	2 390 056	23.2	12.6	34.2	94.1	3.2	918 437	73.2	33.0	62.1	27.7	8.3	4.1	2.53	2.98
Georgia	4 543 425	24.1	11.3	33.5	93.4	2.2	1 740 452	72.4	34.0	61.5	28.6	8.3	4.2	2.56	3.03
Florida	9 475 326	19.3	21.7	39.4	91.2	2.1	4 033 989	66.7	24.0	56.4	19.1	7.6	3.8	2.30	2.78
East South Central	11 990 018	24.1	13.5	34.4	90.8	2.3	4 619 625	73.5	33.8	61.8	28.1	9.1	4.6	2.54	3.01
Kentucky	3 378 022	25.4	13.0	33.5	90.4	2.4	1 274 678	74.0	35.8	61.1	29.1	10.1	5.5	2.59	3.06
Tennessee	4 027 631	23.4	13.5	34.8	90.7	2.4	1 569 905	73.0	32.7	61.1	27.0	9.2	4.6	2.51	2.98
Alabama	2 960 167	23.5	13.9	35.0	91.0	2.0	1 154 468	73.4	32.9	62.8	28.0	8.2	3.9	2.52	2.99
Mississippi	1 624 198	24.5	14.1	34.6	91.3	2.6	620 574	73.9	34.3	63.0	29.1	8.3	4.1	2.55	3.03
West South Central	17 548 372	24.3	13.4	34.2	92.5	2.4	6 950 894	70.0	32.6	59.4	26.9	8.1	4.5	2.48	3.01
Arkansas	1 933 082	24.3	15.8	35.5	90.5	2.3	757 117	73.4	32.9	62.9	27.3	8.0	4.4	2.50	2.97
Louisiana	2 776 022	25.8	12.5	33.2	92.0	2.3	1 048 479	72.0	35.2	60.5	29.4	8.7	4.6	2.59	3.11
Oklahoma	2 547 588	24.4	14.9	35.0	90.8	2.4	1 017 927	70.6	32.9	59.6	26.5	8.5	5.1	2.47	2.99
Texas	10 291 680	23.9	12.8	34.1	93.5	2.4	4 127 371	68.7	31.9	58.4	26.4	7.8	4.4	2.46	3.00
Mountain	10 642 155	26.1	12.7	33.5	95.4	2.1	4 150 892	68.2	32.7	57.2	26.2	8.2	5.1	2.54	3.09
Montana	733 878	26.6	14.1	34.8	95.2	2.9	288 053	68.7	33.7	58.3	27.0	7.7	5.2	2.49	3.04
Idaho	928 661	29.9	12.7	32.4	94.8	2.0	339 756	72.7	37.1	62.4	30.3	7.7	5.2	2.69	3.20
Wyoming	412 711	29.0	10.9	32.8	97.9	2.2	156 722	70.7	37.6	60.2	30.5	7.7	5.5	2.60	3.13
Colorado	2 658 945	24.2	11.0	33.9	95.0	2.0	1 079 056	65.7	31.9	54.9	25.4	8.1	5.1	2.43	3.00
New Mexico	764 164	23.3	14.5	36.2	93.8	2.0	317 576	67.9	30.8	57.0	24.3	8.1	4.9	2.42	2.95
Arizona	2 626 185	22.3	16.2	35.6	94.0	2.1	1 084 721	66.3	27.9	55.3	21.7	8.2	4.8	2.40	2.93
Utah	1 571 254	36.1	9.1	26.7	94.3	1.5	496 808	76.5	44.7	65.5	37.7	8.6	5.8	3.14	3.66
Nevada	946 357	22.6	12.2	35.2	102.7	1.8	388 200	64.8	28.4	52.3	21.6	8.7	5.0	2.42	2.95
Pacific	24 584 846	22.1	13.9	35.3	95.9	2.5	9 992 069	65.2	28.8	53.3	22.4	8.7	4.9	2.44	2.97
Washington	4 221 622	24.5	12.9	34.3	95.2	2.3	1 684 243	67.1	31.9	55.6	24.8	8.6	5.5	2.48	3.00
Oregon	2 579 732	24.5	14.7	35.6	92.5	2.1	1 028 739	67.6	31.2	56.1	23.9	8.8	5.5	2.48	2.98
California	17 029 126	20.9	14.4	35.7	95.7	2.5	6 995 757	64.2	27.3	52.2	21.3	8.7	4.6	2.42	2.95
Alaska	406 722	28.9	4.1	30.8	116.7	3.3	150 833	69.3	41.3	58.1	33.2	7.5	5.7	2.69	3.21
Hawaii	347 644	22.2	9.5	32.8	118.0	5.5	132 497	66.7	32.6	55.7	26.4	7.6	4.6	2.61	3.09

U.S. Department of Commerce
Economics and Statistics Administration
BUREAU OF THE CENSUS

CENSUS '90

1990 CP-2-1

1990 Census of Population

**Social and Economic
Characteristics**

United States

Table 1. Summary of Social Characteristics: 1990

[Data based on sample and subject to sampling variability, see text. For definitions of terms and meanings of symbols, see text]

United States Urban and Rural and Size of Place Inside and Outside Metropolitan Area	All persons		Foreign born persons—Percent entered 1980 to 1990	Native persons—Percent born in State of residence	Persons 5 years and over				Persons enrolled in elementary or high school—Percent in private school	Persons 16 to 19 years—Percent not enrolled in school and not high school graduate	Persons 18 to 24 years—Percent enrolled in college	Persons 25 years and over		Persons under 18 years—Percent living with two parents	Children ever born per 1,000 women 35 to 44 years
	Total	Percent foreign born			Percent living in different house in 1985	Percent living in different State or abroad in 1985	Percent who speak a language other than English at home Total	And do not speak English "very well"				Percent high school graduate or higher	Percent with bachelor's degree or higher		
United States	248 709 873	7.9	43.8	67.1	46.7	11.6	13.8	6.1	9.8	11.2	34.4	75.2	20.3	71.8	1 960
URBAN AND RURAL AND SIZE OF PLACE															
Urban	187 051 543	9.9	44.7	64.6	49.2	12.8	16.4	7.3	11.2	11.3	37.1	76.6	22.6	68.9	1 904
Inside urbanized area	158 258 042	11.0	45.0	63.5	49.1	13.0	17.6	8.0	12.2	11.4	36.6	77.4	23.7	68.6	1 868
Central place	78 847 231	12.5	48.8	64.5	50.5	13.1	21.0	10.0	12.7	13.4	38.3	73.1	21.9	60.0	1 884
Urban fringe	79 410 811	9.6	40.2	62.6	47.6	12.9	14.4	6.0	11.6	9.3	34.5	81.6	25.5	77.2	1 854
Outside urbanized area	28 793 501	3.6	39.8	69.8	49.7	11.7	9.5	3.8	5.9	10.6	39.8	71.8	16.0	70.1	2 122
Place of 10,000 or more	13 826 325	4.1	41.9	68.7	52.4	12.5	10.1	4.1	6.4	10.1	46.7	73.0	17.7	69.2	2 093
Place of 2,500 to 9,999	14 967 176	3.2	37.2	70.9	47.3	10.9	8.9	3.5	5.5	11.2	31.3	70.8	14.6	70.8	2 149
Rural	61 658 330	2.0	30.5	74.3	39.3	7.9	6.0	2.2	6.3	11.0	23.4	71.2	13.6	79.9	2 128
Place of 1,000 to 2,499	7 047 131	2.4	33.0	74.2	41.9	8.4	7.2	2.7	4.6	11.2	24.1	70.0	13.1	73.7	2 172
Place of less than 1,000	3 802 263	1.1	29.3	77.8	37.4	6.8	5.8	2.0	4.0	10.5	18.8	67.6	9.9	74.7	2 300
Other rural	50 808 936	2.1	30.2	74.0	39.0	7.9	5.9	2.2	6.7	11.0	23.6	71.6	13.9	81.1	2 112
Rural farm	3 871 583	1.5	28.6	82.9	20.5	2.9	6.5	2.6	9.7	9.0	26.7	73.7	13.2	89.6	2 403
INSIDE AND OUTSIDE METROPOLITAN AREA															
Inside metropolitan area	192 726 330	9.7	44.3	65.0	48.0	12.3	15.9	7.1	11.3	11.2	35.2	77.0	22.5	70.9	1 901
In central city	77 844 025	12.5	48.9	64.7	50.3	13.0	21.0	10.1	12.8	13.4	38.2	73.0	21.9	59.8	1 881
Not in central city	114 882 305	7.8	39.4	65.3	46.4	11.8	12.4	5.1	10.3	9.7	32.7	79.6	22.8	78.1	1 914
Urban	88 439 931	9.2	40.3	63.1	48.1	12.8	14.2	5.9	11.1	9.5	34.3	80.8	24.6	76.8	1 878
Inside urbanized area	79 754 528	9.7	40.3	62.7	47.8	12.9	14.5	6.0	11.6	9.3	34.3	81.5	25.5	77.1	1 856
Outside urbanized area	8 685 403	5.2	40.3	67.1	50.8	12.2	11.4	4.8	6.4	11.3	33.7	74.0	16.8	73.7	2 098
Rural	26 442 374	2.8	30.3	72.1	40.9	8.3	6.6	2.5	7.9	10.1	26.5	75.6	16.8	82.3	2 030
Outside metropolitan area	55 983 543	2.0	35.3	73.7	42.3	9.2	6.7	2.5	5.4	11.1	31.1	69.2	12.9	74.7	2 183
Urban	20 850 368	3.0	39.0	70.0	49.6	12.0	8.5	3.2	5.7	10.3	42.9	71.3	16.0	68.6	2 127
Inside urbanized area	1 520 613	3.9	35.8	56.0	55.8	19.0	7.1	2.3	6.3	8.8	52.1	78.7	21.9	71.0	1 986
Outside urbanized area	19 329 755	2.9	39.3	71.0	49.1	11.4	8.6	3.3	5.7	10.4	42.0	70.8	15.6	68.4	2 139
Place of 10,000 or more	9 873 735	3.4	41.9	69.7	51.8	12.4	9.2	3.6	6.4	9.5	49.9	72.6	17.5	68.2	2 100
Place of 2,500 to 9,999	9 456 020	2.4	35.5	72.5	46.4	10.4	8.1	3.0	5.0	11.5	30.5	68.9	13.6	68.6	2 179
Rural	35 133 175	1.4	30.8	75.9	38.0	7.6	5.6	2.0	5.2	11.7	21.0	67.9	11.1	78.1	2 214

Table 2. Summary of Labor Force and Commuting Characteristics: 1990

[Data based on sample and subject to sampling variability, see text. For definitions of terms and meanings of symbols, see text]

United States Urban and Rural and Size of Place Inside and Outside Metropolitan Area	Persons 16 years and over—Percent in labor force				Own children under 6 years in families and subfamilies		Civilian labor force—Percent unemployed	Employed persons 16 years and over					Workers 16 years and over		
			Female		Living with two parents—Percent with both parents in labor force	Living with one parent—Percent with parent in labor force		Percent at work 35 or more hours in reference week			Percent government workers (local, State, or Federal)	Percent in manufacturing industries	Percent in carpools	Percent using public transportation	Mean travel time to work (minutes)
	Total	Male	Total	With own children under 6 years				Total	Male	Female					
United States --------------	65.3	74.4	56.8	59.7	55.5	60.0	6.3	77.3	84.5	68.7	15.2	17.7	13.4	5.3	22.3
URBAN AND RURAL AND SIZE OF PLACE															
Urban ----------------------	65.9	75.1	57.6	59.6	55.6	59.2	6.4	77.3	84.3	69.3	15.3	16.5	12.9	6.7	22.2
Inside urbanized area ----------------	66.8	75.9	58.5	59.4	55.3	58.9	6.3	77.7	84.5	69.9	15.0	16.0	12.7	7.7	23.0
Central place -----------------	64.7	73.3	57.0	58.2	55.2	54.9	7.8	77.1	82.8	70.7	16.3	15.1	13.4	11.7	22.4
Urban fringe ------------------	68.9	78.4	60.1	60.5	55.4	67.0	4.9	78.3	86.1	69.3	13.8	16.9	12.0	4.0	23.6
Outside urbanized area --------------	60.8	70.4	52.5	61.2	57.1	60.8	7.1	74.7	82.7	65.4	17.3	19.3	14.6	.9	17.2
Place of 10,000 or more-----------	61.6	70.7	53.5	61.5	57.4	60.6	7.1	73.8	81.7	64.9	17.9	18.7	14.1	1.0	16.2
Place of 2,500 to 9,999-----------	60.2	70.1	51.5	60.9	56.8	61.0	7.1	75.5	83.7	65.9	16.6	19.8	15.1	.8	18.1
Rural-----------------------	63.3	72.6	54.2	59.9	55.2	64.1	6.0	77.3	85.3	66.8	14.8	21.5	14.7	.6	23.0
Place of 1,000 to 2,499-----------	59.6	69.6	50.9	61.6	57.6	61.8	6.6	76.1	84.6	66.0	16.4	20.8	15.3	.6	19.8
Place of less than 1,000-----------	58.3	68.4	49.4	61.7	57.8	61.0	7.2	75.8	84.3	65.4	17.1	21.5	16.1	.4	20.6
Other rural ------------------	64.2	73.3	55.1	59.6	54.7	65.0	5.8	77.5	85.5	67.0	14.4	21.6	14.6	.6	23.6
Rural farm-----------------------	65.2	77.4	52.3	61.3	56.4	67.4	3.1	75.4	82.8	63.6	12.3	12.9	10.2	.4	21.0
INSIDE AND OUTSIDE METROPOLITAN AREA															
Inside metropolitan area --------------	66.7	75.8	58.2	59.4	55.2	59.7	6.1	77.7	84.8	69.4	14.9	16.8	12.9	6.5	23.2
In central city -----------------	64.7	73.3	57.0	58.2	55.2	54.8	7.8	77.1	82.8	70.7	16.3	15.1	13.3	11.8	22.3
Not in central city -----------------	68.0	77.5	59.1	60.2	55.2	66.5	5.0	78.1	86.0	68.6	13.9	17.9	12.6	3.1	23.7
Urban ----------------------	68.4	78.0	59.5	60.3	55.4	66.2	5.0	78.2	85.9	69.1	13.9	17.1	12.4	3.8	23.5
Inside urbanized area ----------	68.9	78.4	60.1	60.4	55.4	66.8	4.9	78.4	86.1	69.3	13.8	16.9	12.1	4.0	23.7
Outside urbanized area ----------	63.8	74.0	54.5	59.7	55.1	62.4	6.4	76.5	84.7	66.8	15.5	19.2	15.2	1.0	21.6
Rural-----------------------	66.7	75.9	57.5	59.6	54.8	67.5	5.1	77.8	86.2	66.7	13.9	20.7	13.4	.7	24.7
Outside metropolitan area --------------	60.4	69.6	51.8	60.8	56.4	61.4	6.9	75.7	83.5	66.0	16.5	21.0	15.2	.6	19.2
Urban ----------------------	59.7	68.8	51.8	61.9	58.1	60.5	7.3	73.7	81.7	64.8	18.1	19.0	14.2	.9	15.3
Inside urbanized area ----------	62.3	70.2	55.0	62.3	57.7	62.1	6.3	72.5	80.1	64.0	18.1	14.9	12.6	1.7	17.0
Outside urbanized area ----------	59.5	68.6	51.5	61.9	58.1	60.3	7.4	73.8	81.8	64.8	18.1	19.3	14.3	.8	15.1
Place of 10,000 or more--------	60.6	69.3	52.9	61.9	58.0	60.2	7.3	72.7	80.6	63.9	18.7	18.6	13.6	1.0	14.6
Place of 2,500 to 9,999--------	58.3	67.9	50.0	61.9	58.3	60.5	7.5	75.0	83.1	65.8	17.4	20.2	15.1	.6	15.8
Rural-----------------------	60.8	70.1	51.8	60.1	55.5	62.2	6.7	76.9	84.6	66.8	15.5	22.2	15.8	.5	21.5

Table 3. **Summary of Occupation, Income, and Poverty Characteristics: 1990**

[Data based on sample and subject to sampling variability, see text. For definitions of terms and meanings of symbols, see text]

United States Urban and Rural and Size of Place Inside and Outside Metropolitan Area	Percent of employed persons 16 years and over						Median income in 1989 (dollars)			Median income in 1989 of year-round full-time workers (dollars)		Income in 1989 below poverty level			
	Manageri-al and profes-sional specialty occupa-tions	Technical, sales, and adminis-trative support occupa-tions	Service occupa-tions	Farming, forestry, and fish-ing occu-pations	Precision produc-tion, craft, and repair oc-cupations	Opera-tors, fab-ricators, and labor-ers	House-holds	Families	Per capita income in 1989 (dollars)	Male	Female	Percent of persons for whom poverty status is determined			Percent of families
												All ages	Related children under 18 years	65 years and over	
United States _____	26.4	31.7	13.2	2.5	11.3	14.9	30 056	35 225	14 420	29 237	19 570	13.1	17.9	12.8	10.0
URBAN AND RURAL AND SIZE OF PLACE															
Urban _____	28.3	33.4	13.5	1.2	10.3	13.3	30 782	36 672	15 084	30 302	20 461	13.2	18.5	11.6	9.9
Inside urbanized area _____	29.1	34.1	13.2	1.0	10.0	12.6	32 002	38 233	15 707	30 855	21 042	12.6	17.8	10.8	9.5
Central place _____	27.4	33.1	15.3	1.1	9.5	13.7	26 784	32 146	13 838	27 172	20 122	17.9	26.1	13.9	14.0
Urban fringe _____	30.7	35.1	11.3	1.0	10.5	11.5	37 944	43 680	17 562	33 374	21 840	7.3	9.8	7.6	5.3
Outside urbanized area _____	23.3	29.2	15.5	2.4	11.9	17.8	23 859	29 645	11 661	25 853	16 347	16.6	21.9	15.4	12.5
Place of 10,000 or more_____	24.4	30.0	15.7	2.0	11.1	16.7	23 989	30 149	11 724	25 965	16 534	17.1	22.1	14.7	12.6
Place of 2,500 to 9,999 _____	22.2	28.4	15.4	2.7	12.5	18.8	23 741	29 192	11 602	25 751	16 167	16.1	21.7	15.9	12.4
Rural _____	20.4	26.3	12.3	6.4	14.7	19.9	27 460	31 463	12 408	26 338	16 473	13.0	16.3	16.3	10.1
Place of 1,000 to 2,499 _____	20.8	27.1	15.1	3.3	13.7	20.1	23 503	28 872	11 393	25 356	15 867	15.2	20.1	16.6	11.7
Place of less than 1,000 _____	17.6	24.5	15.7	4.7	14.3	23.3	20 917	25 785	10 128	22 559	14 672	17.1	21.8	19.4	13.2
Other rural_____	20.5	26.4	11.7	7.0	14.8	19.7	28 849	32 217	12 719	26 686	16 676	12.3	15.4	15.8	9.6
Rural farm_____	15.0	18.7	8.1	36.0	8.8	13.4	29 505	31 971	13 672	23 341	15 189	11.6	16.4	10.1	9.0
INSIDE AND OUTSIDE METROPOLITAN AREA															
Inside metropolitan area _____	28.1	33.3	13.0	1.5	10.8	13.4	32 086	37 896	15 442	30 707	20 660	12.1	16.8	11.0	9.0
In central city _____	27.4	33.1	15.3	1.1	9.4	13.8	26 727	32 076	13 839	27 121	20 114	18.0	26.2	14.0	14.1
Not in central city _____	28.5	33.4	11.5	1.8	11.6	13.1	36 314	41 407	16 527	32 073	21 008	8.1	10.7	8.9	6.0
Urban _____	30.0	34.6	11.6	1.1	10.7	11.9	37 007	42 550	17 097	32 748	21 576	7.8	10.6	8.1	5.7
Inside urbanized area _____	30.6	35.1	11.3	1.0	10.5	11.5	38 003	43 726	17 550	33 433	21 861	7.3	9.8	7.6	5.3
Outside urbanized area _____	23.7	30.2	14.0	2.9	12.6	16.6	28 702	33 823	12 934	28 593	17 953	12.6	16.8	12.2	9.4
Rural _____	23.5	29.0	11.3	4.3	14.8	17.2	33 814	37 552	14 624	30 300	18 473	8.9	11.1	12.0	6.7
Outside metropolitan area _____	19.8	25.8	14.2	6.0	13.4	20.7	23 075	27 591	10 904	23 873	15 307	16.8	21.6	17.8	13.0
Urban _____	23.3	28.8	16.2	2.1	11.5	18.1	22 184	27 923	11 200	24 727	15 710	18.2	23.9	16.4	13.7
Inside urbanized area _____	27.2	31.4	15.3	1.7	10.7	13.8	26 132	31 973	12 967	26 304	17 044	15.1	18.3	11.2	10.1
Outside urbanized area _____	23.0	28.6	16.3	2.2	11.5	18.4	21 925	27 599	11 061	24 577	15 594	18.4	24.3	16.7	14.0
Place of 10,000 or more_____	24.3	29.7	16.3	1.8	10.8	17.0	22 483	28 681	11 323	25 061	15 991	18.5	23.8	15.6	13.6
Place of 2,500 to 9,999 _____	21.5	27.4	16.3	2.6	12.3	19.9	21 365	26 712	10 786	24 043	15 162	18.4	24.8	17.8	14.4
Rural _____	17.8	24.1	13.1	8.2	14.6	22.2	23 648	27 430	10 729	23 412	15 063	16.0	20.3	18.7	12.6

Table 40. Age, Sex, Ability to Speak English, and Disability by Race and Hispanic Origin: 1990

[Data based on sample and subject to sampling variability, see text. For definitions of terms and meanings of symbols, see text]

United States	All persons	Race White	Race Black	Race American Indian, Eskimo, or Aleut	Race Asian or Pacific Islander	Race Other race	Hispanic origin (of any race)	White, not of Hispanic origin
AGE AND SEX								
All persons	248 709 873	199 827 064	29 930 524	2 015 143	7 226 986	9 710 156	21 900 089	188 424 773
Under 3 years	10 924 579	8 137 382	1 662 313	119 287	341 957	663 640	1 415 149	7 436 399
3 and 4 years	7 339 517	5 508 560	1 092 604	78 509	232 476	427 368	915 203	5 054 028
5 to 9 years	18 126 901	13 669 939	2 670 822	197 456	587 783	1 000 901	2 174 463	12 573 070
10 to 14 years	17 151 134	12 877 425	2 619 309	188 374	551 483	914 543	1 987 956	11 872 138
15 to 17 years	10 064 413	7 560 166	1 521 906	107 015	338 729	536 597	1 144 623	6 990 196
18 and 19 years	7 589 506	5 753 714	1 106 299	73 262	251 940	404 291	837 275	5 349 956
20 to 24 years	18 645 387	14 296 570	2 496 037	171 619	606 252	1 074 909	2 198 627	13 250 338
25 to 29 years	21 286 297	16 610 575	2 701 217	186 025	688 392	1 100 088	2 310 503	15 480 462
30 to 34 years	22 180 737	17 605 327	2 712 045	181 313	725 669	956 383	2 069 776	16 567 169
35 to 39 years	19 939 682	16 069 470	2 312 577	158 133	674 166	725 336	1 636 937	15 223 585
40 to 44 years	17 679 734	14 539 053	1 884 046	133 719	583 890	539 026	1 281 723	13 847 443
45 to 49 years	13 977 898	11 639 594	1 434 798	102 852	417 981	382 673	949 236	11 109 495
50 to 54 years	11 488 063	9 584 468	1 220 162	80 866	318 170	284 397	756 325	9 140 642
55 to 59 years	10 484 988	8 921 892	1 028 282	64 950	250 248	219 616	627 235	8 536 844
60 to 64 years	10 635 762	9 222 857	967 266	54 040	215 276	176 323	538 862	8 879 428
65 to 74 years	18 218 481	16 138 327	1 511 617	74 320	295 142	199 075	671 012	15 689 368
75 years and over	12 976 794	11 691 745	989 224	43 403	147 432	104 990	385 184	11 424 212
Female	127 537 494	102 305 531	15 817 802	1 016 503	3 701 295	4 696 363	10 771 487	96 623 292
Under 3 years	5 328 627	3 956 694	819 749	58 922	167 228	326 034	693 275	3 613 168
3 and 4 years	3 585 008	2 681 445	543 176	38 017	113 137	209 233	449 551	2 457 989
5 to 9 years	8 836 345	6 644 942	1 317 751	95 616	287 829	490 207	1 065 067	6 107 041
10 to 14 years	8 363 399	6 263 736	1 294 183	91 608	269 165	444 707	967 764	5 773 647
15 to 17 years	4 874 273	3 653 577	746 313	51 737	164 847	257 799	547 169	3 382 174
18 and 19 years	3 719 669	2 819 770	555 371	35 182	121 929	187 417	390 094	2 630 696
20 to 24 years	9 176 002	7 033 354	1 283 452	82 718	294 485	481 993	1 001 048	6 550 571
25 to 29 years	10 614 778	8 245 038	1 423 571	93 206	348 529	504 434	1 081 233	7 707 614
30 to 34 years	11 142 783	8 772 495	1 448 810	93 440	376 686	451 352	994 960	8 266 185
35 to 39 years	10 061 512	8 028 495	1 241 709	81 726	358 888	350 694	810 547	7 601 326
40 to 44 years	8 950 913	7 289 209	1 013 806	68 479	313 599	265 820	646 454	6 934 813
45 to 49 years	7 118 795	5 878 242	779 837	52 636	216 538	191 542	485 743	5 603 315
50 to 54 years	5 920 436	4 897 954	670 976	41 593	163 257	146 656	395 396	4 664 698
55 to 59 years	5 481 587	4 618 879	574 781	34 377	137 951	115 599	331 414	4 415 272
60 to 64 years	5 682 160	4 884 968	551 034	28 618	122 240	95 300	291 234	4 699 786
65 to 74 years	10 225 733	9 005 443	899 776	41 334	165 103	114 077	381 222	8 751 993
75 years and over	8 455 474	7 631 290	653 507	27 294	79 884	63 499	239 316	7 463 004
Median age for all persons	33.0	34.4	28.3	26.9	30.1	24.2	25.6	34.9
Male	31.8	33.2	26.7	25.9	29.0	24.0	25.0	33.7
Female	34.2	35.7	29.7	27.9	31.1	24.5	26.3	36.2
ABILITY TO SPEAK ENGLISH								
Persons 5 years and over	230 445 777	186 181 122	27 175 607	1 817 347	6 652 553	8 619 148	19 569 737	175 934 346
Speak a language other than English	31 844 979	17 693 779	1 707 777	432 761	4 878 530	7 132 132	15 216 298	10 084 653
5 to 17 years	6 322 934	3 107 817	397 181	94 960	896 940	1 826 036	3 596 267	1 434 470
18 to 64 years	21 707 874	11 543 098	1 215 904	301 226	3 618 339	5 029 307	10 708 585	6 213 758
65 to 74 years	2 118 454	1 618 067	60 312	21 970	236 355	181 750	579 816	1 238 535
75 years and over	1 695 717	1 424 797	34 380	14 605	126 806	95 039	331 630	1 197 890
Do not speak English "very well"	13 982 502	6 879 734	658 044	167 612	2 555 424	3 721 688	7 716 795	3 119 561
5 to 17 years	2 388 243	1 075 134	142 328	41 375	379 325	750 081	1 450 237	415 420
18 to 64 years	9 793 186	4 525 143	473 811	107 532	1 011 768	2 774 932	5 045 348	1 831 438
65 to 74 years	992 887	661 778	26 677	10 579	167 973	125 880	378 432	420 624
75 years and over	808 186	617 679	15 228	8 126	96 358	70 795	242 778	452 081
ABILITY TO SPEAK ENGLISH IN HOUSEHOLD								
Linguistically isolated households	2 936 596	1 548 004	131 793	32 310	542 402	682 087	1 512 726	709 053
Persons 5 years and over in households	223 812 984	181 218 716	25 920 682	1 755 292	6 500 628	8 417 666	19 091 096	171 199 300
In linguistically isolated households	7 741 259	3 603 368	298 152	81 800	1 672 006	2 185 933	4 540 077	1 373 213
5 to 17 years	1 763 173	709 670	70 700	22 760	366 366	593 677	1 150 203	183 082
18 to 64 years	4 968 023	2 153 631	207 110	49 303	1 070 211	1 487 768	3 041 240	693 029
65 to 74 years	556 681	384 249	12 926	5 317	88 226	65 963	216 067	240 469
75 years and over	453 382	355 818	7 416	4 420	47 203	38 525	141 167	256 633
DISABILITY STATUS OF CIVILIAN NONINSTITUTIONALIZED PERSONS								
Males 16 to 64 years	76 669 407	62 558 308	8 043 162	596 490	2 345 354	3 126 093	6 884 794	59 021 646
With a mobility or self-care limitation	3 421 889	2 258 730	771 523	44 526	140 796	206 314	445 469	2 041 812
With a mobility limitation	1 565 915	1 145 473	283 620	20 642	42 130	74 050	167 763	1 059 483
In labor force	412 111	292 919	65 746	5 135	18 942	29 369	65 944	259 694
With a self-care limitation	2 637 472	1 659 977	646 931	34 652	123 424	172 488	369 377	1 482 783
With a work disability	6 705 899	5 372 745	936 599	86 393	98 088	212 074	480 648	5 122 754
In labor force	3 084 402	2 594 567	313 386	37 442	47 301	91 706	207 120	2 486 871
Prevented from working	3 158 993	2 411 001	555 266	42 949	42 009	107 768	243 703	2 284 452
No work disability	69 963 508	57 185 563	7 106 563	510 097	2 247 266	2 914 019	6 404 146	53 898 892
In labor force	61 702 250	51 120 120	5 791 404	415 582	1 829 622	2 545 522	5 594 547	48 241 121
Females 16 to 64 years	80 654 515	64 591 783	9 916 909	639 701	2 557 858	2 948 264	6 755 403	61 035 815
With a mobility or self-care limitation	3 792 873	2 395 678	986 090	50 370	156 843	203 892	447 922	2 177 387
With a mobility limitation	1 886 716	1 346 099	376 463	25 431	54 083	84 640	192 885	1 248 506
In labor force	377 913	265 978	71 176	4 823	16 377	19 559	45 915	242 154
With a self-care limitation	2 746 467	1 612 160	805 810	36 745	131 581	160 171	348 793	1 444 298
With a work disability	6 120 550	4 677 967	1 049 814	81 873	107 524	203 372	455 520	4 448 858
In labor force	1 959 588	1 579 008	272 134	25 239	34 339	48 868	118 146	1 515 967
Prevented from working	3 435 036	2 515 794	679 582	47 533	58 754	133 373	289 037	2 374 468
No work disability	74 533 965	59 913 816	8 867 095	557 828	2 450 334	2 744 892	6 299 883	56 586 957
In labor force	52 950 611	42 876 124	6 417 430	359 877	1 623 106	1 674 074	3 960 490	40 741 124
Males 65 to 74 years	7 871 539	7 030 646	595 410	32 295	129 251	83 937	286 026	6 837 502
With a mobility or self-care limitation	924 691	756 966	126 143	6 814	19 675	15 093	46 830	727 198
With a mobility limitation	589 834	486 632	77 345	4 921	10 883	10 053	30 086	467 657
With a self-care limitation	633 166	511 089	92 867	4 419	14 603	10 188	32 611	490 206
Females 65 to 74 years	10 062 013	8 862 482	881 761	40 569	163 946	113 255	377 840	8 611 400
With a mobility or self-care limitation	1 467 398	1 175 213	226 766	9 282	29 251	26 886	80 052	1 126 011
With a mobility limitation	1 041 816	835 172	160 167	7 214	18 780	20 483	58 737	799 718
With a self-care limitation	876 053	689 269	147 099	5 402	18 900	15 383	47 050	660 033
Males 75 years and over	4 215 939	3 783 747	312 633	15 082	65 182	39 295	138 377	3 689 511
With a mobility or self-care limitation	1 021 930	878 921	106 907	5 021	18 211	12 870	42 980	850 410
With a mobility limitation	796 959	684 954	83 550	4 092	13 825	10 538	34 234	662 465
With a self-care limitation	649 092	552 092	73 382	3 336	11 860	8 422	28 108	533 538
Females 75 years and over	7 414 020	6 656 961	596 112	25 106	75 767	60 074	225 543	6 498 705
With a mobility or self-care limitation	2 529 422	2 203 167	261 704	10 188	27 320	27 043	96 349	2 136 927
With a mobility limitation	2 183 311	1 904 321	223 076	8 787	23 108	24 019	83 985	1 847 013
With a self-care limitation	1 365 773	1 165 353	162 428	5 844	15 531	16 617	58 100	1 126 009

Table 41. Fertility and Household and Family Composition by Race and Hispanic Origin: 1990

[Data based on sample and subject to sampling variability, see text. For definitions of terms and meanings of symbols, see text]

United States	All persons	Race White	Race Black	Race American Indian, Eskimo, or Aleut	Race Asian or Pacific Islander	Race Other race	Hispanic origin (of any race)	White, not of Hispanic origin
FERTILITY								
Women 15 to 24 years	17 769 944	13 506 701	2 585 136	169 637	581 261	927 209	1 938 311	12 563 441
Children ever born	5 420 229	3 425 411	1 334 675	90 637	91 653	477 853	901 379	3 034 019
Per 1,000 women	305	254	516	534	158	515	465	241
Women ever married	3 726 372	3 038 939	303 504	38 482	82 769	262 678	521 219	2 794 858
Children ever born	3 462 487	2 654 608	379 107	49 917	67 530	311 325	601 407	2 380 981
Per 1,000 women	929	874	1 249	1 297	816	1 185	1 154	852
Women 25 to 34 years	21 757 561	17 017 533	2 872 381	186 646	725 215	955 786	2 076 193	15 973 799
Children ever born	28 942 178	21 391 915	4 634 379	352 449	779 523	1 783 912	3 607 708	19 694 202
Per 1,000 women	1 330	1 257	1 613	1 888	1 075	1 866	1 738	1 233
Women ever married	16 431 453	13 482 011	1 536 979	136 936	550 528	724 999	1 577 448	12 680 774
Children ever born	26 088 416	20 568 607	2 943 416	294 715	749 218	1 532 429	3 151 021	19 047 492
Per 1,000 women	1 588	1 526	1 915	2 152	1 361	2 114	1 998	1 502
Women 35 to 44 years	19 012 425	15 317 704	2 255 515	150 205	672 487	616 514	1 457 001	14 536 139
Children ever born	37 260 340	28 769 752	5 075 478	372 668	1 299 946	1 742 496	3 769 710	26 883 666
Per 1,000 women	1 960	1 878	2 250	2 481	1 933	2 826	2 587	1 849
No children	3 459 251	2 928 170	326 498	19 659	123 120	61 804	176 433	2 822 064
1 child	3 196 133	2 554 439	435 387	22 464	115 288	68 555	185 369	2 445 965
2 children	6 589 685	5 523 130	628 185	41 220	244 357	152 793	397 944	5 294 225
3 children	3 605 811	2 861 816	443 449	31 929	119 176	149 441	337 560	2 687 114
4 children	1 357 031	978 612	227 256	18 226	41 685	91 252	187 143	889 572
5 or more children	804 514	471 537	194 740	16 707	28 861	92 669	172 552	397 199
Women ever married	17 154 920	14 092 322	1 764 689	134 368	617 501	546 040	1 298 473	13 390 046
Children ever born	36 033 647	28 477 832	4 299 316	351 771	1 285 080	1 619 648	3 548 525	26 676 224
Per 1,000 women	2 100	2 021	2 436	2 618	2 081	2 966	2 733	1 992
HOUSEHOLD TYPE AND RELATIONSHIP								
All persons	248 709 873	199 827 064	29 930 524	2 015 143	7 226 986	9 710 156	21 900 089	188 424 773
In households	242 050 161	194 852 135	28 665 816	1 952 539	7 074 394	9 505 277	21 415 135	183 679 704
Family householder	65 049 428	53 845 200	7 055 063	463 968	1 577 820	2 107 377	4 776 075	51 337 479
Male	51 091 846	44 381 844	3 583 213	309 410	1 308 673	1 508 706	3 500 984	42 479 130
Female	13 957 582	9 463 356	3 471 850	154 558	269 147	598 671	1 275 091	8 858 349
Nonfamily householder	26 944 154	23 061 780	2 886 787	161 399	442 678	391 510	1 095 965	22 410 268
Male	11 534 397	9 683 509	1 291 687	83 327	244 905	230 969	590 050	9 351 069
Female	15 409 757	13 378 271	1 595 100	78 072	197 773	160 541	505 915	13 059 199
Spouse	51 549 544	44 921 347	3 403 863	310 579	1 504 756	1 408 999	3 436 174	42 985 787
Child	77 059 019	58 988 886	10 921 567	751 748	2 505 467	3 891 351	8 539 818	54 625 916
Other relatives	11 647 867	6 680 709	3 074 395	146 374	686 998	1 059 391	2 212 753	5 617 630
Nonrelatives	9 800 149	7 354 213	1 324 141	118 471	356 675	646 649	1 354 350	6 702 624
In group quarters	6 659 712	4 974 929	1 264 708	62 604	152 592	204 879	484 954	4 745 069
Persons per household	2.63	2.54	2.87	3.08	3.29	3.82	3.52	2.51
Persons per family	3.16	3.06	3.46	3.57	3.74	4.06	3.84	3.03
FAMILY TYPE BY PRESENCE OF OWN CHILDREN								
Families	65 049 428	53 845 200	7 055 063	463 968	1 577 820	2 107 377	4 776 075	51 337 479
With own children under 18 years	31 364 670	24 687 700	3 985 084	281 698	938 105	1 472 083	3 081 169	23 183 692
With own children under 6 years	14 646 378	11 433 634	1 806 391	138 756	445 422	822 175	1 655 314	10 654 479
Married-couple families	51 718 214	45 178 672	3 521 382	305 156	1 295 099	1 417 905	3 339 694	43 342 946
With own children under 18 years	24 224 117	20 338 573	1 865 571	178 736	815 582	1 025 655	2 201 368	19 218 899
With own children under 6 years	11 806 198	9 857 980	862 387	88 960	402 836	594 035	1 228 508	9 253 420
Female householder, no husband present	10 381 654	6 540 382	3 045 283	121 370	185 926	488 693	1 029 646	6 058 841
With own children under 18 years	5 865 147	3 443 573	1 901 114	80 840	94 498	345 122	682 929	3 146 813
With own children under 6 years	2 300 192	1 222 520	840 827	38 040	32 582	166 223	313 076	1 095 480
Subfamilies	2 572 170	1 425 738	783 745	37 017	125 397	200 273	422 272	1 218 744
With own children under 18 years	2 193 137	1 169 266	757 249	34 535	65 285	166 802	347 753	1 001 121
Married-couple subfamilies	611 488	420 134	48 619	4 994	79 014	58 727	127 763	354 488
With own children under 18 years	232 455	163 662	22 123	2 512	18 902	25 256	53 244	136 865
Mother-child subfamilies	1 586 814	810 006	608 623	23 985	34 966	109 234	228 045	700 195
Persons under 18 years	63 606 544	47 753 472	9 566 954	690 641	2 052 428	3 543 049	7 637 394	43 925 831
Percent living with two parents	71.8	79.3	36.8	55.7	82.2	62.1	63.9	80.4
UNMARRIED-PARTNER HOUSEHOLDS								
Total	3 187 772	2 473 499	460 087	45 554	48 517	160 115	319 670	2 327 672
Male and female	3 042 642	2 348 349	447 983	44 191	46 325	155 794	309 138	2 208 275
Both male	81 343	72 485	4 619	588	1 300	2 351	5 704	69 315
Both female	63 787	52 665	7 485	775	892	1 970	4 828	50 082
SELECTED LIVING ARRANGEMENTS								
Households	91 993 582	76 906 980	9 941 850	625 367	2 020 498	2 498 887	5 872 040	73 747 747
With one or more subfamilies	2 416 716	1 358 998	725 413	33 550	115 178	183 577	382 501	1 173 474
With related members 15 and over other than spouse, children, parents, or parents-in-law of householder	4 488 360	2 788 518	999 031	49 173	239 073	412 565	833 952	2 398 111
With roomer, boarder, or foster child 15 years and over	905 979	663 925	149 992	8 106	30 025	53 931	113 447	610 147
LABOR FORCE STATUS OF FAMILY MEMBERS								
Married-couple families	51 718 214	45 178 672	3 521 382	305 156	1 295 099	1 417 905	3 339 694	43 342 946
Husband employed or in Armed Forces	39 286 822	34 232 358	2 598 174	218 614	1 068 819	1 168 857	2 705 020	32 764 255
Wife employed or in Armed Forces	25 799 947	22 440 348	1 874 907	135 797	715 004	633 891	1 507 531	21 609 186
Wife unemployed	1 071 291	835 895	124 728	10 678	31 496	68 494	139 805	768 679
Wife not in labor force	12 415 584	10 956 115	598 539	72 139	322 319	466 472	1 057 684	10 386 390
Husband unemployed	1 364 119	1 076 953	151 968	21 205	33 315	80 678	166 465	996 311
Wife employed or in Armed Forces	790 277	627 582	97 365	10 191	19 141	35 998	77 407	589 102
Wife unemployed	127 477	92 037	16 663	2 955	4 071	11 751	22 759	81 786
Wife not in labor force	446 365	357 334	37 940	8 059	10 103	32 929	66 299	325 423
Husband not in labor force	11 067 273	9 869 361	771 240	65 337	192 965	168 370	468 209	9 582 380
Wife employed or in Armed Forces	2 383 825	2 010 101	254 030	18 947	53 519	47 228	124 853	1 936 739
Wife unemployed	127 210	97 182	18 464	2 256	3 121	6 187	13 606	90 120
Wife not in labor force	8 556 238	7 762 078	498 746	44 134	136 325	114 955	329 750	7 555 521
Female householder, no husband present	10 381 654	6 540 382	3 045 283	121 370	185 926	488 693	1 029 646	6 058 841
Employed or in Armed Forces	6 031 687	4 011 325	1 617 812	58 613	116 808	227 129	513 905	3 751 641
Unemployed	593 069	270 386	269 634	10 433	6 393	36 223	72 294	239 234
Not in labor force	3 756 898	2 258 671	1 157 837	52 324	62 725	225 341	443 447	2 067 966

Table 42. School Enrollment and Educational Attainment by Race and Hispanic Origin: 1990

[Data based on sample and subject to sampling variability, see text. For definitions of terms and meanings of symbols, see text]

United States	All persons	Race					Hispanic origin (of any race)	White, not of Hispanic origin
		White	Black	American Indian, Eskimo, or Aleut	Asian or Pacific Islander	Other race		
SCHOOL ENROLLMENT AND TYPE OF SCHOOL								
Persons 3 years and over enrolled in school	64 987 101	49 273 838	9 269 910	635 992	2 552 671	3 254 690	7 147 066	45 645 771
Preprimary school	4 503 285	3 619 904	563 019	41 421	132 582	146 359	352 080	3 427 660
Public school	2 679 029	2 033 215	427 560	34 573	67 445	116 236	255 870	1 904 040
Elementary or high school	42 566 788	31 537 361	6 642 519	467 518	1 446 890	2 472 500	5 301 622	28 894 611
Public school	38 379 689	28 071 143	6 259 803	444 226	1 280 058	2 324 459	4 917 208	25 648 132
College	17 917 028	14 116 573	2 064 372	127 053	973 199	635 831	1 493 364	13 323 500
Public college	13 805 534	10 811 273	1 626 861	106 465	729 252	531 683	1 217 421	10 174 247
Persons 3 years and over enrolled in school	64 987 101	49 273 838	9 269 910	635 992	2 552 671	3 254 690	7 147 066	45 645 771
3 and 4 years	2 118 735	1 606 278	338 893	19 813	70 729	83 022	193 611	1 503 875
5 to 14 years	32 655 517	24 605 376	4 878 558	357 150	1 059 662	1 754 771	3 827 362	22 666 265
15 to 17 years	9 294 846	7 030 379	1 382 723	95 485	322 079	464 180	1 004 007	6 524 253
18 and 19 years	4 974 321	3 828 687	684 234	39 683	210 889	210 828	460 462	3 596 690
20 to 24 years	6 267 157	4 905 399	700 969	39 474	355 538	265 777	583 237	4 612 543
25 to 34 years	5 064 093	3 740 005	675 830	43 793	316 058	288 407	618 870	3 433 452
35 years and over	4 612 432	3 557 714	608 703	40 594	217 716	187 705	459 517	3 308 693
Percent enrolled in school:								
3 and 4 years	28.9	29.2	31.0	25.2	30.4	19.4	21.2	29.8
5 to 14 years	92.6	92.7	92.2	92.6	93.0	91.6	92.0	92.7
15 to 17 years	92.4	93.0	90.9	89.2	95.1	86.5	87.7	93.3
18 and 19 years	65.5	66.5	61.8	54.2	83.7	52.1	55.0	67.2
20 to 24 years	33.6	34.3	28.1	23.0	58.6	24.7	26.5	34.8
25 to 34 years	11.7	10.9	12.5	11.9	22.4	14.0	14.1	10.7
35 years and over	4.0	3.6	5.4	5.7	7.5	7.1	6.7	3.5
Persons 18 to 24 years	26 234 893	20 050 284	3 602 336	244 881	858 192	1 479 200	3 035 902	18 600 294
Percent enrolled in college	34.4	35.9	27.1	21.6	55.1	20.5	22.9	36.8
Male	32.7	34.7	23.3	20.2	56.0	18.0	20.4	35.7
Female	36.0	37.2	30.8	23.2	54.1	23.4	25.7	37.9
SCHOOL ENROLLMENT AND LABOR FORCE STATUS								
Persons 16 to 19 years	14 315 448	10 799 495	2 129 072	143 769	480 997	762 115	1 600 482	10 015 571
Enrolled in school	11 073 188	8 441 214	1 595 913	100 668	427 064	508 329	1 107 108	7 881 647
Employed	4 159 951	3 495 880	367 584	25 218	120 911	150 358	337 581	3 318 507
Unemployed	756 835	513 627	166 082	8 994	20 084	48 048	97 075	468 812
Not in labor force	6 136 105	4 416 742	1 058 491	66 322	285 473	309 077	670 487	4 080 305
Not enrolled in school	3 242 260	2 358 281	533 159	43 101	53 933	253 786	493 374	2 133 924
High school graduate	1 636 766	1 281 328	240 977	17 106	27 719	69 636	146 313	1 210 340
Employed	1 042 647	875 028	103 897	8 772	16 221	38 729	84 851	831 527
Unemployed	180 695	124 548	42 283	2 680	2 402	8 782	18 265	115 978
Not in labor force	274 277	181 444	65 728	4 258	6 943	15 904	32 235	166 495
Not high school graduate	1 605 494	1 076 953	292 182	25 995	26 214	184 150	347 061	923 584
Employed	640 453	480 799	61 197	8 231	9 440	80 786	151 252	413 238
Unemployed	274 320	181 563	57 297	5 039	2 997	27 424	52 700	157 726
Not in labor force	681 990	407 785	172 503	12 596	13 671	75 435	141 978	346 397
EDUCATIONAL ATTAINMENT								
Persons 18 to 24 years	26 234 893	20 050 284	3 602 336	244 881	858 192	1 479 200	3 035 902	18 600 294
High school graduate (includes equivalency)	8 126 562	6 197 735	1 239 271	83 309	213 094	393 153	822 447	5 799 374
Some college or associate degree	9 941 932	8 082 861	1 107 360	67 252	371 306	313 153	720 485	7 705 438
Bachelor's degree or higher	1 991 840	1 722 489	121 791	5 089	112 580	29 891	85 591	1 670 422
Persons 25 years and over	158 868 436	132 023 308	16 761 234	1 079 621	4 316 366	4 687 907	11 226 793	125 898 648
Less than 5th grade	4 271 677	2 399 702	757 676	50 552	296 660	767 188	1 509 387	1 694 096
5th to 8th grade	12 230 534	9 406 967	1 548 870	100 662	261 234	912 801	1 936 545	8 439 213
9th to 12th grade, no diploma	22 841 507	17 355 153	3 881 407	220 900	411 508	972 539	2 188 300	16 220 529
High school graduate (includes equivalency)	47 642 763	40 891 202	4 680 594	313 783	799 206	957 978	2 419 632	39 521 862
Some college, no degree	29 779 777	25 221 246	3 101 292	224 300	634 810	598 129	1 602 472	24 285 302
Associate degree, occupational program	5 233 002	4 442 356	475 567	40 426	169 200	105 453	273 770	4 286 595
Associate degree, academic program	4 558 923	3 861 226	410 551	28 495	165 109	93 542	268 939	3 698 475
Bachelor's degree	20 832 567	18 337 917	1 261 090	65 512	978 338	189 710	658 197	17 902 015
Master's degree	7 520 469	6 594 032	485 573	24 126	365 155	51 583	209 393	6 443 715
Professional school degree	2 751 791	2 462 972	107 144	7 075	143 977	30 623	121 346	2 377 595
Doctorate degree	1 205 426	1 050 535	51 571	3 790	91 169	8 361	38 823	1 021 251
Females 25 years and over	83 654 171	69 252 013	9 257 807	562 703	2 282 675	2 298 973	5 657 519	66 108 006
Less than 5th grade	2 161 459	1 200 562	363 978	26 399	192 850	377 670	760 704	836 966
5th to 8th grade	6 546 831	5 018 665	857 047	51 569	165 589	453 961	989 986	4 512 548
9th to 12th grade, no diploma	12 360 377	9 404 264	2 131 892	117 140	235 312	471 769	1 085 425	8 834 508
High school graduate (includes equivalency)	26 850 606	23 179 568	2 559 021	163 733	464 698	483 586	1 275 286	22 434 508
Some college, no degree	15 520 115	13 060 799	1 738 237	118 641	316 915	285 523	794 048	12 587 768
Associate degree, occupational program	2 920 672	2 473 486	284 688	21 071	88 196	53 231	140 682	2 392 632
Associate degree, academic program	2 538 505	2 142 909	239 853	15 626	92 715	47 402	140 303	2 056 521
Bachelor's degree	10 015 766	8 661 760	717 007	32 661	515 986	88 352	316 611	8 452 135
Master's degree	3 581 055	3 109 749	296 503	11 565	139 879	23 359	98 201	3 039 111
Professional school degree	857 999	740 400	50 116	3 104	52 911	11 468	42 677	711 806
Doctorate degree	300 786	259 851	19 465	1 194	17 624	2 652	13 396	249 503
Persons 25 years and over	158 868 436	132 023 308	16 761 234	1 079 621	4 316 366	4 687 907	11 226 793	125 898 648
Percent:								
Less than 5th grade	2.7	1.8	4.5	4.7	6.9	16.4	13.4	1.3
High school graduate or higher	75.2	77.9	63.1	65.5	77.5	43.4	49.8	79.1
Male	75.7	78.4	62.2	65.8	81.5	43.5	49.8	79.6
Female	74.8	77.4	63.8	65.3	74.0	43.3	49.9	78.5
Some college or higher	45.2	46.9	35.2	36.5	59.0	23.0	28.3	47.7
Bachelor's degree or higher	20.3	21.5	11.4	9.3	36.6	6.0	9.2	22.0
Male	23.3	25.0	11.0	10.1	41.9	6.5	10.0	25.6
Female	17.6	18.4	11.7	8.6	31.8	5.5	8.3	18.8
Males 25 to 34 years	21 709 473	17 198 369	2 540 881	180 692	688 846	1 100 685	2 304 086	16 073 832
Percent:								
High school graduate or higher	82.7	86.0	74.2	71.7	87.2	50.3	55.4	87.8
Bachelor's degree or higher	22.9	25.0	10.9	7.2	43.6	6.7	9.4	25.9
Females 25 to 34 years	21 757 561	17 017 533	2 872 381	186 646	725 215	955 786	2 076 193	15 973 799
Percent:								
High school graduate or higher	85.5	88.5	78.8	74.9	84.7	54.7	60.4	90.0
Bachelor's degree or higher	22.6	24.5	13.3	7.8	39.9	7.2	10.2	25.2

Table 43. Geographic Mobility, Commuting, and Veteran Status by Race and Hispanic Origin: 1990

[Data based on sample and subject to sampling variability, see text. For definitions of terms and meanings of symbols, see text]

United States	All persons	White	Black	American Indian, Eskimo, or Aleut	Asian or Pacific Islander	Other race	Hispanic origin (of any race)	White, not of Hispanic origin
PLACE OF BIRTH AND NATIVITY								
All persons	248 709 873	199 827 064	29 930 524	2 015 143	7 226 986	9 710 156	21 900 089	188 424 773
Native	228 942 557	189 804 252	28 475 230	1 968 224	2 668 242	6 026 609	14 058 439	182 257 430
Born in State of residence	153 684 685	125 986 730	20 037 406	1 403 322	1 838 871	4 418 356	10 178 632	120 539 891
Born in a different State	72 011 141	61 816 425	8 193 064	549 140	567 800	884 712	2 344 536	60 450 863
Northeast	16 772 309	15 569 445	912 636	35 981	105 598	148 649	446 803	15 297 629
Midwest	21 287 172	19 959 706	1 004 929	121 546	90 697	110 294	300 286	19 777 290
South	24 366 640	17 785 456	5 955 306	191 222	105 754	328 902	795 769	17 347 095
West	9 585 020	8 501 818	320 193	200 391	265 751	296 867	801 678	8 028 849
Born abroad	3 246 731	2 001 097	244 760	15 762	261 571	723 541	1 535 271	1 266 676
Puerto Rico	1 190 533	560 612	50 215	1 752	4 473	573 481	1 155 977	27 466
U.S. outlying area	191 913	64 754	45 047	1 021	46 977	34 114	79 690	32 590
U.S. Virgin Islands	38 481	5 773	30 434	90	408	1 776	4 602	4 395
American Samoa	15 121	1 409	212	66	13 318	116	244	1 347
Guam	53 293	21 173	1 693	246	29 186	995	6 470	19 975
Northern Marianas	3 117	819	60	7	2 189	42	241	762
Born abroad of American parents	1 864 285	1 375 731	149 498	12 989	210 121	115 946	299 604	1 206 620
Foreign born	19 767 316	10 022 812	1 455 294	46 919	4 558 744	3 683 547	7 841 650	6 167 343
RESIDENCE IN 1985								
Persons 5 years and over	230 445 777	186 181 122	27 175 607	1 817 347	6 652 553	8 619 148	19 569 737	175 934 346
Same house	122 796 970	101 490 046	14 266 121	859 045	2 595 263	3 586 495	8 575 524	96 794 335
Different house in the United States	102 540 097	82 193 690	12 439 981	939 731	2 837 293	4 129 402	9 107 837	77 552 317
Same county	58 675 635	45 061 802	8 435 985	537 202	1 663 664	2 976 982	6 341 105	41 906 824
Different county	43 864 462	37 131 888	4 003 996	402 529	1 173 629	1 152 420	2 766 732	35 645 493
Same State	22 279 165	18 935 004	1 897 409	212 129	566 131	668 492	1 543 112	18 127 262
Different State	21 585 297	18 196 884	2 106 587	190 400	607 498	483 928	1 223 620	17 518 231
Northeast	4 346 471	3 658 880	435 852	12 383	133 491	105 865	294 091	3 492 322
Midwest	4 854 669	4 263 869	391 825	35 222	110 931	52 822	135 647	4 186 391
South	7 588 749	6 180 604	1 018 883	61 434	167 890	159 938	392 298	5 965 552
West	4 795 408	4 093 531	260 027	81 361	195 186	165 303	401 584	3 873 966
Puerto Rico	213 886	108 432	9 521	315	1 106	94 512	201 757	9 953
U.S. outlying area	73 764	31 633	20 084	446	14 172	7 429	16 669	25 872
Elsewhere	4 821 060	2 357 321	439 900	17 810	1 204 719	801 310	1 667 950	1 551 869
PLACE OF WORK								
Workers 16 years and over	...	...	...	...	...	...	...	...
Worked in area of residence	...	...	...	...	...	...	...	...
Worked outside area of residence	...	...	...	...	...	...	...	...
MEANS OF TRANSPORTATION AND CARPOOLING								
Workers 16 years and over	115 070 274	95 708 551	11 414 755	724 223	3 381 333	3 841 412	8 858 023	90 988 092
Car, truck, or van	99 592 932	84 500 232	8 782 909	608 615	2 694 332	3 006 844	7 076 332	80 617 006
Drove alone	84 215 298	72 860 206	6 710 774	472 816	2 077 175	2 094 327	5 174 780	69 913 934
Carpooled	15 377 634	11 640 026	2 072 135	135 799	617 157	912 517	1 901 552	10 703 072
2-person carpool	12 078 175	9 347 722	1 543 297	103 235	469 313	614 608	1 321 943	8 676 678
3-person carpool	2 001 378	1 424 891	307 494	19 932	87 694	161 367	316 887	1 277 331
4-person carpool	702 222	471 948	117 706	6 645	33 342	72 581	137 744	410 053
5- or 6-person carpool	305 976	197 714	51 251	3 556	14 564	38 891	74 811	163 985
7-or-more-person carpool	289 883	197 751	52 387	2 431	12 244	25 070	50 167	175 025
Persons per car, truck, or van	1.09	1.08	1.15	1.14	1.14	1.21	1.18	1.08
Public transportation	6 069 589	3 406 567	1 784 576	30 408	381 611	466 427	971 168	2 980 891
Bus or trolley bus	3 445 000	1 761 847	1 162 263	22 039	195 839	303 012	603 408	1 496 905
Streetcar or trolley car	78 130	49 059	18 801	344	6 178	3 748	8 440	44 933
Subway or elevated	1 755 476	972 246	487 564	5 469	147 967	142 230	310 654	842 418
Railroad	574 052	476 826	61 364	879	24 516	10 467	31 210	458 715
Ferryboat	37 497	31 618	3 079	251	1 596	953	2 540	30 241
Taxicab	179 434	114 971	51 505	1 426	5 515	6 017	14 916	107 679
Motorcycle	237 404	211 514	9 168	2 677	5 246	8 799	20 338	200 490
Bicycle	466 856	382 010	35 109	4 914	17 190	27 633	59 469	351 525
Walked	4 488 886	3 501 785	537 389	44 713	188 293	216 706	457 343	3 281 172
Other means	808 582	583 175	131 759	12 317	25 484	55 847	111 337	530 917
Worked at home	3 406 025	3 123 268	133 845	20 579	69 177	59 156	162 036	3 026 091
TRAVEL TIME TO WORK AND DEPARTURE TIME								
Workers who did not work at home	111 664 249	92 585 283	11 280 910	703 644	3 312 156	3 782 256	8 695 987	87 962 001
Minutes to work:								
Less than 10 minutes	18 257 921	16 081 483	1 186 273	143 753	367 160	479 252	1 107 759	15 482 015
10 to 14 minutes	17 954 128	15 277 811	1 553 625	114 199	459 400	549 093	1 277 201	14 583 039
15 to 19 minutes	19 026 053	15 705 710	1 999 244	117 182	538 281	665 636	1 516 782	14 895 539
20 to 29 minutes	22 436 930	18 645 000	2 303 224	121 299	650 766	716 641	1 691 752	17 721 185
30 to 44 minutes	20 053 109	16 006 085	2 381 755	115 855	745 705	803 709	1 822 595	15 054 215
45 or more minutes	13 936 108	10 869 194	1 856 789	91 356	550 844	567 925	1 279 898	10 226 008
Mean travel time to work (minutes)	22.3	21.8	25.3	21.8	25.5	24.3	24.2	21.7
Workers traveling 45 or more minutes	58.5	58.5	58.5	59.9	57.7	58.7	58.5	58.5
Departure time:								
6:00 to 6:59 a.m.	22 820 464	18 664 821	2 506 559	144 564	589 042	915 478	1 976 297	17 666 344
7:00 to 7:59 a.m.	35 346 620	30 008 459	3 215 600	217 587	885 250	1 019 724	2 457 834	28 651 237
8:00 to 8:59 a.m.	18 867 326	16 147 414	1 531 978	97 324	610 086	480 524	1 244 941	15 428 022
All other times	34 629 839	27 764 589	4 026 773	244 169	1 227 778	1 366 530	3 016 915	26 216 398
VETERAN STATUS								
Male civilian veterans	26 330 011	23 379 529	2 230 013	181 439	236 706	302 324	901 021	22 814 871
Percent of civilian males 16 years and over	29.1	31.4	23.4	27.2	9.3	9.1	12.0	32.4
Female civilian veterans	1 151 044	965 525	144 352	12 072	13 549	15 546	43 879	940 072
Percent of civilian females 16 years and over	1.2	1.2	1.3	1.7	.5	.5	.6	1.2
PERIOD OF SERVICE								
Civilian veterans 16 years and over	27 481 055	24 345 054	2 374 365	193 511	250 255	317 870	944 900	23 754 943
May 1975 or later service only	3 352 156	2 579 697	588 200	37 560	51 366	95 333	223 132	2 464 047
September 1980 or later service only	1 900 833	1 459 713	335 325	20 667	30 547	54 581	127 917	1 393 449
Served 2 or more years	1 603 440	1 222 238	291 189	16 944	26 534	46 535	108 366	1 166 226
Vietnam era, no Korean conflict	7 646 908	6 630 269	742 215	72 458	81 388	120 578	329 415	6 435 190
Vietnam era and Korean conflict	585 506	529 878	42 177	3 575	6 730	3 146	15 172	518 588
February 1955 to July 1964 only	2 944 497	2 678 284	196 789	20 151	23 338	25 935	90 257	2 616 778
Korean conflict, no World War II	3 720 976	3 367 125	271 890	23 084	29 318	29 559	107 495	3 292 410
Korean conflict and World War II	624 683	590 118	25 303	3 751	3 246	2 265	10 799	581 945
World War II, no Korean conflict	8 345 431	7 731 666	490 351	31 712	52 773	38 929	161 874	7 612 311
World War I	62 198	58 553	3 194	162	143	146	593	58 125
Other service	198 700	179 464	14 246	1 058	1 953	1 979	6 163	175 549

Table 44.　Labor Force Characteristics by Race and Hispanic Origin: 1990

[Data based on sample and subject to sampling variability, see text. For definitions of terms and meanings of symbols, see text]

United States	All persons	Race					Hispanic origin (of any race)	White, not of Hispanic origin
		White	Black	American Indian, Eskimo, or Aleut	Asian or Pacific Islander	Other race		
LABOR FORCE STATUS								
Persons 16 years and over	191 829 271	157 119 373	21 386 343	1 395 009	5 403 615	6 524 931	15 025 902	149 164 557
In labor force	125 182 378	102 800 818	13 413 487	865 703	3 645 946	4 456 424	10 139 070	97 467 714
Percent of persons 16 years and over	65.3	65.4	62.7	62.1	67.5	68.3	67.5	65.3
Armed Forces	1 708 928	1 275 082	318 306	14 391	42 866	58 283	117 347	1 224 593
Civilian labor force	123 473 450	101 525 736	13 095 181	851 312	3 603 080	4 398 141	10 021 723	96 243 121
Employed	115 681 202	96 237 561	11 407 803	728 953	3 411 586	3 895 299	8 981 516	91 447 312
At work 35 or more hours	89 428 871	74 240 108	8 873 999	548 730	2 690 953	3 075 081	7 078 492	70 470 721
Unemployed	7 792 248	5 288 175	1 687 378	122 359	191 494	502 842	1 040 207	4 795 809
Percent of civilian labor force	6.3	5.2	12.9	14.4	5.3	11.4	10.4	5.0
Not in labor force	66 646 893	54 318 555	7 972 856	529 306	1 757 669	2 068 507	4 886 832	51 696 843
Institutionalized persons	3 232 910	2 360 364	722 050	31 375	23 391	95 730	240 572	2 245 385
Females 16 years and over	99 803 358	81 541 169	11 597 691	714 654	2 810 588	3 139 256	7 410 116	77 546 546
In labor force	56 672 949	45 947 179	6 901 351	393 437	1 688 145	1 742 837	4 145 686	43 705 520
Percent of females 16 years and over	56.8	56.3	59.5	55.1	60.1	55.5	55.9	56.4
Armed Forces	185 700	120 552	53 709	2 017	4 063	5 359	12 143	115 037
Civilian labor force	56 487 249	45 826 627	6 847 642	391 420	1 684 082	1 737 478	4 133 543	43 590 483
Employed	52 976 623	43 515 117	6 015 288	340 042	1 590 897	1 515 279	3 669 186	41 499 763
At work 35 or more hours	36 418 960	29 467 638	4 470 242	235 857	1 174 018	1 071 205	2 605 432	28 036 488
Unemployed	3 510 626	2 311 510	832 354	51 378	93 185	222 199	464 357	2 090 720
Percent of civilian labor force	6.2	5.0	12.2	13.1	5.5	12.8	11.2	4.8
Not in labor force	43 130 409	35 593 990	4 696 340	321 217	1 122 443	1 396 419	3 264 430	33 841 026
Institutionalized persons	1 487 110	1 309 391	149 200	7 261	8 954	12 304	39 187	1 285 589
Males 16 to 19 years	7 342 263	5 543 693	1 072 640	74 536	247 569	403 825	848 933	5 127 602
Employed	2 962 432	2 453 192	256 572	21 985	73 407	157 276	327 922	2 290 734
Unemployed	670 528	460 692	137 333	9 190	14 626	48 687	97 373	415 598
Not in labor force	3 562 362	2 521 228	650 894	41 984	157 048	191 208	411 580	2 317 348
Males 20 to 24 years	9 469 385	7 263 216	1 212 585	88 901	311 767	592 916	1 197 579	6 699 767
Employed	6 419 967	5 154 588	611 066	48 798	179 585	425 930	854 007	4 749 099
Unemployed	768 405	507 787	170 514	13 825	16 824	59 455	117 795	453 974
Not in labor force	1 806 836	1 248 963	343 341	21 626	105 474	87 432	189 444	1 158 783
Males 25 to 54 years	52 743 194	42 937 054	5 686 136	411 828	1 630 771	2 077 405	4 590 167	40 590 845
Employed	44 842 502	37 589 632	3 921 380	284 470	1 382 945	1 664 075	3 705 608	35 660 537
Unemployed	2 450 753	1 691 210	501 719	44 164	56 378	157 282	322 083	1 540 404
Not in labor force	4 553 238	2 966 583	1 114 548	76 893	165 205	230 009	505 969	2 726 457
Males 55 to 64 years	9 957 003	8 640 902	869 733	55 995	205 333	185 040	543 449	8 301 214
Employed	6 377 542	5 620 921	471 369	27 507	145 196	112 549	346 982	5 397 856
Unemployed	294 523	236 665	34 837	3 085	7 962	11 974	29 897	219 790
Not in labor force	3 279 732	2 779 018	362 965	25 359	51 987	60 403	166 292	2 679 426
Males 65 to 69 years	4 555 259	4 046 612	356 341	20 108	76 895	55 303	182 651	3 925 161
In labor force	1 269 464	1 141 235	81 965	4 363	26 527	15 374	55 077	1 103 791
Not in labor force	3 285 795	2 905 377	274 376	15 745	50 368	39 929	127 574	2 821 370
Did not work in 1989	2 675 255	2 346 126	239 385	13 416	41 780	34 548	107 631	2 276 120
Males 70 years and over	7 958 809	7 146 727	591 217	28 987	120 692	71 186	253 007	6 973 422
In labor force	930 288	843 331	60 825	2 505	15 548	8 079	31 464	820 989
Not in labor force	7 028 521	6 303 396	530 392	26 482	105 144	63 107	221 543	6 152 433
Did not work in 1989	6 289 799	5 613 410	495 995	24 303	97 104	58 987	205 592	5 473 801
Females 16 to 19 years	6 973 185	5 255 002	1 050 432	69 233	233 428	358 290	751 549	4 887 969
Employed	2 880 619	2 398 515	276 106	20 236	73 165	112 597	245 762	2 272 538
Unemployed	541 322	359 046	128 329	7 523	10 857	35 567	70 667	326 918
Not in labor force	3 530 010	2 484 743	645 828	41 192	149 039	209 208	433 120	2 275 849
Females 20 to 24 years	9 176 002	7 033 354	1 283 452	82 718	294 485	481 993	1 001 048	6 550 571
Employed	5 946 615	4 822 335	662 335	39 895	168 071	253 715	547 862	4 546 923
Unemployed	605 852	368 091	171 765	9 552	13 326	43 118	85 076	329 885
Not in labor force	2 564 910	1 805 452	431 333	32 551	111 900	103 000	363 779	1 638 321
Females 25 to 54 years	53 809 217	43 111 433	6 578 709	431 080	1 777 497	1 910 498	4 414 333	40 777 951
Employed	37 761 559	30 815 968	4 424 857	251 698	1 203 710	1 065 326	2 588 841	29 393 493
Unemployed	2 079 910	1 361 135	494 029	31 853	59 948	132 945	280 510	1 226 933
Not in labor force	13 863 239	10 865 027	1 630 433	146 514	511 318	709 947	1 539 234	10 091 082
Females 55 to 64 years	11 163 747	9 503 847	1 125 815	62 995	260 191	210 899	622 648	9 115 058
Employed	4 894 548	4 173 827	505 641	22 406	121 478	71 196	237 979	4 016 959
Unemployed	199 774	155 951	26 502	1 953	6 890	8 478	21 939	143 442
Not in labor force	6 068 702	5 173 539	593 541	38 636	131 768	131 218	362 666	4 954 178
Females 65 to 69 years	5 604 849	4 904 414	507 624	24 292	98 240	70 279	228 685	4 754 245
In labor force	944 717	822 170	91 626	3 744	18 228	8 949	34 580	797 974
Not in labor force	4 660 132	4 082 244	415 998	20 548	80 012	61 330	194 105	3 956 271
Did not work in 1989	4 202 287	3 675 743	377 408	18 589	73 041	57 506	179 969	3 559 605
Females 70 years and over	13 076 358	11 732 319	1 045 659	44 336	146 747	107 297	391 853	11 460 752
In labor force	632 342	549 334	66 452	2 560	8 409	5 587	20 327	535 427
Not in labor force	12 444 016	11 182 985	979 207	41 776	138 338	101 710	371 526	10 925 325
Did not work in 1989	11 840 761	10 628 686	939 939	39 694	133 512	98 930	359 792	10 379 637
PRESENCE OF OWN CHILDREN IN FAMILIES AND SUBFAMILIES								
Females 16 years and over	99 803 358	81 541 169	11 597 691	714 654	2 810 588	3 139 256	7 410 116	77 546 546
With own children under 6 years	15 233 818	11 673 162	2 069 059	147 285	515 031	829 281	1 727 350	10 832 368
In labor force	9 095 156	6 981 350	1 321 597	78 910	295 743	417 556	891 044	6 538 068
With own children 6 to 17 years only	16 490 186	12 940 305	2 209 619	142 961	553 642	643 629	1 450 539	12 185 829
In labor force	12 367 705	9 758 938	1 697 017	97 957	404 696	409 097	951 201	9 253 574
Own children under 6 years living with two parents	15 993 967	13 365 043	1 120 631	126 232	582 444	799 617	1 772 746	12 433 972
Both parents in labor force	8 874 102	7 356 865	762 231	61 519	309 547	383 940	869 378	6 894 604
Both at work 35 or more hours	4 433 879	3 551 805	455 328	27 868	197 142	201 736	461 911	3 305 073
Own children under 6 years living with one parent	5 279 645	2 691 801	1 957 353	99 013	92 667	438 811	885 737	2 296 228
Parent in labor force	3 169 479	1 757 315	1 077 653	53 193	52 985	228 333	478 875	1 530 677
At work 35 or more hours	1 936 665	1 151 722	576 138	28 249	38 470	142 086	301 344	1 006 176
Own children 6 to 17 years living with two parents	29 673 627	24 506 771	2 403 582	258 426	1 105 516	1 399 332	3 105 443	22 876 830
Both parents in labor force	19 477 241	16 126 135	1 723 939	149 745	709 041	768 381	1 744 245	15 197 358
Both at work 35 or more hours	10 782 593	8 710 728	1 098 819	78 618	481 480	412 948	965 041	8 187 268
Own children 6 to 17 years living with one parent	9 931 854	5 641 232	3 274 251	153 491	191 540	671 340	1 395 753	4 989 238
Parent in labor force	7 343 393	4 490 361	2 212 058	100 318	133 038	407 618	893 017	4 047 712
At work 35 or more hours	5 231 410	3 369 644	1 423 150	62 936	103 025	272 655	607 654	3 062 492

Table 45. Occupation of Employed Persons by Race and Hispanic Origin: 1990

[Data based on sample and subject to sampling variability, see text. For definitions of terms and meanings of symbols, see text]

United States	All persons	Race White	Black	American Indian, Eskimo, or Aleut	Asian or Pacific Islander	Other race	Hispanic origin (of any race)	White, not of Hispanic origin
Employed persons 16 years and over	**115 681 202**	**96 237 561**	**11 407 803**	**728 953**	**3 411 586**	**3 895 299**	**8 981 516**	**91 447 312**
Managerial and professional specialty occupations	30 533 582	26 877 354	2 066 054	133 555	1 045 160	411 459	1 262 178	26 072 188
Executive, administrative, and managerial occupations	14 227 916	12 651 035	875 835	62 825	428 273	209 948	627 693	12 254 816
Officials and administrators, public administration	578 334	484 939	68 142	6 345	10 748	8 160	25 469	468 576
Management and related occupations	4 140 575	3 606 211	303 762	17 191	149 459	63 952	189 088	3 488 813
Professional specialty occupations	16 305 666	14 226 319	1 190 219	70 730	616 887	201 511	634 485	13 817 372
Engineers and natural scientists	3 000 976	2 635 125	126 864	9 274	201 193	28 520	96 970	2 569 523
Engineers	1 672 559	1 475 994	58 041	4 865	117 858	15 801	52 479	1 440 584
Health diagnosing occupations	869 543	754 907	28 401	1 467	77 501	7 267	35 277	728 482
Health assessment and treating occupations	2 482 553	2 124 802	213 393	10 064	110 659	23 635	76 252	2 077 587
Teachers, librarians, and counselors	5 713 591	4 963 417	512 599	28 766	131 237	77 572	238 263	4 809 953
Teachers, elementary and secondary schools	3 861 446	3 358 038	380 073	19 080	49 959	54 296	165 455	3 251 700
Technical, sales, and administrative support occupations	36 718 398	31 121 238	3 354 120	195 096	1 134 130	913 814	2 321 918	29 799 821
Health technologists and technicians	1 397 189	1 123 408	182 904	8 853	52 383	29 641	77 782	1 079 681
Technologists and technicians, except health	2 860 046	2 445 404	190 994	14 113	155 867	53 668	143 367	2 361 025
Sales occupations	13 634 686	11 984 176	875 576	63 582	400 985	310 367	808 785	11 511 646
Supervisors and proprietors, sales occupations	3 352 054	3 012 184	153 862	13 853	109 710	62 445	172 723	2 907 048
Sales representatives, commodities and finance	3 941 568	3 649 726	151 055	11 351	78 905	50 531	157 289	3 547 155
Other sales occupations	6 341 064	5 322 266	570 659	38 378	212 370	197 391	478 773	5 057 443
Cashiers	2 533 639	1 976 839	327 343	20 049	105 851	103 557	232 840	1 856 694
Administrative support occupations, including clerical	18 826 477	15 568 250	2 104 646	108 548	524 895	520 138	1 291 984	14 847 469
Computer equipment operators	640 982	511 106	86 759	3 554	23 640	15 923	40 615	488 214
Secretaries, stenographers, and typists	4 582 070	3 980 228	393 893	25 649	83 460	98 840	258 327	3 830 459
Financial records processing occupations	2 315 205	2 043 830	147 273	11 484	67 517	45 101	123 119	1 970 166
Mail and message distributing occupations	990 423	715 310	197 530	5 198	41 046	31 339	73 208	677 075
Service occupations	15 295 917	11 354 441	2 522 099	134 744	504 688	779 945	1 719 992	10 481 292
Private household occupations	521 154	312 888	136 283	3 856	14 044	54 083	119 588	251 678
Protective service occupations	1 992 852	1 580 054	312 808	17 198	29 083	53 709	134 930	1 504 544
Police and firefighters	732 609	624 642	78 005	5 930	7 596	16 436	43 644	598 591
Service occupations, except protective and household	12 781 911	9 461 499	2 073 008	113 690	461 561	672 153	1 465 474	8 725 070
Food service occupations	5 167 308	3 981 476	609 088	42 233	250 384	284 127	608 350	3 675 719
Cleaning and building service occupations	3 127 932	2 113 844	660 057	32 043	86 854	235 134	491 540	1 876 092
Farming, forestry, and fishing occupations	2 839 010	2 370 802	166 079	24 405	40 718	237 006	446 133	2 168 116
Farm operators and managers	1 066 944	1 022 746	16 660	4 255	7 679	15 604	33 300	1 005 516
Farm workers and related occupations	1 590 184	1 194 090	133 366	15 449	30 175	217 104	403 200	1 013 742
Precision production, craft, and repair occupations	13 097 963	11 257 116	930 011	99 782	273 473	537 581	1 177 553	10 648 470
Mechanics and repairers	4 080 305	3 554 246	286 565	27 650	74 673	137 171	315 039	3 385 520
Construction trades	4 793 935	4 174 722	310 992	42 638	56 341	209 242	452 936	3 942 128
Precision production occupations	4 047 043	3 368 249	324 809	27 530	141 794	184 661	395 605	3 168 249
Operators, fabricators, and laborers	17 196 332	13 256 610	2 369 440	141 371	413 417	1 015 494	2 053 742	12 277 425
Machine operators and tenders, except precision	4 981 876	3 706 366	721 735	35 625	169 521	348 629	684 988	3 389 822
Fabricators, assemblers, inspectors, and samplers	2 922 321	2 235 775	382 571	24 645	95 890	183 440	362 199	2 066 445
Transportation occupations	3 760 910	3 030 438	511 246	28 763	50 674	139 789	314 362	2 867 043
Motor vehicle operators	3 580 137	2 870 272	495 739	27 380	49 126	137 620	307 684	2 711 162
Material moving equipment operators	968 091	785 824	120 269	10 715	8 046	43 237	87 111	743 694
Handlers, equipment cleaners, helpers, and laborers	4 563 134	3 498 207	633 619	41 623	89 286	300 399	605 082	3 210 421
Construction laborers	948 540	727 176	116 549	10 986	11 419	82 410	162 235	651 253
Freight, stock, and material handlers	1 576 991	1 244 126	221 599	12 327	31 370	67 569	145 346	1 170 890
Employed females 16 years and over	**52 976 623**	**43 515 117**	**6 015 288**	**340 042**	**1 590 897**	**1 515 279**	**3 669 186**	**41 499 763**
Managerial and professional specialty occupations	14 752 659	12 741 104	1 283 844	73 848	448 538	205 325	623 927	12 348 409
Executive, administrative, and managerial occupations	5 993 163	5 202 033	484 659	31 884	179 835	94 752	278 720	5 028 901
Officials and administrators, public administration	251 316	201 382	38 849	2 820	4 454	3 811	11 588	194 171
Management and related occupations	2 156 867	1 835 280	192 955	10 586	82 290	35 756	103 345	1 771 995
Professional specialty occupations	8 759 496	7 539 071	799 185	41 964	268 703	110 573	345 207	7 319 508
Engineers and natural scientists	551 261	461 596	42 566	1 980	38 787	6 332	21 209	447 566
Engineers	151 962	125 956	11 185	541	12 264	2 016	6 190	121 964
Health diagnosing occupations	171 791	137 721	9 596	423	22 310	1 741	7 727	132 394
Health assessment and treating occupations	2 163 863	1 853 159	188 300	8 654	94 913	18 837	61 812	1 815 016
Teachers, librarians, and counselors	3 977 806	3 440 715	392 151	20 144	70 241	54 555	169 075	3 331 338
Teachers, elementary and secondary schools	2 946 061	2 541 887	308 959	14 472	38 662	42 081	128 741	2 459 000
Technical, sales, and administrative support occupations	23 120 191	19 454 638	2 330 616	134 493	636 528	563 916	1 434 647	18 638 286
Health technologists and technicians	1 133 078	920 524	148 650	7 017	35 757	21 130	55 644	889 284
Technologists and technicians, except health	832 879	688 505	76 882	4 297	48 025	15 170	41 899	663 359
Sales occupations	6 584 290	5 633 355	551 297	38 479	197 333	163 826	417 587	5 394 135
Supervisors and proprietors, sales occupations	1 155 921	1 025 665	68 822	6 098	35 101	20 235	56 425	991 276
Sales representatives, commodities and finance	1 314 555	1 192 130	67 358	4 753	31 043	19 271	59 102	1 154 046
Other sales occupations	4 113 814	3 415 560	415 117	27 628	131 189	124 320	302 060	3 248 813
Cashiers	1 995 673	1 562 480	268 886	16 528	71 840	75 939	171 625	1 473 643
Administrative support occupations, including clerical	14 569 944	12 212 254	1 553 787	84 700	355 413	363 790	919 517	11 691 508
Computer equipment operators	394 508	316 845	54 886	2 378	11 366	9 033	23 351	303 446
Secretaries, stenographers, and typists	4 490 363	3 909 921	380 866	24 934	78 838	95 804	250 655	3 764 243
Financial records processing occupations	2 062 414	1 837 858	123 890	10 443	52 787	37 436	102 477	1 776 315
Mail and message distributing occupations	368 423	258 492	83 180	2 288	14 313	10 150	22 607	247 099
Service occupations	8 929 509	6 701 294	1 508 458	79 643	259 244	380 870	863 229	6 254 384
Private household occupations	494 920	296 628	130 525	3 556	12 698	51 513	114 019	238 248
Protective service occupations	310 463	224 472	71 413	2 643	3 923	8 012	20 185	213 290
Police and firefighters	66 355	48 652	14 615	652	699	1 737	4 581	45 958
Service occupations, except protective and household	8 124 126	6 180 194	1 306 520	73 444	242 623	321 345	729 025	5 802 846
Food service occupations	3 062 435	2 507 545	325 529	26 436	106 592	96 333	223 035	2 387 604
Cleaning and building service occupations	1 278 437	814 051	308 521	13 895	40 319	101 651	212 298	710 772
Farming, forestry, and fishing occupations	449 506	383 374	21 048	3 740	8 330	33 014	59 747	357 362
Farm operators and managers	149 675	143 343	2 089	772	1 586	1 885	3 646	141 648
Farm workers and related occupations	290 041	232 000	18 074	2 662	6 561	30 744	55 354	208 059
Precision production, craft, and repair occupations	1 235 327	957 420	143 560	10 609	65 307	58 431	128 792	890 922
Mechanics and repairers	175 669	139 398	25 220	1 332	4 492	5 227	11 970	132 964
Construction trades	131 124	110 834	11 938	1 550	2 178	4 624	9 876	105 794
Precision production occupations	923 593	703 036	105 934	7 648	58 598	48 377	106 538	648 197
Operators, fabricators, and laborers	4 489 431	3 277 287	727 762	37 709	172 950	273 723	558 844	3 010 400
Machine operators and tenders, except precision	2 018 059	1 410 339	355 868	15 613	96 039	140 200	283 994	1 276 251
Fabricators, assemblers, inspectors, and samplers	1 082 797	782 067	174 765	9 008	47 664	69 293	140 821	714 412
Transportation occupations	426 426	345 352	63 642	4 650	3 688	9 094	22 356	333 025
Motor vehicle operators	419 603	340 356	62 240	4 538	3 541	8 928	21 943	328 241
Material moving equipment operators	46 995	35 735	8 228	605	507	1 920	4 332	33 544
Handlers, equipment cleaners, helpers, and laborers	915 154	703 794	125 259	7 833	25 052	53 216	107 341	653 168
Construction laborers	36 177	28 614	4 294	497	562	2 210	4 257	26 708
Freight, stock, and material handlers	359 459	294 616	41 876	2 819	8 021	12 127	27 511	280 178

Table 46. Industry of Employed Persons by Race and Hispanic Origin: 1990

[Data based on sample and subject to sampling variability, see text. For definitions of terms and meanings of symbols, see text]

United States	All persons	Race					Hispanic origin (of any race)	White, not of Hispanic origin
		White	Black	American Indian, Eskimo, or Aleut	Asian or Pacific Islander	Other race		
Employed persons 16 years and over	115 681 202	96 237 561	11 407 803	728 953	3 411 586	3 895 299	8 981 516	91 447 312
Agriculture	2 944 042	2 498 175	142 331	20 168	41 426	241 942	452 473	2 293 573
Forestry and fisheries	171 330	149 627	8 416	5 277	3 880	4 130	9 598	144 470
Mining	723 423	656 731	31 470	8 386	5 845	20 991	47 692	630 499
Construction	7 214 763	6 263 616	476 307	61 635	104 924	308 281	666 765	5 921 492
Manufacturing	20 462 078	16 890 055	1 961 469	117 389	632 058	861 107	1 793 630	16 006 769
Nondurable goods	8 053 234	6 483 339	916 855	44 934	236 568	371 538	769 761	6 106 767
Food and kindred products	1 405 723	1 073 263	181 040	9 855	41 685	99 880	185 749	991 387
Textile mill and finished textile products	1 809 199	1 285 588	305 421	12 325	91 361	114 504	240 243	1 168 280
Printing, publishing, and allied industries	1 941 923	1 705 760	132 120	8 074	44 755	51 214	119 819	1 641 060
Chemicals and allied products	1 196 595	1 000 382	124 820	4 655	30 989	35 749	78 911	959 290
Durable goods	12 408 844	10 406 716	1 044 614	72 455	395 490	489 569	1 023 869	9 900 002
Furniture, lumber, and wood products	1 276 578	1 063 188	128 000	12 545	14 176	58 669	112 525	1 011 586
Primary metal industries	792 239	667 683	82 676	3 902	8 390	29 588	59 423	638 832
Fabricated metal industries, including ordnance	1 172 905	1 004 791	84 946	6 801	19 513	56 854	111 536	952 527
Machinery and computer equipment	2 362 588	2 074 207	131 417	10 910	80 350	65 704	142 968	2 000 374
Electrical equipment and components, except computer	1 899 173	1 555 462	144 908	10 033	117 565	71 205	158 382	1 473 017
Transportation equipment	2 532 532	2 115 135	260 039	13 531	73 424	70 403	155 754	2 034 043
Transportation, communications, and other public utilities	8 205 062	6 668 534	1 058 299	50 969	203 262	223 998	559 009	6 356 416
Air transportation	758 916	627 137	78 581	4 027	30 353	18 818	58 739	589 624
Trucking service and warehousing	1 941 762	1 634 739	207 818	13 516	21 168	64 521	142 487	1 561 041
Other transportation	2 407 325	1 819 568	413 552	14 040	89 759	70 406	178 777	1 721 201
Communications	1 607 009	1 327 802	200 754	8 157	36 354	33 942	91 562	1 273 884
Utilities and sanitary services	1 490 050	1 259 288	157 594	11 229	25 628	36 311	87 444	1 210 666
Wholesale trade	5 071 026	4 394 632	328 670	23 251	145 540	178 933	414 909	4 169 987
Retail trade	19 485 666	16 364 128	1 611 127	118 938	692 411	699 062	1 627 779	15 486 589
General merchandise stores	2 022 380	1 659 971	234 915	11 868	53 978	61 648	151 877	1 574 835
Food, bakery, and dairy stores	3 339 390	2 814 883	268 777	21 323	115 723	118 684	276 636	2 666 533
Automotive dealers and gasoline stations	2 092 880	1 872 502	114 436	12 876	37 802	55 264	134 847	1 796 426
Eating and drinking places	5 463 979	4 274 860	573 498	40 573	288 623	286 425	620 761	3 958 672
Finance, insurance, and real estate	7 984 870	6 861 092	670 697	28 700	253 873	170 508	459 141	6 590 926
Banking and credit agencies	2 374 916	1 965 795	242 159	7 357	101 194	58 411	157 527	1 873 343
Insurance, real estate, and other finance	5 609 954	4 895 297	428 538	21 343	152 679	112 097	301 614	4 717 583
Services	37 880 865	31 122 541	4 271 203	235 768	1 192 364	1 058 989	2 609 580	29 677 459
Business services	3 851 262	3 126 752	437 740	21 471	117 286	148 013	341 635	2 946 163
Repair services	1 726 200	1 471 254	123 872	12 045	33 648	85 381	185 150	1 376 516
Private households	628 510	381 932	163 907	5 073	16 804	60 794	134 272	313 683
Other personal services	3 040 186	2 345 305	366 248	22 619	156 471	149 543	342 906	2 164 676
Entertainment and recreation services	1 636 460	1 405 978	122 681	12 491	44 051	51 259	125 207	1 336 665
Professional and related services	26 998 247	22 391 320	3 056 755	162 069	824 104	563 999	1 480 410	21 539 756
Hospitals	5 204 690	3 974 245	847 519	29 510	231 965	121 511	309 787	3 805 909
Health services, except hospitals	4 477 994	3 688 334	527 437	28 742	135 092	98 389	255 852	3 543 623
Elementary and secondary schools and colleges	9 154 741	7 689 763	989 928	56 849	234 609	183 592	491 516	7 396 551
Other educational services	478 762	406 679	44 479	2 604	15 612	9 388	23 490	393 409
Social services, religious and membership organizations	3 526 197	2 892 979	444 299	29 744	67 294	91 881	220 539	2 774 199
Legal, engineering, and other professional services	4 155 863	3 739 320	203 093	14 620	139 592	59 238	179 226	3 626 085
Public administration	5 538 077	4 368 430	847 814	58 472	136 003	127 358	340 940	4 169 132
Employed females 16 years and over	52 976 623	43 515 117	6 015 288	340 042	1 590 897	1 515 279	3 669 186	41 499 763
Agriculture	612 437	537 096	26 490	4 098	10 878	34 875	65 146	507 751
Forestry and fisheries	36 553	31 322	2 444	1 054	784	949	1 923	30 402
Mining	106 260	94 148	7 152	1 167	1 525	2 268	5 772	90 781
Construction	724 974	645 504	44 956	5 305	14 278	14 931	38 354	623 397
Manufacturing	6 783 022	5 070 527	802 539	43 038	264 121	300 697	644 778	5 049 999
Nondurable goods	3 384 006	2 031 337	446 968	21 179	126 152	158 370	337 170	2 463 282
Food and kindred products	472 089	344 678	74 107	3 683	17 354	32 267	59 894	318 431
Textile mill and finished textile products	1 152 799	801 036	204 822	8 681	60 191	70 169	153 260	723 470
Printing, publishing, and allied industries	856 148	753 081	61 242	4 009	18 833	18 983	45 851	727 926
Chemicals and allied products	377 438	306 406	45 818	1 468	11 338	12 408	27 767	291 899
Durable goods	3 399 916	2 742 190	355 571	21 859	137 969	142 327	307 608	2 586 717
Furniture, lumber, and wood products	285 684	238 798	30 191	2 024	4 376	10 295	20 246	229 247
Primary metal industries	114 107	95 377	12 928	563	1 859	3 380	7 500	91 418
Fabricated metal industries, including ordnance	272 422	230 127	24 730	1 612	4 672	11 281	23 419	218 597
Machinery and computer equipment	556 814	468 443	45 622	2 896	23 462	16 391	37 260	448 589
Electrical equipment and components, except computer	752 836	588 586	76 357	5 132	49 187	33 574	74 948	549 462
Transportation equipment	548 120	435 764	76 313	3 766	17 639	14 638	33 679	417 812
Transportation, communications, and other public utilities	2 399 658	1 899 099	362 524	14 427	68 905	54 703	148 304	1 812 171
Air transportation	267 994	216 599	33 153	1 301	10 954	5 987	20 057	203 406
Trucking service and warehousing	293 817	254 488	25 210	2 154	4 282	7 683	17 932	244 924
Other transportation	786 510	595 426	137 868	4 786	30 308	18 122	49 253	567 044
Communications	740 265	577 569	126 159	3 958	16 003	16 576	44 035	551 953
Utilities and sanitary services	311 072	255 017	40 134	2 228	7 358	6 335	17 027	244 844
Wholesale trade	1 544 115	1 325 107	103 464	7 343	54 734	53 467	120 862	1 255 725
Retail trade	9 969 141	8 477 017	832 578	64 872	317 739	276 935	677 233	8 099 017
General merchandise stores	1 397 288	1 150 985	162 729	8 211	35 519	39 844	98 756	1 095 387
Food, bakery, and dairy stores	1 659 346	1 429 397	125 493	11 554	48 427	44 475	107 173	1 370 365
Automotive dealers and gasoline stations	448 280	406 298	23 058	3 415	7 338	8 171	22 253	392 815
Eating and drinking places	2 991 360	2 442 990	298 125	23 970	125 233	101 042	232 397	2 319 000
Finance, insurance, and real estate	4 759 138	4 046 594	445 779	18 090	146 348	102 327	272 437	3 886 418
Banking and credit agencies	1 705 936	1 407 586	183 457	5 845	65 747	43 301	113 119	1 342 108
Insurance, real estate, and other finance	3 053 202	2 639 008	262 322	12 245	80 601	59 026	159 318	2 544 310
Services	23 663 230	19 318 219	2 924 284	152 072	651 787	616 868	1 538 500	18 461 743
Business services	1 820 459	1 477 813	214 733	10 100	49 864	67 949	158 127	1 393 437
Repair services	226 893	199 743	14 983	1 738	4 553	5 876	14 345	191 563
Private households	576 557	347 492	153 515	4 452	14 955	56 143	124 101	284 468
Other personal services	1 934 944	1 510 244	235 602	15 820	88 455	84 823	195 387	1 406 898
Entertainment and recreation services	691 354	604 667	45 794	6 163	18 836	15 904	40 953	581 165
Professional and related services	18 413 023	15 178 270	2 259 657	113 799	475 124	386 173	1 005 587	14 604 212
Hospitals	3 963 583	3 055 734	644 749	22 000	160 717	80 383	205 880	2 943 904
Health services, except hospitals	3 497 138	2 866 670	444 588	23 938	82 352	79 590	200 480	2 755 922
Elementary and secondary schools and colleges	6 115 006	5 141 479	695 200	37 083	120 554	120 690	327 674	4 944 296
Other educational services	344 215	295 613	30 364	1 888	10 108	6 242	15 424	286 959
Social services, religious and membership organizations	2 515 952	2 061 221	324 508	21 012	42 564	66 647	160 972	1 974 207
Legal, engineering, and other professional services	1 977 129	1 757 553	120 248	7 878	58 829	32 621	95 157	1 698 924
Public administration	2 377 195	1 767 484	464 078	28 576	59 798	57 259	149 877	1 682 359

Table 47. Class of Worker, Work Status in 1989, and Last Occupation of Experienced Unemployed by Race and Hispanic Origin: 1990

[Data based on sample and subject to sampling variability, see text. For definitions of terms and meanings of symbols, see text]

United States	All persons	Race					Hispanic origin (of any race)	White, not of Hispanic origin
		White	Black	American Indian, Eskimo, or Aleut	Asian or Pacific Islander	Other race		
CLASS OF WORKER								
Employed persons 16 years and over	115 681 202	96 237 561	11 407 803	728 953	3 411 586	3 895 299	8 981 516	91 447 312
Private for profit wage and salary workers	81 781 333	68 136 520	7 610 653	473 852	2 449 328	3 110 980	6 987 883	64 474 694
Employees of own corporation	3 118 578	2 852 857	94 427	9 722	115 399	46 173	147 343	2 754 933
Private not-for-profit wage and salary workers	7 760 060	6 588 643	742 351	44 583	218 930	165 553	410 718	6 362 934
Local government workers	8 244 755	6 552 785	1 231 855	66 172	158 495	235 448	577 730	6 235 102
State government workers	5 381 445	4 278 367	757 734	43 141	184 743	117 460	299 289	4 107 997
Federal government workers	3 940 900	2 914 983	726 293	56 132	147 950	95 542	252 848	2 771 167
Self-employed workers	8 067 483	7 318 612	321 516	42 270	227 250	157 835	421 198	7 066 005
In agriculture	1 062 778	1 005 876	21 944	4 614	11 821	18 523	40 993	983 950
Unpaid family workers	505 226	447 651	17 401	2 803	24 890	12 481	31 850	429 413
Employed females 16 years and over	52 976 623	43 515 117	6 015 288	340 042	1 590 897	1 515 279	3 669 186	41 499 763
Private for profit wage and salary workers	35 647 886	29 384 344	3 787 782	206 340	1 128 285	1 141 135	2 703 950	27 917 690
Employees of own corporation	758 589	679 538	29 096	3 056	34 512	12 387	38 445	654 438
Private not-for-profit wage and salary workers	5 045 116	4 318 366	488 904	27 579	123 217	87 050	226 983	4 189 909
Local government workers	4 617 771	3 658 838	718 821	34 311	83 981	121 820	306 212	3 487 920
State government workers	3 002 677	2 328 412	492 672	24 691	90 332	66 570	170 398	2 231 115
Federal government workers	1 663 488	1 137 547	394 015	29 755	61 778	40 393	103 373	1 080 975
Self-employed workers	2 708 708	2 427 162	124 580	16 026	87 877	53 063	143 506	2 340 830
Unpaid family workers	290 977	260 448	8 514	1 340	15 427	5 248	14 764	251 324
WORK STATUS IN 1989								
Persons 16 years and over, worked in 1989	134 529 779	111 350 984	13 914 568	940 172	3 824 000	4 500 055	10 334 670	105 876 755
50 to 52 weeks	84 533 428	71 367 339	8 042 778	472 252	2 309 455	2 341 604	5 647 572	68 256 293
48 and 49 weeks	5 825 217	4 437 724	701 540	39 576	268 951	377 426	765 230	4 075 635
40 to 47 weeks	11 370 482	9 407 780	1 146 309	80 053	321 012	415 328	934 356	8 920 793
27 to 39 weeks	10 110 388	8 200 361	1 135 436	91 517	261 145	421 929	921 507	7 731 591
14 to 26 weeks	11 628 106	9 299 943	1 380 301	117 477	336 256	494 129	1 088 172	8 744 324
1 to 13 weeks	11 062 158	8 637 837	1 508 204	139 297	327 181	449 639	977 833	8 148 119
Usually worked 35 or more hours per week	105 361 883	86 810 887	11 078 912	740 837	3 037 181	3 694 066	8 419 788	82 379 507
40 or more weeks	87 097 175	72 595 060	8 689 678	515 937	2 517 488	2 778 412	6 469 552	69 127 245
50 to 52 weeks	74 660 124	62 809 360	7 239 604	422 031	2 066 573	2 122 556	5 095 863	60 012 196
27 to 39 weeks	6 296 616	5 003 046	762 882	64 503	158 366	307 819	655 046	4 678 059
Usually worked 15 to 34 hours per week	23 491 124	19 822 503	2 235 581	160 366	618 854	653 820	1 559 353	18 967 372
40 or more weeks	12 332 049	10 675 150	975 978	63 650	318 364	298 907	740 363	10 257 858
50 to 52 weeks	8 377 547	7 294 965	651 067	42 253	205 027	184 235	467 792	7 026 526
27 to 39 weeks	3 104 413	2 601 157	305 716	22 452	81 267	93 821	219 994	2 481 609
Usually worked 1 to 14 hours per week	5 676 772	4 717 594	600 075	38 969	167 965	152 169	355 529	4 529 876
40 or more weeks	2 299 903	1 942 033	224 971	12 294	63 566	57 039	137 243	1 867 618
50 to 52 weeks	1 495 757	1 263 014	152 107	7 968	37 855	34 813	83 917	1 217 571
27 to 39 weeks	709 359	596 158	66 838	4 562	21 512	20 289	46 467	571 923
Females 16 years and over, worked in 1989	61 904 615	50 747 988	7 137 050	433 349	1 787 262	1 798 966	4 304 180	48 407 278
50 to 52 weeks	35 419 603	29 347 758	4 003 406	205 888	1 008 791	853 760	2 169 391	28 117 360
48 and 49 weeks	2 692 119	2 046 442	365 603	16 904	124 904	138 266	294 147	1 902 375
40 to 47 weeks	5 996 730	4 993 075	632 882	38 235	165 324	167 214	402 590	4 772 937
27 to 39 weeks	5 569 882	4 572 964	631 517	45 804	139 430	180 167	418 945	4 349 363
14 to 26 weeks	6 241 320	5 061 450	716 379	56 940	176 036	230 515	519 212	4 791 277
1 to 13 weeks	5 984 961	4 726 299	787 263	69 578	172 777	229 044	499 895	4 473 966
Usually worked 35 or more hours per week	42 973 185	34 579 618	5 418 162	311 436	1 333 277	1 330 692	3 169 835	32 866 204
40 or more weeks	34 274 397	27 802 103	4 232 765	212 942	1 075 894	950 693	2 336 251	26 510 719
50 to 52 weeks	28 714 940	23 459 793	3 489 925	173 875	866 664	724 683	1 833 090	22 425 329
27 to 39 weeks	3 061 761	2 440 145	399 557	28 652	78 645	114 762	260 702	2 304 363
Usually worked 15 to 34 hours per week	15 324 105	13 107 704	1 372 271	99 556	360 554	384 020	931 489	12 590 652
40 or more weeks	8 378 004	7 332 452	636 366	41 247	188 914	179 025	454 921	7 071 489
50 to 52 weeks	5 775 176	5 090 201	424 642	27 584	122 002	110 747	290 141	4 920 036
27 to 39 weeks	2 032 961	1 724 536	191 789	14 302	48 252	54 082	131 073	1 651 438
Usually worked 1 to 14 hours per week	3 607 325	3 060 666	346 617	22 357	93 431	84 254	202 856	2 950 422
40 or more weeks	1 456 051	1 252 720	132 760	6 838	34 211	29 522	74 956	1 210 464
50 to 52 weeks	929 487	797 764	88 839	4 429	20 125	18 330	46 160	771 995
27 to 39 weeks	475 160	408 283	40 171	2 850	12 533	11 323	27 170	393 562
WORKERS IN FAMILY IN 1989								
Families	65 049 428	53 845 200	7 055 063	463 968	1 577 820	2 107 377	4 776 075	51 337 479
No workers	8 477 151	6 866 496	1 173 808	67 067	131 352	238 428	533 688	6 598 688
1 worker	18 243 077	14 672 797	2 344 189	153 924	413 200	658 967	1 492 336	13 891 781
2 workers	29 637 580	25 306 415	2 595 101	187 916	720 804	827 344	1 914 539	24 275 747
3 or more workers	8 691 620	6 999 492	941 965	55 061	312 464	382 638	835 512	6 571 263
Married-couple families	51 718 214	45 178 672	3 521 382	305 156	1 295 099	1 417 905	3 339 694	43 342 946
No workers	6 129 613	5 588 666	345 299	29 632	91 301	74 715	219 748	5 449 811
1 worker	11 870 620	10 429 743	692 228	75 213	303 369	370 067	874 426	9 945 895
2 workers	26 129 451	22 829 971	1 832 900	155 414	635 979	675 187	1 579 493	21 967 267
Husband and wife worked	23 856 655	20 926 870	1 642 420	139 524	577 774	570 067	1 339 489	20 194 145
3 or more workers	7 588 530	6 330 292	650 955	44 897	264 450	297 936	666 027	5 979 973
Husband and wife worked	6 742 469	5 686 727	562 299	38 893	226 789	227 761	520 793	5 408 564
Female householder, no husband present	10 381 654	6 540 382	3 045 283	121 370	185 926	488 693	1 029 646	6 058 841
No workers	2 056 800	1 083 218	759 968	32 080	32 120	149 414	283 838	968 480
1 worker	4 929 373	3 194 979	1 404 530	58 200	74 060	197 604	432 787	2 984 183
2 workers	2 557 262	1 760 764	629 390	23 394	50 952	92 762	210 991	1 652 907
3 or more workers	838 219	501 421	251 395	7 696	28 794	48 913	102 030	453 271
LAST OCCUPATION OF EXPERIENCED UNEMPLOYED								
Persons 16 years and over	7 230 647	5 002 542	1 513 845	113 320	164 811	436 129	906 530	4 571 368
Executive, administrative, and managerial occupations	391 241	324 832	42 897	3 482	10 362	9 668	26 103	309 789
Professional specialty occupations	342 022	267 310	47 725	4 176	14 232	8 579	22 713	254 375
Technicians and related support occupations	130 173	99 009	19 379	1 530	6 143	4 112	10 443	93 332
Sales occupations	798 083	578 140	155 774	8 869	20 055	35 245	78 641	538 910
Administrative support occupations, including clerical	879 086	609 262	194 565	10 255	22 984	42 020	92 506	563 522
Private household occupations	42 764	24 092	11 665	611	864	5 532	11 130	18 817
Protective service occupations	91 923	54 149	29 435	2 743	1 229	4 367	9 421	49 715
Service occupations, except protective and household	1 136 953	699 521	323 090	21 143	26 743	66 456	141 022	632 042
Farming, forestry, and fishing occupations	266 385	170 498	37 304	6 550	4 542	47 491	82 144	137 082
Precision production, craft, and repair occupations	933 337	726 356	121 703	16 514	14 506	54 258	113 701	670 790
Machine operators, assemblers, and inspectors	731 307	477 477	159 320	10 118	19 104	65 288	127 420	420 706
Transportation and material moving occupations	369 973	275 887	66 788	6 251	3 450	17 597	36 769	258 122
Handlers, equipment cleaners, helpers, and laborers	679 050	449 139	158 469	13 205	8 975	49 262	98 437	403 422
Last worked 1984 or earlier, or uniquely military occupation	438 350	246 870	145 731	7 873	11 622	26 254	56 080	220 744

Table 48. Income in 1989 of Households, Families, and Persons by Race and Hispanic Origin: 1990

[Data based on sample and subject to sampling variability, see text. For definitions of terms and meanings of symbols, see text]

United States	All persons	Race					Hispanic origin (of any race)	White, not of Hispanic origin
		White	Black	American Indian, Eskimo, or Aleut	Asian or Pacific Islander	Other race		
INCOME IN 1989								
Households	91 993 582	76 906 980	9 941 850	625 367	2 020 498	2 498 887	5 872 040	73 747 747
Less than $5,000	5 684 517	3 726 768	1 513 647	78 140	136 261	229 701	519 528	3 465 190
$5,000 to $9,999	8 529 980	6 610 505	1 412 467	91 731	126 479	288 798	653 488	6 274 975
$10,000 to $14,999	8 133 273	6 540 094	1 089 626	75 537	140 146	287 870	644 179	6 205 647
$15,000 to $24,999	16 123 742	13 295 239	1 878 449	126 456	279 541	544 057	1 205 131	12 675 640
$25,000 to $34,999	14 575 125	12 374 793	1 407 642	91 267	276 512	424 911	963 489	11 867 672
$35,000 to $49,999	16 428 455	14 274 052	1 324 225	83 967	353 574	392 637	937 461	13 758 950
$50,000 to $74,999	13 777 883	12 162 367	928 232	54 774	388 276	244 234	653 931	11 774 378
$75,000 to $99,999	4 704 808	4 203 619	260 092	14 595	168 542	57 960	180 396	4 087 521
$100,000 or more	4 035 799	3 719 543	127 470	8 900	151 167	28 719	114 437	3 637 774
Median (dollars)	30 056	31 435	19 758	20 025	36 784	22 813	24 156	31 672
Mean (dollars)	38 453	40 308	25 872	26 206	46 695	27 843	30 301	40 646
Families	65 049 428	53 845 200	7 055 063	463 968	1 577 820	2 107 377	4 776 075	51 337 479
Less than $5,000	2 582 206	1 419 771	862 062	49 114	70 522	180 737	365 222	1 254 559
$5,000 to $9,999	3 636 361	2 415 421	850 577	60 426	75 072	234 865	483 067	2 186 825
$10,000 to $14,999	4 676 092	3 507 128	762 216	54 908	99 551	252 289	535 520	3 240 989
$15,000 to $24,999	10 658 345	8 549 776	1 341 930	94 195	205 470	466 974	998 207	8 049 852
$25,000 to $34,999	10 729 951	9 043 670	1 043 831	71 009	210 640	360 801	798 318	8 629 800
$35,000 to $49,999	13 270 930	11 519 137	1 060 248	68 493	288 913	334 139	789 353	11 087 614
$50,000 to $74,999	11 857 079	10 467 357	797 643	46 094	339 835	206 150	557 096	10 134 128
$75,000 or more	4 115 468	3 675 722	228 130	12 370	151 611	47 635	152 405	3 576 462
$100,000 or more	3 522 996	3 247 218	108 426	7 359	136 206	23 787	96 887	3 177 250
Median (dollars)	35 225	37 152	22 429	21 750	41 251	22 949	25 064	37 628
Mean (dollars)	43 803	46 330	28 659	28 025	51 102	27 943	31 195	46 930
Married-couple families	51 718 214	45 178 672	3 521 382	305 156	1 295 099	1 417 905	3 339 694	43 342 946
Less than $15,000	5 619 528	4 486 426	601 094	70 912	158 906	302 190	664 507	4 139 565
$15,000 to $24,999	7 734 791	6 575 092	621 592	62 551	154 424	321 132	692 958	6 220 151
$25,000 to $34,999	8 660 211	7 544 938	616 289	54 742	167 491	276 751	612 960	7 223 464
$35,000 to $49,999	11 566 753	10 243 307	745 545	57 587	244 189	276 125	653 998	9 882 640
$50,000 to $74,999	10 895 423	9 726 294	646 514	41 439	302 697	178 479	489 380	9 429 713
$75,000 or more	7 241 508	6 602 615	290 348	17 925	267 392	63 228	225 891	6 447 413
Female householder, no husband present	10 381 654	6 540 382	3 045 283	121 370	185 926	488 693	1 029 646	6 058 841
Less than $5,000	1 530 177	679 291	696 002	28 076	20 848	105 960	206 345	592 849
$5,000 to $9,999	1 636 764	883 985	582 809	29 368	23 576	117 026	224 843	789 442
$10,000 to $14,999	1 379 635	844 016	424 271	18 718	20 000	72 630	151 134	773 575
$15,000 to $24,999	2 286 235	1 531 229	603 978	23 312	34 272	93 444	202 370	1 432 881
$25,000 to $49,999	2 718 497	1 973 670	591 036	18 180	54 590	81 021	194 382	1 870 903
$50,000 or more	830 346	628 191	147 187	3 716	32 640	18 612	50 572	599 191
Males 15 years and over, with income	86 674 947	72 504 525	8 337 527	605 578	2 285 437	2 941 880	6 688 401	68 980 277
Median income (dollars)	20 409	21 695	12 950	12 180	19 396	12 493	13 501	22 065
Percent year-round full-time workers	53.0	54.2	44.9	40.9	52.4	47.5	48.7	54.4
Median income (dollars)	29 237	30 468	21 647	22 080	30 075	18 627	20 316	30 764
Females 15 years and over, with income	84 560 106	69 613 017	9 965 635	587 568	2 125 535	2 268 351	5 473 121	66 627 911
Median income (dollars)	10 371	10 652	8 825	7 310	11 986	7 876	8 354	10 747
Percent year-round full-time workers	33.9	33.6	35.0	29.5	40.6	31.9	33.4	33.6
Median income (dollars)	19 570	19 916	18 005	16 680	21 335	15 362	16 307	20 048
Per capita income (dollars)	14 420	15 687	8 859	8 328	13 638	7 340	8 400	16 074
Persons in households (dollars)	14 649	15 926	9 019	8 367	13 815	7 366	8 444	16 326
Persons in group quarters (dollars)	6 094	6 319	5 226	7 107	5 465	6 162	6 449	6 330
MEDIAN INCOME IN 1989 BY SELECTED CHARACTERISTICS								
Family type and presence of own children:								
Families (dollars)	35 225	37 152	22 429	21 750	41 251	22 949	25 064	37 628
With own children under 18 years (dollars)	34 627	37 303	20 292	20 221	41 025	21 789	23 417	38 074
With own children under 6 years (dollars)	31 580	34 547	16 924	16 856	37 325	20 007	21 230	35 352
Married-couple families (dollars)	39 584	40 396	33 538	28 287	44 965	27 731	29 930	40 723
With own children under 18 years (dollars)	40 693	41 686	35 162	28 124	44 966	27 219	29 208	42 172
With own children under 6 years (dollars)	36 490	37 369	31 268	22 901	40 210	24 138	25 918	37 908
Female householder, no husband present (dollars)	17 414	20 340	12 522	10 742	22 983	11 262	12 406	20 807
With own children under 18 years (dollars)	12 485	15 011	9 539	8 692	15 791	8 915	9 586	15 444
With own children under 6 years (dollars)	7 775	8 942	6 330	6 279	10 838	6 502	6 823	9 117
Workers in family in 1989:								
No workers (dollars)	14 622	17 311	5 308	6 069	9 050	5 431	5 976	17 781
1 worker (dollars)	25 517	27 998	15 764	15 526	27 860	15 776	16 914	28 714
2 or more workers (dollars)	44 500	45 738	36 955	32 978	50 706	32 272	34 879	46 122
Husband and wife worked (dollars)	46 340	47 005	41 557	35 390	52 729	34 166	37 007	47 273
Nonfamily households (dollars)	17 240	17 991	11 624	12 183	21 336	14 905	15 243	18 067
Male householder (dollars)	22 630	24 115	15 368	15 059	23 807	18 095	19 144	24 283
Living alone (dollars)	20 193	21 219	13 160	11 775	21 958	14 185	15 484	21 353
65 years and over (dollars)	11 688	12 574	6 676	6 792	9 295	6 519	7 159	12 726
Female householder (dollars)	13 729	14 294	9 060	9 939	18 405	9 904	10 624	14 369
Living alone (dollars)	12 226	12 737	8 042	8 142	16 190	7 828	8 517	12 837
65 years and over (dollars)	8 639	9 185	5 358	6 179	7 731	5 436	5 721	9 276
INCOME TYPE IN 1989								
Households	91 993 582	76 906 980	9 941 850	625 367	2 020 498	2 498 887	5 872 040	73 747 747
With earnings	73 874 069	61 696 794	7 689 508	509 200	1 799 815	2 178 752	5 058 335	58 989 523
Mean earnings (dollars)	39 143	40 659	28 754	27 324	47 021	29 118	31 542	40 987
With wage or salary income	71 174 232	59 227 199	7 578 431	494 123	1 737 401	2 137 078	4 940 948	56 592 451
Mean wage or salary income (dollars)	37 271	38 633	28 307	26 277	44 129	28 285	30 433	38 933
With nonfarm self-employment income	10 810 605	9 785 727	494 841	60 297	277 492	192 248	519 133	9 473 587
Mean nonfarm self-employment income (dollars)	20 218	20 519	12 852	14 260	27 804	14 801	16 920	20 593
With farm self-employment income	2 020 105	1 931 481	41 044	11 121	19 202	17 257	44 511	1 905 614
Mean farm self-employment income (dollars)	10 064	10 171	5 449	6 235	12 690	8 509	9 047	10 180
With interest, dividend, or net rental income	37 242 801	34 779 342	1 182 252	129 992	856 647	294 568	974 491	34 128 343
Mean interest, dividend, or net rental income (dollars)	6 949	7 180	2 785	3 646	5 211	2 943	4 129	7 227
With Social Security income	24 210 922	21 382 990	2 191 956	115 261	237 518	283 197	857 372	20 836 706
Mean Social Security income (dollars)	7 772	8 007	5 942	6 133	6 819	5 688	6 206	8 046
With public assistance income	6 943 269	4 269 641	1 955 533	116 009	199 127	402 959	839 908	3 878 673
Mean public assistance income (dollars)	4 078	4 059	3 695	4 145	6 852	4 738	4 501	4 041
With retirement income	14 353 202	12 818 402	1 163 375	66 790	157 114	147 521	451 349	12 530 731
Mean retirement income (dollars)	9 216	9 409	7 579	7 640	9 549	5 748	6 889	9 453
With other income	9 344 304	7 844 227	1 043 079	83 317	134 430	239 251	539 080	7 564 340
Mean other income (dollars)	4 093	4 146	3 596	3 641	5 723	3 769	3 978	4 146

Table 49. Poverty Status in 1989 of Families and Persons by Race and Hispanic Origin: 1990

[Data based on sample and subject to sampling variability, see text. For definitions of terms and meanings of symbols, see text]

United States	All persons	Race					Hispanic origin (of any race)	White, not of Hispanic origin
		White	Black	American Indian, Eskimo, or Aleut	Asian or Pacific Islander	Other race		
ALL INCOME LEVELS IN 1989								
Families	65 049 428	53 845 200	7 055 063	463 968	1 577 820	2 107 377	4 776 075	51 337 479
In owner-occupied housing unit	47 221 605	41 666 428	3 488 403	270 377	949 558	846 839	2 234 435	39 843 104
With related children under 18 years	33 536 660	25 929 135	4 699 116	313 592	996 789	1 598 028	3 353 568	24 811 845
With related children under 5 years	14 250 048	10 777 426	2 064 961	144 727	427 763	835 171	1 673 629	10 194 315
Householder worked in 1989	51 357 521	42 948 299	5 055 636	348 200	1 324 838	1 680 548	3 811 513	40 898 459
Householder worked year round full time in 1989	36 318 276	31 057 625	3 169 072	197 646	908 573	985 360	2 344 303	29 625 967
Householder under 65 years with work disability	4 817 701	3 799 301	714 682	64 327	69 169	170 222	364 823	3 600 592
Householder foreign born	5 888 505	3 147 700	441 553	11 812	1 239 508	1 047 932	2 273 032	2 764 656
Householder under 25 years	2 554 838	1 877 270	412 679	31 542	43 244	190 103	352 154	1 722 160
Householder 65 years and over	10 796 925	9 618 752	883 302	44 476	140 075	110 320	375 526	9 058 625
Householder high school graduate or higher	49 435 732	42 422 515	4 519 185	305 619	1 273 900	914 513	2 366 580	40 841 487
With public assistance income in 1989	5 024 146	2 943 001	1 483 805	88 762	171 172	337 406	679 482	2 829 398
With Social Security income in 1989	14 633 024	12 826 264	1 332 865	75 315	183 312	215 268	621 140	12 096 143
Married-couple families	51 718 214	45 178 672	3 521 382	305 156	1 295 099	1 417 905	3 339 694	42 785 906
With related children under 18 years	25 258 549	21 032 242	2 105 944	192 449	846 351	1 081 563	2 329 405	19 979 328
With related children under 5 years	11 134 320	9 165 153	919 135	89 027	377 487	583 518	1 201 491	8 599 942
Householder worked in 1989	42 105 587	36 703 966	2 799 960	245 868	1 116 840	1 238 953	2 867 065	34 802 995
Householder worked year round full time in 1989	30 876 792	27 241 494	1 935 675	151 004	784 751	763 868	1 847 835	25 896 695
Householder high school graduate or higher	40 340 133	36 071 856	2 350 687	207 764	1 069 747	640 079	1 726 727	34 562 667
Householder 65 years and over	8 856 941	8 150 180	492 633	29 148	113 452	71 528	267 232	7 680 962
With public assistance income in 1989	2 196 987	1 595 184	327 404	34 530	116 160	123 709	271 493	1 500 428
With Social Security income in 1989	11 580 548	10 551 848	702 515	48 378	141 343	136 464	423 083	9 945 243
Female householder, no husband present	10 381 654	6 540 382	3 045 283	121 370	185 926	488 693	1 029 646	6 415 256
With related children under 18 years	6 783 155	3 868 218	2 315 622	95 511	111 206	392 598	782 487	3 870 845
With related children under 5 years	2 532 331	1 245 846	1 023 650	42 989	37 058	182 788	345 235	1 260 399
Householder worked in 1989	6 889 101	4 520 231	1 899 466	73 683	127 662	268 059	596 021	4 494 482
Householder worked year round full time in 1989	3 876 706	2 640 115	1 005 228	32 741	73 571	125 051	296 656	2 627 999
Householder high school graduate or higher	7 088 336	4 815 394	1 875 252	75 312	128 201	194 177	461 745	4 808 024
Householder 65 years and over	1 549 529	1 167 361	321 013	12 115	18 962	30 078	84 741	1 095 393
With public assistance income in 1989	2 541 129	1 180 751	1 078 071	47 625	41 385	193 297	366 937	1 169 372
With Social Security income in 1989	2 380 686	1 748 397	522 774	20 903	28 903	59 709	151 265	1 659 943
Unrelated individuals for whom poverty status is determined	36 672 001	30 375 562	4 208 285	278 246	793 413	1 016 495	2 423 197	28 367 481
Nonfamily householder	26 944 154	23 061 780	2 886 787	161 399	442 678	391 510	1 095 965	21 669 520
In owner-occupied housing unit	12 782 991	11 539 278	961 781	64 930	129 766	87 236	309 934	10 919 678
65 years and over	9 752 744	8 681 911	892 690	37 681	70 525	69 937	260 283	8 124 536
Persons for whom poverty status is determined	241 977 859	194 811 704	28 663 173	1 950 915	7 068 454	9 483 613	21 388 017	182 800 924
Persons 18 years and over	179 372 340	147 704 667	19 327 265	1 279 684	5 042 079	6 018 645	13 915 101	139 393 591
Persons 65 years and over	29 562 647	26 333 010	2 385 907	113 052	434 119	296 559	1 027 755	24 950 136
Related children under 18 years	62 278 655	46 880 667	9 284 053	664 454	2 015 646	3 433 835	7 411 310	43 206 797
Related children under 6 years	21 604 123	16 204 013	3 216 863	231 655	683 890	1 267 702	2 717 165	14 863 865
Related children 5 to 17 years	44 300 630	33 408 002	6 599 196	471 750	1 449 657	2 372 025	5 139 867	30 853 463
INCOME IN 1989 BELOW POVERTY LEVEL								
Families	6 487 515	3 787 586	1 852 014	125 432	182 507	539 976	1 067 179	3 572 683
Percent below poverty level	10.0	7.0	26.3	27.0	11.6	25.6	22.3	7.0
In owner-occupied housing unit	2 307 947	1 660 991	454 432	51 562	34 949	106 013	246 971	1 582 305
With related children under 18 years	4 992 845	2 720 709	1 550 105	104 796	138 221	479 014	920 524	2 562 708
With related children under 5 years	2 613 626	1 388 096	817 253	58 315	69 476	280 486	523 812	1 288 796
Householder worked in 1989	3 215 463	2 003 509	777 559	63 196	84 290	286 909	568 434	1 871 711
Householder worked year round full time in 1989	853 067	559 479	179 343	12 167	20 163	81 915	165 164	511 950
Householder under 65 years with work disability	1 073 192	664 549	296 653	23 948	18 003	70 039	136 770	631 518
Householder foreign born	876 281	374 154	73 281	2 515	162 490	263 841	523 594	221 355
Householder under 25 years	763 410	430 358	231 362	15 017	14 894	71 779	128 678	407 022
Householder 65 years and over	762 939	516 038	197 481	11 211	14 090	24 119	67 961	490 610
Householder high school graduate or higher	3 265 377	2 050 477	895 837	62 109	105 940	151 014	318 379	2 045 143
With public assistance income in 1989	2 286 388	1 094 183	888 048	54 404	58 794	190 959	358 515	1 067 904
With Social Security income in 1989	1 094 068	709 269	306 718	18 332	11 910	47 839	112 495	676 032
Mean income deficit (dollars)	5 379	4 856	6 156	5 938	6 099	6 012	5 942	4 875
Married-couple families	2 849 984	2 042 584	387 992	51 812	120 010	247 586	510 211	1 845 075
With related children under 18 years	1 834 332	1 232 264	256 927	39 646	90 804	214 691	424 054	1 085 474
With related children under 5 years	1 011 812	673 129	132 854	23 123	49 199	133 507	256 143	579 634
Householder worked in 1989	1 581 202	1 139 655	178 572	29 345	60 611	173 019	344 303	1 003 200
Householder worked year round full time in 1989	549 131	412 041	56 183	7 005	16 546	57 356	116 186	361 713
Householder high school graduate or higher	1 351 051	1 032 170	161 223	23 835	72 158	61 665	135 971	990 676
Householder 65 years and over	506 426	390 165	85 691	5 732	11 150	13 688	41 868	366 688
With public assistance income in 1989	554 412	356 651	102 309	16 184	34 647	44 621	92 347	329 613
With Social Security income in 1989	635 487	481 923	112 272	9 170	8 076	24 046	60 852	449 875
Mean income deficit (dollars)	4 994	4 720	5 313	5 977	6 266	5 926	5 817	4 669
Female householder, no husband present	3 230 201	1 517 746	1 356 384	61 131	47 873	247 067	470 419	1 517 708
With related children under 18 years	2 866 941	1 327 810	1 216 660	55 054	39 608	227 809	428 177	1 330 290
With related children under 5 years	1 452 618	636 307	645 676	29 124	17 660	123 851	226 184	639 943
Householder worked in 1989	1 403 435	727 287	549 447	26 600	16 518	83 583	166 736	746 303
Householder worked year round full time in 1989	248 472	115 458	110 452	3 922	2 467	16 173	32 943	122 591
Householder high school graduate or higher	1 721 637	902 046	686 327	32 129	24 192	76 943	157 238	938 748
Householder 65 years and over	215 978	104 759	96 037	4 531	2 111	8 540	21 428	103 323
With public assistance income in 1989	1 642 582	692 869	755 527	34 480	21 009	138 697	251 953	694 564
With Social Security income in 1989	390 389	188 630	171 162	7 631	2 967	19 999	43 205	189 180
Mean income deficit (dollars)	5 764	5 068	6 453	5 922	5 786	6 215	6 176	5 155
Unrelated individuals	8 873 475	6 492 447	1 593 404	113 823	258 514	415 287	927 545	6 003 223
Percent below poverty level	24.2	21.4	37.9	40.9	32.6	40.9	38.3	21.2
Nonfamily householder	5 210 297	3 956 178	980 884	53 431	104 308	115 496	307 943	3 734 887
In owner-occupied housing unit	1 957 191	1 607 889	295 158	21 090	12 380	20 674	68 033	1 533 703
65 years and over	2 494 332	1 959 075	460 486	16 360	22 688	35 723	124 455	1 836 613
Mean income deficit (dollars)	3 311	3 166	3 471	3 714	4 504	4 113	3 969	3 150
Persons	31 742 864	19 025 235	8 441 429	603 188	997 196	2 675 816	5 403 492	16 774 507
Percent below poverty level	13.1	9.8	29.5	30.9	14.1	28.2	25.3	9.2
Persons 18 years and over	20 313 948	13 148 968	4 724 301	342 785	650 705	1 447 189	2 996 026	11 950 741
Persons 65 years and over	3 780 585	2 854 161	761 623	33 219	52 129	79 453	246 362	2 673 031
Related children under 18 years	11 161 836	5 695 183	3 671 536	254 431	337 128	1 203 558	2 356 825	4 663 625
Related children under 6 years	4 331 825	2 231 488	1 410 273	102 229	120 474	467 361	909 240	1 840 047
Related children 5 to 17 years	7 544 737	3 836 033	2 489 090	168 816	237 862	812 936	1 598 712	3 129 318
Persons below 125 percent of poverty level	42 246 073	26 422 974	10 325 165	747 713	1 274 873	3 475 348	7 028 410	23 368 486
Persons below 200 percent of poverty level	74 909 296	50 983 766	15 137 833	1 099 251	2 151 021	5 537 425	11 306 861	45 758 478

Table 50. **Selected Characteristics of Persons 60 Years and Over by Age by Race and Hispanic Origin: 1990**

[Data based on sample and subject to sampling variability, see text. For definitions of terms and meanings of symbols, see text]

United States	All persons	Race — White	Black	American Indian, Eskimo, or Aleut	Asian or Pacific Islander	Other race	Hispanic origin (of any race)	White, not of Hispanic origin
LIVING ARRANGEMENTS								
Persons 60 to 64 years	10 635 762	9 222 857	967 266	54 040	215 276	176 323	538 862	8 879 428
In households	10 521 298	9 129 708	950 133	53 196	213 796	174 465	532 660	8 789 983
In group quarters	114 464	93 149	17 133	844	1 480	1 858	6 202	89 445
Nursing homes	59 648	49 488	8 460	459	507	734	2 196	48 124
Persons 65 to 74 years	18 218 481	16 138 327	1 511 617	74 320	295 142	199 075	671 012	15 689 368
In households	17 884 074	15 849 192	1 473 298	72 706	292 155	196 723	661 652	15 406 503
In group quarters	334 407	289 135	38 319	1 614	2 987	2 352	9 360	282 865
Nursing homes	247 973	216 156	27 637	1 211	1 526	1 443	5 434	212 476
Persons 75 years and over	12 976 794	11 691 745	989 224	43 403	147 432	104 990	385 184	11 424 212
In households	11 580 219	10 394 133	906 761	40 038	140 077	99 210	362 620	10 142 768
In group quarters	1 396 575	1 297 612	82 463	3 365	7 355	5 780	22 564	1 281 444
Nursing homes	1 305 978	1 216 973	75 047	3 026	5 688	5 244	19 882	1 202 833
EDUCATIONAL ATTAINMENT								
Persons 60 to 64 years	10 635 762	9 222 857	967 266	54 040	215 276	176 323	538 862	8 879 428
Less than 9th grade	1 627 746	1 178 437	269 444	18 368	52 212	109 285	257 784	1 037 848
9th to 12th grade, no diploma	2 111 592	1 737 520	300 300	12 667	29 774	31 331	104 178	1 668 702
High school graduate (includes equivalency)	3 429 376	3 133 885	207 190	11 091	56 331	20 879	88 651	3 069 262
Some college or associate degree	1 884 132	1 716 401	115 056	8 131	34 205	10 339	53 721	1 675 049
Bachelor's degree or higher	1 582 916	1 456 614	75 276	3 783	42 754	4 489	34 528	1 428 567
Persons 65 to 74 years	18 218 481	16 138 327	1 511 617	74 320	295 142	199 075	671 012	15 689 368
Less than 9th grade	3 636 494	2 770 848	602 045	28 536	99 123	135 942	363 069	2 554 840
9th to 12th grade, no diploma	3 789 423	3 267 541	430 385	17 347	43 146	31 004	123 118	3 180 054
High school graduate (includes equivalency)	5 774 343	5 398 514	268 099	14 298	73 375	20 057	100 040	5 322 349
Some college or associate degree	2 897 366	2 715 353	126 189	9 630	38 129	8 065	50 825	2 674 456
Bachelor's degree or higher	2 120 855	1 986 071	84 899	4 509	41 369	4 007	33 960	1 957 669
Persons 75 years and over	12 976 794	11 691 745	989 224	43 403	147 432	104 990	385 184	11 424 212
Less than 9th grade	4 453 073	3 705 588	570 377	22 788	73 358	80 962	253 500	3 540 182
9th to 12th grade, no diploma	2 709 473	2 456 934	212 268	8 732	19 361	12 178	58 718	2 412 805
High school graduate (includes equivalency)	2 961 417	2 809 591	112 772	6 188	25 595	7 271	40 321	2 778 057
Some college or associate degree	1 616 777	1 544 620	52 176	3 664	13 434	2 883	18 455	1 530 042
Bachelor's degree or higher	1 236 054	1 175 012	41 631	2 031	15 684	1 696	14 190	1 163 126
INCOME AND POVERTY STATUS IN 1989								
Married-couple families, householder 60 to 64 years	3 863 733	3 488 671	239 742	17 231	64 957	53 132	172 855	3 282 559
Less than $5,000	77 968	62 175	10 233	1 037	1 918	2 605	7 052	57 264
$5,000 to $9,999	151 376	123 305	19 109	1 913	2 231	4 818	12 383	114 569
$10,000 to $14,999	239 904	206 430	22 805	2 037	2 775	5 857	15 988	192 695
$15,000 to $24,999	639 545	572 447	45 170	3 616	7 488	10 824	34 135	536 167
$25,000 to $34,999	671 469	611 710	39 677	2 821	7 716	9 545	29 607	574 157
$35,000 to $49,999	788 016	720 604	43 877	2 630	11 469	9 436	31 979	676 548
$50,000 or more	1 295 455	1 192 000	58 871	3 177	31 360	10 047	41 711	1 131 159
Percent with income in 1989 below poverty level	5.1	4.3	12.9	17.7	7.3	16.4	12.2	4.2
Persons 60 to 64 years living alone	1 637 721	1 384 341	206 669	9 561	17 243	19 907	64 508	1 295 398
Less than $5,000	282 378	198 467	71 238	3 184	2 671	6 818	18 766	187 694
$5,000 to $9,999	341 892	277 250	52 242	2 848	2 825	6 727	10 431	257 288
$10,000 to $14,999	254 933	223 101	26 007	1 163	2 373	2 289	8 768	208 817
$15,000 to $24,999	356 102	317 937	30 588	1 315	3 770	2 492	9 839	296 796
$25,000 to $34,999	186 922	168 805	14 299	521	2 287	1 010	4 314	158 847
$35,000 or more	215 494	198 781	12 295	530	3 317	671	4 090	186 856
Percent with income in 1989 below poverty level	24.6	21.1	45.2	45.3	20.9	50.2	41.6	21.2
Married-couple families, householder 65 to 74 years	6 105 480	5 607 732	344 141	21 183	80 457	51 967	192 250	5 285 558
Less than $5,000	105 626	83 632	15 289	1 046	3 201	2 458	7 419	78 609
$5,000 to $9,999	377 532	310 633	50 250	3 160	5 545	7 944	25 403	291 046
$10,000 to $14,999	683 471	608 600	54 655	3 823	7 357	9 036	30 205	570 662
$15,000 to $24,999	1 565 961	1 450 842	84 386	5 632	12 494	12 607	46 953	1 366 436
$25,000 to $34,999	1 168 869	1 093 356	52 278	3 265	11 995	7 975	30 530	1 030 540
$35,000 to $49,999	1 006 332	938 300	44 844	2 329	14 461	6 398	25 776	886 401
$50,000 or more	1 197 689	1 122 369	42 439	1 928	25 404	5 549	25 964	1 061 864
Percent with income in 1989 below poverty level	4.8	3.9	15.2	17.6	9.4	17.9	14.1	3.9
Persons 65 to 74 years living alone	4 238 144	3 724 122	430 259	18 762	31 951	33 050	121 743	3 484 726
Less than $5,000	673 028	496 672	153 485	5 199	6 586	11 086	37 711	469 343
$5,000 to $9,999	1 351 851	1 155 260	163 614	7 608	9 745	15 624	49 628	1 076 453
$10,000 to $14,999	783 518	721 399	52 172	2 364	4 494	3 089	14 168	675 492
$15,000 to $24,999	792 343	742 747	39 690	2 214	5 526	2 166	12 509	694 260
$25,000 to $34,999	315 489	298 602	12 903	778	2 653	553	4 008	279 497
$35,000 or more	321 915	309 442	8 395	599	2 947	532	3 719	289 681
Percent with income in 1989 below poverty level	22.6	19.4	46.8	39.4	25.8	49.0	43.7	19.5
Married-couple families, householder 75 years and over	2 751 461	2 542 448	148 492	7 965	32 995	19 561	74 982	2 395 404
Less than $5,000	73 814	60 830	9 935	512	1 326	1 211	3 832	57 953
$5,000 to $9,999	311 762	263 707	37 150	2 215	3 964	4 726	17 194	248 211
$10,000 to $14,999	488 925	444 636	32 231	1 676	5 737	4 645	17 407	416 606
$15,000 to $24,999	754 492	706 952	34 701	1 704	6 714	4 421	17 448	665 932
$25,000 to $34,999	427 153	403 886	15 729	839	4 688	2 011	7 967	381 170
$35,000 to $49,999	323 881	307 237	10 085	513	4 614	1 432	5 919	289 441
$50,000 or more	371 434	355 200	8 661	506	5 952	1 115	5 215	336 091
Percent with income in 1989 below poverty level	7.7	6.7	22.5	25.0	11.0	22.5	19.8	6.7
Persons 75 years and over living alone	4 751 106	4 338 947	351 051	14 618	23 059	23 431	94 854	4 062 720
Less than $5,000	896 651	719 314	157 644	5 268	5 380	9 045	36 488	677 911
$5,000 to $9,999	1 870 393	1 701 222	140 919	6 178	10 591	11 483	41 233	1 585 707
$10,000 to $14,999	790 052	755 439	28 830	1 513	2 577	1 693	8 647	707 020
$15,000 to $24,999	654 606	633 951	16 429	1 071	2 444	711	5 169	594 867
$25,000 to $34,999	256 210	250 267	4 379	299	1 006	259	1 600	234 991
$35,000 or more	283 194	278 754	2 850	289	1 061	240	1 717	262 224
Percent with income in 1989 below poverty level	27.0	24.3	57.7	48.2	32.9	53.1	51.2	24.4

Table 105. Age, Fertility, and Household and Family Composition for Selected Racial Groups: 1990

[Data based on sample and subject to sampling variability, see text. For definitions of terms and meanings of symbols, see text]

United States	American Indian, Eskimo, or Aleut				Asian or Pacific Islander	Asian					
	Total	American Indian	Eskimo	Aleut	Total	Total	Chinese	Filipino	Japanese	Asian Indian	Korean
AGE											
All persons	2 015 143	1 937 391	55 674	22 078	7 226 986	6 876 394	1 648 696	1 419 711	866 160	786 694	797 304
Under 3 years	119 287	112 910	5 029	1 348	341 957	320 113	66 720	60 957	28 454	38 656	40 258
3 and 4 years	78 509	74 923	2 785	801	232 476	217 707	41 741	41 591	18 732	26 363	29 882
5 to 9 years	197 456	189 240	6 122	2 094	587 783	550 739	102 295	107 032	46 752	67 703	70 337
10 to 14 years	188 374	181 699	4 937	1 738	551 483	516 781	107 327	110 178	40 128	65 878	63 066
15 to 17 years	107 015	103 053	2 787	1 175	338 729	319 884	66 708	67 386	24 003	34 320	41 989
18 and 19 years	73 262	70 520	2 033	709	251 940	238 247	55 149	50 504	20 842	23 222	32 257
20 to 24 years	171 619	164 091	5 543	1 985	606 252	572 578	132 055	116 755	60 847	66 362	63 995
25 to 29 years	186 025	178 043	5 634	2 348	688 392	652 469	170 735	121 851	78 698	80 586	70 049
30 to 34 years	181 313	174 381	4 702	2 230	725 669	693 487	175 395	132 710	89 564	82 979	83 781
35 to 39 years	158 133	152 528	3 786	1 819	674 166	647 958	167 318	132 309	81 342	80 224	67 125
40 to 44 years	133 719	129 577	2 731	1 411	583 890	562 945	144 460	121 676	68 654	75 175	61 987
45 to 49 years	102 852	99 406	2 201	1 245	417 981	402 052	87 523	92 915	51 365	54 613	53 673
50 to 54 years	80 866	78 318	1 635	913	318 170	305 560	76 587	68 860	42 492	35 957	41 839
55 to 59 years	64 950	62 425	1 793	732	250 248	240 240	64 911	49 339	52 879	20 470	25 675
60 to 64 years	54 040	52 281	1 229	530	215 276	207 438	58 000	44 653	55 204	13 333	17 407
65 to 74 years	74 320	72 116	1 574	630	295 142	285 497	86 899	60 877	74 220	15 422	24 066
75 years and over	43 403	41 880	1 153	370	147 432	142 699	44 873	40 118	31 984	5 431	9 918
Median age	26.9	27.0	23.7	27.5	30.1	30.4	32.3	31.3	36.5	29.4	29.1
FERTILITY											
Women 15 to 24 years	169 637	162 849	4 932	1 856	581 261	548 629	123 363	116 621	53 062	58 696	71 257
Children ever born	90 637	86 798	3 047	792	91 653	79 829	6 312	21 252	4 114	7 736	5 125
Per 1,000 women	534	533	618	427	158	146	51	182	78	132	72
Women ever married	38 482	37 122	915	445	82 769	76 390	9 695	18 129	4 779	12 826	7 578
Children ever born	49 917	48 069	1 337	511	67 530	60 647	4 678	15 563	2 837	6 798	3 794
Per 1,000 women	1 297	1 295	1 461	1 148	816	794	483	858	594	530	501
Women 25 to 34 years	186 646	179 423	5 050	2 173	725 215	691 570	174 604	145 766	86 488	74 682	90 249
Children ever born	352 449	338 102	10 647	3 700	779 523	721 784	120 512	160 930	60 317	84 985	96 251
Per 1,000 women	1 888	1 884	2 108	1 703	1 075	1 044	690	1 104	697	1 138	1 067
Women ever married	136 936	131 976	3 321	1 639	550 528	525 790	121 550	109 880	58 096	66 188	76 935
Children ever born	294 715	282 984	8 430	3 301	749 218	698 140	117 387	153 271	58 761	83 976	95 008
Per 1,000 women	2 152	2 144	2 538	2 014	1 361	1 328	966	1 395	1 011	1 269	1 235
Women 35 to 44 years	150 205	145 497	3 143	1 565	672 487	648 858	161 907	149 480	77 695	71 604	79 718
Children ever born	372 668	359 290	9 547	3 831	1 299 946	1 238 665	275 684	283 702	114 191	145 634	141 576
Per 1,000 women	2 481	2 448	3 038	2 448	1 933	1 909	1 703	1 898	1 470	2 034	1 776
No children	19 659	19 179	354	126	123 120	119 662	32 941	30 895	21 260	7 012	11 515
1 child	22 464	21 809	337	318	115 288	112 329	31 772	24 887	15 185	10 224	14 416
2 children	41 220	40 064	696	460	244 357	238 471	61 320	47 343	28 258	35 644	37 836
3 children	31 929	30 935	636	358	119 176	114 432	26 346	30 002	10 321	13 679	13 093
4 children	18 226	17 598	472	156	41 685	38 279	6 913	10 961	2 121	3 405	2 233
5 or more children	16 707	15 912	648	147	28 861	25 685	2 615	5 392	550	1 640	625
Women ever married	134 368	130 212	2 688	1 468	617 501	596 355	147 073	133 601	68 649	69 383	77 343
Children ever born	351 771	339 213	8 826	3 732	1 285 080	1 225 885	274 153	279 108	113 351	145 185	141 097
Per 1,000 women	2 618	2 605	3 283	2 542	2 081	2 056	1 864	2 089	1 651	2 093	1 824
HOUSEHOLD TYPE AND RELATIONSHIP											
All persons	2 015 143	1 937 391	55 674	22 078	7 226 986	6 876 394	1 648 696	1 419 711	866 160	786 694	797 304
In households	1 952 539	1 878 153	53 058	21 328	7 074 394	6 734 211	1 609 368	1 393 874	844 890	771 046	778 929
Family householder	463 968	449 281	10 049	4 638	1 577 820	1 506 724	389 818	293 229	208 165	192 836	163 149
Male	309 410	299 482	6 634	3 294	1 308 673	1 255 352	332 525	229 676	173 501	176 538	137 582
Female	154 558	149 799	3 415	1 344	269 147	251 372	57 293	63 553	34 664	16 298	25 567
Nonfamily householder	161 399	155 619	3 688	2 092	442 678	425 340	119 577	63 146	107 714	40 856	38 619
Male	83 327	79 713	2 451	1 163	244 905	234 658	65 119	28 603	55 070	31 648	16 827
Female	78 072	75 906	1 237	929	197 773	190 682	54 458	34 543	52 644	9 208	21 792
Spouse	310 579	299 422	7 428	3 729	1 504 756	1 450 499	347 014	296 970	230 246	166 021	192 115
Child	751 748	720 078	23 742	7 928	2 505 467	2 369 069	513 578	485 654	221 140	271 509	303 696
Other relatives	146 374	140 048	4 909	1 417	686 998	648 410	158 452	182 077	35 407	69 350	54 318
Nonrelatives	118 471	113 705	3 242	1 524	356 675	334 169	80 929	72 798	42 218	30 474	27 032
In group quarters	62 604	59 238	2 616	750	152 592	142 183	39 328	25 837	21 270	15 648	18 375
Persons per household	3.08	3.07	3.52	2.99	3.29	3.28	3.12	3.63	2.47	3.37	3.16
Persons per family	3.57	3.55	4.19	3.58	3.74	3.73	3.58	3.97	3.07	3.73	3.55
FAMILY TYPE BY PRESENCE OF OWN CHILDREN											
Families	463 968	449 281	10 049	4 638	1 577 820	1 506 724	389 818	293 229	208 165	192 836	163 149
With own children under 18 years	281 698	271 938	6 806	2 954	938 105	892 633	208 745	176 289	86 852	132 489	102 325
With own children under 6 years	138 756	133 017	4 193	1 546	445 422	421 773	95 746	77 657	41 632	62 677	44 281
Married-couple families	305 156	295 600	6 260	3 296	1 295 099	1 242 237	330 606	231 168	174 211	174 768	137 178
With own children under 18 years	178 736	172 271	4 424	2 041	815 582	780 862	190 024	148 411	76 414	125 577	89 775
With own children under 6 years	88 960	85 091	2 766	1 103	402 836	384 494	90 784	67 793	38 850	60 511	41 545
Female householder, no husband present	121 370	117 790	2 636	944	185 926	172 861	36 708	44 304	24 765	8 587	18 419
With own children under 18 years	80 840	78 372	1 764	704	94 498	86 336	14 056	21 930	8 465	4 684	10 011
With own children under 6 years	38 040	36 647	1 036	357	32 582	28 544	3 549	7 540	2 072	1 406	2 176
Subfamilies	37 017	35 361	1 411	245	125 397	116 108	29 291	35 957	7 098	13 482	9 434
With own children under 18 years	34 535	32 982	1 339	214	65 285	57 357	11 647	18 803	4 928	4 664	4 191
Married-couple subfamilies	4 994	4 794	144	56	79 014	75 634	21 916	22 421	3 436	10 745	6 429
With own children under 18 years	2 512	2 415	72	25	18 902	16 883	4 272	5 267	1 266	1 927	1 186
Mother-child subfamilies	23 985	22 976	865	144	34 966	30 308	5 081	10 188	2 913	1 910	2 366
Persons under 18 years	690 641	661 825	21 660	7 156	2 052 428	1 925 224	384 791	387 144	158 069	232 920	245 532
Percent living with two parents	55.7	55.4	60.8	63.8	82.2	83.3	86.8	79.7	85.2	90.9	88.0
UNMARRIED-PARTNER HOUSEHOLDS											
Total	45 554	43 868	1 156	530	48 517	43 187	8 206	11 448	9 232	2 514	3 492
Male and female	44 191	42 564	1 118	509	46 325	41 266	7 750	10 854	8 913	2 317	3 446
Both male	588	564	19	5	1 300	1 181	218	361	232	151	28
Both female	775	740	19	16	892	740	238	233	87	46	18
SELECTED LIVING ARRANGEMENTS											
Households	625 367	604 900	13 737	6 730	2 020 498	1 932 064	509 395	356 375	315 879	233 692	201 768
With one or more subfamilies	33 550	32 008	1 333	209	115 178	107 511	27 343	32 923	7 152	12 699	8 401
With related members 15 years and over other than spouse, children, parents, or parents-in-law of householder	49 173	47 168	1 477	528	239 073	228 074	53 702	59 842	13 920	25 879	15 881
With roomer, boarder, or foster child 15 years and over	8 106	7 878	100	128	30 025	28 387	6 642	8 645	2 571	2 081	2 115

SOCIAL AND ECONOMIC CHARACTERISTICS

UNITED STATES SUMMARY **105**

Table 105. Age, Fertility, and Household and Family Composition for Selected Racial Groups: 1990—Con.

[Data based on sample and subject to sampling variability, see text. For definitions of terms and meanings of symbols, see text]

United States	Asian—Con.						Pacific Islander				
	Vietnamese	Cambodian	Hmong	Laotian	Thai	Other Asian	Total	Hawaiian	Samoan	Guamanian	Other Pacific Islander
AGE											
All persons	593 213	149 047	94 439	147 375	91 360	282 395	350 592	205 501	57 679	47 754	39 658
Under 3 years	29 266	10 851	11 760	9 946	2 876	20 369	21 844	11 974	4 585	2 447	2 838
3 and 4 years	19 858	8 830	8 871	7 126	1 805	12 908	14 769	8 035	3 127	1 901	1 706
5 to 9 years	53 748	26 075	19 966	20 361	5 994	30 476	37 044	20 986	7 221	4 413	4 424
10 to 14 years	53 952	14 923	11 245	18 517	7 107	24 460	34 702	19 949	6 386	4 637	3 730
15 to 17 years	42 519	8 799	5 500	10 380	4 923	13 357	18 845	10 855	3 335	2 585	2 070
18 and 19 years	28 144	5 704	2 995	5 999	3 150	10 281	13 693	7 310	2 559	2 178	1 646
20 to 24 years	61 885	12 401	6 886	12 525	7 541	31 326	33 674	18 678	5 895	4 806	4 295
25 to 29 years	61 595	10 665	6 603	13 360	8 183	30 144	35 923	20 283	5 784	5 314	4 542
30 to 34 years	59 700	12 181	4 835	13 394	8 988	29 960	32 182	18 528	4 451	5 188	4 015
35 to 39 years	56 270	11 343	4 088	10 663	12 160	25 116	26 208	15 458	3 722	4 051	2 977
40 to 44 years	41 256	7 900	2 912	7 588	13 359	17 978	20 945	12 688	2 839	3 269	2 149
45 to 49 years	27 258	6 511	2 163	5 958	8 659	11 414	15 929	10 532	2 007	1 772	1 618
50 to 54 years	18 807	4 084	1 790	4 116	3 538	7 490	12 610	7 967	1 901	1 517	1 225
55 to 59 years	12 764	3 332	1 339	2 442	1 225	5 864	10 008	6 760	1 175	1 131	942
60 to 64 years	9 606	1 809	828	1 637	784	4 177	7 838	5 432	1 074	830	502
65 to 74 years	11 237	2 779	1 932	2 354	879	4 832	9 645	6 668	1 109	1 199	669
75 years and over	5 348	860	726	1 009	189	2 243	4 733	3 398	509	516	310
Median age	25.6	19.7	12.7	20.5	32.3	24.7	25.1	26.2	21.3	25.9	23.9
FERTILITY											
Women 15 to 24 years	58 149	13 597	7 052	14 025	8 119	24 688	32 632	18 107	5 696	4 807	4 022
Children ever born	8 911	5 423	8 778	6 629	1 008	4 541	11 824	7 242	2 089	1 565	928
Per 1,000 women	153	399	1 245	473	124	184	362	400	367	326	231
Women ever married	7 471	2 752	3 514	3 745	1 222	4 679	6 379	3 404	1 138	1 003	834
Children ever born	6 165	3 362	8 083	5 099	751	3 517	6 883	3 856	1 363	958	706
Per 1,000 women	825	1 222	2 300	1 362	615	752	1 079	1 133	1 198	955	847
Women 25 to 34 years	52 783	12 927	5 427	13 197	9 891	25 556	33 645	19 227	5 087	5 020	4 311
Children ever born	75 243	29 844	25 060	31 255	7 782	29 605	57 739	32 067	9 970	8 311	7 391
Per 1,000 women	1 426	2 309	4 618	2 368	787	1 158	1 716	1 668	1 960	1 656	1 714
Women ever married	39 027	10 545	5 123	11 678	7 030	19 738	24 738	13 549	3 727	4 010	3 452
Children ever born	71 714	27 605	24 755	30 281	7 501	27 881	51 078	27 471	9 009	7 659	6 939
Per 1,000 women	1 838	2 618	4 832	2 593	1 067	1 413	2 065	2 028	2 417	1 910	2 010
Women 35 to 44 years	50 250	10 141	3 503	8 520	17 645	18 395	23 629	14 034	3 265	3 657	2 673
Children ever born	126 003	34 528	21 288	29 722	29 734	36 603	61 281	33 440	10 256	9 565	8 020
Per 1,000 women	2 508	3 405	6 077	3 488	1 685	1 990	2 593	2 383	3 141	2 616	3 000
No children	6 965	874	121	663	3 922	3 494	3 458	2 347	390	435	286
1 child	7 302	918	146	683	3 758	3 038	2 959	1 827	447	365	320
2 children	13 097	1 800	163	1 327	5 819	5 864	5 886	3 633	544	1 061	648
3 children	10 230	2 155	206	1 922	2 841	3 637	4 744	2 932	536	833	443
4 children	6 795	1 595	356	1 582	872	1 446	3 406	1 945	496	558	407
5 or more children	5 861	2 799	2 511	2 343	433	916	3 176	1 350	852	405	569
Women ever married	45 831	9 546	3 419	8 246	16 506	16 758	21 146	12 229	2 970	3 398	2 549
Children ever born	123 081	33 789	21 249	29 377	29 655	35 840	59 195	31 911	9 968	9 345	7 971
Per 1,000 women	2 686	3 540	6 215	3 563	1 797	2 139	2 799	2 609	3 356	2 750	3 127
HOUSEHOLD TYPE AND RELATIONSHIP											
All persons	593 213	149 047	94 439	147 375	91 360	282 395	350 592	205 501	57 679	47 754	39 658
In households	583 554	148 247	93 947	146 455	89 396	274 505	340 183	200 624	55 111	46 121	38 327
Family householder	118 309	28 185	14 374	28 592	16 710	53 357	71 096	43 080	10 279	10 314	7 423
Male	93 545	19 064	11 637	23 947	12 353	44 984	53 321	31 364	7 670	8 355	5 932
Female	24 764	9 121	2 737	4 645	4 357	8 373	17 775	11 716	2 609	1 959	1 491
Nonfamily householder	22 004	1 009	441	2 210	6 946	21 578	17 338	12 573	1 216	2 327	1 222
Male	16 099	1 179	242	1 774	3 354	14 743	10 247	7 213	788	1 472	774
Female	6 285	690	199	436	3 592	6 835	7 091	5 360	428	855	448
Spouse	94 937	19 755	11 985	23 670	25 287	42 499	54 257	31 137	7 771	8 448	6 901
Child	232 582	72 907	57 542	71 328	25 704	113 429	136 398	78 470	24 857	17 659	15 412
Other relatives	75 763	17 242	8 417	15 958	7 800	23 626	38 588	21 582	8 252	3 777	4 977
Nonrelatives	39 579	8 289	1 188	4 697	6 949	20 016	22 506	13 782	2 736	3 596	2 392
In group quarters	9 659	800	492	920	1 964	7 890	10 409	4 877	2 568	1 633	1 331
Persons per household	3.99	4.91	6.29	4.75	2.91	3.10	3.63	3.40	4.51	3.50	4.06
Persons per family	4.26	4.90	6.38	4.90	3.40	3.62	4.02	3.82	4.76	3.82	4.38
FAMILY TYPE BY PRESENCE OF OWN CHILDREN											
Families	118 309	28 185	14 374	28 592	16 710	53 357	71 096	43 080	10 279	10 314	7 423
With own children under 18 years	81 614	23 614	12 956	23 662	10 737	33 350	45 472	25 634	7 680	6 911	5 247
With own children under 6 years	40 828	13 702	9 847	12 066	4 342	18 995	23 649	12 652	4 452	3 429	3 116
Married-couple families	84 819	19 374	11 838	23 369	12 437	42 469	52 862	31 302	7 676	8 003	5 881
With own children under 18 years	65 090	17 132	11 022	20 070	8 534	28 813	34 720	18 812	5 947	5 547	4 414
With own children under 6 years	34 502	10 256	8 834	10 387	3 700	17 246	18 342	9 302	3 507	2 797	2 736
Female householder, no husband present	18 815	7 165	1 952	3 238	3 189	5 719	13 065	8 620	1 984	1 530	931
With own children under 18 years	12 101	5 805	1 622	2 482	1 868	3 312	8 162	5 177	1 404	952	629
With own children under 6 years	4 983	3 136	847	1 177	404	1 254	4 038	2 602	758	418	260
Subfamilies	9 350	3 051	1 452	2 598	1 045	3 350	9 289	5 974	1 720	772	823
With own children under 18 years	5 591	2 324	1 004	1 657	585	1 963	7 928	5 346	1 409	616	557
Married-couple subfamilies	5 082	1 162	691	1 274	557	1 921	3 380	1 915	750	292	423
With own children under 18 years	1 323	435	243	333	97	534	2 019	1 287	439	136	157
Mother-child subfamilies	3 242	1 576	527	993	428	1 084	4 658	3 195	763	393	307
Persons under 18 years	199 343	69 478	57 342	66 330	22 705	101 570	127 204	71 799	24 654	15 983	14 768
Percent living with two parents	74.4	68.0	84.1	79.9	76.5	83.3	66.2	63.0	67.0	71.1	75.1
UNMARRIED-PARTNER HOUSEHOLDS											
Total	3 536	662	134	899	942	2 122	5 330	3 804	477	777	272
Male and female	3 401	645	129	889	910	2 012	5 059	3 592	453	756	258
Both male	103	–	–	6	15	67	119	84	–	21	14
Both female	32	17	5	4	17	43	152	128	24	–	–
SELECTED LIVING ARRANGEMENTS											
Households	140 693	30 054	14 815	30 802	23 656	74 935	88 434	55 653	11 495	12 641	8 645
With one or more subfamilies	8 597	2 953	1 374	2 623	686	2 760	7 667	4 910	1 403	686	668
With related members 15 years and over other than spouse, children, parents, or parents-in-law of householder	30 773	6 238	2 762	5 766	3 355	9 956	10 999	5 882	2 116	1 354	1 647
With roomer, boarder, or foster child 15 years and over	3 754	642	120	367	359	1 091	1 638	1 081	170	320	67

Table 106. **Education, Ability to Speak English, and Disability for Selected Racial Groups: 1990**

[Data based on sample and subject to sampling variability, see text. For definitions of terms and meanings of symbols, see text]

United States	American Indian, Eskimo, or Aleut				Asian or Pacific Islander						
						Asian					
	Total	American Indian	Eskimo	Aleut	Total	Total	Chinese	Filipino	Japanese	Asian Indian	Korean
SCHOOL ENROLLMENT AND TYPE OF SCHOOL											
Persons 3 years and over enrolled in school	**635 992**	**611 639**	**17 445**	**6 908**	**2 552 671**	**2 431 694**	**589 888**	**444 857**	**228 551**	**285 362**	**302 447**
Preprimary school	41 421	38 725	2 163	533	132 582	125 410	28 304	18 889	16 483	16 049	21 457
Public school	34 573	32 091	2 043	439	67 445	62 710	12 720	9 966	6 887	7 170	9 557
Elementary or high school	467 518	450 325	12 596	4 597	1 446 890	1 361 373	280 846	272 277	103 598	160 454	168 850
Public school	444 226	427 501	12 394	4 331	1 280 058	1 201 675	250 404	222 589	89 427	138 347	148 898
College	127 053	122 589	2 686	1 778	973 199	944 911	280 738	153 691	108 470	108 859	112 140
Public college	106 465	103 016	2 022	1 427	729 252	707 703	211 875	111 533	82 453	74 125	78 834
Persons 3 years and over enrolled in school	**635 992**	**611 639**	**17 445**	**6 908**	**2 552 671**	**2 431 694**	**589 888**	**444 857**	**228 551**	**285 362**	**302 447**
3 and 4 years	19 813	18 398	1 122	293	70 729	67 044	17 228	9 092	8 696	9 088	10 942
5 to 14 years	357 150	343 436	10 233	3 481	1 059 662	993 103	198 265	201 521	82 176	126 525	123 642
15 to 17 years	95 485	91 909	2 514	1 062	322 079	304 487	64 391	63 791	22 936	32 975	40 009
18 and 19 years	39 683	38 368	938	377	210 889	203 085	50 790	39 331	17 825	20 658	28 312
20 to 24 years	39 474	37 922	1 005	547	355 538	345 483	93 166	54 169	38 611	41 423	42 305
25 to 34 years	43 793	42 329	816	648	316 058	307 629	105 274	36 792	33 023	34 966	36 272
35 years and over	40 594	39 277	817	500	217 716	210 863	60 774	40 161	25 284	19 727	20 965
Persons 18 to 24 years	**244 881**	**234 611**	**7 576**	**2 694**	**858 192**	**810 825**	**187 204**	**167 259**	**81 689**	**89 584**	**96 252**
Percent enrolled in college	21.6	21.7	17.1	25.9	55.1	56.6	66.5	47.1	63.5	61.9	60.3
Persons 16 to 19 years	**143 769**	**138 346**	**3 911**	**1 512**	**480 997**	**454 607**	**100 286**	**96 754**	**37 434**	**45 605**	**60 352**
Percent not enrolled, not high school graduate	18.1	18.2	14.4	16.1	5.4	5.1	3.2	5.7	3.3	4.1	4.3
EDUCATIONAL ATTAINMENT											
Persons 18 to 24 years	**244 881**	**234 611**	**7 576**	**2 694**	**858 192**	**810 825**	**187 204**	**167 259**	**81 689**	**89 584**	**96 252**
High school graduate (includes equivalency)	83 309	78 714	3 602	993	213 094	194 060	42 411	44 233	20 214	17 995	24 980
Some college or associate degree	67 252	64 729	1 733	790	371 306	354 919	83 216	78 697	43 600	36 655	42 649
Bachelor's degree or higher	5 089	4 816	140	133	112 580	110 835	32 771	17 306	10 886	22 961	11 844
Persons 25 years and over	**1 079 621**	**1 040 955**	**26 438**	**12 228**	**4 316 366**	**4 140 345**	**1 076 701**	**865 308**	**626 402**	**464 190**	**455 520**
Less than 5th grade	50 552	46 590	3 074	888	296 660	291 895	101 115	36 410	8 924	17 546	21 099
5th to 8th grade	100 662	95 874	3 553	1 235	261 234	252 175	79 748	53 724	25 940	16 405	25 143
9th to 12th grade, no diploma	220 900	215 408	3 759	1 733	411 508	383 310	103 390	60 368	43 500	36 885	43 782
High school graduate (includes equivalency)	313 783	301 261	8 852	3 670	799 206	735 752	156 447	141 155	162 642	53 639	113 207
Some college, no degree	224 300	217 344	4 600	2 356	634 810	595 600	124 603	157 862	106 932	45 194	63 620
Associate degree, occupational program	40 426	39 221	734	471	169 200	162 702	34 996	36 274	31 620	13 476	15 035
Associate degree, academic program	28 495	27 806	426	263	165 109	159 268	37 909	39 578	30 468	11 491	16 571
Bachelor's degree	65 512	63 496	958	1 058	978 338	964 587	232 531	274 033	153 455	116 174	101 092
Graduate or professional degree	34 991	33 955	482	554	600 301	595 056	205 962	65 904	62 921	153 380	55 971
Females 25 years and over	**562 703**	**543 444**	**13 161**	**6 098**	**2 282 675**	**2 194 033**	**551 414**	**492 955**	**350 125**	**207 657**	**269 165**
Less than 5th grade	26 399	24 336	1 572	491	192 850	190 171	64 830	21 416	5 636	11 867	16 178
5th to 8th grade	51 569	49 119	1 799	651	165 589	160 860	44 948	34 848	17 790	11 306	20 674
9th to 12th grade, no diploma	117 140	114 411	1 880	849	235 312	220 591	54 584	35 540	27 058	20 449	32 840
High school graduate (includes equivalency)	163 733	157 679	4 256	1 798	464 698	431 735	89 139	76 976	103 124	28 991	77 526
Some college, no degree	118 641	115 051	2 347	1 243	316 915	297 653	63 531	76 352	59 923	21 795	34 262
Associate degree, occupational program	21 071	20 511	370	190	88 196	85 149	19 273	20 189	18 314	6 492	8 615
Associate degree, academic program	15 626	15 226	276	124	92 715	89 966	22 167	22 611	19 547	5 705	9 489
Bachelor's degree	32 661	31 630	493	538	515 986	509 714	121 227	170 295	74 937	55 630	52 744
Graduate or professional degree	15 863	15 481	168	214	210 414	208 194	71 715	34 728	23 796	45 422	16 837
Persons 25 years and over	**1 079 621**	**1 040 955**	**26 438**	**12 228**	**4 316 366**	**4 140 345**	**1 076 701**	**865 308**	**626 402**	**464 190**	**455 520**
Percent less than 5th grade	4.7	4.5	11.6	7.3	6.9	7.1	9.4	4.2	1.4	3.8	4.6
Percent high school graduate or higher	65.5	65.6	60.7	68.5	77.5	77.6	73.6	82.6	87.5	84.7	80.2
Percent some college or higher	36.5	36.7	27.2	38.5	59.0	59.8	59.1	66.3	61.5	73.2	55.4
Percent bachelor's degree or higher	9.3	9.4	5.4	13.2	36.6	37.7	40.7	39.3	34.5	58.1	34.5
Males 25 to 34 years	**180 692**	**173 001**	**5 286**	**2 405**	**688 846**	**654 386**	**171 526**	**108 795**	**81 774**	**88 883**	**63 581**
Percent high school graduate or higher	71.7	71.5	75.4	79.0	87.2	87.4	88.3	91.2	96.4	90.8	94.2
Percent bachelor's degree or higher	7.2	7.2	5.0	14.3	43.6	45.3	56.2	31.9	50.4	62.9	49.4
Females 25 to 34 years	**186 646**	**179 423**	**5 050**	**2 173**	**725 215**	**691 570**	**174 604**	**145 766**	**86 488**	**74 682**	**90 249**
Percent high school graduate or higher	74.9	74.6	79.5	82.4	84.7	84.8	86.4	90.4	97.1	88.0	88.2
Percent bachelor's degree or higher	7.8	7.8	4.5	14.0	39.9	41.3	50.4	41.6	46.6	55.2	34.6
ABILITY TO SPEAK ENGLISH											
Persons 5 years and over	**1 817 347**	**1 749 558**	**47 860**	**19 929**	**6 652 553**	**6 338 574**	**1 540 235**	**1 317 163**	**818 974**	**721 675**	**727 164**
Speak a language other than English	432 761	403 139	24 163	5 459	4 878 530	4 780 516	1 294 375	900 675	360 415	561 249	593 529
5 to 17 years	94 960	88 696	5 269	995	896 940	875 932	214 178	103 067	38 440	104 448	107 665
18 to 64 years	301 226	280 361	16 883	3 982	3 618 339	3 546 899	960 758	704 974	256 542	439 058	454 737
65 to 74 years	21 970	20 424	1 229	317	236 355	232 580	78 242	56 373	41 052	13 086	21 879
75 years and over	14 605	13 658	782	165	126 896	125 105	41 197	36 261	24 381	4 657	9 248
Do not speak English "very well"	167 612	155 441	9 546	2 625	2 555 424	2 520 810	777 442	318 305	206 213	169 363	375 527
5 to 17 years	41 375	38 643	2 311	421	379 325	372 464	89 982	31 979	20 841	24 711	39 507
18 to 64 years	107 532	99 696	5 902	1 934	1 911 768	1 886 903	589 497	227 702	147 663	132 899	307 853
65 to 74 years	10 579	9 660	768	151	167 973	166 071	63 520	34 464	20 756	8 530	19 717
75 years and over	8 126	7 442	565	119	96 358	95 372	34 443	24 160	16 953	3 223	8 450
ABILITY TO SPEAK ENGLISH IN HOUSEHOLD											
Linguistically isolated households	32 310	30 276	1 496	538	542 402	538 111	184 240	42 535	61 106	27 683	90 937
Persons 5 years and over in households	**1 755 292**	**1 690 836**	**45 277**	**19 179**	**6 500 628**	**6 196 953**	**1 501 025**	**1 291 425**	**797 740**	**706 066**	**708 875**
In linguistically isolated households	81 800	76 446	3 856	1 498	1 572 006	1 558 272	522 225	125 328	118 176	79 410	248 570
5 to 17 years	22 760	21 339	1 008	413	366 366	362 075	95 366	24 558	18 358	18 655	51 683
18 to 64 years	49 303	45 956	2 373	974	1 070 211	1 061 728	365 612	83 562	80 174	58 106	178 368
65 to 74 years	5 317	4 993	283	41	88 226	87 584	39 943	10 178	10 876	1 940	13 487
75 years and over	4 420	4 158	192	70	47 203	46 885	21 304	7 030	8 768	709	5 032
DISABILITY STATUS OF CIVILIAN NONINSTITUTIONALIZED PERSONS											
Persons 16 to 64 years	**1 236 191**	**1 190 130**	**31 787**	**14 274**	**4 903 212**	**4 690 859**	**1 172 550**	**951 750**	**613 490**	**553 287**	**542 642**
With a mobility or self-care limitation	94 896	92 006	2 044	846	297 639	285 841	63 025	56 260	22 360	32 470	38 663
With a mobility limitation	46 073	44 871	868	334	96 213	91 684	16 447	13 103	8 665	8 182	15 757
In labor force	9 958	9 587	246	125	35 319	34 158	6 531	5 121	3 010	3 272	8 948
With a self-care limitation	71 397	69 090	1 587	720	255 005	245 333	56 159	50 035	17 973	28 619	33 055
With a work disability	168 266	163 704	3 281	1 281	205 612	189 923	37 379	34 216	25 328	15 483	22 980
In labor force	62 681	60 998	1 184	499	81 640	75 218	15 612	15 821	10 855	6 946	11 368
Prevented from working	90 482	88 195	1 667	620	100 763	93 081	17 368	15 207	11 053	7 073	8 833
No work disability	1 067 925	1 026 426	28 506	12 993	4 697 600	4 500 936	1 135 171	917 534	588 162	537 804	519 662
In labor force	775 459	749 009	17 610	8 840	3 452 728	3 302 105	827 902	757 447	431 192	405 170	349 349
Persons 65 to 74 years	**72 864**	**70 746**	**1 495**	**623**	**293 197**	**283 706**	**86 314**	**60 611**	**73 675**	**15 271**	**23 902**
With a mobility or self-care limitation	16 096	15 700	303	93	48 926	47 073	13 313	11 514	8 099	3 256	4 895
With a mobility limitation	12 135	11 833	222	80	29 663	28 364	7 152	7 392	3 935	2 425	3 252
With a self-care limitation	9 821	9 607	178	36	33 503	32 334	10 150	7 159	6 028	1 730	3 601
Persons 75 years and over	**40 188**	**38 845**	**994**	**349**	**140 949**	**136 794**	**43 300**	**39 084**	**29 599**	**5 147**	**9 553**
With a mobility or self-care limitation	15 209	14 738	327	144	45 531	44 212	13 346	12 955	8 272	1 885	3 474
With a mobility limitation	12 879	12 482	275	122	36 933	35 806	10 413	10 641	6 812	1 646	2 610
With a self-care limitation	9 180	8 949	179	52	27 391	26 512	8 335	7 529	4 789	959	2 423

SOCIAL AND ECONOMIC CHARACTERISTICS UNITED STATES SUMMARY 107

446

Table 106. Education, Ability to Speak English, and Disability for Selected Racial Groups: 1990—Con.

[Data based on sample and subject to sampling variability, see text. For definitions of terms and meanings of symbols, see text]

United States	Asian—Con.						Pacific Islander				
	Vietnamese	Cambodian	Hmong	Laotian	Thai	Other Asian	Total	Hawaiian	Samoan	Guamanian	Other Pacific Islander
SCHOOL ENROLLMENT AND TYPE OF SCHOOL											
Persons 3 years and over enrolled in school	252 144	65 221	46 318	64 310	33 645	118 951	120 977	68 369	21 571	16 429	14 608
Preprimary school	7 379	2 402	2 509	2 369	1 346	8 223	7 172	4 606	1 037	779	750
Public school	5 082	1 978	2 357	2 119	660	4 214	4 735	2 935	721	553	526
Elementary or high school	158 233	49 581	35 928	50 368	18 303	62 935	85 517	48 583	15 995	11 288	9 651
Public school	148 642	48 110	35 020	49 292	15 703	55 243	78 383	43 528	15 155	10 638	9 062
College	86 532	13 238	7 881	11 573	13 996	47 793	28 288	15 180	4 539	4 362	4 207
Public college	74 715	11 767	7 279	10 368	9 808	34 946	21 549	11 724	3 455	3 401	2 969
Persons 3 years and over enrolled in school	252 144	65 221	46 318	64 310	33 645	118 951	120 977	68 369	21 571	16 429	14 608
3 and 4 years	3 745	1 079	1 133	1 157	672	4 212	3 685	2 360	600	405	320
5 to 14 years	98 328	36 364	28 059	35 351	12 220	50 652	66 559	38 522	12 485	8 256	7 296
15 to 17 years	40 347	8 174	5 112	9 604	4 598	12 550	17 592	10 190	3 131	2 365	1 906
18 and 19 years	23 921	4 603	2 344	4 460	2 536	8 305	7 804	3 903	1 422	1 325	1 154
20 to 24 years	36 795	6 315	3 293	4 720	4 520	20 166	10 055	5 130	1 660	1 435	1 830
25 to 34 years	28 658	4 144	3 505	4 796	5 149	15 050	8 429	4 151	1 263	1 599	1 416
35 years and over	20 350	4 542	2 872	4 222	3 950	8 016	6 853	4 113	1 010	1 044	686
Persons 18 to 24 years	90 029	18 105	9 881	18 524	10 691	41 607	47 367	25 988	8 454	6 984	5 941
Percent enrolled in college	49.3	36.3	31.7	26.3	53.1	60.9	30.4	28.9	29.7	30.6	37.5
Persons 16 to 19 years	57 395	11 635	6 547	12 637	6 402	19 560	26 390	14 493	4 870	3 969	3 058
Percent not enrolled, not high school graduate	6.5	10.3	11.1	12.2	6.2	6.7	11.0	10.3	13.0	10.9	11.2
EDUCATIONAL ATTAINMENT											
Persons 18 to 24 years	90 029	18 105	9 881	18 524	10 691	41 607	47 367	25 988	8 454	6 984	5 941
High school graduate (includes equivalency)	20 037	4 674	2 212	5 067	2 928	9 309	19 034	11 365	3 494	2 384	1 791
Some college or associate degree	34 599	4 657	2 444	4 051	4 127	20 224	16 387	8 768	2 706	2 390	2 523
Bachelor's degree or higher	6 978	412	177	274	1 551	5 675	1 745	1 005	202	410	128
Persons 25 years and over	303 841	61 464	27 216	62 521	57 964	139 218	176 021	107 714	24 571	24 787	18 949
Less than 5th grade	34 773	25 015	14 950	21 184	5 001	5 878	4 765	1 418	1 050	1 159	1 138
5th to 8th grade	27 151	6 127	1 569	7 146	4 022	5 200	9 059	4 568	1 328	1 942	1 221
9th to 12th grade, no diploma	56 080	8 893	2 235	9 182	6 049	12 946	28 198	16 147	4 848	3 773	3 430
High school graduate (includes equivalency)	53 023	7 232	2 844	11 968	9 653	23 942	63 454	41 562	8 797	7 758	5 337
Some college, no degree	49 456	7 606	2 930	6 910	7 692	22 795	39 210	23 481	5 124	6 086	4 519
Associate degree, occupational program	18 010	1 814	839	1 759	3 843	5 036	6 498	4 276	768	779	675
Associate degree, academic program	12 402	1 285	507	1 027	2 669	5 361	5 841	3 496	698	809	838
Bachelor's degree	39 477	2 530	929	2 410	11 264	30 692	13 751	9 297	1 373	1 807	1 274
Graduate or professional degree	13 469	962	413	935	7 771	27 368	5 245	3 469	585	674	517
Females 25 years and over	146 899	33 463	14 078	29 888	37 699	60 690	88 642	54 694	12 251	12 158	9 539
Less than 5th grade	22 183	17 021	10 023	13 165	4 350	3 502	2 679	662	708	675	634
5th to 8th grade	16 800	3 330	589	3 672	3 766	3 137	4 729	2 513	646	981	589
9th to 12th grade, no diploma	29 601	4 633	797	4 157	4 636	6 296	14 721	8 323	2 749	1 916	1 733
High school graduate (includes equivalency)	27 442	3 299	973	4 866	7 244	12 155	32 963	21 489	4 486	4 023	2 965
Some college, no degree	21 097	3 060	941	2 231	4 333	10 128	19 262	12 083	2 225	2 914	2 040
Associate degree, occupational program	6 314	546	190	451	2 473	2 292	3 047	2 026	405	298	318
Associate degree, academic program	5 570	494	140	296	1 525	2 422	2 749	1 739	282	357	371
Bachelor's degree	14 244	859	271	863	5 984	12 660	6 272	4 332	563	704	673
Graduate or professional degree	3 648	221	154	187	3 388	8 098	2 220	1 527	187	290	216
Persons 25 years and over	303 841	61 464	27 216	62 521	57 964	139 210	170 021	107 714	24 571	24 787	18 949
Percent less than 5th grade	11.4	40.7	54.9	33.9	8.6	4.2	2.7	1.3	4.3	4.7	6.0
Percent high school graduate or higher	61.2	34.9	31.1	40.0	74.0	82.7	76.1	79.5	70.6	72.3	69.4
Percent some college or higher	43.7	23.1	20.6	20.9	57.3	65.5	40.1	40.9	34.8	41.0	41.3
Percent bachelor's degree or higher	17.4	5.7	4.9	5.4	32.8	41.7	10.8	11.0	8.0	10.0	9.5
Males 25 to 34 years	68 512	9 919	6 011	13 557	7 280	34 548	34 460	19 584	5 148	5 482	4 246
Percent high school graduate or higher	71.9	50.9	58.6	56.7	88.5	87.3	83.7	86.5	80.0	79.9	80.0
Percent bachelor's degree or higher	23.8	8.6	7.5	6.0	44.5	43.9	11.9	13.1	9.8	12.0	8.6
Females 25 to 34 years	52 783	12 927	5 427	13 197	9 891	25 556	33 645	19 227	5 087	5 020	4 311
Percent high school graduate or higher	64.6	31.6	24.9	38.6	79.8	86.1	83.7	87.1	76.2	82.1	79.3
Percent bachelor's degree or higher	17.5	3.6	3.3	4.3	35.0	40.4	10.2	11.5	5.8	9.9	10.3
ABILITY TO SPEAK ENGLISH											
Persons 5 years and over	544 089	129 366	73 808	130 303	86 679	249 118	313 979	185 492	49 967	43 406	35 114
Speak a language other than English	510 240	124 211	71 891	126 136	69 421	168 374	98 014	18 601	33 165	20 052	26 196
5 to 17 years	135 480	46 762	35 710	46 915	10 504	32 763	21 008	3 405	8 396	2 927	6 280
18 to 64 years	358 714	73 870	33 668	75 992	57 900	130 686	71 440	12 789	23 566	16 032	19 053
65 to 74 years	10 930	2 728	1 839	2 236	835	3 380	3 775	1 410	909	844	612
75 years and over	5 116	851	674	993	182	1 545	1 791	997	294	249	251
Do not speak English "very well"	330 837	90 614	56 152	88 347	40 078	67 932	34 614	5 034	10 933	7 072	11 575
5 to 17 years	67 031	30 886	26 354	26 880	3 541	10 752	6 861	976	2 568	1 056	2 261
18 to 64 years	249 244	56 492	27 496	58 510	35 629	53 918	24 865	3 277	7 471	5 490	8 627
65 to 74 years	9 910	2 512	1 706	2 068	763	2 125	1 902	406	645	380	471
75 years and over	4 652	724	596	889	145	1 137	986	375	249	146	216
ABILITY TO SPEAK ENGLISH IN HOUSEHOLD											
Linguistically isolated households	66 043	17 287	9 176	16 868	8 865	13 371	4 291	735	969	1 066	1 521
Persons 5 years and over in households	534 502	128 588	73 316	129 404	84 715	241 297	303 675	180 649	47 432	41 782	33 812
In linguistically isolated households	224 938	70 306	43 862	66 633	22 521	36 303	13 734	1 807	3 422	3 376	5 129
5 to 17 years	64 282	28 652	22 124	26 369	4 419	7 609	4 291	623	1 281	805	1 582
18 to 64 years	152 363	39 655	20 254	38 473	17 670	27 491	8 483	921	1 912	2 422	3 228
65 to 74 years	5 912	1 528	1 135	1 302	376	907	642	160	160	95	227
75 years and over	2 381	471	349	489	56	296	318	103	69	54	92
DISABILITY STATUS OF CIVILIAN NONINSTITUTIONALIZED PERSONS											
Persons 16 to 64 years	403 537	81 589	37 916	84 017	70 012	180 069	212 353	126 782	31 485	29 339	24 747
With a mobility or self-care limitation	30 765	12 394	5 896	10 006	3 916	10 086	11 798	5 588	2 600	2 076	1 534
With a mobility limitation	12 080	6 962	2 339	4 424	912	2 813	4 529	2 386	896	655	592
In labor force	3 605	969	336	975	462	929	1 161	512	168	262	219
With a self-care limitation	25 366	8 907	4 790	8 156	3 510	8 763	9 672	4 274	2 269	1 842	1 287
With a work disability	22 538	10 939	4 433	7 713	2 188	6 726	15 689	10 065	2 355	1 926	1 343
In labor force	6 846	1 463	505	1 724	1 260	2 818	6 422	4 173	780	915	554
Prevented from working	12 895	8 421	3 317	5 031	702	3 181	7 682	4 909	1 373	746	654
No work disability	380 999	70 650	33 483	76 304	67 824	173 343	196 664	116 717	29 130	27 413	23 404
	263 336	38 040	11 272	48 783	49 334	120 280	150 623	92 137	20 190	20 961	17 335
Persons 65 to 74 years	11 162	2 779	1 932	2 354	879	4 827	9 491	6 581	1 055	1 192	663
With a mobility or self-care limitation	2 841	961	526	636	196	836	1 853	1 122	273	317	141
With a mobility limitation	2 036	803	310	463	141	455	1 299	696	207	255	141
With a self-care limitation	1 743	557	334	401	123	508	1 169	715	169	171	114
Persons 75 years and over	5 208	849	720	997	182	2 155	4 155	3 126	330	415	284
With a mobility or self-care limitation	2 236	474	226	427	80	837	1 319	999	104	116	100
With a mobility limitation	1 984	434	154	353	73	686	1 127	848	94	89	96
With a self-care limitation	1 283	293	129	305	30	437	879	655	78	79	67

Table 107. Geographic Mobility, Commuting, and Industry of Employed Persons for Selected Racial Groups: 1990

[Data based on sample and subject to sampling variability, see text. For definitions of terms and meanings of symbols, see text]

United States	American Indian, Eskimo, or Aleut				Asian or Pacific Islander						
						Asian					
	Total	American Indian	Eskimo	Aleut	Total	Total	Chinese	Filipino	Japanese	Asian Indian	Korean
PLACE OF BIRTH, NATIVITY, AND CITIZENSHIP											
All persons	2 015 143	1 937 391	55 674	22 078	7 226 986	6 876 394	1 648 696	1 419 711	866 160	786 694	797 304
Native	1 968 224	1 895 383	54 602	18 239	2 668 242	2 363 047	506 116	505 988	585 474	193 271	218 031
Born in State of residence	1 403 322	1 342 974	47 401	12 947	1 838 871	1 645 667	377 045	350 086	434 032	130 914	103 405
Born in a different State	549 140	537 488	6 916	4 736	567 800	500 982	109 495	100 808	127 077	51 793	38 850
Northeast	35 981	35 072	554	355	105 598	102 863	34 592	18 992	7 932	19 760	8 656
Midwest	121 546	120 312	752	482	90 697	87 331	19 107	14 149	13 836	15 055	8 383
South	191 222	189 756	949	517	105 754	99 067	20 512	21 932	11 273	11 698	10 732
West	200 391	192 348	4 661	3 382	265 751	211 721	35 284	45 735	94 036	5 280	11 079
Born abroad	15 762	14 921	285	556	261 571	216 398	19 576	55 094	24 365	10 564	75 776
Puerto Rico	1 752	1 556	73	123	4 473	4 203	764	828	167	404	109
U.S. outlying area	1 021	830	28	163	46 977	8 676	535	5 653	831	342	306
Born abroad of American parents	12 989	12 535	184	270	210 121	203 519	18 277	48 613	23 367	9 818	75 361
Foreign born	46 919	42 008	1 072	3 839	4 558 744	4 513 347	1 142 580	913 723	280 686	593 423	579 273
Naturalized citizen	16 885	15 242	392	1 251	1 830 508	1 814 047	496 209	491 646	72 194	203 614	232 488
Not a citizen	30 034	26 766	680	2 588	2 728 236	2 699 300	646 371	422 077	208 492	389 809	346 785
RESIDENCE IN 1985											
Persons 5 years and over	1 817 347	1 749 558	47 860	19 929	6 652 553	6 338 574	1 540 235	1 317 163	818 974	721 675	727 164
Same house	859 045	824 305	26 113	8 627	2 595 263	2 453 606	630 724	535 276	444 113	251 057	233 613
Different house in the United States	939 731	908 184	21 258	10 289	2 837 293	2 685 879	603 060	565 661	255 510	309 698	332 214
Same county	537 202	518 203	13 274	5 725	1 663 664	1 569 416	345 839	350 230	159 620	154 553	181 848
Different county	402 529	389 981	7 984	4 564	1 173 629	1 116 463	257 221	215 431	95 890	155 145	150 366
Same State	212 129	204 515	5 178	2 436	566 131	543 345	134 163	114 117	45 719	69 387	69 086
Different State	190 400	185 466	2 806	2 128	607 498	573 118	123 058	101 314	50 171	85 758	81 280
Northeast	12 383	11 931	204	248	133 491	131 609	38 239	18 420	7 027	29 296	18 797
Midwest	35 222	34 702	329	191	110 931	108 791	21 795	15 501	7 397	20 586	15 170
South	61 434	60 493	537	404	167 890	161 736	31 705	25 397	9 129	25 118	24 550
West	81 361	78 340	1 736	1 285	195 186	170 982	31 319	41 996	26 618	10 758	22 763
Puerto Rico	315	300	–	15	1 106	1 043	206	376	56	117	25
U.S. outlying area	446	376	6	64	14 172	7 684	950	4 308	473	303	696
Elsewhere	17 810	16 393	483	934	1 204 719	1 190 362	305 295	211 542	118 822	160 500	160 616
MEANS OF TRANSPORTATION TO WORK AND TRAVEL TIME TO WORK											
Workers 16 years and over	724 223	700 800	15 180	8 243	3 381 333	3 231 358	804 329	756 142	447 370	384 980	341 088
Car, truck, or van	608 615	595 447	7 022	6 146	2 694 332	2 566 985	566 496	617 457	381 831	295 113	283 352
Drove alone	472 816	463 155	4 997	4 664	2 077 175	1 983 476	432 563	459 219	317 515	239 459	205 220
Carpooled	135 799	132 292	2 025	1 482	617 157	583 509	133 933	158 238	64 316	55 654	78 132
Persons per car, truck, or van	1.14	1.14	1.19	1.15	1.14	1.14	1.15	1.17	1.10	1.12	1.17
Public transportation	30 408	28 781	1 154	473	381 611	372 248	141 302	81 699	31 354	51 318	28 812
Bus or trolley bus	22 039	21 019	702	318	195 839	187 897	62 339	53 170	18 307	20 157	12 598
Streetcar or trolley car	344	327	9	8	6 178	6 116	2 888	1 525	402	451	376
Subway or elevated	5 469	5 292	101	76	147 967	147 130	67 642	21 496	7 795	23 722	13 150
Railroad	879	865	–	14	24 516	24 356	7 157	3 789	4 010	5 824	2 030
Ferryboat	251	220	5	26	1 596	1 493	465	517	193	197	50
Taxicab	1 426	1 058	337	31	5 515	5 256	811	1 202	647	967	608
Motorcycle	2 677	2 522	92	63	5 246	4 664	1 115	1 214	1 118	196	399
Bicycle	4 914	4 699	85	130	17 190	16 236	6 587	2 270	2 419	1 553	1 139
Walked	44 713	39 660	4 230	823	188 293	181 230	68 029	31 922	17 532	24 764	17 668
Other means	12 317	9 717	2 208	392	25 484	24 064	4 445	7 940	2 076	2 842	1 976
Worked at home	20 579	19 974	389	216	69 177	65 931	16 355	13 640	11 040	9 194	7 742
Mean travel time to work (minutes)	21.8	22.0	14.2	20.2	25.5	25.6	27.3	25.5	24.2	26.4	24.8
INDUSTRY											
Employed persons 16 years and over	728 953	705 518	15 108	8 327	3 411 586	3 264 268	819 932	750 613	452 005	391 949	345 655
Agriculture, forestry, and fisheries	25 445	24 771	272	402	45 306	41 838	3 650	12 008	14 242	2 869	2 611
Mining	8 386	8 045	279	62	5 845	5 602	1 689	1 122	528	899	335
Construction	61 635	60 164	957	514	104 924	93 127	19 774	21 571	17 314	10 982	11 068
Manufacturing	117 389	115 051	1 230	1 108	632 058	614 451	152 484	116 036	61 998	72 390	52 281
Nondurable goods	44 934	43 988	552	394	236 568	230 086	73 332	40 016	19 971	25 146	24 752
Food and kindred products	9 855	9 572	137	146	41 685	39 464	6 727	10 404	4 666	3 312	2 999
Textile mill and finished textile products	12 325	12 142	102	81	91 361	90 213	44 281	8 687	4 403	4 972	13 431
Printing, publishing, and allied industries	8 074	7 818	165	91	44 755	43 329	10 643	9 150	5 706	5 127	4 212
Durable goods	72 455	71 063	678	714	395 490	384 365	79 152	76 020	42 027	47 244	27 529
Furniture, lumber, and wood products	12 545	12 343	102	100	14 176	13 213	1 974	2 378	1 271	1 288	1 249
Metal industries	10 703	10 538	101	64	27 903	26 679	3 600	5 071	2 715	4 142	1 990
Machinery and computer equipment	10 910	10 693	99	118	80 350	78 868	19 874	11 230	6 912	11 976	4 907
Electrical equipment and components, except computer	10 033	9 852	76	105	117 565	115 557	22 599	26 865	9 420	13 368	7 871
Transportation equipment	13 531	13 227	138	166	73 424	70 328	14 284	13 888	14 618	7 298	4 815
Transportation	31 583	30 059	954	570	141 280	130 268	30 623	35 682	23 429	14 328	10 585
Communications and other public utilities	19 386	18 683	511	192	61 982	58 107	15 982	14 101	11 103	7 052	2 907
Wholesale trade	23 251	22 703	292	256	145 540	139 804	39 374	24 293	26 289	14 516	15 573
Retail trade	118 938	115 083	2 359	1 496	692 411	665 657	199 170	114 967	76 231	62 806	107 979
Food, bakery, and dairy stores	21 323	20 566	480	277	115 723	111 440	23 542	16 745	12 309	12 391	26 593
Eating and drinking places	40 573	39 501	591	481	288 623	279 026	123 503	37 550	23 806	15 466	33 241
Banking and credit agencies	7 357	7 099	107	151	101 194	97 753	26 961	28 953	13 106	12 627	6 418
Insurance, real estate, and other finance	21 343	20 790	376	177	152 679	146 944	42 913	38 315	22 747	16 126	12 374
Business and repair services	33 516	32 638	432	446	150 934	142 929	33 039	30 516	19 611	17 577	18 578
Private households	5 073	4 925	80	68	16 804	15 868	3 340	6 207	1 783	1 449	1 036
Other personal services	22 619	21 959	417	243	156 471	147 842	25 497	37 639	16 459	13 304	30 530
Entertainment and recreation services	12 491	12 163	175	153	44 051	40 424	8 439	10 894	7 262	2 702	4 952
Professional and related services	162 069	155 516	4 694	1 859	824 104	798 675	188 953	222 034	110 198	130 947	62 065
Hospitals	29 510	28 625	516	369	231 905	226 842	32 493	107 003	17 645	37 769	13 766
Health services, except hospitals	28 742	27 879	589	274	135 092	131 195	24 596	43 457	15 351	24 445	10 166
Educational services	59 453	56 183	2 592	678	250 221	241 179	76 092	30 697	45 585	40 056	19 441
Public administration	58 472	55 869	1 973	630	136 003	124 979	28 044	36 275	29 705	11 375	6 363

Table 107. Geographic Mobility, Commuting, and Industry of Employed Persons for Selected Racial Groups: 1990—Con.

[Data based on sample and subject to sampling variability, see text. For definitions of terms and meanings of symbols, see text]

United States	Asian or Pacific Islander—Con.										
	Asian—Con.						Pacific Islander				
	Vietnamese	Cambodian	Hmong	Laotian	Thai	Other Asian	Total	Hawaiian	Samoan	Guamanian	Other Pacific Islander
PLACE OF BIRTH, NATIVITY, AND CITIZENSHIP											
All persons	593 213	149 047	94 439	147 375	91 360	282 395	350 592	205 501	57 679	47 754	39 658
Native	119 360	31 190	32 865	30 394	22 385	117 973	305 195	202 910	44 593	42 293	15 399
Born in State of residence	89 325	25 041	25 607	23 509	12 911	73 792	193 204	150 640	21 889	11 629	9 046
Born in a different State	20 563	4 973	6 688	5 735	5 066	29 934	66 818	49 406	8 256	6 012	3 144
Northeast	2 797	769	835	751	1 140	6 639	2 735	1 578	341	618	198
Midwest	4 682	1 057	2 713	1 397	1 137	5 815	3 366	1 938	568	654	206
South	8 381	1 742	1 014	1 318	1 465	9 000	6 687	3 330	1 229	1 780	348
West	4 703	1 405	2 126	2 269	1 324	8 480	54 030	42 560	6 118	2 960	2 392
Born abroad	9 472	1 176	570	1 150	4 408	14 247	45 173	2 864	14 448	24 652	3 209
Puerto Rico	232	20	–	194	24	1 461	270	79	45	108	38
U.S. outlying area	434	72	–	13	60	430	38 301	466	12 841	23 396	1 598
Born abroad of American parents	8 806	1 084	570	943	4 324	12 356	6 602	2 319	1 562	1 148	1 573
Foreign born	473 853	117 857	61 574	116 981	68 975	164 422	45 397	2 591	13 086	5 461	24 259
Naturalized citizen	200 069	20 181	5 668	20 279	21 405	50 294	16 461	1 252	6 857	1 556	6 796
Not a citizen	273 784	97 676	55 906	96 702	47 570	114 128	28 936	1 339	6 229	3 905	17 463
RESIDENCE IN 1985											
Persons 5 years and over	544 089	129 366	73 808	130 303	86 679	249 118	313 979	185 492	49 967	43 406	35 114
Same house	159 100	36 492	14 773	35 080	32 687	80 691	141 657	94 919	19 963	15 528	11 247
Different house in the United States	288 747	73 830	39 833	69 608	37 923	109 795	151 414	88 379	26 065	20 717	16 253
Same county	186 125	45 916	24 888	40 540	21 344	58 513	94 248	57 486	15 393	11 117	10 252
Different county	102 622	27 914	14 945	29 068	16 579	51 282	57 166	30 893	10 672	9 600	6 001
Same State	49 939	10 889	7 213	12 319	7 185	23 328	22 786	12 505	3 814	3 925	2 542
Different State	52 683	17 025	7 732	16 749	9 394	27 954	34 380	18 388	6 858	5 675	3 459
Northeast	6 877	3 068	833	2 204	1 127	5 721	1 882	885	381	407	209
Midwest	10 077	3 410	3 652	3 976	1 777	5 450	2 140	996	547	387	210
South	22 036	5 946	610	4 586	3 450	9 209	6 154	2 892	1 074	1 587	601
West	13 693	4 601	2 637	5 983	3 040	7 574	24 204	13 615	4 856	3 294	2 439
Puerto Rico	31	18	–	14	–	200	63	38	16	–	9
U.S. outlying area	285	64	13	11	264	317	6 488	118	1 593	4 239	538
Elsewhere	95 926	18 962	19 189	25 590	15 805	58 115	14 357	2 038	2 330	2 922	7 067
MEANS OF TRANSPORTATION TO WORK AND TRAVEL TIME TO WORK											
Workers 16 years and over	245 312	34 960	9 559	45 453	47 551	114 614	149 975	91 665	19 947	21 909	16 454
Car, truck, or van	216 822	30 480	8 560	42 180	39 754	84 940	127 347	78 998	16 410	18 617	13 322
Drove alone	170 573	21 763	6 833	29 968	31 255	69 108	93 699	58 857	11 174	14 296	9 372
Carpooled	46 249	8 717	1 727	12 212	8 499	15 832	33 648	20 141	5 236	4 321	3 950
Persons per car, truck, or van	1.13	1.19	1.13	1.19	1.13	1.11	1.17	1.16	1.21	1.15	1.19
Public transportation	13 247	2 177	433	1 453	3 837	16 616	9 363	5 004	1 651	1 570	1 130
Bus or trolley bus	9 369	1 693	402	1 259	1 714	6 889	7 942	4 414	1 482	1 052	994
Streetcar or trolley car	155	32	8	8	70	201	62	51	5	–	6
Subway or elevated	3 218	376	–	153	1 713	7 865	837	261	95	387	94
Railroad	327	70	15	21	259	904	160	62	31	60	11
Ferryboat	16	–	–	–	–	55	103	52	–	45	6
Taxicab	162	56	8	12	81	702	259	168	38	26	27
Motorcycle	214	32	7	28	46	295	582	435	29	102	16
Bicycle	912	106	31	60	204	920	954	577	235	70	72
Walked	8 401	1 114	308	809	2 410	8 273	7 063	3 958	1 060	916	1 129
Other means	2 184	545	97	531	350	1 078	1 420	752	295	196	177
Worked at home	3 532	506	123	363	950	2 486	3 246	1 941	267	438	600
Mean travel time to work (minutes)	24.0	22.9	19.3	21.7	23.7	25.2	23.9	24.2	24.0	23.6	21.8
INDUSTRY											
Employed persons 16 years and over	248 881	35 623	9 756	46 010	48 028	115 816	147 318	91 543	19 041	20 298	16 436
Agriculture, forestry, and fisheries	3 456	542	267	706	371	1 116	3 468	2 123	290	295	760
Mining	627	33	7	73	42	247	243	162	27	45	9
Construction	5 604	745	112	966	823	4 168	11 797	8 345	1 349	1 040	1 063
Manufacturing	91 263	13 890	3 582	24 853	8 725	16 949	17 607	8 667	3 106	3 233	2 601
Nondurable goods	22 451	4 245	1 258	8 672	4 025	6 218	6 482	3 484	961	1 025	1 012
Food and kindred products	4 941	1 047	182	3 501	719	966	2 221	1 326	320	208	367
Textile mill and finished textile products	7 301	1 446	433	2 219	1 785	1 255	1 148	505	138	266	239
Printing, publishing, and allied industries	4 309	506	261	835	662	1 918	1 426	868	144	226	188
Durable goods	68 812	9 645	2 324	16 181	4 700	10 731	11 125	5 183	2 145	2 208	1 589
Furniture, lumber, and wood products	2 573	591	179	956	293	461	963	399	212	213	139
Metal industries	4 523	991	292	1 890	389	1 076	1 224	598	239	154	233
Machinery and computer equipment	15 957	1 649	423	2 977	802	2 161	1 482	603	254	347	278
Electrical equipment and components, except computer	23 277	3 164	510	4 456	1 212	2 815	2 008	790	425	494	299
Transportation equipment	10 107	729	250	1 548	770	2 021	3 096	1 661	627	629	179
Transportation	5 995	881	227	692	1 597	6 229	11 012	7 429	1 425	1 260	898
Communications and other public utilities	3 801	261	112	446	456	1 886	3 875	2 881	282	551	161
Wholesale trade	9 382	1 988	333	2 229	1 594	4 233	5 736	3 378	830	874	654
Retail trade	48 719	6 961	1 391	6 578	14 488	26 367	26 754	16 390	3 390	3 793	3 181
Food, bakery, and dairy stores	9 378	2 004	179	1 223	1 860	5 216	4 283	2 690	533	610	450
Eating and drinking places	20 714	2 747	796	3 069	8 688	9 446	9 597	5 609	1 323	1 159	1 506
Banking and credit agencies	4 497	529	76	262	893	3 431	3 441	1 865	583	691	302
Insurance, real estate, and other finance	6 744	547	177	732	1 354	4 915	5 735	3 867	602	766	500
Business and repair services	12 131	1 382	779	1 648	2 061	5 607	8 005	4 446	1 268	1 301	990
Private households	684	177	15	106	261	810	936	285	114	318	219
Other personal services	13 148	1 401	301	1 610	3 443	4 510	8 629	6 079	715	571	1 264
Entertainment and recreation services	2 544	365	66	421	1 336	1 443	3 627	2 323	560	313	431
Professional and related services	33 760	5 130	1 979	4 195	9 447	29 967	25 429	16 000	3 224	3 308	2 897
Hospitals	6 324	937	143	838	3 418	6 506	5 063	2 570	1 035	844	614
Health services, except hospitals	5 123	755	276	713	1 803	4 510	3 897	2 220	500	561	616
Educational services	11 593	2 020	827	1 462	1 950	11 456	9 042	6 358	907	898	879
Public administration	6 526	791	332	493	1 137	3 938	11 024	7 303	1 276	1 939	506

Table 108. Labor Force Characteristics for Selected Racial Groups: 1990

[Data based on sample and subject to sampling variability, see text. For definitions of terms and meanings of symbols, see text]

United States	American Indian, Eskimo, or Aleut				Asian or Pacific Islander	Asian					
	Total	American Indian	Eskimo	Aleut	Total	Total	Chinese	Filipino	Japanese	Asian Indian	Korean
LABOR FORCE STATUS											
Persons 16 years and over	1 395 009	1 343 392	35 892	15 725	5 403 615	5 167 530	1 309 042	1 078 817	724 683	576 157	579 867
In labor force	865 703	836 656	19 472	9 575	3 645 946	3 480 409	863 285	813 766	467 346	416 404	367 146
Percent of persons 16 years and over	62.1	62.3	54.3	60.9	67.5	67.4	65.9	75.4	64.5	72.3	63.3
Armed Forces	14 391	13 723	530	138	42 866	36 221	2 597	22 897	3 576	1 058	2 466
Civilian labor force	851 312	822 933	18 942	9 437	3 603 080	3 444 188	860 688	790 869	463 770	415 346	364 680
Employed	728 953	705 518	15 108	8 327	3 411 586	3 264 268	819 932	750 613	452 005	391 949	345 655
At work 35 or more hours	548 730	533 109	9 629	5 992	2 690 953	2 576 028	640 061	609 190	354 996	314 243	266 184
Unemployed	122 359	117 415	3 834	1 110	191 494	179 920	40 756	40 256	11 765	23 397	19 025
Percent of civilian labor force	14.4	14.3	20.2	11.8	5.3	5.2	4.7	5.1	2.5	5.6	5.2
Not in labor force	529 306	506 736	16 420	6 150	1 757 669	1 687 121	445 757	265 051	257 337	159 753	212 721
Institutionalized persons	31 375	29 948	1 086	341	23 391	19 950	4 281	4 475	4 343	1 394	1 304
Females 16 years and over	714 654	689 287	17 619	7 748	2 810 588	2 692 480	664 384	599 208	399 585	260 532	333 225
In labor force	393 437	380 664	8 558	4 215	1 688 145	1 614 323	393 077	433 262	221 857	152 718	185 078
Percent of females 16 years and over	55.1	55.2	48.6	54.4	60.1	60.0	59.2	72.3	55.5	58.6	55.5
Armed Forces	2 017	1 949	47	21	4 063	3 417	381	1 698	558	97	359
Civilian labor force	391 420	378 715	8 511	4 194	1 684 082	1 610 906	392 696	431 564	221 299	152 621	184 719
Employed	340 042	329 185	7 122	3 735	1 590 897	1 522 768	373 165	411 393	215 319	141 028	173 422
At work 35 or more hours	235 857	229 324	4 168	2 365	1 174 018	1 125 063	272 176	322 832	153 330	100 477	124 492
Unemployed	51 378	49 530	1 389	459	93 185	88 138	19 531	20 171	5 980	11 593	11 297
Percent of civilian labor force	13.1	13.1	16.3	10.9	5.5	5.5	5.0	4.7	2.7	7.6	6.1
Not in labor force	321 217	308 623	9 061	3 533	1 122 443	1 078 157	271 307	165 946	177 728	107 814	148 147
Institutionalized persons	7 261	6 967	221	73	8 954	7 912	1 709	1 860	2 580	435	707
Males 16 to 19 years	74 536	71 723	2 066	747	247 569	233 951	52 996	49 034	17 993	23 675	29 247
Employed	21 985	21 238	499	248	73 407	68 639	13 495	17 937	5 972	7 057	7 783
Unemployed	9 190	8 938	185	67	14 626	13 460	2 384	3 635	785	1 242	1 392
Not in labor force	41 984	40 267	1 298	419	157 048	149 692	36 885	26 513	11 065	15 307	19 730
Males 20 to 24 years	88 901	84 871	2 930	1 100	311 767	294 787	66 375	58 222	30 828	35 417	31 040
Employed	48 798	46 991	1 176	631	179 585	168 301	35 424	39 015	17 411	21 620	15 050
Unemployed	13 825	13 237	507	81	16 824	15 393	3 074	3 306	959	1 587	1 555
Not in labor force	21 626	20 225	1 043	358	105 474	102 722	27 196	11 433	11 814	11 944	13 624
Males 25 to 54 years	411 828	396 102	10 604	5 122	1 630 717	1 558 256	403 836	284 128	194 208	228 244	155 418
Employed	284 470	275 415	5 617	3 438	1 382 945	1 325 851	345 662	242 149	174 469	205 954	132 506
Unemployed	44 164	42 039	1 653	472	56 378	52 803	12 588	10 326	3 334	7 807	3 979
Not in labor force	76 893	72 608	3 147	1 138	165 205	157 504	44 305	15 962	14 227	13 888	17 985
Males 55 to 64 years	55 995	53 942	1 479	574	205 333	196 737	60 261	40 311	35 906	18 580	18 818
Employed	27 507	26 673	608	226	145 196	140 078	41 945	30 530	26 488	14 038	14 607
Unemployed	3 085	2 976	85	24	7 962	7 688	2 541	1 899	476	994	511
Not in labor force	25 359	24 257	778	324	51 987	48 796	15 753	7 791	8 917	3 517	3 694
Males 65 to 69 years	20 108	19 425	495	188	76 895	74 271	24 452	14 084	19 375	4 469	5 554
In labor force	4 363	4 268	53	42	26 527	25 951	7 342	6 207	7 567	1 677	1 781
Not in labor force	15 745	15 157	442	146	50 368	48 320	17 110	7 877	11 808	2 792	3 773
Did not work in 1989	13 416	12 951	350	115	41 780	40 062	14 381	6 220	9 214	2 493	3 171
Males 70 years and over	28 987	28 042	699	246	120 692	117 048	36 738	33 830	26 788	5 240	6 565
In labor force	2 505	2 443	48	14	15 548	15 118	3 537	4 301	5 010	749	797
Not in labor force	26 482	25 599	651	232	105 144	101 930	33 201	29 529	21 778	4 491	5 768
Did not work in 1989	24 303	23 531	562	210	97 104	94 135	31 004	27 428	19 064	4 277	5 453
Females 16 to 19 years	69 233	66 623	1 845	765	233 428	220 656	47 290	47 720	19 441	21 930	31 105
Employed	20 236	19 457	533	246	73 165	68 346	13 013	18 945	6 381	6 345	9 891
Unemployed	7 523	7 295	184	44	10 857	9 802	1 635	2 622	624	832	1 345
Not in labor force	41 192	39 597	1 120	475	149 039	142 174	32 592	26 002	12 417	14 738	19 825
Females 20 to 24 years	82 718	79 220	2 613	885	294 485	277 791	65 680	58 533	30 019	30 945	32 955
Employed	39 895	38 302	1 118	475	168 071	157 871	37 096	40 630	16 886	16 369	17 133
Unemployed	9 552	9 208	286	58	13 326	12 312	2 242	2 807	738	1 637	1 504
Not in labor force	32 551	31 020	1 189	342	111 968	106 702	26 231	14 677	12 282	12 916	14 186
Females 25 to 54 years	431 080	416 151	10 085	4 844	1 777 497	1 706 215	418 182	386 193	217 907	181 290	223 036
Employed	251 698	243 939	5 004	2 755	1 203 710	1 155 580	289 220	314 635	146 476	112 752	135 095
Unemployed	31 853	30 651	880	322	59 948	57 151	13 214	11 796	3 429	8 473	7 643
Not in labor force	146 514	140 576	4 182	1 756	511 318	491 362	115 539	58 652	67 602	60 006	80 115
Females 55 to 64 years	62 995	60 764	1 543	688	260 191	250 941	62 650	53 681	72 177	15 223	24 264
Employed	22 406	21 769	420	217	121 478	117 314	28 131	30 943	36 651	4 908	10 101
Unemployed	1 953	1 879	39	35	6 890	6 734	1 850	2 093	968	501	622
Not in labor force	38 636	37 116	1 084	436	131 768	126 838	32 658	20 627	34 532	9 814	13 541
Females 65 to 69 years	24 292	23 609	505	178	98 240	94 962	25 781	22 075	25 300	5 179	8 596
In labor force	3 744	3 669	43	32	18 228	17 715	4 264	5 003	6 279	531	902
Not in labor force	20 548	19 940	462	146	80 012	77 247	21 517	17 072	19 021	4 648	7 694
Did not work in 1989	18 589	18 087	389	113	73 041	70 458	19 649	15 408	16 395	4 484	7 431
Females 70 years and over	44 336	42 920	1 028	388	146 747	141 915	44 801	31 006	34 741	5 965	13 269
In labor force	2 560	2 546	4	10	8 409	8 081	2 031	2 090	2 867	273	483
Not in labor force	41 776	40 374	1 024	378	138 338	133 834	42 770	28 916	31 874	5 692	12 786
Did not work in 1989	39 694	38 370	949	375	133 512	129 263	41 422	28 019	30 166	5 593	12 523
PRESENCE OF OWN CHILDREN IN FAMILIES AND SUBFAMILIES											
Females 16 years and over	714 654	689 287	17 619	7 748	2 810 588	2 692 480	664 384	599 208	399 585	260 532	333 225
With own children under 6 years	147 285	140 590	4 980	1 715	515 031	488 929	102 824	110 095	49 337	60 446	61 371
In labor force	78 910	75 591	2 492	827	295 743	280 944	61 796	83 728	25 584	33 234	29 667
With own children 6 to 17 years only	142 961	138 631	2 938	1 392	553 642	530 728	117 442	119 621	54 309	65 855	76 747
In labor force	97 957	95 307	1 757	893	404 696	387 502	85 964	103 866	36 553	47 724	54 105
Own children under 6 years living with two parents	126 232	119 223	5 364	1 645	582 444	554 372	115 878	98 373	50 758	71 730	78 092
Both parents in labor force	61 519	58 456	2 339	724	309 547	294 767	64 951	74 125	23 807	37 181	39 275
Both at work 35 or more hours	27 868	26 837	709	322	197 142	188 789	42 170	52 083	14 461	22 116	23 140
Own children under 6 years living with one parent	99 013	94 806	3 478	729	92 667	78 703	10 888	21 519	5 095	5 533	5 688
Parent in labor force	53 193	50 924	1 937	332	52 985	45 614	7 109	16 247	3 805	3 607	3 891
At work 35 or more hours	28 249	27 210	894	145	38 470	33 548	5 426	12 485	2 796	2 612	3 043
Own children 6 to 17 years living with two parents	258 426	247 703	7 802	2 921	1 105 516	1 049 388	218 237	210 102	83 909	139 960	137 986
Both parents in labor force	149 745	144 512	3 720	1 513	709 041	672 689	143 115	173 030	48 981	92 445	92 132
Both at work 35 or more hours	78 618	76 508	1 360	750	481 480	458 753	97 140	129 023	30 490	60 066	60 002
Own children 6 to 17 years living with one parent	153 491	148 573	3 556	1 362	191 540	170 803	27 395	41 983	13 615	10 691	17 918
Parent in labor force	100 318	97 312	2 123	883	133 038	118 413	20 092	35 475	11 734	8 025	15 015
At work 35 or more hours	62 936	61 300	1 032	604	103 025	92 598	15 793	29 392	9 440	6 258	11 966

Table 108. Labor Force Characteristics for Selected Racial Groups: 1990—Con.

[Data based on sample and subject to sampling variability, see text. For definitions of terms and meanings of symbols, see text]

United States	Asian or Pacific Islander—Con.										
	Asian—Con.						Pacific Islander				
	Vietnamese	Cambodian	Hmong	Laotian	Thai	Other Asian	Total	Hawaiian	Samoan	Guamanian	Other Pacific Islander
LABOR FORCE STATUS											
Persons 16 years and over	**423 121**	**85 500**	**40 649**	**87 683**	**71 907**	**190 104**	**236 085**	**140 885**	**35 336**	**33 562**	**26 302**
In labor force	273 098	39 793	11 923	50 869	51 359	125 420	165 537	100 328	22 523	24 225	18 461
Percent of persons 16 years and over	64.5	46.5	29.3	58.0	71.4	66.0	70.1	71.2	63.7	72.2	70.2
Armed Forces	1 511	89	33	166	642	1 186	6 645	2 627	1 381	2 212	425
Civilian labor force	271 587	39 704	11 890	50 703	50 717	124 234	158 892	97 701	21 142	22 013	18 036
Employed	248 881	35 623	9 756	46 010	48 028	115 816	147 318	91 543	19 041	20 298	16 436
At work 35 or more hours	193 924	27 884	6 534	38 156	37 318	87 538	114 925	71 278	15 057	16 056	12 534
Unemployed	22 706	4 081	2 134	4 693	2 689	8 418	11 574	6 158	2 101	1 715	1 600
Percent of civilian labor force	8.4	10.3	17.9	9.3	5.3	6.8	7.3	6.3	9.9	7.8	8.9
Not in labor force	150 023	45 707	28 726	36 814	20 548	64 684	70 548	40 557	12 813	9 337	7 841
Institutionalized persons	1 703	194	48	149	192	1 867	3 441	1 769	1 085	404	183
Females 16 years and over	**199 310**	**45 754**	**20 265**	**42 044**	**44 917**	**83 256**	**118 108**	**70 907**	**17 393**	**16 590**	**13 218**
In labor force	111 282	17 080	4 039	20 799	30 268	44 863	73 822	45 715	9 524	10 404	8 179
Percent of females 16 years and over	55.8	37.3	19.9	49.5	67.4	53.9	62.5	64.5	54.8	62.7	61.9
Armed Forces	112	–	–	13	67	132	646	291	119	187	49
Civilian labor force	111 170	17 080	4 039	20 786	30 201	44 731	73 176	45 424	9 405	10 217	8 130
Employed	101 304	15 391	3 273	18 847	28 339	41 287	68 129	42 760	8 394	9 557	7 418
At work 35 or more hours	74 015	11 603	2 287	15 157	20 998	27 696	48 955	30 578	6 292	6 866	5 219
Unemployed	9 866	1 689	766	1 939	1 862	3 444	5 047	2 664	1 011	660	712
Percent of civilian labor force	8.9	9.9	19.0	9.3	6.2	7.7	6.9	5.9	10.7	6.5	8.8
Not in labor force	88 028	28 674	16 226	21 245	14 649	38 393	44 286	25 192	7 869	6 186	5 039
Institutionalized persons	340	32	6	12	50	181	1 042	560	341	111	30
Males 16 to 19 years	**31 651**	**5 943**	**3 572**	**6 635**	**3 065**	**10 140**	**13 618**	**7 550**	**2 650**	**1 899**	**1 519**
Employed	8 227	1 189	524	1 776	1 176	3 503	4 768	2 895	682	686	505
Unemployed	1 917	396	312	485	177	735	1 166	682	202	169	113
Not in labor force	21 321	4 332	2 728	4 318	1 671	5 822	7 356	3 823	1 689	956	888
Males 20 to 24 years	**35 218**	**5 802**	**3 674**	**6 371**	**3 660**	**18 180**	**16 980**	**9 408**	**2 973**	**2 444**	**2 155**
Employed	20 087	3 247	1 361	4 169	1 784	9 133	11 284	6 623	1 863	1 461	1 337
Unemployed	2 445	446	352	517	150	1 002	1 431	726	278	188	230
Not in labor force	11 983	2 065	1 954	1 611	1 387	7 711	2 752	1 438	519	332	463
Males 25 to 54 years	**138 622**	**24 054**	**11 358**	**28 902**	**19 395**	**70 091**	**72 515**	**42 886**	**10 514**	**10 950**	**8 165**
Employed	111 379	15 046	4 416	20 341	16 280	57 649	57 094	35 205	7 454	7 885	6 550
Unemployed	7 778	1 422	696	1 604	484	2 785	3 575	1 841	564	659	511
Not in labor force	18 955	7 567	6 228	6 934	2 436	9 017	7 701	4 282	1 630	932	857
Males 55 to 64 years	**11 276**	**2 500**	**987**	**2 315**	**578**	**5 205**	**8 596**	**5 831**	**1 096**	**924**	**745**
Employed	6 966	648	135	733	416	3 572	5 118	3 436	543	636	503
Unemployed	655	108	8	130	16	350	274	192	37	30	15
Not in labor force	3 655	1 744	844	1 452	146	1 283	3 191	2 196	510	258	227
Males 65 to 69 years	**3 114**	**726**	**271**	**643**	**151**	**1 432**	**2 624**	**1 812**	**308**	**333**	**171**
In labor force	657	72	16	110	18	504	576	385	69	59	63
Not in labor force	2 457	654	255	533	133	928	2 048	1 427	239	274	108
Did not work in 1989	2 254	650	255	505	120	799	1 710	1 154	223	248	93
Males 70 years and over	**3 930**	**721**	**522**	**773**	**141**	**1 800**	**3 644**	**2 491**	**402**	**422**	**329**
In labor force	306	50	31	52	15	270	430	292	45	23	70
Not in labor force	3 624	671	491	721	126	1 530	3 214	2 199	357	399	259
Did not work in 1989	3 526	649	488	704	113	1 429	2 969	2 037	333	348	251
Females 16 to 19 years	**25 744**	**5 692**	**2 975**	**6 002**	**3 337**	**9 420**	**12 772**	**6 943**	**2 220**	**2 070**	**1 539**
Employed	6 711	1 058	377	1 383	1 173	3 069	4 819	2 774	610	828	560
Unemployed	1 249	261	133	358	232	511	1 055	519	177	234	125
Not in labor force	17 752	4 373	2 465	4 256	1 920	5 834	6 865	3 639	1 377	1 008	841
Females 20 to 24 years	**26 667**	**6 599**	**3 212**	**6 154**	**3 881**	**13 146**	**16 694**	**9 270**	**2 022**	**2 362**	**2 140**
Employed	14 214	2 881	852	3 297	1 989	6 524	10 200	5 873	1 538	1 538	1 251
Unemployed	1 580	419	129	370	262	624	1 014	495	249	85	185
Not in labor force	10 825	3 299	2 231	2 479	1 624	5 952	5 266	2 811	1 080	696	679
Females 25 to 54 years	**126 264**	**28 630**	**11 033**	**26 177**	**35 492**	**52 011**	**71 282**	**42 570**	**10 190**	**10 161**	**8 361**
Employed	76 741	11 087	1 860	13 897	24 433	29 384	48 130	30 231	5 786	6 812	5 301
Unemployed	6 553	956	470	1 153	1 313	2 151	2 797	1 530	559	327	381
Not in labor force	42 938	16 587	8 703	11 127	9 697	20 396	19 956	10 620	3 798	2 878	2 660
Females 55 to 64 years	**11 094**	**2 641**	**1 180**	**1 764**	**1 431**	**4 836**	**9 250**	**6 361**	**1 153**	**1 037**	**699**
Employed	3 274	308	123	252	654	1 969	4 164	3 187	363	330	284
Unemployed	406	31	29	42	55	137	156	101	26	8	21
Not in labor force	7 414	2 302	1 028	1 470	722	2 730	4 930	3 073	764	699	394
Females 65 to 69 years	**3 747**	**988**	**693**	**700**	**386**	**1 517**	**3 278**	**2 313**	**337**	**405**	**223**
In labor force	309	79	39	7	51	251	513	455	6	38	14
Not in labor force	3 438	909	654	693	335	1 266	2 765	1 858	331	367	209
Did not work in 1989	3 350	909	647	693	306	1 186	2 583	1 748	294	352	189
Females 70 years and over	**5 794**	**1 204**	**1 172**	**1 247**	**390**	**2 326**	**4 832**	**3 450**	**571**	**555**	**256**
In labor force	133	–	27	27	39	111	328	259	52	17	–
Not in labor force	5 661	1 204	1 145	1 220	351	2 215	4 504	3 191	519	538	256
Did not work in 1989	5 581	1 171	1 118	1 209	351	2 110	4 249	2 979	519	495	256
PRESENCE OF OWN CHILDREN IN FAMILIES AND SUBFAMILIES											
Females 16 years and over	**199 310**	**45 754**	**20 265**	**42 044**	**44 917**	**83 256**	**118 108**	**70 907**	**17 393**	**16 590**	**13 218**
With own children under 6 years	42 517	14 942	10 156	12 592	6 366	18 283	26 102	14 157	4 797	3 705	3 443
In labor force	22 759	5 077	1 626	5 865	3 889	7 719	14 799	8 390	2 369	2 091	1 949
With own children 6 to 17 years only	45 352	10 170	3 349	11 469	12 331	14 083	22 914	13 496	3 383	3 482	2 553
In labor force	29 344	4 343	814	6 625	9 087	9 077	17 194	10 484	2 253	2 617	1 840
Own children under 6 years living with two parents	**46 198**	**15 716**	**21 895**	**16 433**	**4 699**	**34 600**	**28 072**	**14 271**	**5 873**	**3 628**	**4 300**
Both parents in labor force	23 788	4 912	2 697	6 416	2 902	14 713	14 780	7 813	2 768	1 977	2 222
Both at work 35 or more hours	15 648	3 494	1 444	4 781	1 906	7 546	8 353	4 357	1 659	1 041	1 296
Own children under 6 years living with one parent	**11 113**	**7 018**	**2 530**	**3 841**	**994**	**4 664**	**13 964**	**8 749**	**2 948**	**1 280**	**987**
Parent in labor force	4 341	1 206	447	1 350	732	2 879	7 371	4 776	1 322	733	540
At work 35 or more hours	2 957	629	170	875	522	2 033	4 922	3 303	772	516	331
Own children 6 to 17 years living with two parents	**102 104**	**31 528**	**26 324**	**36 533**	**12 668**	**50 037**	**56 128**	**30 965**	**10 650**	**7 729**	**6 784**
Both parents in labor force	53 840	11 271	4 173	17 095	8 809	27 798	36 352	21 082	5 859	5 198	4 213
Both at work 35 or more hours	36 422	8 090	2 659	12 800	5 894	16 167	22 727	13 494	3 554	3 194	2 485
Own children 6 to 17 years living with one parent	**26 126**	**10 642**	**4 224**	**6 157**	**3 033**	**9 019**	**20 737**	**13 446**	**3 454**	**2 228**	**1 609**
Parent in labor force	13 762	2 362	497	2 306	2 622	6 523	14 625	9 569	2 134	1 703	1 219
At work 35 or more hours	9 224	1 516	302	1 638	2 101	4 968	10 427	6 669	1 534	1 293	931

Table 109. Additional Labor Force Characteristics and Veteran Status for Selected Racial Groups: 1990

[Data based on sample and subject to sampling variability, see text. For definitions of terms and meanings of symbols, see text]

United States	American Indian, Eskimo, or Aleut				Asian or Pacific Islander	Asian					
	Total	American Indian	Eskimo	Aleut	Total	Total	Chinese	Filipino	Japanese	Asian Indian	Korean
LABOR FORCE STATUS OF FAMILY MEMBERS											
Married-couple families	305 156	295 600	6 260	3 296	1 295 099	1 242 237	330 606	231 168	174 211	174 768	137 178
Husband employed or in Armed Forces	218 614	212 558	3 722	2 334	1 068 819	1 025 777	267 143	196 217	137 592	161 458	117 547
Wife employed or in Armed Forces	135 797	132 208	2 147	1 442	715 004	686 197	180 817	160 402	80 627	98 151	72 923
Wife unemployed	10 678	10 337	203	138	31 496	30 359	7 529	4 886	1 935	7 013	2 874
Husband unemployed	21 205	20 365	613	227	33 315	31 516	8 289	6 311	1 413	4 739	2 837
Wife employed or in Armed Forces	10 191	9 815	290	86	19 141	18 057	4 906	4 761	908	2 846	1 441
Wife unemployed	2 955	2 816	100	39	4 071	3 892	1 061	553	69	550	447
Husband not in labor force	65 337	62 677	1 925	735	192 965	184 944	55 174	28 640	35 206	8 571	16 794
Wife employed or in Armed Forces	18 947	18 150	611	186	53 519	50 489	15 453	13 385	9 076	3 342	4 064
Wife unemployed	2 256	2 158	84	14	3 121	2 987	1 156	464	149	235	350
Female householder, no husband present	121 370	117 790	2 636	944	185 926	172 861	36 708	44 304	24 765	8 587	18 419
Employed or in Armed Forces	58 613	57 265	891	457	116 808	109 728	23 244	34 334	16 149	5 744	13 015
Unemployed	10 433	10 172	211	50	6 393	5 674	942	1 286	437	427	678
SCHOOL ENROLLMENT AND LABOR FORCE STATUS											
Persons 16 to 19 years	143 769	138 346	3 911	1 512	480 997	454 607	100 286	96 754	37 434	45 605	60 352
Enrolled in school	100 668	96 983	2 591	1 094	427 064	407 708	94 190	82 838	33 613	42 029	54 945
Employed	25 218	24 342	569	307	120 911	115 040	24 011	29 032	10 349	11 712	15 177
Unemployed	8 994	8 790	139	65	20 084	18 764	3 532	4 691	1 122	1 711	2 287
Not in labor force	66 322	63 723	1 877	722	285 473	273 359	66 589	48 883	22 080	28 592	37 405
Not enrolled in school	43 101	41 363	1 320	418	53 933	46 899	6 096	13 916	3 821	3 576	5 407
High school graduate	17 106	16 176	756	174	27 719	23 593	2 906	8 417	2 587	1 700	2 825
Employed	8 772	8 363	298	111	16 221	13 654	1 428	5 345	1 569	947	1 573
Unemployed	2 680	2 556	115	9	2 402	2 016	200	726	189	157	225
Not in labor force	4 258	3 954	262	42	6 943	6 080	1 054	1 533	720	530	739
Not high school graduate	25 995	25 187	564	244	26 214	23 306	3 190	5 499	1 234	1 876	2 582
Employed	8 231	7 990	165	76	9 440	8 291	1 069	2 505	435	743	924
Unemployed	5 039	4 887	115	37	2 997	2 482	287	840	98	206	225
Not in labor force	12 596	12 187	279	130	13 671	12 427	1 834	2 099	682	923	1 411
CLASS OF WORKER											
Employed persons 16 years and over	728 953	705 518	15 108	8 327	3 411 586	3 264 268	819 932	750 613	452 005	391 949	345 655
Private wage and salary workers	518 435	504 118	8 375	5 942	2 668 258	2 554 858	644 039	603 695	330 869	307 264	248 703
Local government workers	66 172	62 186	3 118	868	158 495	150 415	36 265	40 426	26 940	18 488	7 094
State government workers	43 141	40 734	1 911	496	184 743	175 366	49 437	29 623	37 791	28 712	11 059
Federal government workers	56 132	54 537	1 171	424	147 950	137 905	28 359	51 440	22 674	11 263	10 940
Self-employed workers	42 270	41 227	485	558	227 250	221 163	55 287	23 819	31 840	24 031	58 728
Unpaid family workers	2 803	2 716	48	39	24 890	24 561	6 545	1 610	1 891	2 191	9 131
Employed females 16 years and over	340 042	329 185	7 122	3 735	1 590 897	1 522 768	373 165	411 393	215 319	141 028	173 422
Private wage and salary workers	233 919	227 653	3 614	2 652	1 251 502	1 198 731	295 722	336 584	154 291	111 435	129 002
Local government workers	34 311	32 434	1 479	398	83 981	80 836	19 581	23 741	15 586	7 889	4 076
State government workers	24 691	23 241	1 166	284	90 332	84 861	21 506	18 191	23 426	9 183	4 539
Federal government workers	29 755	28 907	605	243	61 778	57 613	11 914	20 647	8 964	4 145	6 176
Self-employed workers	16 026	15 659	224	143	87 877	85 456	20 470	11 236	11 804	7 054	23 801
Unpaid family workers	1 340	1 291	34	15	15 427	15 271	3 972	994	1 248	1 322	5 828
WORK STATUS IN 1989											
Persons 16 years and over, worked in 1989	940 172	903 858	24 806	11 508	3 824 000	3 649 619	917 514	837 450	506 554	433 287	388 884
50 to 52 weeks	472 252	459 553	7 734	4 965	2 309 455	2 203 468	552 196	505 524	336 371	265 518	212 707
48 and 49 weeks	39 576	38 335	722	519	268 951	258 147	58 220	84 225	29 745	22 952	27 846
40 to 47 weeks	80 053	77 262	1 962	829	321 012	307 937	83 204	63 798	41 245	36 181	37 234
27 to 39 weeks	91 517	87 657	2 740	1 120	261 145	249 029	64 257	51 921	31 473	31 204	30 131
14 to 26 weeks	117 477	111 585	3 845	2 047	336 256	320 219	81 674	66 809	34 731	40 843	40 232
1 to 13 weeks	139 297	129 466	7 803	2 028	327 181	310 819	77 963	65 173	32 989	36 589	40 734
Usually worked 35 or more hours per week	740 837	714 373	17 779	8 685	3 037 181	2 897 092	716 599	689 989	401 533	348 217	299 659
40 or more weeks	515 937	502 275	8 437	5 225	2 517 488	2 403 267	591 993	583 315	347 454	286 347	237 567
50 to 52 weeks	422 031	411 234	6 554	4 243	2 066 573	1 970 805	488 842	460 314	297 293	240 974	187 541
27 to 39 weeks	64 503	62 075	1 669	759	158 366	150 732	37 930	33 473	17 738	19 764	18 141
Females 16 years and over, worked in 1989	433 349	417 504	10 795	5 050	1 787 262	1 708 124	422 090	447 375	244 602	161 844	196 680
50 to 52 weeks	205 888	200 655	3 184	2 049	1 008 791	964 184	234 840	263 267	150 717	84 925	101 197
48 and 49 weeks	16 904	16 371	294	239	124 904	120 168	26 766	43 444	13 926	8 523	13 074
40 to 47 weeks	38 235	36 855	969	411	165 324	158 973	43 230	36 574	23 429	15 507	19 602
27 to 39 weeks	45 804	43 806	1 491	507	139 430	133 082	34 190	29 845	18 573	14 675	17 039
14 to 26 weeks	56 940	54 474	1 597	869	176 036	167 656	42 190	37 877	19 349	19 744	22 981
1 to 13 weeks	69 578	65 343	3 260	975	172 777	164 061	40 874	36 368	18 608	18 470	22 787
Usually worked 35 or more hours per week	311 436	301 169	6 930	3 337	1 333 277	1 275 125	309 595	356 252	177 451	117 051	142 425
40 or more weeks	212 942	207 541	3 336	2 065	1 075 894	1 029 932	247 764	298 831	149 413	88 964	108 977
50 to 52 weeks	173 875	169 682	2 559	1 634	866 664	828 390	199 421	234 071	125 716	72 253	85 683
27 to 39 weeks	28 652	27 543	815	294	78 645	75 035	18 946	18 313	9 381	8 467	9 714
WORKERS IN FAMILY IN 1989											
Families	463 968	449 281	10 049	4 638	1 577 820	1 506 724	389 818	293 229	208 165	192 836	163 149
No workers	67 067	65 548	1 115	404	131 352	125 147	30 715	12 108	18 026	5 366	12 354
1 worker	153 924	149 259	3 219	1 446	413 200	394 651	99 427	53 068	69 167	53 402	51 860
2 workers	187 916	182 003	3 931	1 982	720 804	688 469	185 555	141 283	89 205	99 833	73 021
3 or more workers	55 061	52 471	1 784	806	312 464	298 457	74 121	86 770	31 767	34 235	25 914
Married-couple families	305 156	295 600	6 260	3 296	1 295 099	1 242 237	330 606	231 168	174 211	174 768	137 178
No workers	29 632	29 029	379	224	91 301	88 550	24 299	8 237	15 020	3 508	9 252
1 worker	75 213	73 192	1 306	715	303 369	292 710	76 454	29 165	54 839	46 704	39 602
2 or more workers	200 311	193 379	4 575	2 357	900 429	860 977	229 853	193 766	104 352	124 556	88 324
Husband and wife worked	178 417	172 627	3 704	2 086	804 563	770 325	204 526	175 730	92 444	112 823	79 543
Female householder, no husband present	121 370	117 790	2 636	944	185 926	172 861	36 708	44 304	24 765	8 587	18 419
No workers	32 080	31 306	615	159	32 120	29 080	4 703	3 177	2 215	1 357	2 462
1 worker	58 200	56 415	1 275	510	74 060	68 676	14 690	17 810	10 406	3 779	9 091
2 or more workers	31 090	30 069	746	275	79 746	75 105	17 315	23 317	12 144	3 451	6 866
VETERAN STATUS AND PERIOD OF SERVICE											
Civilian veterans 16 years and over	193 511	188 412	3 426	1 673	250 255	222 097	38 568	72 065	76 071	4 979	14 428
Male	181 439	176 602	3 235	1 602	236 706	210 908	37 087	68 346	73 655	4 320	13 044
May 1975 or later service only	37 560	36 316	878	366	51 366	44 415	5 215	18 847	6 174	2 361	7 273
September 1980 or later service only	20 667	19 962	491	214	30 547	26 652	3 497	11 460	3 195	1 518	3 858
Served 2 or more years	16 944	16 375	396	173	26 534	23 173	2 876	10 233	2 699	1 371	3 395
Vietnam-era service	76 033	74 090	1 253	690	88 118	75 842	10 422	30 535	20 543	1 518	3 838
World War II service	35 463	34 841	384	238	56 019	52 905	12 340	13 697	24 383	470	1 082

Table 109. Additional Labor Force Characteristics and Veteran Status for Selected Racial Groups: 1990—Con.

[Data based on sample and subject to sampling variability, see text. For definitions of terms and meanings of symbols, see text]

United States	Asian—Con.						Asian or Pacific Islander—Con. Pacific Islander				
	Vietnamese	Cambodian	Hmong	Laotian	Thai	Other Asian	Total	Hawaiian	Samoan	Guamanian	Other Pacific Islander
LABOR FORCE STATUS OF FAMILY MEMBERS											
Married-couple families	84 819	19 374	11 838	23 369	12 437	42 469	52 862	31 302	7 676	8 003	5 881
Husband employed or in Armed Forces	68 067	11 021	3 996	14 975	11 385	36 376	43 042	25 251	6 065	6 752	4 974
Wife employed or in Armed Forces	45 290	7 566	1 628	11 284	8 283	19 226	28 807	17 878	3 527	4 305	3 097
Wife unemployed	2 999	386	319	718	376	1 324	1 137	548	238	178	173
Husband unemployed	3 683	886	704	1 200	216	1 238	1 799	849	360	377	213
Wife employed or in Armed Forces	1 566	327	84	469	166	583	1 084	473	219	244	148
Wife unemployed	665	96	114	207	11	119	179	85	31	33	30
Husband not in labor force	13 069	7 467	7 138	7 194	836	4 855	8 021	5 202	1 251	874	694
Wife employed or in Armed Forces	2 237	327	244	586	441	1 334	3 030	1 986	437	321	286
Wife unemployed	272	97	79	117	6	62	134	71	40	16	7
Female householder, no husband present	18 815	7 165	1 952	3 238	3 189	5 719	13 065	8 620	1 984	1 530	931
Employed or in Armed Forces	8 919	1 310	138	992	2 503	3 380	7 080	4 671	894	905	610
Unemployed	928	284	73	178	131	310	719	418	156	97	48
SCHOOL ENROLLMENT AND LABOR FORCE STATUS											
Persons 16 to 19 years	57 395	11 635	6 547	12 637	6 402	19 560	26 390	14 493	4 870	3 969	3 058
Enrolled in school	51 550	10 010	5 624	10 474	5 513	16 922	19 356	10 498	3 536	2 915	2 407
Employed	12 772	1 750	720	2 360	1 899	5 258	5 871	3 412	758	936	765
Unemployed	2 625	489	369	670	306	962	1 320	715	167	256	182
Not in labor force	36 109	7 765	4 535	7 422	3 300	10 679	12 114	6 345	2 606	1 714	1 449
Not enrolled in school	5 845	1 625	923	2 163	889	2 638	7 034	3 995	1 334	1 054	651
High school graduate	2 095	426	199	616	489	1 333	4 126	2 499	700	620	307
Employed	1 067	230	82	310	290	813	2 567	1 685	339	374	169
Unemployed	178	57	24	55	48	157	386	226	107	42	11
Not in labor force	676	119	85	212	106	306	863	453	165	125	120
Not high school graduate	3 750	1 199	724	1 547	400	1 305	2 908	1 496	634	434	344
Employed	1 099	267	99	489	160	501	1 149	572	234	204	139
Unemployed	363	111	52	118	55	127	515	260	105	105	45
Not in labor force	2 288	821	573	940	185	671	1 244	664	295	125	160
CLASS OF WORKER											
Employed persons 16 years and over	248 881	35 623	9 756	46 010	48 028	115 816	147 318	91 543	19 041	20 298	16 436
Private wage and salary workers	208 372	30 168	7 841	41 711	39 448	92 748	113 400	69 634	14 899	15 024	13 843
Local government workers	9 897	2 087	1 114	1 913	1 516	4 675	8 080	5 554	1 153	1 010	363
State government workers	7 787	960	391	790	1 450	7 366	9 377	7 250	839	695	593
Federal government workers	6 721	664	134	507	1 907	3 296	10 045	5 043	1 593	2 883	526
Self-employed workers	14 239	1 558	218	939	3 349	7 155	6 087	3 834	513	651	1 089
Unpaid family workers	1 865	186	58	150	358	576	329	228	44	35	22
Employed females 16 years and over	101 304	15 391	3 273	18 847	28 339	41 287	68 129	42 760	8 394	9 557	7 418
Private wage and salary workers	83 278	12 995	2 539	17 121	23 210	32 554	52 771	32 608	6 512	7 250	6 401
Local government workers	4 572	903	416	780	1 075	2 217	3 145	1 962	549	452	182
State government workers	3 453	479	193	289	842	2 760	5 471	4 477	388	335	271
Federal government workers	2 709	241	41	203	1 324	1 249	4 165	1 987	696	1 252	230
Self-employed workers	6 173	634	71	373	1 669	2 171	2 421	1 622	226	250	323
Unpaid family workers	1 119	139	13	81	219	336	156	104	23	18	11
WORK STATUS IN 1989											
Persons 16 years and over, worked in 1989	277 575	39 846	12 438	50 792	53 385	131 894	174 381	106 741	23 450	25 360	18 830
50 to 52 weeks	166 027	23 934	5 375	30 394	31 901	73 521	105 987	66 736	13 654	15 037	10 560
48 and 49 weeks	16 507	2 430	850	4 050	3 842	7 480	10 804	6 275	1 633	1 837	1 059
40 to 47 weeks	21 510	3 046	621	3 608	4 762	12 528	13 075	7 930	1 090	1 891	1 555
27 to 39 weeks	18 428	2 276	1 006	3 273	3 929	11 131	12 116	7 306	1 751	1 715	1 344
14 to 26 weeks	27 141	3 823	1 859	4 655	4 579	13 873	16 037	9 368	2 229	2 492	1 948
1 to 13 weeks	27 962	4 337	2 427	4 912	4 372	13 361	16 362	9 120	2 490	2 388	2 364
Usually worked 35 or more hours per week	215 711	31 926	8 125	42 990	42 161	100 182	140 089	85 508	19 194	20 534	14 853
40 or more weeks	175 650	25 872	5 612	34 508	35 226	79 723	114 221	70 954	15 228	16 570	11 469
50 to 52 weeks	147 831	21 613	4 395	28 198	28 493	65 311	95 768	60 152	12 459	13 675	9 482
27 to 39 weeks	10 602	1 307	611	2 397	2 323	6 446	7 634	4 491	1 145	1 101	897
Females 16 years and over, worked in 1989	113 011	17 544	4 222	21 013	31 561	48 182	79 138	49 441	10 089	11 173	8 435
50 to 52 weeks	63 556	9 969	1 788	12 027	18 019	23 879	44 607	28 758	5 372	6 083	4 394
48 and 49 weeks	6 779	1 069	254	1 601	2 074	2 658	4 736	2 871	780	660	425
40 to 47 weeks	9 350	1 454	310	1 655	2 925	4 937	6 351	3 960	803	895	693
27 to 39 weeks	8 516	1 238	408	1 395	2 682	4 521	6 348	3 996	813	915	624
14 to 26 weeks	12 173	1 708	767	2 037	3 003	5 827	8 380	4 906	1 070	1 364	1 040
1 to 13 weeks	12 637	2 106	695	2 298	2 858	6 360	8 716	4 950	1 251	1 256	1 259
Usually worked 35 or more hours per week	82 439	13 401	2 794	17 201	23 905	32 611	58 152	36 249	7 738	8 164	6 001
40 or more weeks	65 670	10 761	1 841	13 630	19 303	24 778	45 962	29 397	5 992	6 119	4 454
50 to 52 weeks	54 471	8 830	1 475	10 963	15 584	19 923	38 274	24 723	4 742	5 111	3 698
27 to 39 weeks	4 475	661	260	976	1 550	2 292	3 610	2 229	438	584	359
WORKERS IN FAMILY IN 1989											
Families	118 309	28 185	14 374	28 592	16 710	53 357	71 096	43 080	10 279	10 314	7 423
No workers	16 085	10 745	7 172	7 648	834	4 094	6 205	4 106	1 144	612	343
1 worker	29 722	5 831	4 021	5 352	4 385	18 416	18 549	10 680	3 036	2 830	2 003
2 workers	47 277	7 801	2 216	10 195	8 904	23 179	32 335	19 663	4 085	4 902	3 685
3 or more workers	25 225	3 808	965	5 397	2 587	7 668	14 007	8 631	2 014	1 970	1 392
Married-couple families	84 819	19 374	11 838	23 369	12 437	42 469	52 862	31 302	7 676	8 003	5 881
No workers	8 092	6 105	5 669	5 770	258	2 340	2 751	1 845	460	276	170
1 worker	18 502	3 667	3 401	3 673	2 556	14 147	10 659	5 639	1 950	1 793	1 277
2 or more workers	58 225	9 602	2 768	13 926	9 623	25 982	39 452	23 818	5 266	5 934	4 434
Husband and wife worked	50 400	8 283	2 112	12 694	9 179	22 591	34 238	20 940	4 295	5 154	3 849
Female householder, no husband present	18 815	7 165	1 952	3 238	3 189	5 719	13 065	8 620	1 984	1 530	931
No workers	6 384	4 234	1 308	1 539	425	1 276	3 040	1 977	642	268	153
1 worker	6 100	1 660	427	875	1 426	2 412	5 384	3 480	803	619	482
2 or more workers	6 331	1 271	217	824	1 338	2 031	4 641	3 163	539	643	296
VETERAN STATUS AND PERIOD OF SERVICE											
Civilian veterans 16 years and over	6 602	701	1 156	1 133	713	5 681	28 158	19 484	2 998	4 783	893
Male	5 968	650	1 093	1 057	531	5 157	25 798	17 999	2 709	4 381	709
May 1975 or later service only	1 451	229	197	258	536	1 874	6 951	3 534	1 442	1 582	393
September 1980 or later service only	1 274	113	116	170	433	1 018	3 895	2 008	722	911	254
Served 2 or more years	1 085	103	93	119	323	876	3 361	1 747	610	776	228
Vietnam-era service	4 559	342	872	696	132	2 385	12 276	8 512	1 149	2 336	279
World War II service	250	32	19	51	21	560	3 114	2 554	146	332	82

Table 110. **Occupation of Employed Persons for Selected Racial Groups: 1990**

[Data based on sample and subject to sampling variability, see text. For definitions of terms and meanings of symbols, see text]

United States	American Indian, Eskimo, or Aleut				Asian or Pacific Islander						
						Asian					
	Total	American Indian	Eskimo	Aleut	Total	Total	Chinese	Filipino	Japanese	Asian Indian	Korean
Employed persons 16 years and over	**728 953**	**705 518**	**15 108**	**8 327**	**3 411 586**	**3 264 268**	**819 932**	**750 613**	**452 005**	**391 949**	**345 655**
Managerial and professional specialty occupations	133 555	128 790	3 014	1 751	1 045 160	1 018 546	293 565	199 949	167 153	170 844	87 974
Executive, administrative, and managerial occupations	62 825	60 681	1 262	882	428 273	413 944	123 859	77 127	79 278	54 687	41 482
Officials and administrators, public administration	6 345	6 031	271	43	10 748	10 165	2 695	2 211	2 983	882	591
Management and related occupations	17 191	16 607	288	296	149 459	145 056	41 341	39 647	25 849	16 451	9 185
Professional specialty occupations	70 730	68 109	1 752	869	616 887	604 602	169 706	122 822	87 875	116 157	46 492
Engineers and natural scientists	9 274	8 941	147	186	201 193	199 186	71 834	22 346	24 887	45 479	9 821
Engineers	4 865	4 678	84	103	117 858	116 842	40 073	12 551	14 603	27 237	5 798
Health diagnosing occupations	1 467	1 408	27	32	77 501	77 171	17 035	14 183	6 746	25 595	6 624
Health assessment and treating occupations	10 064	9 829	95	140	110 659	109 289	14 296	58 616	8 813	13 329	7 480
Teachers, librarians, and counselors	28 766	27 329	1 079	358	131 237	126 978	40 988	13 947	27 127	22 643	10 498
Teachers, elementary and secondary schools	19 080	18 000	879	201	49 959	47 377	11 478	8 083	15 855	5 094	2 296
Technical, sales, and administrative support occupations	195 096	188 174	4 512	2 410	1 134 130	1 086 905	255 598	275 123	155 543	130 182	128 210
Health technologists and technicians	8 853	8 657	115	81	52 383	51 102	8 423	23 323	5 078	7 863	2 242
Technologists and technicians, except health	14 113	13 636	291	186	155 867	152 822	49 630	25 296	17 623	23 091	9 476
Sales occupations	63 582	61 424	1 250	908	400 985	386 108	86 457	68 584	52 214	47 367	80 791
Supervisors and proprietors, sales occupations	13 853	13 380	257	216	109 710	106 880	23 907	11 461	15 229	14 234	30 094
Sales representatives, commodities and finance	11 351	11 003	190	158	78 905	76 267	23 234	12 848	14 265	8 301	10 212
Other sales occupations	38 378	37 041	803	534	212 370	202 961	39 316	44 275	22 720	24 832	40 485
Cashiers	20 049	19 419	446	184	105 851	100 715	20 783	23 237	7 969	12 909	18 087
Administrative support occupations, including clerical	108 548	104 457	2 856	1 235	524 895	496 873	111 088	157 920	80 628	51 861	35 701
Computer equipment operators	3 554	3 416	62	76	23 640	22 729	5 207	6 724	2 864	2 983	1 422
Secretaries, stenographers, and typists	25 649	24 835	561	253	83 460	77 823	16 142	22 456	19 965	5 784	5 797
Financial records processing occupations	11 484	11 021	298	165	67 517	65 110	15 417	21 835	10 494	6 031	4 199
Mail and message distributing occupations	5 198	4 955	151	92	41 046	39 536	9 069	15 265	3 324	3 647	3 688
Service occupations	134 744	129 834	3 308	1 602	504 688	476 433	135 154	125 785	50 382	31 579	52 138
Private household occupations	3 856	3 724	66	66	14 044	13 297	2 858	5 092	1 529	1 100	913
Protective service occupations	17 198	16 718	329	151	29 083	24 280	4 175	8 254	4 836	2 819	1 312
Police and firefighters	5 930	5 765	127	38	7 596	6 041	1 357	1 280	2 270	213	334
Service occupations, except protective and household	113 690	109 392	2 913	1 385	461 561	438 856	128 121	112 439	44 017	27 660	49 913
Food service occupations	42 233	40 861	848	524	250 384	240 840	99 079	40 545	22 675	11 220	26 165
Cleaning and building service occupations	32 043	30 387	1 168	488	86 854	80 357	11 098	30 751	6 924	4 351	11 556
Farming, forestry, and fishing occupations	24 405	23 707	296	402	40 718	37 059	2 893	11 248	12 058	2 304	2 284
Farm operators and managers	4 255	4 180	49	26	7 679	7 274	888	1 166	3 848	357	524
Farm workers and related occupations	15 449	15 235	118	96	30 175	27 172	1 823	9 759	7 942	1 875	1 639
Precision production, craft, and repair occupations	99 782	97 200	1 646	936	273 473	255 901	46 042	55 706	35 462	20 276	30 738
Mechanics and repairers	27 650	26 815	510	325	74 673	69 026	12 153	16 121	12 584	5 526	6 503
Construction trades	42 638	41 668	655	315	56 341	49 183	8 157	12 086	9 485	3 157	7 731
Precision production occupations	27 530	26 823	433	274	141 794	137 091	25 635	27 330	13 309	11 500	16 489
Operators, fabricators, and laborers	141 371	137 813	2 332	1 226	413 417	389 424	86 680	82 802	31 407	36 764	44 311
Machine operators and tenders, except precision	35 625	34 964	422	239	169 521	164 617	49 385	28 208	9 217	12 353	22 448
Fabricators, assemblers, inspectors, and samplers	24 645	24 261	232	152	95 890	92 840	12 555	20 356	5 705	9 566	9 146
Transportation occupations	28 763	27 924	581	258	50 674	44 748	9 106	10 816	5 754	6 039	4 077
Motor vehicle operators	27 380	26 595	547	238	49 126	43 403	8 795	10 444	5 583	5 886	4 033
Material moving equipment operators	10 715	10 425	186	104	8 046	6 081	586	2 615	800	549	284
Handlers, equipment cleaners, helpers, and laborers	41 623	40 239	911	473	89 286	81 138	15 048	20 807	9 931	8 257	8 356
Construction laborers	10 986	10 703	181	102	11 419	9 478	2 452	2 428	1 056	819	960
Freight, stock, and material handlers	12 327	11 886	305	136	31 370	28 911	4 984	7 209	4 225	2 844	3 618
Employed females 16 years and over	**340 042**	**329 185**	**7 122**	**3 735**	**1 590 897**	**1 522 768**	**373 165**	**411 393**	**215 319**	**141 028**	**173 422**
Managerial and professional specialty occupations	73 848	71 187	1 813	848	448 538	434 860	118 919	122 312	71 716	49 322	35 699
Executive, administrative, and managerial occupations	31 884	30 809	677	398	179 835	172 732	55 464	40 841	30 158	14 660	16 386
Officials and administrators, public administration	2 820	2 644	153	23	4 454	4 174	1 099	1 039	1 262	222	278
Management and related occupations	10 586	10 240	169	177	82 290	79 674	25 761	22 355	13 231	6 366	4 996
Professional specialty occupations	41 964	40 378	1 136	450	268 703	262 128	63 455	81 471	41 558	34 662	19 313
Engineers and natural scientists	1 980	1 942	29	9	38 787	38 278	16 469	6 090	4 523	5 125	1 947
Engineers	541	529	8	4	12 264	12 147	5 144	1 699	1 553	1 111	716
Health diagnosing occupations	423	397	11	15	22 310	22 219	4 270	5 610	1 423	7 700	1 347
Health assessment and treating occupations	8 654	8 441	86	127	94 913	93 770	10 800	53 520	6 906	10 504	6 721
Teachers, librarians, and counselors	20 144	19 150	766	228	70 241	67 358	19 972	10 046	19 183	8 022	4 427
Teachers, elementary and secondary schools	14 472	13 681	625	166	38 662	36 727	8 851	6 681	12 907	3 674	1 643
Technical, sales, and administrative support occupations	134 493	129 843	3 066	1 584	636 528	604 122	142 357	170 529	94 030	59 194	68 379
Health technologists and technicians	7 017	6 850	95	72	35 757	34 811	5 658	16 785	3 647	4 563	1 556
Technologists and technicians, except health	4 297	4 116	132	49	48 025	47 096	18 217	7 996	5 416	5 913	2 694
Sales occupations	38 479	37 189	760	530	197 333	187 919	41 410	41 627	24 633	17 709	39 034
Supervisors and proprietors, sales occupations	6 098	5 912	102	84	35 101	33 696	7 538	5 283	4 207	2 903	10 164
Sales representatives, commodities and finance	4 753	4 616	80	57	31 043	29 753	9 679	5 880	5 003	2 523	4 007
Other sales occupations	27 628	26 661	578	389	131 189	124 470	24 193	30 464	15 423	12 283	24 863
Cashiers	16 528	15 981	373	174	71 840	67 736	14 472	17 176	6 109	6 733	12 411
Administrative support occupations, including clerical	84 700	81 688	2 079	933	355 413	334 296	77 072	104 121	60 334	31 009	25 095
Computer equipment operators	2 378	2 267	54	57	11 366	10 740	2 593	3 202	1 437	1 159	802
Secretaries, stenographers, and typists	24 934	24 142	549	243	78 838	73 485	15 203	21 224	19 313	5 344	5 408
Financial records processing occupations	10 443	10 058	258	127	52 787	50 640	12 467	16 723	8 818	3 832	3 540
Mail and message distributing occupations	2 288	2 145	100	43	14 313	13 767	3 663	4 159	1 052	1 495	1 936
Service occupations	79 643	77 071	1 704	868	259 244	244 776	50 893	71 390	29 682	16 153	35 427
Private household occupations	3 556	3 424	66	66	12 698	11 984	2 407	4 767	1 386	975	863
Protective service occupations	2 643	2 583	21	39	3 923	3 213	713	1 013	592	321	212
Police and firefighters	652	652	–	–	699	604	180	111	164	37	23
Service occupations, except protective and household	73 444	71 064	1 617	763	242 623	229 579	47 773	65 610	27 704	14 857	34 352
Food service occupations	26 436	25 659	503	274	106 592	101 510	29 805	19 127	13 167	3 676	17 956
Cleaning and building service occupations	13 895	13 324	384	187	40 319	37 293	4 749	14 578	3 653	1 841	6 245
Farming, forestry, and fishing occupations	3 740	3 680	32	28	8 330	7 815	720	3 082	1 770	436	718
Farm operators and managers	772	767	3	2	1 586	1 550	228	317	617	59	172
Farm workers and related occupations	2 662	2 625	22	15	6 561	6 086	473	2 758	1 141	361	518
Precision production, craft, and repair occupations	10 609	10 365	120	124	65 307	63 650	11 959	13 312	6 633	3 721	9 576
Mechanics and repairers	1 332	1 307	9	16	4 492	4 168	766	1 142	686	200	462
Construction trades	1 550	1 501	41	8	2 178	2 062	226	383	392	73	362
Precision production occupations	7 648	7 478	70	100	58 598	57 381	10 958	11 775	5 549	3 442	8 752
Operators, fabricators, and laborers	37 709	37 039	387	283	172 950	167 545	48 317	30 768	11 488	12 202	23 623
Machine operators and tenders, except precision	15 613	15 326	177	110	96 039	94 011	36 664	13 877	5 426	5 229	14 033
Fabricators, assemblers, inspectors, and samplers	9 008	8 902	66	40	47 664	46 594	6 668	10 684	2 840	4 433	5 958
Transportation occupations	4 650	4 570	43	37	3 688	2 867	473	810	515	154	352
Motor vehicle operators	4 538	4 464	37	37	3 541	2 729	455	737	497	154	344
Material moving equipment operators	605	591	–	14	507	408	84	118	63	30	45
Handlers, equipment cleaners, helpers, and laborers	7 833	7 650	101	82	25 052	23 665	4 428	5 279	2 644	2 356	3 235
Construction laborers	497	490	2	5	562	495	118	122	52	23	122
Freight, stock, and material handlers	2 819	2 727	46	46	8 021	7 462	1 165	1 768	947	707	1 175

Table 110. Occupation of Employed Persons for Selected Racial Groups: 1990—Con.

[Data based on sample and subject to sampling variability, see text. For definitions of terms and meanings of symbols, see text]

United States	Asian or Pacific Islander—Con.										
	Asian—Con.						Pacific Islander				
	Vietnamese	Cambodian	Hmong	Laotian	Thai	Other Asian	Total	Hawaiian	Samoan	Guamanian	Other Pacific Islander
Employed persons 16 years and over	248 881	35 623	9 756	46 010	48 028	115 816	147 318	91 543	19 041	20 298	16 436
Managerial and professional specialty occupations	43 774	3 504	1 247	2 322	11 322	36 892	26 614	18 478	2 567	3 496	2 073
Executive, administrative, and managerial occupations	15 237	1 424	333	824	4 617	15 076	14 329	9 905	1 248	2 147	1 029
Officials and administrators, public administration	267	49	14	24	84	365	583	411	38	105	29
Management and related occupations	5 729	413	128	267	1 342	4 704	4 403	2 843	390	813	357
Professional specialty occupations	28 537	2 080	914	1 498	6 705	21 816	12 285	8 573	1 319	1 349	1 044
Engineers and natural scientists	15 708	478	67	227	1 579	6 760	2 007	1 317	158	421	111
Engineers	11 357	295	29	160	794	3 945	1 016	653	71	206	86
Health diagnosing occupations	2 041	31	13	9	1 134	3 760	330	208	33	61	28
Health assessment and treating occupations	2 155	141	45	177	2 052	2 185	1 370	777	199	220	174
Teachers, librarians, and counselors	3 648	622	290	431	944	5 840	4 259	3 185	385	392	297
Teachers, elementary and secondary schools	1 574	279	168	241	277	2 032	2 582	2 045	176	201	160
Technical, sales, and administrative support occupations	73 460	8 309	1 848	6 971	12 716	38 945	47 225	29 366	6 148	7 289	4 422
Health technologists and technicians	1 731	297	38	148	392	1 567	1 281	672	238	246	125
Technologists and technicians, except health	19 426	1 250	188	715	1 428	4 699	3 045	1 939	284	564	258
Sales occupations	22 968	2 941	490	2 318	5 423	16 555	14 877	9 384	1 656	2 322	1 515
Supervisors and proprietors, sales occupations	5 192	635	65	431	1 295	4 337	2 830	1 843	294	443	250
Sales representatives, commodities and finance	3 037	221	73	336	761	2 979	2 638	1 861	253	349	175
Other sales occupations	14 739	2 085	352	1 551	3 367	9 239	9 409	5 680	1 109	1 530	1 090
Cashiers	8 477	1 175	260	976	2 000	4 842	5 136	2 886	778	780	692
Administrative support occupations, including clerical	29 335	3 821	1 132	3 790	5 473	16 124	28 022	17 371	3 970	4 157	2 524
Computer equipment operators	2 076	259	19	142	348	685	911	542	128	118	123
Secretaries, stenographers, and typists	3 404	448	108	294	608	2 817	5 637	3 492	916	745	484
Financial records processing occupations	3 255	413	82	318	943	2 123	2 407	1 644	179	376	208
Mail and message distributing occupations	2 521	353	82	295	515	777	1 510	866	217	285	142
Service occupations	37 280	6 372	1 952	6 739	12 866	16 186	28 255	17 037	3 809	3 373	4 036
Private household occupations	577	127	15	86	247	753	747	240	67	301	139
Protective service occupations	851	195	72	136	193	1 437	4 803	3 327	850	325	301
Police and firefighters	130	27	21	43	44	322	1 555	1 316	123	59	57
Service occupations, except protective and household	35 852	6 050	1 865	6 517	12 426	13 996	22 705	13 470	2 892	2 747	3 596
Food service occupations	18 366	2 726	839	3 099	8 076	8 050	9 544	5 849	1 095	1 166	1 434
Cleaning and building service occupations	6 626	2 139	627	2 578	1 719	1 988	6 497	3 653	830	808	1 206
Farming, forestry, and fishing occupations	3 474	620	224	685	329	940	3 659	2 242	274	350	793
Farm operators and managers	140	40	30	79	56	146	405	285	8	15	97
Farm workers and related occupations	1 880	520	194	534	242	764	3 003	1 801	238	286	678
Precision production, craft, and repair occupations	38 991	6 143	1 353	9 117	3 605	8 468	17 572	10 798	2 106	2 769	1 899
Mechanics and repairers	9 715	995	357	1 497	972	2 603	5 647	3 463	537	1 129	518
Construction trades	4 190	624	111	909	532	2 201	7 158	4 969	836	739	614
Precision production occupations	25 010	4 514	878	6 701	2 101	3 624	4 703	2 326	721	889	767
Operators, fabricators, and laborers	51 902	10 675	3 132	20 176	7 190	14 385	23 993	13 622	4 137	3 021	3 213
Machine operators and tenders, except precision	21 026	4 447	1 409	9 020	3 273	3 831	4 904	2 035	945	776	1 148
Fabricators, assemblers, inspectors, and samplers	19 417	3 840	1 034	7 365	1 677	2 179	3 050	1 423	561	522	544
Transportation occupations	2 714	418	132	336	850	4 506	5 926	4 039	914	505	468
Motor vehicle operators	2 573	414	132	336	841	4 366	5 723	3 913	907	449	454
Material moving equipment operators	558	92	34	249	38	276	1 965	1 373	305	174	113
Handlers, equipment cleaners, helpers, and laborers	8 187	1 878	523	3 206	1 352	3 593	8 148	4 752	1 412	1 044	940
Construction laborers	760	101	38	190	40	634	1 941	1 232	282	137	290
Freight, stock, and material handlers	2 653	632	164	742	566	1 274	2 459	1 434	463	295	267
Employed females 16 years and over	101 304	15 391	3 273	18 847	28 339	41 287	68 129	42 760	8 394	9 557	7 418
Managerial and professional specialty occupations	16 139	1 258	353	894	5 955	12 293	13 678	9 751	1 124	1 834	969
Executive, administrative, and managerial occupations	7 322	490	92	296	2 225	4 798	7 103	4 970	569	1 121	443
Officials and administrators, public administration	100	10	7	5	41	111	280	189	27	58	6
Management and related occupations	3 735	256	28	123	864	1 959	2 616	1 707	218	469	222
Professional specialty occupations	8 817	768	261	598	3 730	7 495	6 575	4 781	555	713	526
Engineers and natural scientists	2 807	91	–	41	361	824	509	370	23	108	8
Engineers	1 543	63	–	7	58	253	117	73	3	41	–
Health diagnosing occupations	573	11	13	9	347	916	91	63	–	20	8
Health assessment and treating occupations	1 640	79	28	120	1 961	1 491	1 143	612	179	189	163
Teachers, librarians, and counselors	1 711	293	69	191	606	2 838	2 883	2 293	182	256	152
Teachers, elementary and secondary schools	940	161	35	115	220	1 500	1 935	1 535	96	160	109
Technical, sales, and administrative support occupations	35 377	4 431	765	3 673	7 772	17 615	32 406	20 379	4 194	4 791	3 042
Health technologists and technicians	1 115	197	17	90	266	917	946	513	178	181	74
Technologists and technicians, except health	4 907	263	15	145	540	990	929	666	61	94	108
Sales occupations	11 265	1 712	210	1 306	3 207	5 806	9 414	5 852	1 166	1 417	979
Supervisors and proprietors, sales occupations	1 885	209	8	163	510	826	1 405	945	155	189	116
Sales representatives, commodities and finance	1 055	118	8	133	356	991	1 290	939	114	159	78
Other sales occupations	8 325	1 385	194	1 010	2 341	3 989	6 719	3 968	897	1 069	785
Cashiers	5 257	887	150	686	1 561	2 294	4 104	2 333	669	605	497
Administrative support occupations, including clerical	18 090	2 259	523	2 132	3 759	9 902	21 117	13 348	2 789	3 099	1 881
Computer equipment operators	960	98	7	52	180	250	626	362	97	67	100
Secretaries, stenographers, and typists	3 064	413	86	283	542	2 605	5 353	3 336	864	680	473
Financial records processing occupations	2 565	277	33	263	737	1 385	2 147	1 454	155	351	187
Mail and message distributing occupations	909	84	10	82	172	205	546	353	51	94	48
Service occupations	19 293	2 733	614	2 864	8 739	6 988	14 468	8 679	1 863	1 797	2 129
Private household occupations	508	100	7	72	247	652	714	228	67	280	139
Protective service occupations	135	18	–	11	80	118	710	449	175	28	58
Police and firefighters	22	–	–	11	14	42	95	72	23	–	–
Service occupations, except protective and household	18 650	2 615	607	2 781	8 412	6 218	13 044	8 002	1 621	1 489	1 932
Food service occupations	7 847	1 044	288	1 191	4 888	2 521	5 082	3 438	578	547	519
Cleaning and building service occupations	2 243	745	69	1 056	1 340	774	3 026	1 783	286	346	611
Farming, forestry, and fishing occupations	301	199	13	204	235	137	515	319	38	66	92
Farm operators and managers	52	–	8	18	43	36	36	33	–	2	1
Farm workers and related occupations	207	187	5	171	164	101	475	284	38	62	91
Precision production, craft, and repair occupations	10 299	2 014	328	3 081	1 431	1 296	1 657	763	259	351	284
Mechanics and repairers	501	60	29	167	79	76	324	155	22	111	36
Construction trades	298	56	24	89	56	103	116	79	14	19	4
Precision production occupations	9 500	1 898	275	2 819	1 296	1 117	1 217	529	223	221	244
Operators, fabricators, and laborers	19 895	4 756	1 200	8 131	4 207	2 958	5 405	2 869	916	718	902
Machine operators and tenders, except precision	8 683	2 045	594	3 681	2 435	1 344	2 028	854	358	290	526
Fabricators, assemblers, inspectors, and samplers	8 642	1 931	448	3 257	1 021	712	1 070	476	204	181	209
Transportation occupations	240	26	–	3	74	220	821	715	66	18	22
Motor vehicle operators	230	26	–	3	74	209	812	706	66	18	22
Material moving equipment operators	26	–	–	14	16	12	99	56	5	29	9
Handlers, equipment cleaners, helpers, and laborers	2 304	754	158	1 176	661	670	1 387	768	283	200	136
Construction laborers	8	4	–	15	22	9	67	52	–	3	12
Freight, stock, and material handlers	688	230	52	183	241	306	559	288	122	62	87

Table 111. Income in 1989 of Households, Families, and Persons for Selected Racial Groups: 1990

[Data based on sample and subject to sampling variability, see text. For definitions of terms and meanings of symbols, see text]

United States	American Indian, Eskimo, or Aleut				Asian or Pacific Islander	Asian					
	Total	American Indian	Eskimo	Aleut	Total	Total	Chinese	Filipino	Japanese	Asian Indian	Korean
INCOME IN 1989											
Households	625 367	604 900	13 737	6 730	2 020 498	1 932 064	509 395	356 375	315 879	233 692	201 768
Less than $5,000	78 140	75 984	1 600	556	136 261	131 236	38 298	10 732	17 715	11 525	21 597
$5,000 to $9,999	91 731	89 368	1 675	688	126 479	120 467	36 108	13 446	15 079	9 605	16 594
$10,000 to $14,999	75 537	73 203	1 720	614	140 146	132 944	37 428	17 701	16 521	11 802	16 617
$15,000 to $24,999	126 456	122 700	2 632	1 124	279 541	264 262	68 686	42 610	39 816	26 025	31 939
$25,000 to $34,999	91 267	88 205	2 014	1 048	276 512	262 220	65 596	50 041	40 605	30 033	28 011
$35,000 to $49,999	83 967	81 020	1 768	1 179	353 574	336 607	82 962	71 904	58 378	42 128	31 725
$50,000 to $74,999	54 774	52 366	1 548	860	388 276	373 018	93 902	87 187	68 279	50 568	30 790
$75,000 to $99,999	14 595	13 762	488	345	168 542	163 106	44 891	37 255	31 115	23 243	11 573
$100,000 or more	8 900	8 292	292	316	151 167	148 204	41 524	25 499	28 371	28 763	12 922
Median (dollars)	20 025	19 900	21 891	28 781	36 784	37 007	36 259	43 780	41 626	44 696	30 184
Mean (dollars)	26 206	26 012	29 286	37 421	46 695	47 080	46 780	50 713	50 367	59 777	41 331
Families	463 968	449 281	10 049	4 638	1 577 820	1 506 724	389 818	293 229	208 165	192 836	163 149
Less than $5,000	49 114	47 942	926	246	70 522	67 035	17 381	5 847	3 597	5 861	12 357
$5,000 to $9,999	60 426	59 005	1 089	332	75 072	70 701	19 888	7 447	3 938	5 388	9 856
$10,000 to $14,999	54 908	53 253	1 249	406	99 551	94 075	27 491	12 543	6 614	7 885	12 446
$15,000 to $24,999	94 195	91 502	1 919	774	205 470	193 631	51 692	31 868	20 249	19 365	25 361
$25,000 to $34,999	71 009	68 796	1 502	711	210 640	199 280	49 026	39 499	23 761	23 850	23 528
$35,000 to $49,999	68 493	66 203	1 408	882	288 913	274 807	65 542	61 909	40 991	35 537	28 357
$50,000 to $74,999	46 094	44 067	1 279	748	339 835	326 635	80 605	78 580	56 183	46 020	28 330
$75,000 to $99,999	12 370	11 680	420	270	151 611	146 785	40 447	33 444	27 646	21 800	10 772
$100,000 or more	7 359	6 833	257	269	136 206	133 775	37 746	22 092	25 186	27 130	12 142
Median (dollars)	21 750	21 619	24 054	32 477	41 251	41 583	41 316	46 698	51 550	49 309	33 909
Mean (dollars)	28 025	27 796	31 676	42 298	51 102	51 632	51 931	53 474	60 305	65 381	45 760
Married-couple families	305 156	295 600	6 260	3 296	1 295 099	1 242 237	330 606	231 168	174 211	174 768	137 178
Less than $15,000	70 912	69 133	1 332	447	158 906	153 115	49 088	13 711	8 810	14 191	25 220
$15,000 to $24,999	62 551	60 919	1 152	480	154 424	146 349	41 807	20 613	14 521	16 321	19 831
$25,000 to $34,999	54 742	53 187	1 063	492	167 491	158 646	40 246	28 658	18 025	20 831	19 361
$35,000 to $49,999	57 587	55 820	1 033	734	244 189	232 043	55 559	50 074	33 444	32 551	24 837
$50,000 to $74,999	41 439	39 717	1 077	645	302 697	291 169	71 400	68 086	50 003	43 551	26 202
$75,000 or more	17 925	16 824	603	498	267 392	260 915	72 506	50 026	49 408	47 323	21 727
Female householder, no husband present	121 370	117 790	2 636	944	185 926	172 861	36 708	44 304	24 765	8 587	18 419
Less than $5,000	28 076	27 513	436	127	20 848	19 178	3 730	2 608	1 161	1 231	2 594
$5,000 to $9,999	29 368	28 707	485	176	23 576	21 181	3 419	3 236	1 333	1 034	2 399
$10,000 to $14,999	18 718	18 051	507	160	20 000	17 935	3 489	3 751	1 961	838	2 333
$15,000 to $24,999	23 312	22 572	533	207	34 272	31 617	6 588	7 964	4 592	1 463	4 116
$25,000 to $49,999	18 180	17 467	490	223	54 590	51 753	11 388	15 695	9 889	2 504	5 024
$50,000 or more	3 716	3 480	185	51	32 640	31 217	8 094	11 050	5 829	1 517	1 953
Males 15 years and over, with income	605 578	580 600	17 555	7 423	2 285 437	2 179 613	564 351	433 697	302 985	284 374	204 812
Median income (dollars)	12 180	12 226	9 078	16 185	19 396	19 503	18 375	18 612	28 563	25 046	18 101
Percent year-round full-time workers	40.9	41.5	22.7	35.1	52.4	52.4	52.3	51.2	52.1	56.6	49.5
Median income (dollars)	22 080	22 005	25 076	26 959	30 075	30 300	30 300	31 746	26 094	37 334	28 256
Females 15 years and over, with income	587 568	563 678	17 024	6 866	2 125 535	2 030 196	509 317	499 621	311 417	178 982	219 073
Median income (dollars)	7 310	7 327	5 981	8 318	11 986	12 040	11 455	15 046	15 155	11 746	10 570
Percent year-round full-time workers	29.5	30.1	15.0	23.6	40.6	40.6	38.9	46.8	40.3	40.2	38.2
Median income (dollars)	16 680	16 613	21 139	21 547	21 335	21 492	23 277	21 690	24 133	21 590	18 760
Per capita income (dollars)	8 328	8 284	7 891	13 290	13 638	13 806	14 877	13 616	19 373	17 777	11 178
Persons in households (dollars)	8 367	8 340	7 871	12 029	13 815	13 990	15 133	13 709	19 761	18 054	11 374
Persons in group quarters (dollars)	7 107	6 523	8 288	49 140	5 465	5 113	4 386	8 600	3 993	4 168	2 872
MEDIAN INCOME IN 1989 BY SELECTED CHARACTERISTICS											
Family type and presence of own children:											
Families (dollars)	21 750	21 619	24 054	32 477	41 251	41 583	41 316	46 698	51 550	49 309	33 909
With own children under 18 years (dollars)	20 221	20 040	23 639	32 920	41 025	41 534	42 684	47 268	53 494	51 063	35 126
With own children under 6 years (dollars)	16 856	16 658	21 413	27 188	37 325	38 260	42 424	43 797	50 696	45 531	31 354
Married-couple families (dollars)	28 287	28 119	30 817	38 327	44 965	45 261	43 764	50 705	54 733	51 503	36 915
With own children under 18 years (dollars)	28 124	27 928	30 131	41 331	44 966	45 399	45 477	51 529	57 546	52 531	37 769
With own children under 6 years (dollars)	22 901	22 683	26 653	33 417	40 210	40 538	42 424	45 151	50 982	43 470	29 561
Female householder, no husband present (dollars)	10 742	10 635	13 761	15 341	22 983	23 686	26 928	30 950	32 675	22 245	19 127
With own children under 18 years (dollars)	8 692	8 579	11 968	12 353	15 791	16 278	19 469	22 731	21 473	16 281	15 860
With own children under 6 years (dollars)	6 279	6 205	8 070	10 208	10 838	11 338	14 760	19 558	15 965	13 558	11 431
Workers in family in 1989:											
No workers (dollars)	6 069	6 040	7 949	9 285	9 050	9 170	9 293	10 623	21 688	5 000-	5 000-
1 worker (dollars)	15 526	15 473	16 595	20 920	27 860	28 499	28 776	25 707	42 599	36 839	22 969
2 or more workers (dollars)	32 978	32 844	34 193	42 179	50 706	51 044	50 881	53 521	60 174	55 477	43 409
Husband and wife worked (dollars)	35 390	35 273	36 815	45 000	52 729	53 162	52 953	55 651	61 953	57 290	45 463
Nonfamily households (dollars)	12 183	12 129	13 290	16 553	21 336	21 319	20 888	25 238	23 840	23 533	12 456
Male householder (dollars)	15 059	15 023	14 353	20 780	23 807	23 772	23 351	25 154	29 475	25 373	15 902
Living alone (dollars)	11 775	11 750	10 922	15 532	21 958	22 068	22 401	21 258	27 138	25 393	14 516
65 years and over (dollars)	6 792	6 790	6 072	10 187	9 295	9 319	7 859	7 515	15 803	10 750	6 585
Female householder (dollars)	9 939	9 888	11 587	11 005	18 405	18 425	17 455	25 325	19 677	17 702	10 774
Living alone (dollars)	8 142	8 112	10 032	8 535	16 190	16 260	15 696	21 681	17 970	17 074	8 921
65 years and over (dollars)	6 179	6 139	8 930	7 826	7 731	7 680	6 877	7 423	11 751	6 410	5 342
INCOME TYPE IN 1989											
Households	625 367	604 900	13 737	6 730	2 020 498	1 932 064	509 395	356 375	315 879	233 692	201 768
With earnings	509 200	491 708	11 732	5 760	1 799 815	1 720 256	450 265	336 684	270 646	223 914	178 561
Mean earnings (dollars)	27 324	27 184	28 010	37 852	47 021	47 459	46 355	49 568	50 036	58 903	43 215
With wage or salary income	494 123	477 241	11 451	5 431	1 737 401	1 659 270	435 302	332 969	261 035	216 916	160 004
Mean wage or salary income (dollars)	26 277	26 195	26 396	33 246	44 129	44 497	43 600	47 599	47 754	53 850	37 063
With nonfarm self-employment income	60 297	56 944	2 194	1 159	277 492	268 745	71 797	33 850	41 938	36 730	51 979
Mean nonfarm self-employment income (dollars)	14 260	14 030	11 125	31 528	27 804	28 173	25 829	24 108	23 441	40 165	33 720
With farm self-employment income	11 121	10 884	180	57	19 202	18 330	4 154	2 435	5 529	2 277	2 058
Mean farm self-employment income (dollars)	6 235	6 107	10 793	16 180	12 690	12 934	9 246	9 793	16 918	14 462	16 295
With interest, dividend, or net rental income	129 992	115 467	10 716	3 809	856 647	834 132	283 380	123 036	176 453	114 396	60 611
Mean interest, dividend, or net rental income (dollars)	3 646	3 736	2 650	3 735	5 211	5 241	6 428	3 159	5 880	5 006	5 425
With Social Security income	115 261	112 116	2 180	965	237 518	225 072	66 080	46 718	73 430	8 663	12 994
Mean Social Security income (dollars)	6 133	6 152	5 461	5 458	6 819	6 832	6 291	6 562	8 209	5 083	5 379
With public assistance income	116 009	112 118	2 933	958	199 127	188 658	42 043	35 729	9 022	10 663	15 692
Mean public assistance income (dollars)	4 145	4 100	5 516	5 269	6 852	6 914	6 188	5 388	4 589	5 205	5 376
With retirement income	66 790	64 280	1 780	730	157 114	145 166	30 414	41 910	49 624	5 657	6 839
Mean retirement income (dollars)	7 640	7 654	6 814	8 419	9 549	9 483	10 068	8 179	11 240	7 601	8 246
With other income	83 317	80 834	1 626	857	134 430	125 633	26 882	29 497	22 058	10 901	9 746
Mean other income (dollars)	3 641	3 651	3 122	3 654	5 723	5 817	5 730	5 206	5 811	5 960	8 559

Table 111. Income in 1989 of Households, Families, and Persons for Selected Racial Groups: 1990—Con.

[Data based on sample and subject to sampling variability, see text. For definitions of terms and meanings of symbols, see text]

United States	Asian or Pacific Islander—Con.										
	Asian—Con.						Pacific Islander				
	Vietnamese	Cambodian	Hmong	Laotian	Thai	Other Asian	Total	Hawaiian	Samoan	Guamanian	Other Pacific Islander
INCOME IN 1989											
Households	140 693	30 054	14 815	30 802	23 656	74 935	88 434	55 653	11 495	12 641	8 645
Less than $5,000	11 991	3 457	2 232	2 658	2 497	8 534	5 025	2 617	972	713	723
$5,000 to $9,999	12 564	4 450	2 448	3 199	1 438	5 536	6 012	3 839	914	665	594
$10,000 to $14,999	13 354	4 359	3 178	4 186	1 801	5 997	7 202	4 171	1 173	947	911
$15,000 to $24,999	22 964	6 127	3 827	6 702	3 818	11 748	15 279	8 709	2 216	2 496	1 858
$25,000 to $34,999	20 541	4 645	1 820	6 148	3 461	11 319	14 292	8 609	1 813	2 328	1 542
$35,000 to $49,999	23 741	3 541	862	4 829	4 081	12 456	16 967	10 912	2 091	2 497	1 467
$50,000 to $74,999	22 219	2 645	362	2 226	3 923	10 917	15 258	10 626	1 564	1 974	1 094
$75,000 to $99,999	8 194	517	52	594	1 392	4 280	5 436	3 931	561	670	274
$100,000 or more	5 125	313	34	260	1 245	4 148	2 963	2 239	191	351	182
Median (dollars)	29 772	18 837	14 276	23 019	31 632	30 010	31 980	34 830	27 511	30 786	26 263
Mean (dollars)	36 177	24 952	17 198	26 304	40 342	39 795	38 273	40 748	32 323	37 154	31 888
Families	118 309	28 185	14 374	28 592	16 710	53 357	71 096	43 080	10 279	10 314	7 423
Less than $5,000	9 454	3 232	2 145	2 356	894	3 911	3 487	1 638	844	480	525
$5,000 to $9,999	10 493	4 346	2 377	3 042	733	3 193	4 371	2 668	784	510	409
$10,000 to $14,999	11 269	4 253	3 068	3 825	904	3 777	5 476	2 917	1 108	669	782
$15,000 to $24,999	18 743	5 925	3 747	6 304	2 467	7 910	11 839	6 331	1 990	1 932	1 586
$25,000 to $34,999	16 870	4 211	1 774	5 726	2 632	8 403	11 360	6 472	1 581	1 890	1 417
$35,000 to $49,999	20 722	3 244	843	4 567	3 257	9 838	14 106	8 655	1 876	2 266	1 309
$50,000 to $74,999	19 542	2 265	343	2 034	3 400	9 333	13 200	9 081	1 470	1 618	1 031
$75,000 to $99,999	6 990	446	43	527	1 241	3 429	4 826	3 491	487	631	217
$100,000 or more	4 226	263	34	211	1 182	3 563	2 431	1 827	139	318	147
Median (dollars)	30 550	18 126	14 327	23 101	37 257	34 242	33 955	37 269	27 228	33 020	27 473
Mean (dollars)	36 783	24 185	17 168	26 202	47 716	45 316	39 877	43 067	32 204	39 226	32 893
Married-couple families	84 819	19 374	11 838	23 369	12 437	42 469	52 862	31 302	7 676	8 003	5 881
Less than $15,000	16 080	5 934	5 739	6 460	1 101	6 781	5 791	2 588	1 507	663	1 033
$15,000 to $24,999	12 827	4 567	3 296	5 122	1 502	5 942	8 075	4 015	1 445	1 424	1 191
$25,000 to $34,999	12 656	3 506	1 625	5 167	1 911	6 660	8 845	4 840	1 234	1 597	1 174
$35,000 to $49,999	16 895	2 775	788	4 194	2 673	8 253	12 146	7 244	1 649	2 023	1 230
$50,000 to $74,999	16 546	1 981	313	1 811	2 985	8 291	11 528	7 894	1 286	1 437	911
$75,000 or more	9 815	611	77	615	2 265	6 542	6 477	4 721	555	859	342
Female householder, no husband present	18 815	7 165	1 952	3 238	3 189	5 719	13 065	8 620	1 984	1 530	931
Less than $5,000	3 819	1 529	515	549	343	1 099	1 670	904	328	272	166
$5,000 to $9,999	4 443	2 444	683	994	406	790	2 395	1 664	375	194	162
$10,000 to $14,999	2 493	1 176	358	466	413	657	2 065	1 327	372	260	106
$15,000 to $24,999	3 170	1 080	274	613	723	1 034	2 655	1 649	384	336	286
$25,000 to $49,999	3 495	770	102	490	894	1 482	2 857	1 957	399	324	177
$50,000 or more	1 395	166	20	126	410	657	1 423	1 119	126	144	34
Males 15 years and over, with income	188 116	32 667	16 432	38 747	22 783	90 649	105 824	64 513	14 879	15 477	10 955
Median income (dollars)	14 897	10 920	8 661	12 294	18 000	16 690	17 690	19 445	15 318	17 839	13 825
Percent year-round full-time workers	49.5	39.1	17.8	44.4	56.6	50.0	54.3	54.9	51.8	55.3	52.8
Median (dollars)	24 258	18 552	16 276	17 296	25 261	26 990	24 746	26 438	21 390	24 772	19 933
Females 15 years and over, with income	144 630	34 095	12 908	30 702	33 633	55 818	95 339	60 332	12 740	12 925	9 342
Median income (dollars)	9 626	7 805	6 675	9 342	11 587	10 106	10 978	11 028	9 620	10 542	9 072
Percent year-round full-time workers	37.5	25.8	11.4	35.7	46.1	35.6	40.1	41.0	37.2	39.5	39.6
Median (dollars)	18 771	14 027	12 068	13 902	17 864	20 453	18 079	18 930	16 170	18 018	15 876
Per capita income (dollars)	9 033	5 121	2 692	5 597	11 970	11 001	10 342	11 447	7 690	10 834	7 882
Persons in households (dollars)	9 057	5 098	2 694	5 606	12 140	11 189	10 344	11 576	7 101	10 804	8 005
Persons in group quarters (dollars)	7 599	9 297	2 304	4 223	4 243	4 450	10 284	6 138	20 342	11 692	4 344
MEDIAN INCOME IN 1989 BY SELECTED CHARACTERISTICS											
Family type and presence of own children:											
Families (dollars)	30 550	18 126	14 327	23 101	37 257	34 242	33 955	37 269	27 228	33 020	27 473
With own children under 18 years (dollars)	29 369	17 245	14 245	22 533	37 683	34 240	30 894	33 306	25 755	31 302	27 412
With own children under 6 years (dollars)	29 199	16 383	14 193	20 326	35 883	31 426	26 451	28 448	21 887	26 507	26 126
Married-couple families (dollars)	35 586	22 830	15 412	25 188	43 586	38 036	39 177	43 276	31 365	37 128	30 341
With own children under 18 years (dollars)	34 614	22 157	15 337	24 801	45 658	37 703	36 856	40 977	30 398	35 456	29 789
With own children under 6 years (dollars)	37 890	27 477	12 086	24 782	35 922	30 767	31 014	33 763	25 272	31 115	26 412
Female householder, no husband present (dollars)	11 926	8 687	7 578	10 638	20 729	18 068	16 317	17 280	13 814	15 799	16 544
With own children under 18 years (dollars)	9 257	7 709	7 824	8 929	16 296	14 031	11 835	11 495	12 083	12 204	14 461
With own children under 6 years (dollars)	6 609	6 196	5 983	6 938	11 429	13 036	8 395	7 812	10 230	11 250	8 620
Workers in family in 1989:											
No workers (dollars)	6 328	9 442	11 032	10 614	5 000-	5 000-	7 562	8 901	5 080	6 976	5 150
1 worker (dollars)	18 080	14 977	14 662	15 351	24 221	24 908	21 067	22 611	18 269	21 022	17 010
2 or more workers (dollars)	42 796	34 153	27 153	32 551	45 762	43 992	43 986	47 646	38 701	41 329	34 328
Husband and wife worked (dollars)	46 156	35 895	30 528	33 051	49 406	46 694	44 680	48 472	38 863	41 506	35 545
Nonfamily households (dollars)	19 989	10 643	7 363	14 603	15 642	17 314	21 648	22 707	19 967	19 844	15 929
Male householder (dollars)	21 701	13 020	6 913	15 078	16 634	17 991	24 464	25 704	21 350	23 159	15 200
Living alone (dollars)	18 281	11 032	6 885	12 234	14 507	16 307	19 355	20 536	17 139	19 187	11 477
65 years and over (dollars)	5 546	5 138	5 360	20 417	5 000-	11 143	8 867	9 782	7 150	15 083	5 289
Female householder (dollars)	15 102	7 116	7 927	13 190	14 565	16 049	17 874	19 026	16 528	15 175	17 619
Living alone (dollars)	11 678	6 375	7 437	9 324	13 283	13 297	14 658	15 441	10 486	11 512	16 250
65 years and over (dollars)	5 185	5 090	7 453	5 000-	5 000-	6 786	10 081	10 133	10 250	10 417	5 000-
INCOME TYPE IN 1989											
Households	140 693	30 054	14 815	30 802	23 656	74 935	88 434	55 653	11 495	12 641	8 645
With earnings	122 518	19 227	7 488	22 926	21 577	66 450	79 559	49 570	10 204	11 682	8 103
Mean earnings (dollars)	37 839	28 699	15 904	28 752	42 027	41 528	37 557	39 813	32 880	35 875	32 073
With wage or salary income	118 833	18 882	7 435	22 713	20 795	64 386	78 131	48 604	10 125	11 527	7 875
Mean wage or salary income (dollars)	36 481	27 500	15 526	28 297	39 188	38 832	36 314	38 497	32 019	35 263	29 903
With nonfarm self-employment income	16 200	1 817	421	1 296	3 206	9 511	8 747	6 078	712	910	1 047
Mean nonfarm self-employment income (dollars)	18 213	17 027	8 006	12 138	28 189	26 738	16 481	16 015	15 757	13 222	22 508
With farm self-employment income	728	161	98	203	145	542	872	613	69	79	111
Mean farm self-employment income (dollars)	7 827	9 907	2 813	3 536	10 494	9 239	7 575	8 311	1 410	7 320	7 522
With interest, dividend, or net rental income	35 136	4 198	1 012	3 896	7 607	24 407	22 515	16 580	1 693	2 897	1 345
Mean interest, dividend, or net rental income (dollars)	2 243	1 916	1 916	1 578	3 112	4 256	4 114	4 520	2 132	3 596	2 718
With Social Security income	7 001	2 001	896	1 718	783	4 788	12 446	9 281	1 256	1 284	625
Mean Social Security income (dollars)	5 033	6 201	6 583	6 092	5 508	6 371	6 567	6 939	5 684	5 801	4 377
With public assistance income	34 416	15 358	9 946	10 894	808	4 087	10 469	6 513	2 031	1 214	711
Mean public assistance income (dollars)	7 683	10 248	10 974	10 547	4 874	5 042	5 734	5 668	6 016	5 643	5 682
With retirement income	4 301	1 170	384	855	587	3 425	11 948	8 566	1 014	1 942	426
Mean retirement income (dollars)	6 289	6 333	6 612	5 436	6 615	7 296	10 352	10 893	7 428	10 124	7 470
With other income	11 523	2 922	2 506	2 834	1 364	5 400	8 797	5 847	964	1 399	587
Mean other income (dollars)	4 207	4 400	6 454	5 250	8 581	7 876	4 383	4 215	5 749	4 431	3 699

Table 112. **Poverty Status in 1989 of Families and Persons for Selected Racial Groups: 1990**

[Data based on sample and subject to sampling variability, see text. For definitions of terms and meanings of symbols, see text]

United States	American Indian, Eskimo, or Aleut				Asian or Pacific Islander						
						Asian					
	Total	American Indian	Eskimo	Aleut	Total	Total	Chinese	Filipino	Japanese	Asian Indian	Korean
ALL INCOME LEVELS IN 1989											
Families	**463 968**	**449 281**	**10 049**	**4 638**	**1 577 820**	**1 506 724**	**389 818**	**293 229**	**208 165**	**192 836**	**163 149**
In owner-occupied housing unit	270 377	261 082	6 416	2 879	949 558	914 752	260 186	191 220	149 444	122 997	80 693
With related children under 18 years	313 592	302 610	7 802	3 180	996 789	945 251	220 521	192 395	92 412	136 544	106 333
With related children under 5 years	144 727	138 535	4 690	1 502	427 763	402 166	90 001	78 489	39 944	57 349	41 289
Householder worked in 1989	348 200	336 905	7 410	3 885	1 324 838	1 267 056	326 315	258 339	169 326	180 678	141 225
Householder worked year round full time in 1989	197 646	193 380	2 539	1 727	908 573	868 801	221 474	175 386	121 552	133 283	88 753
Householder under 65 years with work disability	64 327	63 004	914	409	69 169	63 201	11 893	10 306	6 987	5 198	7 442
Householder foreign born	11 812	10 602	188	1 022	1 239 508	1 227 216	327 946	245 538	61 271	187 916	156 541
Householder under 25 years	31 542	30 512	749	281	43 244	39 044	6 794	8 192	2 509	3 984	3 656
Householder 65 years and over	44 476	42 966	1 233	277	140 075	134 705	42 649	28 919	42 539	3 510	8 413
Householder high school graduate or higher	305 619	296 455	5 936	3 228	1 273 900	1 219 362	297 006	253 801	184 195	173 862	143 232
With public assistance income in 1989	88 762	85 809	2 291	662	171 172	162 203	34 036	30 930	6 223	9 493	11 543
With Social Security income in 1989	75 315	73 190	1 600	525	183 312	173 588	49 934	38 846	52 777	7 440	10 200
Married-couple families	**305 156**	**295 600**	**6 260**	**3 296**	**1 295 099**	**1 242 237**	**330 606**	**231 168**	**174 211**	**174 768**	**137 178**
With related children under 18 years	192 449	185 400	4 866	2 183	846 351	808 448	196 173	157 660	79 553	128 095	92 034
With related children under 5 years	89 027	84 928	3 017	1 082	377 487	358 258	83 885	66 229	36 354	54 807	38 246
Householder worked in 1989	245 868	237 923	5 082	2 863	1 116 840	1 071 440	281 761	206 403	144 547	165 899	120 780
Householder worked year round full time in 1989	151 004	147 688	1 929	1 387	784 751	752 282	195 204	143 697	105 813	124 504	77 485
Householder high school graduate or higher	207 764	201 613	3 763	2 388	1 069 747	1 027 971	254 052	202 292	156 571	159 470	123 742
Householder 65 years and over	29 148	28 301	654	193	113 452	109 871	36 035	22 692	34 786	2 963	7 211
With public assistance income in 1989	34 530	33 186	1 015	329	116 160	111 737	25 586	20 780	3 710	7 380	8 692
With Social Security income in 1989	48 378	47 199	847	332	141 343	134 697	40 020	29 501	41 031	6 177	7 801
Female householder, no husband present	**121 370**	**117 790**	**2 636**	**944**	**185 926**	**172 861**	**36 708**	**44 304**	**24 765**	**8 587**	**18 419**
With related children under 18 years	95 511	92 611	2 148	752	111 206	100 996	17 276	26 535	10 193	5 303	11 152
With related children under 5 years	42 989	41 439	1 196	354	37 058	32 189	4 151	9 189	2 626	1 453	2 390
Householder worked in 1989	73 683	71 558	1 445	680	127 662	119 538	25 786	36 704	17 711	6 206	14 046
Householder worked year round full time in 1989	32 741	32 161	375	205	73 571	69 137	14 336	22 354	10 822	3 616	7 669
Householder high school graduate or higher	75 312	73 214	1 490	608	128 201	119 113	25 233	36 652	19 921	6 336	13 016
Householder 65 years and over	12 115	11 602	458	55	18 962	17 604	4 841	3 989	5 596	387	943
With public assistance income in 1989	47 625	46 253	1 072	300	41 385	37 375	5 541	7 765	1 948	1 500	2 127
With Social Security income in 1989	20 903	20 155	594	154	28 903	26 537	6 519	6 550	7 970	768	1 807
Unrelated individuals for whom poverty status is determined	**278 246**	**267 530**	**7 140**	**3 576**	**793 413**	**753 933**	**202 171**	**134 740**	**150 041**	**71 576**	**65 044**
Nonfamily householder	161 399	155 619	3 688	2 092	442 678	425 340	119 577	63 146	107 714	40 856	38 619
In owner-occupied housing unit	64 930	62 674	1 469	787	129 766	125 102	40 097	18 052	41 875	7 267	6 900
65 years and over	37 681	36 640	636	405	70 525	67 691	23 584	11 379	20 948	1 577	6 034
Persons for whom poverty status is determined	**1 950 915**	**1 876 359**	**53 268**	**21 288**	**7 068 454**	**6 728 635**	**1 611 033**	**1 392 670**	**844 999**	**771 292**	**778 322**
Persons 18 years and over	1 279 684	1 233 057	32 254	14 373	5 042 079	4 826 731	1 230 058	1 010 562	688 576	539 917	534 590
Persons 65 years and over	113 052	109 591	2 489	972	434 119	420 473	129 597	99 685	103 274	20 418	33 455
Related children under 18 years	664 454	636 723	20 867	6 864	2 015 646	1 892 101	379 496	380 453	154 977	230 828	242 834
Related children under 6 years	231 655	220 267	8 973	2 415	683 890	640 775	127 936	121 969	56 223	77 772	84 338
Related children 5 to 17 years	471 750	453 693	13 256	4 801	1 449 657	1 361 861	272 119	279 647	108 289	166 222	173 144
INCOME IN 1989 BELOW POVERTY LEVEL											
Families	**125 432**	**122 237**	**2 604**	**591**	**182 507**	**171 816**	**43 184**	**15 267**	**7 131**	**13 964**	**24 037**
Percent below poverty level	27.0	27.2	25.9	12.7	11.6	11.4	11.1	5.2	3.4	7.2	14.7
In owner-occupied housing unit	51 562	49 885	1 434	243	34 949	33 105	12 238	4 553	2 348	3 311	4 398
With related children under 18 years	104 796	102 090	2 217	489	138 221	128 638	27 143	11 155	4 383	10 099	15 836
With related children under 5 years	58 315	56 506	1 511	298	69 476	63 509	10 858	5 514	2 149	5 044	7 308
Householder worked in 1989	63 196	61 305	1 526	365	84 290	78 978	22 390	8 051	3 410	8 384	13 207
Householder worked year round full time in 1989	12 167	12 021	111	35	20 163	18 531	5 698	1 388	759	2 173	3 144
Householder under 65 years with work disability	23 948	23 592	299	57	18 003	16 620	2 427	1 132	489	1 079	1 398
Householder foreign born	2 515	2 336	29	150	162 490	159 742	41 243	11 300	4 266	13 372	23 643
Householder under 25 years	15 017	14 642	302	73	14 894	13 504	2 481	1 728	538	1 050	1 243
Householder 65 years and over	11 211	10 942	242	27	14 090	13 490	5 465	2 203	785	574	2 036
Householder high school graduate or higher	62 109	60 523	1 274	312	105 940	99 486	25 492	10 406	5 953	10 029	19 585
With public assistance income in 1989	54 404	53 494	790	120	58 794	54 716	7 758	3 568	825	2 216	2 407
With Social Security income in 1989	18 332	17 968	303	61	11 910	11 020	3 437	2 100	786	543	1 103
Mean income deficit (dollars)	5 938	5 938	5 931	5 981	6 099	6 117	5 462	5 155	5 580	6 108	6 118
Married-couple families	**51 812**	**50 330**	**1 222**	**260**	**120 010**	**115 146**	**32 648**	**7 571**	**4 293**	**10 293**	**17 976**
With related children under 18 years	39 646	38 389	1 063	194	90 804	86 569	20 847	5 112	2 389	7 726	11 834
With related children under 5 years	23 123	22 236	764	123	49 199	46 432	9 046	2 647	1 333	4 131	6 357
Householder worked in 1989	29 345	28 345	829	171	60 611	57 663	17 901	4 029	2 095	6 654	10 235
Householder worked year round full time in 1989	7 005	6 906	70	29	16 546	15 351	5 021	955	534	1 924	2 645
Householder high school graduate or higher	23 835	23 143	552	140	72 158	69 205	18 781	5 173	3 672	7 567	15 621
Householder 65 years and over	5 732	5 593	112	27	11 150	10 813	4 688	1 701	606	480	1 703
With public assistance income in 1989	16 184	15 871	288	25	34 647	33 364	5 811	1 221	206	1 375	1 494
With Social Security income in 1989	9 170	9 009	126	35	8 076	7 593	2 692	1 321	482	395	739
Mean income deficit (dollars)	5 977	5 959	6 522	6 837	6 266	6 276	5 356	5 172	5 846	6 106	6 279
Female householder, no husband present	**61 131**	**59 816**	**1 020**	**295**	**47 873**	**43 035**	**7 288**	**6 303**	**2 367**	**2 354**	**4 768**
With related children under 18 years	55 054	53 885	896	273	39 608	35 046	4 886	5 282	1 826	1 861	3 395
With related children under 5 years	29 124	28 390	562	172	17 660	14 852	1 489	2 575	704	694	829
Householder worked in 1989	26 600	25 962	467	171	16 518	14 702	2 927	3 236	1 091	919	2 311
Householder worked year round full time in 1989	3 922	3 888	34	–	2 467	2 189	405	338	178	156	427
Householder high school graduate or higher	32 129	31 457	523	149	24 192	21 229	4 388	4 181	1 912	1 447	3 006
Householder 65 years and over	4 531	4 437	94	–	2 111	1 933	550	321	129	77	271
With public assistance income in 1989	34 480	33 943	443	94	21 009	18 457	1 599	2 139	598	743	775
With Social Security income in 1989	7 631	7 467	138	26	2 967	2 639	567	628	217	118	247
Mean income deficit (dollars)	5 922	5 933	5 409	5 449	5 786	5 808	5 773	5 149	5 197	6 385	5 610
Unrelated individuals	**113 823**	**109 853**	**2 861**	**1 109**	**258 514**	**246 383**	**72 555**	**32 228**	**37 220**	**23 672**	**27 522**
Percent below poverty level	40.9	41.1	40.1	31.0	32.6	32.7	35.9	23.9	24.8	33.1	42.3
Nonfamily householder	53 431	51 899	1 030	502	104 308	100 919	31 868	9 829	19 154	9 627	13 747
In owner-occupied housing unit	21 090	20 475	452	163	12 380	11 746	3 697	1 853	3 427	602	1 026
65 years and over	16 360	16 071	178	111	22 688	21 872	8 663	3 958	3 790	692	2 961
Mean income deficit (dollars)	3 714	3 705	4 043	3 737	4 504	4 519	4 559	4 097	4 718	4 478	4 554
Persons	**603 188**	**585 273**	**14 335**	**3 580**	**997 196**	**938 930**	**225 777**	**89 081**	**59 127**	**74 972**	**106 822**
Percent below poverty level	30.9	31.2	26.9	16.8	14.1	14.0	14.0	6.4	7.0	9.7	13.7
Persons 18 years and over	342 785	332 399	8 194	2 192	650 705	619 784	172 608	63 715	50 074	53 763	80 578
Persons 65 years and over	33 219	32 526	542	151	52 129	50 264	19 750	8 270	5 317	1 901	7 190
Related children under 18 years	254 431	247 092	6 002	1 337	337 128	310 567	51 838	23 999	7 701	20 755	25 435
Related children under 6 years	102 229	98 741	2 933	555	120 474	109 691	16 165	8 547	3 168	7 460	10 180
Related children 5 to 17 years	168 816	164 449	3 495	872	237 862	220 271	38 254	16 879	5 109	14 547	16 757
Persons below 125 percent of poverty level	747 713	724 648	18 233	4 832	1 274 873	1 198 715	295 707	124 788	73 408	97 375	140 891
Persons below 200 percent of poverty level	1 099 251	1 061 694	28 896	8 661	2 151 021	2 019 832	507 858	277 426	128 289	177 590	247 142

Table 112. **Poverty Status in 1989 of Families and Persons for Selected Racial Groups: 1990**—Con.

[Data based on sample and subject to sampling variability, see text. For definitions of terms and meanings of symbols, see text]

United States	Asian or Pacific Islander—Con.										
	Asian—Con.						Pacific Islander				
	Vietnamese	Cambodian	Hmong	Laotian	Thai	Other Asian	Total	Hawaiian	Samoan	Guamanian	Other Pacific Islander
ALL INCOME LEVELS IN 1989											
Families	**118 309**	**28 185**	**14 374**	**28 592**	**16 710**	**53 357**	**71 096**	**43 080**	**10 279**	**10 314**	**7 423**
In owner-occupied housing unit	56 720	6 863	1 596	8 473	10 437	26 123	34 806	23 582	3 019	5 036	3 169
With related children under 18 years	87 406	24 935	13 486	25 020	11 232	34 967	51 538	29 603	8 688	7 521	5 726
With related children under 5 years	38 776	13 301	9 751	11 716	3 838	17 712	25 597	14 148	4 893	3 471	3 085
Householder worked in 1989	92 238	14 104	5 323	18 246	15 298	45 964	57 782	34 552	7 881	8 890	6 459
Householder worked year round full time in 1989	62 693	9 555	2 261	12 224	10 540	31 080	39 772	24 172	5 290	6 216	4 094
Householder under 65 years with work disability	8 415	4 917	2 109	3 036	602	2 296	5 968	3 600	981	772	615
Householder foreign born	116 777	27 843	14 205	28 233	16 360	44 586	12 292	463	4 021	1 346	6 462
Householder under 25 years	5 726	1 460	1 670	1 647	605	2 801	4 200	2 348	668	675	509
Householder 65 years and over	3 970	976	619	824	150	2 136	5 370	3 962	561	606	241
Householder high school graduate or higher	76 891	11 200	5 890	13 171	14 135	45 979	54 538	34 099	7 500	7 655	5 284
With public assistance income in 1989	30 951	14 674	9 754	10 484	691	3 424	8 969	5 293	1 894	1 129	653
With Social Security income in 1989	5 931	1 785	839	1 616	644	3 576	9 724	7 067	1 109	1 019	529
Married-couple families	**84 819**	**19 374**	**11 838**	**23 369**	**12 437**	**42 469**	**52 862**	**31 302**	**7 676**	**8 003**	**5 881**
With related children under 18 years	66 839	17 665	11 257	20 868	8 742	29 562	37 903	20 897	6 479	5 815	4 712
With related children under 5 years	31 528	9 555	8 539	9 971	3 286	15 858	19 229	10 079	3 753	2 713	2 684
Householder worked in 1989	70 564	11 428	4 745	15 591	11 800	37 922	45 400	26 694	6 291	7 131	5 284
Householder worked year round full time in 1989	49 785	8 193	2 067	10 804	8 296	26 434	32 469	19 482	4 370	5 172	3 445
Householder high school graduate or higher	57 963	8 695	5 219	11 255	11 206	37 506	41 776	25 516	5 826	6 272	4 162
Householder 65 years and over	2 850	616	337	594	132	1 655	3 581	2 555	341	464	221
With public assistance income in 1989	18 562	8 841	7 904	7 937	348	1 997	4 423	2 403	1 008	636	376
With Social Security income in 1989	3 908	1 207	651	1 336	375	2 690	6 646	4 668	810	779	389
Female householder, no husband present	**18 815**	**7 165**	**1 952**	**3 238**	**3 189**	**5 719**	**13 065**	**8 620**	**1 984**	**1 530**	**931**
With related children under 18 years	13 825	6 339	1 795	2 764	2 067	3 747	10 210	6 572	1 754	1 170	714
With related children under 5 years	5 178	3 361	992	1 184	400	1 265	4 869	3 212	943	479	235
Householder worked in 1989	9 730	1 622	235	1 130	2 587	3 781	8 124	5 337	1 076	1 061	650
Householder worked year round full time in 1989	5 037	729	72	567	1 703	2 232	4 434	2 939	581	553	361
Householder high school graduate or higher	8 807	1 625	399	926	2 031	4 167	9 088	6 257	1 245	908	678
Householder 65 years and over	779	286	246	180	13	344	1 358	1 090	150	113	5
With public assistance income in 1989	8 511	5 082	1 498	1 975	266	1 162	4 010	2 551	830	415	214
With Social Security income in 1989	1 293	473	152	188	233	584	2 366	1 849	230	181	106
Unrelated individuals for whom poverty status is determined	**59 466**	**8 117**	**1 252**	**6 340**	**13 724**	**41 462**	**39 480**	**25 884**	**3 855**	**5 874**	**3 867**
Nonfamily householder	22 384	1 869	441	2 210	6 946	21 578	17 338	12 573	1 216	2 327	1 222
In owner-occupied housing unit	5 207	209	19	230	1 484	3 762	4 664	3 684	207	580	193
65 years and over	2 024	407	150	122	128	1 338	2 834	2 231	147	299	157
Persons for whom poverty status is determined	**581 057**	**146 206**	**93 570**	**145 888**	**89 225**	**274 373**	**339 819**	**200 153**	**55 014**	**46 072**	**38 580**
Persons 18 years and over	386 248	78 938	36 649	80 449	66 927	173 817	215 348	129 968	30 908	30 465	24 007
Persons 65 years and over	16 370	3 628	2 652	3 351	1 061	6 982	13 646	9 707	1 385	1 607	947
Related children under 18 years	192 637	66 903	56 658	65 123	22 089	100 103	123 545	69 618	24 023	15 501	14 403
Related children under 6 years	58 275	23 272	24 748	20 757	5 794	39 691	43 115	23 613	9 084	5 018	5 400
Related children 5 to 17 years	145 088	48 291	36 146	48 296	17 488	67 131	87 796	50 087	16 504	11 239	9 966
INCOME IN 1989 BELOW POVERTY LEVEL											
Families	**28 131**	**11 072**	**8 885**	**9 207**	**1 806**	**8 332**	**10 691**	**5 453**	**2 522**	**1 266**	**1 450**
Percent below poverty level	23.8	42.1	61.8	32.2	10.8	15.6	15.0	12.7	24.5	12.3	19.5
In owner-occupied housing unit	3 003	460	314	506	521	1 453	1 844	1 017	265	237	325
With related children under 18 years	23 988	11 259	8 627	8 814	1 297	6 037	9 583	4 921	2 397	1 026	1 239
With related children under 5 years	10 858	6 615	6 613	4 689	511	3 350	5 967	2 938	1 660	620	749
Householder worked in 1989	11 515	2 410	2 115	2 297	931	4 268	5 312	2 467	1 124	711	1 010
Householder worked year round full time in 1989	2 376	693	415	655	229	1 001	1 632	646	434	183	369
Householder under 65 years with work disability	3 763	2 693	1 443	1 404	113	679	1 383	691	319	171	202
Householder foreign born	27 696	11 776	8 793	9 061	1 747	8 845	2 748	123	1 051	334	1 240
Householder under 25 years	2 438	826	1 056	746	223	1 175	1 390	768	264	185	173
Householder 65 years and over	1 126	334	318	290	41	318	600	298	179	84	39
Householder high school graduate or higher	11 425	2 952	3 287	3 121	1 213	6 023	6 454	3 325	1 485	664	980
With public assistance income in 1989	15 089	8 665	6 584	6 051	197	1 356	4 078	2 421	1 027	412	218
With Social Security income in 1989	1 172	594	364	364	68	489	890	508	225	103	54
Mean income deficit (dollars)	6 501	6 669	8 359	6 722	5 910	6 656	5 813	5 282	6 826	5 384	6 426
Married-couple families	**15 686**	**6 506**	**7 157**	**6 858**	**823**	**5 335**	**4 864**	**1 932**	**1 516**	**496**	**920**
With related children under 18 years	14 006	6 307	7 034	6 587	588	4 139	4 235	1 601	1 425	385	824
With related children under 5 years	6 631	3 923	5 731	3 712	337	2 584	2 767	966	990	257	554
Householder worked in 1989	7 689	1 643	1 922	1 792	515	3 188	2 948	1 119	823	303	703
Householder worked year round full time in 1989	1 719	572	394	541	147	899	1 195	433	365	99	298
Householder high school graduate or higher	6 476	1 899	2 910	2 502	612	3 992	2 953	1 112	954	281	606
Householder 65 years and over	800	175	153	246	23	238	337	154	102	42	39
With public assistance income in 1989	8 309	4 596	5 223	4 430	58	641	1 283	675	413	123	72
With Social Security income in 1989	720	354	276	281	24	309	483	250	156	51	26
Mean income deficit (dollars)	6 930	7 371	8 656	7 152	6 642	6 507	6 036	5 466	6 877	4 647	6 596
Female householder, no husband present	**9 228**	**4 753**	**1 479**	**1 817**	**791**	**1 887**	**4 838**	**2 993**	**899**	**587**	**359**
With related children under 18 years	7 959	4 527	1 365	1 759	652	1 534	4 562	2 848	884	520	310
With related children under 5 years	3 660	2 539	758	799	154	651	2 808	1 741	632	296	139
Householder worked in 1989	2 371	539	93	283	372	560	1 816	1 094	255	282	185
Householder worked year round full time in 1989	391	77	21	74	82	40	278	130	62	35	51
Householder high school graduate or higher	3 202	809	297	461	418	1 108	2 963	1 931	483	317	232
Householder 65 years and over	228	130	152	29	13	33	178	84	60	34	–
With public assistance income in 1989	5 549	3 689	1 173	1 362	126	704	2 552	1 592	579	248	133
With Social Security income in 1989	367	199	76	57	39	124	328	206	60	44	18
Mean income deficit (dollars)	5 972	5 858	7 197	5 511	4 828	7 377	5 592	5 181	6 500	6 030	6 030
Unrelated individuals	**23 873**	**3 782**	**812**	**2 292**	**5 480**	**16 947**	**12 131**	**6 879**	**1 474**	**2 020**	**1 758**
Percent below poverty level	40.1	46.6	64.9	36.2	39.9	40.9	30.7	26.6	38.2	34.4	45.5
Nonfamily householder	5 828	683	207	546	2 204	7 226	3 389	2 219	279	542	349
In owner-occupied housing unit	492	30	19	18	147	435	634	466	8	116	44
65 years and over	968	176	49	81	75	459	816	581	56	102	77
Mean income deficit (dollars)	4 410	4 373	4 789	4 539	4 868	4 772	4 205	3 922	4 521	4 402	4 822
Persons	**149 567**	**62 312**	**59 530**	**50 580**	**11 178**	**49 984**	**58 266**	**28 642**	**14 210**	**7 036**	**8 378**
Percent below poverty level	25.7	42.6	63.6	34.7	12.5	18.2	17.1	14.3	25.8	15.3	21.7
Persons 18 years and over	84 637	27 970	20 882	22 453	8 898	34 206	30 921	15 085	6 733	4 192	4 911
Persons 65 years and over	3 288	1 098	1 183	1 019	167	1 081	1 865	1 107	335	224	199
Related children under 18 years	62 893	34 065	38 477	27 855	2 108	15 441	26 561	13 062	7 412	2 757	3 330
Related children under 6 years	17 652	12 482	17 321	9 546	620	6 550	10 783	5 306	3 109	1 085	1 283
Related children 5 to 17 years	48 729	24 149	24 187	20 235	1 572	9 853	17 591	8 671	4 823	1 845	2 252
Persons below 125 percent of poverty level	181 374	76 662	70 785	61 779	13 790	62 156	76 158	37 486	18 000	9 415	11 257
Persons below 200 percent of poverty level	271 012	105 126	86 087	93 903	24 414	100 985	131 189	65 658	28 413	17 426	19 692

Table 113. Selected Characteristics of Persons 60 Years and Over by Age for Selected Racial Groups: 1990

[Data based on sample and subject to sampling variability, see text. For definitions of terms and meanings of symbols, see text]

United States	American Indian, Eskimo, or Aleut				Asian or Pacific Islander	Asian					
	Total	American Indian	Eskimo	Aleut	Total	Total	Chinese	Filipino	Japanese	Asian Indian	Korean
LIVING ARRANGEMENTS											
Persons 60 to 64 years	54 040	52 281	1 229	530	215 276	207 438	58 000	44 653	55 204	13 333	17 407
In households	53 196	51 494	1 189	513	213 796	206 155	57 487	44 268	54 977	13 273	17 388
In group quarters	844	787	40	17	1 480	1 283	513	385	227	60	19
Nursing homes	459	438	10	11	507	459	102	202	82	15	14
Persons 65 to 74 years	74 320	72 116	1 574	630	295 142	285 497	86 899	60 877	74 220	15 422	24 066
In households	72 706	70 600	1 483	623	292 155	282 700	85 628	60 437	73 576	15 235	23 896
In group quarters	1 614	1 516	91	7	2 987	2 797	1 271	440	644	187	170
Nursing homes	1 211	1 144	60	7	1 526	1 403	502	215	403	69	139
Persons 75 years and over	43 403	41 880	1 153	370	147 432	142 699	44 873	40 118	31 984	5 431	9 918
In households	40 038	38 726	963	349	140 077	135 951	42 660	38 962	29 559	5 141	9 524
In group quarters	3 365	3 154	190	21	7 355	6 748	2 213	1 156	2 425	290	394
Nursing homes	3 026	2 857	148	21	5 688	5 171	1 402	842	2 096	278	343
EDUCATIONAL ATTAINMENT											
Persons 60 to 64 years	54 040	52 281	1 229	530	215 276	207 438	58 000	44 653	55 204	13 333	17 407
Less than 9th grade	18 368	17 267	866	235	52 212	50 685	20 861	10 805	2 817	3 439	4 266
9th to 12th grade, no diploma	12 667	12 439	111	117	29 774	27 609	8 233	5 074	6 916	1 852	2 527
High school graduate (includes equivalency)	11 091	10 887	109	95	56 331	53 804	10 759	8 362	25 497	2 052	4 389
Some college or associate degree	8 131	7 958	126	47	34 205	33 120	7 670	7 805	11 446	1 374	2 453
Bachelor's degree or higher	3 783	3 730	17	36	42 754	42 220	10 477	12 607	8 528	4 616	3 772
Persons 65 to 74 years	74 320	72 116	1 574	630	295 142	285 497	86 899	60 877	74 220	15 422	24 066
Less than 9th grade	28 536	26 947	1 238	351	99 123	96 076	33 442	23 583	10 403	6 002	9 282
9th to 12th grade, no diploma	17 347	17 191	85	71	43 146	40 658	12 255	6 773	12 213	2 297	3 591
High school graduate (includes equivalency)	14 298	14 025	142	131	73 375	70 784	16 397	10 773	31 814	2 345	6 117
Some college or associate degree	9 630	9 509	73	48	38 129	37 026	10 567	8 691	11 599	1 510	2 401
Bachelor's degree or higher	4 509	4 444	36	29	41 369	40 953	14 238	11 057	8 191	3 268	2 675
Persons 75 years and over	43 403	41 880	1 153	370	147 432	142 699	44 873	40 118	31 984	5 431	9 918
Less than 9th grade	22 788	21 711	846	231	73 358	71 346	23 666	20 007	14 030	2 220	4 936
9th to 12th grade, no diploma	8 732	8 611	77	44	19 361	18 439	5 213	4 678	4 856	809	1 401
High school graduate (includes equivalency)	6 188	6 026	101	61	25 595	24 564	6 167	6 282	8 163	852	1 866
Some college or associate degree	3 664	3 566	79	19	13 434	12 973	3 905	4 329	2 739	485	794
Bachelor's degree or higher	2 031	1 966	50	15	15 684	15 377	5 922	4 822	2 196	1 065	921
INCOME AND POVERTY STATUS IN 1989											
Married-couple families, householder 60 to 64 years	17 231	16 722	390	119	64 957	62 406	19 690	12 755	15 215	3 806	5 312
Less than $5,000	1 037	988	41	8	1 918	1 859	696	174	85	108	316
$5,000 to $9,999	1 913	1 890	18	5	2 231	2 130	880	168	142	98	335
$10,000 to $14,999	2 037	1 992	41	4	2 775	2 678	998	486	232	126	294
$15,000 to $24,999	3 616	3 516	73	27	7 488	7 071	2 592	1 441	1 145	275	638
$25,000 to $34,999	2 821	2 743	40	38	7 716	7 436	2 691	1 433	1 575	365	666
$35,000 to $49,999	2 630	2 555	64	11	11 469	10 900	3 380	2 319	2 792	565	935
$50,000 or more	3 177	3 038	113	26	31 360	30 332	8 453	6 734	9 244	2 269	2 128
Percent with income in 1989 below poverty level	17.7	17.7	22.8	9.2	7.3	7.3	8.5	3.3	1.1	6.8	12.1
Persons 60 to 64 years living alone	9 561	9 304	152	105	17 243	16 562	3 771	2 396	7 492	813	1 149
Less than $5,000	3 184	3 058	81	45	2 671	2 555	694	343	737	121	384
$5,000 to $9,999	2 848	2 801	40	7	2 825	2 727	699	358	1 145	78	197
$10,000 to $14,999	1 163	1 129	13	21	2 373	2 224	455	328	1 219	53	112
$15,000 to $24,999	1 315	1 281	10	24	3 770	3 668	655	563	1 939	159	219
$25,000 to $34,999	521	515	6	–	2 287	2 197	479	296	1 100	115	79
$35,000 or more	530	520	2	8	3 317	3 191	789	508	1 352	287	158
Percent with income in 1989 below poverty level	45.3	45.1	57.9	42.9	20.9	20.8	26.0	19.1	13.9	16.9	41.0
Married-couple families, householder 65 to 74 years	21 183	20 566	464	153	80 457	77 755	26 232	12 036	26 341	2 522	5 635
Less than $5,000	1 046	1 032	9	5	3 201	3 074	1 352	354	131	244	622
$5,000 to $9,999	3 160	3 081	58	21	5 545	5 383	2 562	582	538	201	908
$10,000 to $14,999	3 823	3 734	62	27	7 357	7 174	2 861	1 163	1 134	181	900
$15,000 to $24,999	5 632	5 471	119	42	12 494	12 003	4 025	1 772	3 964	290	876
$25,000 to $34,999	3 265	3 149	91	25	11 995	11 537	3 523	1 926	4 466	311	587
$35,000 to $49,999	2 329	2 239	70	20	14 461	13 963	3 988	2 283	6 055	378	700
$50,000 or more	1 928	1 860	55	13	25 404	24 621	7 921	3 956	10 053	917	1 042
Percent with income in 1989 below poverty level	17.6	17.7	19.0	8.5	9.4	9.3	12.3	5.9	1.4	15.4	22.5
Persons 65 to 74 years living alone	18 762	18 297	288	177	31 951	30 716	9 619	3 399	11 790	724	3 359
Less than $5,000	5 199	5 135	49	15	6 586	6 333	2 339	727	1 132	204	1 349
$5,000 to $9,999	7 608	7 431	142	35	9 745	9 379	3 364	1 174	2 453	158	1 489
$10,000 to $14,999	2 364	2 245	54	65	4 494	4 228	1 130	557	2 178	92	124
$15,000 to $24,999	2 214	2 170	23	21	5 526	5 349	1 308	532	3 039	94	157
$25,000 to $34,999	778	744	4	30	2 653	2 549	643	199	1 439	49	139
$35,000 or more	599	572	16	11	2 947	2 878	835	210	1 549	127	101
Percent with income in 1989 below poverty level	39.4	39.9	25.3	10.7	25.8	25.8	30.7	27.1	12.3	33.3	48.3
Married-couple families, householder 75 years and over	7 965	7 735	190	40	32 995	32 116	9 803	10 656	8 445	441	1 576
Less than $5,000	512	497	7	8	1 326	1 288	583	292	111	44	169
$5,000 to $9,999	2 215	2 191	18	6	3 964	3 901	1 581	1 105	452	80	422
$10,000 to $14,999	1 676	1 640	34	2	5 737	5 653	2 065	1 908	903	86	471
$15,000 to $24,999	1 704	1 643	43	18	6 714	6 553	1 603	2 298	2 196	62	152
$25,000 to $34,999	839	797	42	–	4 688	4 549	988	1 696	1 577	47	119
$35,000 to $49,999	513	482	28	3	4 614	4 399	1 246	1 506	1 390	60	89
$50,000 or more	506	485	18	3	5 952	5 773	1 737	1 851	1 816	62	154
Percent with income in 1989 below poverty level	25.0	25.3	12.6	35.0	11.0	11.1	14.9	9.3	2.8	20.9	27.5
Persons 75 years and over living alone	14 618	14 183	239	196	23 059	22 247	9 121	2 790	7 310	382	1 863
Less than $5,000	5 268	5 148	58	62	5 380	5 212	2 308	618	1 167	128	697
$5,000 to $9,999	6 178	5 985	91	102	10 591	10 323	4 375	1 439	3 020	157	988
$10,000 to $14,999	1 513	1 417	73	23	2 577	2 455	781	410	1 092	39	59
$15,000 to $24,999	1 071	1 063	5	3	2 444	2 296	812	234	1 151	13	66
$25,000 to $34,999	299	289	8	2	1 006	941	381	44	461	21	21
$35,000 or more	289	281	4	4	1 061	1 020	464	45	419	24	32
Percent with income in 1989 below poverty level	48.2	48.6	30.1	44.4	32.9	33.1	37.6	29.6	24.0	47.4	42.9

Table 113. Selected Characteristics of Persons 60 Years and Over by Age for Selected Racial Groups: 1990—Con.

[Data based on sample and subject to sampling variability, see text. For definitions of terms and meanings of symbols, see text]

United States	Asian or Pacific Islander—Con.										
	Asian—Con.						Pacific Islander				
	Vietnamese	Cambodian	Hmong	Laotian	Thai	Other Asian	Total	Hawaiian	Samoan	Guamanian	Other Pacific Islander
LIVING ARRANGEMENTS											
Persons 60 to 64 years	9 606	1 809	828	1 637	784	4 177	7 838	5 432	1 074	830	502
In households	9 582	1 803	828	1 637	784	4 128	7 641	5 336	1 037	766	502
In group quarters	24	6	–	–	–	49	197	96	37	64	–
Nursing homes	7	–	–	–	–	37	48	18	13	17	–
Persons 65 to 74 years	11 237	2 779	1 932	2 354	879	4 832	9 645	6 668	1 109	1 199	669
In households	11 161	2 775	1 932	2 354	879	4 827	9 455	6 581	1 048	1 163	663
In group quarters	76	4	–	–	–	5	190	87	61	36	6
Nursing homes	75	–	–	–	–	–	123	65	45	7	6
Persons 75 years and over	5 348	860	726	1 009	189	2 243	4 733	3 398	509	516	310
In households	5 202	849	720	997	182	2 155	4 126	3 118	313	411	284
In group quarters	146	11	6	12	7	88	607	280	196	105	26
Nursing homes	140	11	6	12	7	34	517	228	171	92	26
EDUCATIONAL ATTAINMENT											
Persons 60 to 64 years	9 606	1 809	828	1 637	784	4 177	7 838	5 432	1 074	830	502
Less than 9th grade	4 106	1 329	742	1 152	257	911	1 527	833	305	230	159
9th to 12th grade, no diploma	1 934	211	–	115	150	597	2 165	1 444	374	214	133
High school graduate (includes equivalency)	1 479	108	13	206	107	832	2 527	1 934	261	214	118
Some college or associate degree	1 254	107	54	98	108	751	1 085	817	82	124	62
Bachelor's degree or higher	833	54	19	66	162	1 086	534	404	52	48	30
Persons 65 to 74 years	11 237	2 779	1 932	2 354	879	4 832	9 645	6 668	1 109	1 199	669
Less than 9th grade	5 956	2 187	1 788	1 781	361	1 291	3 047	1 844	365	569	269
9th to 12th grade, no diploma	2 005	235	35	260	223	771	2 488	1 765	275	274	174
High school graduate (includes equivalency)	1 636	158	49	170	94	1 231	2 591	2 000	295	139	157
Some college or associate degree	1 002	154	46	75	137	844	1 103	763	132	155	53
Bachelor's degree or higher	638	45	14	68	64	695	416	296	42	62	16
Persons 75 years and over	5 348	860	726	1 009	189	2 243	4 733	3 398	509	516	310
Less than 9th grade	3 280	708	668	818	112	901	2 012	1 378	209	243	182
9th to 12th grade, no diploma	835	41	25	98	35	448	922	685	102	120	15
High school graduate (includes equivalency)	714	80	16	67	21	336	1 031	780	114	68	69
Some college or associate degree	358	22	11	17	13	300	461	374	41	35	11
Bachelor's degree or higher	161	9	6	9	8	258	307	181	43	50	33
INCOME AND POVERTY STATUS IN 1989											
Married-couple families, householder 60 to 64 years	2 851	456	294	585	127	1 315	2 551	1 809	337	215	190
Less than $5,000	233	56	37	50	–	104	59	35	8	–	16
$5,000 to $9,999	288	35	51	98	10	25	101	45	50	–	6
$10,000 to $14,999	222	111	58	73	–	78	97	63	19	–	15
$15,000 to $24,999	467	164	82	134	–	133	417	258	70	25	64
$25,000 to $34,999	309	43	42	105	–	207	280	197	30	25	28
$35,000 to $49,999	502	33	13	50	60	251	569	435	69	51	14
$50,000 or more	830	14	11	75	57	517	1 028	776	91	114	47
Percent with income in 1989 below poverty level	24.5	34.4	62.9	35.7	7.9	9.8	8.0	4.5	27.0	–	16.8
Persons 60 to 64 years living alone	463	16	7	40	35	380	681	533	24	95	29
Less than $5,000	190	–	7	13	6	60	116	71	15	30	–
$5,000 to $9,999	110	16	–	27	–	97	98	74	3	20	1
$10,000 to $14,999	30	–	–	–	–	27	119	115	–	26	8
$15,000 to $24,999	47	–	–	–	8	78	102	80	–	19	3
$25,000 to $34,999	45	–	–	–	6	77	90	90	–	–	–
$35,000 or more	41	–	–	–	15	41	126	103	6	–	17
Percent with income in 1989 below poverty level	49.7	–	100.0	52.5	17.1	23.4	23.2	18.9	75.0	40.0	3.4
Married-couple families, householder 65 to 74 years	2 236	548	294	548	127	1 236	2 702	1 837	300	381	184
Less than $5,000	228	30	40	7	9	57	127	46	40	24	17
$5,000 to $9,999	279	51	40	110	14	98	162	80	44	33	5
$10,000 to $14,999	390	149	64	157	–	175	183	115	14	9	45
$15,000 to $24,999	418	165	69	163	30	231	491	309	43	88	51
$25,000 to $34,999	286	80	70	50	30	208	458	307	68	63	20
$35,000 to $49,999	257	27	6	29	25	215	498	370	42	61	25
$50,000 or more	378	46	5	32	19	252	783	610	49	103	21
Percent with income in 1989 below poverty level	28.0	28.3	47.6	39.6	18.1	11.4	9.8	5.2	31.7	11.0	17.4
Persons 65 to 74 years living alone	846	84	63	33	73	726	1 235	1 004	75	84	72
Less than $5,000	356	36	10	12	36	132	253	195	11	32	15
$5,000 to $9,999	353	48	23	12	14	291	366	275	34	13	44
$10,000 to $14,999	28	–	30	–	12	77	266	252	14	–	–
$15,000 to $24,999	57	–	–	9	11	142	177	130	9	25	13
$25,000 to $34,999	30	–	–	–	–	50	104	100	–	4	–
$35,000 or more	22	–	–	–	–	34	69	52	7	10	–
Percent with income in 1989 below poverty level	49.1	66.7	15.9	36.4	60.3	27.7	24.5	24.3	14.7	38.1	20.8
Married-couple families, householder 75 years and over	614	68	43	46	5	419	879	718	41	83	37
Less than $5,000	66	14	–	–	–	9	38	31	–	–	7
$5,000 to $9,999	139	6	17	11	–	88	63	54	–	9	–
$10,000 to $14,999	115	4	9	24	–	68	84	61	16	7	–
$15,000 to $24,999	108	21	7	8	–	98	161	121	8	9	23
$25,000 to $34,999	63	7	–	–	5	47	139	134	5	–	–
$35,000 to $49,999	42	12	10	–	–	44	215	178	5	25	7
$50,000 or more	81	4	–	3	–	65	179	139	7	33	–
Percent with income in 1989 below poverty level	28.5	29.4	30.2	63.0	–	23.2	8.2	8.1	17.1	–	18.9
Persons 75 years and over living alone	300	25	37	14	14	391	812	669	30	88	25
Less than $5,000	147	7	3	14	14	109	168	133	13	4	18
$5,000 to $9,999	129	18	34	–	–	163	268	228	5	28	7
$10,000 to $14,999	–	–	–	–	–	74	122	106	–	16	–
$15,000 to $24,999	–	–	–	–	–	20	148	121	–	27	–
$25,000 to $34,999	–	–	–	–	–	13	65	52	–	13	–
$35,000 or more	24	–	–	–	–	12	41	29	12	–	–
Percent with income in 1989 below poverty level	62.0	28.0	24.3	100.0	100.0	36.1	25.6	24.8	43.3	4.5	100.0

Table 114. Age, Fertility, and Household and Family Composition for Selected Hispanic Origin Groups: 1990

[Data based on sample and subject to sampling variability, see text. For definitions of terms and meanings of symbols, see text]

| United States | All persons | Hispanic origin (of any race) | | | | Other Hispanic | | | | | | |
| | | Total | Mexican | Puerto Rican | Cuban | Total | Dominican (Dominican Republic) | Central American | | | | |
								Total	Costa Rican	Guatemalan	Honduran	Nicaraguan
AGE												
All persons	248 709 873	21 900 089	13 393 208	2 651 815	1 053 197	4 801 869	520 151	1 323 830	57 223	268 779	131 066	202 658
Under 3 years	10 924 579	1 415 149	949 530	170 014	34 735	260 870	30 833	68 962	2 159	13 750	7 074	9 171
3 and 4 years	7 339 517	915 203	616 679	111 003	23 114	164 407	19 739	41 065	1 661	7 870	4 052	5 904
5 to 9 years	18 126 901	2 174 463	1 466 494	266 030	51 288	390 651	46 117	99 584	4 234	20 089	9 655	17 974
10 to 14 years	17 151 134	1 987 956	1 303 808	260 660	49 512	373 976	42 683	101 067	4 174	19 173	10 220	17 980
15 to 17 years	10 064 413	1 144 623	746 766	138 810	33 289	225 758	24 609	65 068	2 573	12 251	5 858	11 513
18 and 19 years	7 589 506	837 275	542 849	99 687	24 538	170 201	18 707	50 469	1 977	10 327	4 578	7 773
20 to 24 years	18 645 387	2 198 627	1 404 641	252 235	68 492	473 259	48 758	160 983	5 845	34 955	14 899	21 451
25 to 29 years	21 286 297	2 310 503	1 412 744	262 669	95 928	539 162	54 313	181 457	6 666	39 526	18 040	23 059
30 to 34 years	22 180 737	2 069 776	1 233 260	239 759	87 723	509 034	57 622	161 743	5 954	33 303	16 113	22 908
35 to 39 years	19 939 682	1 636 937	958 688	195 262	74 336	408 651	48 544	122 050	5 282	25 737	12 657	17 143
40 to 44 years	17 679 734	1 281 723	723 755	166 881	64 526	326 561	36 796	87 017	4 650	18 932	8 126	13 041
45 to 49 years	13 977 898	949 236	511 583	127 713	65 008	244 932	25 974	58 277	3 396	11 428	5 632	9 652
50 to 54 years	11 488 063	756 325	392 404	100 500	74 452	189 329	20 984	39 014	2 261	7 470	4 347	7 360
55 to 59 years	10 484 988	627 235	323 415	83 243	70 069	150 508	14 025	27 986	1 936	4 720	3 369	5 702
60 to 64 years	10 635 762	538 862	282 487	63 963	69 624	122 788	11 097	20 845	1 620	3 454	2 668	4 145
65 to 74 years	18 218 481	671 012	339 208	75 252	97 878	158 674	13 389	25 553	1 902	4 000	2 608	4 958
75 years and over	12 976 794	385 184	185 257	38 134	68 685	93 108	5 961	12 690	933	1 794	1 170	2 924
Median age	33.0	25.6	23.8	25.5	38.9	28.2	27.6	27.1	29.5	27.0	27.5	27.1
FERTILITY												
Women 15 to 24 years	17 769 944	1 938 311	1 226 036	242 045	61 037	409 193	46 679	122 246	4 990	24 433	12 451	18 718
Children ever born	5 420 229	901 379	615 298	126 880	13 567	145 634	17 513	55 752	1 156	12 032	5 406	6 610
Per 1,000 women	305	465	502	524	222	356	375	456	232	492	434	353
Women ever married	3 726 372	521 219	357 430	54 919	15 251	93 619	11 319	32 317	1 176	6 688	3 057	4 713
Children ever born	3 462 487	601 407	436 233	63 041	10 959	91 174	10 519	34 418	858	7 361	3 088	4 392
Per 1,000 women	929	1 154	1 220	1 148	719	974	929	1 065	730	1 101	1 010	932
Women 25 to 34 years	21 757 561	2 076 193	1 214 061	258 850	86 665	516 617	59 988	166 898	6 454	33 217	18 371	23 417
Children ever born	28 942 178	3 607 708	2 307 002	445 257	97 441	758 008	99 333	280 071	8 489	56 436	30 344	36 733
Per 1,000 women	1 330	1 738	1 900	1 720	1 124	1 467	1 656	1 678	1 315	1 699	1 652	1 569
Women ever married	16 431 453	1 577 448	955 596	175 150	66 705	379 997	45 320	119 348	4 974	23 008	13 099	17 316
Children ever born	26 088 416	3 151 021	2 076 421	333 455	91 728	649 417	84 101	224 971	7 569	45 344	24 017	31 710
Per 1,000 women	1 588	1 998	2 173	1 904	1 375	1 709	1 856	1 885	1 522	1 971	1 833	1 831
Women 35 to 44 years	19 012 425	1 457 001	814 828	190 698	66 913	384 562	46 651	110 951	5 315	22 742	12 139	16 368
Children ever born	37 260 340	3 769 710	2 321 011	467 192	117 673	863 834	116 561	278 614	11 420	58 081	30 655	40 895
Per 1,000 women	1 960	2 587	2 848	2 450	1 759	2 246	2 499	2 511	2 149	2 554	2 525	2 498
No children	3 459 251	176 433	85 443	22 326	12 028	56 636	5 205	12 709	738	2 274	1 493	1 939
1 child	3 196 133	185 369	87 659	25 475	13 518	58 717	5 961	15 101	812	3 133	1 746	2 207
2 children	6 589 685	397 944	198 290	56 625	26 159	116 870	12 675	30 647	1 711	6 200	3 123	4 539
3 children	3 605 811	337 560	193 922	47 014	11 216	85 408	12 729	27 014	1 333	5 718	2 928	3 878
4 children	1 357 031	187 143	121 867	22 128	2 743	40 405	5 956	14 894	546	3 306	1 547	2 227
5 or more children	804 514	172 552	127 647	17 130	1 249	26 526	4 125	10 586	175	2 111	1 302	1 578
Women ever married	17 154 920	1 298 473	740 255	159 729	60 969	337 520	41 780	92 093	4 958	19 234	10 201	13 953
Children ever born	36 033 647	3 548 525	2 225 881	406 669	114 907	801 068	108 319	242 163	11 165	51 672	26 664	36 810
Per 1,000 women	2 100	2 733	3 007	2 546	1 885	2 373	2 593	2 630	2 252	2 686	2 614	2 638
HOUSEHOLD TYPE AND RELATIONSHIP												
All persons	248 709 873	21 900 089	13 393 208	2 651 815	1 053 197	4 801 869	520 151	1 323 830	57 223	268 779	131 066	202 658
In households	242 050 161	21 415 135	13 129 449	2 562 403	1 028 430	4 694 853	511 714	1 305 950	56 112	265 208	128 970	200 354
Family householder	65 049 428	4 776 075	2 776 147	627 527	295 380	1 077 021	126 991	284 787	13 279	56 978	27 445	42 608
Male	51 091 846	3 500 984	2 147 605	354 082	234 789	764 508	62 523	204 567	9 316	43 668	17 397	31 533
Female	13 957 582	1 275 091	628 542	273 445	60 591	312 513	64 468	80 220	3 963	13 310	10 048	11 075
Nonfamily householder	26 944 154	1 095 965	525 979	170 282	96 820	302 884	20 725	51 744	3 792	9 419	5 981	6 589
Male	11 534 397	590 050	304 059	85 274	46 007	154 710	9 847	29 585	1 995	5 948	3 216	3 476
Female	15 409 757	505 915	221 920	85 008	50 813	148 174	10 878	22 159	1 797	3 471	2 765	3 113
Spouse	51 549 544	3 436 174	2 067 768	349 905	223 108	795 393	66 579	208 548	11 781	40 387	22 290	33 104
Child	77 059 019	8 539 818	5 554 628	1 068 498	274 033	1 642 659	200 275	409 680	18 408	79 890	41 756	69 102
Other relatives	11 647 867	2 212 753	1 403 021	205 983	97 107	506 642	63 941	196 988	4 860	39 517	15 710	32 198
Nonrelatives	9 800 149	1 354 350	801 906	140 208	41 982	370 254	33 203	154 203	3 992	39 017	15 788	16 753
In group quarters	6 659 712	484 954	263 759	89 412	24 767	107 016	8 437	17 880	1 111	3 571	2 096	2 304
Persons per household	2.63	3.52	3.81	3.14	2.79	3.27	3.67	3.92	3.15	4.12	3.64	4.07
Persons per family	3.16	3.84	4.08	3.51	3.21	3.61	3.85	3.97	3.52	4.04	3.79	4.19
FAMILY TYPE BY PRESENCE OF OWN CHILDREN												
Families	65 049 428	4 776 075	2 776 147	627 527	295 380	1 077 021	126 991	284 787	13 279	56 978	27 445	42 608
With own children under 18 years	31 364 670	3 081 169	1 884 075	410 584	123 727	662 783	87 974	196 082	8 475	40 148	18 423	28 773
With own children under 6 years	14 646 378	1 655 314	1 050 976	203 456	56 906	343 976	48 238	111 208	4 221	23 196	10 750	14 303
Married-couple families	51 718 214	3 339 694	2 027 520	353 483	230 617	728 074	63 556	180 231	9 279	36 976	16 240	28 534
With own children under 18 years	24 224 117	2 201 366	1 427 380	217 774	97 838	458 376	44 754	135 204	6 330	28 548	11 409	21 035
With own children under 6 years	11 806 198	1 228 508	821 966	111 308	47 499	247 735	25 359	80 533	3 365	16 950	6 897	11 004
Female householder, no husband present	10 381 654	1 029 646	505 042	229 639	48 072	246 893	52 333	64 344	3 104	10 846	8 080	8 851
With own children under 18 years	5 865 147	682 929	338 612	167 705	20 183	156 429	37 548	40 947	1 798	7 199	5 406	5 207
With own children under 6 years	2 300 192	313 076	158 016	79 589	6 865	68 606	19 564	17 667	667	3 198	2 795	1 890
Subfamilies	2 572 170	422 272	275 048	45 895	19 882	81 447	10 729	28 047	940	5 437	2 271	5 272
With own children under 18 years	2 193 137	347 753	229 737	41 252	12 274	64 490	8 938	21 998	672	4 112	1 898	4 095
Married-couple subfamilies	611 488	127 763	84 785	7 705	9 820	25 453	2 551	9 487	371	2 119	615	1 782
With own children under 18 years	232 455	53 244	39 474	3 062	2 212	8 496	760	3 438	103	794	242	605
Mother-child subfamilies	1 586 814	228 045	146 563	29 875	8 225	43 382	6 574	14 506	456	2 616	1 290	2 706
Persons under 18 years	63 606 544	7 637 394	5 083 277	946 517	191 938	1 415 662	163 981	375 746	14 801	73 133	36 859	62 542
Percent living with two parents	71.8	63.9	67.5	45.1	70.0	62.5	44.1	61.5	70.8	64.1	58.1	63.7
UNMARRIED-PARTNER HOUSEHOLDS												
Total	3 187 772	319 670	173 333	56 220	12 857	77 260	8 805	26 502	796	5 200	2 716	3 165
Male and female	3 042 642	309 138	167 919	54 797	11 948	74 474	8 581	25 704	764	5 089	2 637	3 030
Both male	81 343	5 704	3 070	701	476	1 457	79	377	15	57	16	42
Both female	63 787	4 828	2 344	722	433	1 329	145	421	17	54	63	93
SELECTED LIVING ARRANGEMENTS												
Households	91 993 582	5 872 040	3 302 126	797 809	392 200	1 379 905	147 716	336 531	17 071	66 397	33 426	49 197
With one or more subfamilies	2 416 716	382 501	245 456	43 275	20 580	73 190	10 508	25 743	872	4 836	2 102	4 747
With related members 15 years and over other than spouse, children, parents, or parents-in-law of householder	4 488 360	833 952	514 811	76 152	39 647	203 342	28 749	85 642	1 947	17 490	6 892	12 807
With roomer, boarder, or foster child 15 years and over	905 979	113 447	64 469	11 308	4 959	32 711	5 323	12 111	274	2 811	1 071	1 420

Table 114. Age, Fertility, and Household and Family Composition for Selected Hispanic Origin Groups: 1990—Con.

[Data based on sample and subject to sampling variability, see text. For definitions of terms and meanings of symbols, see text]

Hispanic origin (of any race)—Con. / Other Hispanic—Con.

United States	Panamanian	Salvadoran	Other Central American	Total (South American)	Argentinean	Chilean	Colombian	Ecuadorian	Peruvian	Venezuelan	Other South American	All other Hispanic origin	Not of Hispanic origin
AGE													
All persons	92 013	565 081	7 010	1 035 602	100 921	68 799	378 726	191 198	175 035	47 997	72 926	1 922 286	226 809 784
Under 3 years	3 606	32 801	401	45 378	2 744	3 118	17 364	7 967	8 451	2 293	3 441	115 697	9 509 430
3 and 4 years	2 660	18 684	234	28 136	2 082	2 035	10 952	4 876	4 897	1 505	1 789	75 467	6 424 314
5 to 9 years	5 952	41 171	509	67 218	5 109	4 662	25 389	12 717	10 669	4 198	4 474	177 732	15 952 438
10 to 14 years	6 086	42 922	512	68 698	5 675	4 286	25 928	12 573	12 014	3 295	4 927	161 528	15 163 178
15 to 17 years	3 769	28 757	347	43 877	4 292	3 154	15 868	7 959	7 471	1 780	3 353	92 204	8 919 790
18 and 19 years	3 667	21 920	227	32 685	3 399	1 931	10 823	6 476	5 734	1 686	2 636	68 340	6 752 231
20 to 24 years	9 029	74 153	651	92 779	8 439	5 487	32 728	19 248	15 938	4 571	6 368	170 739	16 446 760
25 to 29 years	10 028	83 052	1 086	121 025	9 714	6 466	46 420	23 199	19 572	7 522	8 132	182 367	18 975 794
30 to 34 years	9 054	73 765	646	119 654	10 155	7 063	45 173	20 422	21 252	6 961	8 628	170 015	20 110 961
35 to 39 years	8 298	52 321	612	97 274	9 022	6 009	35 408	16 907	18 470	4 484	6 974	140 783	18 302 745
40 to 44 years	7 900	33 791	577	84 256	8 635	6 310	30 233	15 353	14 448	3 099	6 178	118 492	16 398 011
45 to 49 years	6 254	21 560	355	70 271	7 852	6 053	25 421	12 886	10 780	2 007	5 272	90 410	13 028 662
50 to 54 years	4 203	13 047	326	52 902	6 795	3 816	19 183	9 804	7 909	1 525	3 870	76 429	10 731 738
55 to 59 years	3 113	9 000	146	40 778	6 349	3 163	14 256	7 648	5 891	959	2 512	67 719	9 857 753
60 to 64 years	2 677	6 156	125	28 222	4 644	2 178	9 362	4 863	4 538	886	1 751	62 624	10 096 900
65 to 74 years	3 971	7 955	159	29 254	4 278	1 981	9 935	5 629	4 743	813	1 875	90 478	17 547 469
75 years and over	1 746	4 026	97	13 195	1 737	1 087	4 283	2 671	2 258	413	746	61 262	12 591 610
Median age	30.7	26.3	27.9	30.8	34.4	32.3	30.4	30.1	30.7	28.1	30.8	27.7	33.8
FERTILITY													
Women 15 to 24 years	8 617	52 431	606	81 414	8 009	4 992	28 895	15 158	14 450	3 911	5 999	158 854	15 831 633
Children ever born	2 262	28 085	201	17 084	1 060	725	7 075	3 994	2 543	673	1 014	55 285	4 518 850
Per 1,000 women	263	536	332	210	132	145	245	263	176	172	169	348	285
Women ever married	1 733	14 811	139	16 668	1 385	808	6 229	3 473	2 784	872	1 117	33 315	3 205 153
Children ever born	1 444	17 083	192	12 501	841	544	4 880	3 035	1 806	564	831	33 736	2 861 080
Per 1,000 women	833	1 153	1 381	750	607	673	783	874	649	647	744	1 013	893
Women 25 to 34 years	11 273	73 435	731	117 283	9 201	6 554	45 998	20 497	20 199	6 914	7 920	172 448	19 681 368
Children ever born	14 657	132 133	1 279	132 516	9 231	7 510	50 137	28 020	21 133	6 714	9 771	246 088	25 334 470
Per 1,000 women	1 300	1 799	1 750	1 130	1 003	1 146	1 090	1 367	1 046	971	1 234	1 427	1 287
Women ever married	8 678	51 757	516	88 914	7 292	5 141	34 183	15 547	15 128	5 356	6 267	126 415	14 854 005
Children ever born	13 158	102 108	1 065	121 928	9 009	7 235	45 213	25 381	19 627	6 427	9 036	218 417	22 937 395
Per 1,000 women	1 516	1 973	2 064	1 371	1 235	1 407	1 323	1 633	1 297	1 200	1 442	1 728	1 544
Women 35 to 44 years	9 588	44 162	637	94 588	8 430	6 271	36 861	16 611	15 820	4 050	6 545	132 372	17 555 424
Children ever born	19 392	116 428	1 743	179 498	15 713	11 843	66 563	36 854	28 410	7 462	12 653	289 161	33 490 630
Per 1,000 women	2 023	2 636	2 736	1 898	1 864	1 889	1 806	2 219	1 796	1 842	1 933	2 184	1 908
No children	1 685	4 533	47	17 134	1 559	940	7 196	2 168	3 372	826	1 073	21 588	3 282 818
1 child	1 665	5 449	89	17 517	1 393	1 127	7 405	2 548	3 109	799	1 136	20 138	3 010 764
2 children	3 231	11 670	173	32 203	3 145	2 570	12 411	5 519	4 894	1 242	2 422	41 345	6 191 741
3 children	1 752	11 267	138	18 191	1 635	1 139	6 643	3 737	2 957	741	1 339	27 474	3 268 251
4 children	723	6 443	102	6 592	502	352	2 219	1 737	1 053	325	404	12 963	1 169 888
5 or more children	532	4 800	88	2 951	196	143	987	902	435	117	171	8 864	631 962
Women ever married	8 392	34 813	542	85 209	7 867	5 915	32 778	15 051	13 814	3 710	6 074	118 438	15 856 447
Children ever born	18 293	96 061	1 498	173 871	15 579	11 730	64 007	35 389	27 466	7 314	12 386	276 715	32 485 122
Per 1,000 women	2 180	2 759	2 764	2 041	1 980	1 983	1 953	2 351	1 988	1 971	2 039	2 336	2 049
HOUSEHOLD TYPE AND RELATIONSHIP													
All persons	92 013	565 081	7 010	1 035 602	100 921	68 799	378 726	191 198	175 035	47 997	72 926	1 922 286	226 809 784
In households	88 600	559 767	6 939	1 015 476	98 778	67 781	369 021	188 897	172 427	46 871	71 701	1 861 713	220 635 026
Family householder	21 622	121 115	1 740	251 987	28 463	17 167	88 617	47 058	41 918	10 634	18 130	413 256	60 273 353
Male	12 759	88 870	1 024	193 260	23 842	13 006	66 163	34 856	32 651	8 135	14 617	304 158	47 590 862
Female	8 863	32 245	716	58 727	4 621	3 171	23 454	12 200	9 267	2 499	3 513	109 098	12 682 491
Nonfamily householder	8 666	16 831	466	68 463	10 254	5 232	23 610	9 326	10 817	4 402	4 822	161 952	25 848 189
Male	3 681	11 015	254	37 556	5 613	2 767	12 528	5 098	6 294	2 484	2 772	77 722	10 944 347
Female	4 985	5 816	212	30 907	4 641	2 465	11 082	4 228	4 523	1 918	2 050	84 230	14 903 842
Spouse	19 096	80 850	1 040	202 739	23 228	14 694	71 527	35 596	32 925	9 615	15 154	317 527	48 113 370
Child	27 014	171 128	2 382	314 935	26 680	21 564	116 544	61 022	52 644	14 950	21 531	717 769	68 519 201
Other relatives	7 302	96 651	750	102 016	4 843	4 786	38 332	23 068	21 142	3 454	6 391	143 697	9 435 114
Nonrelatives	4 900	73 192	561	75 336	5 310	4 338	30 391	12 827	12 981	3 816	5 673	107 512	8 445 799
In group quarters	3 413	5 314	71	20 126	2 143	1 018	9 705	2 301	2 608	1 126	1 225	60 573	6 174 758
Persons per household	2.85	4.19	3.55	3.21	2.80	3.03	3.23	3.55	3.32	2.81	2.80	2.82	2.57
Persons per family	3.39	4.05	3.80	3.54	3.25	3.41	3.51	3.78	3.64	3.32	3.20	3.33	3.10
FAMILY TYPE BY PRESENCE OF OWN CHILDREN													
Families	21 622	121 115	1 740	251 987	28 463	17 167	88 617	47 058	41 918	10 634	18 130	413 256	60 273 353
With own children under 18 years	13 125	85 899	1 239	153 108	15 495	10 146	54 316	29 350	25 704	6 682	11 415	225 619	28 283 501
With own children under 6 years	6 011	52 073	654	75 504	6 940	4 423	27 188	14 549	13 061	3 883	5 460	109 026	12 991 064
Married-couple families	13 027	75 170	1 005	183 855	23 810	13 589	60 828	32 957	30 418	8 201	14 052	300 432	48 378 520
With own children under 18 years	8 250	58 874	758	118 447	13 305	8 336	39 953	22 033	20 250	5 348	9 222	159 971	22 022 749
With own children under 6 years	4 253	37 630	434	61 742	6 205	3 872	21 421	11 392	10 798	3 397	4 657	80 101	10 577 690
Female householder, no husband present	7 270	25 684	509	45 334	3 084	2 230	19 004	9 742	6 989	1 763	2 522	84 882	9 352 008
With own children under 18 years	4 284	16 717	336	25 684	1 590	1 253	10 675	5 805	3 745	1 046	1 570	52 250	5 182 218
With own children under 6 years	1 489	7 496	132	9 046	503	302	3 775	2 320	1 335	349	462	22 329	1 987 116
Subfamilies	1 406	12 567	154	15 444	719	726	5 997	3 585	2 979	533	905	27 227	2 149 898
With own children under 18 years	1 298	9 789	134	10 686	378	435	4 518	2 554	1 890	403	508	22 868	1 845 384
Married-couple subfamilies	193	4 348	59	6 715	424	415	2 171	1 443	1 520	266	476	6 700	483 725
With own children under 18 years	85	1 570	39	1 957	83	124	692	412	431	136	79	2 341	179 211
Mother-child subfamilies	1 039	6 338	61	6 912	246	285	3 076	1 597	1 103	234	371	15 390	1 358 769
Persons under 18 years	22 073	164 335	2 003	253 307	19 902	17 255	95 501	46 092	43 502	13 071	17 984	622 628	55 969 150
Percent living with two parents	61.8	59.4	58.3	71.9	81.5	79.9	68.7	69.0	73.6	72.6	73.8	64.1	72.9
UNMARRIED-PARTNER HOUSEHOLDS													
Total	1 367	13 090	168	14 457	1 607	1 004	5 678	2 388	2 239	594	947	27 496	2 868 102
Male and female	1 270	12 746	168	13 971	1 525	975	5 485	2 296	2 204	562	924	26 218	2 733 504
Both male	47	200	–	272	42	8	108	52	23	16	23	729	75 639
Both female	50	144	–	214	40	21	85	40	12	16	–	549	58 959
SELECTED LIVING ARRANGEMENTS													
Households	30 288	137 946	2 206	320 450	38 717	22 399	112 227	56 384	52 735	15 036	22 952	575 208	86 121 542
With one or more subfamilies	1 461	11 609	116	14 758	943	783	5 761	3 326	2 814	332	799	22 181	2 034 215
With related members 15 years and over other than spouse, children, parents, or parents-in-law of householder	2 829	43 318	359	45 786	2 389	1 992	17 644	10 134	9 181	1 267	3 179	43 165	3 654 408
With roomer, boarder, or foster child 15 years and over	449	5 967	119	7 740	443	357	3 317	1 539	1 300	249	535	7 537	792 532

Table 115. Education, Ability to Speak English, and Disability for Selected Hispanic Origin Groups: 1990

[Data based on sample and subject to sampling variability, see text. For definitions of terms and meanings of symbols, see text]

United States		Hispanic origin (of any race)										
						Other Hispanic						
								Central American				
	All persons	Total	Mexican	Puerto Rican	Cuban	Total	Dominican (Dominican Republic)	Total	Costa Rican	Guate-malan	Honduran	Nicaraguan
SCHOOL ENROLLMENT AND TYPE OF SCHOOL												
Persons 3 years and over enrolled in school	**64 987 101**	**7 147 066**	**4 500 307**	**871 101**	**232 790**	**1 542 868**	**165 269**	**436 368**	**19 262**	**84 359**	**42 810**	**74 355**
Preprimary school	4 503 285	352 080	220 224	45 933	13 777	72 146	6 304	15 531	1 022	2 991	1 726	2 466
Public school	2 679 029	255 870	171 088	33 587	5 504	45 691	4 857	10 237	511	2 092	1 112	1 619
Elementary or high school	42 566 788	5 301 622	3 491 515	653 989	134 134	1 021 984	118 496	301 884	11 056	60 314	28 457	50 908
Public school	38 379 689	4 917 208	3 304 973	594 756	106 258	911 221	103 943	278 987	9 395	55 758	26 083	47 051
College	17 917 028	1 493 364	788 568	171 179	84 879	448 738	40 469	118 953	7 184	21 054	12 627	20 981
Public college	13 805 534	1 217 421	687 953	124 027	62 265	343 176	29 749	96 515	5 616	16 978	9 657	17 077
Persons 3 years and over enrolled in school	**64 987 101**	**7 147 066**	**4 500 307**	**871 101**	**232 790**	**1 542 868**	**165 269**	**436 368**	**19 262**	**84 359**	**42 810**	**74 355**
3 and 4 years	2 118 735	193 611	117 646	26 461	7 562	41 942	4 104	9 906	553	1 949	1 138	1 427
5 to 14 years	32 655 517	3 827 362	2 544 325	487 588	93 724	701 725	80 960	182 567	7 889	35 063	17 920	33 376
15 to 17 years	9 294 846	1 004 007	647 686	121 782	30 574	203 965	22 220	56 533	2 380	10 542	5 280	10 412
18 and 19 years	4 974 321	460 462	279 779	54 295	17 768	108 620	12 119	29 501	1 375	5 493	2 866	5 283
20 to 24 years	6 267 157	583 237	327 323	62 876	28 399	164 639	16 074	49 949	2 585	9 660	4 965	8 197
25 to 34 years	5 064 093	618 870	341 124	64 494	29 917	183 335	16 792	64 455	2 647	13 067	6 403	9 076
35 years and over	4 612 432	459 517	242 424	53 605	24 846	138 642	13 000	43 457	1 833	8 585	4 238	6 584
Persons 18 to 24 years	**26 234 893**	**3 035 902**	**1 947 490**	**351 922**	**93 030**	**643 460**	**67 465**	**211 452**	**7 822**	**45 282**	**19 477**	**29 224**
Percent enrolled in college	34.4	22.9	19.5	22.8	40.5	30.5	27.5	23.0	42.3	19.7	26.3	28.3
Persons 16 to 19 years	**14 315 448**	**1 600 482**	**1 040 760**	**190 684**	**46 695**	**322 343**	**35 312**	**94 772**	**3 659**	**18 439**	**8 633**	**15 590**
Percent not enrolled, not high school graduate	11.2	21.7	24.0	20.9	11.5	16.0	16.6	23.1	11.3	26.3	18.3	16.0
EDUCATIONAL ATTAINMENT												
Persons 18 to 24 years	**26 234 893**	**3 035 902**	**1 947 490**	**351 922**	**93 030**	**643 460**	**67 465**	**211 452**	**7 822**	**45 282**	**19 477**	**29 224**
High school graduate (includes equivalency)	8 126 562	822 447	512 290	109 137	25 001	176 019	18 282	47 443	2 274	9 535	4 865	7 777
Some college or associate degree	9 941 932	720 485	404 839	90 123	37 070	188 453	17 112	43 463	3 043	8 118	4 938	7 302
Bachelor's degree or higher	1 991 840	85 591	35 525	12 309	7 866	29 891	2 579	5 745	602	1 111	576	930
Persons 25 years and over	**158 868 436**	**11 226 793**	**6 362 441**	**1 353 376**	**768 229**	**2 742 747**	**288 705**	**736 632**	**34 600**	**150 364**	**74 730**	**110 892**
Less than 5th grade	4 271 677	1 509 367	1 074 408	122 200	62 244	250 515	41 116	112 350	1 745	25 229	9 237	10 165
5th to 8th grade	12 230 534	1 936 545	1 248 634	182 484	138 142	367 285	61 470	141 097	3 692	37 012	14 055	13 691
9th to 12th grade, no diploma	22 841 507	2 188 309	1 227 051	326 305	132 896	502 057	63 073	146 254	5 877	30 413	13 766	19 894
High school graduate (includes equivalency)	47 642 763	2 419 632	1 302 671	331 922	147 156	637 883	54 784	136 643	7 512	25 071	15 667	23 668
Some college, no degree	29 779 777	1 602 472	844 971	198 803	112 098	446 600	33 452	94 600	7 443	16 197	10 354	18 979
Associate degree, occupational program	5 233 002	273 770	140 651	31 140	20 215	81 764	5 551	19 604	1 277	3 559	2 536	3 613
Associate degree, academic program	4 558 923	268 939	125 795	32 622	28 609	81 913	6 679	19 279	1 449	3 206	2 250	3 693
Bachelor's degree	20 832 567	658 197	269 373	85 237	71 863	231 724	13 894	42 977	3 590	5 893	4 761	10 307
Graduate or professional degree	11 477 686	369 562	128 887	42 663	55 006	143 006	8 686	23 828	2 015	3 784	2 104	6 882
Females 25 years and over	**83 654 171**	**5 657 519**	**3 095 462**	**717 571**	**396 722**	**1 447 764**	**160 988**	**393 179**	**19 492**	**75 904**	**43 482**	**61 078**
Less than 5th grade	2 161 459	760 704	515 663	69 278	34 307	141 456	24 896	63 173	1 047	13 699	5 759	6 314
5th to 8th grade	6 546 831	989 986	611 245	98 877	74 762	205 102	36 610	77 633	2 371	19 156	7 837	8 683
9th to 12th grade, no diploma	12 360 377	1 085 425	590 457	165 406	66 111	263 451	33 528	74 818	3 536	14 610	7 632	11 108
High school graduate (includes equivalency)	26 850 606	1 275 286	667 065	174 966	80 843	352 412	30 431	76 441	4 429	12 825	9 732	14 339
Some college, no degree	15 520 115	794 048	406 684	104 389	55 009	227 966	17 319	49 353	4 175	7 727	6 031	9 735
Associate degree, occupational program	2 920 672	140 882	68 185	18 342	10 572	43 783	3 086	10 940	646	1 923	1 609	2 023
Associate degree, academic program	2 538 505	140 303	61 595	18 700	16 059	43 949	3 804	10 450	764	1 788	1 395	1 942
Bachelor's degree	10 015 766	316 611	122 341	46 172	34 987	113 111	7 444	20 751	1 784	2 638	2 414	4 618
Graduate or professional degree	4 739 840	154 274	52 227	21 441	24 072	56 534	3 870	9 620	740	1 538	1 073	2 316
Persons 25 years and over	**158 868 436**	**11 226 793**	**6 362 441**	**1 353 376**	**768 229**	**2 742 747**	**288 705**	**736 632**	**34 600**	**150 364**	**74 730**	**110 892**
Percent less than 5th grade	2.7	13.4	16.9	9.0	8.1	9.1	14.2	15.3	5.0	16.8	12.4	9.2
Percent high school graduate or higher	75.2	49.8	44.2	53.4	56.6	59.2	42.6	45.7	67.3	38.4	50.4	60.5
Percent some college or higher	45.2	28.3	23.7	28.9	37.5	35.9	23.6	27.2	45.6	21.7	29.4	39.2
Percent bachelor's degree or higher	20.3	9.2	6.3	9.5	16.5	13.7	7.8	9.1	16.2	6.4	9.2	15.5
Males 25 to 34 years	**21 709 473**	**2 304 086**	**1 431 943**	**243 578**	**96 986**	**531 579**	**51 947**	**176 302**	**6 166**	**39 612**	**15 782**	**22 550**
Percent high school graduate or higher	82.7	55.4	48.9	65.4	77.2	64.5	58.4	46.3	76.0	40.5	51.4	67.2
Percent bachelor's degree or higher	22.9	9.4	6.5	10.6	21.3	14.7	10.8	8.6	19.9	6.6	10.5	16.3
Females 25 to 34 years	**21 757 561**	**2 076 193**	**1 214 061**	**258 850**	**86 665**	**516 617**	**59 988**	**166 898**	**6 454**	**33 217**	**18 371**	**23 417**
Percent high school graduate or higher	85.5	60.4	54.3	67.9	84.1	66.9	58.7	49.2	81.8	42.1	56.8	68.6
Percent bachelor's degree or higher	22.6	10.2	7.0	12.2	23.9	14.3	10.5	8.3	17.5	6.1	9.3	13.5
ABILITY TO SPEAK ENGLISH												
Persons 5 years and over	**230 445 777**	**19 569 737**	**11 826 999**	**2 370 798**	**995 348**	**4 376 592**	**469 579**	**1 213 803**	**53 403**	**247 159**	**119 940**	**187 583**
Speak a language other than English	31 844 979	15 216 298	9 054 572	1 920 231	890 183	3 351 312	442 719	1 115 116	44 809	233 138	106 526	173 008
5 to 17 years	6 322 934	3 596 267	2 342 725	472 843	106 316	674 383	105 599	233 759	7 861	47 314	21 331	42 824
18 to 64 years	21 707 874	10 708 585	6 248 832	1 347 195	626 799	2 485 759	319 138	847 204	34 492	180 508	81 954	122 943
65 to 74 years	2 118 454	579 816	299 843	66 870	92 421	120 682	12 473	22 759	1 621	3 671	2 228	4 575
75 years and over	1 695 717	331 630	163 172	33 323	64 647	70 488	5 509	11 394	835	1 645	1 013	2 666
Do not speak English "very well"	13 982 502	7 716 795	4 605 389	794 283	484 106	1 833 017	281 491	730 075	19 941	161 117	65 906	111 569
5 to 17 years	2 388 243	1 450 237	988 238	169 387	25 420	267 192	47 464	109 827	2 042	21 787	9 380	22 118
18 to 64 years	9 793 186	5 645 348	3 324 798	553 717	320 853	1 445 980	218 770	594 414	16 438	134 833	54 155	83 511
65 to 74 years	992 887	378 432	178 856	46 890	79 425	73 261	10 582	16 868	897	3 126	1 594	3 670
75 years and over	808 186	242 778	113 497	24 289	58 408	46 584	4 675	8 966	564	1 371	777	2 270
ABILITY TO SPEAK ENGLISH IN HOUSEHOLD												
Linguistically isolated households	2 936 596	1 512 726	813 291	181 704	139 823	377 908	64 125	143 033	3 677	31 655	12 831	20 109
Persons 5 years and over in households	**223 812 984**	**19 091 096**	**11 567 198**	**2 282 394**	**970 647**	**4 270 857**	**461 259**	**1 196 153**	**52 292**	**243 625**	**117 865**	**185 312**
In linguistically isolated households	7 741 259	4 548 677	2 743 044	410 624	277 794	1 117 215	182 577	482 092	9 358	108 448	41 695	73 465
5 to 17 years	1 763 173	1 150 203	773 152	113 255	23 025	240 771	44 589	101 338	1 546	20 914	8 393	20 167
18 to 64 years	4 968 023	3 041 240	1 811 895	254 878	161 347	813 120	129 086	368 274	7 101	85 421	32 042	50 476
65 to 74 years	556 681	216 067	95 157	28 181	54 086	38 643	6 068	8 205	435	1 438	825	1 766
75 years and over	453 382	141 167	62 840	14 310	39 336	24 681	2 834	4 275	276	675	435	1 056
DISABILITY STATUS OF CIVILIAN NONINSTITUTIONALIZED PERSONS												
Persons 16 to 64 years	**157 323 922**	**13 640 197**	**8 111 181**	**1 612 700**	**700 511**	**3 215 805**	**346 644**	**943 366**	**40 673**	**196 288**	**93 423**	**138 757**
With a mobility or self-care limitation	7 214 762	893 909	473 290	150 637	47 681	222 301	34 113	64 718	2 077	13 961	6 639	9 353
With a mobility limitation	3 452 631	360 648	179 444	77 759	22 348	81 097	13 074	19 890	912	4 101	2 136	2 831
In labor force	790 024	111 859	58 120	14 728	5 996	33 015	4 767	10 905	375	2 470	1 035	1 370
With a self-care limitation	5 383 939	718 170	386 876	110 543	36 718	184 033	28 225	56 345	1 656	12 475	5 783	8 105
With a work disability	12 826 449	936 168	508 387	188 938	49 457	189 386	23 866	35 287	2 189	6 952	3 847	5 727
In labor force	5 043 990	325 266	188 378	46 849	14 801	75 238	6 305	16 740	1 111	3 425	1 634	2 515
Prevented from working	6 594 029	532 740	278 607	125 387	31 018	97 728	15 326	15 441	923	2 899	1 854	2 759
No work disability	144 497 473	12 704 029	7 602 794	1 423 762	651 054	3 026 419	322 778	908 079	38 484	189 336	89 576	133 030
In labor force	114 652 861	9 555 037	5 704 812	999 241	528 013	2 322 971	224 452	708 262	29 185	148 247	66 637	104 119
Persons 65 to 74 years	**17 933 552**	**663 866**	**335 483**	**74 139**	**97 328**	**156 916**	**13 376**	**25 424**	**1 867**	**4 000**	**2 601**	**4 950**
With a mobility or self-care limitation	2 392 089	126 882	62 133	19 753	17 525	27 471	3 057	4 340	342	644	458	867
With a mobility limitation	1 631 650	88 823	44 150	15 032	11 687	17 954	2 195	2 816	210	396	306	541
With a self-care limitation	1 509 219	79 661	38 792	11 549	11 394	17 926	1 942	2 631	242	385	269	588
Persons 75 years and over	**11 629 959**	**363 920**	**172 837**	**35 940**	**66 195**	**88 948**	**5 871**	**12 502**	**915**	**1 794**	**1 145**	**2 885**
With a mobility or self-care limitation	3 551 352	139 329	66 449	16 179	25 140	31 561	2 153	4 434	302	473	325	1 119
With a mobility limitation	2 980 270	118 219	57 490	14 043	20 739	25 947	1 836	3 738	258	378	255	1 034
With a self-care limitation	2 014 865	86 208	40 988	9 906	15 716	19 598	1 454	2 814	205	308	196	715

SOCIAL AND ECONOMIC CHARACTERISTICS UNITED STATES SUMMARY 125

464

Table 115. **Education, Ability to Speak English, and Disability for Selected Hispanic Origin Groups: 1990**—Con.

[Data based on sample and subject to sampling variability, see text. For definitions of terms and meanings of symbols, see text]

United States	Hispanic origin (of any race)—Con.												
	Other Hispanic—Con.												
	Central American—Con.			South American									
	Panamanian	Salvadoran	Other Central American	Total	Argentinean	Chilean	Colombian	Ecuadorian	Peruvian	Venezuelan	Other South American	All other Hispanic origin	Not of Hispanic origin
SCHOOL ENROLLMENT AND TYPE OF SCHOOL													
Persons 3 years and over enrolled in school	**30 250**	**183 010**	**2 322**	**330 776**	**29 044**	**21 995**	**120 594**	**58 779**	**58 395**	**18 256**	**23 713**	**610 455**	**57 840 035**
Preprimary school	1 344	5 882	100	15 362	1 347	1 461	5 768	2 346	2 468	1 059	913	34 949	4 151 205
Public school	692	4 140	71	7 849	503	671	3 099	1 437	1 261	421	457	22 748	2 423 159
Elementary or high school	15 960	133 648	1 541	184 896	15 068	12 050	69 665	35 061	30 801	8 904	13 347	416 708	37 265 166
Public school	13 846	125 474	1 380	152 832	12 454	10 093	58 084	27 730	25 678	7 489	11 304	375 459	33 462 481
College	12 946	43 480	681	130 518	12 629	8 484	45 161	21 372	25 126	8 293	9 453	158 798	16 423 664
Public college	9 231	37 396	560	93 426	8 893	6 477	31 785	15 282	18 663	5 504	6 822	123 486	12 588 113
Persons 3 years and over enrolled in school	**30 250**	**183 010**	**2 322**	**330 776**	**29 044**	**21 995**	**120 594**	**58 779**	**58 395**	**18 256**	**23 713**	**610 455**	**57 840 035**
3 and 4 years	940	3 829	70	8 984	819	811	3 335	1 446	1 563	520	490	18 948	1 925 124
5 to 14 years	11 084	76 249	986	126 511	10 285	8 507	47 237	23 411	21 073	7 097	8 901	311 687	28 828 155
15 to 17 years	3 487	24 096	336	41 240	4 057	3 073	14 823	7 447	7 026	1 648	3 166	83 972	8 290 839
18 and 19 years	2 741	11 592	151	24 436	2 664	1 484	8 018	4 715	4 240	1 342	1 973	42 564	4 513 859
20 to 24 years	4 291	20 040	211	41 924	4 148	2 635	13 965	7 974	7 679	2 359	3 164	56 692	5 683 920
25 to 34 years	3 854	29 035	373	49 440	3 940	2 673	18 942	7 912	9 039	3 642	3 292	52 648	4 445 223
35 years and over	3 853	18 169	195	38 241	3 131	2 812	14 274	5 874	7 775	1 648	2 727	43 944	4 152 915
Persons 18 to 24 years	**12 696**	**96 073**	**878**	**125 464**	**11 838**	**7 418**	**43 551**	**25 724**	**21 672**	**6 257**	**9 004**	**239 079**	**23 198 991**
Percent enrolled in college	45.4	17.8	30.1	43.3	50.7	47.4	39.5	39.1	46.8	51.6	45.9	31.3	35.9
Persons 16 to 19 years	**6 222**	**41 772**	**457**	**61 801**	**6 202**	**4 021**	**21 141**	**11 829**	**10 931**	**2 843**	**4 834**	**130 458**	**12 714 966**
Percent not enrolled, not high school graduate	7.8	28.6	17.5	8.3	5.9	6.4	9.6	9.1	7.0	7.1	8.5	14.4	9.9
EDUCATIONAL ATTAINMENT													
Persons 18 to 24 years	**12 696**	**96 073**	**878**	**125 464**	**11 838**	**7 418**	**43 551**	**25 724**	**21 672**	**6 257**	**9 004**	**239 079**	**23 198 991**
High school graduate (includes equivalency)	3 657	19 060	275	37 288	3 446	2 309	12 757	7 642	7 077	1 470	2 587	73 006	7 304 115
Some college or associate degree	5 586	14 269	207	48 829	5 077	3 200	15 556	9 360	9 026	3 091	3 519	79 049	9 221 447
Bachelor's degree or higher	995	1 487	44	9 628	1 593	577	3 075	1 407	1 553	712	711	11 939	1 906 249
Persons 25 years and over	**57 244**	**304 673**	**4 129**	**656 831**	**69 181**	**44 126**	**239 674**	**119 382**	**109 861**	**28 669**	**45 938**	**1 060 579**	**147 641 643**
Less than 5th grade	788	64 737	449	30 874	1 991	1 127	14 754	7 215	3 633	661	1 493	66 175	2 762 310
5th to 8th grade	3 417	68 494	736	55 190	5 742	2 379	21 011	15 320	5 594	1 139	4 005	109 528	10 293 989
9th to 12th grade, no diploma	6 809	68 676	819	106 032	9 241	6 206	43 065	23 872	14 413	2 272	6 963	186 698	20 653 198
High school graduate (includes equivalency)	15 093	48 707	925	165 509	15 261	10 738	64 088	29 501	30 569	4 958	10 394	280 947	45 223 131
Some college, no degree	14 208	26 798	621	121 265	13 135	9 044	40 050	21 075	23 244	5 729	8 988	197 283	28 177 305
Associate degree, occupational program	2 304	6 234	81	24 282	2 037	2 055	9 076	3 760	4 235	1 285	1 834	32 327	4 959 232
Associate degree, academic program	2 881	5 683	117	25 279	2 017	1 684	9 024	3 925	4 816	1 855	1 958	30 676	4 289 984
Bachelor's degree	7 517	10 659	250	74 400	9 103	5 690	23 831	9 536	14 030	6 677	5 533	100 453	20 174 370
Graduate or professional degree	4 227	4 685	131	54 000	10 654	5 203	14 775	5 178	9 327	4 093	4 770	56 492	11 108 124
Females 25 years and over	**35 277**	**155 796**	**2 150**	**342 464**	**33 945**	**22 861**	**130 686**	**61 191**	**55 637**	**14 909**	**23 235**	**551 133**	**77 996 652**
Less than 5th grade	607	35 529	218	18 555	1 170	706	9 215	4 025	2 155	392	892	34 832	1 400 755
5th to 8th grade	2 526	36 664	396	32 206	3 336	1 560	12 847	7 962	3 587	771	2 143	58 653	5 556 845
9th to 12th grade, no diploma	4 404	33 099	429	57 073	4 584	3 240	24 180	12 577	7 420	1 333	3 739	98 032	11 274 952
High school graduate (includes equivalency)	9 447	25 192	477	91 232	7 943	5 887	35 800	16 012	16 853	2 970	5 767	154 308	25 575 320
Some college, no degree	8 534	12 849	302	60 000	6 172	4 598	20 783	10 193	10 945	2 912	4 397	101 294	14 726 067
Associate degree, occupational program	1 462	3 237	40	13 011	1 041	1 056	5 012	1 988	2 327	686	901	16 746	2 779 790
Associate degree, academic program	1 822	2 701	38	13 959	1 104	940	5 285	2 009	2 719	906	910	15 736	2 398 202
Bachelor's degree	4 346	4 779	172	36 355	4 688	2 975	11 908	4 603	6 385	3 125	2 671	48 561	9 699 155
Graduate or professional degree	2 129	1 746	78	20 073	3 907	1 899	5 656	1 822	3 246	1 734	1 809	22 971	4 585 566
Persons 25 years and over	**57 244**	**304 673**	**4 129**	**656 831**	**69 181**	**44 126**	**239 674**	**119 382**	**109 861**	**28 669**	**45 938**	**1 060 579**	**147 641 643**
Percent less than 5th grade	1.4	21.2	10.9	4.7	2.9	2.6	6.2	6.0	3.3	2.3	3.3	6.2	1.9
Percent high school graduate or higher	80.8	33.7	51.5	70.8	75.5	78.0	67.1	61.1	78.5	85.8	72.9	65.8	77.2
Percent some college or higher	54.4	17.7	29.1	45.6	53.4	53.7	40.4	36.4	50.7	68.5	50.2	39.3	46.5
Percent bachelor's degree or higher	20.5	5.0	9.2	19.5	28.6	24.7	16.1	12.3	21.3	37.6	22.4	11.8	21.2
Males 25 to 34 years	**7 809**	**83 382**	**1 001**	**123 396**	**10 668**	**6 975**	**45 595**	**23 124**	**20 625**	**7 569**	**8 840**	**179 934**	**19 405 387**
Percent high school graduate or higher	89.9	36.1	52.6	79.8	87.5	84.4	76.5	71.7	86.0	90.7	80.4	73.7	86.0
Percent bachelor's degree or higher	23.2	4.9	3.8	22.8	36.2	28.6	19.2	14.8	24.3	42.1	22.2	16.2	24.5
Females 25 to 34 years	**11 273**	**73 435**	**731**	**117 283**	**9 201**	**6 554**	**45 998**	**20 497**	**20 199**	**6 914**	**7 920**	**172 448**	**19 681 368**
Percent high school graduate or higher	88.7	35.3	60.1	81.1	88.0	86.1	77.9	75.4	86.3	89.9	81.9	77.3	88.1
Percent bachelor's degree or higher	22.6	4.4	7.3	21.6	35.7	26.9	18.5	15.7	19.4	39.1	23.8	16.4	23.9
ABILITY TO SPEAK ENGLISH													
Persons 5 years and over	**85 747**	**513 596**	**6 375**	**962 088**	**96 095**	**63 646**	**350 410**	**178 355**	**161 687**	**44 199**	**67 696**	**1 731 122**	**210 876 040**
Speak a language other than English	63 820	488 718	5 097	862 589	83 370	54 214	317 046	164 947	146 026	36 742	60 244	930 888	16 628 681
5 to 17 years	8 747	104 617	1 065	147 402	12 173	8 758	54 698	29 104	24 997	7 265	10 407	187 623	2 726 667
18 to 64 years	50 510	372 936	3 861	676 231	65 747	42 692	249 337	127 934	114 552	28 492	47 477	643 186	10 999 289
65 to 74 years	3 131	7 411	122	26 778	3 881	1 804	8 979	5 412	4 338	634	1 730	58 672	1 538 638
75 years and over	1 432	3 754	49	12 178	1 569	960	4 032	2 497	2 139	351	630	41 407	1 364 087
Do not speak English "very well"	20 659	348 291	2 592	469 391	34 967	26 396	185 673	94 577	81 741	15 179	30 858	352 060	6 265 707
5 to 17 years	3 158	50 897	445	44 593	2 776	2 343	16 619	8 736	8 595	2 759	2 765	65 308	938 006
18 to 64 years	15 860	287 560	2 057	393 563	28 310	21 881	158 264	79 094	67 984	11 843	26 187	239 233	4 147 838
65 to 74 years	1 057	6 470	54	21 157	2 704	1 444	7 302	4 514	3 401	368	1 424	24 654	614 455
75 years and over	584	3 364	36	10 078	1 177	728	3 488	2 233	1 761	209	482	22 865	565 408
ABILITY TO SPEAK ENGLISH IN HOUSEHOLD													
Linguistically isolated households	3 714	70 464	583	104 242	9 121	5 883	42 030	19 560	17 614	3 060	6 974	66 508	1 423 870
Persons 5 years and over in households	**82 362**	**508 393**	**6 304**	**942 028**	**93 952**	**62 654**	**340 740**	**176 054**	**159 084**	**43 073**	**66 471**	**1 671 417**	**204 721 888**
In linguistically isolated households	7 954	239 515	1 657	268 522	19 154	13 541	109 082	53 935	46 673	8 669	17 468	184 024	3 192 582
5 to 17 years	1 670	48 284	364	45 636	2 853	2 068	18 199	9 167	7 952	2 447	2 950	49 208	612 970
18 to 64 years	5 504	186 477	1 253	206 940	14 080	10 506	85 066	41 285	36 513	5 879	13 611	108 820	1 926 783
65 to 74 years	555	3 157	29	10 807	1 517	685	3 943	2 321	1 438	212	691	13 563	340 614
75 years and over	225	1 597	11	5 139	704	282	1 874	1 162	770	131	216	12 433	312 215
DISABILITY STATUS OF CIVILIAN NONINSTITUTIONALIZED PERSONS													
Persons 16 to 64 years	**63 853**	**405 433**	**4 939**	**757 383**	**77 210**	**50 091**	**272 426**	**140 772**	**128 601**	**34 376**	**53 907**	**1 168 412**	**143 683 725**
With a mobility or self-care limitation	3 072	29 279	337	47 336	3 904	2 777	16 779	11 291	8 159	1 403	3 023	76 134	6 320 853
With a mobility limitation	899	8 883	128	16 522	1 228	741	5 953	4 239	2 732	447	1 182	31 611	3 091 983
In labor force	386	5 198	71	8 580	625	358	3 141	2 087	1 661	121	587	8 763	678 165
With a self-care limitation	2 599	25 426	301	39 388	3 290	2 500	13 916	9 231	6 884	1 101	2 466	60 075	4 665 769
With a work disability	3 189	13 055	328	29 888	2 856	1 816	11 026	7 026	4 269	1 165	1 730	100 345	11 890 281
In labor force	1 519	6 402	134	13 603	1 245	812	5 037	2 850	2 311	469	879	38 590	4 718 724
Prevented from working	1 290	5 533	183	13 840	1 362	835	5 136	3 667	1 579	574	687	53 121	6 061 289
No work disability	60 664	392 378	4 611	727 495	74 354	48 275	261 400	133 746	124 332	33 211	52 177	1 068 067	131 793 444
In labor force	46 610	309 920	3 544	569 533	58 435	37 862	205 099	104 834	98 652	23 922	40 729	820 724	105 097 824
Persons 65 to 74 years	**3 945**	**7 902**	**159**	**29 123**	**4 230**	**1 976**	**9 892**	**5 616**	**4 743**	**791**	**1 875**	**88 993**	**17 269 686**
With a mobility or self-care limitation	659	1 342	28	5 057	776	377	1 735	1 048	699	97	325	15 017	2 265 207
With a mobility limitation	476	859	28	3 154	399	218	1 208	708	364	46	211	9 789	1 542 827
With a self-care limitation	379	768	–	3 407	559	257	1 084	661	530	87	229	9 946	1 429 558
Persons 75 years and over	**1 726**	**3 945**	**92**	**12 892**	**1 650**	**1 048**	**4 171**	**2 650**	**2 238**	**400**	**735**	**57 683**	**11 266 039**
With a mobility or self-care limitation	706	1 469	40	4 616	665	437	1 473	901	784	108	248	20 358	3 412 023
With a mobility limitation	582	1 207	24	3 753	488	362	1 200	743	646	98	216	16 620	2 862 051
With a self-care limitation	467	890	33	2 693	408	233	755	651	435	73	138	12 637	1 928 657

Table 116. Geographic Mobility, Commuting, and Industry of Employed Persons for Selected Hispanic Origin Groups: 1990

[Data based on sample and subject to sampling variability, see text. For definitions of terms and meanings of symbols, see text]

United States	All persons	Hispanic origin (of any race) Total	Mexican	Puerto Rican	Cuban	Other Hispanic Total	Dominican (Dominican Republic)	Central American Total	Costa Rican	Guatemalan	Honduran	Nicaraguan
PLACE OF BIRTH, NATIVITY, AND CITIZENSHIP												
All persons	248 709 873	21 900 089	13 393 208	2 651 815	1 053 197	4 801 869	520 151	1 323 830	57 223	268 779	131 066	202 658
Native	228 942 557	14 058 439	8 933 371	2 618 963	298 481	2 207 624	153 078	277 731	17 785	52 783	30 076	38 363
Born in State of residence	153 684 685	10 178 632	7 314 939	1 085 173	204 508	1 574 012	117 692	207 477	11 142	41 402	20 722	29 384
Born in a different State	72 011 141	2 344 536	1 429 999	340 824	79 785	493 928	21 870	40 079	3 540	6 113	5 410	5 929
Northeast	16 772 309	446 803	37 105	241 802	40 544	127 352	17 328	11 505	1 262	1 759	2 230	1 120
Midwest	21 287 172	300 286	210 037	32 396	8 370	49 483	892	4 350	455	1 019	615	611
South	24 366 640	795 769	602 945	41 425	23 709	127 690	2 551	13 852	912	1 768	1 797	2 148
West	9 585 020	801 678	579 912	25 201	7 162	189 403	1 099	10 372	911	1 567	768	2 050
Born abroad	3 246 731	1 535 271	188 433	1 192 966	14 188	139 684	13 516	30 175	3 103	5 268	3 944	3 050
Puerto Rico	1 190 533	1 155 977	6 102	1 128 207	3 772	17 896	2 832	437	58	20	117	83
U.S. outlying area	191 913	79 690	7 390	48 066	2 137	22 097	2 679	1 965	54	638	279	247
Born abroad of American parents	1 864 285	299 604	174 941	16 693	8 279	99 691	8 005	27 773	2 991	4 610	3 548	2 720
Foreign born	19 767 316	7 841 650	4 459 837	32 852	754 716	2 594 245	367 073	1 046 099	39 438	215 996	100 990	164 295
Naturalized citizen	7 996 998	2 056 296	999 849	12 795	379 864	663 788	99 132	193 401	11 999	34 159	24 150	24 653
Not a citizen	11 770 318	5 785 354	3 459 988	20 057	374 852	1 930 457	267 941	852 698	27 439	181 837	76 840	139 642
RESIDENCE IN 1985												
Persons 5 years and over	230 445 777	19 569 737	11 826 999	2 370 798	995 348	4 376 592	469 579	1 213 803	53 403	247 159	119 940	187 583
Same house	122 796 970	8 575 524	5 249 712	1 075 655	486 325	1 763 832	205 481	370 218	21 549	75 545	37 628	48 571
Different house in the United States	102 540 097	9 107 837	5 624 943	1 071 424	459 690	1 951 780	175 439	546 145	22 746	108 925	51 874	74 936
Same county	58 675 635	6 341 105	4 073 244	677 203	324 077	1 266 581	111 333	403 215	14 132	85 811	35 443	51 827
Different county	43 864 462	2 766 732	1 551 699	394 221	135 613	685 199	64 106	142 930	8 614	23 114	16 431	23 109
Same State	22 279 165	1 543 112	957 886	180 933	54 018	350 275	34 254	72 215	4 536	12 052	7 265	12 159
Different State	21 585 297	1 223 620	593 813	213 288	81 595	334 924	29 852	70 715	4 078	11 062	9 166	10 950
Northeast	4 346 471	294 091	20 391	128 345	34 136	111 219	23 272	17 954	1 283	2 741	3 423	2 298
Midwest	4 854 669	135 647	79 233	20 315	7 299	28 800	823	5 199	425	1 293	549	629
South	7 588 749	392 298	221 257	41 973	28 238	100 830	4 031	27 984	1 359	3 190	3 745	4 734
West	4 795 408	401 584	272 932	22 655	11 922	94 075	1 726	19 578	1 011	3 838	1 449	3 289
Puerto Rico	213 886	201 757	1 249	187 251	3 696	9 561	5 425	622	66	54	102	173
U.S. outlying area	73 764	16 669	2 260	7 861	567	5 981	1 066	795	108	150	158	65
Elsewhere	4 821 060	1 667 950	948 835	28 607	45 070	645 438	82 168	296 023	8 934	62 485	30 178	63 838
MEANS OF TRANSPORTATION TO WORK AND TRAVEL TIME TO WORK												
Workers 16 years and over	115 070 274	8 858 023	5 239 127	928 100	522 453	2 168 343	192 182	643 289	28 089	134 136	59 280	95 451
Car, truck, or van	99 592 932	7 076 332	4 454 908	606 553	451 052	1 563 819	88 902	431 778	21 332	87 344	37 202	69 084
Drove alone	84 215 298	5 174 780	3 176 961	457 185	366 289	1 174 345	58 914	292 713	16 571	58 139	25 641	48 160
Carpooled	15 377 634	1 901 552	1 277 947	149 368	84 763	389 474	29 988	139 065	4 761	29 205	11 561	20 924
Persons per car, truck, or van	1.09	1.18	1.20	1.16	1.11	1.16	1.26	1.22	1.14	1.24	1.21	1.21
Public transportation	6 069 589	971 168	327 107	218 740	37 342	387 979	77 754	145 101	3 787	31 052	14 781	17 290
Bus or trolley bus	3 445 000	603 408	287 184	86 537	18 847	210 840	24 137	111 521	1 795	25 657	9 406	13 512
Streetcar or trolley car	78 130	8 440	3 203	1 496	358	3 383	632	1 088	21	193	61	142
Subway or elevated	1 755 476	310 654	26 995	116 519	14 736	152 404	48 225	28 156	1 740	4 449	4 706	3 156
Railroad	574 052	31 210	5 818	9 076	2 355	13 961	2 564	2 970	142	541	316	317
Ferryboat	37 497	2 540	421	1 009	179	931	131	234	11	39	84	35
Taxicab	179 434	14 916	3 486	4 103	867	6 460	2 065	1 132	78	173	208	128
Motorcycle	237 404	20 338	13 449	1 317	596	4 976	86	1 257	41	365	122	180
Bicycle	466 856	59 469	40 959	4 098	1 696	12 716	350	5 142	230	1 195	635	789
Walked	4 488 886	457 343	242 393	74 326	18 052	122 572	19 293	36 353	1 599	8 079	3 898	4 841
Other means	808 582	111 337	74 474	9 443	3 984	23 436	2 155	9 053	307	2 080	884	1 467
Worked at home	3 406 025	162 036	85 837	13 623	9 731	52 845	3 642	14 605	793	4 021	1 758	1 800
Mean travel time to work (minutes)	22.3	24.2	22.6	27.1	24.9	26.4	30.4	28.7	25.7	29.3	28.4	27.0
INDUSTRY												
Employed persons 16 years and over	115 681 202	8 981 516	5 323 210	925 893	531 023	2 201 390	196 988	656 495	28 432	137 291	60 560	97 402
Agriculture, forestry, and fisheries	3 115 372	462 071	398 813	12 090	7 324	43 844	961	17 236	458	4 189	1 205	1 459
Mining	723 423	47 692	38 788	1 185	724	6 995	116	866	77	114	146	120
Construction	7 214 763	666 765	450 363	37 760	31 892	146 750	8 033	54 128	1 529	11 697	5 280	7 031
Manufacturing	20 462 078	1 793 630	1 104 048	185 453	90 796	413 333	50 505	133 409	4 540	32 037	11 286	18 973
Nondurable goods	8 053 234	769 761	461 122	78 269	44 268	186 102	25 293	63 178	2 008	14 867	5 125	9 772
Food and kindred products	1 405 723	185 749	139 393	12 713	6 098	27 545	2 256	8 964	311	1 587	907	1 279
Textile mill and finished textile products	1 809 199	240 243	126 111	21 993	18 590	73 549	13 530	28 659	571	7 013	2 129	4 516
Printing, publishing, and allied industries	1 941 923	119 819	63 197	16 154	7 830	32 638	2 826	9 414	358	2 373	813	1 654
Durable goods	12 408 844	1 023 869	642 926	107 184	46 528	227 231	25 212	70 231	2 532	17 170	6 161	9 201
Furniture, lumber, and wood products	1 276 578	112 525	78 103	8 048	5 536	20 838	1 602	8 814	147	2 041	951	1 422
Metal industries	1 965 144	170 959	116 781	19 331	5 737	29 110	2 824	9 428	335	2 382	833	1 127
Machinery and computer equipment	2 362 588	142 968	90 474	14 516	6 336	31 642	2 144	8 246	317	2 256	650	1 097
Electrical equipment and components, except computer	1 899 173	158 382	94 273	18 180	8 514	37 415	3 341	11 124	537	2 376	805	1 518
Transportation equipment	2 532 532	155 754	104 144	13 736	6 875	30 999	1 658	8 275	453	1 972	885	1 271
Transportation	5 108 003	380 003	192 343	53 832	31 555	102 273	11 263	23 757	1 647	4 263	2 345	4 565
Communications and other public utilities	3 097 059	179 006	109 694	20 554	12 450	36 308	2 136	6 845	384	1 171	707	1 041
Wholesale trade	5 071 026	414 909	244 822	40 264	34 809	95 014	9 669	27 497	1 090	5 786	2 618	5 239
Retail trade	19 485 666	1 627 779	991 713	140 262	85 193	410 611	39 516	125 801	5 046	23 623	10 462	21 219
Food, bakery, and dairy stores	3 339 390	276 636	168 495	25 195	14 693	68 253	11 200	17 211	648	3 294	1 765	3 901
Eating and drinking places	5 463 979	620 761	404 968	39 978	18 584	157 231	12 004	59 625	1 750	11 416	4 053	7 667
Banking and credit agencies	2 374 916	157 527	68 825	23 823	18 878	46 001	3 396	11 073	693	1 418	966	2 723
Insurance, real estate, and other finance	5 609 964	301 614	138 682	47 861	29 154	85 917	7 712	21 032	1 427	3 571	2 344	3 674
Business and repair services	5 577 462	526 785	282 635	52 333	31 755	160 062	14 089	58 349	1 991	13 534	4 929	8 109
Private households	628 510	134 272	62 452	4 967	2 571	64 282	3 008	37 685	592	10 690	3 937	2 635
Other personal services	3 040 186	342 906	188 469	31 490	22 278	100 669	8 717	34 158	1 176	6 276	3 459	4 667
Entertainment and recreation services	1 636 460	125 207	71 933	14 281	7 257	31 736	2 375	7 731	451	1 655	625	1 106
Professional and related services	26 998 247	1 480 410	778 273	207 895	107 037	387 205	31 414	86 114	6 547	15 577	9 054	13 204
Hospitals	5 204 690	309 787	147 346	56 029	22 145	84 267	7 356	21 378	1 473	3 533	2 157	2 846
Health services, except hospitals	4 477 994	255 852	128 023	34 254	21 507	72 068	7 286	17 152	1 001	2 913	2 067	3 288
Educational services	9 633 503	515 006	304 730	62 017	32 829	115 430	7 376	20 633	2 059	3 758	2 272	2 806
Public administration	5 538 077	340 940	201 357	51 843	17 350	70 390	4 078	10 814	784	1 690	1 197	1 637

Table 116. Geographic Mobility, Commuting, and Industry of Employed Persons for Selected Hispanic Origin Groups: 1990—Con.

[Data based on sample and subject to sampling variability, see text. For definitions of terms and meanings of symbols, see text]

United States	Central American—Con. Panamanian	Central American—Con. Salvadoran	Central American—Con. Other Central American	South American Total	South American Argentinean	South American Chilean	South American Colombian	South American Ecuadorian	South American Peruvian	South American Venezuelan	South American Other South American	All other Hispanic origin	Not of Hispanic origin
PLACE OF BIRTH, NATIVITY, AND CITIZENSHIP													
All persons	92 013	565 081	7 010	1 035 602	100 921	68 799	378 726	191 198	175 035	47 997	72 926	1 922 286	226 809 784
Native	30 317	106 405	2 002	259 566	22 935	18 477	97 657	49 859	40 530	12 783	17 325	1 517 249	214 884 118
Born in State of residence	14 571	88 790	1 466	166 099	14 368	10 847	59 708	37 361	27 398	5 888	10 529	1 082 744	143 506 053
Born in a different State	8 047	10 771	269	59 414	6 724	4 356	23 266	8 559	8 373	3 833	4 303	372 565	69 666 605
Northeast	2 799	2 254	81	29 622	3 379	1 680	13 060	5 330	3 371	1 549	1 253	68 897	16 325 506
Midwest	992	620	38	6 720	822	582	2 414	688	1 071	543	600	37 521	20 986 886
South	2 688	4 416	123	14 874	1 476	1 109	5 090	1 665	2 533	1 190	1 811	96 413	23 570 871
West	1 568	3 481	27	8 198	1 047	985	2 702	876	1 398	551	639	169 734	8 783 342
Born abroad	7 699	6 844	267	34 053	1 843	3 274	14 683	3 939	4 759	3 062	2 493	61 940	1 711 460
Puerto Rico	17	133	9	929	116	36	329	228	106	28	86	13 698	34 556
U.S. outlying area	127	566	54	1 749	67	54	726	630	211	37	24	15 704	112 223
Born abroad of American parents	7 555	6 145	204	31 375	1 660	3 184	13 628	3 081	4 442	2 997	2 383	32 538	1 564 681
Foreign born	61 696	458 676	5 008	776 036	77 986	50 322	281 069	141 339	134 505	35 214	55 601	405 037	11 925 666
Naturalized citizen	28 919	68 044	1 477	219 984	30 985	15 738	79 091	36 277	34 285	6 197	17 411	151 271	5 940 702
Not a citizen	32 777	390 632	3 531	556 052	47 001	34 584	201 978	105 062	100 220	29 017	38 190	253 766	5 984 964
RESIDENCE IN 1985													
Persons 5 years and over	85 747	513 596	6 375	962 088	96 095	63 646	350 410	178 355	161 687	44 199	67 696	1 731 122	210 876 040
Same house	33 926	150 772	2 227	359 745	38 403	25 351	126 153	81 965	52 656	11 661	23 556	828 388	114 221 446
Different house in the United States	35 763	248 852	3 049	423 237	41 631	26 932	164 703	69 671	70 187	20 324	29 789	806 959	93 432 260
Same county	18 256	195 541	2 205	262 968	25 188	16 680	101 097	45 526	45 109	11 192	18 176	489 065	52 334 530
Different county	17 507	53 311	844	160 269	16 443	10 252	63 606	24 145	25 078	9 132	11 613	317 894	41 097 730
Same State	6 616	29 162	425	74 122	7 687	4 765	26 991	12 804	12 990	3 625	5 260	169 684	20 736 053
Different State	10 891	24 149	419	86 147	8 756	5 487	36 615	11 341	12 088	5 507	6 353	148 210	20 361 677
Northeast	3 621	4 482	106	40 112	4 041	1 619	19 194	7 119	4 619	1 322	2 198	29 881	4 052 380
Midwest	1 067	1 228	8	7 508	835	747	2 869	789	1 090	581	597	15 270	4 719 022
South	3 918	10 844	194	24 736	2 185	1 527	9 946	2 135	4 032	2 358	2 553	44 079	7 196 451
West	2 285	7 595	111	13 791	1 695	1 594	4 606	1 298	2 347	1 246	1 005	58 980	4 393 824
Puerto Rico	147	80	–	1 174	130	76	551	220	80	98	19	2 340	12 129
U.S. outlying area	87	154	73	662	19	76	240	158	83	60	26	3 458	57 095
Elsewhere	15 824	113 738	1 026	177 270	15 912	11 211	58 763	26 341	38 681	12 056	14 306	89 977	3 153 110
MEANS OF TRANSPORTATION TO WORK AND TRAVEL TIME TO WORK													
Workers 16 years and over	45 402	277 725	3 206	535 642	56 930	36 537	191 140	97 125	92 569	22 645	38 696	797 230	106 212 251
Car, truck, or van	30 522	184 127	2 167	378 565	44 457	28 775	136 632	65 506	66 761	17 568	28 866	664 574	92 516 600
Drove alone	24 338	118 371	1 493	289 838	36 479	23 147	102 963	41 086	49 881	13 944	22 338	532 880	79 040 518
Carpooled	6 184	65 756	674	88 727	7 978	5 628	33 669	14 420	16 880	3 624	6 528	131 694	13 476 082
Persons per car, truck, or van	1.12	1.26	1.20	1.15	1.11	1.12	1.16	1.17	1.16	1.13	1.14	1.12	1.09
Public transportation	11 048	66 388	755	104 228	6 634	4 099	36 433	32 145	16 354	2 728	5 835	60 896	5 098 421
Bus or trolley bus	4 014	56 623	514	39 271	2 476	1 814	13 191	9 614	8 413	1 084	2 679	35 911	2 841 592
Streetcar or trolley car	63	607	11	701	73	18	242	110	16	24	072	00 000	00 000
Subway or elevated	6 124	7 760	221	56 785	3 356	1 838	20 308	20 416	6 898	1 224	2 745	19 238	1 444 822
Railroad	586	1 063	5	5 101	511	210	1 812	1 262	719	305	282	3 326	542 842
Ferryboat	18	47	–	243	29	57	49	80	6	17	5	323	34 957
Taxicab	243	298	4	2 037	189	132	831	533	199	53	100	1 226	164 518
Motorcycle	49	472	28	1 048	119	101	301	50	265	103	109	2 585	217 066
Bicycle	173	2 090	30	2 785	254	252	944	379	652	149	155	4 439	407 387
Walked	2 472	15 310	154	30 566	3 205	1 721	10 508	6 434	5 406	1 087	2 205	36 360	4 031 543
Other means	297	4 004	14	4 001	295	303	1 406	818	766	151	262	8 227	697 245
Worked at home	841	5 334	58	14 449	1 966	1 286	4 916	1 793	2 365	859	1 264	20 149	3 243 989
Mean travel time to work (minutes)	29.1	29.2	30.4	26.8	25.9	24.9	26.5	30.2	26.0	24.7	26.0	23.3	22.2
INDUSTRY													
Employed persons 16 years and over	44 617	284 923	3 270	545 925	57 951	36 949	195 240	98 957	94 445	22 924	39 459	801 982	106 699 686
Agriculture, forestry, and fisheries	251	9 600	74	4 935	431	458	1 688	567	1 111	200	480	20 712	2 653 301
Mining	57	345	7	1 158	90	111	314	123	255	123	142	4 855	675 731
Construction	1 552	26 841	198	28 001	3 416	2 203	8 882	4 721	4 628	1 166	2 985	56 588	6 547 998
Manufacturing	5 033	60 889	651	111 037	9 499	5 732	42 938	26 683	17 396	3 219	5 570	118 382	18 668 448
Nondurable goods	2 076	29 045	285	50 346	3 840	2 372	19 777	12 627	8 026	1 295	2 409	47 285	7 283 473
Food and kindred products	297	4 546	37	5 448	496	360	2 093	874	1 126	128	371	10 877	1 219 974
Textile mill and finished textile products	569	13 707	154	20 263	1 198	781	7 877	6 691	2 695	297	724	11 097	1 568 956
Printing, publishing, and allied industries	674	3 503	39	9 380	872	525	3 662	1 861	1 698	403	359	11 018	1 822 104
Durable goods	2 957	31 844	366	60 691	5 659	3 360	23 161	14 056	9 370	1 924	3 161	71 097	11 384 975
Furniture, lumber, and wood products	138	4 071	44	4 321	418	225	1 530	1 013	794	92	249	6 101	1 164 053
Metal industries	364	4 357	30	6 849	552	380	2 846	1 519	999	218	335	10 009	1 794 185
Machinery and computer equipment	437	3 435	54	10 000	1 213	552	3 852	1 949	1 419	406	609	11 252	2 219 620
Electrical equipment and components, except computer	667	5 189	32	10 719	1 065	774	4 408	1 886	1 687	326	573	12 231	1 740 791
Transportation equipment	526	3 087	81	7 296	994	547	2 576	1 457	1 072	257	393	13 770	2 376 778
Transportation	2 663	8 227	47	29 647	2 966	2 170	11 013	5 643	4 603	1 251	2 001	37 606	4 728 000
Communications and other public utilities	1 290	2 195	57	7 136	827	519	2 298	1 220	1 068	542	662	20 191	2 918 053
Wholesale trade	1 386	11 237	141	25 993	2 560	1 484	10 065	4 806	4 330	1 254	1 494	31 855	4 656 117
Retail trade	6 653	58 141	657	95 863	9 973	6 238	33 300	18 144	17 201	4 088	6 919	149 431	17 857 887
Food, bakery, and dairy stores	816	6 689	98	13 720	1 222	875	5 197	2 515	2 387	544	980	26 122	3 062 754
Eating and drinking places	1 910	32 580	249	35 916	3 465	2 177	11 719	7 308	7 167	1 426	2 654	49 686	4 843 218
Banking and credit agencies	1 981	3 253	39	14 266	1 510	905	4 471	3 075	2 640	578	1 087	17 266	2 217 389
Insurance, real estate, and other finance	2 711	7 202	103	23 658	2 878	1 687	8 302	4 271	3 928	1 220	1 372	33 515	5 308 340
Business and repair services	2 540	26 958	288	43 571	4 017	2 442	17 106	7 149	8 041	1 579	3 237	44 053	5 050 677
Private households	482	19 204	145	14 174	770	1 165	5 558	1 242	3 228	326	1 885	9 415	494 238
Other personal services	1 581	16 860	139	26 611	2 517	1 828	10 150	3 953	5 166	783	2 214	31 183	2 697 280
Entertainment and recreation services	762	3 098	34	8 214	1 063	723	3 013	1 048	1 439	342	586	13 416	1 511 253
Professional and related services	12 803	28 338	591	100 425	14 034	8 440	32 883	14 213	17 415	5 514	7 926	169 252	25 517 837
Hospitals	3 881	7 315	173	20 672	2 326	1 518	7 335	2 921	3 999	1 026	1 547	34 861	4 894 903
Health services, except hospitals	2 213	5 555	115	18 889	2 069	1 354	6 837	2 587	3 665	770	1 607	28 741	4 222 142
Educational services	3 534	6 099	105	29 744	5 083	2 966	8 709	4 255	4 517	1 916	2 298	57 677	9 118 497
Public administration	2 872	2 535	99	11 236	1 400	844	3 259	2 099	1 996	739	899	44 262	5 197 137

Table 117. **Labor Force Characteristics for Selected Hispanic Origin Groups: 1990**

[Data based on sample and subject to sampling variability, see text. For definitions of terms and meanings of symbols, see text]

United States	All persons	Hispanic origin (of any race)										
						Other Hispanic						
								Central American				
		Total	Mexican	Puerto Rican	Cuban	Total	Dominican (Dominican Republic)	Total	Costa Rican	Guate-malan	Honduran	Nicaraguan
LABOR FORCE STATUS												
Persons 16 years and over	**191 829 271**	**15 025 902**	**8 807 842**	**1 796 295**	**883 416**	**3 538 349**	**372 775**	**992 387**	**44 104**	**203 758**	**98 262**	**147 933**
In labor force	125 182 378	10 139 070	6 017 646	1 085 454	574 136	2 461 834	235 389	736 840	31 179	153 637	69 540	108 499
Percent of persons 16 years and over	65.3	67.5	68.3	60.4	65.0	69.6	63.1	74.2	70.7	75.4	70.8	73.3
Armed Forces	1 708 928	117 347	59 631	28 137	3 513	26 066	2 107	5 041	448	709	551	558
Civilian labor force	123 473 450	10 021 723	5 958 015	1 057 317	570 623	2 435 768	233 282	731 799	30 731	152 928	68 989	107 941
Employed	115 681 202	8 981 516	5 323 210	925 893	531 023	2 201 390	196 988	656 495	28 432	137 291	60 560	97 402
At work 35 or more hours	89 428 871	7 078 492	4 177 397	738 909	437 563	1 724 623	157 134	521 271	21 707	109 809	47 632	76 976
Unemployed	7 792 248	1 040 207	634 805	131 424	39 600	234 378	36 294	75 304	2 299	15 637	8 429	10 539
Percent of civilian labor force	6.3	10.4	10.7	12.4	6.9	9.6	15.6	10.3	7.5	10.2	12.2	9.8
Not in labor force	66 646 893	4 886 832	2 790 196	710 841	309 280	1 076 515	137 386	255 547	12 925	50 121	28 722	39 434
Institutionalized persons	3 232 910	240 572	128 710	45 379	15 869	50 614	4 777	6 054	201	967	542	783
Females 16 years and over	**99 803 358**	**7 410 116**	**4 199 653**	**935 918**	**452 536**	**1 822 009**	**203 648**	**506 073**	**24 100**	**98 435**	**55 088**	**78 197**
In labor force	56 672 949	4 145 686	2 323 688	470 521	251 522	1 099 955	107 662	322 914	14 383	62 053	33 994	50 166
Percent of females 16 years and over	56.8	55.9	55.3	50.3	55.6	60.4	52.9	63.8	59.7	63.0	61.7	64.2
Armed Forces	185 700	12 143	6 022	2 671	357	3 093	213	606	39	129	52	76
Civilian labor force	56 487 249	4 133 543	2 317 666	467 850	251 165	1 096 862	107 449	322 308	14 344	61 924	33 942	50 090
Employed	52 976 623	3 669 186	2 046 146	409 485	232 782	980 773	89 286	284 211	13 053	54 385	29 346	44 457
At work 35 or more hours	36 418 960	2 605 432	1 429 586	298 722	179 265	697 859	66 954	205 800	8 830	38 893	21 224	32 941
Unemployed	3 510 626	464 357	271 520	58 365	18 383	116 089	18 163	38 097	1 291	7 539	4 596	5 633
Percent of civilian labor force	6.2	11.2	11.7	12.5	7.3	10.6	16.9	11.8	9.0	12.2	13.5	11.2
Not in labor force	43 130 409	3 264 430	1 875 965	465 397	201 014	722 054	95 986	183 159	9 717	36 382	21 094	28 031
Institutionalized persons	1 487 110	39 187	21 234	6 606	3 070	8 277	413	777	59	111	64	62
Males 16 to 19 years	**7 342 263**	**848 933**	**557 417**	**97 749**	**24 659**	**169 108**	**17 640**	**52 881**	**1 806**	**10 455**	**4 356**	**9 033**
Employed	2 962 432	327 922	225 961	29 046	10 301	62 614	4 743	21 606	748	4 412	1 425	3 834
Unemployed	670 528	97 373	64 866	12 787	2 349	17 371	2 206	5 484	105	1 075	579	941
Not in labor force	3 562 362	411 580	259 779	53 503	11 669	86 629	10 448	25 394	919	4 883	2 315	4 210
Males 20 to 24 years	**9 469 385**	**1 197 579**	**783 793**	**126 823**	**34 714**	**252 249**	**23 770**	**89 980**	**3 090**	**20 408**	**7 570**	**10 889**
Employed	6 419 967	854 007	582 611	74 498	24 528	172 370	13 640	67 527	2 056	15 958	5 156	8 145
Unemployed	768 405	117 795	76 420	15 481	2 500	23 394	3 356	8 480	240	1 917	822	913
Not in labor force	1 806 836	189 444	104 193	29 860	6 574	48 817	6 078	12 545	645	2 308	1 437	1 677
Males 25 to 54 years	**52 743 194**	**4 590 167**	**2 750 099**	**522 601**	**236 767**	**1 080 700**	**111 743**	**314 857**	**13 001**	**69 428**	**28 002**	**43 928**
Employed	44 842 502	3 705 608	2 255 627	368 983	195 630	885 368	81 630	267 464	11 315	59 498	22 926	37 680
Unemployed	2 450 753	322 083	199 386	41 023	12 234	69 440	11 571	21 552	592	4 914	2 223	2 644
Not in labor force	4 553 238	505 969	269 034	96 574	27 207	113 154	17 587	23 239	868	4 754	2 546	3 324
Males 55 to 64 years	**9 957 003**	**543 449**	**289 119**	**68 119**	**66 992**	**119 219**	**10 045**	**17 743**	**1 347**	**3 066**	**2 163**	**3 786**
Employed	6 377 542	346 982	176 782	37 860	50 749	81 591	6 501	12 890	1 048	2 379	1 442	2 791
Unemployed	294 523	29 897	17 766	3 117	2 865	6 149	804	1 299	64	130	188	329
Not in labor force	3 279 732	166 292	94 416	27 094	13 370	31 412	2 740	3 546	235	549	533	666
Males 65 to 69 years	**4 555 259**	**182 651**	**99 026**	**19 845**	**25 737**	**38 043**	**2 574**	**4 950**	**373**	**922**	**500**	**845**
In labor force	1 269 464	55 077	26 628	4 325	11 283	12 841	737	2 159	178	421	171	416
Not in labor force	3 285 795	127 574	72 398	15 520	14 454	25 202	1 837	2 791	195	501	329	429
Did not work in 1989	2 675 255	107 631	61 524	13 888	11 386	20 833	1 565	2 372	161	428	277	342
Males 70 years and over	**7 958 809**	**253 007**	**128 735**	**25 240**	**42 011**	**57 021**	**3 355**	**5 903**	**387**	**1 044**	**583**	**1 255**
In labor force	930 288	31 464	14 324	2 347	7 019	7 774	645	1 030	41	300	115	158
Not in labor force	7 028 521	221 543	114 411	22 893	34 992	49 247	2 710	4 873	346	744	468	1 097
Did not work in 1989	6 289 799	205 592	106 293	21 771	32 306	45 222	2 531	4 487	332	721	417	1 023
Females 16 to 19 years	**6 973 185**	**751 549**	**483 343**	**92 935**	**22 036**	**153 235**	**17 672**	**41 891**	**1 853**	**7 984**	**4 277**	**6 557**
Employed	2 880 619	245 762	156 411	26 808	9 217	53 326	5 170	13 142	747	2 500	1 130	2 254
Unemployed	541 322	70 667	46 224	9 490	1 766	13 187	1 824	3 599	111	673	408	485
Not in labor force	3 530 010	433 120	279 550	56 305	11 026	86 239	10 663	24 992	979	4 795	2 718	3 787
Females 20 to 24 years	**9 176 002**	**1 001 048**	**620 848**	**125 412**	**33 778**	**221 010**	**24 988**	**71 003**	**2 755**	**14 547**	**7 329**	**10 562**
Employed	5 946 615	547 862	333 439	59 998	23 829	130 596	12 515	41 133	1 687	8 220	4 023	6 542
Unemployed	605 852	85 076	53 262	11 410	1 648	18 756	2 733	7 075	259	1 487	791	996
Not in labor force	2 564 310	363 779	232 037	53 104	8 173	70 465	9 661	22 555	789	4 758	2 515	2 993
Females 25 to 54 years	**53 809 217**	**4 414 333**	**2 481 975**	**570 183**	**225 206**	**1 136 969**	**132 490**	**334 701**	**15 208**	**66 968**	**36 913**	**49 235**
Employed	37 761 559	2 588 841	1 425 465	294 585	155 453	713 338	64 947	212 369	9 279	40 716	22 021	32 393
Unemployed	2 079 910	280 510	158 298	34 686	11 449	76 077	12 482	25 479	794	5 067	3 167	3 718
Not in labor force	13 863 239	1 539 234	895 494	239 481	58 116	346 143	54 948	96 645	5 132	21 154	11 694	13 110
Females 55 to 64 years	**11 163 747**	**622 648**	**316 783**	**79 087**	**72 701**	**154 077**	**15 077**	**31 088**	**2 209**	**5 108**	**3 874**	**6 061**
Employed	4 894 548	237 979	109 605	24 191	35 506	68 677	5 763	14 542	1 154	2 487	1 818	2 654
Unemployed	199 774	21 939	11 067	2 127	2 790	5 955	872	1 361	97	239	152	315
Not in labor force	6 068 702	362 666	196 075	52 761	34 391	79 439	8 436	15 185	958	2 382	1 904	3 092
Females 65 to 69 years	**5 604 849**	**228 685**	**115 202**	**26 570**	**30 782**	**56 131**	**5 409**	**10 370**	**746**	**1 454**	**1 109**	**2 025**
In labor force	944 717	34 580	15 379	2 719	6 227	10 255	723	1 971	130	200	255	349
Not in labor force	4 660 132	194 105	99 823	23 851	24 555	45 876	4 686	8 399	616	1 254	854	1 676
Did not work in 1989	4 202 287	179 969	93 261	22 630	22 364	41 714	4 430	7 692	564	1 119	788	1 512
Females 70 years and over	**13 076 358**	**391 853**	**181 502**	**41 731**	**68 033**	**100 587**	**8 012**	**17 020**	**1 329**	**2 374**	**1 586**	**3 757**
In labor force	632 342	20 327	8 516	1 836	3 280	6 695	420	1 637	86	335	177	384
Not in labor force	12 444 016	371 526	172 986	39 895	64 753	93 892	7 592	15 383	1 243	2 039	1 409	3 373
Did not work in 1989	11 840 761	359 792	167 554	38 958	63 140	90 140	7 427	14 797	1 167	1 910	1 336	3 304
PRESENCE OF OWN CHILDREN IN FAMILIES AND SUBFAMILIES												
Females 16 years and over	**99 803 358**	**7 410 116**	**4 199 653**	**935 918**	**452 536**	**1 822 009**	**203 648**	**506 073**	**24 100**	**98 435**	**55 088**	**78 197**
With own children under 6 years	15 233 818	1 727 350	1 097 914	209 075	54 890	365 471	49 833	115 922	4 856	23 074	12 943	16 017
In labor force	9 095 156	891 044	562 818	90 779	35 256	202 191	21 728	67 899	2 655	12 228	6 976	10 071
With own children 6 to 17 years only	16 490 186	1 450 539	849 856	200 512	65 160	335 011	40 142	93 720	4 996	17 493	9 269	15 886
In labor force	12 367 705	951 201	553 753	114 915	47 591	234 942	23 455	68 683	3 333	12 050	6 636	11 931
Own children under 6 years living with two parents	**15 993 967**	**1 772 746**	**1 252 793**	**149 687**	**49 457**	**320 809**	**26 297**	**82 092**	**3 466**	**16 431**	**7 787**	**12 010**
Both parents in labor force	8 874 102	869 378	594 535	75 117	29 401	170 325	12 621	44 473	1 793	8 165	3 812	7 089
Both at work 35 or more hours	4 433 879	461 911	314 887	40 398	18 199	88 427	6 922	22 979	836	3 998	1 946	3 856
Own children under 6 years living with one parent	**5 279 645**	**885 737**	**536 817**	**169 117**	**17 213**	**162 590**	**30 737**	**40 315**	**1 057**	**7 517**	**4 513**	**5 422**
Parent in labor force	3 169 479	478 875	310 500	61 773	10 793	95 809	11 571	29 431	793	5 356	2 961	4 002
At work 35 or more hours	1 936 665	301 344	196 285	35 532	7 657	61 870	6 820	20 347	539	3 603	1 934	2 909
Own children 6 to 17 years living with two parents	**29 673 627**	**3 105 443**	**2 179 356**	**277 358**	**84 854**	**563 875**	**45 980**	**148 891**	**7 015**	**30 451**	**13 639**	**27 805**
Both parents in labor force	19 477 241	1 744 245	1 187 982	154 803	55 925	345 535	25 017	93 863	3 883	17 131	7 887	19 090
Both at work 35 or more hours	10 782 593	965 041	645 517	89 021	36 803	193 700	14 515	52 801	2 075	8 913	4 429	11 457
Own children 6 to 17 years living with one parent	**9 931 854**	**1 395 753**	**798 517**	**289 069**	**31 682**	**276 485**	**51 125**	**70 614**	**2 574**	**12 248**	**8 045**	**11 579**
Parent in labor force	7 343 393	893 017	544 944	131 817	23 244	193 012	23 450	57 774	2 001	9 869	6 065	9 679
At work 35 or more hours	5 231 410	607 654	369 685	85 795	17 396	134 778	14 991	42 110	1 548	6 870	4 178	7 444

Table 117. Labor Force Characteristics for Selected Hispanic Origin Groups: 1990—Con.

[Data based on sample and subject to sampling variability, see text. For definitions of terms and meanings of symbols, see text]

United States	Central American—Con.			South American								All other Hispanic origin	Not of Hispanic origin
	Panamanian	Salvadoran	Other Central American	Total	Argentinean	Chilean	Colombian	Ecuadorian	Peruvian	Venezuelan	Other South American		
LABOR FORCE STATUS													
Persons 16 years and over	72 495	420 598	5 237	811 411	83 822	53 634	293 543	150 459	136 730	36 083	57 140	1 361 776	176 803 369
In labor force	51 138	319 089	3 758	596 160	61 456	39 711	214 553	109 995	102 968	24 914	42 563	893 445	115 043 308
Percent of persons 16 years and over	70.5	75.9	71.8	73.5	73.3	74.0	73.1	73.1	75.3	69.0	74.5	65.6	65.1
Armed Forces	2 002	739	34	4 277	393	361	1 441	888	569	259	366	14 641	1 591 581
Civilian labor force	49 136	318 350	3 724	591 883	61 063	39 350	213 112	109 107	102 399	24 655	42 197	878 804	113 451 727
Employed	44 617	284 923	3 270	545 925	57 951	36 949	195 240	98 957	94 445	22 924	39 459	801 982	106 699 686
At work 35 or more hours	34 880	227 688	2 579	431 879	45 674	28 616	153 794	80 704	74 736	17 605	30 750	614 339	82 350 379
Unemployed	4 519	33 427	454	45 958	3 112	2 401	17 872	10 150	7 954	1 731	2 738	76 822	6 752 041
Percent of civilian labor force	9.2	10.5	12.2	7.8	5.1	6.1	8.4	9.3	7.8	7.0	6.5	8.7	6.0
Not in labor force	21 357	101 509	1 479	215 251	22 366	13 923	78 990	40 464	33 762	11 169	14 577	468 331	61 760 061
Institutionalized persons	969	2 579	13	7 736	339	158	5 613	533	579	257	257	32 047	2 992 338
Females 16 years and over	43 286	204 286	2 681	416 800	41 227	27 348	157 060	74 996	68 938	18 477	28 754	695 488	92 393 242
In labor force	28 203	132 464	1 651	264 351	25 353	17 212	100 921	46 657	44 828	10 797	18 583	405 028	52 527 263
Percent of females 16 years and over	65.2	64.8	61.6	63.4	61.5	62.9	64.3	62.2	65.0	58.4	64.6	58.2	56.9
Armed Forces	270	32	8	359	87	47	72	46	47	26	34	1 915	173 557
Civilian labor force	27 933	132 432	1 643	263 992	25 266	17 165	100 849	46 611	44 781	10 771	18 549	403 113	52 353 706
Employed	25 121	116 446	1 403	239 071	23 702	15 971	90 467	41 345	40 580	9 772	17 234	368 205	49 307 437
At work 35 or more hours	18 502	84 358	1 052	169 421	16 122	11 033	64 310	30 805	28 647	6 718	11 786	255 684	33 813 528
Unemployed	2 812	15 986	240	24 921	1 564	1 194	10 382	5 266	4 201	999	1 315	34 908	3 046 269
Percent of civilian labor force	10.1	12.1	14.6	9.4	6.2	7.0	10.3	11.3	9.4	9.3	7.1	8.7	5.8
Not in labor force	15 083	71 822	1 030	152 449	15 874	10 136	56 139	28 339	24 110	7 680	10 171	290 460	39 865 979
Institutionalized persons	109	367	5	1 278	95	56	860	68	84	44	71	5 809	1 447 923
Males 16 to 19 years	2 939	24 024	268	32 039	3 166	2 011	10 891	6 451	5 617	1 459	2 444	66 548	6 493 330
Employed	883	10 200	104	11 850	1 265	773	4 150	2 205	2 047	530	880	24 415	2 634 510
Unemployed	347	2 404	33	2 638	190	172	901	667	502	78	128	7 043	573 155
Not in labor force	1 594	11 342	131	16 997	1 668	1 045	5 655	3 456	2 971	845	1 357	33 790	3 150 782
Males 20 to 24 years	4 303	43 411	309	48 205	4 193	3 010	16 604	10 821	7 951	2 387	3 239	90 294	8 271 806
Employed	2 343	33 653	216	33 426	2 833	2 103	11 701	7 607	5 666	1 450	2 066	57 777	5 565 960
Unemployed	361	4 214	13	3 535	277	186	1 143	962	587	127	253	8 023	650 610
Not in labor force	1 179	5 224	75	9 952	988	624	3 335	1 904	1 530	717	854	20 242	1 617 392
Males 25 to 54 years	18 287	140 372	1 839	268 643	27 525	17 911	94 179	49 455	46 910	12 674	19 989	385 457	48 153 027
Employed	14 555	119 992	1 498	232 284	24 819	15 783	79 326	42 617	41 629	10 573	17 537	303 990	41 136 894
Unemployed	826	10 198	155	12 728	862	763	4 680	2 803	2 218	508	894	23 589	2 128 670
Not in labor force	1 709	9 873	165	21 572	1 683	1 169	9 414	3 664	2 806	1 459	1 377	50 756	4 047 269
Males 55 to 64 years	1 956	5 355	70	31 407	5 472	2 380	10 361	5 823	4 864	672	1 835	60 024	9 413 554
Employed	1 362	3 819	49	25 004	4 560	1 984	8 262	4 517	3 767	454	1 460	37 196	6 030 560
Unemployed	103	485	—	1 722	175	68	645	344	355	10	125	2 324	264 626
Not in labor force	491	1 051	21	4 668	730	328	1 454	962	742	208	244	20 458	3 113 440
Males 65 to 69 years	812	1 464	34	6 371	1 029	413	1 912	1 317	1 145	160	395	24 148	4 372 608
In labor force	372	588	13	3 161	522	238	949	559	613	85	195	6 784	1 214 387
Not in labor force	440	876	21	3 210	507	175	963	758	532	75	200	17 364	3 158 221
Did not work in 1989	381	762	21	2 542	383	161	771	642	386	61	138	14 354	2 567 624
Males 70 years and over	912	1 686	36	7 946	1 210	561	2 536	1 596	1 305	254	484	39 817	7 705 802
In labor force	51	365	—	1 543	294	115	506	215	234	69	110	4 556	898 824
Not in labor force	861	1 321	36	6 403	916	446	2 030	1 381	1 071	185	374	35 261	6 806 978
Did not work in 1989	742	1 216	36	5 836	828	420	1 859	1 262	966	163	338	32 368	6 084 207
Females 16 to 19 years	3 283	17 748	189	29 762	3 036	2 010	10 230	5 378	5 314	1 384	2 390	63 510	6 221 638
Employed	1 072	6 410	29	11 022	1 209	833	3 852	1 844	1 956	446	882	23 992	2 634 857
Unemployed	317	1 585	20	2 146	235	149	809	337	421	77	118	5 618	470 655
Not in labor force	1 842	10 731	140	16 545	1 572	1 020	5 573	3 197	2 932	861	1 390	34 039	3 096 890
Females 20 to 24 years	4 726	30 742	342	44 574	4 246	2 477	16 124	8 427	7 987	2 184	3 129	80 445	8 174 954
Employed	2 487	17 980	194	27 979	2 744	1 608	10 340	5 186	4 991	1 131	1 979	48 969	5 398 753
Unemployed	451	3 066	25	3 012	191	153	1 059	713	585	132	179	5 936	520 776
Not in labor force	1 699	9 686	115	13 391	1 253	704	4 674	2 515	2 369	913	963	24 858	2 200 531
Females 25 to 54 years	27 450	137 164	1 763	276 739	24 648	17 806	107 659	49 116	45 521	12 924	19 065	393 039	49 394 884
Employed	19 078	87 819	1 063	177 366	16 070	11 639	68 271	30 529	30 356	7 648	12 853	258 656	35 172 718
Unemployed	1 868	10 670	195	17 485	910	735	7 578	3 769	2 875	713	905	20 631	1 799 400
Not in labor force	6 375	38 675	505	81 770	7 659	5 405	31 805	14 785	12 290	4 545	5 281	112 780	12 324 005
Females 55 to 64 years	3 834	9 801	201	37 593	5 521	2 961	13 257	6 688	5 565	1 173	2 428	70 319	10 541 099
Employed	1 974	4 371	84	19 062	3 138	1 582	6 635	3 209	2 769	458	1 271	29 310	4 656 569
Unemployed	102	456	—	1 877	202	143	784	375	239	56	78	1 845	177 835
Not in labor force	1 758	4 974	117	16 654	2 181	1 236	5 838	3 104	2 557	659	1 079	39 164	5 706 036
Females 65 to 69 years	1 465	3 522	49	11 245	1 465	788	4 047	2 078	1 811	319	737	29 107	5 376 164
In labor force	395	633	9	2 801	347	198	1 102	463	433	70	188	4 760	910 137
Not in labor force	1 070	2 889	40	8 444	1 118	590	2 945	1 615	1 378	249	549	24 347	4 466 027
Did not work in 1989	1 002	2 667	40	7 666	988	570	2 702	1 450	1 197	223	536	21 926	4 022 318
Females 70 years and over	2 528	5 309	137	16 887	2 311	1 306	5 723	3 309	2 740	493	1 005	58 668	12 684 505
In labor force	189	442	24	1 242	220	125	419	186	156	40	96	3 396	612 015
Not in labor force	2 339	4 867	113	15 645	2 091	1 181	5 304	3 123	2 584	453	909	55 272	12 072 490
Did not work in 1989	2 249	4 723	108	15 046	2 012	1 150	5 115	3 038	2 444	443	844	52 870	11 480 969
PRESENCE OF OWN CHILDREN IN FAMILIES AND SUBFAMILIES													
Females 16 years and over	43 286	204 286	2 681	416 800	41 227	27 348	157 060	74 996	68 938	18 477	28 754	695 488	92 393 242
With own children under 6 years	8 086	50 445	501	80 397	6 545	4 896	30 159	14 954	13 844	4 296	5 703	119 319	13 506 468
In labor force	5 070	30 581	318	44 947	3 397	2 518	16 845	8 209	8 191	2 283	3 504	67 617	8 204 112
With own children 6 to 17 years only	8 898	36 520	658	80 174	7 532	5 380	29 890	15 813	12 687	2 958	5 914	120 975	15 039 647
In labor force	7 115	27 119	499	56 066	4 880	4 041	21 126	10 989	9 006	1 791	4 233	86 738	11 416 504
Own children under 6 years living with two parents	5 016	36 932	450	65 470	4 919	5 119	24 127	10 903	12 025	3 657	4 720	146 950	14 221 221
Both parents in labor force	2 981	20 364	269	34 426	2 408	2 515	12 763	5 736	6 356	1 838	2 810	78 805	8 004 724
Both at work 35 or more hours	1 542	10 664	137	17 548	1 207	1 283	6 468	3 102	3 369	820	1 299	40 978	3 971 968
Own children under 6 years living with one parent	2 344	19 192	270	18 775	747	826	8 093	4 014	3 141	845	1 109	72 763	4 393 908
Parent in labor force	1 631	14 471	217	12 861	468	600	5 601	2 340	2 322	623	907	41 946	2 690 604
At work 35 or more hours	1 018	10 190	154	9 005	313	404	3 895	1 547	1 670	397	779	25 698	1 635 321
Own children 6 to 17 years living with two parents	8 633	60 631	717	116 741	11 293	8 669	41 468	20 918	20 012	5 832	8 549	252 263	26 568 184
Both parents in labor force	5 807	39 545	520	72 256	6 361	5 631	25 431	13 346	12 809	3 185	5 493	154 399	17 732 996
Both at work 35 or more hours	3 499	22 089	339	40 224	3 473	3 103	13 975	7 612	7 172	1 713	3 176	86 160	9 817 552
Own children 6 to 17 years living with one parent	4 874	30 786	508	40 165	2 261	2 069	16 616	8 309	6 198	2 116	2 596	114 581	8 536 101
Parent in labor force	4 096	25 621	443	31 640	1 857	1 827	13 445	5 597	5 224	1 590	2 100	80 148	6 450 376
At work 35 or more hours	3 066	18 701	303	23 194	1 386	1 354	9 953	3 853	3 821	1 122	1 705	54 483	4 623 756

Table 118. **Additional Labor Force Characteristics and Veteran Status for Selected Hispanic Origin Groups: 1990**

[Data based on sample and subject to sampling variability, see text. For definitions of terms and meanings of symbols, see text]

United States		Hispanic origin (of any race)										
						Other Hispanic						
								Central American				
	All persons	Total	Mexican	Puerto Rican	Cuban	Total	Dominican (Dominican Republic)	Total	Costa Rican	Guate-malan	Honduran	Nicaraguan
LABOR FORCE STATUS OF FAMILY MEMBERS												
Married-couple families	**51 718 214**	**3 339 694**	**2 027 520**	**353 483**	**230 617**	**728 074**	**63 556**	**180 231**	**9 279**	**36 976**	**16 240**	**28 534**
Husband employed or in Armed Forces	39 286 822	2 705 020	1 649 212	274 503	181 107	600 198	50 179	159 218	8 202	32 795	13 733	25 270
Wife employed or in Armed Forces	25 799 947	1 507 531	873 731	159 219	113 179	361 402	27 177	93 538	4 892	17 752	7 579	15 686
Wife unemployed	1 071 291	139 805	86 574	14 333	7 063	31 835	3 909	10 736	292	2 302	964	1 646
Husband unemployed	1 364 119	166 465	109 722	18 187	7 127	31 429	4 687	8 721	317	1 816	871	1 280
Wife employed or in Armed Forces	790 277	77 407	47 001	8 617	4 107	17 682	2 350	5 219	195	933	506	791
Wife unemployed	127 477	22 759	16 288	1 894	760	3 817	782	994	46	275	83	103
Husband not in labor force	11 067 273	468 209	268 586	60 793	42 383	96 447	8 690	12 292	760	2 365	1 636	1 984
Wife employed or in Armed Forces	2 383 825	124 853	69 397	15 543	10 898	29 015	2 976	5 043	225	1 114	698	776
Wife unemployed	127 210	13 606	8 207	1 773	807	2 819	519	497	32	105	30	117
Female householder, no husband present	**10 381 654**	**1 029 646**	**505 042**	**229 639**	**48 072**	**246 893**	**52 333**	**64 344**	**3 104**	**10 846**	**8 080**	**8 851**
Employed or in Armed Forces	6 031 687	513 905	264 713	78 675	28 414	142 103	18 614	44 581	2 011	7 441	5 135	6 196
Unemployed	593 069	72 294	37 136	15 166	2 370	17 622	4 318	4 652	172	850	656	618
SCHOOL ENROLLMENT AND LABOR FORCE STATUS												
Persons 16 to 19 years	**14 315 448**	**1 600 482**	**1 040 760**	**190 684**	**46 695**	**322 343**	**35 312**	**94 772**	**3 659**	**18 439**	**8 633**	**15 590**
Enrolled in school	11 073 188	1 107 108	695 537	130 883	37 704	242 984	26 728	66 827	2 947	12 292	6 470	12 167
Employed	4 159 951	337 581	210 994	35 009	14 894	76 684	6 435	19 682	1 077	3 442	1 671	4 196
Unemployed	756 835	97 075	61 978	12 242	2 942	19 913	2 801	5 538	157	1 009	607	1 103
Not in labor force	6 136 105	670 487	421 525	83 335	19 773	145 854	17 430	41 527	1 697	7 812	4 181	6 868
Not enrolled in school	3 242 260	493 374	345 223	59 801	8 991	79 359	8 584	27 945	712	6 147	2 163	3 423
High school graduate	1 636 766	146 313	95 051	19 949	3 614	27 699	2 714	6 085	298	1 294	582	936
Employed	1 042 647	84 851	57 043	9 889	2 296	15 623	1 284	3 381	217	734	233	558
Unemployed	180 695	18 265	11 832	2 603	363	3 467	427	738	1	111	96	91
Not in labor force	274 277	32 235	19 948	5 144	703	6 440	820	1 527	53	404	206	208
Not high school graduate	1 605 494	347 061	250 172	39 852	5 377	51 660	5 870	21 860	414	4 853	1 581	2 487
Employed	640 453	151 252	114 335	10 956	2 328	23 633	2 194	11 685	201	2 736	651	1 334
Unemployed	274 320	52 700	37 280	7 432	810	7 178	802	2 807	58	628	284	232
Not in labor force	681 990	141 978	97 856	21 329	2 219	20 574	2 861	7 332	148	1 462	646	921
CLASS OF WORKER												
Employed persons 16 years and over	**115 681 202**	**8 981 516**	**5 323 210**	**925 893**	**531 023**	**2 201 390**	**196 988**	**656 495**	**28 432**	**137 291**	**60 560**	**97 402**
Private wage and salary workers	89 541 393	7 398 601	4 410 646	726 160	433 905	1 827 890	167 969	579 318	23 407	122 768	52 668	86 462
Local government workers	8 244 755	577 730	331 241	93 698	36 525	116 266	12 078	23 918	1 747	3 946	2 542	3 209
State government workers	5 381 445	299 289	179 887	36 018	13 761	69 623	3 792	10 780	936	1 810	1 219	1 571
Federal government workers	3 940 900	252 848	146 025	41 135	9 275	56 413	2 771	9 342	523	1 219	860	1 217
Self-employed workers	8 067 483	421 198	236 264	26 379	35 693	122 862	9 363	31 061	1 719	7 130	3 023	4 556
Unpaid family workers	505 226	31 850	19 147	2 503	1 864	8 336	1 015	2 076	100	418	248	387
Employed females 16 years and over	**52 976 623**	**3 669 186**	**2 046 146**	**409 485**	**232 782**	**980 773**	**89 286**	**284 211**	**13 053**	**54 385**	**29 346**	**44 457**
Private wage and salary workers	40 693 002	2 930 933	1 624 640	313 800	191 747	800 746	75 529	243 194	10 376	46 821	24 855	39 011
Local government workers	4 617 771	306 212	174 150	48 522	19 574	63 966	7 039	13 737	1 171	2 101	1 605	1 866
State government workers	3 002 677	170 398	104 555	20 156	7 527	38 160	2 242	6 312	520	1 053	744	884
Federal government workers	1 663 488	103 373	58 507	16 844	4 002	24 020	1 316	4 269	170	516	431	373
Self-employed workers	2 708 708	143 506	76 101	8 965	8 798	49 642	2 826	15 574	753	3 648	1 574	2 049
Unpaid family workers	290 977	14 764	8 193	1 198	1 134	4 239	334	1 125	63	246	137	274
WORK STATUS IN 1989												
Persons 16 years and over, worked in 1989	**134 529 779**	**10 334 670**	**6 139 622**	**1 107 071**	**594 506**	**2 493 471**	**230 483**	**716 602**	**31 646**	**148 595**	**67 669**	**105 992**
50 to 52 weeks	84 533 428	5 647 572	3 223 303	649 301	385 665	1 389 303	125 698	380 427	18 537	77 386	35 107	57 124
48 and 49 weeks	5 825 217	765 230	476 442	64 783	35 965	188 040	14 681	70 422	2 035	15 823	5 127	9 536
40 to 47 weeks	11 370 482	934 356	562 624	89 363	49 406	232 963	20 641	71 416	3 200	15 295	6 979	10 286
27 to 39 weeks	10 110 388	921 507	584 538	85 107	39 721	212 141	20 586	62 871	2 547	13 031	6 272	8 848
14 to 26 weeks	11 628 106	1 088 172	679 291	108 472	45 727	254 682	26 516	74 304	3 079	15 617	8 027	10 531
1 to 13 weeks	11 062 158	977 833	613 424	110 045	38 022	216 342	22 361	57 162	2 248	11 443	6 157	9 667
Usually worked 35 or more hours per week	105 361 883	8 419 788	4 998 591	909 241	496 888	2 015 068	193 485	591 286	24 816	123 850	54 978	85 958
40 or more weeks	87 097 175	6 469 552	3 758 471	712 896	416 696	1 581 489	143 568	460 194	20 342	96 069	41 083	67 238
50 to 52 weeks	74 660 124	5 095 863	2 907 960	590 879	350 067	1 246 957	114 467	342 949	16 422	69 771	31 308	51 159
27 to 39 weeks	6 296 616	655 046	421 752	60 564	27 165	145 565	15 821	44 869	1 464	9 332	4 456	6 320
Females 16 years and over, worked in 1989	**61 904 615**	**4 304 180**	**2 432 824**	**485 691**	**261 189**	**1 124 476**	**106 281**	**316 720**	**14 825**	**60 824**	**32 991**	**49 171**
50 to 52 weeks	35 419 603	2 169 391	1 168 094	262 306	159 472	579 519	52 730	158 522	8 028	29 888	16 235	24 658
48 and 49 weeks	2 692 119	294 147	169 919	26 968	15 678	81 582	6 803	29 493	820	6 008	2 525	4 234
40 to 47 weeks	5 996 730	402 590	224 060	43 470	24 256	110 804	10 339	31 832	1 665	6 076	3 541	4 792
27 to 39 weeks	5 569 882	418 945	250 043	42 887	19 898	106 117	10 360	28 881	1 437	5 562	2 979	4 293
14 to 26 weeks	6 241 320	519 212	310 361	54 244	23 025	131 582	14 078	37 294	1 492	7 559	4 187	5 758
1 to 13 weeks	5 984 961	499 895	310 347	55 816	18 860	114 872	11 971	30 698	1 383	5 731	3 524	5 436
Usually worked 35 or more hours per week	42 973 185	3 169 835	1 770 796	365 284	205 001	828 754	85 062	239 536	10 469	45 883	24 753	37 246
40 or more weeks	34 274 397	2 336 251	1 265 114	275 833	167 644	627 660	59 749	180 457	8 281	34 335	18 309	27 805
50 to 52 weeks	28 714 940	1 833 090	979 525	225 964	138 480	489 121	46 340	134 322	6 639	25 166	13 739	21 008
27 to 39 weeks	3 061 761	260 702	155 873	27 800	12 533	64 496	7 757	18 369	705	3 378	1 841	2 955
WORKERS IN FAMILY IN 1989												
Families	**65 049 428**	**4 776 075**	**2 776 147**	**627 527**	**295 380**	**1 077 021**	**126 991**	**284 787**	**13 279**	**56 978**	**27 445**	**42 608**
No workers	8 477 151	533 688	250 352	142 023	33 459	107 854	26 104	15 649	806	2 897	2 429	1 915
1 worker	18 243 077	1 492 336	879 383	201 754	82 809	328 390	40 535	88 099	4 140	17 805	9 413	11 992
2 workers	29 637 580	1 914 539	1 125 132	213 368	127 374	448 665	39 626	118 720	5 882	23 557	11 050	18 197
3 or more workers	8 691 620	835 512	521 280	70 382	51 738	192 112	20 726	62 319	2 451	12 719	4 553	10 504
Married-couple families	**51 718 214**	**3 339 694**	**2 027 520**	**353 483**	**230 617**	**728 074**	**63 556**	**180 231**	**9 279**	**36 976**	**16 240**	**28 534**
No workers	6 129 613	219 748	117 337	33 576	22 054	46 781	3 984	5 498	281	875	767	880
1 worker	11 870 620	874 426	547 194	93 178	53 966	180 088	18 463	43 563	2 347	9 872	4 344	6 065
2 or more workers	33 717 981	2 245 520	1 362 989	226 729	154 597	501 205	41 109	131 170	6 651	26 229	11 129	21 589
Husband and wife worked	30 599 124	1 860 282	1 103 527	192 757	131 069	432 929	33 429	111 626	5 692	21 599	9 328	18 383
Female householder, no husband present	**10 381 654**	**1 029 646**	**505 042**	**229 639**	**48 072**	**246 893**	**52 333**	**64 344**	**3 104**	**10 846**	**8 080**	**8 851**
No workers	2 056 800	283 838	117 880	101 598	9 640	54 720	20 992	8 522	477	1 688	1 428	814
1 worker	4 929 373	432 787	224 041	85 576	20 592	102 578	17 000	27 341	1 391	4 213	3 571	3 689
2 or more workers	3 395 481	313 021	163 121	42 465	17 840	89 595	14 341	28 481	1 236	4 945	3 081	4 348
VETERAN STATUS AND PERIOD OF SERVICE												
Civilian veterans 16 years and over	**27 481 055**	**944 900**	**571 144**	**147 292**	**32 485**	**193 979**	**7 237**	**20 426**	**1 722**	**2 476**	**2 388**	**3 137**
Male	26 330 011	901 021	548 339	138 663	30 855	183 164	6 672	18 535	1 594	2 208	2 156	2 910
May 1975 or later service only	3 352 156	223 132	122 578	43 891	9 950	46 713	3 624	8 331	668	992	880	1 175
September 1980 or later service only	1 900 833	127 917	68 561	25 170	6 259	27 927	2 162	5 304	388	711	471	813
Served 2 or more years	1 603 440	108 366	58 140	21 426	5 491	23 309	1 762	4 413	325	568	399	697
Vietnam-era service	8 232 414	344 587	215 931	54 425	10 468	63 763	2 335	7 438	651	876	794	987
World War II service	8 970 114	172 673	108 689	17 452	4 386	42 146	391	1 457	135	189	252	226

Table 118. Additional Labor Force Characteristics and Veteran Status for Selected Hispanic Origin Groups: 1990—Con.

[Data based on sample and subject to sampling variability, see text. For definitions of terms and meanings of symbols, see text]

United States	Central American—Con. Panamanian	Salvadoran	Other Central American	South American Total	Argentinean	Chilean	Colombian	Ecuadorian	Peruvian	Venezuelan	Other South American	All other Hispanic origin	Not of Hispanic origin
LABOR FORCE STATUS OF FAMILY MEMBERS													
Married-couple families	13 027	75 170	1 005	183 855	23 810	13 589	60 828	32 957	30 418	8 201	14 052	300 432	48 378 520
Husband employed or in Armed Forces	11 259	67 099	860	162 454	21 214	12 158	53 945	28 512	27 099	6 979	12 547	228 347	36 581 802
Wife employed or in Armed Forces	7 821	39 271	537	97 128	12 530	7 491	31 677	16 880	16 368	4 322	7 860	143 559	24 292 416
Wife unemployed	586	4 910	36	9 095	795	493	3 219	1 987	1 584	389	628	8 095	931 486
Husband unemployed	410	3 942	85	6 834	546	394	2 415	1 470	1 357	229	423	11 187	1 197 654
Wife employed or in Armed Forces	273	2 488	33	4 014	320	284	1 389	819	804	163	235	6 099	712 870
Wife unemployed	75	391	21	801	51	13	343	137	195	8	54	1 240	104 718
Husband not in labor force	1 358	4 129	60	14 567	2 050	1 037	4 468	2 975	1 962	993	1 082	60 898	10 599 064
Wife employed or in Armed Forces	454	1 757	19	5 515	678	383	1 864	1 113	763	283	431	15 481	2 258 972
Wife unemployed	12	201	–	627	44	56	244	120	82	46	35	1 176	113 604
Female householder, no husband present	7 270	25 684	509	45 334	3 084	2 230	19 004	9 742	6 989	1 763	2 522	84 882	9 352 008
Employed or in Armed Forces	5 204	18 268	326	30 988	2 287	1 698	13 222	5 577	5 092	1 112	2 000	47 920	5 517 782
Unemployed	462	1 859	35	3 150	141	126	1 501	796	443	94	49	5 502	520 775
SCHOOL ENROLLMENT AND LABOR FORCE STATUS													
Persons 16 to 19 years	6 222	41 772	457	61 801	6 202	4 021	21 141	11 829	10 931	2 843	4 834	130 458	12 714 966
Enrolled in school	5 036	27 545	370	51 501	5 282	3 509	17 505	9 711	9 081	2 405	4 008	97 928	9 966 080
Employed	1 506	7 695	95	17 650	2 046	1 351	6 135	3 029	3 014	751	1 324	32 917	3 822 370
Unemployed	438	2 197	27	3 443	288	232	1 223	687	719	120	174	8 131	659 760
Not in labor force	3 073	17 648	248	30 308	2 923	1 918	10 115	5 977	5 331	1 534	2 510	56 589	5 465 618
Not enrolled in school	1 186	14 227	87	10 300	920	512	3 636	2 118	1 850	438	826	32 530	2 748 886
High school graduate	699	2 269	7	5 181	551	254	1 603	1 037	1 085	236	415	13 719	1 490 453
Employed	303	1 329	7	2 834	294	142	937	530	612	114	205	8 124	957 796
Unemployed	149	290	–	613	52	42	198	158	91	26	46	1 689	162 430
Not in labor force	99	557	–	1 280	172	62	310	244	302	90	100	2 813	242 042
Not high school graduate	487	11 958	80	5 119	369	258	2 033	1 081	765	202	411	18 811	1 258 433
Employed	146	6 586	31	2 388	134	113	930	490	377	111	233	7 366	489 201
Unemployed	77	1 502	26	728	85	47	289	159	113	9	26	2 841	221 620
Not in labor force	264	3 868	23	1 954	145	85	803	432	270	82	137	8 427	540 012
CLASS OF WORKER													
Employed persons 16 years and over	44 617	284 923	3 270	545 925	57 951	36 949	195 240	98 957	94 445	22 924	39 459	801 982	106 699 686
Private wage and salary workers	33 299	257 857	2 857	461 923	45 610	30 026	168 047	86 144	80 693	18 546	32 857	618 680	82 142 792
Local government workers	4 762	7 616	96	22 607	2 853	1 658	7 311	4 565	3 559	1 101	1 560	57 663	7 667 025
State government workers	1 995	3 125	124	13 973	2 184	1 318	4 107	1 805	2 402	1 057	1 100	41 078	5 082 156
Federal government workers	3 108	2 344	71	9 219	1 183	742	2 635	1 795	1 611	548	705	35 081	3 688 052
Self-employed workers	1 406	13 105	122	35 879	5 791	3 095	12 234	4 315	5 840	1 550	3 054	46 559	7 646 285
Unpaid family workers	47	876	–	2 324	330	110	906	333	340	122	183	2 921	473 376
Employed females 16 years and over	25 121	116 446	1 403	239 071	23 702	15 971	90 467	41 345	40 580	9 772	17 234	368 205	49 307 437
Private wage and salary workers	18 380	102 599	1 152	199 627	18 247	12 928	77 287	35 140	34 178	7 756	14 091	282 396	37 762 069
Local government workers	3 022	3 906	66	13 342	1 893	1 000	4 356	2 589	1 954	638	912	29 848	4 311 559
State government workers	1 368	1 696	47	7 083	1 043	640	2 156	1 165	1 204	404	482	22 523	2 832 279
Federal government workers	1 597	1 111	71	4 004	461	320	1 149	842	699	230	303	14 431	1 560 115
Self-employed workers	714	6 769	67	13 697	1 847	1 090	4 979	1 467	2 366	618	1 324	17 545	2 565 202
Unpaid family workers	40	365	–	1 318	211	78	540	142	179	46	122	1 462	276 213
WORK STATUS IN 1989													
Persons 16 years and over, worked in 1989	52 658	306 432	3 610	606 318	63 993	41 155	218 112	110 570	103 435	25 786	43 267	940 068	124 195 109
50 to 52 weeks	30 880	159 350	2 043	343 678	37 685	24 064	124 023	62 611	56 429	14 489	24 377	539 500	78 885 856
48 and 49 weeks	3 726	33 917	258	48 956	4 836	3 260	16 619	9 425	9 080	2 020	3 716	53 981	5 059 987
40 to 47 weeks	4 324	31 066	266	59 553	6 333	3 887	21 981	10 675	10 182	2 304	4 191	81 763	10 436 126
27 to 39 weeks	4 039	27 836	298	49 549	4 576	3 428	17 584	9 056	9 339	2 178	3 388	79 135	9 188 881
14 to 26 weeks	4 837	31 840	373	58 745	5 834	3 500	21 753	10 666	10 383	2 558	4 051	95 117	10 539 934
1 to 13 weeks	4 852	22 423	372	45 837	4 729	3 016	16 152	8 137	8 022	2 237	3 544	90 982	10 084 325
Usually worked 35 or more hours per week	42 621	256 053	3 010	491 256	51 043	32 515	176 788	92 131	83 799	20 270	34 710	739 041	96 942 095
40 or more weeks	34 164	199 026	2 272	395 800	42 509	27 093	141 686	73 705	66 340	16 342	28 125	581 927	80 627 623
50 to 52 weeks	27 995	144 449	1 845	310 342	33 976	21 588	111 289	57 311	51 210	13 045	21 923	479 199	69 564 261
27 to 39 weeks	2 585	20 491	221	33 031	2 691	2 162	12 046	6 376	6 253	1 298	2 205	51 844	5 641 570
Females 16 years and over, worked in 1989	28 938	128 372	1 599	270 070	26 859	18 143	102 506	47 264	45 144	11 208	18 946	431 405	57 600 435
50 to 52 weeks	15 991	62 836	886	138 708	13 938	9 618	52 709	24 556	22 517	5 678	9 692	229 559	33 250 212
48 and 49 weeks	2 109	13 677	120	20 349	1 922	1 353	7 383	3 811	3 532	757	1 591	24 937	2 397 972
40 to 47 weeks	2 654	12 997	107	28 492	3 113	1 855	11 112	4 688	4 618	1 092	2 014	40 141	5 594 140
27 to 39 weeks	2 488	11 985	137	25 868	2 437	1 640	9 801	4 592	4 606	1 136	1 656	41 008	5 150 937
14 to 26 weeks	2 691	15 403	204	31 911	3 097	1 974	12 405	5 338	5 547	1 378	2 172	48 299	5 722 108
1 to 13 weeks	3 005	11 474	145	24 742	2 352	1 703	9 096	4 279	4 324	1 167	1 821	47 461	5 485 066
Usually worked 35 or more hours per week	22 217	97 732	1 236	198 089	18 753	12 867	75 809	36 401	32 863	7 902	13 494	306 067	39 803 350
40 or more weeks	17 426	73 385	916	152 306	14 965	10 316	57 935	27 656	24 857	6 087	10 490	235 148	31 938 146
50 to 52 weeks	14 002	53 026	742	117 822	11 623	8 036	44 708	21 446	19 206	4 798	8 005	190 637	26 881 850
27 to 39 weeks	1 565	7 831	94	15 049	1 184	864	5 899	2 920	2 665	610	907	23 321	2 801 059
WORKERS IN FAMILY IN 1989													
Families	21 622	121 115	1 740	251 987	28 463	17 167	88 617	47 058	41 918	10 634	18 130	413 256	60 273 353
No workers	1 704	5 711	187	13 811	1 427	581	4 572	3 743	1 794	865	829	52 290	7 943 463
1 worker	6 892	37 296	561	73 815	8 736	5 054	26 848	12 386	12 018	3 526	5 247	125 941	16 750 741
2 workers	9 740	49 577	717	114 736	13 775	8 394	39 868	19 717	19 137	5 199	8 646	175 583	27 723 041
3 or more workers	3 286	28 531	275	49 625	4 525	3 138	17 329	11 212	8 969	1 044	3 408	59 442	7 856 108
Married-couple families	13 027	75 170	1 005	183 855	23 810	13 589	60 828	32 957	30 418	8 201	14 052	300 432	48 378 520
No workers	662	1 995	38	6 348	886	344	1 850	1 436	915	496	421	30 951	5 909 865
1 worker	2 579	18 095	261	45 875	6 627	3 305	15 384	7 491	7 300	2 313	3 455	72 187	10 996 194
2 or more workers	9 786	55 080	706	131 632	16 297	9 940	43 594	24 030	22 203	5 392	10 176	197 294	31 472 461
Husband and wife worked	9 044	46 932	648	113 850	14 386	8 728	37 292	19 913	19 491	5 020	9 020	174 024	28 738 842
Female householder, no husband present	7 270	25 684	509	45 334	3 084	2 230	19 004	9 742	6 989	1 763	2 522	84 882	9 352 008
No workers	929	3 062	124	6 369	401	203	2 295	2 151	723	283	313	18 837	1 772 962
1 worker	3 602	10 667	208	18 612	1 348	1 106	7 814	3 348	3 036	855	1 105	39 625	4 496 586
2 or more workers	2 739	11 955	177	20 353	1 335	921	8 895	4 243	3 230	625	1 104	26 420	3 082 460
VETERAN STATUS AND PERIOD OF SERVICE													
Civilian veterans 16 years and over	5 884	4 581	238	20 978	1 947	1 645	7 331	4 474	3 372	890	1 319	145 338	26 536 155
Male	5 369	4 098	200	19 742	1 826	1 562	6 865	4 282	3 202	791	1 214	138 215	25 428 990
May 1975 or later service only	2 328	2 220	68	8 388	583	564	3 374	1 811	1 199	359	498	26 370	3 129 024
September 1980 or later service only	1 340	1 543	38	5 298	380	377	2 140	1 080	743	219	359	15 163	1 772 916
Served 2 or more years	1 195	1 191	38	4 498	268	316	1 860	915	614	200	325	12 624	1 495 074
Vietnam-era service	2 573	1 415	142	7 081	694	472	2 359	1 630	1 174	320	432	46 909	7 887 827
World War II service	341	307	7	1 828	221	184	584	254	350	112	123	38 470	8 797 441

Table 119. **Occupation of Employed Persons for Selected Hispanic Origin Groups: 1990**

[Data based on sample and subject to sampling variability, see text. For definitions of terms and meanings of symbols, see text]

United States		Hispanic origin (of any race)										
						Other Hispanic						
								Central American				
	All persons	Total	Mexican	Puerto Rican	Cuban	Total	Dominican (Dominican Republic)	Total	Costa Rican	Guate-malan	Honduran	Nicaraguan
Employed persons 16 years and over	**115 681 202**	**8 981 516**	**5 323 210**	**925 893**	**531 023**	**2 201 390**	**196 988**	**656 495**	**28 432**	**137 291**	**60 560**	**97 402**
Managerial and professional specialty occupations	30 533 582	1 262 178	617 500	158 799	123 158	362 721	21 928	64 589	5 497	10 651	6 292	12 512
Executive, administrative, and managerial occupations	14 227 916	627 693	313 569	74 536	63 492	176 096	11 377	33 883	2 447	5 623	3 156	7 062
Officials and administrators, public administration	578 334	25 469	14 478	3 386	1 433	6 172	176	757	52	174	98	144
Management and related occupations	4 140 575	189 088	93 557	24 350	19 464	51 717	3 236	9 873	663	1 459	832	2 256
Professional specialty occupations	16 305 666	634 485	303 931	84 263	59 666	186 625	10 551	30 706	3 050	5 028	3 136	5 450
Engineers and natural scientists	3 000 976	96 970	40 982	11 349	10 200	34 439	1 389	4 976	563	612	549	1 021
Engineers	1 672 559	52 479	22 608	5 737	5 568	18 566	725	2 693	349	359	289	525
Health diagnosing occupations	869 543	35 277	8 994	4 190	7 520	14 573	1 096	1 829	126	366	211	453
Health assessment and treating occupations	2 482 553	76 252	34 251	12 529	6 373	23 099	1 070	4 383	416	548	471	794
Teachers, librarians, and counselors	5 713 591	238 263	130 463	30 216	18 210	59 374	3 066	9 277	1 143	1 538	868	1 293
Teachers, elementary and secondary schools	3 861 446	165 455	95 434	21 244	12 799	35 978	1 900	5 915	689	1 026	563	707
Technical, sales, and administrative support occupations	36 718 398	2 321 918	1 256 799	295 286	181 129	588 704	51 145	135 770	8 768	22 691	13 450	27 756
Health technologists and technicians	1 397 189	77 782	39 910	11 375	6 173	20 324	1 506	4 803	276	744	564	841
Technologists and technicians, except health	2 860 046	143 367	73 666	16 737	11 345	41 619	2 498	7 732	672	1 256	798	1 366
Sales occupations	13 634 686	808 785	442 449	83 954	66 440	215 942	21 522	50 248	2 923	8 128	4 770	11 989
Supervisors and proprietors, sales occupations	3 352 054	172 723	90 768	18 403	17 595	45 957	5 215	9 085	667	1 527	932	2 351
Sales representatives, commodities and finance	3 941 568	157 289	75 521	16 203	19 970	45 595	3 168	8 492	700	1 065	810	2 168
Other sales occupations	6 341 064	478 773	276 160	49 348	28 875	124 390	13 139	32 671	1 556	5 536	3 028	7 470
Cashiers	2 533 639	232 840	139 974	24 092	10 372	58 402	7 381	16 784	559	2 979	1 458	3 959
Administrative support occupations, including clerical	18 826 477	1 291 984	700 774	183 220	97 171	310 819	25 619	72 987	4 897	12 563	7 318	13 560
Computer equipment operators	640 982	40 615	19 599	6 358	3 261	11 397	921	2 644	152	477	281	493
Secretaries, stenographers, and typists	4 582 070	258 327	135 212	40 738	21 389	60 988	5 227	12 120	1 015	1 961	1 511	2 078
Financial records processing occupations	2 315 205	123 119	63 748	14 994	12 112	32 265	2 129	7 134	464	1 208	762	1 550
Mail and message distributing occupations	990 423	73 208	37 383	14 264	4 248	17 313	1 474	4 078	147	664	352	709
Service occupations	15 295 917	1 719 992	987 215	170 934	69 970	491 873	44 300	191 937	6 145	41 699	17 418	21 614
Private household occupations	521 154	119 588	54 955	3 370	2 170	59 093	1 890	36 127	537	10 406	3 658	2 463
Protective service occupations	1 992 852	134 930	69 045	28 075	8 979	28 831	2 744	5 839	344	932	652	1 193
Police and firefighters	732 609	43 644	23 934	9 101	3 039	7 570	512	877	104	161	123	88
Service occupations, except protective and household	12 781 911	1 465 474	863 215	139 489	58 821	403 949	39 666	149 971	5 264	30 361	13 108	17 958
Food service occupations	5 167 308	608 350	395 711	42 392	17 072	153 175	11 433	58 905	1 825	10 987	4 203	6 448
Cleaning and building service occupations	3 127 932	491 540	276 822	48 612	22 430	143 676	14 936	60 156	1 522	13 108	5 339	7 083
Farming, forestry, and fishing occupations	2 839 010	446 133	383 859	12 584	6 680	43 010	962	17 428	401	4 327	1 272	1 413
Farm operators and managers	1 066 944	33 300	26 947	879	923	4 551	50	910	28	198	64	121
Farm workers and related occupations	1 590 184	403 200	350 088	11 383	4 947	36 782	912	16 135	358	4 056	1 143	1 237
Precision production, craft, and repair occupations	13 097 963	1 177 553	754 241	94 160	62 306	266 846	20 782	88 408	3 424	20 536	8 195	11 556
Mechanics and repairers	4 080 305	315 039	188 924	31 605	19 739	74 771	6 225	22 916	998	5 744	2 108	3 157
Construction trades	4 793 935	452 936	303 565	26 827	22 176	100 368	5 650	37 981	1 240	8 629	3 506	4 758
Precision production occupations	4 047 043	395 605	249 881	35 480	20 288	89 956	8 876	27 340	1 186	6 120	2 535	3 620
Operators, fabricators, and laborers	17 196 332	2 053 742	1 323 596	194 130	87 780	448 236	57 871	158 363	4 197	37 387	13 933	22 551
Machine operators and tenders, except precision	4 981 876	684 988	421 146	68 616	30 594	164 632	24 835	61 451	1 549	15 429	5 105	8 319
Fabricators, assemblers, inspectors, and samplers	2 922 321	362 199	242 266	33 231	13 641	73 061	9 286	25 794	629	6 584	2 115	3 526
Transportation occupations	3 760 910	314 362	181 501	35 771	19 695	77 395	9 694	22 374	977	4 897	2 107	3 756
Motor vehicle operators	3 580 137	307 684	177 637	34 891	19 422	75 734	9 655	22 003	955	4 881	1 914	3 713
Material moving equipment operators	968 091	87 111	65 619	6 895	2 665	11 932	1 095	2 816	106	569	240	422
Handlers, equipment cleaners, helpers, and laborers	4 563 134	605 082	413 064	49 617	21 185	121 216	12 961	45 928	936	9 908	4 366	6 528
Construction laborers	948 540	162 235	119 263	7 301	4 959	30 712	1 769	13 919	214	3 088	1 394	1 421
Freight, stock, and material handlers	1 576 991	145 346	94 702	15 499	5 711	29 434	3 592	8 252	334	1 707	900	1 616
Employed females 16 years and over	**52 976 623**	**3 669 186**	**2 046 146**	**409 485**	**232 782**	**980 773**	**89 286**	**284 211**	**13 053**	**54 385**	**29 346**	**44 457**
Managerial and professional specialty occupations	14 752 659	623 927	310 839	86 241	56 121	170 726	10 510	30 582	2 574	4 567	3 312	5 757
Executive, administrative, and managerial occupations	5 993 163	278 720	140 519	36 280	25 999	75 922	4 815	14 215	1 013	2 095	1 475	2 888
Officials and administrators, public administration	251 316	11 588	6 344	1 849	666	2 729	100	338	29	37	62	55
Management and related occupations	2 156 867	103 345	50 518	14 438	10 606	27 783	1 914	5 023	321	787	454	1 131
Professional specialty occupations	8 759 496	345 207	170 320	49 961	30 122	94 804	5 695	16 367	1 561	2 472	1 837	2 869
Engineers and natural scientists	551 261	21 209	8 753	2 981	2 202	7 273	301	990	93	106	152	186
Engineers	151 962	6 190	2 550	908	706	2 026	67	264	39	49	40	32
Health diagnosing occupations	171 791	7 727	2 253	1 303	1 398	2 773	250	328	14	41	36	90
Health assessment and treating occupations	2 163 863	61 812	27 305	10 147	4 858	19 502	946	3 845	366	390	419	736
Teachers, librarians, and counselors	3 977 806	169 075	93 315	22 315	13 825	39 620	2 099	6 422	777	1 077	632	830
Teachers, elementary and secondary schools	2 946 061	128 741	73 731	17 114	10 554	27 342	1 464	4 616	541	787	458	573
Technical, sales, and administrative support occupations	23 120 191	1 434 647	791 491	183 864	105 910	353 382	28 410	78 998	5 231	12 246	8 814	16 080
Health technologists and technicians	1 133 078	55 644	29 213	8 020	3 979	14 432	1 076	3 171	211	510	415	529
Technologists and technicians, except health	832 879	41 899	21 199	5 004	3 294	12 402	686	2 123	209	330	300	352
Sales occupations	6 584 290	417 587	236 037	44 082	27 198	110 270	9 532	26 257	1 448	3 924	2 711	6 267
Supervisors and proprietors, sales occupations	1 155 921	56 425	30 658	6 135	4 331	15 301	1 135	2 999	193	370	338	816
Sales representatives, commodities and finance	1 314 555	59 102	27 410	6 695	7 049	17 948	1 318	3 522	330	457	384	871
Other sales occupations	4 113 814	302 060	177 969	31 252	15 818	77 021	7 079	19 736	925	3 097	1 989	4 580
Cashiers	1 995 673	171 625	104 844	18 277	7 409	41 095	4 259	11 336	410	1 838	1 066	2 765
Administrative support occupations, including clerical	14 569 944	919 517	505 042	126 758	71 439	216 278	17 116	47 447	3 363	7 482	5 388	8 932
Computer equipment operators	394 508	23 351	11 785	3 838	2 001	5 727	412	1 409	68	256	205	210
Secretaries, stenographers, and typists	4 490 363	250 655	131 387	39 501	20 906	58 861	5 042	11 590	1 004	1 870	1 424	1 996
Financial records processing occupations	2 062 414	102 477	54 458	12 280	9 803	25 936	1 701	5 383	392	895	645	1 120
Mail and message distributing occupations	368 423	22 607	12 279	3 844	1 086	5 398	327	1 328	56	207	119	145
Service occupations	8 929 509	863 229	483 756	72 003	31 826	275 644	22 217	113 433	3 621	24 848	11 485	12 942
Private household occupations	494 920	114 019	52 320	2 955	1 967	56 777	1 765	34 999	496	10 100	3 544	2 394
Protective service occupations	310 463	20 185	10 168	4 218	1 131	4 668	423	867	67	114	144	143
Police and firefighters	66 355	4 581	2 299	1 111	335	836	38	122	–	18	26	6
Service occupations, except protective and household	8 124 126	729 025	421 268	64 830	28 728	214 199	20 029	77 567	3 058	14 634	7 797	10 405
Food service occupations	3 062 435	223 035	144 381	14 797	6 742	57 115	3 176	19 329	628	2 817	1 673	2 910
Cleaning and building service occupations	1 278 437	212 298	120 490	13 989	8 060	69 759	5 760	32 147	858	6 572	2 996	3 783
Farming, forestry, and fishing occupations	449 506	59 747	51 856	1 640	733	5 518	99	1 953	46	404	205	188
Farm operators and managers	149 675	3 646	2 776	104	132	634	–	115	–	5	18	18
Farm workers and related occupations	290 041	55 354	48 547	1 477	541	4 789	99	1 810	46	392	175	170
Precision production, craft, and repair occupations	1 235 327	128 792	75 838	12 086	8 294	32 574	3 829	10 071	410	2 100	971	1 540
Mechanics and repairers	175 669	11 970	6 986	1 250	675	3 059	218	713	67	172	54	137
Construction trades	131 124	9 876	6 285	860	389	2 342	250	693	23	137	73	120
Precision production occupations	923 593	106 538	62 267	9 956	7 223	27 092	3 350	8 651	320	1 782	844	1 278
Operators, fabricators, and laborers	4 489 431	558 844	332 366	53 651	29 898	142 929	24 221	49 174	1 171	10 220	4 559	7 950
Machine operators and tenders, except precision	2 018 059	283 994	159 360	26 420	18 233	79 981	14 205	29 414	659	5 886	2 763	4 785
Fabricators, assemblers, inspectors, and samplers	1 082 797	140 821	88 479	14 289	6 253	31 800	5 183	10 285	326	2 572	855	1 488
Transportation occupations	426 426	22 356	13 384	2 242	1 200	5 530	507	1 332	75	294	146	251
Motor vehicle operators	419 603	21 943	13 136	2 196	1 162	5 449	496	1 307	75	294	126	251
Material moving equipment operators	46 995	4 332	2 313	602	220	1 197	394	244	7	71	–	46
Handlers, equipment cleaners, helpers, and laborers	915 154	107 341	68 830	10 098	3 992	24 421	3 932	7 899	104	1 397	795	1 380
Construction laborers	36 177	4 257	2 772	194	232	1 059	36	426	–	64	56	38
Freight, stock, and material handlers	359 459	27 511	18 416	2 328	781	5 986	576	1 452	27	207	250	288

Table 119. **Occupation of Employed Persons for Selected Hispanic Origin Groups: 1990**—Con.

[Data based on sample and subject to sampling variability, see text. For definitions of terms and meanings of symbols, see text]

United States	Hispanic origin (of any race)—Con.												
	Other Hispanic—Con.												
	Central American—Con.			South American									
	Panamanian	Salvadoran	Other Central American	Total	Argentinean	Chilean	Colombian	Ecuadorian	Peruvian	Venezuelan	Other South American	All other Hispanic origin	Not of Hispanic origin
Employed persons 16 years and over	**44 617**	**284 923**	**3 270**	**545 925**	**57 951**	**36 949**	**195 240**	**98 957**	**94 445**	**22 924**	**39 459**	**801 982**	**106 699 686**
Managerial and professional specialty occupations	11 188	17 972	477	110 186	18 577	10 151	33 419	14 470	17 662	7 700	8 207	166 018	29 271 404
Executive, administrative, and managerial occupations	5 031	10 357	207	50 406	7 691	4 421	15 779	7 431	8 036	3 443	3 605	80 430	13 600 223
Officials and administrators, public administration	150	129	10	1 112	194	115	315	125	141	127	95	4 127	552 865
Management and related occupations	1 990	2 624	49	14 099	1 847	1 126	4 496	2 633	2 203	922	872	24 509	3 951 487
Professional specialty occupations	6 157	7 615	270	59 780	10 886	5 730	17 640	7 039	9 626	4 257	4 602	85 588	15 671 181
Engineers and natural scientists	831	1 375	25	13 160	2 353	1 160	3 842	1 541	1 978	1 309	977	14 914	2 904 006
Engineers	443	717	11	7 180	1 221	606	2 237	804	1 055	767	490	7 968	1 620 080
Health diagnosing occupations	309	358	6	7 041	1 655	533	2 046	560	1 208	285	754	4 607	834 266
Health assessment and treating occupations	1 157	900	97	5 753	551	578	1 992	737	1 145	326	424	11 893	2 406 301
Teachers, librarians, and counselors	2 206	2 144	85	16 680	3 159	1 845	4 580	2 212	2 538	1 157	1 189	30 351	5 475 328
Teachers, elementary and secondary schools	1 520	1 373	37	8 607	1 394	781	2 678	1 340	1 319	502	593	19 556	3 695 991
Technical, sales, and administrative support occupations	17 006	45 246	853	152 456	16 361	9 905	54 635	27 825	25 869	7 447	10 414	249 333	34 396 480
Health technologists and technicians	606	1 734	38	4 767	487	315	1 942	707	773	193	350	9 248	1 319 407
Technologists and technicians, except health	1 124	2 449	67	13 119	1 925	1 053	4 663	1 585	2 114	965	814	18 270	2 716 679
Sales occupations	4 596	17 561	281	56 065	6 701	3 795	20 100	9 617	9 221	3 082	3 549	88 107	12 825 901
Supervisors and proprietors, sales occupations	963	2 585	60	12 398	1 431	952	4 481	2 124	1 783	811	816	19 259	3 179 331
Sales representatives, commodities and finance	996	2 718	35	14 067	2 098	803	5 008	2 265	2 203	940	750	19 868	3 784 279
Other sales occupations	2 637	12 258	186	29 600	3 172	2 040	10 611	5 228	5 235	1 331	1 983	48 980	5 862 291
Cashiers	1 069	6 652	108	11 853	1 025	745	4 111	2 322	2 321	452	877	22 384	2 300 799
Administrative support occupations, including clerical	10 680	23 502	467	78 505	7 248	4 742	27 930	15 916	13 761	3 207	5 701	133 708	17 534 493
Computer equipment operators	390	834	17	3 567	234	121	1 348	924	574	101	265	4 265	600 367
Secretaries, stenographers, and typists	2 078	3 396	81	15 457	1 338	886	5 460	2 692	2 955	715	1 411	28 184	4 323 743
Financial records processing occupations	1 202	1 916	32	8 385	984	474	2 962	1 593	1 443	303	626	14 617	2 192 086
Mail and message distributing occupations	852	1 354	–	3 698	308	196	1 247	984	686	74	203	8 063	917 215
Service occupations	8 380	95 908	773	111 450	8 682	7 038	42 207	18 749	22 399	3 245	9 130	144 186	13 575 925
Private household occupations	423	18 501	139	13 076	713	1 096	5 215	1 107	2 952	286	1 707	8 000	401 566
Protective service occupations	981	1 669	68	4 792	528	347	1 589	1 013	820	207	288	15 456	1 857 922
Police and firefighters	217	184	–	926	138	59	330	188	132	45	34	5 255	688 965
Service occupations, except protective and household	6 976	75 738	566	93 582	7 441	5 595	35 403	16 629	18 627	2 752	7 135	120 730	11 316 437
Food service occupations	2 071	33 164	207	35 167	2 994	2 186	11 825	7 317	7 048	1 284	2 513	47 670	4 558 958
Cleaning and building service occupations	1 736	31 161	207	33 639	1 824	1 881	14 118	5 472	7 169	602	2 573	34 945	2 636 392
Farming, forestry, and fishing occupations	226	9 691	98	4 783	362	460	1 499	617	1 166	168	511	19 837	2 392 877
Farm operators and managers	10	485	4	474	23	47	170	40	140	37	17	3 117	1 033 644
Farm workers and related occupations	216	9 031	94	4 195	333	399	1 285	556	1 011	129	482	15 540	1 186 984
Precision production, craft, and repair occupations	3 360	40 939	398	64 135	7 566	4 300	22 782	12 116	10 251	2 001	5 119	93 521	11 920 410
Mechanics and repairers	1 249	9 489	171	19 119	2 210	1 336	7 223	3 405	2 838	749	1 358	26 511	3 765 266
Construction trades	965	18 773	110	19 109	2 402	1 523	6 028	2 959	3 291	717	2 189	37 628	4 340 999
Precision production occupations	1 146	12 616	117	25 798	2 952	1 441	9 500	5 746	4 089	510	1 560	27 942	3 651 438
Operators, fabricators, and laborers	4 457	75 167	671	102 915	6 403	5 095	40 698	25 180	17 098	2 363	6 078	129 087	15 142 590
Machine operators and tenders, except precision	1 353	29 398	298	41 954	2 097	1 621	17 135	11 575	6 744	778	2 004	36 392	4 296 888
Fabricators, assemblers, inspectors, and samplers	809	12 066	65	17 334	1 171	881	7 081	4 145	2 833	386	837	20 647	2 560 122
Transportation occupations	803	9 751	83	19 597	1 608	1 293	7 571	3 911	3 118	570	1 526	25 730	3 446 548
Motor vehicle operators	755	9 702	83	19 390	1 562	1 275	7 491	3 911	3 074	559	1 518	24 686	3 272 453
Material moving equipment operators	101	1 365	13	1 862	87	114	748	498	270	57	88	6 159	880 980
Handlers, equipment cleaners, helpers, and laborers	1 391	22 587	212	22 168	1 440	1 186	8 163	5 051	4 133	572	1 623	40 159	3 958 052
Construction laborers	251	7 524	27	4 337	512	365	1 068	1 036	760	134	462	10 687	786 305
Freight, stock, and material handlers	470	3 173	52	5 798	335	374	2 323	1 188	1 012	165	401	11 792	1 431 645
Employed females 16 years and over	**25 121**	**116 446**	**1 403**	**239 071**	**23 702**	**15 971**	**90 467**	**41 345**	**40 580**	**9 772**	**17 234**	**368 205**	**49 307 437**
Managerial and professional specialty occupations	6 427	7 696	249	47 138	7 416	4 308	15 048	6 474	7 230	3 323	3 339	82 496	14 128 732
Executive, administrative, and managerial occupations	2 579	4 048	117	19 655	2 652	1 684	6 579	3 040	3 016	1 278	1 406	37 237	5 714 443
Officials and administrators, public administration	69	76	10	475	94	31	110	73	68	37	62	1 816	239 728
Management and related occupations	1 067	1 231	32	7 239	947	553	2 357	1 362	1 098	480	442	13 607	2 053 522
Professional specialty occupations	3 848	3 648	132	27 483	4 764	2 624	8 469	3 434	4 214	2 045	1 933	45 259	8 414 289
Engineers and natural scientists	166	282	5	2 653	463	230	826	252	403	333	146	3 329	530 052
Engineers	41	63	–	793	62	62	288	84	112	154	31	902	145 772
Health diagnosing occupations	86	61	–	1 157	322	66	304	98	131	83	153	1 038	164 064
Health assessment and treating occupations	1 083	787	64	4 750	432	519	1 637	627	942	259	334	9 961	2 102 051
Teachers, librarians, and counselors	1 678	1 388	40	10 790	2 158	1 086	3 186	1 406	1 509	754	691	20 309	3 808 731
Teachers, elementary and secondary schools	1 245	983	29	6 821	1 181	619	2 198	1 039	994	402	388	14 441	2 817 320
Technical, sales, and administrative support occupations	11 313	24 780	534	87 572	8 936	5 725	32 022	15 660	15 180	3 817	6 232	158 402	21 685 544
Health technologists and technicians	405	1 074	27	3 284	333	245	1 402	475	461	149	219	6 901	1 077 434
Technologists and technicians, except health	377	548	7	3 639	567	253	1 401	410	561	261	186	5 954	790 980
Sales occupations	2 815	8 904	188	27 376	2 906	1 941	10 289	4 603	4 637	1 247	1 753	47 105	6 166 703
Supervisors and proprietors, sales occupations	433	827	22	4 255	396	374	1 610	730	602	238	305	6 912	1 099 496
Sales representatives, commodities and finance	459	994	27	5 244	685	306	2 047	718	846	358	284	7 864	1 255 453
Other sales occupations	1 923	7 083	139	17 877	1 825	1 261	6 632	3 155	3 189	651	1 164	32 329	3 811 754
Cashiers	886	4 263	108	8 386	710	494	2 933	1 698	1 734	269	548	17 114	1 824 048
Administrative support occupations, including clerical	7 716	14 254	312	53 273	5 130	3 286	18 930	10 172	9 521	2 160	4 074	98 442	13 650 427
Computer equipment operators	212	447	11	1 471	91	48	501	382	319	39	91	2 435	371 157
Secretaries, stenographers, and typists	2 012	3 231	53	14 993	1 289	862	5 334	2 558	2 888	687	1 375	27 236	4 239 708
Financial records processing occupations	880	1 426	25	6 390	799	343	2 305	1 215	1 069	227	432	12 462	1 959 937
Mail and message distributing occupations	329	472	–	1 047	88	88	318	239	217	13	84	2 696	345 816
Service occupations	5 280	54 842	415	59 962	4 627	4 052	24 731	7 708	11 722	1 729	5 393	80 032	8 066 280
Private household occupations	423	17 922	120	12 438	629	1 043	4 976	1 054	2 853	274	1 609	7 575	380 901
Protective service occupations	191	208	–	932	150	56	251	182	202	44	47	2 446	290 278
Police and firefighters	45	27	–	94	6	7	32	31	10	6	2	582	61 774
Service occupations, except protective and household	4 666	36 712	295	46 592	3 848	2 953	19 504	6 472	8 667	1 411	3 737	70 011	7 395 101
Food service occupations	1 027	10 219	55	11 049	1 165	738	4 397	1 386	2 116	485	762	23 561	2 839 400
Cleaning and building service occupations	909	16 938	91	16 019	784	970	7 513	2 010	3 117	312	1 313	15 833	1 066 139
Farming, forestry, and fishing occupations	70	1 026	14	635	44	60	167	93	176	51	44	2 831	389 759
Farm operators and managers	2	70	2	104	2	16	24	8	28	26	–	415	146 029
Farm workers and related occupations	68	947	12	508	42	44	135	85	133	25	44	2 372	234 687
Precision production, craft, and repair occupations	441	4 600	9	8 693	780	461	3 565	1 980	1 146	226	535	9 981	1 106 535
Mechanics and repairers	65	218	–	733	55	26	327	139	105	37	44	1 395	163 699
Construction trades	19	321	–	504	45	30	216	79	85	18	31	895	121 248
Precision production occupations	357	4 061	9	7 451	680	405	3 022	1 762	956	166	460	7 640	817 055
Operators, fabricators, and laborers	1 590	23 502	182	35 071	1 899	1 365	14 934	9 430	5 126	626	1 691	34 463	3 930 587
Machine operators and tenders, except precision	806	14 390	125	20 156	829	707	8 486	5 999	2 843	325	967	16 206	1 734 065
Fabricators, assemblers, inspectors, and samplers	377	4 661	6	8 247	645	431	3 609	1 841	1 149	170	402	8 085	941 976
Transportation occupations	61	498	7	999	111	29	397	169	184	42	67	2 692	404 070
Motor vehicle operators	61	493	7	999	111	29	397	169	184	42	67	2 647	397 660
Material moving equipment operators	6	114	–	248	4	11	68	160	5	–	–	311	42 663
Handlers, equipment cleaners, helpers, and laborers	340	3 839	44	5 421	310	187	2 374	1 261	945	89	255	7 169	807 813
Construction laborers	27	241	–	262	39	16	53	55	70	7	22	335	31 920
Freight, stock, and material handlers	113	567	–	1 167	90	69	474	205	212	24	93	2 791	331 948

Table 120. **Income in 1989 of Households, Families, and Persons for Selected Hispanic Origin Groups: 1990**

[Data based on sample and subject to sampling variability, see text. For definitions of terms and meanings of symbols, see text]

United States

		Hispanic origin (of any race)										
						Other Hispanic						
								Central American				
	All persons	Total	Mexican	Puerto Rican	Cuban	Total	Dominican (Dominican Republic)	Total	Costa Rican	Guate-malan	Honduran	Nicaraguan
INCOME IN 1989												
Households	**91 993 582**	**5 872 040**	**3 302 126**	**797 809**	**392 200**	**1 379 905**	**147 716**	**336 531**	**17 071**	**66 397**	**33 426**	**49 197**
Less than $5,000	5 684 517	519 528	268 253	104 495	36 309	110 471	19 391	21 767	1 026	4 052	3 343	2 810
$5,000 to $9,999	8 529 980	653 488	355 255	122 111	40 231	135 891	23 187	29 677	1 398	5 325	3 286	4 148
$10,000 to $14,999	8 133 273	644 179	388 806	79 704	36 039	139 630	15 821	39 380	1 549	7 981	4 095	5 653
$15,000 to $24,999	16 123 742	1 205 131	717 597	147 107	65 469	274 958	29 365	79 499	2 884	16 454	7 993	11 214
$25,000 to $34,999	14 575 125	963 489	561 475	116 505	57 557	227 952	22 415	60 332	3 005	12 243	5 709	8 882
$35,000 to $49,999	16 428 455	937 461	526 955	114 224	65 921	230 361	19 871	55 078	3 426	11 573	4 613	7 748
$50,000 to $74,999	13 777 883	653 931	348 884	81 330	54 647	169 070	12 668	35 427	2 532	6 177	3 132	6 000
$75,000 to $99,999	4 704 808	180 396	87 451	21 249	19 470	52 226	3 165	9 443	675	1 513	736	1 746
$100,000 or more	4 035 799	114 437	47 450	11 084	16 557	39 346	1 833	5 928	576	1 079	519	996
Median (dollars)	30 056	24 156	23 694	21 056	27 741	26 067	20 006	24 695	30 785	24 569	22 109	25 717
Mean (dollars)	38 453	30 301	29 151	26 903	36 944	33 130	25 579	30 359	36 282	30 152	27 671	31 758
Families	**65 049 428**	**4 776 075**	**2 776 147**	**627 527**	**295 380**	**1 077 021**	**126 991**	**284 787**	**13 279**	**56 978**	**27 445**	**42 608**
Less than $5,000	2 582 206	365 222	199 635	78 436	12 846	74 305	16 664	18 475	613	3 554	2 641	2 413
$5,000 to $9,999	3 636 361	483 067	278 974	89 878	22 186	92 029	19 542	25 799	938	5 007	2 879	3 391
$10,000 to $14,999	4 676 092	535 520	338 065	62 805	25 707	108 943	14 433	36 410	1 057	7 760	3 493	5 227
$15,000 to $24,999	10 658 345	998 207	617 115	113 724	50 386	216 982	25 333	69 700	2 165	14 802	6 557	10 151
$25,000 to $34,999	10 729 951	798 318	477 513	91 417	47 215	182 173	19 352	50 221	2 496	10 093	4 765	7 635
$35,000 to $49,999	13 270 930	789 353	451 378	94 947	56 414	186 614	17 088	44 362	2 803	9 190	3 542	6 439
$50,000 to $74,999	11 857 079	557 096	299 323	68 976	48 597	140 200	10 671	27 721	2 159	4 584	2 517	5 099
$75,000 to $99,999	4 115 468	152 405	73 997	18 227	17 436	42 745	2 398	7 334	553	1 103	604	1 453
$100,000 or more	3 522 996	96 887	40 147	9 117	14 593	33 030	1 510	4 765	495	885	447	800
Median (dollars)	35 225	25 064	24 119	21 941	32 417	27 151	19 726	23 619	32 072	22 862	21 761	25 136
Mean (dollars)	43 803	31 195	29 564	27 869	41 619	34 480	25 236	29 451	38 409	28 581	27 351	31 277
Married-couple families	**51 718 214**	**3 339 694**	**2 027 520**	**353 483**	**230 617**	**728 074**	**63 556**	**180 231**	**9 279**	**36 976**	**16 240**	**28 534**
Less than $15,000	5 619 528	664 507	447 890	62 393	36 673	117 551	13 587	34 771	1 169	7 599	3 373	5 143
$15,000 to $24,999	7 734 791	692 958	450 734	66 058	36 160	140 006	13 721	43 793	1 313	9 575	3 901	6 629
$25,000 to $34,999	8 660 211	612 960	378 177	65 007	36 904	132 872	12 664	35 299	1 706	7 239	3 299	5 522
$35,000 to $49,999	11 566 753	653 998	381 436	75 672	47 450	149 440	12 386	33 392	2 204	7 070	2 700	4 947
$50,000 to $74,999	10 895 423	489 380	265 563	59 979	43 749	120 089	8 067	22 669	1 879	3 761	2 080	4 291
$75,000 or more	7 241 508	225 891	103 720	24 374	29 681	68 116	3 131	10 307	1 008	1 732	887	2 002
Female householder, no husband present	**10 381 654**	**1 029 646**	**505 042**	**229 639**	**48 072**	**246 893**	**52 333**	**64 344**	**3 104**	**10 846**	**8 080**	**8 851**
Less than $5,000	1 530 177	206 345	98 058	59 125	6 113	43 049	12 268	9 028	335	1 612	1 404	1 082
$5,000 to $9,999	1 636 764	224 843	106 113	64 394	6 850	47 486	14 363	11 816	509	1 964	1 739	1 364
$10,000 to $14,999	1 379 635	151 134	80 382	29 216	6 093	35 443	6 797	10 668	422	1 930	1 203	1 484
$15,000 to $24,999	2 286 235	202 370	104 174	36 937	10 043	51 216	8 716	14 719	619	2 630	1 852	2 046
$25,000 to $49,999	2 718 497	194 382	94 236	32 170	14 087	53 889	7 992	14 579	1 023	2 298	1 611	2 233
$50,000 or more	830 346	50 572	22 079	7 797	4 886	15 810	2 197	3 534	196	412	271	642
Males 15 years and over, with income	**86 674 947**	**6 688 401**	**4 054 638**	**738 492**	**396 199**	**1 499 072**	**136 297**	**414 786**	**17 956**	**90 481**	**36 630**	**59 170**
Median income (dollars)	20 409	13 501	12 456	15 290	16 506	15 079	13 410	12 294	18 423	11 883	12 171	12 776
Percent year-round full-time workers	53.0	48.7	47.5	49.4	53.3	50.5	49.9	50.3	54.4	49.3	47.9	50.9
Median income (dollars)	29 237	20 316	18 847	22 197	24 671	21 331	18 954	16 515	24 300	15 772	17 574	17 489
Females 15 years and over, with income	**84 560 106**	**5 473 121**	**2 990 119**	**743 796**	**370 213**	**1 368 993**	**151 831**	**353 589**	**17 646**	**66 824**	**37 983**	**55 035**
Median income (dollars)	10 371	8 354	7 975	7 769	9 469	9 220	7 722	8 807	10 227	8 428	8 293	8 773
Percent year-round full-time workers	33.9	33.4	32.7	30.3	37.4	35.6	30.5	37.9	37.6	37.6	36.1	38.0
Median income (dollars)	19 570	16 307	15 478	18 717	18 283	16 415	15 001	12 831	17 344	11 903	13 607	13 822
Per capita income (dollars)	**14 420**	**8 400**	**7 447**	**8 403**	**13 786**	**9 873**	**7 381**	**8 005**	**11 019**	**7 761**	**7 650**	**7 995**
Persons in households (dollars)	14 649	8 444	7 472	8 470	13 965	9 938	7 393	8 027	11 126	7 785	7 581	8 030
Persons in group quarters (dollars)	6 094	6 449	6 229	6 468	6 328	7 003	6 683	6 432	5 625	6 000	11 918	4 938
MEDIAN INCOME IN 1989 BY SELECTED CHARACTERISTICS												
Family type and presence of own children:												
Families (dollars)	35 225	25 064	24 119	21 941	32 417	27 151	19 726	23 619	32 072	22 862	21 761	25 136
With own children under 18 years (dollars)	34 627	23 417	22 917	19 587	34 644	25 428	17 311	22 403	31 250	22 070	20 304	23 867
With own children under 6 years (dollars)	31 580	21 230	20 827	17 089	34 893	23 049	15 701	21 274	29 511	20 382	18 689	23 362
Married-couple families (dollars)	39 584	29 930	27 664	32 111	36 471	32 568	28 252	27 706	37 592	26 531	26 788	29 294
With own children under 18 years (dollars)	40 693	29 208	27 129	32 068	40 211	31 825	27 921	26 991	37 033	26 043	26 260	27 798
With own children under 6 years (dollars)	36 490	25 918	23 687	29 483	39 326	28 175	26 365	24 335	33 333	22 871	23 361	28 086
Female householder, no husband present (dollars)	17 414	12 406	12 714	8 912	19 511	14 576	9 724	15 358	19 323	14 715	13 482	17 177
With own children under 18 years (dollars)	12 485	9 586	10 276	7 366	14 645	10 816	7 568	12 042	13 060	11 673	10 583	14 413
With own children under 6 years (dollars)	7 775	6 823	6 820	6 045	11 340	7 839	6 684	9 471	9 553	8 834	9 928	12 290
Workers in family in 1989:												
No workers (dollars)	14 622	5 976	6 120	5 477	7 883	6 072	5 124	5 000–	6 463	5 000–	5 000–	5 000–
1 worker (dollars)	25 517	16 914	15 973	18 057	21 997	18 023	15 672	14 548	21 679	14 441	14 841	15 260
2 or more workers (dollars)	44 500	34 879	32 646	38 486	43 025	36 547	33 187	30 740	40 210	29 695	29 659	31 278
Husband and wife worked (dollars)	46 340	37 007	34 658	40 825	45 252	39 503	35 910	32 814	43 131	31 608	32 459	33 520
Nonfamily households (dollars)	**17 240**	**15 243**	**15 355**	**13 193**	**11 870**	**16 834**	**11 921**	**16 983**	**19 397**	**17 434**	**15 441**	**16 482**
Male householder (dollars)	22 630	19 144	18 930	17 327	16 758	21 063	17 026	20 197	24 232	20 034	18 103	20 521
Living alone (dollars)	20 193	15 484	15 153	14 234	13 530	17 229	13 011	15 662	22 059	15 783	14 847	16 862
65 years and over (dollars)	11 688	7 159	6 972	6 672	6 331	8 977	6 611	8 683	27 946	9 491	11 667	11 250
Female householder (dollars)	13 729	10 624	10 352	9 306	8 204	12 480	8 299	13 022	14 595	13 160	12 562	11 975
Living alone (dollars)	12 226	8 517	8 185	7 896	6 919	10 373	7 016	10 451	12 349	9 927	9 403	10 025
65 years and over (dollars)	8 639	5 721	5 490	5 783	5 000–	6 575	5 651	6 578	7 577	6 090	5 199	6 643
INCOME TYPE IN 1989												
Households	**91 993 582**	**5 872 040**	**3 302 126**	**797 809**	**392 200**	**1 379 905**	**147 716**	**336 531**	**17 071**	**66 397**	**33 426**	**49 197**
With earnings	73 874 069	5 058 335	2 930 732	602 728	321 917	1 202 958	117 002	314 526	15 546	62 656	30 310	46 304
Mean earnings (dollars)	39 143	31 542	29 722	30 973	39 455	34 146	28 771	30 610	36 954	30 364	28 257	31 680
With wage or salary income	71 174 232	4 940 948	2 865 006	594 276	310 755	1 170 911	114 212	308 711	15 204	61 380	29 608	45 413
Mean wage or salary income (dollars)	37 271	30 433	28 804	30 301	37 445	32 623	27 808	29 541	35 241	29 166	27 600	30 296
With nonfarm self-employment income	10 810 605	519 133	280 926	39 618	48 277	150 312	11 904	34 678	2 075	7 480	3 070	5 244
Mean nonfarm self-employment income (dollars)	20 218	16 920	15 402	16 199	21 540	18 464	15 519	14 262	17 911	14 719	12 668	17 062
With farm self-employment income	2 020 105	44 511	27 799	2 715	2 507	11 490	764	2 252	80	352	185	326
Mean farm self-employment income (dollars)	10 064	9 047	9 203	6 992	9 932	8 961	7 136	6 057	18 916	6 197	2 063	4 902
With interest, dividend, or net rental income	37 242 801	974 491	477 032	111 022	103 558	282 879	14 624	44 198	4 109	7 271	4 362	7 589
Mean interest, dividend, or net rental income (dollars)	6 949	4 129	3 490	3 324	5 580	4 992	2 966	3 371	3 796	2 861	3 015	3 688
With Social Security income	24 210 922	857 372	459 546	116 953	93 340	187 533	14 326	23 993	1 833	3 875	2 844	3 976
Mean Social Security income (dollars)	7 772	6 206	6 146	5 715	6 651	6 438	5 142	5 453	6 170	5 157	5 553	5 734
With public assistance income	6 943 269	839 908	413 944	214 281	59 497	152 186	40 049	27 550	1 465	5 567	3 794	4 031
Mean public assistance income (dollars)	4 078	4 501	4 376	4 843	4 286	4 442	5 097	4 501	4 539	4 556	4 471	4 476
With retirement income	14 353 202	451 349	248 439	57 291	37 856	107 763	6 588	15 382	973	2 625	1 671	2 291
Mean retirement income (dollars)	9 216	6 889	6 782	6 814	5 825	7 547	5 240	5 759	6 200	5 222	6 049	5 554
With other income	9 344 304	539 080	320 803	79 921	24 333	114 023	12 398	20 932	1 161	4 000	2 485	3 224
Mean other income (dollars)	4 093	3 978	3 643	4 127	4 693	4 662	4 560	4 616	4 557	4 912	5 008	4 327

Table 120. **Income in 1989 of Households, Families, and Persons for Selected Hispanic Origin Groups: 1990**—Con.

[Data based on sample and subject to sampling variability, see text. For definitions of terms and meanings of symbols, see text]

United States	Hispanic origin (of any race)—Con.												Not of Hispanic origin
	Other Hispanic—Con.												
	Central American—Con.			South American								All other Hispanic origin	
	Panamanian	Salvadoran	Other Central American	Total	Argentinean	Chilean	Colombian	Ecuadorian	Peruvian	Venezuelan	Other South American		
INCOME IN 1989													
Households	**30 288**	**137 946**	**2 206**	**320 450**	**38 717**	**22 399**	**112 227**	**56 384**	**52 735**	**15 036**	**22 952**	**575 208**	**86 121 542**
Less than $5,000	2 243	8 002	291	19 405	2 004	1 032	6 964	3 741	2 999	1 448	1 217	49 908	5 164 989
$5,000 to $9,999	2 682	12 607	231	22 444	2 206	1 516	8 172	4 580	3 480	1 122	1 368	60 583	7 876 492
$10,000 to $14,999	2 671	17 196	235	26 521	2 865	1 516	10 082	4 499	4 496	1 228	1 835	57 908	7 489 094
$15,000 to $24,999	5 703	34 754	497	58 617	6 121	3 996	21 772	9 947	10 107	2 534	4 140	107 477	14 918 611
$25,000 to $34,999	4 985	25 198	310	56 217	6 039	3 630	20 420	9 896	9 575	2 465	4 192	88 988	13 611 636
$35,000 to $49,999	5 051	22 315	352	60 918	7 596	4 349	21 300	10 956	9 723	2 820	4 174	94 494	15 490 994
$50,000 to $74,999	4 544	12 835	207	47 735	6 606	3 934	15 295	8 413	7 851	2 041	3 595	73 240	13 123 952
$75,000 to $99,999	1 398	3 305	70	15 732	2 373	1 166	4 639	2 822	2 545	778	1 409	23 886	4 524 412
$100,000 or more	1 011	1 734	13	12 861	2 907	1 260	3 583	1 530	1 959	600	1 022	18 724	3 921 362
Median (dollars)	27 872	23 729	22 304	30 716	35 202	33 391	29 171	30 383	30 453	29 686	31 394	26 121	30 447
Mean (dollars)	35 206	28 832	29 229	38 254	45 881	41 448	36 102	35 718	38 065	37 652	39 857	33 836	39 009
Families	**21 622**	**121 115**	**1 740**	**251 987**	**28 463**	**17 167**	**88 617**	**47 058**	**41 918**	**10 634**	**18 130**	**413 256**	**60 273 353**
Less than $5,000	1 237	7 811	206	11 922	1 020	444	4 398	2 644	1 846	874	696	27 244	2 216 984
$5,000 to $9,999	1 366	12 042	176	13 989	1 072	840	5 525	3 110	2 206	539	697	32 699	3 153 294
$10,000 to $14,999	1 696	16 950	227	19 605	1 551	980	7 845	3 780	3 273	829	1 347	38 495	4 140 572
$15,000 to $24,999	3 827	31 822	376	46 140	4 238	2 999	17 107	8 465	8 291	1 793	3 247	75 809	9 660 138
$25,000 to $34,999	3 455	21 560	217	45 858	4 612	3 035	16 657	8 691	7 571	1 723	3 569	66 742	9 931 633
$35,000 to $49,999	4 167	17 900	321	50 755	6 014	3 591	17 673	9 421	8 518	2 070	3 468	74 409	12 481 577
$50,000 to $74,999	3 798	9 407	157	40 007	5 432	3 260	12 549	7 310	6 564	1 771	3 121	61 801	11 299 983
$75,000 to $99,999	1 222	2 352	47	12 731	2 014	968	3 719	2 343	1 983	561	1 143	20 282	3 963 063
$100,000 or more	854	1 271	13	10 980	2 510	1 050	3 144	1 294	1 666	474	842	15 775	3 426 109
Median (dollars)	32 185	22 006	21 415	32 087	39 044	36 128	30 384	31 074	31 828	32 078	33 162	29 683	36 028
Mean (dollars)	38 934	27 014	29 763	40 251	50 690	44 228	37 761	36 517	39 922	41 483	41 996	37 267	44 802
Married-couple families	**13 027**	**75 170**	**1 005**	**183 855**	**23 810**	**13 589**	**60 828**	**32 957**	**30 418**	**8 201**	**14 052**	**300 432**	**48 378 520**
Less than $15,000	1 188	16 075	224	22 308	2 335	1 232	7 731	4 185	3 998	1 290	1 537	46 885	4 955 021
$15,000 to $24,999	1 805	20 362	208	30 359	3 227	2 208	10 793	5 408	5 272	1 222	2 229	52 133	7 041 833
$25,000 to $34,999	2 111	15 300	122	33 993	3 752	2 336	11 744	6 387	5 539	1 393	2 842	50 916	8 047 251
$35,000 to $49,999	2 989	13 200	282	41 384	5 243	3 077	14 035	7 479	6 842	1 782	2 926	62 278	10 912 755
$50,000 to $74,999	3 194	7 355	109	34 349	4 983	2 905	10 362	6 244	5 518	1 586	2 751	55 004	10 406 043
$75,000 or more	1 740	2 878	60	21 462	4 270	1 831	6 163	3 254	3 249	928	1 767	33 216	7 015 617
Female householder, no husband present	**7 270**	**25 684**	**509**	**45 334**	**3 084**	**2 230**	**19 004**	**9 742**	**6 989**	**1 763**	**2 522**	**84 882**	**9 352 008**
Less than $5,000	883	3 588	124	5 671	391	187	2 191	1 463	792	385	262	16 082	1 323 832
$5,000 to $9,999	959	5 219	62	6 314	284	305	2 654	1 785	845	161	280	14 993	1 411 921
$10,000 to $14,999	849	4 690	90	6 100	327	250	2 925	1 241	855	164	338	11 878	1 228 501
$15,000 to $24,999	1 819	5 637	116	10 213	608	483	4 260	1 974	1 789	451	648	17 568	2 083 865
$25,000 to $49,999	1 983	5 352	79	12 586	1 069	682	5 249	2 512	1 983	389	702	18 732	2 524 115
$50,000 or more	777	1 198	38	4 450	405	323	1 725	767	725	213	292	5 629	779 774
Males 15 years and over, with income	**25 970**	**182 412**	**2 167**	**353 735**	**39 302**	**24 193**	**121 427**	**67 044**	**60 796**	**15 353**	**25 620**	**594 254**	**79 986 546**
Median income (dollars)	18 568	11 874	12 509	17 469	22 329	20 224	16 991	16 304	16 587	18 860	19 117	16 183	21 028
Percent year-round full-time workers	53.9	50.1	50.9	54.4	56.8	56.0	54.7	53.4	52.6	53.7	54.3	48.5	53.3
Median income (dollars)	25 660	14 954	19 447	23 857	30 708	26 609	22 347	21 677	22 325	26 446	25 722	25 021	30 096
Females 15 years and over, with income	**34 352**	**139 814**	**1 935**	**306 549**	**30 811**	**20 541**	**115 913**	**55 768**	**49 922**	**12 528**	**21 066**	**557 024**	**79 086 985**
Median income (dollars)	12 011	8 554	9 362	10 495	11 716	10 975	10 246	10 156	10 450	11 187	10 812	9 396	10 533
Percent year-round full-time workers	40.7	37.8	38.3	38.3	37.5	39.0	38.5	38.4	38.3	38.3	37.9	34.2	33.9
Median income (dollars)	20 472	11 608	17 132	17 610	21 190	19 296	16 835	17 219	17 128	20 050	18 243	18 183	19 809
Per capita income (dollars)	**12 223**	**7 201**	**9 191**	**12 119**	**17 447**	**13 663**	**11 150**	**10 889**	**11 640**	**12 168**	**12 662**	**10 623**	**15 002**
Persons in households (dollars)	12 427	7 222	9 213	12 196	17 721	13 800	11 215	10 809	11 733	12 334	12 796	10 747	15 252
Persons in group quarters (dollars)	0 947	5 035	7 010	0 249	4 045	4 524	0 713	17 400	5 501	5 202	4 851	0 803	0 000
MEDIAN INCOME IN 1989 BY SELECTED CHARACTERISTICS													
Family type and presence of own children:													
Families (dollars)	32 185	22 006	21 415	32 087	39 044	36 128	30 384	31 074	31 828	32 078	33 162	29 683	36 028
With own children under 18 years (dollars)	30 821	21 291	21 006	30 910	37 481	35 766	28 613	29 226	30 903	31 544	32 230	27 773	35 856
With own children under 6 years (dollars)	28 155	20 665	20 172	28 619	35 296	32 985	26 471	26 850	28 945	31 151	30 280	25 020	32 837
Married-couple families (dollars)	41 500	25 585	30 687	36 515	41 665	40 141	35 124	35 782	35 610	36 339	36 722	35 058	40 284
With own children under 18 years (dollars)	41 602	25 365	31 125	35 639	41 021	40 216	33 778	34 664	35 006	36 041	36 495	35 421	41 646
With own children under 6 years (dollars)	32 072	23 056	24 625	31 304	36 808	32 715	29 799	29 786	31 705	35 331	31 418	31 092	37 389
Female householder, no husband present (dollars)	20 214	14 061	13 464	19 272	24 000	22 523	18 696	16 670	20 481	20 069	20 254	14 760	18 022
With own children under 18 years (dollars)	16 844	11 555	11 193	13 992	17 177	16 845	14 027	10 850	15 623	15 833	16 489	10 941	13 027
With own children under 6 years (dollars)	10 046	8 739	9 507	10 940	21 161	12 031	10 712	8 190	11 723	14 336	10 833	6 917	7 942
Workers in family in 1989:													
No workers (dollars)	7 559	5 000–	5 000–	5 283	7 620	6 548	5 153	5 191	5 000–	5 000–	5 150	8 676	15 406
1 worker (dollars)	21 011	12 970	15 087	21 477	29 052	23 956	19 744	20 522	20 524	23 102	23 877	20 421	26 385
2 or more workers (dollars)	42 799	28 641	30 833	39 655	45 866	42 784	37 707	39 142	38 217	40 960	40 794	40 529	45 284
Husband and wife worked (dollars)	46 514	30 216	37 572	41 878	47 471	44 138	40 238	41 769	40 774	42 166	42 657	42 884	46 910
Nonfamily households (dollars)	**19 599**	**15 945**	**17 386**	**19 633**	**22 325**	**20 998**	**19 027**	**17 298**	**19 327**	**20 398**	**19 500**	**16 310**	**17 322**
Male householder (dollars)	22 754	18 746	20 789	23 147	25 193	26 585	22 773	21 367	21 962	24 583	23 103	21 052	22 894
Living alone (dollars)	21 173	12 983	15 208	19 047	21 260	21 656	18 323	16 711	17 516	22 354	18 776	17 516	20 401
65 years and over (dollars)	7 987	6 340	–	9 469	13 510	8 698	7 597	7 626	10 962	13 750	15 909	9 166	11 847
Female householder (dollars)	16 431	11 285	15 750	15 495	18 884	16 493	14 969	12 936	15 676	15 029	15 018	12 128	13 834
Living alone (dollars)	14 560	7 986	7 109	12 270	16 070	12 235	11 888	9 584	12 163	12 450	12 363	10 313	12 331
65 years and over (dollars)	7 284	6 297	8 077	6 331	8 326	6 752	5 866	5 718	6 130	7 222	6 784	6 767	8 747
INCOME TYPE IN 1989													
Households	**30 288**	**137 946**	**2 206**	**320 450**	**38 717**	**22 399**	**112 227**	**56 384**	**52 735**	**15 036**	**22 952**	**575 208**	**86 121 542**
With earnings	26 759	131 009	1 942	296 261	35 822	20 982	104 365	50 638	49 662	13 343	21 449	475 169	68 815 734
Mean earnings (dollars)	36 026	29 035	30 671	38 615	45 583	41 478	36 323	37 142	38 027	38 826	40 041	35 024	39 702
With wage or salary income	26 376	128 837	1 893	287 316	34 236	20 058	101 443	49 663	48 388	12 895	20 633	460 672	66 233 284
Mean wage or salary income (dollars)	35 167	28 068	29 935	36 547	42 336	39 251	34 394	35 726	35 856	36 939	38 246	33 434	37 781
With nonfarm self-employment income	2 279	14 373	157	43 271	7 313	3 622	14 757	5 260	6 813	1 949	3 557	60 459	10 291 472
Mean nonfarm self-employment income (dollars)	15 634	12 558	17 904	21 314	24 808	22 528	19 969	19 700	22 023	21 269	19 527	19 413	20 384
With farm self-employment income	241	1 033	35	1 925	203	150	733	335	368	68	68	6 549	1 975 594
Mean farm self-employment income (dollars)	3 411	6 834	2 439	9 052	9 928	9 300	9 701	8 764	9 371	3 869	3 780	10 146	10 086
With interest, dividend, or net rental income	6 682	13 940	245	72 596	11 940	5 784	22 698	10 573	11 865	4 323	5 413	151 461	36 268 310
Mean interest, dividend, or net rental income (dollars)	4 295	3 024	2 347	4 608	6 340	3 993	4 440	3 623	3 924	6 343	4 181	5 845	7 025
With Social Security income	3 483	7 705	277	29 420	4 291	2 211	9 828	5 845	4 407	954	1 884	119 794	23 353 550
Mean Social Security income (dollars)	6 667	4 708	5 255	5 673	6 416	5 760	5 546	5 557	5 392	6 118	5 329	6 979	7 830
With public assistance income	2 600	9 804	289	22 761	1 777	1 216	8 303	6 501	3 155	601	1 208	61 826	6 103 361
Mean public assistance income (dollars)	4 301	4 554	3 950	4 286	4 712	3 849	4 132	4 565	4 311	3 263	4 094	4 048	4 019
With retirement income	3 068	4 642	112	13 631	1 894	1 145	4 560	2 562	1 944	483	1 043	72 162	13 901 853
Mean retirement income (dollars)	8 293	4 307	5 153	6 840	7 219	9 131	6 127	5 872	8 138	5 630	7 276	8 273	9 292
With other income	2 753	7 086	223	21 648	2 350	1 358	7 724	4 090	3 466	1 031	1 629	59 045	8 805 224
Mean other income (dollars)	4 994	4 285	5 230	5 834	7 766	5 257	5 600	4 303	5 524	9 839	6 602	4 271	4 100

Table 121. **Poverty Status in 1989 of Families and Persons for Selected Hispanic Origin Groups: 1990**

[Data based on sample and subject to sampling variability, see text. For definitions of terms and meanings of symbols, see text]

United States	All persons	Hispanic origin (of any race)										
						Other Hispanic						
								Central American				
		Total	Mexican	Puerto Rican	Cuban	Total	Dominican (Dominican Republic)	Total	Costa Rican	Guate-malan	Honduran	Nicaraguan
ALL INCOME LEVELS IN 1989												
Families	**65 049 428**	**4 776 075**	**2 776 147**	**627 527**	**295 380**	**1 077 021**	**126 991**	**284 787**	**13 279**	**56 978**	**27 445**	**42 608**
In owner-occupied housing unit	47 221 605	2 234 435	1 415 359	188 870	176 222	453 984	19 490	70 764	5 601	13 141	7 413	11 302
With related children under 18 years	33 536 660	3 353 568	2 051 177	447 015	137 970	717 406	96 234	213 408	9 063	43 071	19 997	32 073
With related children under 5 years	14 250 048	1 673 629	1 067 258	207 577	57 615	341 179	48 410	111 521	4 020	23 050	10 684	14 842
Householder worked in 1989	51 357 521	3 811 513	2 283 364	413 234	235 618	879 297	83 485	250 909	11 444	50 874	22 715	37 859
Householder worked year round full time in 1989	36 318 276	2 344 303	1 362 661	271 839	164 584	545 219	49 275	144 169	7 273	28 597	12 872	22 813
Householder under 65 years with work disability	4 817 701	364 823	202 419	75 850	16 439	70 115	10 749	12 371	774	2 474	1 417	1 730
Householder foreign born	5 888 505	2 273 032	1 270 594	6 191	265 316	730 931	119 613	269 792	11 865	54 933	25 712	39 581
Householder under 25 years	2 554 838	352 154	226 746	54 368	8 060	62 980	7 486	23 045	606	4 577	1 974	2 958
Householder 65 years and over	10 796 925	375 526	203 981	38 321	53 547	79 677	6 173	8 737	749	1 265	1 087	1 843
Householder high school graduate or higher	49 435 732	2 366 580	1 215 666	328 238	174 523	648 153	53 632	135 386	9 085	23 136	14 032	27 164
With public assistance income in 1989	5 024 146	679 482	344 357	173 572	40 320	121 233	35 154	22 508	1 189	4 563	3 073	3 296
With Social Security income in 1989	14 633 024	621 140	345 965	81 223	67 024	126 928	10 817	17 644	1 272	2 879	2 193	3 014
Married-couple families	**51 718 214**	**3 339 694**	**2 027 520**	**353 483**	**230 617**	**728 074**	**63 556**	**180 231**	**9 279**	**36 976**	**16 240**	**28 534**
With related children under 18 years	25 258 549	2 329 405	1 510 320	231 408	106 951	480 726	47 286	140 987	6 518	29 670	11 950	22 193
With related children under 5 years	11 134 320	1 201 491	808 031	109 000	47 246	237 214	24 552	77 063	3 108	16 161	6 663	10 767
Householder worked in 1989	42 105 587	2 867 065	1 760 690	286 608	190 964	628 803	51 720	164 962	8 415	34 169	14 270	26 235
Householder worked year round full time in 1989	30 876 792	1 847 835	1 095 102	202 960	137 073	412 700	33 138	100 601	5 623	20 133	8 878	16 839
Householder high school graduate or higher	40 340 133	1 726 727	913 510	208 406	137 722	467 089	30 649	92 278	6 651	16 446	8 707	19 606
Householder 65 years and over	8 856 941	267 232	142 609	24 215	43 081	57 327	2 962	5 158	431	861	645	1 048
With public assistance income in 1989	2 196 987	271 493	159 650	43 658	23 014	45 171	8 553	8 969	451	1 933	978	1 396
With Social Security income in 1989	11 580 548	423 083	234 506	49 313	51 434	87 830	5 543	10 679	753	1 818	1 288	1 784
Female householder, no husband present	**10 381 654**	**1 029 646**	**505 042**	**229 639**	**48 072**	**246 893**	**52 333**	**64 344**	**3 104**	**10 846**	**8 080**	**8 851**
With related children under 18 years	6 783 155	782 487	392 662	187 065	24 116	178 644	42 185	47 949	2 135	8 088	6 178	6 529
With related children under 5 years	2 532 331	345 235	178 410	85 244	7 645	73 936	20 226	20 415	735	3 631	2 932	2 424
Householder worked in 1989	6 889 101	596 021	311 152	92 918	31 151	160 800	22 750	48 882	2 230	8 217	5 752	6 794
Householder worked year round full time in 1989	3 876 706	296 656	149 397	47 570	18 468	81 221	10 893	23 520	1 161	3 853	2 617	3 396
Householder high school graduate or higher	7 088 336	461 745	208 323	98 576	27 463	127 383	18 192	27 771	1 913	3 499	3 935	4 656
Householder 65 years and over	1 549 529	84 741	47 130	11 349	8 248	18 014	2 743	3 053	278	287	385	687
With public assistance income in 1989	2 541 129	366 937	163 782	121 161	14 113	67 881	24 919	11 582	668	2 169	1 864	1 611
With Social Security income in 1989	2 380 686	151 265	83 863	25 600	11 656	30 146	4 308	5 201	436	702	688	942
Unrelated individuals for whom poverty status is determined	**36 672 001**	**2 423 197**	**1 309 279**	**312 746**	**139 991**	**661 181**	**52 000**	**198 674**	**7 764**	**47 523**	**21 121**	**22 157**
Nonfamily householder	26 944 154	1 095 965	525 979	170 282	96 820	302 884	20 725	51 744	3 792	9 419	5 981	6 589
In owner-occupied housing unit	12 782 991	309 934	169 301	25 756	26 149	88 728	1 896	7 960	877	1 281	830	1 349
65 years and over	9 752 744	260 283	118 794	35 386	38 811	67 292	4 581	8 398	679	1 356	824	1 376
Persons for whom poverty status is determined	**241 977 859**	**21 388 017**	**13 110 843**	**2 564 659**	**1 029 619**	**4 682 896**	**509 786**	**1 298 677**	**56 092**	**264 295**	**128 322**	**199 169**
Persons 18 years and over	179 372 340	13 915 101	8 135 095	1 639 887	840 573	3 299 546	348 930	935 117	41 490	193 715	92 612	138 487
Persons 65 years and over	29 562 647	1 027 755	508 299	110 079	163 523	245 854	19 247	37 926	2 782	5 794	3 746	7 835
Related children under 18 years	62 278 655	7 411 310	4 934 858	917 968	187 917	1 370 567	160 013	358 189	14 514	69 451	35 376	59 823
Related children under 6 years	21 604 123	2 717 165	1 827 310	328 062	67 759	494 034	58 685	125 305	4 630	24 443	12 530	17 884
Related children 5 to 17 years	44 300 630	5 139 867	3 407 886	643 574	131 096	957 311	110 807	253 223	10 721	48 990	24 779	45 304
INCOME IN 1989 BELOW POVERTY LEVEL												
Families	**6 487 515**	**1 067 179**	**649 920**	**185 631**	**33 607**	**198 021**	**42 446**	**59 652**	**1 785**	**12 029**	**6 986**	**8 551**
Percent below poverty level	10.0	22.3	23.4	29.6	11.4	18.4	33.4	20.9	13.4	21.1	25.5	20.1
In owner-occupied housing unit	2 307 947	246 971	191 438	13 331	8 253	33 949	2 085	5 324	195	1 090	803	667
With related children under 18 years	4 992 845	920 524	569 554	163 577	19 662	167 731	38 068	52 336	1 542	10 738	5 981	7 692
With related children under 5 years	2 613 626	523 812	338 531	86 008	8 665	90 608	20 817	29 600	689	6 445	3 503	3 893
Householder worked in 1989	3 215 463	568 434	404 627	46 779	13 939	103 089	12 762	41 141	1 036	8 500	4 269	6 311
Householder worked year round full time in 1989	853 067	165 164	123 123	9 773	4 026	28 242	3 296	12 882	153	2 663	1 191	2 076
Householder under 65 years with work disability	1 073 192	136 770	74 500	35 455	4 271	22 544	5 019	3 899	209	794	577	548
Householder foreign born	876 281	523 594	348 259	1 685	30 571	143 079	40 555	57 746	1 718	11 731	6 692	8 182
Householder under 25 years	763 410	128 678	81 464	26 867	1 480	18 867	2 937	6 122	85	1 290	662	760
Householder 65 years and over	762 939	67 961	41 617	7 546	8 137	10 661	1 761	1 300	138	170	161	307
Householder high school graduate or higher	3 265 377	318 379	164 379	61 555	11 729	80 716	14 443	18 972	911	3 167	2 565	3 945
With public assistance income in 1989	2 286 388	358 515	177 003	112 252	11 334	57 926	21 384	8 662	480	1 772	1 429	1 077
With Social Security income in 1989	1 094 068	112 495	69 884	18 769	7 032	16 810	2 863	2 125	145	341	332	322
Mean income deficit (dollars)	5 379	5 942	5 947	6 294	4 570	5 825	6 237	5 644	5 401	5 682	5 862	5 978
Married-couple families	**2 849 984**	**510 211**	**366 615**	**43 094**	**18 899**	**81 603**	**11 130**	**27 256**	**832**	**6 095**	**2 673**	**4 265**
With related children under 18 years	1 834 332	424 054	316 350	33 144	8 826	65 734	9 341	24 147	657	5 508	2 196	3 890
With related children under 5 years	1 011 812	256 143	196 466	17 843	4 139	37 695	5 115	14 729	341	3 531	1 466	2 073
Householder worked in 1989	1 581 202	344 303	266 512	18 072	8 156	51 563	5 490	20 707	589	4 793	1 850	3 398
Householder worked year round full time in 1989	549 131	116 186	91 534	5 350	2 669	16 633	1 683	7 341	94	1 666	695	1 201
Householder high school graduate or higher	1 351 051	135 971	80 490	15 442	6 073	33 966	4 032	8 786	453	1 768	844	2 187
Householder 65 years and over	506 426	41 868	25 832	3 466	6 552	6 018	779	622	84	76	102	120
With public assistance income in 1989	554 412	92 347	59 311	16 345	5 062	11 629	2 880	2 082	91	484	265	311
With Social Security income in 1989	635 487	60 852	39 764	7 618	4 935	8 535	1 042	1 037	70	166	149	139
Mean income deficit (dollars)	4 994	5 817	5 905	5 974	4 028	5 754	6 254	5 704	5 393	5 784	5 972	5 794
Female householder, no husband present	**3 230 201**	**470 419**	**229 153**	**131 634**	**12 184**	**97 448**	**28 936**	**23 779**	**867**	**4 103**	**3 483**	**2 928**
With related children under 18 years	2 866 941	428 177	209 591	121 845	9 238	87 503	26 867	21 424	822	3 768	3 149	2 625
With related children under 5 years	1 452 618	226 184	114 445	63 612	3 717	44 410	14 523	10 714	322	2 019	1 674	1 172
Householder worked in 1989	1 403 435	166 736	99 549	24 123	4 291	38 773	6 012	13 765	392	2 284	1 834	1 815
Householder worked year round full time in 1989	248 472	32 943	20 418	3 465	837	8 223	1 246	3 604	38	563	365	504
Householder high school graduate or higher	1 721 637	157 238	70 118	42 938	4 719	39 463	9 443	7 785	444	944	1 396	1 213
Householder 65 years and over	215 978	21 428	12 794	3 459	1 291	3 884	862	599	54	62	59	173
With public assistance income in 1989	1 642 582	251 953	110 501	91 829	5 707	43 916	17 872	6 180	378	1 204	1 113	671
With Social Security income in 1989	390 389	43 205	24 777	9 658	1 735	7 035	1 630	955	69	157	144	155
Mean income deficit (dollars)	5 764	6 176	6 161	6 433	5 377	5 965	6 244	5 746	5 407	5 792	5 859	6 320
Unrelated individuals	**8 873 475**	**927 545**	**513 171**	**125 128**	**52 799**	**236 447**	**22 568**	**84 198**	**2 352**	**21 080**	**9 662**	**9 740**
Percent below poverty level	24.2	38.3	39.2	40.0	37.7	35.8	43.4	42.4	30.3	44.4	45.7	44.0
Nonfamily householder	5 210 297	307 943	139 302	59 560	34 343	74 738	7 745	12 440	800	2 317	1 736	1 544
In owner-occupied housing unit	1 957 191	68 033	42 450	4 217	4 727	16 639	337	942	108	143	57	139
65 years and over	2 494 332	124 455	54 295	20 212	22 904	27 044	2 911	3 444	248	564	323	606
Mean income deficit (dollars)	3 311	3 969	4 063	3 667	2 985	4 147	4 167	4 473	4 165	4 495	4 374	4 507
Persons	**31 742 864**	**5 403 492**	**3 447 149**	**812 798**	**149 825**	**993 720**	**168 277**	**309 028**	**8 452**	**66 806**	**34 897**	**45 654**
Percent below poverty level	13.1	25.3	26.3	31.7	14.6	21.2	33.0	23.8	15.1	25.3	27.2	22.9
Persons 18 years and over	20 313 948	2 996 026	1 836 019	424 389	117 121	618 497	97 599	207 690	5 744	45 968	23 820	28 661
Persons 65 years and over	3 780 585	246 362	125 659	32 701	39 522	48 480	6 372	7 361	442	1 175	797	1 401
Related children under 18 years	11 161 836	2 356 825	1 577 800	382 665	31 898	364 462	69 984	96 939	2 648	19 851	10 784	16 248
Related children under 6 years	4 331 825	909 240	614 744	144 298	11 916	138 282	26 615	34 354	822	7 015	3 812	5 021
Related children 5 to 17 years	7 544 737	1 598 712	1 064 558	262 112	22 240	249 802	48 051	68 344	2 038	13 983	7 607	12 198
Persons below 125 percent of poverty level	42 246 073	7 028 410	4 559 235	965 021	198 673	1 305 481	206 614	422 909	10 922	91 740	45 591	63 793
Persons below 200 percent of poverty level	74 909 296	11 306 861	7 411 141	1 365 093	345 208	2 185 419	307 317	729 840	20 112	156 083	73 618	108 468

Table 121. **Poverty Status in 1989 of Families and Persons for Selected Hispanic Origin Groups: 1990**—Con.

[Data based on sample and subject to sampling variability, see text. For definitions of terms and meanings of symbols, see text]

United States	Hispanic origin (of any race)—Con.												
	Other Hispanic—Con.												
	Central American—Con.			South American									
	Panamanian	Salvadoran	Other Central American	Total	Argentinean	Chilean	Colombian	Ecuadorian	Peruvian	Venezuelan	Other South American	All other Hispanic origin	Not of Hispanic origin
ALL INCOME LEVELS IN 1989													
Families	**21 622**	**121 115**	**1 740**	**251 987**	**28 463**	**17 167**	**88 617**	**47 058**	**41 918**	**10 634**	**18 130**	**413 256**	**60 273 353**
In owner-occupied housing unit	9 103	23 751	453	106 202	15 867	8 718	35 424	16 896	16 190	4 543	8 564	257 528	44 987 170
With related children under 18 years	14 482	93 392	1 330	163 316	16 103	10 693	58 449	31 620	27 599	6 954	11 898	244 448	30 183 092
With related children under 5 years	5 899	52 358	668	73 218	6 512	4 117	26 809	14 077	12 707	3 737	5 259	108 030	12 576 419
Householder worked in 1989	18 566	108 097	1 354	222 716	25 622	15 753	78 256	39 844	37 869	8 953	16 419	322 187	47 546 008
Householder worked year round full time in 1989	12 041	59 650	923	142 651	17 412	10 315	49 804	25 091	23 721	5 589	10 719	209 124	33 973 973
Householder under 65 years with work disability	1 179	4 742	55	10 771	1 063	603	3 969	2 593	1 518	386	639	36 224	4 452 878
Householder foreign born	18 186	117 977	1 538	235 885	26 659	15 784	83 244	44 418	39 364	9 288	17 128	105 641	3 615 473
Householder under 25 years	1 117	11 734	79	9 979	672	480	3 710	2 211	1 580	618	708	22 470	2 202 684
Householder 65 years and over	1 503	2 219	71	11 149	1 662	749	3 693	2 363	1 719	364	599	53 618	10 421 399
Householder high school graduate or higher	17 860	43 115	994	182 957	21 576	13 837	60 900	29 298	34 218	9 332	13 796	276 178	47 069 152
With public assistance income in 1989	1 987	8 186	214	17 892	1 282	819	6 548	5 278	2 577	427	961	45 679	4 344 664
With Social Security income in 1989	2 047	6 092	147	21 202	2 997	1 438	7 198	4 325	3 257	636	1 351	77 265	14 011 884
Married-couple families	**13 027**	**75 170**	**1 005**	**183 855**	**23 810**	**13 589**	**60 828**	**32 957**	**30 418**	**8 201**	**14 052**	**300 432**	**48 378 520**
With related children under 18 years	8 814	61 073	769	123 085	13 691	8 563	41 671	23 110	21 104	5 480	9 466	169 368	22 929 144
With related children under 5 years	3 990	35 958	416	58 267	5 753	3 475	20 461	10 622	10 264	3 232	4 460	77 332	9 932 829
Householder worked in 1989	11 684	69 333	856	167 928	21 851	12 658	55 667	29 452	28 124	7 188	12 988	244 193	39 238 522
Householder worked year round full time in 1989	8 027	40 485	616	112 372	15 154	8 618	37 523	19 417	18 329	4 653	8 678	166 589	29 028 957
Householder high school graduate or higher	11 237	29 013	618	137 529	18 064	11 180	43 528	21 394	25 226	7 355	10 782	206 633	38 613 406
Householder 65 years and over	894	1 234	45	7 965	1 413	548	2 451	1 611	1 201	273	468	41 242	8 589 709
With public assistance income in 1989	587	3 564	60	8 344	848	493	2 729	2 297	1 288	165	524	19 305	1 925 494
With Social Security income in 1989	1 236	3 716	84	14 556	2 344	1 023	4 555	2 939	2 268	442	985	57 052	11 157 465
Female householder, no husband present	**7 270**	**25 684**	**509**	**45 334**	**3 084**	**2 230**	**19 004**	**9 742**	**6 989**	**1 763**	**2 522**	**84 882**	**9 352 008**
With related children under 18 years	4 938	19 674	407	29 241	1 739	1 446	12 264	6 587	4 367	1 141	1 697	59 269	6 000 668
With related children under 5 years	1 640	8 904	149	9 688	505	339	4 122	2 495	1 423	364	440	23 607	2 187 096
Householder worked in 1989	5 682	19 889	318	34 039	2 375	1 844	14 602	6 395	5 591	1 197	2 035	55 129	6 293 080
Householder worked year round full time in 1989	3 221	9 116	156	18 124	1 369	1 003	7 549	3 424	2 942	615	1 222	28 684	3 580 050
Householder high school graduate or higher	5 589	7 911	268	29 711	2 344	1 653	11 606	5 371	5 373	1 417	1 947	51 709	6 626 591
Householder 65 years and over	552	852	12	2 578	192	176	1 007	616	411	91	85	9 640	1 464 788
With public assistance income in 1989	1 257	3 872	141	7 874	355	252	3 053	2 672	985	233	324	23 506	2 174 192
With Social Security income in 1989	685	1 705	43	5 022	485	322	2 024	1 076	704	165	246	15 615	2 229 421
Unrelated individuals for whom poverty status is determined	**13 546**	**85 549**	**1 014**	**142 233**	**15 630**	**9 489**	**53 149**	**22 016**	**23 661**	**8 121**	**10 167**	**268 274**	**34 248 804**
Nonfamily householder	8 666	16 831	466	68 463	10 254	5 232	23 610	9 326	10 817	4 402	4 822	161 952	25 848 189
In owner-occupied housing unit	1 869	1 645	109	14 827	2 765	1 300	4 943	1 710	1 965	965	1 179	64 045	12 473 057
65 years and over	1 832	2 236	95	10 076	1 595	800	3 469	1 839	1 298	391	684	44 237	9 492 461
Persons for whom poverty status is determined	**88 580**	**555 293**	**6 926**	**1 013 910**	**98 844**	**67 700**	**368 169**	**188 760**	**172 290**	**46 774**	**71 373**	**1 860 523**	**220 589 842**
Persons 18 years and over	66 901	396 976	4 936	764 784	79 164	50 656	274 632	143 177	129 363	33 964	53 828	1 250 715	165 457 239
Persons 65 years and over	5 671	11 847	251	42 006	5 880	3 015	14 063	8 266	6 981	1 191	2 610	146 675	28 534 892
Related children under 18 years	21 532	155 518	1 975	247 432	19 561	16 946	92 868	45 270	42 691	12 758	17 338	604 933	54 867 345
Related children under 6 years	7 417	57 681	720	85 663	5 750	6 010	32 842	15 228	15 390	4 532	5 911	224 381	18 886 958
Related children 5 to 17 years	15 389	106 693	1 347	175 258	14 790	11 862	65 181	32 621	29 502	9 036	12 266	418 023	39 160 763
INCOME IN 1989 BELOW POVERTY LEVEL													
Families	**2 837**	**26 969**	**495**	**30 353**	**2 206**	**1 409**	**11 617**	**6 851**	**4 913**	**1 639**	**1 718**	**65 570**	**5 420 336**
Percent below poverty level	13.1	22.3	28.4	12.0	7.8	8.2	13.1	14.6	11.7	15.4	9.5	15.9	9.0
In owner-occupied housing unit	300	2 216	53	5 016	444	328	2 198	759	785	252	250	21 524	2 060 976
With related children under 18 years	2 353	23 654	376	24 705	1 502	1 060	9 425	5 992	4 097	1 297	1 332	52 622	4 072 321
With related children under 5 years	1 109	13 799	162	12 425	776	498	4 731	2 984	2 031	661	744	27 766	2 089 814
Householder worked in 1989	1 591	19 170	204	17 147	1 270	857	6 908	3 060	3 160	871	1 004	32 039	2 647 029
Householder worked year round full time in 1989	285	6 436	78	4 329	195	233	1 921	766	806	147	261	7 735	687 903
Householder under 65 years with work disability	232	1 512	27	2 595	178	114	927	798	326	140	112	11 031	936 422
Householder foreign born	2 530	26 459	434	28 712	2 047	1 334	11 008	6 558	4 688	1 465	1 612	16 066	352 687
Householder under 25 years	410	2 915	–	1 882	120	72	713	340	358	162	117	7 926	634 732
Householder 65 years and over	137	358	29	1 305	178	106	507	264	174	13	63	6 295	694 978
Householder high school graduate or higher	2 019	6 145	220	18 010	1 350	944	6 355	3 274	3 596	1 311	1 180	29 291	2 946 998
With public assistance income in 1989	686	3 104	114	5 815	290	220	2 157	2 217	526	179	226	22 065	1 927 873
With Social Security income in 1989	110	838	37	1 967	242	132	743	433	230	58	129	9 855	981 573
Mean income deficit (dollars)	5 668	5 475	5 809	5 740	5 922	5 006	5 464	6 126	5 800	6 606	5 431	5 764	5 268
Married-couple families	**699**	**12 496**	**196**	**14 810**	**1 352**	**808**	**5 139**	**2 970**	**2 660**	**941**	**940**	**28 407**	**2 339 773**
With related children under 18 years	574	11 188	134	11 869	873	578	4 135	2 551	2 239	779	714	20 377	1 410 278
With related children under 5 years	326	6 924	68	6 768	457	299	2 408	1 410	1 249	485	460	11 083	755 669
Householder worked in 1989	451	9 510	116	9 556	913	547	3 459	1 594	1 883	563	597	15 810	1 236 899
Householder worked year round full time in 1989	95	3 557	33	2 728	146	175	1 181	437	539	113	137	4 881	432 945
Householder high school graduate or higher	475	2 963	96	9 225	758	582	2 963	1 432	2 045	751	694	11 923	1 215 080
Householder 65 years and over	55	156	29	797	141	67	264	186	93	13	33	3 820	464 558
With public assistance income in 1989	71	825	35	1 416	141	76	408	532	158	38	63	5 251	462 065
With Social Security income in 1989	33	451	29	981	126	68	320	266	128	17	56	5 475	574 635
Mean income deficit (dollars)	5 670	5 607	5 264	5 825	5 542	4 805	5 620	6 221	5 913	6 885	5 658	5 570	4 814
Female householder, no husband present	**1 961**	**10 214**	**223**	**12 601**	**653**	**471**	**5 167**	**3 411**	**1 782**	**538**	**579**	**32 132**	**2 759 782**
With related children under 18 years	1 705	9 171	184	10 846	540	408	4 376	3 090	1 521	410	501	28 366	2 438 764
With related children under 5 years	749	4 718	60	4 676	264	138	1 887	1 411	614	137	225	14 497	1 226 434
Householder worked in 1989	1 051	6 292	97	5 765	279	228	2 607	1 159	991	217	284	13 231	1 236 699
Householder worked year round full time in 1989	178	1 942	14	1 204	44	51	549	217	230	13	100	2 169	215 529
Householder high school graduate or higher	1 432	2 267	89	7 133	452	290	2 776	1 593	1 195	427	400	15 102	1 564 399
Householder 65 years and over	82	169	–	419	37	39	185	66	67	–	25	2 004	194 550
With public assistance income in 1989	573	2 162	79	4 033	144	122	1 519	1 623	338	141	146	15 831	1 390 629
With Social Security income in 1989	77	345	8	816	110	64	347	157	72	29	37	3 634	347 184
Mean income deficit (dollars)	5 699	5 546	6 485	5 635	6 377	5 233	5 361	6 025	5 480	6 361	5 062	6 005	5 694
Unrelated individuals	**3 771**	**37 161**	**432**	**43 837**	**3 987**	**2 668**	**17 258**	**6 972**	**6 997**	**2 724**	**3 231**	**85 844**	**7 945 930**
Percent below poverty level	27.8	43.4	42.6	30.8	25.5	28.1	32.5	31.7	29.6	33.5	31.8	32.0	23.2
Nonfamily householder	1 742	4 165	136	14 887	1 824	981	5 595	2 312	2 187	945	1 043	39 666	4 902 354
In owner-occupied housing unit	274	182	39	1 887	253	151	659	188	267	202	167	13 473	1 889 158
65 years and over	721	933	49	4 644	545	275	1 754	1 028	586	172	284	16 045	2 369 877
Mean income deficit (dollars)	4 061	4 539	4 408	4 131	4 088	4 076	4 137	4 037	4 068	4 438	4 283	3 830	3 234
Persons	**13 248**	**137 813**	**2 158**	**145 867**	**10 838**	**6 966**	**55 737**	**30 053**	**24 216**	**9 117**	**8 940**	**370 548**	**26 339 372**
Percent below poverty level	15.0	24.8	31.2	14.4	11.0	10.3	15.1	15.9	14.1	19.5	12.5	19.9	11.9
Persons 18 years and over	9 152	92 913	1 432	103 140	8 332	5 364	39 385	19 905	17 284	6 178	6 692	210 068	17 317 922
Persons 65 years and over	998	2 444	104	7 682	942	498	2 872	1 547	1 130	230	463	27 065	3 534 223
Related children under 18 years	3 994	42 703	711	41 283	2 407	1 512	15 800	9 873	6 725	2 891	2 075	156 256	8 805 011
Related children under 6 years	1 553	15 905	226	15 071	868	580	6 110	3 528	2 347	870	768	62 242	3 422 585
Related children 5 to 17 years	2 697	29 304	517	28 885	1 644	1 026	10 777	7 034	4 734	2 214	1 456	104 522	5 946 025
Persons below 125 percent of poverty level	17 546	190 550	2 767	197 333	14 628	9 397	75 643	39 807	33 876	11 717	12 265	478 625	35 217 663
Persons below 200 percent of poverty level	31 765	335 741	4 053	361 749	26 841	19 285	136 774	73 102	63 806	18 002	23 939	786 513	63 602 435

Table 122. Selected Characteristics of Persons 60 Years and Over by Age for Selected Hispanic Origin Groups: 1990

[Data based on sample and subject to sampling variability, see text. For definitions of terms and meanings of symbols, see text]

United States	All persons	Hispanic origin (of any race) — Total	Mexican	Puerto Rican	Cuban	Other Hispanic — Total	Dominican (Dominican Republic)	Central American — Total	Costa Rican	Guatemalan	Honduran	Nicaraguan
LIVING ARRANGEMENTS												
Persons 60 to 64 years	10 635 762	538 862	282 487	63 963	69 624	122 788	11 097	20 845	1 620	3 454	2 668	4 145
In households	10 521 298	532 660	279 069	62 752	69 024	121 815	11 060	20 692	1 620	3 381	2 668	4 105
In group quarters	114 464	6 202	3 418	1 211	600	973	37	153	–	73	–	40
Nursing homes	59 648	2 196	1 169	523	177	327	8	23	–	–	–	13
Persons 65 to 74 years	18 218 481	671 012	339 208	75 252	97 878	158 674	13 389	25 553	1 902	4 000	2 608	4 958
In households	17 884 074	661 652	334 239	73 773	97 153	156 487	13 376	25 320	1 867	3 913	2 601	4 937
In group quarters	334 407	9 360	4 969	1 479	725	2 187	13	233	35	87	7	21
Nursing homes	247 973	5 434	3 135	769	408	1 122	13	94	35	–	7	8
Persons 75 years and over	12 976 794	385 184	185 257	38 134	68 685	93 108	5 961	12 690	933	1 794	1 170	2 924
In households	11 580 219	362 620	172 316	35 772	65 800	88 732	5 859	12 484	915	1 786	1 145	2 880
In group quarters	1 396 575	22 564	12 941	2 362	2 885	4 376	102	206	18	8	25	44
Nursing homes	1 305 978	19 882	11 701	1 929	2 391	3 861	74	156	18	–	18	25
EDUCATIONAL ATTAINMENT												
Persons 60 to 64 years	10 635 762	538 862	282 487	63 963	69 624	122 788	11 097	20 845	1 620	3 454	2 668	4 145
Less than 9th grade	1 627 746	257 784	159 049	31 131	27 092	40 512	7 297	9 159	564	1 979	1 090	1 508
9th to 12th grade, no diploma	2 111 592	104 178	52 390	13 752	13 031	25 005	1 744	3 432	322	479	439	767
High school graduate (includes equivalency)	3 429 376	88 651	39 423	10 973	11 595	26 660	1 232	3 659	261	482	581	776
Some college or associate degree	1 884 132	53 721	22 518	5 014	8 802	17 387	359	2 888	323	347	304	617
Bachelor's degree or higher	1 582 916	34 528	9 107	3 093	9 104	13 224	465	1 707	150	167	254	477
Persons 65 to 74 years	18 218 481	671 012	339 208	75 252	97 878	158 674	13 389	25 553	1 902	4 000	2 608	4 958
Less than 9th grade	3 636 494	363 069	214 251	43 672	43 309	61 837	9 107	12 766	646	2 289	1 324	2 321
9th to 12th grade, no diploma	3 789 423	123 118	58 032	13 135	19 039	32 912	2 099	4 200	374	560	479	966
High school graduate (includes equivalency)	5 774 343	100 040	40 273	10 643	15 157	33 967	1 525	4 361	286	584	422	774
Some college or associate degree	2 897 366	50 825	19 364	4 806	8 921	17 734	358	2 526	288	332	253	511
Bachelor's degree or higher	2 120 855	33 960	7 288	2 996	11 452	12 224	300	1 700	308	235	130	386
Persons 75 years and over	12 976 794	385 184	185 257	38 134	68 685	93 108	5 961	12 690	933	1 794	1 170	2 924
Less than 9th grade	4 453 073	253 500	142 707	24 716	37 362	48 715	4 155	6 722	377	1 017	640	1 393
9th to 12th grade, no diploma	2 709 473	58 718	21 883	6 285	12 589	17 961	819	2 268	186	249	176	545
High school graduate (includes equivalency)	2 961 417	40 321	12 400	4 241	8 949	14 731	559	2 156	168	291	226	617
Some college or associate degree	1 616 777	18 455	5 519	1 991	4 203	6 742	291	922	144	142	66	195
Bachelor's degree or higher	1 236 054	14 190	2 748	901	5 582	4 959	137	622	58	95	62	174
INCOME AND POVERTY STATUS IN 1989												
Married-couple families, householder 60 to 64 years	3 863 733	172 855	94 333	18 200	24 298	36 024	2 464	4 073	477	548	654	972
Less than $5,000	77 968	7 052	4 539	882	532	1 099	113	151	22	17	48	29
$5,000 to $9,999	151 376	12 383	7 710	1 546	1 203	1 924	115	201	17	15	30	55
$10,000 to $14,999	239 904	15 988	10 093	1 839	1 565	2 491	228	285	21	86	23	64
$15,000 to $24,999	639 545	34 135	19 807	3 676	4 646	6 006	572	631	55	78	123	133
$25,000 to $34,999	671 469	29 607	15 731	3 293	4 398	6 185	371	733	105	70	109	189
$35,000 to $49,999	788 016	31 979	17 126	3 113	4 838	6 902	425	816	94	141	123	157
$50,000 or more	1 295 455	41 711	19 327	3 851	7 116	11 417	640	1 256	163	141	198	345
Percent with income in 1989 below poverty level	5.1	12.2	14.9	13.3	6.8	8.4	14.6	9.8	8.2	11.3	11.8	10.0
Persons 60 to 64 years living alone	1 637 721	64 508	28 376	12 041	8 495	15 596	1 098	1 838	165	311	316	235
Less than $5,000	282 378	18 766	8 678	3 745	2 529	3 814	348	438	44	80	107	31
$5,000 to $9,999	341 892	18 431	7 916	4 631	1 928	3 956	413	646	52	72	69	130
$10,000 to $14,999	254 933	8 768	4 152	1 071	1 268	2 277	132	207	–	24	33	19
$15,000 to $24,999	356 102	9 839	4 292	1 482	1 313	2 752	133	292	41	56	62	29
$25,000 to $34,999	186 922	4 314	1 770	558	710	1 276	38	128	9	43	45	18
$35,000 or more	215 494	4 390	1 568	554	747	1 521	34	127	19	36	–	8
Percent with income in 1989 below poverty level	24.6	41.6	40.1	55.7	39.1	35.0	54.4	32.3	26.7	30.9	46.5	15.7
Married-couple families, householder 65 to 74 years	6 105 480	192 250	104 066	17 986	29 659	40 539	2 275	3 889	299	664	458	827
Less than $5,000	105 626	7 419	4 411	774	1 003	1 231	237	181	14	23	42	52
$5,000 to $9,999	377 532	25 403	14 902	2 874	3 851	3 776	294	299	42	17	29	43
$10,000 to $14,999	683 471	30 205	17 606	3 033	4 168	5 398	317	443	30	89	34	117
$15,000 to $24,999	1 565 961	46 953	25 931	4 342	6 697	9 983	562	864	57	176	118	185
$25,000 to $34,999	1 168 869	30 530	16 252	2 402	4 632	7 244	273	714	66	81	114	164
$35,000 to $49,999	1 006 332	25 776	13 359	2 179	4 176	6 062	285	665	9	189	47	146
$50,000 or more	1 197 689	25 964	11 605	2 382	5 132	6 845	307	723	81	89	74	120
Percent with income in 1989 below poverty level	4.8	14.1	16.6	13.9	11.6	9.3	25.5	12.6	21.4	10.2	15.1	12.3
Persons 65 to 74 years living alone	4 238 144	121 743	54 956	19 257	16 968	30 562	2 288	3 637	372	465	437	416
Less than $5,000	673 028	37 711	18 385	5 250	6 806	7 270	702	815	52	100	179	95
$5,000 to $9,999	1 351 851	49 628	22 533	9 986	5 554	11 555	1 223	1 460	137	197	97	187
$10,000 to $14,999	783 518	14 168	6 551	1 631	1 788	4 198	140	520	77	43	52	74
$15,000 to $24,999	792 343	12 509	4 840	1 413	1 753	4 503	146	576	55	98	93	53
$25,000 to $34,999	315 489	4 008	1 406	486	514	1 602	24	146	32	17	14	–
$35,000 or more	321 915	3 719	1 241	491	553	1 434	53	120	19	10	2	7
Percent with income in 1989 below poverty level	22.6	43.7	41.7	56.1	51.4	35.2	64.6	31.8	24.2	24.9	47.1	32.2
Married-couple families, householder 75 years and over	2 751 461	74 982	38 543	6 229	13 422	16 788	687	1 269	132	197	187	221
Less than $5,000	73 814	3 832	2 160	319	657	696	44	31	–	8	6	–
$5,000 to $9,999	311 762	17 194	9 077	1 418	3 886	2 813	179	124	28	–	20	24
$10,000 to $14,999	488 925	17 407	9 226	1 632	3 010	3 539	101	274	46	37	23	50
$15,000 to $24,999	754 492	17 448	9 177	1 414	2 595	4 262	134	271	18	49	42	44
$25,000 to $34,999	427 153	7 967	3 862	687	1 354	2 064	87	181	7	13	29	44
$35,000 to $49,999	323 881	5 919	2 656	450	921	1 892	110	225	17	65	31	17
$50,000 or more	371 434	5 215	2 385	309	999	1 522	32	163	16	25	36	42
Percent with income in 1989 below poverty level	7.7	19.8	22.1	15.6	13.3		29.1	10.5	15.2	4.1	17.6	8.1
Persons 75 years and over living alone	4 751 106	94 854	44 227	10 959	14 565	25 103	1 260	1 988	163	273	172	365
Less than $5,000	896 651	36 488	18 082	3 244	7 840	7 322	356	614	55	82	73	78
$5,000 to $9,999	1 870 393	41 233	18 850	6 254	4 861	11 268	781	977	53	158	69	195
$10,000 to $14,999	790 052	8 647	3 920	727	991	3 009	44	194	30	10	18	50
$15,000 to $24,999	654 606	5 169	2 041	535	495	2 098	11	112	13	8	–	34
$25,000 to $34,999	256 210	1 600	621	124	153	702	54	49	–	11	4	8
$35,000 or more	283 194	1 717	713	75	225	704	14	42	12	4	8	–
Percent with income in 1989 below poverty level	27.0	51.2	49.9	59.5	65.7	41.6	60.8	40.5	51.5	32.6	42.4	26.8

Table 122. Selected Characteristics of Persons 60 Years and Over by Age for Selected Hispanic Origin Groups: 1990 —Con.

[Data based on sample and subject to sampling variability, see text. For definitions of terms and meanings of symbols, see text]

United States	Panamanian	Salvadoran	Other Central American	South American Total	Argentinean	Chilean	Colombian	Ecuadorian	Peruvian	Venezuelan	Other South American	All other Hispanic origin	Not of Hispanic origin
LIVING ARRANGEMENTS													
Persons 60 to 64 years	2 677	6 156	125	28 222	4 644	2 178	9 362	4 863	4 538	886	1 751	62 624	10 096 900
In households	2 658	6 135	125	28 098	4 638	2 176	9 300	4 863	4 498	881	1 742	61 965	9 988 638
In group quarters	19	21	–	124	6	2	62	–	40	5	9	659	108 262
Nursing homes	–	10	–	7	–	2	5	–	–	–	–	289	57 452
Persons 65 to 74 years	3 971	7 955	159	29 254	4 278	1 981	9 935	5 629	4 743	813	1 875	90 478	17 547 469
In households	3 945	7 898	159	29 013	4 224	1 965	9 823	5 604	4 733	789	1 875	88 778	17 222 422
In group quarters	26	57	–	241	54	16	112	25	10	24	–	1 700	325 047
Nursing homes	26	18	–	90	27	5	36	–	–	22	–	925	242 539
Persons 75 years and over	1 746	4 026	97	13 195	1 737	1 087	4 283	2 671	2 258	413	746	61 262	12 591 610
In households	1 726	3 940	92	12 866	1 650	1 048	4 155	2 647	2 231	400	735	57 523	11 217 599
In group quarters	20	86	5	329	87	39	128	24	27	13	11	3 739	1 374 011
Nursing homes	13	77	5	287	87	39	96	21	20	13	11	3 344	1 286 096
EDUCATIONAL ATTAINMENT													
Persons 60 to 64 years	2 677	6 156	125	28 222	4 644	2 178	9 362	4 863	4 538	886	1 751	62 624	10 096 900
Less than 9th grade	497	3 483	38	7 596	1 045	439	2 998	1 535	908	190	481	16 460	1 369 962
9th to 12th grade, no diploma	530	878	17	5 655	783	446	1 943	1 254	780	117	332	14 174	2 007 414
High school graduate (includes equivalency)	676	859	24	6 469	1 058	430	2 035	1 077	1 329	280	260	15 300	3 340 725
Some college or associate degree	602	665	30	4 178	746	405	1 258	550	764	138	317	9 962	1 830 411
Bachelor's degree or higher	372	271	16	4 324	1 012	458	1 128	447	757	161	361	6 728	1 548 388
Persons 65 to 74 years	3 971	7 955	159	29 254	4 278	1 981	9 935	5 629	4 743	813	1 875	90 478	17 547 469
Less than 9th grade	1 033	5 049	104	9 684	1 178	515	3 752	2 161	1 271	174	633	30 280	3 273 425
9th to 12th grade, no diploma	684	1 125	12	6 146	842	368	2 015	1 364	1 124	124	309	20 467	3 666 305
High school graduate (includes equivalency)	1 189	1 076	30	6 436	861	476	2 140	1 094	1 187	228	450	21 645	5 674 303
Some college or associate degree	665	464	13	3 771	689	398	1 125	589	605	145	220	11 079	2 846 541
Bachelor's degree or higher	400	241	–	3 217	708	224	903	421	556	142	263	7 007	2 086 895
Persons 75 years and over	1 746	4 026	97	13 195	1 737	1 087	4 283	2 671	2 258	413	746	61 262	12 591 610
Less than 9th grade	616	2 626	53	6 020	660	387	2 091	1 512	897	187	286	31 818	4 199 573
9th to 12th grade, no diploma	466	622	24	2 636	377	222	882	503	477	54	121	12 238	2 650 755
High school graduate (includes equivalency)	396	455	3	2 681	356	289	775	401	590	135	135	9 335	2 921 096
Some college or associate degree	137	231	7	990	129	104	336	144	157	24	96	4 539	1 598 322
Bachelor's degree or higher	131	92	10	868	215	85	199	111	137	13	108	3 332	1 221 864
INCOME AND POVERTY STATUS IN 1989													
Married-couple families, householder 60 to 64 years	542	870	10	8 724	1 703	676	2 758	1 538	1 274	198	577	20 763	3 690 070
Less than $5,000	1	34	–	173	40	5	44	23	40	9	12	662	70 916
$5,000 to $9,999	28	56	–	238	50	23	64	45	49	7	–	1 370	138 993
$10,000 to $14,999	20	71	–	463	70	31	126	122	39	26	49	1 515	223 916
$15,000 to $24,999	63	179	–	1 080	239	129	261	175	159	30	87	3 723	605 410
$25,000 to $34,999	117	143	–	1 563	292	111	536	296	214	15	99	3 518	641 862
$35,000 to $49,999	140	161	–	1 911	340	156	718	296	253	66	82	3 750	756 037
$50,000 or more	173	226	10	3 296	672	221	1 009	581	520	45	248	6 225	1 253 744
Percent with income in 1989 below poverty level	7.0	9.9	–	4.9	5.0	3.1	3.4	7.0	6.8	8.1	3.3	8.9	4.8
Persons 60 to 64 years living alone	359	411	41	3 163	666	257	996	449	434	184	177	9 497	1 573 213
Less than $5,000	43	115	18	734	130	71	234	141	119	14	25	2 294	263 612
$5,000 to $9,999	156	152	15	664	94	61	203	119	96	57	34	2 233	323 461
$10,000 to $14,999	35	96	–	460	101	35	154	77	61	26	6	1 478	246 165
$15,000 to $24,999	57	39	8	601	136	45	206	65	83	38	28	1 726	346 263
$25,000 to $34,999	13	–	–	297	49	10	127	35	41	9	26	813	182 608
$35,000 or more	55	9	–	407	156	35	72	12	34	40	58	953	211 104
Percent with income in 1989 below poverty level	21.7	42.3	43.9	31.7	25.7	33.5	33.0	39.9	39.2	19.6	18.1	34.4	23.9
Married-couple families, householder 65 to 74 years	679	932	30	6 376	1 171	397	1 944	1 279	997	190	398	27 999	5 913 230
Less than $5,000	17	33	–	174	55	10	57	28	7	7	10	639	98 207
$5,000 to $9,999	46	102	20	521	101	38	193	138	35	–	16	2 662	352 129
$10,000 to $14,999	61	112	–	587	75	50	171	120	115	–	56	4 051	653 266
$15,000 to $24,999	143	185	–	1 270	255	40	393	217	229	39	97	7 287	1 519 008
$25,000 to $34,999	120	169	–	1 208	182	91	347	289	182	51	66	5 049	1 138 339
$35,000 to $49,999	80	184	10	1 075	182	53	345	202	192	20	81	4 037	980 556
$50,000 or more	212	147	–	1 541	321	115	438	285	237	73	72	4 274	1 171 725
Percent with income in 1989 below poverty level	6.8	12.9	66.7	8.4	9.1	6.5	10.5	10.7	3.6	3.7	5.0	7.8	4.5
Persons 65 to 74 years living alone	1 113	817	17	4 824	799	416	1 509	920	603	229	348	19 813	4 116 401
Less than $5,000	175	212	2	1 220	103	83	489	291	135	47	72	4 533	635 317
$5,000 to $9,999	439	398	5	1 784	264	175	521	388	229	56	151	7 088	1 302 223
$10,000 to $14,999	172	102	–	499	83	54	176	110	37	14	25	3 039	769 350
$15,000 to $24,999	198	69	10	723	174	63	197	58	100	57	74	3 058	779 834
$25,000 to $34,999	79	4	–	230	44	8	68	49	18	29	14	1 202	311 481
$35,000 or more	50	32	–	368	131	33	58	24	84	26	12	893	318 196
Percent with income in 1989 below poverty level	29.1	35.0	11.8	40.1	28.4	26.0	49.0	53.3	28.4	31.4	36.2	31.2	22.0
Married-couple families, householder 75 years and over	215	302	15	1 589	242	151	507	332	204	83	70	13 243	2 676 479
Less than $5,000	9	8	–	98	6	7	23	21	27	6	8	523	69 982
$5,000 to $9,999	–	43	9	325	60	34	103	56	57	9	6	2 185	294 568
$10,000 to $14,999	50	68	–	242	51	22	23	92	28	14	12	2 922	471 518
$15,000 to $24,999	36	82	–	444	30	54	174	74	71	14	27	3 413	737 044
$25,000 to $34,999	42	40	6	148	48	5	41	10	9	25	10	1 648	419 186
$35,000 to $49,999	48	47	–	128	12	18	45	42	8	–	3	1 429	317 962
$50,000 or more	30	14	–	204	35	11	98	37	4	15	4	1 123	366 219
Percent with income in 1989 below poverty level	4.2	11.9	60.0	16.4	14.0	27.2	11.8	14.8	27.9	7.2	18.6	12.4	7.4
Persons 75 years and over living alone	482	499	34	2 690	445	186	872	509	355	132	191	19 165	4 656 252
Less than $5,000	177	144	5	925	89	68	349	134	156	65	64	5 427	860 163
$5,000 to $9,999	232	251	19	1 196	207	78	391	326	110	43	41	8 314	1 829 160
$10,000 to $14,999	39	47	–	245	66	34	34	23	32	19	37	2 526	781 405
$15,000 to $24,999	27	30	–	248	58	–	92	22	37	5	34	1 727	649 437
$25,000 to $34,999	7	9	10	52	18	–	–	4	20	–	10	547	254 610
$35,000 or more	–	18	–	24	7	6	6	–	–	–	5	624	281 477
Percent with income in 1989 below poverty level	55.4	35.7	47.1	48.0	31.5	36.6	53.3	48.3	62.3	59.8	38.2	39.5	26.5

Table 123. **Age, Fertility, and Household and Family Composition for Race and Hispanic Origin: 1990**

[Data based on sample and subject to sampling variability, see text. For definitions of terms and meanings of symbols, see text]

United States	All persons	White		Black		American Indian, Eskimo, or Aleut		Asian or Pacific Islander		Other race	
		Total	Not of Hispanic origin	Total	Not of Hispanic origin	Total	Not of Hispanic origin	Total	Not of Hispanic origin	Total	Not of Hispanic origin
AGE											
All persons	**248 709 873**	**199 827 064**	**188 424 773**	**29 930 524**	**29 284 596**	**2 015 143**	**1 866 807**	**7 226 986**	**6 994 302**	**9 710 156**	**239 306**
Under 3 years	10 924 579	8 137 382	7 436 399	1 662 313	1 613 323	119 287	107 108	341 957	325 043	663 640	27 557
3 and 4 years	7 339 517	5 508 560	5 054 028	1 092 604	1 061 897	78 509	71 080	232 476	221 708	427 368	15 601
5 to 9 years	18 126 901	13 669 939	12 573 070	2 670 822	2 605 216	197 456	178 977	587 783	563 154	1 000 901	32 021
10 to 14 years	17 151 134	12 877 425	11 872 138	2 619 309	2 562 150	188 374	172 776	551 483	528 391	914 543	27 723
15 to 17 years	10 064 413	7 560 166	6 990 196	1 521 906	1 491 018	107 015	98 354	338 729	326 380	536 597	13 842
18 and 19 years	7 589 506	5 753 714	5 349 956	1 106 299	1 083 071	73 262	67 352	251 940	242 969	404 291	8 883
20 to 24 years	18 645 387	14 296 570	13 250 338	2 496 037	2 435 366	171 619	157 678	606 252	584 387	1 074 909	18 991
25 to 29 years	21 286 297	16 610 575	15 480 462	2 701 217	2 637 967	186 025	171 694	688 392	667 202	1 100 088	18 469
30 to 34 years	22 180 737	17 605 327	16 567 169	2 712 045	2 651 166	181 313	168 422	725 669	705 995	956 383	18 209
35 to 39 years	19 939 682	16 069 470	15 223 585	2 312 577	2 261 352	158 133	147 739	674 166	656 197	725 336	13 872
40 to 44 years	17 679 734	14 539 053	13 847 443	1 884 046	1 845 354	133 719	125 062	583 890	568 991	539 026	11 161
45 to 49 years	13 977 898	11 639 594	11 109 495	1 434 798	1 407 402	102 852	97 177	417 981	407 218	382 673	7 370
50 to 54 years	11 488 063	9 584 468	9 140 642	1 220 162	1 197 605	80 866	76 887	318 170	310 181	284 397	6 423
55 to 59 years	10 484 988	8 921 892	8 536 844	1 028 282	1 010 470	64 950	61 694	250 248	243 858	219 616	4 887
60 to 64 years	10 635 762	9 222 857	8 879 428	967 266	951 528	54 040	51 577	215 276	210 124	176 323	4 243
65 to 74 years	18 218 481	16 138 327	15 689 368	1 511 617	1 491 442	74 320	71 373	295 142	288 994	199 075	6 292
75 years and over	12 976 794	11 691 745	11 424 212	989 224	978 269	43 403	41 857	147 432	143 510	104 990	3 762
Median age	33.0	34.4	34.9	28.3	28.4	26.9	27.3	30.1	30.3	24.2	18.7
FERTILITY											
Women 15 to 24 years	**17 769 944**	**13 506 701**	**12 563 441**	**2 585 136**	**2 531 473**	**169 637**	**156 643**	**581 261**	**559 320**	**927 209**	**20 756**
Children ever born	5 420 229	3 425 411	3 034 019	1 334 675	1 308 909	90 637	84 044	91 653	84 825	477 853	7 053
Per 1,000 women	305	254	241	516	517	534	537	158	152	515	340
Women ever married	3 726 372	3 038 939	2 794 858	303 504	292 179	38 482	35 682	82 769	78 779	262 678	3 655
Children ever born	3 462 487	2 654 608	2 380 981	379 107	366 628	49 917	46 340	67 530	63 303	311 325	3 828
Per 1,000 women	929	874	852	1 249	1 255	1 297	1 299	816	804	1 185	1 047
Women 25 to 34 years	**21 757 561**	**17 017 533**	**15 973 799**	**2 872 381**	**2 811 676**	**186 646**	**173 632**	**725 215**	**704 174**	**955 786**	**18 087**
Children ever born	28 942 178	21 391 915	19 694 202	4 634 379	4 535 251	352 449	329 016	779 523	749 205	1 783 912	26 796
Per 1,000 women	1 330	1 257	1 233	1 613	1 613	1 888	1 895	1 075	1 064	1 866	1 482
Women ever married	16 431 453	13 482 011	12 680 774	1 536 979	1 498 537	136 936	127 319	550 528	534 855	724 999	12 520
Children ever born	26 088 416	20 568 607	19 047 492	2 943 447	2 869 935	294 715	274 789	749 218	722 289	1 532 429	22 890
Per 1,000 women	1 588	1 526	1 502	1 915	1 915	2 152	2 158	1 361	1 350	2 114	1 828
Women 35 to 44 years	**19 012 425**	**15 317 704**	**14 536 139**	**2 255 515**	**2 211 454**	**150 205**	**140 872**	**672 487**	**654 577**	**616 514**	**12 382**
Children ever born	37 260 340	28 769 752	26 883 666	5 075 478	4 969 828	372 668	349 489	1 299 946	1 260 234	1 742 496	27 413
Per 1,000 women	1 960	1 878	1 849	2 250	2 247	2 481	2 481	1 933	1 925	2 826	2 214
No children	3 459 251	2 928 170	2 822 064	326 498	320 130	19 659	18 326	123 120	120 088	61 804	2 210
1 child	3 196 133	2 554 439	2 445 965	435 387	428 785	22 464	21 189	115 288	112 744	68 555	2 081
2 children	6 589 685	5 523 130	5 294 225	628 185	616 441	41 220	38 803	244 357	238 961	152 793	3 311
3 children	3 605 811	2 861 816	2 687 114	443 449	433 628	31 929	29 828	119 176	115 298	149 441	2 383
4 children	1 357 031	978 612	889 572	227 256	222 008	18 226	17 019	41 685	39 967	91 252	1 322
5 or more children	804 514	471 537	397 199	194 740	190 462	16 707	15 707	28 861	27 519	92 669	1 075
Women ever married	17 154 920	14 092 322	13 390 046	1 764 689	1 728 328	134 368	125 980	617 501	601 397	546 040	10 696
Children ever born	36 033 647	28 477 832	26 676 224	4 299 316	4 206 169	351 771	330 056	1 285 080	1 246 848	1 619 648	25 825
Per 1,000 women	2 100	2 021	1 992	2 436	2 434	2 618	2 620	2 081	2 073	2 966	2 414
HOUSEHOLD TYPE AND RELATIONSHIP											
All persons	**248 709 873**	**199 827 064**	**188 424 773**	**29 930 524**	**29 284 596**	**2 015 143**	**1 866 807**	**7 226 986**	**6 994 302**	**9 710 156**	**239 306**
In households	242 050 161	194 852 135	183 679 704	28 665 816	28 064 805	1 952 539	1 811 093	7 074 394	6 847 828	9 505 277	231 596
Family householder	65 049 428	53 845 200	51 337 479	7 055 063	6 927 208	463 968	436 752	1 577 820	1 535 190	2 107 377	36 724
Male	51 091 846	44 381 844	42 479 130	3 583 213	3 517 631	309 410	291 768	1 308 673	1 277 756	1 508 706	24 577
Female	13 957 582	9 463 356	8 858 349	3 471 850	3 409 577	154 558	144 984	269 147	257 434	598 671	12 147
Nonfamily householder	26 944 154	23 061 780	22 410 268	2 886 787	2 840 175	161 399	152 074	442 678	429 889	391 510	15 783
Male	11 534 397	9 683 509	9 351 069	1 291 687	1 268 394	83 327	78 214	244 905	238 269	230 969	8 401
Female	15 409 757	13 378 271	13 059 199	1 595 100	1 571 781	78 072	73 860	197 773	191 620	160 541	7 382
Spouse	51 549 544	44 921 347	42 985 787	3 403 863	3 339 637	310 579	292 848	1 504 756	1 468 718	1 408 999	26 380
Child	77 059 019	58 988 886	54 625 916	10 921 567	10 675 551	751 748	687 750	2 505 467	2 408 808	3 891 351	121 176
Other relatives	11 647 867	6 680 709	5 617 630	3 074 395	3 002 296	146 374	133 707	686 998	662 547	1 059 391	18 934
Nonrelatives	9 800 149	7 354 213	6 702 624	1 324 141	1 279 938	118 471	107 962	356 675	342 676	646 649	12 599
In group quarters	6 659 712	4 974 929	4 745 069	1 264 708	1 219 791	62 604	55 714	152 592	146 474	204 879	7 710
Persons per household	2.63	2.54	2.51	2.87	2.87	3.08	3.07	3.29	3.29	3.82	669.76
Persons per family	3.16	3.06	3.03	3.46	3.46	3.57	3.56	3.74	3.74	4.06	84.54
FAMILY TYPE BY PRESENCE OF OWN CHILDREN											
Families	**65 049 428**	**53 845 200**	**51 337 479**	**7 055 063**	**6 927 208**	**463 968**	**436 752**	**1 577 820**	**1 535 190**	**2 107 377**	**36 724**
With own children under 18 years	31 364 670	24 687 700	23 183 692	3 985 084	3 901 825	281 698	264 035	938 105	911 455	1 472 083	22 494
With own children under 6 years	14 646 378	11 433 634	10 654 479	1 806 391	1 762 562	138 756	129 501	445 422	432 822	822 175	11 700
Married-couple families	**51 718 214**	**45 178 672**	**43 342 946**	**3 521 382**	**3 458 050**	**305 156**	**288 308**	**1 295 099**	**1 265 101**	**1 417 905**	**24 115**
With own children under 18 years	24 224 117	20 338 573	19 218 899	1 865 571	1 824 964	178 736	167 980	815 582	796 352	1 025 655	14 554
With own children under 6 years	11 806 198	9 857 980	9 253 420	862 387	840 031	88 960	83 086	402 836	393 402	594 035	7 751
Female householder, no husband present	**10 381 654**	**6 540 382**	**6 058 841**	**3 045 283**	**2 993 086**	**121 370**	**113 658**	**185 926**	**176 964**	**488 693**	**9 459**
With own children under 18 years	5 865 147	3 443 573	3 146 813	1 901 114	1 864 585	80 840	75 511	94 498	88 771	345 122	6 538
With own children under 6 years	2 300 192	1 222 520	1 095 480	840 827	822 969	38 040	35 406	32 582	30 114	166 223	3 147
Subfamilies	**2 572 170**	**1 425 738**	**1 218 744**	**783 745**	**772 397**	**37 017**	**34 537**	**125 397**	**121 270**	**200 273**	**2 950**
With own children under 18 years	2 193 137	1 169 266	1 001 121	757 249	747 132	34 535	32 328	65 285	62 242	166 802	2 561
Married-couple subfamilies	**611 488**	**420 134**	**354 488**	**48 619**	**46 655**	**4 994**	**4 540**	**79 014**	**77 404**	**58 727**	**638**
With own children under 18 years	232 455	163 662	136 865	22 123	21 390	2 512	2 331	18 902	18 376	25 256	249
Mother-child subfamilies	**1 586 814**	**810 006**	**700 195**	**608 623**	**601 140**	**23 985**	**22 446**	**34 966**	**33 117**	**109 234**	**1 871**
Persons under 18 years	**63 606 544**	**47 753 472**	**43 925 831**	**9 566 954**	**9 333 604**	**690 641**	**628 295**	**2 052 428**	**1 964 676**	**3 543 049**	**116 744**
Percent living with two parents	71.8	79.3	80.4	36.8	36.7	55.7	55.9	82.2	82.9	62.1	59.3
UNMARRIED-PARTNER HOUSEHOLDS											
Total	**3 187 772**	**2 473 499**	**2 327 672**	**460 087**	**449 538**	**45 554**	**42 571**	**48 517**	**45 398**	**160 115**	**2 923**
Male and female	3 042 642	2 348 349	2 208 275	447 983	437 683	44 191	41 382	46 325	43 375	155 794	2 789
Both male	81 343	72 485	69 315	4 619	4 525	588	517	1 300	1 183	2 351	99
Both female	63 787	52 665	50 082	7 485	7 330	775	672	892	840	1 970	35
SELECTED LIVING ARRANGEMENTS											
Households	**91 993 582**	**76 906 980**	**73 747 747**	**9 941 850**	**9 767 383**	**625 367**	**588 826**	**2 020 498**	**1 965 079**	**2 498 887**	**52 507**
With one or more subfamilies	2 416 716	1 358 998	1 173 474	725 413	715 385	33 550	31 616	115 178	111 578	183 577	2 162
With related members 15 years and over other than spouse, children, parents, or parents-in-law of householder	4 488 360	2 788 518	2 398 111	999 031	974 950	49 173	45 124	239 073	231 419	412 565	4 804
With roomer, boarder, or foster child 15 years and over	905 979	663 925	610 147	149 992	145 667	8 106	7 247	30 025	28 631	53 931	840

Table 124. Education, Ability to Speak English, and Disability for Race and Hispanic Origin: 1990

[Data based on sample and subject to sampling variability, see text. For definitions of terms and meanings of symbols, see text]

United States	All persons	White		Black		American Indian, Eskimo, or Aleut		Asian or Pacific Islander		Other race	
		Total	Not of Hispanic origin	Total	Not of Hispanic origin	Total	Not of Hispanic origin	Total	Not of Hispanic origin	Total	Not of Hispanic origin
SCHOOL ENROLLMENT AND TYPE OF SCHOOL											
Persons 3 years and over enrolled in school	**64 987 101**	**49 273 838**	**45 645 771**	**9 269 910**	**9 050 487**	**635 992**	**581 667**	**2 552 671**	**2 468 194**	**3 254 690**	**93 916**
Preprimary school	4 503 285	3 619 904	3 427 660	563 019	549 510	41 421	38 054	132 582	127 807	146 359	8 174
Public school	2 679 029	2 033 215	1 904 040	427 560	417 528	34 573	32 015	67 445	64 475	116 236	5 101
Elementary or high school	42 566 788	31 537 361	28 894 611	6 642 519	6 486 700	467 518	426 488	1 446 890	1 389 391	2 472 500	67 976
Public school	38 379 689	28 071 143	25 648 132	6 259 803	6 118 646	444 226	405 984	1 280 058	1 229 058	2 324 459	60 661
College	17 917 028	14 116 573	13 323 500	2 064 372	2 014 277	127 053	117 125	973 199	950 996	635 831	17 766
Public college	13 805 534	10 811 273	10 174 247	1 626 861	1 590 032	106 465	98 281	729 252	712 444	531 683	13 109
Persons 3 years and over enrolled in school	**64 987 101**	**49 273 838**	**45 645 771**	**9 269 910**	**9 050 487**	**635 992**	**581 667**	**2 552 671**	**2 468 194**	**3 254 690**	**93 916**
3 and 4 years	2 118 735	1 606 278	1 503 875	338 893	330 438	19 813	18 155	70 729	68 182	83 022	4 474
5 to 14 years	32 655 517	24 605 376	22 666 265	4 878 558	4 765 882	357 150	325 790	1 059 662	1 015 756	1 754 771	54 462
15 to 17 years	9 294 846	7 030 379	6 524 253	1 382 723	1 355 356	95 485	87 979	322 079	310 791	464 180	12 460
18 and 19 years	4 974 321	3 828 687	3 596 690	684 234	670 103	39 683	36 630	210 889	204 866	210 828	5 570
20 to 24 years	6 267 157	4 905 399	4 612 543	700 969	681 566	39 474	36 044	355 538	347 155	265 777	6 612
25 to 34 years	5 064 093	3 740 005	3 433 452	675 830	656 192	43 793	39 652	316 058	309 877	288 407	6 050
35 years and over	4 612 432	3 557 714	3 308 693	608 703	590 950	40 594	37 417	217 716	211 567	187 705	4 288
Persons 18 to 24 years	**26 234 893**	**20 050 284**	**18 600 294**	**3 602 336**	**3 518 437**	**244 881**	**225 030**	**858 192**	**827 356**	**1 479 200**	**27 874**
Percent enrolled in college	34.4	35.9	36.8	27.1	27.1	21.6	21.7	55.1	55.8	20.5	31.9
Persons 16 to 19 years	**14 315 448**	**10 799 495**	**10 015 571**	**2 129 072**	**2 085 687**	**143 769**	**132 311**	**480 997**	**463 731**	**762 115**	**17 666**
Percent not enrolled, not high school graduate	11.2	10.0	9.2	13.7	13.6	18.1	17.9	5.4	5.2	24.2	14.6
EDUCATIONAL ATTAINMENT											
Persons 18 to 24 years	**26 234 893**	**20 050 284**	**18 600 294**	**3 602 336**	**3 518 437**	**244 881**	**225 030**	**858 192**	**827 356**	**1 479 200**	**27 874**
High school graduate (includes equivalency)	8 126 562	6 197 735	5 799 374	1 239 271	1 215 500	83 309	77 269	213 094	203 513	393 153	8 459
Some college or associate degree	9 941 932	8 082 861	7 705 438	1 107 360	1 084 627	67 252	62 292	371 306	360 084	313 153	9 006
Bachelor's degree or higher	1 991 840	1 722 489	1 670 422	121 791	119 287	5 089	4 790	112 580	110 607	29 891	1 143
Persons 25 years and over	**158 868 436**	**132 023 308**	**125 898 648**	**16 761 234**	**16 432 555**	**1 079 621**	**1 013 482**	**4 316 366**	**4 202 270**	**4 687 907**	**94 688**
Less than 5th grade	4 271 677	2 399 702	1 694 096	757 575	725 663	50 552	45 082	296 660	289 301	767 188	8 168
5th to 8th grade	12 230 534	9 406 967	8 439 213	1 548 870	1 501 132	100 662	93 071	261 234	251 184	912 801	9 389
9th to 12th grade, no diploma	22 841 507	17 355 153	16 228 529	3 881 407	3 805 008	220 900	206 924	411 508	395 822	972 539	16 915
High school graduate (includes equivalency)	47 642 763	40 891 202	39 521 862	4 680 594	4 607 134	313 783	297 883	799 206	773 144	957 978	23 108
Some college, no degree	29 779 777	25 221 246	24 285 302	3 101 292	3 050 083	224 300	210 661	634 810	613 664	598 129	17 595
Associate degree, occupational program	5 233 002	4 442 356	4 286 595	475 567	467 177	40 426	38 086	169 200	164 602	105 453	2 772
Associate degree, academic program	4 558 923	3 861 226	3 698 475	410 551	401 896	28 495	26 529	165 109	160 613	93 542	2 471
Bachelor's degree	20 832 567	18 337 917	17 902 015	1 261 090	1 241 290	65 512	62 330	978 338	959 816	189 710	8 919
Graduate or professional degree	11 477 686	10 107 539	9 842 561	644 288	633 172	34 991	32 916	600 301	594 124	90 567	5 351
Females 25 years and over	**83 654 171**	**69 252 013**	**66 108 006**	**9 257 807**	**9 088 653**	**562 703**	**529 782**	**2 282 675**	**2 221 712**	**2 298 973**	**48 499**
Less than 5th grade	2 161 459	1 200 562	836 966	363 978	346 642	26 399	23 751	192 850	188 958	377 670	4 438
5th to 8th grade	6 546 831	5 018 665	4 512 548	857 047	831 437	51 569	47 923	165 589	159 895	453 961	5 042
9th to 12th grade, no diploma	12 360 377	9 404 264	8 834 508	2 131 892	2 094 616	117 140	110 218	235 312	226 748	471 769	8 862
High school graduate (includes equivalency)	26 850 606	23 179 568	22 434 508	2 559 021	2 522 038	163 733	155 365	464 698	451 280	483 586	12 129
Some college, no degree	15 520 115	13 060 799	12 587 768	1 738 237	1 711 863	118 641	111 837	316 915	306 105	285 523	8 494
Associate degree, occupational program	2 920 672	2 473 486	2 392 632	284 688	280 113	21 071	19 880	88 196	85 694	53 231	1 471
Associate degree, academic program	2 538 505	2 142 909	2 056 521	239 853	235 204	15 626	14 648	92 715	90 347	47 402	1 482
Bachelor's degree	10 015 766	8 661 760	8 452 135	717 007	706 327	32 661	31 178	515 986	505 169	88 352	4 346
Graduate or professional degree	4 739 840	4 110 000	4 000 420	366 084	360 413	15 863	14 982	210 414	207 516	37 479	2 235
Persons 25 years and over	**158 868 436**	**132 023 308**	**125 898 648**	**16 761 234**	**16 432 555**	**1 079 621**	**1 013 482**	**4 316 366**	**4 202 270**	**4 687 907**	**94 688**
Percent less than 5th grade	2.7	1.8	1.3	4.5	4.4	4.7	4.4	6.9	6.9	16.4	8.6
Percent high school graduate or higher	75.2	77.9	79.1	63.1	63.3	65.5	66.0	77.5	77.7	43.4	63.6
Percent some college or higher	45.2	46.9	47.7	35.2	35.3	36.5	36.6	59.0	59.3	23.0	39.2
Percent bachelor's degree or higher	20.3	21.5	22.0	11.4	11.4	9.3	9.4	36.6	37.0	6.0	15.1
Males 25 to 34 years	**21 709 473**	**17 198 369**	**16 073 832**	**2 540 881**	**2 477 457**	**180 692**	**166 484**	**690 046**	**669 023**	**1 100 685**	**18 691**
Percent high school graduate or higher	82.7	86.0	87.8	74.2	74.6	71.7	72.6	87.2	87.6	50.3	71.6
Percent bachelor's degree or higher	22.9	25.0	25.9	10.9	11.0	7.2	7.3	43.6	44.4	6.7	15.8
Females 25 to 34 years	**21 757 561**	**17 017 533**	**15 973 799**	**2 872 381**	**2 811 676**	**186 646**	**173 632**	**725 215**	**704 174**	**955 786**	**18 087**
Percent high school graduate or higher	85.5	88.5	90.0	78.8	79.1	74.9	75.4	84.7	84.9	54.7	73.0
Percent bachelor's degree or higher	22.6	24.5	25.2	13.3	13.3	7.8	7.9	39.9	40.4	7.2	15.2
ABILITY TO SPEAK ENGLISH											
Persons 5 years and over	**230 445 777**	**186 181 122**	**175 934 346**	**27 175 607**	**26 609 376**	**1 817 347**	**1 688 619**	**6 652 553**	**6 447 551**	**8 619 148**	**196 148**
Speak a language other than English	31 844 979	17 693 779	10 084 653	1 707 777	1 319 051	432 761	375 375	4 878 530	4 761 884	7 132 132	87 718
5 to 17 years	6 322 934	3 107 817	1 434 470	397 181	310 572	94 960	82 089	896 940	875 203	1 826 036	24 333
18 to 64 years	21 707 874	11 543 098	6 213 758	1 215 904	935 540	301 226	259 830	3 618 339	3 531 931	5 029 307	58 230
65 to 74 years	2 118 454	1 618 067	1 238 535	60 312	45 753	21 970	19 887	236 355	231 122	181 750	3 341
75 years and over	1 695 717	1 424 797	1 197 890	34 380	27 186	14 605	13 569	126 896	123 628	95 039	1 814
Do not speak English "very well"	13 982 502	6 879 734	3 119 561	658 044	459 701	167 612	142 348	2 555 424	2 506 659	3 721 688	37 438
5 to 17 years	2 388 243	1 075 134	415 420	142 328	106 669	41 375	36 207	379 325	371 597	750 081	8 113
18 to 64 years	9 793 186	4 525 143	1 831 436	473 811	325 170	107 532	88 858	1 911 768	1 875 817	2 774 932	26 557
65 to 74 years	992 887	661 778	420 624	26 677	17 415	10 579	9 701	167 973	165 009	125 880	1 706
75 years and over	808 186	617 679	452 081	15 228	10 447	8 126	7 582	96 358	94 236	70 795	1 062
ABILITY TO SPEAK ENGLISH IN HOUSEHOLD											
Linguistically isolated households	2 936 596	1 548 004	769 053	131 793	86 770	32 310	27 563	542 402	533 602	682 087	6 882
Persons 5 years and over in households	**223 812 984**	**181 218 716**	**171 199 300**	**25 920 682**	**25 398 919**	**1 755 292**	**1 633 389**	**6 500 628**	**6 301 727**	**8 417 666**	**188 553**
In linguistically isolated households	7 741 259	3 603 368	1 373 213	298 152	183 581	81 800	67 785	1 572 006	1 546 963	2 185 933	21 040
5 to 17 years	1 763 173	709 670	183 082	70 700	43 943	22 760	19 059	366 366	360 073	593 677	6 813
18 to 64 years	4 968 023	2 153 631	693 029	207 110	127 621	49 303	39 739	1 070 211	1 053 533	1 487 768	12 861
65 to 74 years	556 681	384 249	240 469	12 926	7 474	5 317	4 871	88 226	86 928	65 963	872
75 years and over	453 382	355 818	256 633	7 416	4 543	4 420	4 116	47 203	46 429	38 525	494
DISABILITY STATUS OF CIVILIAN NONINSTITUTIONALIZED PERSONS											
Persons 16 to 64 years	**157 323 922**	**127 150 091**	**120 057 461**	**17 960 071**	**17 591 009**	**1 236 191**	**1 154 181**	**4 903 212**	**4 764 439**	**6 074 357**	**116 635**
With a mobility or self-care limitation	7 214 762	4 654 408	4 219 199	1 757 613	1 716 953	94 896	88 161	297 639	287 549	410 206	8 991
With a mobility limitation	3 452 631	2 491 572	2 307 989	660 083	644 755	46 073	42 965	96 213	92 813	158 690	3 461
In labor force	790 024	558 897	501 848	136 922	132 315	9 958	8 901	35 319	33 941	48 928	1 160
With a self-care limitation	5 383 939	3 272 137	2 927 081	1 452 741	1 418 663	71 397	66 190	255 005	246 569	332 659	7 266
With a work disability	12 826 449	10 050 712	9 571 612	1 986 413	1 953 042	168 266	158 712	205 612	197 051	415 446	9 864
In labor force	5 043 990	4 173 575	4 002 838	585 520	575 222	62 681	58 617	81 640	78 084	140 574	3 963
Prevented from working	6 594 029	4 926 795	4 658 920	1 234 848	1 215 005	90 482	85 933	100 763	96 503	241 141	4 928
No work disability	144 497 473	117 099 379	110 485 849	15 973 658	15 637 967	1 067 925	995 469	4 697 600	4 567 388	5 658 911	106 771
In labor force	114 652 861	93 996 244	88 982 245	12 208 834	11 964 202	775 459	721 132	3 452 728	3 350 642	4 219 596	79 603
Persons 65 to 74 years	**17 933 552**	**15 893 128**	**15 448 902**	**1 477 171**	**1 457 487**	**72 864**	**69 937**	**293 197**	**287 110**	**197 192**	**6 250**
With a mobility or self-care limitation	2 392 089	1 932 179	1 853 209	352 909	347 949	16 096	15 439	48 926	47 398	41 979	1 212
With a mobility limitation	1 631 650	1 321 804	1 267 375	237 512	234 224	12 135	11 675	29 663	28 801	30 536	752
With a self-care limitation	1 509 219	1 200 358	1 150 239	239 966	236 675	9 821	9 379	33 503	32 420	25 571	845
Persons 75 years and over	**11 629 959**	**10 440 708**	**10 188 216**	**908 745**	**898 448**	**40 188**	**38 705**	**140 949**	**137 126**	**99 369**	**3 544**
With a mobility or self-care limitation	3 551 352	3 082 088	2 987 337	368 611	364 427	15 209	14 609	45 531	44 356	39 913	1 294
With a mobility limitation	2 980 270	2 589 275	2 509 478	306 626	303 246	12 879	12 352	36 933	35 992	34 557	983
With a self-care limitation	2 014 865	1 717 445	1 659 547	235 810	232 865	9 180	8 807	27 391	26 669	25 039	769

Table 125. Geographic Mobility, Commuting, and Industry of Employed Persons for Race and Hispanic Origin: 1990

[Data based on sample and subject to sampling variability, see text. For definitions of terms and meanings of symbols, see text]

United States	All persons	White Total	White Not of Hispanic origin	Black Total	Black Not of Hispanic origin	American Indian, Eskimo, or Aleut Total	American Indian, Eskimo, or Aleut Not of Hispanic origin	Asian or Pacific Islander Total	Asian or Pacific Islander Not of Hispanic origin	Other race Total	Other race Not of Hispanic origin
PLACE OF BIRTH, NATIVITY, AND CITIZENSHIP											
All persons	248 709 873	199 827 064	188 424 773	29 930 524	29 284 596	2 015 143	1 866 807	7 226 986	6 994 302	9 710 156	239 306
Native	228 942 557	189 804 252	182 257 430	28 475 230	28 081 782	1 968 224	1 839 625	2 668 242	2 524 043	6 026 609	181 238
Born in State of residence	153 684 685	125 986 730	120 539 891	20 037 406	19 785 650	1 403 322	1 312 371	1 838 871	1 735 464	4 418 356	132 677
Born in a different State	72 011 141	61 816 425	60 450 863	8 193 064	8 115 666	549 140	516 232	567 800	542 732	884 712	41 112
Northeast	16 772 309	15 569 445	15 297 629	912 636	882 337	35 981	34 263	105 598	101 467	148 649	9 810
Midwest	21 287 172	19 959 706	19 777 290	1 004 929	996 568	121 546	116 782	90 697	88 640	110 294	7 606
South	24 366 640	17 785 456	17 347 095	5 955 306	5 926 107	191 222	182 763	105 754	100 097	328 902	14 809
West	9 585 020	8 501 818	8 028 849	320 193	310 654	200 391	182 424	265 751	252 528	296 867	8 887
Born abroad	3 246 731	2 001 097	1 266 676	244 760	180 466	15 762	11 022	261 571	245 847	723 541	7 449
Puerto Rico	1 190 533	560 612	27 466	50 215	4 182	1 752	194	4 473	776	573 481	1 938
U.S. outlying area	191 913	64 754	32 590	45 047	36 702	1 021	556	46 977	41 753	34 114	622
Born abroad of American parents	1 864 285	1 375 731	1 206 620	149 498	139 582	12 989	10 272	210 121	203 318	115 946	4 889
Foreign born	19 767 316	10 022 812	6 167 343	1 455 294	1 202 814	46 919	27 182	4 558 744	4 470 259	3 683 547	58 068
Naturalized citizen	7 996 998	4 843 090	3 717 537	485 672	403 344	16 885	11 870	1 830 508	1 790 657	820 843	17 294
Not a citizen	11 770 318	5 179 722	2 449 806	969 622	799 470	30 034	15 312	2 728 236	2 679 602	2 862 704	40 774
RESIDENCE IN 1985											
Persons 5 years and over	230 445 777	186 181 122	175 934 346	27 175 607	26 609 376	1 817 347	1 688 619	6 652 553	6 447 551	8 619 148	196 148
Same house	122 796 970	101 490 046	96 794 335	14 266 121	14 024 481	859 045	809 059	2 595 263	2 508 503	3 586 495	85 068
Different house in the United States	102 540 097	82 193 690	77 552 317	12 439 981	12 176 997	939 731	867 020	2 837 293	2 740 846	4 129 402	95 080
Same county	58 675 635	45 061 802	41 906 824	8 435 985	8 275 366	537 202	491 506	1 663 664	1 601 810	2 976 982	59 024
Different county	43 864 462	37 131 888	35 645 493	4 003 996	3 901 631	402 529	375 514	1 173 629	1 139 036	1 152 420	36 056
Same State	22 279 165	18 935 004	18 127 262	1 897 409	1 844 512	212 129	197 618	566 131	548 541	668 492	18 120
Different State	21 585 297	18 196 884	17 518 231	2 106 587	2 057 119	190 400	177 896	607 498	590 495	483 928	17 936
Northeast	4 346 471	3 658 880	3 492 322	435 852	413 270	12 383	11 460	133 491	130 600	105 865	4 728
Midwest	4 854 669	4 263 869	4 186 391	391 825	387 454	35 222	33 602	110 931	109 056	52 822	2 519
South	7 588 749	6 180 604	5 965 552	1 018 883	1 003 783	61 434	58 050	167 890	163 366	159 938	5 700
West	4 795 408	4 093 531	3 873 966	260 027	252 612	81 361	74 784	195 186	187 473	165 303	4 989
Puerto Rico	213 886	108 432	9 953	9 521	1 264	315	51	1 106	579	94 512	282
U.S. outlying area	73 764	31 633	25 872	20 084	17 890	446	342	14 172	12 858	7 429	133
Elsewhere	4 821 060	2 357 321	1 551 869	439 900	388 744	17 810	12 147	1 204 719	1 184 765	801 310	15 585
MEANS OF TRANSPORTATION TO WORK AND TRAVEL TIME TO WORK											
Workers 16 years and over	115 070 274	95 708 551	90 988 092	11 414 755	11 192 416	724 223	673 406	3 381 333	3 281 943	3 841 412	76 394
Car, truck, or van	99 592 932	84 500 232	80 617 006	8 782 909	8 658 063	608 615	569 007	2 694 332	2 615 255	3 006 844	57 269
Drove alone	84 215 298	72 860 206	69 913 934	6 710 774	6 621 310	472 816	443 683	2 077 175	2 017 780	2 094 327	43 811
Carpooled	15 377 634	11 640 026	10 703 072	2 072 135	2 036 753	135 799	125 324	617 157	597 475	912 517	13 458
Persons per car, truck, or van	1.09	1.08	1.08	1.15	1.15	1.14	1.14	1.14	1.14	1.21	1.15
Public transportation	6 069 589	3 406 567	2 980 891	1 784 576	1 711 951	30 408	25 390	381 611	370 442	466 427	9 747
Bus or trolley bus	3 445 000	1 761 847	1 496 905	1 162 263	1 131 510	22 039	18 671	195 839	188 868	303 012	5 638
Streetcar or trolley car	78 130	49 059	44 933	18 801	18 214	344	296	6 178	6 070	3 748	177
Subway or elevated	1 755 476	972 246	842 418	487 564	450 492	5 469	4 081	147 967	144 464	142 230	3 367
Railroad	574 052	476 826	458 715	61 364	58 822	879	764	24 516	24 196	10 467	345
Ferryboat	37 497	31 618	30 241	3 079	2 915	251	247	1 596	1 515	953	39
Taxicab	179 434	114 971	107 679	51 505	49 998	1 426	1 331	5 515	5 329	6 017	181
Motorcycle	237 404	211 514	200 490	9 168	8 957	2 677	2 417	5 246	5 002	8 799	200
Bicycle	466 856	382 010	351 525	35 109	34 194	4 914	4 331	17 190	16 748	27 633	589
Walked	4 488 886	3 501 785	3 281 172	537 389	520 053	44 713	41 501	188 293	183 332	216 706	5 485
Other means	808 582	583 175	530 917	131 759	129 445	12 317	11 507	25 484	24 166	55 847	1 210
Worked at home	3 406 025	3 123 268	3 026 091	133 845	129 753	20 579	19 253	69 177	66 998	59 156	1 894
Mean travel time to work (minutes)	22.3	21.8	21.7	25.3	25.2	21.8	21.6	25.5	25.5	24.3	24.0
INDUSTRY											
Employed persons 16 years and over	115 681 202	96 237 561	91 447 312	11 407 803	11 184 939	728 953	677 843	3 411 586	3 312 806	3 895 299	76 786
Agriculture, forestry, and fisheries	3 115 372	2 647 802	2 438 043	150 747	147 020	25 445	23 293	45 306	43 327	246 072	1 618
Mining	723 423	656 731	630 499	31 470	31 161	8 386	8 155	5 845	5 630	20 991	286
Construction	7 214 763	6 263 616	5 921 492	476 307	464 973	61 635	57 268	104 924	100 070	308 281	4 195
Manufacturing	20 462 078	16 890 055	16 006 769	1 961 469	1 922 160	117 389	109 085	632 058	616 500	861 107	13 934
Nondurable goods	8 053 234	6 483 339	6 106 767	916 855	898 660	44 934	41 897	236 568	230 617	371 538	5 532
Food and kindred products	1 405 723	1 073 263	991 387	181 040	178 228	9 855	9 092	41 685	40 107	99 880	1 160
Textile mill and finished textile products	1 809 199	1 285 588	1 168 280	305 421	297 912	12 325	11 512	91 361	89 764	114 504	1 488
Printing, publishing, and allied industries	1 941 923	1 705 760	1 641 060	132 120	128 836	8 074	7 494	44 755	43 535	51 214	1 179
Durable goods	12 408 844	10 406 716	9 900 002	1 044 614	1 023 500	72 455	67 188	395 490	385 883	489 569	8 402
Furniture, lumber, and wood products	1 276 578	1 063 188	1 011 586	128 000	126 256	12 545	11 903	14 176	13 620	58 669	688
Metal industries	1 965 144	1 672 474	1 591 359	167 622	164 609	10 703	9 967	27 903	27 063	86 442	1 187
Machinery and computer equipment	2 362 588	2 074 207	2 000 374	131 417	129 121	10 910	10 213	80 350	78 797	65 704	1 115
Electrical equipment and components, except computer	1 899 173	1 555 462	1 473 017	144 908	141 925	10 033	9 180	117 565	115 284	71 205	1 385
Transportation equipment	2 532 532	2 115 135	2 034 043	260 039	257 252	13 531	12 664	73 424	71 487	70 403	1 332
Transportation	5 108 003	4 081 444	3 871 866	699 951	687 167	31 583	29 159	141 280	136 363	153 745	3 445
Communications and other public utilities	3 097 059	2 587 090	2 484 550	358 348	353 752	19 386	18 148	61 982	59 753	70 253	1 850
Wholesale trade	5 071 026	4 394 632	4 169 987	328 670	320 104	23 251	21 176	145 540	141 898	178 933	2 952
Retail trade	19 485 666	16 364 128	15 486 589	1 611 127	1 574 195	118 938	109 046	692 411	673 522	699 062	14 535
Food, bakery, and dairy stores	3 339 390	2 814 883	2 666 533	268 777	261 597	21 323	19 423	115 723	112 645	118 684	2 556
Eating and drinking places	5 463 979	4 274 860	3 958 672	573 498	560 893	40 573	36 835	288 623	281 611	286 425	5 207
Banking and credit agencies	2 374 916	1 965 795	1 873 343	242 159	237 184	7 357	6 869	101 194	98 441	58 411	1 552
Insurance, real estate, and other finance	5 609 954	4 895 297	4 717 583	428 538	419 466	21 343	19 842	152 679	148 523	112 097	2 926
Business and repair services	5 577 462	4 598 006	4 322 679	561 612	546 651	33 516	30 606	150 934	145 930	233 394	4 811
Private households	628 510	381 932	313 683	163 907	159 532	5 073	4 385	16 804	15 704	60 794	934
Other personal services	3 040 186	2 345 305	2 164 676	366 248	357 583	22 619	20 770	156 471	151 503	149 543	2 748
Entertainment and recreation services	1 636 460	1 405 978	1 336 665	122 681	119 261	12 491	11 600	44 051	42 382	51 259	1 345
Professional and related services	26 998 247	22 391 320	21 539 756	3 056 755	3 006 719	162 069	152 650	824 104	802 488	563 999	16 224
Hospitals	5 204 690	3 974 245	3 805 909	847 519	832 843	29 510	27 631	231 905	224 970	121 511	3 550
Health services, except hospitals	4 477 994	3 688 334	3 543 623	527 437	517 554	28 742	27 133	135 092	131 066	98 389	2 766
Educational services	9 633 503	8 096 442	7 789 960	1 034 407	1 021 801	59 453	56 415	250 221	245 083	192 980	5 238
Public administration	5 538 077	4 368 430	4 169 132	847 814	838 011	58 472	55 791	136 003	130 772	127 358	3 431

Table 126. Labor Force Characteristics for Race and Hispanic Origin: 1990

[Data based on sample and subject to sampling variability, see text. For definitions of terms and meanings of symbols, see text]

United States	All persons	White		Black		American Indian, Eskimo, or Aleut		Asian or Pacific Islander		Other race	
		Total	Not of Hispanic origin	Total	Not of Hispanic origin	Total	Not of Hispanic origin	Total	Not of Hispanic origin	Total	Not of Hispanic origin
LABOR FORCE STATUS											
Persons 16 years and over	**191 829 271**	**157 119 373**	**149 164 557**	**21 386 343**	**20 953 608**	**1 395 009**	**1 303 471**	**5 403 615**	**5 250 388**	**6 524 931**	**131 345**
In labor force	125 182 378	102 800 818	97 467 714	13 413 487	13 148 010	865 703	805 342	3 645 946	3 535 560	4 456 424	86 682
Percent of persons 16 years and over	65.3	65.4	65.3	62.7	62.7	62.1	61.8	67.5	67.3	68.3	66.0
Armed Forces	1 708 928	1 275 082	1 224 593	318 306	312 409	14 391	13 070	42 866	39 799	58 283	1 710
Civilian labor force	123 473 450	101 525 736	96 243 121	13 095 181	12 835 601	851 312	792 272	3 603 080	3 495 761	4 398 141	84 972
Employed	115 681 202	96 237 561	91 447 312	11 407 803	11 184 939	728 953	677 843	3 411 586	3 312 806	3 895 299	76 786
At work 35 or more hours	89 428 871	74 240 108	70 470 721	8 873 999	8 698 736	548 730	510 624	2 690 953	2 613 609	3 075 081	56 689
Unemployed	7 792 248	5 288 175	4 795 809	1 687 378	1 650 662	122 359	114 429	191 494	182 955	502 842	8 186
Percent of civilian labor force	6.3	5.2	5.0	12.9	12.9	14.4	14.4	5.3	5.2	11.4	9.6
Not in labor force	66 646 893	54 318 555	51 696 843	7 972 856	7 805 598	529 306	498 129	1 757 669	1 714 828	2 068 507	44 663
Institutionalized persons	3 232 910	2 360 364	2 245 385	722 050	694 255	31 375	27 578	23 391	21 914	95 730	3 206
Females 16 years and over	**99 803 358**	**81 541 169**	**77 546 546**	**11 597 691**	**11 380 034**	**714 654**	**670 320**	**2 810 588**	**2 729 681**	**3 139 256**	**66 661**
In labor force	56 672 949	45 947 179	43 705 520	6 901 351	6 780 080	393 437	367 687	1 688 145	1 634 863	1 742 837	39 113
Percent of females 16 years and over	56.8	56.3	56.4	59.5	59.6	55.1	54.9	60.1	59.9	55.5	58.7
Armed Forces	185 700	120 552	115 037	53 709	52 756	2 017	1 791	4 063	3 791	5 359	182
Civilian labor force	56 487 249	45 826 627	43 590 483	6 847 642	6 727 324	391 420	365 896	1 684 082	1 631 072	1 737 478	38 931
Employed	52 976 623	43 515 117	41 499 763	6 015 288	5 912 329	340 042	317 921	1 590 897	1 542 268	1 515 279	35 156
At work 35 or more hours	36 418 960	29 467 638	28 036 488	4 470 242	4 394 169	235 857	220 995	1 174 018	1 138 449	1 071 205	23 427
Unemployed	3 510 626	2 311 510	2 090 720	832 354	814 995	51 378	47 975	93 185	88 804	222 199	3 775
Percent of civilian labor force	6.2	5.0	4.8	12.2	12.1	13.1	13.1	5.5	5.4	12.8	9.7
Not in labor force	43 130 409	35 593 990	33 841 026	4 696 340	4 599 954	321 217	302 633	1 122 443	1 094 818	1 396 419	27 548
Institutionalized persons	1 487 110	1 309 391	1 285 589	149 200	146 195	7 261	6 760	8 954	8 646	12 304	733
Males 16 to 19 years	**7 342 263**	**5 543 693**	**5 127 602**	**1 072 640**	**1 049 522**	**74 536**	**68 324**	**247 569**	**239 106**	**403 825**	**8 776**
Employed	2 962 432	2 453 192	2 290 734	256 572	250 508	21 985	19 893	73 407	70 119	157 276	3 256
Unemployed	670 528	460 692	415 598	137 333	134 514	9 190	8 396	14 626	13 828	48 687	819
Not in labor force	3 562 362	2 521 228	2 317 348	650 894	637 250	41 984	38 838	157 048	152 885	191 208	4 461
Males 20 to 24 years	**9 469 385**	**7 263 216**	**6 699 767**	**1 212 585**	**1 180 150**	**88 901**	**81 127**	**311 767**	**301 043**	**592 916**	**9 719**
Employed	6 419 967	5 154 588	4 749 099	611 066	594 380	48 798	44 125	179 585	172 303	425 930	6 053
Unemployed	768 405	507 787	453 974	170 514	166 944	13 825	12 836	16 824	16 091	59 455	765
Not in labor force	1 806 836	1 248 963	1 158 783	343 341	332 834	21 626	19 916	105 474	103 534	87 432	2 325
Males 25 to 54 years	**52 743 194**	**42 937 054**	**40 590 845**	**5 686 136**	**5 553 288**	**411 828**	**383 430**	**1 630 771**	**1 587 581**	**2 077 405**	**37 883**
Employed	44 842 502	37 589 632	35 660 537	3 921 380	3 835 381	284 470	264 104	1 382 945	1 347 821	1 664 075	29 051
Unemployed	2 450 753	1 691 210	1 540 404	501 719	489 990	44 164	41 618	56 378	54 087	157 282	2 571
Not in labor force	4 553 238	2 966 583	2 726 457	1 114 548	1 082 109	76 893	71 913	165 205	161 225	230 009	5 565
Males 55 to 64 years	**9 957 003**	**8 640 902**	**8 301 214**	**869 733**	**854 668**	**55 995**	**53 202**	**205 333**	**200 301**	**185 040**	**4 169**
Employed	6 377 542	5 620 921	5 397 856	471 369	462 491	27 507	25 948	145 196	141 691	112 549	2 574
Unemployed	294 523	236 665	219 790	34 837	33 927	3 085	2 945	7 962	7 737	11 974	227
Not in labor force	3 279 732	2 779 018	2 679 426	362 965	357 688	25 359	24 272	51 987	50 702	60 403	1 352
Males 65 to 69 years	**4 555 259**	**4 046 612**	**3 925 161**	**356 341**	**351 373**	**20 108**	**19 298**	**76 895**	**75 140**	**55 303**	**1 636**
In labor force	1 269 464	1 141 235	1 103 791	81 965	80 248	4 363	4 095	26 527	25 847	15 374	406
Not in labor force	3 285 795	2 905 377	2 821 370	274 376	271 125	15 745	15 203	50 368	49 293	39 929	1 230
Did not work in 1989	2 675 255	2 346 126	2 276 120	239 385	236 573	13 416	12 987	41 780	40 902	34 548	1 042
Males 70 years and over	**7 958 809**	**7 146 727**	**6 973 422**	**591 217**	**584 573**	**28 987**	**27 770**	**120 692**	**117 536**	**71 186**	**2 501**
In labor force	930 288	843 331	820 989	60 825	59 935	2 505	2 416	15 548	15 165	8 079	319
Not in labor force	7 028 521	6 303 396	6 152 433	530 392	524 638	26 482	25 354	105 144	102 371	63 107	2 182
Did not work in 1989	6 289 799	5 613 410	5 473 801	495 995	490 680	24 303	23 274	97 104	94 511	58 987	1 941
Females 16 to 19 years	**6 973 185**	**5 255 802**	**4 887 969**	**1 056 432**	**1 036 165**	**69 233**	**63 987**	**233 428**	**224 625**	**358 290**	**8 890**
Employed	2 880 619	2 398 515	2 272 538	276 106	270 698	20 236	18 442	73 165	69 861	112 597	3 318
Unemployed	541 322	359 046	326 918	128 329	126 027	7 523	6 982	10 857	10 038	35 567	690
Not in labor force	3 530 010	2 484 743	2 275 849	645 828	633 450	41 192	38 323	149 039	144 386	209 208	4 882
Females 20 to 24 years	**9 176 002**	**7 033 354**	**6 550 571**	**1 283 452**	**1 255 216**	**82 718**	**76 551**	**294 485**	**283 344**	**481 993**	**9 272**
Employed	5 946 615	4 822 599	4 546 923	662 335	648 666	39 895	36 680	168 071	161 052	253 715	5 132
Unemployed	605 852	368 091	329 885	171 765	168 572	9 552	8 888	13 326	12 688	43 118	743
Not in labor force	2 564 310	1 805 452	1 638 321	431 333	420 277	32 551	30 360	111 968	108 546	183 006	3 027
Females 25 to 54 years	**53 809 217**	**43 111 433**	**40 777 951**	**6 578 709**	**6 447 558**	**431 080**	**403 551**	**1 777 497**	**1 728 203**	**1 910 498**	**37 621**
Employed	37 761 559	30 815 968	29 393 493	4 424 857	4 350 497	251 698	235 816	1 203 710	1 169 360	1 065 326	23 552
Unemployed	2 079 910	1 361 135	1 226 933	494 029	483 205	31 853	29 831	59 948	57 327	132 945	2 104
Not in labor force	13 863 239	10 865 027	10 091 082	1 630 433	1 584 916	146 514	136 976	511 318	499 178	709 947	11 853
Females 55 to 64 years	**11 163 747**	**9 503 847**	**9 115 058**	**1 125 815**	**1 107 330**	**62 995**	**60 069**	**260 191**	**253 681**	**210 899**	**4 961**
Employed	4 894 548	4 173 827	4 016 959	505 641	497 887	22 406	21 447	121 478	118 038	71 196	2 238
Unemployed	199 774	155 951	143 442	26 502	25 737	1 953	1 798	6 890	6 685	8 478	173
Not in labor force	6 068 702	5 173 539	4 954 178	593 541	583 581	38 636	36 824	131 768	128 903	131 218	2 550
Females 65 to 69 years	**5 604 849**	**4 904 414**	**4 754 245**	**507 624**	**500 406**	**24 292**	**23 219**	**98 240**	**96 264**	**70 279**	**2 030**
In labor force	944 717	822 170	797 974	91 626	90 408	3 744	3 557	18 228	17 866	8 949	332
Not in labor force	4 660 132	4 082 244	3 956 271	415 998	409 998	20 548	19 662	80 012	78 398	61 330	1 698
Did not work in 1989	4 202 287	3 675 743	3 559 605	377 408	371 844	18 589	17 755	73 041	71 625	57 506	1 489
Females 70 years and over	**13 076 358**	**11 732 319**	**11 460 752**	**1 045 659**	**1 033 359**	**44 336**	**42 943**	**146 747**	**143 564**	**107 297**	**3 887**
In labor force	632 342	549 334	535 427	66 452	65 627	2 560	2 455	8 409	8 157	5 587	349
Not in labor force	12 444 016	11 182 985	10 925 325	979 207	967 732	41 776	40 488	138 338	135 407	101 710	3 538
Did not work in 1989	11 840 761	10 628 686	10 379 637	939 939	928 887	39 694	38 449	133 512	130 683	98 930	3 313
PRESENCE OF OWN CHILDREN IN FAMILIES AND SUBFAMILIES											
Females 16 years and over	**99 803 358**	**81 541 169**	**77 546 546**	**11 597 691**	**11 380 034**	**714 654**	**670 320**	**2 810 588**	**2 729 681**	**3 139 256**	**66 661**
With own children under 6 years	15 233 818	11 673 162	10 832 368	2 069 059	2 023 998	147 285	137 386	515 031	499 425	829 281	13 291
In labor force	9 095 156	6 981 350	6 538 068	1 321 597	1 298 650	78 910	73 761	295 743	286 438	417 556	7 195
With own children 6 to 17 years only	16 490 186	12 940 335	12 185 829	2 209 619	2 170 146	142 961	134 340	553 642	538 274	643 629	11 058
In labor force	12 367 705	9 758 938	9 253 574	1 697 017	1 670 465	97 957	92 263	404 696	392 531	409 097	7 671
Own children under 6 years living with two parents	**15 993 967**	**13 365 043**	**12 433 972**	**1 120 631**	**1 083 154**	**126 232**	**114 286**	**582 444**	**560 032**	**799 617**	**29 777**
Both parents in labor force	8 874 102	7 356 865	6 894 604	762 231	741 478	61 519	55 453	309 547	296 321	383 940	16 868
Both at work 35 or more hours	4 433 879	3 551 805	3 305 073	455 328	443 414	27 868	25 127	197 142	189 326	201 736	9 028
Own children under 6 years living with one parent	**5 279 645**	**2 691 801**	**2 296 228**	**1 957 353**	**1 906 960**	**99 013**	**88 953**	**92 667**	**83 536**	**438 811**	**18 231**
Parent in labor force	3 169 479	1 757 315	1 530 677	1 077 653	1 053 462	53 193	48 069	52 985	47 702	228 333	10 694
At work 35 or more hours	1 936 665	1 151 722	1 006 176	576 138	562 417	28 249	25 410	38 470	34 802	142 086	6 516
Own children 6 to 17 years living with two parents	**29 673 627**	**24 506 771**	**22 876 830**	**2 403 582**	**2 346 780**	**258 426**	**236 978**	**1 105 516**	**1 068 090**	**1 399 332**	**39 506**
Both parents in labor force	19 477 241	16 126 135	15 197 358	1 723 939	1 689 605	149 745	137 696	709 041	682 858	768 381	25 479
Both at work 35 or more hours	10 782 593	8 710 728	8 187 268	1 098 819	1 079 051	78 618	72 393	481 480	464 423	412 948	14 417
Own children 6 to 17 years living with one parent	**9 931 854**	**5 641 232**	**4 989 238**	**3 274 251**	**3 206 326**	**153 491**	**139 897**	**191 540**	**177 634**	**671 340**	**23 006**
Parent in labor force	7 343 393	4 490 361	4 047 712	2 212 058	2 171 735	100 318	91 996	133 038	122 995	407 618	15 938
At work 35 or more hours	5 231 410	3 369 644	3 062 492	1 423 150	1 396 679	62 936	57 810	103 025	95 603	272 655	11 172

Table 127. **Additional Labor Force Characteristics and Veteran Status for Race and Hispanic Origin: 1990**

[Data based on sample and subject to sampling variability, see text. For definitions of terms and meanings of symbols, see text]

United States	All persons	White: Total	White: Not of Hispanic origin	Black: Total	Black: Not of Hispanic origin	American Indian, Eskimo, or Aleut: Total	American Indian, Eskimo, or Aleut: Not of Hispanic origin	Asian or Pacific Islander: Total	Asian or Pacific Islander: Not of Hispanic origin	Other race: Total	Other race: Not of Hispanic origin
LABOR FORCE STATUS OF FAMILY MEMBERS											
Married-couple families	**51 718 214**	**45 178 672**	**43 342 946**	**3 521 382**	**3 458 050**	**305 156**	**288 308**	**1 295 099**	**1 265 101**	**1 417 905**	**24 115**
Husband employed or in Armed Forces	39 286 822	34 232 358	32 764 255	2 598 174	2 549 409	218 614	205 383	1 068 819	1 043 965	1 168 857	18 790
Wife employed or in Armed Forces	25 799 947	22 440 348	21 609 186	1 874 907	1 845 532	135 797	128 071	715 004	697 912	633 891	11 715
Wife unemployed	1 071 291	835 895	768 679	124 728	121 551	10 678	9 894	31 496	30 572	68 494	790
Husband unemployed	1 364 119	1 076 953	996 311	151 968	147 935	21 205	20 187	33 315	32 115	80 678	1 106
Wife employed or in Armed Forces	790 277	627 582	589 102	97 365	95 142	10 191	9 653	19 141	18 443	35 998	530
Wife unemployed	127 477	92 037	81 786	16 663	16 088	2 955	2 822	4 071	3 891	11 751	131
Husband not in labor force	11 067 273	9 869 361	9 582 380	771 240	760 706	65 337	62 738	192 965	189 021	168 370	4 219
Wife employed or in Armed Forces	2 383 825	2 010 101	1 936 739	254 030	250 688	18 947	18 064	53 519	52 102	47 228	1 379
Wife unemployed	127 210	97 182	90 120	18 464	18 090	2 256	2 166	3 121	3 058	6 187	170
Female householder, no husband present	**10 381 654**	**6 540 382**	**6 058 841**	**3 045 283**	**2 993 086**	**121 370**	**113 658**	**185 926**	**176 964**	**488 693**	**9 459**
Employed or in Armed Forces	6 031 687	4 011 325	3 751 641	1 617 812	1 594 622	58 613	54 902	116 808	111 551	227 129	5 066
Unemployed	593 069	270 386	239 234	269 634	265 223	10 433	9 754	6 393	5 814	36 223	750
SCHOOL ENROLLMENT AND LABOR FORCE STATUS											
Persons 16 to 19 years	**14 315 448**	**10 799 495**	**10 015 571**	**2 129 072**	**2 085 687**	**143 769**	**132 311**	**480 997**	**463 731**	**762 115**	**17 666**
Enrolled in school	11 073 188	8 441 214	7 881 647	1 595 913	1 564 533	100 668	92 985	427 064	413 628	508 329	13 287
Employed	4 159 951	3 495 880	3 318 507	367 584	360 110	25 218	23 012	120 911	116 254	150 358	4 487
Unemployed	756 835	513 627	468 812	166 082	162 750	8 994	8 230	20 084	19 013	48 048	955
Not in labor force	6 136 105	4 416 742	4 080 305	1 058 491	1 038 052	66 322	61 625	285 473	277 818	309 077	7 818
Not enrolled in school	3 242 260	2 358 281	2 133 924	533 159	521 154	43 101	39 326	53 933	50 103	253 786	4 379
High school graduate	1 636 766	1 281 328	1 210 340	240 977	236 839	17 106	15 620	27 719	25 858	69 636	1 796
Employed	1 042 647	875 028	831 527	103 897	102 225	8 772	7 940	16 221	15 117	38 729	987
Unemployed	180 695	124 548	115 978	42 283	41 600	2 680	2 510	2 402	2 189	8 782	153
Not in labor force	274 277	181 444	166 495	65 728	64 535	4 258	3 975	6 943	6 587	15 904	450
Not high school graduate	1 605 494	1 076 953	923 584	292 182	284 315	25 995	23 706	26 214	24 245	184 150	2 583
Employed	640 453	480 799	413 238	61 197	58 871	8 231	7 383	9 440	8 609	80 786	1 100
Unemployed	274 320	181 563	157 726	57 297	56 191	5 039	4 638	2 997	2 664	27 424	401
Not in labor force	681 990	407 785	346 397	172 503	168 113	12 596	11 561	13 671	12 866	75 435	1 075
CLASS OF WORKER											
Employed persons 16 years and over	**115 681 202**	**96 237 561**	**91 447 312**	**11 407 803**	**11 184 939**	**728 953**	**677 843**	**3 411 586**	**3 312 806**	**3 895 299**	**76 786**
Private wage and salary workers	89 541 393	74 725 163	70 837 628	8 353 004	8 175 859	518 435	478 560	2 668 258	2 588 989	3 276 533	61 756
Local government workers	8 244 755	6 552 785	6 235 102	1 231 855	1 211 194	66 172	62 430	158 495	153 304	235 448	4 995
State government workers	5 381 445	4 278 367	4 107 997	757 734	749 216	43 141	40 966	184 743	180 615	117 460	3 362
Federal government workers	3 940 900	2 914 983	2 771 167	726 293	718 347	56 132	53 802	147 950	142 083	95 542	2 653
Self-employed workers	8 067 483	7 318 612	7 066 005	321 516	313 660	42 270	39 468	227 250	223 343	157 835	3 809
Unpaid family workers	505 226	447 651	429 413	17 401	16 663	2 803	2 617	24 890	24 472	12 481	211
Employed females 16 years and over	**52 976 623**	**43 515 117**	**41 499 763**	**6 015 288**	**5 912 329**	**340 042**	**317 921**	**1 590 897**	**1 542 268**	**1 515 279**	**35 156**
Private wage and salary workers	40 693 002	33 702 710	32 107 599	4 276 686	4 197 058	233 919	217 251	1 251 502	1 212 468	1 228 185	27 693
Local government workers	4 617 771	3 658 838	3 487 920	718 821	707 269	34 311	32 401	83 981	81 215	121 820	2 754
State government workers	3 002 677	2 328 412	2 231 115	492 672	487 781	24 691	23 534	90 332	87 962	66 570	1 887
Federal government workers	1 663 488	1 137 547	1 080 975	394 015	390 003	29 755	28 609	61 778	59 212	40 393	1 316
Self-employed workers	2 708 708	2 427 162	2 340 830	124 580	121 902	16 026	14 865	87 877	86 222	53 063	1 383
Unpaid family workers	290 977	260 448	251 324	8 514	8 316	1 340	1 261	15 427	15 189	5 248	123
WORK STATUS IN 1989											
Persons 16 years and over, worked in 1989	**134 529 779**	**111 350 984**	**105 876 755**	**13 914 568**	**13 641 643**	**940 172**	**875 245**	**3 824 000**	**3 709 730**	**4 500 055**	**91 736**
50 to 52 weeks	84 533 428	71 367 339	68 256 293	8 042 778	7 895 001	472 252	440 108	2 309 455	2 244 707	2 341 604	49 747
48 and 49 weeks	5 825 217	4 437 724	4 075 635	701 540	683 858	39 576	35 671	268 951	259 583	377 426	5 240
40 to 47 weeks	11 370 482	9 407 780	8 920 793	1 146 309	1 121 466	80 053	74 196	321 012	311 656	415 328	8 015
27 to 39 weeks	10 110 388	8 200 361	7 731 591	1 135 436	1 111 443	91 517	85 461	261 145	252 666	421 929	7 720
14 to 26 weeks	11 628 106	9 299 943	8 744 324	1 380 301	1 350 530	117 477	109 381	336 256	325 124	494 129	10 575
1 to 13 weeks	11 062 158	8 637 837	8 148 119	1 508 204	1 479 345	139 297	130 428	327 181	315 994	449 639	10 439
Usually worked 35 or more hours per week	105 361 883	86 810 887	82 379 507	11 078 912	10 855 309	740 837	690 617	3 037 181	2 946 039	3 694 066	70 623
40 or more weeks	87 097 175	72 595 660	69 127 245	8 689 678	8 521 915	515 937	479 695	2 517 488	2 444 674	2 778 412	54 094
50 to 52 weeks	74 660 124	62 809 360	60 012 196	7 239 604	7 105 899	422 031	393 441	2 066 573	2 008 823	2 122 556	43 902
27 to 39 weeks	6 296 616	5 003 046	4 678 059	762 882	745 094	64 503	60 671	158 366	152 769	307 819	4 977
Females 16 years and over, worked in 1989	**61 904 615**	**50 747 988**	**48 407 278**	**7 137 050**	**7 014 551**	**433 349**	**405 400**	**1 787 262**	**1 731 175**	**1 798 966**	**42 031**
50 to 52 weeks	35 419 603	29 347 758	28 117 360	4 003 406	3 939 490	205 888	192 949	1 008 791	978 925	853 760	21 488
48 and 49 weeks	2 692 119	2 046 442	1 902 375	365 603	357 499	16 904	15 438	124 904	120 365	138 266	2 295
40 to 47 weeks	5 996 730	4 993 075	4 772 937	632 882	621 222	38 235	35 666	165 324	160 434	167 214	3 881
27 to 39 weeks	5 569 882	4 572 964	4 349 363	631 517	620 019	45 804	42 963	139 430	134 822	180 167	3 770
14 to 26 weeks	6 241 320	5 061 450	4 791 277	716 379	702 384	56 940	53 115	176 036	169 972	230 515	5 360
1 to 13 weeks	5 984 961	4 726 299	4 473 966	787 263	773 937	69 578	65 269	172 777	166 657	229 044	5 237
Usually worked 35 or more hours per week	42 973 185	34 579 618	32 866 204	5 418 162	5 324 066	311 436	291 965	1 333 277	1 291 783	1 330 692	29 332
40 or more weeks	34 274 397	27 802 103	26 510 719	4 232 765	4 162 622	212 942	199 356	1 075 894	1 043 473	950 693	21 976
50 to 52 weeks	28 714 940	23 459 793	22 425 329	3 489 925	3 434 384	173 875	163 072	866 664	841 393	724 683	17 672
27 to 39 weeks	3 061 761	2 440 145	2 304 363	399 557	391 611	28 652	27 067	78 645	75 875	114 762	2 143
WORKERS IN FAMILY IN 1989											
Families	**65 049 428**	**53 845 200**	**51 337 479**	**7 055 063**	**6 927 208**	**463 968**	**436 752**	**1 577 820**	**1 535 190**	**2 107 377**	**36 724**
No workers	8 477 151	6 866 496	6 598 688	1 173 808	1 148 809	67 067	63 723	131 352	127 668	238 428	4 575
1 worker	18 243 077	14 672 797	13 891 781	2 344 189	2 300 702	153 924	144 695	413 200	401 771	658 967	11 792
2 workers	29 637 580	25 306 415	24 275 747	2 595 101	2 553 077	187 916	176 866	720 804	702 219	827 344	15 132
3 or more workers	8 691 620	6 999 492	6 571 263	941 965	924 620	55 061	51 468	312 464	303 532	382 638	5 225
Married-couple families	**51 718 214**	**45 178 672**	**43 342 946**	**3 521 382**	**3 458 050**	**305 156**	**288 308**	**1 295 099**	**1 265 101**	**1 417 905**	**24 115**
No workers	6 129 613	5 588 666	5 449 811	345 299	339 840	29 632	28 638	91 301	89 699	74 715	1 877
1 worker	11 870 620	10 429 743	9 945 895	692 228	675 800	75 213	70 982	303 369	297 502	370 067	6 015
2 or more workers	33 717 981	29 160 263	27 947 240	2 483 855	2 442 410	200 311	188 688	900 429	877 900	973 123	16 223
Husband and wife worked	30 599 124	26 613 597	25 602 709	2 204 719	2 169 062	178 417	168 223	804 563	784 660	797 828	14 188
Female householder, no husband present	**10 381 654**	**6 540 382**	**6 058 841**	**3 045 283**	**2 993 086**	**121 370**	**113 658**	**185 926**	**176 964**	**488 693**	**9 459**
No workers	2 056 800	1 083 218	968 480	759 968	741 878	32 080	29 977	32 120	30 208	149 414	2 419
1 worker	4 929 373	3 194 979	2 984 183	1 404 530	1 383 377	58 200	54 555	74 060	70 178	197 604	4 293
2 or more workers	3 395 481	2 262 185	2 106 178	880 785	867 831	31 090	29 126	79 746	76 578	141 675	2 747
VETERAN STATUS AND PERIOD OF SERVICE											
Civilian veterans 16 years and over	**27 481 055**	**24 345 054**	**23 754 943**	**2 374 365**	**2 348 256**	**193 511**	**184 227**	**250 255**	**238 793**	**317 870**	**9 936**
Male	26 330 011	23 379 529	22 814 871	2 230 013	2 206 111	181 439	172 807	236 706	226 002	302 324	9 199
May 1975 or later service only	3 352 156	2 579 697	2 464 047	588 200	578 655	37 560	35 323	51 366	48 450	95 333	2 549
September 1980 or later service only	1 900 833	1 459 713	1 393 449	335 325	329 723	20 667	19 498	30 547	28 720	54 581	1 526
Served 2 or more years	1 603 440	1 222 238	1 166 226	291 189	286 438	16 944	16 016	26 534	25 029	46 535	1 365
Vietnam-era service	8 232 414	7 160 147	6 953 778	784 392	775 449	76 033	72 000	88 118	83 229	123 724	3 371
World War II service	8 970 114	8 321 784	8 194 256	515 654	512 466	35 463	34 287	56 019	54 375	41 194	2 057

Table 128. **Occupation of Employed Persons for Race and Hispanic Origin: 1990**

[Data based on sample and subject to sampling variability, see text. For definitions of terms and meanings of symbols, see text]

United States	All persons	White		Black		American Indian, Eskimo, or Aleut		Asian or Pacific Islander		Other race	
		Total	Not of Hispanic origin	Total	Not of Hispanic origin	Total	Not of Hispanic origin	Total	Not of Hispanic origin	Total	Not of Hispanic origin
Employed persons 16 years and over	**115 681 202**	**96 237 561**	**91 447 312**	**11 407 803**	**11 184 939**	**728 953**	**677 843**	**3 411 586**	**3 312 806**	**3 895 299**	**76 786**
Managerial and professional specialty occupations	30 533 582	26 877 354	26 072 188	2 066 054	2 032 688	133 555	126 731	1 045 160	1 025 274	411 459	14 523
Executive, administrative, and managerial occupations	14 227 916	12 651 035	12 254 816	875 835	860 559	62 825	59 504	428 273	418 746	209 948	6 598
Officials and administrators, public administration	578 334	484 939	468 576	68 142	67 546	6 345	6 117	10 748	10 351	8 160	275
Management and related occupations	4 140 575	3 606 211	3 488 813	303 762	298 542	17 191	16 318	149 459	145 741	63 952	2 073
Professional specialty occupations	16 305 666	14 226 319	13 817 372	1 190 219	1 172 129	70 730	67 227	616 887	606 528	201 511	7 925
Engineers and natural scientists	3 000 976	2 635 125	2 569 523	126 864	124 739	9 274	8 815	201 193	199 300	28 520	1 629
Engineers	1 672 559	1 475 994	1 440 584	58 041	57 092	4 865	4 625	117 858	116 898	15 801	881
Health diagnosing occupations	869 543	754 907	728 482	28 401	27 636	1 467	1 339	77 501	76 453	7 267	356
Health assessment and treating occupations	2 482 553	2 124 802	2 077 587	213 393	210 158	10 064	9 566	110 659	107 878	23 635	1 112
Teachers, librarians, and counselors	5 713 591	4 963 417	4 809 953	512 599	506 466	28 766	27 405	131 237	128 933	77 572	2 571
Teachers, elementary and secondary schools	3 861 446	3 358 038	3 251 700	380 073	375 988	19 080	18 295	49 959	48 552	54 296	1 456
Technical, sales, and administrative support occupations	36 718 398	31 121 238	29 799 821	3 354 120	3 291 652	195 096	181 102	1 134 130	1 101 220	913 814	22 685
Health technologists and technicians	1 397 189	1 123 408	1 079 681	182 904	180 100	8 853	8 353	52 383	50 543	29 641	730
Technologists and technicians, except health	2 860 046	2 445 404	2 361 025	190 994	187 310	14 113	13 170	155 867	153 383	53 668	1 791
Sales occupations	13 634 686	11 984 176	11 511 646	875 576	856 437	63 582	58 901	400 985	390 770	310 367	8 147
Supervisors and proprietors, sales occupations	3 352 054	3 012 184	2 907 048	153 862	150 105	13 853	12 800	109 710	107 843	62 445	1 535
Sales representatives, commodities and finance	3 941 568	3 649 726	3 547 155	151 055	147 767	11 351	10 738	78 905	77 030	50 531	1 589
Other sales occupations	6 341 064	5 322 266	5 057 443	570 659	558 565	38 378	35 363	212 370	205 897	197 391	5 023
Cashiers	2 533 639	1 976 839	1 856 694	327 343	320 690	20 049	18 550	105 851	102 496	103 557	2 369
Administrative support occupations, including clerical	18 826 477	15 568 250	14 847 469	2 104 646	2 067 805	108 548	100 678	524 895	506 524	520 138	12 017
Computer equipment operators	640 982	511 106	488 214	86 759	85 304	3 554	3 405	23 640	22 996	15 923	448
Secretaries, stenographers, and typists	4 582 070	3 980 228	3 830 459	393 893	386 652	25 649	24 129	83 460	80 374	98 840	2 129
Financial records processing occupations	2 315 205	2 043 830	1 970 166	147 273	144 406	11 484	10 750	67 517	65 463	45 101	1 301
Mail and message distributing occupations	990 423	715 310	677 075	197 530	194 934	5 198	4 758	41 046	39 600	31 339	848
Service occupations	15 295 917	11 354 441	10 481 292	2 522 099	2 469 434	134 744	124 364	504 688	485 820	779 945	15 015
Private household occupations	521 154	312 888	251 678	136 283	132 825	3 856	3 276	14 044	13 032	54 083	755
Protective service occupations	1 992 852	1 580 054	1 504 544	312 808	307 911	17 198	16 218	29 083	27 627	53 709	1 622
Police and firefighters	732 609	624 642	598 591	78 005	77 078	5 930	5 656	7 596	7 157	16 436	483
Service occupations, except protective and household	12 781 911	9 461 499	8 725 070	2 073 008	2 028 698	113 690	104 870	461 561	445 161	672 153	12 638
Food service occupations	5 167 308	3 981 476	3 675 719	609 088	596 169	42 233	38 717	250 384	243 374	284 127	4 979
Cleaning and building service occupations	3 127 932	2 113 844	1 876 092	660 057	644 739	32 043	29 454	86 854	82 388	235 134	3 719
Farming, forestry, and fishing occupations	2 839 010	2 370 802	2 168 116	166 079	162 334	24 405	22 217	40 718	38 693	237 006	1 517
Farm operators and managers	1 066 944	1 022 746	1 005 516	16 660	16 374	4 255	4 044	7 679	7 520	15 604	190
Farm workers and related occupations	1 590 184	1 194 090	1 013 742	133 366	130 058	15 449	13 552	30 175	28 407	217 104	1 225
Precision production, craft, and repair occupations	13 097 963	11 257 116	10 648 470	930 011	907 230	99 782	92 918	273 473	263 497	537 581	8 295
Mechanics and repairers	4 080 305	3 554 246	3 385 520	286 565	279 626	27 650	25 909	74 673	71 689	137 171	2 522
Construction trades	4 793 935	4 174 722	3 942 128	310 992	303 102	42 638	39 637	56 341	53 208	209 242	2 924
Precision production occupations	4 047 043	3 368 249	3 168 249	324 809	316 991	27 530	25 452	141 794	137 977	184 661	2 769
Operators, fabricators, and laborers	17 196 332	13 256 610	12 277 425	2 369 440	2 321 601	141 371	130 511	413 417	398 302	1 015 494	14 751
Machine operators and tenders, except precision	4 981 876	3 706 366	3 389 822	721 735	704 732	35 625	32 840	169 521	164 804	348 629	4 690
Fabricators, assemblers, inspectors, and samplers	2 922 321	2 235 775	2 066 445	382 571	375 257	24 645	22 762	95 890	92 909	183 440	2 749
Transportation occupations	3 760 910	3 030 438	2 867 043	511 246	502 019	28 763	26 748	50 674	48 251	139 789	2 487
Motor vehicle operators	3 580 137	2 870 272	2 711 162	495 739	486 693	27 380	25 432	49 126	46 766	137 620	2 400
Material moving equipment operators	968 091	785 824	743 694	120 269	119 166	10 715	10 117	8 046	7 468	43 237	535
Handlers, equipment cleaners, helpers, and laborers	4 563 134	3 498 207	3 210 421	633 619	620 427	41 623	38 041	89 286	84 870	300 309	4 290
Construction laborers	948 540	727 176	651 253	116 549	113 865	10 986	9 950	11 419	10 531	82 410	706
Freight, stock, and material handlers	1 576 991	1 244 126	1 170 890	221 599	217 931	12 327	11 398	31 370	29 973	67 569	1 453
Employed females 16 years and over	**52 976 623**	**43 515 117**	**41 499 763**	**6 015 288**	**5 912 329**	**340 042**	**317 921**	**1 590 897**	**1 542 268**	**1 515 279**	**35 156**
Managerial and professional specialty occupations	14 752 659	12 741 104	12 348 409	1 283 844	1 265 252	73 848	70 233	448 538	437 732	205 325	7 106
Executive, administrative, and managerial occupations	5 993 163	5 202 033	5 028 901	484 659	477 335	31 884	30 164	179 835	174 990	94 752	3 053
Officials and administrators, public administration	251 316	201 382	194 171	38 849	38 493	2 820	2 729	4 454	4 246	3 811	89
Management and related occupations	2 156 867	1 835 200	1 771 995	192 955	190 154	10 580	10 038	82 290	80 191	35 756	1 144
Professional specialty occupations	8 759 496	7 539 071	7 319 508	799 185	787 917	41 964	40 069	268 703	262 742	110 573	4 053
Engineers and natural scientists	551 261	461 596	447 566	42 566	41 900	1 980	1 886	38 787	38 356	6 332	344
Engineers	151 962	125 956	121 964	11 185	11 041	541	507	12 264	12 155	2 016	105
Health diagnosing occupations	171 791	137 721	132 394	9 596	9 300	423	385	22 310	21 909	1 741	76
Health assessment and treating occupations	2 163 863	1 853 159	1 815 016	188 300	185 401	8 654	8 247	94 913	92 445	18 837	942
Teachers, librarians, and counselors	3 977 806	3 440 715	3 331 338	392 151	387 839	20 144	19 226	70 241	68 700	54 555	1 628
Teachers, elementary and secondary schools	2 946 061	2 541 887	2 459 000	308 959	305 779	14 472	13 848	38 662	37 588	42 081	1 105
Technical, sales, and administrative support occupations	23 120 191	19 454 638	18 638 286	2 330 616	2 292 576	134 493	125 160	636 528	615 438	563 916	14 084
Health technologists and technicians	1 133 078	920 524	889 284	148 650	146 507	7 017	6 641	35 757	34 478	21 130	524
Technologists and technicians, except health	832 879	688 505	663 359	76 882	75 714	4 297	4 037	48 025	47 263	15 170	607
Sales occupations	6 584 290	5 633 355	5 394 135	551 297	541 271	38 479	35 674	197 333	191 235	163 826	4 388
Supervisors and proprietors, sales occupations	1 155 921	1 025 665	991 276	68 822	67 643	6 098	5 637	35 101	34 323	20 235	617
Sales representatives, commodities and finance	1 314 555	1 192 130	1 154 046	67 358	65 983	4 753	4 590	31 043	30 174	19 271	660
Other sales occupations	4 113 814	3 415 560	3 248 813	415 117	407 645	27 628	25 447	131 189	126 738	124 320	3 111
Cashiers	1 995 673	1 562 480	1 473 643	268 886	264 124	16 528	15 311	71 840	69 361	75 939	1 609
Administrative support occupations, including clerical	14 569 944	12 212 254	11 691 508	1 553 787	1 529 084	84 700	78 808	355 413	342 462	363 790	8 565
Computer equipment operators	394 508	316 845	303 446	54 886	54 087	2 378	2 297	11 366	11 068	9 033	259
Secretaries, stenographers, and typists	4 490 363	3 909 921	3 764 243	380 866	374 080	24 934	23 471	78 838	75 909	95 804	2 005
Financial records processing occupations	2 062 414	1 837 858	1 776 315	123 890	121 669	10 443	9 793	52 787	51 138	37 436	1 022
Mail and message distributing occupations	368 423	258 492	247 099	83 180	82 410	2 288	2 110	14 313	13 877	10 150	320
Service occupations	8 929 509	6 701 294	6 254 384	1 508 458	1 480 332	79 643	74 202	259 244	249 272	380 870	8 090
Private household occupations	494 920	296 628	238 248	130 525	127 261	3 556	2 991	12 698	11 734	51 513	667
Protective service occupations	310 463	224 472	213 290	71 413	70 451	2 643	2 480	3 923	3 733	8 012	324
Police and firefighters	66 355	48 652	45 958	14 615	14 438	652	644	699	688	1 737	46
Service occupations, except protective and household	8 124 126	6 180 194	5 802 846	1 306 520	1 282 620	73 444	68 731	242 623	233 805	321 345	7 099
Food service occupations	3 062 435	2 507 545	2 387 604	325 529	320 957	26 436	24 961	106 592	103 566	96 333	2 312
Cleaning and building service occupations	1 278 437	814 051	710 772	308 521	302 521	13 895	12 821	40 319	38 382	101 651	1 643
Farming, forestry, and fishing occupations	449 506	383 374	357 362	21 048	20 682	3 740	3 460	8 330	7 966	33 014	289
Farm operators and managers	149 675	143 343	141 648	2 089	2 050	772	740	1 586	1 569	1 885	22
Farm workers and related occupations	290 041	232 000	208 059	18 074	17 747	2 662	2 419	6 561	6 214	30 744	248
Precision production, craft, and repair occupations	1 235 327	957 420	890 922	143 560	140 655	10 609	9 990	65 307	63 801	58 431	1 167
Mechanics and repairers	175 669	139 398	132 964	25 220	24 905	1 332	1 259	4 492	4 313	5 227	258
Construction trades	131 124	110 834	105 794	11 938	11 758	1 550	1 471	2 178	2 088	4 624	137
Precision production occupations	923 593	703 036	648 197	105 934	103 535	7 648	7 190	58 598	57 361	48 377	772
Operators, fabricators, and laborers	4 489 431	3 277 287	3 010 400	727 762	712 832	37 709	34 876	172 950	168 059	273 723	4 420
Machine operators and tenders, except precision	2 018 059	1 410 339	1 276 251	355 868	347 611	15 613	14 560	96 039	93 650	140 200	1 993
Fabricators, assemblers, inspectors, and samplers	1 082 797	782 067	714 412	174 765	171 716	9 008	8 271	47 664	46 396	69 293	1 181
Transportation occupations	426 426	345 352	333 025	63 642	62 870	4 650	4 408	3 688	3 500	9 094	267
Motor vehicle operators	419 603	340 356	328 241	62 240	61 489	4 538	4 305	3 541	3 367	8 928	258
Material moving equipment operators	46 995	35 735	33 544	8 228	8 030	605	582	507	461	1 920	46
Handlers, equipment cleaners, helpers, and laborers	915 154	703 794	653 168	125 259	122 605	7 833	7 055	25 052	24 052	53 216	933
Construction laborers	36 177	28 614	26 708	4 294	4 231	497	446	562	528	2 210	7
Freight, stock, and material handlers	359 459	294 616	280 178	41 876	41 199	2 819	2 567	8 021	7 674	12 127	330

Table 129. **Income in 1989 of Households, Families, and Persons for Race and Hispanic Origin: 1990**

[Data based on sample and subject to sampling variability, see text. For definitions of terms and meanings of symbols, see text]

United States	All persons	White		Black		American Indian, Eskimo, or Aleut		Asian or Pacific Islander		Other race	
		Total	Not of Hispanic origin	Total	Not of Hispanic origin	Total	Not of Hispanic origin	Total	Not of Hispanic origin	Total	Not of Hispanic origin
INCOME IN 1989											
Households	**91 993 582**	**76 906 980**	**73 747 747**	**9 941 850**	**9 767 383**	**625 367**	**588 826**	**2 020 498**	**1 965 079**	**2 498 887**	**52 507**
Less than $5,000	5 684 517	3 726 768	3 465 190	1 513 647	1 487 389	78 140	74 375	136 261	132 442	229 701	5 593
$5,000 to $9,999	8 529 980	6 610 505	6 274 975	1 412 467	1 386 108	91 731	87 230	126 479	121 817	288 798	6 362
$10,000 to $14,999	8 133 273	6 540 094	6 205 647	1 089 626	1 070 901	75 537	71 514	140 146	135 790	287 870	5 242
$15,000 to $24,999	16 123 742	13 295 239	12 675 640	1 878 449	1 843 736	126 456	118 701	279 541	270 653	544 057	9 881
$25,000 to $34,999	14 575 125	12 374 793	11 867 672	1 407 642	1 382 464	91 267	85 226	276 512	267 884	424 911	8 390
$35,000 to $49,999	16 428 455	14 274 052	13 758 950	1 324 225	1 302 720	83 967	78 343	353 574	342 927	392 637	8 054
$50,000 to $74,999	13 777 883	12 162 367	11 774 378	928 232	912 943	54 774	51 517	388 276	378 978	244 234	6 136
$75,000 to $99,999	4 704 808	4 203 619	4 087 521	260 092	256 037	14 595	13 590	168 542	165 547	57 960	1 717
$100,000 or more	4 035 799	3 719 543	3 637 774	127 470	125 085	8 900	8 330	151 167	149 041	28 719	1 132
Median (dollars)	30 056	31 435	31 672	19 758	19 766	20 025	19 857	36 784	36 943	22 813	24 049
Mean (dollars)	38 453	40 308	40 646	25 872	25 881	26 206	26 065	46 695	46 925	27 843	30 542
Families	**65 049 428**	**53 845 200**	**51 337 479**	**7 055 063**	**6 927 208**	**463 968**	**436 752**	**1 577 820**	**1 535 190**	**2 107 377**	**36 724**
Less than $5,000	2 582 206	1 419 771	1 254 559	862 062	844 939	49 114	46 289	70 522	68 095	180 737	3 102
$5,000 to $9,999	3 636 361	2 415 421	2 186 825	850 577	833 239	60 426	57 371	75 072	72 163	234 865	3 696
$10,000 to $14,999	4 676 092	3 507 128	3 240 989	762 216	748 084	54 908	52 006	99 551	96 391	252 289	3 102
$15,000 to $24,999	10 658 345	8 549 776	8 049 852	1 341 930	1 316 011	94 195	88 444	205 470	198 835	466 974	6 996
$25,000 to $34,999	10 729 951	9 043 670	8 629 800	1 043 831	1 024 870	71 009	66 688	210 640	203 954	360 801	6 321
$35,000 to $49,999	13 270 930	11 519 137	11 087 614	1 060 248	1 043 358	68 493	64 029	288 913	280 272	334 139	6 304
$50,000 to $74,999	11 857 079	10 467 357	10 134 128	797 643	785 388	46 094	43 488	339 835	332 073	206 150	4 906
$75,000 to $99,999	4 115 468	3 675 722	3 576 462	228 130	224 793	12 370	11 524	151 611	148 968	47 635	1 316
$100,000 or more	3 522 996	3 247 218	3 177 250	108 426	106 526	7 359	6 913	136 206	134 439	23 787	981
Median (dollars)	35 225	37 152	37 628	22 429	22 466	21 750	21 661	41 251	41 446	22 949	27 104
Mean (dollars)	43 803	46 330	46 930	28 659	28 695	28 025	27 941	51 102	51 383	27 943	33 606
Married-couple families	**51 718 214**	**45 178 672**	**43 342 946**	**3 521 382**	**3 458 050**	**305 156**	**288 308**	**1 295 099**	**1 265 101**	**1 417 905**	**24 115**
Less than $15,000	5 619 528	4 486 426	4 139 565	601 094	588 034	70 912	67 772	158 906	155 404	302 190	4 246
$15,000 to $24,999	7 734 791	6 575 092	6 220 151	621 592	608 185	62 551	59 107	154 424	150 187	321 132	4 203
$25,000 to $34,999	8 660 211	7 544 938	7 223 464	616 289	605 107	54 742	51 467	167 491	162 789	276 751	4 424
$35,000 to $49,999	11 566 753	10 243 307	9 882 640	745 545	733 716	57 587	54 097	244 189	237 225	276 125	5 077
$50,000 to $74,999	10 895 423	9 726 294	9 429 713	646 514	636 976	41 439	39 133	302 697	296 136	178 479	4 085
$75,000 or more	7 241 508	6 602 615	6 447 413	290 348	286 032	17 925	16 732	267 392	263 360	63 228	2 080
Female householder, no husband present	**10 381 654**	**6 540 382**	**6 058 841**	**3 045 283**	**2 993 086**	**121 370**	**113 658**	**185 926**	**176 964**	**488 693**	**9 459**
Less than $5,000	1 530 177	679 291	592 849	696 002	683 442	28 076	26 298	20 848	19 494	105 960	1 749
$5,000 to $9,999	1 636 764	883 985	789 442	582 809	570 876	29 368	27 586	23 576	22 051	117 026	1 966
$10,000 to $14,999	1 379 635	844 016	773 575	424 271	417 425	18 718	17 648	20 000	18 802	72 630	1 051
$15,000 to $24,999	2 286 235	1 531 229	1 432 881	603 978	594 506	23 312	21 735	34 272	32 699	93 444	2 044
$25,000 to $49,999	2 718 497	1 973 670	1 870 903	591 036	582 098	18 180	16 847	54 590	52 217	81 021	2 050
$50,000 or more	830 346	628 191	599 191	147 187	144 739	3 716	3 544	32 640	31 701	18 612	599
Males 15 years and over, with income	**86 674 947**	**72 504 525**	**68 980 277**	**8 337 527**	**8 164 632**	**605 578**	**564 538**	**2 285 437**	**2 220 753**	**2 941 880**	**56 346**
Median income (dollars)	20 409	21 695	22 065	12 950	12 971	12 180	12 162	19 396	19 526	12 493	14 857
Percent year-round full-time workers	53.0	54.2	54.4	44.9	44.9	40.9	40.8	52.4	52.5	47.5	46.5
Median income (dollars)	29 237	30 468	30 764	21 647	21 691	22 080	22 162	30 075	30 223	18 627	22 305
Females 15 years and over, with income	**84 560 106**	**69 613 017**	**66 627 911**	**9 965 635**	**9 793 651**	**587 568**	**552 086**	**2 125 535**	**2 060 212**	**2 268 351**	**53 125**
Median income (dollars)	10 371	10 652	10 747	8 825	8 835	7 310	7 278	11 986	12 013	7 876	9 068
Percent year-round full-time workers	33.9	33.6	33.6	35.0	35.1	29.5	29.5	40.6	40.6	31.9	33.3
Median income (dollars)	19 570	19 916	20 048	18 005	18 015	16 680	16 667	21 335	21 386	15 362	17 941
Per capita income (dollars)	**14 420**	**15 687**	**16 074**	**8 859**	**8 885**	**8 328**	**8 372**	**13 638**	**13 754**	**7 340**	**7 403**
Persons in households (dollars)	14 649	15 926	16 326	9 019	9 049	8 367	8 439	13 815	13 938	7 366	7 333
Persons in group quarters (dollars)	6 094	6 319	6 330	5 226	5 118	7 107	6 199	5 465	5 178	6 162	9 483
MEDIAN INCOME IN 1989 BY SELECTED CHARACTERISTICS											
Family type and presence of own children:											
Families (dollars)	35 225	37 152	37 628	22 429	22 466	21 750	21 661	41 251	41 446	22 949	27 104
With own children under 18 years (dollars)	34 627	37 303	38 074	20 292	20 332	20 221	20 142	41 025	41 256	21 789	25 560
With own children under 6 years (dollars)	31 580	34 547	35 352	16 924	16 941	16 856	16 730	37 325	37 647	20 007	23 607
Married-couple families (dollars)	39 584	40 396	40 723	33 538	33 626	28 287	28 134	44 965	45 115	27 731	32 573
With own children under 18 years (dollars)	40 693	41 686	42 172	35 162	35 281	28 124	27 982	44 966	45 128	27 219	32 565
With own children under 6 years (dollars)	36 490	37 369	37 908	31 268	31 401	22 901	22 769	40 210	40 313	24 138	30 434
Female householder, no husband present (dollars)	17 414	20 340	20 807	12 522	12 559	10 742	10 716	22 983	23 319	11 262	14 762
With own children under 18 years (dollars)	12 485	15 011	15 444	9 539	9 571	8 692	8 671	15 791	15 989	8 915	10 805
With own children under 6 years (dollars)	7 775	8 942	9 117	6 330	6 320	6 279	6 252	10 838	10 898	6 502	8 203
Workers in family in 1989:											
No workers (dollars)	14 622	17 311	17 781	5 308	5 313	6 069	6 103	9 050	9 215	5 431	5 826
1 worker (dollars)	25 517	27 998	28 714	15 764	15 757	15 526	15 474	27 860	28 257	15 776	19 343
2 or more workers (dollars)	44 500	45 738	46 122	36 955	36 986	32 978	32 917	50 706	50 899	32 272	37 848
Husband and wife worked (dollars)	46 340	47 005	47 273	41 557	41 609	35 390	35 324	52 729	52 909	34 166	40 468
Nonfamily households (dollars)	**17 240**	**17 991**	**18 067**	**11 624**	**11 617**	**12 183**	**12 023**	**21 336**	**21 396**	**14 905**	**15 038**
Male householder (dollars)	22 630	24 115	24 283	15 368	15 372	15 059	14 775	23 807	23 903	18 095	18 993
Living alone (dollars)	20 193	21 219	21 353	13 160	13 177	11 775	11 651	21 958	22 087	14 185	16 155
65 years and over (dollars)	11 688	12 574	12 726	6 676	6 680	6 792	6 723	9 295	9 425	6 519	7 538
Female householder (dollars)	13 729	14 294	14 369	9 060	9 057	9 939	9 792	18 405	18 454	9 904	11 183
Living alone (dollars)	12 226	12 737	12 837	8 042	8 044	8 142	8 069	16 190	16 277	7 828	9 361
65 years and over (dollars)	8 639	9 185	9 276	5 358	5 356	6 179	6 169	7 731	7 757	5 436	6 800
INCOME TYPE IN 1989											
Households	**91 993 582**	**76 906 980**	**73 747 747**	**9 941 850**	**9 767 383**	**625 367**	**588 826**	**2 020 498**	**1 965 079**	**2 498 887**	**52 507**
With earnings	73 874 069	61 696 794	58 989 523	7 689 508	7 554 686	509 200	477 720	1 799 815	1 750 123	2 178 752	43 682
Mean earnings (dollars)	39 143	40 659	40 987	28 754	28 749	27 324	27 200	47 021	47 252	29 118	32 431
With wage or salary income	71 174 232	59 227 199	56 592 451	7 578 431	7 446 275	494 123	463 465	1 737 401	1 688 626	2 137 078	42 467
Mean wage or salary income (dollars)	37 271	38 633	38 933	28 307	28 304	26 277	26 172	44 129	44 331	28 285	31 228
With nonfarm self-employment income	10 810 605	9 785 727	9 473 587	494 841	483 999	60 297	56 725	277 492	272 264	192 248	4 897
Mean nonfarm self-employment income (dollars)	20 218	20 519	20 593	12 852	12 845	14 260	14 064	27 804	27 911	14 801	17 742
With farm self-employment income	2 020 105	1 931 481	1 905 614	41 044	40 008	11 121	10 736	19 202	18 700	17 257	536
Mean farm self-employment income (dollars)	10 064	10 171	10 180	5 449	5 463	6 235	6 172	12 690	12 820	8 509	6 733
With interest, dividend, or net rental income	37 242 801	34 779 342	34 128 343	1 182 252	1 163 025	129 992	124 136	856 647	842 714	294 568	10 092
Mean interest, dividend, or net rental income (dollars)	6 949	7 180	7 227	2 785	2 782	3 646	3 639	5 211	5 233	2 943	4 116
With Social Security income	24 210 922	21 382 990	20 836 706	2 191 956	2 167 753	115 261	110 206	237 518	230 472	283 197	8 413
Mean Social Security income (dollars)	7 772	8 007	8 046	5 942	5 946	6 133	6 143	6 819	6 834	5 688	6 431
With public assistance income	6 943 269	4 269 641	3 878 673	1 955 533	1 915 511	116 009	109 567	199 127	192 348	402 959	7 262
Mean public assistance income (dollars)	4 078	4 059	4 041	3 695	3 678	4 145	4 116	6 852	6 910	4 738	4 466
With retirement income	14 353 202	12 818 402	12 530 731	1 163 375	1 150 826	66 790	63 810	157 114	151 643	147 521	4 843
Mean retirement income (dollars)	9 216	9 409	9 453	7 579	7 593	7 640	7 676	9 549	9 599	5 748	7 229
With other income	9 344 304	7 844 227	7 564 340	1 043 079	1 027 919	83 317	78 510	134 430	129 305	239 251	5 150
Mean other income (dollars)	4 093	4 146	4 146	3 596	3 587	3 641	3 621	5 723	5 757	3 769	4 647

Table 130. **Poverty Status in 1989 of Families and Persons for Race and Hispanic Origin: 1990**

[Data based on sample and subject to sampling variability, see text. For definitions of terms and meanings of symbols, see text]

United States	All persons	White		Black		American Indian, Eskimo, or Aleut		Asian or Pacific Islander		Other race	
		Total	Not of Hispanic origin	Total	Not of Hispanic origin	Total	Not of Hispanic origin	Total	Not of Hispanic origin	Total	Not of Hispanic origin
ALL INCOME LEVELS IN 1989											
Families	**65 049 428**	**53 845 200**	**51 337 479**	**7 055 063**	**6 927 208**	**463 968**	**436 752**	**1 577 820**	**1 535 190**	**2 107 377**	**36 724**
In owner-occupied housing unit	47 221 605	41 666 428	39 843 104	3 488 403	3 414 038	270 377	298 057	949 558	881 197	846 839	550 774
With related children under 18 years	33 536 660	25 929 135	24 811 845	4 699 116	3 834 908	313 592	262 314	996 789	721 733	1 598 028	552 292
With related children under 5 years	14 250 048	10 777 426	10 194 315	2 064 961	1 689 052	144 727	120 674	427 763	318 309	835 171	254 069
Householder worked in 1989	51 357 521	42 948 299	40 898 459	5 055 636	4 448 478	348 200	329 660	1 324 838	1 112 247	1 680 548	757 164
Householder worked year round full time in 1989	36 318 276	31 057 625	29 625 967	3 169 072	2 837 297	197 646	203 936	908 573	797 476	985 360	509 297
Householder under 65 years with work disability	4 817 701	3 799 301	3 600 592	714 682	638 558	64 327	44 705	69 169	80 779	170 222	88 244
Householder foreign born	5 888 505	3 147 700	2 764 656	441 553	368 543	11 812	15 808	1 239 508	325 996	1 047 932	140 470
Householder under 25 years	2 554 838	1 877 270	1 722 160	412 679	358 007	31 542	24 139	43 244	45 766	190 103	52 612
Householder 65 years and over	10 796 925	9 618 752	9 058 625	883 302	957 834	44 476	64 870	140 075	190 630	110 320	149 440
Householder high school graduate or higher	49 435 732	42 422 515	40 841 487	4 519 185	4 055 389	305 619	306 874	1 273 900	1 131 659	914 513	733 743
With public assistance income in 1989	5 024 146	2 943 001	2 829 398	1 483 805	1 213 535	88 762	64 154	171 172	106 913	337 406	130 664
With Social Security income in 1989	14 633 024	12 826 264	12 096 143	1 332 865	1 370 606	75 315	91 662	183 312	250 913	215 268	202 560
Married-couple families	**51 718 214**	**45 178 672**	**42 785 906**	**3 521 382**	**3 481 836**	**305 156**	**320 638**	**1 295 099**	**1 092 810**	**1 417 905**	**697 330**
With related children under 18 years	25 258 549	21 032 242	19 979 328	2 105 944	1 847 972	192 449	176 093	846 351	568 773	1 081 563	356 978
With related children under 5 years	11 134 320	9 165 153	8 599 942	919 135	815 937	89 027	81 594	377 487	263 626	583 518	171 730
Householder worked in 1989	42 105 587	36 703 966	34 802 995	2 799 960	2 706 697	245 868	253 278	1 116 840	915 864	1 238 953	559 688
Householder worked year round full time in 1989	30 876 792	27 241 494	25 896 695	1 935 675	1 892 622	151 004	166 643	784 751	676 462	763 868	396 535
Householder high school graduate or higher	40 340 133	36 071 856	34 562 667	2 350 687	2 362 057	207 764	231 793	1 069 747	924 614	640 079	532 275
Householder 65 years and over	8 856 941	8 150 180	7 680 962	492 633	592 464	29 148	49 511	113 452	154 933	71 528	111 839
With public assistance income in 1989	2 196 987	1 595 184	1 500 428	327 404	290 516	34 530	26 974	116 160	58 827	123 709	48 749
With Social Security income in 1989	11 580 548	10 551 848	9 945 243	702 515	803 150	48 378	67 681	141 343	196 379	136 464	145 012
Female householder, no husband present	**10 381 654**	**6 540 382**	**6 415 256**	**3 045 283**	**2 412 843**	**121 370**	**90 450**	**185 926**	**197 247**	**488 693**	**236 212**
With related children under 18 years	6 783 155	3 868 218	3 870 845	2 315 622	1 776 178	95 511	68 098	111 206	121 751	392 598	163 796
With related children under 5 years	2 532 331	1 245 846	1 260 399	1 023 650	783 974	42 989	30 280	37 058	43 152	182 788	69 291
Householder worked in 1989	6 889 101	4 520 231	4 494 482	1 899 466	1 455 323	73 683	55 384	127 662	138 864	268 059	149 027
Householder worked year round full time in 1989	3 876 706	2 640 115	2 627 999	1 005 228	762 033	32 741	26 003	73 571	82 614	125 051	81 401
Householder high school graduate or higher	7 088 336	4 815 394	4 808 024	1 875 252	1 452 915	75 312	57 329	128 201	150 777	194 177	157 546
Householder 65 years and over	1 549 529	1 167 361	1 095 393	321 013	299 684	12 115	12 243	18 962	27 589	30 078	29 879
With public assistance income in 1989	2 541 129	1 180 751	1 169 372	1 078 071	857 671	47 625	32 522	41 385	40 794	193 297	73 833
With Social Security income in 1989	2 380 686	1 748 397	1 659 943	522 774	465 545	20 903	18 705	28 903	40 430	59 709	44 798
Unrelated individuals for whom poverty status is determined	**36 672 001**	**30 375 562**	**28 367 481**	**4 208 285**	**4 079 713**	**278 246**	**275 170**	**793 413**	**912 257**	**1 016 495**	**614 183**
Nonfamily householder	26 944 154	23 061 780	21 669 520	2 886 787	2 875 903	161 399	177 210	442 678	612 651	391 510	512 905
In owner-occupied housing unit	12 782 991	11 539 278	10 919 678	961 781	1 071 828	64 930	84 116	129 766	212 539	87 236	184 896
65 years and over	9 752 744	8 681 911	8 124 536	892 690	1 003 563	37 681	58 182	70 525	153 258	69 937	152 922
Persons for whom poverty status is determined	**241 977 859**	**194 811 704**	**182 800 924**	**28 663 173**	**27 323 464**	**1 950 915**	**1 820 066**	**7 068 454**	**6 624 228**	**9 483 613**	**2 021 160**
Persons 18 years and over	179 372 340	147 704 667	139 393 591	19 327 265	18 326 422	1 279 684	1 211 342	5 042 079	4 659 539	6 018 645	1 866 345
Persons 65 years and over	29 562 647	26 333 010	24 950 136	2 385 907	2 563 380	113 052	153 171	434 119	558 230	296 559	309 975
Related children under 18 years	62 278 655	46 880 667	43 206 797	9 284 053	8 949 914	664 454	603 272	2 015 646	1 956 779	3 433 835	150 583
Related children under 6 years	21 604 123	16 204 013	14 863 865	3 216 863	3 084 878	231 655	212 498	683 890	662 120	1 267 702	63 597
Related children 5 to 17 years	44 300 630	33 408 002	30 853 463	6 599 196	6 376 850	471 750	426 527	1 449 657	1 407 605	2 372 025	96 318
INCOME IN 1989 BELOW POVERTY LEVEL											
Families	**6 487 515**	**3 787 586**	**3 572 683**	**1 852 014**	**1 504 672**	**125 432**	**91 365**	**182 507**	**108 563**	**539 976**	**143 053**
Percent below poverty level	10.0	7.0	7.0	26.3	23.9	27.0	20.8	11.6	8.0	25.6	14.4
In owner-occupied housing unit	2 307 947	1 660 991	1 582 305	454 432	383 419	51 562	43 890	34 949	21 520	106 013	29 842
With related children under 18 years	4 992 845	2 720 709	2 562 708	1 550 105	1 236 502	104 796	74 270	138 221	83 067	479 014	115 774
With related children under 5 years	2 613 626	1 388 096	1 288 796	817 253	650 405	58 315	41 572	69 476	45 332	280 486	63 709
Householder worked in 1989	3 215 463	2 003 509	1 871 711	777 559	618 391	63 196	45 281	84 290	49 472	280 909	62 174
Householder worked year round full time in 1989	853 067	559 479	511 950	179 343	141 524	12 167	9 558	20 163	10 769	81 915	14 102
Householder under 65 years with work disability	1 073 192	664 549	631 518	296 653	250 050	23 948	15 362	18 003	14 688	70 039	24 804
Householder foreign born	876 281	374 154	221 355	73 281	58 602	2 515	2 554	162 490	47 460	263 841	22 716
Householder under 25 years	763 410	430 358	407 022	231 362	186 907	15 017	10 281	14 894	12 097	71 770	18 426
Householder 65 years and over	762 939	516 038	490 610	197 481	170 952	11 211	10 465	14 090	10 255	24 119	12 696
Householder high school graduate or higher	3 265 377	2 050 477	2 045 143	895 837	714 562	62 109	44 628	105 940	65 621	151 014	77 044
With public assistance income in 1989	2 286 388	1 094 183	1 067 904	888 048	720 031	54 404	38 042	58 794	39 347	190 959	62 549
With Social Security income in 1989	1 094 068	709 269	676 032	306 718	260 469	18 332	15 445	11 910	11 409	47 839	18 218
Mean income deficit (dollars)	5 379	4 856	4 875	6 156	6 116	5 938	5 943	6 099	5 539	6 012	5 542
Married-couple families	**2 849 984**	**2 042 584**	**1 845 075**	**387 992**	**347 049**	**51 812**	**41 061**	**120 010**	**56 243**	**247 586**	**50 345**
With related children under 18 years	1 834 332	1 232 264	1 085 474	256 927	221 216	39 646	30 035	90 804	39 004	214 691	34 549
With related children under 5 years	1 011 812	673 129	579 634	132 854	116 365	23 123	17 437	49 199	22 512	133 507	19 721
Householder worked in 1989	1 581 202	1 139 655	1 003 200	178 572	157 984	29 345	22 391	60 611	27 432	173 019	25 892
Householder worked year round full time in 1989	549 131	412 041	361 713	56 183	49 658	7 005	5 817	16 546	7 534	57 356	8 223
Householder high school graduate or higher	1 351 051	1 032 170	990 676	161 223	145 652	23 835	18 724	72 158	33 090	61 665	26 938
Householder 65 years and over	506 426	390 165	366 688	85 691	77 292	5 732	5 963	11 150	7 514	13 688	7 101
With public assistance income in 1989	554 412	356 651	329 613	102 309	91 736	16 184	12 347	34 647	15 259	44 621	13 110
With Social Security income in 1989	635 487	481 923	449 875	112 272	100 695	9 170	8 422	8 076	7 022	24 046	8 621
Mean income deficit (dollars)	4 994	4 720	4 669	5 313	5 206	5 977	5 961	6 266	5 819	5 926	5 379
Female householder, no husband present	**3 230 201**	**1 517 746**	**1 517 708**	**1 356 384**	**1 073 179**	**61 131**	**41 543**	**47 873**	**44 491**	**247 067**	**82 861**
With related children under 18 years	2 866 941	1 327 810	1 330 290	1 216 660	957 672	55 054	37 247	39 608	39 376	227 809	74 179
With related children under 5 years	1 452 618	636 307	639 943	645 676	505 608	29 124	20 009	17 660	20 529	123 851	40 345
Householder worked in 1989	1 403 435	727 287	746 303	549 447	423 095	26 600	18 019	16 518	17 908	83 583	31 374
Householder worked year round full time in 1989	248 472	115 458	122 591	110 452	82 716	3 922	2 898	2 467	2 504	16 173	4 820
Householder high school graduate or higher	1 721 637	902 046	938 748	686 327	531 737	32 129	21 692	24 192	27 359	76 943	44 863
Householder 65 years and over	215 978	104 759	103 323	96 037	80 658	4 531	3 699	2 111	2 218	8 540	4 652
With public assistance income in 1989	1 642 582	692 869	694 564	755 527	603 765	34 480	23 063	21 009	22 326	138 697	46 911
With Social Security income in 1989	390 389	188 630	189 180	171 162	140 483	7 631	5 806	2 967	3 582	19 999	8 133
Mean income deficit (dollars)	5 764	5 068	5 155	6 453	6 465	5 922	5 906	5 786	5 275	6 215	5 686
Unrelated individuals	**8 873 475**	**6 492 447**	**6 003 223**	**1 593 404**	**1 470 988**	**113 823**	**97 221**	**258 514**	**230 404**	**415 287**	**144 094**
Percent below poverty level	24.2	21.4	21.2	37.9	36.1	40.9	35.3	32.6	25.3	40.9	23.5
Nonfamily householder	5 210 297	3 956 178	3 734 887	980 884	914 207	53 431	47 850	104 308	101 661	115 496	103 749
In owner-occupied housing unit	1 957 191	1 607 889	1 533 703	295 158	285 536	21 090	22 014	12 380	18 985	20 674	28 920
65 years and over	2 494 332	1 959 075	1 836 613	460 486	441 674	16 360	19 344	22 688	33 516	35 723	38 730
Mean income deficit (dollars)	3 311	3 166	3 150	3 471	3 414	3 714	3 591	4 504	4 051	4 113	3 349
Persons	**31 742 864**	**19 025 235**	**16 774 507**	**8 441 429**	**7 824 473**	**603 188**	**524 127**	**997 196**	**870 894**	**2 675 816**	**345 371**
Percent below poverty level	13.1	9.8	9.2	29.5	28.6	30.9	28.8	14.1	13.1	28.2	17.1
Persons 18 years and over	20 313 948	13 148 968	11 950 741	4 724 301	4 231 430	342 785	287 907	650 705	540 973	1 447 189	306 871
Persons 65 years and over	3 780 585	2 854 161	2 673 031	761 623	714 994	33 219	35 547	52 129	58 542	79 453	52 109
Related children under 18 years	11 161 836	5 695 183	4 663 625	3 671 536	3 551 697	254 431	231 410	337 128	323 208	1 203 558	35 071
Related children under 6 years	4 331 825	2 231 488	1 840 047	1 410 273	1 358 671	102 229	93 041	120 474	114 793	467 361	16 033
Related children 5 to 17 years	7 544 737	3 836 033	3 129 318	2 489 090	2 413 250	168 816	153 422	237 862	228 557	812 936	21 478
Persons below 125 percent of poverty level	42 246 073	26 422 974	23 368 486	10 325 165	9 605 412	747 713	654 945	1 274 873	1 130 710	3 475 348	458 110
Persons below 200 percent of poverty level	74 909 296	50 983 766	45 758 478	15 137 833	14 175 983	1 099 251	977 366	2 151 021	1 929 446	5 537 425	761 162

Table 131. Selected Characteristics of Persons 60 Years and Over by Age for Race and Hispanic Origin: 1990

[Data based on sample and subject to sampling variability, see text. For definitions of terms and meanings of symbols, see text]

United States	All persons	White Total	White Not of Hispanic origin	Black Total	Black Not of Hispanic origin	American Indian, Eskimo, or Aleut Total	American Indian, Eskimo, or Aleut Not of Hispanic origin	Asian or Pacific Islander Total	Asian or Pacific Islander Not of Hispanic origin	Other race Total	Other race Not of Hispanic origin
LIVING ARRANGEMENTS											
Persons 60 to 64 years	10 635 762	9 222 857	8 879 428	967 266	951 528	54 040	51 577	215 276	210 124	176 323	4 243
In households	10 521 298	9 129 708	8 789 983	950 133	934 932	53 196	50 814	213 796	208 740	174 465	4 169
In group quarters	114 464	93 149	89 445	17 133	16 596	844	763	1 480	1 384	1 858	74
Nursing homes	59 648	49 488	48 124	8 460	8 377	459	400	507	507	734	44
Persons 65 to 74 years	18 218 481	16 138 327	15 689 368	1 511 617	1 491 442	74 320	71 373	295 142	288 994	199 075	6 292
In households	17 884 074	15 849 192	15 406 503	1 473 298	1 453 827	72 706	69 787	292 155	286 094	196 723	6 211
In group quarters	334 407	289 135	282 865	38 319	37 615	1 614	1 586	2 987	2 900	2 352	81
Nursing homes	247 973	216 156	212 476	27 637	27 335	1 211	1 205	1 526	1 493	1 443	30
Persons 75 years and over	12 976 794	11 691 745	11 424 212	989 224	978 269	43 403	41 857	147 432	143 510	104 990	3 762
In households	11 580 219	10 394 133	10 142 768	906 761	896 476	40 038	38 555	140 077	136 265	99 210	3 535
In group quarters	1 396 575	1 297 612	1 281 444	82 463	81 793	3 365	3 302	7 355	7 245	5 780	227
Nursing homes	1 305 978	1 216 973	1 202 833	75 047	74 509	3 026	2 975	5 688	5 610	5 244	169
EDUCATIONAL ATTAINMENT											
Persons 60 to 64 years	10 635 762	9 222 857	8 879 428	967 266	951 528	54 040	51 577	215 276	210 124	176 323	4 243
Less than 9th grade	1 627 746	1 178 437	1 037 848	269 444	262 825	18 368	17 298	52 212	50 696	109 285	1 295
9th to 12th grade, no diploma	2 111 592	1 737 520	1 668 702	300 300	296 632	12 667	12 128	29 774	28 862	31 331	1 090
High school graduate (includes equivalency)	3 429 376	3 133 885	3 069 262	207 190	204 507	11 091	10 626	56 331	55 439	20 879	891
Some college or associate degree	1 884 132	1 716 401	1 675 049	115 056	113 468	8 131	7 863	34 205	33 433	10 339	598
Bachelor's degree or higher	1 582 916	1 456 614	1 428 567	75 276	74 096	3 783	3 662	42 754	41 694	4 489	369
Persons 65 to 74 years	18 218 481	16 138 327	15 689 368	1 511 617	1 491 442	74 320	71 373	295 142	288 994	199 075	6 292
Less than 9th grade	3 636 494	2 770 848	2 554 840	602 045	592 123	28 536	27 069	99 123	96 881	135 942	2 512
9th to 12th grade, no diploma	3 789 423	3 267 541	3 180 054	430 385	425 866	17 347	16 751	43 146	42 111	31 004	1 523
High school graduate (includes equivalency)	5 774 340	5 398 514	5 322 349	268 099	264 635	14 298	13 898	73 375	72 224	20 057	1 197
Some college or associate degree	2 897 366	2 715 353	2 674 456	126 189	124 870	9 630	9 279	38 129	37 348	8 065	588
Bachelor's degree or higher	2 120 855	1 986 071	1 957 669	84 899	83 948	4 509	4 376	41 369	40 430	4 007	472
Persons 75 years and over	12 976 794	11 691 745	11 424 212	989 224	978 269	43 403	41 857	147 432	143 510	104 990	3 762
Less than 9th grade	4 453 073	3 705 588	3 540 182	570 377	564 328	22 788	21 841	73 358	71 400	80 962	1 822
9th to 12th grade, no diploma	2 709 473	2 456 934	2 412 805	212 268	209 953	8 732	8 450	19 361	18 844	12 178	703
High school graduate (includes equivalency)	2 961 417	2 809 591	2 778 057	112 772	111 389	6 188	6 027	25 595	24 953	7 271	670
Some college or associate degree	1 616 777	1 544 620	1 530 042	52 176	51 462	3 664	3 590	13 434	12 938	2 883	290
Bachelor's degree or higher	1 236 054	1 175 012	1 163 126	41 631	41 137	2 031	1 949	15 684	15 375	1 696	277
INCOME AND POVERTY STATUS IN 1989											
Married-couple families, householder 60 to 64 years	3 863 733	3 488 671	3 282 559	239 742	264 172	17 231	22 705	64 957	74 498	53 132	46 944
Less than $5,000	77 968	62 175	57 264	10 233	9 991	1 037	1 060	1 918	1 422	2 605	1 179
$5,000 to $9,999	151 376	123 305	114 569	19 109	18 808	1 913	1 819	2 231	1 566	4 818	2 231
$10,000 to $14,999	239 904	206 430	192 695	22 805	22 927	2 037	2 389	2 775	2 566	5 857	3 339
$15,000 to $24,999	639 545	572 447	536 167	45 170	49 222	3 616	4 806	7 488	7 547	10 824	7 668
$25,000 to $34,999	671 469	611 710	574 157	39 677	45 321	2 821	4 113	7 716	9 815	9 545	8 456
$35,000 to $49,999	788 016	720 604	676 548	43 877	51 072	2 630	4 001	11 469	14 817	9 436	9 599
$50,000 or more	1 295 455	1 192 000	1 131 159	58 871	66 831	3 177	4 517	31 360	36 765	10 047	14 472
Percent with income in 1989 below poverty level	5.1	4.3	4.2	12.9	11.0	17.7	12.4	7.3	3.9	16.4	6.5
Persons 60 to 64 years living alone	1 637 721	1 384 341	1 295 398	206 669	207 563	9 561	10 914	17 243	29 234	19 907	30 104
Less than $5,000	282 378	198 467	187 694	71 238	64 331	3 184	2 852	2 671	3 539	6 818	5 196
$5,000 to $9,999	341 892	277 250	257 288	52 242	51 129	2 848	2 709	2 825	4 923	6 727	7 412
$10,000 to $14,999	254 933	223 101	208 817	26 007	27 939	1 163	1 553	2 373	3 742	2 289	4 114
$15,000 to $24,999	356 102	317 937	296 796	30 588	34 111	1 315	1 933	3 770	6 618	2 492	6 805
$25,000 to $34,999	186 922	168 805	158 847	14 299	15 316	521	923	2 287	4 251	1 010	3 271
$35,000 or more	215 494	198 781	185 956	12 295	14 737	530	944	3 317	6 161	571	3 306
Percent with income in 1989 below poverty level	24.6	21.1	21.2	45.2	41.1	45.3	35.7	20.9	17.1	50.2	26.0
Married-couple families, householder 65 to 74 years	6 105 480	5 607 732	5 285 558	344 141	409 687	21 183	33 714	80 457	109 340	51 967	74 931
Less than $5,000	105 626	83 632	78 609	15 289	14 590	1 046	996	3 201	2 245	2 458	1 767
$5,000 to $9,999	377 532	310 633	291 046	50 250	47 971	3 160	3 536	5 545	4 438	7 944	5 138
$10,000 to $14,999	683 471	608 600	570 662	54 655	60 317	3 823	5 326	7 357	7 633	9 036	9 328
$15,000 to $24,999	1 565 961	1 450 842	1 366 436	84 386	103 387	5 632	9 416	12 494	20 001	12 607	19 768
$25,000 to $34,999	1 168 869	1 093 356	1 030 540	52 278	67 944	3 265	6 217	11 995	19 451	7 975	14 187
$35,000 to $49,999	1 006 332	938 300	886 401	44 844	57 101	2 329	4 284	14 461	20 762	6 398	12 008
$50,000 or more	1 197 689	1 122 369	1 061 864	42 439	58 377	1 928	3 939	25 404	34 810	5 549	12 735
Percent with income in 1989 below poverty level	4.8	3.9	3.9	15.2	11.5	17.6	10.7	9.4	4.4	17.9	5.8
Persons 65 to 74 years living alone	4 238 144	3 724 122	3 484 726	430 259	467 081	18 762	26 019	31 951	66 976	33 050	71 599
Less than $5,000	673 028	496 672	469 343	153 485	140 627	5 199	5 570	6 586	8 454	11 086	11 323
$5,000 to $9,999	1 351 851	1 155 260	1 076 453	163 614	171 212	7 608	9 624	9 745	18 871	15 624	26 063
$10,000 to $14,999	783 518	721 399	675 492	52 172	65 335	2 364	4 617	4 494	11 252	3 089	12 654
$15,000 to $24,999	792 343	742 747	694 260	39 690	55 084	2 214	3 838	5 526	14 453	2 166	12 199
$25,000 to $34,999	315 489	298 602	279 497	12 903	19 417	778	1 402	2 653	6 369	553	4 796
$35,000 or more	321 915	309 442	289 681	8 395	15 406	599	968	2 947	7 577	532	4 564
Percent with income in 1989 below poverty level	22.6	19.4	19.5	46.8	40.0	39.4	30.2	25.8	17.9	49.0	23.4
Married-couple families, householder 75 years and over	2 751 461	2 542 448	2 395 404	148 492	182 777	7 965	15 797	32 995	45 593	19 561	36 908
Less than $5,000	73 814	60 830	57 953	9 935	9 198	512	633	1 326	1 040	1 211	1 158
$5,000 to $9,999	311 762	263 707	248 211	37 150	35 949	2 215	2 996	3 964	3 467	4 726	3 945
$10,000 to $14,999	488 925	444 636	416 606	32 231	37 758	1 676	3 352	5 737	6 607	4 645	7 195
$15,000 to $24,999	754 492	706 952	665 932	34 701	46 102	1 704	4 244	6 714	10 313	4 421	10 453
$25,000 to $34,999	427 153	403 886	381 170	15 729	22 821	839	1 952	4 688	7 646	2 011	5 597
$35,000 to $49,999	323 881	307 237	289 441	10 085	15 750	513	1 349	4 614	7 061	1 432	4 361
$50,000 or more	371 434	355 200	336 091	8 661	15 199	506	1 271	5 952	9 459	1 115	4 199
Percent with income in 1989 below poverty level	7.7	6.7	6.7	22.5	16.4	25.0	14.9	11.0	5.9	22.5	7.5
Persons 75 years and over living alone	4 751 106	4 338 947	4 062 720	351 051	426 052	14 618	27 370	23 059	67 471	23 431	72 639
Less than $5,000	896 651	719 314	677 911	157 644	151 993	5 268	6 729	5 380	10 001	9 045	13 529
$5,000 to $9,999	1 870 393	1 701 222	1 585 707	140 919	173 467	6 178	11 916	10 591	25 847	11 483	32 223
$10,000 to $14,999	790 052	755 439	707 020	28 830	47 247	1 513	4 017	2 577	11 616	1 693	11 505
$15,000 to $24,999	654 606	633 951	594 867	16 429	32 583	1 071	2 713	2 444	9 983	711	9 291
$25,000 to $34,999	256 210	250 267	234 991	4 379	11 052	299	1 106	1 006	4 474	259	2 987
$35,000 or more	283 194	278 754	262 224	2 850	9 710	289	889	1 061	5 550	240	3 104
Percent with income in 1989 below poverty level	27.0	24.3	24.4	57.7	47.2	48.2	35.5	32.9	21.4	53.1	27.4

U.S. Department of Commerce
Economics and Statistics Administration
BUREAU OF THE CENSUS

CENSUS '90

1990 CH-1-1

1990 Census of Housing

General Housing Characteristics

United States

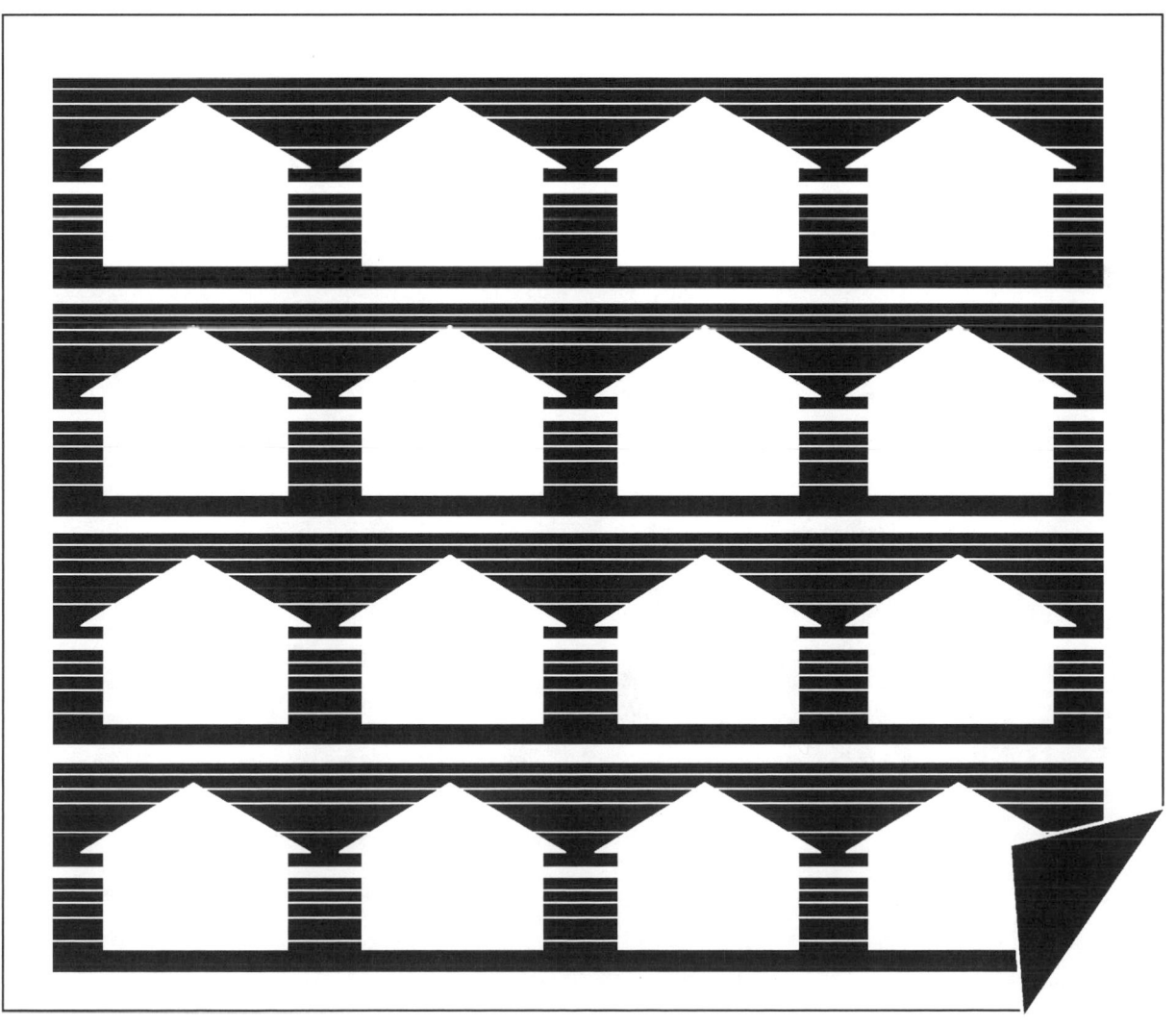

Table 1. **Summary of General Housing Characteristics: 1990**

[For definitions of terms and meanings of symbols, see text]

United States / Urban and Rural and Size of Place / Population Size Class of Urbanized Area / Inside and Outside Metropolitan Area / Population Size Class of Metropolitan Area	All persons	All housing units: Total	All housing units: Median rooms	All housing units: Percent 1 unit, detached or attached	All housing units: Percent In buildings with 10 or more units	Occupied housing units: Total	Occupied: Median persons in unit	Occupied: Mean number of persons per room	Occupied: Percent Owner	Occupied: Percent With 1.01 or more persons per room	Occupied: Percent With householder 65 years and over	Occupied: Percent 1-person households	Occupied: Specified owner, median value (dollars)	Specified renter: Median contract rent (dollars)	Specified renter: Percent with meals included in rent	Vacancy rate: Homeowner	Vacancy rate: Rental
United States	**248 709 873**	**102 263 678**	**5.2**	**64.3**	**12.9**	**91 947 410**	**2.29**	**.49**	**64.2**	**4.9**	**21.7**	**24.6**	**78 300**	**372**	**.9**	**2.1**	**8.5**
URBAN AND RURAL AND SIZE OF PLACE																	
Urban	187 053 487	76 212 052	5.1	60.6	16.8	70 045 167	2.25	.49	59.1	5.4	21.5	26.3	84 200	386	.9	2.2	8.4
Inside urbanized area	158 258 878	64 201 132	5.1	59.1	18.6	59 251 993	2.26	.49	58.4	5.7	20.6	26.2	91 700	407	.9	2.1	8.3
Central place	78 847 406	33 030 250	4.7	51.1	23.0	30 147 116	2.16	.51	49.1	7.3	21.2	30.1	72 300	370	.9	2.4	8.6
Urban fringe	79 411 472	31 170 882	5.5	67.6	14.0	29 104 877	2.35	.47	68.1	4.1	20.0	22.3	109 900	475	1.0	1.9	7.9
Outside urbanized area	28 794 609	12 010 920	5.1	68.3	7.2	10 793 174	2.21	.47	62.6	3.9	26.5	26.9	55 100	267	.6	2.4	8.8
Place of 10,000 or more	13 825 022	5 644 570	5.1	66.6	8.7	5 169 559	2.20	.47	59.1	4.0	25.0	27.4	56 700	280	.6	2.3	8.5
Place of 2,500 to 9,999	14 969 587	6 366 350	5.1	69.7	5.8	5 623 615	2.23	.47	65.8	3.9	27.8	26.4	54 100	253	.6	2.4	9.2
Rural	61 656 386	26 051 626	5.4	75.3	1.3	21 902 243	2.43	.48	80.6	3.4	22.5	18.9	63 300	244	.6	1.9	9.0
Place of 1,000 to 2,499	7 050 858	3 097 406	5.2	73.2	3.5	2 676 603	2.24	.46	71.6	3.4	29.0	25.8	49 700	225	.4	2.3	10.3
Place of less than 1,000	3 801 051	1 740 468	5.3	77.0	1.9	1 464 016	2.22	.46	75.8	3.4	31.3	26.6	35 800	187	.4	2.5	11.7
Other rural	50 804 477	21 213 752	5.4	75.5	.9	17 761 624	2.47	.48	82.3	3.4	20.8	17.2	69 600	260	.7	1.8	8.4
POPULATION SIZE CLASS OF URBANIZED AREA																	
1,000,000 or more	94 016 294	37 658 159	5.0	56.3	22.4	34 897 543	2.28	.50	57.0	7.0	20.0	26.3	116 900	457	.9	2.1	8.1
Central place	41 010 559	17 094 157	4.5	43.5	30.1	15 561 630	2.15	.55	44.3	9.9	20.7	31.2	86 900	409	.8	2.5	8.4
Urban fringe	53 005 735	20 564 002	5.5	66.9	16.1	19 335 913	2.37	.47	67.2	4.7	19.4	22.4	130 000	518	1.0	1.9	7.6
5,000,000 or more	34 239 045	12 967 605	4.7	46.5	28.3	12 213 357	2.34	.56	51.3	10.5	20.5	26.0	184 100	509	.7	1.9	5.8
Central place	16 304 119	6 412 779	4.0	26.8	41.7	5 980 246	2.21	.63	35.1	14.1	20.8	30.9	176 100	460	.6	2.3	5.9
Urban fringe	17 934 926	6 554 826	5.4	65.8	15.2	6 233 111	2.45	.50	66.7	7.0	20.2	21.2	186 400	600	.8	1.7	5.7
2,500,000 to 4,999,999	23 787 767	9 665 903	5.3	61.3	20.1	8 941 231	2.26	.48	59.1	5.4	18.5	26.8	112 600	462	1.0	2.0	9.1
Central place	9 541 204	4 146 422	4.7	50.8	25.9	3 701 940	2.10	.51	47.3	8.0	19.6	32.9	68 200	386	.9	2.6	10.6
Urban fringe	14 246 563	5 519 481	5.7	69.1	15.8	5 239 291	2.37	.46	67.5	3.5	17.7	22.6	135 400	551	1.2	1.7	7.3
1,000,000 to 2,499,999	35 989 482	15 024 651	5.1	61.6	18.9	13 742 955	2.23	.48	60.7	5.1	20.5	26.3	86 600	407	1.1	2.3	9.7
Central place	15 165 236	6 534 956	4.8	55.3	21.4	5 879 444	2.14	.50	51.7	6.8	21.4	30.4	76 600	368	1.1	2.7	10.0
Urban fringe	20 824 246	8 489 695	5.4	66.4	17.0	7 863 511	2.30	.46	67.4	3.7	19.8	23.3	91 200	451	1.2	2.1	9.4
Less than 1,000,000	64 242 584	26 542 973	5.2	63.1	13.3	24 354 450	2.23	.47	60.5	3.8	21.4	26.1	73 300	349	1.0	2.2	8.7
Central place	37 836 847	15 936 093	5.0	59.2	15.5	14 585 486	2.16	.48	54.2	4.5	21.6	28.9	65 300	329	.9	2.3	8.9
Urban fringe	26 405 737	10 606 880	5.4	68.9	9.9	9 768 964	2.33	.46	69.9	2.8	21.1	22.0	83 600	391	1.0	1.9	8.3
500,000 to 999,999	17 955 916	7 510 542	5.2	60.5	16.0	6 886 227	2.22	.47	59.7	3.8	20.8	26.7	77 400	362	.9	2.2	9.2
Central place	9 403 669	4 069 420	4.9	54.6	19.0	3 690 862	2.13	.48	51.6	4.8	20.8	30.4	64 100	332	.8	2.4	9.7
Urban fringe	8 552 247	3 441 122	5.5	67.5	12.5	3 195 365	2.32	.46	69.2	2.7	20.7	22.5	89 800	419	1.2	2.0	8.2
250,000 to 499,999	15 470 005	6 354 909	5.3	64.9	13.0	5 840 087	2.25	.47	61.7	4.0	21.4	25.9	74 400	352	1.0	2.2	8.9
Central place	8 327 127	3 502 161	5.0	61.0	15.5	3 195 892	2.17	.48	54.7	5.0	21.6	29.0	66 100	333	1.1	2.5	9.3
Urban fringe	7 142 878	2 852 748	5.5	69.7	9.9	2 644 195	2.34	.46	70.2	2.7	21.2	22.0	83 400	384	.8	1.9	8.2
100,000 to 249,999	18 879 599	7 734 865	5.1	63.2	12.4	7 100 845	2.24	.48	59.9	3.8	21.0	25.8	73 700	350	.9	2.1	8.3
Central place	11 928 889	4 957 616	5.0	59.6	14.6	4 563 687	2.18	.48	54.5	4.4	21.4	28.2	67 600	336	.9	2.2	8.3
Urban fringe	6 950 710	2 777 249	5.4	69.6	8.6	2 537 158	2.34	.47	69.5	2.9	20.3	21.6	83 000	386	.9	2.0	8.5
Less than 100,000	11 937 064	4 942 657	5.1	64.6	10.8	4 527 291	2.22	.47	61.0	3.5	23.1	26.1	65 000	317	1.0	2.1	8.2
Central place	8 177 162	3 406 896	5.0	62.3	12.7	3 135 045	2.17	.47	56.3	3.8	23.0	28.0	62 700	313	1.0	2.2	8.2
Urban fringe	3 759 902	1 535 761	5.3	69.6	6.5	1 392 246	2.31	.47	71.7	2.8	23.4	21.7	69 500	333	.9	2.0	8.3
INSIDE AND OUTSIDE METROPOLITAN AREA																	
Inside metropolitan area	192 725 741	77 644 313	5.2	62.0	15.9	71 265 264	2.30	.49	61.8	5.3	20.5	24.9	89 100	400	.9	2.1	8.3
In central city	77 843 533	32 641 254	4.7	51.0	23.1	29 793 822	2.16	.51	49.0	7.3	21.2	30.2	71 600	369	.9	2.4	8.6
Not in central city	114 882 208	45 003 059	5.5	69.9	10.7	41 471 442	2.39	.47	71.0	3.9	20.0	21.1	99 000	444	.9	1.9	7.9
Urban	88 439 928	34 761 039	5.4	67.7	13.3	32 340 947	2.35	.47	67.8	4.2	20.3	22.3	105 400	461	1.0	2.0	7.9
Inside urbanized area	79 755 134	31 243 819	5.5	67.6	14.0	29 201 839	2.35	.47	68.0	4.1	19.9	22.2	110 400	476	1.0	1.9	7.8
Outside urbanized area	8 684 794	3 517 220	5.2	68.6	7.3	3 139 108	2.33	.49	65.3	4.7	23.8	23.2	72 700	324	.6	2.4	8.3
Rural	26 442 280	10 242 020	5.6	77.3	1.5	9 130 495	2.52	.47	82.6	3.1	19.0	16.5	82 600	306	.8	1.8	8.2
Outside metropolitan area	55 984 132	24 619 365	5.2	71.7	3.3	20 682 146	2.29	.47	72.4	3.6	25.9	23.5	50 100	235	.6	2.1	9.3
Urban	20 851 951	8 843 531	5.1	67.6	7.3	7 938 898	2.17	.47	61.6	3.6	27.4	28.2	50 600	253	.6	2.4	9.0
Inside urbanized area	1 520 259	662 407	5.1	61.4	10.1	575 362	2.19	.47	60.4	3.1	23.8	25.6	73 800	323	1.0	2.5	8.6
Outside urbanized area	19 331 692	8 181 124	5.1	68.1	7.0	7 363 536	2.16	.47	61.7	3.6	27.7	28.4	49 300	249	.6	2.4	9.1
Place of 10,000 or more	9 873 345	4 084 848	5.1	66.1	8.6	3 735 404	2.16	.47	58.5	3.6	25.7	28.5	51 800	265	.6	2.3	8.8
Place of 2,500 to 9,999	9 458 347	4 096 276	5.1	70.1	5.5	3 628 132	2.17	.46	64.9	3.6	29.7	28.3	46 900	224	.5	2.4	9.5
Rural	35 132 181	15 775 834	5.3	74.0	1.1	12 743 248	2.36	.48	79.2	3.6	25.0	20.6	49 700	211	.5	2.0	9.5
POPULATION SIZE CLASS OF METROPOLITAN AREA																	
1,000,000 or more	124 775 608	49 751 864	5.1	59.6	19.0	45 957 542	2.30	.49	59.9	6.1	19.9	25.2	111 500	444	.9	2.1	8.0
In central city	48 263 927	20 135 413	4.6	45.1	28.0	18 366 553	2.16	.54	45.4	9.0	20.7	30.9	85 100	404	.8	2.4	8.3
Not in central city	76 511 681	29 616 451	5.5	69.4	13.0	27 590 989	2.39	.47	69.6	4.2	19.4	21.4	121 700	495	1.0	1.9	7.6
5,000,000 or more	52 837 069	20 260 608	5.0	54.5	22.6	18 913 934	2.34	.53	56.2	8.8	20.4	25.1	173 600	515	.9	2.0	6.1
In central city	22 256 704	8 793 324	4.3	35.4	35.0	8 179 362	2.21	.60	40.3	12.5	21.0	30.3	157 400	466	.8	2.2	6.1
Not in central city	30 580 365	11 467 284	5.5	69.1	13.1	10 734 572	2.43	.49	68.3	6.0	19.9	21.2	178 000	587	1.0	2.0	6.1
2,500,000 to 4,999,999	31 701 991	12 946 676	5.2	61.0	20.1	11 848 591	2.30	.48	61.3	5.2	18.1	25.3	94 800	422	.9	2.2	9.9
In central city	10 347 206	4 568 534	4.6	48.4	28.2	4 059 898	2.09	.51	46.3	8.0	19.9	32.6	70 500	366	.9	2.6	11.0
Not in central city	21 354 785	8 378 142	5.6	67.9	15.6	7 788 693	2.40	.46	69.1	3.8	17.2	21.5	103 200	478	.9	2.0	8.9
1,000,000 to 2,499,999	40 236 548	16 544 580	5.3	64.7	13.8	15 195 017	2.26	.47	63.5	3.5	20.7	25.2	81 700	377	1.0	2.1	9.2
In central city	15 660 017	6 773 555	4.9	55.4	18.6	6 127 293	2.13	.48	51.6	5.0	20.9	30.4	71 000	356	1.0	2.6	9.8
Not in central city	24 576 531	9 771 025	5.5	71.1	10.6	9 067 724	2.35	.46	71.6	2.6	20.6	21.6	87 100	405	1.1	1.9	8.4
Less than 1,000,000	67 950 133	27 892 449	5.2	66.2	10.3	25 307 722	2.28	.48	65.2	3.9	21.6	24.3	67 800	324	.9	2.1	8.9
In central city	29 579 606	12 505 841	5.0	60.6	15.4	11 427 269	2.16	.48	54.7	4.5	21.9	29.1	61 800	318	.9	2.4	9.2
Not in central city	38 370 527	15 386 608	5.4	70.8	6.2	13 880 453	2.38	.47	73.9	3.4	21.2	20.4	72 300	337	.8	1.9	8.6
500,000 to 999,999	24 905 921	10 259 792	5.2	64.9	12.5	9 345 825	2.28	.48	64.0	4.0	20.7	24.8	73 900	342	.9	2.2	9.1
In central city	10 438 257	4 482 864	4.9	57.8	18.5	4 069 887	2.14	.48	53.0	5.0	21.4	30.0	65 700	327	.9	2.6	9.8
Not in central city	14 467 664	5 776 928	5.4	70.4	7.9	5 275 938	2.38	.47	72.4	3.3	20.3	20.8	79 400	364	.9	1.9	8.3
250,000 to 499,999	21 528 297	8 785 646	5.3	67.3	9.4	7 944 081	2.30	.48	66.2	4.3	22.4	23.6	67 700	329	1.0	2.1	8.7
In central city	8 783 875	3 662 926	5.0	62.3	14.0	3 352 818	2.18	.48	55.5	5.1	22.5	28.3	61 800	322	1.0	2.3	8.7
Not in central city	12 744 422	5 122 720	5.4	70.9	6.1	4 591 263	2.37	.48	74.0	3.6	22.3	20.2	71 400	340	.9	2.0	8.7
100,000 to 249,999	19 403 087	7 981 325	5.2	66.8	8.7	7 224 474	2.27	.47	65.8	3.5	21.7	24.3	61 600	303	.9	1.9	8.9
In central city	9 054 420	3 810 250	5.0	61.9	13.6	3 498 653	2.15	.47	55.5	3.6	21.9	28.7	58 600	306	1.0	2.2	8.8
Not in central city	10 348 667	4 171 075	5.3	71.2	4.2	3 725 821	2.38	.48	75.6	3.3	21.5	20.1	64 100	297	.7	1.7	9.1
Less than 100,000	2 112 828	865 686	5.2	66.9	8.3	793 342	2.26	.46	64.8	2.5	22.0	25.3	57 400	289	.8	1.9	8.4
In central city	1 303 054	549 801	5.1	63.3	11.7	505 911	2.15	.46	57.9	2.8	23.1	28.8	54 900	289	.9	2.2	8.8
Not in central city	809 774	315 885	5.5	73.1	2.5	287 431	2.44	.47	77.0	2.2	20.0	19.1	61 800	288	.4	1.6	7.1

Table 2. Occupied Housing Units by Race and Hispanic Origin of Householder: 1990

[For definitions of terms and meanings of symbols, see text]

United States Urban and Rural and Size of Place	United States	Urban Total	Inside urbanized area Total	Central place	Urban fringe	Outside urbanized area Total	Place of 10,000 or more	Place of 2,500 to 9,999	Rural Total	Place of 1,000 to 2,499	Place of less than 1,000	Other rural
RACE OF HOUSEHOLDER												
Occupied housing units	91 947 410	70 045 167	59 251 993	30 147 116	29 104 877	10 793 174	5 169 559	5 623 615	21 902 243	2 676 603	1 464 016	17 761 624
White	76 880 105	56 613 098	47 112 854	21 600 072	25 512 782	9 500 244	4 486 590	5 013 654	20 267 007	2 452 238	1 346 368	16 468 401
Black	9 976 161	8 836 740	7 996 181	5 970 947	2 025 234	840 559	441 625	398 934	1 139 421	143 168	67 033	929 220
American Indian, Eskimo, or Aleut	591 372	349 899	252 845	155 508	97 337	97 054	42 111	54 943	241 473	31 067	37 317	173 089
American Indian	570 332	338 090	244 718	149 813	94 905	93 372	41 350	52 022	232 242	30 468	30 239	171 535
Eskimo	13 877	6 888	4 082	3 070	1 012	2 806	518	2 288	6 989	287	5 809	893
Aleut	7 163	4 921	4 045	2 625	1 420	876	243	633	2 242	312	1 269	661
Asian or Pacific Islander	2 013 735	1 934 866	1 823 436	995 571	827 865	111 430	62 955	48 475	78 869	17 569	4 208	57 092
Asian	1 922 097	1 852 147	1 756 780	961 132	795 648	95 367	57 310	38 057	69 950	14 525	3 358	52 067
Chinese	504 048	492 808	477 366	277 244	200 122	15 442	10 359	5 083	11 240	1 330	308	9 602
Filipino	348 847	333 089	310 812	164 490	146 322	22 277	10 713	11 564	15 758	4 796	1 135	9 827
Japanese	310 945	293 467	267 566	139 814	127 752	25 901	15 324	10 577	17 478	5 096	1 177	11 205
Asian Indian	237 800	227 406	216 627	100 559	116 068	10 779	6 875	3 904	10 394	1 039	195	9 160
Korean	202 556	197 382	191 109	98 801	92 308	6 273	4 293	1 980	5 174	571	156	4 447
Vietnamese	143 095	139 769	135 497	77 235	58 262	4 272	2 772	1 500	3 326	669	94	2 563
Cambodian	28 957	28 510	27 673	21 172	6 501	837	588	249	447	100	15	332
Hmong	13 742	13 371	12 391	10 883	1 508	980	735	245	371	37	6	328
Laotian	30 188	28 840	26 245	18 848	7 397	2 595	1 528	1 067	1 348	334	77	937
Thai	23 021	22 080	20 943	11 125	9 818	1 137	765	372	941	109	45	787
Other Asian	78 898	75 425	70 551	40 961	29 590	4 874	3 358	1 516	3 473	444	150	2 879
Bangladeshi	3 466	3 396	3 264	2 404	860	132	101	31	70	6	1	63
Burmese	1 757	1 701	1 635	772	863	66	45	21	56	4	2	50
Indonesian	9 793	9 497	8 853	4 424	4 429	644	517	127	296	37	4	255
Malayan	3 941	3 865	3 294	2 414	880	571	479	92	76	13	4	59
Okinawan	751	691	614	316	298	77	33	44	60	13	7	40
Pakistani	23 302	22 572	21 607	11 615	9 992	965	699	266	730	75	22	633
Sri Lankan	3 562	3 423	3 239	1 695	1 544	184	132	52	139	9	1	129
All other Asian	32 326	30 280	28 045	17 321	10 724	2 235	1 352	883	2 046	287	109	1 650
Pacific Islander	91 638	82 719	66 656	34 439	32 217	16 063	5 645	10 418	8 919	3 044	850	5 025
Hawaiian	56 839	49 649	36 413	18 801	17 612	13 236	4 374	8 862	7 190	2 704	751	3 735
Samoan	12 933	12 434	11 361	5 886	5 475	1 073	351	722	499	121	24	354
Guamanian	12 875	12 033	11 168	5 924	5 244	865	511	354	842	109	41	692
Other Pacific Islander	8 991	8 603	7 714	3 828	3 886	889	409	480	388	110	34	244
Tongan	3 383	3 262	2 947	1 325	1 622	315	100	215	121	52	11	58
Tahitian	219	202	174	107	67	28	6	22	17	6	2	9
Northern Mariana Islander	214	206	184	90	94	22	13	9	8	2	1	5
Palauan	298	289	233	147	86	56	41	15	9	2	–	7
Fijian	1 724	1 683	1 625	716	909	58	25	33	41	11	1	29
All other Pacific Islander	3 153	2 961	2 551	1 443	1 108	410	224	186	192	37	19	136
Other race	2 486 037	2 310 564	2 066 677	1 425 018	641 659	243 887	136 278	107 609	175 473	32 561	9 090	133 822
HISPANIC ORIGIN OF HOUSEHOLDER												
Occupied housing units	91 947 410	70 045 167	59 251 993	30 147 116	29 104 877	10 793 174	5 169 559	5 623 615	21 902 243	2 676 603	1 464 016	17 761 624
Hispanic origin (of any race)	6 001 718	5 630 932	4 988 301	3 235 169	1 753 132	542 631	291 255	251 376	470 786	82 639	23 929	364 218
Mexican	3 342 524	3 004 494	2 584 470	1 658 679	925 791	420 024	230 574	189 450	338 030	62 622	16 839	258 569
Puerto Rican	825 933	801 701	776 518	600 150	176 368	25 183	13 874	11 309	24 232	3 172	689	20 371
Cuban	391 261	382 645	376 004	195 845	180 159	6 641	3 747	2 894	8 616	835	160	7 621
Other Hispanic	1 442 000	1 342 092	1 251 309	780 495	470 814	90 783	43 060	47 723	99 908	16 010	6 241	77 657
Not of Hispanic origin	85 945 692	64 514 235	54 263 692	26 911 947	27 351 745	10 250 543	4 878 304	5 372 239	21 431 457	2 593 964	1 440 087	17 397 406
RACE AND HISPANIC ORIGIN OF HOUSEHOLDER												
Occupied housing units	91 947 410	70 045 167	59 251 993	30 147 116	29 104 877	10 793 174	5 169 559	5 623 615	21 902 243	2 676 603	1 464 016	17 761 624
White	76 880 105	56 613 098	47 112 854	21 600 072	25 512 782	9 500 244	4 480 590	5 013 054	20 267 007	2 452 238	1 346 368	16 468 401
Hispanic origin	3 246 356	2 961 558	2 675 539	1 625 453	1 050 086	286 019	148 279	137 740	284 798	48 233	14 059	222 506
Not of Hispanic origin	73 633 749	53 651 540	44 437 315	19 974 619	24 462 696	9 214 225	4 338 311	4 875 914	19 982 209	2 404 005	1 332 309	16 245 895
Black	9 976 161	8 836 740	7 996 181	5 970 947	2 025 234	840 559	441 625	398 934	1 139 421	143 168	67 033	929 220
Hispanic origin	209 390	203 625	196 827	157 052	39 775	6 798	4 004	2 794	5 765	726	240	4 799
Not of Hispanic origin	9 766 771	8 633 115	7 799 354	5 813 895	1 985 459	833 761	437 621	396 140	1 133 656	142 442	66 793	924 421
American Indian, Eskimo, or Aleut	591 372	349 899	252 845	155 508	97 337	97 054	42 111	54 943	241 473	31 067	37 317	173 089
Hispanic origin	39 978	34 430	29 878	19 266	10 612	4 552	2 365	2 187	5 548	836	452	4 260
Not of Hispanic origin	551 394	315 469	222 967	136 242	86 725	92 502	39 746	52 756	235 925	30 231	36 865	168 829
Asian or Pacific Islander	2 013 735	1 934 866	1 823 436	995 571	827 865	111 430	62 955	48 475	78 869	17 569	4 208	57 092
Hispanic origin	75 147	71 292	65 608	40 071	25 537	5 684	2 629	3 055	3 855	1 047	270	2 538
Not of Hispanic origin	1 938 588	1 863 574	1 757 828	955 500	802 328	105 746	60 326	45 420	75 014	16 522	3 938	54 554
Other race	2 486 037	2 310 564	2 066 677	1 425 018	641 659	243 887	136 278	107 609	175 473	32 561	9 090	133 822
Hispanic origin	2 430 847	2 260 027	2 020 449	1 393 327	627 122	239 578	133 978	105 600	170 820	31 797	8 908	130 115
Not of Hispanic origin	55 190	50 537	46 228	31 691	14 537	4 309	2 300	2 009	4 653	764	182	3 707
PERCENT DISTRIBUTION BY RACE OF HOUSEHOLDER												
Occupied housing units	100.0	100.0	100.0	100.0	100.0	100.0	100.0	100.0	100.0	100.0	100.0	100.0
White	83.6	80.8	79.5	71.6	87.7	88.0	86.8	89.2	92.5	91.6	92.0	92.7
Black	10.8	12.6	13.5	19.8	7.0	7.8	8.5	7.1	5.2	5.3	4.6	5.2
American Indian, Eskimo, or Aleut	.6	.5	.4	.5	.3	.9	.8	1.0	1.1	1.2	2.5	1.0
American Indian	.6	.5	.4	.5	.3	.9	.8	.9	1.1	1.1	2.1	1.0
Asian or Pacific Islander	2.2	2.8	3.1	3.3	2.8	1.0	1.2	.9	.4	.7	.3	.3
Asian	2.1	2.6	3.0	3.2	2.7	.9	1.1	.7	.3	.5	.2	.3
Pacific Islander	.1	.1	.1	.1	.1	.1	.1	.2	–	.1	.1	–
Other race	2.7	3.3	3.5	4.7	2.2	2.3	2.6	1.9	.8	1.2	.6	.8
PERCENT DISTRIBUTION BY HISPANIC ORIGIN OF HOUSEHOLDER												
Occupied housing units	100.0	100.0	100.0	100.0	100.0	100.0	100.0	100.0	100.0	100.0	100.0	100.0
Hispanic origin (of any race)	6.5	7.9	8.4	10.7	6.0	5.0	5.6	4.5	2.1	3.1	1.6	2.1
Mexican	3.6	4.3	4.4	5.5	3.2	3.9	4.5	3.4	1.5	2.3	1.2	1.5
Puerto Rican	.9	1.1	1.3	2.0	.6	.2	.3	.2	.1	.1	–	.1
Cuban	.4	.5	.6	.6	.6	.1	.1	.1	–	–	–	–
Other Hispanic	1.6	1.9	2.1	2.6	1.6	.8	.8	.8	.5	.6	.4	.4
Not of Hispanic origin	93.5	92.1	91.6	89.3	94.0	95.0	94.4	95.5	97.9	96.9	98.4	97.9
PERCENT OF HOUSEHOLDERS WHITE, NOT OF HISPANIC ORIGIN												
Occupied housing units	100.0	100.0	100.0	100.0	100.0	100.0	100.0	100.0	100.0	100.0	100.0	100.0
White	83.6	80.8	79.5	71.6	87.7	88.0	86.8	89.2	92.5	91.6	92.0	92.7
Not of Hispanic origin	80.1	76.6	75.0	66.3	84.1	85.4	83.9	86.7	91.2	89.8	91.0	91.5

2 UNITED STATES SUMMARY   GENERAL HOUSING CHARACTERISTICS

Table 3. Occupied Housing Units by Race and Hispanic Origin of Householder: 1990

[For definitions of terms and meanings of symbols, see text]

United States Population Size Class of Urbanized Area	1,000,000 or more — Total			5,000,000 or more			2,500,000 to 4,999,999		
	Total	Central place	Urban fringe	Total	Central place	Urban fringe	Total	Central place	Urban fringe
RACE OF HOUSEHOLDER									
Occupied housing units	34 897 543	15 561 630	19 335 913	12 213 357	5 980 246	6 233 111	8 941 231	3 701 940	5 239 291
White	26 635 557	10 039 879	16 595 678	8 715 609	3 560 593	5 155 016	6 686 811	2 181 437	4 505 374
Black	5 252 282	3 768 376	1 483 906	1 912 046	1 463 187	448 859	1 588 712	1 158 641	430 071
American Indian, Eskimo, or Aleut	128 575	68 687	59 888	36 625	20 455	16 170	28 181	12 718	15 463
American Indian	124 652	66 576	58 076	35 327	19 645	15 682	27 392	12 355	15 037
Eskimo	1 604	882	722	515	330	185	344	167	177
Aleut	2 319	1 229	1 090	783	480	303	445	196	249
Asian or Pacific Islander	1 355 163	686 728	668 435	655 466	344 618	310 848	362 354	166 311	196 043
Asian	1 322 958	672 219	650 739	644 219	339 194	305 025	354 131	163 565	190 566
Chinese	389 443	215 419	174 024	187 567	104 394	83 173	127 669	72 070	55 599
Filipino	240 143	122 819	117 324	108 629	58 675	49 954	63 411	24 999	38 412
Japanese	163 786	72 901	90 885	87 843	37 155	50 688	29 849	12 701	17 148
Asian Indian	167 249	71 285	95 964	86 178	43 513	42 665	45 496	14 261	31 235
Korean	153 034	73 939	79 095	94 903	53 665	41 238	30 049	9 997	20 052
Vietnamese	104 211	54 394	49 817	34 572	13 768	20 804	31 052	16 413	14 639
Cambodian	17 652	12 392	5 260	7 004	5 566	1 438	4 914	3 121	1 793
Hmong	5 163	4 480	683	177	119	58	305	263	42
Laotian	13 573	8 314	5 259	1 725	993	732	3 876	2 015	1 861
Thai	16 082	7 974	8 108	9 376	5 224	4 152	3 358	1 377	1 981
Other Asian	52 622	28 302	24 320	26 245	16 122	10 123	14 152	6 348	7 804
Bangladeshi	2 674	2 002	672	1 860	1 614	246	556	252	304
Burmese	1 356	602	754	614	283	331	509	206	303
Indonesian	6 786	2 902	3 884	3 506	1 403	2 103	1 469	610	859
Malayan	1 657	992	665	605	412	193	492	289	203
Okinawan	201	84	117	79	33	46	47	17	30
Pakistani	17 559	9 120	8 439	9 733	6 183	3 550	4 881	1 898	2 983
Sri Lankan	2 365	1 098	1 267	1 235	661	574	602	213	389
All other Asian	20 024	11 502	8 522	8 613	5 533	3 080	5 596	2 863	2 733
Pacific Islander	32 205	14 509	17 696	11 247	5 424	5 823	8 223	2 746	5 477
Hawaiian	12 622	5 229	7 393	4 290	1 817	2 473	3 112	1 042	2 070
Samoan	7 218	3 449	3 769	3 179	1 478	1 701	1 504	641	863
Guamanian	7 469	3 858	3 611	2 561	1 604	957	1 637	637	1 000
Other Pacific Islander	4 896	1 973	2 923	1 217	525	692	1 970	426	1 544
Tongan	1 731	580	1 151	421	123	298	841	167	674
Tahitian	92	56	36	32	21	11	30	17	13
Northern Mariana Islander	119	55	64	27	13	14	24	5	19
Palauan	108	56	52	19	8	11	21	3	18
Fijian	1 290	447	843	193	114	79	622	61	561
All other Pacific Islander	1 556	779	777	525	246	279	432	173	259
Other race	1 525 966	997 960	528 006	893 611	591 393	302 218	275 173	182 833	92 340
HISPANIC ORIGIN OF HOUSEHOLDER									
Occupied housing units	34 897 543	15 561 630	19 335 913	12 213 357	5 980 246	6 233 111	8 941 231	3 701 940	5 239 291
Hispanic origin (of any race)	3 683 627	2 245 865	1 437 762	1 938 047	1 224 019	714 028	596 053	353 545	242 508
Mexican	1 750 555	999 414	751 141	836 673	406 336	430 337	336 226	210 828	125 398
Puerto Rican	591 527	462 034	129 493	447 455	379 781	67 674	65 703	44 817	20 886
Cuban	343 610	178 594	165 016	86 054	44 147	41 907	14 713	7 341	7 372
Other Hispanic	997 935	605 823	392 112	567 865	393 755	174 110	179 411	90 559	88 852
Not of Hispanic origin	31 213 916	13 315 765	17 898 151	10 275 310	4 756 227	5 519 083	8 345 178	3 348 395	4 996 783
RACE AND HISPANIC ORIGIN OF HOUSEHOLDER									
Occupied housing units	34 897 543	15 561 630	19 335 913	12 213 357	5 980 246	6 233 111	8 941 231	3 701 940	5 239 291
White	26 635 557	10 039 879	16 595 678	8 715 609	3 560 593	5 155 016	6 686 811	2 181 437	4 505 374
Hispanic origin	1 955 421	1 095 261	860 160	912 319	523 520	388 799	291 498	151 294	140 204
Not of Hispanic origin	24 680 136	8 944 618	15 735 518	7 803 290	3 037 073	4 766 217	6 395 313	2 030 143	4 365 170
Black	5 252 282	3 768 376	1 483 906	1 912 046	1 463 187	448 859	1 588 712	1 158 641	430 071
Hispanic origin	164 413	131 382	33 031	112 487	96 983	15 504	24 146	17 639	6 507
Not of Hispanic origin	5 087 869	3 636 994	1 450 875	1 799 559	1 366 204	433 355	1 564 566	1 141 002	423 564
American Indian, Eskimo, or Aleut	128 575	68 687	59 888	36 625	20 455	16 170	28 181	12 718	15 463
Hispanic origin	19 874	11 874	8 000	9 266	5 702	3 564	3 226	1 833	1 393
Not of Hispanic origin	108 701	56 813	51 888	27 359	14 753	12 606	24 955	10 885	14 070
Asian or Pacific Islander	1 355 163	686 728	668 435	655 466	344 618	310 848	362 354	166 311	196 043
Hispanic origin	48 348	28 918	19 430	24 863	16 255	8 608	10 267	5 122	5 145
Not of Hispanic origin	1 306 815	657 810	649 005	630 603	328 363	302 240	352 087	161 189	190 898
Other race	1 525 966	997 960	528 006	893 611	591 393	302 218	275 173	182 833	92 340
Hispanic origin	1 495 571	978 430	517 141	879 112	581 559	297 553	266 916	177 657	89 259
Not of Hispanic origin	30 395	19 530	10 865	14 499	9 834	4 665	8 257	5 176	3 081
PERCENT DISTRIBUTION BY RACE OF HOUSEHOLDER									
Occupied housing units	100.0	100.0	100.0	100.0	100.0	100.0	100.0	100.0	100.0
White	76.3	64.5	85.8	71.4	59.5	82.7	74.8	58.9	86.0
Black	15.1	24.2	7.7	15.7	24.5	7.2	17.8	31.3	8.2
American Indian, Eskimo, or Aleut	.4	.4	.3	.3	.3	.3	.3	.3	.3
American Indian	.4	.4	.3	.3	.3	.3	.3	.3	.3
Asian or Pacific Islander	3.9	4.4	3.5	5.4	5.8	5.0	4.1	4.5	3.7
Asian	3.8	4.3	3.4	5.3	5.7	4.9	4.0	4.4	3.6
Pacific Islander	.1	.1	.1	.1	.1	.1	.1	.1	.1
Other race	4.4	6.4	2.7	7.3	9.9	4.8	3.1	4.9	1.8
PERCENT DISTRIBUTION BY HISPANIC ORIGIN OF HOUSEHOLDER									
Occupied housing units	100.0	100.0	100.0	100.0	100.0	100.0	100.0	100.0	100.0
Hispanic origin (of any race)	10.6	14.4	7.4	15.9	20.5	11.5	6.7	9.6	4.6
Mexican	5.0	6.4	3.9	6.9	6.8	6.9	3.8	5.7	2.4
Puerto Rican	1.7	3.0	.7	3.7	6.4	1.1	.7	1.2	.4
Cuban	1.0	1.1	.9	.7	.7	.7	.2	.2	.1
Other Hispanic	2.9	3.9	2.0	4.6	6.6	2.8	2.0	2.4	1.7
Not of Hispanic origin	89.4	85.6	92.6	84.1	79.5	88.5	93.3	90.4	95.4
PERCENT OF HOUSEHOLDERS WHITE, NOT OF HISPANIC ORIGIN									
Occupied housing units	100.0	100.0	100.0	100.0	100.0	100.0	100.0	100.0	100.0
White	76.3	64.5	85.8	71.4	59.5	82.7	74.8	58.9	86.0
Not of Hispanic origin	70.7	57.5	81.4	63.9	50.8	76.5	71.5	54.8	83.3

Table 3. Occupied Housing Units by Race and Hispanic Origin of Householder: 1990—Con.

[For definitions of terms and meanings of symbols, see text]

United States Population Size Class of Urbanized Area	1,000,000 or more—Con.			Less than 1,000,000					
	1,000,000 to 2,499,999			Total			500,000 to 999,999		
	Total	Central place	Urban fringe	Total	Central place	Urban fringe	Total	Central place	Urban fringe
RACE OF HOUSEHOLDER									
Occupied housing units	13 742 955	5 879 444	7 863 511	24 354 450	14 585 486	9 768 964	6 886 227	3 690 862	3 195 365
White	11 233 137	4 297 849	6 935 288	20 477 297	11 560 193	8 917 104	5 599 143	2 683 850	2 915 293
Black	1 751 524	1 146 548	604 976	2 743 899	2 202 571	541 328	903 037	743 180	159 857
American Indian, Eskimo, or Aleut	63 769	35 514	28 255	124 270	86 821	37 449	31 920	20 534	11 386
American Indian	61 933	34 576	27 357	120 066	83 237	36 829	31 463	20 244	11 219
Eskimo	745	385	360	2 478	2 188	290	207	137	70
Aleut	1 091	553	538	1 726	1 396	330	250	153	97
Asian or Pacific Islander	337 343	175 799	161 544	468 273	308 843	159 430	208 783	132 387	76 396
Asian	324 608	169 460	155 148	433 822	288 913	144 909	188 938	120 028	68 910
Chinese	74 207	38 955	35 252	87 923	61 825	26 098	37 416	26 596	10 820
Filipino	68 103	39 145	28 958	70 669	41 671	28 998	32 241	15 989	16 252
Japanese	46 094	23 045	23 049	103 780	66 913	36 867	68 431	45 968	22 463
Asian Indian	35 575	13 511	22 064	49 378	29 274	20 104	14 376	6 971	7 405
Korean	28 082	10 277	17 805	38 075	24 862	13 213	14 604	9 701	4 903
Vietnamese	38 587	24 213	14 374	31 286	22 841	8 445	9 197	6 066	3 131
Cambodian	5 734	3 705	2 029	10 021	8 780	1 241	2 335	1 792	543
Hmong	4 681	4 098	583	7 228	6 403	825	223	206	17
Laotian	7 972	5 306	2 666	12 672	10 534	2 138	3 040	2 332	708
Thai	3 348	1 373	1 975	4 861	3 151	1 710	1 580	900	680
Other Asian	12 225	5 832	6 393	17 929	12 659	5 270	5 495	3 507	1 988
Bangladeshi	258	136	122	590	402	188	208	127	81
Burmese	233	113	120	279	170	109	67	33	34
Indonesian	1 811	889	922	2 067	1 522	545	541	385	156
Malayan	560	291	269	1 637	1 422	215	430	361	69
Okinawan	75	34	41	413	232	181	301	190	111
Pakistani	2 945	1 039	1 906	4 048	2 495	1 553	1 248	625	623
Sri Lankan	528	224	304	874	597	277	267	165	102
All other Asian	5 815	3 106	2 709	8 021	5 819	2 202	2 433	1 621	812
Pacific Islander	12 735	6 339	6 396	34 451	19 930	14 521	19 845	12 359	7 486
Hawaiian	5 220	2 370	2 850	23 791	13 572	10 219	14 799	9 415	5 384
Samoan	2 535	1 330	1 205	4 143	2 437	1 706	2 590	1 523	1 067
Guamanian	3 271	1 617	1 654	3 699	2 066	1 633	925	512	413
Other Pacific Islander	1 709	1 022	687	2 818	1 855	963	1 531	909	622
Tongan	469	290	179	1 216	745	471	911	515	396
Tahitian	30	18	12	82	51	31	53	34	19
Northern Mariana Islander	68	37	31	65	35	30	28	14	14
Palauan	68	45	23	125	91	34	65	54	11
Fijian	475	272	203	335	269	66	44	28	16
All other Pacific Islander	599	360	239	995	664	331	430	264	166
Other race	357 182	223 734	133 448	540 711	427 058	113 653	143 344	110 911	32 433
HISPANIC ORIGIN OF HOUSEHOLDER									
Occupied housing units	13 742 955	5 879 444	7 863 511	24 354 450	14 585 486	9 768 964	6 886 227	3 690 862	3 195 365
Hispanic origin (of any race)	1 149 527	668 301	481 226	1 304 674	989 304	315 370	368 088	266 701	101 307
Mexican	577 656	382 250	195 406	833 915	659 265	174 650	216 818	174 802	42 016
Puerto Rican	78 369	37 436	40 933	184 991	138 116	46 875	68 314	46 053	22 261
Cuban	242 843	127 106	115 737	32 394	17 251	15 143	15 705	6 929	8 776
Other Hispanic	250 659	121 509	129 150	253 374	174 672	78 702	67 251	38 997	28 254
Not of Hispanic origin	12 593 428	5 211 143	7 382 285	23 049 776	13 596 182	9 453 594	6 518 139	3 424 081	3 094 058
RACE AND HISPANIC ORIGIN OF HOUSEHOLDER									
Occupied housing units	13 742 955	5 879 444	7 863 511	24 354 450	14 585 486	9 768 964	6 886 227	3 690 862	3 195 365
White	11 233 137	4 297 849	6 935 288	20 477 297	11 560 193	8 917 104	5 599 143	2 683 850	2 915 293
Hispanic origin	751 604	420 447	331 157	720 118	530 192	189 926	208 754	145 019	63 735
Not of Hispanic origin	10 481 533	3 877 402	6 604 131	19 757 179	11 030 001	8 727 178	5 390 389	2 538 831	2 851 558
Black	1 751 524	1 146 548	604 976	2 743 899	2 202 571	541 328	903 037	743 180	159 857
Hispanic origin	27 780	16 760	11 020	32 414	25 670	6 744	11 171	8 411	2 760
Not of Hispanic origin	1 723 744	1 129 788	593 956	2 711 485	2 176 901	534 584	891 866	734 769	157 097
American Indian, Eskimo, or Aleut	63 769	35 514	28 255	124 270	86 821	37 449	31 920	20 534	11 386
Hispanic origin	7 382	4 339	3 043	10 004	7 392	2 612	2 548	1 782	766
Not of Hispanic origin	56 387	31 175	25 212	114 266	79 429	34 837	29 372	18 752	10 620
Asian or Pacific Islander	337 343	175 799	161 544	468 273	308 843	159 430	208 783	132 387	76 396
Hispanic origin	13 218	7 541	5 677	17 260	11 153	6 107	6 906	3 875	3 031
Not of Hispanic origin	324 125	168 258	155 867	451 013	297 690	153 323	201 877	128 512	73 365
Other race	357 182	223 734	133 448	540 711	427 058	113 653	143 344	110 911	32 433
Hispanic origin	349 543	219 214	130 329	524 878	414 897	109 981	138 709	107 694	31 015
Not of Hispanic origin	7 639	4 520	3 119	15 833	12 161	3 672	4 635	3 217	1 418
PERCENT DISTRIBUTION BY RACE OF HOUSEHOLDER									
Occupied housing units	100.0	100.0	100.0	100.0	100.0	100.0	100.0	100.0	100.0
White	81.7	73.1	88.2	84.1	79.3	91.3	81.3	72.7	91.2
Black	12.7	19.5	7.7	11.3	15.1	5.5	13.1	20.1	5.0
American Indian, Eskimo, or Aleut	.5	.6	.4	.5	.6	.4	.5	.6	.4
American Indian	.5	.6	.3	.5	.6	.4	.5	.5	.4
Asian or Pacific Islander	2.5	3.0	2.1	1.9	2.1	1.6	3.0	3.6	2.4
Asian	2.4	2.9	2.0	1.8	2.0	1.5	2.7	3.3	2.2
Pacific Islander	.1	.1	.1	.1	.1	.1	.3	.3	.2
Other race	2.6	3.8	1.7	2.2	2.9	1.2	2.1	3.0	1.0
PERCENT DISTRIBUTION BY HISPANIC ORIGIN OF HOUSEHOLDER									
Occupied housing units	100.0	100.0	100.0	100.0	100.0	100.0	100.0	100.0	100.0
Hispanic origin (of any race)	8.4	11.4	6.1	5.4	6.8	3.2	5.3	7.2	3.2
Mexican	4.2	6.5	2.5	3.4	4.5	1.8	3.1	4.7	1.3
Puerto Rican	.6	.6	.5	.8	.9	.5	1.0	1.2	.7
Cuban	1.8	2.2	1.5	.1	.1	.2	.2	.2	.3
Other Hispanic	1.8	2.1	1.6	1.0	1.2	.8	1.0	1.1	.9
Not of Hispanic origin	91.6	88.6	93.9	94.6	93.2	96.8	94.7	92.8	96.8
PERCENT OF HOUSEHOLDERS WHITE, NOT OF HISPANIC ORIGIN									
Occupied housing units	100.0	100.0	100.0	100.0	100.0	100.0	100.0	100.0	100.0
White	81.7	73.1	88.2	84.1	79.3	91.3	81.3	72.7	91.2
Not of Hispanic origin	76.3	65.9	84.0	81.1	75.6	89.3	78.3	68.8	89.2

Table 3. Occupied Housing Units by Race and Hispanic Origin of Householder: 1990—Con.

[For definitions of terms and meanings of symbols, see text]

United States Population Size Class of Urbanized Area	Less than 1,000,000—Con.								
	250,000 to 499,999			100,000 to 249,999			Less than 100,000		
	Total	Central place	Urban fringe	Total	Central place	Urban fringe	Total	Central place	Urban fringe
RACE OF HOUSEHOLDER									
Occupied housing units	5 840 087	3 195 892	2 644 195	7 100 845	4 563 687	2 537 158	4 527 291	3 135 045	1 392 246
White	4 836 001	2 445 935	2 390 066	6 064 730	3 744 783	2 319 947	3 977 423	2 685 625	1 291 798
Black	722 006	546 266	175 740	735 786	596 970	138 816	383 070	316 155	66 915
American Indian, Eskimo, or Aleut	35 206	24 057	11 149	32 531	23 458	9 073	24 613	18 772	5 841
American Indian	34 673	23 728	10 945	29 711	20 798	8 913	24 219	18 467	5 752
Eskimo	269	170	99	1 814	1 734	80	188	147	41
Aleut	264	159	105	1 006	926	80	206	158	48
Asian or Pacific Islander	89 710	59 159	30 551	116 100	75 703	40 397	53 680	41 594	12 086
Asian	86 487	57 430	29 057	106 798	71 369	35 429	51 599	40 086	11 513
Chinese	16 077	10 311	5 766	22 942	15 572	7 370	11 488	9 346	2 142
Filipino	13 948	9 042	4 906	17 085	11 174	5 911	7 395	5 466	1 929
Japanese	10 261	6 056	4 205	18 116	9 441	8 675	6 972	5 448	1 524
Asian Indian	12 384	6 635	5 749	14 942	10 166	4 776	7 676	5 502	2 174
Korean	8 058	4 271	3 787	10 727	7 315	3 412	4 686	3 575	1 111
Vietnamese	9 174	7 135	2 039	9 102	6 603	2 499	3 813	3 037	776
Cambodian	3 833	3 609	224	3 000	2 718	282	853	661	192
Hmong	3 505	3 255	250	811	695	116	2 689	2 247	442
Laotian	3 826	3 501	325	3 392	2 765	627	2 414	1 936	478
Thai	1 102	681	421	1 430	994	436	749	576	173
Other Asian	4 319	2 934	1 385	5 251	3 926	1 325	2 864	2 292	572
Bangladeshi	131	85	46	161	121	40	90	69	21
Burmese	76	46	30	88	59	29	48	32	16
Indonesian	485	332	153	722	547	175	319	258	61
Malayan	353	288	65	527	468	59	327	305	22
Okinawan	18	10	8	85	24	61	9	8	1
Pakistani	1 034	598	436	1 135	793	342	631	479	152
Sri Lankan	173	102	71	272	214	58	162	116	46
All other Asian	2 049	1 473	576	2 261	1 700	561	1 278	1 025	253
Pacific Islander	3 223	1 729	1 494	9 302	4 334	4 968	2 081	1 508	573
Hawaiian	1 483	804	679	6 475	2 581	3 894	1 034	772	262
Samoan	594	335	259	767	445	322	192	134	58
Guamanian	867	401	466	1 240	685	555	667	468	199
Other Pacific Islander	279	189	90	820	623	197	188	134	54
Tongan	44	29	15	239	186	53	22	15	7
Tahitian	6	4	2	20	11	9	3	2	1
Northern Mariana Islander	13	5	8	15	9	6	9	7	2
Palauan	26	15	11	22	14	8	12	8	4
Fijian	44	36	8	224	192	32	23	13	10
All other Pacific Islander	146	100	46	300	211	89	119	89	30
Other race	157 164	120 475	36 689	151 698	122 773	28 925	88 505	72 899	15 606
HISPANIC ORIGIN OF HOUSEHOLDER									
Occupied housing units	5 840 087	3 195 892	2 644 195	7 100 845	4 563 687	2 537 158	4 527 291	3 135 045	1 392 246
Hispanic origin (of any race)	370 419	275 064	95 355	356 836	281 217	75 619	209 331	166 242	43 089
Mexican	244 719	184 308	60 411	226 025	181 622	44 403	146 353	118 533	27 820
Puerto Rican	44 641	35 380	9 261	53 053	42 229	10 824	18 983	14 454	4 529
Cuban	6 050	3 578	2 472	7 145	4 774	2 371	3 494	1 970	1 524
Other Hispanic	75 009	51 798	23 211	70 613	52 592	18 021	40 501	31 285	9 216
Not of Hispanic origin	5 469 668	2 920 828	2 548 840	6 744 009	4 282 470	2 461 539	4 317 960	2 968 803	1 349 157
RACE AND HISPANIC ORIGIN OF HOUSEHOLDER									
Occupied housing units	5 840 087	3 195 892	2 644 195	7 100 845	4 563 687	2 537 158	4 527 291	3 135 045	1 392 246
White	4 836 001	2 445 935	2 390 066	6 064 730	3 744 783	2 319 947	3 977 423	2 685 625	1 291 798
Hispanic origin	201 822	145 747	56 075	194 478	150 744	43 734	115 064	88 682	26 382
Not of Hispanic origin	4 634 179	2 300 188	2 333 991	5 870 252	3 594 039	2 276 213	3 862 359	2 596 943	1 265 416
Black	722 006	546 266	175 740	735 786	596 970	138 816	383 070	316 155	66 915
Hispanic origin	8 003	6 394	1 609	9 385	7 749	1 636	3 855	3 116	739
Not of Hispanic origin	714 003	539 872	174 131	726 401	589 221	137 180	379 215	313 039	66 176
American Indian, Eskimo, or Aleut	35 206	24 057	11 149	32 531	23 458	9 073	24 613	18 772	5 841
Hispanic origin	2 968	2 191	777	2 647	1 915	732	1 841	1 504	337
Not of Hispanic origin	32 238	21 866	10 372	29 884	21 543	8 341	22 772	17 268	5 504
Asian or Pacific Islander	89 710	59 159	30 551	116 100	75 703	40 397	53 680	41 594	12 086
Hispanic origin	3 720	2 651	1 069	4 419	2 913	1 506	2 215	1 714	501
Not of Hispanic origin	85 990	56 508	29 482	111 681	72 790	38 891	51 465	39 880	11 585
Other race	157 164	120 475	36 689	151 698	122 773	28 925	88 505	72 899	15 606
Hispanic origin	153 906	118 081	35 825	145 907	117 896	28 011	86 356	71 226	15 130
Not of Hispanic origin	3 258	2 394	864	5 791	4 877	914	2 149	1 673	476
PERCENT DISTRIBUTION BY RACE OF HOUSEHOLDER									
Occupied housing units	100.0	100.0	100.0	100.0	100.0	100.0	100.0	100.0	100.0
White	82.8	76.5	90.4	85.4	82.1	91.4	87.9	85.7	92.8
Black	12.4	17.1	6.6	10.4	13.1	5.5	8.5	10.1	4.8
American Indian, Eskimo, or Aleut	.6	.8	.4	.5	.5	.4	.5	.6	.4
American Indian	.6	.7	.4	.4	.5	.4	.5	.6	.4
Asian or Pacific Islander	1.5	1.9	1.2	1.6	1.7	1.6	1.2	1.3	.9
Asian	1.5	1.8	1.1	1.5	1.6	1.4	1.1	1.3	.8
Pacific Islander	.1	.1	.1	.1	.1	.2	—	—	—
Other race	2.7	3.8	1.4	2.1	2.7	1.1	2.0	2.3	1.1
PERCENT DISTRIBUTION BY HISPANIC ORIGIN OF HOUSEHOLDER									
Occupied housing units	100.0	100.0	100.0	100.0	100.0	100.0	100.0	100.0	100.0
Hispanic origin (of any race)	6.3	8.6	3.6	5.0	6.2	3.0	4.6	5.3	3.1
Mexican	4.2	5.8	2.3	3.2	4.0	1.8	3.2	3.8	2.0
Puerto Rican	.8	1.1	.4	.7	.9	.4	.4	.5	.3
Cuban	.1	.1	.1	.1	.1	.1	.1	.1	.1
Other Hispanic	1.3	1.6	.9	1.0	1.2	.7	.9	1.0	.7
Not of Hispanic origin	93.7	91.4	96.4	95.0	93.8	97.0	95.4	94.7	96.9
PERCENT OF HOUSEHOLDERS WHITE, NOT OF HISPANIC ORIGIN									
Occupied housing units	100.0	100.0	100.0	100.0	100.0	100.0	100.0	100.0	100.0
White	82.8	76.5	90.4	85.4	82.1	91.4	87.9	85.7	92.8
Not of Hispanic origin	79.4	72.0	88.3	82.7	78.8	89.7	85.3	82.8	90.9

Table 4. Occupied Housing Units by Race and Hispanic Origin of Householder: 1990

[For definitions of terms and meanings of symbols, see text]

United States Inside and Outside Metropolitan Area	United States	Inside metropolitan area						Outside metropolitan area				
		Total	In central city	Not in central city Total	Urban Inside urbanized area	Outside urbanized area	Rural	Total	Urban Inside urbanized area	Outside urbanized area Place of 10,000 or more	Place of 2,500 to 9,999	Rural
RACE OF HOUSEHOLDER												
Occupied housing units	91 947 410	71 265 264	29 793 822	41 471 442	29 201 839	3 139 108	9 130 495	20 682 146	575 362	3 735 404	3 628 132	12 743 248
White	76 880 105	58 333 897	21 323 382	37 010 515	25 573 614	2 817 272	8 619 629	18 546 208	495 534	3 234 124	3 194 329	11 622 221
Black	9 976 161	8 455 952	5 925 383	2 530 569	2 028 435	173 038	329 096	1 520 209	65 249	341 554	305 713	807 693
American Indian, Eskimo, or Aleut	591 372	323 542	154 315	169 227	98 568	19 657	51 002	267 830	2 815	32 868	42 013	190 134
American Indian	570 332	314 711	148 658	166 053	96 107	19 411	50 535	255 621	2 767	32 210	39 263	181 381
Eskimo	13 877	4 446	3 049	1 397	1 024	133	240	9 431	29	463	2 196	6 743
Aleut	7 163	4 385	2 608	1 777	1 437	113	227	2 778	19	195	554	2 010
Asian or Pacific Islander	2 013 735	1 896 281	982 551	913 730	838 502	32 146	43 082	117 454	6 234	47 167	28 410	35 643
Asian	1 922 097	1 820 726	949 822	870 904	804 624	26 342	39 938	101 371	5 983	42 310	23 185	29 893
Chinese	504 048	488 259	274 980	213 279	201 391	4 036	7 852	15 789	1 723	7 818	2 884	3 364
Filipino	348 847	326 574	161 086	165 488	149 542	8 205	7 741	22 273	696	6 953	6 631	7 993
Japanese	310 945	280 084	136 848	143 236	130 348	4 994	7 894	30 861	951	12 740	7 606	9 564
Asian Indian	237 800	227 152	99 700	127 452	116 683	3 444	7 325	10 648	946	4 587	2 067	3 048
Korean	202 556	195 843	98 092	97 751	92 699	1 674	3 378	6 713	574	3 295	1 054	1 790
Vietnamese	143 095	138 440	76 620	61 820	58 645	1 237	1 938	4 655	383	2 023	872	1 377
Cambodian	28 957	28 145	21 062	7 083	6 540	228	315	812	107	416	157	132
Hmong	13 742	13 108	10 997	2 111	1 499	345	267	634	26	381	123	104
Laotian	30 188	27 744	18 943	8 801	7 450	654	697	2 444	131	985	679	649
Thai	23 021	21 734	10 983	10 751	9 907	281	563	1 287	106	575	230	376
Other Asian	78 898	73 643	40 511	33 132	29 920	1 244	1 968	5 255	340	2 537	882	1 496
Bangladeshi	3 466	3 325	2 395	930	868	22	40	141	8	83	21	29
Burmese	1 757	1 688	747	941	879	21	41	69	9	36	9	15
Indonesian	9 793	9 142	4 321	4 821	4 498	129	194	651	48	447	55	101
Malayan	3 941	3 397	2 392	1 005	880	82	43	544	32	408	71	33
Okinawan	751	660	309	351	306	13	32	91	–	28	35	28
Pakistani	23 302	22 357	11 567	10 790	10 039	266	485	945	75	489	138	243
Sri Lankan	3 562	3 370	1 652	1 718	1 577	43	98	192	25	89	37	41
All other Asian	32 326	29 704	17 128	12 576	10 873	668	1 035	2 622	143	957	516	1 006
Pacific Islander	91 638	75 555	32 729	42 826	33 878	5 804	3 144	16 083	251	4 857	5 225	5 750
Hawaiian	56 839	43 074	17 369	25 705	19 010	4 518	2 177	13 765	136	3 961	4 662	5 006
Samoan	12 933	12 251	5 801	6 450	5 552	617	281	682	26	260	183	213
Guamanian	12 875	11 980	5 789	6 191	5 370	343	478	895	48	328	168	351
Other Pacific Islander	8 991	8 250	3 770	4 480	3 946	326	208	741	41	308	212	180
Tongan	3 383	3 158	1 302	1 856	1 641	134	81	225	9	81	95	40
Tahitian	219	200	105	95	68	20	7	19	1	4	4	10
Northern Mariana Islander	214	195	90	105	93	6	6	19	1	12	4	2
Palauan	298	246	144	102	89	9	4	52	–	37	10	5
Fijian	1 724	1 685	695	990	932	31	27	39	3	13	9	14
All other Pacific Islander	3 153	2 766	1 434	1 332	1 123	126	83	387	27	161	90	109
Other race	2 486 037	2 255 592	1 408 191	847 401	662 720	96 995	87 686	230 445	5 530	79 691	57 667	87 557
HISPANIC ORIGIN OF HOUSEHOLDER												
Occupied housing units	91 947 410	71 265 264	29 793 822	41 471 442	29 201 839	3 139 108	9 130 495	20 682 146	575 362	3 735 404	3 628 132	12 743 248
Hispanic origin (of any race)	6 001 718	5 427 548	3 196 572	2 230 976	1 794 407	200 303	236 266	574 170	14 034	177 936	148 244	233 956
Mexican	3 342 524	2 922 489	1 632 699	1 289 790	957 135	159 304	173 351	420 035	6 578	139 748	109 340	164 369
Puerto Rican	825 933	803 501	596 764	206 737	180 144	11 649	14 944	22 432	1 705	6 991	4 565	9 171
Cuban	391 261	383 828	195 045	188 783	180 708	2 291	5 784	7 433	415	2 465	1 743	2 810
Other Hispanic	1 442 000	1 317 730	772 064	545 666	476 420	27 059	42 187	124 270	5 336	28 732	32 596	57 606
Not of Hispanic origin	85 945 692	65 837 716	26 597 250	39 240 466	27 407 432	2 938 805	8 894 229	20 107 976	561 328	3 557 468	3 479 888	12 509 292
RACE AND HISPANIC ORIGIN OF HOUSEHOLDER												
Occupied housing units	91 947 410	71 265 264	29 793 822	41 471 442	29 201 839	3 139 108	9 130 495	20 682 146	575 362	3 735 404	3 628 132	12 743 248
White	76 880 105	58 333 897	21 323 382	37 010 515	25 573 614	2 817 272	8 619 629	18 546 208	495 534	3 234 124	3 194 329	11 622 221
Hispanic origin	3 246 356	2 917 034	1 604 834	1 312 200	1 069 057	98 740	144 403	329 322	8 194	94 096	86 942	140 090
Not of Hispanic origin	73 633 749	55 416 863	19 718 548	35 698 315	24 504 557	2 718 532	8 475 226	18 216 886	487 340	3 140 028	3 107 387	11 482 131
Black	9 976 161	8 455 952	5 925 383	2 530 569	2 028 435	173 038	329 096	1 520 209	65 249	341 554	305 713	807 693
Hispanic origin	209 390	201 376	156 395	44 981	40 143	2 511	2 327	8 014	508	2 358	1 730	3 418
Not of Hispanic origin	9 766 771	8 254 576	5 768 988	2 485 588	1 988 292	170 527	326 769	1 512 195	64 741	339 196	303 983	804 275
American Indian, Eskimo, or Aleut	591 372	323 542	154 315	169 227	98 568	19 657	51 002	267 830	2 815	32 868	42 013	190 134
Hispanic origin	39 978	33 567	18 881	14 686	10 982	1 465	2 239	6 411	199	1 526	1 382	3 304
Not of Hispanic origin	551 394	289 975	135 434	154 541	87 586	18 192	48 763	261 419	2 616	31 342	40 631	186 830
Asian or Pacific Islander	2 013 735	1 896 281	982 551	913 730	838 502	32 146	43 082	117 454	6 234	47 167	28 410	35 643
Hispanic origin	75 147	69 536	39 405	30 131	26 203	2 068	1 860	5 611	166	1 725	1 734	1 986
Not of Hispanic origin	1 938 588	1 826 745	943 146	883 599	812 299	30 078	41 222	111 843	6 068	45 442	26 676	33 657
Other race	2 486 037	2 255 592	1 408 191	847 401	662 720	96 995	87 686	230 445	5 530	79 691	57 667	87 557
Hispanic origin	2 430 847	2 206 035	1 377 057	828 978	648 022	95 519	85 437	224 812	4 967	78 231	56 456	85 158
Not of Hispanic origin	55 190	49 557	31 134	18 423	14 698	1 476	2 249	5 633	563	1 460	1 211	2 399
PERCENT DISTRIBUTION BY RACE OF HOUSEHOLDER												
Occupied housing units	100.0	100.0	100.0	100.0	100.0	100.0	100.0	100.0	100.0	100.0	100.0	100.0
White	83.6	81.9	71.6	89.2	87.6	89.7	94.4	89.7	86.1	86.6	88.0	91.2
Black	10.8	11.9	19.9	6.1	6.9	5.5	3.6	7.4	11.3	9.1	8.4	6.3
American Indian, Eskimo, or Aleut	.6	.5	.5	.4	.3	.6	.6	1.3	.5	.9	1.2	1.5
American Indian	.6	.4	.5	.4	.3	.6	.6	1.2	.5	.9	1.1	1.4
Asian or Pacific Islander	2.2	2.7	3.3	2.2	2.9	1.0	.5	.6	1.1	1.3	.8	.3
Asian	2.1	2.6	3.2	2.1	2.8	.8	.4	.5	1.0	1.1	.6	.2
Pacific Islander	.1	.1	.1	.1	.1	.2	–	.1	–	.1	.1	–
Other race	2.7	3.2	4.7	2.0	2.3	3.1	1.0	1.1	1.0	2.1	1.6	.7
PERCENT DISTRIBUTION BY HISPANIC ORIGIN OF HOUSEHOLDER												
Occupied housing units	100.0	100.0	100.0	100.0	100.0	100.0	100.0	100.0	100.0	100.0	100.0	100.0
Hispanic origin (of any race)	6.5	7.6	10.7	5.4	6.1	6.4	2.6	2.8	2.4	4.8	4.1	1.8
Mexican	3.6	4.1	5.5	3.1	3.3	5.1	1.9	2.0	1.1	3.7	3.0	1.3
Puerto Rican	.9	1.1	2.0	.5	.6	.4	.2	.1	.3	.2	.1	.1
Cuban	.4	.5	.7	.5	.6	.1	.1	–	.1	.1	–	–
Other Hispanic	1.6	1.8	2.6	1.3	1.6	.9	.5	.6	.9	.8	.9	.5
Not of Hispanic origin	93.5	92.4	89.3	94.6	93.9	93.6	97.4	97.2	97.6	95.2	95.9	98.2
PERCENT OF HOUSEHOLDERS WHITE, NOT OF HISPANIC ORIGIN												
Occupied housing units	100.0	100.0	100.0	100.0	100.0	100.0	100.0	100.0	100.0	100.0	100.0	100.0
White	83.6	81.9	71.6	89.2	87.6	89.7	94.4	89.7	86.1	86.6	88.0	91.2
Not of Hispanic origin	80.1	77.8	66.2	86.1	83.9	86.6	92.8	88.1	84.7	84.1	85.6	90.1

Table 5. Occupied Housing Units by Race and Hispanic Origin of Householder: 1990

[For definitions of terms and meanings of symbols, see text]

United States Population Size Class of Metropolitan Area	1,000,000 or more — Total			5,000,000 or more			2,500,000 to 4,999,999		
	Total	In central city	Not in central city	Total	In central city	Not in central city	Total	In central city	Not in central city
RACE OF HOUSEHOLDER									
Occupied housing units	45 957 542	18 366 553	27 590 989	18 913 934	8 179 362	10 734 572	11 848 591	4 059 898	7 788 693
White	36 587 278	12 266 573	24 320 705	14 132 945	5 024 912	9 108 033	9 420 776	2 639 642	6 781 134
Black	5 981 262	4 204 163	1 777 099	2 580 861	1 909 758	671 103	1 844 955	1 129 432	715 523
American Indian, Eskimo, or Aleut	173 535	80 394	93 141	65 905	30 249	35 656	39 230	15 312	23 918
American Indian	168 755	78 041	90 714	63 811	29 166	34 645	37 768	14 679	23 089
Eskimo	2 037	1 008	1 029	868	460	408	629	276	353
Aleut	2 743	1 345	1 398	1 226	623	603	833	357	476
Asian or Pacific Islander	1 485 853	735 860	749 993	992 516	507 210	485 306	258 229	99 951	158 278
Asian	1 447 459	719 412	728 047	969 794	497 675	472 119	252 870	97 946	154 924
Chinese	416 311	225 471	190 840	303 890	170 931	132 959	65 132	27 316	37 816
Filipino	260 556	129 136	131 420	186 416	91 824	94 592	28 665	10 838	17 827
Japanese	181 927	78 741	103 186	126 149	53 060	73 089	24 943	10 031	14 912
Asian Indian	188 492	78 292	110 200	115 280	52 588	62 692	45 329	13 806	31 523
Korean	165 195	78 180	87 015	116 275	62 273	54 002	29 621	8 008	21 613
Vietnamese	112 728	58 247	54 481	59 207	29 644	29 563	29 464	13 850	15 614
Cambodian	22 186	16 216	5 970	10 565	8 461	2 104	6 889	4 191	2 698
Hmong	5 570	4 727	843	324	164	160	449	307	142
Laotian	17 737	11 005	6 732	4 995	2 971	2 024	4 764	2 436	2 328
Thai	17 548	8 462	9 086	11 304	5 962	5 342	3 709	1 340	2 369
Other Asian	59 209	30 935	28 274	35 389	19 797	15 592	13 905	5 823	8 082
Bangladeshi	2 856	2 073	783	2 029	1 675	354	614	282	332
Burmese	1 488	634	854	1 015	462	553	290	88	202
Indonesian	7 562	3 196	4 366	5 133	1 966	3 167	1 172	505	667
Malayan	1 956	1 181	775	839	511	328	574	333	241
Okinawan	227	92	135	132	56	76	50	15	35
Pakistani	19 295	9 705	9 590	11 794	6 882	4 912	5 276	1 892	3 384
Sri Lankan	2 718	1 229	1 489	1 644	796	848	574	193	381
All other Asian	23 107	12 825	10 282	12 803	7 449	5 354	5 355	2 515	2 840
Pacific Islander	38 394	16 448	21 946	22 722	9 535	13 187	5 359	2 005	3 354
Hawaiian	15 280	5 970	9 310	8 862	3 371	5 491	2 405	791	1 614
Samoan	8 215	3 770	4 445	5 416	2 513	2 903	1 029	527	502
Guamanian	8 843	4 297	4 546	5 058	2 608	2 450	1 212	411	801
Other Pacific Islander	6 056	2 411	3 645	3 386	1 043	2 343	713	276	437
Tongan	2 452	900	1 552	1 293	319	974	212	66	146
Tahitian	114	64	50	67	41	26	17	8	9
Northern Mariana Islander	133	56	77	60	21	39	29	11	18
Palauan	127	63	64	56	21	35	26	9	17
Fijian	1 395	470	925	968	238	730	95	38	57
All other Pacific Islander	1 835	858	977	942	403	539	334	144	190
Other race	1 729 614	1 079 563	650 051	1 141 707	707 233	434 474	285 401	175 561	109 840
HISPANIC ORIGIN OF HOUSEHOLDER									
Occupied housing units	45 957 542	18 366 553	27 590 989	18 913 934	8 179 362	10 734 572	11 848 591	4 059 898	7 788 693
Hispanic origin (of any race)	4 154 630	2 414 004	1 740 626	2 489 327	1 458 170	1 031 157	893 130	480 869	412 261
Mexican	2 003 309	1 061 763	941 546	1 176 236	534 526	641 710	329 075	200 075	129 000
Puerto Rican	693 138	525 252	167 886	523 467	430 869	92 598	84 115	44 493	39 622
Cuban	357 851	182 876	174 975	95 338	48 009	47 329	234 560	121 442	113 118
Other Hispanic	1 100 332	644 113	456 219	694 286	444 766	249 520	245 380	114 859	130 521
Not of Hispanic origin	41 802 912	15 952 549	25 850 363	16 424 607	6 721 192	9 703 415	10 955 461	3 579 029	7 376 432
RACE AND HISPANIC ORIGIN OF HOUSEHOLDER									
Occupied housing units	45 957 542	18 366 553	27 590 989	18 913 934	8 179 362	10 734 572	11 848 591	4 059 898	7 788 693
White	36 587 278	12 266 573	24 320 705	14 132 945	5 024 912	9 108 033	9 420 776	2 639 642	6 781 134
Hispanic origin	2 206 844	1 173 312	1 033 532	1 191 228	628 590	562 638	572 782	284 308	288 474
Not of Hispanic origin	34 380 434	11 093 261	23 287 173	12 941 717	4 396 322	8 545 395	8 847 994	2 355 334	6 492 660
Black	5 981 262	4 204 163	1 777 099	2 580 861	1 909 758	671 103	1 844 955	1 129 432	715 523
Hispanic origin	178 261	140 285	37 976	125 737	105 552	20 185	33 360	20 964	12 396
Not of Hispanic origin	5 803 001	4 063 878	1 739 123	2 455 124	1 804 206	650 918	1 811 595	1 108 468	703 127
American Indian, Eskimo, or Aleut	173 535	80 394	93 141	65 905	30 249	35 656	39 230	15 312	23 918
Hispanic origin	23 858	13 040	10 818	13 983	7 441	6 542	3 258	1 827	1 431
Not of Hispanic origin	149 677	67 354	82 323	51 922	22 808	29 114	35 972	13 485	22 487
Asian or Pacific Islander	1 485 853	735 860	749 993	992 516	507 210	485 306	258 229	99 951	158 278
Hispanic origin	53 247	30 749	22 498	36 492	21 660	14 832	7 265	3 478	3 787
Not of Hispanic origin	1 432 606	705 111	727 495	956 024	485 550	470 474	250 964	96 473	154 491
Other race	1 729 614	1 079 563	650 051	1 141 707	707 233	434 474	285 401	175 561	109 840
Hispanic origin	1 692 420	1 056 618	635 802	1 121 887	694 927	426 960	276 465	170 292	106 173
Not of Hispanic origin	37 194	22 945	14 249	19 820	12 306	7 514	8 936	5 269	3 667
PERCENT DISTRIBUTION BY RACE OF HOUSEHOLDER									
Occupied housing units	100.0	100.0	100.0	100.0	100.0	100.0	100.0	100.0	100.0
White	79.6	66.8	88.1	74.7	61.4	84.8	79.5	65.0	87.1
Black	13.0	22.9	6.4	13.6	23.3	6.3	15.6	27.8	9.2
American Indian, Eskimo, or Aleut	.4	.4	.3	.3	.4	.3	.3	.4	.3
American Indian	.4	.4	.3	.3	.4	.3	.3	.4	.3
Asian or Pacific Islander	3.2	4.0	2.7	5.2	6.2	4.5	2.2	2.5	2.0
Asian	3.1	3.9	2.6	5.1	6.1	4.4	2.1	2.4	2.0
Pacific Islander	.1	.1	.1	.1	.1	.1	—	—	—
Other race	3.8	5.9	2.4	6.0	8.6	4.0	2.4	4.3	1.4
PERCENT DISTRIBUTION BY HISPANIC ORIGIN OF HOUSEHOLDER									
Occupied housing units	100.0	100.0	100.0	100.0	100.0	100.0	100.0	100.0	100.0
Hispanic origin (of any race)	9.0	13.1	6.3	13.2	17.8	9.6	7.5	11.8	5.3
Mexican	4.4	5.8	3.4	6.2	6.5	6.0	2.8	4.9	1.7
Puerto Rican	1.5	2.9	.6	2.8	5.3	.9	.7	1.1	.5
Cuban	.8	1.0	.6	.5	.6	.4	2.0	3.0	1.5
Other Hispanic	2.4	3.5	1.7	3.7	5.4	2.3	2.1	2.8	1.7
Not of Hispanic origin	91.0	86.9	93.7	86.8	82.2	90.4	92.5	88.2	94.7
PERCENT OF HOUSEHOLDERS WHITE, NOT OF HISPANIC ORIGIN									
Occupied housing units	100.0	100.0	100.0	100.0	100.0	100.0	100.0	100.0	100.0
White	79.6	66.8	88.1	74.7	61.4	84.8	79.5	65.0	87.1
Not of Hispanic origin	74.8	60.4	84.4	68.4	53.7	79.6	74.7	58.0	83.4

Table 5. Occupied Housing Units by Race and Hispanic Origin of Householder: 1990—Con.

[For definitions of terms and meanings of symbols, see text]

United States Population Size Class of Metropolitan Area	1,000,000 or more—Con. 1,000,000 to 2,499,999 Total	In central city	Not in central city	Less than 1,000,000 Total Total	In central city	Not in central city	500,000 to 999,999 Total	In central city	Not in central city
RACE OF HOUSEHOLDER									
Occupied housing units	15 195 017	6 127 293	9 067 724	25 307 722	11 427 269	13 880 453	9 345 825	4 069 887	5 275 938
White	13 033 557	4 602 019	8 431 538	21 746 619	9 056 809	12 689 810	7 697 165	2 959 624	4 737 541
Black	1 555 446	1 164 973	390 473	2 474 690	1 721 220	753 470	1 136 147	814 418	321 729
American Indian, Eskimo, or Aleut	68 400	34 833	33 567	150 007	73 921	76 086	61 285	28 664	32 621
American Indian	67 176	34 196	32 980	145 956	70 617	75 339	60 706	28 331	32 375
Eskimo	540	272	268	2 409	2 041	368	267	150	117
Aleut	684	365	319	1 642	1 263	379	312	183	129
Asian or Pacific Islander	235 108	128 699	106 409	410 428	246 691	163 737	250 038	141 894	108 144
Asian	224 795	123 791	101 004	373 267	230 410	142 857	220 220	129 756	90 464
Chinese	47 289	27 224	20 065	71 948	49 509	22 439	41 916	28 562	13 354
Filipino	45 475	26 474	19 001	66 018	31 950	34 068	40 462	16 963	23 499
Japanese	30 835	15 650	15 185	98 157	58 107	40 050	79 241	46 707	32 534
Asian Indian	27 883	11 898	15 985	38 660	21 408	17 252	16 040	8 079	7 961
Korean	19 299	7 899	11 400	30 648	19 912	10 736	15 626	10 201	5 425
Vietnamese	24 057	14 753	9 304	25 712	18 373	7 339	10 287	7 188	3 099
Cambodian	4 732	3 564	1 168	5 959	4 846	1 113	2 083	1 579	504
Hmong	4 797	4 256	541	7 538	6 270	1 268	2 801	2 546	255
Laotian	7 978	5 598	2 380	10 007	7 938	2 069	3 691	3 011	680
Thai	2 535	1 160	1 375	4 186	2 521	1 665	1 763	973	790
Other Asian	9 915	5 315	4 600	14 434	9 576	4 858	6 310	3 947	2 363
Bangladeshi	213	116	97	469	322	147	211	137	74
Burmese	183	84	99	200	113	87	87	55	32
Indonesian	1 257	725	532	1 580	1 125	455	664	458	206
Malayan	543	337	206	1 441	1 211	230	523	414	109
Okinawan	45	21	24	433	217	216	378	187	191
Pakistani	2 225	931	1 294	3 062	1 862	1 200	1 299	700	599
Sri Lankan	500	240	260	652	423	229	299	182	117
All other Asian	4 949	2 861	2 088	6 597	4 303	2 294	2 849	1 814	1 035
Pacific Islander	10 313	4 908	5 405	37 161	16 281	20 880	29 818	12 138	17 680
Hawaiian	4 013	1 808	2 205	27 794	11 399	16 395	24 418	9 494	14 924
Samoan	1 770	730	1 040	4 036	2 031	2 005	3 125	1 513	1 612
Guamanian	2 573	1 278	1 295	3 137	1 492	1 645	1 106	517	589
Other Pacific Islander	1 957	1 092	865	2 194	1 359	835	1 169	614	555
Tongan	947	515	432	706	402	304	472	214	258
Tahitian	30	15	15	86	41	45	63	29	34
Northern Mariana Islander	44	24	20	62	34	28	34	16	18
Palauan	45	33	12	119	81	38	78	57	21
Fijian	332	194	138	290	225	65	64	34	30
All other Pacific Islander	559	311	248	931	576	355	458	264	194
Other race	302 506	196 769	105 737	525 978	328 628	197 350	201 190	125 287	75 903
HISPANIC ORIGIN OF HOUSEHOLDER									
Occupied housing units	15 195 017	6 127 293	9 067 724	25 307 722	11 427 269	13 880 453	9 345 825	4 069 887	5 275 938
Hispanic origin (of any race)	772 173	474 965	297 208	1 272 918	782 568	490 350	460 666	289 670	170 996
Mexican	497 998	327 162	170 836	919 180	570 936	348 244	325 972	212 246	113 726
Puerto Rican	85 556	49 890	35 666	110 363	71 512	38 851	51 068	34 719	16 349
Cuban	27 953	13 425	14 528	25 977	12 169	13 808	14 207	6 286	7 921
Other Hispanic	160 666	84 488	76 178	217 398	127 951	89 447	69 419	36 419	33 000
Not of Hispanic origin	14 422 844	5 652 328	8 770 516	24 034 804	10 644 701	13 390 103	8 885 159	3 780 217	5 104 942
RACE AND HISPANIC ORIGIN OF HOUSEHOLDER									
Occupied housing units	15 195 017	6 127 293	9 067 724	25 307 722	11 427 269	13 880 453	9 345 825	4 069 887	5 275 938
White	13 033 557	4 602 019	8 431 538	21 740 019	9 050 009	12 690 010	7 607 166	2 060 624	4 737 541
Hispanic origin	442 834	260 414	182 420	710 190	431 522	278 668	240 265	153 229	87 036
Not of Hispanic origin	12 590 723	4 341 605	8 249 118	21 036 429	8 625 287	12 411 142	7 456 900	2 806 395	4 650 505
Black	1 555 446	1 164 973	390 473	2 474 690	1 721 220	753 470	1 136 147	814 418	321 729
Hispanic origin	19 164	13 769	5 395	23 115	16 110	7 005	9 967	7 015	2 952
Not of Hispanic origin	1 536 282	1 151 204	385 078	2 451 575	1 705 110	746 465	1 126 180	807 403	318 777
American Indian, Eskimo, or Aleut	68 400	34 833	33 567	150 007	73 921	76 086	61 285	28 664	32 621
Hispanic origin	6 617	3 772	2 845	9 709	5 841	3 868	3 825	2 217	1 608
Not of Hispanic origin	61 783	31 061	30 722	140 298	68 080	72 218	57 460	26 447	31 013
Asian or Pacific Islander	235 108	128 699	106 409	410 428	246 691	163 737	250 038	141 894	108 144
Hispanic origin	9 490	5 611	3 879	16 289	8 656	7 633	9 393	4 320	5 073
Not of Hispanic origin	225 618	123 088	102 530	394 139	238 035	156 104	240 645	137 574	103 071
Other race	302 506	196 769	105 737	525 978	328 628	197 350	201 190	125 287	75 903
Hispanic origin	294 068	191 399	102 669	513 615	320 439	193 176	197 216	122 889	74 327
Not of Hispanic origin	8 438	5 370	3 068	12 363	8 189	4 174	3 974	2 398	1 576
PERCENT DISTRIBUTION BY RACE OF HOUSEHOLDER									
Occupied housing units	100.0	100.0	100.0	100.0	100.0	100.0	100.0	100.0	100.0
White	85.8	75.1	93.0	85.9	79.3	91.4	82.4	72.7	89.8
Black	10.2	19.0	4.3	9.8	15.1	5.4	12.2	20.0	6.1
American Indian, Eskimo, or Aleut	.5	.6	.4	.6	.6	.5	.7	.7	.6
American Indian	.4	.6	.4	.6	.6	.5	.6	.7	.6
Asian or Pacific Islander	1.5	2.1	1.2	1.6	2.2	1.2	2.7	3.5	2.0
Asian	1.5	2.0	1.1	1.5	2.0	1.0	2.4	3.2	1.7
Pacific Islander	.1	.1	.1	.1	.1	.2	.3	.3	.3
Other race	2.0	3.2	1.2	2.1	2.9	1.4	2.2	3.1	1.4
PERCENT DISTRIBUTION BY HISPANIC ORIGIN OF HOUSEHOLDER									
Occupied housing units	100.0	100.0	100.0	100.0	100.0	100.0	100.0	100.0	100.0
Hispanic origin (of any race)	5.1	7.8	3.3	5.0	6.8	3.5	4.9	7.1	3.2
Mexican	3.3	5.3	1.9	3.6	5.0	2.5	3.5	5.2	2.2
Puerto Rican	.6	.8	.4	.4	.6	.3	.5	.9	.3
Cuban	.2	.2	.2	.1	.1	.1	.2	.2	.2
Other Hispanic	1.1	1.4	.8	.9	1.1	.6	.7	.9	.6
Not of Hispanic origin	94.9	92.2	96.7	95.0	93.2	96.5	95.1	92.9	96.8
PERCENT OF HOUSEHOLDERS WHITE, NOT OF HISPANIC ORIGIN									
Occupied housing units	100.0	100.0	100.0	100.0	100.0	100.0	100.0	100.0	100.0
White	85.8	75.1	93.0	85.9	79.3	91.4	82.4	72.7	89.8
Not of Hispanic origin	82.9	70.9	91.0	83.1	75.5	89.4	79.8	69.0	88.1

Table 5. Occupied Housing Units by Race and Hispanic Origin of Householder: 1990—Con.

[For definitions of terms and meanings of symbols, see text]

United States Population Size Class of Metropolitan Area	Less than 1,000,000—Con.								
	250,000 to 499,999			100,000 to 249,999			Less than 100,000		
	Total	In central city	Not in central city	Total	In central city	Not in central city	Total	In central city	Not in central city
RACE OF HOUSEHOLDER									
Occupied housing units	7 944 081	3 352 818	4 591 263	7 224 474	3 498 653	3 725 821	793 342	505 911	287 431
White	6 910 423	2 689 303	4 221 120	6 413 108	2 958 245	3 454 863	725 923	449 637	276 286
Black	704 863	468 127	236 736	588 034	400 177	187 857	45 646	38 498	7 148
American Indian, Eskimo, or Aleut	37 521	18 844	18 677	44 976	21 739	23 237	6 225	4 674	1 551
American Indian	36 940	18 508	18 432	42 144	19 145	22 999	6 166	4 633	1 533
Eskimo	313	174	139	1 792	1 688	104	37	29	8
Aleut	268	162	106	1 040	906	134	22	12	10
Asian or Pacific Islander	91 094	57 307	33 787	63 758	42 912	20 846	5 538	4 578	960
Asian	86 728	54 819	31 909	60 971	41 398	19 573	5 348	4 437	911
Chinese	15 823	10 150	5 673	12 654	9 411	3 243	1 555	1 386	169
Filipino	17 692	10 521	7 171	7 364	4 121	3 243	500	345	155
Japanese	11 079	6 635	4 444	7 197	4 256	2 941	640	509	131
Asian Indian	11 762	6 224	5 538	10 013	6 465	3 548	845	640	205
Korean	7 483	4 123	3 360	6 964	5 119	1 845	575	469	106
Vietnamese	9 141	6 657	2 484	5 969	4 261	1 708	315	267	48
Cambodian	2 953	2 612	341	905	639	266	18	16	2
Hmong	1 838	1 597	241	2 579	1 812	767	320	315	5
Laotian	3 592	2 867	725	2 639	1 981	658	85	79	6
Thai	1 268	763	505	1 032	680	352	123	105	18
Other Asian	4 097	2 670	1 427	3 655	2 653	1 002	372	306	66
Bangladeshi	118	75	43	124	96	28	16	14	2
Burmese	60	28	32	46	24	22	7	6	1
Indonesian	477	327	150	393	298	95	46	42	4
Malayan	303	258	45	561	486	75	54	53	1
Okinawan	23	12	11	31	17	14	1	1	—
Pakistani	1 014	657	357	684	464	220	65	41	24
Sri Lankan	136	79	57	189	140	49	28	22	6
All other Asian	1 966	1 234	732	1 627	1 128	499	155	127	28
Pacific Islander	4 366	2 488	1 878	2 787	1 514	1 273	190	141	49
Hawaiian	1 931	1 074	857	1 346	765	581	99	66	33
Samoan	524	285	239	373	222	151	14	11	3
Guamanian	1 191	583	608	798	358	440	42	34	8
Other Pacific Islander	720	546	174	270	169	101	35	30	5
Tongan	180	142	38	49	41	8	5	5	—
Tahitian	14	7	7	9	5	4	—	—	—
Northern Mariana Islander	8	4	4	20	14	6	—	—	—
Palauan	29	17	12	11	6	5	1	1	—
Fijian	212	184	28	14	7	7	—	—	—
All other Pacific Islander	277	192	85	167	96	71	29	24	5
Other race	200 180	119 237	80 943	114 598	75 580	39 018	10 010	8 524	1 486
HISPANIC ORIGIN OF HOUSEHOLDER									
Occupied housing units	7 944 081	3 352 818	4 591 263	7 224 474	3 498 653	3 725 821	793 342	505 911	287 431
Hispanic origin (of any race)	506 839	293 970	212 869	281 793	179 215	102 578	23 620	19 713	3 907
Mexican	375 002	214 588	160 414	199 237	128 060	71 177	18 969	16 042	2 927
Puerto Rican	38 747	22 376	16 371	19 822	13 869	5 953	726	548	178
Cuban	6 549	3 329	3 220	5 010	2 409	2 601	211	145	66
Other Hispanic	86 541	53 677	32 864	57 724	34 877	22 847	3 714	2 978	736
Not of Hispanic origin	7 437 242	3 058 848	4 378 394	6 942 681	3 319 438	3 623 243	769 722	486 198	283 524
RACE AND HISPANIC ORIGIN OF HOUSEHOLDER									
Occupied housing units	7 944 081	3 352 818	4 591 263	7 224 474	3 498 653	3 725 821	793 342	505 911	287 431
White	6 910 423	2 689 303	4 221 120	6 413 108	2 958 245	3 454 863	725 923	449 637	276 286
Hispanic origin	294 700	166 775	127 925	162 234	100 846	61 388	12 991	10 672	2 319
Not of Hispanic origin	6 615 723	2 522 528	4 093 195	6 250 874	2 857 399	3 393 475	712 932	438 965	273 967
Black	704 863	468 127	236 736	588 034	400 177	187 857	45 646	38 498	7 148
Hispanic origin	7 667	5 248	2 419	5 120	3 544	1 576	361	303	58
Not of Hispanic origin	697 196	462 879	234 317	582 914	396 633	186 281	45 285	38 195	7 090
American Indian, Eskimo, or Aleut	37 521	18 844	18 677	44 976	21 739	23 237	6 225	4 674	1 551
Hispanic origin	3 343	2 051	1 292	2 253	1 340	913	288	233	55
Not of Hispanic origin	34 178	16 793	17 385	42 723	20 399	22 324	5 937	4 441	1 496
Asian or Pacific Islander	91 094	57 307	33 787	63 758	42 912	20 846	5 538	4 578	960
Hispanic origin	4 385	2 815	1 570	2 326	1 370	956	185	151	34
Not of Hispanic origin	86 709	54 492	32 217	61 432	41 542	19 890	5 353	4 427	926
Other race	200 180	119 237	80 943	114 598	75 580	39 018	10 010	8 524	1 486
Hispanic origin	196 744	117 081	79 663	109 860	72 115	37 745	9 795	8 354	1 441
Not of Hispanic origin	3 436	2 156	1 280	4 738	3 465	1 273	215	170	45
PERCENT DISTRIBUTION BY RACE OF HOUSEHOLDER									
Occupied housing units	100.0	100.0	100.0	100.0	100.0	100.0	100.0	100.0	100.0
White	87.0	80.2	91.9	88.8	84.6	92.7	91.5	88.9	96.1
Black	8.9	14.0	5.2	8.1	11.4	5.0	5.8	7.6	2.5
American Indian, Eskimo, or Aleut	.5	.6	.4	.6	.6	.6	.8	.9	.5
American Indian	.5	.6	.4	.6	.5	.6	.8	.9	.5
Asian or Pacific Islander	1.1	1.7	.7	.9	1.2	.6	.7	.9	.3
Asian	1.1	1.6	.7	.8	1.2	.5	.7	.9	.3
Pacific Islander	.1	.1		—	—		—	—	—
Other race	2.5	3.6	1.8	1.6	2.2	1.0	1.3	1.7	.5
PERCENT DISTRIBUTION BY HISPANIC ORIGIN OF HOUSEHOLDER									
Occupied housing units	100.0	100.0	100.0	100.0	100.0	100.0	100.0	100.0	100.0
Hispanic origin (of any race)	6.4	8.8	4.6	3.9	5.1	2.8	3.0	3.9	1.4
Mexican	4.7	6.4	3.5	2.8	3.7	1.9	2.4	3.2	1.0
Puerto Rican	.5	.7	.4	.3	.4	.2	.1	.1	.1
Cuban	.1	.1	.1	.1	.1	.1	—	—	—
Other Hispanic	1.1	1.6	.7	.8	1.0	.6	.5	.6	.3
Not of Hispanic origin	93.6	91.2	95.4	96.1	94.9	97.2	97.0	96.1	98.6
PERCENT OF HOUSEHOLDERS WHITE, NOT OF HISPANIC ORIGIN									
Occupied housing units	100.0	100.0	100.0	100.0	100.0	100.0	100.0	100.0	100.0
White	87.0	80.2	91.9	88.8	84.6	92.7	91.5	88.9	96.1
Not of Hispanic origin	83.3	75.2	89.2	86.5	81.7	91.1	89.9	86.8	95.3

Table 6. Summary of General Housing Characteristics of Housing Units With a White Householder: 1990

[For definitions of terms and meanings of symbols, see text]

United States Urban and Rural and Size of Place Population Size Class of Urbanized Area Inside and Outside Metropolitan Area Population Size Class of Metropolitan Area	All persons: Total	All persons: White: Total	All persons: White: Percent of all persons	Housing units with a White householder: Total	Median persons in unit	Median rooms	Percent: Owner	Percent: With 1.01 or more persons per room	Percent: With householder 65 years and over	Percent: 1-person households	Percent: 1 unit, detached or attached	Percent: In buildings with 10 or more units	Specified owner, median value (dollars)	Specified renter: Median contract rent (dollars)	Specified renter: Percent with meals included in rent
United States	**248 709 873**	**199 686 070**	**80.3**	**76 880 105**	**2.24**	**5.4**	**68.2**	**2.8**	**23.2**	**25.1**	**68.3**	**10.9**	**80 200**	**382**	**1.0**
URBAN AND RURAL AND SIZE OF PLACE															
Urban	187 053 487	143 807 279	76.9	56 613 098	2.17	5.3	63.5	2.9	23.4	27.4	65.1	14.5	86 700	401	1.0
Inside urbanized area	158 258 878	119 359 248	75.4	47 112 854	2.18	5.3	63.2	3.0	22.6	27.3	64.0	16.1	94 900	424	1.1
Central place	78 847 406	52 192 735	66.2	21 600 072	2.03	5.0	54.4	3.8	23.7	32.4	55.8	20.8	76 500	392	1.1
Urban fringe	79 411 472	67 166 513	84.6	25 512 782	2.29	5.7	70.7	2.4	21.6	23.0	70.8	12.1	110 100	474	1.2
Outside urbanized area	28 794 609	24 448 031	84.9	9 500 244	2.16	5.3	64.7	2.4	27.6	27.6	70.5	6.5	57 000	276	.6
Place of 10,000 or more	13 825 022	11 562 503	83.6	4 486 590	2.15	5.2	61.6	2.4	26.2	28.2	68.8	8.3	58 500	291	.7
Place of 2,500 to 9,999	14 969 587	12 885 528	86.1	5 013 654	2.18	5.3	67.6	2.4	28.8	27.1	72.1	5.0	55 500	262	.6
Rural	61 656 386	55 878 791	90.6	20 267 007	2.40	5.6	81.5	2.5	22.6	18.8	77.2	1.0	65 000	254	.6
Place of 1,000 to 2,499	7 050 858	6 299 526	89.3	2 452 238	2.20	5.4	72.9	2.3	29.7	26.2	75.2	2.9	50 600	234	.4
Place of less than 1,000	3 801 051	3 402 922	89.5	1 346 368	2.18	5.4	76.8	2.2	32.0	27.0	79.0	1.4	36 100	194	.3
Other rural	50 804 477	46 176 343	90.9	16 468 401	2.45	5.7	83.1	2.6	20.8	17.1	77.4	.7	71 500	268	.7
POPULATION SIZE CLASS OF URBANIZED AREA															
1,000,000 or more	94 016 294	67 356 421	71.6	26 635 557	2.18	5.3	62.6	3.6	22.3	27.7	61.9	19.4	122 200	486	1.1
Central place	41 010 559	23 700 299	57.8	10 039 879	1.97	4.7	50.2	5.2	24.0	34.9	47.8	28.3	96 400	449	1.0
Urban fringe	53 005 735	43 656 122	82.4	16 595 678	2.30	5.7	70.2	2.6	21.2	23.4	70.3	14.0	130 500	519	1.2
5,000,000 or more	34 239 045	22 461 002	65.6	8 715 609	2.19	5.1	58.7	5.2	23.8	28.2	53.1	24.4	189 900	550	.8
Central place	16 304 119	8 468 435	51.9	3 560 593	1.95	4.2	41.6	7.6	25.6	36.2	30.3	40.2	198 600	507	.7
Urban fringe	17 934 926	13 992 567	78.0	5 155 016	2.35	5.7	70.5	3.6	22.6	22.7	68.9	13.5	187 800	610	.9
2,500,000 to 4,999,999	23 787 767	16 834 101	70.8	6 686 811	2.18	5.6	64.1	2.5	20.2	27.8	66.1	17.0	123 500	507	1.3
Central place	9 541 204	4 983 496	52.2	2 181 437	1.90	4.9	51.6	3.6	22.0	37.2	53.3	24.6	82 900	449	1.1
Urban fringe	14 246 563	11 850 605	83.2	4 505 374	2.31	5.8	70.1	2.0	19.4	23.3	72.3	13.3	136 800	548	1.4
1,000,000 to 2,499,999	35 989 482	28 061 318	78.0	11 233 137	2.16	5.4	64.8	3.0	22.3	27.3	66.1	17.0	89 100	428	1.3
Central place	15 165 236	10 248 368	67.6	4 297 849	2.02	5.0	56.5	4.0	23.8	32.6	59.6	20.4	81 800	398	1.3
Urban fringe	20 824 246	17 812 950	85.5	6 935 288	2.25	5.6	70.0	2.4	21.5	23.9	70.1	14.8	92 200	456	1.3
Less than 1,000,000	64 242 584	52 002 827	80.9	20 477 297	2.18	5.4	63.9	2.2	22.9	26.8	66.7	11.8	75 800	363	1.1
Central place	37 836 847	28 492 436	75.3	11 560 193	2.08	5.2	58.0	2.5	23.4	30.2	62.8	14.2	68 400	348	1.1
Urban fringe	26 405 737	23 510 391	89.0	8 917 104	2.29	5.6	71.6	1.9	22.2	22.4	71.7	8.6	84 500	397	1.1
500,000 to 999,999	17 955 916	14 060 661	78.3	5 599 143	2.17	5.4	63.5	2.1	22.1	27.4	64.7	13.8	80 300	380	1.1
Central place	9 403 669	6 435 430	68.4	2 683 850	2.03	5.1	55.7	2.6	22.5	32.2	58.7	17.0	68 100	354	1.0
Urban fringe	8 552 247	7 625 231	89.2	2 915 293	2.28	5.6	70.7	1.8	21.8	23.0	70.2	10.9	90 100	422	1.3
250,000 to 499,999	15 470 005	12 264 139	79.3	4 836 001	2.18	5.5	65.6	2.2	23.1	26.7	68.8	11.6	77 500	367	1.2
Central place	8 327 127	5 969 730	71.7	2 445 935	2.07	5.3	59.2	2.6	23.9	30.9	64.9	14.5	69 700	353	1.4
Urban fringe	7 142 878	6 294 409	88.1	2 390 066	2.30	5.7	72.2	1.8	22.3	22.4	72.7	8.7	85 100	392	.9
100,000 to 249,999	18 879 599	15 534 992	82.3	6 064 730	2.18	5.3	63.1	2.4	22.4	26.6	66.4	11.3	76 100	364	1.1
Central place	11 928 889	9 346 512	78.4	3 744 783	2.11	5.2	58.0	2.6	23.0	29.4	62.7	13.7	70 500	354	1.1
Urban fringe	6 950 710	6 188 480	89.0	2 319 947	2.31	5.5	71.3	2.0	21.3	22.0	72.3	7.4	84 000	393	1.0
Less than 100,000	11 937 064	10 143 035	85.0	3 977 423	2.17	5.3	63.7	2.2	24.3	26.7	67.4	9.8	66 600	328	1.1
Central place	8 177 162	6 740 764	82.4	2 685 625	2.11	5.2	59.2	2.3	24.4	28.9	65.0	11.9	64 600	325	1.2
Urban fringe	3 759 902	3 402 271	90.5	1 291 798	2.28	5.4	73.1	2.0	24.3	22.1	72.4	6.1	70 200	338	1.0
INSIDE AND OUTSIDE METROPOLITAN AREA															
Inside metropolitan area	192 725 741	150 863 170	78.3	58 333 897	2.23	5.4	66.3	2.9	22.1	25.6	66.5	13.4	91 700	414	1.1
In central city	77 843 533	51 452 071	66.1	21 323 382	2.03	5.0	54.3	3.7	23.7	32.5	55.8	20.9	75 800	390	1.1
Not in central city	114 882 208	99 411 099	86.5	37 010 515	2.34	5.7	73.3	2.4	21.2	21.6	72.7	9.2	99 400	443	1.1
Urban	88 439 928	74 886 399	84.7	28 390 886	2.29	5.6	70.3	2.5	21.8	23.1	70.8	11.6	105 700	460	1.1
Inside urbanized area	79 755 134	67 365 275	84.5	25 573 614	2.30	5.7	70.6	2.4	21.5	23.0	70.8	12.2	110 600	475	1.2
Outside urbanized area	8 684 794	7 521 124	86.6	2 817 272	2.28	5.4	67.3	2.9	24.8	23.9	70.8	6.4	74 100	335	.7
Rural	26 442 280	24 524 700	92.7	8 619 629	2.50	5.8	83.2	2.4	19.0	16.5	78.9	1.1	84 000	310	.8
Outside metropolitan area	55 984 132	48 822 900	87.2	18 546 208	2.26	5.4	74.0	2.4	26.5	23.7	73.8	3.0	51 400	246	.6
Urban	20 851 951	17 538 683	84.1	6 923 987	2.12	5.2	63.8	2.2	28.6	29.0	70.1	6.7	52 000	263	.7
Inside urbanized area	1 520 259	1 267 155	83.4	495 534	2.15	5.2	63.6	2.1	25.1	26.0	65.1	8.8	76 800	349	1.1
Outside urbanized area	19 331 692	16 271 528	84.2	6 428 453	2.11	5.2	63.8	2.2	28.9	29.2	70.4	6.5	50 700	258	.6
Place of 10,000 or more	9 873 345	8 245 260	83.5	3 234 124	2.11	5.2	61.0	2.2	26.9	29.3	68.3	8.2	53 200	274	.7
Place of 2,500 to 9,999	9 458 347	8 026 268	84.9	3 194 329	2.11	5.3	66.7	2.2	30.9	29.1	72.6	4.7	48 200	236	.5
Rural	35 132 181	31 284 217	89.0	11 622 221	2.34	5.5	80.1	2.6	25.3	20.6	76.0	.9	51 000	218	.5
POPULATION SIZE CLASS OF METROPOLITAN AREA															
1,000,000 or more	124 775 608	94 402 349	75.7	36 587 278	2.22	5.4	65.2	3.2	21.8	26.1	64.8	16.1	115 500	466	1.1
In central city	48 263 927	29 171 220	60.4	12 266 573	1.99	4.8	51.2	4.7	23.8	34.1	49.6	25.8	93 200	436	1.1
Not in central city	76 511 681	65 231 129	85.3	24 320 705	2.34	5.7	72.2	2.5	20.8	22.0	72.4	11.2	122 000	494	1.1
5,000,000 or more	52 837 069	36 734 791	69.5	14 132 945	2.22	5.3	62.7	4.4	23.1	26.8	60.2	19.3	178 800	554	1.0
In central city	22 256 704	12 050 920	54.1	5 024 912	1.98	4.5	46.7	6.5	25.3	34.9	39.3	33.2	178 400	514	.9
Not in central city	30 580 365	24 683 871	80.7	9 108 033	2.34	5.8	71.5	3.2	21.9	22.3	71.8	11.6	178 900	594	1.1
2,500,000 to 4,999,999	31 701 991	24 218 918	76.4	9 420 776	2.24	5.5	66.1	3.0	19.7	25.8	66.1	16.8	101 100	454	1.0
In central city	10 347 206	6 113 253	59.1	2 639 642	1.93	4.8	51.0	4.6	22.6	35.9	51.9	26.4	84 200	409	1.1
Not in central city	21 354 785	18 105 665	84.8	6 781 134	2.35	5.8	72.0	2.4	18.7	21.9	71.6	13.0	106 300	483	1.0
1,000,000 to 2,499,999	40 236 548	33 448 640	83.1	13 033 557	2.22	5.5	67.2	2.2	21.9	25.5	68.7	12.2	83 900	394	1.2
In central city	15 660 017	11 007 047	70.3	4 602 019	2.03	5.1	56.3	2.7	22.9	32.2	59.7	17.4	75 000	379	1.2
Not in central city	24 576 531	22 441 593	91.3	8 431 538	2.32	5.7	73.1	1.9	21.4	21.9	73.6	9.3	87 600	408	1.2
Less than 1,000,000	67 950 133	56 460 821	83.1	21 746 619	2.24	5.4	68.3	2.4	22.6	24.7	69.5	8.9	69 800	338	1.0
In central city	29 579 606	22 280 851	75.3	9 056 809	2.08	5.2	58.4	2.5	23.6	30.4	64.1	14.1	64 700	335	1.1
Not in central city	38 370 527	34 179 970	89.1	12 689 810	2.35	5.6	75.4	2.3	21.9	20.7	73.3	5.2	73 200	344	.9
500,000 to 999,999	24 905 921	19 725 324	79.2	7 697 165	2.22	5.4	67.8	2.2	21.9	25.3	68.6	10.6	76 400	360	1.1
In central city	10 438 257	7 114 029	68.2	2 959 624	2.03	5.2	57.5	2.5	23.3	31.9	62.2	16.6	69 800	351	1.1
Not in central city	14 467 664	12 611 295	87.2	4 737 541	2.34	5.6	74.2	2.0	21.0	21.2	72.6	6.9	80 200	370	1.0
250,000 to 499,999	21 528 297	18 093 596	84.0	6 910 423	2.25	5.4	69.1	2.7	23.6	24.1	70.5	8.1	69 700	343	1.1
In central city	8 783 875	6 679 010	76.0	2 689 303	2.10	5.2	59.1	3.0	24.5	29.7	65.3	13.2	64 700	341	1.2
Not in central city	12 744 422	11 414 586	89.6	4 221 120	2.34	5.6	75.5	2.6	23.1	20.5	73.9	4.9	72 600	346	1.0
100,000 to 249,999	19 403 087	16 745 333	86.3	6 413 108	2.24	5.3	68.3	2.3	22.5	24.6	69.5	7.8	63 300	314	1.0
In central city	9 054 420	7 361 451	81.3	2 958 245	2.10	5.2	58.4	2.2	23.2	29.7	64.7	12.9	61 100	320	1.1
Not in central city	10 348 667	9 383 882	90.7	3 454 863	2.36	5.5	76.9	2.4	22.0	20.3	73.6	3.4	65 100	303	.7
Less than 100,000	2 112 828	1 896 568	89.8	725 923	2.23	5.3	66.7	1.8	22.5	25.5	68.6	7.8	59 000	297	.8
In central city	1 303 054	1 126 361	86.4	449 637	2.11	5.2	59.9	1.8	24.0	29.4	65.1	11.1	56 900	299	1.0
Not in central city	809 774	770 207	95.1	276 286	2.43	5.6	77.7	1.9	20.0	19.1	74.4	2.3	62 300	291	.4

Table 7. **Summary of General Housing Characteristics of Housing Units With a Black Householder: 1990**

[For definitions of terms and meanings of symbols, see text]

United States Urban and Rural and Size of Place Population Size Class of Urbanized Area Inside and Outside Metropolitan Area Population Size Class of Metropolitan Area	All persons	All persons: Black		Housing units with a Black householder			Percent							Specified renter	
	Total	Total	Percent of all persons	Total	Median persons in unit	Median rooms	Owner	With 1.01 or more persons per room	With householder 65 years and over	1-person households	1 unit, detached or attached	In buildings with 10 or more units	Specified owner, median value (dollars)	Median contract rent (dollars)	Percent with meals included in rent
United States	**248 709 873**	**29 986 060**	**12.1**	**9 976 161**	**2.52**	**4.8**	**43.4**	**9.8**	**17.0**	**25.4**	**52.6**	**19.3**	**50 700**	**312**	**.4**
URBAN AND RURAL AND SIZE OF PLACE															
Urban	187 053 487	26 153 444	14.0	8 836 740	2.49	4.7	39.7	9.7	16.0	25.9	50.6	21.6	53 100	319	.4
Inside urbanized area	158 258 878	23 533 536	14.9	7 996 181	2.48	4.7	39.1	9.7	15.4	26.0	49.2	23.3	56 300	332	.4
Central place	78 847 406	17 308 291	22.0	5 970 947	2.42	4.6	36.6	10.0	17.2	27.6	47.0	23.9	47 900	307	.4
Urban fringe	79 411 472	6 225 245	7.8	2 025 234	2.69	5.0	46.4	8.7	10.1	21.3	55.7	21.3	79 300	445	.3
Outside urbanized area	28 794 609	2 619 908	9.1	840 559	2.57	4.8	45.7	9.8	21.7	25.1	63.9	6.3	35 600	182	.4
Place of 10,000 or more	13 825 022	1 366 724	9.9	441 625	2.52	4.8	41.6	9.3	20.4	25.6	62.8	7.6	36 500	203	.4
Place of 2,500 to 9,999	14 969 587	1 253 184	8.4	398 934	2.62	4.8	50.3	10.4	23.1	24.6	65.2	4.8	34 800	159	.4
Rural	61 656 386	3 832 616	6.2	1 139 421	2.79	5.1	71.9	10.6	24.5	21.7	68.2	1.3	38 900	153	.6
Place of 1,000 to 2,499	7 050 858	447 585	6.3	143 168	2.62	4.9	58.0	11.0	25.5	24.9	66.7	3.2	32 100	137	.4
Place of less than 1,000	3 801 051	205 368	5.4	67 033	2.59	4.9	66.2	11.3	28.5	25.6	68.1	1.5	27 700	113	.4
Other rural	50 804 477	3 179 663	6.3	929 220	2.82	5.2	74.4	10.5	24.0	20.9	68.4	1.0	40 800	162	.6
POPULATION SIZE CLASS OF URBANIZED AREA															
1,000,000 or more	94 016 294	15 387 703	16.4	5 252 282	2.47	4.6	37.7	10.6	15.3	26.5	45.1	27.9	66 500	368	.4
Central place	41 010 559	10 879 622	26.5	3 768 376	2.40	4.5	34.7	11.2	17.5	28.4	41.8	29.3	52 700	335	.5
Urban fringe	53 005 735	4 508 081	8.5	1 483 906	2.66	4.9	45.5	9.0	9.7	21.7	53.7	24.5	90 100	484	.3
5,000,000 or more	34 239 045	5 705 341	16.7	1 912 046	2.49	4.3	30.8	13.3	15.9	26.8	29.7	38.7	114 900	415	.4
Central place	16 304 119	4 293 698	26.3	1 463 187	2.43	4.1	26.4	14.2	17.0	28.4	23.7	43.0	94 200	391	.4
Urban fringe	17 934 926	1 411 643	7.9	448 859	2.71	4.8	45.0	10.3	12.0	21.5	49.1	24.9	140 100	547	.3
2,500,000 to 4,999,999	23 787 767	4 536 123	19.1	1 588 712	2.41	5.0	43.7	8.4	15.6	27.4	55.2	23.8	52 400	359	.4
Central place	9 541 204	3 267 559	34.2	1 158 641	2.35	4.9	43.0	9.0	18.1	29.2	55.1	22.3	39 000	316	.5
Urban fringe	14 246 563	1 268 564	8.9	430 071	2.58	5.1	45.7	7.0	8.7	22.5	55.3	27.9	99 400	548	.3
1,000,000 to 2,499,999	35 989 482	5 146 239	14.3	1 751 524	2.50	4.8	39.9	9.5	14.4	25.4	52.9	19.8	59 100	323	.4
Central place	15 165 236	3 318 365	21.9	1 146 548	2.42	4.7	36.8	9.6	17.4	27.5	51.2	18.8	50 900	286	.5
Urban fringe	20 824 246	1 827 874	8.8	604 976	2.69	4.9	45.8	9.5	8.7	21.3	56.0	21.7	70 000	412	.3
Less than 1,000,000	64 242 584	8 145 833	12.7	2 743 899	2.52	4.8	41.6	8.0	15.6	25.0	56.9	14.4	46 700	273	.4
Central place	37 836 847	6 428 669	17.0	2 202 571	2.47	4.8	39.9	8.1	16.7	26.2	55.9	14.8	43 700	262	.4
Urban fringe	26 405 737	1 717 164	6.5	541 328	2.75	5.0	48.8	7.9	11.3	20.2	61.3	12.5	59 600	339	.3
500,000 to 999,999	17 955 916	2 594 678	14.5	903 037	2.46	4.9	42.0	7.5	15.7	26.2	54.4	17.1	48 200	284	.4
Central place	9 403 669	2 108 473	22.4	743 180	2.41	4.8	40.7	7.5	16.9	27.4	53.3	17.4	44 500	269	.4
Urban fringe	8 552 247	486 205	5.7	159 857	2.71	5.0	47.9	7.9	9.9	20.4	59.6	16.0	68 200	382	.3
250,000 to 499,999	15 470 005	2 166 471	14.0	722 006	2.57	4.9	42.7	8.4	15.1	24.4	58.4	14.4	48 000	282	.4
Central place	8 327 127	1 614 142	19.4	546 266	2.51	4.8	40.5	8.6	16.2	25.7	57.4	14.8	44 400	269	.4
Urban fringe	7 142 878	552 329	7.7	175 740	2.76	5.1	49.4	7.8	11.5	20.4	61.3	13.1	59 300	335	.3
100,000 to 249,999	18 879 599	2 218 683	11.8	735 786	2.54	4.8	40.1	8.2	15.3	24.5	56.8	13.1	46 300	270	.3
Central place	11 928 889	1 762 876	14.8	596 970	2.49	4.7	38.6	8.2	16.3	25.5	55.8	13.6	44 400	262	.3
Urban fringe	6 950 710	455 807	6.6	138 816	2.77	5.0	46.5	8.0	11.4	20.2	60.9	10.9	54 000	315	.3
Less than 100,000	11 937 064	1 166 001	9.8	383 070	2.55	4.8	41.8	8.2	17.1	24.4	60.3	10.3	41 100	239	.3
Central place	8 177 162	943 178	11.5	316 155	2.50	4.8	39.2	8.2	17.7	25.5	59.2	11.1	39 100	232	.3
Urban fringe	3 759 902	222 823	5.9	66 915	2.82	5.1	53.7	8.1	14.3	19.5	65.6	6.2	49 000	284	.3
INSIDE AND OUTSIDE METROPOLITAN AREA															
Inside metropolitan area	192 725 741	25 122 054	13.0	8 455 952	2.50	4.7	40.6	9.7	15.7	25.7	50.3	22.2	55 500	329	.4
In central city	77 843 533	17 169 430	22.1	5 925 383	2.42	4.6	36.6	10.0	17.2	27.6	46.9	24.0	47 800	307	.4
Not in central city	114 882 208	7 952 624	6.9	2 530 569	2.71	5.0	50.0	8.9	12.3	21.2	58.3	17.9	72 900	420	.3
Urban	88 439 928	6 790 086	7.7	2 201 473	2.69	4.9	46.3	8.8	10.8	21.4	56.2	20.3	77 100	430	.3
Inside urbanized area	79 755 134	6 235 478	7.8	2 028 435	2.69	5.0	46.3	8.7	10.1	21.3	55.7	21.4	79 800	446	.3
Outside urbanized area	8 684 794	554 608	6.4	173 038	2.69	4.8	46.5	10.3	19.1	22.5	62.7	8.2	45 500	237	.3
Rural	26 442 280	1 162 538	4.4	329 096	2.84	5.3	74.5	9.1	22.4	19.9	72.3	1.9	50 800	212	.5
Outside metropolitan area	55 984 132	4 864 006	8.7	1 520 209	2.65	4.9	58.9	10.5	23.8	23.9	65.2	3.3	34 400	161	.4
Urban	20 851 951	2 203 157	10.6	712 516	2.53	4.8	45.3	9.6	22.0	25.6	63.7	5.9	34 400	173	.4
Inside urbanized area	1 520 259	201 221	13.2	65 249	2.56	4.8	41.3	8.6	17.9	23.7	58.1	7.6	45 500	218	.3
Outside urbanized area	19 331 692	2 001 936	10.4	647 267	2.53	4.8	45.7	9.7	22.5	25.8	64.3	5.7	33 500	169	.4
Place of 10,000 or more	9 873 345	1 052 836	10.7	341 554	2.50	4.8	41.5	9.1	21.0	26.2	63.1	7.0	34 600	190	.4
Place of 2,500 to 9,999	9 458 347	949 100	10.0	305 713	2.57	4.8	50.4	10.5	24.1	25.4	65.7	4.2	32 500	147	.4
Rural	35 132 181	2 660 849	7.6	807 693	2.76	5.0	70.8	11.2	25.3	22.4	66.5	1.1	34 500	134	.6
POPULATION SIZE CLASS OF METROPOLITAN AREA															
1,000,000 or more	124 775 608	17 638 128	14.1	5 981 262	2.48	4.7	38.4	10.2	15.2	26.2	46.3	26.3	65 500	363	.4
In central city	48 263 927	12 140 180	25.2	4 204 163	2.41	4.6	34.9	10.8	17.2	28.2	42.4	28.0	52 400	331	.5
Not in central city	76 511 681	5 497 948	7.2	1 777 099	2.68	5.0	46.9	8.9	10.7	21.5	55.6	22.4	87 400	469	.3
5,000,000 or more	52 837 069	7 705 099	14.6	2 580 861	2.48	4.4	35.0	12.0	16.2	26.5	37.3	33.2	94 400	416	.4
In central city	22 256 704	5 585 464	25.1	1 909 758	2.42	4.3	31.1	12.9	17.5	28.3	32.0	36.7	72 200	387	.5
Not in central city	30 580 365	2 119 635	6.9	671 103	2.68	4.9	45.9	9.4	12.3	21.5	52.6	23.3	129 400	534	.3
2,500,000 to 4,999,999	31 701 991	5 368 985	16.9	1 844 955	2.47	4.9	42.1	9.7	13.7	26.0	52.8	24.5	59 100	352	.4
In central city	10 347 206	3 202 461	31.0	1 129 432	2.36	4.8	39.2	9.9	17.1	28.9	51.0	24.3	42 800	304	.5
Not in central city	21 354 785	2 166 524	10.1	715 523	2.68	5.0	46.7	9.3	8.5	21.5	55.6	24.8	77 800	462	.3
1,000,000 to 2,499,999	40 236 548	4 564 044	11.3	1 555 446	2.48	4.8	39.8	7.9	15.5	25.9	53.7	17.0	53 800	302	.4
In central city	15 660 017	3 352 255	21.4	1 164 973	2.42	4.8	36.8	8.1	16.7	27.4	51.3	17.3	49 900	288	.4
Not in central city	24 576 531	1 211 789	4.9	390 473	2.67	5.0	48.9	7.2	11.9	21.3	60.9	16.3	66 600	368	.3
Less than 1,000,000	67 950 133	7 483 926	11.0	2 474 690	2.56	4.9	45.8	8.4	16.9	24.5	60.0	12.2	44 500	258	.4
In central city	29 579 606	5 029 250	17.0	1 721 220	2.47	4.8	40.8	8.2	17.2	26.2	57.9	14.3	42 200	252	.4
Not in central city	38 370 527	2 454 676	6.4	753 470	2.77	5.1	57.2	8.9	16.2	20.6	64.7	7.5	50 300	285	.3
500,000 to 999,999	24 905 921	3 351 612	13.5	1 136 147	2.50	4.8	44.8	8.0	16.7	25.3	57.4	15.0	48 300	271	.4
In central city	10 438 257	2 336 258	22.4	814 418	2.43	4.7	40.7	7.9	17.3	27.0	55.3	17.0	45 100	262	.4
Not in central city	14 467 664	1 015 354	7.0	321 729	2.73	5.0	55.2	8.3	15.2	20.9	62.8	10.0	56 200	310	.3
250,000 to 499,999	21 528 297	2 174 861	10.1	704 863	2.62	4.9	46.5	8.9	16.4	23.6	62.5	10.4	43 300	257	.4
In central city	8 783 875	1 387 488	15.8	468 127	2.52	4.8	41.4	8.7	16.8	25.4	60.5	12.4	40 300	250	.4
Not in central city	12 744 422	787 373	6.2	236 736	2.81	5.1	56.7	9.2	15.5	20.3	66.3	6.5	49 300	287	.3
100,000 to 249,999	19 403 087	1 819 417	9.4	588 034	2.59	4.9	46.8	8.9	17.7	24.0	61.5	9.3	40 400	236	.3
In central city	9 054 420	1 191 268	13.2	400 177	2.49	4.8	40.1	8.5	17.4	25.6	59.6	11.6	39 300	235	.3
Not in central city	10 348 667	628 149	6.1	187 857	2.80	5.0	61.1	9.7	18.4	20.5	65.5	4.5	42 400	237	.4
Less than 100,000	2 112 828	138 036	6.5	45 646	2.48	5.0	47.0	7.1	20.5	26.3	65.6	8.9	33 900	221	.4
In central city	1 303 054	114 236	8.8	38 498	2.47	4.9	44.1	7.1	19.3	26.7	64.1	10.1	33 500	222	.3
Not in central city	809 774	23 800	2.9	7 148	2.60	5.2	63.0	7.2	27.0	24.1	73.5	2.6	36 400	213	.5

Table 8. Summary of General Housing Characteristics of Housing Units With an American Indian, Eskimo, or Aleut Householder: 1990

[For definitions of terms and meanings of symbols, see text]

United States — Urban and Rural and Size of Place / Population Size Class of Urbanized Area / Inside and Outside Metropolitan Area / Population Size Class of Metropolitan Area	All persons Total	American Indian, Eskimo, or Aleut Total	Percent of all persons	Total	Median persons in unit	Median rooms	Owner	With 1.01 or more persons per room	With householder 65 years and over	1-person households	1 unit, detached or attached	In buildings with 10 or more units	Specified owner, median value (dollars)	Median contract rent (dollars)	Percent with meals included in rent
United States	248 709 873	1 959 234	.8	591 372	2.80	4.7	53.8	15.2	13.1	19.6	62.1	9.9	51 900	300	.5
URBAN AND RURAL AND SIZE OF PLACE															
Urban	187 053 487	1 100 534	.6	349 899	2.58	4.6	42.6	12.1	11.4	21.8	54.9	16.2	64 500	338	.5
Inside urbanized area	158 258 878	768 135	.5	252 845	2.50	4.6	40.7	10.9	10.4	22.5	52.2	19.8	74 200	371	.6
Central place	78 847 406	468 915	.6	155 508	2.43	4.4	34.0	12.2	10.8	24.9	46.3	23.1	64 200	345	.6
Urban fringe	79 411 472	299 220	.4	97 337	2.65	5.0	51.3	8.8	9.7	18.7	61.6	14.5	87 300	447	.5
Outside urbanized area	28 794 609	332 399	1.2	97 054	2.81	4.6	47.7	15.2	14.0	20.0	61.8	6.7	44 300	240	.4
Place of 10,000 or more	13 825 022	134 735	1.0	42 111	2.55	4.6	42.5	10.4	13.7	22.6	58.6	9.6	46 500	264	.4
Place of 2,500 to 9,999	14 969 587	197 664	1.3	54 943	3.02	4.6	51.6	18.8	14.2	17.9	64.3	4.5	42 800	215	.3
Rural	61 656 386	858 700	1.4	241 473	3.12	4.7	69.9	19.6	15.6	16.5	72.5	.9	39 300	165	.6
Place of 1,000 to 2,499	7 050 858	108 037	1.5	31 067	3.05	4.7	54.9	16.8	15.3	18.0	71.0	2.7	39 200	167	.5
Place of less than 1,000	3 801 051	140 600	3.7	37 317	3.38	4.5	64.7	26.6	16.1	16.8	82.4	1.0	33 800	125	.5
Other rural	50 804 477	610 063	1.2	173 089	3.08	4.8	73.8	18.6	15.5	16.1	70.7	.6	40 900	178	.6
POPULATION SIZE CLASS OF URBANIZED AREA															
1,000,000 or more	94 016 294	389 044	.4	128 575	2.51	4.5	39.3	12.9	10.0	22.7	49.5	24.8	97 700	429	.7
Central place	41 010 559	207 148	.5	68 687	2.43	4.2	30.4	15.7	10.7	25.8	40.0	30.8	79 000	386	.8
Urban fringe	53 005 735	181 896	.3	59 888	2.64	4.9	49.6	9.6	9.2	19.1	60.5	17.9	112 200	508	.5
5,000,000 or more	34 239 045	113 011	.3	36 625	2.60	4.1	35.0	18.3	11.8	22.8	40.3	32.1	177 300	513	1.0
Central place	16 304 119	62 270	.4	20 455	2.50	3.8	25.7	21.7	12.3	25.9	26.5	42.9	172 100	460	1.1
Urban fringe	17 934 926	50 741	.3	16 170	2.72	4.7	46.7	14.1	11.1	18.9	57.8	18.4	180 100	614	.8
2,500,000 to 4,999,999	23 787 767	79 264	.3	28 181	2.38	4.9	45.1	8.6	10.6	24.9	56.5	21.4	86 500	451	.6
Central place	9 541 204	34 199	.4	12 718	2.20	4.5	36.1	11.0	12.4	30.5	47.3	26.7	58 700	383	.8
Urban fringe	14 246 563	45 065	.3	15 463	2.53	5.2	52.4	6.7	9.0	20.3	64.1	17.1	104 400	539	.5
1,000,000 to 2,499,999	35 989 482	196 769	.5	63 769	2.55	4.6	39.3	11.6	8.8	21.7	51.7	22.1	81 600	387	.6
Central place	15 165 236	110 679	.7	35 514	2.48	4.3	31.1	13.8	9.2	24.1	45.0	25.2	70 400	358	.6
Urban fringe	20 824 246	86 090	.4	28 255	2.65	5.0	49.6	8.7	8.3	18.6	60.1	18.0	89 700	447	.4
Less than 1,000,000	64 242 584	379 091	.6	124 270	2.49	4.7	42.1	8.9	10.7	22.3	55.0	14.6	61 200	319	.4
Central place	37 836 847	261 767	.7	86 821	2.43	4.6	36.9	9.5	10.8	24.2	51.4	17.0	57 600	311	.5
Urban fringe	26 405 737	117 324	.4	37 449	2.68	5.0	54.0	7.5	10.4	18.0	63.4	9.1	66 000	354	.3
500,000 to 999,999	17 955 916	95 114	.5	31 920	2.44	4.8	43.5	9.0	11.2	23.6	55.5	15.9	57 900	308	.4
Central place	9 403 669	59 119	.6	20 534	2.34	4.6	37.9	9.4	11.6	26.3	51.0	18.2	52 500	291	.4
Urban fringe	8 552 247	35 995	.4	11 386	2.66	5.0	53.6	8.1	10.4	18.8	63.8	11.8	64 800	362	.3
250,000 to 499,999	15 470 005	105 896	.7	35 206	2.48	4.8	44.3	8.6	11.3	22.4	58.2	15.3	60 700	320	.5
Central place	8 327 127	71 368	.9	24 057	2.41	4.6	39.2	9.5	11.5	24.7	54.5	18.5	56 800	312	.5
Urban fringe	7 142 878	34 528	.5	11 149	2.69	5.1	55.3	6.8	10.8	17.6	66.1	8.5	65 900	354	.3
100,000 to 249,999	18 879 599	100 675	.5	32 531	2.50	4.6	40.5	8.8	9.5	21.9	51.9	14.3	68 000	351	.5
Central place	11 928 889	72 491	.6	23 458	2.46	4.5	35.4	9.5	9.4	23.3	48.1	16.6	66 500	346	.5
Urban fringe	6 950 710	28 184	.4	9 073	2.65	4.9	53.6	6.9	9.7	18.2	61.6	8.4	70 000	370	.3
Less than 100,000	11 937 064	77 406	.6	24 613	2.57	4.6	39.0	9.4	10.9	20.9	54.0	12.4	58 300	299	.4
Central place	8 177 162	58 789	.7	18 772	2.52	4.5	34.7	9.7	11.0	22.2	52.0	14.3	56 500	295	.4
Urban fringe	3 759 902	18 617	.5	5 841	2.74	4.9	53.0	8.5	10.6	16.9	60.3	6.4	62 600	312	.3
INSIDE AND OUTSIDE METROPOLITAN AREA															
Inside metropolitan area	192 725 741	1 002 984	.5	323 542	2.58	4.7	46.5	10.9	11.1	21.2	56.3	16.0	69 000	361	.6
In central city	77 843 533	465 364	.6	154 315	2.43	4.4	34.1	12.2	10.9	25.0	46.5	23.0	62 800	343	.6
Not in central city	114 882 208	537 620	.5	169 227	2.74	5.0	57.8	9.7	11.2	17.7	65.1	9.5	73 300	397	.5
Urban	88 439 928	366 132	.4	118 225	2.67	4.9	51.5	9.2	10.4	18.5	62.6	13.2	82 200	423	.4
Inside urbanized area	79 755 134	302 903	.4	98 568	2.65	5.0	51.3	8.9	9.7	18.6	61.7	14.5	88 600	450	.5
Outside urbanized area	8 684 794	63 229	.7	19 657	2.78	4.9	52.5	10.7	13.9	18.0	67.0	6.4	54 700	304	.4
Rural	26 442 280	171 488	.6	51 002	2.91	5.1	72.5	10.9	13.2	15.9	71.0	1.1	56 700	254	.6
Outside metropolitan area	55 984 132	956 250	1.7	267 830	3.07	4.6	62.5	20.3	15.5	17.7	69.1	2.7	36 800	187	.5
Urban	20 851 951	270 174	1.3	77 696	2.81	4.5	46.1	16.3	13.8	20.5	59.8	7.0	41 700	229	.3
Inside urbanized area	1 520 259	8 925	.6	2 815	2.54	4.5	38.5	9.5	10.3	21.2	51.3	11.1	64 800	284	.3
Outside urbanized area	19 331 692	261 249	1.4	74 881	2.82	4.5	46.4	16.5	13.9	20.4	60.2	6.8	41 100	226	.3
Place of 10,000 or more	9 873 345	106 069	1.1	32 868	2.51	4.6	41.1	10.7	13.7	23.4	56.3	9.9	43 100	255	.4
Place of 2,500 to 9,999	9 458 347	155 180	1.6	42 013	3.08	4.5	50.5	21.1	14.1	18.1	63.2	4.4	39 500	203	.3
Rural	35 132 181	686 076	2.0	190 134	3.18	4.6	69.2	22.0	16.3	16.6	73.0	.9	34 700	151	.6
POPULATION SIZE CLASS OF METROPOLITAN AREA															
1,000,000 or more	124 775 608	530 902	.4	173 535	2.57	4.6	42.8	12.1	10.2	21.7	52.3	20.8	92 900	416	.7
In central city	48 263 927	241 540	.5	80 394	2.43	4.2	30.7	14.7	10.6	25.6	40.8	28.8	77 100	380	.8
Not in central city	76 511 681	289 362	.4	93 141	2.70	5.0	53.3	9.9	9.8	18.3	62.3	13.9	100 300	473	.5
5,000,000 or more	52 837 069	201 590	.4	65 905	2.60	4.4	41.0	15.1	11.6	21.7	49.8	24.0	160 500	520	.8
In central city	22 256 704	91 201	.4	30 249	2.49	4.0	30.1	18.9	12.1	25.2	35.1	35.4	160 200	473	1.0
Not in central city	30 580 365	110 309	.4	35 656	2.70	4.8	50.2	12.0	11.1	18.8	62.3	14.3	160 600	583	.6
2,500,000 to 4,999,999	31 701 991	114 976	.4	39 230	2.47	4.9	46.9	8.4	9.4	22.5	56.4	19.7	77 300	396	.6
In central city	10 347 206	42 873	.4	15 312	2.23	4.4	33.4	10.5	11.2	29.4	46.1	27.6	61 200	355	.7
Not in central city	21 354 785	72 103	.3	23 918	2.66	5.2	55.6	7.1	8.2	18.0	62.9	14.7	83 900	440	.5
1,000,000 to 2,499,999	40 236 548	214 336	.5	68 400	2.61	4.7	42.2	11.4	9.4	21.1	52.5	18.3	71 900	358	.6
In central city	15 660 017	107 466	.7	34 833	2.48	4.4	30.1	12.9	9.1	24.2	43.4	23.7	63 600	342	.6
Not in central city	24 576 531	106 870	.4	33 567	2.74	5.0	54.8	9.8	9.7	17.9	61.9	12.8	77 900	393	.5
Less than 1,000,000	67 950 133	472 082	.7	150 007	2.60	4.8	50.8	9.5	12.1	20.6	60.8	10.4	53 800	300	.4
In central city	29 579 606	223 824	.8	73 921	2.42	4.7	37.8	9.5	11.2	24.3	52.8	16.7	54 000	304	.5
Not in central city	38 370 527	248 258	.6	76 086	2.79	5.0	63.4	9.4	12.9	17.1	68.6	4.2	53 600	290	.4
500,000 to 999,999	24 905 921	188 446	.8	61 285	2.51	4.9	54.0	8.9	13.2	21.6	64.6	10.7	52 300	298	.4
In central city	10 438 257	82 651	.8	28 664	2.34	4.7	42.3	8.5	12.7	25.7	57.0	17.3	52 000	296	.4
Not in central city	14 467 664	105 795	.7	32 621	2.73	5.0	64.3	9.2	13.7	17.9	71.2	4.8	52 600	302	.4
250,000 to 499,999	21 528 297	115 866	.5	37 521	2.62	4.8	48.8	10.0	11.4	20.1	59.4	11.3	60 700	320	.4
In central city	8 783 875	56 851	.6	18 844	2.47	4.5	36.2	11.0	10.5	23.4	51.9	17.8	61 700	322	.4
Not in central city	12 744 422	59 015	.5	18 677	2.78	5.0	61.5	8.9	12.3	16.9	67.1	4.8	60 000	317	.3
100,000 to 249,999	19 403 087	146 185	.8	44 976	2.67	4.8	50.2	9.8	11.2	19.9	58.2	9.0	52 400	291	.5
In central city	9 054 420	68 103	.8	21 739	2.45	4.5	35.4	9.3	9.8	23.8	49.2	15.2	54 300	308	.6
Not in central city	10 348 667	78 082	.8	23 237	2.89	5.0	64.1	10.1	12.5	16.2	66.6	3.2	51 300	258	.5
Less than 100,000	2 112 828	21 585	1.0	6 225	2.74	4.6	35.9	10.3	10.9	20.0	50.9	12.8	45 700	264	.3
In central city	1 303 054	16 219	1.2	4 674	2.71	4.4	28.5	10.9	10.9	21.2	47.4	16.4	43 700	265	.4
Not in central city	809 774	5 366	.7	1 551	2.85	5.1	58.2	8.4	11.0	16.2	61.4	2.0	50 500	255	—

Table 9. Summary of General Housing Characteristics of Housing Units With an Asian or Pacific Islander Householder: 1990

[For definitions of terms and meanings of symbols, see text]

United States Urban and Rural and Size of Place Population Size Class of Urbanized Area Inside and Outside Metropolitan Area Population Size Class of Metropolitan Area	All persons			Housing units with an Asian or Pacific Islander householder											
		Asian or Pacific Islander					Percent							Specified renter	
	Total	Total	Percent of all persons	Total	Median persons in unit	Median rooms	Owner	With 1.01 or more persons per room	With householder 65 years and over	1-person households	1 unit, detached or attached	In buildings with 10 or more units	Specified owner, median value (dollars)	Median contract rent (dollars)	Percent with meals included in rent
United States	**248 709 873**	**7 273 662**	**2.9**	**2 013 735**	**3.13**	**4.2**	**52.2**	**23.6**	**10.0**	**16.3**	**55.3**	**23.9**	**178 300**	**484**	**.6**
URBAN AND RURAL AND SIZE OF PLACE															
Urban	187 053 487	6 934 689	3.7	1 934 866	3.13	4.2	51.4	24.0	9.8	16.4	54.3	24.7	180 900	487	.6
Inside urbanized area	158 258 878	6 507 391	4.1	1 823 436	3.14	4.2	51.3	24.2	9.6	16.3	53.6	25.4	186 400	497	.6
Central place	78 847 406	3 421 439	4.3	995 571	2.89	3.7	40.7	27.6	11.8	20.0	41.3	32.9	170 100	448	.6
Urban fringe	79 411 472	3 085 952	3.9	827 865	3.41	4.8	63.9	20.1	6.8	11.9	68.3	16.5	196 000	590	.5
Outside urbanized area	28 794 609	427 298	1.5	111 430	2.98	4.5	53.3	20.0	13.4	17.6	66.1	12.6	113 600	339	.4
Place of 10,000 or more	13 825 022	227 888	1.6	62 955	2.76	4.3	48.2	18.0	12.5	19.8	59.4	16.6	103 100	324	.3
Place of 2,500 to 9,999	14 969 587	199 410	1.3	48 475	3.27	4.6	59.9	22.7	14.6	14.7	74.9	7.3	126 000	374	.6
Rural	61 656 386	338 973	.5	78 869	3.13	5.2	71.0	14.1	14.7	14.4	79.4	3.7	129 500	334	.5
Place of 1,000 to 2,499	7 050 858	65 784	.9	17 569	2.96	4.7	64.3	18.2	23.5	17.0	79.3	3.9	103 500	304	.4
Place of less than 1,000	3 801 051	17 286	.5	4 208	2.79	4.8	58.3	17.1	25.3	18.8	81.0	3.1	87 400	220	.1
Other rural	50 804 477	255 903	.5	57 092	3.21	5.5	74.0	12.7	11.2	13.2	79.3	3.7	144 700	366	.6
POPULATION SIZE CLASS OF URBANIZED AREA															
1,000,000 or more	94 016 294	4 815 262	5.1	1 355 163	3.21	4.1	51.6	25.4	8.9	15.8	53.3	26.1	196 500	535	.6
Central place	41 010 559	2 347 588	5.7	686 728	2.95	3.6	40.0	29.8	11.5	19.7	39.2	34.6	184 000	486	.7
Urban fringe	53 005 735	2 467 674	4.7	668 435	3.44	4.8	63.5	20.8	6.2	11.8	67.9	17.3	203 700	619	.5
5,000,000 or more	34 239 045	2 297 774	6.7	655 466	3.25	3.9	48.7	27.9	8.9	15.2	47.8	29.9	227 500	582	.7
Central place	16 304 119	1 143 533	7.0	344 618	2.95	3.3	35.0	32.5	11.3	19.5	29.0	42.4	211 400	524	.8
Urban fringe	17 934 926	1 154 241	6.4	310 848	3.55	4.7	63.8	22.8	6.4	10.5	68.6	16.0	235 000	675	.4
2,500,000 to 4,999,999	23 787 767	1 270 383	5.3	362 354	3.14	4.3	54.3	22.3	9.9	16.8	55.9	24.1	195 800	519	.6
Central place	9 541 204	548 749	5.8	166 311	2.73	3.6	39.7	26.4	14.3	22.9	39.7	32.1	179 200	436	.6
Urban fringe	14 246 563	721 634	5.1	196 043	3.43	5.0	66.7	18.9	6.1	11.6	69.5	17.3	200 400	630	.6
1,000,000 to 2,499,999	35 989 482	1 247 105	3.5	337 343	3.19	4.3	54.4	23.7	7.9	15.8	61.4	20.8	144 800	453	.6
Central place	15 165 236	655 306	4.3	175 799	3.16	4.1	50.0	27.7	9.5	17.3	58.5	21.8	154 100	411	.6
Urban fringe	20 824 246	591 799	2.8	161 544	3.21	4.7	59.2	19.4	6.1	14.2	64.4	19.7	138 300	494	.5
Less than 1,000,000	64 242 584	1 692 129	2.6	468 273	2.96	4.2	50.2	20.9	11.4	17.8	54.2	23.6	148 000	388	.5
Central place	37 836 847	1 073 851	2.8	308 843	2.76	3.9	42.4	22.7	12.5	20.5	46.1	29.0	135 000	372	.5
Urban fringe	26 405 737	618 278	2.3	159 430	3.30	5.0	65.5	17.3	9.2	12.5	70.0	13.1	161 200	442	.4
500,000 to 999,999	17 955 916	698 114	3.9	208 783	2.79	4.2	54.9	19.3	16.8	19.3	53.9	26.9	213 200	424	.3
Central place	9 403 669	410 967	4.4	132 387	2.46	3.7	46.7	20.0	20.0	23.7	44.0	35.3	248 800	411	.4
Urban fringe	8 552 247	287 147	3.4	76 396	3.34	4.9	69.0	18.2	11.3	11.7	71.0	12.4	190 700	469	.2
250,000 to 499,999	15 470 005	352 353	2.3	89 710	3.24	4.3	46.6	25.0	7.5	15.8	55.7	20.4	97 100	362	.6
Central place	8 327 127	232 973	2.8	59 159	3.26	4.0	38.0	30.6	8.2	16.5	48.6	23.5	88 500	348	.6
Urban fringe	7 142 878	119 380	1.7	30 551	3.21	5.2	63.2	14.1	6.0	14.5	69.4	14.5	113 300	416	.3
100,000 to 249,999	18 879 599	433 880	2.3	116 100	3.04	4.4	49.1	19.9	7.2	16.4	56.2	20.4	142 000	387	.6
Central place	11 928 889	274 240	2.3	75 703	2.91	4.1	41.3	21.4	6.4	18.6	48.6	24.0	125 000	369	.5
Urban fringe	6 950 710	159 640	2.3	40 397	3.28	5.0	63.6	17.2	8.7	12.3	70.4	13.5	165 100	459	.7
Less than 100,000	11 937 064	207 782	1.7	53 680	2.94	4.1	40.8	22.2	5.8	18.1	49.1	22.8	99 800	348	.5
Central place	8 177 162	155 671	1.9	41 594	2.83	4.0	36.7	22.8	5.8	19.6	44.9	25.9	97 600	341	.5
Urban fringe	3 759 902	52 111	1.4	12 086	3.29	4.7	54.9	20.0	5.9	13.3	63.4	12.3	106 700	376	.4
INSIDE AND OUTSIDE METROPOLITAN AREA															
Inside metropolitan area	192 725 741	6 823 859	3.5	1 896 281	3.15	4.2	52.0	24.0	9.6	16.1	54.6	24.6	184 000	495	.6
In central city	77 843 533	3 373 675	4.3	982 551	2.89	3.7	40.4	27.8	11.8	20.1	40.9	33.1	169 100	447	.6
Not in central city	114 882 208	3 450 184	3.0	913 730	3.41	4.9	64.5	19.9	7.3	11.9	69.2	15.5	191 700	579	.5
Urban	88 439 928	3 262 758	3.7	870 648	3.41	4.8	63.9	20.3	7.1	11.9	68.6	16.1	193 000	583	.5
Inside urbanized area	79 755 134	3 125 833	3.9	838 502	3.41	4.8	64.1	20.1	6.9	11.9	68.5	16.4	196 000	590	.5
Outside urbanized area	8 684 794	136 925	1.6	32 146	3.45	4.6	59.1	24.7	12.1	13.3	72.6	8.9	113 700	392	.4
Rural	26 442 280	187 426	.7	43 082	3.33	5.7	75.5	13.0	11.0	12.1	81.0	3.8	162 200	401	.5
Outside metropolitan area	55 984 132	449 803	.8	117 454	2.80	4.5	54.6	17.1	15.2	19.0	66.6	11.6	106 900	319	.4
Urban	20 851 951	298 962	1.4	81 811	2.76	4.3	49.8	17.7	13.5	19.8	61.8	15.0	112 200	325	.4
Inside urbanized area	1 520 259	23 044	1.5	6 234	2.50	3.9	35.0	15.0	4.8	23.7	41.0	26.7	87 000	375	.5
Outside urbanized area	19 331 692	275 918	1.4	75 577	2.78	4.4	51.0	18.0	14.2	19.5	63.5	14.1	113 700	321	.4
Place of 10,000 or more	9 873 345	165 504	1.7	47 167	2.62	4.2	46.0	17.0	13.3	21.1	57.5	18.1	104 200	314	.3
Place of 2,500 to 9,999	9 458 347	110 414	1.2	28 410	3.05	4.6	59.1	19.6	15.7	16.7	73.6	7.5	128 500	355	.7
Rural	35 132 181	150 841	.4	35 643	2.89	4.9	65.7	15.5	19.2	17.1	77.4	3.6	97 600	286	.5
POPULATION SIZE CLASS OF METROPOLITAN AREA															
1,000,000 or more	124 775 608	5 317 229	4.3	1 485 853	3.21	4.2	52.1	24.6	8.7	15.7	54.1	25.2	191 400	525	.6
In central city	48 263 927	2 524 580	5.2	735 860	2.96	3.6	39.9	29.3	11.1	19.6	39.5	33.9	179 100	480	.7
Not in central city	76 511 681	2 792 649	3.6	749 993	3.43	4.8	64.1	20.0	6.3	11.9	68.5	16.6	197 500	607	.5
5,000,000 or more	52 837 069	3 518 730	6.7	992 516	3.24	4.1	52.1	26.4	9.6	15.3	52.9	25.8	234 500	582	.7
In central city	22 256 704	1 724 860	7.7	507 210	3.00	3.5	39.8	31.2	12.4	19.2	36.7	35.6	224 200	522	.8
Not in central city	30 580 365	1 793 870	5.9	485 306	3.47	4.8	64.9	21.4	6.7	11.3	69.7	15.5	240 200	665	.5
2,500,000 to 4,999,999	31 701 991	910 401	2.9	258 229	3.13	4.4	52.4	20.2	6.2	16.5	54.7	27.2	124 300	457	.4
In central city	10 347 206	322 412	3.1	99 951	2.62	3.6	34.8	24.1	8.5	23.4	36.9	39.4	89 100	389	.5
Not in central city	21 354 785	587 989	2.8	158 278	3.41	5.0	63.6	17.7	4.7	12.2	65.9	19.4	136 300	527	.4
1,000,000 to 2,499,999	40 236 548	888 098	2.2	235 108	3.14	4.4	51.9	21.7	7.4	16.5	58.8	20.4	115 000	404	.5
In central city	15 660 017	477 308	3.0	128 699	3.05	4.1	44.3	25.6	8.2	18.5	52.4	23.2	113 900	381	.5
Not in central city	24 576 531	410 790	1.7	106 409	3.23	5.0	61.1	17.1	6.5	14.1	66.6	17.1	115 700	439	.4
Less than 1,000,000	67 950 133	1 506 630	2.2	410 428	2.96	4.2	51.6	21.9	13.1	17.7	56.1	22.7	147 000	373	.5
In central city	29 579 606	849 095	2.9	246 691	2.69	3.8	41.8	23.4	13.9	21.4	45.1	30.7	128 400	360	.5
Not in central city	38 370 527	657 535	1.7	163 737	3.34	4.9	66.3	19.6	11.9	12.3	72.7	10.5	160 000	416	.4
500,000 to 999,999	24 905 921	875 741	3.5	250 038	2.93	4.2	56.0	21.2	16.9	17.8	57.9	24.1	207 100	412	.4
In central city	10 438 257	454 580	4.4	141 894	2.53	3.7	45.5	21.9	19.2	22.8	44.3	34.8	233 200	396	.4
Not in central city	14 467 664	421 161	2.9	108 144	3.40	4.9	69.6	20.4	13.9	11.3	75.7	10.1	195 500	455	.3
250,000 to 499,999	21 528 297	358 684	1.7	91 094	3.16	4.4	48.8	23.6	8.8	16.4	58.4	18.1	98 500	367	.6
In central city	8 783 875	220 522	2.5	57 307	3.12	4.0	40.6	27.8	9.1	17.8	51.9	22.2	94 000	354	.6
Not in central city	12 744 422	138 162	1.1	33 787	3.22	5.0	62.6	16.6	8.5	14.0	69.5	11.2	106 000	408	.7
100,000 to 249,999	19 403 087	251 215	1.3	63 758	2.88	4.1	40.1	21.9	5.2	19.1	47.5	22.9	78 700	314	.5
In central city	9 054 420	157 629	1.7	42 912	2.73	3.8	32.5	22.6	4.2	21.2	39.9	28.4	73 600	309	.6
Not in central city	10 348 667	93 586	.9	20 846	3.19	4.7	55.6	20.5	7.1	14.7	63.1	11.5	84 800	333	.5
Less than 100,000	2 112 828	20 990	1.0	5 538	2.57	3.7	31.6	20.6	3.5	22.2	37.1	28.8	77 100	290	.4
In central city	1 303 054	16 364	1.3	4 578	2.49	3.5	27.6	22.5	3.7	23.5	33.2	32.6	73 300	284	.5
Not in central city	809 774	4 626	.6	960	2.95	5.0	50.4	11.7	2.8	15.6	55.9	10.8	89 400	338	–

Table 10. Summary of General Housing Characteristics of Housing Units With an Hispanic Origin Householder: 1990

[Householders of Hispanic origin may be of any race. For definitions of terms and meanings of symbols, see text]

United States Urban and Rural and Size of Place Population Size Class of Urbanized Area Inside and Outside Metropolitan Area Population Size Class of Metropolitan Area	All persons			Housing units with an Hispanic origin householder											
		Hispanic origin					Percent							Specified renter	
	Total	Total	Percent of all persons	Total	Median persons in unit	Median rooms	Owner	With 1.01 or more persons per room	With householder 65 years and over	1-person households	1 unit, detached or attached	In buildings with 10 or more units	Specified owner, median value (dollars)	Median contract rent (dollars)	Percent with meals included in rent
United States	**248 709 873**	**22 354 059**	**9.0**	**6 001 718**	**3.29**	**4.2**	**42.4**	**27.1**	**11.3**	**14.8**	**51.3**	**21.5**	**77 200**	**393**	**.7**
URBAN AND RURAL AND SIZE OF PLACE															
Urban	187 053 487	20 426 228	10.9	5 530 932	3.28	4.2	40.6	27.4	11.1	15.0	50.0	23.2	80 200	399	.7
Inside urbanized area	158 258 878	18 355 980	11.6	4 988 301	3.27	4.1	39.3	27.8	10.9	15.1	48.2	24.9	87 500	410	.7
Central place	78 847 406	11 671 728	14.8	3 235 169	3.20	4.0	33.6	28.6	11.5	16.7	41.9	29.1	67 200	374	.8
Urban fringe	79 411 472	6 684 252	8.4	1 753 132	3.39	4.4	49.9	26.3	9.7	12.3	59.9	17.2	121 400	510	.6
Outside urbanized area	28 794 609	2 070 248	7.2	542 631	3.37	4.5	52.7	24.1	13.7	13.9	67.0	6.8	47 500	267	.5
Place of 10,000 or more	13 825 022	1 102 447	8.0	291 255	3.34	4.5	49.2	23.6	13.2	14.1	65.6	8.4	50 000	278	.5
Place of 2,500 to 9,999	14 969 587	967 801	6.5	251 376	3.40	4.5	56.8	24.6	14.3	13.6	68.5	5.0	44 900	251	.5
Rural	61 656 386	1 927 831	3.1	470 786	3.43	4.7	63.5	23.2	12.5	12.5	66.7	1.4	50 600	238	.6
Place of 1,000 to 2,499	7 050 858	318 036	4.5	82 639	3.42	4.6	62.5	22.9	14.9	13.4	69.4	2.5	37 600	222	.5
Place of less than 1,000	3 801 051	89 028	2.3	23 929	3.13	4.8	65.7	17.2	17.6	16.6	70.4	1.4	29 300	186	.4
Other rural	50 804 477	1 520 767	3.0	364 218	3.46	4.7	63.6	23.6	11.6	12.1	65.9	1.2	58 900	252	.6
POPULATION SIZE CLASS OF URBANIZED AREA															
1,000,000 or more	94 016 294	13 600 190	14.5	3 683 627	3.29	4.0	36.8	30.2	10.7	15.1	44.7	28.7	111 000	434	.8
Central place	41 010 559	8 108 012	19.8	2 245 865	3.21	3.8	29.2	31.7	11.5	16.9	35.6	35.0	79 100	395	.8
Urban fringe	53 005 735	5 492 178	10.4	1 437 762	3.41	4.3	48.6	27.7	9.6	12.1	58.9	18.8	137 000	527	.7
5,000,000 or more	34 239 045	7 469 886	21.8	1 938 047	3.48	3.8	29.0	35.0	9.7	14.0	34.4	33.7	168 000	466	.8
Central place	16 304 119	4 558 322	28.0	1 224 019	3.36	3.6	20.4	35.7	9.9	15.8	21.5	43.6	157 600	423	.8
Urban fringe	17 934 926	2 911 564	16.2	714 028	3.67	4.1	43.9	33.8	9.3	10.8	56.4	16.8	173 100	562	.7
2,500,000 to 4,999,999	23 787 767	2 189 445	9.2	596 053	3.26	4.2	39.3	28.1	8.2	15.8	51.2	26.4	70 400	378	.9
Central place	9 541 204	1 286 752	13.5	353 545	3.24	3.9	32.9	31.5	8.6	17.6	46.4	29.6	46 900	331	1.0
Urban fringe	14 246 563	902 693	6.3	242 508	3.30	4.6	48.5	23.1	7.7	13.2	58.3	21.9	121 100	542	.8
1,000,000 to 2,499,999	35 989 482	3 940 859	11.0	1 149 527	3.02	4.2	48.5	23.1	13.8	16.5	58.7	21.3	80 900	399	.6
Central place	15 165 236	2 262 938	14.9	668 301	2.94	4.1	43.6	24.6	15.9	18.7	55.7	22.1	67 000	359	.7
Urban fringe	20 824 246	1 677 921	8.1	481 226	3.12	4.5	55.5	21.1	10.8	13.5	62.8	20.3	94 700	474	.5
Less than 1,000,000	64 242 584	4 755 790	7.4	1 304 674	3.19	4.5	46.4	21.1	11.2	15.3	58.1	14.4	61 900	337	.6
Central place	37 836 847	3 563 716	9.4	989 304	3.16	4.4	43.4	21.5	11.5	16.1	56.0	15.8	57 900	324	.6
Urban fringe	26 405 737	1 192 074	4.5	315 370	3.28	4.7	56.0	19.9	10.2	12.8	64.5	10.1	72 000	389	.5
500,000 to 999,999	17 955 916	1 284 790	7.2	368 088	3.08	4.5	44.8	19.0	11.1	16.5	53.4	18.4	60 900	334	.7
Central place	9 403 669	923 451	9.8	266 781	3.06	4.4	41.2	19.6	11.7	17.5	51.3	20.3	54 700	311	.7
Urban fringe	8 552 247	361 339	4.2	101 307	3.14	4.7	54.3	17.4	9.3	13.9	59.0	13.7	76 900	419	.5
250,000 to 499,999	15 470 005	1 344 597	8.7	370 419	3.18	4.6	49.1	20.5	12.0	15.4	61.9	12.8	61 700	333	.6
Central place	8 327 127	982 762	11.8	275 064	3.13	4.5	45.5	20.5	12.0	16.3	59.0	14.4	60 700	328	.6
Urban fringe	7 142 878	361 835	5.1	95 355	3.32	4.7	59.6	20.7	11.8	12.6	70.3	8.3	64 200	362	.5
100,000 to 249,999	18 879 599	1 348 272	7.1	356 836	3.30	4.4	45.0	23.0	10.4	14.3	58.1	13.2	62 600	351	.6
Central place	11 928 889	1 049 745	8.8	281 217	3.29	4.4	42.9	23.6	10.9	14.8	56.2	14.0	55 100	334	.7
Urban fringe	6 950 710	298 527	4.3	75 019	3.35	4.7	52.9	21.0	0.7	12.1	64.0	9.9	81 900	416	.5
Less than 100,000	11 937 064	778 131	6.5	209 331	3.21	4.4	47.0	22.5	11.5	14.8	59.6	12.3	63 600	329	.6
Central place	8 177 162	607 758	7.4	166 242	3.17	4.4	44.2	22.6	11.5	15.6	58.4	14.0	62 900	328	.6
Urban fringe	3 759 902	170 373	4.5	43 089	3.37	4.6	57.8	22.1	11.7	12.0	64.1	5.8	66 500	335	.5
INSIDE AND OUTSIDE METROPOLITAN AREA															
Inside metropolitan area	192 725 741	20 204 818	10.5	5 427 548	3.30	4.1	40.8	27.9	10.9	14.7	49.8	23.3	84 600	405	.7
In central city	77 843 533	11 514 262	14.8	3 106 672	3.10	4.0	33.3	28.6	11.5	16.7	41.7	29.3	66 300	373	.8
Not in central city	114 882 208	8 690 566	7.6	2 230 976	3.45	4.4	51.4	26.9	9.9	11.9	61.4	14.7	107 100	479	.6
Urban	88 439 928	7 669 637	8.7	1 994 710	3.42	4.4	49.9	27.0	9.9	12.0	60.5	16.3	113 300	491	.6
Inside urbanized area	79 755 134	6 854 456	8.6	1 794 407	3.40	4.4	49.9	26.5	9.7	12.2	59.9	17.2	121 500	509	.6
Outside urbanized area	8 684 794	815 181	9.4	200 303	3.66	4.3	50.2	31.2	11.6	10.8	65.8	8.2	61 600	308	.6
Rural	26 442 280	1 020 929	3.9	236 266	3.63	4.7	63.8	26.4	10.3	10.4	68.7	1.6	65 900	270	.7
Outside metropolitan area	55 984 132	2 149 241	3.8	574 170	3.18	4.6	58.1	19.6	14.8	15.4	66.4	4.0	39 900	229	.5
Urban	20 851 951	1 244 669	6.0	340 214	3.16	4.6	54.5	19.4	15.0	15.9	67.5	6.0	40 500	241	.5
Inside urbanized area	1 520 259	51 453	3.4	14 034	2.73	4.7	48.5	11.4	10.8	18.1	58.3	11.0	68 200	340	.6
Outside urbanized area	19 331 692	1 193 216	6.2	326 180	3.18	4.6	54.8	19.7	15.2	15.8	67.9	5.8	39 500	237	.5
Place of 10,000 or more	9 873 345	655 690	6.6	177 936	3.20	4.5	51.0	20.3	14.3	15.5	66.6	7.3	42 800	256	.5
Place of 2,500 to 9,999	9 458 347	537 526	5.7	148 244	3.15	4.6	59.3	19.0	16.3	16.0	69.5	3.9	36 200	213	.4
Rural	35 132 181	904 572	2.6	233 956	3.22	4.7	63.3	20.0	14.6	14.8	64.8	1.3	38 800	209	.5
POPULATION SIZE CLASS OF METROPOLITAN AREA															
1,000,000 or more	124 775 608	15 435 936	12.4	4 154 630	3.30	4.0	37.9	29.4	10.6	14.8	45.9	26.8	108 500	431	.8
In central city	48 263 927	8 724 237	18.1	2 414 004	3.21	3.8	29.4	31.1	11.3	16.8	35.8	33.8	79 600	396	.8
Not in central city	76 511 681	6 711 699	8.8	1 740 626	3.42	4.4	49.7	27.1	9.5	12.0	59.8	17.1	129 900	513	.7
5,000,000 or more	52 837 069	9 646 762	18.3	2 489 327	3.47	3.9	33.0	33.4	9.7	13.7	40.2	29.3	163 700	474	.8
In central city	22 256 704	5 470 682	24.6	1 458 170	3.37	3.7	23.6	34.8	10.0	15.6	26.8	39.1	154 200	430	.8
Not in central city	30 580 365	4 176 080	13.7	1 031 157	3.60	4.3	46.4	31.5	9.4	11.1	59.1	15.5	168 200	557	.7
2,500,000 to 4,999,999	31 701 991	3 047 711	9.6	893 130	3.08	4.0	42.9	27.0	11.8	16.3	50.1	28.6	74 100	373	.8
In central city	10 347 206	1 607 576	15.5	480 869	2.97	3.6	32.8	30.6	13.8	19.1	42.1	33.7	59 200	338	.9
Not in central city	21 354 785	1 440 135	6.7	412 261	3.21	4.4	54.7	22.8	9.6	12.9	59.4	22.6	84 600	460	.6
1,000,000 to 2,499,999	40 236 548	2 741 463	6.8	772 173	3.06	4.5	47.6	19.3	11.8	16.6	59.3	16.7	67 200	362	.6
In central city	15 660 017	1 645 979	10.5	474 965	3.00	4.4	43.6	20.3	12.9	18.3	57.0	17.6	54 900	335	.6
Not in central city	24 576 531	1 095 484	4.5	297 208	3.13	4.8	54.1	17.6	9.9	13.8	63.0	15.2	83 400	416	.5
Less than 1,000,000	67 950 133	4 768 882	7.0	1 272 918	3.28	4.5	50.2	23.0	11.9	14.5	62.4	11.9	55 100	305	.6
In central city	29 579 606	2 790 015	9.4	782 568	3.13	4.4	45.6	20.9	12.2	16.5	59.6	15.4	53 700	303	.6
Not in central city	38 370 527	1 978 867	5.2	490 350	3.54	4.6	57.5	26.3	11.3	11.4	66.8	6.2	58 300	311	.6
500,000 to 999,999	24 905 921	1 696 135	6.8	460 666	3.23	4.5	46.5	22.1	11.0	15.1	58.5	15.4	60 500	319	.6
In central city	10 438 257	1 020 275	9.8	289 670	3.11	4.4	43.1	20.4	11.6	16.8	55.6	19.1	56 000	310	.6
Not in central city	14 467 664	675 860	4.7	170 996	3.44	4.5	52.4	25.1	10.1	12.1	63.3	9.3	68 100	343	.6
250,000 to 499,999	21 528 297	1 941 524	9.0	506 839	3.38	4.5	52.7	25.1	12.8	13.7	66.3	10.1	53 300	310	.6
In central city	8 783 875	1 065 089	12.1	293 970	3.18	4.4	46.9	22.7	12.8	15.9	62.0	13.8	55 900	315	.6
Not in central city	12 744 422	876 435	6.9	212 869	3.64	4.6	60.9	28.4	12.7	10.6	72.3	4.8	50 000	299	.6
100,000 to 249,999	19 403 087	1 048 036	5.4	281 793	3.23	4.5	51.3	21.2	11.5	15.0	61.2	9.4	50 700	274	.5
In central city	9 054 420	636 781	7.0	179 215	3.09	4.5	46.9	19.3	12.1	16.7	61.3	12.6	47 700	274	.6
Not in central city	10 348 667	411 255	4.0	102 578	3.47	4.6	59.1	24.6	10.5	12.0	61.1	3.9	55 900	275	.5
Less than 100,000	2 112 828	83 187	3.9	23 620	3.01	4.6	52.2	15.2	12.7	17.1	67.7	9.6	39 600	257	.3
In central city	1 303 054	67 870	5.2	19 713	2.95	4.6	50.3	15.5	13.2	18.0	68.0	11.1	38 500	257	.4
Not in central city	809 774	15 317	1.9	3 907	3.27	5.0	62.0	13.7	10.3	12.1	65.8	1.9	50 100	264	.2

Table 11. **Summary of General Housing Characteristics of Housing Units With a White, Not of Hispanic Origin Householder: 1990**

[For definitions of terms and meanings of symbols, see text]

United States / Urban and Rural and Size of Place / Population Size Class of Urbanized Area / Inside and Outside Metropolitan Area / Population Size Class of Metropolitan Area	All persons: Total	All persons: White, not of Hispanic origin: Total	All persons: White, not of Hispanic origin: Percent of all persons	Housing units with a White, not of Hispanic origin householder: Total	Median persons in unit	Median rooms	Percent: Owner	Percent: With 1.01 or more persons per room	Percent: With householder 65 years and over	Percent: 1-person households	Percent: 1 unit, detached or attached	Percent: In buildings with 10 or more units	Specified owner, median value (dollars)	Specified renter: Median contract rent (dollars)	Specified renter: Percent with meals included in rent
United States	**248 709 873**	**188 128 296**	**75.6**	**73 633 749**	**2.21**	**5.4**	**69.1**	**2.0**	**23.6**	**25.5**	**68.8**	**10.5**	**80 300**	**381**	**1.0**
URBAN AND RURAL AND SIZE OF PLACE															
Urban	187 053 487	133 375 398	71.3	53 651 540	2.15	5.4	64.4	1.9	23.9	27.9	65.7	14.1	86 800	400	1.1
Inside urbanized area	158 258 878	109 975 510	69.5	44 437 315	2.15	5.4	64.3	1.8	23.0	27.9	64.7	15.7	95 100	424	1.2
Central place	78 847 406	46 619 577	59.1	19 974 619	1.99	5.0	55.6	2.2	24.4	33.4	56.6	20.3	77 000	393	1.1
Urban fringe	79 411 472	63 355 933	79.8	24 462 696	2.27	5.7	71.4	1.6	22.0	23.4	71.2	11.9	109 800	471	1.2
Outside urbanized area	28 794 609	23 399 888	81.3	9 214 225	2.15	5.3	65.0	1.9	27.9	28.0	70.6	6.5	57 200	277	.6
Place of 10,000 or more	13 825 022	11 020 682	79.7	4 338 311	2.13	5.3	61.9	1.9	26.5	28.6	68.8	8.3	58 700	291	.7
Place of 2,500 to 9,999	14 969 587	12 379 206	82.7	4 875 914	2.16	5.3	67.7	2.0	29.1	27.4	72.2	5.0	55 800	263	.6
Rural	61 656 386	54 752 898	88.8	19 982 209	2.40	5.6	81.6	2.3	22.7	18.9	77.4	1.0	65 100	254	.6
Place of 1,000 to 2,499	7 050 858	6 119 686	86.8	2 404 005	2.19	5.4	73.0	2.0	29.9	26.4	75.3	2.9	50 800	235	.4
Place of less than 1,000	3 801 051	3 352 640	88.2	1 332 309	2.18	5.4	76.9	2.0	32.1	27.1	79.1	1.4	36 200	194	.3
Other rural	50 804 477	45 280 572	89.1	16 245 895	2.44	5.7	83.3	2.4	20.9	17.1	77.5	.7	71 600	268	.7
POPULATION SIZE CLASS OF URBANIZED AREA															
1,000,000 or more	94 016 294	60 537 603	64.4	24 680 136	2.14	5.4	64.2	2.0	22.9	28.5	62.9	18.8	122 700	491	1.2
Central place	41 010 559	19 991 801	48.7	8 944 618	1.90	4.8	52.1	2.6	25.1	36.7	48.9	27.7	97 800	457	1.1
Urban fringe	53 005 735	40 545 802	76.5	15 735 518	2.27	5.8	71.1	1.6	21.7	23.9	70.9	13.8	130 300	518	1.3
5,000,000 or more	34 239 045	19 120 102	55.8	7 803 290	2.12	5.2	61.5	2.5	25.1	29.5	54.8	23.7	191 100	566	.8
Central place	16 304 119	6 619 612	40.6	3 037 073	1.84	4.3	44.6	3.7	27.8	39.1	31.3	40.0	203 600	520	.7
Urban fringe	17 934 926	12 500 490	69.7	4 766 217	2.30	5.8	72.3	1.8	23.4	23.4	69.8	13.2	188 400	616	.9
2,500,000 to 4,999,999	23 787 767	15 815 595	66.5	6 395 313	2.16	5.6	65.0	1.6	20.7	28.3	66.7	16.6	124 300	511	1.3
Central place	9 541 204	4 469 665	46.8	2 030 143	1.85	5.0	52.7	2.0	22.7	38.4	53.8	24.1	84 600	459	1.1
Urban fringe	14 246 563	11 345 930	79.6	4 365 170	2.30	5.9	70.7	1.4	19.7	23.6	72.7	13.1	136 900	548	1.4
1,000,000 to 2,499,999	35 989 482	25 601 906	71.1	10 481 533	2.13	5.4	65.8	1.8	22.7	27.9	66.6	16.6	89 500	431	1.4
Central place	15 165 236	8 902 524	58.7	3 877 402	1.97	5.1	57.7	2.1	24.2	33.9	60.1	20.0	83 200	404	1.4
Urban fringe	20 824 246	16 699 382	80.2	6 604 131	2.23	5.6	70.5	1.6	21.9	24.4	70.4	14.6	92 100	454	1.4
Less than 1,000,000	64 242 584	49 437 907	77.0	19 757 179	2.16	5.4	64.3	1.7	23.2	27.2	66.9	11.7	76 200	364	1.1
Central place	37 836 847	26 627 776	70.4	11 030 001	2.06	5.2	58.4	1.8	23.8	30.8	62.9	14.2	68 800	349	1.2
Urban fringe	26 405 737	22 810 131	86.4	8 727 178	2.28	5.6	71.8	1.6	22.4	22.6	71.9	8.6	84 700	397	1.1
500,000 to 999,999	17 955 916	13 340 475	74.3	5 390 389	2.15	5.4	63.9	1.6	22.4	27.8	64.9	13.7	81 100	382	1.1
Central place	9 403 669	5 938 917	63.2	2 538 831	2.00	5.2	56.1	1.8	22.9	32.9	58.8	16.9	68 900	356	1.0
Urban fringe	8 552 247	7 401 558	86.5	2 851 558	2.27	5.7	70.9	1.5	22.0	23.2	70.4	10.9	90 400	422	1.3
250,000 to 499,999	15 470 005	11 544 438	74.6	4 634 179	2.16	5.5	66.1	1.6	23.5	27.1	68.9	11.6	78 100	369	1.2
Central place	8 327 127	5 459 291	65.6	2 300 188	2.03	5.3	59.7	1.7	24.5	31.7	65.0	14.5	70 300	355	1.5
Urban fringe	7 142 878	6 085 147	85.2	2 333 991	2.29	5.7	72.3	1.5	22.5	22.6	72.7	8.7	85 500	393	.9
100,000 to 249,999	18 879 599	14 821 260	78.5	5 870 252	2.17	5.3	63.5	1.8	22.7	26.9	66.5	11.3	76 400	365	1.1
Central place	11 928 889	8 799 544	73.8	3 594 039	2.09	5.2	58.4	1.9	23.4	29.9	62.8	13.7	70 900	355	1.1
Urban fringe	6 950 710	6 021 716	86.6	2 276 213	2.30	5.5	71.5	1.7	21.5	22.1	72.4	7.4	84 000	393	1.0
Less than 100,000	11 937 064	9 731 734	81.5	3 862 359	2.16	5.3	64.1	1.7	24.6	27.0	67.6	9.8	66 700	328	1.1
Central place	8 177 162	6 430 024	78.6	2 596 943	2.10	5.2	59.5	1.8	24.7	29.3	65.2	11.9	64 700	325	1.2
Urban fringe	3 759 902	3 301 710	87.8	1 265 416	2.27	5.4	73.3	1.7	24.5	22.2	72.5	5.4	70 300	338	1.0
INSIDE AND OUTSIDE METROPOLITAN AREA															
Inside metropolitan area	192 725 741	140 496 200	72.9	55 416 863	2.20	5.5	67.4	1.9	22.5	26.0	67.2	13.0	91 900	414	1.1
In central city	77 843 533	45 957 707	59.0	19 718 548	1.99	5.0	55.5	2.1	24.4	33.6	56.6	20.3	76 200	392	1.1
Not in central city	114 882 208	94 538 493	82.3	35 698 315	2.32	5.7	73.9	1.8	21.5	21.9	73.0	9.0	99 200	440	1.1
Urban	88 439 928	70 615 050	79.8	27 223 089	2.27	5.7	71.0	1.7	22.2	23.5	71.2	11.4	105 400	457	1.1
Inside urbanized area	79 755 134	63 480 467	79.6	24 504 557	2.27	5.7	71.3	1.6	21.9	23.4	71.2	11.9	110 300	472	1.2
Outside urbanized area	8 684 794	7 134 583	82.2	2 718 532	2.26	5.4	67.7	2.1	25.1	24.3	70.9	6.4	74 300	336	.7
Rural	26 442 280	23 923 443	90.5	8 475 226	2.49	5.8	83.5	2.1	19.2	16.6	79.0	1.1	84 100	311	.8
Outside metropolitan area	55 984 132	47 632 096	85.1	18 216 886	2.25	5.4	74.2	2.2	26.7	23.8	73.9	3.0	51 600	246	.6
Urban	20 851 951	16 871 318	80.9	6 734 755	2.10	5.3	63.9	1.8	28.9	29.3	70.1	6.7	52 200	263	.7
Inside urbanized area	1 520 259	1 238 190	81.4	487 340	2.15	5.3	63.8	2.0	25.3	26.1	65.2	8.8	76 900	349	1.1
Outside urbanized area	19 331 692	15 633 128	80.9	6 247 415	2.10	5.3	64.0	1.8	29.2	29.5	70.5	6.5	50 900	259	.6
Place of 10,000 or more	9 873 345	7 910 296	80.1	3 140 028	2.10	5.2	61.2	1.8	27.2	29.6	68.3	8.3	53 400	275	.7
Place of 2,500 to 9,999	9 458 347	7 722 832	81.7	3 107 387	2.10	5.3	66.8	1.8	31.3	29.4	72.7	4.7	48 500	237	.5
Rural	35 132 181	30 760 778	87.6	11 482 131	2.33	5.5	80.3	2.4	25.4	20.6	76.1	.9	51 100	218	.5
POPULATION SIZE CLASS OF METROPOLITAN AREA															
1,000,000 or more	124 775 608	86 629 788	69.4	34 380 434	2.19	5.5	66.5	1.9	22.3	26.6	65.7	15.6	115 700	469	1.1
In central city	48 263 927	25 186 606	52.2	11 093 261	1.93	4.9	53.0	2.4	24.7	35.5	50.7	25.2	94 100	442	1.1
Not in central city	76 511 681	61 443 182	80.3	23 287 173	2.32	5.8	73.0	1.7	21.2	22.4	72.8	11.0	121 700	492	1.2
5,000,000 or more	52 837 069	32 330 913	61.2	12 941 717	2.17	5.4	64.9	2.3	24.1	27.7	61.7	18.6	179 200	566	1.1
In central city	22 256 704	9 809 198	44.1	4 396 322	1.89	4.6	49.4	3.3	27.0	37.2	40.7	32.7	179 800	525	.9
Not in central city	30 580 365	22 521 715	73.6	8 545 395	2.31	5.8	72.8	1.8	22.6	22.9	72.5	11.4	179 100	598	1.2
2,500,000 to 4,999,999	31 701 991	22 373 259	70.6	8 847 994	2.21	5.6	67.3	1.7	20.0	26.3	67.0	16.0	102 800	460	1.1
In central city	10 347 206	5 237 387	50.6	2 355 334	1.87	4.9	52.8	2.0	23.0	37.5	53.0	25.4	86 600	419	1.1
Not in central city	21 354 785	17 135 872	80.2	6 492 660	2.33	5.8	72.6	1.6	19.0	22.2	72.0	12.6	107 300	483	1.0
1,000,000 to 2,499,999	40 236 548	31 925 616	79.3	12 590 723	2.21	5.5	67.7	1.7	22.2	25.8	68.9	12.1	84 400	396	1.3
In central city	15 660 017	10 140 021	64.8	4 341 605	2.00	5.1	56.7	1.8	23.3	32.9	59.6	17.4	76 000	382	1.2
Not in central city	24 576 531	21 785 595	88.6	8 249 118	2.31	5.7	73.4	1.6	21.6	22.0	73.8	9.2	87 700	407	1.3
Less than 1,000,000	67 950 133	53 866 412	79.3	21 036 429	2.22	5.4	68.7	1.8	22.9	25.0	69.6	8.8	70 200	340	1.1
In central city	29 579 606	20 771 101	70.2	8 625 287	2.05	5.2	58.7	1.8	24.0	31.0	64.1	14.1	65 200	337	1.2
Not in central city	38 370 527	33 095 311	86.3	12 411 142	2.33	5.6	75.7	1.9	22.1	20.8	73.4	5.2	73 500	345	.9
500,000 to 999,999	24 905 921	18 869 756	75.8	7 456 900	2.21	5.5	68.2	1.7	22.1	25.6	68.8	10.5	76 900	361	1.1
In central city	10 438 257	6 584 313	63.1	2 806 395	2.00	5.2	58.0	1.7	23.7	32.6	62.3	16.5	70 500	354	1.1
Not in central city	14 467 664	12 285 443	84.9	4 650 505	2.33	5.6	74.5	1.7	21.2	21.3	72.8	6.8	80 300	370	1.0
250,000 to 499,999	21 528 297	16 985 792	78.9	6 615 723	2.22	5.5	69.6	1.9	24.0	24.5	70.6	8.1	70 300	346	1.1
In central city	8 783 875	6 084 575	69.3	2 522 528	2.06	5.3	59.5	1.9	25.0	30.5	65.3	13.2	65 200	343	1.3
Not in central city	12 744 422	10 901 217	85.5	4 093 195	2.32	5.6	75.9	1.9	23.3	20.8	73.8	4.9	73 100	349	1.0
100,000 to 249,999	19 403 087	16 159 512	83.3	6 250 874	2.23	5.4	68.6	1.9	22.7	24.8	69.6	7.8	63 500	315	1.0
In central city	9 054 420	7 012 007	77.4	2 857 399	2.08	5.2	58.6	1.7	23.5	30.0	64.7	12.9	61 400	321	1.1
Not in central city	10 348 667	9 147 505	88.4	3 393 475	2.35	5.5	77.1	2.1	22.1	20.4	73.8	3.4	65 200	303	.8
Less than 100,000	2 112 828	1 851 352	87.6	712 932	2.23	5.4	66.9	1.6	22.6	25.6	68.6	7.8	59 300	298	.9
In central city	1 303 054	1 090 206	83.7	438 965	2.10	5.2	60.1	1.5	24.2	29.6	65.0	11.1	57 300	300	1.0
Not in central city	809 774	761 146	94.0	273 967	2.43	5.6	77.8	1.8	20.1	19.1	74.4	2.3	62 400	291	.4

Table 12. **Occupancy, Structural Characteristics, and Age of Householder: 1990**

[For definitions of terms and meanings of symbols, see text]

United States Urban and Rural and Size of Place	United States	Urban							Rural			
			Inside urbanized area			Outside urbanized area						
		Total	Total	Central place	Urban fringe	Total	Place of 10,000 or more	Place of 2,500 to 9,999	Total	Place of 1,000 to 2,499	Place of less than 1,000	Other rural
All housing units	**102 263 678**	**76 212 052**	**64 201 132**	**33 030 250**	**31 170 882**	**12 010 920**	**5 644 570**	**6 366 350**	**26 051 626**	**3 097 406**	**1 740 468**	**21 213 752**
POPULATION												
All persons	**248 709 873**	**187 053 487**	**158 258 878**	**78 847 406**	**79 411 472**	**28 794 609**	**13 825 022**	**14 969 587**	**61 656 386**	**7 050 858**	**3 801 051**	**50 804 477**
Persons in occupied housing units	242 012 129	181 566 153	154 151 248	76 257 971	77 893 277	27 414 905	13 041 963	14 372 942	60 445 976	6 868 558	3 747 973	49 829 445
Per occupied housing unit	2.63	2.59	2.60	2.53	2.68	2.54	2.52	2.56	2.76	2.57	2.56	2.81
Owner-occupied housing units	162 303 028	113 221 832	95 499 999	39 777 078	55 722 921	17 721 833	8 007 767	9 714 066	49 081 196	5 027 233	2 866 865	41 187 098
Per owner-occupied housing unit	2.75	2.74	2.76	2.69	2.81	2.62	2.62	2.62	2.78	2.62	2.58	2.82
Renter-occupied housing units	79 709 101	68 344 321	58 651 249	36 480 893	22 170 356	9 693 072	5 034 196	4 658 876	11 364 780	1 841 325	881 108	8 642 347
Per renter-occupied housing unit	2.42	2.38	2.38	2.38	2.39	2.40	2.38	2.42	2.67	2.43	2.49	2.75
TENURE BY RACE AND HISPANIC ORIGIN OF HOUSEHOLDER												
Occupied housing units	**91 947 410**	**70 045 167**	**59 251 993**	**30 147 116**	**29 104 877**	**10 793 174**	**5 169 559**	**5 623 615**	**21 902 243**	**2 676 603**	**1 464 016**	**17 761 624**
Owner-occupied housing units	59 024 811	41 375 627	34 617 648	14 793 984	19 823 664	6 757 979	3 057 179	3 700 800	17 649 184	1 917 463	1 110 269	14 621 452
Percent of occupied housing units	64.2	59.1	58.4	49.1	68.1	62.6	59.1	65.8	80.6	71.6	75.8	82.3
White	52 432 648	35 924 502	29 773 538	11 741 509	18 032 029	6 150 964	2 764 077	3 386 887	16 508 146	1 787 351	1 033 619	13 687 176
Black	4 327 265	3 508 536	3 124 200	2 184 832	939 368	384 336	183 697	200 639	818 729	82 978	44 403	691 348
American Indian, Eskimo, or Aleut	318 001	149 128	102 837	52 925	49 912	46 291	17 914	28 377	168 873	17 062	24 157	127 654
Asian or Pacific Islander	1 050 182	994 175	934 822	405 674	529 148	59 353	30 326	29 027	56 007	11 291	2 452	42 264
Other race	896 715	799 286	682 251	409 044	273 207	117 035	61 165	55 870	97 429	18 781	5 638	73 010
Hispanic origin (of any race)	2 545 584	2 246 472	1 960 595	1 085 656	874 939	285 877	143 219	142 658	299 112	51 680	15 724	231 708
White, not of Hispanic origin	50 860 725	34 548 244	28 560 872	11 103 806	17 457 066	5 987 372	2 684 453	3 302 919	16 312 481	1 755 329	1 023 962	13 533 190
Renter-occupied housing units	32 922 599	28 669 540	24 634 345	15 353 132	9 281 213	4 035 195	2 112 380	1 922 815	4 253 059	759 140	353 747	3 140 172
White	24 447 457	20 688 596	17 339 316	9 858 563	7 480 753	3 349 280	1 722 513	1 626 767	3 758 861	664 887	312 749	2 781 225
Black	5 648 896	5 328 204	4 871 981	3 786 115	1 085 866	456 223	257 928	198 295	320 692	60 190	22 630	237 872
American Indian, Eskimo, or Aleut	273 371	200 771	150 008	102 583	47 425	50 763	24 197	26 566	72 600	14 005	13 160	45 435
Asian or Pacific Islander	963 553	940 691	888 614	589 897	298 717	52 077	32 629	19 448	22 862	6 278	1 756	14 828
Other race	1 589 322	1 511 278	1 384 426	1 015 974	368 452	126 852	75 113	51 739	78 044	13 780	3 452	60 812
Hispanic origin (of any race)	3 456 134	3 284 460	3 027 706	2 149 513	878 193	256 754	148 036	108 718	171 674	30 959	8 205	132 510
White, not of Hispanic origin	22 773 024	19 103 296	15 876 443	8 870 813	7 005 630	3 226 853	1 653 858	1 572 995	3 669 728	648 676	308 347	2 712 705
VACANCY STATUS												
Vacant housing units	**10 316 268**	**6 166 885**	**4 949 139**	**2 883 134**	**2 066 005**	**1 217 746**	**475 011**	**742 735**	**4 149 383**	**420 803**	**276 452**	**3 452 128**
For sale only	1 260 233	916 676	752 695	367 678	385 017	163 981	72 522	91 459	343 557	46 060	28 830	268 667
For rent	3 046 638	2 623 596	2 232 655	1 441 752	790 903	390 941	196 426	194 515	423 042	87 129	46 661	289 252
Rented or sold, not occupied	807 631	555 594	456 455	273 406	183 049	99 139	43 227	55 912	252 037	31 222	19 826	200 989
For seasonal, recreational, or occasional use	3 081 923	909 091	612 225	202 096	410 129	296 866	50 758	246 108	2 172 832	162 182	97 098	1 913 552
For migrant workers	34 944	7 015	4 152	2 192	1 960	2 863	1 000	1 863	27 929	1 200	980	25 749
Other vacant	2 084 899	1 154 913	890 957	596 010	294 947	263 956	111 078	152 878	929 986	93 010	83 057	753 919
Boarded up	207 626	160 758	143 029	119 624	23 405	17 729	8 608	9 121	46 868	5 042	4 233	37 593
UNITS IN STRUCTURE												
All housing units	**102 263 678**	**76 212 052**	**64 201 132**	**33 030 250**	**31 170 882**	**12 010 920**	**5 644 570**	**6 366 350**	**26 051 626**	**3 097 406**	**1 740 468**	**21 213 752**
1, detached	60 383 409	41 163 092	33 401 637	14 472 312	18 929 325	7 761 455	3 554 496	4 206 959	19 220 317	2 190 637	1 315 230	15 714 450
1, attached	5 378 243	4 986 653	4 550 575	2 402 962	2 147 613	436 078	204 566	231 512	391 590	75 259	24 667	291 664
2	4 948 118	4 522 135	3 781 840	2 567 052	1 214 788	740 295	384 650	355 645	425 983	135 615	45 123	245 245
3 or 4	4 928 289	4 584 771	3 900 677	2 541 063	1 359 614	684 094	358 416	325 678	343 518	120 134	47 319	176 065
5 to 9	4 935 041	4 057 423	4 000 410	2 450 200	1 036 147	571 007	304 145	266 062	270 410	91 043	32 070	154 306
10 to 19	4 905 888	4 710 080	4 276 859	2 418 830	1 858 029	433 221	244 617	188 604	195 808	61 643	20 588	113 577
20 to 49	3 868 056	3 777 737	3 520 836	2 228 479	1 292 357	256 901	145 358	111 543	90 319	31 958	8 445	49 916
50 or more	4 394 825	4 345 913	4 175 362	2 964 986	1 210 376	170 551	101 894	68 657	48 912	15 203	3 825	29 884
Mobile home or trailer	7 399 855	2 663 747	1 844 170	593 984	1 250 186	819 577	286 885	532 692	4 736 108	337 673	221 437	4 176 998
Other	1 121 154	800 501	662 760	390 313	272 447	137 741	59 543	78 198	320 653	37 341	21 755	261 557
Owner-occupied housing units	**59 024 811**	**41 375 627**	**34 617 648**	**14 793 984**	**19 823 664**	**6 757 979**	**3 057 179**	**3 700 800**	**17 649 184**	**1 917 463**	**1 110 269**	**14 621 452**
1, detached	47 535 989	33 403 161	27 579 701	11 293 694	16 286 007	5 823 460	2 683 555	3 139 905	14 132 828	1 622 062	941 612	11 569 154
1, attached	2 979 548	2 796 103	2 623 483	1 311 993	1 311 490	172 620	77 473	95 147	183 445	31 569	10 554	141 322
2	1 173 856	1 090 979	983 394	662 272	321 122	107 585	55 182	52 403	82 877	21 484	6 945	54 448
3 or 4	515 553	487 843	451 390	268 755	182 635	36 453	18 385	18 068	27 710	6 939	2 167	18 604
5 or more	1 516 246	1 480 107	1 438 122	725 886	712 236	41 985	19 027	22 958	36 139	6 775	2 046	27 318
Mobile home or trailer	4 896 741	1 831 287	1 303 520	408 681	894 839	527 767	183 466	344 301	3 065 454	214 646	137 920	2 712 888
Other	406 878	286 147	238 038	122 703	115 335	48 109	20 091	28 018	120 731	13 988	9 025	97 718
Renter-occupied housing units	**32 922 599**	**28 669 540**	**24 634 345**	**15 353 132**	**9 281 213**	**4 035 195**	**2 112 380**	**1 922 815**	**4 253 059**	**759 140**	**353 747**	**3 140 172**
1, detached	8 030 262	5 680 169	4 349 447	2 422 432	1 927 015	1 330 722	648 012	682 710	2 350 093	316 532	190 786	1 842 775
1, attached	1 862 737	1 747 946	1 542 166	875 140	667 026	205 780	104 438	101 342	114 791	27 295	7 419	80 077
2	3 264 856	2 985 535	2 441 682	1 645 349	796 333	543 853	286 328	257 525	279 321	92 877	30 314	156 130
3 or 4	3 846 455	3 593 386	3 033 938	1 979 754	1 054 184	559 448	297 998	261 450	253 069	94 339	34 455	124 275
5 to 9	3 949 553	3 752 218	3 280 316	2 006 938	1 273 378	471 902	258 285	213 617	197 335	72 111	22 392	102 832
10 to 19	3 934 394	3 799 388	3 442 731	1 987 746	1 454 985	356 657	208 735	147 922	135 006	47 535	14 140	73 331
20 to 49	3 029 921	2 976 447	2 773 906	1 824 827	949 079	202 541	124 070	78 471	53 474	21 752	4 718	27 004
50 or more	3 288 738	3 268 933	3 141 176	2 292 266	848 910	127 757	87 162	40 595	19 805	5 116	914	13 775
Mobile home or trailer	1 237 256	460 981	286 796	100 909	185 887	174 185	67 484	106 701	776 275	67 341	41 822	667 112
Other	478 427	404 537	342 187	217 771	124 416	62 350	29 868	32 482	73 890	14 242	6 787	52 861
Occupied housing units	**91 947 410**	**70 045 167**	**59 251 993**	**30 147 116**	**29 104 877**	**10 793 174**	**5 169 559**	**5 623 615**	**21 902 243**	**2 676 603**	**1 464 016**	**17 761 624**
AGE OF HOUSEHOLDER												
Owner-occupied housing units	**59 024 811**	**41 375 627**	**34 617 648**	**14 793 984**	**19 823 664**	**6 757 979**	**3 057 179**	**3 700 800**	**17 649 184**	**1 917 463**	**1 110 269**	**14 621 452**
Under 25 years	862 169	527 856	422 942	202 579	220 363	104 914	46 189	58 725	334 313	31 473	20 662	282 178
25 to 34 years	9 000 394	6 249 324	5 298 037	2 170 060	3 127 977	951 287	431 755	519 532	2 751 070	267 658	155 878	2 327 534
35 to 44 years	13 502 988	9 448 913	8 069 880	3 244 889	4 824 991	1 379 033	637 450	741 583	4 054 075	380 248	203 490	3 470 337
45 to 54 years	10 773 931	7 472 536	6 390 191	2 562 256	3 827 935	1 082 345	492 404	589 941	3 301 395	307 339	169 396	2 824 660
55 to 64 years	9 864 090	6 950 259	5 840 221	2 520 945	3 319 276	1 110 038	503 736	606 302	2 913 831	313 554	177 469	2 422 808
65 to 74 years	9 071 906	6 480 924	5 281 405	2 429 118	2 852 287	1 199 519	535 956	663 563	2 590 982	339 541	200 450	2 050 991
75 years and over	5 949 333	4 245 815	3 314 972	1 664 137	1 650 835	930 843	409 689	521 154	1 703 518	277 650	182 924	1 242 944
Renter-occupied housing units	**32 922 599**	**28 669 540**	**24 634 345**	**15 353 132**	**9 281 213**	**4 035 195**	**2 112 380**	**1 922 815**	**4 253 059**	**759 140**	**353 747**	**3 140 172**
Under 25 years	4 187 189	3 705 033	3 078 118	2 005 724	1 072 394	626 915	374 071	252 844	482 156	89 787	40 376	351 993
25 to 34 years	10 849 257	9 460 220	8 229 960	4 956 145	3 273 815	1 230 260	652 475	577 785	1 389 037	224 125	104 256	1 060 656
35 to 44 years	6 890 085	5 954 656	5 188 849	3 183 814	2 005 035	765 807	393 316	372 491	935 429	148 098	68 440	718 891
45 to 54 years	3 529 283	3 049 172	2 659 302	1 677 877	981 425	389 870	197 391	192 479	480 111	77 182	36 597	366 332
55 to 64 years	2 515 323	2 180 651	1 884 539	1 241 157	643 382	296 112	147 430	148 682	334 672	60 430	28 866	245 376
65 to 74 years	2 444 676	2 133 672	1 797 845	1 162 948	634 897	335 827	162 619	173 208	311 004	71 419	32 187	207 398
75 years and over	2 506 786	2 186 136	1 795 732	1 125 467	670 265	390 404	185 078	205 326	320 650	88 099	43 025	189 526

Table 13. **Utilization Characteristics: 1990**

[For definitions of terms and meanings of symbols, see text]

United States Urban and Rural and Size of Place	United States	Urban							Rural			
			Inside urbanized area			Outside urbanized area						
		Total	Total	Central place	Urban fringe	Total	Place of 10,000 or more	Place of 2,500 to 9,999	Total	Place of 1,000 to 2,499	Place of less than 1,000	Other rural
ROOMS												
All housing units	**102 263 678**	**76 212 052**	**64 201 132**	**33 030 250**	**31 170 882**	**12 010 920**	**5 644 570**	**6 366 350**	**26 051 626**	**3 097 406**	**1 740 468**	**21 213 752**
1 room	1 941 253	1 678 241	1 532 544	1 149 105	383 439	145 697	76 937	68 760	263 012	26 129	15 787	221 096
2 rooms	4 219 329	3 631 879	3 205 837	2 167 514	1 038 323	426 042	220 842	205 200	587 450	80 591	40 751	466 108
3 rooms	10 695 285	9 074 066	7 881 160	4 958 524	2 922 636	1 192 906	592 000	600 906	1 621 219	255 156	128 324	1 237 739
4 rooms	19 149 396	14 311 821	11 847 180	6 623 065	5 224 115	2 464 641	1 159 267	1 305 374	4 837 575	619 002	349 990	3 868 583
5 rooms	22 136 448	15 775 046	12 906 242	6 678 128	6 228 114	2 868 804	1 317 907	1 550 897	6 361 402	767 609	445 880	5 147 913
6 rooms	18 990 381	13 630 140	11 347 183	5 477 189	5 869 994	2 282 957	1 054 448	1 228 509	5 360 241	616 192	352 470	4 391 579
7 rooms	11 592 274	8 306 875	7 027 220	2 911 535	4 115 685	1 279 655	591 469	688 186	3 285 399	357 671	203 759	2 723 969
8 rooms	7 059 472	5 124 173	4 412 849	1 593 800	2 819 049	711 324	331 450	379 874	1 935 299	199 753	110 800	1 624 746
9 or more rooms	6 479 840	4 679 811	4 040 917	1 471 390	2 569 527	638 894	300 250	338 644	1 800 029	175 303	92 707	1 532 019
Median	5.2	5.1	5.1	4.7	5.5	5.1	5.1	5.1	5.4	5.2	5.3	5.4
Owner-occupied housing units	**59 024 811**	**41 375 627**	**34 617 648**	**14 793 984**	**19 823 664**	**6 757 979**	**3 057 179**	**3 700 800**	**17 649 184**	**1 917 463**	**1 110 269**	**14 621 452**
1 room	138 128	85 145	74 147	47 303	26 844	10 998	4 105	6 893	52 983	3 816	3 335	45 832
2 rooms	553 871	396 694	347 395	192 816	154 579	49 299	20 569	28 730	157 177	14 178	9 586	133 413
3 rooms	1 951 092	1 397 713	1 211 371	613 312	598 059	186 342	78 891	107 451	553 379	54 756	35 155	463 468
4 rooms	6 712 441	4 237 704	3 396 888	1 599 551	1 797 337	840 816	356 495	484 321	2 474 737	267 722	171 358	2 035 657
5 rooms	13 455 461	9 055 881	7 301 780	3 411 541	3 890 239	1 754 101	780 112	973 989	4 399 580	504 875	298 571	3 596 134
6 rooms	14 450 417	10 297 148	8 599 857	3 880 919	4 718 938	1 697 291	778 217	919 074	4 153 269	467 154	264 661	3 421 454
7 rooms	9 783 837	7 084 205	6 033 099	2 384 539	3 648 560	1 051 106	487 172	563 934	2 699 632	290 997	162 219	2 246 416
8 rooms	6 199 624	4 575 988	3 965 244	1 372 825	2 592 419	610 744	286 447	324 297	1 623 636	166 472	89 809	1 367 355
9 or more rooms	5 779 940	4 245 149	3 687 867	1 291 178	2 396 689	557 282	265 171	292 111	1 534 791	147 493	75 575	1 311 723
Median	6.0	6.0	6.1	5.9	6.2	5.8	5.9	5.8	5.8	5.7	5.6	5.8
Renter-occupied housing units	**32 922 599**	**28 669 540**	**24 634 345**	**15 353 132**	**9 281 213**	**4 035 195**	**2 112 380**	**1 922 815**	**4 253 059**	**759 140**	**353 747**	**3 140 172**
1 room	1 450 705	1 390 136	1 288 587	973 319	315 268	101 549	59 398	42 151	60 569	12 360	4 346	43 863
2 rooms	3 049 832	2 848 651	2 540 999	1 748 314	792 685	307 652	172 057	135 595	201 181	46 934	17 461	136 786
3 rooms	7 116 936	6 568 508	5 749 453	3 744 604	2 004 849	819 055	433 669	385 386	548 428	145 600	58 924	343 904
4 rooms	9 558 092	8 326 731	7 056 798	4 233 843	2 822 955	1 269 933	663 174	606 759	1 231 361	237 757	103 244	890 360
5 rooms	6 390 435	5 385 990	4 553 588	2 689 299	1 864 289	832 402	430 844	401 558	1 004 445	161 204	80 055	763 186
6 rooms	3 211 247	2 589 178	2 162 340	1 278 939	883 401	426 838	216 818	210 020	622 069	87 813	47 562	486 694
7 rooms	1 218 088	912 916	751 156	409 362	341 794	161 760	79 932	81 828	305 172	37 300	23 017	244 855
8 rooms	537 441	379 067	311 789	160 366	151 423	67 278	32 776	34 502	158 374	17 289	11 200	129 885
9 or more rooms	389 823	268 363	219 635	115 086	104 549	48 728	23 712	25 016	121 460	12 883	7 938	100 639
Median	4.0	3.9	3.9	3.8	4.0	4.1	4.1	4.2	4.6	4.2	4.4	4.7
DURATION OF VACANCY												
Vacant-for-sale-only housing units	**1 260 233**	**916 676**	**752 695**	**367 678**	**385 017**	**163 981**	**72 522**	**91 459**	**343 557**	**46 060**	**28 830**	**268 667**
Less than 2 months	202 327	158 120	133 514	59 652	73 862	24 606	11 212	13 394	44 207	5 901	2 701	35 605
2 up to 6 months	456 667	353 692	298 960	137 450	161 510	54 732	25 726	29 006	102 975	12 718	6 422	83 835
6 or more months	601 239	404 864	320 221	170 576	149 645	84 643	35 584	49 059	196 375	27 441	19 707	149 227
Vacant-for-rent housing units	**3 046 638**	**2 623 596**	**2 232 655**	**1 441 752**	**790 903**	**390 941**	**196 426**	**194 515**	**423 042**	**87 129**	**46 661**	**289 252**
Less than 2 months	1 085 916	975 903	840 322	511 709	328 613	135 581	70 786	64 795	110 013	24 332	10 435	75 246
2 up to 6 months	1 173 045	1 019 907	878 120	566 630	311 490	141 787	71 482	70 305	153 138	30 159	15 214	107 765
6 or more months	787 677	627 786	514 213	363 413	150 800	113 573	54 158	59 415	159 891	32 638	21 012	106 241
PERSONS IN UNIT												
Owner-occupied housing units	**59 024 811**	**41 375 627**	**34 617 648**	**14 793 984**	**19 823 664**	**6 757 979**	**3 057 179**	**3 700 800**	**17 649 184**	**1 917 463**	**1 110 269**	**14 621 452**
1 person	11 005 717	8 046 727	6 589 849	3 257 404	3 332 445	1 456 878	655 954	800 924	2 958 990	419 196	266 473	2 273 321
2 persons	20 459 188	14 219 936	11 772 868	5 038 928	6 733 940	2 447 068	1 107 211	1 339 857	6 239 252	688 685	392 802	5 157 765
3 persons	10 758 497	7 468 272	6 347 071	2 568 507	3 778 564	1 121 201	511 275	609 926	3 290 225	315 790	172 145	2 802 290
4 persons	10 015 908	6 884 139	5 838 407	2 208 229	3 630 178	1 045 732	477 579	568 153	3 131 769	294 981	161 993	2 674 795
5 persons	4 333 756	2 992 199	2 543 134	1 005 914	1 537 220	449 065	201 495	247 570	1 341 557	130 664	75 533	1 135 360
6 persons	1 507 407	1 063 830	913 524	400 521	513 003	150 306	65 814	84 492	443 577	43 686	26 572	373 319
7 or more persons	944 338	700 524	612 795	314 481	298 314	87 729	37 851	49 878	243 814	24 461	14 751	204 602
Median	2.40	2.39	2.41	2.32	2.48	2.29	2.29	2.28	2.44	2.28	2.23	2.48
Renter-occupied housing units	**32 922 599**	**28 669 540**	**24 634 345**	**15 353 132**	**9 281 213**	**4 035 195**	**2 112 380**	**1 922 815**	**4 253 059**	**759 140**	**353 747**	**3 140 172**
1 person	11 574 703	10 402 862	8 960 493	5 808 954	3 151 539	1 442 369	758 577	683 792	1 171 841	270 377	122 961	778 503
2 persons	8 994 405	7 868 104	6 816 775	4 086 100	2 730 675	1 051 329	561 036	490 293	1 126 301	191 581	85 374	849 346
3 persons	5 211 772	4 444 372	3 783 587	2 286 670	1 496 917	660 785	344 438	316 347	767 400	125 117	58 436	583 847
4 persons	3 844 186	3 188 988	2 690 935	1 616 374	1 074 561	498 053	253 794	244 259	655 198	97 137	47 920	510 141
5 persons	1 855 182	1 531 757	1 300 891	818 851	482 040	230 866	117 119	113 747	323 425	46 002	23 936	253 487
6 persons	793 113	667 239	576 627	383 251	193 376	90 612	46 218	44 394	125 874	17 641	9 220	99 013
7 or more persons	649 238	566 218	505 037	352 932	152 105	61 181	31 198	29 983	83 020	11 285	5 900	65 835
Median	2.04	2.00	1.99	1.96	2.05	2.05	2.03	2.07	2.35	2.07	2.13	2.43
PERSONS PER ROOM												
Owner-occupied housing units	**59 024 811**	**41 375 627**	**34 617 648**	**14 793 984**	**19 823 664**	**6 757 979**	**3 057 179**	**3 700 800**	**17 649 184**	**1 917 463**	**1 110 269**	**14 621 452**
0.50 or less	41 557 203	29 696 862	24 818 807	10 509 894	14 308 913	4 878 055	2 228 877	2 649 178	11 860 341	1 362 620	785 339	9 712 382
0.51 to 0.75	10 485 276	7 093 305	5 973 852	2 425 549	3 548 303	1 119 453	503 002	616 451	3 391 971	326 015	183 844	2 882 112
0.76 to 1.00	5 371 931	3 441 048	2 843 623	1 330 630	1 512 993	597 425	256 920	340 505	1 930 883	183 282	111 839	1 635 762
1.01 to 1.50	1 103 951	759 480	644 959	340 004	304 955	114 521	48 187	66 334	344 471	33 440	21 076	289 955
1.51 or more	506 450	384 932	336 407	187 907	148 500	48 525	20 193	28 332	121 518	12 106	8 171	101 241
Mean	.45	.44	.44	.44	.44	.43	.43	.44	.46	.44	.44	.47
Renter-occupied housing units	**32 922 599**	**28 669 540**	**24 634 345**	**15 353 132**	**9 281 213**	**4 035 195**	**2 112 380**	**1 922 815**	**4 253 059**	**759 140**	**353 747**	**3 140 172**
0.50 or less	18 283 341	15 905 368	13 568 354	8 250 634	5 317 720	2 337 014	1 220 316	1 116 698	2 377 973	450 624	212 196	1 715 153
0.51 to 0.75	6 208 119	5 318 796	4 525 981	2 709 331	1 816 650	792 815	415 471	377 344	889 323	148 578	68 452	672 293
0.76 to 1.00	5 492 741	4 784 272	4 138 992	2 725 468	1 413 524	645 280	340 639	304 641	708 469	115 779	52 946	539 744
1.01 to 1.50	1 532 981	1 345 976	1 185 061	809 665	375 396	160 915	83 259	77 656	187 005	29 844	14 103	143 058
1.51 or more	1 405 417	1 315 128	1 215 957	858 034	357 923	99 171	52 695	46 476	90 289	14 315	6 050	69 924
Mean	.59	.60	.60	.62	.58	.57	.57	.56	.56	.55	.54	.56
Occupied housing units	**91 947 410**	**70 045 167**	**59 251 993**	**30 147 116**	**29 104 877**	**10 793 174**	**5 169 559**	**5 623 615**	**21 902 243**	**2 676 603**	**1 464 016**	**17 761 624**
HOUSEHOLDER 65 YEARS AND OVER												
Occupied housing units	**19 972 701**	**15 046 547**	**12 189 954**	**6 381 670**	**5 808 284**	**2 856 593**	**1 293 342**	**1 563 251**	**4 926 154**	**776 709**	**458 586**	**3 690 859**
1-person households	8 824 845	6 892 466	5 483 431	3 089 599	2 393 832	1 409 035	640 021	769 014	1 932 379	379 237	227 594	1 325 548
Mean number of persons per room	.80	.80	.82	.81	.83	.70	.72	.69	.79	.65	.62	.84
Units in structure:												
1, detached or attached	13 628 399	9 671 278	7 594 709	3 706 493	3 888 216	2 076 569	934 822	1 141 747	3 957 121	595 307	374 916	2 986 898
2 or more	4 786 910	4 526 451	3 947 613	2 437 092	1 510 521	578 838	284 361	294 477	260 459	112 347	42 188	105 924
Mobile home, trailer, or other	1 557 392	848 818	647 632	238 085	409 547	201 186	74 159	127 027	708 574	69 055	41 482	598 037
Specified owner	10 877 683	8 353 285	6 602 108	3 166 831	3 435 277	1 751 177	789 146	962 031	2 524 398	505 657	314 096	1 704 645
Mean value (dollars)	94 200	102 100	112 800	94 200	130 000	61 500	61 100	61 800	68 200	57 500	39 600	76 700
Specified renter	4 809 275	4 274 110	3 559 667	2 268 882	1 290 785	714 443	342 465	371 978	535 165	156 721	72 982	305 462
Mean contract rent (dollars)	344	356	379	345	441	234	246	222	221	197	161	255
With meals included in rent	176 860	167 290	153 080	83 237	69 843	14 210	8 179	6 031	9 570	1 542	461	7 567
Mean contract rent (dollars)	895	898	911	856	976	758	760	755	848	552	476	930
No meals included in rent	4 304 135	3 910 175	3 262 434	2 108 333	1 154 101	647 741	312 366	335 375	393 960	136 980	59 841	197 139
No cash rent	328 280	196 645	144 153	77 312	66 841	52 492	21 920	30 572	131 635	18 199	12 680	100 756

Table 14. Financial Characteristics: 1990

[For definitions of terms and meanings of symbols, see text]

United States Urban and Rural and Size of Place	United States	Urban — Total	Inside urbanized area — Total	Central place	Urban fringe	Outside urbanized area — Total	Place of 10,000 or more	Place of 2,500 to 9,999	Rural — Total	Place of 1,000 to 2,499	Place of less than 1,000	Other rural
VALUE												
Specified owner-occupied housing units	44 918 000	34 134 878	28 520 962	11 890 617	16 630 345	5 613 916	2 595 663	3 018 253	10 783 122	1 534 953	865 863	8 382 306
Less than $20,000	1 937 962	1 030 104	612 936	471 322	141 614	417 168	169 048	248 120	907 858	169 184	202 341	536 333
$20,000 to $29,999	2 251 761	1 413 089	894 450	658 260	236 190	518 639	227 938	290 701	838 672	175 275	144 640	518 757
$30,000 to $39,999	3 309 485	2 227 322	1 499 472	1 017 510	481 962	727 850	332 002	395 848	1 082 163	218 495	143 795	719 873
$40,000 to $49,999	3 903 314	2 750 026	1 992 068	1 198 525	793 543	757 958	349 702	408 256	1 153 288	210 277	117 625	825 386
$50,000 to $59,999	3 940 018	2 881 430	2 235 243	1 183 144	1 052 099	646 187	306 325	339 862	1 058 588	168 372	80 879	809 337
$60,000 to $69,999	4 070 534	3 056 262	2 482 017	1 175 431	1 306 586	574 245	277 642	296 603	1 014 272	139 816	58 228	816 228
$70,000 to $79,999	3 633 633	2 771 422	2 327 466	981 021	1 346 445	443 956	216 265	227 691	862 211	103 251	37 667	721 293
$80,000 to $89,999	2 895 172	2 247 109	1 931 385	753 572	1 177 813	315 724	154 692	161 032	648 063	70 100	21 930	556 033
$90,000 to $99,999	2 418 101	1 912 155	1 673 446	608 602	1 064 844	238 709	116 295	122 414	505 946	51 252	13 808	440 886
$100,000 to $124,999	3 808 158	3 021 118	2 695 314	889 488	1 805 826	325 804	155 820	169 984	787 040	71 526	17 275	698 239
$125,000 to $149,999	2 965 099	2 422 544	2 206 693	656 261	1 550 432	215 851	102 826	113 025	542 555	45 932	8 907	487 716
$150,000 to $174,999	2 316 164	1 926 285	1 783 450	503 880	1 279 570	142 835	66 063	76 772	389 879	32 323	5 628	351 928
$175,000 to $199,999	1 700 998	1 456 148	1 370 258	382 511	987 747	85 890	39 684	46 206	244 850	19 978	2 988	221 884
$200,000 to $249,999	2 084 263	1 795 949	1 704 841	489 021	1 215 820	91 108	41 121	49 987	288 314	22 959	3 452	261 903
$250,000 to $299,999	1 292 638	1 122 453	1 073 665	315 833	757 832	48 788	20 688	28 100	170 185	13 595	1 930	154 660
$300,000 to $399,999	1 206 814	1 058 113	1 021 983	297 879	724 104	36 130	12 441	23 689	148 701	11 364	1 692	135 645
$400,000 to $499,999	501 342	442 628	430 397	126 641	303 756	12 231	3 506	8 725	58 714	4 516	850	53 348
$500,000 or more	682 544	600 721	585 878	181 716	404 162	14 843	3 605	11 238	81 823	6 738	2 228	72 857
Median (dollars)	78 300	84 200	91 700	72 300	109 900	55 100	56 700	54 100	63 300	49 700	35 800	69 600
Mean (dollars)	111 700	119 800	129 400	106 000	146 100	71 300	70 700	71 800	85 800	67 000	44 900	93 500
Specified vacant-for-sale-only housing units	906 113	676 666	545 415	256 780	288 635	131 251	59 331	71 920	229 447	36 154	22 907	170 386
Less than $20,000	82 803	46 251	25 133	20 274	4 859	21 118	8 935	12 183	36 552	8 126	9 719	18 707
$20,000 to $39,999	150 734	105 469	70 703	51 606	19 097	34 766	15 647	19 119	45 265	9 853	6 645	28 767
$40,000 to $59,999	151 755	115 175	90 001	52 390	37 611	25 174	11 861	13 313	36 580	6 411	3 121	27 048
$60,000 to $79,999	125 770	97 554	81 292	39 075	42 217	16 262	7 726	8 536	28 216	3 529	1 470	23 217
$80,000 to $99,999	81 653	63 046	53 592	21 999	31 593	9 454	4 471	4 983	18 607	1 894	613	16 100
$100,000 to $149,999	115 455	89 642	78 179	27 449	50 730	11 463	5 295	6 168	25 813	2 493	605	22 715
$150,000 to $199,999	75 706	60 112	53 683	16 832	36 851	6 429	2 932	3 497	15 594	1 553	279	13 762
$200,000 to $249,999	39 829	32 281	29 611	8 790	20 821	2 670	1 266	1 404	7 548	745	107	6 696
$250,000 to $299,999	26 475	21 472	19 929	5 650	14 279	1 543	616	927	5 003	465	72	4 466
$300,000 or more	55 933	45 664	43 292	12 715	30 577	2 372	582	1 790	10 269	1 085	276	8 908
Median (dollars)	69 800	73 900	81 900	61 800	108 700	46 500	47 500	45 600	57 300	40 200	24 600	68 500
Mean (dollars)	108 300	114 300	125 100	96 400	150 500	69 400	66 800	71 600	90 700	68 900	39 900	102 200
Owner-occupied mobile homes or trailers	4 896 741	1 831 287	1 303 520	408 681	894 839	527 767	183 466	344 301	3 065 454	214 646	137 920	2 712 888
Median (dollars)	18 600	18 500	19 200	17 000	20 200	16 700	14 900	17 700	18 700	16 100	13 600	19 200
Mean (dollars)	28 100	27 800	28 500	26 700	29 300	26 200	24 900	26 800	28 300	25 100	19 900	28 900
CONTRACT RENT												
Specified renter-occupied housing units	31 966 779	28 374 269	24 398 534	15 220 402	9 178 132	3 975 735	2 085 413	1 890 322	3 592 510	743 598	342 109	2 506 803
Less than $100	1 405 990	1 097 458	772 347	599 797	172 550	325 111	143 142	181 969	308 532	81 739	46 117	180 676
$100 to $149	1 557 814	1 220 362	890 935	692 107	198 828	329 427	151 854	177 573	337 452	83 020	52 814	201 618
$150 to $199	1 961 716	1 522 006	1 061 392	825 579	235 813	460 614	224 910	235 704	439 710	106 907	61 189	271 614
$200 to $249	2 552 687	2 080 613	1 538 954	1 181 288	357 666	541 669	278 803	262 856	472 074	111 067	50 777	310 230
$250 to $299	3 046 821	2 660 070	2 107 951	1 583 614	524 337	552 119	307 537	244 582	386 751	90 900	34 581	261 851
$300 to $349	3 213 961	2 916 889	2 474 048	1 762 306	711 742	442 841	258 658	184 183	297 072	62 674	20 163	214 235
$350 to $399	3 189 292	2 976 458	2 628 834	1 753 835	874 999	347 624	208 894	138 730	212 834	43 301	11 623	157 910
$400 to $449	2 709 613	2 555 233	2 326 600	1 413 545	913 064	228 624	134 396	94 228	154 380	28 716	6 263	119 401
$450 to $499	2 212 210	2 115 267	1 967 114	1 115 397	851 717	148 153	87 656	60 497	96 943	17 037	3 172	76 734
$500 to $549	1 903 134	1 817 939	1 715 227	917 147	798 080	102 712	56 501	46 211	85 195	13 939	2 422	68 834
$550 to $599	1 404 012	1 351 426	1 285 975	643 414	642 561	65 451	36 080	29 371	52 586	8 632	1 261	42 693
$600 to $649	1 231 731	1 182 393	1 127 710	550 305	577 405	54 683	29 418	25 265	49 338	7 580	1 088	40 670
$650 to $699	942 169	909 005	870 564	404 177	466 387	38 441	20 297	18 144	33 164	5 134	665	27 365
$700 to $749	707 321	683 330	657 587	301 209	356 378	25 743	12 979	12 764	23 991	3 863	469	19 659
$750 to $999	1 626 608	1 573 678	1 520 485	703 418	817 067	53 193	25 958	27 235	52 930	8 005	1 077	43 848
$1,000 or more	825 456	796 977	776 320	401 699	374 621	20 657	9 023	11 634	28 479	3 739	704	24 036
No cash rent	1 476 244	915 165	676 482	371 565	304 917	238 683	99 307	139 376	561 079	67 926	47 724	445 429
Median (dollars)	372	386	407	370	475	267	280	253	244	225	187	260
Mean (dollars)	414	429	450	412	513	293	302	283	283	258	206	302
Specified vacant-for-rent housing units	3 011 342	2 615 381	2 225 944	1 437 440	788 504	389 437	195 758	193 679	395 961	86 588	46 147	263 226
Less than $100	116 862	81 146	56 827	47 833	8 994	24 319	10 331	13 988	35 716	8 186	6 473	21 057
$100 to $199	372 097	263 806	173 571	141 136	32 435	90 235	42 709	47 526	108 291	25 278	17 785	65 228
$200 to $299	632 342	523 104	407 674	320 743	86 931	115 430	62 207	53 223	109 238	24 024	11 859	73 355
$300 to $399	623 909	568 126	497 991	357 633	140 358	70 135	39 946	30 189	55 783	11 195	4 180	40 408
$400 to $499	429 832	402 625	368 889	219 899	148 990	33 736	18 326	15 410	27 207	5 208	1 763	20 236
$500 to $599	288 992	272 249	253 912	128 054	125 858	18 337	8 602	9 735	16 743	2 946	1 049	12 748
$600 to $749	256 745	242 378	229 120	104 963	124 157	13 258	6 295	6 963	14 367	2 573	615	11 179
$750 to $999	146 135	138 430	131 217	60 997	70 220	7 213	3 144	4 069	7 705	1 692	457	5 556
$1,000 or more	144 428	123 517	106 743	56 182	50 561	16 774	4 198	12 576	20 911	5 486	1 966	13 459
Median (dollars)	359	374	395	357	483	265	268	261	239	230	192	254
Mean (dollars)	421	436	455	412	533	331	314	349	322	323	258	333
MEALS INCLUDED IN RENT												
Specified renter-occupied housing units	31 966 779	28 374 269	24 398 534	15 220 402	9 178 132	3 975 735	2 085 413	1 890 322	3 592 510	743 598	342 109	2 506 803
With meals included in rent	261 001	243 161	220 902	131 006	89 896	22 259	12 528	9 731	17 840	2 990	1 058	13 792
Mean (dollars)	747	758	773	698	882	611	622	597	596	432	331	651
No meals included in rent	30 229 534	27 215 943	23 501 150	14 717 831	8 783 319	3 714 793	1 973 578	1 741 215	3 013 591	672 682	293 327	2 047 582
No cash rent	1 476 244	915 165	676 482	371 565	304 917	238 683	99 307	139 376	561 079	67 926	47 724	445 429

Table 15. Occupancy, Structural Characteristics, and Age of Householder: 1990

[For definitions of terms and meanings of symbols, see text]

United States Inside and Outside Metropolitan Area	United States	Inside metropolitan area						Outside metropolitan area				
				Not in central city					Urban			
					Urban					Outside urbanized area		
		Total	In central city	Total	Inside urbanized area	Outside urbanized area	Rural	Total	Inside urbanized area	Place of 10,000 or more	Place of 2,500 to 9,999	Rural
All housing units	**102 263 678**	**77 644 313**	**32 641 254**	**45 003 059**	**31 243 819**	**3 517 220**	**10 242 020**	**24 619 365**	**662 407**	**4 084 848**	**4 096 276**	**15 775 834**
POPULATION												
All persons	**248 709 873**	**192 725 741**	**77 843 533**	**114 882 208**	**79 755 134**	**8 684 794**	**26 442 280**	**55 984 132**	**1 520 259**	**9 873 345**	**9 458 347**	**35 132 181**
Persons in occupied housing units	242 012 129	187 811 251	75 285 754	112 525 497	78 238 718	8 377 576	25 909 203	54 200 878	1 440 821	9 260 687	9 042 315	34 457 055
Per occupied housing unit	2.63	2.64	2.53	2.71	2.68	2.67	2.84	2.62	2.50	2.48	2.49	2.70
Owner-occupied housing units	162 303 028	122 337 371	39 185 972	83 151 399	55 909 860	5 622 507	21 619 032	39 965 657	901 138	5 644 424	6 017 655	27 402 440
Per owner-occupied housing unit	2.75	2.78	2.69	2.82	2.81	2.74	2.87	2.67	2.59	2.58	2.56	2.72
Renter-occupied housing units	79 709 101	65 473 880	36 099 782	29 374 098	22 328 858	2 755 069	4 290 171	14 235 221	539 683	3 616 263	3 024 660	7 054 615
Per renter-occupied housing unit	2.42	2.41	2.37	2.44	2.39	2.53	2.69	2.50	2.37	2.34	2.37	2.66
TENURE BY RACE AND HISPANIC ORIGIN OF HOUSEHOLDER												
Occupied housing units	**91 947 410**	**71 265 264**	**29 793 822**	**41 471 442**	**29 201 839**	**3 139 108**	**9 130 495**	**20 682 146**	**575 362**	**3 735 404**	**3 628 132**	**12 743 248**
Owner-occupied housing units	59 024 811	44 045 859	14 588 932	29 456 927	19 870 564	2 049 137	7 537 226	14 978 952	347 794	2 187 044	2 353 704	10 090 410
Percent of occupied housing units	64.2	61.8	49.0	71.0	68.0	65.3	82.6	72.4	60.4	58.5	64.9	79.2
White	52 432 648	38 700 331	11 570 173	27 130 158	18 061 482	1 894 779	7 173 897	13 732 317	315 110	1 972 846	2 129 806	9 314 555
Black	4 327 265	3 432 514	2 168 204	1 264 310	938 482	80 544	245 284	894 751	26 920	141 755	154 098	571 978
American Indian, Eskimo, or Aleut	318 001	150 530	52 656	97 874	50 558	10 329	36 987	167 471	1 085	13 524	21 233	131 629
Asian or Pacific Islander	1 050 182	986 071	397 014	589 057	537 544	18 985	32 528	64 111	2 184	21 715	16 803	23 409
Other race	896 715	776 413	400 885	375 528	282 498	44 500	48 530	120 302	2 495	37 204	31 764	48 839
Hispanic origin (of any race)	2 545 584	2 211 987	1 065 612	1 146 375	894 991	100 560	150 824	333 597	6 807	90 797	87 938	148 055
White, not of Hispanic origin	50 860 725	37 334 955	10 943 814	26 391 141	17 476 344	1 840 758	7 074 039	13 525 770	310 892	1 920 721	2 075 245	9 218 912
Renter-occupied housing units	32 922 599	27 219 405	15 204 890	12 014 515	9 331 275	1 089 971	1 593 269	5 703 194	227 568	1 548 360	1 274 428	2 652 838
White	24 447 457	19 633 566	9 753 209	9 880 357	7 512 132	922 493	1 445 732	4 813 891	180 424	1 261 278	1 064 523	2 307 666
Black	5 648 896	5 023 438	3 757 179	1 266 259	1 089 953	92 494	83 812	625 458	38 329	199 799	151 615	235 715
American Indian, Eskimo, or Aleut	273 371	173 012	101 659	71 353	48 010	9 328	14 015	100 359	1 730	19 344	20 780	58 505
Asian or Pacific Islander	963 553	910 210	585 537	324 673	300 958	13 161	10 554	53 343	4 050	25 452	11 607	12 234
Other race	1 589 322	1 479 179	1 007 306	471 873	380 222	52 495	39 156	110 143	3 035	42 487	25 903	38 718
Hispanic origin (of any race)	3 456 134	3 215 561	2 130 960	1 084 601	899 416	99 743	85 442	240 573	7 227	87 139	60 306	85 901
White, not of Hispanic origin	22 773 024	18 081 908	8 774 734	9 307 174	7 028 213	877 774	1 401 187	4 691 116	176 448	1 219 307	1 032 142	2 263 219
VACANCY STATUS												
Vacant housing units	**10 316 268**	**6 379 049**	**2 847 432**	**3 531 617**	**2 041 980**	**378 112**	**1 111 525**	**3 937 219**	**87 045**	**349 444**	**468 144**	**3 032 586**
For sale only	1 260 233	937 317	360 230	577 087	387 656	51 163	138 268	322 916	9 080	50 379	58 909	204 548
For rent	3 046 638	2 463 752	1 429 003	1 034 749	793 250	98 996	142 503	582 886	21 308	148 677	133 240	279 661
Rented or sold, not occupied	807 631	568 049	270 026	298 023	183 368	27 447	87 208	239 582	5 581	31 844	37 671	164 486
For seasonal, recreational, or occasional use	3 081 923	1 206 243	193 221	1 013 022	381 656	135 415	495 951	1 875 680	40 335	34 995	125 780	1 674 570
For migrant workers	34 944	13 310	2 200	11 110	1 962	1 288	7 860	21 634	33	450	1 097	20 054
Other vacant	2 084 899	1 190 378	592 752	597 626	294 088	63 803	239 735	894 521	10 708	83 099	111 447	689 267
Boarded up	207 626	161 344	119 422	41 922	23 538	4 436	13 948	46 282	614	6 382	6 419	32 867
UNITS IN STRUCTURE												
All housing units	**102 263 678**	**77 644 313**	**32 641 254**	**45 003 059**	**31 243 819**	**3 517 220**	**10 242 020**	**24 619 365**	**662 407**	**4 084 848**	**4 096 276**	**15 775 834**
1, detached	60 383 409	43 191 173	14 263 355	28 927 818	18 974 834	2 236 541	7 716 443	17 192 236	379 224	2 579 007	2 754 575	11 479 430
1, attached	5 378 243	4 923 926	2 390 451	2 533 475	2 155 653	175 806	202 016	454 317	27 714	120 511	117 382	188 710
2	4 948 118	4 156 864	2 552 438	1 604 426	1 214 640	202 528	187 258	791 254	37 241	283 945	231 800	238 268
3 or 4	4 928 289	4 194 597	2 510 334	1 684 263	1 370 997	183 106	130 160	733 692	39 733	268 188	212 943	212 828
5 to 9	4 935 841	4 335 504	2 420 809	1 914 695	1 645 366	161 742	107 587	600 337	38 596	224 167	167 835	169 739
10 to 19	4 905 888	4 474 036	2 389 998	2 084 038	1 866 408	129 845	87 785	431 852	33 932	175 174	114 913	107 833
20 to 49	3 868 056	3 626 189	2 211 731	1 414 458	1 297 693	76 587	40 178	241 867	19 789	104 750	67 720	49 608
50 or more	4 394 825	4 244 246	2 949 885	1 294 361	1 218 575	49 931	25 855	150 579	13 498	72 905	41 184	22 992
Mobile home or trailer	7 399 855	3 695 585	565 385	3 130 200	1 226 041	261 433	1 642 726	3 704 270	66 822	212 529	336 807	3 088 112
Other	1 121 154	802 193	386 868	415 325	273 612	39 701	102 012	318 961	5 858	43 672	51 117	218 314
Owner-occupied housing units	**59 024 811**	**44 045 859**	**14 588 932**	**29 456 927**	**19 870 564**	**2 049 137**	**7 537 226**	**14 978 952**	**347 794**	**2 187 044**	**2 353 704**	**10 090 410**
1, detached	47 535 989	35 349 556	11 128 848	24 220 708	16 333 270	1 716 928	6 170 510	12 186 433	280 338	1 933 179	2 027 989	7 944 927
1, attached	2 979 548	2 807 336	1 306 893	1 500 443	1 317 911	78 328	104 204	172 212	9 524	40 440	43 199	79 049
2	1 173 856	1 054 789	660 190	394 599	321 032	33 010	40 557	119 067	5 422	39 976	31 416	42 253
3 or 4	515 553	474 332	265 947	208 385	183 418	11 972	12 995	41 221	2 914	13 120	10 498	14 689
5 or more	1 516 246	1 468 925	717 977	750 948	712 109	17 390	21 449	47 321	8 608	12 721	11 336	14 656
Mobile home or trailer	4 896 741	2 597 510	387 466	2 210 044	887 334	178 180	1 144 530	2 299 231	38 929	132 727	210 387	1 917 188
Other	406 878	293 411	121 611	171 800	115 490	13 329	42 981	113 467	2 059	14 881	18 879	77 648
Renter-occupied housing units	**32 922 599**	**27 219 405**	**15 204 890**	**12 014 515**	**9 331 275**	**1 089 971**	**1 593 269**	**5 703 194**	**227 568**	**1 548 360**	**1 274 428**	**2 652 838**
1, detached	8 030 262	5 487 878	2 390 142	3 097 736	1 935 515	331 245	830 976	2 542 384	63 176	482 492	481 157	1 515 559
1, attached	1 862 737	1 674 696	869 317	805 379	668 846	74 785	61 748	188 041	14 721	65 505	55 166	52 649
2	3 264 856	2 698 345	1 633 935	1 064 410	797 042	145 224	122 144	566 511	27 359	211 188	171 088	156 876
3 or 4	3 846 455	3 264 230	1 954 981	1 309 249	1 063 988	148 054	97 207	582 225	32 153	222 809	171 847	155 416
5 to 9	3 949 553	3 475 298	1 983 906	1 491 392	1 282 488	131 584	77 320	474 255	29 733	190 526	134 804	119 192
10 to 19	3 934 394	3 597 302	1 966 161	1 631 141	1 464 752	105 123	61 266	337 092	23 755	149 849	89 868	73 620
20 to 49	3 029 921	2 850 853	1 812 108	1 038 745	955 358	59 027	24 360	179 068	13 597	89 047	47 504	28 920
50 or more	3 288 738	3 184 182	2 281 090	903 092	857 882	33 873	11 337	104 556	8 160	61 624	26 361	8 411
Mobile home or trailer	1 237 256	599 525	96 977	502 548	180 420	43 908	278 220	637 731	11 983	53 311	75 320	497 117
Other	478 427	387 096	216 273	170 823	124 984	17 148	28 691	91 331	2 931	22 009	21 313	45 078
Occupied housing units	**91 947 410**	**71 265 264**	**29 793 822**	**41 471 442**	**29 201 839**	**3 139 108**	**9 130 495**	**20 682 146**	**575 362**	**3 735 404**	**3 628 132**	**12 743 248**
AGE OF HOUSEHOLDER												
Owner-occupied housing units	**59 024 811**	**44 045 859**	**14 588 932**	**29 456 927**	**19 870 564**	**2 049 137**	**7 537 226**	**14 978 952**	**347 794**	**2 187 044**	**2 353 704**	**10 090 410**
Under 25 years	862 169	575 954	198 057	377 897	220 913	31 844	125 140	286 215	6 431	33 903	37 031	208 850
25 to 34 years	9 000 394	6 846 605	2 129 389	4 717 216	3 146 520	330 546	1 240 150	2 153 789	48 805	293 215	304 110	1 507 659
35 to 44 years	13 502 988	10 411 140	3 197 000	7 214 140	4 842 616	457 608	1 913 916	3 091 848	71 243	442 337	443 445	2 134 823
45 to 54 years	10 773 931	8 238 231	2 530 846	5 707 385	3 836 656	346 040	1 524 689	2 535 700	55 442	347 861	360 454	1 771 943
55 to 64 years	9 864 090	7 338 708	2 492 017	4 846 691	3 321 283	320 834	1 204 574	2 525 382	58 454	368 514	392 916	1 705 498
65 to 74 years	9 071 906	6 538 422	2 396 809	4 141 613	2 851 312	327 226	963 075	2 533 484	64 999	396 094	447 190	1 625 201
75 years and over	5 949 333	4 096 799	1 644 814	2 451 985	1 651 264	235 039	565 682	1 852 534	42 420	305 120	368 558	1 136 436
Renter-occupied housing units	**32 922 599**	**27 219 405**	**15 204 890**	**12 014 515**	**9 331 275**	**1 089 971**	**1 593 269**	**5 703 194**	**227 568**	**1 548 360**	**1 274 428**	**2 652 838**
Under 25 years	4 187 189	3 374 756	1 973 133	1 401 623	1 078 971	148 521	174 131	812 433	46 683	287 658	170 848	307 244
25 to 34 years	10 849 257	9 094 740	4 905 087	4 189 653	3 291 873	349 803	547 977	1 754 517	74 067	471 288	370 924	838 238
35 to 44 years	6 890 085	5 759 912	3 156 077	2 603 835	2 015 286	220 849	367 700	1 130 173	43 210	280 366	240 401	566 196
45 to 54 years	3 529 283	2 942 741	1 664 573	1 278 168	987 496	109 417	181 255	586 542	20 021	141 157	127 299	298 065
55 to 64 years	2 515 323	2 075 068	1 232 844	842 224	646 970	77 745	117 509	440 255	13 898	108 158	101 540	216 659
65 to 74 years	2 444 676	1 983 618	1 154 271	829 347	638 147	87 209	103 991	461 058	15 015	120 658	118 672	206 713
75 years and over	2 506 786	1 988 570	1 118 905	869 665	672 532	96 427	100 706	518 216	14 674	139 075	144 744	219 723

Table 16. **Utilization Characteristics: 1990**

[For definitions of terms and meanings of symbols, see text]

United States Inside and Outside Metropolitan Area	United States	Inside metropolitan area						Outside metropolitan area				
				Not in central city					Urban			
					Urban					Outside urbanized area		
		Total	In central city	Total	Inside urbanized area	Outside urbanized area	Rural	Total	Inside urbanized area	Place of 10,000 or more	Place of 2,500 to 9,999	Rural
ROOMS												
All housing units	**102 263 678**	**77 644 313**	**32 641 254**	**45 003 059**	**31 243 819**	**3 517 220**	**10 242 020**	**24 619 365**	**662 407**	**4 084 848**	**4 096 276**	**15 775 834**
1 room	1 941 253	1 638 797	1 140 106	498 691	386 367	40 988	71 336	302 456	10 285	56 611	44 283	191 277
2 rooms	4 219 329	3 504 157	2 145 468	1 358 689	1 044 957	119 249	194 483	715 172	27 175	162 397	133 642	391 958
3 rooms	10 695 285	8 717 412	4 914 070	3 803 342	2 938 441	327 105	537 796	1 977 873	62 599	436 884	397 320	1 081 070
4 rooms	19 149 396	14 119 434	6 536 846	7 582 588	5 228 252	693 894	1 660 442	5 029 962	147 273	852 120	858 864	3 171 705
5 rooms	22 136 448	15 998 139	6 600 460	9 397 679	6 234 735	829 593	2 333 351	6 138 309	150 170	953 428	1 014 340	4 020 371
6 rooms	18 990 381	14 156 601	5 412 127	8 744 474	5 887 050	688 160	2 169 264	4 833 780	117 880	751 497	780 254	3 184 149
7 rooms	11 592 274	8 838 090	2 867 438	5 970 652	4 130 345	396 166	1 444 141	2 754 184	68 621	420 000	428 867	1 836 696
8 rooms	7 059 472	5 544 577	1 569 787	3 974 790	2 826 514	225 667	922 609	1 514 895	39 207	233 471	232 163	1 010 054
9 or more rooms	6 479 840	5 127 106	1 454 952	3 672 154	2 567 158	196 398	908 598	1 352 734	39 197	218 440	206 543	888 554
Median	5.2	5.2	4.7	5.5	5.5	5.2	5.6	5.2	5.1	5.1	5.1	5.3
Owner-occupied housing units	**59 024 811**	**44 045 859**	**14 588 932**	**29 456 927**	**19 870 564**	**2 049 137**	**7 537 226**	**14 978 952**	**347 794**	**2 187 044**	**2 353 704**	**10 090 410**
1 room	138 128	92 883	46 845	46 038	27 019	3 160	15 859	45 245	533	2 958	4 732	37 022
2 rooms	553 871	418 924	189 942	228 982	155 429	16 278	57 275	134 947	3 104	13 996	18 216	99 631
3 rooms	1 951 092	1 467 769	602 083	865 686	603 338	61 274	201 074	483 323	10 223	54 445	67 023	351 632
4 rooms	6 712 441	4 507 263	1 573 487	2 933 776	1 796 052	237 101	900 623	2 205 178	45 621	265 118	322 758	1 571 681
5 rooms	13 455 461	9 480 456	3 367 769	6 112 687	3 896 204	511 963	1 704 520	3 975 005	83 183	563 358	638 028	2 690 436
6 rooms	14 450 417	10 861 648	3 832 703	7 028 945	4 736 001	518 532	1 774 412	3 588 769	82 369	551 028	581 558	2 373 814
7 rooms	9 783 837	7 590 632	2 347 845	5 242 787	3 661 907	330 608	1 250 272	2 193 205	55 373	343 750	348 412	1 445 670
8 rooms	6 199 624	4 964 907	1 351 828	3 613 079	2 599 451	196 575	817 053	1 234 717	33 307	200 556	196 491	804 363
9 or more rooms	5 779 940	4 661 377	1 276 430	3 384 947	2 395 163	173 646	816 138	1 118 563	34 081	191 835	176 486	716 161
Median	6.0	6.1	5.9	6.1	6.2	5.9	6.0	5.7	5.9	5.9	5.7	5.6
Renter-occupied housing units	**32 922 599**	**27 219 405**	**15 204 890**	**12 014 515**	**9 331 275**	**1 089 971**	**1 593 269**	**5 703 194**	**227 568**	**1 548 360**	**1 274 428**	**2 652 838**
1 room	1 450 705	1 337 381	965 801	371 580	318 517	28 345	24 718	113 324	7 536	43 457	26 564	35 767
2 rooms	3 049 832	2 695 521	1 731 438	964 083	800 433	83 221	80 429	354 311	18 450	126 743	88 652	120 466
3 rooms	7 116 936	6 153 689	3 715 439	2 438 250	2 017 920	214 725	205 605	963 247	41 024	321 739	258 334	342 150
4 rooms	9 558 092	7 835 477	4 183 997	3 651 480	2 836 534	348 028	466 918	1 722 615	75 303	484 306	400 219	762 787
5 rooms	6 390 435	5 134 806	2 663 455	2 471 351	1 872 279	227 702	371 370	1 255 629	45 659	312 363	266 635	630 972
6 rooms	3 211 247	2 499 436	1 266 713	1 232 723	886 175	116 494	230 054	711 811	24 522	157 811	138 630	390 848
7 rooms	1 218 088	901 792	404 768	497 024	343 244	42 300	111 480	316 296	8 789	59 270	55 091	193 146
8 rooms	537 441	385 552	158 936	226 616	151 802	17 434	57 380	151 889	3 542	24 436	23 130	100 781
9 or more rooms	389 823	275 751	114 343	161 408	104 371	11 722	45 315	114 072	2 743	18 235	17 173	75 921
Median	4.0	3.9	3.8	4.1	4.0	4.1	4.6	4.3	4.1	4.1	4.2	4.6
DURATION OF VACANCY												
Vacant-for-sale-only housing units	**1 260 233**	**937 317**	**360 230**	**577 087**	**387 656**	**51 163**	**138 268**	**322 916**	**9 080**	**50 379**	**58 909**	**204 548**
Less than 2 months	202 327	161 804	57 971	103 833	74 701	8 545	20 587	40 523	1 582	7 428	8 018	23 495
2 up to 6 months	456 667	366 631	133 621	233 010	163 392	19 590	50 028	90 036	3 513	16 745	17 118	52 660
6 or more months	601 239	408 882	168 638	240 244	149 563	23 028	67 653	192 357	3 985	26 206	33 773	128 393
Vacant-for-rent housing units	**3 046 638**	**2 463 752**	**1 429 003**	**1 034 749**	**793 250**	**98 996**	**142 503**	**582 886**	**21 308**	**148 677**	**133 240**	**279 661**
Less than 2 months	1 085 916	913 187	505 927	407 260	330 780	36 922	39 558	172 729	7 608	52 521	42 377	70 223
2 up to 6 months	1 173 045	964 528	560 923	403 605	312 282	36 072	55 251	208 517	8 773	53 567	48 605	97 572
6 or more months	787 677	586 037	362 153	223 884	150 188	26 002	47 694	201 640	4 927	42 589	42 258	111 866
PERSONS IN UNIT												
Owner-occupied housing units	**59 024 811**	**44 045 859**	**14 588 932**	**29 456 927**	**19 870 564**	**2 049 137**	**7 537 226**	**14 978 952**	**347 794**	**2 187 044**	**2 353 704**	**10 090 410**
1 person	11 005 717	8 028 743	3 223 493	4 805 250	3 334 758	378 855	1 091 637	2 976 974	70 899	489 512	552 421	1 864 142
2 persons	20 459 188	15 005 596	4 967 156	10 038 440	6 738 798	722 668	2 576 974	5 453 592	136 027	799 646	863 597	3 654 322
3 persons	10 758 497	8 172 734	2 533 344	5 639 390	3 789 217	362 691	1 487 482	2 585 763	57 407	358 542	371 386	1 798 428
4 persons	10 015 908	7 636 004	2 173 555	5 462 449	3 644 578	350 904	1 466 967	2 379 904	50 606	329 867	338 441	1 660 990
5 persons	4 333 756	3 300 655	988 901	2 311 754	1 545 532	151 714	614 508	1 033 101	20 833	138 854	147 905	725 509
6 persons	1 507 407	1 157 721	393 278	764 443	516 470	51 477	196 496	349 686	7 540	45 180	50 348	246 618
7 or more persons	944 338	744 406	309 205	435 201	301 211	30 828	103 162	199 932	4 482	25 443	29 606	140 401
Median	2.40	2.43	2.32	2.49	2.48	2.39	2.57	2.33	2.26	2.26	2.22	2.37
Renter-occupied housing units	**32 922 599**	**27 219 405**	**15 204 890**	**12 014 515**	**9 331 275**	**1 089 971**	**1 593 269**	**5 703 194**	**227 568**	**1 548 360**	**1 274 428**	**2 652 838**
1 person	11 574 703	9 692 783	5 765 867	3 926 916	3 162 185	349 987	414 744	1 881 920	76 469	575 227	474 613	755 611
2 persons	8 994 405	7 509 812	4 042 070	3 467 742	2 742 437	286 836	438 469	1 484 593	66 415	412 299	319 844	686 035
3 persons	5 211 772	4 249 135	2 260 747	1 988 388	1 505 957	187 535	294 896	962 637	38 415	247 865	205 136	471 221
4 persons	3 844 186	3 075 048	1 598 037	1 477 011	1 082 257	147 050	247 704	769 138	27 598	179 063	156 443	406 034
5 persons	1 855 182	1 485 645	809 838	675 807	487 141	69 660	119 006	369 537	11 647	81 828	72 259	203 803
6 persons	793 113	649 799	378 893	270 906	196 254	28 018	46 634	143 314	4 394	31 791	28 065	79 064
7 or more persons	649 238	557 183	349 438	207 745	155 044	20 885	31 816	92 055	2 630	20 287	18 068	51 070
Median	2.04	2.02	1.95	2.10	2.05	2.18	2.37	2.15	2.06	1.98	2.01	2.33
PERSONS PER ROOM												
Owner-occupied housing units	**59 024 811**	**44 045 859**	**14 588 932**	**29 456 927**	**19 870 564**	**2 049 137**	**7 537 226**	**14 978 952**	**347 794**	**2 187 044**	**2 353 704**	**10 090 410**
0.50 or less	41 557 203	31 209 613	10 373 936	20 835 677	14 326 062	1 428 665	5 080 950	10 347 590	259 100	1 611 957	1 712 121	6 764 412
0.51 to 0.75	10 485 276	7 825 860	2 386 350	5 439 510	3 562 304	368 784	1 508 422	2 659 416	56 099	350 376	373 336	1 879 605
0.76 to 1.00	5 371 931	3 801 493	1 309 664	2 491 829	1 521 890	193 951	775 988	1 570 438	26 795	179 770	211 127	1 152 746
1.01 to 1.50	1 103 951	810 891	334 132	476 759	308 885	38 670	129 204	293 060	4 492	32 770	40 870	214 928
1.51 or more	506 450	398 002	184 850	213 152	151 423	19 067	42 662	108 448	1 308	12 171	16 250	78 719
Mean	.45	.44	.44	.44	.44	.45	.46	.45	.42	.42	.43	.46
Renter-occupied housing units	**32 922 599**	**27 219 405**	**15 204 890**	**12 014 515**	**9 331 275**	**1 089 971**	**1 593 269**	**5 703 194**	**227 568**	**1 548 360**	**1 274 428**	**2 652 838**
0.50 or less	18 283 341	14 981 232	8 178 563	6 802 669	5 333 624	593 111	875 934	3 302 109	130 217	913 649	759 690	1 498 553
0.51 to 0.75	6 208 119	5 069 783	2 678 986	2 390 797	1 826 157	222 013	342 627	1 138 336	46 884	301 986	244 283	545 183
0.76 to 1.00	5 492 741	4 574 179	2 696 829	1 877 350	1 424 853	185 240	267 257	918 562	38 239	244 343	196 253	439 727
1.01 to 1.50	1 532 981	1 300 919	800 738	500 181	381 138	50 490	68 553	232 062	8 162	56 842	48 933	118 125
1.51 or more	1 405 417	1 293 292	849 774	443 518	365 503	39 117	38 898	112 125	4 066	31 540	25 269	51 250
Mean	.59	.60	.62	.58	.58	.60	.56	.55	.56	.56	.55	.55
Occupied housing units	**91 947 410**	**71 265 264**	**29 793 822**	**41 471 442**	**29 201 839**	**3 139 108**	**9 130 495**	**20 682 146**	**575 362**	**3 735 404**	**3 628 132**	**12 743 248**
HOUSEHOLDER 65 YEARS AND OVER												
Occupied housing units	**19 972 701**	**14 607 409**	**6 314 799**	**8 292 610**	**5 813 255**	**745 901**	**1 733 454**	**5 365 292**	**137 108**	**960 947**	**1 079 164**	**3 188 073**
1-person households	8 824 845	6 436 294	3 064 396	3 371 898	2 397 622	344 054	630 222	2 388 551	57 910	483 224	546 764	1 300 653
Mean number of persons per room	.80	.83	.81	.84	.83	.80	.90	.71	.71	.69	.64	.73
Units in structure:												
1, detached or attached	13 628 399	9 455 288	3 667 516	5 787 772	3 888 690	517 485	1 381 597	4 173 111	93 670	700 163	807 553	2 571 725
2 or more	4 786 910	4 181 072	2 420 995	1 760 077	1 514 142	153 369	92 566	605 838	28 330	211 560	198 145	167 803
Mobile home, trailer, or other	1 557 392	971 049	226 288	744 761	410 423	75 047	259 291	586 343	15 108	49 224	73 466	448 545
Specified owner	10 877 683	7 938 029	3 132 428	4 805 601	3 435 118	437 405	933 078	2 939 654	80 256	590 604	679 758	1 589 036
Mean value (dollars)	94 200	108 400	93 700	118 000	130 100	79 700	91 300	55 900	94 500	56 900	53 400	54 700
Specified renter	4 809 275	3 906 385	2 253 717	1 652 668	1 296 274	180 625	175 769	902 890	29 230	255 848	258 811	359 001
Mean contract rent (dollars)	344	372	344	410	441	277	293	209	314	234	200	185
With meals included in rent	176 860	161 832	82 187	79 645	69 822	4 217	5 606	15 028	1 505	5 936	3 625	3 962
Mean contract rent (dollars)	895	911	856	968	976	837	972	720	836	744	687	671
No meals included in rent	4 304 135	3 546 469	2 094 699	1 451 770	1 159 844	163 484	128 442	757 666	25 635	233 409	233 354	265 268
No cash rent	328 280	198 084	76 831	121 253	66 608	12 924	41 721	130 196	2 090	16 503	21 832	89 771

Table 17. Financial Characteristics: 1990

[For definitions of terms and meanings of symbols, see text]

United States Inside and Outside Metropolitan Area

	United States	Inside metropolitan area: Total	In central city	Not in central city: Total	Urban: Inside urbanized area	Urban: Outside urbanized area	Rural	Outside metropolitan area: Total	Urban: Inside urbanized area	Outside urbanized area: Place of 10,000 or more	Outside urbanized area: Place of 2,500 to 9,999	Rural
VALUE												
Specified owner-occupied housing units	44 918 000	35 118 012	11 725 643	23 392 369	16 683 355	1 681 000	5 028 014	9 799 988	272 555	1 853 252	1 932 418	5 741 763
Less than $20,000	1 937 962	845 131	475 157	369 974	140 492	55 989	173 493	1 092 831	5 912	142 423	210 474	734 022
$20,000 to $29,999	2 251 761	1 179 496	662 122	517 374	233 612	79 191	204 571	1 072 265	9 730	191 470	237 321	633 744
$30,000 to $39,999	3 309 485	1 937 133	1 021 163	915 970	476 193	129 907	309 870	1 372 352	19 181	272 717	308 736	771 718
$40,000 to $49,999	3 903 314	2 553 200	1 197 723	1 355 477	784 907	173 341	397 229	1 350 114	28 287	273 379	293 171	755 277
$50,000 to $59,999	3 940 018	2 829 676	1 176 215	1 653 461	1 045 022	179 812	428 627	1 110 342	30 876	226 686	223 895	628 885
$60,000 to $69,999	4 070 534	3 110 044	1 164 106	1 945 938	1 302 239	178 786	464 913	960 490	31 570	197 440	183 372	548 108
$70,000 to $79,999	3 633 633	2 908 408	968 238	1 940 170	1 346 097	153 647	440 426	725 225	26 645	147 077	130 801	420 702
$80,000 to $89,999	2 895 172	2 405 826	740 475	1 665 351	1 181 821	122 035	361 495	489 346	19 296	99 401	85 098	285 551
$90,000 to $99,999	2 418 101	2 070 210	594 764	1 475 446	1 071 315	101 163	302 968	347 891	15 118	71 301	59 368	202 104
$100,000 to $124,999	3 808 158	3 331 910	862 952	2 468 958	1 820 128	151 005	497 825	476 248	23 895	89 580	75 051	287 722
$125,000 to $149,999	2 965 099	2 680 655	630 566	2 050 089	1 564 705	112 291	373 093	284 444	20 260	52 819	42 989	168 376
$150,000 to $174,999	2 316 164	2 136 998	485 466	1 651 532	1 290 200	79 341	281 991	179 166	13 583	31 371	27 076	107 136
$175,000 to $199,999	1 700 998	1 601 440	370 103	1 231 337	996 385	48 927	186 025	99 558	7 930	18 287	15 013	58 328
$200,000 to $249,999	2 084 263	1 977 996	473 173	1 504 823	1 228 010	51 003	225 810	106 267	8 661	19 147	16 629	61 830
$250,000 to $299,999	1 292 638	1 235 762	308 295	927 467	763 584	27 132	136 751	56 876	4 683	9 653	9 582	32 958
$300,000 to $399,999	1 206 814	1 164 584	291 052	873 532	728 645	21 066	123 821	42 230	3 752	6 420	7 612	24 446
$400,000 to $499,999	501 342	486 984	124 186	362 798	305 299	7 430	50 069	14 358	1 334	1 972	2 598	8 454
$500,000 or more	682 544	662 559	179 887	482 672	404 701	8 934	69 037	19 985	1 842	2 109	3 632	12 402
Median (dollars)	78 300	89 100	71 600	99 000	110 400	72 700	82 600	50 100	73 800	51 800	46 900	49 700
Mean (dollars)	111 700	125 300	105 200	135 400	146 400	93 800	112 600	62 700	97 300	63 300	58 700	62 300
Specified vacant-for-sale-only housing units	906 113	680 455	251 051	429 404	291 565	40 146	97 693	225 658	6 311	40 895	47 258	131 194
Less than $20,000	82 803	33 947	20 569	13 378	4 855	2 530	5 993	48 856	233	7 499	10 582	30 542
$20,000 to $39,999	150 734	87 574	51 668	35 906	18 928	5 794	11 184	63 160	862	12 730	15 527	34 041
$40,000 to $59,999	151 755	109 239	52 017	57 222	37 381	6 866	12 975	42 516	1 235	8 610	9 131	23 540
$60,000 to $79,999	125 770	99 762	38 556	61 206	42 231	5 995	12 980	26 008	949	4 946	4 966	15 147
$80,000 to $99,999	81 653	67 426	21 340	46 086	31 864	4 240	9 982	14 227	655	2 647	2 348	8 577
$100,000 to $149,999	115 455	99 872	25 812	74 060	51 753	6 328	15 979	15 583	1 058	2 511	2 284	9 730
$150,000 to $199,999	75 706	68 328	15 259	53 069	38 025	4 185	10 859	7 378	603	1 002	1 105	4 668
$200,000 to $249,999	39 829	36 740	8 013	28 727	21 364	1 744	5 619	3 089	321	426	439	1 903
$250,000 to $299,999	26 475	24 646	5 391	19 255	14 457	976	3 822	1 829	138	247	294	1 150
$300,000 or more	55 933	52 921	12 426	40 495	30 707	1 488	8 300	3 012	257	277	582	1 896
Median (dollars)	69 800	82 600	60 600	100 600	110 000	76 000	90 700	40 300	77 200	40 400	36 800	40 700
Mean (dollars)	108 300	124 600	94 800	142 000	150 900	103 700	130 900	59 300	108 000	54 800	53 100	60 500
Owner-occupied mobile homes or trailers	4 896 741	2 597 510	387 466	2 210 044	887 334	178 180	1 144 530	2 299 231	38 929	132 727	210 387	1 917 188
Median (dollars)	18 600	20 300	16 600	21 100	20 400	22 700	21 400	16 900	19 000	13 600	15 000	17 300
Mean (dollars)	28 100	30 400	26 100	31 200	29 600	32 400	32 200	25 500	27 500	21 900	23 500	25 900
CONTRACT RENT												
Specified renter-occupied housing units	31 966 779	26 749 099	15 072 174	11 676 925	9 227 959	1 072 574	1 376 392	5 217 680	224 852	1 528 919	1 253 461	2 210 448
Less than $100	1 405 990	891 941	595 376	296 565	171 993	58 504	66 068	514 049	11 014	116 132	144 667	242 236
$100 to $149	1 557 814	1 022 946	685 589	337 357	199 899	58 502	78 956	534 868	12 832	123 021	140 714	258 301
$150 to $199	1 961 716	1 247 819	819 337	428 482	234 526	78 083	115 873	713 897	18 710	185 201	186 454	323 532
$200 to $249	2 552 687	1 799 017	1 175 371	623 646	354 116	109 606	159 924	753 670	24 192	223 891	193 887	311 700
$250 to $299	3 046 821	2 384 064	1 579 003	805 061	520 225	129 647	155 189	662 757	27 219	235 933	168 411	231 194
$300 to $349	3 213 961	2 732 905	1 755 028	977 877	711 828	126 671	139 378	481 056	23 777	187 485	112 662	157 132
$350 to $399	3 189 292	2 848 488	1 742 384	1 106 104	878 512	117 122	110 470	340 804	22 683	141 199	75 231	101 691
$400 to $449	2 709 613	2 494 315	1 398 449	1 095 866	920 166	88 871	86 829	215 298	18 123	84 703	45 392	67 080
$450 to $499	2 212 210	2 082 581	1 098 588	983 993	861 178	64 518	58 297	129 629	13 725	51 907	25 585	38 412
$500 to $549	1 903 134	1 809 781	902 324	907 457	806 329	47 583	53 545	93 353	10 464	32 545	18 902	31 442
$550 to $599	1 404 012	1 349 547	631 358	718 189	650 193	32 723	35 273	54 465	6 900	19 545	10 815	17 205
$600 to $649	1 231 731	1 184 637	541 024	643 613	582 417	27 625	33 571	47 094	6 362	15 562	9 528	15 642
$650 to $699	942 169	912 064	397 580	514 484	470 506	20 631	23 347	30 105	4 139	9 995	6 257	9 714
$700 to $749	707 321	686 219	295 698	390 521	359 811	13 667	17 043	21 102	3 094	6 378	4 749	6 881
$750 to $999	1 626 608	1 582 906	690 221	892 685	826 088	27 239	39 358	43 702	6 374	13 434	10 472	13 422
$1,000 or more	825 456	805 154	396 312	408 842	377 440	9 237	22 165	20 302	3 211	5 507	5 375	6 209
No cash rent	1 476 244	914 715	368 532	546 183	302 732	62 345	181 106	561 529	12 033	76 481	94 360	378 655
Median (dollars)	372	400	369	444	476	324	306	235	323	265	224	211
Mean (dollars)	414	442	411	482	514	354	352	260	361	283	249	238
Specified vacant-for-rent housing units	3 011 342	2 449 887	1 424 676	1 025 211	790 846	98 568	135 797	561 455	21 250	148 180	132 697	259 328
Less than $100	116 862	66 383	47 584	18 799	8 901	3 333	6 565	50 479	705	8 847	11 797	29 130
$100 to $199	372 097	208 298	140 884	67 414	31 817	12 080	23 517	163 799	2 827	36 260	39 988	84 724
$200 to $299	632 342	465 052	321 040	144 012	85 715	22 800	35 497	167 290	4 454	49 303	39 950	73 583
$300 to $399	623 909	541 656	356 302	185 354	140 214	20 733	24 407	82 253	4 006	28 510	18 564	31 173
$400 to $499	429 832	394 864	216 592	178 272	150 927	13 543	13 802	34 968	2 686	11 490	7 555	13 237
$500 to $599	288 992	271 368	125 276	146 092	127 535	8 806	9 751	17 624	1 642	4 974	4 088	6 920
$600 to $749	256 745	243 767	102 499	141 268	124 997	6 912	9 359	12 978	2 013	3 583	2 488	4 894
$750 to $999	146 135	138 964	59 818	79 146	70 728	3 591	4 827	7 171	801	2 005	1 515	2 850
$1,000 or more	144 428	119 535	54 681	64 854	50 012	6 770	8 072	24 893	2 116	3 208	6 752	12 817
Median (dollars)	359	388	355	453	484	350	306	230	364	256	227	213
Mean (dollars)	421	449	410	504	534	426	390	299	459	298	301	286
MEALS INCLUDED IN RENT												
Specified renter-occupied housing units	31 966 779	26 749 099	15 072 174	11 676 925	9 227 959	1 072 574	1 376 392	5 217 680	224 852	1 528 919	1 253 461	2 210 448
With meals included in rent	261 001	234 982	129 522	105 460	90 024	6 406	9 030	26 019	2 041	9 079	6 101	8 798
Mean (dollars)	747	769	697	858	882	686	745	543	718	608	535	442
No meals included in rent	30 229 534	25 599 402	14 574 120	11 025 282	8 835 203	1 003 823	1 186 256	4 630 132	210 778	1 443 359	1 153 000	1 822 995
No cash rent	1 476 244	914 715	368 532	546 183	302 732	62 345	181 106	561 529	12 033	76 481	94 360	378 655

Table 176. Summary of General Housing Characteristics: 1990

[For definitions of terms and meanings of symbols, see text]

United States Region and Division State	All persons	All housing units Total	Median rooms	Percent 1 unit, detached or attached	Percent In buildings with 10 or more units	Occupied Total	Median persons in unit	Mean number of persons per room	Owner	With 1.01 or more persons per room	With householder 65 years and over	1-person households	Specified owner, median value (dollars)	Specified renter Median contract rent (dollars)	Percent with meals included in rent	Vacancy rate Homeowner	Rental
United States	248 709 873	102 263 678	5.2	64.3	12.9	91 947 410	2.29	.49	64.2	4.9	21.7	24.6	78 300	372	.9	2.1	8.5
REGION AND DIVISION																	
Northeast	50 809 229	20 810 637	5.3	57.2	16.6	18 872 713	2.29	.47	61.3	3.9	23.4	25.6	124 400	427	.6	1.9	6.3
New England	13 206 943	5 570 296	5.3	58.5	11.1	4 942 714	2.29	.46	63.1	2.3	22.5	24.8	153 100	473	.6	1.8	7.5
Middle Atlantic	37 602 286	15 240 341	5.3	56.8	18.7	13 929 999	2.29	.48	60.7	4.5	23.8	25.9	106 700	415	.6	1.9	5.9
Midwest	59 668 632	24 492 718	5.4	69.3	10.1	22 316 975	2.28	.46	68.1	2.5	22.4	25.0	62 300	316	.9	1.5	7.8
East North Central	42 008 942	17 027 966	5.4	68.0	10.3	15 596 590	2.30	.47	67.7	2.6	21.9	24.7	64 200	324	.9	1.4	7.4
West North Central	17 659 690	7 464 752	5.4	72.1	9.5	6 720 385	2.23	.45	69.2	2.2	23.6	25.8	57 800	294	.9	1.9	9.0
South	85 445 930	36 065 102	5.1	65.8	11.3	31 822 254	2.30	.48	66.2	4.8	21.7	24.0	65 800	321	.8	2.5	11.1
South Atlantic	43 566 853	18 718 982	5.2	63.3	12.6	16 503 063	2.26	.47	66.8	4.1	22.5	24.1	76 700	368	1.0	2.5	10.4
East South Central	15 176 284	6 213 714	5.2	69.9	6.5	5 651 671	2.33	.48	69.6	3.4	22.7	23.6	52 600	248	.6	1.9	9.2
West South Central	26 702 793	11 132 406	5.0	67.7	11.8	9 667 520	2.34	.52	63.3	6.8	19.9	24.1	56 000	303	.7	3.1	12.9
West	52 786 082	20 895 221	4.9	62.9	15.2	18 935 468	2.31	.53	59.0	9.1	19.1	23.9	126 200	471	1.1	2.2	7.3
Mountain	13 658 776	5 863 976	5.0	63.5	12.8	5 033 336	2.27	.49	64.3	5.4	19.4	24.4	75 200	348	1.0	3.0	11.7
Pacific	39 127 306	15 031 245	4.8	62.7	16.1	13 902 132	2.33	.55	57.1	10.5	19.0	23.7	165 500	518	1.1	1.9	5.9
STATE																	
New England	13 206 943	5 570 296	5.3	58.5	11.1	4 942 714	2.29	.46	63.1	2.3	22.5	24.8	153 100	473	.6	1.8	7.5
Maine	1 227 928	587 045	5.2	66.5	4.5	465 312	2.28	.46	70.5	1.7	22.3	23.3	86 800	357	.8	1.8	8.4
New Hampshire	1 109 252	503 904	5.3	63.7	9.1	411 186	2.34	.47	68.2	1.6	18.8	22.0	129 400	477	.6	2.7	11.8
Vermont	562 758	271 214	5.4	65.5	3.8	210 650	2.29	.45	69.0	1.7	20.1	23.4	95 400	375	.2	2.1	7.5
Massachusetts	6 016 425	2 472 711	5.3	53.6	13.7	2 247 110	2.28	.47	59.3	2.5	23.0	25.8	162 800	504	.5	1.7	6.9
Rhode Island	1 003 464	414 572	5.2	55.5	10.4	377 977	2.26	.47	59.5	2.3	25.0	26.2	133 500	412	.7	1.5	7.9
Connecticut	3 287 116	1 320 850	5.5	61.7	11.8	1 230 479	2.30	.45	65.6	2.3	22.4	24.2	177 800	508	.9	1.9	6.9
Middle Atlantic	37 602 286	15 240 341	5.3	56.8	18.7	13 929 999	2.29	.48	60.7	4.5	23.8	25.9	106 700	415	.6	1.9	5.9
New York	17 990 455	7 226 891	4.9	44.7	27.6	6 639 322	2.28	.51	52.2	6.5	22.6	27.2	131 600	423	.5	1.9	4.9
New Jersey	7 730 188	3 075 310	5.5	60.9	14.7	2 794 711	2.38	.47	64.9	3.9	22.9	23.1	162 300	517	.6	2.5	7.4
Pennsylvania	11 881 643	4 938 140	5.7	71.8	8.0	4 495 966	2.26	.44	70.6	1.8	26.1	25.6	69 500	319	1.1	1.5	7.2
East North Central	42 008 942	17 027 966	5.4	68.0	10.3	15 596 590	2.30	.47	67.7	2.6	21.9	24.7	64 200	324	.9	1.4	7.4
Ohio	10 847 115	4 371 945	5.6	69.6	9.5	4 087 546	2.29	.45	67.5	1.8	22.3	25.0	63 200	296	1.1	1.3	7.5
Indiana	5 544 159	2 246 046	5.4	72.6	7.5	2 065 355	2.30	.46	70.2	2.2	21.9	24.1	53 300	290	.9	1.5	8.3
Illinois	11 430 602	4 506 275	5.3	60.2	14.7	4 202 240	2.30	.48	64.2	4.0	21.9	25.7	80 300	367	.8	1.5	8.0
Michigan	9 295 297	3 847 926	5.4	72.9	8.8	3 419 331	2.33	.47	71.0	2.6	21.0	23.7	60 600	341	.8	1.3	7.2
Wisconsin	4 891 769	2 055 774	5.3	67.7	8.5	1 822 118	2.28	.46	66.7	2.1	22.8	24.3	62 300	329	.8	1.2	4.7
West North Central	17 659 690	7 464 752	5.4	72.1	9.5	6 720 385	2.23	.45	69.2	2.2	23.6	25.8	57 800	294	.9	1.9	9.0
Minnesota	4 375 099	1 848 445	5.5	70.3	15.0	1 647 853	2.26	.44	71.8	2.1	21.3	25.1	74 000	384	1.1	1.5	7.9
Iowa	2 776 755	1 143 669	5.5	76.1	6.7	1 064 325	2.20	.43	70.0	1.5	25.8	25.9	45 900	260	.8	1.5	6.4
Missouri	5 117 073	2 199 129	5.2	70.3	7.8	1 961 206	2.23	.46	68.8	2.5	23.9	26.0	59 700	281	.9	2.2	10.7
North Dakota	638 800	276 340	5.3	66.3	11.0	240 878	2.22	.44	65.6	2.0	24.5	26.5	50 700	266	.6	2.8	9.0
South Dakota	696 004	292 436	5.3	70.9	7.4	259 034	2.22	.46	66.1	3.0	25.7	26.4	45 200	241	.7	1.8	7.3
Nebraska	1 578 385	660 621	5.5	74.9	8.9	602 363	2.21	.43	66.5	1.7	24.0	26.5	50 400	282	.8	1.7	7.7
Kansas	2 477 574	1 044 112	5.4	74.9	7.2	944 726	2.22	.44	67.9	2.5	23.4	25.9	52 000	283	1.1	2.3	11.1
South Atlantic	43 566 853	18 718 982	5.2	63.3	12.6	16 503 063	2.26	.47	66.8	4.1	22.5	24.1	76 700	368	1.0	2.5	10.4
Delaware	666 168	289 919	5.8	67.7	11.2	247 497	2.32	.43	70.2	2.3	20.6	23.2	100 100	424	1.1	2.3	7.8
Maryland	4 781 468	1 891 917	5.9	70.4	15.6	1 748 991	2.37	.44	65.0	3.0	18.5	22.6	116 500	472	1.1	1.6	6.8
District of Columbia	606 900	278 489	4.0	38.0	42.5	249 634	1.82	.50	38.9	8.2	21.0	41.5	123 900	439	1.0	3.1	7.9
Virginia	6 187 358	2 496 334	5.6	70.0	11.5	2 291 830	2.33	.44	66.3	2.8	18.4	22.9	89 600	410	.9	2.1	8.1
West Virginia	1 793 477	781 295	5.3	71.4	3.7	688 557	2.29	.45	74.1	1.9	26.6	24.5	47 900	217	.3	2.2	10.1
North Carolina	6 628 637	2 818 193	5.1	67.6	5.4	2 517 026	2.28	.47	68.0	2.9	20.8	23.7	65 500	282	.8	1.8	9.2
South Carolina	3 486 703	1 424 155	5.2	65.4	5.6	1 258 044	2.37	.49	69.8	4.1	20.6	22.4	61 100	273	.6	1.7	11.5
Georgia	6 478 216	2 638 418	5.3	64.9	8.8	2 366 615	2.37	.48	64.9	4.0	17.8	22.7	71 300	343	.7	2.5	12.2
Florida	12 937 926	6 100 262	4.8	55.2	18.5	5 134 869	2.15	.49	67.2	5.8	28.8	25.5	76 600	402	1.4	3.4	12.4
East South Central	15 176 284	6 213 714	5.2	69.9	6.5	5 651 671	2.33	.48	69.6	3.4	22.7	23.6	52 600	248	.6	1.9	9.2
Kentucky	3 685 296	1 506 845	5.2	68.8	6.4	1 379 782	2.34	.47	69.6	2.6	22.6	23.3	50 400	250	.7	1.6	8.2
Tennessee	4 877 185	2 026 067	5.2	69.8	8.2	1 853 725	2.29	.46	68.0	2.7	21.8	23.9	58 000	272	.7	2.1	9.6
Alabama	4 040 587	1 670 379	5.3	69.8	6.1	1 506 790	2.32	.47	70.5	3.5	23.1	23.8	53 100	226	.4	1.8	9.3
Mississippi	2 573 216	1 010 423	5.2	72.0	4.1	911 374	2.40	.51	71.5	5.8	23.8	23.4	45 600	213	.7	1.9	9.5
West South Central	26 702 793	11 132 406	5.0	67.7	11.8	9 667 520	2.34	.52	63.3	6.8	19.9	24.1	56 000	303	.7	3.1	12.9
Arkansas	2 350 725	1 000 667	5.0	72.6	4.4	891 179	2.27	.50	69.6	3.7	25.9	24.0	46 300	226	.7	2.4	10.4
Louisiana	4 219 973	1 716 241	5.0	67.8	7.3	1 499 269	2.41	.52	65.9	6.0	20.7	23.7	58 200	259	.5	2.7	12.5
Oklahoma	3 145 585	1 406 499	5.1	73.8	7.1	1 206 135	2.23	.48	68.1	3.3	23.2	25.6	48 100	258	.6	3.7	14.7
Texas	16 986 510	7 008 999	4.9	65.7	14.8	6 070 937	2.37	.53	60.9	8.1	18.2	23.9	59 600	325	.7	3.2	13.0
Mountain	13 658 776	5 863 976	5.0	63.5	12.8	5 033 336	2.27	.49	64.3	5.4	19.4	24.4	75 200	348	1.0	3.0	11.7
Montana	799 065	361 155	5.1	68.1	4.7	306 163	2.20	.46	67.3	2.9	22.7	26.3	56 100	251	1.9	2.9	9.6
Idaho	1 006 749	413 327	5.3	71.4	4.2	360 723	2.31	.47	70.1	4.2	21.8	22.4	57 900	260	1.0	2.0	7.3
Wyoming	453 588	203 411	5.2	66.6	5.1	168 839	2.29	.45	67.8	2.8	18.5	24.5	61 600	267	.6	3.9	14.4
Colorado	3 294 394	1 477 349	5.3	65.8	16.9	1 282 489	2.21	.44	62.2	3.0	16.6	26.6	81 700	361	1.0	3.3	11.4
New Mexico	1 515 069	632 058	4.9	65.8	7.6	542 709	2.37	.53	67.4	7.9	19.6	23.0	69 900	310	.7	2.3	11.4
Arizona	3 665 228	1 659 430	4.7	58.9	15.5	1 368 843	2.23	.49	64.2	7.4	22.1	24.7	79 300	369	1.4	3.6	15.3
Utah	1 722 850	598 388	5.5	69.7	10.4	537 273	2.67	.52	68.1	5.5	18.0	18.9	68 700	300	.7	2.4	8.6
Nevada	1 201 833	518 858	4.7	50.6	17.3	466 297	2.19	.52	54.8	6.4	17.3	25.7	95 500	445	.6	2.3	9.1
Pacific	39 127 306	15 031 245	4.8	62.7	16.1	13 902 132	2.33	.55	57.1	10.5	19.0	23.7	165 500	518	1.1	1.9	5.9
Washington	4 866 692	2 032 378	5.2	65.0	13.5	1 872 431	2.21	.46	62.6	3.9	19.7	25.4	92 800	382	1.3	1.3	5.8
Oregon	2 842 321	1 193 567	5.2	66.7	9.9	1 103 313	2.19	.44	63.1	3.6	22.8	25.3	66 600	344	1.7	1.4	5.3
California	29 760 021	11 182 882	4.8	62.0	17.0	10 381 206	2.35	.57	55.6	12.3	18.7	23.4	195 500	561	1.0	2.0	5.9
Alaska	550 043	232 608	4.6	60.3	9.1	188 915	2.46	.56	56.1	8.6	7.5	22.1	94 400	502	.3	4.5	8.5
Hawaii	1 108 229	389 810	4.3	60.8	25.7	356 267	2.60	.67	53.9	15.9	20.2	19.4	245 300	599	.4	.8	5.4

U.S. Department of Commerce
Economics and Statistics Administration
BUREAU OF THE CENSUS

CENSUS '90

1990 CP-S-1-2

1990 Census of Population

Detailed Ancestry Groups for States

Table 2. Persons Who Reported at Least One Specific Ancestry Group: 1990

United States	Persons who reported at least one specific ancestry		Persons who reported first ancestry	Persons who reported second ancestry	Percent	
	Total	Percent of total[1]			First ancestry	Second ancestry
Total --	**248 709 873**	**100.0**	**224 788 502**	**73 771 208**	**90.4**	**29.7**

WESTERN EUROPE (NON-HISPANIC GROUPS)

Alsatian	16 465	0.0	9 683	6 782	58.8	41.2
Austrian[2]	864 783	0.3	542 138	322 645	62.7	37.3
Basque	47 956	0.0	37 842	10 114	78.9	21.1
Basque, French	6 001	0.0	4 961	1 040	82.7	17.3
Basque, Spanish	7 620	0.0	6 681	939	87.7	12.3
Basque, n.e.c.	34 335	0.0	26 200	8 135	76.3	23.7
Bavarian	4 348	0.0	2 833	1 515	65.2	34.8
Belgian[3]	380 498	0.2	239 439	141 059	62.9	37.1
British	1 119 154	0.4	867 255	251 899	77.5	22.5
Celtic	29 652	0.0	22 966	6 686	77.5	22.5
Cornish	3 991	0.0	2 237	1 754	56.1	43.9
Cypriot	4 897	0.0	4 678	219	95.5	4.5
Cypriot, Greek	2 197	0.0	2 161	36	98.4	1.6
Cypriot, Turkish	289	0.0	289	0	100.0	0.0
Cypriot, n.e.c.	2 411	0.0	2 228	183	92.4	7.6
Danish	1 634 669	0.7	980 868	653 801	60.0	40.0
Dutch	6 227 089	2.5	3 475 410	2 751 679	55.8	44.2
English	32 651 788	13.1	21 834 160	10 817 628	66.9	33.1
Finnish	658 870	0.3	465 070	193 800	70.6	29.4
Flemish	14 157	0.0	8 636	5 521	61.0	39.0
French[4]	10 320 935	4.1	6 194 501	4 126 434	60.0	40.0
German[5]	57 947 374	23.3	45 555 748	12 391 626	78.6	21.4
Greek[6]	1 110 373	0.4	921 782	188 591	83.0	17.0
Icelander	40 529	0.0	27 171	13 358	67.0	33.0
Irish[7]	38 735 539	15.6	22 695 454	16 040 085	58.6	41.4
Italian[8]	14 664 550	5.9	11 246 781	3 417 769	76.7	23.3
Luxemburger	49 061	0.0	28 846	20 215	58.8	41.2
Maltese	39 600	0.0	30 292	9 308	76.5	23.5
Manx	6 317	0.0	3 806	2 511	60.3	39.7
Northern Irish	4 009	0.0	2 832	1 177	70.6	29.4
Norwegian	3 869 395	1.6	2 517 760	1 351 635	65.1	34.9
Portuguese	1 153 351	0.5	900 060	253 291	78.0	22.0
Azores Islander	4 310	0.0	2 873	1 437	66.7	33.3
Madeira Islander	184	0.0	106	78	57.6	42.4
Portuguese, n.e.c.	1 148 857	0.5	897 081	251 776	78.1	21.9
Prussian	25 469	0.0	19 184	6 285	75.3	24.7
Saxon	4 519	0.0	2 658	1 861	58.8	41.2
Scandinavian	678 880	0.3	480 646	198 234	70.8	29.2
Scotch-Irish[9]	5 617 773	2.3	4 334 197	1 283 576	77.2	22.8
Scottish	5 393 581	2.2	3 315 306	2 078 275	61.5	38.5
Sicilian	50 389	0.0	40 034	10 355	79.4	20.6
Swedish	4 680 863	1.9	2 881 950	1 798 913	61.6	38.4
Swiss	1 045 495	0.4	607 833	437 662	58.1	41.9
Tirol	5 748	0.0	3 718	2 030	64.7	35.3
Welsh	2 033 893	0.8	1 038 603	995 290	51.1	48.9
West German	3 885	0.0	3 509	376	90.3	9.7
Western European*	42 409	0.0	41 664	745	98.2	1.8
Other Western European, n.e.c.	2 005	0.0	1 328	677	66.2	33.8

EASTERN EUROPE AND SOVIET UNION

Albanian	47 710	0.0	38 361	9 349	80.4	19.6
Belorussian	4 277	0.0	3 471	806	81.2	18.8
Bulgarian	29 595	0.0	20 894	8 701	70.6	29.4
Carpath Rusyn	7 602	0.0	6 927	675	91.1	8.9
Central European	5 604	0.0	5 434	170	97.0	3.0
Croatian	544 270	0.2	409 458	134 812	75.2	24.8
Czech[10]	1 296 411	0.5	769 427	526 984	59.4	40.6
Czechoslovakian	315 285	0.1	240 489	74 796	76.3	23.7
Estonian	26 762	0.0	20 996	5 766	78.5	21.5
European*	466 718	0.2	444 107	22 611	95.2	4.8
German Russian/Volga	10 153	0.0	9 833	320	96.8	3.2
Hungarian	1 582 302	0.6	997 545	584 757	63.0	37.0
Latvian	100 331	0.0	75 747	24 584	75.5	24.5
Lithuanian	811 865	0.3	526 089	285 776	64.8	35.2
Macedonian	20 365	0.0	16 113	4 252	79.1	20.9
Moravian	3 781	0.0	2 660	1 121	70.4	29.6
Northern European*	65 993	0.0	64 758	1 235	98.1	1.9
Polish	9 366 106	3.8	6 542 844	2 823 262	69.9	30.1
Rom	5 693	0.0	3 353	2 340	58.9	41.1
Romanian	365 544	0.1	235 774	129 770	64.5	35.5
Russian[11]	2 952 987	1.2	2 115 232	837 755	71.6	28.4
Ruthenian	3 776	0.0	3 010	766	79.7	20.3
Serbian	116 795	0.0	89 583	27 212	76.7	23.3
Slavic*	76 931	0.0	43 301	33 630	56.3	43.7
Slovak	1 882 897	0.8	1 210 652	672 245	64.3	35.7
Slovene	124 437	0.1	87 500	36 937	70.3	29.7
Soviet Union	7 729	0.0	6 080	1 649	78.7	21.3
Ukrainian	740 803	0.3	514 085	226 718	69.4	30.6
Windish	3 189	0.0	1 935	1 254	60.7	39.3
Yugoslavian*	257 994	0.1	184 952	73 042	71.7	28.3
Other Eastern European and Soviet Union, n.e.c.	132 332	0.1	123 717	8 615	93.5	6.5

Table 2. Persons Who Reported at Least One Specific Ancestry Group: 1990—Con.

United States	Persons who reported at least one specific ancestry		Persons who reported first ancestry	Persons who reported second ancestry	Percent	
	Total	Percent of total[1]			First ancestry	Second ancestry

CENTRAL AND SOUTH AMERICA (HISPANIC GROUPS) AND SPAIN

Argentinean	63 176	0.0	54 324	8 852	86.0	14.0
Bolivian	33 738	0.0	31 035	2 703	92.0	8.0
Central American*	10 310	0.0	9 755	555	94.6	5.4
Chilean	61 465	0.0	54 842	6 623	89.2	10.8
Colombian	351 717	0.1	329 160	22 557	93.6	6.4
Costa Rican	51 771	0.0	45 601	6 170	88.1	11.9
Cuban	859 739	0.3	805 204	54 535	93.7	6.3
Dominican	505 690	0.2	484 893	20 797	95.9	4.1
Ecuadorian	197 374	0.1	182 904	14 470	92.7	7.3
Guatemalan	241 559	0.1	229 479	12 080	95.0	5.0
Hispanic*	1 113 259	0.4	1 059 910	53 349	95.2	4.8
Honduran	116 635	0.0	108 364	8 271	92.9	7.1
Latin American^	43 521	0.0	39 446	4 075	90.6	9.4
Mexican	11 586 983	4.7	11 165 939	421 044	96.4	3.6
Nicaraguan	177 077	0.1	167 395	9 682	94.5	5.5
Panamanian	88 649	0.0	76 829	11 820	86.7	13.3
Paraguayan	5 415	0.0	4 916	499	90.8	9.2
Peruvian	161 866	0.1	147 504	14 362	91.1	8.9
Puerto Rican	1 955 323	0.8	1 813 122	142 201	92.7	7.3
Salvadoran	499 153	0.2	479 977	19 176	96.2	3.8
South American*	10 867	0.0	9 075	1 792	83.5	16.5
Spaniard[12]	360 935	0.1	312 865	48 070	86.7	13.3
Spanish*	2 024 004	0.8	1 625 866	398 138	80.3	19.7
Uruguayan	14 641	0.0	13 418	1 223	91.6	8.4
Venezuelan	40 331	0.0	34 046	6 285	84.4	15.6
Other Hispanic, n.e.c.	5 259	0.0	3 940	1 319	74.9	25.1

CENTRAL AND SOUTH AMERICA (NON-HISPANIC GROUPS)

Belizean	22 922	0.0	21 205	1 717	92.5	7.5
Brazilian	65 875	0.0	57 108	8 767	86.7	13.3
Guyanese	81 665	0.0	75 765	5 900	92.8	7.2
Other Central and South American, n.e.c.	1 217	0.0	1 078	139	88.6	11.4

WEST INDIES (NON-HISPANIC GROUPS)

Bahamian	21 081	0.0	18 752	2 329	89.0	11.0
Barbadian	35 455	0.0	33 178	2 277	93.6	6.4
Bermudan	4 941	0.0	4 007	934	81.1	18.9
British West Indian	37 819	0.0	35 446	2 373	93.7	6.3
Antigua and Barbuda	7 364	0.0	6 891	473	93.6	6.4
Grenadian	11 188	0.0	10 737	451	96.0	4.0
Kitts-Nevis Islander	2 811	0.0	2 564	247	91.2	8.8
St. Lucia Islander	3 415	0.0	3 113	302	91.2	8.8
Vincent-Grenadine Islander	5 773	0.0	5 487	286	95.0	5.0
British West Indian, n.e.c.	7 268	0.0	6 654	614	91.6	8.4
Dutch West Indian	61 530	0.0	33 473	28 057	54.4	45.6
Haitian	289 521	0.1	280 874	8 647	97.0	3.0
Jamaican	435 024	0.2	410 933	24 091	94.5	5.5
Trinidadian and Tobagonian	76 270	0.0	71 720	4 550	94.0	6.0
US Virgin Islander	7 621	0.0	6 831	790	89.6	10.4
West Indian*	159 167	0.1	138 521	20 646	87.0	13.0
Other West Indian, n.e.c.	4 139	0.0	3 405	734	82.3	17.7

NORTH AFRICA AND SOUTHWEST ASIA

Algerian	3 215	0.0	2 537	678	78.9	21.1
Arab*	127 364	0.1	112 411	14 953	88.3	11.7
Armenian	308 096	0.1	267 975	40 121	87.0	13.0
Assyrian	51 765	0.0	46 099	5 666	89.1	10.9
Egyptian	78 574	0.0	73 097	5 477	93.0	7.0
Iranian	235 521	0.1	220 714	14 807	93.7	6.3
Iraqi	23 212	0.0	20 657	2 555	89.0	11.0
Israeli	81 677	0.0	69 018	12 659	84.5	15.5
Jordanian	20 656	0.0	19 657	999	95.2	4.8
Lebanese	394 180	0.2	309 578	84 602	78.5	21.5
Middle Eastern*	7 656	0.0	6 654	1 002	86.9	13.1
Moroccan	19 089	0.0	15 015	4 074	78.7	21.3
Palestinian	48 019	0.0	44 651	3 368	93.0	7.0
Saudi Arabian	4 486	0.0	4 257	229	94.9	5.1
Syrian	129 606	0.1	95 155	34 451	73.4	26.6
Turkish	83 850	0.0	66 492	17 358	79.3	20.7
Yemeni	4 011	0.0	3 497	514	87.2	12.8
Other North African and Southwest Asian, n.e.c.	10 670	0.0	9 225	1 445	86.5	13.5

SUBSAHARAN AFRICA

African*	245 845	0.1	224 740	21 105	91.4	8.6
Cape Verdean	50 772	0.0	46 552	4 220	91.7	8.3
Eritrean	4 270	0.0	4 231	39	99.1	0.9
Ethiopian[13]	30 581	0.0	29 637	944	96.9	3.1
Ghanian	20 066	0.0	19 695	371	98.2	1.8
Kenyan	4 639	0.0	4 460	179	96.1	3.9
Liberian	8 797	0.0	8 309	488	94.5	5.5
Nigerian	91 688	0.0	86 875	4 813	94.8	5.2
Sierra Leonean^	4 627	0.0	4 441	186	96.0	4.0
South African*	17 992	0.0	15 347	2 645	85.3	14.7
Sudanese	3 623	0.0	3 341	282	92.2	7.8
Ugandan	2 681	0.0	2 475	206	92.3	7.7
Other Subsaharan African, n.e.c.	20 607	0.0	19 182	1 425	93.1	6.9

SOUTH ASIA

Afghanistan	31 301	0.0	30 600	701	97.8	2.2
Asian Indian	570 322	0.2	549 669	20 653	96.4	3.6
Bangladeshi	12 486	0.0	11 901	585	95.3	4.7
Nepali	2 516	0.0	2 369	147	94.2	5.8
Pakistani	99 974	0.0	95 301	4 673	95.3	4.7
Sri Lankan	14 448	0.0	13 541	907	93.7	6.3
Other South Asian, n.e.c.	116	0.0	116	0	100.0	0.0

Table 2. **Persons Who Reported at Least One Specific Ancestry Group: 1990**—Con.

United States	Persons who reported at least one specific ancestry		Persons who reported first ancestry	Persons who reported second ancestry	Percent	
	Total	Percent of total[1]			First ancestry	Second ancestry

OTHER ASIA

United States	Total	Percent of total[1]	First ancestry	Second ancestry	First ancestry	Second ancestry
Amerasian*	15 523	0.0	15 449	74	99.5	0.5
Asian*	107 172	0.0	98 776	8 396	92.2	7.8
Burmese	8 646	0.0	7 196	1 450	83.2	16.8
Cambodian[14]	134 955	0.1	132 157	2 798	97.9	2.1
Cantonese	25 020	0.0	24 926	94	99.6	0.4
Chinese[15]	1 505 245	0.6	1 404 634	100 611	93.3	6.7
Eurasian*	14 177	0.0	13 553	624	95.6	4.4
Filipino	1 450 512	0.6	1 333 521	116 991	91.9	8.1
Hmong	84 823	0.0	81 194	3 629	95.7	4.3
Hong Kong	5 774	0.0	4 541	1 233	78.6	21.4
Indonesian	43 969	0.0	27 936	16 033	63.5	36.5
Japanese	1 004 645	0.4	908 599	96 046	90.4	9.6
Khmer	2 979	0.0	2 979	0	100.0	0.0
Korean	836 987	0.3	798 595	38 392	95.4	4.6
Laotian	146 930	0.1	142 640	4 290	97.1	2.9
Malaysian	27 800	0.0	25 317	2 483	91.1	8.9
Mongolian	3 507	0.0	2 554	953	72.8	27.2
Okinawan	10 554	0.0	8 498	2 056	80.5	19.5
Singaporean	2 419	0.0	2 230	189	92.2	7.8
Taiwanese	192 973	0.1	187 012	5 961	96.9	3.1
Thai	112 117	0.0	102 941	9 176	91.8	8.2
Vietnamese	535 825	0.2	519 200	16 625	96.9	3.1
Other Asian, n.e.c.	2 185	0.0	1 887	298	86.4	13.6

PACIFIC

United States	Total	Percent of total[1]	First ancestry	Second ancestry	First ancestry	Second ancestry
Australian	52 133	0.0	36 290	15 843	69.6	30.4
Chamorro	4 427	0.0	4 065	362	91.8	8.2
Fijian	7 472	0.0	6 928	544	92.7	7.3
Guamanian	39 237	0.0	33 053	6 184	84.2	15.8
Hawaiian	256 081	0.1	205 802	50 279	80.4	19.6
Micronesian	3 406	0.0	3 171	235	93.1	6.9
New Zealander	7 742	0.0	5 997	1 745	77.5	22.5
Pacific Islander*	11 330	0.0	10 289	1 041	90.8	9.2
Polynesian	10 854	0.0	8 303	2 551	76.5	23.5
Samoan	55 419	0.0	49 503	5 916	89.3	10.7
Tongan	16 019	0.0	14 971	1 048	93.5	6.5
Other Pacific Islander, n.e.c.	8 674	0.0	7 258	1 416	83.7	16.3

NORTH AMERICA

United States	Total	Percent of total[1]	First ancestry	Second ancestry	First ancestry	Second ancestry
Acadian/ Cajun	668 271	0.3	597 729	70 542	89.4	10.6
Afro-American[16]	23 777 098	9.6	23 541 280	235 818	99.0	1.0
Aleut	15 816	0.0	13 232	2 584	83.7	16.3
American Indian[17]	8 708 220	3.5	4 864 263	3 843 957	55.9	44.1
American	12 395 999	5.0	12 395 999	0	100.0	0.0
Canadian[18]	549 990	0.2	354 656	195 334	64.5	35.5
Eskimo	52 920	0.0	48 523	4 397	91.7	8.3
French Canadian	2 167 127	0.9	1 698 394	468 733	78.4	21.6
Newfoundland	5 412	0.0	3 636	1 776	67.2	32.8
North American*	12 618	0.0	12 618	0	100.0	0.0
Nova Scotian	5 489	0.0	3 320	2 169	60.5	39.5
Pennsylvania German	305 841	0.1	246 461	59 380	80.6	19.4
United States	643 561	0.3	643 561	0	100.0	0.0
White[19]	1 799 711	0.7	1 799 711	0	100.0	0.0
Other North America, n.e.c.	309	0.0	185	124	59.9	40.1

OTHER GROUPS, N.E.C., NOT CLASSIFIED AND NOT REPORTED

United States	Total	Percent of total[1]	First ancestry	Second ancestry	First ancestry	Second ancestry
Other groups, n.e.c. and not classified[20]	3 389 599	1.4	3 088 188	301 411	91.1	8.9
Not reported	23 921 371	9.6	23 921 371		n.a.	n.a.

Note: Some individuals reported a single ancestry group; others reported more than one group. All first (or single) and second responses were coded. Since persons who reported two ancestries were included in more than one group, the sum of persons reporting the ancestry groups is greater than the total. The ancestry data include groups that correspond to those identified separately in the race and Hispanic origin items. In the 1990 census, separate questions were asked on race and Hispanic origin. The race item provides the primary source of data for White; Black; American Indian, Eskimo, and Aleut; and Asian and Pacific Islander. The 1990 census Hispanic origin question is the primary identifier for Mexican, Puerto Rican, Cuban and those who indicated that they were of "other" Spanish/ Hispanic origin.

*This category represents a general type response, which may encompass several ancestry groups.

[1]Numbers and percents by ancestry group do not add to total because persons reporting a multiple ancestry are included in more than one group.
[2]Excludes Tirol.
[3]Excludes Flemish.
[4]Excludes French Basque.
[5]Excludes Bavarian, Prussian, Saxon and West German.
[6]Excludes Greek Cypriot.
[7]Excludes Northern Irish and Celtic.
[8]Excludes Sicilian.
[9]Includes persons who reported "Scotch-Irish."
[10]Excludes Moravian.
[11]Includes persons who reported "Rusyn," "Cossack," "Black Russian," "Great Russian," "Red Russian," "Rossiya," and "Muscovite."
[12]Excludes Spanish Basque.
[13]Excludes Eritrean.
[14]Excludes Khmer.
[15]Excludes Cantonese.
[16]Includes persons who reported "African American," "Afro-American," "Afro," "Black," "Negro," "Colored," "Creole," and other related groups.
[17]Includes persons who reported "Native American," "Centraal American Indian," "South American Indian," and "Cherokee," and other related groups.
[18]Excludes Newfoundland and Nova Scotia.
[19]Includes persons who reported "White," "Caucasian," "Anglo," "Wasp," "Appalachian," "Aryan," and other related groups.
[20]Includes persons who reported "Mixture," "Adopted," "Don't know," and other unclassifiable responses, as well as responses indicating religious groups.

DETAILED ANCESTRY GROUPS FOR STATES   5

Table 3. Persons Who Reported at Least One Specific Ancestry Group: 1990

United States Region Division State	United States	Region Northeast	Midwest	South	West
Total	248 709 873	50 809 229	59 668 632	85 445 930	52 786 082
WESTERN EUROPE (NON-HISPANIC GROUPS)					
Alsatian	16 465	4 300	3 466	5 417	3 282
Austrian[2]	864 783	329 401	183 307	165 340	186 735
Basque	47 956	2 855	1 671	4 192	39 238
Basque, French	6 001	287	233	459	5 022
Basque, Spanish	7 620	556	210	901	5 953
Basque, n.e.c.	34 335	2 012	1 228	2 832	28 263
Bavarian	4 348	624	1 430	1 197	1 097
Belgian[3]	380 498	18 023	84 353	17 040	21 643
British	1 119 154	188 052	195 956	440 352	294 794
Celtic	29 652	5 679	4 516	9 340	10 117
Cornish	3 991	435	1 656	553	1 347
Cypriot	4 897	2 700	583	1 147	467
Cypriot, Greek	2 197	1 139	357	496	205
Cypriot, Turkish	289	143	20	69	57
Cypriot, n.e.c.	2 411	1 418	206	582	205
Danish	1 634 669	146 046	555 346	194 769	738 508
Dutch	6 227 089	1 020 383	2 123 623	1 780 043	1 303 040
English	32 651 788	5 873 052	7 293 707	11 375 464	8 109 565
Finnish	658 870	95 408	310 855	73 761	178 846
Flemish	14 157	2 280	4 029	3 843	4 005
French[4]	10 320 935	2 637 321	2 640 874	2 964 481	2 078 259
German[5]	57 947 374	9 928 722	22 477 450	14 630 411	10 910 791
Greek[6]	1 110 373	413 246	255 780	234 530	206 817
Icelander	40 529	4 140	10 904	5 594	19 891
Irish[7]	38 735 539	9 420 118	9 643 261	12 950 799	6 721 361
Italian[8]	14 664 550	7 503 740	2 429 651	2 473 371	2 257 788
Luxemburger	49 061	2 503	34 408	4 174	7 976
Maltese	39 600	10 829	14 769	4 657	9 345
Manx	6 317	492	2 448	1 212	2 165
Northern Irish	4 009	1 468	666	1 029	846
Norwegian	3 869 395	241 229	2 000 129	369 485	1 258 552
Portuguese	1 153 351	563 801	29 814	90 924	468 812
Azores Islander	4 310	1 991	112	297	1 910
Madeira Islander	184	78	29	24	53
Portuguese, n.e.c.	1 148 857	561 732	29 673	90 603	466 849
Prussian	25 469	3 695	7 691	6 434	7 649
Saxon	4 519	647	1 670	1 275	927
Scandinavian	678 880	52 958	221 666	100 981	303 275
Scotch-Irish[9]	5 617 773	772 250	1 078 883	2 616 155	1 150 485
Scottish	5 393 581	1 088 462	1 135 343	1 768 494	1 401 282
Sicilian	50 389	14 061	13 353	9 274	13 701
Swedish	4 680 863	669 531	1 858 855	671 099	1 481 378
Swiss	1 045 495	170 618	378 239	181 425	315 213
Tirol	5 748	426	4 313	619	390
Welsh	2 033 893	446 623	493 214	545 082	548 974
West German	3 885	942	755	1 301	887
Western European*	42 409	5 526	7 986	12 724	16 173
Other Western European, n.e.c.	2 005	254	429	596	726
EASTERN EUROPE AND SOVIET UNION					
Albanian	47 710	28 730	10 822	4 381	3 777
Belorussian	4 277	1 818	1 120	758	581
Bulgarian	29 595	4 986	10 326	4 984	9 299
Carpath Rusyn	7 602	5 651	1 053	646	278
Central European	5 604	2 019	1 108	1 173	1 304
Croatian	544 270	114 681	236 134	106 302	87 153
Czech[10]	1 296 411	129 325	671 371	290 732	204 983
Czechoslovakian	315 285	72 008	103 162	69 313	70 802
Estonian	26 762	9 760	4 212	5 441	7 349
European*	466 718	64 179	77 638	144 257	180 644
German Russian/ Volga	10 153	1 452	3 503	1 817	3 381
Hungarian	1 582 302	564 216	504 619	261 688	251 779
Latvian	100 331	32 870	26 830	18 548	22 083
Lithuanian	811 865	352 523	228 210	127 266	103 866
Macedonian	20 365	3 438	12 770	1 644	2 513
Moravian	3 781	431	1 192	1 660	498
Northern European*	65 993	7 975	14 258	13 378	30 382
Polish	9 366 106	3 499 502	3 468 832	1 361 537	1 036 235
Rom	5 693	890	1 176	1 467	2 160
Romanian	365 544	122 949	96 318	64 601	81 676
Russian[11]	2 952 987	1 292 472	473 588	545 671	641 256
Ruthenian	3 776	1 945	900	528	403
Serbian	116 795	26 349	58 782	13 727	17 937
Slavic*	76 931	21 581	22 076	12 388	20 886
Slovak	1 882 897	759 264	648 461	272 131	203 041
Slovene	124 437	19 697	81 163	10 701	12 876
Soviet Union	7 729	3 895	877	1 221	1 736
Ukrainian	740 803	374 282	163 133	104 695	98 693
Windish	3 189	2 896	44	148	101
Yugoslavian*	257 994	59 941	72 606	30 553	94 894
Other Eastern European and Soviet Union, n.e.c.	132 332	68 773	14 756	24 484	24 319

DETAILED ANCESTRY GROUPS FOR STATES

Table 3. Persons Who Reported at Least One Specific Ancestry Group: 1990—Con.

United States Region Division State		Region			
	United States	Northeast	Midwest	South	West
CENTRAL AND SOUTH AMERICA (HISPANIC GROUPS) AND SPAIN					
Argentinean	63 176	22 252	4 015	15 867	21 042
Bolivian	33 738	7 053	2 879	14 476	9 330
Central American*	10 310	1 800	464	2 026	6 020
Chilean	61 465	18 828	4 144	18 252	20 241
Colombian	351 717	173 173	17 862	113 859	46 823
Costa Rican	51 771	16 109	2 911	13 968	18 783
Cuban	859 739	157 247	29 269	594 106	79 117
Dominican	505 690	436 478	6 083	53 021	10 108
Ecuadorian	197 374	124 318	11 745	30 356	30 955
Guatemalan	241 559	38 449	17 922	36 218	148 970
Hispanic*	1 113 259	149 104	61 715	347 411	555 029
Honduran	116 635	35 254	5 590	46 298	29 493
Latin American*	43 521	5 342	3 448	17 193	17 538
Mexican	11 586 983	142 829	1 021 049	3 774 379	6 648 726
Nicaraguan	177 077	15 620	3 125	90 541	67 791
Panamanian	88 649	33 302	6 179	31 049	18 119
Paraguayan	5 415	2 357	556	1 642	860
Peruvian	161 866	61 788	8 350	43 312	48 416
Puerto Rican	1 955 323	1 289 858	209 974	293 124	162 367
Salvadoran	499 153	66 537	8 709	114 707	309 200
South American*	10 867	4 547	690	2 817	2 813
Spaniard[12]	360 935	78 181	17 160	131 738	133 856
Spanish*	2 024 004	331 319	158 061	614 708	919 916
Uruguayan	14 641	8 044	573	3 806	2 218
Venezuelan	40 331	10 646	2 685	20 696	6 304
Other Hispanic, n.e.c.	5 259	672	271	3 706	610
CENTRAL AND SOUTH AMERICA (NON-HISPANIC GROUPS)					
Belizean	22 922	6 230	2 456	2 956	11 280
Brazilian	65 875	31 099	4 997	17 234	12 545
Guyanese	81 665	65 127	2 031	11 306	3 201
Other Central and South American, n.e.c.	1 217	590	12	347	268
WEST INDIES (NON-HISPANIC GROUPS)					
Bahamian	21 081	3 142	1 145	16 001	793
Barbadian	35 455	29 229	627	4 202	1 397
Bermudan	4 941	2 507	430	1 627	377
British West Indian	37 819	28 199	807	7 346	1 467
Antigua and Barbuda	7 364	5 625	189	1 367	183
Grenadian	11 188	8 819	118	1 921	330
Kitts-Nevis Islander	2 811	1 937	115	677	82
St. Lucia Islander	3 415	2 315	48	934	118
Vincent-Grenadine Islander	5 773	4 841	117	664	151
British West Indian, n.e.c.	7 268	4 662	220	1 783	603
Dutch West Indian	61 530	1 668	2 856	49 492	7 514
Haitian	289 521	158 470	7 201	117 261	6 589
Jamaican	435 024	256 637	20 861	133 259	24 267
Trinidadian and Tobagonian	76 270	52 473	1 760	18 215	3 822
US Virgin Islander	7 621	3 546	360	2 988	727
West Indian*	159 167	104 248	7 132	35 373	12 414
Other West Indian, n.e.c.	4 139	1 897	180	1 627	435
NORTH AFRICA AND SOUTHWEST ASIA					
Algerian	3 215	1 007	368	1 035	805
Arab*	127 364	25 583	36 498	29 670	35 613
Armenian	308 096	89 331	32 365	23 625	162 775
Assyrian	51 765	3 799	29 403	1 897	16 666
Egyptian	78 574	32 478	8 844	15 063	22 189
Iranian	235 521	34 693	22 283	55 109	123 436
Iraqi	23 212	4 273	9 015	2 989	6 935
Israeli	81 677	38 015	7 221	12 924	23 517
Jordanian	20 656	4 543	4 884	5 016	6 213
Lebanese	394 180	111 321	100 783	108 312	73 764
Middle Eastern*	7 656	2 612	985	1 785	2 274
Moroccan	19 089	6 794	2 880	5 472	3 943
Palestinian	48 019	8 642	13 023	12 681	13 673
Saudi Arabian	4 486	563	820	1 792	1 311
Syrian	129 606	55 996	24 526	26 162	22 922
Turkish	83 850	34 003	10 295	21 168	18 384
Yemeni	4 011	1 820	991	562	638
Other North African and Southwest Asian, n.e.c.	10 670	2 421	1 843	3 098	3 308
SUBSAHARAN AFRICA					
African*	245 845	71 442	39 542	91 605	43 256
Cape Verdean	50 772	44 528	636	2 839	2 769
Eritrean	4 270	420	618	1 506	1 726
Ethiopian[13]	30 581	152	161	225	406
Ghanian	20 066	9 206	2 303	6 388	2 169
Kenyan	4 639	1 081	748	1 555	1 255
Liberian	8 797	3 819	1 488	2 819	671
Nigerian	91 688	18 961	15 852	43 354	13 521
Sierra Leonean	4 627	1 487	356	2 460	324
South African*	17 992	4 570	2 118	5 898	5 406
Sudanese	3 623	1 732	448	925	518
Ugandan	2 681	515	574	1 003	589
Other Subsaharan African, n.e.c.	20 607	6 131	2 997	7 808	3 671

Table 3. **Persons Who Reported at Least One Specific Ancestry Group: 1990**—Con.

United States Region Division State	United States	Northeast	Midwest	South	West
			Region		

SOUTH ASIA

Afghanistan	31 301	6 560	1 938	7 619	15 184
Asian Indian	570 322	180 513	108 383	145 791	135 635
Bangladeshi	12 486	7 211	1 097	2 631	1 547
Nepali	2 516	809	408	718	581
Pakistani	99 974	31 691	19 809	27 305	21 169
Sri Lankan	14 448	4 124	2 220	3 167	4 937
Other South Asian, n.e.c.	116	43	13	20	40

OTHER ASIA

Amerasian*	15 523	2 195	2 578	5 076	5 674
Asian*	107 172	19 279	15 837	27 252	44 804
Burmese	8 646	1 644	975	1 794	4 233
Cambodian[14]	134 955	25 543	11 470	18 572	79 370
Cantonese	25 020	7 393	1 338	1 572	14 717
Chinese[15]	1 505 245	374 410	118 844	185 231	826 760
Eurasian*	14 177	1 937	1 452	2 921	7 867
Filipino	1 450 512	149 972	127 070	181 898	991 572
Hmong	84 823	1 619	36 530	1 141	45 533
Hong Kong	5 774	1 627	493	607	3 047
Indonesian	43 969	6 669	4 156	6 631	26 513
Japanese	1 004 645	89 521	84 897	107 527	722 700
Khmer	2 979	814	108	481	1 576
Korean	836 987	180 288	119 455	169 025	368 219
Laotian	146 930	14 481	28 597	27 401	76 451
Malaysian	27 800	4 569	4 424	6 523	12 284
Mongolian	3 507	1 082	377	784	1 264
Okinawan	10 554	305	575	1 166	8 508
Singaporean	2 419	538	325	494	1 062
Taiwanese	192 973	44 141	20 748	37 565	90 519
Thai	112 117	14 773	16 842	32 396	48 106
Vietnamese	535 825	50 348	45 010	148 704	291 763
Other Asian, n.e.c.	2 185	372	192	410	1 211

PACIFIC

Australian	52 133	9 613	8 559	13 360	20 601
Chamorro	4 427	159	175	901	3 192
Fijian	7 472	191	95	193	6 993
Guamanian	39 237	1 997	1 900	7 204	28 112
Hawaiian	256 081	6 822	9 079	18 121	222 059
Micronesian	3 406	79	289	482	2 556
New Zealander	7 742	1 153	751	1 741	4 097
Pacific Islander*	11 330	787	1 014	1 974	7 555
Polynesian	10 854	676	959	2 185	7 034
Samoan	55 419	901	1 695	3 498	49 325
Tongan	16 019	122	249	676	14 972
Other Pacific Islander, n.e.c.	8 674	600	842	1 513	5 719

NORTH AMERICA

Acadian/Cajun	668 271	9 653	16 484	609 427	32 707
Afro-American[16]	23 777 098	3 658 088	4 875 147	12 936 066	2 307 797
Aleut	15 816	332	408	574	14 502
American Indian[17]	8 708 220	754 051	1 907 001	4 086 342	1 960 826
American	12 395 999	1 275 211	2 204 709	7 558 114	1 357 965
Canadian[18]	549 990	184 979	100 717	112 858	151 436
Eskimo	52 920	981	1 864	2 004	48 071
French Canadian	2 167 127	973 230	436 548	423 497	333 852
Newfoundland	5 412	3 899	432	742	339
North American*	12 618	1 338	2 140	6 520	2 620
Nova Scotian	5 489	3 107	317	1 400	665
Pennsylvania German	305 841	164 385	77 033	32 402	32 021
United States	643 561	101 193	114 282	341 677	86 409
White[19]	1 799 711	121 033	230 641	946 103	501 934
Other North America, n.e.c.	309	6	100	109	94

OTHER GROUPS, N.E.C., NOT CLASSIFIED AND NOT REPORTED

Other groups, n.e.c. and not classified[20]	3 389 599	867 916	845 996	997 282	678 405
Not reported	23 921 371	3 855 120	4 832 528	11 101 628	4 132 095

Table 3. Persons Who Reported at Least One Specific Ancestry Group: 1990—Con.

United States Region Division State	Division								
	New England	Middle Atlantic	East North Central	West North Central	South Atlantic	East South Central	West South Central	Mountain	Pacific
Total	13 206 943	37 602 286	42 008 942	17 659 690	43 566 853	15 176 284	26 702 793	13 658 776	39 127 306

WESTERN EUROPE (NON-HISPANIC GROUPS)

Alsatian	999	3 301	2 728	738	2 153	343	2 921	745	2 537
Austrian[2]	50 435	278 966	138 405	44 902	122 996	10 327	32 017	50 440	136 295
Basque	771	2 084	1 175	496	2 214	295	1 683	15 675	23 563
Basque, French	61	226	152	81	227	41	191	1 262	3 760
Basque, Spanish	158	398	145	65	508	73	320	1 926	4 027
Basque, n.e.c.	552	1 460	878	350	1 479	181	1 172	12 487	15 776
Bavarian[3]	114	510	918	512	724	157	316	218	879
Belgian[3]	5 126	12 897	69 300	15 053	10 276	1 328	5 436	6 347	15 296
British	65 793	122 259	141 990	53 966	260 839	70 500	109 013	83 313	211 481
Celtic	2 080	3 599	3 029	1 487	4 792	1 628	2 920	2 166	7 951
Comish	125	310	1 501	155	331	34	188	316	1 031
Cypriot	178	2 522	520	63	931	54	162	65	402
Cypriot, Greek	75	1 064	332	25	412	46	38	21	184
Cypriot, Turkish	0	143	9	11	69	0	0	0	57
Cypriot, n.e.c.	103	1 315	179	27	450	8	124	44	161
Danish	50 410	95 636	239 081	316 265	107 478	18 971	68 320	336 938	401 570
Dutch	136 755	883 628	1 496 951	626 672	886 239	313 043	580 761	389 819	913 221
English	2 329 864	3 543 188	5 082 750	2 210 957	6 306 540	1 977 550	3 091 374	2 843 048	5 266 517
Finnish	57 165	38 243	190 625	120 230	49 808	6 902	17 051	42 262	136 584
Flemish	856	1 424	3 215	814	2 455	332	1 056	927	3 078
French[4]	1 590 707	1 046 614	1 816 430	824 444	1 264 676	384 360	1 315 445	573 581	1 504 678
German[5]	1 307 116	8 621 606	14 775 614	7 701 836	7 881 678	2 177 176	4 571 557	3 477 358	7 433 433
Greek[6]	137 313	275 933	218 564	37 216	170 102	20 231	44 197	50 961	155 856
Icelander	1 668	2 472	3 360	7 544	3 538	578	1 478	5 945	13 946
Irish[7]	2 948 634	6 471 484	6 655 116	2 988 145	6 376 855	2 580 937	3 993 007	1 921 297	4 800 064
Italian[8]	1 835 919	5 667 821	2 044 546	385 105	1 671 248	217 775	584 348	541 972	1 715 816
Luxemburger	762	1 741	18 996	15 412	2 647	407	1 120	2 471	5 505
Maltese	944	9 885	14 338	431	3 379	397	881	916	8 429
Manx	181	311	1 845	603	774	79	359	600	1 565
Northern Irish	606	862	436	230	706	146	177	188	658
Norwegian	72 934	168 295	713 424	1 286 705	207 706	31 994	129 785	357 392	901 160
Portuguese	443 753	120 048	21 409	8 405	64 692	5 991	20 241	28 980	439 832
Azores Islander	1 902	89	42	70	226	5	66	149	1 761
Madeira Islander	53	25	29	0	17	0	7	12	41
Portuguese, n.e.c.	441 798	119 934	21 338	8 335	64 449	5 986	20 168	28 819	438 030
Prussian	1 015	2 680	5 120	2 571	3 647	641	2 146	2 430	5 219
Saxon	117	530	1 526	144	665	271	339	206	721
Scandinavian	20 446	32 612	80 025	141 041	57 025	11 733	31 623	102 203	201 072
Scotch-Irish[9]	249 130	523 120	705 146	373 737	1 374 240	503 642	738 273	330 609	819 876
Scottish	465 724	622 738	822 675	312 668	1 047 924	277 659	442 911	430 824	970 458
Sicilian	3 073	10 188	11 378	1 977	5 753	911	2 610	3 275	10 426
Swedish	305 290	364 235	885 338	973 517	380 329	70 863	219 907	482 921	998 457
Swiss	29 424	141 194	273 152	105 087	104 653	27 497	49 275	102 233	212 980
Tirol	145	4 168	332	94	662	32	35	212	178
Welsh	73 965	372 658	356 125	137 089	325 604	77 293	142 185	190 595	358 379
West German	176	766	547	208	828	174	299	229	658
Western European*	1 970	3 556	4 958	3 028	6 700	1 701	4 323	3 520	12 653
Other Western European, n.e.c.	65	189	264	165	359	37	200	162	564

EASTERN EUROPE AND SOVIET UNION

Albanian	12 225	16 505	9 926	896	3 414	289	678	778	2 999
Belorussian	253	1 565	1 065	55	628	49	81	62	519
Bulgarian	953	4 033	8 267	2 059	3 126	536	1 322	2 038	7 261
Carpath Rusyn	298	5 353	954	99	563	7	76	100	178
Central European	386	1 633	735	373	899	134	140	250	1 054
Croatian	7 241	107 440	190 979	45 155	59 161	20 581	26 560	23 900	63 253
Czech[10]	26 310	103 015	354 871	316 500	88 635	12 010	190 087	71 967	133 016
Czechoslovakian	13 467	58 541	66 621	36 541	35 244	4 106	29 963	20 587	50 215
Estonian	2 428	7 332	3 145	1 067	4 373	291	777	1 209	6 140
European*	16 497	47 682	48 038	29 600	81 274	27 760	35 223	45 439	135 205
German Russian/ Volga	213	1 239	1 753	1 750	969	169	679	1 032	2 349
Hungarian	82 828	481 388	461 975	42 644	199 238	18 747	43 703	60 254	191 525
Latvian	10 592	22 278	21 061	5 769	14 217	1 231	3 100	3 905	18 178
Lithuanian	128 984	223 539	205 529	22 681	100 431	7 356	19 479	24 446	79 420
Macedonian	600	2 838	12 288	482	1 158	115	371	695	1 818
Moravian	166	265	794	398	337	55	1 268	130	368
Northern European*	2 958	5 017	7 162	7 096	7 037	1 959	4 382	6 917	23 465
Polish	809 571	2 689 931	2 979 889	488 943	962 041	92 364	307 132	289 648	746 587
Rom	155	735	822	354	580	298	589	437	1 723
Romanian	17 040	105 909	84 360	11 958	51 189	3 703	9 709	13 537	68 139
Russian[11]	250 307	1 042 165	353 972	119 616	448 460	24 106	73 105	112 096	529 160
Ruthenian	103	1 842	747	153	421	28	79	95	308
Serbian	1 184	25 165	52 620	6 162	10 011	984	2 732	5 209	12 728
Slavic*	2 787	18 794	15 385	6 691	8 389	1 071	2 928	6 156	14 730
Slovak	76 273	682 991	568 825	79 636	189 227	19 775	63 129	69 900	133 141
Slovene	1 522	18 175	72 316	8 847	7 100	890	2 711	5 685	7 191
Soviet Union	792	3 103	687	190	1 049	33	139	319	1 417
Ukrainian	49 481	324 801	139 059	24 074	81 661	5 710	17 324	23 252	75 441
Windish	9	2 887	30	14	73	0	75	31	70
Yugoslavian*	6 358	53 583	58 586	14 020	19 528	3 162	7 863	21 706	73 188
Other Eastern European and Soviet Union, n.e.c.	13 708	55 065	11 662	3 094	20 100	1 253	3 131	3 254	21 065

DETAILED ANCESTRY GROUPS FOR STATES

9

Table 3. **Persons Who Reported at Least One Specific Ancestry Group: 1990**—Con.

United States Region Division State	New England	Middle Atlantic	East North Central	West North Central	South Atlantic	East South Central	West South Central	Mountain	Pacific
CENTRAL AND SOUTH AMERICA (HISPANIC GROUPS) AND SPAIN									
Argentinean	3 170	19 082	3 278	737	12 472	378	3 017	1 772	19 270
Bolivian	1 311	5 742	2 142	737	12 527	170	1 779	887	8 443
Central American*	110	1 690	462	2	942	49	1 035	240	5 780
Chilean	2 977	15 851	3 059	1 085	14 861	419	2 972	2 580	17 661
Colombian	20 305	152 868	14 531	3 331	93 814	1 905	18 140	4 918	41 905
Costa Rican	2 846	13 263	2 331	580	10 044	473	3 451	1 568	17 215
Cuban	13 768	143 479	24 322	4 947	564 962	4 102	25 042	11 365	67 752
Dominican	43 237	393 241	5 196	887	46 620	1 432	4 969	1 780	8 328
Ecuadorian	6 339	117 979	10 392	1 353	24 442	905	5 009	1 428	29 527
Guatemalan	10 826	27 623	16 915	1 007	22 705	477	13 036	4 285	144 685
Hispanic*	28 364	120 740	47 285	14 430	79 639	4 479	263 293	227 602	327 427
Honduran	4 177	31 077	4 599	991	27 188	779	18 331	1 734	27 759
Latin American*	1 013	4 329	2 868	665	6 174	464	10 555	1 296	16 242
Mexican	25 929	116 900	838 617	182 432	254 785	31 276	3 488 318	1 108 796	5 539 930
Nicaraguan	1 198	14 422	2 460	665	78 636	506	11 399	2 378	65 413
Panamanian	2 364	30 938	4 188	1 991	21 759	1 812	7 478	3 260	14 859
Paraguayan	315	2 042	381	175	1 325	36	281	175	685
Peruvian	7 373	54 415	6 967	1 383	35 533	683	7 096	3 897	44 519
Puerto Rican	209 670	1 080 188	199 870	10 104	237 662	9 343	46 119	21 768	140 599
Salvadoran	9 854	56 683	7 323	1 386	59 670	351	54 686	6 712	302 488
South American*	529	4 018	593	97	2 137	176	504	424	2 389
Spaniard[12]	8 203	69 978	13 221	3 939	91 834	2 749	37 155	52 062	81 794
Spanish*	67 919	263 400	115 087	42 974	310 304	32 973	271 431	415 896	504 020
Uruguayan	920	7 124	325	248	3 090	49	667	283	1 935
Venezuelan	2 299	8 347	1 993	692	15 952	672	4 072	1 235	5 069
Other Hispanic, n.e.c.	167	505	220	51	3 125	84	497	120	490
CENTRAL AND SOUTH AMERICA (NON-HISPANIC GROUPS)									
Belizean	245	5 985	2 359	97	1 775	30	1 151	318	10 962
Brazilian	10 960	20 139	3 799	1 198	13 902	642	2 690	2 049	10 496
Guyanese	1 349	63 778	1 445	586	9 969	283	1 054	210	2 991
Other Central and South American, n.e.c.	32	558	12	0	280	0	67	0	268
WEST INDIES (NON-HISPANIC GROUPS)									
Bahamian	376	2 766	831	314	15 019	514	468	206	587
Barbadian	4 483	24 746	539	88	3 474	122	606	125	1 272
Bermudan	682	1 825	367	63	1 273	192	162	27	350
British West Indian	1 918	26 281	661	146	5 998	221	1 127	261	1 206
Antigua and Barbuda	398	5 227	133	56	1 002	54	311	44	139
Grenadian	168	8 651	86	32	1 589	37	295	28	302
Kitts-Nevis Islander	97	1 840	105	10	633	15	29	19	63
St. Lucia Islander	249	2 066	48	0	611	14	309	3	115
Vincent-Grenadine Islander	175	4 666	88	29	582	19	63	80	71
British West Indian, n.e.c.	831	3 831	201	19	1 581	82	120	87	516
Dutch West Indian	211	1 457	1 319	1 537	2 915	3 381	43 196	2 606	4 908
Haitian	30 156	128 314	6 327	874	113 998	710	2 553	806	5 783
Jamaican	33 327	223 310	18 163	2 698	121 260	2 882	9 117	2 696	21 571
Trinidadian and Tobagonian	3 746	48 727	1 523	237	15 096	549	2 570	446	3 376
US Virgin Islander	359	3 187	252	108	2 317	102	569	138	589
West Indian*	11 811	92 437	5 688	1 444	27 531	1 875	5 967	1 636	10 778
Other West Indian, n.e.c.	180	1 717	164	16	1 337	89	201	63	372
NORTH AFRICA AND SOUTHWEST ASIA									
Algerian	321	686	287	81	651	20	364	115	690
Arab*	4 495	21 088	33 302	3 196	17 668	2 571	9 431	4 932	30 681
Armenian	44 314	45 017	29 465	2 900	18 017	1 309	4 299	7 242	155 533
Assyrian	1 952	1 847	29 154	249	1 043	198	656	571	16 095
Egyptian	3 492	28 986	6 838	2 006	10 257	1 020	3 786	1 624	20 565
Iranian	7 492	27 201	15 465	6 818	33 293	4 217	17 599	8 232	115 204
Iraqi	528	3 745	8 629	386	2 055	220	714	549	6 386
Israeli	4 633	33 382	5 747	1 474	9 835	598	2 491	2 081	21 436
Jordanian	470	4 073	4 361	523	2 473	756	1 787	432	5 781
Lebanese	48 737	62 584	81 635	19 148	61 709	12 839	33 764	16 810	56 954
Middle Eastern*	327	2 285	613	372	1 047	166	572	214	2 060
Moroccan	843	5 951	2 200	680	4 607	167	698	694	3 249
Palestinian	1 356	7 286	11 871	1 152	7 804	1 154	3 723	1 314	12 359
Saudi Arabian	231	332	289	531	1 000	130	662	446	865
Syrian	13 482	42 514	19 819	4 707	16 225	1 923	8 014	4 352	18 570
Turkish	4 669	29 334	8 192	2 103	15 204	1 617	4 347	2 804	15 580
Yemeni	38	1 782	907	84	443	46	73	34	604
Other North African and Southwest Asian, n.e.c.	476	1 945	1 288	555	1 789	487	822	556	2 752
SUBSAHARAN AFRICA									
African*	10 701	60 741	29 313	10 229	59 483	10 160	21 962	6 270	36 986
Cape Verdean	42 647	1 881	473	163	2 227	153	459	196	2 573
Eritrean	158	262	465	153	1 208	0	298	54	1 672
Ethiopian[13]	36	116	124	37	178	22	25	62	344
Ghanian	1 182	8 024	1 902	401	4 983	152	1 253	270	1 899
Kenyan	220	861	494	254	909	85	561	104	1 151
Liberian	1 081	2 738	924	564	2 227	120	472	23	648
Nigerian	3 037	15 924	10 986	4 866	22 592	4 153	16 609	2 115	11 406
Sierra Leonean	182	1 305	259	97	2 012	32	416	0	324
South African*	1 321	3 249	1 800	318	3 625	358	1 915	742	4 664
Sudanese	112	1 620	340	108	733	76	116	150	368
Ugandan	236	279	375	199	834	23	146	76	513
Other Subsaharan African, n.e.c.	1 091	5 040	2 027	970	5 973	306	1 529	697	2 974

DETAILED ANCESTRY GROUPS FOR STATES

Table 3. **Persons Who Reported at Least One Specific Ancestry Group: 1990**—Con.

United States Region Division State	Division								
	New England	Middle Atlantic	East North Central	West North Central	South Atlantic	East South Central	West South Central	Mountain	Pacific
SOUTH ASIA									
Afghanistan	665	5 895	1 068	870	6 239	157	1 223	1 154	14 030
Asian Indian	26 275	154 238	91 737	16 646	83 491	12 397	49 903	12 191	123 444
Bangladeshi	381	6 830	872	225	1 683	277	671	237	1 310
Nepali	231	578	341	67	521	35	162	152	429
Pakistani	3 551	28 140	17 201	2 608	15 901	1 162	10 242	2 179	18 990
Sri Lankan	590	3 534	1 327	893	2 191	172	804	575	4 362
Other South Asian, n.e.c.	9	34	6	7	20	0	0	0	40
OTHER ASIA									
Amerasian*	577	1 618	1 453	1 125	3 024	544	1 508	1 279	4 395
Asian*	3 696	15 583	12 270	3 567	14 667	2 748	9 837	4 261	40 543
Burmese	294	1 350	881	94	1 385	91	318	248	3 985
Cambodian[14]	17 586	7 957	6 293	5 177	10 688	1 520	6 364	3 402	75 968
Cantonese	1 105	6 288	1 146	192	822	83	667	339	14 378
Chinese[15]	64 558	309 852	91 281	27 563	103 888	14 246	67 097	39 312	787 448
Eurasian*	578	1 359	1 124	328	1 927	295	699	926	6 941
Filipino	19 475	130 497	106 092	20 978	119 096	10 913	51 889	38 683	952 889
Hmong	1 060	559	18 815	17 715	906	26	209	1 395	44 138
Hong Kong	292	1 335	364	129	315	17	275	86	2 961
Indonesian	1 327	5 342	3 068	1 088	3 864	611	2 156	1 889	24 624
Japanese	19 563	69 958	64 460	20 437	62 157	13 102	32 268	46 807	675 893
Khmer	545	269	62	46	326	5	150	18	1 558
Korean	23 256	157 032	85 743	33 712	108 266	14 906	45 853	31 888	336 331
Laotian	9 369	5 112	14 993	13 604	10 955	3 602	12 844	6 031	70 420
Malaysian	983	3 586	3 081	1 343	3 344	917	2 262	879	11 405
Mongolian	108	974	326	51	383	95	306	304	960
Okinawan	65	240	422	153	680	157	329	445	8 063
Singaporean	130	408	236	89	252	43	199	69	993
Taiwanese	6 169	37 972	15 240	5 508	19 243	2 922	15 400	4 556	85 963
Thai	3 609	11 164	11 326	5 516	19 613	2 366	10 417	7 854	40 252
Vietnamese	18 626	31 722	22 644	22 366	56 586	8 737	83 381	17 977	273 786
Other Asian, n.e.c.	48	324	104	88	272	19	119	106	1 105
PACIFIC									
Australian	2 869	6 744	6 063	2 496	8 271	1 557	3 532	4 548	16 053
Chamorro	61	98	127	48	607	82	212	204	2 988
Fijian	33	158	41	54	120	8	66	103	9 090
Guamanian	492	1 505	1 068	832	3 550	726	2 928	2 078	20 034
Hawaiian	1 786	5 036	5 740	3 339	9 742	2 163	6 216	10 200	211 859
Micronesian	15	64	78	211	200	42	240	357	2 199
New Zealander	305	750	477	274	1 191	77	473	865	3 232
Pacific Islander*	170	617	828	186	1 155	185	634	816	6 739
Polynesian	159	517	489	470	1 046	278	861	1 480	5 554
Samoan	213	688	606	1 089	1 981	507	1 010	3 254	46 071
Tongan	38	84	70	179	145	10	521	4 147	10 825
Other Pacific Islander, n.e.c.	122	478	577	265	964	132	417	854	4 865
NORTH AMERICA									
Acadian/ Cajun	4 738	4 915	10 196	6 288	37 241	24 461	547 725	9 153	23 554
Afro-American[16]	392 392	3 265 696	4 107 796	767 351	7 105 744	2 510 316	3 320 006	316 954	1 990 843
Aleut	80	252	281	127	286	62	226	477	14 025
American Indian[17]	227 371	526 680	1 244 276	662 725	1 557 713	862 348	1 666 281	725 235	1 235 591
American	404 788	870 423	1 577 339	627 370	3 598 563	2 243 648	1 715 903	409 847	948 118
Canadian[18]	115 597	69 382	84 666	16 051	79 517	10 177	23 164	29 541	121 895
Eskimo	325	656	965	899	948	291	765	1 280	46 791
French Canadian	755 924	217 306	335 442	101 106	223 732	35 977	163 788	86 830	247 022
Newfoundland	2 809	1 090	291	141	625	31	86	70	269
North American*	399	939	1 535	605	3 506	1 465	1 549	565	2 055
Nova Scotian	2 878	229	172	145	636	50	714	119	546
Pennsylvania German	2 988	161 397	55 213	21 820	23 079	2 554	6 769	10 730	21 291
United States	23 548	77 645	85 824	28 458	177 391	80 387	83 899	21 866	64 543
White[19]	52 962	68 071	154 394	76 247	355 622	214 413	376 068	135 335	366 599
Other North America, n.e.c.	0	6	40	60	59	13	37	35	59
OTHER GROUPS, N.E.C., NOT CLASSIFIED AND NOT REPORTED									
Other groups, n.e.c. and not classified[20]	192 036	675 880	671 844	174 152	494 720	189 800	312 762	190 589	487 816
Not reported	885 147	2 969 973	3 416 040	1 416 488	5 693 245	2 576 733	2 831 650	1 048 171	3 083 924

Table 3. Persons Who Reported at Least One Specific Ancestry Group: 1990—Con.

United States Region Division State	State								
	Alabama	Alaska	Arizona	Arkansas	California	Colorado	Connecticut	Delaware	District of Columbia
Total	4 040 587	550 043	3 665 228	2 350 725	29 760 021	3 294 394	3 287 116	666 168	606 900

WESTERN EUROPE (NON-HISPANIC GROUPS)

	Alabama	Alaska	Arizona	Arkansas	California	Colorado	Connecticut	Delaware	District of Columbia
Alsatian	31	12	251	68	1 865	215	368	77	68
Austrian[2]	2 497	1 695	12 212	1 746	104 645	16 568	20 333	2 203	2 533
Basque	82	245	1 316	104	19 122	937	319	13	37
Basque, French	24	37	53	20	3 387	148	22	0	0
Basque, Spanish	44	38	298	21	3 508	110	64	7	16
Basque, n.e.c.	14	170	965	63	12 227	679	233	6	21
Bavarian	59	0	74	29	634	43	42	0	33
Belgian[3]	290	172	1 651	359	10 229	2 055	1 196	219	147
British	19 913	3 012	18 034	9 383	151 050	19 730	17 547	4 378	3 803
Celtic	500	107	590	205	5 420	746	529	57	76
Cornish	8	0	86	36	681	93	55	0	14
Cypriot	0	10	44	34	324	0	36	13	22
Cypriot, Greek	0	0	0	0	157	0	22	13	6
Cypriot, Turkish	0	0	0	0	57	0	0	0	0
Cypriot, n.e.c.	0	10	44	34	110	0	14	0	16
Danish	5 180	5 993	36 859	5 014	262 101	42 801	16 739	1 732	1 264
Dutch	76 037	14 365	95 326	72 670	591 618	100 024	37 183	14 956	3 768
English	479 499	76 600	586 458	290 462	3 645 975	581 886	462 919	122 759	34 266
Finnish	1 759	3 773	10 395	983	64 302	8 632	7 486	872	479
Flemish	68	35	219	53	2 130	304	190	39	96
French[4]	93 104	23 844	155 951	75 026	1 032 843	148 950	260 064	19 190	8 566
German[5]	430 442	127 103	878 088	400 234	4 935 147	1 063 694	450 247	138 128	39 218
Greek[6]	6 895	1 665	12 799	2 734	125 792	11 999	26 646	3 203	2 279
Icelander	210	131	759	95	6 512	939	444	29	91
Irish[7]	617 065	74 322	529 575	464 287	3 425 089	537 945	613 765	139 180	34 392
Italian[8]	52 969	14 467	159 140	30 199	1 439 778	155 844	628 232	63 467	11 662
Luxemburger	113	79	924	104	3 487	629	234	7	72
Maltese	107	15	435	63	8 029	144	280	40	61
Manx	28	13	67	37	1 048	102	22	0	17
Northern Irish	12	0	73	22	538	51	159	0	0
Norwegian	8 489	23 087	70 940	8 778	411 282	75 646	19 004	3 036	2 620
Portuguese	1 408	1 628	7 338	1 337	356 495	4 654	43 098	1 127	870
Azores Islander	5	0	27	6	1 630	16	99	0	7
Madeira Islander	0	0	0	0	26	0	5	0	0
Portuguese, n.e.c.	1 403	1 628	7 311	1 331	354 839	4 638	42 994	1 127	863
Prussian	167	77	569	97	3 430	707	368	18	17
Saxon	35	0	47	6	527	45	48	0	0
Scandinavian	2 845	4 814	16 735	2 343	102 310	17 002	5 029	966	736
Scotch-Irish[9]	127 826	12 850	82 552	67 388	546 496	95 012	45 742	13 847	5 943
Scottish	76 020	16 996	93 835	36 231	646 674	100 952	82 319	16 796	8 194
Sicilian	297	124	1 157	142	8 654	763	991	101	29
Swedish	18 235	17 716	92 248	16 168	587 772	125 097	79 374	7 659	3 531
Swiss	4 107	2 902	16 700	5 280	140 351	20 288	10 558	1 860	1 632
Tirol	15	0	14	0	138	78	64	161	0
Welsh	18 809	5 774	38 340	12 436	238 134	41 520	19 018	9 759	2 477
West German	50	0	35	20	514	58	98	19	14
Western European*	524	187	419	401	8 666	1 167	399	114	86
Other Western European, n.e.c.	13	28	32	10	343	72	21	0	0

EASTERN EUROPE AND SOVIET UNION

	Alabama	Alaska	Arizona	Arkansas	California	Colorado	Connecticut	Delaware	District of Columbia
Albanian	26	197	189	36	2 261	198	2 745	123	60
Belorussian	15	0	30	23	368	24	71	18	27
Bulgarian	197	110	431	54	5 277	591	181	13	57
Carpath Rusyn	0	0	60	14	128	40	262	0	0
Central European	96	8	43	16	874	93	120	0	22
Croatian	5 336	518	6 769	3 145	47 822	6 437	2 669	542	547
Czech[10]	3 031	2 834	18 043	4 175	88 286	24 184	10 682	1 449	1 034
Czechoslovakian	1 109	878	5 374	1 115	35 510	6 662	6 162	736	483
Estonian	110	95	323	33	4 101	391	1 088	123	48
European*	8 769	3 598	8 645	3 422	89 777	10 921	3 689	906	1 777
German Russian/ Volga	23	24	283	47	1 563	469	116	40	85
Hungarian	4 117	2 200	22 433	2 300	159 121	16 861	49 508	3 468	2 518
Latvian	252	179	1 029	198	13 652	1 772	2 389	438	552
Lithuanian	1 809	1 267	9 353	1 456	63 871	7 232	41 747	2 695	1 789
Macedonian	18	2	243	21	1 498	122	285	13	38
Moravian	19	0	13	8	260	95	47	0	0
Northern European*	777	611	1 081	348	14 188	2 131	670	38	167
Polish	21 907	12 294	102 405	17 600	578 256	82 257	312 587	38 286	9 879
Rom	11	0	112	130	1 213	89	57	0	0
Romanian	816	549	5 714	427	57 417	3 211	6 359	680	987
Russian[11]	5 157	6 032	35 508	2 595	447 752	36 134	79 884	6 839	12 353
Ruthenian	0	0	28	0	270	19	65	16	0
Serbian	182	274	1 772	155	10 605	1 271	374	183	163
Slavic*	162	254	1 456	146	10 803	2 225	1 106	193	73
Slovak	5 022	1 895	21 335	3 752	101 328	24 257	49 891	4 697	1 378
Slovene	247	97	1 104	76	5 546	3 194	864	79	169
Soviet Union	2	0	78	0	1 262	147	107	7	67
Ukrainian	1 585	962	8 471	870	56 211	6 984	23 711	4 950	1 082
Windish	0	0	0	0	55	0	9	3	0
Yugoslavian*	656	1 374	4 869	450	53 442	4 840	2 786	364	386
Other Eastern European and Soviet Union, n.e.c.	368	337	1 017	120	18 469	1 335	3 347	342	1 272

Table 3. **Persons Who Reported at Least One Specific Ancestry Group: 1990**—Con.

United States Region Division State	State								
	Alabama	Alaska	Arizona	Arkansas	California	Colorado	Connecticut	Delaware	District of Columbia
CENTRAL AND SOUTH AMERICA (HISPANIC GROUPS) AND SPAIN									
Argentinean	63	54	413	15	18 390	391	1 407	43	300
Bolivian	70	42	198	41	7 989	179	182	36	764
Central American*	19	3	148	22	5 712	39	3	0	29
Chilean	95	138	655	68	16 124	466	1 183	98	316
Colombian	574	421	1 517	270	39 427	810	7 098	369	822
Costa Rican	177	47	441	21	16 379	325	942	67	128
Cuban	1 260	366	2 314	331	64 152	2 049	5 377	649	911
Dominican	326	394	383	183	7 032	547	4 253	245	1 568
Ecuadorian	150	20	364	32	28 698	456	3 212	41	688
Guatemalan	108	56	1 359	137	143 017	640	1 304	59	1 053
Hispanic*	1 151	1 232	50 573	919	303 271	53 798	12 428	1 229	1 147
Honduran	278	40	693	90	26 834	209	593	55	365
Latin American*	58	0	358	70	15 631	339	410	20	176
Mexican	7 556	6 888	520 009	10 835	5 322 170	198 902	7 555	2 515	2 361
Nicaraguan	137	113	606	102	64 285	244	420	41	850
Panamanian	540	203	733	219	13 015	1 272	543	341	581
Paraguayan	36	0	30	9	634	66	133	75	165
Peruvian	119	246	950	65	42 322	1 264	3 897	39	933
Puerto Rican	2 659	1 623	6 840	1 069	113 548	6 020	93 608	5 246	1 089
Salvadoran	80	161	1 697	179	300 102	595	1 018	115	8 547
South American*	49	0	126	21	2 134	126	168	27	24
Spaniard[12]	631	442	6 385	501	74 787	14 052	3 599	291	529
Spanish*	9 366	4 252	44 059	5 668	434 759	121 029	23 222	2 514	3 628
Uruguayan	16	0	70	0	1 837	75	216	0	80
Venezuelan	221	20	363	63	4 575	391	599	18	104
Other Hispanic, n.e.c.	31	2	11	0	471	38	60	0	5
CENTRAL AND SOUTH AMERICA (NON-HISPANIC GROUPS)									
Belizean	8	0	154	9	10 848	44	82	0	0
Brazilian	188	64	617	18	9 357	307	2 489	89	524
Guyanese	133	72	42	0	2 671	85	698	38	757
Other Central and South American, n.e.c.	0	0	0	0	233	0	0	0	0
WEST INDIES (NON-HISPANIC GROUPS)									
Bahamian	167	20	70	14	398	24	154	48	48
Barbadian	64	6	26	22	1 160	36	972	74	102
Bermudan	97	0	0	20	176	7	127	32	70
British West Indian	62	33	80	22	994	43	493	22	298
Antigua and Barbuda	24	16	14	0	91	15	76	6	34
Grenadian	0	0	0	15	265	0	8	0	117
Kitts-Nevis Islander	7	0	12	0	63	0	83	0	19
St. Lucia Islander	0	6	0	0	97	0	147	0	5
Vincent-Grenadine Islander	10	0	34	0	55	13	37	13	95
British West Indian, n.e.c.	21	11	20	7	423	7	142	3	28
Dutch West Indian	583	51	782	2 679	3 841	421	89	14	0
Haitian	188	91	319	39	5 054	198	5 004	242	937
Jamaican	814	186	1 005	180	19 237	819	20 219	1 118	3 184
Trinidadian and Tobagonian	225	41	250	24	3 100	58	899	158	1 012
US Virgin Islander	28	0	67	0	517	71	63	9	131
West Indian*	692	140	649	211	9 136	409	3 842	289	1 164
Other West Indian, n.e.c.	22	0	51	10	315	0	139	8	23
NORTH AFRICA AND SOUTHWEST ASIA									
Algerian	2	11	0	0	579	108	38	0	26
Arab*	757	148	1 600	303	27 688	1 394	815	250	493
Armenian	353	138	2 519	185	151 340	1 686	5 218	294	369
Assyrian	42	0	302	111	15 736	106	1 212	0	62
Egyptian	279	0	568	43	19 597	489	735	221	291
Iranian	1 118	144	2 351	343	108 871	2 105	1 669	254	1 144
Iraqi	45	0	243	47	6 080	158	85	39	44
Israeli	135	14	966	26	20 651	423	1 320	162	146
Jordanian	287	0	195	13	5 503	71	57	24	16
Lebanese	3 672	279	6 296	817	49 776	3 544	8 612	533	1 070
Middle Eastern*	18	0	99	2	1 836	55	53	0	43
Moroccan	73	5	163	20	2 981	118	187	74	353
Palestinian	367	15	497	144	11 566	489	322	94	186
Saudi Arabian	33	0	143	128	517	224	93	11	75
Syrian	270	76	1 820	301	15 803	801	1 843	202	116
Turkish	592	66	772	166	12 929	792	1 329	327	309
Yemeni	0	0	18	0	525	0	0	0	16
Other North African and Southwest Asian, n.e.c.	36	7	239	36	2 168	151	78	22	50
SUBSAHARAN AFRICA									
African*	3 120	361	2 073	1 125	32 413	1 566	3 064	774	4 750
Cape Verdean	0	20	104	67	2 433	29	3 047	0	145
Eritrean	0	0	0	0	1 438	34	21	0	180
Ethiopian[13]	0	0	43	0	315	0	0	0	11
Ghanian	17	5	148	45	1 681	84	375	6	168
Kenyan	11	0	5	23	942	21	28	9	33
Liberian	33	0	0	0	639	23	83	22	101
Nigerian	1 401	53	557	894	10 027	730	803	231	1 762
Sierra Leonean	0	0	0	0	275	0	26	0	167
South African*	78	0	265	19	4 299	227	496	36	129
Sudanese	57	0	85	0	305	40	50	7	126
Ugandan	13	0	0	8	436	45	20	17	26
Other Subsaharan African, n.e.c.	95	20	260	44	2 377	270	314	93	662

DETAILED ANCESTRY GROUPS FOR STATES   **13**

Table 3. **Persons Who Reported at Least One Specific Ancestry Group: 1990**—Con.

United States Region Division State	Alabama	Alaska	Arizona	Arkansas	California	Colorado	Connecticut	Delaware	District of Columbia
SOUTH ASIA									
Afghanistan	19	0	220	58	13 018	456	131	30	42
Asian Indian	3 686	466	4 642	1 202	112 560	2 764	8 866	1 518	1 150
Bangladeshi	116	0	85	12	1 256	40	75	27	67
Nepali	13	0	30	26	224	84	15	6	8
Pakistani	365	21	549	226	17 729	666	1 301	217	228
Sri Lankan	26	14	171	0	3 827	184	234	92	110
Other South Asian, n.e.c.	0	0	0	0	34	0	0	0	0
OTHER ASIA									
Amerasian*	130	100	343	110	3 022	331	143	21	96
Asian*	738	288	1 273	393	34 715	1 232	966	170	290
Burmese	22	3	79	0	3 636	18	0	23	77
Cambodian[14]	363	75	958	81	63 431	929	1 217	65	92
Cantonese	11	0	110	19	13 457	103	37	27	63
Chinese[15]	3 529	1 549	12 542	1 575	641 250	9 117	10 217	1 813	2 574
Eurasian*	133	40	291	53	5 728	193	176	27	34
Filipino	2 305	8 584	10 069	2 166	709 599	7 270	6 272	1 479	2 035
Hmong	0	0	24	0	42 843	1 080	0	0	0
Hong Kong	0	0	24	0	2 761	36	31	8	35
Indonesian	110	56	506	64	21 767	608	323	50	223
Japanese	3 516	3 009	8 430	1 586	353 251	15 198	5 000	989	1 260
Khmer	5	0	0	0	1 317	12	9	0	0
Korean	3 969	4 349	7 300	1 470	260 822	12 490	5 427	1 463	943
Laotian	746	233	581	2 004	59 976	1 771	2 720	122	33
Malaysian	202	62	245	170	9 755	132	498	14	89
Mongolian	6	44	49	0	828	82	21	0	0
Okinawan	64	10	237	0	1 799	110	8	0	9
Singaporean	0	0	4	0	890	27	74	0	17
Taiwanese	1 003	193	1 704	342	79 658	1 062	1 127	444	278
Thai	674	432	1 800	368	33 654	1 645	710	270	335
Vietnamese	2 136	429	4 511	1 788	242 946	6 679	3 671	475	663
Other Asian, n.e.c.	0	0	21	16	709	51	0	9	9
PACIFIC									
Australian	442	197	869	95	12 006	786	976	96	129
Chamorro	8	0	61	0	1 851	64	35	0	0
Fijian	8	2	31	0	5 866	43	13	0	0
Guamanian	141	234	571	175	19 820	697	82	21	31
Hawaiian	436	985	2 324	318	43 418	1 931	353	96	121
Micronesian	5	28	104	21	615	101	0	0	0
New Zealander*	12	32	117	35	2 460	144	92	0	25
Pacific Islander*	40	188	242	0	4 869	163	49	23	21
Polynesian	43	152	189	48	3 545	171	23	0	0
Samoan	34	533	374	36	26 444	295	48	0	8
Tongan	0	121	244	2	7 056	0	0	0	0
Other Pacific Islander, n.e.c.	8	48	183	54	2 031	102	34	17	33
NORTH AMERICA									
Acadian/Cajun	5 780	852	2 459	5 237	18 337	2 528	784	247	167
Afro-American[16]	838 689	18 834	91 580	307 292	1 784 171	115 008	189 181	94 890	315 318
Aleut	29	10 244	57	44	1 091	67	0	0	29
American Indian[17]	236 720	50 506	255 131	228 070	838 458	107 287	40 309	16 278	7 331
American	687 394	22 350	96 176	305 459	658 879	91 998	70 810	27 697	10 639
Canadian[18]	2 650	1 440	9 644	1 306	86 341	6 191	13 768	1 248	603
Eskimo	50	42 024	263	133	1 854	303	24	8	0
French Canadian	9 185	5 335	25 248	5 981	156 625	21 859	110 426	2 990	1 717
Newfoundland	6	0	23	7	186	12	62	0	23
North American*	334	35	139	163	1 712	202	79	14	13
Nova Scotian	14	17	13	23	369	39	107	0	0
Pennsylvania German	395	354	2 645	682	12 742	3 569	904	2 396	59
United States	18 179	615	5 177	8 582	48 851	4 410	5 598	1 373	999
White[19]	60 705	7 445	37 431	37 817	267 505	27 241	11 125	2 910	2 258
Other North America, n.e.c.	0	8	0	0	39	25	0	0	0
OTHER GROUPS, N.E.C., NOT CLASSIFIED AND NOT REPORTED									
Other groups, n.e.c. and not classified[20]	27 612	8 091	49 752	27 446	331 630	42 904	36 781	8 097	5 539
Not reported	662 139	39 866	322 159	403 077	2 332 327	219 721	226 842	61 228	72 395

Table 3. Persons Who Reported at Least One Specific Ancestry Group: 1990—Con.

United States Region Division State	Florida	Georgia	Hawaii	Idaho	Illinois	Indiana	Iowa	Kansas
Total	12 937 926	6 478 216	1 108 229	1 006 749	11 430 602	5 544 159	2 776 755	2 477 574
WESTERN EUROPE (NON-HISPANIC GROUPS)								
Alsatian	805	155	76	28	888	286	138	100
Austrian[2]	63 932	9 396	1 943	2 759	49 970	8 330	4 516	6 541
Basque	1 189	128	169	5 587	445	190	59	70
Basque, French	117	11	19	166	49	55	20	10
Basque, Spanish	334	27	29	353	75	0	8	24
Basque, n.e.c.	738	90	121	5 068	321	135	31	36
Bavarian	227	29	13	34	184	102	48	126
Belgian[3]	4 636	1 099	171	310	13 131	5 180	2 997	1 719
British	76 630	39 724	2 882	5 121	34 734	24 749	7 960	10 028
Celtic	1 172	738	114	122	564	470	228	252
Cornish	109	62	4	10	160	28	44	0
Cypriot	330	55	9	0	177	68	8	0
Cypriot, Greek	140	29	9	0	131	29	4	0
Cypriot, Turkish	28	0	0	0	0	0	0	0
Cypriot, n.e.c.	162	26	0	0	46	39	4	0
Danish	46 654	10 404	3 455	40 297	70 586	14 918	84 202	18 878
Dutch	279 077	112 322	9 839	35 881	264 339	198 589	175 769	99 645
English	1 845 667	889 698	71 569	290 516	1 140 917	767 070	389 466	405 709
Finnish	25 031	4 978	1 422	3 937	20 636	4 470	2 401	1 717
Flemish	634	315	63	44	849	414	144	115
French[4]	508 205	155 250	21 674	45 801	355 629	209 181	103 265	109 945
German[5]	2 410 257	810 165	102 714	278 615	3 326 248	2 004 667	1 394 542	968 078
Greek[6]	66 861	14 795	1 589	2 525	93 046	18 978	6 233	3 986
Icelander	1 348	353	127	408	981	224	310	169
Irish[7]	1 898 822	970 713	65 473	141 901	1 860 989	965 080	527 428	435 784
Italian[8]	784 770	111 940	21 535	23 736	729 000	124 581	45 213	44 528
Luxemburger	1 259	192	162	207	9 249	685	6 153	361
Maltese	2 190	182	41	28	314	121	80	49
Manx	351	85	4	149	634	78	95	81
Northern Irish	285	39	0	6	118	52	26	79
Norwegian	90 375	21 388	9 054	32 956	167 003	25 978	152 084	21 878
Portuguese	32 345	4 925	57 125	2 717	6 810	2 476	1 097	1 414
Azores Islander	120	0	7	43	2	8	0	8
Madeira Islander	4	0	0	29	0	0	0	0
Portuguese, n.e.c.	32 221	4 925	57 111	2 674	6 779	2 468	1 097	1 406
Prussian	1 270	558	126	162	1 093	455	273	588
Saxon	258	56	30	2	68	147	25	12
Scandinavian	20 067	6 970	1 748	10 349	23 446	6 528	13 221	4 700
Scotch-Irish[9]	320 217	192 187	10 628	26 230	173 035	113 568	64 500	74 643
Scottish	316 732	141 833	13 784	39 890	176 096	111 535	53 694	57 460
Sicilian	2 887	538	157	127	2 824	716	182	102
Swedish	171 780	39 612	10 396	52 892	374 965	69 619	120 470	79 188
Swiss	37 877	9 210	1 948	12 680	47 057	44 511	18 886	18 105
Tirol	93	28	22	8	20	28	0	4
Welsh	103 115	37 811	4 596	20 746	63 144	42 004	29 060	27 031
West German	360	53	0	38	174	116	35	16
Western European*	1 327	1 255	168	387	1 330	735	680	632
Other Western European, n.e.c.	164	37	0	0	68	53	26	21
EASTERN EUROPE AND SOVIET UNION								
Albanian	1 812	202	63	21	2 837	255	86	66
Belorussian	232	15	8	0	627	42	12	0
Bulgarian	1 396	205	137	80	2 136	944	437	219
Carpath Rusyn	220	10	0	0	75	78	0	11
Central European	449	53	25	4	266	13	36	3
Croatian	18 020	9 651	679	981	61 284	18 633	5 295	8 511
Czech[10]	35 993	7 199	1 553	5 252	131 503	11 582	58 690	21 629
Czechoslovakian	15 085	2 817	703	1 260	23 927	3 458	6 142	3 564
Estonian	1 501	236	48	71	1 164	315	93	78
European*	22 179	14 216	1 622	3 757	14 040	7 263	4 071	6 333
German Russian/ Volga	145	59	40	29	464	167	67	659
Hungarian	99 822	13 418	2 631	2 455	68 439	40 828	3 710	4 058
Latvian	5 725	1 035	224	47	6 978	1 622	965	384
Lithuanian	41 713	6 751	1 411	831	109 417	11 098	3 090	2 079
Macedonian	583	74	6	74	1 264	3 210	17	17
Moravian	134	21	0	5	438	21	27	90
Northern European*	1 920	732	170	785	1 807	1 078	1 250	689
Polish	410 666	67 171	11 795	11 540	962 827	179 501	32 502	34 844
Rom	306	30	29	115	275	147	24	34
Romanian	29 675	3 850	610	470	23 202	7 725	917	940
Russian[11]	232 298	29 235	5 246	4 155	144 656	18 288	7 669	16 484
Ruthenian	65	57	16	6	120	67	21	0
Serbian	4 082	558	188	161	15 503	8 418	639	454
Slavic*	3 136	755	164	207	3 658	1 252	454	479
Slovak	74 335	13 110	2 087	2 582	120 400	44 412	10 599	8 085
Slovene	2 733	726	73	112	11 743	1 495	397	1 085
Soviet Union	350	65	0	11	322	91	14	76
Ukrainian	33 792	4 967	1 234	906	38 414	6 379	1 356	2 075
Windish	16	11	6	0	13	0	8	0
Yugoslavian*	9 462	1 317	678	1 137	19 145	4 214	1 047	1 425
Other Eastern European and Soviet Union, n.e.c.	5 900	1 699	95	53	4 901	549	226	371

DETAILED ANCESTRY GROUPS FOR STATES

15

Table 3. **Persons Who Reported at Least One Specific Ancestry Group: 1990**—Con.

United States Region Division State	State							
	Florida	Georgia	Hawaii	Idaho	Illinois	Indiana	Iowa	Kansas
CENTRAL AND SOUTH AMERICA (HISPANIC GROUPS) AND SPAIN								
Argentinean	8 356	455	89	68	1 759	199	79	75
Bolivian	2 904	352	8	41	1 423	154	55	145
Central American*	548	35	24	0	285	19	0	0
Chilean	8 856	441	55	106	1 580	237	129	172
Colombian	78 183	3 308	244	120	9 747	667	200	505
Costa Rican	7 130	510	84	36	1 000	241	111	159
Cuban	541 011	6 530	314	140	14 625	1 537	388	1 111
Dominican	36 116	1 301	259	19	2 518	426	162	108
Ecuadorian	16 377	778	176	32	9 009	272	70	537
Guatemalan	12 137	962	60	92	15 263	203	132	336
Hispanic*	54 960	4 071	1 133	3 018	22 248	3 287	1 547	4 895
Honduran	21 682	789	161	74	3 212	224	208	174
Latin American*	4 188	327	73	70	1 338	433	140	121
Mexican	134 161	37 267	10 720	35 591	557 536	60 593	21 255	65 729
Nicaraguan	70 374	694	101	127	1 366	101	103	117
Panamanian	10 907	2 133	241	93	1 903	567	304	444
Paraguayan	269	60	0	3	207	46	18	77
Peruvian	21 784	1 581	143	170	4 821	273	95	256
Puerto Rican	174 445	11 512	16 432	512	121 871	13 164	762	2 342
Salvadoran	10 502	1 783	111	114	5 951	156	299	306
South American*	1 031	167	43	0	253	19	17	22
Spaniard[12]	78 656	2 703	1 332	767	6 845	1 246	367	1 067
Spanish*	201 059	21 116	12 998	8 159	41 586	11 734	4 211	10 046
Uruguayan	2 039	254	15	0	183	15	29	10
Venezuelan	12 362	697	45	4	654	191	21	285
Other Hispanic, n.e.c.	2 644	125	0	0	117	23	21	0
CENTRAL AND SOUTH AMERICA (NON-HISPANIC GROUPS)								
Belizean	1 334	63	31	3	2 118	129	10	33
Brazilian	7 788	742	67	129	1 729	419	153	243
Guyanese	4 497	530	49	0	679	81	60	5
Other Central and South American, n.e.c.	247	7	0	0	0	0	0	0
WEST INDIES (NON-HISPANIC GROUPS)								
Bahamian	13 668	462	5	8	286	64	68	44
Barbadian	1 770	287	30	0	195	62	6	21
Bermudan	400	203	56	0	92	22	7	7
British West Indian	3 678	341	24	0	191	11	16	29
Antigua and Barbuda	685	58	12	0	35	0	0	6
Grenadian	850	39	0	0	7	0	16	0
Kitts-Nevis Islander	417	66	0	0	19	0	0	0
St. Lucia Islander	344	84	12	0	10	0	0	0
Vincent-Grenadine Islander	331	21	0	0	47	11	0	12
British West Indian, n.e.c.	1 051	73	0	0	73	0	0	11
Dutch West Indian	903	600	46	176	232	256	79	476
Haitian	105 495	1 183	215	32	4 597	316	50	85
Jamaican	86 231	6 262	443	78	7 734	1 368	104	442
Trinidadian and Tobagonian	7 500	616	63	43	444	157	31	71
US Virgin Islander	1 353	213	6	0	53	63	2	0
West Indian*	13 350	2 064	268	53	2 093	494	75	326
Other West Indian, n.e.c.	861	41	0	0	32	17	0	2
NORTH AFRICA AND SOUTHWEST ASIA								
Algerian	169	133	0	0	89	10	15	10
Arab*	7 233	1 198	254	183	10 468	1 513	391	579
Armenian	7 424	1 122	478	147	8 431	1 052	304	358
Assyrian	414	101	9	59	13 759	398	0	66
Egyptian	3 119	1 043	125	40	2 407	571	221	228
Iranian	6 088	3 279	352	366	6 458	1 230	787	1 155
Iraqi	696	90	0	26	1 638	47	30	74
Israeli	5 518	415	74	45	2 528	521	125	137
Jordanian	615	300	0	7	1 833	170	130	103
Lebanese	24 322	5 792	504	285	8 299	3 610	2 180	2 937
Middle Eastern*	324	82	35	8	283	23	58	75
Moroccan	1 400	89	24	10	690	138	44	81
Palestinian	2 786	420	10	23	5 534	471	165	270
Saudi Arabian	324	45	11	13	157	49	33	7
Syrian	8 225	1 032	152	145	3 367	1 773	660	450
Turkish	5 809	1 478	229	103	2 778	842	301	205
Yemeni	152	8	13	0	25	0	0	0
Other North African and Southwest Asian, n.e.c.	621	195	33	0	330	117	77	57
SUBSAHARAN AFRICA								
African*	13 065	10 212	308	80	10 106	3 108	926	1 628
Cape Verdean	718	204	50	0	111	53	0	69
Eritrean	91	163	0	0	129	0	0	0
Ethiopian[13]	14	32	0	0	14	21	0	4
Ghanian	415	531	17	0	1 167	111	51	94
Kenyan	76	134	6	4	171	12	31	62
Liberian	199	563	0	0	282	39	9	32
Nigerian	2 922	5 040	13	96	4 455	720	423	344
Sierra Leonean*	210	146	0	0	17	19	0	0
South African*	1 379	700	13	43	599	109	35	18
Sudanese	47	8	0	0	147	9	18	38
Ugandan	41	143	8	0	137	30	31	69
Other Subsaharan African, n.e.c.	786	931	33	16	675	201	225	100

Table 3. **Persons Who Reported at Least One Specific Ancestry Group: 1990**—Con.

United States Region Division State	State							
	Florida	Georgia	Hawaii	Idaho	Illinois	Indiana	Iowa	Kansas
SOUTH ASIA								
Afghanistan	196	503	44	6	557	129	37	175
Asian Indian	22 240	9 868	719	382	45 778	6 093	2 438	3 280
Bangladeshi	425	165	24	0	233	98	46	109
Nepali	67	21	79	0	16	13	27	0
Pakastani	3 835	1 665	192	92	11 237	1 035	356	623
Sri Lankan	422	73	186	14	405	267	53	152
Other South Asian, n.e.c.	0	0	0	0	0	0	0	0
OTHER ASIA								
Amerasian*	633	494	153	48	301	290	185	202
Asian*	3 760	1 858	1 903	104	5 655	1 012	525	714
Burmese	267	50	145	14	482	40	11	28
Cambodian[14]	1 347	1 860	133	73	2 720	277	586	662
Cantonese	274	73	394	0	748	49	56	22
Chinese[15]	28 787	11 180	95 899	1 469	44 077	6 128	3 727	4 298
Eurasian*	691	190	289	16	488	55	21	38
Filipino	37 531	7 527	176 370	1 586	66 984	5 354	2 156	2 974
Hmong	22	320	0	0	483	134	325	483
Hong Kong	141	11	76	10	197	27	2	35
Indonesian	1 211	340	474	97	723	406	270	236
Japanese	15 401	9 450	262 113	3 865	26 579	6 338	2 189	3 360
Khmer	7	6	0	0	3	0	25	0
Korean	14 722	16 580	28 887	1 214	42 167	6 298	4 959	5 406
Laotian	2 365	3 306	1 554	430	4 191	699	2 860	2 049
Malaysian	904	426	634	40	972	421	132	315
Mongolian	66	60	42	5	106	40	7	0
Okinawan	142	114	5 998	17	77	75	0	23
Singaporean	35	20	47	0	70	8	16	0
Taiwanese	4 509	2 364	1 632	82	7 163	1 168	1 025	1 246
Thai	6 295	2 224	1 753	279	5 963	1 056	1 305	1 073
Vietnamese	14 586	6 864	5 277	572	8 550	2 420	2 128	6 001
Other Asian, n.e.c.	28	13	48	0	15	11	7	64
PACIFIC								
Australian	2 791	1 065	409	375	1 539	826	231	645
Chamorro	94	69	416	2	18	30	0	13
Fijian	30	33	371	0	0	0	0	8
Guamanian	935	545	1 954	148	410	113	27	257
Hawaiian	3 075	1 156	156 812	695	1 535	1 008	430	631
Micronesian	31	41	999	49	10	6	0	77
New Zealander*	388	134	137	36	160	65	63	74
Pacific Islander*	340	53	691	65	397	44	10	0
Polynesian	390	154	1 083	53	103	123	40	76
Samoan	602	332	14 971	130	136	164	25	268
Tongan	136	0	3 283	78	9	26	33	43
Other Pacific Islander, n.e.c.	264	113	1 887	101	148	31	10	74
NORTH AMERICA								
Acadian/ Cajun	12 114	7 893	800	374	3 175	1 860	498	1 474
Afro-American[16]	1 194 537	1 420 631	23 864	3 190	1 425 762	370 476	41 013	121 451
Aleut	131	17	86	41	61	11	0	35
American Indian[17]	426 108	292 003	14 835	42 043	254 707	246 891	57 866	122 760
American[18]	678 601	804 672	7 013	41 831	301 671	373 498	82 295	112 285
Canadian[18]	43 958	6 425	1 699	2 323	12 794	6 451	2 385	2 793
Eskimo	319	147	237	202	254	184	24	155
French Canadian	110 221	20 430	3 176	7 529	47 059	20 094	11 030	11 512
Newfoundland	288	43	3	3	88	37	2	10
North American*	741	515	6	18	433	374	63	126
Nova Scotian	406	83	0	0	9	13	30	42
Pennsylvania German	9 451	1 027	149	930	7 208	9 684	6 580	5 042
United States	45 577	31 997	553	1 419	16 966	21 625	4 396	6 242
White[19]	62 393	82 402	13 442	9 138	29 455	32 446	9 644	17 117
Other North America, n.e.c.	12	18	0	0	2	18	2	0
OTHER GROUPS, N.E.C., NOT CLASSIFIED AND NOT REPORTED								
Other groups, n.e.c. and not classified[20]	179 096	55 318	6 182	21 968	154 153	142 902	24 282	29 779
Not reported	1 408 110	989 612	55 494	82 392	859 335	654 787	209 967	269 654

Table 3. Persons Who Reported at Least One Specific Ancestry Group: 1990—Con.

United States Region Division State	State							
	Kentucky	Louisiana	Maine	Maryland	Massachusetts	Michigan	Minnesota	Mississippi
Total	3 685 296	4 219 973	1 227 928	4 781 468	6 016 425	9 295 297	4 375 099	2 573 216

WESTERN EUROPE (NON-HISPANIC GROUPS)

Alsatian	133	133	41	308	444	342	204	38
Austrian[2]	2 945	3 445	1 910	18 028	20 733	24 899	16 361	1 171
Basque	94	226	36	268	337	236	130	28
Basque, French	11	73	2	60	37	7	24	4
Basque, Spanish	15	38	21	45	73	47	15	0
Basque, n.e.c.	68	115	13	163	227	182	91	24
Bavarian	29	26	8	116	41	79	172	16
Belgian[3]	309	1 203	250	1 152	2 263	22 559	6 328	134
British	18 006	10 837	6 646	28 992	28 905	31 204	11 596	8 537
Celtic	354	281	280	689	792	721	372	208
Cornish	24	0	2	45	49	292	55	0
Cypriot	25	52	0	231	120	193	37	0
Cypriot, Greek	25	11	0	66	42	131	21	0
Cypriot, Turkish	0	0	0	41	0	7	0	0
Cypriot, n.e.c.	0	41	0	124	78	55	16	0
Danish	3 888	5 713	6 979	12 563	18 172	51 184	98 373	2 454
Dutch	79 575	43 259	15 416	80 433	53 062	560 792	103 757	31 860
English	552 802	335 620	372 042	670 915	920 850	1 315 444	356 574	253 741
Finnish	1 405	1 590	6 326	5 547	31 529	109 357	103 603	1 250
Flemish	132	123	32	357		414	278	52
French[4]	92 588	550 440	223 653	125 278	634 833	652 465	236 268	84 955
German[5]	798 001	507 453	108 859	1 218 257	497 462	2 666 179	2 020 975	224 674
Greek[6]	4 060	5 964	5 341	32 203	81 769	42 678	8 924	2 215
Icelander	108	81	110	425	719	756	3 165	84
Irish[7]	695 853	518 124	217 226	769 312	1 570 742	1 320 458	573 755	392 864
Italian[8]	55 423	196 904	51 397	252 428	843 524	409 573	88 812	36 304
Luxemburger	83	59	42	340	326	907	5 898	70
Maltese	114	61	30	184	401	13 446	104	88
Manx	32	20	9	113	103	343	206	19
Northern Irish	79	59	39	48	360	141	56	5
Norwegian	7 355	9 510	7 256	22 520	30 726	72 261	757 212	4 052
Portuguese	1 275	2 988	4 523	6 898	289 424	4 203	1 386	1 306
Azores Islander	0	0	0	20	1 276	4	22	0
Madeira Islander	0	0	0	0	36	0	0	0
Portuguese, n.e.c.	1 275	2 988	4 523	6 878	288 112	4 199	1 364	1 306
Prussian	157	297	77	584	421	1 130	662	29
Saxon	91	22	19	86	44	126	27	43
Scandinavian	2 696	2 774	2 217	7 012	8 804	16 514	91 712	1 755
Scotch-Irish[9]	89 822	79 491	41 310	89 223	108 407	157 483	52 423	88 052
Scottish	65 638	40 417	72 320	108 427	199 489	252 104	63 996	35 921
Sicilian	159	874	219	849	1 908	2 636	351	195
Swedish	16 447	15 908	24 131	40 456	143 841	194 063	536 203	8 629
Swiss	10 901	4 217	2 227	14 405	10 670	27 146	25 524	2 237
Tirol	9	0	11	153	55	79	60	0
Welsh	21 128	12 408	10 124	47 236	26 621	55 588	22 753	8 611
West German	74	0	21	156	27	108	18	12
Western European*	339	283	147	921	907	1 206	561	211
Other Western European, n.e.c.	9	21	12	71	17	51	55	11

EASTERN EUROPE AND SOVIET UNION

Albanian	53	81	597	429	7 710	4 955	148	23
Belorussian	0	0	35	239	99	189	33	18
Bulgarian	106	124	95	588	532	2 232	635	50
Carpath Rusyn	0	6	0	146	36	174	82	7
Central European	23	27	4	207	210	171	101	7
Croatian	3 140	5 081	645	5 869	2 535	29 356	11 020	7 428
Czech[10]	2 832	3 883	1 833	18 130	9 285	40 242	87 718	1 271
Czechoslovakian	1 073	1 666	746	6 686	4 569	14 485	11 466	400
Estonian	71	55	86	1 487	977	478	558	0
European*	7 385	2 820	1 443	9 881	6 787	10 523	6 247	3 563
German Russian/ Volga	101	77	8	90	86	338	385	0
Hungarian	5 819	5 722	3 234	26 726	19 989	109 178	12 349	1 462
Latvian	240	285	455	3 398	6 479	5 485	2 612	116
Lithuanian	1 726	1 899	4 678	23 608	68 447	38 384	7 033	569
Macedonian	61	33	3	198	181	4 106	115	15
Moravian	13	27	18	47	50	114	30	2
Northern European*	198	685	161	1 070	1 249	2 153	2 871	122
Polish	24 487	22 456	23 838	200 570	359 677	889 527	238 039	10 645
Rom	41	70	10	114	56	145	99	77
Romanian	1 081	858	421	7 672	7 809	24 832	4 903	445
Russian[11]	6 435	7 328	8 122	95 964	133 080	76 121	31 945	1 892
Ruthenian	2	5	6	137	29	137	79	7
Serbian	333	236	85	1 196	595	7 439	3 292	115
Slavic*	241	364	195	1 398	957	3 713	4 169	323
Slovak	5 017	5 133	3 518	33 597	16 321	84 864	31 190	2 319
Slovene	321	166	67	1 018	393	3 002	6 614	66
Soviet Union	11	11	0	362	513	128	27	0
Ukrainian	1 582	1 391	1 328	15 872	17 500	43 914	10 691	480
Windish	0	0	0	18	0	0	0	0
Yugoslavian*	860	1 818	339	2 505	2 390	15 878	7 765	952
Other Eastern European and Soviet Union, n.e.c.	256	472	405	6 577	8 381	2 376	1 049	107

Table 3. Persons Who Reported at Least One Specific Ancestry Group: 1990—Con.

United States Region Division State	State							
	Kentucky	Louisiana	Maine	Maryland	Massachusetts	Michigan	Minnesota	Mississippi
CENTRAL AND SOUTH AMERICA (HISPANIC GROUPS) AND SPAIN								
Argentinean	112	392	96	1 432	1 421	595	132	14
Bolivian	53	131	24	2 879	717	226	196	0
Central American*	11	175	0	205	105	35	2	0
Chilean	76	341	45	2 231	1 493	545	268	90
Colombian	678	1 421	219	4 332	7 795	1 623	1 295	201
Costa Rican	143	628	24	762	1 739	313	115	59
Cuban	931	6 048	262	5 254	6 468	3 890	1 116	309
Dominican	502	657	190	3 342	29 065	1 053	186	211
Ecuadorian	526	781	67	2 632	2 437	471	192	63
Guatemalan	159	1 890	75	4 042	5 866	475	227	85
Hispanic*	1 255	4 325	363	5 999	13 516	10 461	2 437	635
Honduran	145	8 268	30	1 910	3 155	525	204	122
Latin American*	123	444	9	488	535	579	160	95
Mexican	6 823	21 046	1 990	14 948	11 421	118 424	28 512	4 900
Nicaraguan	95	3 635	19	3 279	591	237	158	74
Panamanian	531	982	79	2 243	1 497	638	358	236
Paraguayan	0	14	13	483	157	44	79	0
Peruvian	180	410	51	4 396	2 817	487	338	78
Puerto Rican	2 692	4 089	939	13 004	103 792	13 698	2 668	880
Salvadoran	96	1 118	78	16 449	7 835	345	315	85
South American*	14	69	7	272	311	195	12	84
Spaniard[12]	591	4 099	119	3 326	3 812	2 426	584	588
Spanish*	5 810	65 125	2 947	22 255	32 495	26 094	7 584	8 555
Uruguayan	5	0	5	316	525	87	151	0
Venezuelan	65	481	45	1 257	1 403	589	119	142
Other Hispanic, n.e.c.	9	219	0	82	107	41	18	11
CENTRAL AND SOUTH AMERICA (NON-HISPANIC GROUPS)								
Belizean	10	331	0	150	102	80	20	6
Brazilian	98	290	113	2 551	7 483	887	403	120
Guyanese	47	80	0	3 106	541	126	414	5
Other Central and South American, n.e.c.	0	0	0	0	32	0	0	0
WEST INDIES (NON-HISPANIC GROUPS)								
Bahamian	32	50	2	295	192	250	66	50
Barbadian	28	87	8	626	3 393	128	50	12
Bermudan	21	3	47	168	390	126	15	37
British West Indian	41	76	56	1 196	1 268	296	65	5
Antigua and Barbuda	26	15	2	141	320	62	20	0
Grenadian	6	11	8	508	138	55	14	0
Kitts-Nevis Islander	0	0	0	87	14	67	5	0
St. Lucia Islander	0	44	22	84	80	0	0	0
Vincent-Grenadine Islander	3	0	0	102	101	30	11	0
British West Indian, n.e.c.	6	6	24	274	615	82	6	5
Dutch West Indian	434	339	1	178	100	212	48	225
Haitian	276	633	157	3 837	23 692	614	237	80
Jamaican	600	1 105	198	15 456	11 990	3 777	696	318
Trinidadian and Tobagonian	111	349	40	4 493	2 590	294	63	24
US Virgin Islander	25	110	0	277	281	38	75	0
West Indian*	315	829	156	5 424	7 271	1 357	498	274
Other West Indian, n.e.c.	11	32	6	249	35	50	9	9
NORTH AFRICA AND SOUTHWEST ASIA								
Algerian	0	36	0	128	283	63	40	10
Arab*	569	1 271	156	2 160	2 782	14 842	751	160
Armenian	258	530	908	3 076	28 714	14 263	714	158
Assyrian	3	78	11	157	663	14 724	66	46
Egyptian	147	269	14	1 817	2 197	1 785	760	141
Iranian	962	1 123	143	9 644	4 659	3 117	1 922	235
Iraqi	17	98	0	468	383	6 668	80	9
Israeli	136	184	76	2 254	2 899	1 150	452	83
Jordanian	229	123	9	467	326	1 441	111	37
Lebanese	3 153	6 705	2 623	5 771	29 700	39 673	6 096	3 177
Middle Eastern*	20	59	2	266	256	161	116	29
Moroccan	49	58	37	1 303	550	758	70	27
Palestinian	231	454	67	1 038	903	2 695	368	92
Saudi Arabian	0	38	0	84	106	178	74	40
Syrian	639	1 659	490	1 845	7 552	7 656	1 114	314
Turkish	290	449	152	2 366	2 336	1 776	597	206
Yemeni	0	0	0	156	23	840	35	0
Other North African and Southwest Asian, n.e.c.	93	93	0	359	341	310	170	48
SUBSAHARAN AFRICA								
African*	1 601	5 604	168	12 107	5 841	6 219	2 129	2 459
Cape Verdean	60	84	57	484	29 326	85	37	12
Eritrean	0	82	8	419	120	106	137	0
Ethiopian[13]	9	0	5	53	26	77	33	7
Ghanian	59	68	7	2 502	661	330	181	0
Kenyan	20	0	5	408	166	53	102	0
Liberian	0	19	0	720	385	312	452	0
Nigerian	445	1 430	44	6 515	1 620	2 103	1 714	1 225
Sierra Leonean	8	0	0	975	156	53	78	0
South African*	59	58	33	568	750	360	119	19
Sudanese	6	24	0	170	57	82	22	13
Ugandan	10	0	0	317	211	46	99	0
Other Subsaharan African, n.e.c.	103	102	25	1 929	601	556	280	19

DETAILED ANCESTRY GROUPS FOR STATES

19

Table 3. **Persons Who Reported at Least One Specific Ancestry Group: 1990**—Con.

United States Region Division State	State							
	Kentucky	Louisiana	Maine	Maryland	Massachusetts	Michigan	Minnesota	Mississippi
SOUTH ASIA								
Afghanistan	18	9	304	488	214	217	225	0
Asian Indian	2 367	4 385	449	21 262	13 603	18 100	5 308	1 793
Bangladeshi	62	23	15	487	256	250	0	26
Nepali	0	3	15	241	197	167	25	22
Pakastani	228	485	16	3 342	1 814	2 524	446	99
Sri Lankan	57	129	24	844	297	158	497	35
Other South Asian, n.e.c.	0	0	0	0	9	0	0	0
OTHER ASIA								
Amerasian*	108	207	49	448	264	223	283	138
Asian*	557	1 095	165	2 358	1 944	2 688	1 012	463
Burmese	0	30	9	513	237	85	31	27
Cambodian[14]	190	173	809	1 798	11 821	687	2 981	14
Cantonese	67	63	0	186	952	232	29	0
Chinese[15]	3 137	5 321	1 269	26 479	47 245	17 100	8 850	2 532
Eurasian*	75	54	7	407	335	300	155	11
Filipino	2 587	5 981	1 438	21 086	8 024	16 086	5 210	2 120
Hmong	0	0	0	0	90	2 013	16 785	0
Hong Kong	0	0	0	63	244	24	80	0
Indonesian	307	224	41	770	808	876	164	39
Japanese	3 275	2 681	1 202	10 067	10 662	13 309	5 330	1 576
Khmer	0	37	0	83	528	0	21	0
Korean	4 264	3 643	1 225	29 471	12 878	17 738	12 922	1 610
Laotian	308	862	44	639	3 953	2 753	7 252	54
Malaysian	63	120	33	400	310	503	76	198
Mongolian	55	19	13	76	52	53	13	6
Okinawan	22	0	27	61	17	67	34	71
Singaporean	5	15	0	47	56	31	16	0
Taiwanese	356	968	48	5 303	4 401	2 892	1 179	297
Thai	625	1 032	221	3 202	1 996	1 803	883	283
Vietnamese	1 340	14 696	809	7 809	13 101	5 229	8 698	3 340
Other Asian, n.e.c.	14	0	19	40	23	20	4	0
PACIFIC								
Australian	475	350	191	1 251	1 198	1 388	607	162
Chamorro	49	13	2	69	24	6	32	0
Fijian	0	9	0	50	20	35	0	0
Guamanian	180	307	85	390	256	216	140	83
Hawaiian	539	779	276	986	637	1 333	493	303
Micronesian	0	50	0	33	0	50	21	0
New Zealander	7	67	18	201	206	144	36	8
Pacific Islander*	57	32	43	101	56	227	101	7
Polynesian	74	60	19	85	66	48	69	42
Samoan	181	98	23	87	115	148	72	56
Tongan	10	0	2	0	23	8	39	0
Other Pacific Islander, n.e.c.	60	47	37	141	41	179	83	11
NORTH AMERICA								
Acadian/ Cajun	2 086	432 549	2 365	2 298	1 162	1 954	645	11 097
Afro-American[16]	222 428	1 097 499	4 882	965 573	170 439	1 099 751	78 891	774 950
Aleut	7	38	9	21	33	22	68	1
American Indian[17]	208 938	154 511	48 617	121 765	67 157	282 695	70 252	114 236
American	586 090	272 108	84 120	167 320	150 550	316 566	63 517	317 021
Canadian[18]	2 200	2 435	13 648	6 606	66 007	47 488	4 495	1 357
Eskimo	71	98	41	77	128	150	240	65
French Canadian	8 033	86 569	110 209	21 206	310 636	174 138	46 719	7 487
Newfoundland	7	21	107	58	2 333	87	48	0
North American*	193	164	29	254	200	286	83	249
Nova Scotian	21	485	182	61	2 206	41	48	7
Pennsylvania German	818	469	374	3 581	1 025	10 758	2 185	181
United States	23 512	7 871	2 677	11 126	10 519	15 615	2 884	11 006
White[19]	42 777	34 343	7 603	18 457	18 700	38 556	8 890	44 108
Other North America, n.e.c.	13	0	0	5	0	11	0	0
OTHER GROUPS, N.E.C., NOT CLASSIFIED AND NOT REPORTED								
Other groups, n.e.c. and not classified[20]	60 667	35 710	23 291	63 168	94 050	127 760	29 622	36 803
Not reported	688 555	405 322	87 649	439 105	390 044	722 977	217 550	367 941

Table 3. **Persons Who Reported at Least One Specific Ancestry Group: 1990**—Con.

United States Region Division State	Missouri	Montana	Nebraska	Nevada	New Hampshire	New Jersey	New Mexico	New York	North Carolina
Total	5 117 073	799 065	1 578 385	1 201 833	1 109 252	7 730 188	1 515 069	17 990 455	6 628 637
WESTERN EUROPE (NON-HISPANIC GROUPS)									
Alsatian	228	8	40	46	49	717	156	1 977	165
Austrian[2]	11 764	5 556	3 152	4 401	2 851	58 912	3 299	156 994	6 859
Basque	151	469	45	4 840	53	534	502	1 300	119
Basque, French	27	66	0	472	0	72	63	131	16
Basque, Spanish	10	46	0	776	0	143	61	242	6
Basque, n.e.c.	114	357	45	3 592	53	319	378	927	97
Bavarian	116	5	8	32	0	70	18	227	97
Belgian[3]	1 930	994	1 017	469	688	2 978	283	5 115	813
British	18 492	2 135	3 997	5 368	6 716	27 217	6 397	58 197	34 868
Celtic	404	73	126	165	230	784	186	1 920	517
Cornish	15	6	41	52	16	48	13	104	29
Cypriot	11	7	0	7	12	659	7	1 734	17
Cypriot, Greek	0	7	0	7	3	315	7	687	17
Cypriot, Turkish	11	0	0	0	0	9	0	134	0
Cypriot, n.e.c.	0	0	0	0	9	335	0	913	0
Danish	20 695	16 752	59 860	19 170	4 156	27 703	7 122	47 058	9 848
Dutch	153 961	27 018	46 237	30 751	14 238	159 165	29 401	369 807	147 469
English	743 232	137 181	208 616	207 010	265 668	702 504	188 934	1 566 019	986 683
Finnish	3 583	7 324	1 651	3 582	8 294	8 343	2 266	21 288	3 830
Flemish	166	41	72	47	97	272	90	801	299
French[4]	268 116	43 073	54 459	60 172	205 455	157 195	43 970	625 459	141 803
German[5]	1 843 299	285 305	794 911	279 693	118 033	1 407 956	234 000	2 898 888	1 110 581
Greek[6]	13 294	1 920	3 266	6 490	15 507	60 899	3 108	159 876	14 927
Icelander	304	334	226	342	166	522	149	1 427	245
Irish[7]	1 037 658	138 828	272 185	199 772	232 409	1 415 489	163 690	2 800 128	841 276
Italian[8]	161 173	21 322	35 014	86 785	81 310	1 457 013	36 204	2 837 904	111 983
Luxemburger	417	216	922	225	90	425	132	915	83
Maltese	98	0	45	193	84	1 252	11	8 245	268
Manx	133	87	67	45	23	57	32	130	50
Northern Irish	55	5	0	16	9	175	0	411	87
Norwegian	29 531	86 460	30 533	23 229	8 401	46 991	13 936	90 158	20 184
Portuguese	3 086	1 421	744	8 246	10 199	63 188	1 768	44 090	4 970
Azores Islander	40	0	0	42	19	31	8	46	9
Madeira Islander	0	0	0	0	8	0	12	18	7
Portuguese, n.e.c.	3 046	1 421	744	8 204	10 172	63 157	1 748	44 026	4 954
Prussian	633	109	183	286	77	487	153	1 366	373
Saxon	35	31	45	29	0	76	29	76	77
Scandinavian	7 156	9 971	5 988	6 112	2 428	7 921	4 098	17 092	6 678
Scotch-Irish[9]	129 228	25 369	34 701	27 950	27 747	86 869	33 977	165 952	343 345
Scottish	94 211	27 904	26 278	32 601	56 864	132 882	29 082	266 312	177 699
Sicilian	949	139	301	740	386	2 284	174	5 968	434
Swedish	69 039	36 784	99 263	31 301	25 464	72 647	19 999	165 333	35 861
Swiss	26 697	5 754	10 408	7 392	2 608	25 402	4 281	46 873	10 716
Tirol	23	0	0	8	0	287	1	385	9
Welsh	40 516	9 704	11 998	14 266	7 868	47 015	11 275	103 679	36 229
West German	109	24	30	12	13	238	28	322	92
Western European*	879	174	195	328	284	759	251	1 693	1 103
Other Western European, n.e.c.	34	16	19	9	0	23	14	154	29
EASTERN EUROPE AND SOVIET UNION									
Albanian	531	45	50	158	849	3 339	30	10 628	191
Belorussian	10	8	0	0	24	629	0	703	45
Bulgarian	361	246	123	206	2	815	61	2 208	240
Carpath Rusyn	6	0	0	0	0	614	0	1 038	38
Central European	187	0	25	35	4	454	53	913	44
Croatian	16 519	3 119	3 283	2 560	682	8 173	1 842	20 517	8 189
Czech[10]	24 529	7 607	90 043	5 518	1 693	23 473	4 245	50 014	6 156
Czechoslovakian	4 550	1 967	7 871	1 615	799	13 686	1 811	28 402	2 355
Estonian	155	66	58	148	128	2 623	67	3 982	304
European*	9 436	2 652	2 271	2 626	1 481	9 531	3 229	27 446	11 253
German Russian/ Volga	202	30	172	89	3	328	88	598	179
Hungarian	14 843	2 750	3 318	7 100	4 093	141 627	4 337	186 898	12 749
Latvian	760	223	869	278	713	5 393	257	12 038	843
Lithuanian	6 283	915	3 557	2 722	7 953	49 870	1 943	70 397	5 602
Macedonian	265	36	42	145	31	460	62	1 570	29
Moravian	54	1	179	0	3	65	7	118	71
Northern European*	798	588	472	427	270	1 010	710	2 854	920
Polish	95 900	15 736	61 199	33 591	48 767	626 506	19 523	1 181 077	59 722
Rom	114	20	48	53	17	284	34	225	12
Romanian	3 733	572	900	1 745	937	21 177	713	66 977	2 007
Russian[11]	27 516	7 776	10 136	13 241	11 066	229 449	7 912	596 875	17 688
Ruthenian	7	8	46	0	0	330	3	277	16
Serbian	1 285	522	443	871	68	1 718	307	3 534	639
Slavic*	1 084	556	342	475	131	4 171	384	5 969	751
Slovak	17 261	3 907	9 156	6 311	2 671	117 562	4 469	118 045	12 313
Slovene	515	264	190	238	80	972	189	2 619	537
Soviet Union	41	0	32	63	56	469	12	2 150	28
Ukrainian	4 766	1 478	1 161	2 434	2 434	73 935	1 512	121 113	4 897
Windish	6	11	0	20	0	29	0	31	7
Yugoslavian*	2 668	3 355	483	2 483	359	12 682	903	30 455	1 315
Other Eastern European and Soviet Union, n.e.c.	1 275	97	151	315	511	11 075	243	34 778	913

DETAILED ANCESTRY GROUPS FOR STATES   **21**

Table 3. **Persons Who Reported at Least One Specific Ancestry Group: 1990**—Con.

United States Region Division State	Missouri	Montana	Nebraska	Nevada	New Hampshire	New Jersey	New Mexico	New York	North Carolina
CENTRAL AND SOUTH AMERICA (HISPANIC GROUPS) AND SPAIN									
Argentinean	318	17	119	415	43	5 789	116	12 087	410
Bolivian	276	6	65	165	10	1 052	67	4 406	127
Central American*	0	0	0	53	2	369	0	1 300	31
Chilean	307	24	143	374	99	4 640	306	10 288	456
Colombian	1 011	49	124	1 262	436	47 809	469	99 935	1 707
Costa Rican	144	0	42	443	103	4 612	90	7 939	433
Cuban	1 845	145	383	5 430	641	72 373	772	64 741	3 296
Dominican	314	29	105	429	756	51 138	246	337 867	999
Ecuadorian	467	24	53	286	129	27 486	101	89 040	1 008
Guatemalan	259	46	27	852	103	6 694	681	20 293	471
Hispanic*	2 752	553	2 083	5 022	369	26 265	105 892	78 843	2 795
Honduran	224	36	97	384	204	7 241	87	23 014	457
Latin American*	118	9	35	228	6	934	144	2 843	213
Mexican	35 860	7 037	25 814	72 281	2 334	24 703	215 576	71 284	24 685
Nicaraguan	240	37	44	957	31	3 663	270	10 036	408
Panamanian	585	75	143	361	45	3 063	434	26 491	1 890
Paraguayan	1	0	0	28	10	413	13	1 552	34
Peruvian	476	62	197	430	119	22 962	175	30 011	462
Puerto Rican	2 894	368	916	3 829	2 528	219 942	2 183	762 429	10 161
Salvadoran	232	34	192	3 121	88	14 766	498	40 992	863
South American*	41	12	5	24	16	547	20	3 168	153
Spaniard[12]	1 351	229	406	2 435	247	23 666	24 861	42 309	1 620
Spanish*	13 993	3 351	4 686	20 156	3 051	71 596	190 700	156 310	15 957
Uruguayan	49	0	9	36	142	3 297	5	3 742	58
Venezuelan	215	66	46	150	62	2 130	95	5 559	430
Other Hispanic, n.e.c.	12	0	0	18	0	77	53	334	130
CENTRAL AND SOUTH AMERICA (NON-HISPANIC GROUPS)									
Belizean	29	0	5	61	14	304	50	5 520	74
Brazilian	254	7	103	408	289	7 482	184	11 145	469
Guyanese	79	27	28	23	39	6 697	33	56 462	308
Other Central and South American, n.e.c.	0	0	0	0	0	45	0	489	17
WEST INDIES (NON-HISPANIC GROUPS)									
Bahamian	71	0	37	97	21	562	4	1 986	114
Barbadian	3	0	0	25	32	1 687	26	22 298	211
Bermudan	29	0	0	7	58	529	5	1 050	110
British West Indian	29	2	5	106	24	1 857	8	23 799	149
Antigua and Barbuda	21	0	0	7	0	421	0	4 659	8
Grenadian	2	0	0	12	0	483	8	7 916	52
Kitts-Nevis Islander	0	0	5	0	0	172	0	1 617	22
St. Lucia Islander	0	0	0	3	0	139	0	1 906	16
Vincent-Grenadine Islander	6	0	0	26	0	282	0	4 335	9
British West Indian, n.e.c.	0	2	0	58	24	360	0	3 366	42
Dutch West Indian	778	37	97	169	0	152	899	1 153	550
Haitian	414	0	55	128	281	18 854	66	107 207	542
Jamaican	1 202	26	158	369	324	26 690	261	186 429	2 639
Trinidadian and Tobagonian	54	0	8	73	53	4 245	16	42 973	391
US Virgin Islander	27	0	4	0	9	338	0	2 743	71
West Indian*	394	10	117	238	147	8 935	179	80 075	1 634
Other West Indian, n.e.c.	5	0	0	0	0	320	12	1 330	51
NORTH AFRICA AND SOUTHWEST ASIA									
Algerian	12	0	0	7	0	94	0	523	62
Arab*	1 090	52	310	553	307	5 311	712	12 884	1 348
Armenian	1 058	158	210	1 224	2 710	14 664	525	23 590	1 060
Assyrian	70	9	15	66	0	845	13	680	14
Egyptian	520	37	186	253	185	11 704	143	15 211	903
Iranian	2 208	106	479	1 118	499	5 804	667	18 183	2 094
Iraqi	119	18	23	30	51	632	31	2 814	124
Israeli	566	24	172	339	51	6 569	144	24 091	253
Jordanian	122	19	15	33	0	1 234	41	2 408	265
Lebanese	4 973	816	1 682	2 219	3 777	12 261	1 974	31 089	5 619
Middle Eastern*	85	2	13	0	0	491	44	1 618	45
Moroccan	437	34	43	214	12	811	61	4 043	124
Palestinian	291	23	14	57	8	2 367	112	4 098	894
Saudi Arabian	75	0	59	0	6	46	54	46	68
Syrian	1 230	164	749	789	628	11 722	269	18 201	1 114
Turkish	632	52	218	404	379	7 579	336	19 325	1 046
Yemeni	40	0	0	0	0	141	9	1 564	0
Other North African and Southwest Asian, n.e.c.	178	0	7	51	33	359	42	1 338	72
SUBSAHARAN AFRICA									
African*	4 607	36	740	1 045	239	10 922	872	41 452	7 650
Cape Verdean	36	0	21	22	114	436	21	1 099	211
Eritrean	16	0	0	20	0	33	0	192	0
Ethiopian[13]	0	0	0	12	0	26	7	74	9
Ghanian	59	0	16	19	68	1 466	8	6 158	205
Kenyan	59	0	0	54	12	493	20	272	87
Liberian	54	0	17	0	0	952	0	1 422	220
Nigerian	1 644	67	466	188	49	4 330	95	9 610	2 083
Sierra Leonean	19	0	0	0	0	384	0	710	103
South African*	88	0	58	8	25	716	106	1 884	217
Sudanese	23	0	7	0	5	158	0	1 221	23
Ugandan	0	14	0	0	0	46	9	231	64
Other Subsaharan African, n.e.c.	283	19	53	56	31	734	29	3 408	686

Table 3. **Persons Who Reported at Least One Specific Ancestry Group: 1990**—Con.

United States Region Division State	State								
	Missouri	Montana	Nebraska	Nevada	New Hampshire	New Jersey	New Mexico	New York	North Carolina
SOUTH ASIA									
Afghanistan	158	0	275	196	9	659	223	4 675	118
Asian Indian	4 030	213	948	1 236	1 871	54 039	1 566	80 430	7 091
Bangladeshi	55	0	15	22	17	548	63	5 989	69
Nepali	0	11	15	25	4	36	0	441	123
Pakastani	908	28	145	380	217	7 053	203	19 163	787
Sri Lankan	136	7	55	99	9	898	61	1 923	180
Other South Asian, n.e.c.	0	0	7	0	0	27	0	7	8
OTHER ASIA									
Amerasian*	231	18	100	249	55	366	166	777	420
Asian*	981	64	200	909	149	4 234	346	9 117	1 521
Burmese	14	3	0	40	25	196	29	970	112
Cambodian[14]	695	6	125	290	289	476	59	3 326	1 493
Cantonese	76	0	9	84	5	632	10	5 366	0
Chinese[15]	8 006	811	1 908	7 001	2 218	47 068	2 400	236 876	8 078
Eurasian*	45	13	49	164	0	335	38	715	123
Filipino	7 181	908	1 699	12 734	1 304	51 821	2 539	64 202	6 181
Hmong	0	123	117	13	0	16	0	184	551
Hong Kong	6	0	6	0	0	133	6	1 090	19
Indonesian	268	22	92	180	47	916	175	3 680	273
Japanese	6 233	1 391	2 307	5 111	1 153	19 948	3 482	39 859	8 069
Khmer	0	0	0	0	0	12	0	153	92
Korean	6 452	842	2 600	4 693	1 635	38 087	1 756	93 145	8 572
Laotian	637	171	675	950	475	526	444	2 658	1 731
Malaysian	535	42	173	223	51	718	118	2 471	203
Mongolian	20	48	5	83	9	362	37	301	21
Okinawan	66	0	21	53	9	45	18	78	150
Singaporean	0	0	0	22	0	82	0	315	57
Taiwanese	1 500	16	378	605	200	11 391	476	21 956	2 076
Thai	1 433	126	525	2 408	285	2 284	655	6 991	1 982
Vietnamese	3 652	239	1 242	1 978	281	5 480	1 374	12 116	4 406
Other Asian, n.e.c.	8	8	5	14	0	39	5	271	137
PACIFIC									
Australian	763	268	140	576	241	1 573	129	3 688	698
Chamorro	3	0	0	22	0	26	12	43	202
Fijian	46	7	0	0	0	52	4	68	7
Guamanian	216	44	145	245	40	363	249	776	380
Hawaiian	1 202	269	342	2 060	308	1 260	583	1 876	1 428
Micronesian	76	7	29	27	5	9	0	3	39
New Zealander	46	45	0	96	39	219	34	386	107
Pacific Islander*	55	6	2	150	9	353	27	188	117
Polynesian	211	56	28	130	19	52	46	339	183
Samoan	621	91	87	384	0	147	100	335	390
Tongan	56	0	0	177	0	4	18	25	0
Other Pacific Islander, n.e.c.	58	19	14	219	10	92	81	302	103
NORTH AMERICA									
Acadian/ Cajun	3 074	235	483	1 278	257	1 047	1 308	2 219	4 478
Afro-American[16]	469 075	2 071	51 226	67 797	5 181	750 914	25 288	1 620 890	1 227 936
Aleut	6	80	15	42	9	94	163	133	10
American Indian[17]	306 254	55 858	31 998	55 723	30 114	88 728	144 936	271 105	265 777
American	316 691	22 699	30 722	39 377	48 993	156 379	46 290	426 740	752 901
Canadian[18]	4 359	1 469	1 077	3 354	12 913	12 783	1 643	45 274	6 621
Eskimo	335	131	44	161	34	71	31	388	95
French Canadian	17 860	7 780	6 503	9 662	118 857	30 768	6 260	155 531	20 308
Newfoundland	65	0	6	20	257	201	12	688	51
North American*	252	31	62	60	48	207	50	517	689
Nova Scotian	22	28	0	11	267	32	7	113	23
Pennsylvania German	3 013	1 040	3 709	752	355	7 886	664	10 503	1 747
United States	12 952	1 458	1 323	1 799	1 985	13 853	3 771	41 497	34 210
White[19]	34 484	3 669	3 766	9 093	7 417	11 325	29 880	33 624	76 652
Other North America, n.e.c.	52	0	6	0	0	6	0	0	17
OTHER GROUPS, N.E.C., NOT CLASSIFIED AND NOT REPORTED									
Other groups, n.e.c. and not classified[20]	67 918	12 369	14 494	20 711	14 963	105 831	16 118	431 474	63 639
Not reported	569 213	51 238	90 353	91 206	77 320	568 460	124 805	1 556 551	1 037 704

Table 3. Persons Who Reported at Least One Specific Ancestry Group: 1990—Con.

United States Region Division State	North Dakota	Ohio	Oklahoma	Oregon	Pennsylvania	Rhode Island	South Carolina	South Dakota	Tennessee
Total	638 800	10 847 115	3 145 585	2 842 321	11 881 643	1 003 464	3 486 703	696 004	4 877 185
WESTERN EUROPE (NON-HISPANIC GROUPS)									
Alsatian	19	868	47	292	607	49	86	9	141
Austrian[2]	1 178	29 810	3 379	9 582	63 060	2 695	3 166	1 390	3 714
Basque	11	203	105	2 257	250	24	48	30	91
Basque, French	0	33	0	172	23	0	4	0	2
Basque, Spanish	0	15	23	298	13	0	14	8	14
Basque, n.e.c.	11	155	82	1 787	214	24	30	22	75
Bavarian	18	226	57	92	213	0	31	24	53
Belgian[3]	441	3 085	589	1 862	4 804	554	247	621	595
British	853	41 342	11 932	19 028	36 845	3 181	15 548	1 040	24 044
Celtic	45	1 028	176	1 048	895	117	199	60	566
Cornish	0	99	52	110	158	0	20	0	2
Cypriot	0	74	0	6	129	0	29	7	29
Cypriot, Greek	0	35	0	6	62	0	0	0	21
Cypriot, Turkish	0	0	0	0	0	0	0	0	0
Cypriot, n.e.c.	0	39	0	0	67	0	29	7	8
Danish	10 801	21 602	9 938	47 806	20 875	1 978	5 307	23 456	7 449
Dutch	10 459	310 765	140 457	118 089	354 656	6 933	55 860	36 844	125 571
English	39 015	1 449 303	441 391	575 183	1 274 665	161 001	436 149	68 345	691 508
Finnish	3 807	21 044	1 844	22 977	8 612	1 562	1 849	3 468	2 488
Flemish	20	442	125	373	351	62	70	19	80
French[4]	27 901	360 151	118 804	160 967	263 960	134 128	87 527	24 490	113 713
German[5]	324 929	4 067 840	714 184	878 555	4 314 762	73 425	500 089	355 102	724 059
Greek[6]	608	49 496	4 451	8 535	55 158	6 208	8 119	905	7 061
Icelander	3 161	590	155	1 200	523	185	127	209	176
Irish[7]	53 678	1 896 231	641 733	466 887	2 255 867	213 653	485 804	87 657	875 155
Italian[8]	4 255	637 143	44 951	83 093	1 372 904	199 028	56 291	6 110	73 079
Luxemburger	419	867	253	606	401	65	108	1 242	141
Maltese	36	294	55	107	388	104	87	19	88
Manx	21	632	57	208	124	6	7	0	0
Northern Irish	6	112	1	20	276	31	45	8	50
Norwegian	189 106	31 911	17 401	124 216	31 146	4 010	9 170	106 361	12 098
Portuguese	256	6 151	2 612	11 369	12 770	94 650	2 252	422	2 002
Azores Islander	0	24	0	67	12	508	9	0	0
Madeira Islander	0	0	0	0	7	4	0	0	0
Portuguese, n.e.c.	256	6 127	2 612	11 302	12 751	94 138	2 243	422	2 002
Prussian	53	1 075	364	540	827	48	197	179	288
Saxon	0	1 147	65	57	378	0	46	0	102
Scandinavian	11 074	9 046	4 305	28 021	7 499	924	3 874	7 790	4 437
Scotch-Irish[9]	8 262	217 478	95 508	95 336	270 299	13 638	159 534	9 980	197 942
Scottish	8 557	224 351	59 409	110 314	223 544	24 144	77 111	8 472	100 080
Sicilian	46	3 274	142	688	1 936	162	210	46	260
Swedish	35 933	87 475	32 638	124 620	126 255	22 373	18 534	33 421	27 552
Swiss	2 036	88 523	7 474	30 984	68 919	1 459	5 546	3 431	10 252
Tirol	0	141	0	0	3 496	15	8	7	8
Welsh	1 697	165 494	21 894	40 781	221 964	3 253	17 190	4 034	28 745
West German	0	99	77	29	206	9	41	0	38
Western European*	55	1 092	204	1 361	1 104	37	337	26	627
Other Western European, n.e.c.	6	31	27	69	12	15	25	4	4
EASTERN EUROPE AND SOVIET UNION									
Albanian	15	1 107	22	139	2 538	223	52	0	187
Belorussian	0	146	19	99	233	24	0	0	16
Bulgarian	175	2 408	277	768	1 010	105	117	109	183
Carpath Rusyn	0	620	15	2	3 701	0	0	0	0
Central European	4	183	16	37	266	18	49	17	8
Croatian	246	59 315	2 592	3 804	78 750	461	4 585	281	4 677
Czech[10]	15 298	67 389	15 215	16 470	29 528	1 262	3 183	18 593	4 876
Czechoslovakian	1 565	15 864	3 451	5 202	16 453	640	1 087	1 383	1 524
Estonian	115	852	47	641	727	56	194	10	110
European*	327	10 902	5 156	16 311	10 705	1 017	4 958	915	8 043
German Russian/ Volga	228	441	222	127	313	0	67	37	45
Hungarian	3 005	218 145	3 797	10 776	152 863	2 902	6 111	1 361	7 349
Latvian	64	3 973	338	1 197	4 847	377	252	115	623
Lithuanian	383	29 840	2 090	4 341	103 272	4 580	2 673	256	3 252
Macedonian	9	3 452	38	135	808	66	28	17	21
Moravian	4	98	24	47	82	25	7	14	21
Northern European*	219	1 271	509	2 724	1 153	161	406	797	862
Polish	17 320	442 226	29 519	48 414	882 348	47 227	29 762	9 139	35 325
Rom	18	224	143	206	226	13	16	17	169
Romanian	339	25 950	860	4 439	17 755	1 102	936	226	1 361
Russian[11]	18 544	81 618	7 580	28 735	215 841	12 412	6 483	7 322	10 622
Ruthenian	0	417	15	0	1 235	0	15	0	19
Serbian	27	15 545	160	466	19 913	7	262	22	354
Slavic*	85	4 165	298	917	8 654	192	382	78	345
Slovak	1 557	273 380	5 781	8 939	447 384	2 231	6 926	1 788	7 417
Slovene	24	49 598	215	343	14 584	73	290	22	256
Soviet Union	0	127	9	43	484	90	18	0	20
Ukrainian	3 634	43 569	1 969	6 220	129 753	3 530	2 266	391	2 063
Windish	0	17	9	0	2 827	0	7	0	0
Yugoslavian*	272	13 172	652	4 968	10 446	251	769	360	694
Other Eastern European and Soviet Union, n.e.c.	8	2 876	95	871	9 212	519	356	14	522

24

DETAILED ANCESTRY GROUPS FOR STATES

Table 3. Persons Who Reported at Least One Specific Ancestry Group: 1990—Con.

United States Region Division State	North Dakota	Ohio	Oklahoma	Oregon	Pennsylvania	Rhode Island	South Carolina	South Dakota	Tennessee
CENTRAL AND SOUTH AMERICA (HISPANIC GROUPS) AND SPAIN									
Argentinean	0	544	162	251	1 206	153	107	14	189
Bolivian	0	153	108	132	284	361	65	0	47
Central American*	0	107	14	25	21	0	0	0	19
Chilean	4	409	121	448	923	146	165	62	158
Colombian	152	1 584	780	722	5 124	4 617	888	44	452
Costa Rican	0	423	138	381	712	13	127	9	94
Cuban	70	2 826	905	1 197	6 365	811	1 204	34	1 602
Dominican	2	840	254	186	4 236	8 902	544	10	393
Ecuadorian	28	515	163	148	1 453	457	292	6	166
Guatemalan	14	770	277	992	636	3 463	118	12	125
Hispanic*	287	7 884	3 847	6 957	15 632	1 537	1 307	429	1 438
Honduran	65	503	359	404	822	152	322	19	234
Latin American*	6	381	132	236	552	29	91	0	188
Mexican	2 311	50 725	53 069	71 680	20 913	1 994	8 316	2 951	11 997
Nicaraguan	3	370	100	412	723	130	151	0	200
Panamanian	42	814	711	346	1 384	170	625	115	505
Paraguayan	0	66	18	13	77	0	21	0	0
Peruvian	12	1 080	486	612	1 442	440	192	9	306
Puerto Rican	263	35 644	3 444	2 180	97 817	8 366	4 282	259	3 112
Salvadoran	30	615	312	800	925	826	119	12	90
South American*	0	94	39	38	303	18	123	0	29
Spaniard[12]	47	2 056	1 329	1 745	4 003	301	817	117	939
Spanish*	1 158	26 408	13 880	18 692	35 494	3 679	8 497	1 296	9 242
Uruguayan	0	13	38	16	85	32	22	0	28
Venezuelan	6	416	233	148	658	162	146	0	244
Other Hispanic, n.e.c.	0	12	4	0	94	0	29	0	33
CENTRAL AND SOUTH AMERICA (NON-HISPANIC GROUPS)									
Belizean	0	10	18	23	161	47	58	0	6
Brazilian	36	531	235	394	1 512	529	298	6	236
Guyanese	0	476	70	60	619	69	73	0	98
Other Central and South American, n.e.c.	0	5	8	0	24	0	0	0	0
WEST INDIES (NON-HISPANIC GROUPS)									
Bahamian	23	154	68	71	218	5	147	5	265
Barbadian	0	114	31	26	761	72	75	8	18
Bermudan	5	88	7	11	246	47	37	0	37
British West Indian	0	128	30	9	625	77	42	2	113
Antigua and Barbuda	0	30	7	9	147	0	19	0	4
Grenadian	0	24	4	0	252	14	0	0	31
Kitts-Nevis Islander	0	19	7	0	51	0	0	0	8
St. Lucia Islander	0	16	7	0	21	0	13	0	14
Vincent-Grenadine Islander	0	0	5	0	49	37	0	0	6
British West Indian, n.e.c.	0	39	0	0	105	20	10	2	50
Dutch West Indian	32	539	23 465	604	152	21	220	27	2 139
Haitian	25	703	208	105	2 253	958	300	8	166
Jamaican	67	3 841	332	223	10 191	483	1 135	29	1 150
Trinidadian and Tobagonian	0	469	179	4	1 509	147	189	10	189
US Virgin Islander	0	65	30	17	106	6	47	0	49
West Indian*	18	1 499	414	357	3 427	332	752	16	594
Other West Indian, n.e.c.	0	35	22	25	67	0	20	0	47
NORTH AFRICA AND SOUTHWEST ASIA									
Algerian	0	116	64	36	69	0	7	4	8
Arab*	26	5 340	790	866	2 893	380	608	49	1 085
Armenian	174	2 948	401	1 308	6 763	6 345	455	82	540
Assyrian	6	159	14	139	322	57	55	26	107
Egyptian	28	1 654	328	255	2 071	306	279	63	453
Iranian	117	3 399	2 494	2 208	3 214	378	570	150	1 902
Iraqi	28	267	74	104	299	9	11	32	149
Israeli	13	1 158	167	249	2 722	194	198	9	244
Jordanian	26	723	153	43	431	78	118	16	203
Lebanese	563	27 226	4 308	2 611	19 234	2 666	3 732	717	2 837
Middle Eastern*	25	96	42	67	176	6	39	0	99
Moroccan	5	449	66	142	1 097	41	180	0	18
Palestinian	20	2 436	181	317	821	44	140	24	464
Saudi Arabian	0	75	83	152	240	21	0	41	57
Syrian	204	6 145	732	1 350	12 591	2 796	637	300	700
Turkish	80	2 147	459	673	2 430	399	828	70	529
Yemeni	0	42	0	34	77	15	7	9	46
Other North African and Southwest Asian, n.e.c.	59	336	85	310	248	8	17	7	310
SUBSAHARAN AFRICA									
African*	66	8 035	1 604	1 109	8 367	1 179	3 390	133	2 980
Cape Verdean	0	214	44	19	346	10 080	78	0	81
Eritrean	0	196	20	11	37	9	0	0	0
Ethiopian[13]	0	2	19	6	16	0	0	0	6
Ghanian	0	215	215	24	400	67	103	0	76
Kenyan	0	245	7	109	96	9	0	0	54
Liberian	0	251	49	9	364	611	20	0	87
Nigerian	147	2 329	1 132	541	1 984	508	1 582	128	1 082
Sierra Leonean	0	150	10	10	211	0	0	0	24
South African*	0	630	52	116	649	14	149	0	202
Sudanese	0	37	0	14	241	0	45	0	0
Ugandan	0	133	0	23	48	5	112	0	0
Other Subsaharan African, n.e.c.	0	309	131	164	898	108	96	29	89

DETAILED ANCESTRY GROUPS FOR STATES

25

Table 3. Persons Who Reported at Least One Specific Ancestry Group: 1990—Con.

United States Region Division State	North Dakota	Ohio	Oklahoma	Oregon	Pennsylvania	Rhode Island	South Carolina	South Dakota	Tennessee
SOUTH ASIA									
Afghanistan	0	100	11	272	561	0	46	0	120
Asian Indian	428	17 633	3 810	2 726	19 769	1 227	3 500	214	4 551
Bangladeshi	0	191	108	16	293	16	20	0	73
Nepali	0	76	20	88	101	0	0	0	0
Pakastani	59	1 683	610	333	1 924	116	182	71	470
Sri Lankan	0	341	26	211	713	26	24	0	54
Other South Asian, n.e.c.	0	6	0	0	0	0	0	0	0
OTHER ASIA									
Amerasian*	92	471	135	286	475	43	173	32	168
Asian*	33	2 006	764	680	2 232	325	670	102	990
Burmese	0	250	3	72	184	19	7	10	42
Cambodian[14]	74	2 165	451	2 255	4 155	3 417	248	54	953
Cantonese	0	40	10	196	290	103	24	0	5
Chinese[15]	364	16 829	5 178	14 796	25 908	3 037	2 872	410	5 048
Eurasian*	3	210	93	284	309	40	83	17	76
Filipino	934	12 726	3 689	9 114	14 474	2 032	6 028	824	3 901
Hmong	5	243	76	516	359	970	6	0	26
Hong Kong	0	74	13	65	112	11	12	0	17
Indonesian	33	659	313	1 239	746	52	57	25	155
Japanese	560	13 999	4 272	14 142	10 151	1 010	3 279	458	4 735
Khmer	0	41	0	5	104	8	0	0	0
Korean	687	13 041	5 459	9 355	25 800	1 293	3 198	686	5 063
Laotian	42	2 053	821	3 287	1 928	2 040	393	89	2 494
Malaysian	14	861	322	192	397	72	176	98	454
Mongolian	0	84	10	8	311	11	0	6	28
Okinawan	2	162	54	92	117	0	26	7	0
Singaporean	33	50	8	34	11	0	42	24	38
Taiwanese	127	3 032	1 010	939	4 625	300	450	53	1 266
Thai	159	1 965	1 087	1 144	1 889	348	965	138	784
Vietnamese	256	4 121	6 248	8 130	14 126	587	1 379	389	1 921
Other Asian, n.e.c.	0	29	6	55	14	6	5	0	5
PACIFIC									
Australian	25	1 489	410	1 429	1 483	170	379	85	478
Chamorro	0	49	27	131	29	0	41	0	25
Fijian	0	0	9	256	38	0	0	0	0
Guamanian	14	209	329	746	367	11	230	33	322
Hawaiian	86	1 225	983	3 437	1 900	158	799	155	885
Micronesian	8	11	8	297	52	0	18	0	37
New Zealander	7	54	25	250	153	15	17	48	50
Pacific Islander*	10	121	100	234	76	8	136	8	81
Polynesian	36	178	95	292	126	25	110	10	119
Samoan	16	106	128	488	206	0	108	0	236
Tongan	0	14	7	181	55	0	0	8	0
Other Pacific Islander, n.e.c.	16	163	64	460	84	0	101	10	53
NORTH AMERICA									
Acadian/Cajun[16]	49	2 614	3 957	1 061	1 649	96	5 086	65	5 498
Afro-American[16]	3 082	997 269	194 597	38 914	893 892	21 098	869 786	2 613	674 249
Aleut	3	120	55	439	25	23	9	0	25
American Indian[17]	26 597	383 689	468 588	141 079	166 847	12 731	117 321	46 998	302 454
American	9 669	512 979	257 655	98 355	287 304	19 137	347 488	12 191	653 143
Canadian[18]	438	13 508	2 306	10 553	11 325	5 338	3 438	504	3 970
Eskimo	15	231	195	694	197	79	47	86	105
French Canadian	4 194	38 709	10 961	29 161	31 007	72 747	9 923	3 288	11 272
Newfoundland	1	69	0	25	201	38	19	9	18
North American*	0	327	174	102	215	33	425	19	689
Nova Scotian	3	60	16	76	84	83	5	0	8
Pennsylvania German	518	24 872	1 810	3 556	143 008	182	797	773	1 160
United States	325	27 685	8 559	4 895	22 295	1 824	15 882	336	27 690
White[19]	661	45 819	53 971	27 747	23 122	3 308	40 027	1 685	66 823
Other North America, n.e.c.	0	7	4	0	0	0	0	0	0
OTHER GROUPS, N.E.C., NOT CLASSIFIED AND NOT REPORTED									
Other groups, n.e.c. and not classified[20]	2 636	219 731	40 140	61 015	138 575	11 329	27 035	5 421	64 718
Not reported	20 484	942 442	465 868	260 154	844 962	59 999	564 832	39 267	858 098

Table 3. Persons Who Reported at Least One Specific Ancestry Group: 1990—Con.

United States Region Division State	Texas	Utah	Vermont	Virginia	Washington	West Virginia	Wisconsin	Wyoming
Total	16 986 510	1 722 850	562 758	6 187 358	4 866 692	1 793 477	4 891 769	453 588

WESTERN EUROPE (NON-HISPANIC GROUPS)

	Texas	Utah	Vermont	Virginia	Washington	West Virginia	Wisconsin	Wyoming
Alsatian	2 673	29	48	456	292	33	344	12
Austrian[2]	23 447	3 903	1 913	14 886	18 430	1 993	25 396	1 742
Basque	1 248	1 422	2	403	1 770	9	101	602
Basque, French	98	148	0	19	145	0	8	146
Basque, Spanish	238	261	0	59	154	0	8	21
Basque, n.e.c.	912	1 013	2	325	1 471	9	85	435
Bavarian	204	12	23	151	140	40	327	0
Belgian[3]	3 285	425	175	1 564	2 862	399	25 345	160
British	76 861	24 527	2 798	49 823	35 509	7 073	9 961	2 001
Celtic	2 258	268	132	1 109	1 262	235	246	16
Cornish	100	46	3	27	236	25	922	10
Cypriot	76	0	10	234	53	0	8	0
Cypriot, Greek	27	0	8	141	12	0	6	0
Cypriot, Turkish	0	0	0	0	0	0	2	0
Cypriot, n.e.c.	49	0	2	93	41	0	0	0
Danish	47 655	163 048	2 386	18 374	82 215	1 332	80 791	10 889
Dutch	324 375	55 770	9 923	117 477	179 310	74 877	162 466	15 648
English	2 023 901	749 665	147 384	1 050 605	897 190	269 798	410 016	101 398
Finnish	12 634	3 718	1 968	6 770	44 110	452	35 118	2 408
Flemish	755	127	61	595	477	50	818	55
French[4]	571 175	53 902	132 574	178 732	265 350	40 125	239 004	21 762
German[5]	2 949 686	299 414	59 090	1 186 056	1 389 014	468 927	2 630 680	158 489
Greek[6]	31 048	10 439	1 842	23 390	18 275	4 325	14 366	1 681
Icelander	1 147	2 970	44	814	5 976	106	809	44
Irish[7]	2 368 863	136 645	100 839	888 908	768 293	348 448	612 358	72 941
Italian[8]	312 294	45 857	32 428	207 023	156 943	71 684	144 249	13 084
Luxemburger	704	39	5	564	1 171	22	7 288	99
Maltese	702	84	45	360	237	7	163	21
Manx	245	108	18	135	292	16	158	10
Northern Irish	95	27	8	199	100	3	13	10
Norwegian	94 096	36 178	3 537	35 815	333 521	2 598	416 271	18 047
Portuguese	13 304	1 954	1 859	10 818	13 215	487	1 769	882
Azores Islander	60	13	0	54	57	7	4	0
Madeira Islander	7	0	0	6	8	0	0	0
Portuguese, n.e.c.	13 237	1 941	1 059	10 758	13 150	480	1 765	882
Prussian	1 388	377	24	581	1 046	49	1 367	67
Saxon	246	23	6	129	107	13	38	0
Scandinavian	22 201	34 106	1 044	10 366	64 179	958	24 491	3 830
Scotch-Irish[9]	495 886	24 292	12 286	195 722	154 566	54 222	43 582	15 227
Scottish	306 854	89 463	30 588	166 959	182 690	34 173	58 589	17 097
Sicilian	1 452	151	207	554	803	151	1 926	24
Swedish	155 193	103 715	10 113	56 040	257 953	6 856	159 216	20 885
Swiss	32 304	31 737	1 902	19 451	36 795	3 956	65 915	3 401
Tirol	35	58	0	100	10	0	58	45
Welsh	95 447	48 070	7 081	54 891	69 094	16 896	29 895	6 674
West German	202	27	8	89	115	4	50	7
Western European*	3 435	629	196	1 343	2 271	214	595	165
Other Western European, n.e.c.	142	0	0	26	124	7	61	19

EASTERN EUROPE AND SOVIET UNION

	Texas	Utah	Vermont	Virginia	Washington	West Virginia	Wisconsin	Wyoming
Albanian	539	137	101	533	339	12	772	0
Belorussian	39	0	0	45	44	7	61	0
Bulgarian	867	275	38	355	969	155	547	148
Carpath Rusyn	41	0	0	103	48	46	7	0
Central European	81	22	30	75	110	0	102	0
Croatian	15 742	1 446	249	7 543	10 430	4 215	22 391	746
Czech[10]	166 814	3 373	1 555	13 555	23 873	1 936	104 155	3 745
Czechoslovakian	23 731	1 108	551	5 144	7 922	851	8 887	790
Estonian	642	107	93	461	1 255	19	336	36
European*	23 825	11 711	2 080	14 593	23 897	1 511	5 310	1 898
German Russian/ Volga	333	24	0	289	595	15	343	20
Hungarian	31 884	2 944	3 102	25 178	16 797	9 248	25 385	1 374
Latvian	2 279	172	179	1 806	2 926	168	3 003	127
Lithuanian	14 034	1 118	1 579	13 375	8 530	2 225	16 790	332
Macedonian	279	0	34	150	177	45	256	13
Moravian	1 209	9	23	57	61	0	123	0
Northern European*	2 840	935	447	1 643	5 772	141	853	260
Polish	237 557	14 832	17 475	115 121	95 828	30 864	505 808	9 764
Rom	246	0	2	57	275	45	31	14
Romanian	7 564	943	412	4 633	5 124	749	2 651	169
Russian[11]	55 602	4 401	5 743	42 578	41 395	5 022	33 289	2 969
Ruthenian	59	31	3	92	22	23	6	0
Serbian	2 181	220	55	1 563	1 195	1 365	5 715	85
Slavic*	2 120	532	206	1 446	2 592	255	2 597	321
Slovak	48 463	4 167	1 641	31 604	18 892	11 267	45 769	2 872
Slovene	2 254	289	45	1 125	1 132	423	6 478	295
Soviet Union	119	8	26	146	112	6	19	0
Ukrainian	13 094	1 062	978	12 321	10 814	1 514	6 783	405
Windish	66	0	0	6	9	0	0	0
Yugoslavian*	4 943	3 095	233	2 523	12 726	887	6 177	1 024
Other Eastern European and Soviet Union, n.e.c.	2 444	178	545	2 957	1 293	84	960	16

DETAILED ANCESTRY GROUPS FOR STATES

27

Table 3. Persons Who Reported at Least One Specific Ancestry Group: 1990—Con.

United States Region Division State	Texas	Utah	Vermont	Virginia	Washington	West Virginia	Wisconsin	Wyoming
CENTRAL AND SOUTH AMERICA (HISPANIC GROUPS) AND SPAIN								
Argentinean	2 448	332	50	1 350	486	19	181	20
Bolivian	1 499	224	17	5 385	272	15	186	7
Central American*	824	0	0	94	16	0	16	0
Chilean	2 442	649	11	2 195	896	103	288	0
Colombian	15 669	666	140	4 078	1 091	127	910	25
Costa Rican	2 664	233	25	870	324	17	354	0
Cuban	17 758	497	209	5 851	1 723	256	1 444	18
Dominican	3 875	114	71	2 318	457	187	359	13
Ecuadorian	4 033	159	37	2 564	485	62	125	6
Guatemalan	10 732	612	15	3 850	560	13	204	3
Hispanic*	254 202	6 708	151	7 779	14 834	352	3 405	2 038
Honduran	9 614	216	43	1 561	320	47	135	35
Latin American*	9 909	136	24	660	302	11	137	12
Mexican	3 403 368	45 675	635	28 375	128 472	2 157	51 339	13 725
Nicaraguan	7 562	115	7	2 821	502	18	386	22
Panamanian	5 566	258	30	3 000	1 054	39	266	34
Paraguayan	240	35	2	218	38	0	18	0
Peruvian	6 135	829	49	6 105	1 196	41	306	17
Puerto Rican	37 517	1 656	437	17 453	6 816	470	15 493	360
Salvadoran	53 077	629	9	21 170	1 314	122	256	24
South American*	375	103	9	316	174	24	32	13
Spaniard[12]	31 226	2 804	125	3 600	3 488	292	648	529
Spanish*	186 758	21 075	2 525	30 357	33 319	4 921	9 265	7 367
Uruguayan	629	97	0	315	67	6	27	0
Venezuelan	3 295	147	28	912	281	26	143	19
Other Hispanic, n.e.c.	274	0	0	98	17	12	27	0
CENTRAL AND SOUTH AMERICA (NON-HISPANIC GROUPS)								
Belizean	793	6	0	89	60	7	22	0
Brazilian	2 147	386	57	1 382	614	59	233	11
Guyanese	904	0	2	660	139	0	83	0
Other Central and South American, n.e.c.	59	0	0	9	35	0	7	0
WEST INDIES (NON-HISPANIC GROUPS)								
Bahamian	336	3	2	237	93	0	77	0
Barbadian	466	12	6	315	50	14	40	0
Bermudan	132	8	13	237	107	16	39	0
British West Indian	999	22	0	268	146	4	35	0
Antigua and Barbuda	289	8	0	51	11	0	6	0
Grenadian	265	0	0	23	37	0	0	0
Kitts-Nevis Islander	22	7	0	22	0	0	0	0
St. Lucia Islander	258	0	0	65	0	0	22	0
Vincent-Grenadine Islander	58	7	0	11	16	0	0	0
British West Indian, n.e.c.	107	0	0	96	82	4	7	0
Dutch West Indian	16 713	81	0	217	366	233	80	41
Haitian	1 673	63	64	1 398	228	64	97	0
Jamaican	7 500	102	113	4 975	1 482	260	1 443	36
Trinidadian and Tobagonian	2 018	6	17	737	168	0	159	0
US Virgin Islander	429	0	0	216	49	0	33	0
West Indian*	4 513	86	63	2 787	877	67	245	12
Other West Indian, n.e.c.	137	0	0	84	32	0	30	0
NORTH AFRICA AND SOUTHWEST ASIA								
Algerian	264	0	0	121	64	5	9	0
Arab*	7 067	404	55	4 122	1 725	256	1 139	34
Armenian	3 183	928	419	4 078	2 269	139	2 771	55
Assyrian	453	16	9	220	211	20	114	0
Egyptian	3 146	94	55	2 462	588	122	421	0
Iranian	13 639	1 458	144	9 858	3 629	362	1 261	61
Iraqi	495	43	0	570	202	13	9	0
Israeli	2 114	134	93	856	448	33	390	6
Jordanian	1 498	66	0	660	235	8	194	0
Lebanese	21 934	1 534	1 359	10 692	3 784	4 178	2 827	142
Middle Eastern*	469	0	10	248	122	0	50	6
Moroccan	554	89	16	1 076	97	8	165	5
Palestinian	2 944	105	12	2 170	451	76	735	8
Saudi Arabian	413	0	5	363	185	30	72	12
Syrian	5 322	315	173	2 248	1 189	806	878	49
Turkish	3 273	317	74	2 673	1 683	368	649	28
Yemeni	73	7	0	90	32	14	0	0
Other North African and Southwest Asian, n.e.c.	608	73	16	434	234	19	195	0
SUBSAHARAN AFRICA								
African*	13 629	488	210	7 112	2 795	423	1 845	110
Cape Verdean	264	20	23	387	51	0	10	0
Eritrean	196	0	0	355	223	0	34	0
Ethiopian[13]	6	0	5	59	23	0	10	0
Ghanian	925	11	4	1 048	172	5	79	0
Kenyan	531	0	0	162	94	0	13	0
Liberian	404	0	2	382	0	0	40	0
Nigerian	13 153	280	13	2 210	772	247	1 379	102
Sierra Leonean	416	0	0	405	39	6	20	0
South African*	1 786	93	3	437	236	10	102	0
Sudanese	92	17	0	307	49	0	65	8
Ugandan	138	8	0	109	46	5	29	0
Other Subsaharan African, n.e.c.	1 252	47	12	772	380	18	286	0

Table 3. Persons Who Reported at Least One Specific Ancestry Group: 1990—Con.

United States Region Division State	State							
	Texas	Utah	Vermont	Virginia	Washington	West Virginia	Wisconsin	Wyoming
SOUTH ASIA								
Afghanistan	1 145	29	7	4 814	696	2	65	24
Asian Indian	40 506	1 306	259	14 937	6 973	1 925	4 133	82
Bangladeshi	528	27	2	363	14	60	100	0
Nepali	113	2	0	55	38	0	69	0
Pakastani	8 921	132	87	5 278	715	367	722	129
Sri Lankan	649	33	0	405	124	41	156	6
Other South Asian, n.e.c.	0	0	0	12	6	0	0	0
OTHER ASIA								
Amerasian*	1 056	104	23	667	834	72	168	20
Asian*	7 585	263	147	3 696	2 957	344	909	70
Burmese	285	63	4	311	129	25	24	2
Cambodian[14]	5 659	1 050	33	3 761	10 074	24	444	37
Cantonese	575	32	8	159	331	16	77	0
Chinese[15]	55 023	5 487	572	20 857	33 954	1 248	7 147	485
Eurasian*	499	189	20	346	600	26	71	22
Filipino	40 053	2 983	405	35 605	49 222	1 624	4 942	594
Hmong	133	155	0	7	779	0	15 942	0
Hong Kong	262	10	6	26	59	0	42	0
Indonesian	1 555	288	56	894	1 088	46	404	13
Japanese	23 729	8 455	536	12 385	43 378	1 257	4 235	875
Khmer	113	6	0	128	236	10	18	0
Korean	35 281	3 215	798	32 362	32 918	955	6 499	378
Laotian	9 157	1 678	137	2 321	5 370	45	5 297	6
Malaysian	1 650	40	19	1 117	762	15	324	39
Mongolian	277	0	11	148	38	12	43	0
Okinawan	275	10	4	178	164	0	41	0
Singaporean	176	9	0	34	22	0	77	7
Taiwanese	13 080	567	93	3 527	3 541	292	985	44
Thai	7 930	831	49	3 997	3 269	343	539	110
Vietnamese	60 649	2 540	177	20 271	17 004	133	2 324	84
Other Asian, n.e.c.	97	7	0	31	293	0	29	0
PACIFIC								
Australian	2 677	1 372	93	1 651	2 012	211	821	173
Chamorro	172	39	0	132	590	0	24	4
Fijian	47	18	0	0	395	0	0	0
Guamanian	2 117	69	18	1 006	3 280	12	120	55
Hawaiian	4 136	2 102	54	1 901	7 207	180	639	236
Micronesian	161	69	10	38	260	0	1	0
New Zealander	346	390	25	331	353	8	54	3
Pacific Islander*	502	140	5	333	757	31	39	23
Polynesian	658	831	7	119	482	5	37	4
Samoan	748	1 854	27	442	3 635	12	52	26
Tongan	512	3 630	13	9	184	0	13	0
Other Pacific Islander, n.e.c.	252	133	0	188	439	4	56	16
NORTH AMERICA								
Acadian/ Cajun	105 982	519	74	4 581	2 504	377	603	452
Afro-American[10]	1 720 618	9 288	1 611	969 899	125 060	47 174	214 538	2 732
Aleut	89	25	6	69	2 165	0	67	2
American Indian[17]	815 112	43 145	28 443	201 613	190 713	109 517	76 294	21 112
American	000 001	54 004	31 178	549 672	161 521	259 573	72 625	17 472
Canadian[18]	17 117	4 287	3 923	9 597	21 862	1 021	4 425	630
Eskimo	339	173	19	212	1 982	43	146	16
French Canadian	60 277	5 607	33 049	33 641	52 725	3 296	55 442	2 885
Newfoundland	58	0	12	143	58	0	10	0
North American*	1 048	57	10	696	200	159	115	8
Nova Scotian	190	21	33	52	84	6	49	0
Pennsylvania German	3 808	329	148	3 033	4 490	988	2 691	801
United States	58 877	3 207	945	27 923	9 629	8 304	3 933	625
White[19]	249 937	15 055	4 809	56 228	50 460	14 295	8 118	3 828
Other North America, n.e.c.	33	10	0	0	12	7	2	0
OTHER GROUPS, N.E.C., NOT CLASSIFIED AND NOT REPORTED								
Other groups, n.e.c. and not classified[20]	209 466	21 845	11 622	58 132	80 898	34 696	27 298	4 922
Not reported	1 557 383	119 645	43 293	815 350	396 083	304 909	236 499	37 005

Note: Some individuals reported a single ancestry group; others reported more than one group. All first (or single) and second responses were coded. Since persons who reported two ancestries were included in more than one group, the sum of persons reporting the ancestry groups is greater than the total. The ancestry data include groups that correspond to those identified separately in the race and Hispanic origin items. In the 1990 census, separate questions were asked on race and Hispanic origin. The race item provides the primary source of data for White; Black; American Indian, Eskimo, and Aleut; and Asian and Pacific Islander. The 1990 census Hispanic origin question is the primary identifier for Mexican, Puerto Rican, Cuban and those who indicated that they were of "other" Spanish/Hispanic origin.

*This category represents a general type response, which may encompass several ancestry groups.

[1]Numbers and percents by ancestry group do not add to total because persons reporting a multiple ancestry are included in more than one group.
[2]Excludes Tirol.
[3]Excludes Flemish.
[4]Excludes French Basque.
[5]Excludes Bavarian, Prussian, Saxon and West German.
[6]Excludes Greek Cypriot.
[7]Excludes Northern Irish and Celtic.
[8]Excludes Sicilian.
[9]Includes persons who reported "Scotch-Irish."
[10]Excludes Moravian.
[11]Includes persons who reported "Rusyn," "Cossack," "Black Russian," "Great Russian," "Red Russian," "Rossiya," and "Muscovite."
[12]Excludes Spanish Basque.
[13]Excludes Eritrean.
[14]Excludes Khmer.
[15]Excludes Cantonese.
[16]Includes persons who reported "African American," "Afro-American," "Afro," "Black," "Negro," "Colored," "Creole," and other related groups.
[17]Includes persons who reported "Native American," "Centraal American Indian," "South American Indian," and "Cherokee," and other related groups.
[18]Excludes Newfoundland and Nova Scotia.
[19]Includes persons who reported "White," "Caucasian." "Anglo," "Wasp," "Appalachian," "Aryan," and other related groups.
[20]Includes persons who reported "Mixture," "Adopted," "Don't know," and other unclassifiable responses, as well as responses indicating religious groups.

DETAILED ANCESTRY GROUPS FOR STATES   **29**

U.S. Department of Commerce
Economics and Statistics Administration
BUREAU OF THE CENSUS

1990 CP-S-1-1

CENSUS '90

1990 Census of Population

Detailed Occupation and Other Characteristics From the EEO File for the United States

Table 1. Detailed Occupation of the Civilian Labor Force by Sex, Race, and Hispanic Origin: 1990

[Data based on sample and subject to sampling variability, see text. For definitions of terms and meanings of symbols, see text]

United States	All persons Male	All persons Female	Hispanic origin (of any race) Male	Hispanic origin (of any race) Female	Not of Hispanic origin White Male	White Female	Black Male	Black Female	American Indian, Eskimo, or Aleut Male	American Indian, Eskimo, or Aleut Female	Asian or Pacific Islander Male	Asian or Pacific Islander Female	Other race Male	Other race Female
Civilian labor force 16 years and over	66 986 201	56 487 249	5 888 180	4 133 543	52 652 633	43 590 483	6 108 277	6 727 324	426 376	365 896	1 864 689	1 631 072	46 041	38 931
MANAGERIAL AND PROFESSIONAL SPECIALTY OCCUPATIONS														
Executive, administrative, and managerial occupations	8 448 483	6 170 674	362 358	290 938	7 398 764	5 165 841	402 889	499 587	30 880	31 820	249 424	179 300	3 668	3 188
Legislators	7 431	5 285	141	231	6 218	4 309	612	619	331	104	129	52	—	—
Chief executives and general administrators, public administration	13 788	5 235	667	354	11 17?	3 655	1 594	1 033	202	72	154	113	—	8
Administrators and officials, public administration	275 864	230 819	12 068	10 525	230 095	178 035	25 223	35 735	2 680	2 521	5 611	3 917	187	86
Administrators, protective services	35 201	14 072	1 285	803	30 864	10 863	2 422	2 053	288	153	329	190	13	10
Financial managers	343 630	292 281	12 032	12 663	306 454	252 494	12 179	17 516	605	859	12 265	8 614	95	135
Personnel and labor relations managers	141 246	134 249	10 351	8 560	115 315	108 353	10 105	13 227	596	782	4 797	3 247	82	80
Purchasing managers	80 136	40 639	2 500	1 599	72 811	34 562	2 547	3 325	224	250	2 022	881	32	22
Managers, marketing, advertising, and public relations	415 411	193 698	11 326	7 079	384 566	174 468	10 234	7 698	876	581	8 328	3 837	81	35
Administrators, education and related fields	295 274	328 338	11 183	15 427	249 921	264 437	26 389	40 114	1 698	2 141	6 043	6 052	40	167
Managers, medicine and health	78 099	155 522	3 986	7 293	63 205	126 913	8 185	16 874	304	910	2 373	3 424	46	108
Postmasters and mail superintendents	21 614	18 232	874	351	18 472	16 617	1 788	948	198	201	237	108	45	7
Managers, food serving and lodging establishments	572 095	458 556	44 016	26 246	448 799	369 131	38 234	38 947	2 409	2 912	38 057	21 044	580	276
Managers, properties and real estate	221 625	189 841	13 240	10 195	190 785	163 607	11 674	11 667	916	1 169	4 873	3 051	133	152
Funeral directors	39 393	6 093	718	1-4	34 525	4 873	3 898	1 016	116	35	130	19	6	6
Managers, service organizations, n.e.c.	201 002	203 071	9 123	7 824	171 845	171 836	15 000	19 189	1 240	1 464	3 650	2 654	144	104
Managers and administrators, n.e.c., salaried	3 355 970	1 585 636	125 977	70 135	3 024 916	1 383 619	109 449	88 438	10 048	6 715	84 566	35 985	1 014	744
Managers and administrators, n.e.c. self-employed	2 037 105	2 218 319	89 346	107 644	1 759 029	1 817 900	9 429	198 842	1 466	10 508	8 695	82 238	215	61
Management related occupations	751 840	838 338	28 867	38 170	646 664	678 739	37 457	68 589	1 500	3 435	37 092	48 912	955	1 187
Accountants and auditors	328 204	45 818	570	1 964	19 576	38 911	3 457	3 770	45	97	555	1 056	260	493
Underwriters	21 949	351 071	11 329	17 752	293 550	295 804	13 245	25 920	681	1 353	9 267	10 104	132	138
Other financial officers	186 724	95 065	4 672	3 025	170 371	81 846	6 610	7 507	607	507	4 354	2 490	110	66
Management analysts	217 138	296 487	13 411	16 558	177 290	233 612	21 358	1 852	1 321	1 852	3 580	5 926	178	108
Personnel, training, and labor relations specialists	14 336	2 962	820	344	12 648	2 030	617	493	40	42	211	53	—	—
Purchasing agents and buyers, farm products	107 051	121 348	5 741	4 950	94 422	107 777	3 808	5 361	323	387	2 719	2 828	38	65
Buyers, wholesale and retail trade, except farm products	135 474	111 493	5 796	4 676	120 229	95 506	6 461	8 994	495	622	2 433	1 630	60	65
Purchasing agents and buyers, n.e.c.	19 569	16 923	1 375	598	16 686	14 770	1 032	1 057	64	117	387	381	25	—
Business and promotion agents	60 087	4 197	3 358	225	50 978	3 106	3 882	712	481	51	1 365	103	23	—
Construction inspectors	112 130	49 147	7 486	3 773	100 358	33 136	10 871	10 386	775	459	2 560	1 341	80	52
Inspectors and compliance officers, except construction	82 603	285 470	5 921	15 589	36 257	232 663	7 383	28 018	351	1 586	2 642	7 414	49	200
Professional specialty occupations	7 706 256	8 941 432	299 731	357 467	6 619 249	7 452 498	403 176	815 695	28 730	42 451	351 345	269 089	4 025	4 232
Engineers, architects, and surveyors	1 695 690	180 833	54 591	7 693	1 459 852	146 297	51 619	12 209	4 550	579	114 191	13 950	887	105
Architects	133 212	23 662	6 720	1 286	115 733	20 342	3 711	616	250	40	6 719	1 378	79	—
Engineers	1 551 961	156 283	47 539	6 394	1 344 335	125 167	47 728	11 538	4 233	535	107 323	12 544	803	105
Aerospace	131 786	11 648	5 197	437	112 350	9 170	3 648	942	405	65	10 109	1 025	77	9
Metallurgical and materials	17 021	2 209	424	75	15 149	1 816	422	243	34	5	992	70	—	—
Mining	6 063	415	134	—	5 607	370	44	18	54	18	160	—	14	—
Petroleum	22 908	1 657	654	117	21 029	1 373	425	90	69	13	731	67	—	—
Chemical	57 163	7 157	1 501	304	50 001	5 778	1 726	520	86	7	3 830	548	19	—
Nuclear	10 108	693	232	13	9 006	626	186	5	21	8	663	41	—	—
Civil	235 162	17 646	8 466	783	200 217	14 015	6 937	1 047	736	60	18 691	1 708	115	28
Agricultural	2 012	136	83	—	1 838	96	27	18	—	—	64	22	—	—
Electrical and electronic	420 471	46 552	12 999	1 921	358 739	35 622	15 055	4 283	1 086	110	32 383	4 566	209	51
Industrial	151 859	24 474	4 628	1 104	135 998	20 422	4 830	1 645	472	114	5 870	1 185	61	4
Mechanical	176 092	9 780	4 144	254	156 757	8 274	4 516	538	420	17	10 181	697	74	—
Marine and naval architects	176 092	493	199	—	1 623	422	315	52	65	—	568	7	6	—
Engineers, n.e.c.	308 540	33 423	8 828	1 370	266 021	27 183	9 597	2 131	785	118	23 081	2 608	228	13
Surveyors and mapping scientists	10 517	888	332	13	9 734	788	180	55	67	4	149	28	5	—
Mathematical and computer scientists	503 806	275 701	15 089	10 142	430 714	223 505	23 831	24 729	1 412	980	32 419	16 227	341	127
Computer systems analysts and scientists	326 831	144 459	9 069	4 214	278 755	118 604	13 668	11 249	877	432	24 231	9 817	231	100
Operations and systems researchers and analysts	144 484	107 334	5 160	5 157	123 549	85 804	8 927	11 184	464	479	6 291	4 683	93	27
Actuaries	12 416	6 316	163	93	11 304	5 480	195	214	7	—	738	529	9	—
Statisticians	15 744	16 108	604	65	13 317	12 390	888	1 862	64	60	863	1 139	8	—
Mathematical scientists, n.e.c.	4 331	1 484	93	2	3 789	1 184	153	211	—	9	296	59	—	—

Table 1. **Detailed Occupation of the Civilian Labor Force by Sex, Race, and Hispanic Origin: 1990**—Con.

[Data based on sample and subject to sampling variability, see text. For definitions of terms and meanings of symbols, see text]

United States

MANAGERIAL AND PROFESSIONAL SPECIALTY OCCUPATIONS—Con.

Occupation	All persons Male	All persons Female	Hispanic origin (of any race) Male	Hispanic origin (of any race) Female	Not of Hispanic origin White Male	White Female	Black Male	Black Female	American Indian, Eskimo, or Aleut Male	American Indian, Eskimo, or Aleut Female	Asian or Pacific Islander Male	Asian or Pacific Islander Female	Other race Male	Other race Female
Natural scientists	300 573	108 102	8 318	3 991	262 247	87 827	10 686	6 435	1 255	397	17 955	9 328	112	124
Physicists and astronomers	24 238	3 604	541	120	21 688	3 058	470	206	74	10	1 465	210	—	—
Chemists, except biochemists	102 505	38 750	2 803	1 701	84 751	29 179	5 679	2 938	214	93	9 013	4 767	45	72
Atmospheric and space scientists	7 279	1 075	105	68	6 680	883	242	63	37	2	215	55	—	4
Geologists and geodesists	45 501	7 628	989	281	43 093	7 010	421	169	128	27	840	139	30	2
Physical scientists, n.e.c.	13 338	5 444	295	68	12 098	4 745	433	433	44	40	455	158	—	17
Agricultural and food scientists	25 537	9 305	1 128	348	22 702	7 911	849	597	57	52	793	380	8	17
Biological and life scientists	36 207	25 930	1 127	848	31 327	21 599	1 149	1 285	161	72	2 435	2 119	8	7
Forestry and conservation scientists	30 205	4 610	756	123	27 757	4 191	919	185	540	56	225	55	8	7
Medical scientists	15 763	11 756	574	434	12 151	9 251	524	559	—	45	2 514	1 445	—	22
Health diagnosing occupations	700 419	174 106	27 833	8 007	597 992	133 951	18 579	9 491	965	387	54 770	22 188	280	82
Physicians	465 468	121 247	22 978	5 803	383 033	89 318	13 707	7 167	654	214	44 881	18 671	215	74
Dentists	135 588	19 941	2 950	1 059	122 417	15 502	3 549	1 218	137	53	6 494	2 107	41	2
Veterinarians	35 755	12 989	705	262	33 358	12 003	539	296	56	25	1 085	403	12	1
Optometrists	23 463	4 052	370	185	21 938	3 372	205	192	56	11	894	292	—	—
Podiatrists	7 904	1 004	130	58	7 436	726	172	127	6	—	160	93	—	—
Health diagnosing practitioners, n.e.c.	32 241	14 873	700	640	29 810	13 030	407	491	56	84	1 256	622	12	6
Health assessment and treating occupations	322 927	2 191 413	14 799	63 077	265 402	1 834 729	25 593	190 835	1 357	8 447	15 606	93 371	170	954
Registered nurses	107 244	1 777 885	5 998	48 065	84 999	1 488 663	10 444	155 076	520	7 004	5 213	78 314	70	763
Pharmacists	114 949	66 849	2 815	2 869	101 820	54 002	2 771	4 277	267	103	6 594	5 574	13	24
Dietitians	9 629	80 594	830	3 483	5 641	58 633	2 817	14 422	73	475	310	3 539	4	42
Therapists	78 143	253 478	4 284	7 939	62 592	223 139	7 887	16 038	402	737	2 965	5 500	83	125
Respiratory therapists	26 155	33 434	1 895	1 341	19 966	30 119	2 887	4 140	136	157	1 240	996	31	24
Occupational therapists	3 957	33 938	313	874	3 139	30 776	333	1 666	8	50	164	1 213	—	16
Physical therapists	22 540	69 482	962	2 330	18 728	61 697	1 607	3 498	108	189	1 129	1 749	6	19
Speech therapists	5 736	58 977	123	1 385	5 339	54 140	185	2 612	28	100	57	716	4	24
Therapists, n.e.c.	19 755	51 647	991	2 009	15 420	44 407	2 805	4 122	122	241	375	826	42	42
Physicians' assistants	12 962	12 607	872	721	10 350	10 292	1 121	1 022	95	128	524	444	—	—
Teachers, postsecondary	467 429	318 804	14 744	12 333	393 551	269 962	18 666	19 201	1 511	1 294	38 642	15 809	315	205
Earth, environmental, and marine science teachers	889	364	26	16	813	334	26	—	10	—	50	5	—	9
Biological science teachers	4 031	2 070	100	88	3 687	1 837	44	56	10	—	190	89	—	—
Chemistry teachers	4 053	1 393	56	46	3 591	1 180	110	45	7	9	289	113	19	—
Physics teachers	3 876	556	59	2	3 349	487	129	28	7	—	339	39	—	—
Natural science teachers, n.e.c.	292	97	—	8	272	80	7	9	5	—	13	—	—	—
Psychology teachers	2 409	2 109	48	74	2 224	1 880	79	100	7	19	51	36	—	—
Economics teachers	2 650	776	75	17	2 272	709	75	10	7	—	219	40	9	—
History teachers	2 996	1 125	65	26	2 841	1 033	71	59	6	7	12	14	—	—
Political science teachers	752	253	22	23	656	209	53	7	—	7	15	11	6	—
Sociology teachers	905	552	15	4	776	496	39	39	27	2	48	11	42	—
Social science teachers, n.e.c.	548	312	18	—	435	276	65	11	14	11	16	14	—	—
Engineering teachers	6 489	1 288	227	27	5 486	1 158	259	68	12	—	505	35	—	—
Mathematical science teachers	10 639	6 718	334	142	9 021	5 835	515	352	30	57	720	332	19	—
Computer science teachers	1 705	767	93	113	1 427	674	106	73	5	11	282	78	—	3
Medical science teachers	1 976	1 927	39	12	1 777	569	68	38	7	—	85	43	—	—
Health specialties teachers	3 784	2 775	111	254	3 251	2 411	134	882	14	45	274	500	7	—
Business, commerce, and marketing teachers	2 288	302	51	17	1 926	283	148	198	25	22	138	69	—	—
Agriculture and forestry teachers	759	—	17	26	714	11	16	11	2	8	10	—	9	—
Art, drama, and music teachers	10 591	10 802	417	237	9 441	9 698	465	431	40	43	221	387	7	6
Physical education teachers	2 042	2 073	31	91	1 752	1 681	163	255	8	12	54	34	34	—
Education teachers	747	708	64	14	608	589	65	97	15	8	10	14	15	16
English teachers	10 243	14 033	252	516	9 393	12 541	448	620	12	56	120	284	—	—
Foreign language teachers	2 966	7 059	577	1 151	2 075	5 250	128	109	11	7	175	542	—	—
Law teachers	3 158	1 397	63	23	2 882	1 275	173	70	17	—	23	29	—	—
Social work teachers	103	205	16	22	85	159	—	24	5	—	18	—	—	—
Theology teachers	2 001	615	34	4	1 878	588	59	44	8	3	40	2	15	—
Trade and industrial teachers	668	602	51	254	589	539	29	9	7	—	9	19	—	—
Home economics teachers	94	499	17	75	75	354	19	16	—	—	—	16	7	—
Teachers, postsecondary, n.e.c.	8 779	4 676	311	218	7 606	3 972	279	261	19	35	557	187	7	3
Postsecondary teachers, subject not specified	374 022	241 046	11 623	9 094	311 883	202 438	14 920	15 200	1 213	932	34 159	13 214	224	168

Table 1. Detailed Occupation of the Civilian Labor Force by Sex, Race, and Hispanic Origin: 1990—Con.

[Data based on sample and subject to sampling variability, see text. For definitions of terms and meanings of symbols, see text]

United States	All persons Male	All persons Female	Hispanic origin (of any race) Male	Hispanic origin (of any race) Female	Not Hispanic — White Male	White Female	Black Male	Black Female	American Indian, Eskimo, or Aleut Male	Amer. Indian Female	Asian or Pacific Islander Male	Asian Female	Other race Male	Other race Female
MANAGERIAL AND PROFESSIONAL SPECIALTY OCCUPATIONS—Con.														
Teachers, except postsecondary	1 157 678	3 401 848	49 117	148 664	992 885	2 842 142	89 757	345 801	5 983	16 916	19 380	47 036	556	1 309
Teachers, prekindergarten and kindergarten	5 920	263 410	415	15 259	4 167	207 514	1 108	33 882	93	2 126	132	4 393	5	236
Teachers, elementary school	652 015	2 372 174	27 858	104 645	554 541	1 970 664	57 464	254 799	3 442	11 158	8 410	30 097	300	811
Teachers, secondary school	269 533	354 867	9 366	12 056	242 466	311 996	13 842	25 358	1 103	1 451	2 710	3 865	46	101
Teachers, special education	11 047	51 169	573	1 724	9 206	43 136	1 081	5 402	79	341	108	521	–	25
Teachers, n.e.c.	219 163	360 228	10 905	14 900	182 505	308 832	16 262	26 360	1 266	1 840	8 020	8 160	205	136
Counselors, educational and vocational	91 763	146 770	5 230	7 846	72 383	113 282	11 389	21 490	862	1 400	1 825	2 604	74	148
Librarians, archivists, and curators	49 787	178 669	2 227	5 183	41 520	153 974	3 721	13 253	261	846	2 046	5 416	12	67
Librarians	37 522	163 359	1 576	4 568	30 878	140 592	3 093	12 407	157	741	1 812	4 964	6	67
Archivists and curators	12 265	15 310	651	525	10 642	13 382	628	846	104	105	234	452	6	–
Social scientists and urban planners	189 041	196 197	6 293	6 388	157 670	172 717	9 883	11 958	601	789	4 551	4 272	43	73
Economists	85 335	66 902	2 433	1 777	76 409	59 302	3 522	3 519	192	166	2 769	2 138	10	–
Psychologists	79 430	112 532	2 792	3 853	70 276	99 107	5 037	7 200	311	573	988	1 736	26	63
Sociologists	1 152	1 059	102	65	828	829	65	99	31	7	126	59	–	–
Social scientists, n.e.c.	10 649	9 648	361	381	9 628	8 395	398	601	35	26	230	235	7	10
Urban planners	12 475	6 056	615	312	10 529	5 084	861	539	32	17	438	104	–	–
Social, recreation, and religious workers	552 861	580 533	27 998	33 561	443 976	428 592	63 824	103 558	3 818	5 436	12 864	8 994	381	392
Social workers	204 760	454 159	16 388	28 481	142 816	319 329	38 726	94 323	2 292	4 835	4 363	6 876	175	315
Recreation workers	14 811	35 968	1 034	1 851	9 973	29 105	3 322	4 206	154	213	277	551	51	42
Clergy	291 140	33 749	8 710	1 180	234 600	29 439	19 222	2 266	1 222	173	7 244	680	142	11
Religious workers, n.e.c.	42 150	56 657	1 866	2 049	36 587	50 719	2 554	2 763	150	215	980	887	13	24
Lawyers and judges	589 326	190 145	13 130	6 580	552 746	167 094	15 452	11 868	1 082	519	6 822	4 023	94	61
Lawyers	564 332	182 745	12 330	6 282	530 259	161 054	14 061	11 006	972	445	6 616	3 897	94	61
Judges	24 994	7 400	800	298	22 487	6 040	1 391	862	110	74	206	126	–	–
Writers, artists, entertainers, and athletes	1 084 956	998 311	60 362	44 090	928 311	878 426	60 176	44 876	5 073	4 461	30 274	25 871	760	585
Authors	53 863	52 867	1 091	1 355	50 202	49 161	1 402	1 724	235	189	912	816	21	22
Technical writers	37 265	37 027	524	373	34 636	32 876	1 354	2 027	102	188	649	944	16	16
Designers	265 409	331 503	15 570	16 723	225 872	293 142	10 717	9 689	951	1 259	12 013	10 559	176	128
Musicians and composers	99 409	48 611	8 743	3 372	79 614	44 330	8 677	677	417	131	1 827	1 066	131	22
Actors and directors	67 787	41 786	3 390	1 395	58 673	35 682	4 538	3 215	258	176	864	686	64	31
Painters, sculptors, craft-artists, and artist printmakers	101 067	111 695	3 853	3 307	84 913	102 028	4 934	3 526	909	753	3 352	2 785	106	96
Photographers	100 189	43 351	5 808	2 461	85 496	37 148	5 526	2 504	414	219	2 904	972	21	48
Dancers	5 097	16 816	555	1 043	3 698	13 980	557	1 031	57	172	230	561	–	27
Artists, performers, and related workers, n.e.c.	46 865	46 556	4 511	5 389	36 958	35 664	2 914	1 888	318	406	2 058	2 659	106	40
Editors and reporters	131 303	135 240	4 260	5 991	118 006	120 040	5 762	8 115	427	399	2 800	2 625	48	70
Public relations specialists	69 118	98 450	2 963	4 356	60 401	84 347	4 124	7 745	300	338	1 308	1 595	22	69
Announcers	47 752	12 517	2 669	617	40 348	10 202	3 940	1 352	266	114	498	219	31	13
Athletes	59 962	21 892	3 425	692	49 494	19 826	5 731	870	419	117	859	384	34	3
TECHNICAL, SALES, AND ADMINISTRATIVE SUPPORT OCCUPATIONS														
Technicians and related support occupations	2 366 641	2 020 767	129 501	102 091	1 943 965	1 590 073	154 054	232 189	11 643	11 282	126 041	83 958	1 437	1 174
Health technologists and technicians	270 887	1 158 210	22 809	57 699	164 404	905 466	35 148	152 513	1 827	6 942	16 491	35 037	208	553
Clinical laboratory technologists and technicians	82 202	247 690	6 696	11 390	55 684	189 023	11 341	31 108	460	1 019	7 958	15 039	63	111
Dental hygienists	1 174	71 220	108	1 887	859	66 717	124	1 354	6	142	77	1 111	–	9
Health record technologists and technicians	4 663	51 101	648	3 438	3 893	37 922	541	6 510	229	367	852	1 278	39	25
Radiologic technicians	36 176	94 207	2 535	3 238	26 622	82 757	3 541	5 643	196	3 196	1 131	8 501	34	57
Licensed practical nurses	27 569	401 904	1 067	17 245	17 972	299 284	5 643	73 493	254	1 535	4 968	7 622	72	185
Health technologists and technicians, n.e.c.	119 103	292 088	8 929	20 507	90 909	229 763	13 391	32 501	834	—	4 968	—	72	166
Technologists and technicians, except health	2 095 754	862 557	106 692	44 392	1 749 561	684 607	118 906	79 676	9 816	4 340	109 550	48 921	1 229	621
Engineering and related technologists and technicians	899 324	205 111	50 524	11 975	754 306	161 145	48 508	19 376	4 650	1 233	40 791	11 200	545	182
Electrical and electronic technicians	345 626	55 837	19 754	4 126	282 624	40 458	22 064	7 019	1 522	374	19 406	3 793	256	65
Industrial engineering technicians	11 991	3 333	510	128	10 489	2 816	672	332	74	24	235	32	11	–
Mechanical engineering technicians	27 578	3 531	1 154	195	23 938	1 958	1 075	218	77	25	1 318	120	16	11
Engineering technicians, n.e.c.	166 541	73 139	8 542	3 822	139 736	56 919	10 164	7 963	825	378	7 187	3 099	87	58
Drafting occupations	263 940	60 824	16 233	3 280	223 240	51 197	11 680	2 898	1 257	310	11 389	3 099	141	40
Surveying and mapping technicians	83 648	9 447	4 331	417	74 279	7 797	2 853	946	895	122	1 256	157	34	8

Table 1. **Detailed Occupation of the Civilian Labor Force by Sex, Race, and Hispanic Origin: 1990**—Con.

[Data based on sample and subject to sampling variability, see text. For definitions of terms and meanings of symbols, see text]

United States

Occupation	All persons Male	All persons Female	Hispanic origin (of any race) Male	Hispanic origin (of any race) Female	Not of Hispanic origin — White Male	White Female	Black Male	Black Female	Am. Indian, Eskimo, Aleut Male	Am. Indian, Eskimo, Aleut Female	Asian or Pacific Islander Male	Asian or Pacific Islander Female	Other race Male	Other race Female
TECHNICAL, SALES, AND ADMINISTRATIVE SUPPORT OCCUPATIONS—Con.														
Science technicians	141 022	67 966	9 144	4 255	112 916	52 358	11 303	6 886	876	439	6 694	3 951	89	77
Biological technicians	32 467	24 256	2 961	1 877	25 512	19 021	2 362	2 021	230	128	1 355	1 202	47	7
Chemical technicians	57 700	18 939	3 169	697	46 528	14 620	5 674	2 572	325	126	1 977	915	27	9
Science technicians, n.e.c.	50 855	24 771	3 014	1 681	40 876	18 711	3 267	2 293	321	185	3 362	1 834	15	61
Technicians, except health, engineering, and science	1 055 408	589 480	47 024	28 162	882 339	471 104	59 095	53 414	4 290	2 668	62 065	33 770	595	362
Airplane pilots and navigators	105 929	3 897	2 273	88	100 624	3 450	1 594	292	384	19	1 021	48	33	–
Air traffic controllers	36 668	10 495	1 637	638	31 193	8 155	3 088	1 483	147	58	603	161	–	–
Broadcast equipment operators	27 241	8 278	1 626	426	22 280	6 241	2 508	1 248	174	104	629	243	24	16
Computer programmers	447 109	215 650	15 237	7 534	381 021	170 471	20 717	18 567	1 169	535	28 700	18 613	265	108
Tool programmers, numerical control	3 141	529	102	34	2 824	353	102	142	34	–	79	–	–	–
Legal assistants	62 545	195 977	4 906	11 211	49 340	165 588	5 509	13 588	410	1 125	1 961	4 084	49	106
Technicians, n.e.c.	373 145	154 654	21 243	8 409	295 057	116 846	25 577	17 819	1 972	827	29 072	10 621	224	132
Sales occupations	7 334 643	7 098 126	419 068	468 358	6 324 402	5 726 154	353 747	655 224	25 576	41 438	207 803	202 096	4 047	4 856
Supervisors and proprietors, sales occupations, salaried	1 964 716	1 050 658	105 892	53 585	1 715 855	898 017	80 602	69 136	6 430	5 063	55 049	24 300	888	557
Supervisors and proprietors, sales occupations, self-employed	285 593	150 494	15 030	6 098	242 363	128 614	6 896	3 748	1 120	921	20 095	11 018	89	95
Sales representatives, finance and business services	1 475 043	1 013 597	52 432	41 868	1 331 051	888 020	57 618	57 013	3 683	3 748	29 636	22 511	623	437
Insurance sales occupations	431 027	235 515	15 453	11 110	386 662	198 631	19 738	20 356	1 074	899	7 933	4 399	167	120
Real estate sales occupations	397 205	404 033	14 905	14 313	356 763	366 355	12 916	11 258	1 011	1 435	11 401	10 536	209	136
Securities and financial services sales occupations	214 848	82 700	5 737	4 002	197 180	70 452	6 304	5 215	305	211	5 289	2 773	33	47
Advertising and related sales occupations	84 108	89 957	3 434	3 337	74 986	79 924	4 391	5 016	233	403	1 018	1 202	46	75
Sales occupations, other business services	347 855	201 392	12 903	9 106	315 460	172 658	14 269	15 168	1 060	800	3 995	3 601	168	59
Sales representatives, commodities, except retail	1 220 788	350 644	50 142	21 031	1 117 814	303 845	30 757	15 554	2 847	1 258	18 880	8 700	348	256
Sales engineers	41 408	2 208	772	68	39 550	2 041	324	50	34	3	726	46	2	–
Sales representatives, mining, manufacturing, and wholesale	1 179 380	348 436	49 370	20 963	1 078 264	301 804	30 433	15 504	2 813	1 255	18 154	8 654	346	256
Sales workers, retail and personal services	2 363 574	4 484 707	194 411	343 531	1 894 956	3 465 438	176 934	507 447	11 389	30 087	83 796	134 716	2 088	3 488
Sales workers, motor vehicles and boats	314 915	37 364	18 312	1 796	275 531	32 583	15 747	2 025	1 204	212	3 955	741	166	262
Sales workers, apparel	82 914	361 663	8 359	28 966	60 825	288 743	8 883	31 086	263	1 487	4 483	11 119	101	741
Sales workers, shoes	44 534	73 233	5 736	5 943	30 745	56 763	6 148	8 250	147	357	1 688	1 826	70	94
Sales workers, furniture and home furnishings	102 617	84 503	6 418	3 645	89 341	75 874	6 782	3 376	296	333	1 767	1 262	38	13
Sales workers, radio, TV, hi-fi, and appliances	122 032	48 840	6 955	2 836	104 379	41 735	6 905	2 798	387	248	3 429	1 191	100	32
Sales workers, hardware and building supplies	135 593	39 594	7 799	1 475	120 783	36 323	4 757	743	482	133	1 584	587	40	–
Sales workers, parts	118 966	13 127	8 891	755	103 463	11 258	4 905	1 076	641	149	1 347	198	32	24
Sales workers, other commodities	626 278	1 231 579	46 306	78 606	515 251	1 019 766	39 069	91 044	2 740	958	22 487	35 140	425	914
Sales counter clerks	72 545	137 528	5 993	9 866	56 899	110 288	2 678	11 045	467	227	4 119	5 227	76	144
Cashiers	596 364	2 259 316	69 276	199 779	417 781	1 623 658	68 915	340 508	4 020	24 718	35 525	74 654	847	1 881
Street and door-to-door sales workers	77 367	153 560	5 510	7 530	63 136	129 618	6 697	13 213	418	880	1 503	2 223	103	96
News vendors	69 449	44 400	4 856	2 334	56 822	38 829	5 448	2 283	324	385	1 909	548	90	21
Sales related occupations	24 929	48 026	1 161	2 245	22 363	42 220	940	2 326	107	361	347	851	11	23
Demonstrators, promoters and models, sales	8 317	36 948	660	1 725	6 806	32 609	562	1 777	48	276	230	557	11	4
Auctioneers	7 209	1 163	71	18	7 004	1 079	94	55	22	11	18	11	–	–
Sales occupations, n.e.c.	9 403	9 915	430	502	8 553	8 532	284	494	37	74	99	283	–	19
Administrative support occupations, including clerical	4 482 923	15 222 640	401 751	982 739	3 285 948	12 125 043	594 910	1 663 394	24 106	86 112	172 449	356 083	3 759	9 269
Supervisors, administrative support occupations	406 628	517 698	29 078	30 696	318 648	407 604	46 232	65 310	2 133	2 560	10 366	11 229	171	299
Supervisors, general office	214 678	364 947	16 798	22 441	164 808	285 303	25 862	47 437	1 260	1 995	5 756	7 542	74	229
Supervisors, computer equipment operators	21 917	12 631	1 042	635	18 503	10 054	1 734	1 556	77	87	561	299	–	–
Supervisors, financial records processing	33 380	77 006	1 520	4 043	28 348	64 031	2 223	6 533	89	287	1 178	2 080	22	32
Chief communications operators	1 720	2 653	69	171	1 489	2 075	115	346	9	–	38	61	–	–
Supervisors, distribution, scheduling, and adjusting clerks	134 933	60 461	9 649	3 406	105 500	46 141	16 178	9 438	698	191	2 833	1 247	75	38
Computer equipment operators	256 310	410 903	18 184	24 748	191 094	314 087	33 192	57 873	1 188	2 430	12 421	11 465	231	300
Computer operators	253 115	407 203	17 849	24 360	188 887	311 723	32 664	57 083	1 178	2 388	12 306	11 355	231	294
Peripheral equipment operators	3 195	3 700	335	388	2 207	2 364	528	790	10	42	115	110	–	6

Table 1. Detailed Occupation of the Civilian Labor Force by Sex, Race, and Hispanic Origin: 1990—Con.

[Data based on sample and subject to sampling variability, see text. For definitions of terms and meanings of symbols, see text]

United States	All persons		Hispanic origin (of any race)		Not of Hispanic origin									
					White		Black		American Indian, Eskimo, or Aleut		Asian or Pacific Islander		Other race	
	Male	Female	Male	Female	Male	Female	Male	Female	Male	Female	Male	Female	Male	Female
TECHNICAL, SALES, AND ADMINISTRATIVE SUPPORT OCCUPATIONS—Con.														
Secretaries, stenographers, and typists	97 485	4 663 841	8 266	265 703	69 662	3 888 331	13 998	403 270	720	25 682	4 715	78 675	124	2 180
Secretaries	52 492	3 966 179	4 206	219 115	39 213	3 375 482	6 554	288 645	400	20 636	2 064	60 516	50	1 785
Stenographers	7 563	72 317	255	2 989	6 767	62 441	359	5 228	24	5	158	1 315	—	18
Typists	37 430	625 345	3 805	43 599	23 677	450 408	7 085	109 397	296	4 720	2 493	16 844	74	377
Information clerks	230 674	1 347 972	19 916	105 723	171 103	1 067 383	26 968	133 829	1 550	8 652	10 924	31 139	213	1 246
Interviewers	49 781	156 177	3 839	11 634	36 782	117 133	7 203	22 283	700	1 663	1 194	3 311	63	103
Hotel clerks	27 005	69 385	2 366	4 384	20 155	54 367	2 535	7 182	138	592	1 788	2 773	23	87
Transportation ticket and reservation agents	79 758	190 193	7 538	13 658	59 107	153 237	8 361	14 673	305	708	1 799	7 580	100	176
Receptionists	35 037	787 056	3 794	65 014	24 323	633 492	4 874	68 716	220	4 708	1 799	14 425	27	701
Information clerks, n.e.c.	39 093	145 161	2 379	10 973	30 736	109 154	3 995	20 975	187	830	1 796	3 050	—	179
Records processing occupations, except financial	192 809	691 402	18 402	49 731	134 447	512 189	28 888	104 684	1 009	4 100	9 855	20 089	208	609
Classified-ad clerks	910	4 372	74	216	735	3 809	96	285	—	5	5	57	6	167
Correspondence clerks	2 116	10 405	111	436	1 609	8 023	347	702	—	47	43	167	—	—
Order clerks	64 599	164 523	6 963	11 522	46 521	123 015	8 940	25 874	322	856	801	3 115	52	141
Personnel clerks, except payroll and timekeeping	11 771	69 122	1 086	5 257	8 269	52 204	1 837	9 155	83	424	478	953	18	129
Library clerks	31 965	118 510	2 433	6 814	22 664	93 316	3 673	12 852	212	831	936	566	47	131
File clerks	51 924	216 022	5 751	18 238	32 212	149 256	10 336	39 365	274	1 399	3 311	544	40	170
Records clerks	29 524	108 448	1 984	7 158	22 437	82 566	3 659	15 451	118	538	1 281	687	45	38
Financial records processing occupations	264 608	2 136 921	21 900	106 653	201 589	1 833 438	24 772	130 379	1 094	10 365	14 965	53 033	288	1 053
Bookkeepers, accounting, and auditing clerks	200 750	1 721 202	16 669	82 432	153 146	1 497 872	18 397	89 431	733	8 225	11 605	42 452	200	790
Payroll and timekeeping clerks	20 343	159 137	1 524	8 948	15 211	131 392	2 352	14 625	181	752	1 054	3 346	21	74
Billing clerks	15 783	152 693	1 480	9 415	11 511	125 022	1 805	13 697	73	817	882	3 619	32	123
Cost and rate clerks	20 177	58 090	442	4 438	16 250	44 780	399	6 640	90	326	760	875	15	11
Billing, posting, and calculating machine operators	7 555	45 799	785	3 400	5 250	34 372	819	5 986	17	245	664	1 741	20	55
Duplicating, mail and other office machine operators	28 348	40 440	3 332	3 177	18 097	30 676	4 772	7 248	126	278	1 958	1 156	63	9
Duplicating machine operators	13 018	14 848	1 646	1 087	8 039	10 676	2 306	2 411	44	126	959	543	24	5
Mail preparing and paper handling machine operators	2 608	3 588	257	395	1 784	2 485	358	624	46	16	163	68	—	—
Office machine operators, n.e.c.	12 722	22 004	1 429	1 695	8 274	15 411	2 108	4 213	36	136	836	545	39	4
Communications equipment operators	33 799	210 316	3 264	13 706	23 467	152 137	6 148	40 565	203	1 193	700	2 524	17	191
Telephone operators	29 670	203 587	2 883	13 156	20 946	147 199	5 039	39 486	196	1 177	589	2 385	17	184
Communications equipment operators, n.e.c.	4 129	6 729	381	550	2 521	4 938	1 109	1 079	7	16	111	139	—	7
Mail and message distributing occupations	646 568	386 709	53 906	24 070	440 528	254 956	122 144	90 868	2 856	2 300	26 583	14 180	551	335
Postal clerks, except mail carriers	192 895	157 670	14 744	4 725	121 410	86 243	45 430	51 377	664	1 088	10 524	9 463	123	181
Mail carriers, postal service	240 290	87 951	16 706	3 818	181 698	68 842	32 480	12 547	1 092	410	8 189	1 375	125	52
Mail clerks, except postal service	105 987	105 722	11 381	2 898	64 205	71 900	25 127	22 685	504	588	4 605	2 568	165	83
Messengers	107 396	35 366	11 075	2 129	73 215	27 971	19 107	4 259	596	214	3 265	774	138	19
Material recording, scheduling, and distributing clerks	1 332 268	888 638	143 735	67 060	572 972	691 590	172 526	103 671	7 582	6 017	34 387	19 801	1 066	499
Dispatchers	107 747	97 200	6 994	5 000	90 419	78 670	8 501	10 567	556	849	1 242	981	35	55
Production coordinators	133 509	119 150	8 932	7 628	111 165	96 974	9 336	20 926	562	748	3 454	3 179	60	54
Traffic, shipping, and receiving clerks	460 680	187 922	62 977	17 862	316 151	143 973	67 423	33 863	2 434	1 250	11 270	3 797	425	114
Stock and inventory clerks	451 459	260 313	48 722	20 287	319 587	197 087	65 334	41 841	2 918	1 921	14 461	6 974	437	181
Meter readers	42 565	6 971	3 762	357	31 397	5 684	6 694	841	384	48	318	61	10	—
Weighers, measurers, checkers, and samplers	43 126	37 620	4 332	3 653	31 576	27 248	5 948	5 361	280	383	966	972	24	3
Expediters	82 324	156 465	7 062	10 128	64 267	125 650	8 330	16 754	398	684	2 215	3 179	52	70
Material recording, scheduling, and distributing clerks, n.e.c.	10 858	22 997	954	2 165	8 410	16 304	960	3 714	50	134	461	658	23	22
Adjusters and investigators	313 023	826 064	20 146	52 346	253 006	643 107	29 599	107 617	1 511	3 719	8 610	18 605	151	670
Insurance adjusters, examiners, and investigators	101 118	243 521	4 388	11 124	86 104	191 533	7 844	34 468	362	858	2 361	5 332	59	206
Investigators and adjusters, except insurance	151 592	430 238	10 016	28 842	121 749	336 500	14 398	52 127	768	1 827	4 596	10 608	65	334
Eligibility clerks, social welfare	5 150	44 356	965	3 939	2 868	32 190	705	6 914	31	364	581	896	—	53
Bill and account collectors	55 163	107 949	4 777	8 441	42 285	82 884	6 652	14 108	350	670	1 072	1 769	27	77

Table 1. Detailed Occupation of the Civilian Labor Force by Sex, Race, and Hispanic Origin: 1990—Con.

[Data based on sample and subject to sampling variability, see text. For definitions of terms and meanings of symbols, see text]

United States	All persons Male	All persons Female	Hispanic origin (of any race) Male	Hispanic origin (of any race) Female	White Male	White Female	Black Male	Black Female	Not of Hispanic origin — American Indian, Eskimo, or Aleut Male	American Indian, Eskimo, or Aleut Female	Asian or Pacific Islander Male	Asian or Pacific Islander Female	Other race Male	Other race Female
TECHNICAL, SALES, AND ADMINISTRATIVE SUPPORT OCCUPATIONS—Con.														
Miscellaneous administrative support occupations	680 403	3 101 736	61 622	237 126	491 335	2 331 649	85 671	418 080	4 134	18 816	36 965	94 187	676	1 878
General office clerks	264 538	1 226 578	27 030	95 836	185 545	918 998	36 355	166 327	1 459	7 546	13 893	36 991	256	880
Bank tellers	51 882	457 141	6 581	29 649	35 369	369 860	5 639	40 495	183	1 542	4 069	15 343	41	252
Proofreaders	7 304	23 022	302	728	6 220	19 710	546	937	20	66	216	552	–	29
Data-entry keyers	83 043	556 222	8 486	43 085	54 332	387 764	13 522	100 446	585	3 242	6 020	21 352	98	333
Statistical clerks	48 733	99 845	2 966	5 421	37 771	76 991	5 457	14 346	224	614	2 236	2 422	79	51
Teachers' aides	29 662	245 881	3 880	31 964	17 781	172 417	3 907	33 787	445	2 935	3 599	4 619	50	159
Administrative support occupations, n.e.c.	195 241	493 047	12 377	30 443	154 317	385 909	20 245	60 742	1 218	2 871	6 932	12 908	152	174
SERVICE OCCUPATIONS														
Private household occupations	29 077	534 841	6 219	124 499	14 870	255 625	6 184	138 071	309	3 540	1 407	12 394	88	712
Launderers and ironers	291	1 396	37	194	215	867	5	275	–	10	34	50	–	–
Cooks, private household	1 008	8 204	95	1 084	523	4 101	188	2 656	6	30	196	301	–	32
Housekeepers and butlers	2 087	32 329	465	10 800	800	9 853	683	10 132	–	209	128	1 263	11	72
Child care workers, private household	4 428	159 824	585	22 960	3 206	115 450	453	16 595	86	1 295	78	3 396	20	128
Private household cleaners and servants	21 263	333 088	5 037	89 461	10 126	125 354	4 855	108 413	217	1 996	971	7 384	57	480
Protective service occupations	1 754 500	330 275	122 436	21 915	1 330 522	223 737	259 384	77 367	15 866	3 014	24 922	3 879	1 370	363
Supervisors, protective service occupations	121 044	14 162	6 026	824	99 832	9 728	13 225	3 384	690	97	1 236	115	35	14
Supervisors, firefighting and fire prevention occupations	28 466	832	926	38	25 946	697	1 188	97	148	–	258	–	–	–
Supervisors, police and detectives	54 159	7 063	2 471	328	45 669	4 756	5 320	1 856	258	49	435	60	6	14
Supervisors, guards	38 419	6 267	2 629	458	28 217	4 275	6 717	1 431	284	48	543	55	29	3
Firefighting and fire prevention occupations	233 170	8 316	11 351	418	196 263	6 344	20 320	1 201	3 063	315	2 063	35	110	3
Fire inspection and fire prevention occupations	14 407	2 318	623	145	12 104	1 691	1 327	437	208	31	145	11	–	3
Firefighting occupations	218 763	5 998	10 728	273	184 159	4 653	18 993	764	2 855	284	1 918	24	110	3
Police and detectives	702 475	119 808	44 625	7 851	558 783	78 703	86 389	30 978	5 508	1 118	6 672	1 048	498	110
Police and detectives, public service	457 078	62 106	29 165	4 482	374 308	42 260	45 253	14 074	3 457	573	4 568	671	327	46
Sheriffs, bailiffs, and other law enforcement officers	95 561	12 871	5 498	1 425	77 970	9 627	10 463	2 749	740	204	856	249	34	22
Correctional institution officers	149 836	44 831	9 962	1 944	106 505	26 816	30 673	12 749	1 311	341	1 248	128	137	42
Guards	697 811	187 989	60 434	12 822	475 644	128 962	139 450	41 804	6 605	1 484	14 951	2 681	727	236
Crossing guards	12 818	32 495	822	2 124	9 524	22 068	2 309	6 039	78	140	75	95	10	29
Guards and police, except public service	655 141	130 370	57 619	9 734	440 912	82 110	135 332	34 733	6 285	1 262	14 294	2 347	699	184
Protective service occupations, n.e.c.	29 852	25 124	1 993	964	25 208	22 784	3 332	1 032	242	82	582	239	18	23
Service occupations, except protective and household	5 135 444	8 783 420	803 674	802 822	3 171 383	6 185 729	885 789	1 460 372	43 766	80 889	224 700	245 824	6 132	7 784
Food preparation and service occupations	2 369 276	3 369 682	421 287	250 850	1 432 140	2 594 481	346 387	381 696	17 271	30 313	149 191	109 746	3 000	2 596
Supervisors, food preparation and service occupations	117 402	159 018	13 862	9 586	80 141	125 945	14 677	16 894	605	1 185	7 904	5 309	213	99
Bartenders	166 630	164 080	13 781	5 395	140 017	150 210	7 571	4 002	961	1 929	4 170	2 441	130	103
Waiters and waitresses	290 768	1 197 485	48 693	69 295	189 781	1 025 935	25 530	52 830	1 349	9 013	25 102	39 641	313	771
Cooks	1 085 895	987 365	191 390	87 253	615 444	665 954	189 799	190 622	8 706	11 234	79 152	31 587	1 404	715
Food counter, fountain and related occupations	65 491	170 989	7 621	12 840	46 220	134 235	8 043	17 670	427	1 425	3 122	4 599	58	220
Kitchen workers, food preparation	52 183	159 317	8 403	11 591	35 040	122 155	6 309	20 595	273	1 021	2 062	3 803	96	152
Waiters'/waitresses' assistants	217 437	161 121	54 109	15 155	123 673	118 142	28 098	20 723	1 352	1 045	9 999	5 860	206	196
Miscellaneous food preparation occupations	373 470	370 307	83 428	39 735	201 824	251 905	66 360	58 360	3 598	3 461	17 680	16 506	580	340
Health service occupations	287 943	1 974 015	27 244	148 274	169 771	1 247 415	76 495	512 027	3 053	19 460	11 038	44 894	342	1 945
Dental assistants	5 166	174 121	940	14 382	3 950	145 547	291	8 650	21	1 133	577	4 282	–	127
Health aides, except nursing	45 064	177 913	3 775	10 761	26 730	124 471	11 878	36 973	489	1 147	2 215	4 413	37	148
Nursing aides, orderlies, and attendants	237 713	1 621 981	22 529	123 131	140 091	977 397	63 999	466 404	2 543	17 180	8 246	36 199	305	1 670
Cleaning and building service occupations, except household	2 013 354	1 410 347	305 247	234 789	1 243 260	769 461	395 968	348 336	19 802	15 815	46 779	40 168	2 298	1 778
Supervisors, cleaning and building service workers	117 971	49 504	13 241	6 719	83 724	39 297	18 351	9 430	950	432	1 557	1 541	148	85
Maids and housemen	137 337	575 452	30 158	103 022	56 514	282 901	41 849	159 793	1 254	7 379	7 297	21 042	265	815
Janitors and cleaners	1 700 984	780 561	255 573	124 696	1 059 736	453 749	329 540	176 251	17 194	7 946	37 082	17 041	1 859	878
Elevator operators	9 684	1 727	2 216	139	5 065	837	2 162	712	30	30	204	9	7	–
Pest control occupations	47 378	3 103	4 059	213	38 221	2 677	4 066	150	374	28	639	35	19	–
Personal service occupations	464 871	2 029 376	49 896	168 909	326 212	1 574 372	66 939	218 313	3 640	15 301	17 692	51 016	492	1 465
Supervisors, personal service occupations	19 313	43 619	1 653	3 122	14 465	34 045	2 291	5 198	153	364	741	837	10	53
Barbers	66 677	17 949	6 069	1 452	50 091	11 885	9 159	1 680	468	116	875	816	15	53
Hairdressers and cosmetologists	76 143	657 433	9 090	50 613	56 139	529 006	7 713	52 976	362	3 700	2 749	20 712	90	426

Table 1. Detailed Occupation of the Civilian Labor Force by Sex, Race, and Hispanic Origin: 1990—Con.

[Data based on sample and subject to sampling variability, see text. For definitions of terms and meanings of symbols, see text]

Columns under "Not of Hispanic origin": White, Black, American Indian, Eskimo, or Aleut, Asian or Pacific Islander, Other race.

United States	All persons Male	All persons Female	Hispanic Male	Hispanic Female	White Male	White Female	Black Male	Black Female	Am. Ind. Male	Am. Ind. Female	Asian/PI Male	Asian/PI Female	Other race Male	Other race Female
SERVICE OCCUPATIONS—Con.														
Attendants, amusement and recreation facilities	86 248	50 905	7 128	3 826	66 004	36 841	8 094	5 307	982	1 086	4 011	3 792	29	53
Guides	19 281	22 005	1 495	977	13 452	16 609	2 562	2 913	164	123	1 597	1 365	11	18
Ushers	19 853	9 758	1 880	781	14 899	7 237	2 382	1 361	70	76	604	271	18	32
Public transportation attendants	21 801	84 148	2 623	3 541	13 431	68 499	4 433	9 317	71	206	1 193	2 574	50	11
Baggage porters and bellhops	34 558	4 205	4 287	622	19 153	2 282	8 884	988	141	—	2 036	290	52	8
Welfare service aides	7 871	40 319	808	4 588	4 774	24 407	1 825	9 908	214	657	250	756	—	23
Family child care providers	6 234	428 409	508	37 020	4 772	351 312	728	29 940	82	2 723	116	6 870	28	330
Early childhood teacher's assistants	14 059	324 869	1 550	25 733	9 090	244 067	2 921	47 585	127	2 940	360	4 552	11	209
Child care workers, n.e.c.	22 932	188 419	2 318	19 285	14 049	133 125	5 723	30 786	322	1 358	487	3 165	33	118
Personal service occupations, n.e.c.	69 901	157 338	10 487	17 359	45 888	113 057	10 224	20 354	484	—	2 673	5 016	145	184
FARMING, FORESTRY, AND FISHING OCCUPATIONS														
Farming, forestry, and fishing occupations	2 597 829	507 566	443 270	85 037	1 924 614	380 584	170 994	27 812	23 945	4 384	33 464	9 388	1 542	391
Farm operators and managers	933 808	153 557	33 238	4 852	874 322	143 630	16 196	2 558	3 655	806	6 218	1 671	179	30
Farmers, except horticultural	680 512	114 675	11 466	1 814	656 812	110 429	6 660	962	2 378	569	3 105	896	91	5
Horticultural specialty farmers	31 261	3 471	3 289	112	25 398	3 139	1 692	—	134	27	733	122	15	—
Managers, farms, except horticultural	208 114	30 770	16 674	2 639	181 006	26 102	7 179	1 337	1 097	178	2 085	524	73	20
Managers, horticultural specialty farms	13 921	4 641	1 809	327	11 106	3 960	665	—	46	46	295	129	—	—
Other agricultural and related occupations	1 466 828	342 587	399 625	79 232	890 052	228 127	137 216	24 146	14 321	3 181	24 367	7 499	1 247	342
Farm occupations, except managerial	666 460	175 613	227 217	49 533	374 968	106 636	49 127	13 019	6 533	1 672	7 947	4 449	668	254
Supervisors, farm workers	37 273	6 162	11 977	1 337	22 836	3 933	1 473	651	236	57	717	180	34	4
Farm workers	609 123	150 546	207 238	45 638	341 936	88 723	46 484	11 030	6 169	1 430	6 683	3 465	613	240
Marine life cultivation workers	879	354	59	42	695	271	51	41	43	—	31	—	—	—
Nursery workers	19 185	18 551	7 943	2 546	9 501	13 709	1 119	1 127	85	185	516	804	21	10
Related agricultural occupations	800 368	166 974	172 408	29 709	515 084	121 491	88 089	11 127	7 788	1 509	16 420	3 050	579	88
Supervisors, related agricultural occupations	60 452	5 155	7 516	457	49 003	4 265	2 704	318	300	83	845	32	84	—
Groundskeepers and gardeners, except farm	680 843	54 713	151 017	6 403	427 982	41 515	79 988	4 880	6 832	650	14 577	1 234	447	31
Animal caretakers, except farm	40 059	67 146	4 441	217	31 400	62 883	3 256	390	455	390	491	474	16	16
Graders and sorters, agricultural products	16 695	37 964	9 094	20 279	5 018	11 789	1 924	301	181	369	446	1 245	32	41
Inspectors, agricultural products	2 319	1 996	340	453	1 681	1 039	217	422	20	17	61	65	—	—
Forestry and logging occupations	140 463	7 560	7 383	576	113 505	5 737	14 414	900	3 716	248	377	99	70	—
Supervisors, forestry and logging workers	11 529	539	380	21	10 162	500	726	18	233	—	19	—	9	—
Forestry workers, except logging	16 858	3 573	2 661	426	12 355	2 689	104	306	641	120	85	32	8	—
Timber cutting and logging occupations	112 076	3 448	4 342	129	90 988	2 548	13 584	576	2 842	128	273	67	53	19
Fishers, hunters, and trappers	56 730	3 862	3 024	277	46 737	3 090	2 168	208	2 253	149	2 502	119	46	—
Captains and other officers, fishing vessels	6 149	192	320	21	5 452	150	78	17	154	4	136	4	9	—
Fishers	48 813	3 339	2 604	229	39 831	2 672	2 002	166	2 034	141	2 305	112	37	19
Hunters and trappers	1 768	331	100	27	1 454	268	88	25	65	4	61	7	—	—
PRECISION PRODUCTION, CRAFT, AND REPAIR OCCUPATIONS														
Precision production, craft, and repair occupations	12 701 437	1 329 863	1 148 544	142 710	10 370 551	948 709	867 525	158 390	97 173	11 373	209 785	67 455	7 859	1 226
Mechanics and repairers	4 085 908	185 258	323 481	13 002	3 385 468	139 201	277 371	26 837	27 048	1 379	70 082	4 573	2 458	266
Supervisors, mechanics and repairers	247 901	22 681	11 577	1 065	220 556	17 395	11 557	3 689	1 058	143	3 039	377	114	12
Mechanics and repairers, except supervisors	3 838 007	162 577	311 904	11 937	3 164 912	121 806	265 814	23 148	25 990	1 236	67 043	4 196	2 344	254
Vehicle and mobile equipment mechanics and repairers	1 829 964	35 714	169 683	2 860	1 487 194	26 839	126 462	4 990	13 015	310	32 396	675	1 214	40
Automobile mechanics, except apprentices	936 977	17 646	92 946	1 461	747 463	13 404	70 620	2 312	6 590	162	18 644	277	714	30
Automobile mechanic apprentices	1 531	—	125	3	1 207	57	156	—	14	—	29	—	—	—
Bus, truck, and stationary engine mechanics	263 806	2 336	18 918	154	221 670	1 581	18 559	504	1 957	27	2 595	30	107	—
Aircraft engine mechanics	129 256	5 416	11 435	490	103 155	3 913	9 661	799	911	45	4 012	169	82	—
Small engine repairers	60 914	4 719	3 686	—	53 315	812	2 726	190	561	7	592	22	34	10
Automobile body and related repairers	223 437	2 377	28 132	364	177 785	1 691	12 849	482	1 333	29	3 661	32	231	—
Aircraft mechanics, except engine	155 764	1 731	10 071	133	123 858	1 315	2 515	421	191	37	1 263	95	14	—
Heavy equipment mechanics	29 288	321	1 074	63	25 260	204	954	249	1 345	—	187	29	32	—
Farm equipment mechanics	28 984	—	—	—	23 412	—	422	33	113	3	1 413	21	10	—
Industrial machinery repairers	318 984	13 795	21 235	1 124	239 412	10 407	23 333	1 807	1 825	93	4 021	318	158	46
Machinery maintenance occupations	24 140	1 133	1 522	115	19 356	800	2 624	181	419	2	208	27	11	—
Electrical and electronic equipment repairers	573 064	62 461	36 835	4 298	478 230	45 971	41 405	9 738	3 251	487	13 016	1 882	327	85
Electronic repairers, communications and industrial equipment	164 678	14 551	12 306	1 062	133 637	11 039	12 877	1 777	947	132	4 782	525	129	16
Data processing equipment repairers	79 736	11 921	4 378	782	66 433	9 149	5 759	1 381	340	69	2 795	540	31	—
Household appliance and power tool repairers	50 935	2 190	3 455	243	43 639	1 637	2 534	236	311	11	981	58	15	—

Table 1. Detailed Occupation of the Civilian Labor Force by Sex, Race, and Hispanic Origin: 1990—Con.

[Data based on sample and subject to sampling variability, see text. For definitions of terms and meanings of symbols, see text]

United States	All persons		Hispanic origin (of any race)		White		Black		American Indian, Eskimo, or Aleut		Asian or Pacific Islander		Other race	
									Not of Hispanic origin					
	Male	Female	Male	Female	Male	Female	Male	Female	Male	Female	Male	Female	Male	Female
PRECISION PRODUCTION, CRAFT, AND REPAIR OCCUPATIONS—Con.														
Telephone line installers and repairers	47 211	3 422	2 676	355	40 852	2 387	2 855	512	327	33	467	114	34	21
Telephone installers and repairers	164 418	26 509	9 029	1 522	139 554	19 118	12 494	5 177	856	141	2 430	503	55	48
Miscellaneous electrical and electronic equipment repairers	66 086	3 868	4 991	329	54 115	2 641	4 886	655	470	101	1 561	142	63	11
Heating, air conditioning, and refrigeration mechanics	190 412	2 571	13 102	130	164 475	1 977	9 184	410	1 201	18	2 357	25	93	64
Miscellaneous mechanics and repairers	901 443	46 903	69 527	3 410	746 245	35 812	63 806	6 022	6 279	326	15 045	1 269	541	—
Camera, watch, and musical instrument repairers	27 311	3 786	1 730	291	23 582	2 917	799	344	61	22	1 121	212	18	5
Locksmiths and safe repairers	25 360	1 777	1 541	86	22 014	1 547	1 251	254	173	27	361	27	20	5
Office machine repairers	39 540	2 348	1 565	169	32 749	1 829	2 979	239	200	—	1 033	96	14	—
Mechanical controls and valve repairers	19 393	1 015	1 434	6	15 211	734	1 184	72	96	20	204	16	30	—
Elevator installers and repairers	25 207	427	2 721	53	22 119	302	647	408	140	—	292	—	38	—
Millwrights	92 874	266	4 794	214	84 512	549	4 647	1 938	519	52	464	43	11	6
Specified mechanics and repairers, n.e.c.	199 247	14 702	14 794	124	166 286	11 159	13 107	2 682	1 421	87	3 533	388	106	53
Not specified mechanics and repairers	472 511	19 582	43 177	1 467	379 772	14 775	37 552	—	3 669	118	8 037	487	304	—
Construction trades	5 170 054	147 946	502 639	11 534	4 210 711	117 870	350 888	14 278	47 798	1 843	54 807	2 278	3 211	143
Supervisors, construction occupations	815 303	22 697	52 707	1 307	711 202	18 634	37 932	2 209	5 254	206	7 857	324	351	17
Supervisors, brickmasons, stonemasons, and tile setters	12 880	88	957	9	10 542	62	1 163	9	81	16	137	8	—	—
Supervisors, carpenters and related workers	45 096	529	3 155	50	40 100	436	948	27	352	—	514	—	27	—
Supervisors, electricians and power transmission installers	71 958	1 598	3 226	106	65 083	1 343	2 497	114	318	11	782	24	52	—
Supervisors, painters, paperhangers, and plasterers	30 759	1 610	2 678	68	25 480	1 388	1 853	117	324	11	409	26	15	—
Supervisors, plumbers, pipefitters, and steamfitters	20 103	415	938	17	18 108	363	741	19	120	16	196	—	—	—
Supervisors, construction n.e.c.	634 507	18 457	41 753	1 057	551 889	15 042	30 730	1 923	4 059	152	5 819	266	257	17
Construction trades, except supervisors	4 354 751	125 249	449 932	10 227	3 499 509	99 236	312 956	12 069	42 544	1 637	46 950	1 954	2 860	126
Brickmasons and stonemasons	194 480	2 459	20 325	229	142 932	1 582	28 187	621	1 455	24	1 465	3	116	—
Brickmason and stonemason apprentices	685	42	55	—	535	37	87	5	—	—	8	—	—	—
Tile setters, hard and soft	54 356	1 286	9 009	209	41 053	983	3 008	61	346	34	894	33	46	—
Carpet installers	109 426	2 410	13 312	240	88 434	1 926	6 053	173	821	342	709	29	97	—
Carpenters	1 337 544	23 163	119 732	1 799	1 124 393	18 744	65 242	1 923	13 751	22	13 618	299	808	31
Carpenter apprentices	4 600	253	436	4	3 725	150	224	77	57	86	151	—	7	—
Drywall installers	146 761	3 793	22 763	449	111 386	2 975	8 923	283	2 587	200	1 007	7	95	—
Electricians	619 358	15 659	37 073	1 193	533 493	11 705	35 050	2 102	3 970	7	437	450	335	7
Electrician apprentices	14 888	684	881	22	12 853	580	891	75	124	11	139	—	—	—
Electrical power installers and repairers	118 543	1 689	5 161	66	102 000	1 395	9 672	189	1 108	—	575	28	27	15
Painters, construction and maintenance	515 697	43 329	83 618	3 451	372 083	35 944	46 459	2 671	4 425	484	8 479	748	633	31
Paperhangers	12 811	399	918	73	11 318	226	302	49	87	29	170	22	16	—
Plasterers	42 260	849	11 650	170	24 627	521	5 356	142	281	16	305	—	41	—
Plumbers, pipefitters, and steamfitters	481 639	7 219	37 868	484	401 484	5 732	33 134	846	4 179	58	4 694	92	280	7
Plumber, pipefitter, and steamfitter apprentices	6 426	153	415	—	5 546	134	306	19	52	—	107	—	33	—
Concrete and terrazzo finishers	74 944	1 001	14 033	225	44 668	448	14 971	314	876	14	363	—	15	—
Glaziers	43 142	2 453	3 820	163	36 884	893	7 236	299	237	35	443	63	26	—
Insulation workers	71 460	2 952	11 212	428	51 326	826	1 744	623	859	59	801	16	10	8
Paving, surfacing, and tamping equipment operators	12 777	333	1 472	15	9 360	247	1 744	71	132	90	59	8	154	—
Roofers	194 098	3 085	28 440	326	142 984	2 224	18 328	437	2 833	3	1 359	7	4	—
Sheetmetal duct installers	29 541	421	701	59	26 039	326	1 455	26	193	21	149	21	22	8
Structural metal workers	73 885	1 453	5 068	121	62 829	1 092	4 040	198	1 284	6	642	—	—	—
Drillers, earth	19 983	508	1 612	69	17 095	364	893	69	309	96	74	135	95	15
Construction trades, n.e.c.	175 447	5 656	19 358	432	132 462	4 182	19 652	796	2 578	—	1 302	—	82	—
Extractive occupations	187 451	5 411	14 935	440	161 685	4 298	7 864	537	2 265	89	620	39	89	8
Supervisors, extractive occupations	47 578	1 741	2 505	79	43 143	1 484	1 239	150	403	7	279	21	12	—
Drillers, oil well	36 539	533	3 916	4	30 220	503	1 669	8	665	18	57	—	6	—
Explosives workers	8 872	505	608	91	7 373	313	700	74	165	19	20	18	31	8
Mining machine operators	60 613	1 705	3 708	138	53 461	1 340	2 627	178	581	31	205	—	24	—
Mining occupations, n.e.c.	33 849	927	4 198	128	27 488	658	1 629	127	451	14	59	—	50	13
Precision production occupations	3 258 024	991 248	307 489	117 734	2 612 687	687 340	231 402	116 738	20 062	8 062	84 276	60 565	2 108	809
Supervisors, production occupations	1 069 504	230 133	81 527	25 386	888 132	172 129	77 393	24 829	5 145	1 483	16 818	6 123	489	183
Precision metal working occupations	973 271	79 163	72 101	9 255	818 433	55 458	53 191	9 581	6 727	1 708	22 158	3 047	601	114
Tool and die makers, except apprentices	139 502	3 312	5 186	283	129 264	2 533	3 377	322	448	12	1 207	162	20	—
Tool and die maker apprentices	2 267	109	67	—	2 130	91	40	9	10	—	10	—	—	—
Precision assemblers, metal	31 912	9 047	3 780	1 419	23 167	4 998	3 621	1 915	222	96	1 072	606	50	13
Machinists, except apprentices	543 172	25 909	39 106	2 918	454 867	18 035	32 245	4 168	3 093	239	13 507	527	354	22

Table 1. Detailed Occupation of the Civilian Labor Force by Sex, Race, and Hispanic Origin: 1990—Con.

[Data based on sample and subject to sampling variability, see text. For definitions of terms and meanings of symbols see text]

United States	All persons Male	All persons Female	Hispanic origin (of any race) Male	Hispanic origin (of any race) Female	Not of Hispanic origin — White Male	White Female	Black Male	Black Female	American Indian, Eskimo, or Aleut Male	American Indian, Eskimo, or Aleut Female	Asian or Pacific Islander Male	Asian or Pacific Islander Female	Other race Male	Other race Female
PRECISION PRODUCTION, CRAFT, AND REPAIR OCCUPATIONS—Con.														
Machinist apprentices	1 436	107	101	12	1 224	75	57	18	11	2	39	—	4	—
Boilermakers	23 706	587	1 415	23	19 843	445	2 089	106	223	13	136	—	—	—
Precision grinders, filers, and tool sharpeners	21 378	1 691	1 039	52	19 165	1 412	799	201	165	—	191	26	19	—
Patternmakers and model makers, metal	5 177	265	191	33	4 782	192	169	30	12	—	23	10	—	—
Lay-out workers	14 834	2 153	629	6	11 694	1 577	2 044	833	149	31	312	83	6	3
Precious stones and metals workers (Jewelers)	40 995	20 835	8 746	3 340	26 865	14 137	1 226	343	1 499	1 194	2 579	1 257	80	74
Engravers, metal	10 659	8 499	899	495	9 082	5 580	422	216	41	25	215	142	—	—
Sheet metal workers, except apprentices	135 431	8 060	10 702	654	114 112	443	6 917	1 216	812	87	2 820	221	68	2
Sheet metal worker apprentices	1 877	86	100	—	682	60	58	47	11	—	14	13	—	—
Miscellaneous precision metal workers		503	140	634	1 556	267	127	771	21	91	33	84	69	21
Precision woodworking occupations	97 016	13 643	10 627	—	79 681	11 042	4 904	48	615	—	1 120	8	—	—
Patternmakers and model makers, wood	2 976	323	159	274	2 694	354	82	343	10	9	31	25	42	—
Cabinet makers and bench carpenters	67 251	4 620	6 531	343	56 826	3 958	2 739	1 343	412	52	701	51	27	21
Furniture and wood finishers	25 035	8 396	3 796	7	18 727	6 586	1 972	26	149	97	364	404	—	—
Miscellaneous precision woodworkers	1 754	304	141	—	1 434	231	111	—	44	30	24	—	—	—
Precision textile, apparel, and furnishings machine workers	119 539	152 981	25 999	21 560	75 990	100 509	10 794	14 333	635	827	6 010	15 685	111	47
Dressmakers	6 421	90 837	1 883	13 586	3 164	57 918	544	8 336	51	565	771	10 141	8	21
Tailors	29 538	27 269	7 903	1 269	15 675	15 208	3 169	2 862	52	57	2 688	3 928	51	5
Upholsterers	57 167	16 771	11 605	1 200	39 754	13 890	4 483	409	349	112	743	155	33	5
Shoe repairers	20 178	7 850	3 601	865	12 712	901	2 103	685	129	50	1 618	404	15	5
Miscellaneous precision apparel and fabric workers		10 254	807	510	685	6 592	495	1 041	54	43	190	1 057	4	11
Precision workers, assorted materials	265 293	303 078	34 376	39 155	190 347	199 764	20 531	34 034	1 527	2 052	277	822	235	251
Hand molders and shapers, except jewelers	16 892	3 165	2 249	350	13 402	2 398	892	232	117	36	204	109	28	—
Patternmakers, lay-out workers, and cutters	17 388	5 502	992	864	15 440	3 419	509	414	73	9	363	842	11	14
Optical goods workers	33 171	41 736	2 983	1 417	26 933	34 050	1 858	767	140	206	1 231	486	26	15
Dental laboratory and medical appliance technicians	34 394	22 570	3 922	857	25 645	18 152	1 920	1 539	210	95	679	1 335	18	32
Bookbinders	13 964	15 969	1 273	1 311	11 008	11 252	1 282	347	77	59	320	465	4	9
Electrical and electronic equipment assemblers	104 105	205 301	16 168	30 164	54 041	124 165	11 109	25 831	691	591	11 990	23 357	106	173
Miscellaneous precision workers, n.e.c.	45 379	8 335	6 789	1 311	33 878	6 328	2 961	904	219	56	1 490	228	42	8
Precision food production occupations	331 632	160 280	59 404	17 605	225 771	110 260	32 693	24 977	2 276	1 419	11 096	5 876	392	143
Butchers and meat cutters	224 107	54 795	36 788	6 712	159 350	29 948	19 938	14 752	1 671	677	6 155	629	205	77
Bakers	86 076	73 096	18 436	6 408	52 020	55 960	10 585	7 941	468	488	4 424	2 277	143	32
Food batchmakers	21 449	32 835	4 180	4 485	14 401	24 362	2 170	4 758	137	254	517	970	44	34
Precision inspectors, testers, and related workers	105 820	32 044	6 958	3 108	36 840	25 073	7 821	517	576	252	3 565	614	60	32
Inspectors, testers, and graders	99 861	2 791	6 587	2 672	31 823	25 073	7 517	473	529	234	3 353	1 559	52	20
Adjusters and calibrators	5 959	17 135	371	434	5 017	1 799	304	18	47	18	212	55	8	12
Plant and system operators	296 009	3 095	16 497	1 013	247 493	13 105	24 075	2 455	2 561	230	5 232	314	151	18
Water and sewage treatment plant operators	58 174	2 253	2 952	89	49 091	2 434	5 103	468	530	50	483	54	15	—
Power plant operators	34 759	7 602	1 717	143	29 878	1 704	2 403	332	418	62	335	12	8	7
Stationary engineers	153 639	4 185	7 358	538	129 657	5 715	11 615	1 028	1 128	97	3 812	217	69	7
Miscellaneous plant and system operators	49 437		4 470	243	38 867	3 252	4 954	627	485	21	602	31	59	11
OPERATORS, FABRICATORS, AND LABORERS														
Machine operators, assemblers, and inspectors	5 185 397	3 450 107	681 514	493 093	3 760 481	2 176 492	635 330	599 509	37 875	27 011	125 506	150 422	4 691	3 580
Machine operators and tenders, except precision	3 176 768	2 231 958	437 314	327 447	2 242 513	1 388 448	397 125	396 711	21 208	17 065	75 594	100 049	3 014	2 238
Metal working and plastic working machine operators	317 227	70 805	30 605	5 655	251 726	54 094	28 776	9 439	1 887	556	4 085	994	148	66
Lathe and turning machine set-up operators	26 770	2 690	2 389	213	22 164	2 108	1 799	337	85	7	331	25	—	—
Lathe and turning machine operators	32 088	4 442	2 568	319	27 916	3 561	1 643	477	178	13	478	72	5	—
Milling and planing machine operators	5 806	983	399	43	4 868	769	331	129	31	15	168	22	9	—
Punching and stamping press machine operators	79 351	31 976	7 418	2 442	62 117	23 872	8 392	4 251	572	257	830	271	22	22
Rolling machine operators	11 767	1 976	897	123	9 538	1 477	1 216	339	46	15	70	13	—	9
Drilling and boring machine operators	17 201	4 375	1 034	328	14 713	3 407	1 236	558	71	50	129	26	18	6
Grinding, abrading, buffing, and polishing machine operators	105 876	19 582	13 934	1 775	78 869	14 596	10 687	2 587	713	170	1 586	425	87	29
Forging machine operators	16 076	970	1 043	46	13 108	796	1 688	114	81	—	156	14	—	—
Numerical control machine operators	1 363	273	133	23	1 102	189	85	24	—	—	43	37	—	—
Miscellaneous metal, plastic, stone, and glass working machine operators														
Fabricating machine operators, n.e.c.	20 929	4 399	1 490	339	17 331	3 319	1 699	623	110	29	294	89	5	—
Metal and plastic processing machine operators	18 127	8 535	2 568	744	13 056	6 290	1 993	1 206	70	45	414	244	26	25
Molding and casting machine operators	132 690	29 677	16 811	2 670	58 959	22 270	13 828	3 992	947	221	1 994	499	151	25
Metal plating machine operators	68 281	21 187	7 238	1 855	52 925	15 960	6 806	2 881	500	132	754	334	58	—
Heat treating equipment operators	31 109	4 288	5 817	499	21 106	3 171	3 045	845	214	50	857	99	70	—
Miscellaneous metal and plastic processing machine operators	17 323	1 220	1 124	8	14 314	849	1 731	266	64	2	90	22	—	—
operators	15 977	2 982	2 632	235	10 614	2 290	2 246	376	169	37	293	44	23	—

Table 1. **Detailed Occupation of the Civilian Labor Force by Sex, Race, and Hispanic Origin: 1990**—Con.

[Data based on sample and subject to sampling variability, see text. For definitions of terms and meanings of symbols, see text]

United States	All persons		Hispanic origin (of any race)		Not of Hispanic origin									
					White		Black		American Indian, Eskimo, or Aleut		Asian or Pacific Islander		Other race	
	Male	Female	Male	Female	Male	Female	Male	Female	Male	Female	Male	Female	Male	Female
OPERATORS, FABRICATORS, AND LABORERS—Con.														
Woodworking machine operators	132 205	23 432	10 003	2 038	105 724	18 062	13 432	2 746	1 749	277	1 197	293	100	16
Wood lathe, routing, and planing machine operators	7 157	1 054	396	32	6 085	850	510	135	100	29	66	8	–	–
Sawing machine operators	82 788	12 117	5 821	1 355	65 402	8 955	9 641	1 445	1 241	134	610	212	73	16
Shaping and joining machine operators	4 180	1 864	392	75	3 417	1 563	283	199	54	15	34	12	–	–
Nailing and tacking machine operators	2 345	874	350	92	1 670	681	256	97	33	4	33	–	3	–
Miscellaneous woodworking machine operators	35 735	7 523	3 044	484	29 150	6 013	2 742	870	321	95	454	61	24	–
Printing machine operators	374 529	157 616	34 109	10 844	301 683	130 559	27 810	12 262	1 676	854	8 939	2 998	312	99
Printing press operators	293 657	66 124	28 472	6 173	232 614	50 983	23 741	7 166	1 358	373	7 184	1 372	288	57
Photoengravers and lithographers	35 861	13 245	2 528	797	31 245	11 235	1 371	900	102	81	608	219	7	13
Typesetters and compositors	21 641	50 712	1 277	1 920	18 625	45 618	941	2 107	90	215	697	836	11	16
Miscellaneous printing machine operators	23 370	27 535	1 832	1 954	19 199	22 723	1 757	2 089	126	185	450	571	6	13
Textile, apparel, and furnishings machine operators	341 153	1 076 419	68 986	167 869	192 812	615 037	59 766	215 752	2 008	8 815	17 176	68 013	405	933
Winding and twisting machine operators	19 579	51 041	530	686	14 098	33 929	4 600	15 510	109	395	242	516	–	5
Knitting, looping, taping, and weaving machine operators	21 250	38 973	2 216	1 496	13 893	26 721	4 587	9 384	216	427	314	914	24	31
Textile cutting machine operators	4 549	3 290	840	448	2 758	2 167	824	602	28	22	95	51	4	–
Textile sewing machine operators	93 074	690 725	32 621	123 539	39 485	383 544	14 820	120 961	500	5 460	5 508	56 632	140	589
Shoe machine operators	10 052	24 192	1 355	1 701	7 788	20 447	736	1 722	66	115	100	156	7	51
Pressing machine operators	54 543	93 868	10 597	15 651	30 018	47 429	9 242	27 448	310	662	4 295	2 589	81	89
Laundering and dry cleaning machine operators	82 729	136 368	15 090	21 840	46 523	75 314	14 618	31 095	464	1 290	5 952	6 666	82	163
Miscellaneous textile machine operators	55 377	37 962	5 737	2 508	38 249	25 486	10 339	9 030	315	444	670	489	67	5
Machine operators, assorted materials	1 860 837	865 474	274 232	137 626	1 278 553	542 130	251 520	151 314	12 871	6 297	41 789	27 008	1 872	1 099
Cementing and gluing machine operators	20 070	12 316	3 569	1 280	12 421	8 893	3 510	1 819	240	118	262	206	68	–
Packaging and filling machine operators	112 546	168 699	23 926	34 395	64 667	94 970	19 511	32 183	851	1 113	3 433	5 782	158	256
Extruding and forming machine operators	23 668	4 233	1 755	348	19 181	3 402	2 237	425	168	12	294	46	33	–
Mixing and blending machine operators	97 976	13 165	10 883	1 349	67 044	8 844	17 772	2 425	677	90	1 531	426	69	31
Separating, filtering, and clarifying machine operators	61 822	7 808	5 105	845	48 174	5 391	7 414	1 418	311	85	810	58	8	11
Compressing and compacting machine operators	17 356	4 997	1 713	443	12 841	3 404	2 428	1 036	138	65	225	38	11	11
Painting and paint spraying machine operators	116 325	19 852	21 267	2 257	80 609	14 068	11 799	2 925	795	172	1 800	397	55	33
Roasting and baking machine operators, food	3 796	952	564	112	2 678	593	508	238	33	3	13	6	–	–
Washing, cleaning, and pickling machine operators	7 229	3 209	1 086	509	5 143	2 084	837	523	70	28	93	59	–	6
Folding machine operators	6 699	13 730	900	1 647	4 959	8 542	660	3 076	34	87	146	335	–	43
Furnace, kiln, and oven operators, except food	90 357	5 919	5 583	352	71 653	4 339	11 681	1 034	733	92	674	100	33	2
Crushing and grinding machine operators	36 554	8 653	4 335	672	27 337	6 238	4 084	1 500	412	121	370	122	16	–
Slicing and cutting machine operators	133 879	54 070	23 332	9 493	90 601	33 194	16 108	9 100	1 234	491	2 480	1 753	124	39
Motion picture projectionists	8 811	1 546	579	46	7 671	1 344	424	69	13	8	118	71	6	8
Photographic process machine operators	49 210	52 729	4 596	4 031	37 094	41 828	4 439	4 593	288	392	2 720	1 879	73	6
Miscellaneous machine operators, n.e.c.	411 563	199 707	63 723	31 383	277 687	123 345	56 416	37 093	2 744	1 538	10 516	6 059	477	289
Manufacturing, nondurable goods	164 760	72 060	21 210	11 669	113 627	43 143	25 345	14 613	1 099	559	3 294	2 001	185	75
Manufacturing, durable goods	189 490	87 622	34 156	15 493	124 564	52 709	23 738	15 571	1 132	659	5 650	3 024	250	166
Nonmanufacturing industries	57 313	40 025	8 357	4 221	39 496	27 493	7 333	6 909	513	320	1 572	1 034	42	48
Machine operators, not specified	662 976	293 889	101 316	48 464	448 793	181 651	91 692	51 857	4 130	1 882	16 304	9 671	741	364
Manufacturing, nondurable goods	190 549	118 677	29 434	18 792	126 017	74 093	29 680	21 551	1 029	710	4 143	3 452	246	79
Manufacturing, durable goods	314 293	125 191	47 520	20 918	215 776	78 000	40 502	20 776	1 879	778	8 282	4 502	334	217
Nonmanufacturing industries	158 134	50 021	24 362	8 754	107 000	29 558	21 510	9 530	1 222	394	3 879	1 717	161	68
Fabricators, assemblers, and hand working occupations	1 611 743	780 910	207 631	105 905	1 156 126	503 227	195 348	129 907	14 155	6 436	37 060	34 534	1 423	901
Welders and cutters	613 596	30 382	67 814	3 677	478 483	20 511	51 767	5 297	6 770	378	8 346	476	416	43
Solderers and brazers	9 320	18 917	3 009	3 118	4 954	12 566	729	1 888	54	191	555	1 128	19	26
Assemblers	892 566	681 413	123 232	93 822	602 851	434 129	133 334	116 006	6 467	5 304	25 835	31 390	847	762
Hand cutting and trimming occupations	10 378	6 127	2 313	909	6 110	2 876	1 385	1 779	149	92	404	471	17	–
Hand molding, casting, and forming occupations	18 792	7 617	2 252	841	14 391	5 730	1 707	775	126	61	289	199	27	11
Hand painting, coating, and decorating occupations	30 865	14 193	3 986	1 255	23 221	11 319	2 676	1 148	321	164	607	286	54	21
Hand engraving and printing occupations	8 417	6 437	1 088	504	6 556	5 400	474	411	52	38	247	84	–	–
Miscellaneous hand working occupations	27 809	15 824	3 937	1 779	19 560	10 696	3 276	2 603	216	208	777	500	43	38
Production inspectors, testers, samplers, and weighers	396 886	437 239	36 569	59 741	301 842	284 817	42 857	72 891	2 512	3 510	12 852	15 839	254	441
Production inspectors, checkers, and examiners	294 026	330 982	22 684	34 393	231 636	227 642	29 069	54 976	1 664	2 476	8 789	11 218	184	277
Production testers	40 360	19 784	2 720	1 704	31 592	13 859	3 310	2 501	173	162	2 554	1 525	11	33
Production samplers and weighers	5 285	5 505	706	2 125	3 894	2 577	552	499	34	24	88	271	11	9
Graders and sorters, except agricultural	57 215	80 968	10 459	21 519	34 720	40 739	9 926	14 915	641	848	1 421	2 825	48	122

Table 1. Detailed Occupation of the Civilian Labor Force by Sex, Race, and Hispanic Origin: 1990—Con.

[Data based on sample and subject to sampling variability, see text. For definitions of terms and meanings of symbols, see text]

United States	All persons Male	All persons Female	Hispanic origin (of any race) Male	Hispanic origin (of any race) Female	Not of Hispanic origin White Male	White Female	Black Male	Black Female	American Indian, Eskimo, or Aleut Male	American Indian, Eskimo, or Aleut Female	Asian or Pacific Islander Male	Asian or Pacific Islander Female	Other race Male	Other race Female
OPERATORS, FABRICATORS, AND LABORERS—Con.														
Transportation and material moving occupations	4 594 570	504 404	408 847	29 395	3 481 397	387 462	609 410	77 409	37 247	5 568	54 689	4 199	2 980	371
Motor vehicle operators	3 392 948	444 959	310 262	23 8?3	2 540 950	345 474	469 292	67 099	24 434	4 770	45 699	3 503	2 311	300
Supervisors, motor vehicle operators	67 709	12 642	4 652	671	54 538	10 181	7 268	1 589	325	81	920	120	6	—
Truck drivers	2 733 620	175 332	240 989	10 690	2 106 910	140 885	337 125	19 707	19 792	2 044	27 157	1 892	1 647	114
Driver-sales workers	128 937	14 416	8 332	850	110 556	12 430	7 879	837	503	133	1 593	145	74	21
Bus drivers	232 404	215 166	19 176	8 967	143 330	163 415	64 209	39 669	2 324	2 126	3 168	833	197	156
Taxicab drivers and chauffeurs	184 894	22 439	27 911	2 088	101 972	15 515	42 642	4 274	1 262	306	10 831	256	276	9
Parking lot attendants	41 776	4 783	8 641	541	21 280	2 916	9 555	985	184	75	2 005	257	111	9
Motor transportation occupations, n.e.c.	3 608	181	561	—	2 364	132	614	38	44	5	25	—	—	—
Transportation occupations, except motor vehicles	183 732	7 375	6 675	431	158 956	5 229	15 200	1 438	1 326	117	1 495	151	80	9
Rail transportation occupations	117 319	4 527	4 209	283	100 804	3 032	11 163	1 061	577	57	522	94	44	—
Railroad conductors and yardmasters	35 140	2 433	1 066	173	31 142	1 617	2 528	561	114	30	276	52	14	—
Locomotive operating occupations	44 744	1 222	1 540	64	37 888	841	4 881	248	257	27	152	42	26	—
Railroad brake, signal, and switch operators	32 689	570	1 352	40	27 882	440	3 227	90	149	—	75	—	4	—
Rail vehicle operators, n.e.c.	4 746	302	251	6	3 892	134	527	162	57	—	19	—	—	—
Water transportation occupations	66 413	2 848	2 466	148	58 152	2 197	4 037	377	749	60	973	57	36	9
Ship captains and mates, except fishing boats	31 956	1 041	756	58	29 645	907	796	81	395	—	353	15	11	—
Sailors and deckhands	24 992	953	1 399	65	20 199	708	2 586	104	250	29	533	27	25	—
Marine engineers	4 103	49	109	—	3 712	40	199	9	23	—	60	—	—	—
Bridge, lock, and lighthouse tenders	5 362	805	202	25	4 596	542	456	183	81	31	27	15	9	9
Material moving equipment operators	1 017 890	52 070	91 910	5 151	781 491	36 759	124 918	8 872	11 487	681	7 495	545	589	62
Supervisors, material moving equipment operators	22 365	1 438	1 377	55	18 860	1 177	1 801	168	153	18	161	40	13	—
Operating engineers	236 996	4 816	15 325	462	200 053	3 406	16 415	706	3 467	161	1 625	91	111	—
Longshore equipment operators	4 331	72	446	8	2 476	64	1 226	—	83	—	100	—	4	—
Hoist and winch operators	19 831	469	2 454	55	15 667	328	1 230	106	370	—	91	40	19	—
Crane and tower operators	79 850	1 975	4 795	196	53 491	1 354	10 358	458	680	7	502	12	24	40
Excavating and loading machine operators	94 408	1 575	4 622	78	83 036	1 285	5 257	187	1 074	13	365	12	54	12
Grader, dozer, and scraper operators	63 758	1 122	2 561	51	55 979	901	4 035	114	910	39	261	17	12	17
Industrial truck and tractor equipment operators	414 030	27 829	53 657	1 974	278 034	20 163	74 605	5 119	3 753	331	3 693	210	288	32
Miscellaneous material moving equipment operators	82 321	12 774	6 673	2 402	53 895	8 081	9 991	2 014	997	112	697	152	68	13
Handlers, equipment cleaners, helpers, and laborers	4 203 264	1 038 920	575 949	127 570	2 831 706	722 137	623 288	152 681	41 478	9 119	66 885	26 330	3 958	1 083
Supervisors, handlers, equipment cleaners, and laborers, n.e.c.	13 990	1 678	1 650	129	9 866	1 147	2 010	342	106	25	332	35	26	—
Helpers, mechanics, and repairers	20 613	1 258	4 191	162	13 300	883	2 426	143	274	48	400	22	22	—
Helpers, construction, and extractive occupations	88 032	4 680	15 313	343	60 841	3 788	10 028	460	965	64	850	28	35	—
Helpers, construction trades	81 768	3 836	14 956	317	55 460	3 036	9 629	417	862	45	816	21	35	—
Helpers, surveyor	4 221	454	179	7	3 766	387	180	43	62	10	34	7	—	—
Helpers, extractive occupations	2 043	390	168	15	1 615	365	219	9	41	9	10	9	7	—
Construction laborers	1 103 482	46 298	188 082	5 365	744 189	33 252	145 635	6 256	13 235	843	11 392	575	949	7
Production helpers	29 835	8 148	6 115	1 453	18 353	4 959	4 225	1 194	280	92	831	444	31	7
Freight, stock, and material handlers	1 364 220	397 396	134 220	31 233	976 326	304 056	217 669	50 193	10 934	3 135	24 143	8 391	1 232	388
Garbage collectors	57 407	2 502	6 535	213	31 823	779	18 060	46	561	6	347	18	81	8
Stevedores	11 133	350	1 611	65	5 737	186	3 316	92	160	—	287	—	22	—
Stock handlers and baggers	726 754	303 608	67 611	22 911	547 294	239 602	90 148	31 671	4 907	2 353	16 246	6 780	695	288
Machine feeders and offbearers	56 986	30 223	5 167	2 940	40 304	20 457	10 069	5 971	607	233	832	572	7	50
Freight, stock, and material handlers, n.e.c.	512 244	60 713	53 443	5 097	351 168	42 376	96 076	10 069	4 699	497	6 431	1 021	427	42
Garage and service station related occupations	241 429	28 798	22 703	2 164	187 379	23 142	23 987	2 586	2 309	335	4 847	549	204	25
Vehicle washers and equipment cleaners	203 731	28 785	34 295	3 643	125 739	18 613	38 980	5 342	1 553	335	2 935	802	229	50
Hand packers and packagers	130 183	238 158	30 814	44 227	71 818	148 174	22 446	36 442	964	1 628	3 948	7 387	193	300
Laborers, except construction	1 007 445	283 721	138 566	38 848	683 895	184 123	155 882	49 723	10 858	2 617	17 207	8 097	1 037	313
Manufacturing, durable goods	156 302	74 247	23 170	9 585	102 384	45 976	26 372	14 896	1 233	571	2 999	2 148	144	71
Manufacturing, nondurable goods	238 225	69 630	31 066	9 393	169 227	47 932	32 933	10 029	1 922	530	2 898	1 638	179	108
Transportation, communications, and other public utilities	119 224	14 387	14 906	1 794	78 184	8 398	22 843	3 552	1 623	296	1 502	332	166	15
Wholesale and retail trade	278 875	69 948	37 501	9 343	157 159	47 425	35 472	10 291	2 238	431	6 206	2 372	299	86
All other industries	214 819	55 509	31 923	7 733	156 941	34 392	38 262	10 955	3 842	789	3 602	1 607	249	33
EXPERIENCED UNEMPLOYED NOT CLASSIFIED BY OCCUPATION														
Unemployed, no recent civilian work experience	445 737	554 214	84 818	104 939	154 786	250 399	141 597	169 624	7 782	7 895	16 269	20 655	485	702

Table 2. Detailed Occupation of the Civilian Labor Force by Sex and Race: 1990

[Data based on sample and subject to sampling variability, see text. For definitions of terms and meanings of symbols, see text]

United States	All persons Male	All persons Female	White Male	White Female	Black Male	Black Female	American Indian, Eskimo, or Aleut Male	American Indian, Eskimo, or Aleut Female	Asian or Pacific Islander Male	Asian or Pacific Islander Female	Other race Male	Other race Female
Civilian labor force 16 years and over	66 986 201	56 487 249	55 699 109	45 826 627	6 247 539	6 847 642	459 892	391 420	1 918 998	1 684 082	2 660 663	1 737 478
MANAGERIAL AND PROFESSIONAL SPECIALTY OCCUPATIONS												
Executive, administrative, and managerial occupations	8 448 483	6 170 674	7 630 041	5 345 826	411 472	507 260	32 624	33 683	254 287	184 348	120 059	99 557
Legislators	7 431	5 285	6 302	4 399	612	631	335	115	129	58	53	82
Chief executives and general administrators, public administration	13 788	5 235	11 591	3 869	1 617	1 039	202	77	154	120	224	130
Administrators and officials, public administration	275 864	230 819	238 091	184 657	25 425	36 056	2 813	2 610	5 777	4 119	3 758	3 377
Administrators, protective services	35 201	14 072	31 659	11 348	2 449	2 070	288	155	354	190	451	309
Financial managers	343 630	292 281	315 117	260 880	12 417	17 858	637	895	12 488	8 842	2 971	3 806
Personnel and labor relations managers	141 246	134 249	121 111	113 557	10 413	13 498	618	821	4 861	3 355	4 243	3 018
Purchasing managers	80 136	40 639	74 513	35 500	2 592	3 381	256	283	2 032	938	743	537
Managers, marketing, advertising, and public relations	415 411	193 698	393 106	179 343	10 360	7 798	914	653	8 412	3 983	2 619	1 921
Administrators, education and related fields	295 274	328 338	257 136	274 088	26 745	40 565	1 748	2 287	6 101	6 226	3 544	5 172
Managers, medicine and health	78 099	155 522	65 703	131 261	8 360	17 170	348	946	2 430	3 523	1 258	2 622
Postmasters and mail superintendents	21 614	18 232	18 973	16 869	1 824	957	209	203	249	116	359	87
Managers, food serving and lodging establishments	572 095	458 556	473 859	384 362	39 149	39 419	2 600	3 088	38 685	21 413	17 802	10 274
Managers, properties and real estate	221 625	189 841	198 794	169 631	12 334	11 876	1 010	1 254	4 974	3 156	4 513	3 924
Funeral directors	39 393	6 093	34 994	4 978	3 917	1 016	116	35	140	19	226	45
Managers, service organizations, n.e.c.	201 002	203 071	177 228	176 341	15 195	19 562	1 307	1 561	3 857	2 802	3 415	2 805
Managers and administrators, n.e.c., salaried	3 355 970	1 585 636	3 107 913	1 428 336	111 904	90 208	10 608	7 165	85 999	37 094	39 546	22 833
Managers and administrators, n.e.c., self-employed	313 599	90 788	288 654	82 753	9 657	2 369	1 555	464	8 819	3 950	4 914	1 252
Management related occupations	2 037 105	2 218 319	1 815 297	1 883 654	116 502	201 787	7 060	11 071	68 826	84 444	29 420	37 363
Accountants and auditors	751 840	838 338	666 140	702 298	38 187	69 768	1 589	3 614	37 734	49 971	8 190	12 687
Underwriters	21 949	45 818	19 893	40 235	1 237	3 823	45	115	575	1 099	199	546
Other financial officers	328 204	351 071	301 317	306 963	13 565	26 293	727	1 415	9 478	10 372	3 117	6 028
Management analysts	186 724	95 065	173 726	83 900	6 725	7 231	627	522	4 441	2 562	1 205	850
Personnel, training, and labor relations specialists	217 138	296 487	184 670	243 372	21 800	38 857	1 406	1 942	3 781	6 191	5 481	6 125
Purchasing agents and buyers, farm products	14 336	2 962	13 025	2 188	617	510	40	42	226	53	428	169
Buyers, wholesale and retail trade, except farm products	107 051	121 348	97 931	110 781	3 874	5 427	326	433	2 868	2 861	2 052	1 846
Purchasing agents and buyers, n.e.c.	135 474	111 493	123 680	98 479	6 587	9 055	533	644	2 547	1 728	2 127	1 587
Business and promotion agents	19 569	16 923	17 428	15 131	1 125	1 073	95	117	414	381	507	221
Construction inspectors	60 087	4 197	53 044	3 229	4 000	721	493	51	1 414	103	1 136	93
Inspectors and compliance officers, except construction	112 130	49 147	94 987	35 219	11 131	10 545	789	459	2 651	1 434	2 572	1 490
Management related occupations, n.e.c.	82 603	285 470	69 456	241 859	7 654	28 484	390	1 717	2 697	7 689	2 406	5 721
Professional specialty occupations	7 706 256	8 941 432	6 814 728	7 678 901	410 505	827 439	30 475	44 431	355 851	275 268	94 697	115 393
Engineers, architects, and surveyors	1 695 690	180 833	1 507 087	151 469	52 577	12 376	4 793	621	115 218	14 064	16 015	2 303
Architects	133 212	23 662	120 541	21 365	3 790	639	274	48	6 834	1 378	1 773	232
Engineers	1 551 961	156 283	1 376 473	129 303	48 607	11 682	4 452	569	108 235	12 658	14 194	2 071
Aerospace	131 786	11 648	115 649	9 435	3 705	942	431	65	10 249	1 034	1 752	172
Metallurgical and materials	17 021	2 209	15 430	1 856	422	243	34	5	992	70	143	35
Mining	6 063	415	5 731	373	44	24	54	18	160	–	74	–
Petroleum	22 908	1 657	21 477	1 470	449	90	75	13	742	67	165	17
Chemical	57 163	7 157	51 104	6 004	1 754	520	86	7	3 848	555	371	71
Nuclear	10 108	693	9 172	629	186	5	21	8	668	41	61	10
Civil	235 162	17 646	206 163	14 523	7 113	1 094	771	64	18 843	1 710	2 272	255
Agricultural	2 012	136	1 903	96	27	18	–	–	64	22	18	–
Electrical and electronic	420 471	46 552	367 566	36 935	15 370	4 320	1 156	133	32 634	4 618	3 745	546
Industrial	151 859	24 474	139 045	21 086	4 851	1 659	472	114	5 945	1 213	1 546	402
Mechanical	176 092	9 780	159 458	8 359	4 627	559	448	17	10 295	703	1 264	142
Marine and naval architects	12 776	493	11 742	434	323	52	65	–	574	7	72	–
Engineers, n.e.c.	308 540	33 423	272 033	28 103	9 736	2 156	839	125	23 221	2 618	2 711	421
Surveyors and mapping scientists	10 517	888	10 073	801	180	55	67	4	149	28	48	–
Mathematical and computer scientists	503 806	275 701	440 712	230 099	24 338	25 127	1 483	1 013	32 708	16 447	4 565	3 015
Computer systems analysts and scientists	326 831	144 459	284 776	121 555	13 964	11 406	915	446	24 390	9 925	2 786	1 127
Operations and systems researchers and analysts	144 484	107 334	126 926	88 938	9 111	11 416	497	498	6 414	4 773	1 536	1 709
Actuaries	12 416	6 316	11 416	5 542	195	214	7	–	745	529	53	31
Statisticians	15 744	16 108	13 736	12 865	915	1 880	64	60	863	1 161	166	142
Mathematical scientists, n.e.c.	4 331	1 484	3 858	1 199	153	211	–	9	296	59	24	6
Natural scientists	300 573	108 102	267 943	90 489	10 776	6 539	1 333	418	18 162	9 436	2 359	1 220
Physicists and astronomers	24 238	3 604	22 096	3 137	479	206	85	14	1 480	210	98	37
Chemists, except biochemists	102 505	38 750	86 661	30 240	5 732	3 008	228	93	9 115	4 853	769	556
Atmospheric and space scientists	7 279	1 075	6 751	934	242	63	37	2	215	61	34	15
Geologists and geodesists	45 501	7 628	43 720	7 191	421	183	128	36	848	139	384	79
Physical scientists, n.e.c.	13 338	5 444	12 281	4 813	433	433	44	40	467	158	113	–
Agricultural and food scientists	25 537	9 305	23 444	8 132	869	597	87	55	814	387	323	134
Biological and life scientists	36 207	25 930	32 176	22 216	1 151	1 292	168	72	2 468	2 128	244	222
Forestry and conservation scientists	30 205	4 610	28 218	4 245	919	191	556	61	231	55	281	58
Medical scientists	15 763	11 756	12 596	9 581	530	566	–	45	2 524	1 445	113	119
Health diagnosing occupations	700 419	174 106	619 287	139 436	19 068	9 803	1 055	425	55 417	22 589	5 592	1 853
Physicians	465 468	121 247	400 756	93 271	14 130	7 408	727	252	45 483	19 052	4 372	1 264
Dentists	135 588	19 941	124 507	16 274	3 604	1 262	149	53	6 519	2 107	809	245
Veterinarians	35 755	12 989	33 945	12 219	550	302	56	25	1 099	413	105	30
Optometrists	23 463	4 052	22 250	3 521	205	200	56	11	900	292	52	28
Podiatrists	7 904	1 004	7 487	784	172	127	6	–	160	93	79	–
Health diagnosing practitioners, n.e.c.	32 241	14 873	30 342	13 367	407	504	61	84	1 256	632	175	286
Health assessment and treating occupations	322 927	2 191 413	274 643	1 873 530	25 935	193 847	1 479	8 871	15 919	95 884	4 951	19 281
Registered nurses	107 244	1 777 885	88 579	1 517 912	10 550	157 515	598	7 363	5 386	80 494	2 131	14 601
Pharmacists	114 949	66 849	104 015	56 134	3 487	4 349	267	111	6 616	5 606	564	649
Dietitians	9 629	80 594	6 096	60 634	2 806	14 639	88	475	315	3 612	324	1 234
Therapists	78 143	253 978	65 050	228 181	7 923	16 292	425	794	3 065	5 690	1 680	2 521
Respiratory therapists	26 155	39 434	21 014	33 643	2 934	4 167	154	157	1 305	1 028	748	439
Occupational therapists	3 957	33 938	3 271	30 677	343	1 711	8	71	172	1 213	163	266
Physical therapists	22 540	69 482	19 333	63 197	1 623	3 531	108	198	1 156	1 823	320	733
Speech therapists	5 736	58 977	5 415	55 114	185	2 650	28	102	57	737	51	374
Therapists, n.e.c.	19 755	51 647	16 017	45 550	2 838	4 233	127	266	375	889	398	709
Physicians' assistants	12 962	12 607	10 903	10 669	1 169	1 052	101	128	537	482	252	276

Table 2. Detailed Occupation of the Civilian Labor Force by Sex and Race: 1990—Con.

[Data based on sample and subject to sampling variability, see text. For definitions of terms and meanings of symbols, see text]

United States	All persons		White		Black		American Indian, Eskimo, or Aleut		Asian or Pacific Islander		Other race	
	Male	Female	Male	Female	Male	Female	Male	Female	Male	Female	Male	Female
MANAGERIAL AND PROFESSIONAL SPECIALTY OCCUPATIONS—Con.												
Teachers, postsecondary	467 429	318 804	403 626	278 755	19 052	19 489	1 599	1 362	38 856	15 988	4 296	3 210
Earth, environmental, and marine science teachers	889	364	839	342	–	–	–	–	50	5	8	17
Biological science teachers	4 031	2 070	3 768	1 917	44	56	10	–	201	97	8	–
Chemistry teachers	4 053	1 393	3 634	1 204	110	45	7	9	289	113	13	22
Physics teachers	3 876	556	3 389	489	129	28	–	–	339	39	19	–
Natural science teachers, n.e.c.	292	97	272	80	7	9	–	–	13	–	–	8
Psychology teachers	2 409	2 109	2 249	1 926	79	100	7	19	51	36	23	28
Economics teachers	2 650	776	2 323	726	84	10	–	–	219	40	24	–
History teachers	2 996	1 125	2 883	1 054	82	59	7	7	12	–	12	5
Political science teachers	752	253	678	222	53	–	6	7	15	14	–	10
Sociology teachers	905	552	782	500	39	39	27	2	48	11	9	–
Social science teachers, n.e.c.	548	312	453	276	65	11	14	11	16	14	–	–
Engineering teachers	6 489	1 288	5 644	1 180	271	68	12	–	510	40	52	–
Mathematical science teachers	10 639	6 718	9 229	5 899	522	363	30	57	728	332	130	67
Computer science teachers	2 679	1 705	2 255	1 498	106	82	5	11	282	78	31	36
Medical science teachers	1 976	767	1 816	686	68	38	7	–	85	43	–	–
Health specialties teachers	3 784	11 927	3 320	10 760	151	882	14	45	284	177	15	63
Business, commerce, and marketing teachers	2 288	2 775	1 946	2 475	148	198	25	22	138	69	31	11
Agriculture and forestry teachers	759	302	724	283	16	11	2	8	10	–	7	–
Art, drama, and music teachers	10 591	10 802	9 681	9 870	493	431	40	49	221	387	156	65
Physical education teachers	2 042	2 073	1 767	1 755	163	255	8	12	54	34	50	17
Education teachers	747	708	661	603	65	97	–	8	10	–	11	–
English teachers	10 243	14 033	9 498	12 869	448	627	15	56	120	295	162	186
Foreign language teachers	2 966	7 059	2 495	6 146	128	109	11	7	188	556	144	241
Law teachers	3 158	1 397	2 921	1 291	173	70	17	–	31	29	16	7
Social work teachers	103	205	85	181	–	24	–	–	18	–	–	–
Theology teachers	2 001	615	1 894	592	59	18	8	3	40	2	–	–
Trade and industrial teachers	668	602	605	539	37	44	7	–	9	19	10	–
Home economics teachers	94	499	75	390	19	93	–	–	–	16	–	–
Teachers, postsecondary, n.e.c.	8 779	4 676	7 823	4 105	286	273	19	35	561	190	90	73
Postsecondary teachers, subject not specified	374 022	241 046	319 917	208 897	15 207	15 449	1 301	994	34 314	13 352	3 283	2 354
Teachers, except postsecondary	1 157 678	3 401 848	1 024 154	2 937 371	91 025	349 480	6 307	17 646	19 856	48 360	16 336	48 991
Teachers, prekindergarten and kindergarten	5 920	263 410	4 350	216 097	1 142	34 299	95	2 294	154	4 587	179	6 133
Teachers, elementary school	652 015	2 372 174	572 473	2 038 535	58 147	257 434	3 540	11 547	8 602	30 932	9 253	33 726
Teachers, secondary school	269 533	354 867	248 376	320 240	14 074	25 549	1 168	1 518	2 843	3 967	3 072	3 593
Teachers, special education	11 047	51 169	9 584	44 183	1 081	5 439	79	349	108	535	195	663
Teachers, n.e.c.	219 163	360 228	189 371	318 316	16 581	26 759	1 425	1 938	8 149	8 339	3 637	4 876
Counselors, educational and vocational	91 763	146 770	75 142	117 990	11 546	21 814	898	1 473	1 890	2 668	2 287	2 825
Librarians, archivists, and curators	49 787	178 669	42 834	157 333	3 789	13 372	278	920	2 075	5 462	811	1 582
Librarians	37 522	163 359	31 840	143 646	3 137	12 504	163	781	1 823	5 003	559	1 425
Archivists and curators	12 265	15 310	10 994	13 687	652	868	115	139	252	459	252	157
Social scientists and urban planners	189 041	196 197	171 835	177 232	10 055	12 145	639	849	4 695	4 340	1 817	1 631
Economists	85 035	66 902	78 211	60 649	3 565	3 552	197	166	2 151		574	384
Psychologists	79 430	112 532	72 014	101 696	5 151	7 345	337	624	1 038	1 774	890	1 093
Sociologists	1 152	1 059	913	888	53	105	31	7	126	59	17	–
Social scientists, n.e.c.	10 649	9 648	9 819	8 687	404	604	42	29	261	242	123	86
Urban planners	12 475	6 066	10 878	5 012	870	539	32	23	482	114	213	68
Social, recreation, and religious workers	552 861	580 533	459 625	446 915	64 827	105 240	3 988	5 670	13 196	9 336	11 225	13 372
Social workers	204 760	454 159	151 512	334 472	39 357	95 808	2 379	5 055	4 556	7 140	6 956	11 684
Recreation workers	14 811	36 068	10 456	00 170	3 005	4 312	168	221	280	583	542	715
Clergy	291 140	33 749	259 894	30 205	19 446	2 306	1 257	179	7 364	699	3 179	360
Religious workers, n.e.c.	42 150	56 657	37 763	52 101	2 659	2 814	184	215	996	914	548	613
Lawyers and judges	589 326	190 145	562 660	171 754	15 767	12 181	1 146	547	6 960	4 102	2 793	1 561
Lawyers	564 332	182 745	539 582	165 478	14 360	11 310	1 029	473	6 744	3 976	2 617	1 508
Judges	24 994	7 400	23 078	6 276	1 407	871	117	74	216	126	176	53
Writers, artists, entertainers, and athletes	1 084 956	998 311	965 180	906 528	61 750	46 026	5 477	4 616	30 899	26 592	21 650	14 549
Authors	53 863	52 867	50 948	49 829	1 429	1 733	270	200	937	834	279	271
Technical writers	37 265	37 027	35 092	33 547	1 354	2 042	102	196	656	964	61	278
Designers	265 299	331 503	235 215	303 185	11 059	10 145	1 016	1 324	12 246	10 852	5 763	5 997
Musicians and composers	99 409	48 611	84 442	44 986	8 969	2 197	434	146	1 912	1 073	3 652	209
Actors and directors	67 787	41 786	61 024	37 086	4 622	3 329	300	178	892	705	949	488
Painters, sculptors, craft-artists, and artist printmakers	101 067	111 695	89 022	104 373	5 086	2 610	1 001	784	3 400	2 854	2 558	1 074
Photographers	100 169	43 351	89 125	38 533	5 591	2 576	446	223	2 938	991	2 069	1 028
Dancers	5 097	16 816	4 008	14 641	576	1 056	57	185	230	637	226	297
Artists, performers, and related workers, n.e.c.	46 865	46 556	39 635	39 574	3 025	1 987	344	406	2 082	2 704	1 779	1 885
Editors and reporters	131 303	135 240	120 883	122 708	5 884	8 232	441	399	2 860	2 709	1 235	1 192
Public relations specialists	69 118	98 450	62 338	87 234	4 179	7 843	314	342	1 323	1 650	964	1 381
Announcers	47 752	12 517	41 978	10 574	4 061	1 373	285	116	518	233	910	221
Athletes	59 962	21 892	51 470	20 258	5 915	903	467	117	905	386	1 205	228
TECHNICAL, SALES, AND ADMINISTRATIVE SUPPORT OCCUPATIONS												
Technicians and related support occupations	2 366 641	2 020 767	2 019 015	1 648 806	157 491	235 786	12 494	12 002	128 344	86 049	49 297	38 124
Health technologists and technicians	270 887	1 158 210	207 248	937 792	35 874	154 752	1 955	7 348	17 057	36 339	8 753	21 979
Clinical laboratory technologists and technicians	82 202	247 690	59 477	195 726	11 648	31 598	517	1 071	8 192	15 491	2 368	3 804
Dental hygienists	1 174	71 220	937	68 024	124	1 413	6	151	87	1 118	20	514
Health record technologists and technicians	4 663	51 101	2 718	39 761	1 123	7 684	45	709	527	1 548	250	1 399
Radiologic technicians	36 176	94 207	28 922	84 812	3 599	6 612	262	380	1 913	1 308	1 480	1 095
Licensed practical nurses	27 569	401 904	19 260	308 561	5 785	74 292	263	3 328	1 195	8 912	1 066	6 811
Health technologists and technicians, n.e.c.	119 103	292 088	95 934	240 908	13 595	33 153	862	1 709	5 143	7 962	3 569	8 356

Table 2. Detailed Occupation of the Civilian Labor Force by Sex and Race: 1990—Con.

[Data based on sample and subject to sampling variability, see text. For definitions of terms and meanings of symbols, see text]

United States	All persons		White		Black		American Indian, Eskimo, or Aleut		Asian or Pacific Islander		Other race	
	Male	Female	Male	Female	Male	Female	Male	Female	Male	Female	Male	Female
TECHNICAL, SALES, AND ADMINISTRATIVE SUPPORT OCCUPATIONS—Con.												
Technologists and technicians, except health	2 095 754	862 557	1 811 767	711 014	121 617	81 034	10 539	4 654	111 287	49 710	40 544	16 145
Engineering and related technologists and technicians	899 324	205 111	783 355	168 147	49 743	19 778	5 010	1 328	41 556	11 423	19 660	4 435
Electrical and electronic technicians	345 626	55 837	293 759	42 781	22 597	7 121	1 664	389	19 717	3 883	7 889	1 663
Industrial engineering technicians	11 991	3 333	10 785	2 891	680	332	74	24	241	32	211	54
Mechanical engineering technicians	27 578	2 531	24 616	2 034	1 085	238	81	35	1 337	145	459	79
Engineering technicians, n.e.c.	166 541	73 139	144 841	59 086	10 380	8 098	872	407	7 274	4 092	3 174	1 456
Drafting occupations	263 940	60 824	232 525	53 309	12 108	3 037	1 371	330	11 701	3 114	6 235	1 034
Surveying and mapping technicians	83 648	9 447	76 829	8 046	2 893	952	948	143	1 286	157	1 692	149
Science technicians	141 022	67 966	117 702	54 586	11 393	7 001	959	439	6 848	4 022	4 120	1 918
Biological technicians	32 467	24 256	26 917	19 922	2 378	2 043	241	128	1 388	1 218	1 543	945
Chemical technicians	57 700	18 939	48 232	15 046	5 708	2 572	351	126	2 054	930	1 355	265
Science technicians, n.e.c.	50 855	24 771	42 553	19 618	3 307	2 386	367	185	3 406	1 874	1 222	708
Technicians, except health, engineering, and science	1 055 408	589 480	910 710	488 281	60 481	54 255	4 570	2 887	62 883	34 265	16 764	9 792
Airplane pilots and navigators	105 929	3 897	102 328	3 504	1 644	292	402	19	1 054	48	501	34
Air traffic controllers	36 668	10 495	32 199	8 602	3 240	1 495	151	64	628	161	450	173
Broadcast equipment operators	27 241	8 278	23 218	6 514	2 571	1 257	184	104	646	261	622	142
Computer programmers	447 109	215 650	390 605	175 109	21 164	18 813	1 221	565	29 001	18 729	5 118	2 434
Tool programmers, numerical control	3 141	529	2 884	387	102	142	42	–	79	–	34	–
Legal assistants	62 175	195 977	52 237	172 326	5 713	14 243	429	1 253	2 072	4 272	1 724	3 883
Technicians, n.e.c.	373 145	154 654	307 239	121 839	26 047	18 013	2 141	882	29 403	10 794	8 315	3 126
Sales occupations	**7 334 643**	**7 098 126**	**6 572 300**	**5 990 016**	**364 072**	**667 278**	**27 735**	**44 716**	**212 229**	**208 811**	**158 307**	**187 305**
Supervisors and proprietors, sales occupations, salaried	1 964 716	1 050 658	1 779 842	930 236	82 971	70 321	6 995	5 499	56 068	25 062	38 840	19 540
Supervisors and proprietors, sales occupations, self-employed	285 593	150 494	251 597	132 594	7 335	3 800	1 187	966	20 214	11 075	5 260	2 059
Sales representatives, finance and business services	1 475 043	1 013 597	1 366 193	915 753	58 809	58 061	3 914	3 863	30 232	23 165	15 895	12 755
Insurance sales occupations	431 027	235 515	396 881	205 596	20 043	20 651	1 141	925	8 137	4 542	4 825	3 801
Real estate sales occupations	397 205	404 033	366 785	376 528	13 243	11 495	1 085	1 479	11 557	10 789	4 535	3 742
Securities and financial services sales occupations	214 848	82 700	201 192	73 077	6 481	5 372	339	211	5 374	2 856	1 462	1 184
Advertising and related sales occupations	84 108	89 957	77 234	81 987	4 510	5 153	247	411	1 037	1 266	1 080	1 140
Sales occupations, other business services	347 855	201 392	324 101	178 565	14 532	15 390	1 102	837	4 127	3 712	3 993	2 888
Sales representatives, commodities, except retail	1 220 788	350 644	1 149 656	316 248	31 656	16 055	3 095	1 350	19 350	8 942	17 031	8 049
Sales engineers	41 408	2 208	40 083	2 086	324	50	48	3	738	54	215	15
Sales representatives, mining, manufacturing, and wholesale	1 179 380	348 436	1 109 573	314 162	31 332	16 005	3 047	1 347	18 612	8 888	16 816	8 034
Sales workers, retail and personal services	2 363 574	4 484 707	2 001 906	3 651 482	182 328	516 702	12 437	32 656	86 010	139 680	80 893	144 187
Sales workers, motor vehicles and boats	314 915	37 364	286 770	33 682	16 079	2 052	1 331	238	4 167	752	6 568	640
Sales workers, apparel	82 914	361 663	65 320	305 578	9 119	31 843	290	1 689	4 590	11 512	3 595	11 041
Sales workers, shoes	44 534	73 233	33 833	60 180	6 304	8 374	168	422	1 739	1 939	2 490	2 318
Sales workers, furniture and home furnishings	102 617	84 503	93 147	78 201	4 878	3 450	307	350	1 778	1 310	2 507	1 192
Sales workers, radio, TV, hi-fi, and appliances	122 032	48 840	108 517	43 386	7 010	2 852	451	275	3 521	1 243	2 533	1 084
Sales workers, hardware and building supplies	135 593	39 594	125 353	37 250	5 043	1 076	533	143	1 675	618	2 989	507
Sales workers, parts	118 966	13 127	108 297	11 664	4 732	771	702	152	1 412	198	3 823	342
Sales workers, other commodities	626 278	1 231 579	541 817	1 066 418	40 350	92 882	2 980	6 731	23 005	36 372	18 126	29 176
Sales counter clerks	72 545	137 528	60 264	115 696	5 263	11 284	504	1 023	4 171	5 299	2 343	4 226
Cashiers	596 364	2 259 316	452 965	1 725 368	71 149	346 359	4 379	20 287	36 479	77 490	31 392	89 812
Street and door-to-door sales workers	77 367	153 560	66 273	134 091	6 878	13 416	442	944	1 508	2 313	2 266	2 796
News vendors	69 449	44 400	59 350	39 968	5 523	2 343	350	402	1 965	634	2 261	1 053
Sales related occupations	24 929	48 026	23 106	43 703	973	2 339	107	382	355	887	388	715
Demonstrators, promoters and models, sales	8 317	36 948	7 247	33 740	583	1 790	48	296	230	593	209	529
Auctioneers	7 209	1 163	7 043	1 096	94	55	22	12	18	–	32	–
Sales support occupations, n.e.c.	9 403	9 915	8 816	8 867	296	494	37	74	107	294	147	186
Administrative support occupations, including clerical	**4 482 923**	**15 222 640**	**3 499 712**	**12 677 800**	**608 499**	**1 690 712**	**26 338**	**92 465**	**178 185**	**369 694**	**170 189**	**391 969**
Supervisors, administrative support occupations	406 628	517 698	335 646	425 718	47 362	66 458	2 336	2 738	10 770	11 612	10 514	11 172
Supervisors, general office	214 678	364 947	174 720	298 523	26 631	48 203	1 368	2 126	5 985	7 812	5 974	8 283
Supervisors, computer equipment operators	21 917	12 631	19 146	10 440	1 790	1 617	94	99	568	310	319	165
Supervisors, financial records processing	33 380	77 006	29 369	66 534	2 250	6 641	89	309	1 209	2 157	463	1 365
Chief communications operators	1 720	2 653	1 523	2 183	115	356	9	7	38	61	35	46
Supervisors, distribution, scheduling, and adjusting clerks	134 933	60 461	110 888	48 038	16 576	9 641	776	197	2 970	1 272	3 723	1 313
Computer equipment operators	256 310	410 903	201 021	328 122	33 904	58 772	1 270	2 522	12 767	11 767	7 348	9 720
Computer operators	253 115	407 203	198 683	325 605	33 356	57 962	1 258	2 480	12 652	11 657	7 166	9 499
Peripheral equipment operators	3 195	3 700	2 338	2 517	548	810	12	42	115	110	182	221
Secretaries, stenographers, and typists	97 485	4 663 841	74 086	4 041 838	14 463	410 735	777	27 229	4 872	81 793	3 287	102 246
Secretaries	52 492	3 966 179	41 568	3 504 652	6 763	294 437	436	21 870	2 135	62 929	1 590	82 291
Stenographers	7 563	72 317	6 932	64 404	359	5 302	24	371	158	1 389	90	851
Typists	37 430	625 345	25 586	472 782	7 341	110 996	317	4 988	2 579	17 475	1 607	19 104
Information clerks	230 674	1 347 972	182 940	1 125 309	27 672	136 492	1 731	9 606	11 222	32 622	7 109	43 943
Interviewers	49 781	156 177	38 924	123 428	7 353	22 553	754	1 790	1 264	3 415	1 486	4 991
Hotel clerks	27 005	69 385	21 629	56 816	2 602	7 322	158	617	1 839	2 925	777	1 705
Transportation ticket and reservation agents	79 758	190 193	64 092	162 203	8 590	15 093	352	920	4 449	7 819	2 275	4 158
Receptionists	35 037	787 056	26 338	668 110	5 001	70 286	242	5 336	1 852	15 310	1 604	28 014
Information clerks, n.e.c.	39 093	145 161	31 957	114 752	4 126	21 238	225	943	1 818	3 153	967	5 075

Table 2. Detailed Occupation of the Civilian Labor Force by Sex and Race: 1990—Con.

[Data based on sample and subject to sampling variability, see text. For definitions of terms and meanings of symbols, see text]

United States	All persons		White		Black		American Indian, Eskimo, or Aleut		Asian or Pacific Islander		Other race	
	Male	Female	Male	Female	Male	Female	Male	Female	Male	Female	Male	Female
TECHNICAL, SALES, AND ADMINISTRATIVE SUPPORT OCCUPATIONS—Con.												
Records processing occupations, except financial	192 809	691 402	143 988	538 922	29 630	106 186	1 085	4 393	10 078	20 864	8 028	21 037
Classified-ad clerks	910	4 372	792	3 929	96	297	–	5	5	57	17	84
Correspondence clerks	2 116	10 405	1 689	8 272	347	1 722	–	57	43	199	37	155
Order clerks	64 599	164 523	50 148	129 382	9 187	26 173	359	879	1 862	3 249	3 043	4 840
Personnel clerks, except payroll and timekeeping	11 771	69 122	8 816	55 334	1 877	9 263	89	452	493	2 016	496	2 057
Library clerks	31 965	118 510	23 904	97 125	3 778	13 051	218	885	2 942	4 694	1 123	2 755
File clerks	51 924	216 022	35 088	158 355	10 624	39 994	285	1 531	3 409	7 892	2 518	8 250
Records clerks	29 524	108 448	23 551	86 525	3 721	15 686	134	584	1 324	2 757	794	2 896
Financial records processing occupations	264 608	2 136 921	214 409	1 898 405	25 495	132 795	1 184	11 033	15 375	54 734	8 145	39 954
Bookkeepers, accounting, and auditing clerks	200 750	1 721 202	163 051	1 548 980	18 988	91 236	793	8 772	11 888	43 741	6 030	28 473
Payroll and timekeeping clerks	20 343	159 137	16 086	136 119	2 387	14 851	194	819	1 086	3 503	590	3 845
Billing clerks	15 783	152 693	12 343	130 090	1 831	13 886	77	855	946	3 806	586	4 056
Cost and rate clerks	20 177	58 090	17 169	47 081	1 430	6 719	96	342	785	1 891	697	2 057
Billing, posting, and calculating machine operators	7 555	45 799	5 760	36 135	859	6 103	24	245	670	1 793	242	1 523
Duplicating, mail and other office machine operators	28 348	40 440	19 581	30 166	4 947	7 326	133	304	1 998	1 234	1 689	1 410
Duplicating machine operators	13 018	14 848	8 752	11 217	2 416	2 419	51	134	962	552	837	526
Mail preparing and paper handling machine operators	2 608	3 588	1 871	2 700	358	624	46	16	177	82	156	166
Office machine operators, n.e.c.	12 722	22 004	8 958	16 249	2 173	4 283	36	154	859	600	696	718
Communications equipment operators	33 799	210 316	25 117	159 221	6 264	40 945	217	1 367	740	2 636	1 461	6 147
Telephone operators	29 670	203 587	22 392	153 968	5 146	39 856	210	1 351	618	2 497	1 304	5 915
Communications equipment operators, n.e.c.	4 129	6 729	2 725	5 253	1 118	1 089	7	16	122	139	157	232
Mail and message distributing occupations	646 568	386 709	468 811	267 096	124 218	91 679	3 154	2 484	27 625	14 636	22 760	10 814
Postal clerks, except mail carriers	192 895	157 670	129 371	90 960	45 924	51 834	737	1 166	10 895	9 726	5 968	3 984
Mail carriers, postal service	240 290	87 951	190 955	71 359	33 003	12 688	1 172	461	8 541	1 386	6 619	2 057
Mail clerks, except postal service	105 987	105 722	69 754	75 728	25 643	22 878	582	632	4 792	2 692	5 216	3 792
Messengers	107 396	35 366	78 731	29 049	19 648	4 279	663	225	3 397	832	4 957	981
Material recording, scheduling, and distributing clerks	1 332 268	888 638	1 044 650	727 959	176 417	105 180	8 375	6 469	35 912	20 643	66 914	28 387
Dispatchers	107 747	97 200	94 407	81 793	8 820	11 778	602	892	1 302	1 068	2 016	1 669
Production coordinators	133 509	119 150	116 009	101 234	9 479	10 808	580	821	3 548	3 255	3 893	3 032
Traffic, shipping, and receiving clerks	460 680	187 922	346 053	153 417	69 094	21 214	2 791	1 333	11 750	3 990	30 992	7 968
Stock and inventory clerks	451 459	260 313	344 072	208 018	66 751	34 375	3 241	2 070	15 190	7 197	22 205	8 653
Meter readers	42 565	6 971	33 482	5 868	6 792	841	397	65	348	65	1 546	132
Weighers, measurers, checkers, and samplers	43 126	37 620	33 616	28 893	6 047	5 410	285	401	995	1 026	2 183	1 890
Expediters	82 324	156 465	68 072	131 333	8 446	16 970	429	745	2 299	3 359	3 078	4 058
Material recording, scheduling, and distributing clerks, n.e.c.	10 858	22 997	8 939	17 403	988	3 784	50	142	480	683	401	985
Adjusters and investigators	313 023	826 064	264 546	672 624	30 167	109 126	1 645	4 114	8 852	19 507	7 813	20 693
Insurance adjusters, examiners, and investigators	101 118	243 521	88 915	197 901	7 927	34 802	401	956	2 413	5 619	1 462	4 243
Investigators and adjusters, except insurance	151 592	430 238	127 375	352 656	14 760	53 042	832	2 023	4 687	11 054	3 938	11 463
Eligibility clerks, social welfare	5 150	44 356	3 315	34 323	742	6 988	38	417	608	952	447	1 676
Bill and account collectors	55 163	107 949	44 941	87 744	6 738	14 294	374	718	1 144	1 882	1 966	3 311
Miscellaneous administrative support occupations	680 403	3 101 736	524 917	2 462 420	87 960	425 018	4 431	20 206	37 974	97 646	25 121	96 446
General office clerks	264 538	1 226 578	200 101	972 436	37 456	169 735	1 610	8 240	14 362	38 392	11 009	37 775
Bank tellers	51 882	457 141	38 969	386 074	5 827	41 116	187	1 652	4 194	15 832	2 705	12 467
Proofreaders	7 304	23 022	6 443	20 157	554	1 966	20	71	216	563	71	265
Data-entry keyers	83 043	556 222	58 800	410 633	13 834	101 843	625	3 494	6 186	21 999	3 598	18 253
Statistical clerks	48 733	99 845	39 454	79 961	5 588	14 492	240	632	2 259	2 536	1 192	2 224
Teachers' aides	29 662	245 881	19 813	189 264	4 061	34 298	449	3 070	3 659	4 871	1 680	14 378
Administrative support occupations, n.o.c.	195 241	493 047	161 337	403 895	20 640	61 568	1 300	3 047	7 098	13 453	4 866	11 084
SERVICE OCCUPATIONS												
Private household occupations	**29 077**	**534 841**	**18 036**	**318 944**	**6 386**	**141 562**	**324**	**4 143**	**1 455**	**13 453**	**2 876**	**56 739**
Launderers and ironers	291	1 396	224	973	5	281	–	10	34	57	28	75
Cooks, private household	1 008	8 204	572	4 692	188	2 695	6	54	196	301	46	462
Housekeepers and butlers	2 087	32 329	1 028	15 083	691	10 566	–	247	128	1 357	240	5 076
Child care workers, private household	4 428	159 824	3 563	127 303	476	17 204	88	1 459	92	3 557	209	10 301
Private household cleaners and servants	21 263	333 088	12 649	170 893	5 026	110 816	230	2 373	1 005	8 181	2 353	40 825
Protective service occupations	**1 754 500**	**330 275**	**1 398 416**	**235 787**	**263 779**	**78 464**	**16 733**	**3 208**	**26 243**	**4 069**	**49 329**	**8 747**
Supervisors, protective service occupations	121 044	14 162	103 604	10 119	13 334	3 442	690	105	1 305	137	2 111	359
Supervisors, firefighting and fire prevention occupations	28 466	832	26 559	724	1 188	97	148	–	272	–	299	11
Supervisors, police and detectives	54 159	7 063	47 266	4 893	5 373	1 870	258	49	473	75	789	176
Supervisors, guards	38 419	6 267	29 779	4 502	6 773	1 475	284	56	560	62	1 023	172
Firefighting and fire prevention occupations	233 170	8 316	202 814	6 598	20 485	1 223	3 189	318	2 179	45	4 503	132
Fire inspection and fire prevention occupations	14 407	2 318	12 471	1 767	1 337	448	223	31	145	21	231	51
Firefighting occupations	218 763	5 998	190 343	4 831	19 148	775	2 966	287	2 034	24	4 272	81
Police and detectives	702 475	119 808	584 823	83 139	87 471	31 334	5 805	1 179	7 163	1 072	17 213	3 084
Police and detectives, public service	457 078	62 106	391 884	44 874	45 864	14 261	3 637	592	4 895	682	10 798	1 697
Sheriffs, bailiffs, and other law enforcement officers	95 561	22 871	81 253	17 585	10 569	4 207	803	229	916	249	2 020	601
Correctional institution officers	149 836	34 831	111 686	20 680	31 038	12 866	1 365	358	1 352	141	4 395	786
Guards	697 811	187 989	507 175	135 931	142 489	42 465	7 049	1 606	15 596	2 815	25 502	5 172
Crossing guards	12 818	32 495	10 006	25 230	2 336	6 118	78	153	80	100	318	894
Guards and police, except public service	655 141	130 370	470 830	87 221	138 304	35 307	6 688	1 364	14 890	2 474	24 429	4 004
Protective service occupations, n.e.c.	29 852	25 124	26 339	23 480	1 849	1 040	283	89	626	241	755	274

Table 2. Detailed Occupation of the Civilian Labor Force by Sex and Race: 1990—Con.

[Data based on sample and subject to sampling variability, see text. For definitions of terms and meanings of symbols, see text]

United States	All persons		White		Black		American Indian, Eskimo, or Aleut		Asian or Pacific Islander		Other race	
	Male	Female	Male	Female	Male	Female	Male	Female	Male	Female	Male	Female
SERVICE OCCUPATIONS—Con.												
Service occupations, except protective and household	5 135 444	8 783 420	3 562 149	6 598 871	909 017	1 487 081	48 526	86 307	232 863	255 441	382 889	355 720
Food preparation and service occupations	2 369 276	3 369 682	1 635 500	2 728 296	355 959	387 014	19 643	32 082	153 506	113 173	204 668	109 117
Supervisors, food preparation and service occupations	117 402	159 018	87 242	131 257	15 038	17 067	731	1 245	8 158	5 477	6 233	3 972
Bartenders	166 630	164 080	147 583	153 476	7 822	4 087	1 087	2 003	4 338	2 562	5 800	1 952
Waiters and waitresses	290 768	1 197 485	215 510	1 065 475	26 590	54 091	1 484	9 545	25 769	40 722	21 415	27 652
Cooks	1 085 895	987 365	704 865	709 445	194 282	192 620	9 739	11 854	80 976	32 510	96 033	40 936
Food counter, fountain and related occupations	65 491	170 989	50 075	141 262	8 307	18 025	474	1 520	3 254	4 893	3 381	5 289
Kitchen workers, food preparation	52 183	159 317	39 139	128 481	6 578	20 836	373	1 124	2 154	3 896	3 939	4 980
Waiters'/waitresses' assistants	217 437	161 121	150 003	126 431	29 040	20 990	1 640	1 138	10 421	6 076	26 333	6 486
Miscellaneous food preparation occupations	373 470	370 307	241 083	272 469	68 302	59 298	4 115	3 653	18 436	17 037	41 534	17 850
Health service occupations	287 943	1 974 015	183 551	1 320 287	77 960	522 169	3 300	20 579	11 418	47 082	11 714	63 898
Dental assistants	5 166	174 121	3 402	153 539	731	8 929	28	1 185	619	4 445	386	6 023
Health aides, except nursing	45 064	177 913	28 610	129 933	12 046	37 538	519	1 307	2 261	4 555	1 628	4 580
Nursing aides, orderlies, and attendants	237 713	1 621 981	151 539	1 036 815	65 183	475 702	2 753	18 087	8 538	38 082	9 700	53 295
Cleaning and building service occupations, except household	2 013 354	1 410 347	1 389 282	883 545	406 568	355 036	21 572	17 075	49 521	42 268	146 411	112 423
Supervisors, cleaning and building service workers	117 971	49 504	90 692	32 631	18 732	11 557	1 049	483	1 663	1 653	5 835	3 180
Maids and housemen	137 337	575 462	69 943	332 595	43 399	162 870	1 424	7 961	7 620	22 684	14 951	49 342
Janitors and cleaners	1 700 984	780 561	1 182 001	514 627	337 996	179 734	18 672	8 573	39 322	17 887	122 993	59 740
Elevator operators	9 684	1 727	6 038	900	2 315	712	30	30	230	9	1 071	76
Pest control occupations	47 378	3 103	40 608	2 792	4 126	163	397	28	686	35	1 561	85
Personal service occupations	464 871	2 029 376	353 816	1 666 743	68 530	222 862	4 011	16 571	18 418	52 918	20 096	70 282
Supervisors, personal service occupations	19 313	43 619	15 421	35 677	2 328	5 311	157	377	768	884	639	1 370
Barbers	66 677	17 949	53 818	14 623	9 258	1 711	512	121	959	819	2 130	675
Hairdressers and cosmetologists	76 143	657 433	61 875	558 958	7 869	54 212	447	4 008	2 814	21 188	3 138	19 067
Attendants, amusement and recreation facilities	86 248	50 905	69 856	38 787	8 237	5 371	1 042	1 129	4 102	3 861	3 011	1 757
Guides	19 281	22 005	14 298	17 146	2 605	2 953	179	132	1 635	1 387	564	387
Ushers	19 853	9 758	15 853	7 609	2 461	1 425	70	97	643	288	826	339
Public transportation attendants	21 801	84 148	14 925	70 859	4 573	9 452	94	238	1 248	2 692	961	907
Baggage porters and bellhops	34 558	4 205	21 553	2 590	9 084	1 001	153	15	2 215	329	1 553	270
Welfare service aides	7 871	40 319	5 098	26 671	1 838	10 156	232	696	259	825	444	1 971
Family child care providers	6 234	428 409	5 007	371 144	745	30 681	101	3 242	129	7 265	252	16 077
Early childhood teacher's assistants	14 059	324 869	9 898	257 882	2 976	48 351	152	2 920	377	4 744	656	10 972
Child care workers, n.e.c.	22 932	188 419	15 158	142 874	5 795	31 431	346	2 054	499	3 331	1 134	8 729
Personal service occupations, n.e.c.	69 901	157 338	51 056	121 923	10 761	20 807	526	1 542	2 770	5 305	4 788	7 761
FARMING, FORESTRY, AND FISHING OCCUPATIONS												
Farming, forestry, and fishing occupations	2 597 829	507 566	2 124 661	416 639	175 111	28 272	26 224	4 731	35 371	9 889	236 462	48 035
Farm operators and managers	933 808	153 557	891 311	145 849	16 467	2 597	3 852	838	6 379	1 688	15 799	2 585
Farmers, except horticultural	680 512	114 675	663 580	111 413	6 717	971	2 470	583	3 173	898	4 572	810
Horticultural specialty farmers	31 261	3 471	27 130	3 213	1 711	78	174	27	751	129	1 495	24
Managers, farms, except horticultural	208 114	30 770	188 630	27 098	7 355	1 360	1 162	196	2 153	532	8 814	1 584
Managers, horticultural specialty farms	13 921	4 641	11 971	4 125	684	188	46	32	302	129	918	167
Other agricultural and related occupations	1 466 828	342 587	1 067 544	261 529	140 878	24 567	16 292	3 489	26 006	7 983	216 108	45 019
Farm occupations, except managerial	666 460	175 613	470 727	127 224	50 654	13 287	7 598	1 843	8 814	4 693	128 667	28 566
Supervisors, farm workers	37 273	6 162	27 968	4 459	1 500	664	255	62	788	188	6 762	789
Farm workers	609 123	150 546	428 971	107 563	47 910	11 246	7 167	1 580	7 449	3 692	117 626	26 465
Marine life cultivation workers	879	354	721	297	51	41	43	–	31	–	33	16
Nursery workers	19 185	18 551	13 067	14 905	1 193	1 336	133	201	546	813	4 246	1 296
Related agricultural occupations	800 368	166 974	596 817	134 305	90 224	11 280	8 694	1 646	17 192	3 290	87 441	16 453
Supervisors, related agricultural occupations	60 452	5 155	52 419	4 493	2 776	318	356	83	894	44	4 007	217
Groundskeepers and gardeners, except farm	680 843	54 713	499 846	44 695	81 772	4 928	7 598	710	15 267	1 323	76 360	3 057
Animal caretakers, except farm	40 059	67 146	33 822	64 320	3 410	1 241	499	404	507	492	1 821	689
Graders and sorters, agricultural products	16 695	37 964	8 881	19 472	2 041	4 364	221	432	463	1 350	5 089	12 346
Inspectors, agricultural products	2 319	1 996	1 849	1 325	225	429	20	17	61	81	164	144
Forestry and logging occupations	140 463	7 560	116 869	5 998	15 515	900	3 786	255	418	99	3 875	308
Supervisors, forestry and logging workers	11 529	539	10 309	510	738	18	233	–	30	–	219	11
Forestry workers, except logging	16 858	3 573	13 463	2 850	1 134	306	681	127	99	32	1 481	258
Timber cutting and logging occupations	112 076	3 448	93 097	2 638	13 643	576	2 872	128	289	67	2 175	39
Fishers, hunters, and trappers	56 730	3 862	48 937	3 263	2 251	208	2 294	149	2 568	119	680	123
Captains and other officers, fishing vessels	6 149	192	5 664	171	97	17	156	4	172	–	60	–
Fishers	48 813	3 339	41 774	2 804	2 066	166	2 073	141	2 335	112	565	116
Hunters and trappers	1 768	331	1 499	288	88	25	65	4	61	7	55	7
PRECISION PRODUCTION, CRAFT, AND REPAIR OCCUPATIONS												
Precision production, craft, and repair occupations	12 701 437	1 329 863	10 961 761	1 021 711	889 906	161 808	104 169	12 127	218 887	69 092	526 714	65 125
Mechanics and repairers	4 085 908	185 258	3 558 276	146 148	284 567	27 182	28 823	1 452	73 000	4 755	141 242	5 721
Supervisors, mechanics and repairers	247 901	22 681	227 602	18 103	11 805	3 695	1 139	143	3 129	386	4 226	354
Mechanics and repairers, except supervisors	3 838 007	162 577	3 330 674	128 045	272 762	23 487	27 684	1 309	69 871	4 369	137 016	5 367
Vehicle and mobile equipment mechanics and repairers	1 829 964	35 714	1 576 258	28 298	130 544	5 025	13 855	323	33 748	711	75 559	1 357
Automobile mechanics, except apprentices	936 977	17 646	795 669	14 094	73 175	2 332	6 992	169	19 473	298	41 668	753
Automobile mechanic apprentices	1 531	60	1 260	60	167	–	14	–	29	–	61	–
Bus, truck, and stationary engine mechanics	263 806	2 336	231 495	1 660	19 005	504	2 060	27	2 711	30	8 535	115
Aircraft engine mechanics	129 256	5 416	110 442	4 193	9 867	805	975	45	4 161	177	3 811	196
Small engine repairers	60 914	1 108	55 497	855	2 789	199	590	7	592	22	1 446	25
Automobile body and related repairers	223 991	4 719	191 400	4 028	13 352	482	1 445	29	3 834	39	13 960	141
Aircraft mechanics, except engine	29 437	2 377	24 338	1 791	2 579	421	214	43	1 271	95	1 035	27
Heavy equipment mechanics	155 764	1 731	140 073	1 373	8 641	249	1 441	3	1 478	29	4 131	77
Farm equipment mechanics	28 288	321	26 084	244	969	33	124	–	199	21	912	23
Industrial machinery repairers	318 984	13 795	280 212	10 949	22 581	1 839	1 947	96	4 233	335	10 011	576
Machinery maintenance occupations	24 140	1 133	20 169	865	2 649	181	419	2	217	27	686	58

Table 2. Detailed Occupation of the Civilian Labor Force by Sex and Race: 1990—Con.

[Data based on sample and subject to sampling variability, see text. For definitions of terms and meanings of symbols, see text]

United States	All persons		White		Black		American Indian, Eskimo, or Aleut		Asian or Pacific Islander		Other race	
	Male	Female	Male	Female	Male	Female	Male	Female	Male	Female	Male	Female
PRECISION PRODUCTION, CRAFT, AND REPAIR OCCUPATIONS—Con.												
Electrical and electronic equipment repairers	573 064	62 461	499 345	48 270	42 274	9 884	3 520	511	13 585	1 980	14 340	1 816
Electronic repairers, communications and industrial equipment	164 678	14 551	140 835	11 622	13 180	1 827	1 057	132	4 955	548	4 651	422
Data processing equipment repairers	79 736	11 921	68 900	9 523	5 881	1 405	364	69	2 884	552	1 707	372
Household appliance and power tool repairers	50 935	2 190	45 538	1 791	2 612	238	330	11	1 020	58	1 435	92
Telephone line installers and repairers	47 211	3 422	42 328	2 529	2 899	523	346	44	486	143	1 152	183
Telephone installers and repairers	164 418	26 509	144 871	20 033	12 730	5 236	925	154	2 573	537	3 319	549
Miscellaneous electrical and electronic equipment repairers	66 086	3 868	56 873	2 772	4 972	655	498	101	1 667	142	2 076	198
Heating, air conditioning, and refrigeration mechanics	190 412	2 571	171 999	2 068	9 438	410	1 298	18	2 510	25	5 167	50
Miscellaneous mechanics and repairers	901 443	46 903	782 691	37 595	65 276	6 148	6 645	359	15 578	1 291	31 253	1 510
Camera, watch, and musical instrument repairers	27 311	3 786	24 615	3 093	875	356	72	22	1 161	212	588	103
Locksmiths and safe repairers	25 360	1 777	22 943	1 608	1 258	85	183	27	361	27	615	30
Office machine repairers	39 540	2 348	34 232	1 874	3 026	296	200	–	1 065	96	1 017	82
Mechanical controls and valve repairers	19 393	1 015	16 018	736	2 332	239	102	20	204	16	737	4
Elevator installers and repairers	25 207	427	22 910	339	1 215	72	151	–	310	–	621	16
Millwrights	92 874	3 266	85 929	2 678	4 725	408	524	52	467	43	1 229	85
Specified mechanics and repairers, n.e.c.	199 247	14 702	174 158	11 760	13 358	1 991	1 555	93	3 693	392	6 483	466
Not specified mechanics and repairers	472 511	19 582	401 886	15 507	38 487	2 701	3 858	145	8 317	505	19 963	724
Construction trades	5 170 054	147 946	4 467 953	123 701	359 970	14 519	51 156	1 972	58 203	2 385	232 772	5 369
Supervisors, construction occupations	815 303	22 697	739 924	19 374	38 822	2 229	5 653	206	8 360	348	22 544	540
Supervisors, brickmasons, stonemasons, and tile setters	12 880	88	11 053	62	1 168	9	89	–	150	8	420	9
Supervisors, carpenters and related workers	45 096	529	41 867	464	995	28	355	16	573	–	1 306	21
Supervisors, electricians and power transmission installers	71 958	1 598	67 139	1 408	2 533	114	326	11	823	34	1 137	31
Supervisors, painters, paperhangers, and plasterers	30 759	1 610	26 819	1 424	1 986	117	339	11	438	26	1 177	32
Supervisors, plumbers, pipefitters, and steamfitters	20 103	415	18 631	380	764	19	142	16	202	–	364	–
Supervisors, construction n.e.c.	634 507	18 457	574 415	15 636	31 376	1 942	4 402	152	6 174	280	18 140	447
Construction trades, except supervisors	4 354 751	125 249	3 728 029	104 327	321 148	12 290	45 503	1 766	49 843	2 037	210 228	4 829
Brickmasons and stonemasons, except apprentices	194 480	2 459	153 093	1 693	28 581	621	1 601	24	1 521	3	9 684	118
Brickmason and stonemason apprentices	685	42	564	37	89	5	–	–	8	–	24	–
Tile setters, hard and soft	54 356	1 286	46 153	1 102	3 102	61	382	–	923	33	3 796	90
Carpet installers	109 426	2 410	95 030	2 033	6 314	186	967	34	743	29	6 372	128
Carpenters, except apprentices	1 337 544	23 163	1 187 316	19 700	67 358	1 952	14 580	366	14 399	305	53 891	840
Carpenter apprentices	4 600	253	3 975	150	224	77	57	22	157	4	187	–
Drywall installers	146 761	3 793	122 183	3 259	9 174	307	2 751	101	1 116	–	11 537	126
Electricians, except apprentices	619 358	15 659	554 075	12 322	36 069	2 121	4 187	207	9 759	464	15 268	545
Electrician apprentices	14 888	684	13 389	587	897	75	138	7	145	–	319	15
Electrical power installers and repairers	118 543	1 689	104 837	1 425	9 819	189	1 167	11	607	28	2 113	36
Painters, construction and maintenance	515 697	43 329	413 037	37 571	48 231	2 747	4 821	527	9 129	790	40 479	1 694
Paperhangers	12 811	4 399	11 869	4 254	302	49	87	32	170	22	383	42
Plasterers	42 260	849	30 531	613	5 569	142	375	16	362	–	5 423	78
Plumbers, pipefitters, and steamfitters, except apprentices	481 639	7 219	421 671	5 934	33 835	855	4 528	64	5 024	98	16 581	268
Plumber, pipefitter, and steamfitter apprentices	6 426	153	5 760	134	335	19	52	–	107	–	172	–
Concrete and terrazzo finishers	74 944	1 001	50 786	524	15 102	334	944	14	418	–	7 694	129
Glaziers	43 142	2 453	38 490	2 014	1 826	299	246	35	476	74	1 694	31
Insulation workers	71 460	2 952	56 306	2 067	7 489	637	906	75	862	16	5 897	157
Paving, surfacing, and tamping equipment operators	12 777	333	10 067	254	1 000	71	138	–	70	–	669	8
Roofers	194 098	3 085	156 118	2 385	18 629	437	3 025	90	1 509	8	14 817	165
Sheetmetal duct installers	29 541	421	26 971	341	1 474	37	200	10	157	7	739	26
Structural metal workers	73 885	1 453	65 528	1 158	4 090	198	1 309	21	681	21	2 277	55
Drillers, earth	19 983	508	17 974	408	909	69	317	6	89	–	694	25
Construction trades, n.e.c.	175 447	5 656	141 896	4 362	19 897	802	2 725	104	1 411	135	9 518	253
Extractive occupations	187 451	5 411	169 406	4 496	7 987	548	2 352	98	662	39	7 044	230
Supervisors, extractive occupations	47 578	1 741	44 545	1 532	1 246	150	412	7	285	21	1 090	31
Drillers, oil well	36 539	533	32 266	503	1 686	8	700	18	69	–	1 818	4
Explosives workers	8 872	505	7 679	347	718	74	190	28	28	–	257	56
Mining machine operators	60 613	1 705	55 494	1 399	2 684	189	588	31	212	18	1 635	68
Mining occupations, n.e.c.	33 849	927	29 422	715	1 653	127	462	14	68	–	2 244	71
Precision production occupations	3 258 024	991 248	2 766 126	747 366	237 382	119 559	21 838	8 605	87 022	61 913	145 656	53 805
Supervisors, production occupations	1 069 504	230 133	930 804	186 170	78 945	25 297	5 514	1 543	17 491	6 337	36 750	10 786
Precision metal working occupations	973 211	79 163	854 907	59 872	54 434	9 881	7 150	1 748	22 894	3 145	33 826	4 517
Tool and die makers, except apprentices	139 502	3 312	132 233	2 662	3 486	331	455	12	1 260	162	2 068	145
Tool and die maker apprentices	2 267	109	2 177	91	40	9	20	9	10	–	20	–
Precision assemblers, metal	31 912	9 047	24 880	5 583	3 669	1 937	251	109	1 090	629	2 022	789
Machinists, except apprentices	543 172	25 909	473 997	19 342	32 840	4 231	3 341	260	13 971	553	19 023	1 523
Machinist apprentices	1 436	107	1 288	81	57	18	11	2	39	–	41	6
Boilermakers	23 706	587	20 545	460	2 114	106	252	13	149	–	646	8
Precision grinders, filers, and tool sharpeners	21 378	1 691	19 745	1 435	799	201	169	–	197	31	468	24
Patternmakers and model makers, metal	5 177	265	4 914	225	169	30	12	–	23	10	59	–
Lay-out workers	14 834	2 153	12 036	1 638	2 056	356	165	31	312	83	265	45
Precious stones and metals workers (jewelers)	40 995	20 835	31 535	15 840	1 530	1 026	1 532	1 194	2 614	1 289	3 784	1 486
Engravers, metal	10 659	6 499	9 583	5 804	442	347	44	25	235	144	355	179
Sheet metal workers, except apprentices	135 431	8 060	119 610	6 208	7 039	1 216	866	93	2 947	231	4 969	312
Sheet metal worker apprentices	865	86	725	60	58	26	11	–	14	–	57	–
Miscellaneous precision metal workers	1 877	503	1 639	443	135	47	21	–	33	13	49	–
Precision woodworking occupations	97 016	13 643	84 780	11 342	5 137	1 782	698	93	1 174	94	5 227	332
Patternmakers and model makers, wood	2 976	323	2 765	267	82	48	10	–	31	8	88	–
Cabinet makers and bench carpenters	67 251	4 620	60 235	4 087	2 814	354	490	11	747	35	2 965	133
Furniture and wood finishers	25 035	8 396	20 293	6 748	2 107	1 354	154	52	372	51	2 109	191
Miscellaneous precision woodworkers	1 754	304	1 487	240	134	26	44	30	24	–	65	8
Precision textile, apparel, and furnishings machine workers	119 539	152 981	88 215	111 851	11 420	15 147	732	965	6 128	15 943	13 044	9 075
Dressmakers	6 421	90 837	4 080	65 085	612	8 976	51	651	793	10 317	885	5 808
Tailors	29 538	27 269	19 321	18 640	3 479	2 969	74	90	2 728	3 980	3 936	1 590
Upholsterers	57 167	16 771	45 298	14 406	4 567	1 417	409	126	767	166	6 126	656
Shoe repairers	20 178	7 850	14 506	6 321	2 188	724	135	50	1 634	404	1 715	351
Miscellaneous precision apparel and fabric workers	6 235	10 254	5 010	7 399	574	1 061	63	48	206	1 076	382	670

Table 2. Detailed Occupation of the Civilian Labor Force by Sex and Race: 1990—Con.

[Data based on sample and subject to sampling variability, see text. For definitions of terms and meanings of symbols, see text]

United States	All persons Male	All persons Female	White Male	White Female	Black Male	Black Female	American Indian, Eskimo, or Aleut Male	American Indian, Eskimo, or Aleut Female	Asian or Pacific Islander Male	Asian or Pacific Islander Female	Other race Male	Other race Female
PRECISION PRODUCTION, CRAFT, AND REPAIR OCCUPATIONS—Con.												
Precision workers, assorted materials	265 293	303 078	207 154	219 454	21 277	34 842	1 717	2 257	18 778	28 376	16 367	18 149
Hand molders and shapers, except jewelers	16 892	3 165	14 521	2 548	902	245	138	54	204	109	1 127	209
Patternmakers, lay-out workers, and cutters	17 388	5 502	16 033	3 815	525	438	84	9	371	855	375	385
Optical goods workers	33 171	41 736	28 623	35 947	1 902	2 816	162	220	1 289	1 544	1 195	1 209
Dental laboratory and medical appliance technicians	34 394	22 570	28 002	18 928	2 033	1 597	228	111	2 725	1 351	1 406	583
Bookbinders	13 964	15 969	11 672	12 065	1 295	2 384	89	69	321	486	587	965
Electrical and electronic equipment assemblers	104 105	205 301	71 287	139 131	11 467	26 428	756	1 732	12 288	23 803	8 307	14 207
Miscellaneous precision workers, n.e.c.	45 379	8 835	37 016	7 020	3 153	934	260	62	1 580	228	3 370	591
Precision food production occupations	331 632	160 280	252 887	118 237	33 754	25 340	2 680	1 486	11 541	6 031	30 770	9 186
Butchers and meat cutters	224 107	54 795	175 798	32 583	20 576	14 914	1 809	702	6 405	2 694	19 439	3 902
Bakers	86 076	73 096	60 847	59 317	10 980	8 108	650	513	4 575	2 330	9 024	2 828
Food batchmakers	21 449	32 389	16 242	26 337	2 198	2 318	141	271	561	1 007	2 307	2 456
Precision inspectors, testers, and related workers	105 820	34 835	90 773	26 722	7 914	4 777	596	283	3 616	1 651	2 921	1 402
Inspectors, testers, and graders	99 861	32 044	85 543	24 677	7 610	4 304	549	265	3 401	1 592	2 758	1 206
Adjusters and calibrators	5 959	2 791	5 230	2 045	304	473	47	18	215	59	163	196
Plant and system operators	296 009	17 135	256 606	13 718	24 501	2 493	2 751	230	5 400	336	6 751	358
Water and sewage treatment plant operators	58 174	3 095	50 694	2 488	5 217	477	590	50	530	54	1 143	26
Power plant operators	34 759	2 253	30 855	1 789	2 433	348	460	62	364	26	647	28
Stationary engineers	153 639	7 602	133 849	6 040	11 851	1 033	1 210	97	3 856	225	2 873	207
Miscellaneous plant and system operators	49 437	4 185	41 208	3 401	5 000	635	491	21	650	31	2 088	97
OPERATORS, FABRICATORS, AND LABORERS												
Machine operators, assemblers, and inspectors	**5 185 397**	**3 450 107**	**4 010 589**	**2 409 029**	**650 217**	**613 409**	**41 280**	**29 108**	**129 919**	**154 596**	**353 392**	**243 965**
Machine operators and tenders, except precision	3 176 768	2 231 958	2 440 824	1 542 439	407 108	406 917	23 265	18 322	78 163	102 768	227 408	161 512
Metal working and plastic working machine operators	317 227	70 805	265 805	56 614	29 244	9 543	2 029	592	4 274	1 036	15 875	3 020
Lathe and turning machine set-up operators	26 770	2 690	23 375	2 222	1 843	337	102	7	339	25	1 111	99
Lathe and turning machine operators	32 088	4 442	28 829	3 728	1 663	477	188	19	494	84	914	134
Milling and planing machine operators	5 806	983	5 141	784	331	129	31	15	168	22	135	33
Punching and stamping press machine operators	79 351	31 115	65 212	24 989	8 523	4 314	607	287	883	281	4 126	1 244
Rolling machine operators	11 767	1 976	10 088	1 531	1 218	339	53	15	70	13	338	78
Drilling and boring machine operators	17 201	4 375	15 225	3 540	1 236	558	83	50	141	31	516	196
Grinding, abrading, buffing, and polishing machine operators	105 876	19 582	85 145	15 311	10 924	2 611	769	170	1 674	440	7 364	1 050
Forging machine operators	16 076	970	13 534	803	1 715	122	81	–	164	14	582	31
Numerical control machine operators	1 363	273	1 158	212	85	24	–	–	43	37	77	–
Miscellaneous metal, plastic, stone, and glass working machine operators	20 929	4 399	18 098	3 494	1 706	632	115	29	298	89	712	155
Fabricating machine operators, n.e.c.	18 127	8 535	14 123	6 612	2 053	1 284	86	45	414	251	1 451	343
Metal and plastic processing machine operators	132 690	29 677	106 071	23 526	14 141	4 043	1 030	222	2 078	538	9 370	1 348
Molding and casting machine operators	68 281	21 187	56 081	16 868	6 980	2 907	535	133	812	353	3 873	926
Metal plating machine operators	31 109	4 288	23 291	3 345	3 130	482	253	50	861	111	3 574	300
Heat treating equipment operators	17 323	1 220	14 848	897	1 747	266	67	2	106	30	555	25
Miscellaneous metal and plastic processing machine operators	15 977	2 982	11 851	2 416	2 284	388	175	37	299	44	1 368	97
Woodworking machine operators	132 205	23 432	110 177	18 912	13 578	2 851	1 884	291	1 212	329	5 354	1 049
Wood lathe, routing, and planing machine operators	7 157	1 054	6 286	875	518	135	104	29	66	8	183	7
Sawing machine operators	82 788	12 117	68 025	9 532	9 708	1 494	1 304	140	617	248	3 134	703
Shaping and joining machine operators	4 180	1 864	3 560	1 578	283	218	88	15	34	12	215	41
Nailing and tacking machine operators	2 345	874	1 810	709	256	105	40	12	33	–	206	48
Miscellaneous woodworking machine operators	35 735	7 523	30 496	6 218	2 813	899	348	95	462	61	1 616	250
Printing machine operators	374 529	157 616	319 274	136 407	28 546	12 581	1 914	881	9 232	3 162	15 563	4 585
Printing press operators	293 657	66 124	246 964	54 289	24 369	7 384	1 549	397	7 419	1 471	13 356	2 583
Photoengravers and lithographers	35 861	13 245	32 822	11 717	1 426	907	136	81	639	219	838	321
Typesetters and compositors	21 641	50 712	19 409	46 729	977	2 166	100	215	719	877	436	725
Miscellaneous printing machine operators	23 370	27 535	20 079	23 672	1 774	2 124	129	188	455	595	933	956
Textile, apparel, and furnishings machine operators	341 153	1 076 419	223 456	696 541	62 062	221 436	2 267	9 466	17 477	69 431	35 891	79 545
Winding and twisting machine operators	19 579	51 041	14 383	34 262	4 601	15 532	113	397	242	526	240	324
Knitting, looping, taping, and weaving machine operators	21 250	38 973	14 950	27 543	4 636	9 431	223	439	317	916	1 124	644
Textile cutting machine operators	4 549	3 290	3 146	2 349	906	629	33	25	103	51	361	236
Textile sewing machine operators	93 074	690 725	52 638	444 232	15 754	125 412	614	5 856	5 603	57 602	18 465	57 623
Shoe machine operators	10 052	24 192	8 552	21 448	788	1 777	66	115	100	166	546	686
Pressing machine operators	54 543	93 868	34 959	54 512	9 754	27 898	352	729	4 337	2 661	5 141	8 068
Laundering and dry cleaning machine operators	82 729	136 368	53 755	85 643	15 131	31 624	520	1 437	6 061	6 976	7 262	10 688
Miscellaneous textile machine operators	55 377	37 962	41 073	26 552	10 492	9 133	346	468	714	533	2 752	1 276
Machine operators, assorted materials	1 860 837	865 474	1 401 918	603 827	257 484	155 179	14 055	6 825	43 476	28 021	143 904	71 622
Cementing and gluing machine operators	20 070	12 316	13 892	9 361	3 609	1 866	268	124	286	215	2 015	750
Packaging and filling machine operators	112 546	168 699	75 018	109 690	20 177	32 977	952	1 217	3 545	6 047	12 854	18 768
Extruding and forming machine operators	23 658	4 233	20 064	3 586	2 278	431	189	12	294	54	843	150
Mixing and blending machine operators	97 976	13 165	71 871	9 502	17 988	2 425	725	98	1 629	442	5 763	698
Separating, filtering, and clarifying machine operators	61 822	7 808	50 581	5 755	7 461	1 424	381	85	857	58	2 542	486
Compressing and compacting machine operators	17 356	4 997	13 639	3 542	2 492	1 062	150	65	241	38	834	290
Painting and paint spraying machine operators	116 325	19 852	90 444	15 179	12 104	3 069	841	189	1 877	405	11 059	1 010
Roasting and baking machine operators, food	3 796	952	2 946	646	534	238	44	3	13	6	259	59
Washing, cleaning, and pickling machine operators	7 229	3 209	5 596	2 346	867	523	100	35	93	67	573	238
Folding machine operators	6 699	13 730	5 365	9 336	689	3 110	34	95	146	346	465	843
Furnace, kiln, and oven operators, except food	90 357	5 919	74 450	4 495	11 753	1 045	773	99	689	107	2 692	173
Crushing and grinding machine operators	36 554	8 653	29 460	6 543	4 147	1 507	450	121	397	122	2 100	360
Slicing and cutting machine operators	133 879	54 070	100 968	37 221	16 674	9 354	1 293	513	2 603	1 813	12 341	5 169
Motion picture projectionists	8 811	1 546	8 037	1 351	424	69	13	8	126	71	211	47
Photographic process machine operators	49 210	52 729	39 242	44 158	4 567	4 661	331	430	2 781	1 934	2 289	1 546
Miscellaneous machine operators, n.e.c.	411 563	199 707	306 401	137 296	57 755	38 152	3 001	1 702	10 980	6 324	33 426	16 233
Manufacturing, nondurable goods	164 760	72 060	123 429	48 413	25 694	14 873	1 178	597	3 489	2 091	10 970	6 086
Manufacturing, durable goods	189 490	87 622	139 691	59 423	24 531	16 205	1 278	769	5 831	3 115	18 159	8 110
Nonmanufacturing industries	57 313	40 025	43 281	29 460	7 530	7 074	545	336	1 660	1 118	4 297	2 037
Machine operators, not specified	662 976	293 889	493 944	203 820	93 965	53 266	4 510	2 029	16 919	9 972	53 638	24 802
Manufacturing, nondurable goods	190 549	118 677	139 333	82 800	30 425	21 994	1 122	729	4 301	3 586	15 368	9 568
Manufacturing, durable goods	314 293	125 191	236 484	87 544	41 552	21 405	2 060	844	8 558	4 597	25 639	10 801
Nonmanufacturing industries	158 134	50 021	118 127	33 476	21 988	9 867	1 328	456	4 060	1 789	12 631	4 433

Table 2. Detailed Occupation of the Civilian Labor Force by Sex and Race: 1990—Con.

[Data based on sample and subject to sampling variability, see text. For definitions of terms and meanings of symbols, see text]

United States	All persons		White		Black		American Indian, Eskimo, or Aleut		Asian or Pacific Islander		Other race	
	Male	Female	Male	Female	Male	Female	Male	Female	Male	Female	Male	Female
OPERATORS, FABRICATORS, AND LABORERS—Con.												
Fabricators, assemblers, and hand working occupations	1 611 743	780 910	1 250 097	552 806	199 453	132 456	15 282	6 982	38 596	35 464	108 315	53 202
Welders and cutters	613 596	30 382	509 701	22 305	52 709	5 362	7 160	399	8 763	488	35 263	1 828
Solderers and brazers	9 320	18 917	6 427	14 270	774	1 957	74	206	572	1 155	1 473	1 329
Assemblers	892 566	681 413	657 962	477 728	136 189	118 290	7 103	5 782	26 863	32 222	64 449	47 391
Hand cutting and trimming occupations	10 378	6 127	7 145	3 280	1 434	1 805	160	92	420	495	1 219	455
Hand molding, casting, and forming occupations	18 792	7 617	15 252	6 180	1 721	782	143	68	307	208	1 369	379
Hand painting, coating, and decorating occupations	30 865	14 193	25 187	11 929	2 702	1 162	352	169	625	299	1 999	634
Hand engraving and printing occupations	8 417	6 437	7 051	5 672	518	425	52	46	252	84	544	210
Miscellaneous hand working occupations	27 809	15 824	21 372	11 442	3 406	2 673	238	220	794	513	1 999	976
Production inspectors, testers, samplers, and weighers	396 886	437 239	319 668	313 784	43 656	74 036	2 733	3 804	13 160	16 364	17 669	29 251
Production inspectors, checkers, and examiners	294 026	330 982	243 073	245 360	29 582	55 522	1 816	2 701	9 003	11 604	10 552	15 795
Production testers	40 360	19 784	33 037	14 795	3 334	2 548	175	162	2 605	1 537	1 209	742
Production samplers and weighers	5 285	5 505	4 229	3 717	588	611	34	30	88	275	346	872
Graders and sorters, except agricultural	57 215	80 968	39 329	49 912	10 152	15 355	708	911	1 464	2 948	5 562	11 842
Transportation and material moving occupations	**4 594 570**	**504 404**	**3 688 936**	**403 213**	**619 826**	**78 477**	**39 849**	**5 880**	**57 671**	**4 499**	**188 288**	**12 335**
Motor vehicle operators	3 392 948	444 959	2 700 059	358 534	478 493	67 920	26 335	5 035	48 038	3 711	140 023	9 759
Supervisors, motor vehicle operators	67 709	12 642	57 179	10 554	7 363	1 623	368	101	945	126	1 854	238
Truck drivers	2 733 620	175 332	2 231 097	146 749	342 492	20 000	21 247	2 181	28 904	1 977	109 880	4 425
Driver-sales workers	128 937	14 416	115 304	12 926	7 962	866	561	138	1 685	145	3 425	341
Bus drivers	232 404	215 166	153 172	168 370	65 375	40 000	2 492	2 211	3 328	905	8 037	3 680
Taxicab drivers and chauffeurs	184 894	22 439	115 421	16 609	44 877	4 393	1 398	324	11 056	271	12 142	842
Parking lot attendants	41 776	4 783	25 315	3 188	9 804	1 000	219	75	2 085	287	4 353	233
Motor transportation occupations, n.e.c.	3 608	181	2 571	138	620	38	50	5	35	–	332	–
Transportation occupations, except motor vehicles	183 732	7 375	163 262	5 459	15 394	1 459	1 384	126	1 549	165	2 143	166
Rail transportation occupations	117 319	4 527	103 383	3 174	11 241	1 082	620	66	549	104	1 526	101
Railroad conductors and yardmasters	35 140	2 433	31 819	1 682	2 540	575	130	39	286	62	365	75
Locomotive operating occupations	44 744	1 222	38 790	892	4 937	248	259	27	164	42	594	13
Railroad brake, signal, and switch operators	32 689	570	28 685	460	3 229	97	174	–	80	–	521	13
Rail vehicle operators, n.e.c.	4 746	302	4 089	140	535	162	57	–	19	–	46	–
Water transportation occupations	66 413	2 848	59 879	2 285	4 153	377	764	60	1 000	61	617	65
Ship captains and mates, except fishing boats	31 956	1 041	30 266	933	796	81	396	–	370	19	128	8
Sailors and deckhands	24 992	953	21 040	763	2 702	104	264	29	543	27	443	30
Marine engineers	4 103	49	3 791	40	199	9	23	–	60	–	30	–
Bridge, lock, and lighthouse tenders	5 362	805	4 782	549	456	183	81	31	27	15	16	27
Material moving equipment operators	1 017 890	52 070	825 615	39 220	125 939	9 098	12 130	719	8 084	623	46 122	2 410
Supervisors, material moving equipment operators	22 365	1 438	19 601	1 212	1 801	168	173	18	180	40	610	–
Operating engineers	236 996	4 816	207 961	3 615	16 574	722	3 635	161	1 771	121	7 055	197
Longshore equipment operators	4 331	72	2 765	72	1 226	–	83	–	100	–	157	–
Hoist and winch operators	19 831	469	16 772	347	1 256	106	372	–	91	–	1 340	16
Crane and tower operators	79 850	1 975	65 896	1 419	10 459	458	726	7	571	40	2 198	51
Excavating and loading machine operators	94 408	1 575	85 614	1 321	5 271	187	1 098	13	365	12	2 060	42
Grader, dozer, and scraper operators	63 758	1 122	57 434	939	4 042	114	921	39	284	–	1 077	30
Industrial truck and tractor equipment operators	414 030	27 829	302 370	21 230	75 212	5 125	4 098	354	3 993	252	28 357	868
Miscellaneous material moving equipment operators	82 321	12 774	67 202	9 065	10 098	2 218	1 024	127	729	158	3 268	1 206
Handlers, equipment cleaners, helpers, and laborers	**4 203 264**	**1 038 920**	**3 165 746**	**781 600**	**635 951**	**156 137**	**44 826**	**10 002**	**70 799**	**27 462**	**285 942**	**63 719**
Supervisors, handlers, equipment cleaners, and laborers, n.e.c.	13 990	1 678	10 645	1 238	2 044	350	106	25	377	35	818	30
Helpers, mechanics, and repairers	20 613	1 258	15 499	967	2 489	143	277	48	430	28	1 918	72
Helpers, construction, and extractive occupations	88 032	4 680	68 488	3 967	10 244	460	1 019	64	918	34	7 363	155
Helpers, construction trades	81 768	3 836	62 923	3 209	9 845	417	916	45	884	27	7 200	138
Helpers, surveyor	4 221	454	3 863	387	180	43	62	10	34	7	82	7
Helpers, extractive occupations	2 043	390	1 702	371	219	–	41	9	–	–	81	10
Construction laborers	1 103 482	46 298	832 692	35 711	148 861	6 355	14 423	912	12 347	618	95 159	2 702
Production helpers	29 835	8 148	21 019	5 683	4 355	1 264	342	92	847	400	3 272	659
Freight, stock, and material handlers	1 364 524	397 396	1 043 020	320 214	221 369	51 004	11 731	3 418	25 357	8 763	63 047	13 997
Garbage collectors	57 407	2 502	35 065	1 516	18 194	790	614	46	390	23	3 144	127
Stevedores	11 133	350	6 741	224	3 360	92	181	6	322	–	529	28
Stock handlers and baggers	726 754	303 608	582 295	251 561	92 378	32 234	5 341	2 583	16 960	7 078	29 780	10 152
Machine feeders and offbearers	56 986	30 223	42 745	21 921	10 114	6 054	630	262	861	602	2 636	1 384
Freight, stock, and material handlers, n.e.c.	512 244	60 713	376 174	44 992	97 323	11 834	4 965	521	6 824	1 060	26 958	2 306
Garage and service station related occupations	241 429	28 798	199 454	24 396	24 514	2 615	2 421	354	5 111	567	9 929	866
Vehicle washers and equipment cleaners	203 731	28 785	141 481	20 305	39 818	5 416	1 734	386	3 044	849	17 654	1 829
Hand packers and packagers	130 183	238 158	84 657	167 278	23 169	37 636	1 078	1 826	4 137	7 717	17 142	23 701
Laborers, except construction	1 007 445	283 721	748 791	201 841	159 088	50 904	11 695	2 877	18 231	8 391	69 640	19 708
Manufacturing, nondurable goods	156 302	74 247	112 411	50 565	26 883	15 187	1 320	633	3 135	2 199	12 553	5 663
Manufacturing, durable goods	238 225	69 630	183 146	52 229	33 607	10 501	2 103	604	3 060	1 696	16 309	4 600
Transportation, communications, and other public utilities	119 224	14 387	85 363	9 315	23 150	3 609	1 724	311	1 610	345	7 377	807
Wholesale and retail trade	278 875	69 948	215 745	51 876	36 421	10 462	2 495	483	6 500	2 435	17 714	4 692
All other industries	214 819	55 509	152 126	37 856	39 027	11 145	4 053	846	3 926	1 716	15 687	3 946
EXPERIENCED UNEMPLOYED NOT CLASSIFIED BY OCCUPATION												
Unemployed, no recent civilian work experience	445 737	554 214	233 019	299 484	145 307	173 957	8 295	8 617	16 894	21 411	42 222	50 745

Table 3. Educational Attainment of the Civilian Labor Force by Age, Sex, Race, and Hispanic Origin: 1990

[Data based on sample and subject to sampling variability, see text. For definitions of terms and meanings of symbols, see text]

United States	All persons Male	All persons Female	Hispanic origin (of any race) Male	Hispanic origin (of any race) Female	Not Hispanic — White Male	Not Hispanic — White Female	Not Hispanic — Black Male	Not Hispanic — Black Female	Not Hispanic — American Indian, Eskimo, or Aleut Male	Not Hispanic — American Indian, Eskimo, or Aleut Female	Not Hispanic — Asian or Pacific Islander Male	Not Hispanic — Asian or Pacific Islander Female	Not Hispanic — Other race Male	Not Hispanic — Other race Female
Civilian labor force 16 years and over	66 986 201	56 487 249	5 888 180	4 133 543	52 652 638	43 590 483	6 108 277	6 727 324	426 376	365 896	1 864 689	1 631 072	46 041	38 931
Not high school graduate	13 594 875	9 044 223	2 881 037	1 582 557	8 454 569	5 541 218	1 828 444	1 528 158	124 335	85 216	290 890	295 426	15 600	11 648
High school graduate (includes equivalency)	19 142 416	17 580 312	1 302 899	1 069 908	15 424 300	13 994 802	1 951 237	2 070 712	137 479	116 946	314 786	317 916	11 715	10 028
Some college or associate degree	18 382 602	17 990 928	1 178 798	1 071 662	14 986 616	14 164 840	1 600 233	2 173 092	121 297	125 448	483 808	444 251	11 850	11 635
Bachelor's degree	10 031 399	8 122 857	332 936	283 105	8 745 491	6 747 387	493 306	652 021	28 017	26 139	427 462	410 367	4 187	3 838
Graduate or professional degree	5 834 909	3 748 929	192 510	126 311	5 041 662	3 142 236	235 057	303 341	15 248	12 147	347 743	163 112	2 689	1 782
Civilian labor force 16 to 19 years	3 632 960	3 421 941	425 295	316 429	2 706 332	2 599 456	385 022	396 725	28 289	25 424	83 947	79 899	4 075	4 008
Not high school graduate	2 275 324	1 814 905	305 613	189 632	1 649 246	1 358 427	251 815	210 382	18 986	14 607	46 822	39 514	2 842	2 343
High school graduate (includes equivalency)	785 302	819 914	79 139	73 284	592 658	616 081	87 776	104 655	6 119	6 361	18 852	18 662	758	871
Some college or associate degree	569 853	784 526	40 207	53 165	462 770	623 261	45 279	81 355	3 173	4 446	17 949	21 507	475	792
Bachelor's degree	2 256	2 371	297	337	1 504	1 536	140	303	11	10	304	195	–	–
Graduate or professional degree	225	225	39	11	154	151	12	30	–	–	20	21	–	2
Civilian labor force 20 to 24 years	7 188 372	6 552 467	971 802	632 938	5 203 073	4 876 808	761 324	817 238	56 961	45 568	188 394	173 740	6 818	6 175
Not high school graduate	1 422 211	717 839	465 127	184 852	727 778	381 879	187 618	124 811	16 654	9 099	22 985	15 865	2 049	1 333
High school graduate (includes equivalency)	2 461 561	1 989 754	264 785	189 590	1 818 106	1 456 308	308 156	288 853	22 439	16 893	45 738	36 295	2 337	1 815
Some college or associate degree	2 590 360	2 923 850	211 847	222 657	2 043 440	2 254 561	232 485	342 949	16 188	17 580	84 371	83 542	2 029	2 561
Bachelor's degree	674 122	872 207	26 722	32 828	583 493	744 905	30 888	56 835	1 514	1 844	31 149	35 348	356	447
Graduate or professional degree	40 118	48 817	3 321	3 011	30 256	39 155	2 177	3 790	166	152	4 151	2 690	47	19
Civilian labor force 25 to 29 years	9 323 790	7 876 938	1 068 644	694 845	6 989 127	5 886 726	922 305	1 007 800	67 708	54 206	268 105	227 578	7 901	5 783
Not high school graduate	1 551 236	810 144	473 494	207 497	832 517	426 393	194 017	141 668	17 367	10 022	31 661	23 408	2 180	1 156
High school graduate (includes equivalency)	2 976 114	2 246 777	266 095	184 661	2 290 552	1 690 538	345 686	314 152	26 306	18 915	45 170	37 054	2 305	1 457
Some college or associate degree	2 694 503	2 740 378	236 308	213 792	2 082 569	2 044 624	276 510	392 565	19 241	20 022	77 587	67 352	2 288	2 023
Bachelor's degree	1 685 689	1 722 700	70 503	71 597	1 446 902	1 433 306	90 615	136 895	3 850	4 491	73 066	75 533	753	878
Graduate or professional degree	416 248	356 939	22 244	17 298	336 587	291 865	15 477	22 520	944	756	40 621	24 231	375	269
Civilian labor force 30 to 34 years	9 928 799	8 145 404	947 539	644 086	7 662 928	6 116 382	947 553	1 071 242	65 288	57 727	297 910	249 500	7 581	6 467
Not high school graduate	1 476 466	869 236	412 882	214 824	813 364	447 633	196 431	163 367	15 908	10 230	35 747	31 760	2 134	1 422
High school graduate (includes equivalency)	3 052 271	2 410 357	219 548	162 418	2 435 961	1 862 680	325 693	321 846	23 750	18 891	45 546	43 028	1 773	1 692
Some college or associate degree	2 896 180	2 792 453	212 121	182 981	2 293 766	2 112 670	289 221	403 915	19 704	22 216	79 092	68 437	2 276	2 234
Bachelor's degree	1 722 743	1 491 499	68 362	59 097	1 471 922	1 211 569	103 765	140 556	4 368	4 778	73 478	74 712	848	787
Graduate or professional degree	781 139	581 859	34 626	24 766	647 915	482 028	32 443	41 558	1 558	1 612	64 047	31 563	550	332
Civilian labor force 35 to 39 years	8 957 803	7 595 481	730 868	544 077	7 064 328	5 791 880	822 754	950 620	57 672	53 681	276 447	250 298	5 734	4 925
Not high school graduate	1 161 167	784 653	319 763	193 085	622 720	390 510	172 027	151 029	11 141	8 411	33 726	40 409	1 790	1 209
High school graduate (includes equivalency)	2 383 871	2 227 575	152 593	137 906	1 913 076	1 738 872	259 149	290 501	18 407	16 572	39 385	42 429	1 242	1 295
Some college or associate degree	2 769 525	2 537 398	167 074	142 295	2 256 495	1 964 878	254 922	331 599	20 171	20 808	69 237	63 203	1 626	1 329
Bachelor's degree	1 652 440	1 306 935	56 333	45 151	1 426 246	1 078 164	93 332	118 292	5 190	5 303	70 614	72 619	725	692
Graduate or professional degree	990 800	738 920	35 105	25 640	845 791	619 456	43 305	59 199	2 763	2 587	63 485	31 638	351	400
Civilian labor force 40 to 69 years	27 024 277	22 262 685	1 712 574	1 280 841	22 205 919	17 783 813	2 209 408	2 418 072	148 042	126 835	734 721	641 900	13 613	11 224
Not high school graduate	5 378 946	3 822 520	884 472	580 342	3 544 112	2 367 943	788 477	697 547	43 043	31 688	114 377	141 030	4 465	3 970
High school graduate (includes equivalency)	7 261 524	7 682 733	316 146	317 919	6 171 005	6 448 051	614 607	736 873	39 980	38 731	116 566	138 331	3 220	2 828
Some college or associate degree	6 692 153	6 090 904	307 730	254 564	5 690 206	5 041 628	495 379	613 156	42 456	39 900	153 268	139 001	3 114	2 655
Bachelor's degree	4 196 910	2 680 933	109 568	73 292	3 723 573	2 249 373	172 382	196 615	12 940	9 574	176 968	151 053	1 479	1 026
Graduate or professional degree	3 494 744	1 985 595	94 658	54 724	3 077 023	1 676 818	138 563	173 881	9 623	6 942	173 542	72 485	1 335	745
Civilian labor force 70 years and over	930 200	632 333	31 458	20 327	820 931	535 418	59 911	65 627	2 416	2 455	15 165	8 157	319	349
Not high school graduate	329 525	224 926	19 686	12 325	264 832	168 433	38 059	39 354	1 236	1 159	5 572	3 440	140	215
High school graduate (includes equivalency)	221 773	203 202	4 593	4 130	202 942	182 470	10 151	13 832	478	583	3 529	2 117	80	70
Some college or associate degree	170 028	121 419	3 511	2 208	157 370	109 932	6 437	7 553	364	476	2 304	907	42	41
Bachelor's degree	97 239	46 212	1 151	803	91 851	41 820	2 184	2 525	144	149	1 883	907	26	8
Graduate or professional degree	111 635	36 574	2 517	861	103 936	32 763	3 080	2 363	194	88	1 877	484	31	15

Table 4. Educational Attainment of the Civilian Labor Force by Age, Sex, and Race: 1990

[Data based on sample and subject to sampling variability, see text. For definitions of terms and meanings of symbols, see text]

United States	All persons		White		Black		American Indian, Eskimo, or Aleut		Asian or Pacific Islander		Other race	
	Male	Female	Male	Female	Male	Female	Male	Female	Male	Female	Male	Female
Civilian labor force 16 years and over	66 986 201	56 487 249	55 699 109	45 826 627	6 247 539	6 847 642	459 892	391 420	1 918 998	1 684 082	2 660 663	1 737 478
Not high school graduate	13 594 875	9 044 223	9 789 849	6 299 495	1 890 088	1 570 966	138 391	93 181	305 847	307 632	1 470 700	772 949
High school graduate (includes equivalency)	19 142 416	17 580 312	16 114 162	14 587 956	1 984 940	2 099 809	145 379	124 132	328 164	330 045	569 771	438 370
Some college or associate degree	18 382 602	17 990 928	15 651 724	14 777 659	1 631 122	2 207 378	130 358	133 858	499 649	460 743	469 749	411 290
Bachelor's degree	10 031 399	8 122 857	8 963 799	6 930 838	501 704	661 598	29 529	27 407	434 747	420 039	101 620	82 975
Graduate or professional degree	5 834 909	3 748 929	5 179 575	3 230 679	239 685	307 891	16 235	12 842	350 591	165 623	48 823	31 894
Civilian labor force 16 to 19 years	3 632 960	3 421 941	2 913 884	2 757 561	393 905	404 435	31 175	27 759	88 033	84 022	205 963	148 164
Not high school graduate	2 275 324	1 814 905	1 794 690	1 450 925	258 019	214 907	20 999	15 989	49 290	41 541	152 326	91 543
High school graduate (includes equivalency)	785 302	819 914	632 532	653 354	89 519	106 484	6 700	6 986	19 737	19 708	36 814	33 382
Some college or associate degree	569 853	784 526	484 746	651 452	46 215	82 701	3 465	4 774	18 682	22 550	16 745	23 049
Bachelor's degree	2 256	2 371	1 739	1 679	140	313	11	–	304	202	62	177
Graduate or professional degree	225	225	177	151	12	30	–	10	20	21	16	13
Civilian labor force 20 to 24 years	7 188 372	6 552 467	5 662 375	5 190 690	781 580	834 100	62 623	49 447	196 409	181 397	485 385	296 833
Not high school graduate	1 422 211	717 839	928 498	463 703	195 612	128 957	19 211	10 068	24 934	17 001	253 956	98 110
High school graduate (includes equivalency)	2 461 561	1 989 754	1 947 611	1 550 285	314 477	293 522	24 026	18 202	48 317	38 546	127 130	89 199
Some college or associate degree	2 590 360	2 923 850	2 154 495	2 370 658	237 625	349 869	17 611	19 059	87 276	86 930	93 353	97 334
Bachelor's degree	674 122	872 207	599 607	765 255	31 565	57 868	1 589	1 957	31 672	36 176	9 689	10 951
Graduate or professional degree	40 118	48 817	32 164	40 789	2 301	3 884	186	161	4 210	2 744	1 257	1 239
Civilian labor force 25 to 29 years	9 323 790	7 876 938	7 508 525	6 241 584	945 030	1 026 981	73 322	58 525	277 055	235 337	519 858	314 511
Not high school graduate	1 551 236	810 144	1 038 915	518 788	202 042	146 468	19 366	11 006	33 763	24 510	257 150	109 372
High school graduate (includes equivalency)	2 976 114	2 246 777	2 423 577	1 785 329	351 909	318 985	27 858	20 243	47 748	38 991	125 022	83 229
Some college or associate degree	2 694 503	2 740 378	2 205 901	2 157 785	282 748	399 243	20 946	21 695	80 490	70 168	104 418	91 487
Bachelor's degree	1 685 689	1 722 700	1 489 640	1 476 376	92 375	139 269	4 142	4 796	74 147	77 188	25 385	25 071
Graduate or professional degree	416 248	356 939	350 492	303 306	15 956	23 016	1 010	785	40 907	24 480	7 883	5 352
Civilian labor force 30 to 34 years	9 928 799	8 145 404	8 136 271	6 451 324	969 946	1 090 275	70 788	61 648	305 839	256 906	445 955	285 251
Not high school graduate	1 476 466	869 236	995 726	542 656	204 521	168 686	17 978	11 289	37 597	33 153	220 644	113 452
High school graduate (includes equivalency)	3 052 271	2 410 357	2 548 036	1 948 218	331 250	326 114	25 109	19 867	47 868	44 693	100 008	71 465
Some college or associate degree	2 896 180	2 792 453	2 406 848	2 212 921	295 041	410 626	21 399	23 755	81 332	70 991	91 560	74 160
Bachelor's degree	1 722 743	1 491 499	1 514 583	1 248 987	105 794	142 410	4 609	4 978	74 652	76 185	23 105	18 939
Graduate or professional degree	781 139	581 859	671 078	498 542	33 340	42 439	1 693	1 759	64 390	31 884	10 638	7 235
Civilian labor force 35 to 39 years	8 957 803	7 595 481	7 438 355	6 083 680	842 389	966 880	62 140	57 089	283 495	257 610	331 424	230 222
Not high school graduate	1 161 167	784 653	764 201	477 100	179 803	156 174	12 501	9 232	35 522	41 958	169 140	100 189
High school graduate (includes equivalency)	2 383 871	2 227 575	1 992 841	1 814 186	263 424	294 216	19 467	17 359	40 957	43 755	67 182	58 059
Some college or associate degree	2 769 525	2 537 398	2 348 753	2 060 954	260 125	336 349	21 588	22 179	71 438	65 388	67 621	52 528
Bachelor's degree	1 652 440	1 306 935	1 462 737	1 094 213	94 808	120 072	5 558	5 557	63 853	74 436	17 612	12 657
Graduate or professional degree	990 800	738 920	869 823	637 227	44 229	60 069	3 026	2 762	71 725	32 073	9 869	6 789
Civilian labor force 40 to 69 years	27 024 277	22 262 685	23 196 426	18 552 463	2 253 888	2 458 519	157 339	134 392	752 619	660 401	664 005	456 910
Not high school graduate	5 378 946	3 822 520	3 990 241	2 669 901	811 376	715 858	47 045	34 378	118 962	145 944	411 322	256 439
High school graduate (includes equivalency)	7 261 524	7 682 733	6 363 193	6 651 022	624 065	746 556	41 718	40 868	119 949	142 173	112 599	102 114
Some college or associate degree	6 692 153	6 090 904	5 890 687	5 212 419	502 898	620 939	44 985	41 902	158 060	143 447	95 523	72 197
Bachelor's degree	4 196 910	2 680 933	3 802 671	2 301 907	174 828	199 100	13 476	9 970	180 332	154 916	25 603	15 040
Graduate or professional degree	3 494 744	1 985 595	3 149 634	1 717 214	140 721	176 066	10 115	7 274	175 316	73 921	18 958	11 120
Civilian labor force 70 years and over	930 200	632 333	843 273	549 325	60 801	66 452	2 505	2 560	15 548	8 409	8 073	5 587
Not high school graduate	329 525	224 926	277 578	176 422	38 715	39 916	1 291	1 219	5 779	3 525	6 162	3 844
High school graduate (includes equivalency)	221 773	203 202	206 372	185 562	10 296	13 932	501	607	3 588	2 179	1 016	922
Some college or associate degree	170 028	121 419	160 294	111 470	6 470	7 651	364	494	2 371	1 269	529	535
Bachelor's degree	97 239	46 212	92 822	42 421	2 194	2 566	144	149	1 915	936	164	140
Graduate or professional degree	111 635	36 574	106 207	33 450	3 126	2 387	205	91	1 895	500	202	146

| | RESIDENCE, APRIL 1, 1935 | | | | | | | | | | | | | PERSONS 14 YEARS OLD AND OV |

FURTHER READING

16	17	18	19	20	D	21	22	23	24	25	E	26	27	28
	Same House				No	Yes	—	—			1	40	—	Foreman
	Same House				No	No	No	No	No	H		—	—	
	Same House				No	No	No	No	No	S		—	—	
	Same House				No	Yes	—	—			1	—	—	Labore

Adelman, Ken. *Reagan at Reykjavik: Forty-Eight Hours That Ended the Cold War.* New York: HarperCollins, 2014. Print.

Batchelor, Bob, and Scott Stoddart. *The 1980s (American Popular Culture through History).* Connecticut: Greenwood Press, 2006. Print.

Bernstein, Jonathan. *Pretty In Pink: The Golden Age of Teenage Movies.* New York, St. Martin's Press, 1997. Print.

Brown, Archie. *The Rise and Fall of Communism.* New York: Ecco, 2011. Print.

Day, Christine. *A Retro Collection of 70s and 80s Short Stories.* Amazon Digital, 2012.

Ehrman, John. *The Eighties: America in the Age of Reagan.* New Haven, CT: Yale University Press, 2006. Print.

Freed, Les, and Sarah Ishida. *The History of Computers.* Emeryville, CA: Ziff-Davis, 1995. Print.

Grant, James. *Money of the Mind: How the 1980s Got That Way.* New York: Farrar Straus & Giroux, 1994. Print.

Jackson, Michael. *Moonwalk.* New York: Crown, 1988 (reissued 2009). Print.

Jenkins, Philip. *Decade of Nightmares: The End of the Sixties and the Making of Eighties America.* New York: Oxford University Press, 2008. Print.

Johnson, Michael. *A 1980s Childhood: From He-Man to Shell Suits.* South Carolina: History Press, 2013. Print.

Kaufman, Will. *American Culture in the 1980s.* Edinburgh University Press, 2007. Print.

Kengor, Paul. *The Crusader: Ronald Reagan and the Fall of Communism.* New York: Harper, 2007. Print.

Majewski, Lori. *Mad World: An Oral History of New Wave Artists and Songs That Defined the 1980s.* New York: Abrams, 2013. Print.

Mallon, Thomas. *Finale: A Novel of the Reagan Years.* New York: Pantheon, 2015. Print.

Mann, James. *The Rebellion of Ronald Reagan: A History of the End of the Cold War.* New York: Penguin, 2010. Print.

New York Times. *The Times of the Eighties: The Culture, Politics, and Personalities that Shaped the Decade.* The New York Times, 2013. Print.

Pemberton, William. *Exit with Honor: The Life and Presidency of Ronald Reagan.* New York: Routledge, 2015. Print.

Rossinow, Doug. *The Reagan Era: A History of the 1980s.* New York: Columbia University Press, 2015. Print.

Sirota, David. *Back to Our Future: How the 1980s Explain the World We Live in Now-Our Culture, Our Politics, Our Everything.* New York: Ballantine Books, 2011. Print.

Stross, Randall. *Steve Jobs & The NeXT Big Thing.* Amazon Digital, 2012. Print.

Taborrelli, J. Randy. *Madonna: An Intimate Biography.* New York: Simon & Schuster, 2007. Print.

Tannenbaum, Rob. *I Want My MTV: The Uncensored Story of the Music Video Revolution.* New York: Plume, 2013.

Troy, Gil, and Vincent J. Cannato, eds. *Living in the Eighties.* New York: Oxford University Press, 2009. Print.

Troy, Gil. *The Reagan Revolution: A Very Short Introduction.* New York: Oxford University Press, 2009. Print.

Walser, Robert. *Running with the Devil: Power, Gender, and Madness in Heavy Metal Music.* Middletown, CT: Wesleyan, 1993. Print.

INDEX

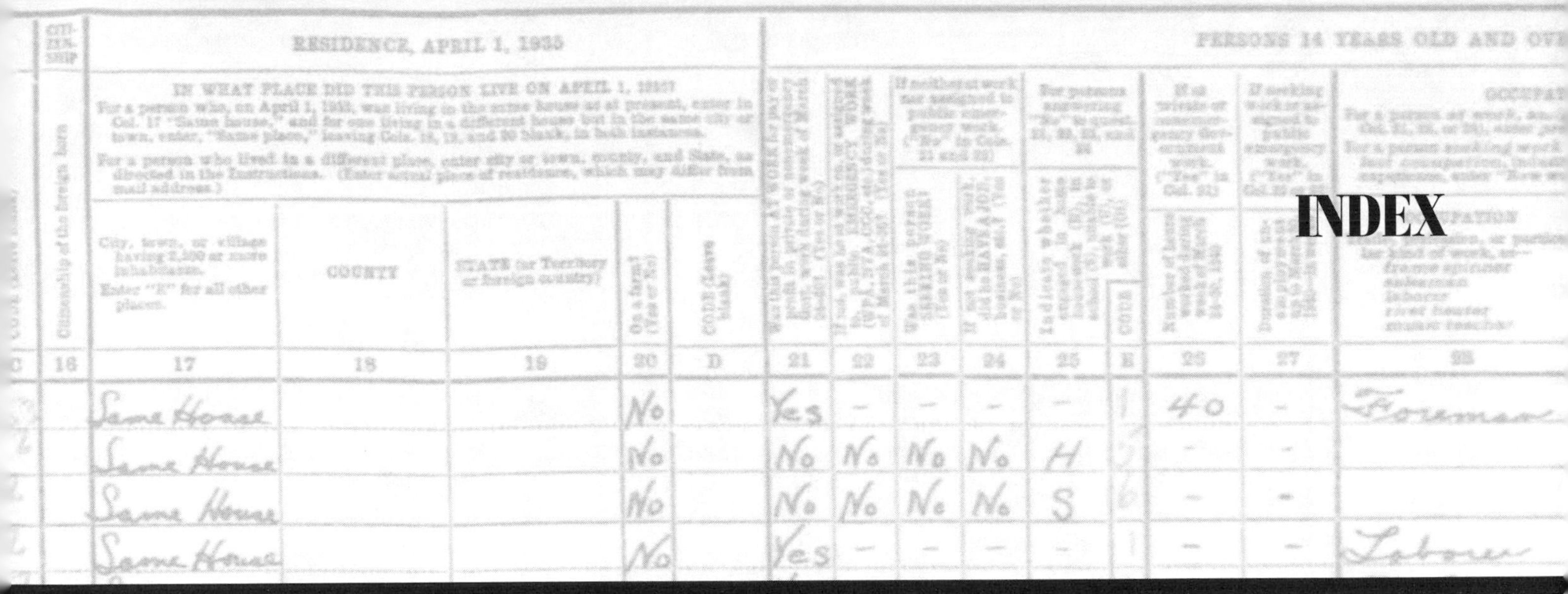
RESIDENCE, APRIL 1, 1935
IN WHAT PLACE DID THIS PERSON LIVE ON APRIL 1, 1935?
COUNTY
Same House
Same House
Same House
Same House

A

AARP News Bulletin, 159
ABBA, 159
ABC, 161
Adams, Bryan, 164
Adler, Mortimer, 108
The Adventures of Huckleberry Finn, 158
Affirmative Action hiring quotas, 166, 171
AIDS
  blood test for, 163
  Haiti and, 74
  New York City and, 117
Albuquerque, New Mexico, 134
Almagest (Ptolemy), 109
Amadeus, 162, 164
American Bandstand, 167
American Bantam Car Company, 130
American Cancer Society, 163
American Federation of Labor (AFL), 149
American Football League, 65
American Furniture Company, 44, 46
American Motors Corporation, 166
American Pro-Freeze rallies, 22
American Revolution, 122
America's Cup, 157
Ameritech, 157
Anchorage Daily News, 168
Andrews, Tommy Lee, 168
Andropov, Yuri, 159
An Dung, 147-152
Animal conservationist, 91-95
Annapolis, Maryland, 110-111
Annual income of standard jobs, 175
Ansell America, 166
Anthony, Susan B., 25
Anti-abortion protesters, 141-146
Apple Computer, 18, 19
Apple Inc., 157
Apple Macintosh, 162, 165
Aristotle, 109
Art Institute of Chicago, 170
Artists, 71-74
ARTnews magazine, 162
Ash-Shiraa, 164
Aspartame, 161
Associated Press, 195-196
Atari, 50
The A-Team, 161
Atkins, Chet, 13
Atlanta Falcons, 66
Atlantic Coast Conference (ACC), 41
AT&T, 158
Austin, Stephen F., 16
Austin, Texas, 15-16
Austin City Limits, 11-14, 15

B

B-2 Stealth bomber, 166
Back to the Future, 162, 163, 164
Bad, 169
Bakker, Jim, 169
Ballard, Robert, 166
Baltimore Colts, 67
Baltimore Orioles, 157
Bankers Trust Company, 116
Barkin, Ellen, 32
Barney Miller, 159
Barr, Stringfellow, 108
Bassett Furniture, 46
Bates, Bill, 67
Batman, 169
"The Battle for Grenada, American Troops Take Charge on the Island but Face Surprisingly Stiff Opposition," 196
Bay Area Woodworkers Association, 61
Beals, Jennifer, 157
Beanfield rifle, 99
Beatles, 87
Bee Gees, 13
Behavioral Science Research Institute of Coral Gables, 74
Behr, Alex, 81-86
Behr, Naomi, 81, 84-85
Beloved (Morrison), 171
Belushi, John, 158
Bendix, 82
Bennett, William, 115, 170
Berbick, Trevor, 164
Berry, Chuck, 87
Better Homes and Gardens, 159
Beverly Hills Cop, 164
Big Mac, 127
The Bill Cosby Show, 162, 165
"Billie Jean," 159
Bill of Rights, 122
Billy Bathgate (Doctrow), 167
Bilotti, Thomas, 163
Birdseye, Clarence, 10
Bishop, Maurice, 36
Bissell, Phil, 65
Blashfeld, Edwin Howland, 122
Blondie, 161
Bloom, Allan, 166
Bluford, Guion S., 160
Boaz, Noel, 46
Bon Appetit, 212-213
The Bonfire of the Vanities, 167
Boom operator, 27-33
Borg, Björn, 157
Bork, Robert H., 141
Born in the U.S.A., 165
Boston Patriots, 65
Boy George, 162
Bradley, Milton, 50
Brain (computer virus), 163
Branch, Taylor, 170
Braniff Incorporated, 167
Braniff International Airlines, 157
Brann, Eva, 109
Brawley, Tawana, 167
BRC (Bantam Reconnaissance Car) 40, 130
The Breakfast Club, 164
British Antarctic Survey, 165
"Broncos, Saints Inspire Opposite in Fans," 204
Broughton, Harold, 99
Buchanan, Scott, 108
Burack, Alicia, 35-40
Burlington Industries, 116
Burns, Beverly Lynn, 162
Burns, Jethro, 13
Burroughs, 165
Bush, George H. W., 141, 145, 166, 168, 170
Business Week, 203
Buster, John, 162
Butler, Pennsylvania, 130
Butler, Richard, 130

2016 Title List

Visit www.GreyHouse.com for Product Information, Table of Contents, and Sample Pages.

General Reference

An African Biographical Dictionary
America's College Museums
American Environmental Leaders: From Colonial Times to the Present
Encyclopedia of African-American Writing
Encyclopedia of Constitutional Amendments
Encyclopedia of Gun Control & Gun Rights
An Encyclopedia of Human Rights in the United States
Encyclopedia of Invasions & Conquests
Encyclopedia of Prisoners of War & Internment
Encyclopedia of Religion & Law in America
Encyclopedia of Rural America
Encyclopedia of the Continental Congress
Encyclopedia of the United States Cabinet, 1789-2010
Encyclopedia of War Journalism
Encyclopedia of Warrior Peoples & Fighting Groups
The Environmental Debate: A Documentary History
The Evolution Wars: A Guide to the Debates
From Suffrage to the Senate: America's Political Women
Global Terror & Political Risk Assessment
Nations of the World
Political Corruption in America
Privacy Rights in the Digital Era
The Religious Right: A Reference Handbook
Speakers of the House of Representatives, 1789-2009
This is Who We Were: 1880-1900
This is Who We Were: A Companion to the 1940 Census
This is Who We Were: In the 1910s
This is Who We Were: In the 1920s
This is Who We Were: In the 1940s
This is Who We Were: In the 1950s
This is Who We Were: In the 1960s
This is Who We Were: In the 1970s
U.S. Land & Natural Resource Policy
The Value of a Dollar 1600-1865: Colonial Era to the Civil War
The Value of a Dollar: 1860-2014
Working Americans 1770-1869 Vol. IX: Revolutionary War to the Civil War
Working Americans 1880-1999 Vol. I: The Working Class
Working Americans 1880-1999 Vol. II: The Middle Class
Working Americans 1880-1999 Vol. III: The Upper Class
Working Americans 1880-1999 Vol. IV: Their Children
Working Americans 1880-2015 Vol. V: Americans At War
Working Americans 1880-2005 Vol. VI: Women at Work
Working Americans 1880-2006 Vol. VII: Social Movements
Working Americans 1880-2007 Vol. VIII: Immigrants
Working Americans 1880-2009 Vol. X: Sports & Recreation
Working Americans 1880-2010 Vol. XI: Inventors & Entrepreneurs
Working Americans 1880-2011 Vol. XII: Our History through Music
Working Americans 1880-2012 Vol. XIII: Education & Educators
World Cultural Leaders of the 20th & 21st Centuries

Education Information

Charter School Movement
Comparative Guide to American Elementary & Secondary Schools
Complete Learning Disabilities Directory
Educators Resource Directory
Special Education: A Reference Book for Policy and Curriculum Development

Health Information

Comparative Guide to American Hospitals
Complete Directory for Pediatric Disorders
Complete Directory for People with Chronic Illness
Complete Directory for People with Disabilities
Complete Mental Health Directory
Diabetes in America: Analysis of an Epidemic
Directory of Drug & Alcohol Residential Rehab Facilities
Directory of Health Care Group Purchasing Organizations
Directory of Hospital Personnel
HMO/PPO Directory
Medical Device Register
Older Americans Information Directory

Business Information

Complete Television, Radio & Cable Industry Directory
Directory of Business Information Resources
Directory of Mail Order Catalogs
Directory of Venture Capital & Private Equity Firms
Environmental Resource Handbook
Food & Beverage Market Place
Grey House Homeland Security Directory
Grey House Performing Arts Directory
Grey House Safety & Security Directory
Grey House Transportation Security Directory
Hudson's Washington News Media Contacts Directory
New York State Directory
Rauch Market Research Guides
Sports Market Place Directory

Statistics & Demographics

American Tally
America's Top-Rated Cities
America's Top-Rated Smaller Cities
America's Top-Rated Small Towns & Cities
Ancestry & Ethnicity in America
The Asian Databook
Comparative Guide to American Suburbs
The Hispanic Databook
Profiles of America
"Profiles of" Series – State Handbooks
Weather America

Financial Ratings Series

TheStreet Ratings' Guide to Bond & Money Market Mutual Funds
TheStreet Ratings' Guide to Common Stocks
TheStreet Ratings' Guide to Exchange-Traded Funds
TheStreet Ratings' Guide to Stock Mutual Funds
TheStreet Ratings' Ultimate Guided Tour of Stock Investing
Weiss Ratings' Consumer Guides
Weiss Ratings' Guide to Banks
Weiss Ratings' Guide to Credit Unions
Weiss Ratings' Guide to Health Insurers
Weiss Ratings' Guide to Life & Annuity Insurers
Weiss Ratings' Guide to Property & Casualty Insurers

Bowker's Books In Print® Titles

American Book Publishing Record® Annual
American Book Publishing Record® Monthly
Books In Print®
Books In Print® Supplement
Books Out Loud™
Bowker's Complete Video Directory™
Children's Books In Print®
El-Hi Textbooks & Serials In Print®
Forthcoming Books®
Large Print Books & Serials™
Law Books & Serials In Print™
Medical & Health Care Books In Print™
Publishers, Distributors & Wholesalers of the US™
Subject Guide to Books In Print®
Subject Guide to Children's Books In Print®

Canadian General Reference

Associations Canada
Canadian Almanac & Directory
Canadian Environmental Resource Guide
Canadian Parliamentary Guide
Canadian Venture Capital & Private Equity Firms
Financial Post Directory of Directors
Financial Services Canada
Governments Canada
Health Guide Canada
The History of Canada
Libraries Canada
Major Canadian Cities

Grey House Publishing | Salem Press | H.W. Wilson | 4919 Route, 22 PO Box 56, Amenia NY 12501-0056

2016 Title List

Visit www.SalemPress.com for Product Information, Table of Contents, and Sample Pages.

Science, Careers & Mathematics

Ancient Creatures
Applied Science
Applied Science: Engineering & Mathematics
Applied Science: Science & Medicine
Applied Science: Technology
Biomes and Ecosystems
Careers in Building Construction
Careers in Business
Careers in Chemistry
Careers in Communications & Media
Careers in Environment & Conservation
Careers in Healthcare
Careers in Hospitality & Tourism
Careers in Human Services
Careers in Law, Criminal Justice & Emergency Services
Careers in Manufacturing
Careers in Physics
Careers in Sales, Insurance & Real Estate
Careers in Science & Engineering
Careers in Technology Services & Repair
Computer Technology Innovators
Contemporary Biographies in Business
Contemporary Biographies in Chemistry
Contemporary Biographies in Communications & Media
Contemporary Biographies in Environment & Conservation
Contemporary Biographies in Healthcare
Contemporary Biographies in Hospitality & Tourism
Contemporary Biographies in Law & Criminal Justice
Contemporary Biographies in Physics
Earth Science
Earth Science: Earth Materials & Resources
Earth Science: Earth's Surface and History
Earth Science: Physics & Chemistry of the Earth
Earth Science: Weather, Water & Atmosphere
Encyclopedia of Energy
Encyclopedia of Environmental Issues
Encyclopedia of Environmental Issues: Atmosphere and Air Pollution
Encyclopedia of Environmental Issues: Ecology and Ecosystems
Encyclopedia of Environmental Issues: Energy and Energy Use
Encyclopedia of Environmental Issues: Policy and Activism
Encyclopedia of Environmental Issues: Preservation/Wilderness Issues
Encyclopedia of Environmental Issues: Water and Water Pollution
Encyclopedia of Global Resources
Encyclopedia of Global Warming
Encyclopedia of Mathematics & Society
Encyclopedia of Mathematics & Society: Engineering, Tech, Medicine
Encyclopedia of Mathematics & Society: Great Mathematicians
Encyclopedia of Mathematics & Society: Math & Social Sciences
Encyclopedia of Mathematics & Society: Math Development/Concepts
Encyclopedia of Mathematics & Society: Math in Culture & Society
Encyclopedia of Mathematics & Society: Space, Science, Environment
Encyclopedia of the Ancient World
Forensic Science
Geography Basics
Internet Innovators
Inventions and Inventors
Magill's Encyclopedia of Science: Animal Life
Magill's Encyclopedia of Science: Plant life
Notable Natural Disasters
Principles of Astronomy
Principles of Chemistry
Principles of Physics
Science and Scientists
Solar System
Solar System: Great Astronomers
Solar System: Study of the Universe
Solar System: The Inner Planets
Solar System: The Moon and Other Small Bodies
Solar System: The Outer Planets
Solar System: The Sun and Other Stars
World Geography

Literature

American Ethnic Writers
Classics of Science Fiction & Fantasy Literature
Critical Insights: Authors
Critical Insights: Film
Critical Insights: Literary Collection Bundles
Critical Insights: Themes
Critical Insights: Works
Critical Survey of Drama
Critical Survey of Graphic Novels: Heroes & Super Heroes
Critical Survey of Graphic Novels: History, Theme & Technique
Critical Survey of Graphic Novels: Independents/Underground Classics
Critical Survey of Graphic Novels: Manga
Critical Survey of Long Fiction
Critical Survey of Mystery & Detective Fiction
Critical Survey of Mythology and Folklore: Heroes and Heroines
Critical Survey of Mythology and Folklore: Love, Sexuality & Desire
Critical Survey of Mythology and Folklore: World Mythology
Critical Survey of Poetry
Critical Survey of Poetry: American Poets
Critical Survey of Poetry: British, Irish & Commonwealth Poets
Critical Survey of Poetry: Cumulative Index
Critical Survey of Poetry: European Poets
Critical Survey of Poetry: Topical Essays
Critical Survey of Poetry: World Poets
Critical Survey of Shakespeare's Plays
Critical Survey of Shakespeare's Sonnets
Critical Survey of Short Fiction
Critical Survey of Short Fiction: American Writers
Critical Survey of Short Fiction: British, Irish, Commonwealth Writers
Critical Survey of Short Fiction: Cumulative Index
Critical Survey of Short Fiction: European Writers
Critical Survey of Short Fiction: Topical Essays
Critical Survey of Short Fiction: World Writers
Critical Survey of Young Adult Literature
Cyclopedia of Literary Characters
Cyclopedia of Literary Places
Holocaust Literature
Introduction to Literary Context: American Poetry of the 20th Century
Introduction to Literary Context: American Post-Modernist Novels
Introduction to Literary Context: American Short Fiction
Introduction to Literary Context: English Literature
Introduction to Literary Context: Plays
Introduction to Literary Context: World Literature
Magill's Literary Annual 2015
Magill's Survey of American Literature
Magill's Survey of World Literature
Masterplots
Masterplots II: African American Literature
Masterplots II: American Fiction Series
Masterplots II: British & Commonwealth Fiction Series
Masterplots II: Christian Literature
Masterplots II: Drama Series
Masterplots II: Juvenile & Young Adult Literature, Supplement
Masterplots II: Nonfiction Series
Masterplots II: Poetry Series
Masterplots II: Short Story Series
Masterplots II: Women's Literature Series
Notable African American Writers
Notable American Novelists
Notable Playwrights
Notable Poets
Recommended Reading: 600 Classics Reviewed
Short Story Writers

Grey House Publishing | Salem Press | H.W. Wilson | 4919 Route, 22 PO Box 56, Amenia NY 12501-0056

2016 Title List

Visit **www.SalemPress.com** for Product Information, Table of Contents, and Sample Pages.

History and Social Science

The 2000s in America
50 States
African American History
Agriculture in History
American First Ladies
American Heroes
American Indian Culture
American Indian History
American Indian Tribes
American Presidents
American Villains
America's Historic Sites
Ancient Greece
The Bill of Rights
The Civil Rights Movement
The Cold War
Countries, Peoples & Cultures
Countries, Peoples & Cultures: Central & South America
Countries, Peoples & Cultures: Central, South & Southeast Asia
Countries, Peoples & Cultures: East & South Africa
Countries, Peoples & Cultures: East Asia & the Pacific
Countries, Peoples & Cultures: Eastern Europe
Countries, Peoples & Cultures: Middle East & North Africa
Countries, Peoples & Cultures: North America & the Caribbean
Countries, Peoples & Cultures: West & Central Africa
Countries, Peoples & Cultures: Western Europe
Defining Documents: American Revolution
Defining Documents: Civil Rights
Defining Documents: Civil War
Defining Documents: Emergence of Modern America
Defining Documents: Exploration & Colonial America
Defining Documents: Manifest Destiny
Defining Documents: Postwar 1940s
Defining Documents: Reconstruction
Defining Documents: 1920s
Defining Documents: 1930s
Defining Documents: 1950s
Defining Documents: 1960s
Defining Documents: 1970s
Defining Documents: American West
Defining Documents: Ancient World
Defining Documents: Middle Ages
Defining Documents: Vietnam War
Defining Documents: World War I
Defining Documents: World War II
The Eighties in America
Encyclopedia of American Immigration
Encyclopedia of Flight
Encyclopedia of the Ancient World
Fashion Innovators
The Fifties in America
The Forties in America
Great Athletes
Great Athletes: Baseball
Great Athletes: Basketball
Great Athletes: Boxing & Soccer
Great Athletes: Cumulative Index
Great Athletes: Football
Great Athletes: Golf & Tennis
Great Athletes: Olympics
Great Athletes: Racing & Individual Sports
Great Events from History: 17th Century
Great Events from History: 18th Century
Great Events from History: 19th Century
Great Events from History: 20th Century (1901-1940)
Great Events from History: 20th Century (1941-1970)
Great Events from History: 20th Century (1971-2000)
Great Events from History: Ancient World
Great Events from History: Cumulative Indexes
Great Events from History: Gay, Lesbian, Bisexual, Transgender Events

Great Events from History: Middle Ages
Great Events from History: Modern Scandals
Great Events from History: Renaissance & Early Modern Era
Great Lives from History: 17th Century
Great Lives from History: 18th Century
Great Lives from History: 19th Century
Great Lives from History: 20th Century
Great Lives from History: African Americans
Great Lives from History: American Women
Great Lives from History: Ancient World
Great Lives from History: Asian & Pacific Islander Americans
Great Lives from History: Cumulative Indexes
Great Lives from History: Incredibly Wealthy
Great Lives from History: Inventors & Inventions
Great Lives from History: Jewish Americans
Great Lives from History: Latinos
Great Lives from History: Middle Ages
Great Lives from History: Notorious Lives
Great Lives from History: Renaissance & Early Modern Era
Great Lives from History: Scientists & Science
Historical Encyclopedia of American Business
Issues in U.S. Immigration
Magill's Guide to Military History
Milestone Documents in African American History
Milestone Documents in American History
Milestone Documents in World History
Milestone Documents of American Leaders
Milestone Documents of World Religions
Music Innovators
Musicians & Composers 20th Century
The Nineties in America
The Seventies in America
The Sixties in America
Survey of American Industry and Careers
The Thirties in America
The Twenties in America
United States at War
U.S.A. in Space
U.S. Court Cases
U.S. Government Leaders
U.S. Laws, Acts, and Treaties
U.S. Legal System
U.S. Supreme Court
Weapons and Warfare
World Conflicts: Asia and the Middle East
World Political Yearbook

Health

Addictions & Substance Abuse
Adolescent Health & Wellness
Cancer
Complementary & Alternative Medicine
Genetics & Inherited Conditions
Health Issues
Infectious Diseases & Conditions
Magill's Medical Guide
Psychology & Behavioral Health
Psychology Basics

Grey House Publishing | Salem Press | H.W. Wilson | 4919 Route, 22 PO Box 56, Amenia NY 12501-0056

2016 Title List

Visit **www.HWWilsonInPrint.com** for Product Information, Table of Contents and Sample Pages

Current Biography
Current Biography Cumulative Index 1946-2013
Current Biography Monthly Magazine
Current Biography Yearbook: 2003
Current Biography Yearbook: 2004
Current Biography Yearbook: 2005
Current Biography Yearbook: 2006
Current Biography Yearbook: 2007
Current Biography Yearbook: 2008
Current Biography Yearbook: 2009
Current Biography Yearbook: 2010
Current Biography Yearbook: 2011
Current Biography Yearbook: 2012
Current Biography Yearbook: 2013
Current Biography Yearbook: 2014
Current Biography Yearbook: 2015

Core Collections
Children's Core Collection
Fiction Core Collection
Graphic Novels Core Collection
Middle & Junior High School Core
Public Library Core Collection: Nonfiction
Senior High Core Collection
Young Adult Fiction Core Collection

The Reference Shelf
Aging in America
American Military Presence Overseas
The Arab Spring
The Brain
The Business of Food
Campaign Trends & Election Law
Conspiracy Theories
The Digital Age
Dinosaurs
Embracing New Paradigms in Education
Faith & Science
Families: Traditional and New Structures
The Future of U.S. Economic Relations: Mexico, Cuba, and Venezuela
Global Climate Change
Graphic Novels and Comic Books
Immigration
Immigration in the U.S.
Internet Safety
Marijuana Reform
The News and its Future
The Paranormal
Politics of the Ocean
Racial Tension in a "Postracial" Age
Reality Television
Representative American Speeches: 2008-2009
Representative American Speeches: 2009-2010
Representative American Speeches: 2010-2011
Representative American Speeches: 2011-2012
Representative American Speeches: 2012-2013
Representative American Speeches: 2013-2014
Representative American Speeches: 2014-2015
Representative American Speeches: 2015-2016
Rethinking Work
Revisiting Gender
Robotics
Russia
Social Networking
Social Services for the Poor
Space Exploration & Development
Sports in America
The Supreme Court
The Transformation of American Cities

U.S. Infrastructure
U.S. National Debate Topic: Surveillance
U.S. National Debate Topic: The Ocean
U.S. National Debate Topic: Transportation Infrastructure
Whistleblowers

Readers' Guide
Abridged Readers' Guide to Periodical Literature
Readers' Guide to Periodical Literature

Indexes
Index to Legal Periodicals & Books
Short Story Index
Book Review Digest

Sears List
Sears List of Subject Headings
Sears: Lista de Encabezamientos de Materia

Facts About Series
Facts About American Immigration
Facts About China
Facts About the 20th Century
Facts About the Presidents
Facts About the World's Languages

Nobel Prize Winners
Nobel Prize Winners: 1901-1986
Nobel Prize Winners: 1987-1991
Nobel Prize Winners: 1992-1996
Nobel Prize Winners: 1997-2001

World Authors
World Authors: 1995-2000
World Authors: 2000-2005

Famous First Facts
Famous First Facts
Famous First Facts About American Politics
Famous First Facts About Sports
Famous First Facts About the Environment
Famous First Facts: International Edition

American Book of Days
The American Book of Days
The International Book of Days

Junior Authors & Illustrators
Eleventh Book of Junior Authors & Illustrations

Monographs
The Barnhart Dictionary of Etymology
Celebrate the World
Guide to the Ancient World
Indexing from A to Z
The Poetry Break
Radical Change: Books for Youth in a Digital Age

Wilson Chronology
Wilson Chronology of Asia and the Pacific
Wilson Chronology of Human Rights
Wilson Chronology of Ideas
Wilson Chronology of the Arts
Wilson Chronology of the World's Religions
Wilson Chronology of Women's Achievements

Grey House Publishing | Salem Press | H.W. Wilson | 4919 Route, 22 PO Box 56, Amenia NY 12501-0056